C

HOWARD SCHAEFFER
Data Processing Consultant

DATA
CENTER
OPERATIONS

a guide
to effective
planning,
processing,
and
performance

Prentice-Hall, Inc., Englewood Cliffs, N.J. 07632

Library of Congress Cataloging in Publication Data

Schaeffer, Howard.
    Data center operations.

    Bibliography: p. 467
    Includes index.
    1. Data processing service centers.
2. Computer service industry. I. Title.
HD9696.C62S3   658'.054   80-15702
ISBN 0-13-196360-0

Editorial/production supervision by Maria McKinnon
    and Ellen De Filippis
Interior design by Lee Cohen and Ellen De Filippis
Cover design by Lee Cohen
Page layout by Peter J. Ticola, Jr.
Manufacturing buyer: Joyce Levatino

Printed in the United States of America

10 9 8 7 6 5 4 3 2

PRENTICE-HALL INTERNATIONAL, INC., *London*
PRENTICE-HALL OF AUSTRALIA PTY. LIMITED, *Sydney*
PRENTICE-HALL OF CANADA, LTD., *Toronto*
PRENTICE-HALL OF INDIA PRIVATE LIMITED, *New Delhi*
PRENTICE-HALL OF JAPAN, INC., *Tokyo*
PRENTICE-HALL OF SOUTHEAST ASIA PTE. LTD., *Singapore*
WHITEHALL BOOKS LIMITED, *Wellington, New Zealand*

TO THOSE WHO HELPED

To my Alice and to my son Rob,
   who innocently accepted many chores and tolerated
   considerable clutter.

To Karl Karlstrom of Prentice-Hall,
   an idea-provoking friend and editor, who occasionally
   prodded during our delightful discussions.

To Len Krauss, a friend and fellow author,
   who remained thoroughly and encouragingly convinced
   of the value of this book.

To the many people at various companies
   who enthusiastically contributed information and ideas.

And finally to our two Siamese cats who, while frantically
   running from our German Shepherd, scattered reference
   material and drafts, unknowingly providing badly
   needed random rest periods.

CONTENTS

REFERENCE AIDS

II DATA CENTER PROCESSING 167

III DATA CENTER PERFORMANCE 301

SELECTED CHECKLISTS

SELECTED TABLES

SELECTED DIAGRAMS

SELECTED FORMS

SELECTED REPORTS

DATA CENTER PERFORMANCE EVALUATION

MEETING THE AUTHOR

Howard Schaeffer, of Howard Schaeffer Associates, Inc., is a consultant for data processing installations. He is a former data center manager, director of data processing, systems designer, and data processing instructor. These varied responsibilities have provided him with empathy for the goals and concerns of data center and user managers and staff.

Working for insurance, manufacturing, medical, educational, and other types of organizations, he has developed and enhanced, as well as corrected, many systems and procedures. His writing experience includes preparing material for Prentice-Hall, Auerbach Publishers, the American Management Association, and others.

Howard is an active member and participant in such organizations as the Data Processing Management Association and the Association for Computing Machinery. Through these organizations and visits to the installations of clients and friends he maintains close contact with the current thoughts, attitudes, and practices in the data processing field.

A FEW WORDS FROM THE AUTHOR

This book results from the author's experiences, the experiences of managers in many data centers, and a wide range of literature. Although this exposure resulted in a comprehensive book, it is certain that useful ideas have been implemented in data centers not visited by the author. One conclusion becomes quickly apparent to anyone visiting data centers: there are innovative, thoughtful individuals in these data centers who have developed ideas of interest to persons in other data centers.

So—to increase the usefulness of future editions of this book, the author would be delighted to receive from readers information on any techniques, aids, recommendations, guidelines, forms, or reports that other readers may want to consider for adoption. Please forward this material to the author in care of Prentice-Hall, Inc., Englewood Cliffs, New Jersey 07632.

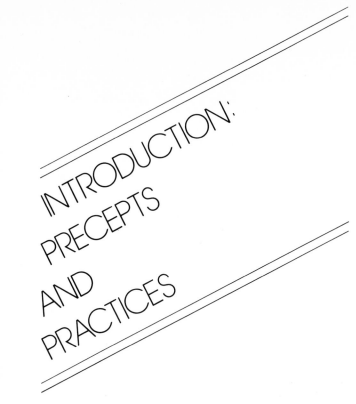

INTRODUCTION:
PRECEPTS
AND
PRACTICES

Although *Data Center Operations* is directly addressed to the data center manager, it is also intended for data center staff personnel and for those who intend to work in a data center. Each reader can expect to obtain from this book:

1. a framework and a perspective for all data center activities;
2. clarification of data center objectives, functions, concepts, and techniques;
3. guidelines and checklists for experienced personnel, as well as for those new to data center activities;
4. tutorial for those approaching aspects of the data center for the first time, or to the depth presented;
5. typical forms and reports used in data centers, which can be adapted to the needs of a specific data center;
6. awareness of the pitfalls and the opportunities present in the various data center activities; and ultimately
7. a guide to help:

- establish standards and procedures
- utilize resources effectively and efficiently
- minimize data center costs
- develop and maintain rapport with users

- coordinate user and data center activities
- control data center activities and performance and
- plan for improvements and for future needs

From this list, it is apparent that this book must cover a considerable number of topics. To provide a comprehensive treatment of data center functions and activities, it is necessary to include such topics as organization structure for effectiveness, managerial rapport with staff, personnel administration, financial control, site security and safety, hardware and software acquisition, documentation of standards and procedures, workflow and scheduling, data communications reliability and security, and performance evaluation of computer processing and data center activities in general. Truly, as intended, this book should be a helpful companion and guide for confident management and staff actions.

Most data center personnel have had no opportunity to become acquainted with many of the topics discussed. They understandably will be hesitant to perform the new techniques introduced without adequate guidelines. This applies also to the very experienced personnel in the data center.

They may be aware of the topics discussed, but have not had the opportunity or time to obtain any depth of knowledge; in fact, they may not even realize the benefits (as well as the difficulties) associated with the various techniques. The explanations in this book should remedy these situations to a large degree and should stimulate confidence.

Some managers may be hasty in rejecting recommended techniques because of poor prior experiences. For example, one recommendation made several times throughout this book is a plea for establishing a data center steering committee. In face-to-face conversations with data center managers, this recommendation has initiated grunts, suspicious side glances, clenched jaws, or other more subtle signs of disagreement. In many instances, their reactions were justifiable. These managers had had bad experiences with committees. However, in most cases, if not all, the problem was not with having committees to coordinate activities, but with how the committees were established and how the committee meetings were conducted. Some of the most common problems were poor selection of members for cooperative effort, poor choice of a chairperson to provide definite leadership without being overly aggressive, and poor or no guidelines for conducting and controlling meetings. In any case, recommendations such as this have been applied and have been effective in some data centers; therefore, they should not be casually rejected.

This brings us to the main point of this introduction. To be of value to a data center, it is not enough to intellectually agree with the worth of what is presented: to be of value, *precepts must be put into practice*. Precepts not put into practice are as useful as a road map locked in the glove compartment of a car.

Putting precepts into practice, however, is more easily said than done. For example, several reviewers of this book enthusiastically agreed with various recommendations—but then continued to manage their data centers as in the past. Their intentions were admirable, but they were too involved in daily operational activities and problems to consider new programs and long-term benefits. As a result, several techniques that they agreed

were desirable were postponed. The techniques often neglected include management by objectives, personnel career paths, zero-base budgeting, charge-out of data center expenses, functional and financial analysis of hardware alternatives for acquisition, and the means for evaluating computer and data center performance.

Thus, a manager's attention must focus on both being aware of precepts and finding the time to put these precepts into practice. A few ideas may be helpful at this time on how others have obtained some control of how they utilize their time. An excellent technique for controlling time utilization is to set aside 1½-hour time periods, possibly as many as four a day, but at least one a day. (This may sound more like prescribing a vitamin, and in fact, it may have the effect of bringing new vitality to the data center.) Each time period is allocated for a specific purpose and is not to be interrupted except for a real emergency. Any noncritical telephone calls and other distracting interruptions should be attended to after each time period. Thus, for example, a half-hour can be set aside following each time period for the purpose of attending to these matters, instead of permitting them to dominate the day's activities.

Another technique used by most data center managers, as well as most people who seek to avoid being overwhelmed by many activities, is the preparation of "To Do" lists. The lists that are usually prepared, however, are not as useful as they could be, because they tend to be merely lists of reminders. These lists can be made more useful by indicating priorities, that is, by indicating which activities must be done before all others, and which may be left uncompleted. But another problem arises. Often, the urgent but unimportant activities receive immediate attention, while the truly important, but less urgent, activities tend to be ignored. Thus, the activities that would provide significant long-term benefits are allowed to slip from day to day, from year to year. Urgent activities cannot be ignored, but they must be put into perspective with the truly important activities that can provide greater overall benefits. The form shown in this introduction suggests a rather formal means for assigning a higher priority to important activities than to urgent activities. If nothing else, this distinction will make managers conscious of the important activities pushed aside because of less-important but urgent activities; this awareness may encourage the delegating of distracting activities to others.

An attitude that helps to limit the number of activities that receive priority attention, reducing hectic activity and at the same time increasing the benefits received, is represented by what is called the "20/80 rule." This rule states that 20 percent of the activities provide approximately 80 percent of the benefits. Thus, if there are 10 activities on a list, it is likely that 2 of these activities will provide 80 percent of the benefits anticipated for all 10 activities. This rule may appear arbitrary, but it is uncanny how accurate it is as a general guide. For example, 20 percent of the computer programs provide about 80 percent of the problems, 20 percent of the systems provide about 80 per-cent of the benefits to the company, and 20 percent of the personnel account for about 80 percent of the productivity, or the problems, or the latenesses, or the absenteeism. Therefore, in the case of time management, the goal is to locate those 20 percent of the activities that provide the most benefits, and to postpone (if not totally avoid) the remaining 80 percent of the activities that consume considerable amounts of time but provide little in return. (Observe that the "To Do" list illustrated includes this suggestion.) The desirable small group of activities are often referred to as the "vital few," and the large group of less-beneficial activities are often referred to as the "trivial many."

Superior performance for managers and staff becomes possible when they know what should be done and how, but it becomes a reality only when time is allocated to take action and then action is taken—to be effective, *precepts must be put into practice.*

To-Do List		Date	

1. List all activities.

2. Enter two asterisks (**) for each important activity, but for no more than 20% of the listed activities.

3. Enter an asterisk (*) for each urgent activity.

Note: The resulting priority categories are:

  *** Important and urgent

  ** Important

  * Urgent

Priority	Activity	Comment

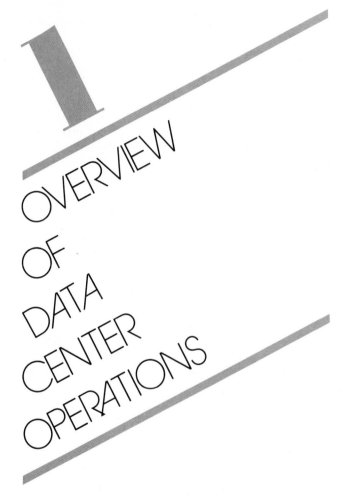

1

OVERVIEW
OF
DATA
CENTER
OPERATIONS

GOAL

To obtain a balanced perspective of data center operations.

HIGHLIGHTS

The Overall Control Cycle

Data center activities can be segmented into three general functions associated with classical control cycles:

- Resource Planning
- Daily Processing
- Performance Evaluation

Frequently Occurring Themes

Despite the individualistic nature of each aspect of data center operations, several themes occur frequently; these themes include:

- Control and Breakthrough
- Effectiveness versus Efficiency
- People Orientation
- Hierarchical Structure
- Checklist Guidelines

- Need for Policies, Standards, and Procedures
- Communication Aids
- Analytic Aids
- Data Center Steering Committee
- Use of Software Packages

A journey starts by first surveying the terrain. The resulting perspective permits locating landmarks and relating details to these landmarks. If this perspective is not obtained, one or more interesting aspects of data center operations may receive immediate attention, postponing for later consideration aspects that receive attention only after they create critical disturbances. It is natural and too easy to attend to aspects of personal interest and not to aspects that should receive priority attention for a particular data center.

For example, a data center manager may be particularly sensitive to access security and thus may immediately proceed to the chapter including this topic. This may be done although the present security measures are excellent and other topics have received little or no attention. Typical topics that often receive inadequate attention are personnel career paths, data center job scheduling, and data center performance evaluation. Therefore, the first step is to obtain a perspective of the topics discussed, and then to decide on the topics requiring priority attention.

The immediacy of daily activities and problems tends to provide a distorted view of data center operations. More is involved than daily activities. Data center operations consist of more than scheduling jobs, operating equipment, and controlling the flow of work. As the overview will show, this perspective ignores most of the planning and performance-evaluation activities. Casual putting aside of planning and performance-evaluation activities can easily occur because they almost always are less urgent than daily activities. At the same time, daily activities cannot be put aside for less urgent, long-range planning and performance-evaluation activities. None of these activities should be ignored; a balance of how much attention each type of activity should receive must be established.

Thus, the first part of this overview will examine the planning, processing, and performance-evaluation aspects of data center operations. The remainder of this overview will introduce several themes that occur frequently. These themes may be techniques such as the use of software packages, or attitudes such as people orientation.

THE OVERALL CONTROL CYCLE

A control cycle (such as used for manufacturing-process control) as explained in classical control methodology consists of three types of activities. The first activity type is planning for the activities to occur and setting standards to evaluate the results obtained. A non-DP manufacturing process will illustrate this and the other two activity types. Planning the manufacture of coffee requires establishing the means for mixing types of coffee beans and placing the mixture in containers, the means for measuring the accuracy of these actions, and the setting of standards for allowable deviations. The second activity type is actually performing the actions planned and at the same time monitoring these actions. Several questions arise. If, for example, considering the stringent requirements of manufacturing-process control, it has been decided to have at least 75 percent Colombian coffee in the mixture, but no more than 78 percent, is this what is actually occurring? As for filling the containers, has the quantity marked on the container been actually added, at least to meet legal requirements, and without adding an excessive amount that would be costly and possibly even cause physical problems in closing the container? Thus, the third and final activity type is using the information obtained from the monitored activities to evaluate performance. If variations are excessive, rejects occur and adjustments must be made to lessen future rejects.

This is the cycle of control activities, repeated constantly. It proceeds from planning and doing to

ILLUSTRATION 1-1. Data Center Control Cycle.

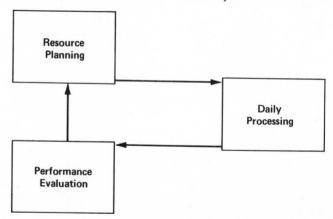

evaluating and adjusting. In terms of data center activities, as shown in Illustration 1–1, the overall cycle is that of planning for utilization of resources, then daily processing of the workload, and finally evaluating performance. All aspects of the data center are located in one of these three general categories.

Resource Planning

The primary focus of Chapters 2 through 6 is on resource planning. It is only natural to assemble the best resources available for the data center's purposes before processing the daily workload and evaluating and optimizing performance. It would be self-defeating to have a sophisticated scheduling system but not the management direction or the personnel and software to support this system. It is also obviously necessary to consider the requirements of the hardware and the limitations and potential of the site. It would be just as capricious to ignore the financial constraints that are always present, and also the operating considerations that should not be ignored. For example, a financial constraint is that no money has been allocated for scheduling software and for the personnel needed to support it. An operating consideration that should not be ignored is that, no matter how impressive a scheduling software package may be, it may not be appropriate for a particular installation. This is true, for example, for a data center that is almost entirely dependent on unscheduled job requests. But even these environments may be able to benefit from scheduling software.

Resource planning can be complex. Many resources are involved and many alternatives exist. At this point, a brief introduction to the resources discussed in Chapters 2 through 6 should be helpful.

Organization Structure. It is inevitable that organizations are structured in a hierarchical manner. In spite of grumblings from some experts (and near experts) on organization structure, it is likely to remain the best means for directing and coordinating activities, as well as for monitoring and evaluating performance. There are several useful principles that have served managers well in the past and are still effective. Organization structure is, in effect, an invisible resource, one

that can be taken lightly because it is not a solid, concrete resource. An important question concerning organization structure, one that is basic and must be answered, is: Would centralization or decentralization be more effective? Many organizations combine both for great effectiveness. This is the basis of the distributed-data-processing philosophy, where data-processing activity is decentralized by function or location and where summary and exception data are transmitted to a single location for centralized management control and planning.

Management. It has been the sad experience of many technically oriented persons to be promoted to management positions, with few guidelines as to how to proceed and how to improve personal performance. Many management experts have given this situation considerable thought. The result has been numerous recommendations and guidelines, many of which have been culled for this book. It is not, however, only newcomers to management responsibilities that will find these guidelines useful. Competent, experienced managers, who have demonstrated their abilities and strengths, will also find these guidelines useful. They may be doing many things right, but it is easy to fall into accustomed ways and not to be aware of policies and procedures that would improve their effectiveness even more. Strong-minded managers, for example, tend to get the work done and to get it done well, but they also tend to ignore the thoughts and morale of personnel. In contrast, democratically oriented managers may have strong empathy for the needs and feelings of others, but may not provide the direction and motivation required.

Personnel. An excellent data center, with all the standards and procedures thoroughly documented, can become a confused, error-ridden site when staffed with poorly selected, poorly trained, poorly motivated personnel. The recruiting process is almost always done in an atmosphere of intuitive judgment, depending on the philosophy and preferences of the interviewer. There are more objective means. Nearly all data centers exist without any job descriptions or clear-cut, documented career paths. Those installations with job descriptions often have to ignore them because they are out of date and thus of only little value. It is just as common for minimum thought to be given to personnel motivation, to using such techniques as job enrichment, where each person when possible is given a wider range of activities. Another important aspect of personnel management is personnel appraisal. This should be done not solely to put people in line and to criticize them, showing them that management is aware of their shortcomings. Instead, periodic personnel appraisals provide opportunities to resolve or at least to lessen an individual's problems, to seek means of helping each person to reach his or her career goals, and to increase each person's efforts to satisfying the data center's goals.

Finances. It is impossible to bypass the budgeting requirements of an organization. More and more organizations are considering, rightfully so, the possibilities of zero-base budgeting. The pros and cons for this approach are examined. Many organizations have considered chargeout or charge-back systems, some enthusiastically implementing one of these systems and others avoiding them like a plague. The pros and cons of these systems are also examined. Zero-base budgeting and charge-back are fascinating in concept and intriguing in technique, but each installation must determine if the time and cost overhead justifies the benefits anticipated. An area that often receives little attention is financial analysis. Only too often the on-going costs of operations are monitored and accepted without considering trends and examining alternatives that will result in less-expensive future operations. Two of the most significant trends are the lowering of equipment costs and the concurrent rise of personnel costs. Observation of these trends strongly suggests that increasing staff size and dependency on a large staff should be done with alert concern, not with casual acceptance. Financial analysis also includes such considerations as the efficiency and appropriateness of current applications. Many applications, in fact, may be of marginal value and may continue in existence because no one has taken the initiative to terminate them. And many of the worthwhile applications are likely to be inefficient. They may be using the wrong means for processing, such as an on-line system when batch processing is adequate, or printing 15 pounds of paper when five or six sheets of summary information is all that is really needed.

Many organizations are replacing paper output, for example, with microfiche. The finances of a data center are resources that concern managers, but they are usually given less attention than they should receive.

Site. A site is associated with a large array of resources that must be considered when selecting a site for a data center, when preparing a site, and when relocating a data center from one site to another. Site preparation, for example, includes the technical considerations of such aspects as layout, power supply, and safety precautions. When the many preventative and detection means advisable for security are also considered, it becomes apparent that site preparation presents many challenges. These challenges increase as the need for contingency plans (with the consideration of backup equipment) and the need for future expansion are examined.

Hardware. The main concern in the selection of hardware is adequate and thorough analysis of alternatives. Many installations have become one-vendor shops. This occurs because of concern about compatibility of components. But with the current existence of compatible components, it is definitely unnecessarily wasteful to ignore cost-reduction alternatives. Some organizations have sophisticated and sound methods for comparing alternatives. These should be considered for adoption. It is also necessary to evaluate the financial alternative for acquiring hardware. Depending on an organization's acquisition policy, primarily that of how often hardware is updated, one method of financing is likely to become predominant. But analysis is necessary. It is also necessary to be aware of the contract provisions that a vendor may casually include and may become troublesome, and those that will be beneficial and a vendor may willingly include. The entire hardware-acquisition process requires a reasonable, well-defined procedure that includes activities such as verifying hardware-performance promises by using benchmarks and judging vendor service by questioning current users.

Software. The basic process for acquiring hardware applies to software acquisition. One point, however, requires special mention. It is all too common for the data center to process a wide variety of sophisticated user applications while almost totally disregarding its own needs. This is seen in the absence of scheduling systems, especially one for all data center activities. Other software often missing include an adequate, trouble-free tape library system and the many performance evaluation packages available. Then there is the peculiar attitude that an installation with minimal knowledge of the intricacies required to develop these packages insists on developing them in-house and surprisingly expects the resulting packages to perform with greater effectiveness than those developed by experts in the various fields. This is a startling attitude and, for those trying to live with the results, a source of daily frustrations. Some of these in-house systems are excellent, but many more are barely functional. Software is an important data center resource that definitely requires considerable attention, with serious second thoughts given to developing them in-house at high expense, especially when software of proven quality is available at lower costs, usually much lower costs.

Daily Processing

Whereas Chapters 2 through 6 focus on resource planning, Chapters 7 through 10 focus on daily processing. In other words, these chapters focus on the actual processing of the data center's workload. The emphasis here is on the techniques and procedures for completing jobs quickly and reliably.

Standards and Procedures. A clear distinction is made between the words "policy," "standards," and "procedures." A policy provides a general guideline for establishing standards; a standard provides the criteria for evaluating performance; and procedures are the sequential activities used to satisfy standards. The absence or deficiencies of standards and procedures account for much of the hectic confusion and embarrassing mistakes occurring in a data center. Even if serious problems do not result, which is unlikely, the absence of adequate standards and procedures inevitably results in inefficient processing. This has the end result of requiring more people and equipment than would otherwise be needed and thus increases the cost of operating the data center.

Documentation. What use are excellently defined standards and procedures if they are not documented? It is a standard (to use the word facetiously) in many data centers not to document standards and procedures. However, by necessity, operating instructions for application systems are documented. But even these are often incomplete and are not updated when changes are made to systems that affect their operation. The situation is even worse when the less-frequent emergency incidents occur. A fire, for example, can create havoc. Even if a contingency plan exists, if it is poorly documented, the staff members may not know what to do, and, as a result, will be dependent on guidance from others. This situation becomes particularly critical if experienced personnel, such as the people who developed the undocumented contingency plan, are not available to guide and the recently hired, inexperienced personnel must act—right or wrong. The documentation needs for the data center must be defined, taken seriously, and criteria must be established for judging documentation.

Workflow and Job Control. For batch processing, a definite sequence for the progress of jobs through the data center is necessary. Not only must this sequence be clearly established, but also controls must exist to avoid misplacing jobs and to report on their status. The arrangement of work areas should match the workflow pattern to avoid inefficiencies and unnecessary traffic and confusion. To answer inquiries about the location and status of jobs, control logs can be located at the various work stations, with a master control log at one location, which is usually in the job and data reception area. Some organizations have an on-line job-control system, and thus they can respond to inquiries about a job's status from a specially equipped control area, possibly a separate room for that purpose.

Computer and Data Center Scheduling and Resource Allocation. In some environments it may be acceptable to pass on the responsibility for scheduling jobs to the operator. A preferred approach is to assign a nonoperator to scheduling jobs, someone who has the time to consider deadlines and priorities. But, except for installations consisting mostly of unscheduled jobs, this is not satisfactory. Scheduling assistance is provided to a minor degree by operating system schedulers, and to a greater degree by separate computer-scheduling software; but the greater challenge of scheduling the data center activities is often forgotten. It is difficult to meet deadline commitments and to attend to job priorities without considering the processing requirements and the time consumption of the precomputer and postcomputer processing activities. Thus, all data center job-processing activities should be scheduled to meet user commitments.

Data Communications. Some data center activities do not apply to data communications, where data are transferred by means of telecommunication links, but the remaining and the additional activities can create more severe problems. It is not required to consider workflow and to a large extent scheduling considerations, but it is much more difficult to assure processing availability, data protection, and data security. Thus, the need for constant monitoring and control of processing becomes more significant than for batch off-line processing. Preliminary to controlling data communications

processing, it is necessary to clear away such underbrush as the confusion between the terms used, such as "data communications," "on-line batch processing," "in-line processing," and "real-time processing." Then it is necessary to obtain a reasonable understanding of the hardware and software components involved. With a precise understanding of the basics of data communications and the establishment of adequate controls, it is possible to provide reliable service and to minimize excessive downtime.

Performance Evaluation

The last two chapters, Chapters 11 and 12, are devoted to performance evaluation. Chapter 11 focuses on monitoring and evaluating computer performance and also examines the overall computer performance evaluation (CPE) process and the means for obtaining approval for a CPE program. Chapter 12 examines the monitoring and evaluating of the overall data center performance. Thus, it includes examination of all data center resources, and it also examines the effects data center activities have on data center costs and

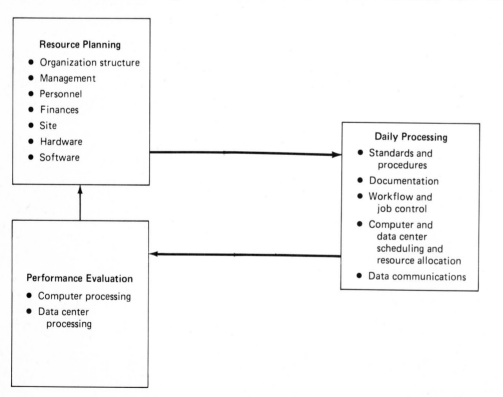

ILLUSTRATION 1-2. Topics in the Data Center.

Resource Planning
- Organization structure
- Management
- Personnel
- Finances
- Site
- Hardware
- Software

Daily Processing
- Standards and procedures
- Documentation
- Workflow and job control
- Computer and data center scheduling and resource allocation
- Data communications

Performance Evaluation
- Computer processing
- Data center processing

user service. For both computer and data center performance evaluation, the performance criteria are segmented into categories of sufficiency, efficiency, and effectiveness. Sufficiency is primarily concerned with the adequacy of capacities for the workloads; efficiency examines how resources are utilized; effectiveness examines the data center's costs and the services provided.

Computer Processing. Evaluation is limited to the adequacy of computer resources for the workload, how efficiently these resources are used, and how effectively the work is completed. Sufficiency is not limited to only present demands, but also anticipates future demands. Resource utilization considers all computer-related resources, such as real memory, disk storage, and tape units. Effectiveness, in contrast to efficiency, is concerned not with how resources are used, but with the effects of resource use, considering such criteria as turnaround and throughput. Software packages are available for monitoring and evaluating computer performance, particularly for analyzing resource utilization. These packages can specify the degree of peripheral usage, disk arm movement, paging activity, and channel usage. Furthermore, significant application-processing improvements are possible from packages that analyze program activity so that the frequently executed instructions can be isolated and optimized.

Data Center Processing. Attending to computer sufficiency, efficiency, and effectiveness does not guarantee data center sufficiency, efficiency, and effectiveness. Although computer processing may be satisfactory, inadequacies in precomputer or postcomputer processing areas can negate all benefits gained. Unfortunately, few data centers evaluate overall data center performance. It is a common occurrence for delays in the data-entry area to delay the processing of jobs, and for delays in the decollating and bursting areas to delay delivery of output. The problem can be insufficient resources, poor utilization of resources, or indifference to the relative importance of jobs, processing jobs on a first-come, first-served basis instead of according to their importance.

Illustration 1–2 shows the preceding data center topics as they occur in each of the three segments of the data center control cycle.

FREQUENTLY OCCURRING THEMES

Several themes occur frequently in the various aspects of data center operations. These themes can also be thought of as techniques, recommendations, or simply as ways of thinking. Checklists, for example, are provided, and their use is a theme occurring throughout this book. They can be considered as techniques since they guide actions and make actions more effective and efficient. (Effectiveness versus efficiency is another theme that occurs frequently.) Checklists are definitely recommendations; they can also be considered as ways of thinking, since they dictate what factors are attended to and how.

These themes can act as threads that tie together the various activities in the data center. Checklists, for example, tie together a series of ideas and actions into single entities. The same is true for the other themes, although in some cases they are much more subtle. The theme of effectiveness versus efficiency, for example, is abstract but extremely important. In all actions in the data center, as well as in an individual's personal life, before attempts are made to act efficiently, to do something in the right manner, one should decide to act effectively, to choose the best thing to do. From these two themes alone, it becomes apparent how awareness and application of themes can be beneficial to data center operations. The major themes are now summarized.

Control Cycles

The concept of control cycles has already been introduced, in terms of the overall activities in the data center. But control cycles occur also within most of these activities. Illustration 1–3 shows that for each of the three overall data center segments of the control cycle, there is at least one control cycle contained within it. The resource-planning segment includes the cycle for planning a budget, implementing it, and evaluating deviations. The daily-processing segment includes the planning needed to establish standards and procedures, and then to implement and evaluate these plans. The performance-evaluation segment includes planning to establish a CPE program, the actual implementa-

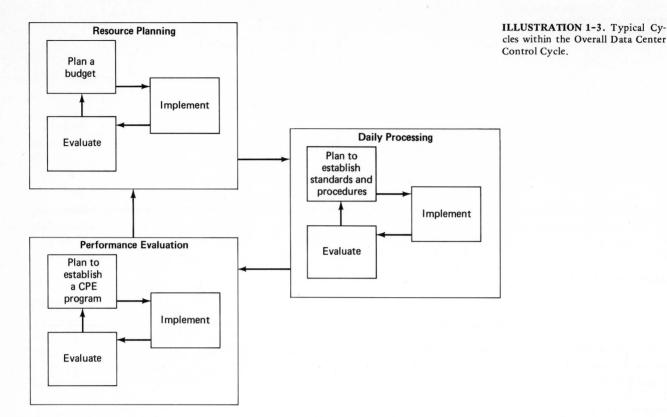

tion of this plan, and finally its evaluation, which can lead to improvements and enhancements. Many other control cycles exist, such as for personnel performance, for benchmarking hardware, for job control, and for the CPE (computer performance evaluation) and DCPE (Data Center Performance Evaluation) processes themselves.

Control and Breakthrough

Control is, or at least should be, only half of the concern of data center personnel. It is fine to control performances so that standards are met, but once these standards are met, what then? It definitely is not appropriate to relax and enjoy the fruits of the effort to maintain the status quo. It is also each person's responsibility to set higher levels of performance standards and to strive to reach these new levels. Once these new levels are attained, performance is controlled to assure a stable

environment—and when that is attained, sights are set to break through to even higher levels of performance. This results in a dynamic environment. Illustration 1-4 indicates how the control and breakthrough phases for performance-level settings and performance-level attainments should alternate. This pattern applies to many aspects of data center performance, such as to personnel productivity, to reduction of job reruns, and to increased job throughput. In fact, all CPE and DCPE criteria can be viewed in terms of this alternating pattern.

Effectiveness Versus Efficiency

These two terms are often confused, and yet clear distinction between them is extremely important. Simply, as already stated, effectiveness involves choosing what should be done, what is really important; efficiency involves doing whatever was chosen in the least wasteful and in the quickest

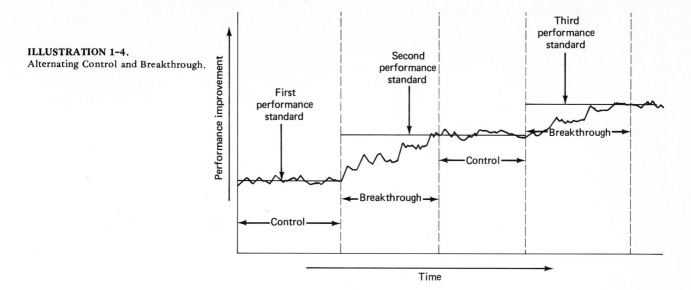

ILLUSTRATION 1–4.
Alternating Control and Breakthrough.

ILLUSTRATION 1–5. The Hierarchical Structure of This Book.

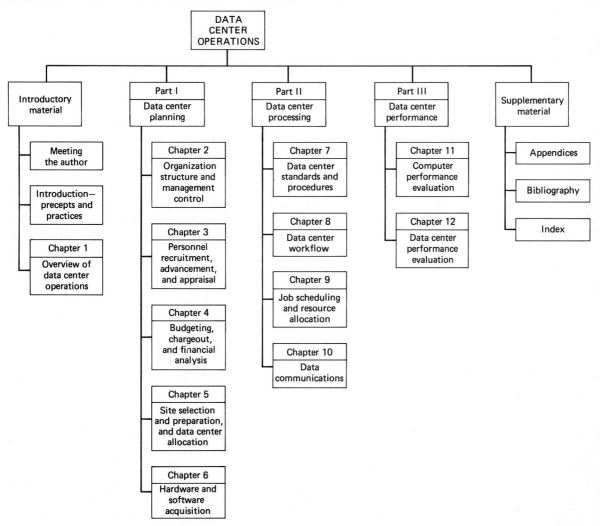

manner. An activity can be done very efficiently, but if it is done while more important activities are ignored, effectiveness is reduced. In contrast, the most important activity may be chosen, which means being effective, but it may be done in a manner that wastes time and resources and is thus being done inefficiently. Data center personnel are continually encountering these situations. Consider the application jobs received in the data center. If processed in an efficient, quick manner in the sequence that they arrive, it is inevitable that this processing will be ineffective. Important jobs would be forced to wait while many trivial jobs are processed, even though these trivial jobs could be delayed a day, a week, or possibly longer.

People Orientation

Rapport between individuals avoids much of the interpersonal conflicts that can arise and thus stimulates a more comfortable, pleasant environment. Improved rapport must be continually encouraged between data center managers and staff, and between data center personnel and users. Rapport between data center managers and staff consists of such actions as consideration of staff career paths and training requirements, of staff motivation through means such as job enrichment, of staff participation in planning and control activities, and of staff goal-setting and performance appraisals. Data center personnel and user rapport results from such means as periodic meetings to learn of one another's problems, which permits working together in seeking solutions. However, this rapport can be obtained only when the concern of the user and data center personnel is sincere. This notion, at first, seems idealistic. But actually enlightened self-interest makes it practical. When rapport and cooperation improve, so does data center performance and service.

Hierarchical Structure

The most familiar hierarchical structure is that for an organization. This book, in fact, has a hierarchical structure. Putting aside the introductory and supplementary material, the remainder of the book is separated into three sections, one for each of the three segments of the data center's overall control cycle. Within each of these sections are chapters, and within these chapters are sections, subsections, and sometimes sub-subsections. This is shown down to the chapter level in Illustration 1–5. In a data center there are many other hierarchies than that for organization structure. There are, for example, hierarchies for career paths and for data center objectives, and there are hierarchies for policies, standards, and procedures. Consider the last hierarchy. For a single general policy, there may be several specific standards, and for each of these standards there are one or more procedures. Thus, a clear and important hierarchy results.

Checklist Guidelines

Most installations have several checklists to guide activities. The availability of these checklists minimizes the likelihood of forgotten actions, that is, if the checklists are referred to. A familiar checklist is the one for releasing a job to production. But many more checklists should be present. This book contains a wide variety of these checklists. There are checklists for evaluating management techniques, for selecting a data center site, and for evaluating an acquisition contract. The absence of checklists in a data center has led to serious and costly mistakes. It is only necessary to forget, or not be aware of, one factor to incur a disastrous situation. Just permitting the unquestioned presence of a significant clause in a contract, for example, can result in having unwanted hardware; this is especially regrettable because many of these clauses are negotiable.

Need For Policies, Standards, and Procedures

Policies, standards, and procedures guide actions. Policies guide decision-making; they consist of general statements of expectations that permit the establishment of compatible standards. Standards are specific performance expectations that guide the definition of procedures to attain the standards, and permit evaluation and control of performance. Procedures should unambiguously direct the actions to be performed to meet the previously established standards and policies. Without these action guidelines, individuals are on their own, doing what they recall as being correct or as commonly accepted, or simply doing whatever seems acceptable at the moment. At one installation of fortunately competent tape librarians, procedures were sketchily defined; as a result, the librarians did some of the activities differently. These librarians were competent, but still they were fortunate that the procedural differences did not seriously conflict and create problems. In many other installations, the absence of adequate procedures results in persons sometimes repeating work done by others, sometimes not doing certain tasks at all, and sometimes having to redo tasks done incorrectly or not done according to the majority opinion.

Communications Aids

The most obvious communication aid is that of documentation. The previously stressed policies, standards, and procedures must be documented; and so must application operating instructions. It is also necessary that documentation be kept up-to-date. The other communication aids stressed throughout this book are reports, forms, and user communication. The importance of reports and forms is stressed, but at the same time the avoidance of unnecessary reports and forms is also stressed. A large number of typical reports and forms occur throughout this book. As for user communication aids, the primary means presented are a "help desk" to provide operational assistance to users, a data center newsletter to inform users of changes and of comparisons between actual and anticipated performance, and a data center steering committee to coordinate user and data center activities, to resolve existing problems, and to anticipate and avoid upcoming problems.

All these user communication aids have proved useful. The greatest difficulty, however, has been in establishing a successful steering committee. These have suffered from all the diseases common to committees, such as weak leadership contrasted

with strong, opposing participants. Many of these committees have suffered from a bad case of anemia, an overall weakness and inability to accomplish anything. This is not a criticism of having a data center steering committee, but it is a criticism of poorly established committees.

Analytic Aids

These aids include such techniques as break-even analysis and weighted-value analysis. Break-even analysis occurs in such diverse instances as determining (1) when increased expenses for security do not justify the protection provided; (2) when hardware purchase instead of leasing or rental is the preferred hardware acquisition method; (3) when resource utilization can be increased to obtain minimum cost per unit of resource utilization without seriously degrading user service. Weighted-value analysis is used for selecting from hardware alternatives and for selecting the security and safety threats that should be tolerated and those that must be minimized. These and other analytic aids are extremely valuable for carefully reasoned decision-making, permitting confidence in the resulting decisions and permitting justification for these decisions if they are questioned.

Data Center Steering Committee

This was already mentioned as a communication aid. Its importance, its absence from most data centers, and its frequent recommendation in this book justify highlighting this theme. A committee of user and data center personnel provides an opportunity for constructive, cooperative discussions. It permits resolution of scheduling difficulties, the transferring of jobs to level demands on resources, and the analysis of other operational problems. Data center personnel become aware of upcoming demands on resources, and users become aware of the services and the limitations existing in the data center. It is possible to replace subjective opinions with objective knowledge and to replace emotional outbursts with calm insight. Just the existence of this committee is enough to convince all but the most belligerent users that the data center personnel are concerned about the user's welfare.

Use of Software Packages

It is surprising that many data center managers heartily agree on the importance of the services that computers provide users, but inadequately utilize the available computer power for their own benefit. A wide variety of software packages are available. They include packages for scheduling, for charging back to users data center expenses, for reporting budgeting deviations, for showing career paths and career-path inadequacies, for controlling jobs and reporting on their status, and for monitoring and evaluating computer performance. In many cases, the personnel time and the resource wastefulness that can be reduced are enough to justify many of these packages. Their use is even more impressive when the qualitative benefits are considered, such as higher data center morale and improved user image of the data center.

part one

DATA CENTER PLANNING

2
ORGANIZATION STRUCTURE AND MANAGEMENT CONTROL

GOAL

To attain user and data center objectives through management control within an effectively structured organization.

HIGHLIGHTS

Organization Characteristics

The improvement of an organization is more likely when the five characteristics of traditional organization structure are understood.

Structuring Guidelines

These guidelines support the evaluation of the existing organization structure, attend to the centralization-versus-decentralization issue, and assist in organization restructuring.

Management Guidelines

The many success and problem indicators listed permit judging the adequacy of management actions, guiding the elimination of deficiencies, and encouraging increased effectiveness.

Management Control

Three means are available for controlling data center activities and developing rapport with users, and these are adequate management reporting, establishment of a *data center steering committee*, and the preparation of *a user/data center handbook.*

Organization structure and management activities directly affect the attainment of data center objectives. From user service objectives (such as meeting deadlines) to data center objectives (such as efficient use of resources), the organization structure establishes paths for communicating objectives and monitoring actual performance. An adequate structure minimizes unassigned responsibilities and hazy or duplicate assignments of responsibilities. Too often, for example, data center security is stated as a major objective, but no one is assigned to periodically monitor adherence to security standards and procedures and to recommend improvements. This crucial objective often receives on-request attention only when a serious deficiency becomes obvious, usually as a result of criticism from outside auditors. Duplicate assignments of responsibility occur most frequently when staff members are supervised by more than one person, resulting in conflicting orders and lack of managerial awareness of each staff member's total activities.

Management activities are even more crucial than organization structure in meeting data center objectives. Managers following good practices can obtain results in spite of organizational deficiencies. Good management practices promote a stimulating progressive environment and avoid its opposite, a bored conformist environment. Whereas a conformist environment focuses on means (adherence to the activities expected to be performed), a progressive environment focuses on ends (attainment of data center objectives through modification of expected activities). Thus, instead of a data-entry supervisor merely reporting production counts, the causes for poor performance can be reported, with recommendations for improvement, stimulating an alert, goal-oriented environment.

Since the basis for discussing organization structure and management guidelines is an understanding of organizations, organization characteristics are examined first; the first characteristic stresses the significance of defining data center objectives. With this background information, the recommendations contained in the structuring and management guidelines can be evaluated and, where applicable, adopted. Although managers may adhere to all relevant recommendations, they cannot be certain that data center objectives are being met unless management control exists. Management control is the concluding topic in this chapter.

ORGANIZATION CHARACTERISTICS

"Organizations are blueprints for human activities," states Edgar H. Schein in his book *Organizational Psychology*.[1] Both a blueprint and an organization structure specify what elements are included and how they are related. If a blueprint for a bridge, for example, is adequate, and if the engineers adhere to it, everything fits and functions as intended. The same is true for an organization. If the organization structure is adequate, and if management adheres to it, all elements of the organization are more likely to operate together smoothly and efficiently to obtain preestablished objectives. Accepting the importance of organization structure, the first question to be answered is, What characteristics affect the adequacy of an organization's structure?

Traditional Organization Structure

The characteristics of organization structure have been stated in various ways in management literature. Those characteristics most frequently identified are referred to as the traditional organization structure. Several attempts have been made by writers on organization structure to deny the effectiveness of traditional organization structure, with little success. These attempts center on the consideration of the psychological factors in an organization; these factors usually fit comfortably within the concepts and practice of the traditional organization structure to be considered. These factors involve the informal structure that exists in an organization for some of its communications, coordination, and decision-making. For those wishing to delve more deeply into the pros and cons of traditional organization structure and its alternatives, one of the worthwhile books that should be of interest is *Organization Theory: A*

[1] Edgar H. Schein, *Organizational Psychology* (Englewood Cliffs, N.J.: Prentice-Hall, Inc., 1965), p. 10.

Structural and Behavioral Analysis by William G. Scott and Terence R. Mitchell.[2]

The characteristics of traditional organization structure are logical and develop naturally when the reason for a structure is examined. It is apparent that organization structure is developed to attain objectives, and to attain these objectives through the coordination of activities. This statement stresses two of its primary characteristics: the establishment of *objectives* and the *coordination* of activities. Now, the obvious questions are, What activities? How should these activities be related? The answer to both of these questions supplies the remaining two concepts of traditional organization structure. The third concept—which answers the question, What activities?—is referred to as division of labor or *specialization*. In most data centers, specialization exists according to functions, grouping activities into such functions as data preparation, file storage, and computer processing. In very large organizations, several data centers may exist, possibly one for the corporation and several for business units; within each of these data centers the structure is still likely to be by function. The fourth and last concept answers the question, How should these activities be related? The answer given is through a *hierarchy of authority and responsibility*. This concept accounts for the appearance of the customary organization chart with its various levels of management and division and delegation of responsibilities.

Although these concepts are discussed as stated, if authority and responsibility are considered as two separate characteristics, as they sometimes are, an acronym results that makes these characteristics easy to recall. The acronym is OSCAR,[3] which when expanded means:

> Objectives
> Specialization
> Coordination
> Authority
> Responsibility

See Illustration 2-1. Thus, the customary and reasonable way to view organization structure is that

[2]William G. Scott and Terrence R. Mitchell, *Organization Theory: A Structural and Behavioral Analysis* (Homewood, Illinois: Richard D. Irwin, Inc., 1976).

[3]Ernest Dale, *Management: Theory and Practice*, 2nd ed. (New York: McGraw-Hill, 1969).

Objectives	Objectives are defined to guide data center activities and to judge and control performance.
Specialization	Specialization concentrates similar functions in one area, avoiding duplication and unnecessary costs, encouraging the use of specialized skills for efficiency and effectiveness.
Coordination	Coordination of activities supports smooth processing, stimulating cooperation in resolving day-to-day problems and anticipating potential problems.
Authority	Authority is allocated for decision making and for acting on those decisions.
Responsibility	Responsibility is assigned for the performance of activities and for the reporting on those activities.

ILLUSTRATION 2-1. The Characteristics of Traditional Organization Structure: OSCAR is an acronym that makes it easy to recall the five characteristics of traditional, formal organization structure, but it does not indicate the informal structure that exists for communication, coordination, and decision making.

an organization attains its objectives through the coordination of specialized activities within a hierarchy of authority and responsibility.

Objectives to be Met

The first step in organization structuring—whether establishing a structure for the first time or evaluating an existing structure for modifications—is precisely stating the objectives to be met. If this is not done first, adequacy of specialization and coordination of activities, and adequacy of the hierarchy of authority and responsibility, cannot be reliably determined. If, for example, the objective, "At least 80 percent of available computer time will be used," is not stated, very likely no one will be assigned to monitor and report on computer time utilization. By stating this objective a void is automatically felt if the means to attain the objective do not exist; and the void receives attention. An unstated objective is an objective not likely to be attained, and instead of managing-by-objectives-and-accomplishments, the result is managing-by-chance-and-regrets. Objectives should be measurable, attainable, comprehensive, and relevant to data center needs.

Measurable and Attainable. The statement "At least 80 percent of available computer time will be used" suggests the advantages of a measurable statement of objective. An "objective" that is not measurable is frequently not an objective but a statement of function or responsibility. The statement "Use as much computer time available as possible" should not be considered a statement of objective, but a vague statement of function or responsibility. As stated, its attainment is always questionable. What if 70 percent, 60 percent, or even less of the available computer time is used? No judgment can be made. However, when 80 percent is given as the minimum acceptable level, a definite judgment is possible—even if only to make the requirement more demanding or less demanding.

This brings us to the second requirement for an objective: it should be attainable. If 80 percent for the above example has proved by performance to be unattainable, the requirement must be lowered to avoid an atmosphere of desperation, frustration, and lowering of morale. If the standard set is attainable with the means provided or with the means that can be provided, although the standard is not met, it should remain as is to provide impetus to improve performance. An unmet but attainable objective stimulates an atmosphere of challenge and initiative.

Comprehensive Statement of Relevant Objectives. Statements of precise, measurable, and attainable objectives are not enough if statements for all significant objectives do not exist. For a data center the primary responsibility is to get the job done. Stated as an objective, this may translate to "Meet the deadlines for all scheduled jobs, and complete unscheduled jobs within six hours from receipt of jobs and data."—definitely a desirable objective. But what if, to meet this objective, it is necessary to skip several verification steps and thus sacrifice the reliability of the results? Again, to assure meeting this objective is it acceptable to obtain whatever additional equipment and personnel needed, no matter what the cost? Obviously, all significant objectives must be explored and established.

Data Center Objectives. Fortunately, the significant objectives for a data center are generally known and can be conveniently placed in two categories: user-oriented objectives and data-center-objectives. Users are concerned about getting their jobs when they want them and getting good output. Thus, user-oriented objectives are timely processing and quality results:

1. *Timeliness.* A possible statement for timely processing has already been given. To that statement the only other standard that may be needed is limits for on-line-processing response time. The appended statement could be "All scheduled jobs should be completed by their deadlines; all unscheduled jobs should be completed within 6 hours of receipt of jobs and data; average response time should not exceed 5 seconds, and maximum response time should not exceed 30 seconds."

2. *Quality.* A statement for quality processing is much more difficult. Many quality criteria cannot be measured. What is frequently done is to state what must be performed and what precautions should be taken. Required actions include assurance of backup for protection of critical files, appropriate response to program messages, and verification of control totals. Precautions include preparation of data according to instructions, use of the indicated files, and proper processing and distribution of output.

Of the data-center-oriented objectives, four are most critical:

1. *Efficiency.* To maximize processing efficiency by getting the greatest amount of productivity from available resources, which include not only hardware and associated software, but also personnel and the procedures they follow. To accomplish this objective, adequate monitoring and reporting procedures must be established and adhered to. Location of inefficiencies is usually the starting point for improving processing efficiency. At the same time, cost must be justified for obtaining the improved efficiency.

2. *Security.* To maximize, within financial limits, the protection of equipment, systems, data, and the personnel and premises. Security is expensive and, as in the case of improving processing efficiency, must be financially justified. Naturally, a minimum acceptable level of security must be established, but expenses to provide security above that level must be examined carefully.

3. *Cost.* To minimize processing cost by documenting the causes for the data center's costs and analyzing how processing methods and user demands can be modified. In many situations an alternate processing approach can reduce processing costs and possibly even improve quality of service. One such approach is preparation and

correction of input by the user department personnel.

4. *Morale.* To maximize personnel morale by stressing and stimulating participation, initiative, and personal improvement. Data center performance is affected by the competency and industry of its personnel. Thus, attention to their needs and interests is an example of data center management's enlightened self-interest. Both management and staff benefit from management's concern for personnel morale.

Specialization of Activities

Many of the specializations in a data center are directly related to processing of application systems. These specializations include data preparation, scheduling, computer operations, and report distribution. These are activities that cannot be ignored and thus are always present.

A large number of specializations, however, are not essential to the operation of a data center, but their absence can delay resolution of problems, elimination of inefficiencies, and correction of unreliable service. Illustration 2–2 lists the major optional specializations present in various data centers. The availability of specialists allows quick resolution of problems, reduction of inefficiencies, and improved reliability of service.

Although the activities for most specializations shown in Illustration 2-2 are easy to envision, the activities for the support specializations may not be clear. The four support groups shown have occurred often in various data centers; these are hardware support, system support, operations support, and documentation support.

Hardware Support. A person in a hardware support group has the primary function of evaluating the value and performance of existing equipment and of equipment being considered for use. If a recommendation to add or change a piece of equipment is approved, that person then becomes responsible for having the equipment function properly and effectively. This person becomes of critical importance if a hardware problem occurs, especially if a data communications system is involved. In fact, if the data center has a data communications system, at least one hardware-support person is an absolute necessity. Delays can be tolerated for batch-processing systems, but not for data communications systems.

System Support. This group evaluates the efficiency of application and system programs. It

User-Data Center Specializations

Data Control	To control the receipt and processing of jobs and data, and to control the distribution of output.
User-Data Center Coordination	To coordinate the delivery of material to and from the data center in order to meet deadlines and to obtain timely correction and reentry of rejected transactions.
System-Data Center Coordination	To coordinate the installation of new systems and the modification of existing systems.

Processing Method Specializations

Data Communications	To attend to all technical matters related to data communications.
Data Base	To support and administer all actions necessary to establish and maintain data bases.
Computer Output Microfilm	To advise and administer microfilm activities.

Support Specializations

Hardware Support	To evaluate existing and new hardware, to resolve hardware problems, and to improve hardware efficiency.
Systems Support	To evaluate existing and new system software, to pinpoint inefficiencies, and to improve system software.
Operations Support	To establish and evaluate standards and procedures, including safety and security, and to recommend improvements.
Documentation Support	To prepare and update documentation.

ILLUSTRATION 2-2. Data Center Specializations: These specialized activities contribute to controlling data center activities, improving efficiency, and encouraging interpersonal rapport.

strives to resolve inefficiencies found in system programs, but only pinpoints the inefficiencies in application programs, which application programmers are expected to remedy. This group also performs a function that in the past was kept in the programming department but is becoming increasingly prevalent in data centers. This group attends to systems programming. In other words, they are responsible for preparing nonapplication programs that serve general purposes as an assistance to programmers, such as programs that aid in debugging application programs and programs that perform utility functions. This group also is available for quick resolution of any system problems that occur. In resolving problems, they usually have the added advantage of being able to quickly isolate and diagnose problems.

Operations Support. Attending to the data center's standards and procedures, the operations support group monitors and supports the smooth flow of the work, the adherence to manual processing standards and procedures, and the attainment of predetermined levels of safety and security. Without this group, not only are standards and procedures likely to be incomplete and ambiguous, but they are also likely to be inadequately and incorrectly documented. It is not uncommon for a data center to have procedure documentation that no one trusts. The staff depends on word of mouth, and when this becomes the accepted means of communicating standards and procedures, a quick survey of the staff's opinions of "correct" standards and procedures reveals conflicting views. Besides monitoring and supporting adherence to standards and procedures, this group is also responsible for establishing standards and procedures, with special emphasis often required on those related to safety and security. Managers have a difficult task maintaining adequate safety and security without such a group (which may actually consist of only one person) frequently monitoring and reporting on the adequacy of safety and security and notifying management of potential dangers.

Documentation Support. It has almost become a standard in data centers that forms are hastily and poorly designed, that all required documents are not always supplied, and that those documents supplied are not updated when required. The docu-mentation support group attempts to eliminate these deficiencies, which the operations support group usually brings to their attention. They also attempt to keep documents as few as possible and as brief as possible. By monitoring the design of forms, they assure that all needed space for information is provided, of the proper size, and in the proper sequence, besides attending to other form design considerations. This group also monitors any changes to standards, procedures, and systems to assure that documentation is updated before the changes become effective. It also may have the educational goal of making others aware of a form's importance, stressing that a form supports and guides procedures throughout the data center—a form establishes, however mutely, a pattern of thinking.

Coordination of Activities

The separate, specialized activities must be coordinated. Lack of coordination of data center activities, in effect, is like a fleet of ships leaving port together, intending to arrive together at a specific destination, but with each ship's captain choosing his own speed and course. Just as these captains must agree on where they are going and how they are going to get there, data center personnel must know their objectives and how they will work together to attain those objectives.

In addition to supporting smooth and efficient attainment of clearly understood objectives, coordination fosters another benefit, an important and usually unanticipated benefit: coordination of activities has a synergistic effect. In other words, the benefits resulting from the coordinated effort of several individuals tends to be greater than the sum of benefits of those individuals working independently. When this principle is applied to the production-line activity within a data center, this is easy to understand and appreciate. If, for example, there is poor coordination between the computer room, data preparation, and the scheduler, correction of rejects may be delayed and rescheduling may be delayed, resulting in jobs missing deadlines. Not only is coordination needed between different processing areas in a data center, but it is also necessary for activities within each processing area and, on a larger scale, between the data center and other departments. Thus, there are three types of coordination: coordination for activities within each processing area, coordination for activities between processing areas, and coordination for activities between the data center and other departments.

Coordination Within Each Processing Area. Someone in each processing area must be responsible for deciding what should be done, initiating and guiding activities, and accounting for results. The preparation of data provides a good example of why this is necessary. The supervisor responsible for this function must decide which jobs should be processed first and by whom. Without this guidance, personnel would choose the easiest jobs first or on the basis of first-come, first-served, treating all jobs as if they were equally important and not giving priority attention to critical jobs.

Coordination Between Processing Areas. The need for coordination between processing areas is dramatically illustrated by the interfacing required between scheduling personnel and data receipt, data preparation, file storage, computer processing, output processing (such as decollating and bursting), and output distribution. Scheduling personnel must know when delays occur, permitting rescheduling of jobs and notification to users of delays. Coordination is also needed between each processing area along the entire production line, such as between data receipt and data preparation. For this purpose, some organizations assign a person in each area to the coordination of activities between work areas. These people are usually called *work coordinators.*

Coordination Between the Data Center and Other Departments. Most organizations provide for coordination between user departments and the data center. Ignoring this need leads to uncertain delivery of data, uncertainty in meeting scheduled deadlines, and, if user intervention is required, confusion in correcting and reentering rejected transactions. Therefore, most organizations have user–data-center coordinators. System–data-center coordinators are not as prevalent. Their absence causes delays and confusion in releasing new systems and in modifying existing systems. System–data-center coordinators are definitely desirable.

Many other coordination problems exist between the data center and other departments that are almost never considered, such as making data center managers aware of expectations of increased demands on data center resources, which can result because of new systems, enhanced systems, or increases in data quantity. In addition, user managers should be made aware of operating inefficiencies and problems in production systems, and user managers should be involved in resolving scheduling conflicts. The only reasonable approach to resolving these and other coordination difficulties is to have a *data center steering committe* consisting of data center and user department representatives. The activities and potential benefits of such a committee are discussed later.

Hierarchy of Authority and Responsibility

First, a precise distinction must be made between the two terms "authority" and "responsibility." A person given authority for a function has been granted the right to make decisions that affect that function and to act on those decisions. A person given responsibility for a function is held accountable for performance of required actions, but may not be given authority to make decisions or to act. Authority to make decisions and perform a function properly should accompany the assignment of responsibilities. Not doing this leads to frustration and poor morale. Consider the situation where the computer-room manager is made responsible for meeting deadlines but does not have the authority to assign personnel to a third shift when necessary.

All organization charts clearly show what is meant by a hierarchy of authority and responsibility. An organization chart shows the downward sequence for the communication of expectancies and the upward sequence for reporting on performance. Decision-making authority and responsibility must be placed at levels in the hierarchy with considerable thought. The higher up in the hierarchy the decisions are made, the better the overall direction, consistency, and control of actions. On the other hand, the lower down the hierarchy the decisions are made, the closer the decision-making, the direction, and control are placed to where decisions and actions are implemented—and in the hands of those with the greatest amount of local information.

Thus, even such a mundane although important authority as deciding when tape heads should be cleaned requires serious thought. The manager of the computer room can set the standard that tape heads should be cleaned every four hours, no matter how heavy or light a tape drive's usage. If, however, the person responsible for this task is given the authority to use this standard as a guideline and to vary from it as the occasions require, tape drives used infrequently may be cleaned once a day, and tape drives used heavily may be cleaned every two hours. Naturally, these qualifications on cleaning every four hours can be and should be included in the standards, but it is apparently wise to place the authority to decide specifically when to vary from this time with the person responsible.

Since the data center is concerned with the overall obligations of the company, the data center manager should have, as already exists in many companies, the status and power associated with a vice-presidency title. If, for whatever reason, this does not occur, the data center manager should report to a high-level nondepartmental vice-president—thus preventing the data center from becoming a servant to a single department such as accounting.

A few words should be said about organization charts, especially since they have received much criticism by theorists and have been ignored or left inadequate by many organizations. Illustration 2–3 shows the organization structure that can exist for a large-size data center. The preparation of organization charts forces managers to establish specializations, their coordination, and lines of command and management reporting. That is all organization charts are intended to accomplish, and that is what they accomplish admirably. But that does not stop the critics. They say that it does not show informal organization structure and requires periodic updating to be accurate. As for the last point, it is obvious that the trivial effort required is worth the benefits of having the organization charts. The first point refers to the informal organization structure formed by friendships that have developed and by coordinating and communicating activities between processing areas. Organization charts are not intended to meet these needs. Documentation of coordinating and communicating activities is needed and should be clearly presented in procedure documentation.

Norman Deunk of IBM provides additional defense for organization charts. He said that without charts, overlapping of authority and responsibility

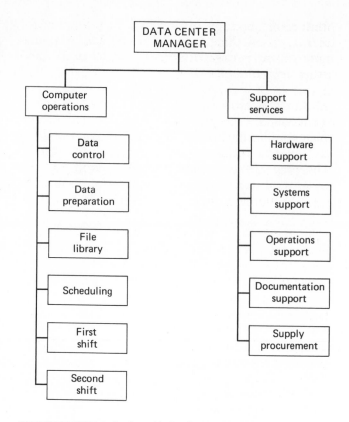

ILLUSTRATION 2–3. Organization for a Data Center.

among middle managers is likely.[4] The avoidance of overlapping authority and responsibility is enough to justify organization charts. Besides stating precisely what the hierarchy of authority and responsibility is, organization charts provide several other benefits. They permit experimentation with several structures; they permit easier discussion of possible changes; they show managers and staff how their work contributes to the functioning of the data center; and finally, they provide a general overview of possible paths for promotion, presented as groups of jobs instead of as individual jobs.

STRUCTURING GUIDELINES

Organization theorists and thoughtful managers have searched through the years for guidelines to structuring organizations. This effort has produced numerous concepts; many are useful and

[4]Franklin G. Moore, *Management: Organization and Practice* (New York: Harper & Row, Pub., 1964), p. 517.

22

productive, and some are contradictory. The guidelines discussed here have received general acceptance. They consist of structuring principles and several related topics. The word "principle" as used in this section should be understood to indicate a concept that has been proved useful, not one that can be blindly accepted as a universal truth, a truth always applicable no matter what the situation.

After the major and most promising structuring principles are presented, several closely related topics are considered: the types of structure, the centralization-versus-decentralization issue, and the reasons and the approach for restructuring an organization. Some of the guidelines and related topics may seem abstract and of little concern to a data center manager, but this is far from true. These considerations have a direct effect on the performance of a data center manager in meeting the data center objectives. They affect user service, reliability of service, data center efficiency, cost reduction, and the morals of data center personnel. These considerations are definitely important.

Structuring Principles

The organization characteristics already discussed are frequently presented as principles:

1. The data center objectives must be precisely stated so that they are consistent with those of the overall organization. These objectives should be stated so that they are measurable, attainable, comprehensive, and relevant to data center needs.
2. Functional specializations must be defined to meet data center needs, and responsibility must be assigned for each functional area along with matching authority to accomplish that responsibility. Responsibility without authority leads to inefficiencies, frustration, and poor morale.
3. Coordination of activities must be established for activities within a functional area, between functional areas, and between the data center and user departments. Procedures should support coordination requirements, and personnel should be assigned to coordination activities.
4. An up-to-date organization chart must be maintained that shows the hierarchy of authority and responsibility for downward direction and control, and for upward management reporting and accountability. The level at which responsibility

and authority are located should consider the benefits of high-level decision-making for direction, consistency, and control of actions, and should consider the benefits of low-level access to detailed information.

Three more principles have received much attention and are the only other principles that will be considered; they are unity of command, span of control, and minimization of levels.

Unity of Command. Simply stated, this principle states that no person should serve two bosses. Stated in the standard jargon of management literature, no subordinate will report to and receive orders from more than one superior. This principle is likely to be violated whenever there is an assistant manager. Frequently the staff under both managers receive orders from and reports to both managers. The problems that can occur are easy to visualize. One manager may commit 80 percent of a person's time; the other manager may commit more than 20 percent of that person's time and possibly a matching 80 percent; and both are likely to complain about poor performance. In some situations the orders are contradictory. In other situations confusion results because each manager may not be informed of all that is happening. If all orders from the higher-level manager are first presented to the assistant manager, the orders can then be relayed with no confusion or conflicts, with both managers having full knowledge of what has been assigned.

Span of Control. The number of subordinates a superior can effectively manage is limited. This limit is usually set from five to eight subordinates. However, surveys have shown that some managers direct much more, in some cases 20 persons or more. A wide span of control seems most successful when the people managed are doing routine work, work that requires little supervision.

Minimization of Levels. This principle and the preceding one, span of control, are contradictory and thus a balance must be sought. The smaller the span of control (which is desirable), the greater the number of organization levels (which is not desirable)—because as the number of levels increases, the less direct, slower, and more error-prone are communications between the higher and the lower

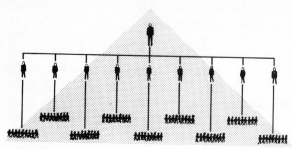

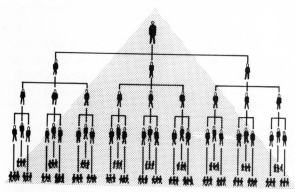

Span of 81 per executive:
1 supervisory level, 1 executive.

Span of 9 per executive:
2 supervisory levels, 10 executives.

Span of 3 per executive:
4 supervisory levels, 40 executives.

ILLUSTRATION 2-4. The Interrelationship of Span of Control and Managerial Levels. *Source:* William H. Newman, *Administrative Action* (Englewood Cliffs, N.J.: Prentice-Hall, Inc., 1963), p. 255.

levels. Each level adds an element of delay and an opportunity for information distortion. Because of these difficulties, many organizations, such as IBM, keep organization levels as few as possible. Other organizations, especially those working on short-term projects that require constant supervision, prefer more levels and a small span of control. The awkwardness of an extremely large span of control and the inefficiency of a very narrow span of control, with many additional managerial levels, are shown in Illustration 2-4.

Another consideration that must be attended to is to determine what effect different organization structures could have on processing procedures and on personnel morale. For example, a structure with few levels and a wide span may provide quick flow of orders and performance reports but may make control more difficult and thus hinder processing workflow. Too many levels, in contrast, clarify specialization of activities and their control but inevitably create coordination difficulties. Lack of control or coordination leads to processing inefficiencies and to lowered personnel morale.

A primary test of an organization's effectiveness is the attainment of its objectives through efficient and frictionless activities.

Structure Types

The structure of an organization is classified by the primary upper-level separation of activities. The separation of activities most apparent in data centers is by function. But in many organizations the primary separation of activities is collectively referred to as separation by division, where "division" can refer to various approaches for grouping activities.

Functional Structure. All data center managers think in terms of the various functional areas in a data center. It is natural and easy to precisely separate such functions as data preparations, computer processing, and support activities.

The primary advantage of this structure, naturally, is specialization by function, which automatically leads to the centralization of specialized facilities, equipment, systems, and personnel. The end results are usually more efficient processing, more reliable service to users, and financial savings.

The benefits of this structure cannot be ignored, and even if a divisional structure is used as the primary high-level separation of activities, the next lower level is almost always by function.

Functional structures have their disadvantages. If they did not, they would be automatically accepted without any need to consider the pros and cons of both approaches. There are two significant difficulties. First, the managers for each functional area become activity-oriented instead of result-oriented. They become more concerned about meeting the performance standards set for their area than with satisfying the data center's objectives. This leads to the second difficulty. The data center manager is held wholly responsible for the total performance of the data center, for the meeting of the data center's objectives. Each person reporting to the data center manager is responsible for a specific functional area, with concern for that area's performance but not for the effect of that area's performance on the overall performance of the data center. The supervisor responsible for decollating and for bursting reports, for example, may stress high productivity, avoiding delayed use of equipment that may be necessary when waiting for a high-priority report to be printed. High productivity benefits the performance shown by that functional area but sacrifices the overall data center performance.

Divisional Structure. The term "divisional" actually applies to separation of activities other than by function. It applies to five types of divisions for activities in an organization.[5] These five types are:

1. *Product.* In a company such as General Foods, the division is by the various types of food products. In an insurance company, it is by types of insurance. This type of structure frequently occurs in large organizations.
2. *Customer.* A typical example of division by customer occurs in banks. They may have separate data centers for the corporation, for domestic business, and for foreign business. In this example the division by customer may be convenient for another reason; it is likely that each customer requires a different processing approach and

must adhere to different scheduling constraints.
3. *Territory.* It is not uncommon for an organization to have operations throughout the United States and possibly in Europe. A common arrangement is to have a data center on the east coast, on the west coast, and in Europe.
4. *Process.* Many large organizations keep the processing equipment and personnel for batch, online, and COM (computer output microfilm) separate. In some situations they are treated as three separate data centers, although possibly located in the same facility; in other situations they are considered as part of a single data center with the primary division occurring by processing type.
5. *Service.* One structure that illustrates division by service is where one data center exists for scheduled jobs, another data center exists for on-request jobs, and possibly another group performs as coordinators and advisors for minicomputers scattered throughout an organization.

Divisional structures have their advantages and disadvantages; they provide benefits and also create problems. The benefits they provide arise from the fact that these types of structures tend to be more result-oriented than activity-oriented. Personnel in each division in the structure are aware of the specific needs of that division, are deeply involved in the division's welfare, and thus create an atmosphere of individual commitment and motivation.

As for the problems created, three are of particular concern. The primary advantage for functional structures becomes the primary disadvantage for divisional structures. First, divisions are not centralized. Duplication of resources—facilities, hardware, systems, and personnel—leads to more costly processing. Since it is usually not economically feasible to duplicate all of the specialized resources that a centralized installation can have, the divisions cannot attain the same efficiency, controls, and reliability. The remaining two problems to be considered are the closely related problems of provincialism and interdivision lack of cooperation. Provincialism results from being aware of only the division's needs, and not being aware of the organization's overall needs. Lack of cooperation develops when each division tries to outdo the other divisions and is thus reluctant to help other divisions by sharing performance-improving techniques.

[5]Joel E. Ross and Robert G. Murdick, *Management Update* (New York: Amacom, 1973), p. 74.

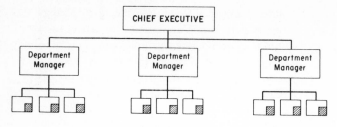

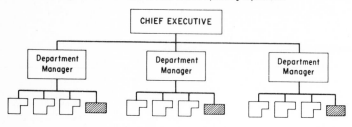

(C) Organization with separate service division.

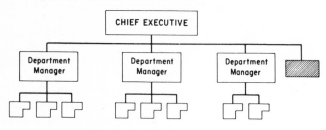

(D) Organization with multiple service units.

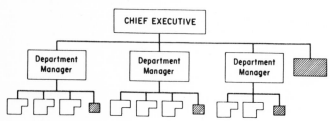

ILLUSTRATION 2-5. Alternative Locations for Data Center Services. *Source:* William H. Newman, *Administrative Action* (Englewood Cliffs, N.J.: Prentice-Hall, Inc., 1963), p. 170.

The choice between organization types is usually not easy and requires careful analysis of the alternatives. In some situations only one choice is acceptable. If large quantities of processing are required in widely separated locations, division by territory is dictated as the primary separation of activities. An organization can have several distinct data centers, each using a different structural type. One data center could serve the corporation needs (customer type), another could service on-line pro-

cessing (process type), a third could serve scheduled batch jobs (process type), and a fourth could receive the on-request jobs (service type). Many combinations can and do exist. Illustration 2–5 shows how a service division such as a data center can be part of an operating department, separate from it, or both.

Centralization versus Decentralization

The preceding discussion of functional and divisional organization types introduced the issue of centralization versus decentralization. Harvey Golub, in his article "Organizing Information System Resources,"[6] provides six criteria that are basic when deciding whether to centralize or decentralize. The criteria are:

1. *Cost:* specifically, costs associated with hardware, systems, personnel, technological changes, and special financial approaches. This includes consideration of long-term operating costs and maintenance.
2. *User service:* considering divisional effectiveness, application design options available, security and control, and the effect of specialized hardware, systems, and personnel. This includes use of such service measurements as job turnaround time.
3. *Management style:* according to whether the prevalent management philosophy is toward centralized or decentralized leadership, with accompanying centralization or delegation of responsibility. Management's plans for the future should also be considered.
4. *Manageability:* operational effectiveness of the organization as a whole. This is the ability of the organization to function in whatever structure is chosen.
5. *Attracting, holding, and utilizing people:* the effect on the general atmosphere and on individual morale in particular, and on whether imagination and initiative are stimulated. Opportunities for advancement and for satisfying personal needs are particularly important.
6. *Adaptability to changes:* how easily can organiza-

[6] Harvey Golub, "Organizing Information System Resources: Centralization vs. Decentralization," in *The Information Systems Handbook,* ed. F. Warren McFarlan and Richard L. Nolan (Homewood, Illinois: Dow Jones-Irwin, 1975), p. 68.

tional or technological changes be adjusted to. Change is to be expected and planned for.

The first two criteria are the most important and are now examined in more detail.

Cost. The costs related to the centralization/ decentralization issue are for hardware, systems, personnel, technological changes, and special financial approaches. It is generally accepted that a saving results when a large centralized computer can do the same amount of work as several smaller computers. This is often expressed by a formula known as Grosch's Law,[7] which approximates the pricing scale used by hardware vendors. The formula is:

$$Cost = constant \times (effectiveness)^{1/2}$$

where effectiveness is the ability to do a number of operations within a specified time.

Thus, the cost of a machine with an effectiveness of 10,000 and with a vendor's constant of 100 is:

$$Cost = 100 \times (10,000)^{1/2} = 100 \times 100 = \$10,000$$

Four of these machines would cost $40,000. But a machine of four times the effectiveness of the smaller machine may cost half as much for the same processing effectiveness, as the following shows:

$$Cost = 100 \times (40,000)^{1/2} = 100 \times 200 = \$20,000$$

As for systems and personnel costs, multiple data centers require duplication of systems and personnel. Consider personnel. If 50 persons at a centralized data center can do the work of 100 persons at four data centers, the money saved is impressive. Consider an average salary of $10,000 per person. The personnel cost at the centralized data center would be $500,000, and the combined personnel costs of the four data centers would be $1,000,000, an additional expense of $500,000. Since personnel costs continually increase, the additional costs incurred because of duplication of personnel also increase.

As for technological changes and special financial approaches, these cost factors are also advantageous to a centralized data center. When a

[7]Harvey Golub, "Organizing Information System Resources," p. 74.

technological change occurs, only one adjustment or conversion is required; however, if there are four data centers, there are that many more adjustments or conversions necessary. The larger, centralized installation is more willing to consider financial approaches that are complex, which the smaller installations are likely to be reluctant to try. These approaches may be long-term and may involve several vendors.

User Service. Decentralized data centers usually provide better service when divisional organization structure is desirable, or when highly specialized user needs are to be met. When divisional organization is not desirable, a centralized data center usually provides better service because it permits more application-design options and better security and control, besides the benefits of specialized hardware, systems, and personnel. Improved user service is usually the reason given for decentralizing, in spite of the likelihood of increased costs. As stated earlier, decentralization may be absolutely necessary, especially in the case of wide territorial separation of operations.

Since decentralized data centers cannot financially justify specialized hardware, systems, and personnel, they cannot obtain the benefits available to centralized data centers that can justify the additional expense. The availability of these specialized resources provides the centralized data center with the benefits mentioned earlier, which include greater efficiency, more control, tighter security, and more-reliable service.

Restructuring the Organization

Organization restructuring may be necessary from time to time. Restructuring usually consists of adjustments rather than major changes. Major changes such as converting from centralization to decentralization or from decentralization to centralization are, fortunately, infrequent. The situations that could lead to restructuring are:

1. Organization philosophy has changed on the centralization/decentralization issue.
2. A new data center manager may prefer a different style of leadership.
3. A new technology may require elimination, modification, or addition of activities.

4. Production bottlenecks may exist because of poor coordination within the data center or between the data center and user departments.
5. Communications between levels in the organization may be inadequate.
6. Decision-making is occurring at the wrong level in the organization.
7. Personnel morale is poor because leadership is either too confining or too vague.

Organization or procedural changes should be done cautiously. Although changes may be beneficial to personnel, personnel may be resistant. Their resistance may occur because they are not certain of how they will be affected; they will be concerned about the effect of changes on their friendships, their prestige, and their job security.

Resistance can be minimized by following the right approach. The first step is to evaluate the tentative restructuring approach against the organization guidelines already provided. Bypassing consideration of a guideline may result in unnecessary problems. The next step is to determine the effect of the restructuring on the informal structure and activities in the organization. Even formal communication, coordination, and control activities may not be apparent from the organization charts and may be hidden in procedure documentation. The data center manager should then obtain the participation of all managerial personnel and should request ideas and comments from all personnel affected. Those persons who participate in examining the proposed restructuring will more willingly accept what is agreed upon. The final step is to gradually restructure the organization, if that is possible. This avoids sudden disruption of harmonious relationships and allows new relationships to develop comfortably. Managers who have attempted the sudden, "earthquake approach" have witnessed the lowering of morale, indicated by lack of cooperation, increase in absenteeism, and loss of personnel.

However, sudden, large-scale changes are sometimes necessary, as was the case for a large bank of over 750 operation personnel, who were switched from 12-hour shifts three days per week to 8-hour shifts five days per week. Thus, changing from four shifts of personnel providing 24-hour service six days a week, to three shifts of personnel providing 24-hour service five days a week. This change eliminated only one day of service but saved the cost of one shift of personnel. (The personnel were actually absorbed in other areas of the company.)

Organization restructuring should occur as infrequently as possible. No matter what precautions are taken, some personnel dissatisfactions and processing inefficiencies are likely to occur.

MANAGEMENT GUIDELINES

Whereas organization guidelines provide assistance when structuring or evaluating the structure for an organization, management guidelines provide assistance in managing a data center or in evaluating the managing of the data center. Attention to management guidelines directly affects the vitality of the data center and the attainment of its objectives. The relationship of management to the organization structure of the data center is similar to the relationship of the human nervous system to the human skeleton. Just as the human skeleton is motionless until the nervous system activates it, the data center depends on the vigor and momentum supplied by management. Without pushing this analogy too far, one other similarity is important: both the human skeleton and the organization structure are limited in what can be accomplished, because of their structure, no matter how much force is used to activate them. For the human skeleton one such limitation is the length of the arms, which limit reach; for the organization structure an excessive span of control limits degree of supervision. Thus, management is critical in bringing the data center to life but, at the same time, is limited by the data center's organization structure.

The management guidelines are separated into success indicators and problem indicators, which are discussed in the following sections.

Success Indicators

Illustration 2–6 shows a comprehensive list of success indicators, indicators of successful data center management. Four of these indicators are particularly representative of good management practices and are described below.

Reliable Management Reporting. Data center managers must be informed of data center perfor-

Related to managers in general:

1. Managers have adequate leadership skills and technical knowledge.
2. Managers balance strong leadership with open-minded discussion.
3. Managers do not bypass a person's immediate superior when giving orders.
4. Managers explain any changes in authority and responsibility to those affected.
5. Managers immediately resolve disputes over authority and responsibility.
6. Managers establish performance standards and monitor performance to determine if standards are attained.
7. Managers accurately perceive what is occurring in the data center.
8. Managers periodically evaluate personnel to correct faulty performance and to aid them along their career paths.
9. Managers provide a means for personnel to evaluate their own work.
10. Managers criticize personnel privately.

Related to specific managers:

11. The data center manager controls data center plans, expenditures, and resources.
12. The data center manager is responsible for strategic decisions and planning, such as setting objectives.

13. The assistant data center manager is responsible for tactical decisions and planning, such as allocation of resources.
14. The manager for each functional area is responsible for operating efficiency and problem resolution.

Related to personnel in general:

15. Personnel selection, training, motivation, and evaluation are precisely defined.
16. Personnel have their needs integrated with data center objectives.
17. Personnel are result-oriented instead of activity-oriented.
18. Each person and immediate superior agrees on that person's career path, required training, and short-range objectives.
19. Personnel morale is high as indicated by low turnover and low absenteeism.
20. Personnel are flexible in solving problems and in adjusting to day-to-day variations.
21. Personnel participate in discussion of changes that affect them.
22. Each person reports to only one superior.

Related to user department personnel:

23. User department personnel participate in coordinating user-data center activities, improving processing efficiency, and resolving interdepartment problems.

ILLUSTRATION 2-6. Management Success Indicators.

mance and problems. If managers are not given reliable performance information for all significant performance standards, they may believe that all is functioning well when processing actually is inefficient, resource capabilities are being wasted, and users are dissatisfied. The managers will be informed eventually, but it may be too late to retain the faith of the users, and delay may make problem resolution more difficult than necessary. To obtain reliable management reporting, requirements should be precisely stated, leaving no room for misunderstanding, and procedures must be established to meet those requirements.

Identification with Data Center Objectives. Data center personnel should have their needs integrated with the data center's objectives. When they realize how achievement of the data center's objectives satisfies their needs, the problems associated with motivation, initiative, and cooperation are greatly reduced. Personnel should be made aware of how their needs for respect and achievement are satisfied by working to meet data center objectives. All this is somewhat idealistic but not unrealistic. Personnel want to participate and feel important. They do not object to a superior-subordinate relationship, but do object to a superior-inferior relationship.

Flexible Problem Solving. Personnel want and need some flexibility and freedom in adjusting their actions to variations in day-to-day situations. Permission to make job-related decisions and permission to solve job-related problems stimulates their initiative and motivation, their interest in doing a good job. The atmosphere generated is progressive instead of restrictive. The emphasis is placed on using the best means available to meet data center objectives—not on adhering in a detached, indifferent manner to what is usually done. Naturally, any deviation from standards and procedures must be justified and approved.

User Participation. Participation from user department personnel is essential in coordinating user-data center activities, improving processing efficiency, and resolving interdepartment conflicts. Good rapport with users usually results, and rapport is unlikely to occur unless user participation is obtained. The ideas that can be discussed and evaluated are many. For example, data center personnel could suggest alternate methods of processing that would provide better user service and at the same time use data center resources more efficiently, such as the use of microfiche for output reports. Users can participate in resolving scheduling conflicts and lessening input-delivery and error-correction difficulties.

Problem Indicators

Illustration 2-7 shows a comprehensive list of problem indicators, which indicate that management problems exist. Four of these problem indicators were selected as representative of management problems and are described below.

Managers Resistant to New Viewpoints and Approaches. When this occurs, the overall environment is stagnant and personnel resist "sticking their necks out" by suggesting improvements. They accept management's demand for conformity. Only too often people in organizations are seen inching through the corridors, glancing cautiously from side to side, quietly moving along, avoiding any suspicion that they may in any way be assertive. Managers who foster this environment attract passive and dependent persons. Those persons who

ILLUSTRATION 2-7. Management Problem Indicators.

Related to managers:

1. Managers are out of touch with broad trends.
2. Managers are unwilling to consider new viewpoints and approaches.
3. Managers do not have precise statements of performance standards.
4. Managers are slow in making and implementing decisions.
5. Managers make frequent serious decision errors.
6. Managers responsible for decision making lack adequate knowledge.
7. Managers are unable to obtain compliance to standards and procedures.
8. Managers are excessively busy with one problem after another.
9. Managers have too many persons reporting to them.
10. Managers attract passive and dependent people.
11. Managers demand conformity from their people.
12. Managers provide little or no guidance to personnel for self-improvement.
13. Managers neither regard merit nor condemn failure.

Related to the environment:

14. Environment has a dull gray look of mediocrity throughout.
15. Deadlines are not met.
16. Overly decentralized decision making is causing lack of policy uniformity and conflicts between objectives.
17. Committee activities are inefficient.
18. Coordination is inadequate within the data center.
19. Coordination is inadequate between the data center and other departments.
20. Interdepartmental and personality clashes occur.
21. One or more persons are critical for the successful operation of the data center.

did fit this pattern when hired usually conform and become mediocre performers. As is to be expected, many persons become discouraged and turnover tends to be high; the most talented persons are lost and the less promising are retained. The more alert become discouraged, grumble, and stay on the job because "a job is a job and pays the rent," which results in indifferent workers.

Managers are Unable to Coordinate Activities. The reason may be simply that the procedures that should provide the coordination required do not exist or are inadequate. The problem, however, may be that procedures are adequate, even if undocumented, but managers make no effort or only half-hearted effort to enforce adherence to them. This is serious. In effect, in this situation the staff is managing the data center, and the managers have lost control. This situation may occur because managers' "span of control" is too wide and they cannot monitor all the activities they are responsible for. The answer to this situation is delegation of responsibility with matching authority. This may require isolating a single person from each functional area for this purpose. Alternatively, another management level can be added in the organization structure; however, an additional management level, while permitting a smaller span of control, delays downward and upward communications.

Managers are not Making Timely or Reliable Decisions. Most managers have the aptitude and ability to make proper decisions in a timely manner—if they know a decision is necessary, have reliable information when they need it, and are not distracted by operating problems. All these hindrances to timely and reliable decision-making are likely to exist unless conscious, firm effort is made. Lack of awareness of a problem and the absence of adequate information can be remedied only through the reporting of performance and problems to managers, where the reports are comprehensive although concise, and information is reliable and permits quick interpretation and evaluation. This is discussed in the next section of this chapter. The distractions created by a continual progression of operating problems are difficult to resolve. They require investigating the causes of the problems and seeking solutions. The most frequent causes of these distractions are inadequate delegation of responsibility and the absence of documented standards and procedures. By eliminating the causes of distracting operating problems, more time becomes available for decision-making.

Personnel are not Provided Job and Personal Goals. In most data centers the computer operator, for example, informally understands that a promotion leads to a senior computer-operator position. But if there are other possibilities, they have not been stated and the operator is not aware of them. The end result is that the operator believes that he is more restricted than he probably is. Making personnel aware and interested in job opportunities must be a serious concern of the data center manager. This includes mapping out the career paths possible for each data center person and also indicating the training required to go from one position to the next. Besides the absence of career paths and training schedules, managers affect personnel effectiveness when accomplishments are not appreciated and when poor performance is ignored and not corrected. When this occurs, personnel accept as a fact, which it may be, that the managers have no interest in them and their futures.

One practice that was not mentioned but can be considered a problem indicator is a manager's inclination to perform data center activities that should be delegated to the staff. This practice diverts the manager's attention from the planning and coordination of activities. A manager, like a ship's captain, cannot steer his ship while stoking the furnace. This very pointed analogy is used by Eric Webster in his article, "Let's Repeal Parkinson's Law." In this article he appropriately states, "If the captain oscillates between bridge and boiler room, a high head of steam won't compensate for steering in circles."[8]

Closely related to management's involvement in operational activities is the freedom given by management to staff to participate in decision-making. As shown in Illustration 2–8, the less authoritarian a manager is, the more the staff is permitted to participate. It is necessary to decide what degree of participation is best to stimulate staff motivation and to attain an efficient, effective data center. A highly authoritarian, task-oriented environment is likely to lower morale, motivation, and productivity, possibly because of personnel indifference, resistance, and turnover. On the other hand, a permissive country-club environment may create a contented but unmotivated staff. Generally, a manager must try to obtain and retain a balance between strong leadership and delegation of responsibility to staff members.

Many attempts have been made to form a comprehensive set of guidelines for management activities. Illustration 2–9 shows one of the most successful. William H. Newman, in his book

[8]Ted W. Engstrom and R. Alec Mackensie, *Managing Your Time* (Grand Rapids, Michigan: Zondervan Publishing House, 1977), p. 177.

ILLUSTRATION 2-8. The Leadership Continuum.

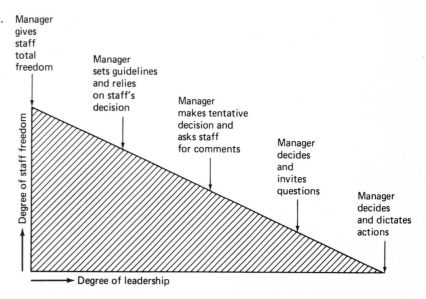

PLAN	ORGANIZE	ASSEMBLE RESOURCES	SUPERVISE	CONTROL

1. Develop integrated and comprehensive structure.
  a. Use all types of plans.
    1) Objectives and sub-goals.
    2) Single-use plans.
    3) Standing plans.
  b. Weigh detail and period covered.
    1) Benefits of planning:
      a) Crises avoided.
      b) Better methods.
      c) Easier delegation.
      d) Basis for control.
    2) Limits on planning:
      a) Unreliable forecasts.
      b) Nonrecurring problems.
      c) Danger of inflexibility.
      d) Expense of planning.
      e) Time required.
      f) Effect on individual.
  c. Incorporate logistics and strategy.
2. Use these steps:
  a. Diagnose problem.
  b. Find creative alternatives.
  c. Project consequences.
  d. Evaluate and choose.
3. Aid planning.
  a. Simplify scope.
  b. Organize for planning.
  c. Simplify with logic.
  d. Consider operations research.
  e. Test choice.
4. Integrate planning structure.
	1. Establish departments which:
	  a. Make use of specialization.
	  b. Facilitate control.
	  c. Aid in coordination.
	  d. Secure adequate attention.
	  e. Recognize local conditions.
	  f. Reduce expense.
	2. Provide staff and service divisions where needed.
	3. Clarify relations between units and men.
	  a. Decentralize where practical.
	    1) Who knows facts?
	    2) Capacity of men.
	    3) Need for speed.
	    4) Need for coordination.
	    5) Importance of decision.
	    6) Executive load.
	    7) Effect on morale.
	  b. Identify staff responsibility.
	  c. Use functional authority cautiously.
	4. Build a sound structure.
	  a. Assign all duties.
	  b. Avoid dual subordination.
	  c. Keep spans of supervision workable.
	  d. Use committees wisely.
	  e. Provide for top-management.
	  f. Seek:
	    1) Even strata.
	    2) Consistent departmentation.
	    3) Parallel departmentation.
	    4) Simple structure.
		1. Build external alliances.
		  a. Informal agreements.
		  b. Formal contracts.
		  c. Partial ownership.
		  d. Serving on board of directors.
		  e. Consortiums for projects.
		2. Select key executives.
		  a. Determine needs through:
		    1) Job analysis.
		    2) Man specifications.
		    3) Promotion programs.
		  b. Appraise and select using:
		    1) Group judgment.
		    2) Performance appraisals.
		    3) Promotion qualifications.
		    4) Trial or series of jobs.
		    5) Psychological tests.
		3. Assist executive to develop by:
		  a. Learning on the job.
		  b. Rotation among jobs.
		  c. Use of committees, courses, etc.
		  d. Support of personal programs.
		4. Compensate executives wisely.
		  a. Build a sound salary structure.
		  b. Recognize individual results.
		  c. Use bonuses, stock options, etc. for special cases.
			1. Give directions that will obtain desired results.
			  a. Issue good instructions.
			  b. Always follow up instructions.
			  c. Simplify through s. o. p. and indoctrination.
			  d. Explain why.
			  e. Use consultative direction in key relationships.
			2. Motivate men through:
			  a. Financial income.
			  b. Social status.
			  c. Security.
			  d. Attractive work.
			  e. Opportunity.
			  f. Worthwhile activity.
			  g. Power.
			  h. Personal attention.
			  i. Participation.
			  j. Just supervision.
			3. Promote coordination in all phases of administration.
			  a. Harmonize programs and policies.
			  b. Organize for coordinated action.
			  c. Design effective means of communication.
			  d. Aid voluntary coordination.
			    1) Instill dominant objectives.
			    2) Develop customs and terms.
			    3) Encourage informal contacts.
			    4) Provide liaison as needed.
			    5) Use committees.
			  e. Coordinate through supervision.
				1. Set standards at strategic points.
				  a. Tie standards to individual responsibility.
				  b. Concentrate on strategic points.
				  c. Use integrated budgets.
				2. Check on performance.
				  a. Use required confirmation sparingly.
				  b. Concentrate on exceptions.
				  c. Observe personally.
				  d. Design reports for action.
				3. Take corrective action.
				  a. Adjust physical and external factors.
				  b. Review direction, training, and selection of men.
				  c. Motivate and discipline.
				  d. Modify plans where necessary.
				4. Balance control structure.
				  a. Check relative emphasis.
				  b. Focus control at suitable organization level.
				  c. Seek speed and simplicity.
				  d. Check motivation effects.
				  e. Detect dynamic changes.
				  f. Provide data for planning.

ILLUSTRATION 2-9. Five Categories of Management Activities. *Source:* William H. Newman, *Administrative Action* (Englewood Cliffs, N.J.: Prentice-Hall, Inc., 1963), p. 475.

Administrative Action, expounds on these management activities at great length; his book is recommended for thorough reading.[9] The management activities are:

- Planning
- Organizing
- Assembling resources
- Supervising
- Controlling

MANAGEMENT CONTROL

Management control means awareness of performance and problems. It means the existence of means not only to know what is happening, but to change, if necessary, what is happening and to provide the guidance personnel require to perform as desired. To control data center activities, managers have used three means that have proved successful: the receipt of management reports, the existence of an active data center steering committee, and availability of a *user/data center handbook.*

Before considering these three management tools, a desirable extension of each manager's concern for controlling data center activities must be stressed. Besides being concerned about controlling data center activities so that performance standards are met, each manager must consider how procedures and technology can be modified to permit the setting of higher performance standards. J. M. Juran, in his book *Managerial Breakthrough,* refers to improvement of performance standards as an attempt to break through to higher levels of performance. He indicates the different end results of breakthrough and control: "Breakthrough is then, the creation of good (or at least, necessary) changes, whereas control is the prevention of bad changes."[10] An example should make these two aspects clear. Consider a process that may consume 20 hours if properly controlled, and much longer if not controlled, possibly 30 hours or more. If, however, the process is improved, only 15 hours may be necessary. In the first case the "improvement," actually the planned-for performance standard,

[9]William H. Newman, *Administrative Action* (Englewood Cliffs, N.J.: Prentice-Hall, Inc., 1963).
[10]J. M. Juran, *Managerial Breakthrough* (New York: McGraw-Hill, 1964), p. 4.

results from control; in the second case the improvement results from a breakthrough to a performance level higher than the performance standard.

For example, one opportunity for significant improvement is in how tapes are handled. The tape-library procedure can be examined, tape storage location can be changed, and the possibility of minimizing tape handling should be considered. Tape handling can be greatly reduced, for example, by adding mass-storage units such as IBM's Mass Storage System (MSS). This system can store many files, which can then be accessed directly. Thus, no preparation, no operator intervention, and no mounting delays occur in making files available.

The data center environment requires both control and breakthrough: control to have a stable, predictable environment; breakthrough to build and improve this environment. Thus, the three tools can both control activities and break through to higher levels of performance.

Management Reporting

Management decision-making and action is dependent on having adequate information. Managers have been divided into three categories: those who make things happen, those who watch things happen, and those who don't know what happened. This statement of categories is facetious, but it provides a real warning. The only method that data center managers have for knowing what is happening, other than attending many time-consuming meetings, actually dedicating large amounts of time to visiting work areas, or looking at detailed activity reports, is to receive management reports. These reports should provide all the critical information needed in a form that makes it quick to review. On the basis of these reports, managers can make reasonable decisions and then "make things happen." Viewed from this perspective, management reports can be readily accepted as the backbone of management control.

The three questions relevant to obtaining adequate management reports are: What information should be included? How should this information be presented? What difficulties should be considered?

What Information Should Be Included? The answer is simply all the information needed to determine if the data center's objectives have been met. Thus, if the objective is to use 80 percent of available computer time for production work, the data center manager must receive information on computer usage. In addition, supplementary detailed information should be available to explain occurrences that affected computer usage.

For this and the other data center objectives, the unanswered question becomes: How can this information be obtained? This question is answered in the chapters on computer performance evaluation and operating performance evaluation.

How Should This Information Be Presented?
The guidelines for formatting and expressing information are discussed in the chapter on documentation standards. Three recommendations particularly relevant to management reporting are:

1. *Management reports should be summary reports.* To make reports easy to review quickly, only summary and exception information should be included. All information presented must relate directly to the data center's performance standards and, where possible, should indicate trends. Supporting detailed reports should be available for reference.

2. *Use forms, tables, and graphs.* Forms provide a consistent method of presenting information succinctly, with convenient separation of information. Tables and graphs also condense information and should be used whenever possible. Graphs are particularly useful for indicating trends.

3. *Use ratios.* Ratios stress the changing relationship between two factors that would not be apparent as isolated entries. For example, a 10 percent increase in machine repairs would look as if a problem is developing. But if the increase is a result of using the machines for two shifts instead of one, the picture is totally different. Repairs have actually decreased per hour of use, nearly in half, as the following ratios show:

$$\text{First case:} \quad \frac{\text{no. of repairs}}{\text{hours used}} = \frac{10}{40} = 0.25$$

$$\text{Second case:} \quad \frac{\text{no. of repairs}}{\text{hours used}} = \frac{11}{80} = 0.1375$$

What Difficulties Should Be Considered?
Two difficulties that should be considered are that an improvement for one performance standard may be responsible for the degeneracy of one or more of the other performance standards, and second, that summary values may be deceptive, especially averages, which may hide excellent performance in one location and poor performance in another. Consider how improvement for one performance criterion, reduced personnel cost because of personnel turnover, may appear satisfactory, since it approaches the standard set for personnel cost. But what if production has become unreliable, more scheduled jobs are late, and processing errors have increased? It is hoped this information will also appear on the management report and that these effects will be related to their cause: loss of personnel.

As for the deceptive nature of averages, consider the statistics obtained on the number of jobs processed by two identical computers. One computer processed 75 jobs on a particular day, and on that same day the other computer processed only 25 jobs. If all that managers see on the management report is an average, they would be informed that an average of 50 jobs were done per machine. This is obviously misleading. Awareness of this difficulty indicates that separate totals for each machine should be shown. Another approach is to show the average on the management report, but to also include reference to a note or to supporting documents, indicating that a problem exists that is not apparent in the report.

Illustration 2–10 shows two management reports that, besides indicating the type of information to be received, stress the use of summarized and interpreted data.

The Data Center Steering Committee

The *data center steering committee* is an excellent channel for bringing data center and user department representatives together for their mutual benefit. The overall effect

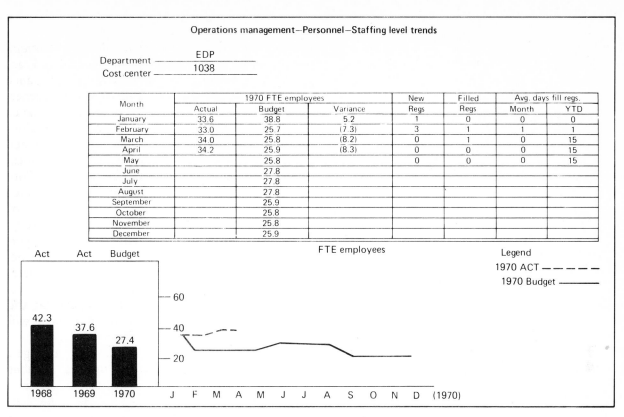

Operations management—Personnel—Staffing level trends

Department — EDP
Cost center — 1038

Month	1970 FTE employees			New	Filled	Avg. days fill regs.	
	Actual	Budget	Variance	Regs	Regs	Month	YTD
January	33.6	38.8	5.2	1	0	0	0
February	33.0	25.7	(7.3)	3	1	1	1
March	34.0	25.8	(8.2)	0	1	0	15
April	34.2	25.9	(8.3)	0	0	0	15
May		25.8		0	0	0	15
June		27.8					
July		27.8					
August		27.8					
September		25.9					
October		25.8					
November		25.8					
December		25.9					

FTE employees

Legend
1970 ACT — — — — —
1970 Budget ————————

Act   Act   Budget

42.3   37.6   27.4
1968   1969   1970

J F M A M J J A S O N D (1970)

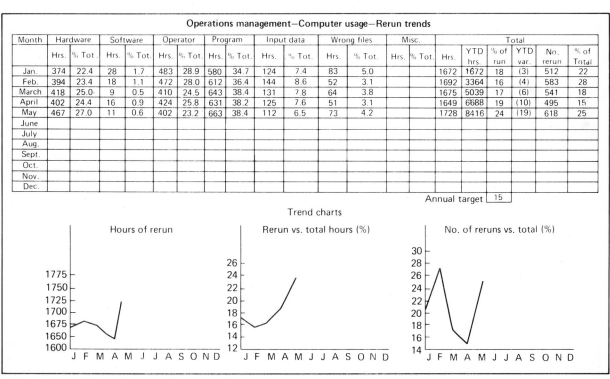

Operations management—Computer usage—Rerun trends

Month	Hardware		Software		Operator		Program		Input data		Wrong files		Misc.		Total					
	Hrs.	% Tot.	Hrs.	% Tot.	Hrs.	% Tot.	Hrs.	% Tot.	Hrs.	% Tot.	Hrs.	% Tot.	Hrs.	% Tot.	Hrs.	YTD hrs.	% of run	YTD var.	No. rerun	% of Total
Jan.	374	22.4	28	1.7	483	28.9	580	34.7	124	7.4	83	5.0			1672	1672	18	(3)	512	22
Feb.	394	23.4	18	1.1	472	28.0	612	36.4	144	8.6	52	3.1			1692	3364	16	(4)	583	28
March	418	25.0	9	0.5	410	24.5	643	38.4	131	7.8	64	3.8			1675	5039	17	(6)	541	18
April	402	24.4	16	0.9	424	25.8	631	38.2	125	7.6	51	3.1			1649	6688	19	(10)	495	15
May	467	27.0	11	0.6	402	23.2	663	38.4	112	6.5	73	4.2			1728	8416	24	(19)	618	25
June																				
July																				
Aug.																				
Sept.																				
Oct.																				
Nov.																				
Dec.																				

Annual target 15

Trend charts

Hours of rerun
1775 1750 1725 1700 1675 1650 1600
J F M A M J J A S O N D

Rerun vs. total hours (%)
26 24 22 20 18 16 14 12
J F M A M J J A S O N D

No. of reruns vs. total (%)
30 28 26 24 22 20 18 16 14
J F M A M J J A S O N D

ILLUSTRATION 2-10. Typical Management Reports. *Source:* "Managing and Reporting on EDP Functions," *EDP Solutions* (N.J.: Data-pro Research Corp., 1976), pp. E40-450-112, and 115.

desired, and one that is attainable, is rapport and mutual assistance; this results from understanding one another's problems and intentions and from striving to avoid conflicts and criticisms.

Specifically, the actual activities recommended for this committee can be conveniently segmented into five categories: coordination of data center and user activities, resolution of scheduling difficulties, data center management's awareness of upcoming resource demands, user department representative's awareness of application processing problems and inefficiencies, and examination of alternative processing approaches.

Coordination of Activities. Data center and user department representatives are able to resolve through the committee any procedural problems that arise. The committee can assign a group of data center and user personnel to the task of analyzing the situation and establishing and documenting procedures. These procedures can include activities such as receipt of input data, inquiry about job status, and distribution of output.

Resolution of Scheduling Difficulties. The most critical scheduling difficulties are (1) receipt of input data so that adequate time is allowed for data preparation to meet the time scheduled for computer processing, and (2) receipt of request for computer processing so that the deadlines indicated can be met using the existing resources. The first is resolved through the establishment of definite procedures for data delivery and the acceptance of the policy that late receipt of input data negates the data center's scheduling commitments for any jobs affected. The contention of jobs for limited resources is a much more difficult situation. This can usually be avoided by preparing computer schedules far enough in advance, but the main brunt of responsibility for resolving this situation is through a sincere effort of users to level the demands for data center resources, thus avoiding peak periods when all deadlines cannot be met and avoiding slack periods when data center resources are used inadequately. Uncontrolled peak periods lead to poor user service; uncontrolled slack periods lead to inefficient use of data center resources.

Awareness of Upcoming Resource Demands. Many times data center managers have been surprised by the unexpected demands on the data center's resources because of the release of a new or modified system, or because of a sharp increase in input data that requires much data preparation, particularly that of keying operations. With communication between data center and user representatives, including systems development personnel, this situation should occur infrequently.

Awareness of Application-Processing Problems and Inefficiencies. User department personnel may be entirely unaware that considerable time and effort are being wasted in the data center because of application system problems and because of wasteful use of data center resources. The problems may include frequent restarts and difficulty in verifying proper completion of jobs. Inefficiencies include poor system design and the printing of reports that may not be needed, particularly large quantity reports of which many copies are printed.

Examination of Alternative Processing Approaches. With rapport established between data center and user personnel, various alternatives to the existing processing method can be considered. For example, the users can prepare input in their department, thus attending to corrections of mistakes where the most-informed persons for the appropriate applications are located. This method has improved user service and data center efficiency, especially when timely receipt of input had been a problem. Many other approaches are also worth consideration, such as on-line processing, the preparation of microfiche, and the use of minicomputers.

Many people are critical of committees. Unfortunately, much criticism is justified. But if careful attention is given to such factors as the selection of members, the preparation of a charter and the agendas, and the means of controlling the meetings and of reporting the results of the meetings, it is likely that the committee meetings will proceed efficiently and productively.

A charter should succinctly and clearly state the goals of the committee; the means for establishing and maintaining the committee; the procedures for preparing for, conducting, and concluding meetings; and the guidelines for chairperson leadership and member participation. A form such as that shown in Illustration 2–11 permits orderly introduction of topics, statement of results, and responsibilities and deadlines assigned

Starting time	Topic	Introduced by	Result	Responsibility and deadline

Data Center Steering Committee Agenda   Date:

Additional comments:

ILLUSTRATION 2-11. Form for Committee Agenda and for Reporting Results.

ILLUSTRATION 2-12. Guidelines for Committee Chairperson and Members.

For the Chairperson

1. Prepare the agenda and distribute it with associated reference material far enough in advance to permit members to prepare.
2. Start each meeting as scheduled, requiring a member who cannot attend the meeting as scheduled to assign another person to appear.
3. Conduct the meeting so that members adhere to the charter, the agenda, and the time limits for each item on the agenda, permitting scheduling of other meetings for those topics requiring more time.
4. Keep the discussion on the topic while keeping all members involved and not permitting one viewpoint or one person to dominate the meeting.
5. Firmly restrain interpersonnel conflicts, possibly insisting on replacement members when conflicts have not been minimized and they have hampered the meetings.
6. Clarify and then report on agreements and on actions to be taken, including deadlines for the actions and who will be responsible.
7. Forward a report of committee actions, agreements, and problems to the members and to upper management.

8. Notify members in a timely manner of changes to scheduled meetings, such as change of time, location, or topics, and also notify members of other meetings that may be of interest, such as those for resolving operational problems or for evaluating new technologies.

For the Members

1. Do all the preparation required for a meeting, including the gathering of data, ideas, and recommendations.
2. Arrive on time, but if this is not possible, have a representative arrive at the scheduled time.
3. Be aware of the time allocated to each topic and keep the discussions within the limits set, arranging for additional meetings if necessary.
4. Be actively involved in discussions to assure that your viewpoints and problems are known, as well as your ideas and recommendations.
5. Avoid interpersonnel conflicts—these conflicts detract from the purposes of the meetings, present a poor image of those involved, and may lead to personnel replacements, thus also eliminating their contributions.

to members. The "Additional Comments" area on this form can be used to state unresolved problems, including committee membership problems. Thus, this agenda also serves as a report to upper management on committee activities and performance. Basic guidelines for the chairperson and for the committee members are listed in Illustration 2-12.

The User/Data Center Handbook

The primary document for guiding and coordinating the activities of the data center and the user departments is the *user/data center handbook*. It explains the structure and functions within the data center, the purposes and procedures of the data center steering committee, and the procedures coordinating the activities of the data center user personnel.

Data Center Structure and Functions. Two types of documentation are basic. The first shows the hierarchical structure of the data center's functions and is accompanied by a short narrative description for each function. This documentation provides users with some insight as to what the data center consists of, and it should stress how the users are related to the various functions. The second type of documentation explains how jobs move through the data center, in other words, the processing workflow. This documentation is accompanied by information on the processing controls used and on the safety and security measures that are taken. Thus this section of the *user/data center handbook* provides a total orientation of how the data center functions and what precautions are taken in the data center to provide reliable service to users.

The Data Center Steering Committee. This section provides all the policies, procedures, and guidelines needed to obtain efficient and productive committee activity. Besides providing specifics on member selection, agenda preparation, the reporting of committee results, this section also should provide leadership guidelines for the chairperson and participation guidelines for the members.

User-Data Center Procedures. All the procedures that involve both data center personnel and user personnel should be precisely defined and documented. Any procedure not documented is almost certain to create confusion and conflict. The procedures that must be present include the procedures for scheduling jobs, for submitting unscheduled jobs, for submitting data, for inquiring about job status, for error correction, for problem resolution, and for installing, maintaining, and discontinuing applications. With smooth-flowing operating procedures for these activities, attention can be diverted from correcting individual processing problems to improving user service and data center efficiency.

The table of contents for the *user/data center handbook* is shown in Illustration 2-13; it provides a good basis for determining what is suitable for a

ILLUSTRATION 2-13. *User-Data Center Handbook* Table of Contents: This handbook coordinates user and data center activities, and encourages rapport between user and data center personnel.

Management Letter of Support

PART 1   The *Handbook's* Purpose and Benefits

PART 2   The Data Center Organization

    2.1   Organization Chart
    2.2   Organization Components
    2.3   Processing Workflow and Controls
    2.4   Safety and Security Precautions
    2.5   Chargeout and Billing Information
    2.6   Data Center Performance Monitoring

PART 3   The Data Center Steering Committee

    3.1   Committee Goals
    3.2   Establishing and Maintaining the Committee
    3.3   Committee Procedures
    3.4   Guidelines for the Chairperson
    3.5   Guidelines for the Members

PART 4   The User-Data Center Procedures

    4.1   Introduction to the Procedures
    4.2   Application Installation
    4.3   Application Maintenance
    4.4   Application Discontinuance
    4.5   Job Scheduling
    4.6   Unscheduled Jobs
    4.7   Data Submission
    4.8   Job Status Inquiry
    4.9   Error Correction
    4.10 Problem Resolution

PART 5   Enforcement of Data Center Procedures

    5.1   Built-in Controls
    5.2   Orientation Seminars
    5.3   "Fire Drills" and Random Tests
    5.4   Continual Monitoring

specific data center. Some data centers, for example, may want to include JCL (job control language) and cataloged procedures information for systems development personnel. Many other topics may also be useful. As shown in the table of contents, it is recommended that a means be established for verifying adherence to the procedures as documented. If deviations do occur, they must be either sternly controlled or, if an improvement, adopted after appropriate updating of documentation—and after reasonable reprimand of personnel who ignored official procedures. Seeking improvements is praiseworthy, but implementing them without managerial awareness and approval can lend to confusion or to varying degrees of havoc.

3 PERSONNEL RECRUITMENT, ADVANCEMENT, AND APPRAISAL

GOAL

To obtain competent personnel who, while obtaining satisfaction from their jobs, strive to attain the objectives of the data center.

HIGHLIGHTS

Career Specifications

The focus is on career paths, supplemented with clarification of job requirements, salary ranges, and responsibilities.

Personnel Recruiting

After clarifying the goals and precautions associated with personnel recruitment, a five-step recruiting process is presented to improve the likelihood of hiring competent, interested, and compatible personnel.

Personnel Planning

Stress is placed on individual commitment for meeting data center objectives and on individual training programs for meeting personal objectives.

Personnel Motivation

The most recent theories and practices are provided to motivate personnel, including the theories of Maslow and Herzberg, followed by job enrichment and other practices.

Performance Appraisal

Positive, progress-oriented interviews are recommended to eliminate or lessen poor personnel performance, always aiming to attain data center and personal objectives.

Recommendations exist for all aspects of personnel administration. Of the ideas and approaches available, many have proved to be useful to data center managers.

All aspects of personnel administration are usually treated as detached topics, independent of one another; however, many of these aspects can be united into a structure that is both dynamic and coordinated. The primary aspects of personnel administration, the aspects discussed in this chapter, are personnel recruiting, training, motivation, appraisal, and performance improvement. The means for unifying these aspects, for making them dynamic and coordinated, is the use of personnel career paths. With the aid of career paths, a person is recruited and trained, motivated and appraised, and if necessary, corrected to proceed along a career path.

The data center manager benefits because oriented and motivated personnel create fewer personnel problems and increase the likelihood of attaining data center objectives. The establishment of career paths is thus a way to achieve effective personnel administration. However, besides career path information, other career-related information should be documented. Career path documentation does not indicate the skills, salary range, and responsibilities associated with each position. When this information is documented, total career specifications are available.

CAREER SPECIFICATIONS

Career specification documentation, to be complete, must answer the questions: What career path can a person follow? What skills are required for each position along a career path? What is the salary range for each position? What responsibilities are associated with each position? The documents recommended to answer these questions are:

1. Career ladders
2. Job/skills matrix
3. Skill level narratives
4. Salary/grade ranges chart
5. Job descriptions

Career Paths

Career paths indicate the possible paths personnel can follow when promoted from one position to another. Some positions on a career path may permit promotion to only one other position, whereas other positions may permit advancement, and sometimes a lateral change, to more than one position. As stated, each of the major aspects of personnel administration benefits from the use of career paths.

Benefits for Personnel Recruitment. The data center manager benefits because it becomes easy to determine the requirements for the immediate position and to determine the requirements appropriate for advancement along the potential career paths. A person who may seem ideal for the present position may not be suitable for advancement along any of the career paths. Unless it is considered acceptable by both manager and applicant to be restricted to one job, that person would be automatically rejected. It is possible that new career paths may develop that are suitable for that person, but this gamble should not be taken. The applicant obviously benefits from knowledge of what positions may eventually be attained. Besides being assured that the job is not a dead-end position, the applicant has the opportunity to decide whether or not the potential career paths are appealing. The data center directly benefits from hiring persons who will be satisfied with their career opportunities.

Benefits for Personnel Planning. Unless the data center manager knows the intended career path for each person, how can training for the next career step be determined? On the other hand, the chosen career path determines what training is needed. The training scheduled for a person assuming more managerial responsibilities is different from that scheduled for a person becoming more and more involved with the technical aspects of the data center. As a person assumes more managerial responsibility, the scope of knowledge and responsibility increases to include such activities as budgeting and managing people. In contrast, a person becoming more and more of a technical specialist decreases scope of knowledge and responsibility to the limited specialty, whether it is hardware-performance evaluation or file library control or any of the many other specialties. One additional benefit the data center manager gains— a very important benefit—is greater assurance of backup personnel for each position. By training persons for advancement to the next position, that person automatically becomes backup to that position. As for benefits for personnel, training requirements to satisfy career path requirements become meaningful, and the usefulness of training for their growth and advancement stimulates interested participation.

Benefits for Personnel Motivation. Managers can use the expectation of progressing along a career path to motivate personnel. The more a man-

ager makes career satisfactions correspond to the needs of each person, the more that person is motivated to contribute to high data center performance. A person becomes more motivated when a direct relationship exists between performance and recognition and advancement. Without a definite career path, only a vague feeling exists that effort is appreciated and that promotions are possible. On the other hand, the existence of a career path and management's attentiveness to adhering to it assure each person that his or her future has been seriously considered and planned for.

Benefits for Performance Appraisal. Managers and personnel can meet and discuss significant and specific plans instead of discussing relatively trivial

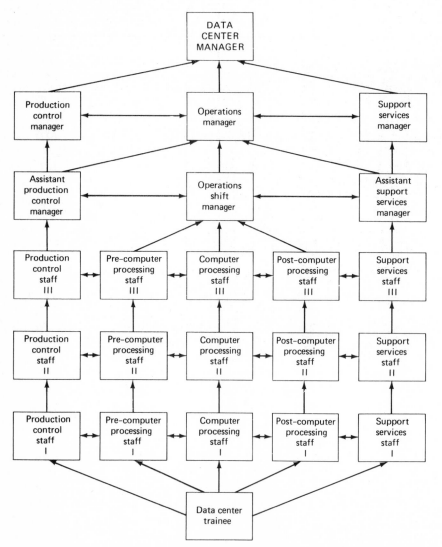

ILLUSTRATION 3-1. Overview of Data Center Career Paths: This overview indicates the possible career paths in a data center, although this chart requires modifications to show the actual titles used in a specific data center, and to show the actual career paths possible.

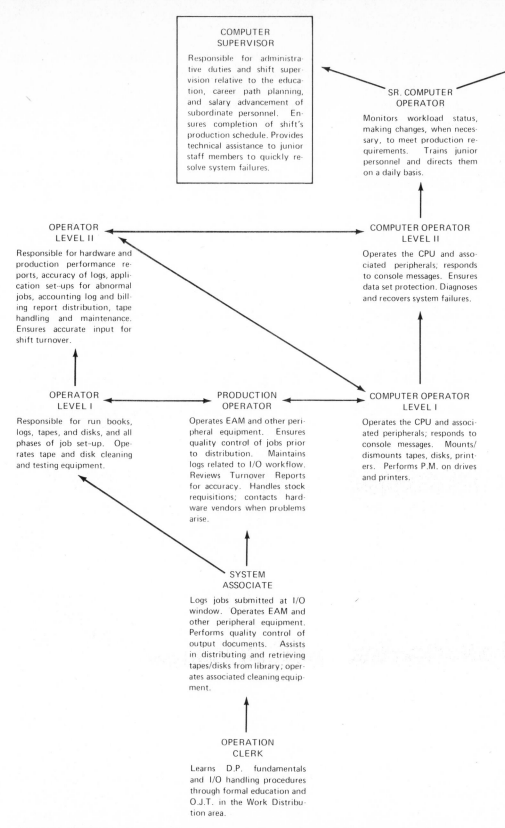

COMPUTER SUPERVISOR

Responsible for administrative duties and shift supervision relative to the education, career path planning, and salary advancement of subordinate personnel. Ensures completion of shift's production schedule. Provides technical assistance to junior staff members to quickly resolve system failures.

SR. COMPUTER OPERATOR

Monitors workload status, making changes, when necessary, to meet production requirements. Trains junior personnel and directs them on a daily basis.

SCHEDULER

Plans and coordinates schedules for shift's production workloads. Interfaces with Systems, Operations and User staff to resolve scheduling problems; ensures maximum productivity of computer resources.

OPERATOR LEVEL II

Responsible for hardware and production performance reports, accuracy of logs, application set-ups for abnormal jobs, accounting log and billing report distribution, tape handling and maintenance. Ensures accurate input for shift turnover.

COMPUTER OPERATOR LEVEL II

Operates the CPU and associated peripherals; responds to console messages. Ensures data set protection. Diagnoses and recovers system failures.

OPERATOR LEVEL I

Responsible for run books, logs, tapes, and disks, and all phases of job set-up. Operates tape and disk cleaning and testing equipment.

PRODUCTION OPERATOR

Operates EAM and other peripheral equipment. Ensures quality control of jobs prior to distribution. Maintains logs related to I/O workflow. Reviews Turnover Reports for accuracy. Handles stock requisitions; contacts hardware vendors when problems arise.

COMPUTER OPERATOR LEVEL I

Operates the CPU and associated peripherals; responds to console messages. Mounts/dismounts tapes, disks, printers. Performs P.M. on drives and printers.

SYSTEM ASSOCIATE

Logs jobs submitted at I/O window. Operates EAM and other peripheral equipment. Performs quality control of output documents. Assists in distributing and retrieving tapes/disks from library; operates associated cleaning equipment.

OPERATION CLERK

Learns D.P. fundamentals and I/O handling procedures through formal education and O.J.T. in the Work Distribution area.

ILLUSTRATION 3-2. Career Ladder: Career paths for a segment of the data center positions are precisely shown with a succinct statement of responsibilities for each position. *Source:* Manufacturers Hanover Trust Company.

side issues. Too often, appraisal interviews at best become unproductive, and at worst have a degenerative effect. With a knowledge of what is expected of a person now and later, discussion can center on how to obtain personal and data center goals. When a person has not performed well or has been disruptive, the discussion can be kept positive, stressing concern about that person's advancement and how to improve the situation. Having the proper techniques and supporting documentation available can set a positive tone to all communications between management and personnel.

Several methods of documenting career paths have been used; some of them appear complex, others simpler and more relevant to individual career paths. A complex chart representing career paths from the entry position of Data Center Trainee to the top position of Data Center Manager is shown on Illustration 3-1. This chart gives a helpful overview of the hierarchy of data center positions, and can be used by the data center manager, with changes for his data center's particular hierarchy of positions, to produce career path charts for individual career paths.

An excellent means of presenting precisely and clearly individual career paths is used by Manufacturers Hanover Trust Company (MHT) and is called a *career ladder.* Illustration 3-2 shows a typical career ladder. A few career ladder documents can easily present all career paths in the data center. As shown, a short narrative explains the primary responsibilities associated with each job title.

Job/Skills Requirements

Instead of promoting a person from one position to another because that person has been in a position for a long period of time, a person should be promoted only if that person has the required skills or can quickly attain the required skills. Preliminary to judging skills competency, definite skill levels must be directly related with each position. MHT provides an excellent means for documenting this with documents that correspond directly to their career ladder documents. They use *job/skills matrices* and *skill level narratives.* Illustrations 3-3 and 3-4 show examples of these. A glance at a job/skills matrix shows how skills must be increased to permit progression from one position to another, and the skill level narratives state specifically what those levels of skills are. No confusion of the skills required for a position can exist.

A career ladder, a job/skills matrix, and skill level narratives thus work together in guiding the career of each person in the data center.

Hardware	Operation clerk	System associate	Production operator	Operator level I	Operator level II	Computer operator level I	Computer operator level II	Sr. computer operator	Computer supervisor	Scheduler	Sr. computer supervisor
UNIVAC hardware and peripheral devices	1	1	2	2	2	2	3	4	4	3	4
IV phase and communications hardware						2	2	2	2	2	2
Work distribution hardware	2	2	4						4	2	2
Installation planning and layout									2		4

ILLUSTRATION 3-3. Job/Skills Matrix: Progression of skill levels are directly related to positions shown on the Career Ladder; the skill level codes are described on the Skill Level Narratives. *Source:* Manufacturers Hanover Trust Company.

UNIVAC Hardware and Peripheral Devices

Level 1: Awareness of the capabilities of the mainframes and the characteristics, speeds, and volumes of the commonly found peripheral devices.

Level 2: Moderate to heavy usage of the CPU and its peripherals. Moderate knowledge of direct access devices, core requirements and cycle time.

Level 3: Knowledge of I/O bound vs. CPU bound processing and its effect on the hardware. Good knowledge of performance and criteria, such as configuration and interface capabilities.

Level 4: Extensive knowledge of the hardware, sequential and direct access devices, configuration optimization and performance criteria. Experience in hardware troubleshooting.

ILLUSTRATION 3-4. Skill Level Narratives: An explanation is provided for each skill level code shown for a skill on the Job/Skills Matrix. *Source:* Manufacturers Hanover Trust Company.

Job/Salary Settings

The salary for each position must be first established and then presented in a form easy to grasp. The resulting salaries should be justified by internal and external criteria. The internal criteria include the organization's financial condition, its reputation, and its fringe benefits. These factors are obvious, but what may not be obvious are some of the fringe benefits that exist but go un-

heralded. One such fringe benefit is the training which prepares persons for career path advancement. The author has seen many persons leave stimulating environments, places where new techniques and experimentation were continually tried, to go to environments that paid a few more dollars, or had prettier work stations, but were monotonous and unprogressive. These persons were unaware of the prior environment's advantages, and the prior managers had failed to stress these advantages. Thus, active capable persons are lost.

The primary external criterion for setting salary scale is the pay scale of other data centers, particularly those of competitors. Although many salary surveys are available from many sources and are helpful, their relevance to local pay scales must be considered. The pay scales in a suburban area, for example, are almost always lower than those in a city. Pay scales also vary according to organization type, which may be educational or manufacturing or insurance, and according to data center size.

After pay scales have been established, this information must be conveyed to personnel. The most direct and easiest representation of this information is shown in Illustration 3-5, a chart of *salary/grade ranges*. Each job is assigned a pay-scale grade, with a minimum and a maximum salary as-

ILLUSTRATION 3-5. Pay Scale Chart: After the salary range for each position in the data center is assigned a pay scale grade, a single pay scale chart shows the salary ranges for all data center positions.

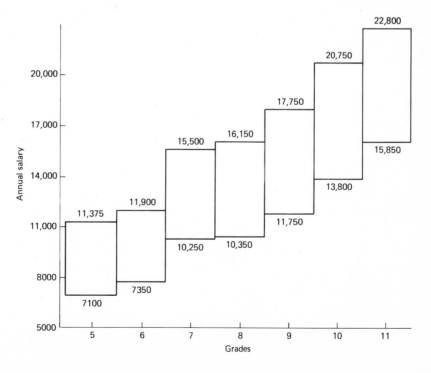

sociated with each grade. By assigning grades instead of displaying job titles, a single chart covers all jobs in the data center. This chart also clearly indicates the pay advantages of advancing along intended career paths, moving from one pay grade to the next.

Job Descriptions

The last document required for career specifications is the *job description.* Basically, this document lists the responsibilities associated with a job. However, it can and should serve more purposes than merely being a reminder of personnel responsibilities. The potential purposes of a job description include:

1. Provide an opportunity to define job-related requirements
2. Clarify job-related requirements to new personnel
3. Provide a means for documenting performance standards
4. Aid the personnel department in determining fair pay scales
5. Guide personnel recruitment and selection
6. Guide determination of training requirements
7. Establish responsibilities, accountability, and authority
8. Document reporting and supervisory responsibilities
9. Permit evaluation of personnel performance, particularly for determining promotions, terminations, or transfers
10. Provide a means for judging work-related grievances
11. Provide clues for job improvements

The number of purposes that job descriptions can serve are impressive. Despite their potential usefulness, most companies prepare them because policy demands their preparation, not because their value is appreciated. This may account for the existence of casually considered and defined standards for preparing job descriptions, if standards were considered and defined at all. Often when job descriptions exist, all jobs are not included, and those that are included are out-of-date, not trusted, and thus not referred to. In many cases trivial information is included while critical information is ignored, formats are confusing,

and the manner of expression tends to be pompous and much too general. Some are too sketchy, and others are too wordy. Illustration 3–6 shows a one-page job description that encourages the inclusion of only critical information and provides a format that clearly separates information. With agreement on a job description's content and format, a third standard is required: how information should be expressed. The following discussion of these three standards refers to the recommended form shown in Illustration 3–6.

Job Description Content. The first item is a statement of primary responsibility. This should be a statement of the primary goal for that job, such as "control the receipt and distribution of all jobs, data, and output" for the job-control personnel. This statement should not be, as is done frequently, a summary of all the responsibilities listed later, which usually requires long, torturous, one-sentence paragraphs. Simply, this statement should answer the question, What does this person do—stated in about five seconds?

The section of the job description entitled "Typical Duties" should include only the major duties, avoiding any attempt to include every trivial duty. This approach actually stimulates the inclusion of the critical job-related duties that may be otherwise left out inadvertently. The information required for "Reporting Responsibility" and "Supervisory Responsibilities" should state by job titles who is the superior and who are the subordinates. As for "Job Qualification," all educational, skill, and aptitude qualifications must be listed; if there are many, the primary ones should be listed and the job/skill matrix should be referred to for details on skill requirements.

Job Description Format. Many of the largest companies, many with competent forms-design personnel, do *not* have a form for job descriptions. The typists supply headings and type as many pages as requested, usually varying from one to four pages. The fill-in information, since it uses the same font used for the headings, does not stand out as it should, giving the overall impression that the job description was prepared as an afterthought. A much more attractive and pleasant approach is to use a form, such as the one recommended. The form shown includes a feature that some managers may want for those jobs requiring

Job Description

Department	Date
Job title	Job code

Primary responsibility

Typical duties

☐ Check this box if continued on the other side.

Reporting responsibilities

Supervisory responsibilities

Job qualifications

ILLUSTRATION 3-6. Job Description.

more space for listing duties. A small box with the instruction "Check this box if continued on the other side" is located at the bottom of the area entitled "Typical Duties."

Job Description Manner of Expression. The final consideration when preparing job descriptions is how the duties should be expressed. General, abstract wording should be avoided. Instead of "control timely receipt of jobs and data," this duty should be stated in specific, measurable terms, such as "telephone user representative if a job or data are not received at least one hour before scheduled time." The word "control" is replaced by the less-abstract phrase "telephone user representative if a job or data are not received," and the general phrase "timely receipt" is replaced by "at least one hour before scheduled time." A person reading the second statement knows precisely what should be performed and can judge whether or not it was performed properly.

Each statement of a duty, however, should stress results to be obtained, not the activities to be performed. To convert the preceding statement to a result-oriented statement, it can be reworded: "To minimize late receipt of jobs and data that may cause deadlines to be missed, telephone user representative if a job or data are not received at least one hour before scheduled time." This statement is what is needed; it is precise, measurable, and result-oriented.

PERSONNEL RECRUITING

The need for concern and care when recruiting is well expressed in Milton Mandell's book *The Selection Process: Choosing the Right Man for the Job.*

> Clearly, no organization can itself survive and grow if it fails to hire employees with the capacity for self-development and to provide an atmosphere conducive to achievement.[1]

This statement returns to the point stressed earlier: Recruitment should center on searching for and selecting personnel according to how well

they fit the career paths available, not merely according to how well they fit the immediate job. With this attitude and all the preparatory work already recommended, recruitment for a career can commence. Many companies have prepared statements to guide the recruiting process, such as the following by the General Motors Corporation:

> The careful selection and placement of employees to make sure that they are physically, mentally and temperamentally fitted to the jobs they are expected to do; to make sure that new employees can reasonably be expected to develop into desirable employees, and so that there will be a minimum of square pegs in round holes.[2]

Before considering the actual recruiting process, a few precautions should be noted:

1. *Avoid bias.* Everyone has preferences as to the type of person wanted which have no relevance to the job requirements. This is one of the few generalizations that most people will accept. It may be a preference for neatly or conservatively dressed persons, or conversely for the casual, lively dresser. Some persons do not like excessive hand motions, cigarette smoking, or long hair. All of these biases usually have nothing to do with the job. If a specific image must be satisfied or if safety standards must be met, such as the elimination of cigarette smoking, then normally irrelevant factors must receive attention.

2. *Avoid the halo effect.* This refers to the tendency of basing a decision on one factor or on a few desirable factors. Many an incompetent keying operator or console operator have been hired because they have "such pleasant personalities." In contrast, some managers place stress on highly motivated, aggressive persons, forgetting that these same persons may cause friction with others and, in their eagerness to get the job done, may skip over critical details that are necessary for proper processing. Each person must be judged by all pertinent characteristics, not by a preferred few.

3. *Avoid false economy.* Do not search for the lowest-priced persons available. A competent computer operator, for example, can and has saved organizations many times their yearly income—besides avoiding embarrassment, loss of user faith, and possibly loss of customers. Less-competent computer operators are not aware when processing is not

[1]Milton M. Mandell, *The Selection Process: Choosing the Right Man for the Job* (New York: American Management Association, 1964).

[2]A. A. Hendrix, "Interviewing Techniques," *Industrial Medicine and Surgery*, vol. 19, 1950.

occurring properly, and to add to their liability, with total lack of awareness they calmly create problems, such as destroying files.

4. *Avoid stereotyped interviews.* Adapt each interview to the person being interviewed. Follow leads suggested by the applicant's interests and hesitancies. These reactions may indicate lack of real interest in the career presented or, in contrast, definite interest and aptitude. If the immediate job requires mostly repetitive, lonely work, watch for hints of persons who become bored quickly or who are very outgoing and require frequent socializing.

The Five-step Personnel-recruiting Process

The personnel-recruiting process has been defined in many ways, most of which are similar to the five-step process shown in Illustration 3–7. This process includes all the activities from the screening of applicants to the assurance of physical fitness for the selected person. Each of these steps is discussed in detail in the following sections. Preceding these steps, however, are several preparatory steps, which include knowing policy decisions on hiring practices, verification of hiring criteria,

ILLUSTRATION 3-7. The 5-Step Personnel Recruiting Process.

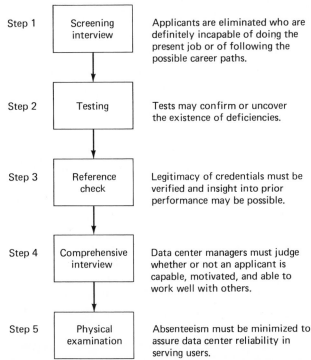

Step 1	Screening interview	Applicants are eliminated who are definitely incapable of doing the present job or of following the possible career paths.
Step 2	Testing	Tests may confirm or uncover the existence of deficiencies.
Step 3	Reference check	Legitimacy of credentials must be verified and insight into prior performance may be possible.
Step 4	Comprehensive interview	Data center managers must judge whether or not an applicant is capable, motivated, and able to work well with others.
Step 5	Physical examination	Absenteeism must be minimized to assure data center reliability in serving users.

awareness of time constraint, and use of all personnel sources permitted.

In a data center, policy decisions that are frequently in effect are to hire, where possible, only for entry-level positions and to promote or transfer from within the organization. These approaches support adherence to career paths. When an opening occurs, persons at the next lower level should be considered first, and rarely if ever should someone be brought into the organization, ignoring the career paths established. With proper attention to setting up career paths and training personnel for those paths, personnel should always be available for filling positions as they appear. Organizations whose thinking is oriented along the lines of career paths almost automatically adopt these two policies.

As for hiring criteria, all the necessary and desirable requirements must be stated and identified as either necessary or desirable. Too often, superior applicants are rejected because they lack a minor desirable skill, such as experience with a particular type of tape drive, or a skill that is easy to acquire. The necessary requirements must be stated as such, and they must be satisfied. The desirable requirements should be considered when evaluating those applicants who have the necessary requirements. Knowledge and skills requirements are well documented if a job/skills matrix and a skill level narrative exist. When requirements are listed, the motivation and personality requirements are almost always forgotten. Does the job require initiative? Does it require perseverance? Must the person be adaptable? What attitude is expected toward irregular hours and overtime? Is leadership ability necessary?

If a time constraint exists, it may be necessary to know what the absolute minimum requirements are. A more satisfactory approach, however, if an applicant who meets the requirements is not expected to be found quickly, is to hire temporary help. This approach provides more time for careful recruiting. The most likely sources for temporary help are employment agencies, service bureaus, and vendors. From these sources a competent person is likely to be found, and a restrictive time constraint becomes less critical and less likely to lead to a hasty selection.

The final preparatory step before the recruiting process commences is to choose the sources for personnel. For most positions, the answer has already been given: from within the organization whenever possible. The obvious sources outside the organization are agencies and through newspaper advertisements. To reduce the amount of time consumed in the recruiting process, the job requirements should be stated to eliminate those applicants definitely not suitable while encouraging those who may be suitable.

Step 1: The Screening Interview

As indicated in Illustration 3-7, the purpose of the screening interview is to eliminate definitely deficient applicants and to become aware of positive and negative tendencies in abilities, interests, and personality. Anyone not satisfying the minimum requirements for education, willingness to work shift hours or overtime when necessary, ability to cooperate with others, and any other minimum requirements established must be eliminated immediately.

This initial interview uses the application form as a point of focus for examining abilities, interests, and personality. Thus, the questions asked should cover these three areas fairly well, although a screening interview is usually short. Before these three areas are examined, the applicant should be introduced to the organization's goals, policies, and benefits. The applicant's response to this introduction may provide insight into what the applicant considers important and what may be found to be frustrating or disturbing. At the same time, this discussion permits the applicant to relax and feel more comfortable in expressing thoughts and reservations more honestly.

The questions that should be asked are similar to those that follow. The following questions are segmented according to ability, interest, and then personality traits—this is a natural sequence. Also, these questions are further separated according to those that can be related directly to the application form and those that go beyond the application form.

1. *For ability.* In prior jobs, how did you perform in activities similar to those required for this job? Was attention to details and thoroughness required? Was supervision of others required? Can you perform the activities required for the job immediately or with some training? Can you perform the activities required for jobs along the various career paths after receiving adequate training?

2. *For interest.* What was interesting or uninteresting in your prior jobs? What were your personal interests? Why are you interested in this job? Are you interested in possible career paths? Do the career paths agree with your one-year, five-year, and career goals? Will you find activities boring or frustrating? What is your attitude toward working on shifts and overtime? What are your personal interests now?

3. *For personality traits.* Did previous jobs provide adequate opportunity for initiative and self-reliance? Did you find the work routine, boring, or frustrating? Was supervision nearly absent or excessive? Were people friendly and cooperative? What do you find more important, freedom and allowance of initiative or well-defined procedures and strong leadership? What are your strong points? Your weak points? What annoys or frustrates you? Have you analyzed your abilities and interests and related them to your career intentions?

Besides asking these questions, naturally, any unusual information on the application form should also be questioned. Of particular interest are indications of job hopping and poor school grades. Both of these situations can be justified in many ways—but look for potential trouble that will affect the applicant's performance. This includes lack of motivation in doing the job, inability to work with others, or simply inability to do the job correctly.

Step 2: Testing

The surest method of testing an applicant's suitability for a job is to observe that person on the job. Since this is not a practical solution, the next best approach is to test a person for the qualities most important for the job and the possible career paths. The reliability of tests, however, has been questioned by many experts. For example, Robert Thorndike and Elizabeth Hagen examined the careers of 10,000 men 10 years after they were tested during World War II. Their conclusion was that the results "would suggest that we should view the long-range prediction of occupational success of aptitude tests with a good bit of skepticism."[3] The attitude is humorously presented in the cartoon in Illustration 3-8. This attitude is widely held for other types of tests.

[3] Franklin G. Moore, *Management: Organization and Practice* (New York: Harper & Row, Pub., 1964), p. 251.

"I took our aptitude test at the plant this morning. Thank heaven, I own the company."

ILLUSTRATION 3-8. Reaction to Aptitude Tests. *Source: The Wall Street Journal,* Oct. 6, 1960. Reproduced by permission of Joe Mirachi.

In spite of this prevailing attitude, another, apparently contradictory, attitude exists: Tests are believed to uncover deficiencies and may confirm suspicion of negative tendencies. The result of a survey showed that 80 percent of United States firms give tests and give them some credence.[4] Considering these reservations and trust in the reliability of testing, tests should be given and judged as indicators, not as absolute guides as to how a person will behave and how effective that person will be on the job.

Before outlining the various types of tests, federal restrictions on the types of tests permitted should be noted. Briefly, the only tests that can be given are those that test for specific characteristics, not for general characteristics that may be affected by a person's environment, such as intelligence tests that are affected by the vocabulary level a person has been exposed to. Misunderstanding of this restriction, even by personnel managers, has caused many organizations to avoid giving tests for specific skills and aptitudes.

Tests fall into four categories: achievement

tests, aptitude tests, interest tests, and personality tests.

1. *Achievement tests.* These tests estimate the knowledge and skills of an applicant. They might include questions on how to operate equipment that an applicant is expected to be familiar with, and they may survey knowledge that an applicant is expected to know.

2. *Aptitude tests.* These tests estimate potential for development, the likelihood of being able to perform specific skills well. They test such aptitudes as the ability to learn, to reason, and to handle machinery. Some tests examine a single aptitude, and general tests examine several aptitudes. Two widely used general aptitude tests are the General Aptitude Test Battery (GATB) and the Army General Classification Test (AGCT).

3. *Interest tests.* Each person has groups of interest that are satisfying—and very likely activities that are dissatisfying. The more activities associated with a job that an applicant finds satisfying, the more likely is that person likely to perform well; and any activities in which an applicant lacks interest or dislikes will detract from performance. Two tests that seek to identify interests are Strongs Vocational Interest Blank and Kuder Preference Record.

4. *Personality tests.* A wide range of personality traits can be examined by tests, indicating with some reliability strong tendencies. These tests attempt to determine such characteristics as motivation, cooperativeness, emotional control and stability, characteristic mood, and personal values. As in the other test types, there are a variety of tests that can be given; in this category three tests are the Rorschach test, the Thematic Apperception Test (TAT), and the Thematic Evaluation of Management Potential test (TEMP).

Step 3: Reference Check

This step can be the most important, but is more often trivial and unreliable. Reference checking is important for checking the legitimacy of credentials. An applicant that presents false credentials knows that he or she may not be suitable for the job, and for that reason the interviewer can use that person's own evaluation to immediately eliminate him or her. Another reason for immediate elimination is the dishonesty inherent in this behavior; an organization is fortunate when dishonest and blatant self-seeking individuals are avoided. Thus, the information provided on an application form about prior employment and schooling must be verified.

[4]Dale Yoder, *Personnel Management and Industrial Relations,* 6th ed. (Englewood Cliffs, N.J.: Prentice-Hall, Inc., 1970), p. 311.

Now for an apparent contradiction. If an applicant has stated prior work experience and education correctly, accomplishments may be significant; but positive and negative comments of others in response to reference checks are totally unreliable. First of all, many organizations refuse to provide any information but verification of employment and attendance. Thus, a person who had been fired, and in some cases has even physically walked off the premises of the organization, will receive a noncommittal recommendation. It may sound like an endorsement, but it is actually a comment only on what was done well and not on deficiencies or the serious wrongs performed. Second, an applicant may receive negative comments from an immediate superior because of personal differences, even though actual performance may have been much above average. Since personal evaluations are usually not permitted by organizations, it is unlikely that more than one person will "slip," accidentally or intentionally, and make a negative or positive statement. If, however, several personal comments are obtained and they are all positive or negative, then these comments become reliable. But be cautious. Even if comments agree, they may only indicate that the applicant has one serious deficiency, possibly one that is irrelevant to the job and the possible careers being considered.

As for gaps in education or employment history, they may indicate reasons for immediately disqualifying an applicant. They can indicate a person's resistance to steady employment or the occurrence of "resignations"—often a euphemism for being fired. The reasons for these gaps may be lack of motivation in working, interpersonal conflicts, or simply incompetency. Therefore, gaps should not be ignored. At the same time, empathy should be shown, and the applicant's quest for the "right job" should be considered.

Step 4: The Comprehensive Interview

All the previous recruiting steps could have been and usually are performed by persons in the personnel department. This step, however, must be performed by data center managers. All the precautions mentioned at the beginning of this section and all the questions introduced in step 1, the screening interview, apply to the comprehensive interview. Since data center managers have less

"He meets all the criteria, Chief, but brown shoes with a blue suit...?"

ILLUSTRATION 3-9. Pitfalls of Job Interviewing. *Source:* Printed with the permission of Joe Mirachi.

training and less exposure in conducting interviews, greater care is necessary to consider all relevant and only relevant criteria for personnel selection. Illustration 3-9 shows a cartoon that exaggerates but indicates the kind of superficial thinking that can occur when evaluating applicants. This relates to the precautions mentioned earlier of biased preconceptions and the halo effect, the rejection or acceptance of an applicant because of one or only a few, possibly irrelevant, criteria.

The author knows of one situation where an attractive woman who was alert, capable, and anxious to do a good job was not hired for a secretarial job because she was too attractive and expected to distract the men in the department and attract men from other departments. This person was rejected, unfairly, because of an unfounded belief.

With the results of the screening interview and the tests in front of them, data center managers can ask very specific questions to confirm or disprove what is indicated. Firm but friendly insistence on definite answers is necessary. Deficiencies and potentialities should be uncovered, and the managers must use judgment in deciding whether or not potentialities offset deficiencies.

With evaluation of each applicant's strengths

and weaknesses, the data center managers are now able to select the applicant who is most likely to be compatible with the job and career possibilities, and they are ready to make a job offer—depending on whether the applicant passes the physical examination.

Step 5:   The Physical Examination

The primary purpose of the examination is to hire persons least likely to be frequently absent from the job. Obviously, excessive absenteeism affects the data center's ability to provide reliable service to users. Not as obvious, but just as necessary, are the secondary reasons: to keep health care and life insurance costs low. To accomplish these goals most companies require applicants to go to a company-approved doctor for the physical examination; many of the larger organizations perform extensive examinations, sometimes requiring four or more hours, at their own physical-examination facilities. Applicants must also satisfy any special physical requirements of the job. These requirements may be strength to lift heavy boxes of supplies; coordination to perform several activities at the same time, such as is often required of computer operators; and the hearing ability needed to attend to sounds emitted from equipment, which indicate either routine or emergency attention.

Finally, a person who passes all the requirements of the recruiting process and is hired should be informed of any probationary requirements, and at the same time it should be made clear that evaluations are intended to help that person perform well and progress along a career path. The only action now required is to introduce the selected person to the staff. Orienting the person to what work is to be done, and introducing the new person to others makes adjustment to the new   environment easier and more comfortable, with less chance for misunderstandings and poor adjustment.

PERSONNEL PLANNING

Personnel planning consists of establishing data center objectives for personnel to meet, and providing training so that personnel can proceed along their career paths. The establishing of data center objectives is best done according to a formalized approach, of which both management by objectives and management by group objectives have been successful. The last of these two approaches is not widely known. Both of these approaches are discussed in some detail. Through personnel planning, data center objectives are set for personnel, and personnel are then responsible for attaining those objectives.

This aspect of personnel planning satisfies the needs of the data center but does not satisfy the needs of each person. The attention of each person should also be focused on a predefined career path, a personal objective. This aspect of personnel planning requires management to set training requirements and to prepare a training schedule.

Thus, besides clarification of data center and career path objectives, plans are established to meet the needs of the data center and of each person. The end result is: a static, nondirective environment is avoided; instead, a dynamic, progressive environment is encouraged.

Management by Objectives

"Perfection of means, and confusion of goals, characterize our age," comments Albert Einstein.[5] Each manager should clearly define objectives and evaluate and alter where necessary the means to meet these objectives. Thus, all actions, all documents, and all standards would be judged from the viewpoint of how well they permit objectives to be attained. Observe that the word "objective" and has been used in preference to the word "goal." The reason is that "goal" suggests a one-time attainment, and also suggests a struggle that is not necessarily true—anyway, not always. On the other hand, the word "objective" suggests something to be attained on a continuous basis, without suggestions of emotional stress. General approaches and specific techniques may be the substance of each manager's day, but they are likely to miss their targets if the targets are not kept in plain view. That is the primary benefit, only one of many benefits, of management by objectives (MBO).

The various benefits of MBO are impressive. The following list indicates the benefits emphasized by various MBO specialists, particularly the

[5]W. L. Howse, "How to Determine Church Objectives," *Church Administrator*, January 1964, p. 8.

insight provided by Karl Albrecht in his stimulating book *Successful Management By Objectives:*[6]

1. Provides structure and direction
2. Provides challenge
3. Increases feeling of worth
4. Increases commitment and interest
5. Clarifies responsibilities and expectations
6. Provides opportunity for managers and staff to identify objectives
7. Provides a means for appraising performance
8. Encourages self-appraisal and self-development
9. Increases productivity
10. Supports "managerial excellence"

The above claims for MBO may appear excessive, but when MBO is conducted in an affirmative atmosphere, with orientation toward objectives rather than toward the means used, these positive results can occur. MBO stimulates assertiveness, for both managers and staff; the absence of MBO, in contrast, results in a reactive environment, where each person waits for something to happen (usually an emergency) and then reacts. A manager who follows the management-by-reaction instead of the management-by-objectives philosophy is usually too busy to plan for improvements; that manager is busy chasing after one emergency after another. He becomes a fire fighter and, in effect, is running a fire-fighting department.

It becomes clear that MBO is desirable. It also becomes clear that MBO is not a set of techniques and forms, although they are necessary, but a way of thinking; it is not an additional task for a manager, but a way of doing his job. Since forms and procedures merely support the frame of mind required for MBO, they can and should be changed whenever the need becomes apparent. Many MBO programs have failed primarily because organizations have confused the techniques of MBO with the purposes of MBO. All too frequently, managers become tangled in the mechanics of MBO when they should be moving directly toward objectives. Many complex interlocking procedures and hierarchies of forms have been established—and have been smothered and crushed under their own weight. The lesson to be learned is that the simpler the mechanics, the more likely attention will remain focused on

[6]Karl Albrecht, *Successful Management by Objectives* (Englewood Cliffs, N.J.: Prentice-Hall, Inc., 1978).

objectives, and the more likely the application of MBO will be successful.

Although the existence of hierarchies of forms has just been criticized, it must exist; but it should be kept simple. Illustration 3–10 shows a clever and simple means of displaying the hierarchy of primary objectives in a middle-size company. A similar means of documentation can be adopted by data center management. Thus, the expectations assigned to the data center manager can be succinctly shown, indicating how they are distributed to the various levels and functional areas. When this is supported by documented commitments between each person and that person's manager, the required documentation has been supplied. The chart recommended to show hierarchy of objectives and the forms to document commitments of each person are merely tools, not a required method for implementing MBO. It may be accepted as suggested, or adapted to the specific structure, policies, and needs of the organization.

The MBO procedure has sometimes been made to seem difficult, tedious, and full of pitfalls. Actually, the procedure as it affects each individual consists of that person meeting with his or her immediate manager and attending to a two-step procedure: first, mutually agreeing on objectives; second, establishing performance criteria for later determination of success.

Mutually Agreeing on Objectives. There are two sets of objectives to be agreed upon, as stated earlier. The first set consists of the data center's objectives. These include such objectives as meeting deadlines and minimizing errors. The second set of objectives is usually treated casually, although stressed several times in this chapter; it consists of the objectives necessary for a person to progress along a career path. Specifically, this refers to agreeing on training objectives. The form shown in Illustration 3–11 satisfies these objectives by providing space for listing data center and training objectives. It also provides space for appraising personal qualities. This form thus becomes critical for stimulating an individual's performance and for evaluating performance.

Establishing Performance Criteria. Too often, a statement of an objective is "fuzzy"; it is not specific and therefore its attainment cannot be

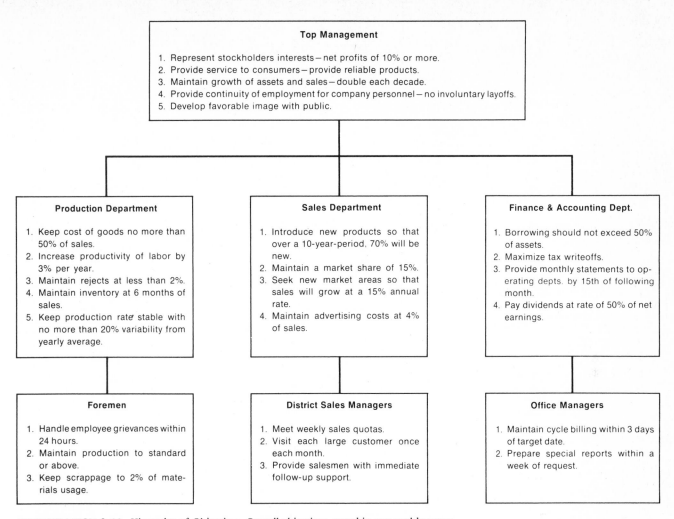

ILLUSTRATION 3-10. Hierarchy of Objectives: Overall objectives, stated in measurable terms when possible, are defined at the highest level in the organization, and then each lower level in the organization defines its objectives to make the overall objectives possible. *Source:* Joseph L. Massie and John Douglas, *Managing: A Contemporary Introduction,* 2nd ed. (Englewood Cliffs, N.J.: Prentice-Hall, 1977), p. 278.

determined. An objective must be specific and measurable. Karl Albrecht lists five characteristics of a nonfuzzy statement of an objective:

Specific—It spells out, in concrete terms, what is to be achieved, to what degree, and the deadline for achieving it. It uses very specific terms instead of abstractions. It focuses on performance, and it uses performance variables whenever possible. It tells how much, how many, how big, how small, etc. Or, it identifies specific qualitative conditions which leave no doubt as to their attainment.

Payoff-oriented—It identifies a set of end conditions which have intrinsic value, or which are associated with something of value. It is clearly a worthwhile thing to achieve; there is an unquestionable element of value in the conditions it identifies.

Intrinsically rewarding—It specifies a desired set of conditions which will bring rewards *to the person who is to strive for them.* That is, there must be associated with the goal a reward which the "action person" wants and is willing to work for. This may be simply a matter of recognition accorded the action person for achieving it; or it may be a payoff associated directly with the goal. But, in any case, it is only a goal in the eyes of the action person if he himself can foresee a personal payoff in accomplishing it.

Realistic—It identifies a target which is reasonably attainable. It accounts for practical experience and various uncertainties, and it allows a reasonable margin for error. It rests upon reasonable assumptions about the future and about the people who will work to achieve the goal.

Personnel Objectives and Performance Review

Name	Date prepared
Department	Prior review date

Data center objectives	Appraisal comment

Training objectives	Date	Comment

Personal quality	Poor	Fair	Good	Exc.
Competency				
Leadership				
Initiative				
Reliability				
Cooperativeness				

Reviewed by	Date

ILLUSTRATION 3-11. Personnel Objectives and Performance Review Form.

Observable—It specifies a set of conditions which can be detected, a target which can be identified to the satisfaction of all concerned, especially the people responsible for its achievement. These conditions will be clearly recognizable when the goal has been achieved.[7]

An example of a fuzzy statement of an objective is "to meet deadlines for all scheduled jobs and to attempt to satisfy unscheduled job requests." How will a manager determine if an attempt to satisfy unscheduled job requests was made? His only means would be frequent, personal observation or reports of frequent observation of another manager. Even then, a precise means of evaluating performance is not provided. However, the situation is completely different if the statement of objective is "to meet deadlines for scheduled jobs, and to complete at least 90 percent of the unscheduled jobs within 24 hours of the receipt of each job and its accompanying data, and to complete the remaining 10 percent of the unscheduled jobs within 48 hours." This is a lengthy statement, but it is comprehensive, precise, and measurable. This statement permits performance appraisal.

Management by Group Objectives

MBO is an excellent means for stimulating action and enthusiasm, but unfortunately it also stimulates aggressiveness. Once the objectives for a person have been clearly defined and the benefits are apparent, especially those for moving that person along a chosen career path, the attainment of the objectives may eliminate any concern for cooperative effort. Aggressiveness may even cause efforts to make others look less competent, thus making that person look more competent. This striving for personal gain, which was intended to result in attainment of data center objectives, may actually result in uncooperativeness that may block attainment of data center objectives. To make a bad situation worse, interpersonal relationships are likely to become strained, if not outwardly hostile.

One approach to avoid this situation is to be cautious when defining objectives so that the

attainment of one objective, or combination of objectives, will not negatively affect the attainment of other objectives. This is frequently impossible to do. If a keypunch supervisor's performance is measured by the quantity of work done, as it is most likely to be, this objective definitely conflicts with that of the scheduler, who may require work on low-priority jobs to be held aside until a priority job arrives. Another approach is either to replace or to supplement MBO with management by group objectives (MBGO). As the name suggests, this involves obtaining a group's agreement on group objectives and making the group responsible for the results. MBGO stresses cooperative teamwork and team spirit instead of self-interest and competitiveness.

MBGO provides another benefit, an important benefit that is often forgotten. MBGO satisfies the social need that each person has, the need to feel like an accepted member of a group. Most jobs make no attempt to satisfy this need. Being a member of a group with common objectives provides a feeling of belonging and worth that is often absent. A person who feels important and part of efforts to meet objectives will inevitably be more motivated to attain those objectives, which is definitely beneficial to the data center. This is discussed further when Maslow's hierarchy of needs is explained.

Training

As soon as a person is hired, training requirements should be established, and a training plan should be documented on the form such as shown in Illustration 3–11. At each performance appraisal interview, training needs should be reviewed and scheduled for the next time period, which coincides with the next performance-appraisal interview. Usually this occurs every 6 or 12 months. Adequate attention to training benefits both the data center and the individual. The data center benefits because training increases the likelihood of developing and retaining competent, efficient, and motivated personnel. The end results will be increased likelihood of meeting data center objectives and decreased turnover of personnel. Personnel, on the other hand, benefit from being prepared to perform competently in their present positions and being prepared to move up to the next step in their career paths.

[7]Karl Albrecht, *Successful Management by Objectives*, pp. 75–76.

Training naturally must correspond to the type of career being followed, whether toward a managerial position or a specialist position. If a person is aiming for a managerial position, the training will increase his scope of knowledge to include knowledge of several specialties as well as managerial skills. In contrast, if a person is aiming for a specialist position, the training will decrease his scope of knowledge and provide depth of understanding in the chosen specialty.

Besides managerial and specialty training, education in the organization's and in the data center's standards and procedures is required. This is usually not attended to at all. The absence of any attempt at formal education in standards and procedures is a continuous cause of errors and confusion and automatically makes attainment of this information an on-the-job learning task. The natural time to convey this information is when a person first joins the organization. The minimal effort for providing this education is to indicate what reference manuals are available and how the contents are structured, thus aiding self-education.

But this is a minimal attempt and should not be considered an adequate approach.

From a person's job/skills matrix and skill level narratives, it should be easy to determine what training each person requires. The training each person requires is:

$$\text{Training required} = \text{job and career requirements} - \text{employee's attainments}$$

Most training for data center personnel, particularly lower-level personnel, is on-the-job training. This is the easiest to implement, because it requires little preparation, but it also is the worst method of training if not accompanied by formal training, as in the situation of learning standards and procedures from manuals. If on-the-job training is not accompanied by formal training, and if adequate supervision and assistance are not provided, this approach becomes training by error. Since data center personnel have their own work to do, they have little time to instruct others. And the poorly trained person who is performing poorly naturally feels incompetent

ILLUSTRATION 3–12. The Four-Step Training Method: This training method proved its effectiveness during World War II when it was used for the Training Within Industry program. *Source:* Robert P. Cort, "Getting an Idea Across," in *Effective Communication on the Job,* rev. ed. Edited by Joseph M. Dooher. (N.Y.: American Management Association, 1963), p. 72. ©1963 by American Management Association, Inc., p. 72. All rights reserved.

THE STEPS	HOW EACH IS ACCOMPLISHED
1. *Preparation.* *Prepare* learner to receive new experience.	1. Put the learner at *ease.* 2. Tell him the *title* of the job. 3. Explain the *purpose* of the job. 4. Explain *why* he has been selected to learn. 5. Help him relate his *past experiences* to the job.

2. *Presentation.*
 Set *pattern* in his mind.
	1. *Introduce* him to tools, materials, equipment, and trade terms.
	 2. *Demonstrate* the job, *explaining* each step slowly and clearly.
	 3. Review with him what he should know up to this point:
	    Title of job
	    Purpose of job
	    Steps to be taken

3. *Tryout performance.* Help him form *habit.*	1. Supervise *his* doing of the job. 2. Question him on *weak* and *key* points. 3. Have him repeat until he has developed the *manual skills* and/or *habits of thought.*
4. *Follow through.* Check the *success* of *your* instruction.	1. Have him do the job *alone.* 2. Inspect job against *standards* of performance. 3. Discuss with him *where he goes from here,* whether to a particular job or to new learning experiences.

Course Critique

Last name	First name	Employee no.	Department	Code	Course no.
Course title			Instructor		Date (YYMMDD)

Years of experience with: COBOL ☐ Assembler ☐ Other _____

Course contents	Poor	Fair	Adeq.	Good	Exc.
Usefulness for your work					
Coverage of subject					
Degree of detail					
Overall					

Comments: _____

Course structure	Poor	Fair	Adeq.	Good	Exc.
Adequacy of introduction					
Sequence of material					
Adequacy of summary					
Overall					

Comments: _____

Course presentation (* for audio-visual only; ** for instructor-presented only)

		Quality					Quantity		
		Poor	Fair	Adeq.	Good	Exc.	Not enough	Just right	Too much
*	Audio tapes								
	Video tapes								
**	Verbal								
	Homework								
	Text								
	Handouts								
	Displays								
	Overall								

Comments: _____

ILLUSTRATION 3–13a. Course Critique: This form permits the course attendees to comment on a course's strong and weak points, thus allowing improvement of future presentations of the course. *Source:* Royal-Globe Insurance Companies.

Did you prefer to attend the course (circle one)

Earlier	When given	Later	Not at all

Do you prefer audio-visual instead of instructor-presented course? (circle one)

Yes	No preference	No

Explain: _____

_____

_____

Please list course topics and check appropriate boxes.

Topic	Helpful		Topic useful		Topic new		More Info. needed	
	Most	Least	Yes	No	Yes	No	Yes	No

What topics should be added, if any? _____

_____

_____

Additional comments and suggested changes: _____

_____

_____

_____

_____

ILLUSTRATION 3-13b. Course Critique.

and uncomfortable—exactly the opposite effect that the data center manager wants to instill in his staff.

The more formal training approaches are packaged material, in-house classes, classes at other installations, and seminars. Packaged material includes instruction through books, audio cassettes, and video tapes. These means of instruction have the advantage that each person can proceed at his own pace. The primary disadvantage is that an instructor is usually not available to answer questions, to clarify points that may be blocking understanding of the material that depends on a point not understood.

Packaged material can be replaced or supplemented by in-house classes. The combination of audio-visual tapes and in-house classes is frequently used and has proved effective—where the tapes were professionally prepared and the instructors were trained. If the organization does not have personnel specially trained in preparing and teaching these in-house classes, the next best approach is to have knowledgeable personnel available to answer trainee questions. For those managers who want to give in-house classes but do not have specially trained personnel, a guide to one of the most effective patterns for instructing a class is outlined in Illustration 3-12. This is the famous four-step process used in the Army's "Training within Industry" program during World War II.

The two remaining means of training, classes at other installations and seminars, provide professionally prepared training material and professional instructors. These classes and seminars are conducted by computer manufacturers, such as IBM and CDC, and by various associations, such as the American Management Association (AMA) and Association for Computing Machinery (ACM). CDC, for example, conducted a three-day seminar on computer operations management that the author found competently prepared and presented. AMA classes are listed in the *American Management Association's Management Development Guide*, which is issued every six months and contains over 1000 entries. In addition, it is possible to learn of courses given at universities by contacting the Data Processing Management Association (DPMA).

For formal classes, each attendee should comment on deficiencies and benefits obtained. These evaluations permit managers to determine how effective the course was and what can be done to improve instruction. Many types of evaluation forms are available, and Illustration 3-13 shows one of the most complete forms available. It requires less time to prepare than is apparent at first glance. Analysis of responses entered on the form permits judgment as to whether the approach should be changed; whether the content, structure, and presentation should be improved; whether the course's timing should be changed; and whether additional courses are needed.

PERSONNEL MOTIVATION

A data center manager's intention is not to motivate personnel for the sake of motivation, but to motivate them for the attainment of data center objectives. Although motivation, its factors, and how it is attained are being considered, it is the attainment of data center objectives that must always be kept in mind and should not be sacrificed. Motivation is a key factor for attaining those objectives. That is why a significant amount of space is now devoted to it. As part of the author's research for this book, many data center managers were asked what their primary concerns were and where they hoped for suggestions and guidance. The problem of how to motivate their people always was mentioned, as were other needs such as meeting deadlines and improving computer performance.

After considering several basic issues (such as manager-staff attitudes), the topics discussed include assumptions underlying personnel motivation, the hierarchy of human needs, the differences between satisfying and dissatisfying factors, and the approaches used to motivate. These are discussed in sufficient detail for a manager to determine their usefulness to his particular environment—with stress on job-enrichment techniques.

Basic Considerations

One gap inevitably exists between a data center manager and staff that cannot be bridged. It can be made less noticeable, but it will always exist and must be accepted. A manager gives orders and has the welfare of the data center foremost in mind;

staff must accept and act on orders and have their personal interest foremost in mind. A manager may strive for and may obtain good rapport with the staff, but their differences of viewpoints will continue to exist. The data center manager's solution is to relate each person's personal interests to the interests of the data center. Thus, satisfaction of each person's personal interests leads to satisfaction of the data center's objectives. The importance of career paths and associated activities becomes increasingly apparent.

Even though the separation between manager and staff concerns cannot be eliminated, the encouragement of trust and rapport must be sincerely attempted, not through mere acceptance of the idea, but through actual actions. Dr. M. Feinberg, in *Effective Psychology for Managers,* provides 17 actions each manager should perform and nine actions he should avoid.[8] These actions demonstrate clear concern for the welfare of personnel and therefore should not be taken lightly. Illustration 3–14 lists these actions.

The data center manager must determine what atmosphere is wanted in the data center and not leave this critical factor to chance. A desirable atmosphere is one in which personnel are free to show initiative within a definite, predictable structure. A predictable structure lets them know

what is expected of them and how their performance will be judged; the freedom to show initiative permits them to contribute to the effectiveness of the data center. To attain this atmosphere, the data center manager is placed in the difficult but stimulating position of obtaining discipline to satisfy standards and objectives and of encouraging original thinking to make personnel feel worthwhile, strive to improve themselves, and ultimately to improve data center effectiveness.

This atmosphere avoids the extremes of country-club and sweat-shop environments. When discipline is too lax (the country-club atmosphere), personnel have a vague sense of direction and purpose; when discipline is too strict (the sweat-shop environment), personnel feel harassed and their sense of direction may be too definite—to escape from the data center at the first opportunity. The country-club atmosphere often leads to bored, unconcerned, slow-motion activities. Objectives are treated casually or totally forgotten, and user dissatisfaction increases. The sweat-shop atmosphere creates other problems. Everyone rushes about, frantic and tense, hurrying to meet demands that may be unreasonable. Users get their jobs and are generally satisfied. Staff, however, is not satisfied. The eventual personnel turnover requires the training of new personnel, which adds to the burden of the work already performed in the data center, which only further increases tension and frustra-

[8] M. M. Feinberg, *Effective Psychology for Managers* (Englewood Cliffs, N. J.: Prentice-Hall, Inc., 1965).

ILLUSTRATION 3–14. Management Actions—Desirable and Undesirable. *Source:* M.M. Feinberg, *Effective Psychology for Managers* (Englewood Cliffs, N.J.: Prentice-Hall, 1966).

DESIRABLE	UNDESIRABLE
1. Communicate standards, and be consistent.	1. Never belittle a subordinate.
2. Be aware of your own biases and prejudices.	2. Never criticize a subordinate in front of others.
3. Let people know where they stand.	3. Never fail to give subordinates your undivided attention.
4. Give praise when it is appropriate.	
5. Keep your employees informed of changes that may affect them.	4. Never seem preoccupied with your own interests.
6. Care about your employees.	5. Never play favorites.
7. Perceive people as ends, not means.	6. Never fail to help your subordinates grow.
8. Go out of your way to help subordinates.	7. Never be insensitive to small things.
9. Take responsibility for your employees.	8. Never embarass weak employees.
10. Build independence.	9. Never vacillate in making a decision.
11. Exhibit personal diligence.	
12. Be tactful with your employees.	
13. Be willing to learn from others.	
14. Demonstrate confidence.	
15. Allow freedom of expression.	
16. Delegate, delegate, delegate.	
17. Encourage ingenuity.	

tion. Sweat-shop management has been referred to as "management by baseball bat," because of the need to obtain results through a constant stream of threats. It has also been called the "KITA theory," where KITA is an acronym for "kick in the ass." In contrast to these two extremes, the goal should be a "challenging climate," an environment that provides direction to attain personal and data center objectives and that provides freedom to show initiative, initiative to prove personal ability and to improve data center service.

Paul Tournier, in his book *The Adventure of Living,* indicates the need for a stimulating climate, where persons can participate and contribute. Consider the following statement from his book:

> When a worker believes that he is looked upon merely as a tool of production, he feels he is becoming just a thing. When he feels that an interest is taken in him as a person, in his personal life, in the adventure of his life, that what is expected of him is not just a mechanical gesture but a personal understanding of his work, intelligence, initiative and lively imagination, as well as a sense of being one of a team engaged in a common adventure, he takes cognizance of himself as a person, engaged in a personal adventure.[9]

Hierarchy of Human Needs

"People who sense in their leader the ability to help them satisfy their needs will follow him willingly and enthusiastically."[10] This is the basis for all attempts to motivate personnel. The obvious questions are: What are a person's needs? Which of these needs are of particular importance for motivating a person? Abraham Maslow, in his book *Motivation and Personality,* addressed himself to these questions, and his answers have been repeated many times and have become a reliable guide to viewing needs, their relationships to one another, and their effect on motivating persons.[11]

Basically, Maslow's theory states that each person has a hierarchy of needs, where each lower

level need must be adequately satisfied before the next higher need becomes significant enough to motivate action. Thus, if the lowest need is not satisfied, attempts to satisfy that need provide motivation, while the needs on levels above it have relatively little motivational value. To understand how this applies, it is necessary to know what needs Maslow identified and the hierarchy he established for them. The needs fall into five categories, and the hierarchy from lowest to highest is:

1. *The physiological need.* This includes, for example, a person's need for food and shelter. If this need is not met, a person has difficulty being concerned about anything else—although the deprivations some people have suffered from seem to throw some doubt on this. Artists, for example, have been known to suffer extremely bad conditions to continue with their struggling aspirations. A contradiction, however, does not really exist; they had the bare essentials, although possibly barely enough to survive. If they did not have the bare essentials, their art would have had to be put aside while they did something to survive. From a data center manager's point of view, his concern is that each person is receiving a salary and receiving benefits that are adequate to meet that person's living requirements. A person who requires more than can be reasonably supplied will become dissatisfied and is likely to become troublesome, particularly if that person is impatient in waiting for advancement on his career path and associated salary increases.

2. *The safety need.* In general terms, this means protection from threats. Although each person may not be actually concerned about physical attack, the effect is similar if that person believes that his job is not secure. Job security is a problem in many environments, particularly in those dependent on the receipt of contracts. Fortunately, personnel in data centers are usually required to do the work that exists no matter what the workload. Thus, security is likely not to be a problem. Concern for security becomes even less of an issue if an adequate career-path program exists, and each person knows that his future has been considered and plans exist to advance him to other positions.

3. *The belongingness need.* Although many people give the impression of independence, they as well as everyone else require a friendly relationship with others. Each person has to have the feeling of being a member, an accepted member, of the data center. Each person has to feel that others are cooperating with him or her in obtaining objectives and in resolving problems. As stated earlier,

[9]Paul Tournier, *The Adventure of Living* (New York: Harper & Row, Pub., 1965).

[10]Ted W. Engstrom and R. Alec Mackensie, *Managing Your Time,* p. 133.

[11]Abraham Maslow, *Motivation and Personality* (New York: Harper & Row, Pub., 1954).

MBGO stimulates cooperativeness and thus is a means for helping persons to satisfy their belongingness need.

4. *The esteem need.* Each person requires respect from others. Usually this results from being an accepted and contributing member of a group. Esteem results from performing effectively in the data center, proving personal worth, and thus receiving respect from others and feeling respect for oneself. It is the manager's responsibility to meet this esteem need by showing appreciation for each person's efforts and accomplishments. To be of any value, however, in fact to avoid a negative reaction, appreciation should be sincere. If appreciation is shown merely to "motivate," it will be received as meaningless, and a barrier of distrust and lack of rapport will be built. Once built, this barrier is difficult to remove.

5. *The self-actualization need.* This is the highest human need. Each person wants to make use of whatever special skills and aptitudes he or she may have. One of the tragedies of many jobs is that persons are not matched to jobs that utilize what they can contribute. Awareness of what provides satisfaction, of what a person enjoys and wants to do, assists a manager in modifying jobs and the career paths to make them more stimulating. Fortunately, many persons merely want to supervise and control their daily activities to some degree. This is usually possible, as is shown when job enrichment is discussed.

According to this theory, only an unsatisfied need can be a motivator, and the lowest unsatisfied need is the primary motivator. From these assumptions it becomes clear that if a person has the physiological and safety needs satisfied, but not the belongingness need, the need for affiliation with others becomes the center of attention for that person, and it becomes the most effective means for a manager to motivate that person. This person may have unsatisfied esteem and self-actualization needs, but they remain secondary in importance because they are secondary in their ability to motivate that person. Illustration 3–15 provides a means of visualizing the hierarchy of needs as just presented.

Human needs have been expressed in various manners, and one that may be useful is based on the statements of Walter W. Lindsey:[12]

1. All of us want security, a feeling that our efforts will provide what we need and want, and an absence of serious concern that those needs and wants are threatened.
2. All of us want to belong, to be an accepted member of a group, which may be a formally or informally organized group.
3. All of us want recognition, to receive approval and confirmation of our worth.
4. All of us want to be important, to feel that the job is significant, that is, of value to others.

One final statement on human needs may further stress the importance assigned to satisfaction of human needs. The following is from Robert Ardrey's book, *The Territorial Imperative.* Observe that Ardrey, who has based his conclusions primarily on his observation of many forms of animal life, creates a hierarchy in which security is of relatively minor importance.

[12]Walter W. Lindsey, "Understanding People on the Job," *Supervisory Management,* June 1972, pp. 34–36.

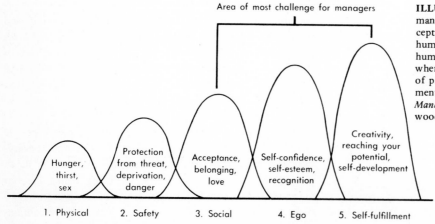

Area of most challenge for managers

| Hunger, thirst, sex | Protection from threat, deprivation, danger | Acceptance, belonging, love | Self-confidence, self-esteem, recognition | Creativity, reaching your potential, self-development |

1. Physical 2. Safety 3. Social 4. Ego 5. Self-fulfillment

ILLUSTRATION 3-15. Maslow's Hierarchy of Human Needs: Maslow's theory is based on the concepts that an unsatisfied human need motivates human behavior, and that the lowest unsatisfied human need becomes the primary motivator, where the lowest human need is for satisfaction of physical needs and the highest is for self-fulfillment. *Source:* Joseph L. Massie and John Douglas, *Managing: A Contemporary Introduction* (Englewood Cliffs, N.J.: Prentice-Hall, 1977), p. 63.

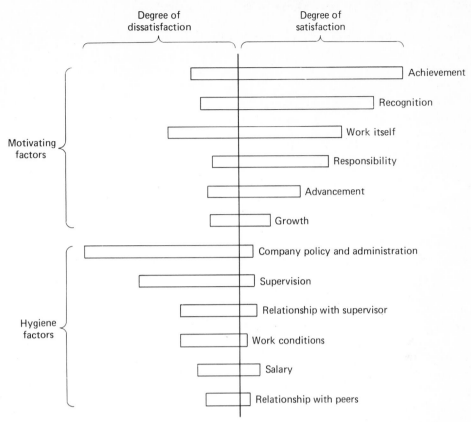

ILLUSTRATION 3-16. The Factors Influencing Job Satisfaction and Dissatisfaction: Frederick Herzberg's studies resulted in his conclusions that the factors primarily influencing job satisfaction are closely related to the work done and that these factors are different from those factors primarily influencing job dissatisfaction, which are tangential to the work done.

We shun anonymity, dread boredom, seek to dispel anxiety. We grasp at identification, yearn for stimulation, conserve or gain security. . . . There are few exceptions to the rule that the need for identity is the most powerful and the most pervasive among all species. The need for stimulation is not far behind. And security, normally, will be sacrified for either of the other two.[13]

Satisfiers and Dissatisfiers

According to the research of Frederick Herzberg, the factors that bring a person satisfaction on the job are different from the factors that bring dissatisfaction. He arrived at this conclusion after interviewing many employees, and his theory is presented in his book, *Work and the Nature of Man.*[14]

The factors that produce satisfaction he termed "motivating factors," or simply "motiva-

tors," and the factors that produce dissatisfaction he termed "hygiene factors," which some who adhere to his theory call maintenance factors or maintenance needs. It is Herzberg's belief that, although satisfaction of the motivating factors brings job satisfaction, the absence of satisfaction for these factors may bring dissatisfaction—but only to a negligible degree. These factors are all closely related to the job itself and have been isolated as those related to achievement, recognition, the work itself, responsibility, advancement, and growth. Herzberg's analysis has shown that, of these six factors, achievement and recognition are the strongest motivators.

As for the hygiene factors, if they are satisfied, job satisfaction occurs to only a slight degree; but if these factors are not satisfied, job dissatisfaction inevitably results to a greater degree. The hygiene factors include company policy and administration, supervision, relationship with supervisor, work conditions, salary, and relationship with peers. Of these factors, company policy and administration, and supervision are the two factors that can create the most dissatisfaction. Observe that these factors are tangential to the job itself,

[13] Robert Ardrey, *The Territorial Imperative* (New York: Atheneum, 1966).

[14] Frederick Herzberg, *Work and the Nature of Man* (New York: Collins Publishers, 1966).

not closely related as are the motivation factors. The degree of satisfaction and dissatisfaction caused by motivators and hygiene factors are indicated in Illustration 3–16.

In accordance with this theory, a person can be both satisfied and dissatisfied at the same time. Consider the situation where supervision is very restrictive and disturbing, but this person is at the same time accomplishing much and feeling worthwhile. That person is dissatisfied with the tangential factor of supervision, but satisfied with his achievements which are closely related to the job. As the illustration shows, salary is primarily a hygiene factor, but it is also a motivator because it increases job satisfaction. This seems reasonable. If adequate income is not received, a person will surely become dissatisfied. On the other hand, satisfaction increases with the receipt of a salary increase, because it indicates reward for achievement and recognition from others.

Herzberg's theory is taken very seriously by many companies. Texas Instruments, for example, uses these factors as a guide in appraising personnel problems. They use an interesting display that distinguishes between motivation and maintenance needs (to use their terms) and indicates those closely related and those tangential to a job. This display is shown in Illustration 3–17.

An interesting experiment and one that should bring valuable insight into personnel values and motivation is to have personnel indicate by numbering from 1 to 10 the importance to them of the following factors, where 1 indicates the most important factor and 10 indicates the least important. Then a manager, without having looked at what personnel prepared, should also number from 1 to 10 what he or she thinks personnel consider important. Supervisors for a study prepared the following list:[15]

1. Good wages
2. Job security
3. Promotion and growth with company
4. Good working conditions
5. Interesting work
6. Management loyalty to workers
7. Tactful disciplining
8. Full appreciation of work done
9. Sympathetic understanding of personal problems.
10. Feeling "in" on things

When staff personnel prepared their list showing which factors were most important to them

[15] Karl Albrecht, *Successful Management by Objectives*, p. 60.

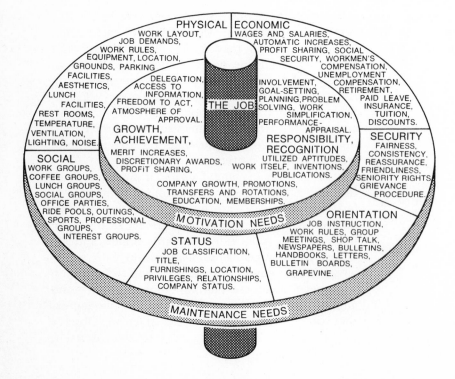

ILLUSTRATION 3–17. Texas Instruments' Representation of Herzberg's Theory: This diagram is a basic tool at Texas Instruments to explain the separation of motivational needs (whose adequate fulfillment provides satisfaction) from maintenance needs (whose adequate fulfillment avoids dissatisfaction.) *Source:* Printed with the permission of Texas Instruments, Incorporated, Dallas, Texas.

and brought them the most satisfaction, they produced a radically different list of preferences, which was:

1. Full appreciation of work done
2. Feeling "in" on things
3. Sympathetic understanding of personal problems
4. Job security
5. Good wages
6. Interesting work
7. Promotion and growth with company
8. Management loyalty to workers
9. Good working conditions
10. Tactful disciplining

Job Enrichment

A primary ingredient in motivating personnel is to define jobs so that they provide the opportunity for obtaining satisfaction and avoiding dissatisfaction. As stated earlier, attainment of data center objectives can result more pleasantly and more reliably by making the job a source of enjoyment instead of a chore. Before considering the assumptions and factors underlying job-enrichment programs, an anecdote may be useful for indicating typical personnel attitudes toward their work.

An elderly gentleman, strolling along a country road in England many years ago, stopped to watch a group of stone cutters who were apparently beginning a construction project. He approached one of the men and inquired off-handedly, "What are you doing?" "I'm working," muttered the man, and said nothing more. The old gentleman wandered about the site a bit and asked the same question of another worker. This one was more willing to talk. He stood up straight and said, with a touch of pride, "Why, I'm doing the best job of stonemasonry in all of England."

The old fellow later inquired about the activity of a third worker. When asked, the man stopped, straightened up, and as he stretched the kinks out of his back he tilted back his head and looked up thoughtfully, as if he were studying something which the visitor could not see. He said quietly, "I'm helping to build a cathedral."[16]

[16] Karl Albrecht, *Successful Management by Objectives*, p. 14.

The point of this story is that some persons, the more fortunate, are working toward an objective that gives them satisfaction, whereas others are doing their job because they were told to or because they take pride in their skill. Workers who take pride in their skill, obtain satisfaction, but lose sight of the objective of their efforts and very likely are not benefiting the data center as much as is possible. Thus, three types of person can be expected to be found in a data center: persons doing their job without concern as to how well it is done, persons concerned with the quality of their work but without any concern or possibly even awareness of the data center's objectives, and persons with their attention directed to the attaining data center's objectives, and obtaining satisfaction from doing just that.

The goal of job-enrichment efforts is to make personnel objective-oriented by making each person a participant in meeting objectives. Louis Allen, among his many other guidelines to managers, clearly indicates the relationship between a person's effort to meet objectives and a person's participation when he states: "Motivation to accomplish results tends to increase as people are given opportunity to participate in the decisions affecting results."[17]

Job-enrichment specialists develop programs on a set of generally accepted assumptions.

1. Most people want to do activities that are significant and give them a feeling of worth.
2. Most jobs do not permit this to the extent possible.
3. Managers should try to make jobs satisfying to staff while attaining the organization's goals.
4. Managers should increase each person's self-management as each person's skill increases.
5. Managers who provide opportunities for utilization of capabilities stimulate self-direction and motivate to attain organization goals.

With these assumptions in mind, job-enrichment specialists have isolated three factors to consider when developing an enriched job or when evaluating how enriched a job is. An enriched job, in accordance with their analysis, must be oriented toward a definite goal, must permit the person involved to make any decisions necessary to doing the job properly, and must provide feedback

[17] Louis Allen, "Leadership Pattern and Organizational Effectiveness." Delivered at a seminar at the Foundation for Research on Human Behavior at Ann Arbor, Michigan, 1954.

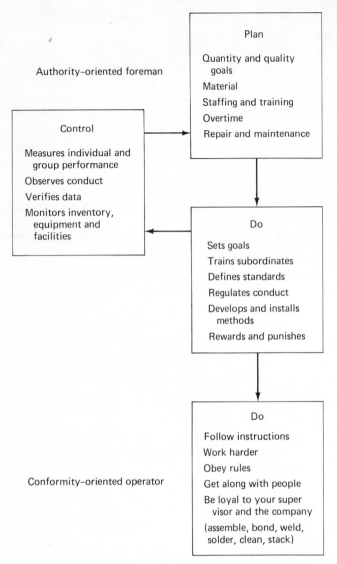

Authority-oriented foreman

Control

Measures individual and group performance

Observes conduct

Verifies data

Monitors inventory, equipment and facilities

Plan

Quantity and quality goals

Material

Staffing and training

Overtime

Repair and maintenance

Do

Sets goals

Trains subordinates

Defines standards

Regulates conduct

Develops and installs methods

Rewards and punishes

Do

Follow instructions

Work harder

Obey rules

Get along with people

Be loyal to your super visor and the company

(assemble, bond, weld, solder, clean, stack)

Conformity-oriented operator

ILLUSTRATION 3-18. Unenriched Job. A person in an unenriched job does no planning or control, but receives orders and performs as ordered. *Source:* M. Scott Myers, "Every Employee a Manager," reprinted from *California Management Review,* vol. 10 (1968), no. 3, p. 14. © 1968 by the Regents of the University of California.

from the job itself so that the person involved can evaluate his or her own performance. In effect, the aim of job enrichment is, as has been well expressed by M. Scott Myers of Texas Instruments, to make "every employee a manager."[18]

Myers presents in his article a set of illustrations that clearly show the nature and differences between jobs that are not enriched and those that are enriched. Illustrations 3-18 and 3-19 show authority-oriented management for an unenriched job and goal-oriented management for an en-

[18]M. Scott Myers, "Every Employee a Manager," *California Management Review,* 10 (1968), no. 3, 9-20.

riched job. In the first case, Illustration 3-18, the person supervised does not plan and control the job's activities, in other words, does not make the decisions affecting the job and does not evaluate and control his or her own performance. In Illustration 3-19, both supervisor and employee perform the functions of a manager; each is in effect a manager. To make a job enriched, a good guide is to answer the question, if that person were self-employed to do that job, what planning and control would be performed?

Thus, a person in an enriched job will do any planning directly related to the actual performance of the job; this includes setting goals, allocating resources, organizing, and problem solving. The actual performance of activities includes implementing plans, coordinating activities, and utilizing any special skills needed. The third and final aspect of an enriched job is controlling performance of activities, which consists of using performance standards established during planning for measuring, evaluating, and if necessary, correcting performance. It is advisable to include these three distinct sets of responsibilities on job descriptions under three separate headings. These three groups of responsibilities should be preceded by a statement of the data center objectives that the job accomplishes. This method of describing a job avoids the dull and unmotivating job descriptions usually prepared and provides instead a description of an enriched job which encourages alertness and participation.

Other Approaches

There are many approaches other than job enrichment for improving job performance and personnel satisfaction. The primary approaches are now listed and briefly discussed.

Job Enlargement. Whereas job enrichment, in effect, expands a job vertically, including more responsibilities for the same activities, job enlargement adds more activities, usually without adding additional decision-making and control responsibilities. Job enlargement thus expands a job horizontally.

Job Rotation. Job rotation, as practiced in some companies, usually refers to changing a person's job activities periodically, such as every six months. Sometimes job rotation is performed by having a person do one job in the morning and another in the afternoon.

Job Sharing. Two or more persons who have different jobs work together and periodically agree among themselves when and for low long to exchange jobs, thus providing a variety of activities and a feeling of camaraderie.

Team Building. As in the case of project teams, several persons work as a group to accomplish a specific job. Jointly they are responsible for

successful completion of assignments and jointly they receive credit for superior performance.

Employee Action Committee. Committees are formed to observe the environment and to recommend changes that employees desire. These committees are concerned with "hygiene" factors, which according to Herzberg's theory attend to avoiding dissatisfaction, not to providing satisfaction.

Personal-development Programs. Programs are provided to improve personal abilities. These programs may attempt to improve interpersonal

ILLUSTRATION 3-19. Enriched Job: A person in an enriched job does all planning and control necessary to perform the job properly. *Source:* M. Scott Myers, "Every Employee a Manager," reprinted from *California Management Review,* vol. 10 (1968), no. 3. p. 17. © 1968 by the Regents of the University of California.

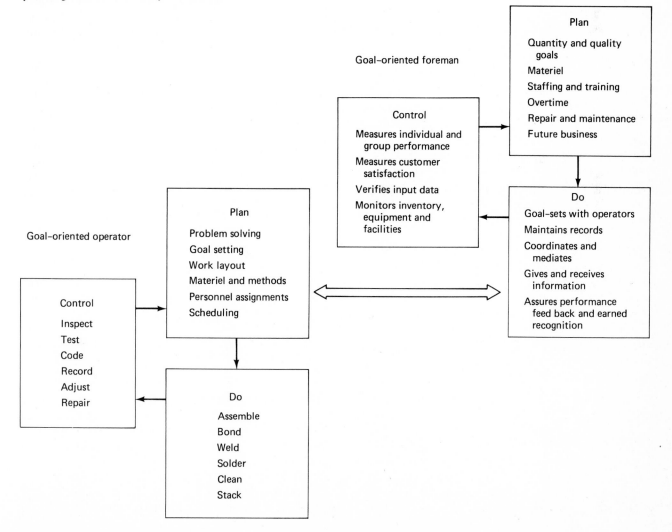

relationships through techniques such as transactional analysis; to improve communications ability, particularly the ability to write memos and reports; and to use time effectively, considering on what time is consumed and how efficiently time is used.

Flexible Work Hours. This includes staggered work hours and such arrangements as a three-day work week.

Incentive Plans. Personnel can receive cash or time-off benefits for superior performance or for recommendations that have been implemented. A particularly effective plan is the Scanlon plan, in which persons making recommendations that improve productivity receive immediate increase in base pay instead of receiving a bonus. The Scanlon plan rewards an entire group when they are responsible for the recommendation.

PERFORMANCE APPRAISAL

The effort dedicated to carefully selecting personnel, to establishing a career path and associated training plan, and to making a job more satisfying cannot have its full effect if periodic performance appraisals are not properly performed. Performance appraisal is not an academic exercise; it provides not only an opportunity to evaluate performance, but also to isolate deficiencies and problems, and then to plan for improvements. These improvements relate directly to attaining data center and personal objectives.

Because performance appraisals have been conducted inadequately, personnel have developed a critical and negative attitude toward them. Instead of their providing an opportunity to benefit the data center and the person, and to stimulate greater effort, they are looked upon as a waste of time, of little constructive value. In a survey of 14 companies, 71 percent of the personnel stated that only the company benefited from performance reviews, and only 3 percent stated that they themselves obtained any benefit at all.[19] The main reasons for these negative views are the atmosphere in which performance-appraisal interviews are conducted and the inadequacies of what

---

[19]Mortimer Feinberg, "Performance Review . . . Threat or Promise," *Supervisory Management*, May 1961.

> ### Why an Appraisal and Development Plan?
>
> The Company's most valuable asset is its employees. One of the most important qualifications of a supervisor, regardless of level, is the ability to train, develop, and treat people in a manner that wins confidence and gets results. A good supervisor knows his employees as individuals. He considers each employee's performance, his interests, his make-up and his environment in developing his work force.
>
> Toward this end, the Company established a number of years ago an Appraisal and Development Plan for use on a uniform basis in all departments. It is a very helpful guide to a highly important aspect of good supervision.
>
> *Primary Purpose of Plan*
>
> To aid the employee in his growth and development by appraising all phases of his performance and then by following through with constructive discussion and guidance.
>
> *Additional Benefits*
>
> When this is done thoughtfully and skillfully, the Plan will accomplish several additional and highly important purposes. It will:
>
> Promote that employee's job satisfaction and morale by letting him know that his supervisor is interested in his progress and development.
>
> Serve as a systematic guide to the supervisor in planning the employee's further training.
>
> Assure considered opinion of employee's performance rather than snap judgment.
>
> Assist in planning personnel moves and placements that will best utilize each employee's capabilities.
>
> Assist in locating and recording special talents and capabilities that might otherwise not be noticed or recognized.
>
> Provide employee an opportunity to talk to supervisor about job problems, interest, future, etc.

ILLUSTRATION 3-20. Company Statement of Benefits of a Personnel Appraisal Plan. *Source:* "Performance Appraisal and Employee Development Guide," Standard Oil Company of California.

are discussed and what are agreed upon. To provide the setting for productive appraisal interviews, many companies have prepared statements of the goals of these interviews. One of the best of these statements is shown in Illustration 3–20.

The Proper Atmosphere

The performance-appraisal interview is not the time for placating personnel with general, noncommittal comments, nor is it the time for destructive criticism. It is a time when a manager can display sincere concern for an employee's well-being and career. Any performance deficiencies are discussed by stating what has been observed or reported and asking for clarification or confirmation. The intention should not be to condemn, but to correct. Through probing, personal problems may be uncovered, and then the manager has an opportunity to demonstrate concern by taking a problem-solving attitude to resolve the problem and to make plans. The intention is to always focus on how the person being appraised can be helped to progress along his intended career path.

The atmosphere throughout the interview should be sincere and creative. Too often, a person is given a distorted picture of what opportunities are available or what pay increases can be attained. The result is loss of trust. Actually, opportunities are usually greater than they may appear at first. Opportunities, for example, should be considered for advancing to other jobs in other departments, if that is what is desired by the person being appraised.

During the appraisal interview three precautions must be taken to increase the objectivity of judgment:

1. *Avoid prejudice.* This can be minimized by being aware of your own preferences. Bernard Baruch expressed this well when he stated, "Only as you know yourself can your brain serve you as a sharp and efficient tool. Know your own failings, passions, and prejudices so that you can separate them from what you see."
2. *Tolerate human differences.* Each manager must accept and make use of the idea that each person has different inherent capabilities, as was expressed by the philosopher Alain: "The power of Caesar or Alexander rested upon the fact that they had a liking for differences and did not expect pear trees to produce plums."
3. *Listen to the other person's views.* The only way to obtain insight into another person's behavior is to listen to that person. Psychologist Carl Rogers stated this idea this way: "The biggest block to personal communication is a man's inability to listen intelligently, understandingly, and skillfully to another person."

The Appraisal Interview

Once the proper atmosphere has been established, the actual conducting of the appraisal interview should progress naturally and friendly, with possible interruptions when it is necessary to discuss sensitive areas, such as deficiencies that are serious or problems that require firm and possibly strict supervision. Even then, the recommendation is to maintain a problem-solving attitude. The problem-solving method of conducting the interview, along with several factors related to interviews, is compared with two other types of interviews in Illustration 3-21. Stress on this type of interview should not be taken to negate the other two types of interviews. It is always necessary to determine when an authoritarian or listening approach should be used, although they should always be subordinated to the more constructive and stimulating problem-solving approach.

An interview can be viewed as separated into three phases, which start with discussion of past performance, continue with discussion of present attitude, and finish with the setting of data center and personal objectives for the next time period.

1. *Discuss past performance.* The manager performing the appraisal interview would have commented on the attainment of previously agreed upon and documented data center and personal objectives. These statements should be on the Personnel Objectives and Performance Review form, Illustration 3-11, from the last time period when an interview was held. Since these objectives were stated carefully so that their attainment could be easily judged, appraisals can be objectively and precisely stated. The interviewee should be shown these comments and asked if he or she agrees with them. Differences of opinions should be resolved if they do not require an excessive amount of time. As shown on the form, the data center objectives are separated from the personal-training objectives. It should be made clear that satisfactory performance in both categories, as well as adequate ratings on personal qualities, affect promotions and progress along the chosen career path.

The stress, as already mentioned, is on agreeing on how the interviewee can move along a career path, not on condemning past actions. The difficulty avoided by stating precisely what objectives should be obtained is not avoided when personal qualities are judged. These judgments frequently elicit responses similar to that shown in the cartoon in Illustration 3-22, although the ambiguous evaluation shown refers to job performance and not to a personal quality. What is entered for these general evaluations of personal qualities should be honest and justifiable. But no matter how honest and how justified the evalua-

METHOD	TELL AND SELL	TELL AND LISTEN	PROBLEM SOLVING
ROLE OF INTERVIEWER	JUDGE	JUDGE	HELPER
Objective	To communicate evaluation To persuade employee to improve	To communicate evaluation To release defensive feelings	To stimulate growth and development in employee
Assumptions	Employee desires to correct weaknesses if he knows them Any person can improve if he so chooses A superior is qualified to evaluate a subordinate	People will change if defensive feelings are removed	Growth can occur without correcting faults Discussing job problems leads to improved performance
Reactions	Defensive behavior suppressed Attempts to cover hostility	Defensive behavior expressed Employee feels accepted	Problem solving behavior
Skills	Salesmanship Patience	Listening and reflecting feelings Summarizing	Listening and reflecting feelings Reflecting ideas Using exploratory questions Summarizing
Attitude	People profit from criticism and appreciate help	One can respect the feelings of others if one understands them	Discussion develops new ideas and mutual interests
Motivation	Use of positive or negative incentives or both (Extrinsic in that motivation is added to the job itself)	Resistance to change reduced Positive incentive (Extrinsic and some intrinsic motivation)	Increased freedom Increased responsibility (Intrinsic motivation in that interest is inherent in the task)
Gains	Success most probable when employee respects interviewer	Develops favorable attitude to superior which increases probability of success	Almost assured of improvement in some respect
Risks	Loss of loyalty Inhibition of independent judgment Face-saving problems created	Need for change may not be developed	Employee may lack ideas Change may be other than what superior had in mind
Values	Perpetuates existing practices and values	Permits interviewer to change his views in the light of employee's responses Some upward communication	Both learn since experience and views are pooled Change is facilitated

ILLUSTRATION 3-21. *Source:* Adapted from Norman R.F. Maier, "The Appraisal Interview: Three Basic Approaches." San Diego, CA: University Associates, 1976, p. 20. Used with permission.

" 'Lousy' is a bit general... specifically, what do you think of my work?"

ILLUSTRATION 3-22. Vague Performance Appraisals. *Source: Personnel Administration,* 27, (Jan.–Feb. 1964), no. 1, pp. 32-33. Reprinted by permission of the cartoonist Bob Weber.

tions, differences of opinions occur—in fact, emotional outbursts are not uncommon. Because of the hard feelings created and the disruptive influence on the remainder of the interview, it may be advisable to eliminate these judgments from the form but to allow space for comments on definitely unsatisfactory or exceptional personal qualities.

2. *Discuss present attitude.* At this point in the interview, the manager is interested in what may be causing dissatisfaction and what may increase the interviewee's satisfaction. The critical question that should be answered is, "Has your satisfaction with your job changed since the last interview, and if so, what event caused that change?" A sincere answer to this question may uncover a situation that may be seriously affecting performance, besides creating unhappiness. The questionnaire shown in Illustration 3-23 is very helpful for isolating dissatisfactions. This form was developed by Frederick Herzberg and Alex Zautra for evaluating the effect of orthodox job-enrichment programs.

The result of this questioning may simply be confirma- , tion that the job and environment are satisfactory. It is also likely that deficiencies may be mentioned that can be easily, or at least with little difficulty, corrected. Unfortunately, it is also possible that a serious personal adjustment problem may exist; this is discussed in the next section on the "problem person."

3. *Discuss future objectives.* At this time, the objectives to be met for the next time period are defined and,

to whatever degree possible, quantified. The data center objectives may be the same, measurements may require adjustment, or objectives may be added, modified, or deleted. As for training objectives, naturally all knowledge and skills needed for the present job take priority over those required for the next position along the career path. It may be necessary to reschedule previously scheduled training programs because they were not completed or because they were completed with poor results.

ILLUSTRATION 3-23. Appraisal Interview Questionnaire: Although this questionnaire was prepared for OJE (Orthodox Job Enrichment) interviews, it is also useful for appraisal interviews; it focuses attention on motivational changes and the causes. *Source:* Frederick Herzberg and Alex Zautra, "Orthodox Job Enrichment: Measuring True Quality in Job Satisfaction," *Personnel,* 53, (Sept.–Oct. 1976) no. 5, p. 60. © 1976 by AMACOM, a division of American Management Associations. All rights reserved.

OJE Interview Format

1. *Have you noticed any changes in your work that you have been asked to do in your job over the last _____ months? (from 6 to 18 months for job enrichment projects—12 months for pre-OJE groups)*

Describe the changes that have taken place.

   a. What were your job assignments before the change(s)?
   b. What are your job assignments now?

2. *Specifically, has there been an increase or decrease in the following:*
   a. *Recognition for achievements*—how much recognition you have received for the work you do? Explain.
   b. *Achievement*—a change in your opportunities to achieve on the job? Explain.
   c. *Work itself*—a change in the type of work you do? Your job assignments? Explain.
   d. *Responsibility*—a change in the amount of responsibility you have for your work? Explain.
   e. *Advancement*—a change in the complexity of the task? A higher-skilled job or a lesser-skilled job? Explain.
   f. *Growth*—a change in your opportunity to learn more or to learn less on the job? Explain.

3. *How did you feel about the change(s) and why did you feel the way you did?*

4. *Because of the change(s), has there been an increase or a decrease in the amount of satisfaction you are getting from your work?*

5. *Did the change(s) affect you personally in any way?*
   a. Did it change the way you get along with people in general or with your family?
   b. Did it affect your sleep, appetite, digestion, general health?

6. *Rate on a scale from one to seven how strongly your feelings about your job were affected by the change(s).*

				Changed a			
No Change				Great Deal			
1	2	3	4	5	6	7	*Positive Feelings*

				Changed a			
No Change				Great Deal			
1	2	3	4	5	6	7	*Negative Feelings*

7. *Further comments?*

After both the manager and the interviewee have agreed on objectives, a copy of the agreement is made for the interviewee. The interviewee now walks away from the appraisal interview knowing what deficiencies and excellences the manager is aware of, what the manager expects in the next time period, and what must be done to progress along his or her career path.

The "Problem Person"

During the interview it may have become apparent that the interviewee has a serious personal problem; in this case it may be advisable to postpone the continuation of the interview for a later time, allowing some time for determining what the cause may be. However, it is more likely that if a person has a serious personal problem, it would have been brought to the manager's attention earlier. Thus, the manager would have automatically investigated to determine the cause and would be prepared to conduct a special interview to attempt to resolve the problem. A problem person must be helped or be eliminated, because this person can affect others, eventually disrupting data center processing activities and performance.

The signs of a person who has a problem are usually only too obvious, and they produce either of two extreme effects: passivity or hostility. The noisy person who is frequently disturbing others is an obvious problem that cannot be ignored and must be resolved. Less apparent and usually ignored is the silent, passive person who does not bother others and is not as productive as can be. Both of these reactions indicate that the person may be troubled.

A rational approach to resolving personnel problems is to determine the cause of the problem, to decide on a means to correct the situation, and then to discuss this means with the troubled person. That is the general outline of the approach to be recommended; the specific steps that should be followed are:

1. *Define the problem* in terms of how the person's behavior differs from what is wanted.
2. *Obtain information* from files and from individuals to isolate the possible causes of the problem.
3. *Define the category of need not satisfied,* as defined by Maslow, starting at the lowest level (the physiological level).

4. *Review your tools,* the opportunities and services that can be provided to satisfy the category of need that is unsatisfied.
5. *Structure environment* to satisfy the need isolated, considering style of leadership, environment, and job development.
6. *Conduct a goal-setting session;* determine initially the person's feelings and then obtain agreement on the goals to be attained.
7. *Later, collect performance information.*
8. *Conduct performance-appraisal interview;* determine the person's feelings and set new goals, if necessary.
9. *Follow-up* through encouragement and, if necessary, with additional correction.

Step 5 refers to "style of leadership," which should be explained. Four styles of leadership are frequently identified: authoritarian, democratic, laissez-faire, and buddy-buddy. The authoritarian leader is also referred to as the "carrot-and-stick" leader, who rewards the person for acceptable performance and punishes the person for unacceptable performance. A reward may be a raise or a promotion; a punishment may be the withholding of a raise or dismissal. The democratic leader would discuss what actions should be taken and then obtain mutual agreement on the course of action. The laissez-faire leader has the most casual approach, indicating what should be accomplished and then permitting the person complete freedom to proceed. The last style of leader is the buddy-buddy type, the leader who depends on close friendship to get a person's cooperation.

Persons differ as to what style of leadership is most effective for them. A major cause of difficulty in managing people is that most managers select a single style and totally ignore the others. To determine what style should be used for a person, a manager should consider what style has proved to be effective in the past and what is most compatible with the unsatisfied need. The style that has been most effective in the past can be determined from the information gathered during step 2 in many cases. As for compatibility with unsatisfied needs, the buddy-buddy style is usually considered best for an unsatisfied social need, the laissez-faire style for a self-actualization need, and the democratic style for an esteem need.

A book that does an excellent job of presenting this approach is M. D. Wadsworth's *The Human Side of Data Processing Management.*[20] Wadsworth examines this approach in great detail, providing many case histories.

As an example, one of the cases discussed is entitled "Silent Silvia, the closet case." The steps followed are basically those outlined for the full approach.

Define the problem: Silvia does an adequate job, but could do more if she tried. She does not volunteer assistance and ideas, and thus does not contribute to the group and to the department to the degree possible.

Obtain information: Her present performance is typical of what it has been in other departments, with comments noted on her difficulty in communicating with others. Her performance under all types of leadership has been the same. She has always kept to herself, has no friends on the job, and appears to have no friends off the job.

Define the category of need: Her manner of dressing and the location of her apartment suggest that physiologically she is not unsatisfied. She appears healthy and has good benefits from the company,

and her job is not threatened. Thus, she should have no security-need difficulty. Since she is quiet and does not bother with anyone on the job, a social problem is indicated as the lowest level of need not satisfied—however, a definite conclusion is withheld until more analysis is performed. As for her needs for esteem and accomplishment, there has been no indication of any effort in these areas. From all of the above, it appears that her semiapathy and detachment are a result of poor social relationships—actually, no social relationships.

Review tools and structure the environment: Review the activities within the company that may provide Silvia with opportunities for meeting others. As for style of leadership, democratic leadership is chosen because it will provide the social environment she may need to resolve her social problem.

Conduct goal-setting session: The session can start by confirming that the problem is social and that the problem also exists outside work. At this time, suggestions may be made about the opportunities available in the company for meeting others.

Follow-up: A friendly relationship should be maintained with Silvia, possibly switching to a buddy-buddy style of leadership, and if at any time she goes to another department, her new manager should be informed of her problem and of previous attempts and their results.

---

[20]M. D. Wadsworth, *The Human Side of Data Processing Management* (Englewood Cliffs, N.J.: Prentice-Hall, Inc., 1973).

BUDGETING, CHARGEOUT, AND FINANCIAL ANALYSIS

GOAL

To budget and control expenditures, while analyzing alternatives.

HIGHLIGHTS

Budgeting Data Center Costs

In contrast to traditional budgeting, which inevitably accepts prior expenditures and increments for inflation, zero-base budgeting is recommended to focus on defining objectives and justifying expenditures.

Chargeout of Data Center Costs

Whereas charging data center costs to company overhead leads to unexamined processing of user applications, irrespective of their cost and worth, chargeout and chargeback systems, in contrast, inform users of application costs and require their approval.

Financial Analysis of Data Center Costs

Awareness of financial trends, alternative processing methods, and cost-benefit trade-offs for user applications permit short-range and long-range savings.

inancially, the data center manager is in a glass fishbowl, because data processing affects nearly every activity in a company. Computer-printed reports are common in all departments; computer-output microfilm and microfiche readers are becoming more and more common, as are computer terminals. This high dependency on data processing makes its results and its problems apparent even to the most casual observer.

Because of this high visibility, economic difficulties such as inflation, shrinking profit margins, competition, and budget squeezes lead to close scrutiny of data-processing expenses, especially those of the data center. Users tend to forget the cost reductions that motivated and, more often than not, resulted from transfer of applications from user departments to the data center. Instead, forgetting the cost reductions in the various departments, users and upper management often look at the data center not as a cost center or a profit center, but as a "burden" center. To reverse this attitude and to place the data center in a positive framework, its objectives and benefits, particularly its cost-consciousness and cost-effectiveness, must be made clear.

The economic activities of the data center can be segmented into three categories:

1. *Budgeting.* The standard budgeting practice is to state the money needed for resources without indicating what benefits will be obtained for that money. More recent budgeting practices attempt to directly relate money allocations to benefits anticipated. Careful selection of a budgeting practice can determine the difference between wasteful and resourceful data center expenditures.
2. *Chargeout.* A chargeout system informs users of the processing costs for their application systems, permitting judgment as to whether or not these systems should be modified or replaced. Thus, a chargeout system encourages users to cost-justify their use of data center resources. With the proper attitude, besides eliminating wasteful applications and increasing the efficiency for those that remain, the development and implementation of new cost-justifiable applications are stimulated.
3. *Financial analysis.* Analysis of financial trends, particularly in the cost of resources, can de-

termine what processing techniques will be stressed. Naturally, the combined awareness of resource cost alternatives and application costs, from chargeout information, permit optimization of benefits received for money spent. Thoughtful analysis reduces the squeeze of financial constraints on data center managers while increasing user satisfaction—goals frequently considered incompatible.

BUDGETING DATA CENTER COSTS

"A budget is a quantitative expression of a plan," states Leonard I. Krauss.[1] This definition diverts attention from a budget as a restraint and instead identifies it as an opportunity to plan for increased processing and cost effectiveness. Focus is placed on eliminating ineffective activities and improving utilization of resources. At the same time, new data center projects can be initiated, permitting the introduction of new ideas and resources. Budget-preparation time, for example, is the time to consider the replacement of keypunching equipment with such innovations as shared key-to-disk equipment. It is also the time to initiate or strengthen a computer performance evaluation program. Opportunities are limited only by a manager's imagination and initiative—and courage.

That a budget is a planning tool is indicated in Illustration 4-1. As shown, a budget is used to both plan activities and to evaluate actual performance. Thus, the customary control cycle of plan-act-evaluate is established. Adequate control is dependent on the existence of an internal accounting system to document plans, report actual performance, and indicate variances, where variances may indicate potential or already-existing problems. But even more important than control is the budget as a quantitative plan for data center activities. As expressed by Charles T. Horngren, "Planning is more vital than control because superior control is fruitless if faulty plans are being implemented."[2]

[1] Leonard I. Krauss, "Cost-Analysis and Controls for the EDP Function," *EDP Solutions* (Delran, N.J.: Datapro Research Corp., 1976), p. E40–300–204.
[2] Charles T. Horngren, *Accounting for Management Control,* 2nd ed. (Englewood Cliffs, N.J.: Prentice-Hall, Inc., 1970), p. 6.

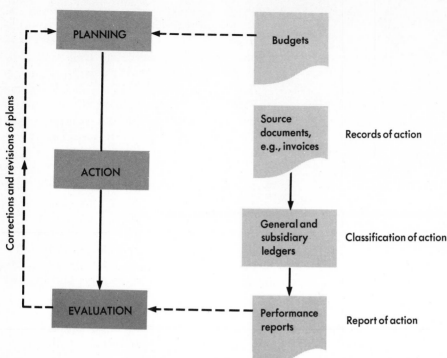

LINE MANAGEMENT   INTERNAL ACCOUNTING SYSTEM

PLANNING

Corrections and revisions of plans

ACTION

EVALUATION

Budgets

Source documents, e.g., invoices — Records of action

General and subsidiary ledgers — Classification of action

Performance reports — Report of action

ILLUSTRATION 4-1. The Budget Control Cycle: A budget, instead of restricting activities, can be viewed as a major tool for planning innovations, and for controlling variances in performance and costs. *Source:* Charles T. Horngren, *Accounting for Management Control,* 3rd ed. (Englewood Cliffs, N.J.: Prentice-Hall, 1974), p. 6.

Budgeting, however, results only in estimates. Many factors can upset the most carefully prepared budget estimates. Computer paper can become scarce, skyrocketing the cost. Personnel overtime may be necessary. Equipment may not perform according to vendor promises. The uncertainty of budget estimates agrees with the whimsical old adage, "Forecasting is very difficult, especially about the future." Consider the expectations at the Ford Motor Corporation. Their design plans are directly related to their estimate of market demands. They put a large amount of planning effort into the designs of both the Edsel and the Thunderbird, the first a disappointment, the second an unqualified success. The same is true for data center budgets. Although some estimates are predictably accurate, others are dependent on the whims of uncontrolled factors, such as the sudden scarcity of material and malfunctioning of equipment.

A manager's ability to set realistic budgets while allowing for uncertainties, to guide expenses, and to account for variances is a measure of that manager's effectiveness. It demonstrates to upper management his ability to control his present responsibilities and to take on more responsibilities.

Traditional Budgeting

The standard budgeting approach is to examine the expenditures for the prior year and to enter these expenditures in the new budget, adding inflation costs and costs for any new needs that have arisen. This is the traditional budgeting approach. The end result is continually increasing budgets, as represented in Illustration 4-2. Besides general acceptance of continually increasing budgets, a critical fault of traditional budgeting is that attention is directed to resources, not to results.

Because attention is directed to resources, prior expenses are accepted as necessary without considering that they may be excessive or applied to the wrong resources. For example, because of the increase in the number of tapes handled, it may be thought necessary to hire more tape librarians. This is the traditional, somewhat casual approach. However, if alternate methods of processing are considered, such as an improved tape library system, fewer people may actually be necessary. The people freed from the tape library can then be reassigned to an area where they are needed (avoiding layoffs, in keeping with the policy of making personnel feel secure in their

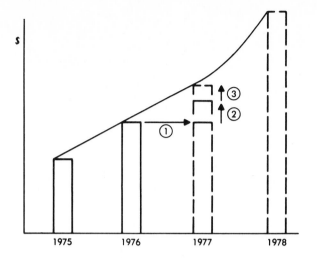

① Extrapolate past spending trend

② Increment for inflation

③ Increment for new programs

ILLUSTRATION 4-2. Traditional Budgeting and Increment of Costs: The traditional budgeting approach tends to accept prior expenditures and increment for inflation, while restricting the substitution or addition of expenditures for more worthwhile resources. *Source:* Logan M. Cheek, *Zero-Base Budgeting Comes of Age* (N.Y.: Amacom, 1977), p. 3. © 1977 by AMACOM, a division of American Management Associations. All rights reserved.

jobs and providing career paths). Another example is consideration of replacing keypunching equipment with a more efficient means of preparing input such as key-to-disk equipment. This new equipment will permit processing an increased workload without increasing the staff, while simultaneously decreasing costs.

The faults of traditional budgeting do not end here. It also hides service costs, since money is budgeted by resource-cost categories and not by services provided. A traditional budget may even provide better service than reasonably expected by users because of excess resources, which results in extra expenses that are avoidable. It also generally relates a manager's status, and salary increases, to the size of the budget, instead of to the benefits received for the money spent. These faults indicate why much dissatisfaction has been felt with traditional budgeting, and why alternate approaches have been sought.

The whole process of agreeing on a budget leads to gamesmanship, uncertainty, and frustration. The data center manager practices gamesmanship by preparing an inflated budget (expecting the inevitable cutting) and then having to spend any excesses that are approved. The chief executives usually do not adequately understand the operating needs of the data center to make decisions with a high degree of certainty. The controller receives the revised budget and has the frustration of having to make it workable. The end results of the activities of the data center manager, the chief executives, and the controller were indicated by Logan Cheek when he stated, "They do know how much is being spent, but they lack an appreciation of specifically what's going on, why, what better ways might be available, and which efforts are really necessary, because everything is functionally buried."[3] Cheek further criticized the traditional approach to budgeting when he humorously stated:

In short, the system has given birth to an elephant with the muscular development of a mouse and the brain of an amoeba. Worse yet, top executives and the budget staff don't understand the creature's physiology. So they are at a loss to efficiently wield a scalpel on its fat without damaging its already overtaxed muscles. Even if he could, the chief executive is wary of stimulating the creature into charging off without purpose and in the wrong direction. And the controller fears it might viciously strike back at its tormentor as it has often been known to do.[4]

Alternatives to Traditional Budgeting

The inadequacies of traditional budgeting has led to the development of several alternative approaches. Three of these approaches are summarized, and then the alternative of zero-base budgeting is examined in greater detail.

Capital Budgeting. For many years capital-expense requests have been accompanied by information on costs, benefits anticipated, and alternative methods. This information has been

---

[3] Logan M. Cheek, *Zero-Base Budgeting Comes of Age* (New York: Amacom, 1977), p. 7.

[4] Ibid., p. 7.

analyzed by using various analytical tools such as return on investment, opportunity cost, and years to break even, to mention only a few. In effect, capital budgeting applies the basic methodology of zero-base budgeting, but it applies this methodology only to capital expenditures, whereas zero-base budgeting applies it to all expenditures.

Program, Planning, and Budgeting (PPB). This approach was initiated in the early 1960s by the Department of Defense's Office of Systems Analysis. It stresses assessing the effects of programs on future expenditures, where the programs are defined in terms of their objectives and are evaluated against alternatives for cost-effectiveness. The outcome of PPB is a budget with emphasis on program planning.

Objectives, Strategies, and Tactics (OST). OST includes zero-base budgeting. Texas Instruments developed this approach by combining the techniques of MBO (management by objectives), zero-base budgeting, and long-range planning. Thus, they have a unified tool for guiding short-range operational activities, anticipating long-range effects, and budgeting to support these activities. This approach is very sophisticated and requires an understanding of zero-base budgeting before it can be considered.

Zero-Base Budgeting

The inadequacies of traditional budgeting and the ideas contained in such approaches as capital budgeting and PPB find a general solution in zero-base budgeting (ZBB). This becomes apparent when the following definition of ZBB is considered: Each manager responsible for budgeting starts with no money budgeted, prepares a "decision package" for each goal required or desired, includes cost-benefit information, and ranks these decision packages according to his or her judgment of their relative worth.

This definition both highlights the principal ideas of ZBB and indicates its basic procedure. The approach of starting with no money budgeted justifies the use of the phrase "zero base." Each manager starts with a zero base and has the responsibility of justifying any budgeting requests

that build on this base. By doing this, each manager is responsible for submitting accurate cost information instead of bloated estimates anticipating upper management cuts. Each manager must justify requests, not merely accept past expenditures and automatically adjust for inflation. This new responsibility should be viewed positively, as an opportunity for improving data center service and efficiency, as an opportunity to consider innovative approaches and new methodology. For example, money can be allocated for personnel who coordinate the receipt and preparation of user input, for a scheduling system that provides the status of all jobs, and for a program that evaluates computer performance.

The use of decision packages is a stimulating and also a disciplining concept. It is usually a one-sheet form that states an approach to meet a goal. Often, several decision packages are prepared for a single goal. They may indicate various approaches to meet a goal and possibly several levels of effort for each approach. Levels of effort are directly related to resource commitments and thus are directly related to cost. Each decision package includes statements of the resources required and their costs, the consequences if accepted or if rejected, and a summary of alternate approaches and levels documented in other decision packages. Obviously, when decision packages are presented to upper management for approval, much more information is provided than in a traditional budget request, permitting upper management to make more reasonable decisions.

Each manager who prepared decision packages then indicates his or her judgment of their relative worth by ranking them, that is, by listing them in order of importance. This listing consists of one-line entries for the decision packages, which include cost information. From this explanation of the ZBB concepts, it becomes apparent that significant information is collected and analyzed and that many critical questions, such as the following, now can be answered.

> What are the present goals?
> Can these goals be justified?
> Which approach for each goal is the most effective?
> Which level for each goal is the most effective?
> Which goals are the most important?

The development of ZBB is credited to Peter

A. Pyhrr, who states that a similar approach was attempted at the Department of Agriculture in the early 1960s, but without much success. He, however, successfully implemented ZBB at Texas Instruments in 1970. He then brought attention to ZBB by describing the process in an article in the November/December 1970 issue of the *Harvard Business Review.* Jimmy Carter, who was then the newly elected governor of Georgia, read this article and asked Pyhrr if he would install ZBB in Georgia. Phyrr left Texas Instruments and helped install ZBB in Georgia for the 1973 fiscal year. The publishing of his book *Zero-Base Budgeting,*[5] speeded the adoption of this approach by many corporations and government agencies.

The Zero-Base Budgeting Procedure

The details of the ZBB procedure are in Pyhrr's book and also in a book written by Logan M.

Cheek, *Zero-Base Budgeting Comes of Age.*[6] Cheek presents the procedure as shown in Illustration 4–3. The six-step procedure is:

1. Defining the objectives
2. Structuring the implementation strategy
3. Developing the supporting system
4. Preparing the decision packages
5. Ranking all decision packages
6. Approving the selected decision packages

Defining the Objectives. At this stage of the procedure, the word "objective" refers to the overall objective or objectives of the ZBB procedure. The objective could be simply to prepare an operating budget, to reduce overall data center costs by 10 percent or both. Attempting to obtain more than two objectives at the same time leads to complexities that may cause frustration and failure. Once the objectives have been defined, it

[5] Peter A. Pyhrr, *Zero-Base Budgeting* (New York: John Wiley, 1973).

[6] Logan M. Cheek, *Zero-Base Budgeting Comes of Age,* p. 7.

ILLUSTRATION 4-3. The Zero-Base Budgeting Procedure: Based on the approach of beginning the budgeting process with no money budgeted, all budget allocations, instead of automatic continuation as in traditional budgeting, require analysis and justification. *Source:* Logan M. Cheek, *Zero-Base Budgeting Comes of Age* (N.Y.: Amacom, 1977), p. 20. © 1977 by AMACOM, a division of American Management Associations. All rights reserved.

should be made clear to upper management levels that the remainder of the ZBB procedure will be directed to attaining those objectives, and that any changes or additions after the entire procedure has been completed are not likely to be compatible with the information gathered and cannot be included unless the entire procedure is repeated.

Structuring the Implementation Strategy. The ground rules must be set. The questions to be

ILLUSTRATION 4-4a. Decision Package Form: At least one sheet is prepared for each request, with additional sheets prepared for alternative approaches and for alternate levels of effort. Most of these forms are only one-sided, while others are two-sided, such as this form used by the State of Georgia. *Source:* Peter A. Pyhrr, *Zero-Base Budgeting* (New York: John Wiley, 1973), pp. 66–69.

(1) **Package Name** Air Quality Laboratory (1 of 3)	(2) **Agency** Health	(3) **Activity** Air Quality Control	(4) **Organization** Ambient Air	(5) **Rank** 3

(6) Statement of Purpose

Ambient air laboratory analysis must be conducted for identification and evaluation of pollutants by type and by volume. Sample analysis enables engineers to determine effect of control and permits use of an emergency warning system.

(7) Description of Actions (Operations)

Use a central lab to conduct all sample testing and analysis: 1 Chemist II, 1 Chemist I, 2 Technicians, and 1 Steno I. This staff could analyze and report on a maximum of 37,300 samples. At 37,300 samples per year, we would only sample the 5 major urban areas of the State (70% of the population). These 5 people are required as a minimum to conduct comprehensive sample analysis of even a few samples on a continuous basis.

(8) Achievements from Actions

Ambient air laboratory analysis yields valuable information for management and field engineers to enable them to evaluate effects of the Air Quality Program, identify new or existing pollutants by type and volume, and maintain an emergency warning system.

(9) Consequences of not Approving Package

Field engineers would be forced to rely on their portable testing equipment which does not provide the desired quantitative data (the portable equipment only identified pollutants by major type, does not measure particle size, and does not provide quantitative chemical analyses to determine the specific chemical compounds in the pollutant), and greatly reduces the effectiveness of the emergency warning system which requires detail quantitative chemical analyses.

(10) **Quantitative Package Measures**	**FY 1971**	**FY 1972**	**FY 1973**	(11) **Resources Required ($ in Thousands)**	**FY 1971**	**FY 1972**	**FY 1973**	**% FY 73/72**
Samples analyzed and reported	38,000	55,000	37,300	**Operational**	160	224	140	63%
Cost per sample	$4.21	$4.07	$3.75	**Grants**				
Samples per man hour	3.8	3.9	3.7	**Capital Outlay**				
				Lease Rentals				
				Total	160	224	140	63%
				People (Positions)	5	7	5	71%

Manager Bill Jones   Prepared By Bill Jones   Date 2-22-71   Page 1 of 2

answered include: Who will be responsible for implementing ZBB? What criteria will be used for stating anticipated benefits? What time schedule would provide adequate time to do a quality job? Responsibility for implementing ZBB can be assigned to individual managers, task forces, outside consultants, or a combination of these. Where management is aggressive and communications flow freely without excessive gamesmanship, individual managers are considered the best ap-

proach. At the other extreme, where interpersonal conflicts and office politics are likely to obstruct objective evaluations, outside consultants are usually best. As for the criteria used to state benefits, multiple criteria are likely to be superior to centering on one criterion, such as cost. Three criteria that are the most promising, since they correspond to an organization's overall objectives, are improved user service, more efficient processing, and reduced cost. The amount of time re-

ILLUSTRATION 4–4b. Decision Package Form.

(1) **Package Name** Air Quality Laboratory (1 of 3)	(2) **Agency** Health	(3) **Activity** Air Quality Control	(4) **Organization** Ambient Air	(5) **Rank** 3

(12) **Alternatives (Different Levels of Effort) and Cost**
Air Quality Laboratory (2 of 3): $61,000—Analyze 27,700 additional samples (totaling 55,000 samples, which is the current level), thereby determining air quality for 5 additional problem urban areas and 8 other counties chosen on the basis of worst pollution (covering 80% of the population).
Air Quality Laboratory (3 of 3): $45,000—Analyze 20,000 additional samples (totaling 75,000 samples), thereby determining air quality for 90% of the population, and leaving only rural areas with little or no pollution problems unsampled.

(13) **Alternatives (Different Ways of Performing the Same Function, Activity, or Operation)**
1. Contract sample analysis work to Georgia Tech—Cost $6 per sample for a total cost of $224K for analyzing 37,300 samples. Emergency warning system would not be as effective due to their time requirement on reporting analysis work done by graduate students.
2. Conduct sample analysis work entirely in regional locations—cost a total of $506K the first year and $385K in subsequent years. Specialized equipment must be purchased in the first year for several locations if central lab is discontinued. Subsequent years would also require lab staffing at several locations at minimum levels which would not fully utilize people.
3. Conduct sample analysis work in central lab for special pollutants only, and set up regional labs to reduce sample mailing costs—cost a total of $305K for analyzing 37,300 samples. Excessive cost would persist due to minimum lab staffing at several locations in addition to the special central lab.

(14) **Source of Funds** ($ in Thousands)		FY 1971	FY 1972	FY 1973	(15) **Projection of Funds Committed by This Package***	**Funds**	FY 1974	FY 1975	FY 1976	FY 1977	FY 1978
Operational:	Federal	20	24	40		State					
	Other					Total					
	State	140	200	100	Reasons:						
Grants:	Federal										
	State										
Capital and Lease	Federal										
	State										

***Projected if Funds increase or decrease more than 10% from the prior year (FY 1973–FY 1978).**

quired to establish and implement both traditional budgeting and ZBB are about the same. The results at some organizations have been that the first year for ZBB it takes about 17 weeks for the entire ZBB process, and 14 weeks thereafter.

Developing the Supporting System. The material needed to support ZBB consists of a procedures manual, decision-package forms, worksheets for alternative approaches and levels, and ranking forms. Cheek's book provides good guidelines for preparing a procedures manual. Basically, the ZBB procedures manual should contain the following:

1. Transmittal letter from upper management
2. Statement of ZBB's purpose
3. Economic overview of the organization and its industry
4. The procedure for preparing decision packages
5. The procedure for ranking decision packages
6. A detailed implementation schedule

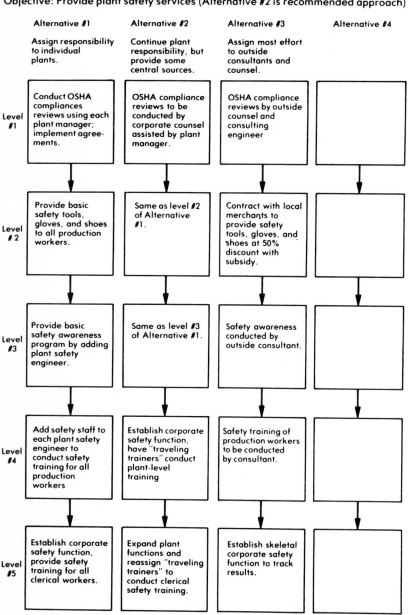

Objective: Provide plant safety services (Alternative #2 is recommended approach)

ILLUSTRATION 4-5. Decision Package Worksheet: This is a convenient "think sheet" for developing alternative approaches and levels before documenting them as decision packages. *Source:* Logan M. Cheek, *Zero-Base Budgeting Comes of Age* (N.Y.: Amacom, 1977), p. 50 © 1977 by AMACOM, a division of American Management Associations. All rights reserved.

R A N K	Package Name	FY 1972 Resources			FY 1973 Resources			Cumulative Level		
		Total $	State $	People	Total $	State $	People	Total $	State $	%*
1	Reviews and Permits	129	129	14	116	116	13	116	116	16%
2	Registrations	113	113	12	103	103	10	219	219	29%
***3	Air Quality Laboratory (1 of 3)	224	200	7	140	100	5	359	319	43%
4	Source Evaluation (1 of 2)	326	204	11	273	253	9	632	572	77%
5	Ambient Air Monitoring	53	43	6	53	43	6	685	615	83%
***6	Air Quality Laboratory (2 of 3)				61	24	2	746	639	**86%
7	Research (1 of 2)	117	56	5	85	56	3	831	695	93%
8	Source Evaluation (2 of 2)				57	38	3	888	733	98%
9	Air Quality Laboratory (3 of 3)				45	25	2	933	758	102%
10	Research (2 of 2)				24	24	1	957	782	105%
	TOTAL	962	745	55	957	782	54			

** See Sample Packages.

**Sample Calculation:

$$\frac{639}{745} = 86\%$$

Agency, Activity, or Organization Ranked	Manager	Prepared By	Date	Page
Air Quality Control	Bob Davis	John Doe	2-28-71	1 of 1

*FY 1973 Cumulative State $ as a % of Total FY 1972 State $ for corresponding organizations.

ILLUSTRATION 4-6. Ranking Form: One-line summary information is entered for each decision package, with each entry in sequence according to the preparer's judgement of their relative importance, with the most important listed first. *Source:* Peter A. Pyhrr, *Zero-Base Budgeting* (New York: John Wiley, 1973), pp. 80-81.

Representative form designs for the decision-package form, the worksheet, and the ranking form are shown in Illustrations 4-4, 4-5, and 4-6. The decision package and ranking forms shown were developed for the State of Georgia and are not likely to be suitable, as is, for anyone else. But they do contain the elements needed and can be modified for the needs of any organization. The worksheet, Illustration 4-5, is a convenience for developing alternative approaches and levels of effort. On the worksheet shown, four approaches can be entered, with up to five levels for each approach. With these support materials, decision packages can be prepared and ranked.

Preparing the Decision Packages. With a properly designed decision-package form and the ZBB procedures manual, the information and actions required are stated clearly and comprehensively. For each objective, many subobjectives are likely, and for each of these subobjectives several decision packages may be prepared, allowing for different approaches and levels of effort. A minimum level of effort decision package is recommended when multiple decision packages are prepared. This makes upper management aware that cuts in cost are possible and also makes them aware of what the effects will be. Levels of effort for next year's budget can be stated as a percentage of the current budget. One decision package could indicate 80 percent of the current budget, the second 95 percent, and another 115 percent.

One precaution that must be taken when preparing decision packages is to avoid making one decision package dependent on another. If a package is dependent on one that is rejected, what happens to the dependent package? If this situation cannot be avoided, a solution is to include cross references so that it would be known that a package cannot be eliminated unless it is acceptable to eliminate all dependent packages.

Ranking All Decision Packages. The difference between efficiency and effectiveness, as defined by management authority Peter Drucker, is the difference between "doing things right" and "doing the right things." Decision packages promote "doing things right." But if relatively unimportant things are being done right, ignoring the important things, the result is being efficiently ineffective. Ranking decision packages assures, as far as judgment permits, "doing the right things." The most important decision package is ranked first, and the least important last.

The person or persons preparing the decision packages are likely to be those responsible for ranking them. However, once they are ranked they will proceed to upper levels for consideration, and reordering is likely. Reordering should be done cautiously and should be kept to a minimum to avoid operational problems; when reordering occurs, data center managers must be conferred with to assure that problems will not arise. Upper management may select scheduling and computer-performance decision packages that will increase throughput, but at the same time select a low level of effort decision package for data preparation, that hampers throughput.

A method suitable for ranking decision packages is to isolate several criteria, to assign a weight to each criterion, and to assign a value for each of these criteria in each decision package. The total value for a decision package results from the following formula:

$$\text{Total value} = (\text{value}_1 \times \text{weight}_1)$$
$$+ (\text{value}_2 \times \text{weight}_2)$$
$$+ \ldots$$

For the sake of illustration, assume that only two criteria will be used, for example, cost and efficiency. Also assume that cost is twice as important as efficiency: a weight of 2 is assigned

to cost, and a weight of 1 is assigned to efficiency. Using a scale of 1 to 10, with 10 being the highest value, approach *A* may have a cost value of 8 and an efficiency value of 4, and approach *B* may have a cost value of 6 and an efficiency value of 5. Inserting these numbers in the preceding formula, we obtain the total values for the two approaches:

$$\text{Total value of } A = (8 \times 2) + (4 \times 1) = 20$$

$$\text{Total value of } B = (6 \times 2) + (5 \times 1) = 17$$

Approach *A* is the higher-ranked decision package in this example. The accuracy of this approach depends on the assignment of the proper weight to each criterion and accurate values to each criterion in each decision package.

Approving the Selected Decision Packages. Upper management receives the decision packages and their ranking and, after reordering discussions, can quickly and intelligently decide what to approve. Upper managers have been delighted by their increased insight into operational activities and by their awareness of the results they can expect from their decisions.

Budgeting Reports

Data center managers must be kept informed of actual expenditures and how they compare with budgeted estimates. Two simple forms that can be used for this purpose are shown in Illustrations 4–7 and 4–8. The detail expenditure report in Illustration 4–7 provides space for dollar variance, for percent of variance, and for comments on variances. Whereas a budget answers the question How much do we intend to spend for specified budget items?, the detail expenditure report answers the question Did we spend as intended?, and If not, why the variance? A variance requires comment if it is above or below a preestablished percentage, usually 5 percent. Some organizations may permit greater variances, and others may require more stringent adherence to budgeted amounts.

The summary expenditure report in Illustration 4–8 can be used to merely record expenditures for historical purposes, but if variance columns are added, it could also be used to study trends. A recommended aid for studying trends is a graph of budgeted and actual expenditures. This approach makes trends immediately apparent, particularly if graphs are prepared for each budget item. Analysis of variances and investigation of their causes have located problems, many of which have been easy to remedy. For example, in one installation management was not aware of excessive personnel overtime. Excessive personnel costs brought this to their attention, and through some rescheduling of the testing schedule, overtime was greatly reduced. In another instance, excessive costs were traced to frequent restarts because of equipment failures. Inquiries pinpointed the problem as inadequate maintenance. The maintenance schedule, which was adequate, was more strictly enforced and equipment failures were reduced.

The budget items can be recorded and controlled in much greater detail than shown in Illustration 4-7. Each budget item is usually referred to as an "account" and a *charter of accounts* can be prepared. An account consists of all the charges for a particular asset or equity—in other words, for a particular budget item. The charter of accounts is a listing of all the accounts. One of the possible charter of accounts is shown in Appendix B.

It is obvious that computer-prepared budget reports are possible, and these can include variance information. This budgeting system can be developed in-house or obtained from a software

ILLUSTRATION 4-7. Monthly Expenditure Report.

Monthly Expenditure Report — Month / Year

Expense		This month	Year-to-date Budgeted	Year-to-date Actual	Year-to-date Variance	Comment
Hardware	Purchase					
	Lease					
	Rental					
	Maintenance					
	Total					
Software	Purchase					
	Lease					
	Total					
Site	Rental					
	Utilities					
	Maintenance					
	Tax					
	Total					
Supplies	Disc					
	Tape					
	Paper					
	Cards					
	Total					
Staff	Management					
	Computer room staff					
	Remaining staff					
	Total					
Grand totals						

Yearly Summary Expenditure Report

Year

Expense		Month												Year's Total
		1	2	3	4	5	6	7	8	9	10	11	12	
Hardware	Purchase														
	Lease														
	Rental														
	Maintenance														
	Total														
Software	Purchase														
	Lease														
	Total														
Site	Rental														
	Utilities														
	Maintenance														
	Tax														
	Total														
Supplies	Disc														
	Tape														
	Paper														
	Cards														
	Total														
Staff	Management														
	Computer room staff														
	Remaining staff														
	Total														
Grand totals															

ILLUSTRATION 4-8. Yearly Expenditure Report.

vendor. Two vendor-supplied packages are Responsibility Accounting System from IBM, and EASY from Financial Computer Services.

CHARGEOUT OF DATA CENTER COSTS

When users are unaware of the cost of executing their applications, the data center is viewed as a "free" service. This results when data center costs are treated as overhead expenses, charged to the company without being directly related to each department and to each application. As a result, some users, sometimes unknowingly and sometimes not, do not hesitate to install or retain marginally useful applications. To run an incomplete job and then to run it several times again

may not concern them, or they may be totally unaware of the expenses incurred and the resources wasted. The solution to this situation is considered by many data center managers to be informing users of the actual costs for executing their jobs, which is known as *chargeout*. Thus, users become definitely aware of the costs for their jobs. When users are actually billed for these costs, the system implemented is referred to as *chargeback*. In this case, users must budget for data center processing costs.

Data center managers must judge the suitability of a chargeout, chargeback, or an alternate approach according to the nature of their environment. Before examining the basic methodologies of the primary alternatives, the pros and cons of chargeout systems are noted, and then guidelines for developing and evaluating a chargeout system are considered.

Pros and Cons of Chargeout Systems

The advantages and disadvantages of chargeout or chargeback systems have been discussed at some length by data center managers, consultants, and vendors of job-accounting packages. The pros and cons that have evolved are fascinating because of the insight they provide and because of their contradictions. The primary contradictions, as the following shows, relate to whether or not users will attempt to use data center resources more efficiently, and whether user and data center personnel will develop better rapport or will alienation be the actual result. Six advantages of these systems are anticipated.

1. *Better allocation of resources.* Since user managers are made responsible for justifying the costs associated with applications, they must relate benefits received to cost. This attitude leads to elimination of worthless applications and reconsideration of marginally useful applications. Being aware of costs for running a job, of the costs of printouts, and of other cost factors would lead to attempts to reduce the number of runs, the amount of paper produced, and such other items as the number of copies printed.

2. *More resource capacity made available.* Removal of wasteful and marginally useful applications frees resource capacity. The availability of extra capacity provides two significant benefits. First, users now have extra capacity to support the development of new systems and the enhancement of existing systems. Second, the need to increase data center resource capacities can be forestalled for longer periods of time, reducing operating expenses and the frequency of upgrading equipment, with all the adjustment confusion that usually occurs.

3. *Reduction of "expensive-overhead" criticism.* Users have transferred their manual processing and their processing costs to the data center processing budget and then have criticized the data center as a high overhead expense. By indicating the processing cost for an application, users are made aware that the cost for processing their work is their expense. Users are also made aware that if they have a less-expensive method of processing, they are welcome to use it. The cost of processing, thus, is directly related to user decisions, and they cannot relinquish responsibility for work that would otherwise be done in their departments.

4. *Quantitative improvement of application processing.* Awareness of processing costs leads users to seek alternate methods to obtain the same or more benefits for less cost. If users are responsible for costs, they will attempt to have programmers make programs more efficient, stimulating the use of such program-analysis software as Boole & Babbage's PPE (Program Performance Evaluator). At the same time, data center personnel can experiment with different equipment configurations to forecast their effect on costs. Job-accounting information is also a generally accepted means of initiating a program for computer performance evaluations and improvements.

5. *Increased user attentiveness to processing.* Users become more careful in submitting jobs. To avoid additional charges because of their oversights, they will attempt to provide accurate and complete input and processing instructions. Naturally, this is true only if there are charges for any delays and reruns for which they are responsible. This should also minimize the requests for intermediary runs of an application with incomplete data merely for curiosity.

6. *Opportunity for rapport of user-data center personnel.* Rapport between user and data center personnel is likely to result if discussions center on how user benefits can be increased and how cost can be reduced. Alternative approaches can be discussed, modification of inefficient and troublesome systems and programs can be implemented, and the sincere concern and interest in the goals and difficulties of one another can be appreciated. A Utopian goal. But with sincere effort, it is possible.

Those are the advantages hoped for from a chargeout or chargeback system. If there were no drawbacks, or only minor drawbacks, they would be more common than they are. Six disadvantages of these systems are prominent.

1. *Wasted resources.* In contrast to those who believe that resources will be used more cautiously, others believe that waste will increase. Several reasons are given. Many organizations relate a person's importance, including salary, to the degree that data center resources are used. This naturally promotes wastefulness. In addition, many managers associate computer usage with their own self-importance; in other words, it is a means of their going on an "ego trip." Increased usage and cost indicate to them that they are important. Bruce Rogow of IBM investigated the effects of chargeback systems and arrived at several conclusions related to waste of resources, two of which are: (1) excessive personnel time was required—33 percent of technical personnel time and up to 50 percent of management time was necessary to update the systems for new hardware and for new software releases; (2) additional overhead—administration and operating costs for a charge-

back system often ranged from 6 percent to 24 percent of the total EDP budget.[7]

2. *Decreased data center efficiencies.* Data center personnel will become less concerned about efficiency because users are responsible for costs. This is possible if data center performance is not monitored, which is not likely. Monitoring of data center personnel's attempts to coordinate and assist users, to schedule jobs for optimum use of resources, will uncover slackness and indifference. If monitoring does not occur, however, this criticism may become justifiable.

3. *Restrictions on data center innovations.* Data center management would attempt to avoid changes that will affect charge rates, even if only temporarily. Changes in rates may suggest instability to users and may lead to user complaints because they would have difficulty predicting expenses and budgeting those expenses. Management, thus, may tend to avoid expenses that have a long-term benefit but do not provide short-term benefits.

4. *Restrictions on user innovations.* Users, particularly those who are overly cost conscious, may not want to gamble on worthwhile applications, fearing difficulty in justifying benefits. This is exactly the opposite of one of the benefits anticipated, the availability of extra resource capacity to permit the inclusion of new applications. Here the stress is improperly placed on cost-cutting and not on using resources when they are beneficial. If this overcautious attitude cannot be eliminated, a real problem exists, and the progress of the affected departments will be halted.

5. *User alienation.* Few users have been found who understand how a chargeout system determines application charges. This feeling of inadequacy plus an uneasiness about fluctuating charges causes alienation. Most chargeout systems are dependent on resource charge rates and resource usage. Without adequate education, users are not likely to understand what resources they are being charged for, and what units are used for rates and to measure usage. When this situation is compounded because of the need to change resource charge rates, the user is lead to doubt the accuracy of the system.

6. *Comparison to lower-priced services.* With application cost made available, users are able to compare in-house data processing costs with those of outside services. When this is done, in-house services are frequently found to be more expensive. Usually the difference is small and can be justified by the additional services provided in-house, such as rapid turnaround and correction of rejected

transactions. However, sometimes the cost difference is large. In one New Jersey county, the Freeholders realized that their data center processed at a much higher cost similar applications to those of a neighboring county, which used an outside service. This realization led to criticism and some embarrassment to data center management. Fortunately, efficiency eventually improved and costs were reduced.

Chargeout Guidelines

The basic justification for chargeout systems is that data center resources will no longer be wasted on worthless applications. At the same time, the critics of these systems comment that this waste is actually encouraged. In either case, the situation is as one senior administrator stated, "We have developed a computer system the equivalent of an atomic reactor powering a Mickey Mouse watch."[8]

There is no doubt that, if applications are not evaluated in terms of their cost and worth, this situation does occur. However, it is not necessarily true that this is avoided when a chargeout system is installed. The success of a chargeout system depends on how compatible the system is with the organization's development and management style and how well the system meets performance standards.

Compatibility with the Organization's Development. Some organizations are not ready for the controls of a chargeout system, particularly for the stringent controls of a chargeback system. Richard L. Nolan states that a basic step in determining the advisability of a chargeout cost-control system is the data center's development in the organization; that is, is it in its initial, introductory stage; in its contagion, growth stage; in its control, consolidation stage; or in its final, integrated stage, a stage where the data center is a coordinated part of the overall organization?[9] In a data center's initial or contagion stages the primary concern is to stimulate use of the data center resources. This is a poor time to hamper and complicate development activities with unnecessary cost controls. However, as resource

---

[7]Bruce Rogow, "Why and How to Use Chargeback Control Systems for EDP Services," *EDP Solutions* (Delran, N.J.: Datapro Research Corp., 1977), p. E40-300-054.

[8]John B. Wallace, "When to Bill for Computer Services," *Data Mangement,* July 1975, p. 13.

[9]Richard I. Nolan, "How to Install Chargeout Control Systems for Computer Services," *EDP Solutions* (Delran, N.J.: Datapro Research Corp., 1977), p. E40-300-153.

Criteria	Development Stages			
	Stage I Initiation	Stage II Contagion	Stage III Control	Stage IV Integration
Data Processing Organization	Get several applications on the computer, with stress on acquiring technical personnel.	Extend range of applications, increase sophistication, and stimulate cooperation between data processing and user personnel.	Apply quality and cost-effectiveness controls, and centralize activities.	Technical competency is balanced with management competency, and management is represented at high levels in the organization.
User Awareness	Anxiety over lack of knowledge and uncertainty of the effects of data processing on user staff and management.	Increased demands on application development and scheduling, and ironically, inadequate involvement in developing systems.	New constraints imposed to attain cost accountability, and to increase the formality of communications.	User acceptance and integrated effort in maintaining effective, cost conscious processing.
Planning and Control	Stress on budgeting, but with few controls and standards implemented.	Stress on increasing the number of applications on the computer, but controls and standards still receiving little attention.	Stress on formalized, central direction and control, with standards aggressively enforced.	Stress on dynamic, flexible planning and control, with documented standards for stable and reliable activities.
Application Portfolio	Persuading users to use the computer, with emphasis on cost savings.	Many applications cross departmental boundaries and coordinate their activities.	Justification required to develop and implement new systems, and existing systems are evaluated for efficiency and worth.	Exploit opportunities for integrated systems by such means as an integrated data base that serves several applications.

ILLUSTRATION 4-9. Organization Development and Its Attributes: The appropriateness and intention of a chargeout system depend on the development stage of the organization. Where in stages I and II a chargeout system is likely to hinder increased use of data processing, stage III can use it advantageously for control, and stage IV can use it for integration. *Source:* Based on table by Richard L. Nolan, "Controlling the Costs of Data Services," *Harvard Business Review.* (July–Aug., 1977).

capacity becomes close to fully used, then cost control and application justification is recommended. Illustration 4–9 provides Nolan's summary of the attributes for each development stage.

Chargeout systems usually are not necessary for decentralized data centers. The reason is that there is no competition for resources between different interest groups, since each data center frequently exists for a specific individual department. In these situations, cost is usually more efficiently controlled through budgeting. But even in these situations a chargeout system has definite benefits. The cost information provided permits cost-benefit analysis and permits user managers to consider less-costly processing alternatives.

Compatibility with Management Style. Success depends partly on management style. An excellent system is likely to be of little value if management is unconcerned, whereas even a basic, unsophisticated chargeout system can obtain dramatic results through active, conscientious administration.

F. Warren McFarlan relates chargeout systems to the management style prevalent in an organization when he comments, "Chargeout frequently offers the more significant advantages where management is vigorous or the EDP department is becoming mature.[10] A potentially effective chargeout system can be installed, but if management is not vigorous in assuring user understanding and profit from it, it becomes merely expensive overhead and consumes personnel time. The chargeout reports can become like so many reports, which data center managers suspect are dispersed in all directions and are ignored.

Chargeout reports provide opportunity for users to evaluate applications and to consider improvements when they receive adequate education and understand these reports. Vigorous management provides this education and also restricts the intentional waste of resources for worthless applications to give individuals a feeling of importance. Usually intentional waste of data center resources is associated with users seeking prestige. In one instance, hopefully not representative of many others, a data center manager intentionally wasted surplus computer capacity so that he could demand a larger computer—and he got it. Situations

of this type, where users are intentionally wasting resources, can be controlled by the data center steering committee. Just the presence of this committee should restrain most intentional wastes. Management style is dependent on the authority that managers and the committee have and on how vigorously they apply that authority.

Performance Criteria. Various chargeout systems offer special features, some that may have strong appeal and others that may not provide any practical value. Each manager must judge which are worthwhile, possibly necessary, and which should have no influence on selecting a package. Software packages used for chargeout or chargeback systems are called job-accounting packages. Each package should be evaluated in terms of five criteria:

1. *Accountability for total costs.* A chargeout system that permits allocation of only 40 percent or even 60 percent of the data center expenditure is of questionable value. It should be possible to charge for all data center costs, including manual processing associated with an application, and also overhead costs.

2. *Consistency of charges.* The charge for a job should be the same, or very close, if it is executed at different times using the same transactions and files. In a multiprogramming environment, job mix affects overall time, and a chargeout system should have the logic needed to make the discrepancies very small—as will soon be explained, the discrepancies presently cannot be totally eliminated.

3. *Equitability of charges.* All users should be treated fairly and charged for all resources they use, and only for the resources they use. Some systems, for example, do not permit charging for priority treatment, for using special forms, or for input preparation.

4. *Simplicity of charging algorithm.* The charging algorithm is the formula that uses resource quantity and rate information to determine the total charge for a job. This algorithm should be reasonably easy to explain to users so that they know precisely what they are being charged for and can determine where excessive costs can be trimmed. Most algorithms in use today are not understood by users, which is another conclusion of Bruce Rogow's research.

[10] F. Warren McFarlan, "Management Audit of the EDP Department," *Harvard Business Review*, May–June 1973, p. 135.

5. *Usefulness of reports.* Reports received by users should contain all the information needed to analyze charges and to consider means of reducing costs. These reports should contain, for example, the printing costs and the costs of repetitive processing steps.

Potential Problems. The most general problem that arises is loss of rapport between data center personnel and users. The usual reasons are related to the performance criteria. Users lose faith in the data center if charges vary considerably for two runs of the same job, if some users are getting "free" resources because they are not part of the charging algorithm, or if users are mystified by the charging algorithm. To add to these disturbances, some installations frequently vary the charge rates, thus making it impossible for users to budget for costs. This last difficulty can be minimized if rates are changed infrequently, possibly no oftener than every six months.

Users should not be charged for additional work required because of an error in the data center. It definitely is not fair to users to be charged for data-preparation errors or for reruns required because of operator errors. If, however, the user supplies incomplete input and one or more reruns are necessary, the user should be charged—this is a mild form of arm twisting to force users to use data center resources conscientiously.

Multiprogramming and virtual memory create technical problems in charging equitably and consistently for resources used. In a nonmultiprogramming environment, storage occupancy time can be measured by elapsed time. This cannot be done in a multiprogramming environment and result in consistent charges. The job mix varies from one run to the next, affecting elapsed time. Therefore "occupancy time" must be used to determine the time a job would have consumed if run alone, unaffected by wait time needed for other jobs. The solution to this problem is to charge for central processing unit (CPU) and input/output (I/O) activity for each job. Apparently this permits charging for storage occupancy only for the time actually required by a job. It is not that simple. Presently, the difficulty is that of not charging for unsuccessful I/O accesses because a shared data set is being used. This difficulty has not been resolved. However, the inconsistency of charges is significantly small and not of serious concern, and it has not invalidated job-accounting systems. Another source of presently uncontrolled charge variations occurs for paging activity for a virtual-memory operating system. This inconsistency of charges can either be accepted, or a fixed charge can be established for paging for each job and used for all runs of those jobs.

Chargeout by Unit Rate

The most precise means for consistent and equitable charging, although not the simplest, is by establishing a unit rate for each resource and measuring resource usage. In a nonmultiprogramming environment, all computer system resources are dedicated to each job as it is executed. Charging by unit rate in this situation is simple. A charge is established for "wall-clock" time. If the charge is $200/hour and if only 6 minutes of elapsed time is required for a job, the charge for the job is 6/60 times $200, or $20. This charging procedure, however, does not account for such items as manual processing and printout costs.

A multiprogramming environment complicates the basic charging formula considerably. The CPU is not used solely for a single job, and thus elapsed time cannot be used. Internal storage and peripheral devices are no longer dedicated to any single job. To account for these considerations, the charging algorithm becomes more complicated, requiring resource usage and rate information for each resource, as shown by the generalized expression:

$$\text{Total charge} = (\text{resource}_1 \times \text{rate}_1)$$
$$+ (\text{resource}_2 \times \text{rate}_2)$$
$$+ \ldots$$

To obtain a better feeling for how a total charge results from a charging algorithm, Illustration 4-10 shows the charge for a Remote Job Entry execution of a small mailing list application. The job-accounting package used was GO-PAC, developed by Grumman Data Systems. The resource identified by SRU is a *system resource unit* that results from such factors as storage allocated and CPU and I/O activity. SRU thus accounts for all the multiprogramming and virtual storage factors that make charging algorithms particularly difficult for users to understand. The simplicity of this approach should make users more comfortable with chargeout information, especially since the other resource-usage information, such as cards read and lines printed, are easy to relate to.

Illustration 4–10 indicates the basic method of using unit costs and suggests such questions as:

What resources should be considered?

How are rates determined?

How is usage measured?

Are there special charge adjustments?

What reports are provided?

How are reports used?

Resources Used for Charging. Vendors of job-accounting packages state what resources are used in their charging algorithms; unfortunately these resources are grouped and identified differently. To avoid this welter of different classifications, with varying degrees of omissions, the author is adding another classification, hopefully one that provides a reference point for relating the other classifications. The total charges for an application result from four resource-cost categories: computer time-related costs, computer volume-related costs, data center support services, and data center overhead costs. Computer time-related costs include CPU and I/O activity costs and storage costs related to these activities, which in turn include core and disk storage used during these activites. Computer volume-related costs refer to such activities as the number of cards read, cards punched, and lines printed. The third category, data center support services, includes computer-operator activities such as tape and disk pack mounting, and includes other support

activities such as input keying, tabulating, and decollating and bursting of reports. The final category of costs is data center overhead costs. This includes administrative and management personnel costs and costs for site rental, taxes, and utilities. Whereas the first three categories are charged according to usage, overhead costs are usually added to each of these resources according to their relative costs. Thus, if one of the three resource categories incurs 40 percent of the cost for all three categories, 40 percent of the overhead cost is added to this category.

Resource-rate Determination. There are various methods for determining rates. The procedure presented provides an understanding of the generally preferred method. Departure may be felt necessary for greater simplicity or precision, or to make the procedure compatible with the job-accounting package chosen. The recommended procedure involves six steps.

1. *Estimate total data center costs for a time period.* The time period chosen initially may be only one or two months. This provides quick zeroing-in on reasonably close rates. Once reasonable rates have been obtained, it may be necessary to adjust rates only once every six months. For illustrative purpose, the total data center cost for two months will be estimated at $150,000.

2. *Determine percentage of costs for nonoverhead resources.* For nonoverhead resources, the percentage of each resource cost to all nonoverhead costs is calculated. Thus, if CPU hardware and supporting software is $40,000 for two months, and if the total nonoverhead costs are $100,000, the percentage would be 40 percent. The resulting percentages could be the following:

ILLUSTRATION 4-10. Job Accounting Charge Report: The total charge for the execution of a RJE job is clearly reported by GO-PAC, a product of Grumman Data Systems, which reports charges by resource unit rates and resource usage. This charge report is the property of Grumman Data Systems Corporation and may not be published or copied for public dissemination unless permission is first obtained from Grumman Data Systems Corporation.

```
******************************** GO*PAC  V08 L08.1 JOB ACCOUNTING BLOCK ********************************
* JOB  Z001104N  RDR STOP = 10.55.56  STARTED = 16.13.21     ENDED = 16.19.34     REMOTE ID = 05           *
*                                                                                                          *
* CPU MIN = 0000.06              CORE        TAPE       2314       3330       3331       3350    *
* CHAN MIN = 00000.08   MOUNTS     --          02         01         00         00         --    *
* PRTY REQ = 02         EXCPS      --      00000024   00000022   00000198   00000000   00000000 *
* PRTY REC = 02         OCC HRS  00001.30   00000.00   00000.00   00000.00   00000.00   00000.00 *
* DATE    = 78.104                                                                               *
* ACCOUNT = 1849001                   AMOUNT      RATE         TOTAL                              *
* SYSTEM  = 370/470  05/01   SRU       0000.46     07.00     000003.22                            *
*                          MOUNTS (T/D) 002/001   02.00/02.00 000006.00                           *
*                          CARDS READ   0001666    01.50/K    000002.49                           *
*                          CARDS PUNCHED 0000000   03.65/K    000000.00                           *
*                          LINES PRINTED 0000669   01.65/K    000001.10                           *
*                        ESTIMATED CHARGE FOR THIS JOB IS $0000012.81                             *
********************************** VS RELEASE  01.7 *********************************B33*(OSREEL)**
```

CPU hardware and supporting software	40%
Tape drives and tapes	6
Disk drives and disks	10
Printers and paper	5
Card readers and cards	5
Input preparation equipment, material, and personnel	25
Tabulating equipment and personnel	2
Decollating and bursting equipment and personnel	7
	100%

3. *Relate percentages to total data center costs.* The percentage obtained in step 2 for each resource is multiplied by the total data center costs. This step adds, in effect, overhead costs to each resource according to the relative cost of each resource. The result would be the following:

CPU hardware and supporting software	$ 60,000
Tape drives and tapes	9,000
Disk drives and disks	15,000
Printers and paper	7,500
Card readers and cards	7,500
Input preparation equipment, material and personnel	37,500
Tabulating equipment and personnel	3,000
Decollating and bursting equipment and personnel	10,500
	$150,000

4. *Translate resource cost to unit rate.* Whereas each resource cost indicates the total cost to be charged out, the unit rate is the cost related to resource usage. In the case of the printer, a unit rate is assigned to how many lines are printed. If 5 million lines were printed in the last time period, which is for two months, the price per line is 7500/5,000,000, which is 0.0015. This is customarily stated in cost per 1000 lines, which becomes $1.50 per 1000 lines. This is the unit rate for the printer.

5. *Obtain total charges allocated for the time period.* The total charges allocated to users for each resource is compared to the actual resource cost in the data center. The differences show what adjustments are necessary to allocate the actual resource costs.

6. *Adjust unit rates for correct allocation of resource costs.* If only $6750 was charged for the printer, which costs $7500, the unit rate must be increased. The discrepancy is 10 percent less than the amount needed; thus, a 10 percent increase in unit rate is necessary. The new unit rate for the printer is increased from $1.50 per 1000 lines to $1.65 per 1000 lines.

Measurement of Resource Usage. Computer equipment vendors usually include as part of their operating systems a facility for gathering and supplying resource usage information. IBM, for example, has the System Management Facility (SMF) for OS (Operating System) and Job Accounting for DOS (Disk Operating System). SMF can provide 31 types of resource usage records, and at the time of system generation, data center personnel decide which of these records are needed. Since programmers in the organization can assess this information, they can develop a chargeout system and produce chargeout reports. But this is not recommended. Errors may occur, the understanding required to code programs that are efficient is usually not present, and the development costs are likely to far exceed the cost of purchasing a proven job-accounting package.

Many excellent job-accounting packages are available. In choosing a package, it should be compatible with the operating system and should be evaluated in terms of the performance criteria introduced earlier. In addition, different charge features are available with the various packages, and these features can have a dramatic effect on resource usage. These features are discussed in the next section. Some of the job-accounting packages available are listed below in alphabetical order, with vendor names in parentheses:

CALCBILL (B & K Associates)
CAS/CPA (Boole & Babbage)
COMPUT-A-CHARGE SYSTEM (Value Computing)
COMPUTER USAGE ACCOUNTING (Hycom)
CONTROL/IMS (Boole & Babbage)
CSAR (Computer Concepts Corp.)
DASD DEVICE INDEPENDENCE ROUTINES (IBM Corp.)
DOS-DOS/VS JOB ACCOUNTING-CIMS (BMS Computer)
DOS TIME ACCOUNTING AND BILLING (IBM Corp.)
FILE CONVERSION AIDS (Univac Division, Sperry Rand Corp.)
JAB (Duquesne Systems)
JASPER (Datachron Corp.)
JOB ACCOUNTING REPORT SYSTEM (Johnson Systems)
JOB ACCOUNTING SYSTEM (Universal Software)
JOBDOC (Gulf Computer Sciences)

JOB MONITOR/JOB ACCOUNTING
   (Westinghouse Electric Corp.)
KOMMAND (Pace Applied Technology)
OS JOB ACCOUNTING-CIMS (BMS Computer)
POWER/VS JOB ACCOUNTING-CIMS
   (BMS Computer)
SYSTEM 1-JOB ACCOUNTING (Value Computing)
TABS (Burroughs Corp.)

Charge Adjustments. Software packages permit various types of charge adjustments. These adjustments relate to user service requirements and to efficient data center resources. First, consider user requirements. When a user demands priority attention, it is natural and acceptable to charge extra for that special service. Many packages permit increase of charge for priority service. This tends to lessen casual user demands for special treatment. In contrast, users may be willing to have their applications executed as low-priority jobs or on the second or third shifts if a charge reduction is obtained. A package that supports this adjustment is definitely beneficial for lessening demand for peak-activity first-shift processing. Users who elect to take advantage of the shift-differential reduction may be able to cost-justify an application whose benefits were difficult to justify at full cost. The request for high- or low-priority treatment therefore places the decision for increased or decreased charges on the user.

Charge adjustments can significantly improve the efficient use of data center resources. The basic idea is to increase unit rates for scarce resources and to decrease unit rates for underutilized resources. For example, if there is excessive sharing of specific types of disk units, the unit rate is increased and the user is made aware that those units are overutilized and that less-expensive resources are available. In line with this approach, penalty charges can be added to jobs that make excessive demands on resources. Thus, for example, an additional charge can be added to a job if more than five minutes of CPU time is required, or if more than one third of available memory is required. For each of these conditions, the additional charge could be 25 percent of the normal charge for the job. These additional charges will cause users to put pressure on system-development personnel to consider efficient use of data center resources when considering alternative system-development approaches.

Job-accounting Reports. The available job-accounting packages provide a rich variety of reports. Most of the information contained is similar, but the differences are critical in deciding what is appropriate for any specific environment. This is particularly true in making the information intelligible to users. Some of the reports produced have the added advantage of being formatted for easy comprehension and for pleasant appearance. Each data center manager must examine what vendors have to offer and decide which vendor provides the information needed in the formats wanted. Selection of representative reports is a difficult task, but three have been chosen. These reports are shown in Illustrations 4-11, 4-12, and 4-13. The reports suggest the variety available and are not necessarily the primary reports for the packages used. The basic reports of the three packages are similar, although each vendor provides different features and presents the information differently.

Use of Job-accounting Reports. Users naturally want to eliminate applications that cannot be cost-justified and to reduce the costs of those that remain. The data center manager, on the other hand, is primarily concerned about allocating data center costs. The data center manager is also concerned about improving computer performance (job-accounting packages can help, but this topic is discussed elsewhere) and leveling workload demands on resources. In an issue of *EDP Performance Review*, several questions are suggested when examining reports to determine how the resources are used:

1. How is the workload distributed throughout day, week, month?
2. Which departments place the heaviest loads on the system?
3. Which programs account for the greatest resource usage?
4. What is the productivity by shift?
5. What is the level of usage of each component?
6. What are the characteristics of the workload?
7. What is the distribution of errors by device?
8. What is the distribution of program-abort causes?
9. What is the distribution of turnaround time by user?[11]

[11] Phillip C. Howard, "Getting the Most of System Usage Accounting," *EDP Performance Review*, April 1973, p. 4.

| JOBNAME TRANS ID | #JOBS #TRANS | ACTIVE TIME | CPU TIME | *----PROCESSING CHARGES----* | | | | | *-OTHER CHARGES-* | | **TOTAL** | PCT TOT |
				RUNTIME	CPUTIME	TAPE	DISK	PRINT	OFFLINE	DEBITS CREDITS		
① JPURO410	60	9.00	176/20	348.64	423.20	124.83	98.04	312.30	218.95		③ $1,525.96	
JPURO420	3	.12	7/16	8.34	17.44		3.89		72.40		$102.07	
JPURO430	21	1.36	45/36	62.14	109.44	11.58	36.19		90.44		$309.79	
JPURO440	6	.24	11/08	14.28	26.72	1.38	7.23	.81	66.97		$117.39	
JPURO500	31	6.00	115/12	232.24	276.48	85.76	52.62	52.53	234.63		$934.26	
JPURO520	9	.44	9/48	27.48	23.52		58.29		67.99		$177.28	
JPURO550	1	.04	/24	1.81	.96		1.03	2.68	7.30		$13.78	
APPL CODE PUR	131	17.59	365/44	694.93	877.76	223.55	257.29	368.32	758.68		④ $3,180.53	5.3
② TPR3	1,109	.08	5/24	4.47	12.96		2.37		7.60		$27.40	
TPR4	6,922	.36	34/16	24.42	82.24		5.56		53.09		$165.31	
TPR5	5,605	.32	29/12	19.82	70.08		2.27		62.48.		$154.65	
APPL CODE TPR	13,636	1.16	68/52	48.71	165.28		10.20		,123.17		$347.36	.6
CHG CODE 9300		19.15	434/36	743.64	1043.04	223.55	267.49	368.32	881.85		⑤ $3,577.89	5.9

```
DEPT NAME = PURCHASING
TOTAL NO. JOBS RUN = 131
TOTAL NO. CICS TRANS = 13,636
BATCH PROCESSING CHARGES = $2,421.85
CICS PROCESSING CHARGES  =   $224.19
OTHER CHARGES            =   $881.85
TOTAL                    = $3,527.89
```

ILLUSTRATION 4-11. Job Accounting Summary Charge Report: For a time period, possibly each month, this report shows (1) the number of jobs executed for each job name, (2) the number of transactions processed for each transaction code, (3) cost by job name, (4) by all jobs, (5) by transaction code, by all transaction codes, and by charge code, which is usually by department. This report is from JASPER, a product of Trans-American Computer Associates, Jericho, N.Y.

ILLUSTRATION 4-12. Revenue Analysis: This report from KOMMAND, a product of Pace Applied Technology, permits analysis of charges to determine if resource unit rates should be adjusted.

K O M A N D DATA ACQUISITION SYSTEM
SYSTEM 21 REVENUE ANALYSIS

RESOURSE DESCRIPTION	QUANTITY MEASURED	BASE REVENUE GENERATED	PRIORITY FACTOR GENERATED	TOTAL REVENUE GENERATED	PERCENT OF SYSTEM REVENUE
CENTRAL PROCESSOR HOURS	0.1458	$51.05	$18.38	$69.43	33.78
SELECTOR CHANNEL HOURS	0.0097	$0.17	$0.18	$0.35	0.17
MULTIPLEXOR CHANNEL HOURS	0.0022	$0.01	$0.00	$0.01	0.00
TAPE OCCUPANCY HOURS	0.0000	$0.00	$0.00	$0.00	0.00
3330 OCCUPANCY HOURS	0.0043	$0.06	$0.07	$0.13	0.06
2311 OCCUPANCY HOURS	0.0000	$0.00	$0.00	$0.00	0.00
2314 OCCUPANCY HOURS	1.1269	$11.19	$6.09	$17.28	6.39
U/P OCCUPANCY HOURS	0.1047	$1.02	$0.28	$1.30	0.63
TP LINE OCCUPANCY HOURS	0.0654	$1.31	$0.37	$1.68	0.81
MAIN CORE KCORE HOURS	27.7040	$13.87	$7.18	$21.05	10.22
DOS CORE KCORE HOURS	0.0000	$0.00	$0.00	$0.00	0.00
TAPE MOUNTS	0.0000	$0.00	$0.00	$0.00	0.00
DISK MOUNTS	1.0000	$1.00	$1.00	$2.00	0.97
CARDS READ LOCAL	875.0000	$0.64	$0.59	$1.23	0.59
CARDS READ REMOTE	0.0000	$0.00	$0.00	$0.00	0.00
LINES PRINTED LOCAL	22,907.0000	$22.92	$15.65	$38.57	18.74
LINES PRINTED REMOTE	0.0000	$0.00	$0.00	$0.00	0.00
CARDS PUNCHED LOCAL	0.0000	$0.00	$0.00	$0.00	0.00
CARDS PUNCHED REMOTE	0.0000	$0.00	$0.00	$0.00	0.00
VIRTUAL CORE KCORE HOURS	0.0000	$0.00	$0.00	$0.00	0.00
SPECIAL FORMS PRINTING	513.0000	$52.75	$0.00	$52.75	25.63
REVENUE TOTALS		$155.99	$49.79	$205.78	100.00

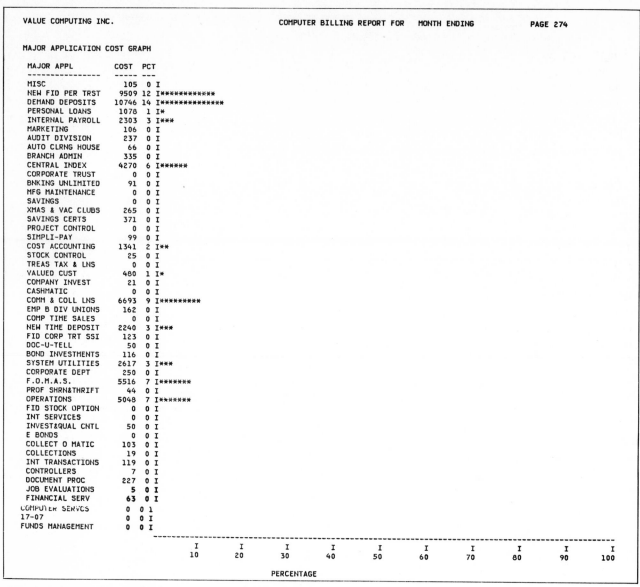

```
MAJOR APPLICATION COST GRAPH

    MAJOR APPL          COST  PCT
    ----------------    ----  ---
    MISC                 105   0  I
    NEW FID PER TRST    9509  12  I************
    DEMAND DEPOSITS    10746  14  I**************
    PERSONAL LOANS      1078   1  I*
    INTERNAL PAYROLL    2303   3  I***
    MARKETING            106   0  I
    AUDIT DIVISION       237   0  I
    AUTO CLRNG HOUSE      66   0  I
    BRANCH ADMIN         335   0  I
    CENTRAL INDEX       4270   6  I******
    CORPORATE TRUST        0   0  I
    BNKING UNLIMITED      91   0  I
    MFG MAINTENANCE        0   0  I
    SAVINGS                0   0  I
    XMAS & VAC CLUBS     265   0  I
    SAVINGS CERTS        371   0  I
    PROJECT CONTROL        0   0  I
    SIMPLI-PAY            99   0  I
    COST ACCOUNTING     1341   2  I**
    STOCK CONTROL         25   0  I
    TREAS TAX & LNS        0   0  I
    VALUED CUST          480   1  I*
    COMPANY INVEST        21   0  I
    CASHMATIC              0   0  I
    COMM & COLL LNS     6693   9  I*********
    EMP B DIV UNIONS     162   0  I
    COMP TIME SALES        0   0  I
    NEW TIME DEPOSIT    2240   3  I***
    FID CORP TRT SSI     123   0  I
    DOC-U-TELL            50   0  I
    BOND INVESTMENTS     116   0  I
    SYSTEM UTILITIES    2617   3  I***
    CORPORATE DEPT       250   0  I
    F.O.M.A.S.          5516   7  I*******
    PROF SHRN&THRIFT      44   0  I
    OPERATIONS          5048   7  I*******
    FID STOCK OPTION       0   0  I
    INT SERVICES           0   0  I
    INVEST&QUAL CNTL      50   0  I
    E BONDS                0   0  I
    COLLECT O MATIC      103   0  I
    COLLECTIONS           19   0  I
    INT TRANSACTIONS     119   0  I
    CONTROLLERS            7   0  I
    DOCUMENT PROC        227   0  I
    JOB EVALUATIONS        5   0  I
    FINANCIAL SERV        63   0  I
    COMPUTER SERVCS        0   0  I
    17-07                  0   0  I
    FUNDS MANAGEMENT       0   0  I
                          -------------------------------------------------------------------------------------
                          I        I        I        I        I        I        I        I        I        I
                          10       20       30       40       50       60       70       80       90      100

                                                    PERCENTAGE
```

ILLUSTRATION 4-13. Application Cost Graph: COMPUT-A-CHARGE is a product of Value Computing that produces this graph to obtain an overview of percentages of total charges associated with major applications and such factors as ABENDS.

Alternative Approaches to Unit-Rate Chargeout

Chargeout by unit rate is the most precise method, but a data center manager may prefer another approach that lessens personnel time and processing-cost overhead, stresses limiting resource usage rather than charging-out costs, or presents usage information in terms the user can relate to easier. Five alternatives are worth considering.

Periodic Job Accounting. Instead of incurring the time and cost overhead of continuous job accounting, the job-accounting process can be performed for applications periodically. This method permits evaluation of applications for discontinuance, modification, or conversion to a different means of processing. Here the stress is on justifying applications rather than charging-out data center costs.

Application-unit Costing. Most applications have a unit measurement built into the application. A payroll system, for example, can be charged by how many people are on the payroll. An insurance system can be charged by how many claimants are processed. This method has the distinct advantage that users can relate to services provided. Since in many applications the actual processing cost for processing one application unit is not much less than the cost for many more application units, a base amount for just executing the job should be part of the charging process.

Fixed Price by Department. A department is charged a fixed price according to estimated usage. This method is similar to facilities management where a department purchases the use of outside data center facilities and services for a fixed price. To make this method usable, a time budget must be also established according to estimated usage. This is necessary to avoid use of resources and services paid for by other departments. Thus, each department would have a fixed number of hours allocated at a fixed cost. If a user requires more time than allocated, the user would have to pay extra and receive approval from another user to use his time.

Budgeted by Money. This method is similar to charging users fixed prices, but it charges only incurred costs, with the budgeted amount used only as an estimate to set maximum limits. The objective of this method is to assure that each user has a fair share of data center resources.

Budgeted by Time. This has the same objective as budgeting by money, except that the high overhead of job accounting is avoided. The approach is direct. CPU time is budgeted for each user, possibly also budgeting data preparation and post-processing times. This approach ignores I/O activity, including such factors as cards read and lines printed, and it also ignores storage used.

FINANCIAL ANALYSIS OF DATA CENTER COSTS

The increased visibility of data center operations and its accompanying costs require that a data center manager be "on top" of what is happening and what can be done to justify costs. This is particularly true if ZBB and chargeout procedures are installed. These progressive techniques, while clarifying where money is spent, also uncover excesses and deficiencies. ZBB may lead to questioning the relatively small amount spent on security, considering the larger losses possible—in contrast, excessive money may be allocated to security, where a significant amount is actually buying very little additional security. A chargeout system makes apparent the cost of reports and stimulates consideration of alternatives, such as microfilm. Increased data center visibility requires increased cost analysis and cost justification.

Several topics that would normally be examined as part of financial analysis are covered in other sections of this book, since they closely relate to topics treated separately. Thus, budgeting approaches and analysis of variances are discussed earlier in this chapter, as is allocation of data center costs to users. The topic of centralization of data center resources and activities, and its benefits, are discussed in the chapter on organization structure (Chapter 2). Acquisition practices for hardware and software, with examination of the benefits and drawbacks of the various practices, are discussed in Chapter 6. The other major cost-analysis topic is discussed in Chapter 11, which is the preparation of a cost-benefit proposal to justify the installation of a computer performance evaluation program.

Three broad areas are examined here: overall data center costs, data center resources costs, and user application costs.

Overall Data Center Costs

Each data center manager must be aware of cost trends and must establish management policies and criteria for evaluating the cost-effectiveness of various methodologies. For example, if a manager is not aware of the resources that will have the greatest effect on future data center costs, cost-reduction analysis and actions may occur in the wrong areas, missing the more promising opportunities. Too often, frantic activity exists to modify operating system software for gains that are relatively minor compared to those possible by improving data preparation methods. This is primarily true, as will be illustrated, because hardware costs have been continually decreasing while personnel costs have been increasing. Besides attending to cost trends, policies must be set for judging alternatives, such as optimum user service versus optimum data center efficiency, and short-term benefits versus long-term benefits.

How could operational strategies be established if the relative values for these factors have not been defined?

Data Center Cost Ratios. A basic measure of overall data center costs is the ratio of total data center costs to total costs for the entire organization served. If the data center budget is $100,000 and the organization budget is $10 million, the ratio as a percentage is 1.0 percent. According to Robert Keston, this would be close to the median percentage of 0.9 percent in 1975.[12] Keston

further states that this value ranged from 0.6 percent to 1.5 percent for data centers between the first and third quartiles, thus this range does not include lower or higher quarter of values recorded. With this value it is possible to judge how a particular data center compares with other data centers.

Other percentages are useful for judging relative cost performances. Variations of the percentage of data center budgets spent on various resources according to industry type are shown in Illustration 4-14. This charge results from a 1976 *Datamation* survey. Observe that in nearly all cases the primary cost is personnel, the secondary cost is hardware, and all the other costs combined fall far behind. *Datamation* included another interesting chart, Illustration 4-15, which shows

[12] Robert Keston, "Handbook for Conducting an Internal Audit of Computer Cost-Effectiveness," Keston Associates, Rockville, Maryland.

ILLUSTRATION 4-14a. Allocation of Expenses by Industry. *Source:* Richard A. McLaughlin, "1976 DP Budgets," *Datamation*, Feb. 1976, 54-55.

	Banking (9 sites)	Construction (6 sites)	Education: universities (37 sites)	Education: school districts (6 sites)	Food processing (4 sites)	Food store chains (5 sites)	Gov't.: city (10 sites)	Gov't.: county (6 sites)	Gov't.: state (4 sites)
PERSONNEL EXPENSES									
Salaries & fringe benefits	35.45%	49.51%	45.78%	48.41%	52.13%	49.77%	53.24%	52.84%	40.40%
Conferences, travel, training	0.94%	0.20%	0.79%	0.27%	1.07%	1.52%	1.00%	0.85%	0.82%
Other	—	—	0.05%	0.62%	0.01%	—	—	0.03%	0.13%
HARDWARE & MAINTENANCE	46.54%	40.13%	43.52%	38.03%	34.70%	33.33%	33.77%	35.16%	41.25%
MEDIA, SUPPLIES & ACCESSORIES	8.51%	7.42%	6.55%	7.53%	5.84%	11.65%	7.66%	5.11%	12.81%
PACKAGED SOFTWARE									
From mainframe vendor	0.83%	0.95%	0.83%	1.09%	2.17%	0.84%	0.78%	0.52%	0.84%
From independent	2.11%	—	0.28%	0.06%	0.48%	0.25%	0.55%	0.41%	2.65%
OUTSIDE SERVICES									
Time-sharing	0.52%	—	0.14%	—	0.69%	—	—	—	—
Batch processing	0.53%	0.12%	—	0.05%	—	—	0.02%	—	—
Remote batch	—	—	0.47%	—	—	—	0.35%	—	—
Microfilm processing	0.05%	0.26%	0.07%	—	—	0.21%	—	0.09%	0.26%
Keypunching	0.03%	—	0.05%	0.21%	0.12%	0.23%	—	0.38%	—
Facilities management	—	—	—	—	—	—	—	—	—
Consultants	0.01%	—	0.03%	—	0.54%	0.35%	1.45%	1.22%	—
Contract programming	0.08%	—	0.16%	—	—	0.58%	—	0.67%	—
Temporary help	0.08%	0.33%	0.14%	0.61%	0.12%	0.07%	0.49%	2.03%	—
VOICE & DATA LINES	3.66%	0.77%	0.99%	3.12%	2.13%	1.11%	0.41%	0.21%	0.54%
MISCELLANEOUS	0.66%	0.31%	0.15%	—	—	0.09%	0.28%	0.48%	0.30%
TOTAL	100.00%	100.00%	100.00%	100.00%	100.00%	100.00%	100.00%	100.00%	100.00%

	Banking (9 sites)	Construction (6 sites)	Education: universities (37 sites)	Education: school districts (6 sites)	Food processing (4 sites)	Food store chains (5 sites)	Gov't.: city (10 sites)	Gov't.: county (6 sites)	Gov't.: state (4 sites)
CENTRAL SITE									
Computers & memory	42.02%	39.90%	51.25%	59.41%	29.91%	32.35%	46.75%	35.06%	60.82%
Peripherals	32.08%	37.75%	30.29%	16.42%	45.82%	41.31%	25.74%	44.45%	24.85%
Data entry	4.30%	16.58%	8.60%	8.77%	7.87%	8.57%	13.11%	9.73%	9.08%
Communications gear	5.86%	1.08%	2.28%	7.22%	1.28%	5.74%	0.32%	6.10%	0.50%
COM equipment	1.59%	—	0.11%	—	—	—	0.12%	—	—
Microfilm readers, etc.	—	—	0.03%	0.23%	—	—	—	0.24%	—
Auxiliary equipment	0.08%	1.98%	2.12%	3.81%	0.80%	0.14%	1.47%	0.70%	0.55%
Other	4.60%	0.94%	—	3.07%	—	—	0.55%	0.92%	—
REMOTE SITES									
Computers	1.62%	0.83%	0.50%	1.07%	—	—	1.88%	2.32%	—
Terminals	7.63%	0.94%	3.80%	—	13.99%	11.89%	8.62%	—	1.66%
Communications gear	0.22%	—	0.69%	—	0.33%	—	0.38%	—	2.54%
Other	—	—	0.33%	—	—	—	1.06%	0.48%	—
TOTAL	100.00%	100.00%	100.00%	100.00%	100.00%	100.00%	100.00%	100.00%	100.00%

the percentage of data center budgets spent on resources according to installation size. In general, less is spent for personnel and more is spent for hardware as the size of the installation increases. The ratio of personnel costs to hardware costs for the IBM installations up to $25,000 budgets is 1.64; for non-IBM installations it is 2.62. These ratios drop for the up to $1 million budgets, to 1.05 for IBM installations and 0.94 for non-IBM installations.

Yearly Trends in Resource Costs. By being aware of trends in resource costs, the data center manager can direct methodology for lower costs in the future. If a choice is available of two alternatives that require the same investment and provide the same savings for the first year, say $100,000, the general rule is that an alternative that affects an accelerating cost should be chosen over one that affects a decelerating cost. For example, if the choice is between eliminating personnel who (as will be soon shown) represent an accelerating cost and eliminating hardware which (as will also be shown) represent a decelerating cost, personnel should be eliminated—putting aside other considerations at this time such as effect on morale. Assume that personnel costs are increasing 12 percent each year and that hardware costs are decreasing 10 percent each year. Further assume that the value of the dollar decreases 15 percent each year. The first five year's savings are shown in the table on page 102.

ILLUSTRATION 4-14b. Allocation of Expenses by Industry.

Insurance (8 sites)	Mfg.: chemicals (10 sites)	Mfg.: electrical & dp equip. (11 sites)	Mfg.: machinery (12 sites)	Mfg.: primary metals (7 sites)	Mfg.: scientific instrument (7 sites)	Mfg.: stone & glass prods. (4 sites)	Mfg.: transport. products (5 sites)	Medical & health (16 sites)	Printing & publishing (7 sites)	Utilities (9 sites)	Wholesale trade (12 sites)
50.61%	48.53%	48.73%	46.96%	51.24%	53.98%	44.84%	45.35%	50.62%	51.00%	49.26%	39.48%
1.18%	1.26%	1.19%	1.00%	1.10%	1.00%	2.43%	0.81%	0.63%	0.56%	0.42%	1.08%
—	0.07%	0.58%	—	—	1.52%	0.34%	—	0.04%	0.03%	—	0.41%
38.49%	38.62%	32.68%	38.76%	35.62%	31.86%	33.50%	43.80%	34.91%	38.02%	36.26%	45.46%
3.93%	6.60%	7.91%	6.46%	7.73%	5.43%	10.84%	5.96%	6.66%	8.73%	9.97%	8.99%
0.39%	1.00%	0.10%	0.56%	0.54%	0.70%	1.01%	0.37%	0.72%	0.42%	0.66%	0.82%
0.80%	0.20%	1.18%	0.91%	0.40%	0.77%	0.93%	1.08%	1.47%	—	0.25%	0.88%
0.22%	0.32%	0.67%	0.46%	0.04%	0.77%	2.44%	—	0.06%	0.23%	—	0.10%
0.23%	—	—	0.20%	—	0.04%	—	—	2.47%	—	0.65%	0.34%
—	0.15%	2.84%	—	—	1.78%	—	—	—	—	—	—
0.35%	0.03%	0.33%	0.13%	0.04%	0.02%	0.27%	—	0.15%	0.34%	0.14%	0.72%
0.25%	0.46%	0.10%	0.20%	—	0.42%	0.02%	—	1.24%	0.07%	—	0.38%
—	—	—	2.12%	—	—	—	—	0.06%	—	—	—
0.03%	0.29%	0.40%	0.61%	—	—	—	0.38%	0.27%	—	1.36%	—
0.13%	0.07%	0.50%	0.35%	0.14%	0.24%	2.02%	0.59%	0.14%	0.18%	—	—
0.08%	0.14%	0.31%	0.02%	0.27%	0.08%	0.22%	0.12%	0.16%	0.04%	0.40%	0.30%
3.23%	2.02%	1.52%	1.24%	2.68%	1.39%	0.81%	0.83%	0.07%	0.36%	0.63%	0.96%
0.08%	0.24%	0.96%	0.02%	0.20%	—	0.33%	0.71%	0.33%	0.02%	—	0.08%
100.00%	100.00%	100.00%	100.00%	100.00%	100.00%	100.00%	100.00%	100.00%	100.00%	100.00%	100.00%

Insurance (8 sites)	Mfg.: chemicals (10 sites)	Mfg.: electrical & dp equip. (11 sites)	Mfg.: machinery (12 sites)	Mfg.: primary metals (7 sites)	Mfg.: scientific instrument (7 sites)	Mfg.: stone & glass prods. (4 sites)	Mfg.: transport. products (5 sites)	Medical & health (16 sites)	Printing & publishing (7 sites)	Utilities (9 sites)	Wholesale trade (12 sites)
35.46%	46.37%	40.39%	44.17%	38.61%	45.98%	34.65%	34.81%	48.70%	33.32%	44.54%	40.05%
37.02%	31.55%	35.65%	35.42%	31.58%	35.44%	37.29%	40.98%	31.03%	38.84%	42.91%	38.25%
10.61%	6.68%	9.62%	4.67%	14.07%	12.20%	10.51%	14.41%	11.82%	9.77%	6.27%	10.32%
2.91%	3.98%	2.98%	4.56%	1.04%	2.46%	3.76%	—	3.75%	1.05%	0.32%	1.42%
0.76%	—	1.00%	0.23%	—	0.32%	—	—	—	0.49%	0.18%	—
0.39%	—	0.19%	—	—	0.03%	0.78%	—	0.01%	0.49%	—	—
0.15%	1.07%	0.78%	3.40%	2.24%	3.38%	2.81%	0.86%	0.55%	3.70%	0.18%	0.11%
1.18%	0.35%	0.36%	1.08%	0.31%	—	0.50%	—	0.63%	2.05%	—	0.66%
0.16%	0.13%	2.80%	—	2.06%	—	2.81%	—	—	5.79%	2.27%	4.25%
10.19%	9.04%	6.23%	5.08%	10.09%	0.19%	5.36%	8.94%	3.22%	4.20%	3.33%	4.27%
0.99%	0.58%	—	1.39%	—	—	0.55%	—	0.29%	0.30%	—	0.57%
0.18%	0.25%	—	—	—	—	0.98%	—	—	—	—	0.10%
100.00%	100.00%	100.00%	100.00%	100.00%	100.00%	100.00%	100.00%	100.00%	100.00%	100.00%	100.00%

	1st YEAR	2nd YEAR	3rd YEAR	4th YEAR	5th YEAR	TOTAL
Accelerating cost item (after 1st year, 12% increase, 15% decrease on value of the dollar)	100K	97K	94K	91K	88K	470K
Decelerating cost item (after 1st year, 10% decrease, and 15% decrease on value of the dollar)	100K	75K	56K	42K	31K	304K

In effect, the accelerating cost item is losing only 3 percent of what was saved in the prior year, whereas the decelerating cost item loses a total of 25 percent of what was saved the prior year. Both of these alternatives saved $100,000 in the first year, but after five years the difference in savings is $166,000, the difference of the total cost savings.

It has just been stated that personnel costs are accelerating and hardware costs are decelerating.

ILLUSTRATION 4-15a. Allocation of Expenses by Installation Size. *Source:* Richard A. McLaughlin, "1976 DP Budget," *Datamation*, Feb. 1976, 56-57.

(Number of sites)	to $25,000 IBM (9)	to $25,000 Others (8)	to $50,000 IBM (25)	to $50,000 Others (18)	to $100,000 IBM (31)	to $100,000 Others (21)
PERSONNEL EXPENSES						
Salaries & fringe benefits	53.14%	62.92%	50.97%	53.78%	47.13%	50.28%
Conferences, travel, training	0.87%	0.49%	0.87%	0.89%	0.85%	0.90%
Other	—	—	0.19%	0.58%	—	0.03%
HARDWARE & MAINTENANCE	32.43%	24.02%	38.73%	33.81%	38.74%	37.16%
MEDIA, SUPPLIES & ACCESSORIES	10.86%	8.32%	7.35%	6.73%	7.99%	7.60%
PACKAGED SOFTWARE						
From mainframe vendor	0.92%	0.13%	0.78%	0.13%	0.68%	1.01%
From independent	0.20%	—	0.29%	0.73%	1.09%	0.30%
OUTSIDE SERVICES						
Time-sharing	—	—	0.15%	—	0.26%	0.49%
Batch processing	—	1.02%	—	0.04%	0.15%	0.29%
Remote batch	0.55%	—	—	0.82%	—	0.62%
Microfilm processing	—	—	0.08%	—	0.10%	0.09%
Keypunching	—	—	0.04%	0.09%	0.12%	0.07%
Facilities management	—	—	—	—	0.82%	—
Consultants	0.19%	2.19%	—	0.03%	0.82%	—
Contract programming	—	—	0.08%	1.07%	0.27%	—
Temporary help	0.20%	0.59%	0.31%	0.13%	0.48%	0.24%
VOICE & DATA LINES	0.55%	0.32%	0.09%	0.54%	0.46%	0.80%
MISCELLANEOUS	0.09%	—	0.07%	0.63%	0.04%	0.12%
TOTAL	100.00%	100.00%	100.00%	100.00%	100.00%	100.00%

(Number of sites)	to $25,000 IBM (9)	to $25,000 Others (8)	to $50,000 IBM (25)	to $50,000 Others (18)	to $100,000 IBM (31)	to $100,000 Others (21)
CENTRAL SITE						
Computers & memory	51.67%	62.41%	36.40%	44.34%	39.81%	43.52%
Peripherals	26.84%	12.74%	46.84%	40.00%	38.34%	33.02%
Data entry	19.34%	16.29%	14.73%	13.32%	10.49%	13.84%
Communications gear	—	4.28%	—	0.85%	1.62%	1.85%
COM equipment	—	—	—	—	—	—
Microfilm readers, etc.	—	—	0.06%	—	—	0.07%
Auxiliary equipment	0.48%	4.28%	0.02%	1.34%	1.06%	2.02%
Other	0.49%	—	0.62%	0.15%	1.38%	0.81%
REMOTE SITES						
Computers	—	—	—	—	1.49%	0.33%
Terminals	—	—	1.33%	—	4.41%	4.35%
Communications gear	—	—	—	—	0.71%	0.19%
Other	1.18%	—	—	—	0.69%	—
TOTAL	100.00%	100.00%	100.00%	100.00%	100.00%	100.00%

This can be easily proved. In 1955, approximately 55 percent of the total data center costs was for hardware and only 38 percent of the cost was for personnel; in 1974, however, only 23 percent of the total data center costs went to hardware, but the amount that was spent for personnel rose to approximately 62%.[13] In 1974, the monthly rental for an IBM System 3 processor, without peripherals, was less than the monthly salary for a clerk, even without including personnel overhead expenses such as facilities and benefits.[14] These trends in hardware and personnel costs are plainly shown in Illustration 4-16.

[13]Montgomery Phister, Jr., *Data Processing Technology and Economics* (California: The Santa Monica Publ. Co., 1976), p. 150.
[14]Ibid., p. 146.

Management Policies. A basic policy concerns the degree to which user demands should be permitted to lessen data center efficiency. Should jobs be reshuffled to execute late-arriving jobs? Should excess capacity be available for peak demands? Should user errors be corrected in the data center so as not to lessen turnaround? The policy decided on can affect the data center's ability to function without continual frustration. If user service is the primary consideration, adequate resource capacity must be available. Some installations have adopted the policy of having excessive capacity to meet any reasonable—or unreasonable—demands.

Opposed to having excess capacity is the policy of obtaining the most performance for the dollar. This conflicts directly with having excess capacity

ILLUSTRATION 4-15b. Allocation of Expenses by Installation Size.

to $150,000 IBM (22)	Others (17)	to $250,000 IBM (23)	Others (17)	to $500,000 IBM (25)	Others (9)	to $1 million IBM (15)	Others (9)	over $1 million IBM (15)	Others (6)
49.48%	50.62%	47.42%	45.53%	44.28%	46.46%	42.90%	42.37%	39.09%	41.73%
0.98%	1.57%	0.92%	0.59%	1.30%	0.62%	1.23%	0.46%	0.86%	0.94%
—	0.22%	—	0.19%	0.67%	—	0.16%	—		
38.67%	35.87%	41.17%	38.66%	37.30%	41.99%	40.97%	45.24%	45.31%	36.90%
6.56%	6.79%	7.47%	6.72%	8.74%	5.14%	6.72%	6.30%	5.28%	7.23%
0.89%	0.33%	1.01%	0.39%	0.95%	0.20%	0.74%	0.40%	0.72%	0.54%
0.66%	0.65%	0.53%	0.42%	0.65%	0.07%	2.32%	0.22%	0.49%	1.07%
0.34%	0.06%	0.16%		0.86%	0.01%	0.33%	2.52%	0.42%	0.02%
—	0.05%	0.01%	2.06%	0.51%	—	—	—	0.45%	0.04%
0.86%	—	0.04%	—	0.43%	2.10%				
0.11%	0.35%	0.06%	0.29%	0.18%	0.09%	0.18%	0.21%	0.20%	0.84%
0.17%	0.23%	0.15%	0.14%	0.31%	0.13%	0.10%	0.17%	1.81%	1.18%
—	0.95%	—		—		0.06%	—	—	—
0.34%	0.16%	—	1.28%	0.64%	0.23%	0.83%	—	0.08%	—
0.35%	0.23%	0.09%	0.64%	0.70%	0.09%	0.79%	0.25%	0.42%	7.45%
0.05%	0.26%	0.04%	0.14%	0.16%	—	0.28%	0.16%	0.02%	0.30%
0.30%	1.54%	0.79%	2.88%	2.12%	2.84%	1.89%	1.35%	4.44%	0.92%
0.24%	0.12%	0.14%	0.07%	0.20%	0.03%	0.50%	0.35%	0.41%	0.84%
100.00%	100.00%	100.00%	100.00%	100.00%	100.00%	100.00%	100.00%	100.00%	100.00%

to $150,000 IBM (22)	Others (17)	to $250,000 IBM (23)	Others (17)	to $500,000 IBM (25)	Others (9)	to $1 million IBM (15)	Others (9)	over $1 million IBM (15)	Others (6)
45.22%	37.87%	44.69%	48.22%	41.98%	43.39%	38.22%	41.10%	49.09%	51.68%
35.22%	36.63%	33.94%	26.57%	31.74%	35.31%	29.93%	37.19%	31.08%	21.05%
9.81%	7.50%	7.97%	8.78%	6.26%	5.74%	8.21%	3.50%	4.11%	2.30%
2.55%	5.53%	3.49%	2.92%	5.78%	2.87%	3.58%	1.87%	2.30%	1.13%
0.12%	0.63%	0.80%	1.29%	0.57%	—	3.28%	1.55%	0.67%	1.47%
	0.08%	0.03%	0.35%	0.15%	0.07%	0.01%	0.02%	0.17%	—
1.27%	1.65%	1.20%	2.09%	0.83%	0.46%	2.20%	0.21%	1.50%	1.47%
—	1.35%	0.19%	0.46%	0.37%	1.41%	0.28%	0.88%	0.58%	1.61%
0.15%	0.72%	2.15%	1.00%	1.22%	—	2.67%	0.32%	3.35%	2.77%
5.15%	7.40%	4.56%	8.24%	9.82%	9.78%	10.34%	12.31%	6.11%	15.68%
0.51%	0.64%	0.98%	0.08%	0.90%	0.97%	0.92%	0.96%	0.79%	0.58%
—	—	—	—	0.38%	—	0.36%	0.09%	0.25%	0.26%
100.00%	100.00%	100.00%	100.00%	100.00%	100.00%	100.00%	100.00%	100.00%	100.00%

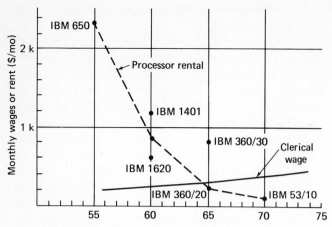

ILLUSTRATION 4-16. Cost Trends of Equipment and Personnel: This chart clearly shows, putting aside several factors that affect but do not invalidate these trends, that equipment costs have decreased dramatically while clerical costs have continued to increase. *Source:* Montgomery Phister, Jr., *Data Processing Technology and Economics,* 2nd ed. (Santa Monica, Calif.: Digital Press and The Santa Monica Publishing Co., 1979), p. 147.

Other organizations prefer to have the surplus capacity, avoiding potential conflicts with users.

Another policy that should be established concerns restrictions on long-term projects. What if an on-line monitoring system for the data center is being considered? The inclusion of the development expenses in the data center budget will not bring short-term benefits but may be justifiable in the long run. Will short-term benefits be stressed? Avoidance of projects that do not deliver short-term benefits hampers progress. Unrestricted funds, however, lead to experimentation on the latest technical gadgets and techniques. A policy is usually necessary to help obtain a balance between stagnation and unbridled experimentation.

Data Center Resource Costs

to assure satisfaction of user demands. A decision must be made as to whether to provide optimum user service, obtain optimum data center efficiency, or find a middle position. Some organizations decide on minimum excess capacity, depending on user cooperation in leveling demands for resources.

With an overview of cost trends in the data center, the next step is to consider the costs of data center resources. Although this information is usually available on lists, usually as part of the budget, it is convenient for uncovering patterns to organize this information into a table. The form prepared

ILLUSTRATION 4-17. Data Center Allocation of Costs: This form is a convenient means of reporting resource costs according to functional areas.

Data Center Allocation of Costs										
By resource \ By function	Data control	Data prep.	Job sched.	Comp. proc.	Post-proc.	D. C. library	Support serv's	Admin.		Total
Facility overhead										
Staff personnel										
Management personnel										
Hardware										
Software										
Total										Full total

for Illustration 4–17 could be used. This form relates the costs of data center resources to data center functional areas. The patterns that result are likely to suggest spending excesses and deficiencies. The form can also be used to examine the financial effects of configuration and functional changes. Cost reduction, however, is not the only criterion for judging the effect of changes. Two other criteria must be considered: effect on the quality of the product and effect on the quality of the service. Will the input contain more errors? Will balancing and control values be ignored? As for the quality of service, will more scheduled jobs be late? Will users receive less cooperation and assistance? For example, the refusal to pay for a good tape library system is one instance where both the product and service suffer.

If the effects on product and service are not considered, the attitude becomes that of the data center manager who stated that his approach to cost cutting was through prayer. The effectiveness of his approach is not documented. However, a secular approach is recommended. To do this, three categories of resources should be considered: personnel, hardware, and supplies.

Personnel Costs. One of the primary causes of excessive personnel costs, ironically, is lack of adequate automation in the data center. There are many instances of this. Either automation is not used when it should be or it is used poorly. In one small data center, four tape librarians were required when two should have been adequate. The cause was a tape library system that required manual transferring of information that should have been done automatically. The effort and salaries of two people were wasted.

Another cause of excessive personnel costs is overtime. This occurs because there are peak workload periods. Thus, the logical method to avoid peak periods is to level the demands for resources and to schedule jobs so that they fit into the normal work hours. Scheduling and user cooperation are the keys. When searching for means of reducing personnel costs, it should be realized that elimination of a needed person can incur more cost than is saved. This is particularly true if an assistant computer operator is eliminated. The delays that result because an operator is not available to supply a response to a program message, to mount a tape, or to fix a paper or card jam can cost much

more than the salary of an operator. Just one hour of delays in one week is more costly than an operator's weekly salary.

Hardware Costs. The savings possible from acquisition alternatives and computer-performance improvements are discussed elsewhere. Only one hardware change will now be considered. It involves the usually unobserved cost giant of the data center: data preparation. As A. H. Rosbury stated, "In a typical data processing installation, 30% to 50% of the installation's budget goes to data preparation—and these costs are rising at an estimated annual rate of 20%."[15] There are several methods of improving the efficiency of data preparation, permitting the preparation of input with less people. These methods include minimizing keying of redundant information and the design of forms to permit efficient keying. There are even more dramatic methods available, including hardware alternatives such as key-to-tape, key-to-disk, optical character recognition, and mark sense reading. One of the most prevalent methods is key-to-disk using a shared-processor keyboard system. Illustration 4–18 shows the basic configuration for this system. For efficiency alone, the estimated saving over keypunching is approximately 50 percent, from $0.94 per 1000 strokes for keypunching and verifying to $0.47 per 1000 strokes for shared-processor keyboard system, which includes verification.[16] The throughput can be expected to improve from 20 percent to 50 percent.[17] At Blue Cross in Massachusetts, just in the cost of cards, a keyboard system saved $60,000.[18]

Supply Costs. When a sudden paper shortage occurs, as has happened in the past, the dramatic increase in cost causes concern. Although paper costs do not compare in magnitude with the cost of personnel or hardware, it is still a large ongoing expense. Actually, the cost of paper and cards is usually close to the lease prices for printers and keypunch units.[19] Surveys have shown that supplies are approximately 20 percent of the CPU

[15] A. H. Rosbury, "Shared Processor Keyboard Data Entry," *Datamation*, June 1970.

[16] Alfonso F. Cardenas, "Data Entry: A Cost Giant," *Journal of Systems Management*, August 1973.

[17] Ibid.

[18] Ibid.

[19] Montgomery Phister, *Data Processing Technology and Economics*, p. 152.

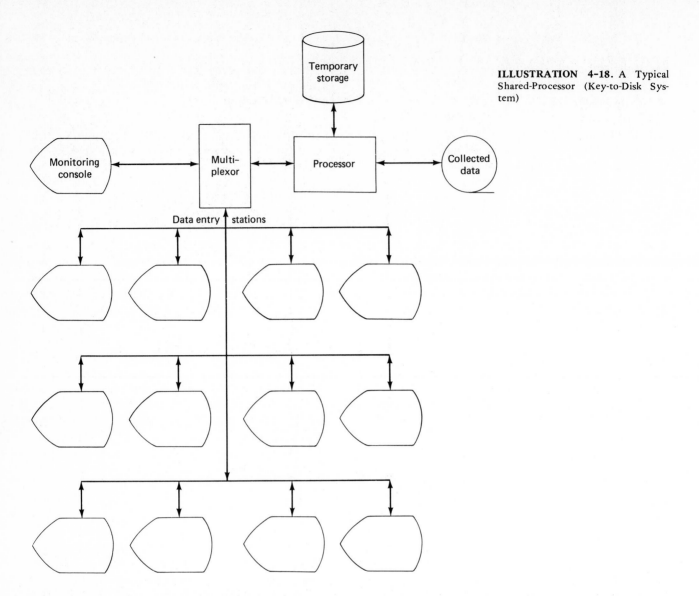

ILLUSTRATION 4-18. A Typical Shared-Processor (Key-to-Disk System)

cost; thus if the rental for a CPU is $1 million, supplies would cost $200,000. This is definitely significant. To reduce waste, users should be questioned periodically about the need for reports, the need for all copies produced, and about the possibility of using microfilm.

Closely associated with supply costs is the cost of inventory, particularly of too much or too little on hand. Inventory has a *carrying cost,* a cost related to the quantity in inventory. Carrying costs become excessive when inventory levels are too high because additional storage space is required, more personnel are needed to handle and administer the inventory, and supplies are wasted through obsolescence, which results from changes in technology or methodology. Carrying costs also become excessive when supplies are ordered in small lots to keep inventory levels low. Because quantity

discounts are not taken advantage of, fortuitous purchasing is ignored, purchasing and transportation costs per unit are higher, and emergency purchasing incurs higher costs, besides occasionally requiring emergency computer runs and overtime expenses.

The total cost for inventory is basically dependent on carrying cost, which increases with quantity on hand, and ordering cost, which decreases with quantity ordered, since fewer orders have to be placed to meet the supply needs of the data center. Consideration of these two costs trends leads to the most economical purchase and inventory levels, as is indicated in Illustration 4-19. As shown, the quantity that can be ordered at a reasonable low total cost actually covers a wide range of order sizes.

Some data center managers have stressed mini-

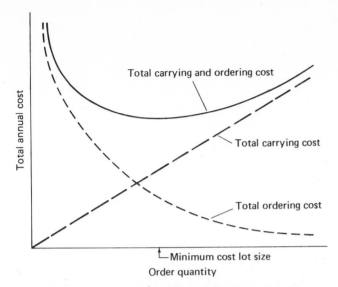

ILLUSTRATION 4-19. Choosing Optimum Order Size: The cost associated with an order decreases with the size of the order, and the carrying cost for retaining supplies in inventory increases with the size of the order; thus, the optimum order size depends on considering both ordering and carrying costs. *Source:* Charles T. Horngren, *Accounting for Management Control* (Englewood Cliffs, N.J.: Prentice-Hall, 1970), p. 546.

mizing facility space cost. This is usually false economy. The cost of additional space for later expansion, which is likely to occur, can be expensive. For every $300 for facility cost, it is common to have $10,000 for hardware costs, which results in facility cost being only 3 percent of hardware costs.[20] Thus, instead of skimping on facility space, it may be advisable not only to have additional space but also to have additional environmental support such as air conditioning.

User Application Costs

When data center management at the University Hospitals of Cleveland decided to evaluate the benefits received from user applications, positive results were obtained. Users were asked to estimate the number of work hours required to prepare the reports produced by the computer. It was calculated that for every dollar spent for data processing, $2.40 must be spent for manual processing.[21] Thus, for a data-processing expense of $1.1 million for 1977, the service provided was the equivalent

[20] Ibid., p. 150.
[21] P. Palaniappan, "A Healthy Look at Return on Investment," *Infosystems*, February 1978, p. 99.

of manual labor at $2.5 million.[22] In addition, many nonfinancial benefits were identified, such as fewer delays for patient admittance, faster processing of laboratory results, earlier preparation of surgery schedules, and quick response to patient inquiries about bills.[23]

This critical attitude of user applications is not to restrict users, but exactly the opposite. The intention is to eliminate wasteful use of data center resources and to add those applications that can be shown to be beneficial and can be cost-justified. When an application was developed there was a need; but the data center manager must be periodically reassured that the need still exists and that the benefits received still justify the cost. The applications should be examined to determine if they can be modified for increased efficiency, lower cost, and possibly the inclusion of additional benefits. Besides the elimination of wasteful applications, alternative processing methods should be considered, even manual processing. Although, considering the increasing cost of personnel, not too many applications will gain from this alternative.

A useful form for performing this evaluation is shown in Illustration 4–20. The benefits can be entered by the user, the costs can be entered by the data center and systems development, and the data center steering committee or a similar committee can then evaluate each application. Observe that the form is similar in many ways to the decision packages prepared for ZBB. Cost information can be obtained from a job-accounting system, supplemented with cost estimates for any alternative approaches being considered, such as computer output microfilm. As in the case of ZBB, quantification of nonfinancial benefits may be difficult. The only goal in these situations is obtaining precise statements that can be evaluated for their worth.

The justification for the hospital applications were positive, and computer use more or less continued as established. Many applications could not survive this scrutiny. A few "war stories" will justify the need to closely examine applications. Illustration 4–21 presents five applications, permitting comparison of the cost for each application as originally executed and its cost using an alternate method. The comparisons are reasonable, although

[22] Ibid., p. 99.
[23] Ibid., p. 100.

Application Cost/Benefit Evaluation

Application name	Evaluation start date

Prepared by user

Purpose: Benefits:	Recommendation ☐ No change ☐ Modify ☐ Discontinue
Signature	Title	Date

Prepared by EDP

Anticipated cost per year	Runs per year	Anticipated cost per run
Inefficiencies and problems:		Alternative methods:
Signature	Title	Date

Prepared by user–EDP evaluation committee

Decision: Reasons:
Signature	Title	Date

ILLUSTRATION 4-20. User Application Evaluation: Periodic use of this or a similar form provides a means for evaluating user applications, for discontinuing valueless applications and for modifying marginal applications.

oversimplified; in some instances, as the cliché states, it is like comparing apples and oranges. The first application shown is a medical batch application. When a Honeywell 1200 was substituted, cost per transaction dropped from $1.60 to $0.22. The remaining four applications show even more dramatic reduction in costs. Note the decrease in transaction cost for the law-enforcement application, which plunged from $36.36 to $0.72—replacing an on-line system with a clerk, file cabinet, and possibly a telephone.

The ready availability of so many more war stories indicates how badly application analysis is needed. Two more such stories should further stress this need. The first involved the use of an EAM Reproducer. This machine was used to punch social security numbers from each lead punch card into the cards that followed, which consisted of one to six cards. Many trays of these cards were prepared for this processing, and once started, processing continued for two or three days, approximately eight hours per day—truly a tedious task for the person feeding this machine. After this, what was done with the tray of cards? Those with a vivid imagination and a cruel twist of mind may have anticipated the answer. They were loaded onto tape for further processing. Obviously, a change to the card-to-tape program eliminated the entire EAM processing. This process had been performed three times a year for five years!

The final war story concerns the frustration of every data center manager: How do you convince managers to discontinue worthless reports? In one organization a "special" report was produced several times a year; it consisted of approximately 400 pages, and 36 copies were printed. To produce 36 copies it was necessary to execute the print program six times, using six-part paper. How

ILLUSTRATION 4-21. Dramatic Improvements through System Changes: The drastic cost reduction for the law enforcement application, for example, from a transaction cost of $36.36 to $0.72 is definitely dramatic—however, various factors are not considered and distort the results shown. *Source:* Montgomery Phister, Jr., *Data Processing Technology and Economics* (Santa Monica, Calif.: Digital Press and The Santa Monica Publishing Co., 1979), p. 161.

		APPLICATION				
	UNITS	MEDICAL	INSURANCE	PERSONNEL	CREDIT	LAW ENFORCEMENT
Described system						
Operating mode		Batch	On-line	On-line	On-line	On-line
Data base						
Number of subjects	M	1.0	3.3	0.010	35.0	0.031
Number of characters	M	3500	3600	20.0	3500	19.0
Characters per subject		3500	1091	2000	100	613
Number of users		50	60,000	45	500,000	5000
Transaction volume						
per year	M	2.5	12.0	0.050	10.0	0.055
per hour	k	1.20	5.77	0.024	4.81	0.026
per user per hour		24	0.096	.53	0.0096	0.0053
Costs						
Total annual	$M	4.0	13.0	0.34	14.0	2.0
per transaction	$	1.60	1.08	6.80	1.40	36.36
per kByte	$	0.46	0.99	3.40	14.00	59.32
Alternative systems						
System		HIS	IBM	One	IBM	One
		1200	360/50	Clerk	360/50	Clerk
Annual cost	$k	550.8	817.2	39.6	817.2	39.6
File capacity, characters	M	3,500	100.0	20.0	100.0	19.0
Transaction volume						
potential, per year	M	3.5	64.0	.125	64.0	.125
Assumed, per year	M	2.5	12.0	.050	10.0	.055
Cost per transaction	$	0.22	0.07*	0.79	0.08*	0.72

*These costs are not strictly comparable with those of the described systems, above, because the file capacity provided is only 100 million bytes compared with the 3500 million of the described systems.

were these reports used? Three of these reports were delivered to one small department. One went to the director, who looked at it twice a year, maybe. Another copy went to his assistant, who wanted to receive a display copy of what his boss received. And the third copy went to a clerk, who filed it. These three desks were about 15 feet from one another. All attempts to eliminate any of these preciously worthless reports were of no avail. At this time, it is likely that these prestigious reports are cluttering the desks, bookcases, and floors of this organization.

5
SITE SELECTION AND PREPARATION, AND DATA CENTER RELOCATION

GOAL

To obtain a data center that will support reliable, efficient, protected processing, and to relocate with minimum confusion and disruption of service.

HIGHLIGHTS

Site Selection

Adequate guidelines can prevent oversights that result in hampered processing, unsatisfactory security and safety, and possibly outright exposure to disasters.

Site Preparation

Reliable processing depends on the adequacy of the data center facilities and on how well environmental needs are satisfied, including "clean" electrical power and possibly electrical power backup; and efficient processing is largely dependent on the layout for equipment, work areas, and storage units.

Security and Safety

Although part of site preparation, security and safety are examined separately and in greater detail because of their critical nature; in fact, the existence of the data center and the continuation of the company may depend on precautions taken and plans made in case of a disaster.

Date Center Relocation

A rational approach to data center relocation requires adherence to a definite procedure, including activities from formation of a relocation committee to the control of the actual relocation.

The data center manager must be cautious and thorough when selecting and preparing a site for a data center. A casual attitude can result in unreliable and inefficient processing and, more important, can leave the data center open to partial or total destruction. And the total destruction of the data center may threaten the survival of the organization.

Unreliable processing occurs, for example, when the communications service is unreliable, the electrical power fluctuates, and no backup electrical power exists to safeguard against brownouts and blackouts. When natural disasters, human destructiveness and carelessness, and the possibility of disabling fires are considered, the threats to a data center's reliability and existence are apparent.

Inefficient processing can start by poor choice of a site, possibly ignoring proximity to good highways, and choosing a building that requires awkward separation and sequencing of processing functions. In one organization the data center is in the basement and the data preparation personnel and equipment are one flight of *stairs* up. All keypunched and keytaped data must be carried down the stairs in small quantities—naturally, carts cannot be used. Even when the chosen building has adequate space for efficient processing, the layout of equipment and supporting worktables and storage units may cause backtracking, excessive crossing of paths, and mixture of jobs at different stages of completion on the same worktables.

Disaster, whether partial or total, has always been foremost in the minds of data center managers. Unfortunately, protection against processing disruptions and disasters often receives only partial attention and merely provides a topic for discussion at meetings. Most organizations have minimal-access security and fire protection, for example, but do not go the few steps further that will buy considerably more protection for relatively little extra cost. But worst of all, few organizations have true disaster plans. Many have no plan at all. And many of the disaster plans in existence have serious defects, such as backup for critical data but not for programs, a backup facility but no periodic verification that the facility is still compatible.

If a site proves unsatisfactory, possibly for one or more of the reasons given, relocation to another site may be considered. These thoughts indicate

the substance of this chapter, which are:

- Site selection
- Site preparation
- Security and safety
- Data center relocation

SITE SELECTION

One reason for changing a site has been stated: the previous site was unsatisfactory. But there are several other reasons. It may be, as has happened for many companies, that a data center at a site other than the main office is being moved to the main office. It is also possible that a company is just starting and thus does not have a data center. These are all reasonable, but there are two other reasons that are reasonable but appear contradictory. Some organizations require a new site because they are combining two or more data centers. The major motivation for this approach is to centralize operations and gain the financial savings resulting from centralization. They also gain the advantage of being able to include more specialized support services and data center tools, such as sophisticated hardware and software. Several smaller data centers are not likely to obtain uninterruptible power systems, nor are they likely to use scheduling or computer performance evaluation software.

Although some organizations are combining data centers, other organizations are doing just the opposite. A data center is sometimes divided into two or more separate data centers. A frequent reason is to decentralize so that divisions have their own data centers. This permits each division to control the service it receives. Another reason for dividing a data center has been becoming more popular. As one data center vice-president put his reason for this decision, "We do not want all our eggs in one basket." The idea is to split the risk of being seriously disabled or possibly put out of business. In this case a large New York City data center was split into two widely separated data centers that were within "trucking" distance of one another and provided total backup for each other. In fact, plans are in the works to have total on-line network backup also.

The same vice-president has many suggestions for those selecting a site, and the most critical, putting aside its apparent simplicity, is, "For God's sake, decide what you want before you select a site!" By this advice he is strongly recommending that before searching for a site, criteria are established and that they are adequate. The oversights made by those setting up expensive data centers are astounding. How many data centers, for example, are dependent on unreliable telephone service for their communications systems, and on a volunteer fire department for fire protection? Sadly, there are many.

The goal, therefore, for thoughtful site selection is the preparation of a checklist. Almost each person preparing a checklist for selecting a site will have different entries. What some consider a threat and a must on the checklist, others consider unimportant and not to be considered. The variation in opinions is astonishing. Items that some data center managers consider trivial have caused others to reject a site outright. For example, several data center managers whom the author knows have rejected sites because of their proximity to an airport. Managers in the New Jersey area frequently refer to the time that an airplane, shortly after leaving the Princeton Airport, crashed into the Applied Data Research building, which housed their data center. Yet there are many data center managers who have consciously located data centers within a very short distance of an airport or even among its buildings. They consider the probability of a crash occurring so small that they refuse to consider it. The primary criteria for site selection will now be listed, and from these each manager can develop a personal checklist of "musts" and "desirable" criteria. For convenience, the criteria are separated into three categories, which correspond to the natural areas of consideration when searching for a site: selection of a general area that is satisfactory; selection of a specific site within this area; and selection of a building or possibly contemplating the construction of a building at the chosen site.

Selection of a General Area

Even before these criteria are examined, usually a map is obtained and the user locations are marked, making it easier to envision physical traveling distance if receipt of input and distribution of output is necessary or may be necessary in case of a communications failure. The location of a single user, dependent on a single data center, may limit the distance to within a five-mile radius. However, a backup data center may be more appropriate if at least 60 miles away, and possibly farther, considering the possibility of a major disaster. Criteria to be considered in selecting a general area are:

1. Proximity to off-line batch-processing users is the first consideration.
2. Availability of a major highway is particularly important when a company wants data centers for mutual backup.
3. Nearby availability of a backup configuration that is compatible with the new data center's equipment and operating system, and is likely to remain available and compatible. When possible, backup availability and compatibility should be guaranteed in writing.
4. Reliable commercial power.
5. Reliable communication services, preferring AT&T to a private company.
6. Appealing rental and tax rates.
7. Absence of threats from natural disasters such as flooding, forest fires, and earthquakes.
8. Full-time police and fire service, not volunteer service.
9. Direct communication facility available to police and fire services, preferably an automatic alarm for fire notification.
10. Unlikeliness of neighborhood civil disorders and crime, which also minimizes the difficulty of having persons working late.
11. A good labor market for data center personnel.
12. A good school system and community facilities that will attract and retain personnel.

Selection of a Specific Site

After general areas have been isolated, the main job of site selection has been completed, but there remain a few significant criteria that should be considered for the specific sites within these areas:

1. High-ground location as protection against flooding; this threat is particularly important if the data center will be located in the basement for increased security.
2. Proximity to airports, considering the possibility of an airplane crash or communication disruption because of radar, which may also result in loss of data.

3. Proximity to a major highway, but with a buffer zone to separate it from the data center.
4. Proximity to commercial transportation as a convenience for employees and visitors.
5. Proximity to electromagnetic interference.
6. Adequacy of parking facilities.
7. Effect of storms on access to site—to avoid the data center's becoming inaccessible after a heavy rain.

Selection of a Specific Building

Whether considering a completed building or the construction of a building, there are several requirements that must be met, and several safety and security criteria to be considered before committing oneself to a final decision. Consider how impossible and potentially expensive, not to say embarrassing, the situation is when corridor widths are inadequate for moving equipment. Fortunately, this does not occur too often—but it can occur. A more frequent oversight is allowing inadequate space for efficient arrangement of equipment and all supporting equipment, worktables, and storage cabinets. How many times has every data center manager observed all the wasted steps—and time—consumed because equipment could not be placed properly, causing personnel to maneuver with twists and turns from one piece of equipment to another. As if this were not bad enough, these cramped quarters obviously do not permit for expansion. Surplus space supports efficient processing and permits later expansion. The criteria to be considered should include:

1. Adequate space for present equipment and personnel, and anticipated expansion, allowing for all the supporting work and storage space required.
2. Absence of site preparation difficulties, having at least eight feet between ceiling and raised flooring for adequate air circulation; appropriate wall material and construction for safety and security protection; and adequate floor strength for supporting heavy equipment.
3. Adequate space to house air conditioning and electrical power backup equipment.
4. A large door permitting receipt or removal of equipment.
5. Adequate corridor width for moving equipment.
6. Able to locate the data center away from areas containing flammable material, such as maintenance rooms with oil and paint.

7. Away from explosives, or potential explosive situations, such as may occur in a boiler room.
8. Able to provide a buffer area to separate visitors from the data center, thus requiring that they pass through this area to enter the data center.
9. Able to control access from stairways and elevators.
10. Able to control access to electric panels, air intakes, and communication switches.
11. For an office building, not locating the data center above the sixth floor, since most of the effective fire-fighting equipment cannot reach beyond the sixth floor.
12. Adequate lounging, eating, and lavatory facilities.

SITE PREPARATION

In general, site preparation is a cut-and-dried procedure. Equipment vendors provide planning guides that state equipment requirements; they also provide equipment templates for experimenting with various layouts before a decision is made. To add to the certainty of success in becoming operational with little difficulty, vendors also supply technical advisors who help select equipment and prepare layouts. However, matters are not quite this simple. The options open to the data center manager are many, and future requirements must also be considered. How much space is needed now and later for expansion? What about power supply? Is the power free from fluctuations, or must it be made "clean" for reliable processing? How about power backup? How much time is adequate for a smooth shutting-down of operations, or is continuous operation necessary? And among the remaining questions that must be considered is, What is the most efficient and adaptable layout?

Satisfactory site preparation thus depends on careful planning, specification of environment requirements, and preparation of layouts. Although security and safety considerations definitely affect the resulting layout, because of the greater degree of flexibility and the critical nature of decisions required in these areas, they will be treated separately, immediately after the other site-preparation topics.

Planning

As in the case of any planning activity, the first step is to state the objectives to be met and the

| Equipment Relocation | | | | | | Relocation coordinator's name | | Date prepared | | | |

Dates				Item relocated		Mover's name	Relocation		
Move		Install		Name	Serial number		From	To	Date accepted
Est	Act	Est	Act						

ILLUSTRATION 5-1. Equipment Relocation Form: This form guides and controls the moving and installation of equipment and the acceptance of equipment installation. It can be wholly or partially replaced by computer-generated reports, such as the report in Illustration 5-14.

constraints guiding decisions, including cost limit, and then to obtain upper-management approval. An objective may be to obtain surplus computer capability, possibly anticipating only 60 percent utilization, for future expansion, to meet schedules when the workload peaks, or to sell computer time for additional revenue. In most cases the equipment wanted may have already been selected. In these cases, cost and environmental requirements can be stated precisely; otherwise, they would have to be presented as constraints to be satisfied. Upper management should also receive alternative approaches where appropriate. For example, several methods are available for lessening electrical power fluctuations and providing backup power. These should be stated, making clear the total costs, benefits, and drawbacks associated with each. The same should be done for alternative security and safety approaches. With this information, management can discuss and decide the approaches acceptable and approve the cost for the

site preparation, or they can request additional information and analysis.

On receipt of approval, personnel are assigned and a schedule is prepared. If a new data center is being prepared with all new equipment, existing processing is not being disrupted and scheduling becomes a relatively easy task. Relocation of a data center, whether a total relocation, combining, or splitting of a data center, is a much more difficult and trying task. What is involved is discussed under data center relocation. A detailed schedule may not give a quick overview of the status for the installation of equipment. To obtain this overview, which is necessary to maintain control and to answer inquiries about status, the form in Illustration 5-1 is recommended. It actually provides considerable detailed information that is not likely to be included on the schedule, although some schedules have this information. It will show scheduled and actual dates for moving, installing, and accepting equipment. Thus, at a glance it informs what

115

equipment has not been accepted, what is on the premises but not installed, and what is not even on the premises—any of which may indicate a problem that could affect the completion date.

The schedule should include the obtaining of approvals and contracts. Approvals are required from the building inspector, fire inspector, electrical inspector, plumbing inspector, insurance inspector, and possibly others. Signed approval must be obtained from each to avoid later disagreements. Several contracts are also necessary. There are the contracts for moving computer equipment and office furniture (which may involve different movers), for maintenance agreements for equip-

ment (usually from the vendors), and for insurance. A special insurance policy is necessary for deinstallation, if necessary, and for moving and installing equipment as financial protection for equipment loss or damage and for personnel injury.

Environmental Requirements

The specifications and schematics for an IBM 2870 multiplexer unit shown in Illustration 5–2 suggest the categories of environmental requirements. In more general and inclusive terms, these categories are space requirements, floor loading and surface types, airflow and air-conditioning requirements,

2870 MULTIPLEXER CHANNEL MODEL 1

PLAN VIEW

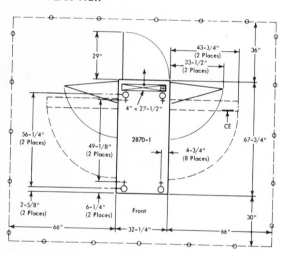

Note: For cabling information, see host processor.

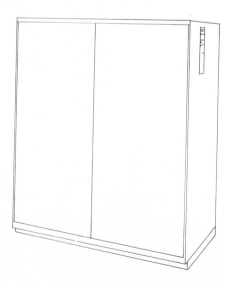

ILLUSTRATION 5–2. Equipment Specifications and Schematics: IBM specifications and schematics include information on space requirements, the maximum floor loading limit, lower and upper limits for operation temperature and airflow, and electrical power limits. *Source: IBM System/370 Installation Manual Physical Planning,* GC22-7004-5.

SPECIFICATIONS

Dimensions:

	F	S	H
Inches	32-1/4*	67-3/4*	70-3/4
(cm)	(82*)	(172*)	(180)

Service Clearances:

	F	R	Rt	L
Inches	30	36	66	66
(cm)	(76)	(91)	(168)	(168)

Weight: 1,450 lb (660 kg)

Heat Output:

	50 Hz	60 Hz
BTU/hr	4,200	4,900
(kcal/hr)	(1 100)	(1 250)

Airflow:

cfm	1,060	1,060
(m^3/min)	(31)	(31)

Power Requirements:

kVA	1.6	1.9
Phases	3	3
Plug	R&S, FS3730**	
Connector	R&S, FS3914**	
Receptacle	R&S, FS3744**	
Power Cord Style	B1	

Notes:

  * Dimensions can be reduced to 29-1/2" (75 cm) x 60" (152 cm) for shipping.

** Applicable to serial number 70502 and higher. Prior units use:

Plug	R&S, FS3760
Connector	R&S, FS3934
Receptacle	R&S, FS3754

| | | Space requirements | | | | | | | Environmental factors | | | | Power requirement |
| | | Dimensions | | | Service clearance | | | | Operating | | Non-operating | | |
Unit	Weight	Front	Side	Height	Front	Rear	Right	Left	Heat output	Max. humidity	Heat output	Max. humidity	

Equipment Requirements

Area	Prepared by	Date

ILLUSTRATION 5-3. Equipment Requirements: The primary equipment specifications for equipment can be collected and entered on this form for convenient documentation and reference.

electrical power requirements, and miscellaneous environmental requirements. For the purposes of indicating equipment in the data center and for providing technicians with summary specifications for equipment, it is advisable to complete a form such as that shown in Illustration 5-3. This form does not replace the details contained in the specifications supplied by vendors, since it does not provide space for airflow, cabling, and miscellaneous information provided. With these specifications, the site can be prepared to satisfy the environmental requirements of equipment. It is also advisable to have surplus air-conditioning and power resources to support later expansion.

Floor Loading and Surface Types. The first decision is whether to use raised flooring, "no-trip" wire conduits, or overhead drop cords. Whichever is chosen, it is desirable to have a minimum distance of eight feet between floor and ceiling. This permits adequate airflow for temperature and humidity control. The minimum height for raised flooring is 12 inches, with 18–24 inches usually recommended by vendors. Whether or not raised flooring is used, the real floor in the building must be able to support the load placed upon it. This load includes equipment, cables, personnel, and, if used, the raised flooring. The floor-loading limits for most office buildings are expressed in limits with and without partitions. The limits, for example, could be 50 lb/sq ft without partitions and 75 lb/sq ft with partitions. The local building department should be consulted as to the limit that can be used.

When selecting floor material, the factors to consider are resistance to static-electricity buildup, ease of maintenance, durability, appearance, and cost. Resistance to static-electricity buildup is the most important consideration. Static-electricity buildup is produced by the motion of people, carts, and furniture across the floor. It can be particularly severe if carpet floor covering is used; in this case, antistatic carpeting must be used. IBM recommends three means for minimizing static-electricity buildup:[1]

[1]*IBM System/370 Installation Manual—Physical Planning,* GC22-7004-5, IBM Corporation, 1977, p. 1.4.

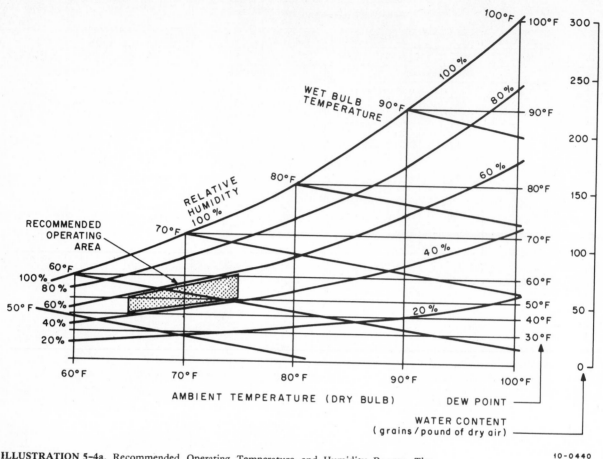

ILLUSTRATION 5-4a. Recommended Operating Temperature and Humidity Ranges: The limits may vary from one piece of equipment to another, but the limits shown are usually accepted as conservatively safe limits. Temperature measurements for this graph given in Fahrenheit (English) degrees. *Source: Computer Site Preparation Handbook,* DEC-00-ICSPA-A-D (Mass.: Digital Equipment Corp.), p. C2.

10-0440

1. Provide a conductive path to the ground from metallic raised floor structure and metal panels.
2. Use floor covering that provides a resistance of at least 150 kilohms from any point on the floor.
3. Maintain relative humidity close to 50 percent, realizing that as relative humidity drops the likelihood of disturbances because of static electricity increases.

More information on this topic, including the method recommended for determining electrical resistance, is published by the National Fire Protection Association Standard (NFPA) in Standard No. 56A. (To obtain a copy of these standards, as well as the many other standards they publish, write to National Fire Protection Association, 60 Batterymarch Street, Boston, Massachusetts 02110.)

Airflow and Air-Conditioning Requirements. Referring to standards in the NFPA Bulletin No.

75 on computer-room construction, Burroughs recommends an airflow of 15 cu ft/min per person for constant occupancy, or one air change per hour, whichever is larger.[2] Burroughs also recommends for the B 7700 processor an ideal temperature of 72°F ±2°F; they also recommend an ideal of 50 percent relative humidity, with ±10 percent being acceptable.[3] These specifications are close to those recommended by IBM for the IBM System/370. They recommend a temperature of 75°F and a relative humidity of 50 percent, in accordance with their design criteria. IBM adds that the automatic air-conditioning controls should respond to ±2°F variations and to ±5 percent relative humidity variations. IBM further adds that equipment should never be used above 90°F and 80 percent

[2]*Burroughs Field Engineering Installation Planning Manual,* Form no. 1060027, August 1973, p. 1.6.
[3]Ibid.

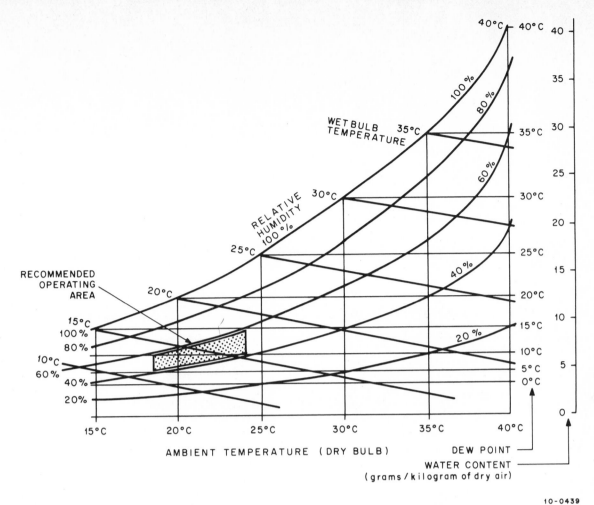

ILLUSTRATION 5–4b. Temperature measurements for this graph given in Celsius (Metric) degrees. *Source: Computer Site Preparation Handbook,* DEC–00–ICSPA–A–D (Mass.: Digital Equipment Corp.), p. C1.

10-0439

relative humidity, nor below 60°F and 20 percent humidity.[4] Considering temperature and humidity factors, Illustration 5–4 shows their generally accepted operating ranges.

To prevent dust from entering the computer room, the room should be kept pressurized, forcing air to leave rather than enter the computer room. This is accomplished by using predominantly recirculated air, with a minimal amount of fresh air introduced for personnel. During cold weather, humidity is likely to be low, and it may be necessary to add moisture to the air. Besides automatic controls for adjusting temperature and humidity, an alarm should be sounded if high or low limits are being approached, and a recording device is recommended to verify the functioning of the control devices. These precautions and controls avoid

[4] *IBM System/370 Installation Manual,* p. 1.7.

damage to equipment and improve the reliability of processing and the comfort of personnel.

Electrical Power Requirements. The total power requirements for the computer room can be obtained by adding the kVA (kilovolt-ampere) of the individual machines. A more detailed analysis can be obtained from such software as the IBM System Power Profile program, which, besides showing power requirements, also shows heat dissipated per hour as well. The power supply situation, unfortunately, is not this simple. There are power voltage and frequency variations that can affect data and cause the system to fail. There are, for example, limits for steady-state voltage, transient voltage, and line frequency. Vendors provide the specifications for their equipment. For the IBM System/370, line-to-line, steady-state voltage must not be 10 percent above or 8 percent below the normal rated voltage; transient

Performance criteria	Desired characteristic	Ultra isolation transformer	Line regulators		Line conditioners	Electro-mechanical		UPS	
			Voltage-regulating transformer	SCR Tap-changing transformer		Motor generator	Roesel generator	Standby	On line
Output voltage regulation									
Response to steady state	Output ± 3% with Input + 10% to - 15%	No regulation or response capability	OK	OK	Varies	Superior response		OK-Brown out Protection depends on charger	
Response to sags/surges	1 cycle or less		5-10 cycle	OK	Varies			No	Superior
Output power continuity									
Energy storage	Short term	None	None	None	None	.15-3 Seconds flywheel	10-30 Seconds flywheel	30 seconds to 60 minutes with batteries	
	Long term						Engine generator		
Noise rejection									
Common mode	65 dB min.	140+dB	0dB	0dB	Usually high (100+dB)	Superior rejection	None		Superior rejection
Normal mode	25 dB min.	0dB	0dB	0dB	Claims vary from 0 to 25 to 125 dB				
Other output characteristics									
Load variation effects	Efficiency constant with partial load	OK	Relatively good	OK	Varies	Relatively good	OK	Not controlled by standby UPS	Varies
	No effect on steady state voltage regulation	adds ±3% voltage variation	OK	OK	OK	OK			OK
	Load power factor effects	OK	Varies	OK	Varies	Handles in-rush and poor power factors		Varies	Varies
Ability to start load	Oversizing not desirable	Oversize	Varies	Varies	Oversize	No	No	Use utility to start, must have static switch option	No
Frequency	Performance not affected by varying input	No	Varies	None	Varies	No	No	No	No
	60 hertz out despite varying input	No	No	No	Usually no	No	Yes	No	Yes
Phase angle	120 electrical degree phase angle fixed	Usually no problem				Phase angle mechanically fixed		Can vary depending on design	
Harmonics	3% rms total harmonics with good wave shape	OK	Adds harmonics	OK	Varies	Superior		Varies	
Overload capacity	110-120% for 30 minutes	No	Varies	Varies	Varies			Most are current-limited	
Output stiffness	Blow fuse or circuit breaker	OK	Varies	OK	Most are current limiting				
Typical prices									
Load: 15 KVA, 120/208 volts, 3 Phase, 60 hertz	Basic equipment	$3300	$3200	$3500	$5300	$6000	$14,000	$16,000	$18,000
	installation	300	300	300	300	500	1,000[1]	3,000[2]	3,000[2]
	energy storage						6,000[1]	3,000[2]	3,000[2]
	Total	$3600	$3500	$3800	$5600	$6500	$21,000	$22,000	$24,000

[1] Unlimited energy storage using engine generator
[2] 30 minutes of batteries

ILLUSTRATION 5-5. Power Protection Equipment: Equipment is available to provide varying degrees of protection from electrical power variations, short-term disruptions, and prolonged power failures. *Source:* Kenneth G. Brill, "Power Protection Equipment: A Survey," *Mini-Micro Systems*, July 1977, p. 41.

voltage must not be 15 percent above or 18 percent below nominal and must return within the accepted steady-state range within 30 cycles; and the line frequency must be maintained at 60 Hz ±0.5 Hz.[5] Vendors explain the meanings of these measurements, but they primarily concern the technicians who will monitor power supply and recommend means for controlling variations.

Variation in voltage and frequency can result from internal and external conditions. Internally, disruptions can result from other equipment (such as a card reader) in the computer room, particularly if both the processor and the card reader are connected to the same power panel. However, the disrupting source need not be in the same room as the processor; it can be elsewhere in the same building. Externally, disruptions can result from machinery in other buildings, electrical storms, or failures and accidents involving power supply equipment.

Many computer installations have no serious power-fluctuation problems, but others suffer daily disruptions. When disruptions are significant, a line monitor should be used to try to isolate its source. At the Con Edison data center, erratic power supply was monitored and isolated as coming from noncomputer equipment on the same power line used for the computer system in the building. The solution implemented was to provide a separate power line for the computer system, and the problem was eliminated. Power problems may not end here, even for those with "clean" power, that is, power without significant variations. Even then, there are always the possibilities of brown-outs, drops in power, and blackouts, that is, total power failures. Illustration 5–5 summarizes the power-protection equipment available and their attributes. Brief definitions of the five categories are:

1. *Isolation transformers* attenuate electrical noise but do not affect normal-mode noise.
2. *Line regulators* maintain a relatively constant output voltage in spite of variations in input voltage, but they do not attenuate electrical noise.
3. *Line conditioners* attend to voltage variations and to electrical noise in varying degrees, but they do not store energy and thus are unable to

supply power during short-duration power interruptions.
4. *Electromechanical equipment* receives commercial power to drive a motor, which absorbs electrical noise, and the motor operates a generator and a flywheel, which provide clean power that bridges short-duration interruptions for up to three seconds.
5. *Uninterruptible power systems (UPS)* receive commercial power to charge batteries which, if an on-line UPS, supply clean power, or if a standby UPS, supply power only when commercial power fails; a generator can be included to keep the batteries charged and to provide indefinite power, in contrast to the 5–15 minutes supplied by the batteries alone.

There is another, more recent, approach not included in Illustration 5–5. It uses a standby UPS and a voltage stabilizer, such as the Automatic Computer Voltage Stabilizer (ACVS) manufactured by the Energy-Saver Division of ABC Marketing. This combination provides the clean power and power backup of on-line UPS at a significant saving. The manufacturer states that the ACVS is 99.6 percent efficient, since no power conversion occurs.[6] Illustration 5–6 compares this approach to on-line UPS and clearly demonstrates its savings. The low efficiency shown for UPS is much lower than the 90 percent advertised by UPS vendors, but the people who performed these calculations believe the lower efficiency represents real-life performance. Several reasons are given for the lower efficiency. The major reason is that the high efficiency rating advertised is based on full loading: but systems are unlikely to be fully loaded, and as load is reduced, efficiency is reduced.

When electrical variations persist in spite of corrective measures such as separate power panels, some form of power protection equipment is necessary; but is UPS needed? This is an individual matter. For most batch systems, delays of five hours or longer can be tolerated. But many on-line systems cannot tolerate interruption. Legal requirements must be considered and the potential loss of revenue must be compared to the total cost of UPS, including its overhead. Only after careful analysis should UPS be accepted or rejected.

---

[5] *Ibid.*, p. 1.10.

[6] Peter N. Budzilovich, "Thinking of Buying a UPS?," *Computer Decisions,* May 1977, p. 88.

The Ultimate UPS?

A couple of months ago, at the request of Federal Energy Administration, a report on a novel voltage stabilizing device was submitted by Bert Neuman. Mr. Neuman is president of Energy-Saver Div., ABC Marketing, Inc., of Passaic Park, N.J. The report is titled "A 2000 megawatt hour energy conservation potential within computer backup power systems."

Designated by the manufacturer as Automatic Computer Voltage Stabilizer, or ACVS, the stabilizer device essentially is a combination fast-response series and autotransformer. According to the specifications, it can handle line-voltage variations up to 18 percent, and maintain stable output within ±0.25 percent. Since no power conversion takes place, 99.6 percent power efficiency is claimed.

There are many possible configurations for the ACVS. For example, assume that a typical UPS installation, operating with a lower power efficiency, is placed into a standby mode. The ACVS is placed in series with the computer load and takes care of various line-voltage problems—dips, surges, transients—that cause data errors and other disruptions. Should a total outage occur, the static switch connects the UPS output to the ACVS input and operates the computer for the time it is capable of supplying the required power.

The advantage of this approach versus a standard online UPS is the power saving. According to Neuman's report, many UPS installations operate at efficiencies as low as 40 to 50 percent. This results from a variety of factors: light loading, redundant UPS module usage, difficulty in attaining balanced loading on all three phases. In other words, a 90 percent efficient UPS, after being placed into an actual installation, may operate at only half of its rated efficiency, because of various practical facts of life and the usual high safety factor introduced by most UPS users.

The report points out that a power saving is possible using an ACVS together with a UPS. The following UPS data is taken from an actual installation:

Standard UPS operating on line 24 hours a day:

1200 kva UPS @ 42 percent loading (loss)	519 kW
Required air conditioning (147 tons)	276 kW
Total system consumption	795 kW
Total for a 8760-hour year	6,964,200 kWh
Cost @ $0.07 New York City 1977 rate	$487,494/year
@ 1.5936 10-year inflation factor	$776,870/year

UPS in a stand-by mode, ACVS on line:

1200 KVA UPS @ 0 percent loading (loss)	169 kW
Required air conditioning (48 tons)	90 kW
Total system consumption	259 kW
Total for a 8760-hour year	2,268,840 KWH
Cost @ $0.07 New York City 1977 rate	$158,819/year
@ 1.5936 10-year inflation factor	$253,094/year

Comparison—online UPS versus UPS plus ACVS:

	kWh	Average 10 years	@ 1977 rates
Standard mode (UPS online 24 hrs)	6,964,200	$776,870	$487,494
ACVS plus a stand-by UPS	2,268,840	253,094	158,819
Annual savings	4,695,360	$523,776	$328,675

This example assumed only 42 percent loading of the UPS, so that the UPS efficiency was very low. You may ask: Does such a low loading actually exist in practice? Let's consider a typical sequence of events in purchasing a UPS.

Computer center managers hire a consulting firm. They get accurate computer center load characteristics—suppose the figure is 100 kVA. The consultant will then ask "What future expression do you anticipate?" The answer is 50 percent. So he jots down 150 kVA. He then asks what kind or redundancy would be desired and gets a reply that nothing less than 100 percent would be acceptable. So he puts down 250 kVA (being conservative). So, even before we start, we have a UPS system that will run at 40 percent capacity with the resulting efficiency very, very low—in spite of the fact that we'll get the best system there is.

ILLUSTRATION 5-6. A Less Expensive Alternative to Online UPS. *Source:* Peter N. Budzilovich, "Thinking of Buying a UPS?", *Computer Decisions*, May 1977, p. 88. Copyright 1977, Hayden Publishing Co.

Miscellaneous Environmental Requirements. Attention must also be given to minimize vibrations, electromagnetic disturbances, and noise, and to obtain adequate lighting and a pleasant atmosphere for personnel. Noise reduction is usually attained by using acoustical ceiling tiles and by distributing noisy equipment throughout the data center, alternating noisy and quiet-running equipment. An IBM recommendation for adequate lighting is a minimum illumination of 50–75 footcandles in the computer room, measured 30 inches above the floor.[7] Light switches should sectionally control lighting, permitting the shutting of lights in areas not being used. Direct sunlight should be avoided because it may affect light-sensing devices such as the magnetic tape units and because it makes console and signal lights difficult to observe.

Considering all the serious variations that can occur—operational situations that can develop in the data center, as well as environmental situations—it is advisable to bring these conditions to someone's attention with a monitoring device such as the System Sentry (manfactured by CRU, a subsidiary of Computer Resources, Inc.). This device has 10 sensors for monitoring such conditions as smoke, temperature limits, humidity limits, and power problems. When a condition exceeds pre-established limits, the System Sentry can sound an alarm, use alternate means of notifying personnel, or record variations.

Layout Preparation

Careful layout of the data center and the computer room can greatly affect processing efficiency and reduce costs. Various workable arrangements are possible, but with different degrees of efficiency. In one installation, management realized that they had a workable data center but that it was inefficient. They decided to invest $50,000 in improving the layout. This one-time expense is reported to provide a $30,000 saving each year. The three reasons given for this saving were increased efficiency, reduced staff, and reduced maintenance costs.

Vendors are usually helpful in providing advisors to examine alternatives and recommend the most efficient layout. Although these advisors have considerably more experience in designing layouts,

[7] *IBM System/370 Installation Manual,* p. 1.6.

their time is limited; so data center managers should obtain equipment templates from vendors and try their own experiments. These templates not only show equipment sizes and shapes, they also indicate working and maintenance space required around each piece of equipment. With adequate guidelines, a manager should be able to design several workable layouts, which can then be shown to a vendor representative for discussion. The layout guidelines recommended are separated into two checklists, one that applies to both the data center and the computer room and another that applies only to the computer room.

The data-center and computer-room layout considerations are:

Does work flow efficiently, with appropriate areas adjacent to one another?

Does the work flow without backtracking?

Does traffic flow interfere with processing?

Is there adequate storage at each working area and between working areas?

What would occur if work collected at one area because of problems at the next area?

Are service areas close to where their services are used?

Are personnel near files and equipment they frequently use?

Are there two exits from each room containing people?

Is there an entrance large enough to permit delivery of equipment?

Is there an area to receive and store bulk supplies?

Is there an area for storage and disposal of discarded paper and other material?

Are aisles wide enough for the traffic, including carriers?

Have the swing of doors, the opening of windows, and the presence of obstructions been considered?

Are there enough electrical outlets and are they conveniently located?

Is there adequate space for desks, chairs, equipment, supplies, and storage?

Are telephones properly located?

Can supervisors easily observe personnel?

Is there a lounge for lunch and coffee breaks?

Are there adequate rest rooms?

Is there space for coat closets or coat racks?

Is there adequate space for air-conditioning units and backup power equipment?

Are all desired security and safety provisions included?

Is modification and expansion possible?

Is the overall appearance attractive?

The additional layout considerations for the computer room are:

Does each piece of equipment have adequate operator and maintenance clearance space?

Is there adequate space for worktables, carriers, and storage cabinets?

Is there adequate space for temporary storage of tapes, disk packs, and printed material?

Is there adequate space for test equipment and maintenance personnel?

Can maintenance personnel see between the system console and at least one of its channels, between each channel and at least one of its control units, and between each control unit and at least one of its I/O devices?

Are all cable lengths within the limits specified by vendors?

Is the power panel accessible and is it in a secure location?

Are noisy units separated so that they alternate with quieter units?

Illustration 5–7 is an example of a data center layout that is excellent and shows how a layout can support the efficient, natural flow of work. The work flows smoothly from receipt of data to data control, to data preparation, back to data control, and continues to the computer room, off-line processing, and output distribution. This layout does not provide enough detail to judge the adequacy of many of the design criteria, such as adequacy of storage space and the adequacy of security on the doors entering the data center.

SECURITY AND SAFETY

"Every company that relies on its computer to conduct day to day business without adequate computer room protection is risking corporate extinction," states Miklos B. Korodi, Director of Corporate Development for the American District Telegraph Security System.[8] This may at first thought seem like an exaggeration, but consider the loss of just the accounts-receivable files. This loss could be large enough to put a company out of business. The disasters that

[8]Miklos B. Korodi, "Computer Room Security," *Data Management*, January 1974, p. 15.

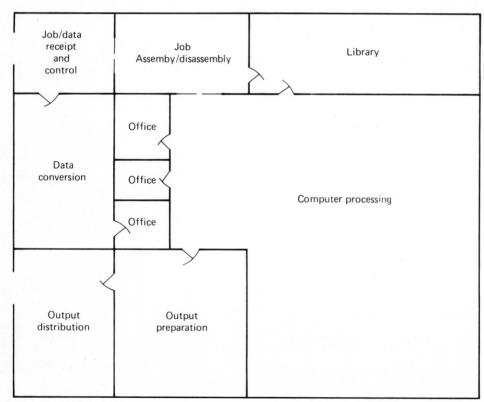

ILLUSTRATION 5-7. Data Center Layout: Jobs and data flow naturally and efficiently from receipt and control area to data conversion, and then to job assembly computer processing output preparation and distribution.

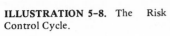

ILLUSTRATION 5–8. The Risk Control Cycle.

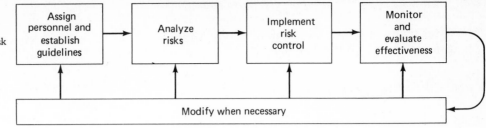

have occurred should stimulate concern about adequate protection. There have been costly fires. The 1959 fire in the Pentagon resulted in approximately $7 million of physical damage and a total loss of about $30 million.[9] There have been considerable losses because of human sabotage and negligence and because of natural disasters such as flooding. Consider the hundreds of data centers buried in water and mud in the mid-Atlantic area as a result of the tropical storm called Agnes. The data center is a compact area that has a high probability of generating high financial losses. In one fire affecting only 650 square feet, for example, the loss was approximately $4 million. Few other areas can cause as much loss per square foot.

The forecasts are not encouraging. The opinion of 30 experts is that losses, injuries, and damage associated with computers will exceed $2 billion annually by 1982.[10] With all the publicity high-loss disasters have received, it becomes apparent that the real threat to a data center is those persons who agree to the importance of a risk-control program but say (or whose lack of effort suggests their belief that), "It will not happen to us!"

Absolute security and safety are unlikely. But not making any attempt to minimize the risks is inviting trouble. What is recommended is that a risk-control program be developed, implemented, and monitored. Further, it is recommended that the entire risk-control program be viewed as part of a control cycle designed to maintain and progressively improve effectiveness. Illustration 5–8 relates the five phases of this cycle, which are:

- Establishing risk-control guidelines
- Performing a risk analysis
- Implementing the risk-control program
- Monitoring and evaluating the program
- Modifying the program

[9] Haig G. Neville, "Insurance for Data Processing," *Datamation*, July 1966.

[10] Jerome Lobel, "Computer Security," in *The Information Systems Handbook*, ed. F. Warren McFarlan and Richard L. Nolan (Homewood, Illinois: Dow Jones-Irwin, 1975), p. 833.

Establishing Risk-Control Guidelines

The first step is the assignment of responsibilities. In a large organization, a few persons may be assigned full time to monitoring and improving safety and security, and possibly also to evaluating computer and data center efficiency. In smaller organizations, only one person may be assigned to these tasks, and that person may be assigned only part time. This part-time person may be the data center manager. How this responsibility is handled is an individual matter for each organization, but at least one person must have the responsibility for auditing and evaluating safety and security, and for recommending improvements. Once personnel have been chosen, guidelines for making the risk-control program effective and for obtaining adherence must be established.

The guidelines consist of documented standards and procedures for each phase of the risk-control program. The objective of each step must be documented, as well as who performs the various tasks (preferably by titles), when each task is done, and how it should be done. For the risk-analysis and the evaluation-reporting phases, forms should be designed to make the process easier to perform quickly, comprehensively, and consistently. Then any constraints that must be adhered to should be stated in definite, measurable terms when possible. These constraints may be legal, such as those for building, health, and safety codes. They may also be financial, personnel, or organization restructions. This includes financial limits for security and safety measures, possibly dependent on cost-benefit tradeoffs: At what point does the investment of more money result in less anticipated savings than the amount spent? And finally, practicality guidelines must be defined, such as ease of implementation, reliability, and timing constraints. Do the means fit into existing procedures? Are they easy to adhere to? Can they be trusted? What is their resistance to being bypassed? How soon must they be available? How soon should response occur after detection of various conditions, such as excessive environmental variation (electrical power, temperature, humidity, etc.) and unauthorized access to the data center?

Performing a Risk Analysis

Risk analysis involves the identification, assessment, and selection of risks to be controlled. Risks can be identified as belonging to one of four categories:

1. *Natural disasters.* Floods, earthquakes, and lightning are in this category. The risk of these occurrences is critical, for example, if the data center is exposed to flooding because it is located in low lands or in the basement of a building or if the data center may experience earthquakes because it is built on a fault.

2. *Accidents.* An accident can result if a careless console operator tips a cup over and spills coffee into the equipment; also, frayed wires or the presence of flammable material can start a fire. These are examples of incidents that could have been avoided by adherence to adequate preventative and operational procedures. Other incidents, such as dropping a disk pack, depend on individual caution.

3. *Vandalism.* Bombing or other acts of destruction can result from civil disorders, a disgruntled employee who wants to get revenge. Damage is not restricted to equipment damage in this or the previous risk categories; damage can also be done to programs, data, and documentation.

4. *Stealing.* Money may be stolen, possibly by obtaining printed and signed checks, or by modifying payroll or accounts-receivable programs and files. There are also many instances where mailing lists or restricted information have been stolen and sold.

Considering these categories, a list of specific risks can now be written for each. It is then necessary to assess these risks in terms of vulnerability and severity. Vulnerability means the probability of a risk occurring. If there is very little probability of a risk occurring, the data center is nearly, but not absolutely, invulnerable to that risk. Severity refers to how disastrous will be the results if that risk occurs. If only a small financial loss or a short processing delay results, the risk has an extremely low severity. Illustration 5-9 shows a form for entering vulnerability and severity evaluations. For

each risk listed, a check mark is placed in one of the boxes for each of the two risk criteria.

To quantify these evaluations, values can be assigned to the various degrees of vulnerability and severity. If the criterion of severity is given twice the importance given to vulnerability, the values could be:

Vulnerability	*Severity*
1 = Extremely unlikely	2 = Very low
2 = Unlikely	4 = Low
3 = Possible	6 = Medium
4 = Probable	8 = High
5 = Highly probable	10 = Very high

If risk A is unlikely and has a medium severity, its total risk value is 2 times 6, or a value of 12. Another risk, B, may be extremely unlikely and have a very high risk; its total risk value is 1 times 10, a value of 10. The conclusion is that either risk A has priority over risk B, or the values assigned are incorrect and should be adjusted. This approach, although resulting in definite values, is still dependent on individual judgments as to the relative vulnerability and severity of each risk.

The preceding approach for assessing risks provides perspective and general direction, but its high dependency on judgment may make it unsatisfactory. Fortunately, a more precise method is available. Lance J. Hoffman, who is with the Computer Science Department at the University of California, recommends the approach indicated in Illustration 5-10. In this approach a dollar value is associated with each anticipated loss, which actually represents degree of severity; probability values are set to represent the nonlinear probability of occurrence, instead of an equal numeric progression such as 1, 2, 3, 4. The highest total risk value in this example is 13,125 for improper disclosure of personal data. Thus, this risk should receive priority attention. The form shown also provides space for recommended actions and their anticipated cost, but in this phase of the risk-control cycle, these decisions cannot be made. They are made in the next phase of the cycle: implementing the risk-control program.

Implementing the Risk-Control Program

Risk analysis results in two general categories of risks: those to be retained and those requiring

Risk Analysis	Vulnerability					Severity				
Risk	Extremely unlikely	Unlikely	Possible	Probable	Highly probable	Very low	Low	Medium	High	Very high

ILLUSTRATION 5-9. Risk Analysis: By using the product of values assigned to the levels of vulnerability and severity, risks can be ranked according to their importance. This approach, however, is largely dependent on the analysts judgement.

DESCRIPTION OF RISK	POTENTIAL EFFECT	POTENTIAL COST OF RISK	PROBABILITY (High = .75) (Average = .50) (Low = .25) (Negligible = .05)	COST-PROBABILITY PRODUCT ($\times 10^3$) (RELATIVE PRIORITY) (High priority is highest product)	PREVENTIVE/REMEDIAL ACTION	COSTS OF SAFEGUARD AND COMMENTS
1. Computer room destroyed	i. Loss of processing capability for production-scheduling, payroll, etc. ii. Replacement of computer iii. Site reconstruction	$ 500,000 200,000 2,000,000	Low	675	i. Ensure adequate backup ii. Maintain fall-back manual system iii. Insure site and equipment iv. Impose fire precautions	Nil. $3000 per year
2. Complete loss of records	i. Unable to bill customers ii. Production line stoppage within four days iii. Unable to continue trading within six weeks	500,000 250,000 25,000,000	Low	6437.5	i. Ensure remote copies kept of all vital files ii. Insure against consequential loss during recovery	$1000 per year
3. Theft of information of use to competitors	i. Erosion of market position ii. Estimated saving to competitor	1,000,000 10,000	Average	505	i. Strict control of access to vital files ii. Personnel bonding	i. Impose system for signing out files
4. Illegal sale of machine time	i. Slightly increased machine costs ii. Possible adverse effect on own systems testing	10,000 5,000	Negligible	0.750	i. Spot checks	No action recommended; risk/small loss outweighed by staff morale considerations
5. Improper disclosure of personal data	i. Lawsuit against firm ii. Loss of goodwill through publicity	10,000,000 7,500,000	High	13125	i. Tighten up controls at areas where information is disseminated ii. Put a legal notice on all forms with personal data specifying laws and sanctions applicable to it.	Intangible effect and cost to data subjects important but not considered here

ILLUSTRATION 5-10. Risk Analysis Using Dollar Values: By substituting anticipated dollar losses for judged severity value used in Illustration 5–9, a more precise analysis results—although actual losses may deviate significantly. *Source:* Lance J. Hoffman, *Modern Methods for Computer Security and Privacy* (Englewood Cliffs, N.J.: Prentice-Hall, 1977), Fig. 13–5.

attention. Attending to a risk may involve merely transferring the risk to another organization in the form of insurance, or it may involve the more active methods of preventing or detecting occurrences, reducing the effect of occurrences, and recovering from disastrous occurrences. Thus, a risk-control decision places each risk in one or more of the following categories:

- Retention of risk
- Transfer of risk
- Prevention of occurrence
- Detection of occurrence
- Reduction of effect
- Recovery from disaster

Retention of risk. The decision to retain a risk may be made because of low severity. For example, it is wasteful to prepare backup for uncritical files, especially files that can be easily recreated. A frequent reason for retaining a risk is the high cost of "total protection." Total protection is generally considered unattainable. A reasonable attitude held by most data center managers is that any attempt to obtain total protection, or even close to total protection, besides being unattainable, is actually financially wasteful. It has been demonstrated in various reports that money spent

for security and safety is justifiable up to a certain point, and beyond that point it provides less cost protection than the price of the protection. A report published by IBM Sweden examines the effect of increased risk-control costs on exposure to losses and on total cost to an organization. Illustration 5-11 shows the results. As is to be expected, exposure to loss decreases as more is spent on risk control; however, at a certain point, indicated by X, the overall financial effect on the organization increases as more is spent on risk control. The conclusion obtained from this study is that each organization must determine the level of risk control providing the lowest expected cost to the organization. And this approach inevitably means retention of risks to some degree.

Another reason for retention of risks is suggested by a data center manager, who said, "Security has an economic cost and a functional cost." The financial cost is obvious and has already been discussed: the more risk control wanted, the more money must be spent—putting aside the possibility of finding less costly means of providing the same protection. But the effect of increasing risk control on data center functions may not be apparent. Extreme levels of security may make it extremely difficult to get work done. Many security measures hamper the movement of personnel, interrupt the flow of data, and thus delay the processing of jobs. Some of the automatic personnel-identification devices, primarily those identifying a person's physiological characteristics, are not totally reliable, requiring a person to be delayed access until someone appears to make positive identification. Another security measure that hampers access to files is the retention of files in secured locations, sometimes in a distant room or in a safe. As this manager continued to comment, "Getting the work down is the first priority . . . there must be a trade-off between security and the ability to do the job efficiently. Total security is not having any doors or windows. Great security, but highly impractical."

Transfer of risk. Severe risks that are expensive to prevent, especially if their occurrences are unlikely, are not reasonable candidates for preventative measures. Furthermore, it may not be possible to retain these risks because of their catastrophic effects. The solution in this situation is to transfer the risk to another organization in the form of insurance. All data centers carry various types of

ILLUSTRATION 5-11. Maximum Financial Benefit from Risk Control: The more spent for risk control the less the organization's exposure to loss, but the trends are that more and more must be spent for risk control to obtain less and less protection–thus, a risk control expenditure point exists, point *X* in the diagram, where lowest financial impact on the organization is anticipated.

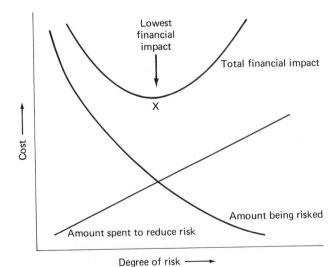

insurance, but it is unlikely that all potentially catastrophic risks are insured. The insurance needs of a data center, which protect against the catastrophic risks as well as the less serious, have been identified as:[11]

1. *Data-processing-equipment* insurance should be adequate to cover replacement. Leased equipment does not automatically pass responsibility for repair or replacement to the lessor or the lessor's insurance company. In either case, the lessee's contract with the lessor should state that either the lessor or the insurance company absorbs the cost. The insurance company accomplishes this by waiving its subrogation recovery rights, the rights to claim damage from the third party who caused the damage. Two precautions are that insurance should be for current replacement cost to purchase new equipment instead of for cash value (replacement cost minus depreciation), because of the rapid obsolescence of data-processing equipment, and that serial numbers should not be included in the insurance policy since a replacement unit, which would have a different serial number, would not be insured.

2. *Storage-media* insurance should cover not only loss of blank tapes and disks, but also the cost to reproduce lost programs and data. In addition, insurance is needed to cover losses in transit or at another site, possibly at a service bureau or an off-site storage area.

3. *Accounts-receivable* insurance avoids dependence on customers to pay their bills promptly, and significant delays can cause a company to go out of business. A discount of 25 percent to 50 percent is possible by stipulating that files will be duplicated and stored off-site, as all critical files should be. This insurance can be obtained as a separate policy or as part of a general policy.

4. *Business-interruption* insurance covers revenue losses because of business disruption resulting from equipment, media, or facility damage, even if the disruption resulted from damage to an adjoining facility. Thus, if a fire on a floor below the data center disrupts the data center's business, its revenue losses are covered.

5. *Extra expenses.* Insurance for expenses such as use of a service bureau, when unable to use data center facilities, can be obtained; this also includes overtime and transportation costs. In the case of a disaster, when another site may have to be used for a long period of time, this extra expense can be high.

6. *Data processors' errors and omissions* insurance protects the data center from liability for any errors, omissions, or negligence resulting from facilities or services it has made available to other organizations. Thus, if excess computer time in the data center is sold to other organizations and if the data center's computer operator causes a customer file to be destroyed, the data center is not held liable. This can be serious if, for example, an accounts-receivable file is destroyed.

As in the case of insurance for accounts-receivable files, reduction in insurance rates is possible when adequate protection measures exist in the data center. In fact, some insurance coverages may be impossible to obtain unless such protective measures exist, particularly adequate backup procedures and off-site storage facilities.

Prevention of occurrence. Where insurance is the last line of defense against risks, prevention is the first line of defense, avoiding loss and damage instead of minimizing the financial effects. The time to first consider prevention of risks is when a site is being selected for the data center. At that time, exposure to natural disasters can be lessened by considering such restrictions as choosing a site not on low ground, in an area in which civil disorders are not likely to occur, and by choosing a building that is easy to secure. Once a site has been selected, the two main concerns are avoidance of fires and blockage of unauthorized access to the data center, programs, and data. Joe Pujals of the Teale Consolidated Data Center in Sacramento, California, states his concept of perfect access security: "Given the choice, I'd specify a reinforced-concrete, windowless building, within a reinforced-concrete, windowless building, security systems on both and a secured perimeter with single-access control. I'd design, in other words, a building for computer use."[12]

This degree of access security is generally not practical, especially when a data center is estab-

[11]Guy R. Migliaccio, "The Ins and Outs of DP Insurance," *Computer Decisions*, February 1978, p. 26.

[12]Lawrence A. Yaggi, Jr., "DP Bureau Establishes 'Secure' Facility," *Computerworld*, September 12, 1977, p. 57.

lished in an office building instead of in a separate building totally dedicated to the data center. The next lower level of total access control is the "man trap." In this approach, a single entry, usually only to the computer room, consists of two doors enclosing a small area. A person enters the first door, which closes and locks behind him, and provides positive identification either to a guard or to an automatic identification device. Thus, a person not receiving positive identification is trapped until a decision is made as to whether or not access should be permitted.

A more frequent procedure is to have either a guard or an identification device without the man trap. Some organizations require identification by two automatic identification devices. These devices avoid the expense of guards and the likelihood of human errors, but they also have their shortcomings, which, when known, can be greatly minimized. These devices fall into three categories: those dependent on a person's special knowledge, those dependent on a person's possessions, and those dependent on a person's physical attributes. The required special knowledge may be a password, a lock combination, or some other information. The fault with this method is that others can learn and then use this information. A means to lessen the likelihood of this information becoming generally known is to periodically change it—some organizations change their password once a month.

The second category of these devices, a person's possessions that permit admittance, can be a key, a magnetic-encoded card, or a card key. These have the deficiency that they can be obtained by another person, possibly even duplicated and returned so that the key or card is not missed and made invalid, thus permitting entry at any time desired. The approach used to lessen this deficiency is similar to that used for protecting special knowledge: the key or card is replaced periodically, usually every six or twelve months. The deficiencies of the first two categories are eliminated by the third category, identification of persons by physical attribute. The attribute used could be represented by a photograph that is verified by a guard, or it could be the voice, fingerprints, or finger lengths. Photographs tend to be poor likenesses and receive only glancing looks before a person is admitted. Other devices, such as those that perform identification by the lengths of fingers, vary in reliability.

If the measurements are made as critical as possible, an extremely small percentage of imposters may be passed, but an increasing number of legitimate persons will also be rejected. A combination of a physical-attribute method and a key or card method should provide as close to absolute access security as is possible.

These devices lose their protective value if a special precaution is not taken: no "tailgating" should be permitted, that is, when one person is positively identified, no one else should be permitted to follow that person without also being positively identified. This is a serious problem. Some organizations are aware of the tailgating problem and warn their employees not to permit it, but the author's observations are that these warnings are ineffective unless employees are threatened with being fired. Many of these apparently foolproof devices and procedures are made nearly worthless by casual human attitudes.

Some installations include in their security programs closed-circuit television (CCTV). If there is a buffer space separating the computer room from the rest of the data center, this area is likely to be closely watched. But security is not limited only to stopping unauthorized persons from entering restricted areas; it must also include control of authorized persons who may want to profit from their access to materials or information or who may be discontented and may want to cause damage. These problems are very difficult to control and actually impossible to control totally. A large step in the right direction, however, is to use CCTV for surveillance.

The remaining preventative measures fall into the category of safety precautions. There are many safety precautions such as not wearing loose clothing near equipment with moving parts. The majority of precautions, however, center on fire prevention. Putting aside fire-detection and loss-reduction devices, fire prevention depends on adequate fire-prevention procedures. And these procedures actually involve the obvious requirements of cleanliness and carefulness. For example, combustible material should not be permitted and the space under the raised flooring should be periodically cleaned—fires under raised flooring because of accumulated dirt is an all-too-frequent occurrence.

Detection of occurrence. No matter how thorough safety and security procedures are and how

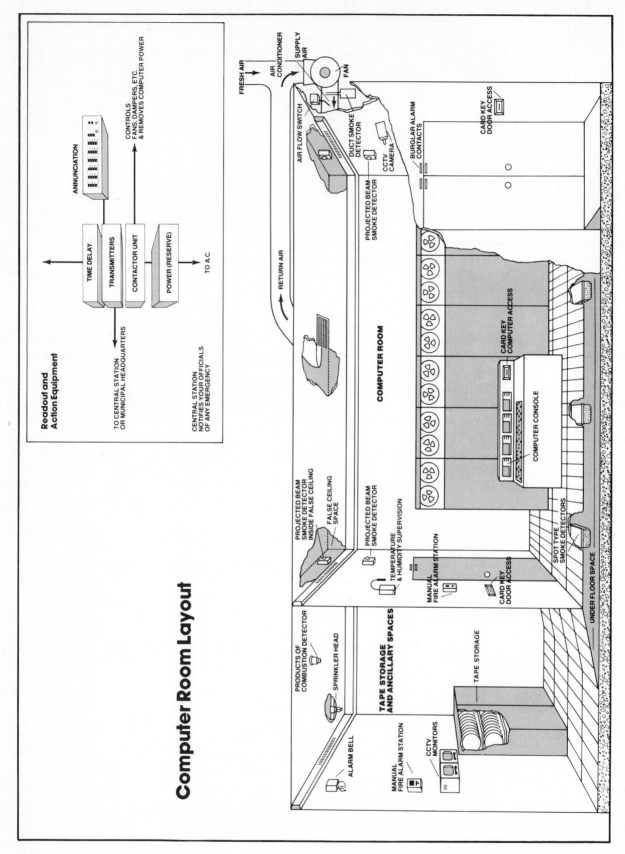

ILLUSTRATION 5-12. Computer Room Security and Safety: Many means are shown for obtaining security, such as card-key door access and CCTV camera surveillance, and for detecting fire, such as smoke detectors in floor, walls, ceiling, and air conditioning ducts. A particularly interesting feature shown is automatic notification to a monitoring station of an emergency. *Source:* ADT Security Systems in New York City.

carefully they are adhered to, a fire could occur or an employee could attempt a criminal act. Illustration 5-12 shows some of the detection devices available. To detect smoke in the computer room, there are smoke detectors of various types in the floor, the walls, the ceiling, and in the air-conditioning duct. The tape storage area shows a combustion-particle detector, a special type of detector that is believed to detect combustion particles that are released into the air before smoke occurs. There is some disagreement among safety experts as to whether or not these particles actually exist. In addition, the illustration shows manual alarms and an automatic alarm to an off-site location. The off-site location may be a fire house or it may be a monitoring control station that monitors many data centers on a 24-hour, 7-day basis. For example, ADT Security Systems, who prepared this illustration, has over 130 of these stations throughout the United States. Notice that, as part of the automatic fire-notification system, the occurrence of a fire is announced on-site and several actions can be performed automatically, such as shutting off electrical power and closing dampers.

Although CCTV was mentioned as a preventive measure, that is actually only its secondary purpose. True, its presence causes potential criminals to think twice, but there are those who will think twice and still commit a crime. The effectiveness of CCTV is dependent partly on the alertness and diligence of the person watching the monitors and partly on the adequacy of coverage. But this monitoring will not catch a person modifying a program or data. The controls for those actions must be built into the system software—a responsibility of the systems-development department.

Reduction of effect. Generally, the most effective means of reducing the effect of a safety or security problem is quick detection. But if quick notification is not followed by quick corrective action, the initial advantage is lost and considerable unnecessary damage can result. The best assurance of quick action is through automatic devices. Fire-extinguishing devices are particularly important. There are four types of fire-extinguishing devices:

1. *Water sprinklers* are inexpensive, easy to install, and effective, but they can cause extensive water damage; if this type is used, it may be best to consider a bifunctional system that releases water when the temperature reaches 165°F and shuts off the water when the temperature drops to 100°F.

2. *Foam types* have the advantages of the water sprinklers without the water flooding problems, but they present a new problem: the extreme difficulty of removing the foam from the interior of the equipment.

3. *Carbon dioxide* extinguishers do little, if any, damage to computer equipment and require no cleanup; but because they are harmful to humans, release must be delayed and safety controls make them expensive.

4. *Halon* extinguishers have all the advantages of carbon dioxide extinguishers, and since they are not harmful to humans, they can be released immediately upon detection of a fire. These are considered the best type and are generally the most expensive.

Next in importance to automatic means for reducing the effect of fires are adequate procedures and well-trained personnel. Procedures should be established for storing backup programs, files, and documentation off-site and for storing critical files in high-temperature-rated safes until off-site delivery can be performed. Personnel must adhere to these procedures and must know the procedure to use in case of a fire, such as the shutting off electrical power and how to use the fire extinguishers.

Recovery from disaster. If a disaster occurs, all preparation for continuing operations with minimal disruption must have been completed. Critical files, programs, and data must be duplicated and stored at an off-site location as an on-going procedure. Also, all special forms and necessary documentation must be stored off-site. All this, however, is a waste of effort if a backup facility is not available with compatible hardware and software. The backup facility could be the data center of another division of the same company, a data center at another company, a service bureau, a vendor, a special data center supported by several companies for disaster backup, or a combination of these. Some companies have formed a consortium that agrees to provide their facilities in case of an emergency. A variation of the backup data center approach is used by 10 manufacturing com-

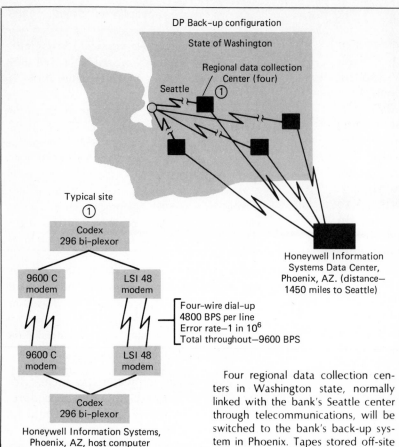

DP Back-up configuration

State of Washington

Regional data collection
Center (four)

Seattle

Typical site
①

Codex
296 bi-plexor

9600 C
modem

LSI 48
modem

Four-wire dial-up
4800 BPS per line
Error rate—1 in 10^6
Total throughout—9600 BPS

9600 C
modem

LSI 48
modem

Codex
296 bi-plexor

Honeywell Information Systems,
Phoenix, AZ, host computer

Honeywell Information
Systems Data Center,
Phoenix, AZ. (distance—
1450 miles to Seattle)

ILLUSTRATION 5-13. Disaster Telecommunication Backup. *Source:* Jack P. Curry, "Planning for Disaster Recovery," *Infosystems*, March 1978, p. 66.

Four regional data collection centers in Washington state, normally linked with the bank's Seattle center through telecommunications, will be switched to the bank's back-up system in Phoenix. Tapes stored off-site from the bank's main computer facility in Seattle will be transported to Phoenix, and personnel from headquarters will be flown there, Thompson explained. The disaster procedures are tested periodically to assure that they will work if the need becomes a reality.

Cost of the plan involves relatively economical dial-up lines to the Honeywell Center and extra equipment costing about $60,000, according to Seattle-First. Development of the plan involved efforts amounting to about three man-years of planning.

A disaster could deal a costly blow to a company's operations and put the firm out of business. But officials at Seattle-First National Bank, Seattle, WA, feel confident their bank would remain solvent in such an event because they have planned for disaster recovery. If the bank's data center in Seattle is knocked out, DP operations will be switched to Honeywell Information Systems' Data Center in Phoenix, AZ, according to Wes Thompson, manager, data communications, Seattle-First.

panies. They have leased 6000 square feet of building space solely for emergency use.[13]

The Seattle-First National Bank in Seattle, Washington, has carried disaster protection to its ultimate. They have their data center in Seattle and a backup center in Phoenix, Arizona, which is 1450 miles away, definitely far enough to be unaffected if a disaster occurs in Seattle. The Seattle data center has telecommunication connections with four data-collection centers throughout Washington. If a disaster occurs at the Seattle data center, the four data-collection centers are switched to the Arizona site. Tapes stored off-site are then transported to Arizona, and personnel are flown there. Dial-up lines and equipment cost for this backup protection was about $60,000. The network is indicated in Illustration 5-13.

Disaster backup cannot be obtained overnight. It requires planning and effort. It starts with the formation of a disaster committee, identification of survival needs, preparation of disaster plans, and

[13]Jack P. Curry, "Planning for Disaster Recovery," *Infosystems*, March 1978, p. 66.

implementation of all necessary procedures, and then it continues by adhering strictly to procedures. The disaster committee's importance cannot be treated lightly; it assigns levels of importance to jobs, develops disaster plans with their standards and procedures, directs the preparation necessary to support the disaster plans, and monitors adherence to standards and procedures. Thus, their first duty is to assign levels of importance to jobs or, to put it another way, to identify survival needs. To do this it is necessary for user department representatives to meet with the disaster committee and decide how critical the various jobs are. If a data center steering committee exists, the task of obtaining user department representatives is already attended to. To avoid undue complexity, but have adequate separation of jobs, a division of the jobs into three categories should be satisfactory. These categories can be defined as follows:

- *High-priority jobs.* Jobs that must be run to meet deadlines or to avoid significant financial losses, such as payroll and accounts receivable.
- *Medium-priority jobs.* Jobs that will be run when time and resources permit.
- *Low-priority jobs.* Jobs that will not be run until the first two categories have been executed.

With this step completed, the committee is ready to develop several disaster plans. Several plans are necessary, since the data center may experience several degrees of disaster. The worst is, naturally, a total destruction of the data center. A less disastrous situation results if only part of the data center is destroyed, possibly only a few critical files in the tape library or one or more pieces of equipment in the computer room. A much less serious situation is disruption because of an environmental failure or a personnel shortage. The first would result if a power failure or air-conditioning failure occurred, and the second, if an epidemic, strike, or riot occurred. Each disaster plan should resolve as many decisions as possible, avoiding on-the-spot decisions at a time of crisis.

After the disaster plans have been precisely defined and adequately documented, all preparation required should be attended to. Of particular importance is to obtain a signed contract from the organization providing the backup facility. The contract should state that the backup facility will be available and that it will remain compatible with the data center's equipment and software, or, if it is to be modified, that the data center management will be notified, permitting it to make similar modification or allowing time to locate another facility. Once the preparation has been completed, personnel must be trained in the necessary backup and off-site storage procedures, and these procedures must be adhered to. Schedules are established and control documents should be available to verify strict adherence to this schedule.

Monitoring and Evaluating the Program

The risk-control program must be monitored to assure that the guidelines for the program are adequate, that the risks have been analyzed properly, and that the security measures implemented are effective. Besides having the person or persons assigned to monitor security observe and record deficiencies, violations to security and safety measures should be attempted to test their adequacy, and likewise, disasters should be simulated to test the disaster plans. These should be performed randomly so that no one will know when a test will occur. In addition, an excellent idea is to prepare a checklist of security and safety conditions that should exist. Many of these checklists are already available. One of the most thorough is the contents of a nearly 300-page book; its title is *SAFE: Security Audit and Field Evaluation Systems,* by Leonard I. Krauss.[14] A shorter and very provocative checklist, one that is certain to stimulate interest in security and to suggest its scope and depth, is included in this book as Appendix C. A checklist can be either used as is or modified for an installation's particular needs. If the resulting checklist is as large as the one Krauss prepared, a portion of the checklist can be used for each audit, possibly completing each total audit every four or eight weeks.

Modifying the Program

To complete the control cycle for the risk-control program, it is necessary to review the evaluations resulting from the monitoring phase and decide if

[14] Leonard I. Krauss, *SAFE: Security Audit and Field Evaluation for Computer Facilities and Information Systems* (New York: Amacom, 1972).

any changes are advisable. The most basic change would be that the person assigned to conduct the evaluation should be replaced. As shown by the control cycle in Illustration 5–8, decisions to modify can also affect the risk analysis, implementation, and evaluation procedures. If it is believed that the wrong risks were identified in the risk analysis, then that phase and all those that follow would have to be repeated. If the implementation of risk control has proven deficient, then that phase will have to be reviewed for modification, and the following evaluation phase may have to be modified, changing either the testing activities, the checklists used, or both.

The subjects of security and safety are vast, and although the most critical concepts have been discussed, more detail may be wanted. To cover the subject adequately requires a book dedicated solely to the subject, as many have been. For those who want to delve more deeply into this subject, an excellent introduction is *Guidelines for Automatic Data Processing Physical Security and Risk Management.*[15]

DATA CENTER RELOCATION

As stated under site selection, relocation occurs when the total data center is moved from one location to another, when a data center is divided and relocated in two or more locations, or when two or more data centers are combined into one. The benefits of relocation are justified by reduced operating costs, improved efficiency, better user service, or better control of safety and security. Normally, when the cost of these locations is analyzed, only the actual relocation costs are considered, and several indirect costs are overlooked.

Two indirect costs are of particular importance: loss of revenue during the disruption of operations, and the diversion of money to the relocation that could have been spent for revenue-increasing projects. These indirect costs should be considered when a cost-benefit analysis is performed.

Once the decision has been made to relocate, the next step is to establish a procedure that provides comprehensive attention to all the details of planning and controlling the relocation. Inadequate planning could lead to inadequate insurance coverage, poor vendor coordination, and uncertain delivery of equipment—all leading to extended schedules and excessive expenses. Poor control could cause inadequate checking of equipment connections, for example, causing processing disruptions and remedial maintenance for an extended period. What is needed is the plan-do-control cycle that has proved its effectiveness in many other situations, such as in establishing and maintaining the risk-control program. The control cycle recommended is shown in Illustration 5–14 and consists of six phases:

- Establishing a relocation committee
- Defining relocation constraints
- Developing a relocation strategy
- Preparing for relocation
- Implementing the relocation schedule
- Controlling deviations

Establishing a Relocation Committee

A data center relocation committee is needed to obtain the coordinated effort of managerial and technical personnel. Lack of leadership in any one area, such as determining all significant constraints, can cause incorrect decisions and their accompanying disruptions and delays. What if relocation timing is treated casually? It is likely that, instead of choosing the least critical time for relocation, a time will be chosen that will delay significant

---

[15]*Guidelines for Automatic Data Processing Physical Security and Risk Management,* Federal Information Processing Standards Publication 31, June 1974.

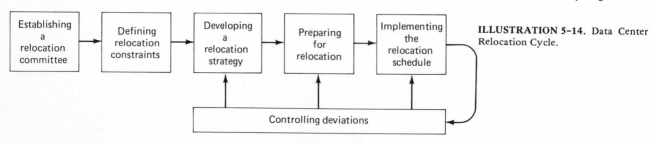

ILLUSTRATION 5-14. Data Center Relocation Cycle.

jobs, or at least create unnecessary inconveniences. If, on the other hand, there is inadequate technical representation, oversights such as no verification of electrical connections will occur—requiring delay of processing until the causes of the equipment malfunctions are found and corrected. The more adequate the managerial and technical representation, the more forethought will occur and the more smoothly the relocation will proceed.

Relocation for a large data center is usually preceded by at least one year of detailed planning and preparation. During this time, many meetings are necessary, and they should be scheduled so that attendance will cause little conflict with daily operating activities. Considering the desire of some personnel to take long weekends, it is recommended that the meetings be scheduled for Tuesday, Wednesday, or Thursday. It is also recommended that the meetings be held first thing in the morning to avoid the possibility that a prior activity will delay someone. To prevent the meetings from affecting daily activities, the purpose of each meeting must be established before it occurs, and agendas should be distributed along with a list of who will be responsible for supplying information. To further minimize disruption of regular responsibilities, the meetings should be limited to one or two hours at most.

Defining Relocation Constraints

This phase requires considerable planning. If a site has not been selected, the first concern is the preparation of constraints in the form of a site-selection checklist, considering the guidelines presented at the beginning of this chapter. The next constraint is setting a limit on relocation cost. The natural tendency is to set this as low as seems feasible. But this may lead to a difficult relocation and disrupted processing, possibly costing more as a result. A low budget for relocation would automatically eliminate relocation alternatives that permit minimal or no disruption of processing and nearly assure a trouble-free move.

If a budget limit is set that necessarily requires processing disruption (although at this point this decision has not been made), the next constraint is the length of time that processing can be disrupted. A constraint that works closely with this consideration is the time that relocation should occur to disrupt processing as little as possible. Obviously, end-of-the-month, end-of-the-quarter, and end-of-the-year times should be avoided. These disruption considerations are not necessary if it is understood that a relocation strategy will be used that will not affect processing at all.

Another critical constraint involves whether or not the final configuration will be upgraded during relocation. Since relocation has been decided upon, this is an excellent time to consider this possibility. A decision on this point may automatically determine the relocation strategy; one possibility is not to relocate existing equipment, but to transfer workload to new equipment.

Developing a Relocation Strategy

There are two basic strategies: one is referred to as "evolutionary" and the other, as "revolutionary." In the evolutionary approach, the workload is gradually transferred to the new data center; in the revolutionary approach, the workload is transferred all at one time, as quickly as possible.

The most appealing and the most expensive of the evolutionary approaches is to install duplicate or upgraded equipment at the new site and then gradually transfer the workload. This approach causes no disruption of processing and allows time for thorough testing of the new configuration. A variation of this approach that provides the same benefits at less cost, but causes crowding at the original site for a while, is to lease duplicate equipment, possibly for three months, and install it at the old site. Jobs can then be run on both machines for about two weeks, and when the leased equipment has proved to be reliable, the original equipment can be transferred and tested. After the original equipment proves satisfactory, the workload is transferred to it.

There is another alternative that is the least expensive but the most troublesome. The new site can be prepared for processing, including raised flooring, all power connections, and air conditioning. The high-workload peripherals and all *new* cables can be installed. (Avoid transferring old cables because of the problems and delays that are almost inevitable from such defects as bent connector pins.) Then part of the computer equipment is transferred, with only the critical jobs being executed on the equipment that remains. In effect, a semidisaster situation has been created and some processing disruption has been accepted.

There is one very attractive variation of the evolutionary approach that may be possible. If an agreement exists with one or more organizations to provide backup facilities, part of the workload can be transferred to that facility before some of the computer equipment is transferred. Thus, although this is the least expensive of the evolutionary approaches, processing is uninterrupted.

If a company is dependent on teleprocessing, it is advisable to install a duplicate network at the new data center before relocation. Both networks should then be run in parallel to assure that the new network is functioning correctly.

The revolutionary approach is simple to explain, but the execution is anything but simple.

One day processing stops, everything is moved to the new site, everything is connected and checked as quickly as possible, and processing is resumed. Some of these moves have been successful, but the potential problems that can occur are legitimate causes for concern. One company that was successful started the move at 5:30 P.M. on a Friday, had the equipment fully installed at the new site 11 blocks away by 9:30 A.M. Saturday, and was fully operational at 3:30 P.M. Sunday. If new cables are used at the new site, if the computer is up to specifications, and if all electrical connections and environmental equipment have been thoroughly checked, this approach is worthy of consideration—for a small data center. The time to move and install a large data center is usually estimated to require at least two weeks, a disruption of processing few companies can tolerate.

ILLUSTRATION 5-15. Relocation Schedule and Checklist: Only the first page of the 12-page report is shown. An *X* in the last column indicates completion of an activity. *Source:* Royal-Globe Insurance Companies in New York City.

```
********** EDP RELOCATION CHECKLIST **********
```

TASK CODE	DATE DUE	DAY	HOUR	DESCRIPTION OF TASK	DEPARTMENT INVOLVED	NAME OF PERSON	MEETING NUMBER	ITEM NUMBER	C
A0223	0378			OBTAIN 6 COPIES OF FLOOR PLANS FOR J. STUBENRAUCH	OPERATIONS	C. FITZGERALD			X
A0229	0378			DETERMINE PRODUCTION SCHEDULE FOR THE WEEK OF THE MOVE	OPERATIONS	J. SQUASHIC	S02	02	X
A5331	0313	MO		CRIPPLE 168 TO 4 MEGS FOR PERFORMANCE TESTING	TECHNICAL SYSTEMS	E. BIRD	M02	11	X
A0222	0378			SUPPLY TECHNICAL WITH NOVEMBER PRODUCTION SCHEDULE	OPERATIONS	J. QUINN			X
A0299	0378			DEVELOP A KEY EVENTS CHART-RELOCATION CHECKLIST	OPERATIONS	J. SQUASHIC	M01	05	X
A04	0378			DETERMINE WHAT PERSONNEL WILL MOVE	ADMINISTRATION		M01	04	
A0410	0378			DETERMINE USER LOCATIONS FOR RJE & REMOTE TSO (GOLD ST.)	ADMINISTRATION	D. FRITTS			X
A07	0405	WE		TOUR TELCO EDP AND GATHER INFO ON THEIR RECENT MOVE	RELOCATION COMMITTEE		M04	03	X
A0180	0420	TH		COMPLETE HARDWARE LAYOUT ON CHANNELS	IBM	J. STUBENRAUCH	M09	01	X
A0180	0427	TH		OBTAIN POWER REQUIREMENTS FOR ALL EQUIP. (WILLIAM ST.)	IBM	J. STUBENRAUCH			X
A0223	0427	TH		REVIEW CIRCUIT LAYOUTS BY WALL PANELS (WILLIAM ST.)	OPERATIONS	C. FITZGERALD			X
A0180	0427	TH		SUPPLY CHECKLIST FOR JUNE'S 3777 RJE INSTALL. (GOLD ST.)	IBM	J. STUBENRAUCH	M09	01	X
A0180	0427	TH		COMPLETE CHRONOLOGY OF I/O INSTALLATIONS (WILLIAM ST.)	IBM	J. STUBENRAUCH	M09	01	X
A0223	0428	FR		ORDER RIBBONS, ETC. FOR 3777 RJE AT GOLD ST. (JUNE)	OPERATIONS	C. FITZGERALD			X
A0180	0428	FR		ORDER 3705 UPGRADE TO SUPPORT 2ND RJE CLUSTER (GOLD ST.)	IBM	J. STUBENRAUCH			X
A0181	0478			SUPPLY MEASUREMENTS OF ALL EQUIPMENT WITH PACKING	IBM	S. DOODY	M09	03	X
A0331	0478			COMPLETE DOCUMENTATION ON THE ABILITY TO TRANSFER IMS	TECHNICAL SYSTEMS	E. BIRD	M07	07	
A0331	0478			SUPPLY COMMITTEE WITH TOTAL EQUIPMENT CONFIGURATION	TECHNICAL SYSTEMS	E. BIRD	M05	01	
A0720	0478			DETERMINE WHETHER TO SPLIT TSO OR NOT	RELOCATION COMMITTEE	W. HAMILTON			X
A0720	0478			DETERMINE WHETHER TO SPLIT SCOPE OR NOT	RELOCATION COMMITTEE	W. HAMILTON	M01	10	X
A0991	0478			DETERMINE SEPARATION REQUIREMENTS FOR IMS/3790 SYSTEMS	FOND	E. CHARNEY	M06	10	X
A0410	0478			INSTITUTE PHYSICAL PLANNING FOR 2ND RJE (GOLD ST.)	ADMINISTRATION	D. FRITTS			X
A0222	0478			DETERMINE TOTAL BACKUP COST OF EQUIPMENT FOR THE MOVE	OPERATIONS	J. QUINN	M02	11	
A0223	0478			ORDER D1 COND. LINE FOR REMOTE TSO AT GOLD ST.	OPERATIONS	C. FITZGERALD			X
A0223	0478			ORDER D1 COND. LINE FOR RJE AT GOLD ST. (2ND)	OPERATIONS	C. FITZGERALD			X
A0223	0478			ORDER (2) 209A DATASETS FOR REMOTE TSO AT GOLD ST.	OPERATIONS	C. FITZGERALD			X
A0223	0478			ORDER (2) 209A DATASETS FOR RJE AT GOLD ST. (2ND)	OPERATIONS	C. FITZGERALD			X
A0181	0505	FR		SUPPLY INSTALLATION TIME FOR EACH BOX TO BE MOVED	IBM	S. DOODY			X

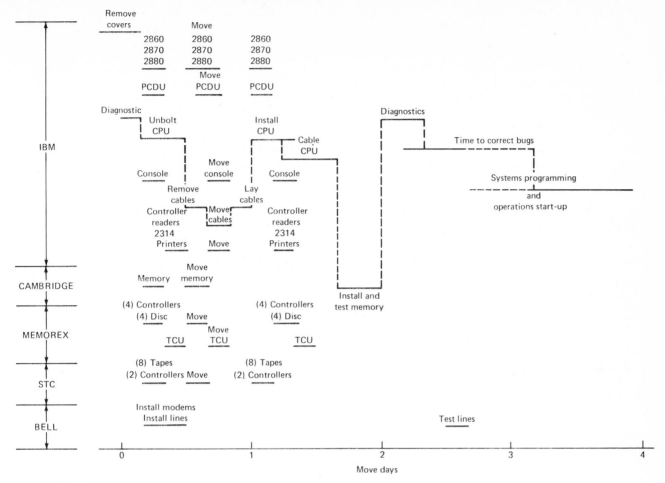

ILLUSTRATION 5-16. Relocation Dependencies and Critical Path: For those time periods that interrelated activities are critical, it is advisable to prepare a PERT-type graph. The graph shown combines the benefits of a PERT chart (that shows dependencies and critical path) and the benefits of a Gannt chart (that shows the schedule and also responsibilities). *Source:* William R. Townsend and Gary E. Whitehouse, "We Used Risk Analysis to Move Our Computer," *Industrial Engineering*, May 1977, p. 36.

Preparing for Relocation

To assure that all activities are known and will be attended to, a schedule must be prepared, personnel must be assigned to each activity, and a means must be developed for indicating what has been completed. Illustration 5-15 shows the first of a 12-page "general" schedule and checklist used by Royal-Globe Insurance Companies in New York City. This is considered a general schedule because many minor steps are not shown but are grouped as a single entry on the schedule. When a step is completed, a data base is updated, and the report can be obtained showing an *x* for completed steps. This listing, besides showing scheduled dates, also shows responsibilities.

Some organizations may prefer a Gantt-type chart, in which black lines indicate scheduled start and end dates, and red lines can be used to indicate actual start and end dates. This permits quick visual checking to determine at any time if all activities are on schedule. If an activity is not on schedule, the length of the black line indicates the amount of time required for the activity.

One problem of listings and Gantt charts is that they normally do not indicate precedence relationships. It is important to know which activities must be completed before another can be started. It is also important to know what the critical path is, that is, what series of activities, if not done as scheduled, would delay completion on schedule. Illustration 5-16 shows a portion of a relocation schedule, indicating precedence relationships only for those activities on a critical path.

The schedule should consist of much more than the activities surrounding the days of moving and installation. The following steps also must be taken:

1. Obtain written permission from leasing companies to move their equipment, as well as any special agreements related to preparation for the move and to actions during and after the move.
2. Obtain a contract from the lessors, vendors, or a service company for deinstallation and reinstallation of the equipment.
3. Obtain a maintenance agreement from the maintenance organization, usually the vendor, to approve the installation and continue maintenance.
4. Inform current and future building managements of the moving schedule, and obtain assurance that utilities will be available when needed.
5. Select a mover with experience in moving computer equipment, and discuss the route to the site and such matters as access to freight elevators.
6. Obtain insurance for the move.
7. Prepare the new data center, considering such factors as equipment layout, raised flooring, air conditioning, electrical power, and security and safety means.

Implementing the Relocation Schedule

If the schedule has been carefully prepared, all that is required next is that everyone does his or her job. The only warning is to never assume that something has been completed properly without checking it. For example, the person responsible for overseeing electrical connections, the activity almost certain to be done improperly, should verify that electrical connections actually work and that they are properly phased. In one data center about 90 percent of the connections were out of phase, making it easier to reverse the remaining 10 percent—

in other words, making all out of phase according to specifications. At this same site, some of the connections had not even been completed.

Controlling Deviations

Through frequent meetings to review progress, the data center relocation committee should become aware of deviations and should be able to control them. Control of these deviations may require modification of strategy, scheduling, or implementation. One organization had to change its relocation strategy when the computer they expected to have delivered to the new site could not be ready for delivery on schedule. Thus, instead of installing an upgraded computer system at the new site and transferring their workload, they had to go to the less satisfactory alternative of relocating one of their existing computers, which would disrupt some of their processing, and then transfer jobs.

Deviations may not affect the overall strategy, but may affect the schedule. If a task on the critical path is delayed or requires more time than anticipated, the entire schedule must be adjusted. Less critical deviations that do not affect the schedule may occur in the implementation phase. For example, equipment may be found to be defective, requiring either repair or replacement. Inadequate services, such as the incorrect electrical connections mentioned earlier, may create additional work and require additional assignment of work, possibly requiring the services of those not originally contracted for in the relocation. Adequate monitoring is the means to correct deviations before they cause extended delays. The most-expert planning can be nullified to a large extent by casual attentiveness to the control phase of the relocation process.

HARDWARE AND SOFTWARE ACQUISITION

GOAL

To place the acquisition of hardware and software in perspective and to proceed rationally in evaluating and financing acquisitions and in negotiating contracts.

HIGHLIGHTS

General Considerations

Basic guidelines and precautions establish a foundation for the acquisition procedures.

Obtaining Proposals

Comprehensive statements of user intentions and requirements permit vendors to respond with realistic proposals.

Evaluating Proposals

Justifiable evaluations result from attention to the worth of many factors, with judgement assisted by quantitative methods, not by "seat of the pants" guesses—and mistakes.

Financing the Acquisition

Techniques are available to make the rent-lease-purchase decision on a sound financial basis.

Negotiating the Contract

Sincere buyer-seller efforts to obtain a "fair" contract minimizes later conflict and frustration, lessening the likelihood of litigation.

Software Acquisition

This procedure is similar to that used for hardware acquisition, but it has its own special guidelines and precautions.

Hardware and software acquisition would seem to be the private responsibility of the data center manager, whose responsibility is to get the work done and to use the expertise in the department to do this. But the pressures on the manager tend to remove this responsibility from him or her—but not the responsibility for productivity. Who exerts the pressures to acquire something? Who does not? There are armies of salesmen from the various vendors. Internally, there are the demands of users for processing power and from the technical staff for the latest advancements. With these pressures, it is tempting to place the vendor salesmen (frequently only those for a favorite vendor) together with several enthusiastic technicians and then to approve and act on their recommendation. In effect, they are deciding the data center's financial and performance effectiveness.

This tendency must be blocked. The data center manager must not delegate the responsibility to others for establishing acquisition policy, determining the evaluation criteria, and controlling the thoroughness of the evaluation. Management control should assure that the entire acquisition process is done with more precision and thoroughness than it customarily receives. That is the goal: to make the progress precise and thorough. In any acquisition, specifications must be prepared, proposals must be evaluated, a financial agreement must be arrived at, and a contract must be signed. The general process does not change when it is converted from a casual, carefree process to one that is cautious and controlled; what changes is the thoroughness and precision applied at each step of the process.

Two factors make rational acquisition even more difficult: one is rapid technological changes and the other is political, the pressure to "keep up with the Joneses." In the early history of computer use, major changes in equipment and operating systems occurred every two or three years. Minor corrections and enhancements were necessary during this time. But present equipment and operating systems usually require several major modifications a year. When changes are made this frequently, adequate evaluation of the latest innovation is practically impossible. But is it really necessary? No doubt advantages are gained: however, can they be delayed a month, a year, maybe two years? If so, who keeps pressuring for changes? It becomes apparent that the problem of frequent technological changes is to a large extent actually part of the second problem, keeping up with the Joneses.

The attitude that what is ordered today and received tomorrow was already obsolete yesterday must be killed—given a quick and permanent death. This attitude makes adherence to a rational acquisition process impossible. It also creates its own particular problems. It results in acquiring unproven, error-prone equipment and software. Those who have used equipment released too soon do not have to be cautioned about hurried acquisitions. Personnel in data centers blessed with hurriedly acquired equipment have observed technicians eyeing the innards of the equipment, holding a soldering iron in one hand and a wiring diagram in the other. It is also common for the programmers in user organizations that have received newly released vendor software to daily notify vendors of software deficiencies. The lesson to be learned from these experiences is that equipment and software must be allowed to mature, and at the vendor's expense.

Two of the culprits fostering the quick acquisition attitude have already been identified. The vendor salesman wants to make sales. Just as a car salesman does not want to know that your present, one-year-old car is running well, and wants to sell the latest available, caring little if it actually functions better or poorer, the computer salesman also wants to make a sale. The second culprit is the technician who wants to use the latest hardware available—after all, how would it look on a resume to be associated with "obsolete" equipment. There is a third culprit: the user department manager who knows little about data processing, but knows enough to affect acquisition decisions, to pressure the acquisition of the latest, talked-about piece of equipment. An editorial in the September 4, 1978, issue of *Computerworld* states, "It does seem shocking that 80 percent of federal computer systems are at least six years old, while the other 20 percent are more than three years old," and attributes this comment to a "major computer vendor." With the all too obvious tint of self-interest, vendor statements of this type have led user departments, possibly with the agreement of data center managers, to swap the latest unproven for the old reliable, to swap what

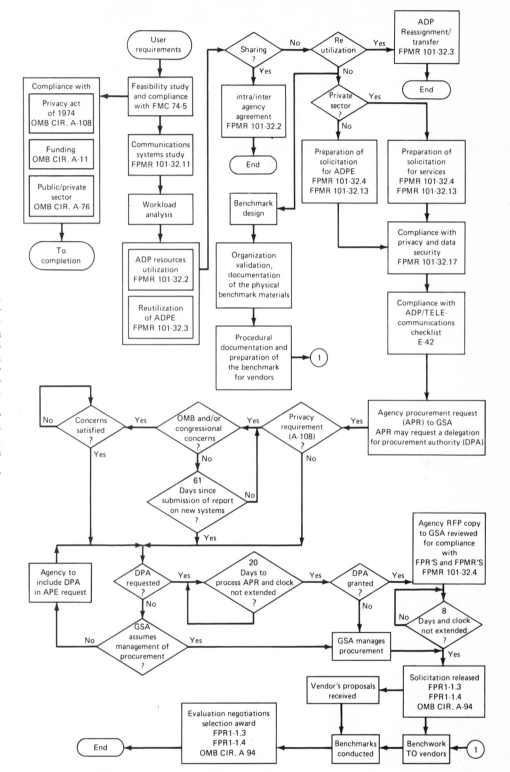

ILLUSTRATION 6–1. Federal Government Acquisition Procedure: This complex procedure does not occur in private industry; however, some of the safeguards indicated are worth considering, particularly the automatically imposed acquisition delay that lessens the likelihood of hasty use of unproven equipment. *Source: Guidelines for Benchmarking ADP Systems in the Competitive Procurement Environment,* Federal Information Processing Standards Publication 42–1, National Bureau of Standards, U.S. Department of Commerce, May 15, 1977, p. 7.

will take three years to have functioning correctly for what took three years and now functions correctly. The same editorial repeats a statement in a report to the U.S. House of Representatives Appropriation Committee: "In the rapidly changing computer industry, three years represents a point of obsolescence." The vendors have performed a good job of brainwashing. A more true statement is that it takes about three years to obtain a reliable computer, and that obsolescence depends on the users' requirements and what is available to meet those requirements—but only what is available that is reliable.

The federal government's slowness in acquiring equipment is due partly to the thoroughness recommended for proper acquisition and partly to all the checks and controls included in their procedure. Illustration 6–1 shows this complexity, which

ILLUSTRATION 6-2. The Acquisition Procedure.

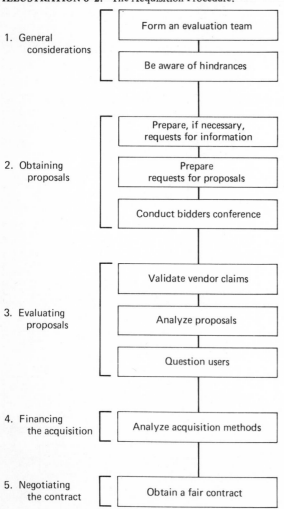

does not exist at nongovernment organizations and which, while frustratingly slow, lessens the likelihood of hasty acquisitions and lengthy regrets. Review of this procedure should stimulate precise definition of a simpler procedure, and one defined in adequate detail. The acquisition procedure consists of five phases:

- General considerations
- Obtaining proposals
- Evaluating proposals
- Financing the acquisition
- Negotiating the contract

In actual practice, financing and contract agreements affect evaluation and selection. For the sake of discussion, they are treated separately. The five phases of the acquisition procedure and their components are shown in Illustration 6-2. These phases are examined from the viewpoint of computer acquisition, and are similar for acquisition of peripherals and software. Because software acquisition has several special considerations, especially because of the increasing attention it is receiving—and should receive—the final section of this chapter reviews these five phases in terms of the special considerations and precautions required for software acquisition.

GENERAL CONSIDERATIONS

The data center manager is responsible for reviewing recommendations and for approving or rejecting these recommendations, but is not responsible for doing the actual analysis. For this purpose the best approach is to form a team to evaluate acquisitions; the minimum approach is to assign only one person to this task. In either case, technical, financial, and legal assistance must be available for consultation and for review of relevant analysis and conclusions. Financial representation is necessary to assure that no significant financial aspects are ignored, and legal representation is necessary for review of contracts. By having one or more persons permanently assigned to this procedure, expertise is developed and the procedure is carried out with increasing smoothness and certainty. Many large organizations have several persons assigned full time to equipment evaluation.

Two evaluation groups that have had outstanding success in selecting computer equipment are the Navy's Automatic Data Processing Equipment Selection Office (ADPESO) and the Air Force's Directorate of Automatic Data Processing Equipment Selection, with the Navy having about 22 persons and the Air Force about 65.[1] The activities and methods of these groups provide a standard that should guide the formation of similar groups and a standard to judge the adequacy of the groups formed. One of the most authoritative guides to computer acquisition was prepared by Dr. Edward O. Joslin, the head of the Techniques and Analysis Division of ADPESO, in his book *Computer Selection.*[2]

Several factors complicate and hinder the evaluation and selection procedure:

1. *Divergence of objectives.* The data center manager is concerned with maximum performance for the dollar; the user wants the best service possible, customarily with little concern for expenses; technicians want exposure to the latest and most interesting technology; and vendors focus on maximum profit. Realizing the different motivations involved provides the data center manager with some perspective when evaluating differing judgments.

2. *Prestige and image.* Pressure generally exists for the data center manager to select equipment that is considered the state-of-the-art, even though less-impressive alternatives may be more reliable and more productive at less cost. Some organizations have taken the attitude that the "bells and whistles" of the latest computers should generally be bypassed, even considering such alternatives as used computers.

3. *Unwarranted preference.* The tendency to remain with one vendor without even considering the relative merits of other vendors is prevalent in the computer industry. The reasons for this attitude are many, such as avoidance of complicating the existing configuration, an attempt to follow the safest route, and the existence of good rapport with the vendor personnel. These reasons are basically emotional, pushing aside the reality that other alternatives may provide more productivity for the money invested.

4. *Choice of vendors.* Because many vendors exist, it is time-consuming to request proposals from all of them and to evaluate those proposals. To minimize this difficulty, an attempt should be made to prescreen vendors as to the absolute unsuitability of their products in meeting present and future "mandatory" requirements. Further

---

[1] E. M. Timmreck, "Computer Selection Methodology," *Computing Surveys,* December 1973, p. 203.
[2] Edward O. Joslin, *Computer Selection* (Reading, Mass.: Addison-Wesley, 1968).

elimination is possible because of doubts about vendor reputation and service facilities.

5. *Incompatibility of vendor measurements.* Vendors use different measurements for stating the characteristics of their equipment; in effect, they speak different languages. In some instances the measurements are the same, but what is measured is different; for example, they may state processing speed in terms of the millions of instructions per second (mips), but the number of instructions required to complete a specific and equivalent task may vary. This explains why many computer evaluators prefer to judge productivity by how long it takes to process a typical workload, instead of comparing nanosecond add-times and transfer rates.

6. *Related costs and delays.* Many costs and activities are not considered when comparing alternatives, causing unexpected difficulties, delays, and expenses. These include the cost and time required for conversion of programs and the training of personnel.

7. *Forecast of future needs.* Forecasts are approximate even with insight into user department's present workload and system changes.

8. *Subjective evaluation.* Many of the criteria used for evaluation require judgment and thus will vary from one evaluator to another. The only protection is to be aware of the items requiring subjective judgment and to proceed cautiously.

OBTAINING PROPOSALS

To obtain proposals to meet user requirements, requests for proposals (RFPs) are prepared by users and submitted to vendors. When many vendors are being considered, an excessive amount of time may be needed to evaluate RFPs. Some vendors are likely to be eliminated because of doubts about their reliability or because of their inability to provide services wanted. Other vendors are eliminated by considering their ability to meet mandatory requirements.

Mandatory requirements must be clearly defined and distinguished from other requirements. A mandatory requirement is a requirement that must be met; it is *not* optional. If a vendor cannot meet a mandatory requirement, that vendor is automatically rejected, no matter how praiseworthy the proposal in other respects. Requirements that are not mandatory are often referred to as desirable requirements. Since the word "desirable" has the connotation of luxury extras, many persons object to its use. Because of this objection, substitute words and phrases have been tried. The Navy uses the phrase "other requirements," and the Air Force uses the phrase "required special optional features"; the first, although acceptable, lacks precision, and the second has contradictory terms. It seems that the phrases "mandatory specifications" and "preferred specifications" would be clearer, especially since, to complicate the matter further, the word "requirements" indicates that something is mandatory and must be present. Putting aside this bickering, the phrases generally accepted and used—"mandatory requirements" and "desirable requirements"—will continue to be used in this chapter.

If too many vendors still qualify, they can be narrowed further by obtaining more information by issuing a request for information (RFI). The RFI will indicate intent and the mandatory requirements. One point should be made about mandatory requirements: they should be kept to an absolute minimum. It would be ridiculous to reject an exceptional proposal because a requirement had been classified as mandatory but is not. It is unlikely, for example, that a maximum cost of $500,000 or a deadline of 20 weeks is mandatory; a bid of $501,000 and a deadline of 21 weeks are likely to be acceptable—and thus, these two criteria should be considered desirable requirements.

With the selection of the vendors most likely to meet the data center's equipment needs, RFPs can be prepared. These should be prepared to provide all the information needed and to guide responses so they will be uniform in format and terminology, making later comparison simple and direct. A good representative RFP is shown in Appendix F. RFPs must include the following:

1. *Statement of purpose.* Vendors should be given a perspective of what is to be accomplished. Should the proposal support only batch processing? Also support remote job entry? How about distributed processing? Is capability to modify the configuration to expand, to include redundancy for reliability, a primary concern? The more precise this statement, the more likely vendors will be to respond with proposals that are adequate for the user's intentions, and the easier the proposals will be to compare. Requirements should be stated so that they are not directed at, and can be met by, only one or a few of the vendors, automatically eliminating potentially excellent proposals.

2. *Deadline for proposals.* A deadline must be established to maintain control of the evaluation and selection procedure and to give all vendors equal time to prepare their proposals. The deadline should be adequate and should be adhered to. Vendors will have an opportunity to comment on the adequacy of this deadline at the "bidders conference." For the sake of fairness to all vendors, the deadline agreed upon must be adhered to, with exceptions only when adequately justified. For example, a proposal lost in the mail justifies waiting a *short* time.

3. *Date for the bidders conference.* Clarification of intentions and requirements may be necessary for vendors, possibly only for confirmation of assumptions. By gathering together all the vendors who will bid on a request, all vendors receive the same information; their doubts, if any, are eliminated, and thus all are treated equally and cannot complain later about discrimination in presenting information and providing guidelines. Anything told to a vendor privately may provide unfair advantage and should be conveyed to the other vendors.

4. *Mandatory requirements.* As stated earlier, mandatory requirements are those requirements that must be met, without any exceptions. Although these should be kept to a minimum to avoid unnecessary restrictions, they nevertheless must include all requirements that, if not met, will make the proposal unsatisfactory. Instead of concentrating on minute measures of nanoseconds, the ability and capacity to do the work intended should be judged. Thus, it should include a statement of the weekly time constraints for completing a workload. In addition, it should include such items as the number of terminals that must be supported now and later, the storage capacity required, and the degree of reliability necessary.

5. *Desirable requirements.* This includes the users' preferences, none of which are indispensable. It may be desirable for whatever is proposed to be compatible with specific peripherals and specific software, but not necessary. If this list becomes extensive, as it sometimes does, it is advisable to segment them into groups of varying importance and to clearly indicate which are most important and which are relatively less important.

6. *Request for proposal specifics.* Naturally, the primary information requested is exactly what products and services the vendor will supply. This should include information on the maintenance and backup provided and on vendor responsibility and action if the user is dissatisfied with the products or service. The financial information provided should include the costs for the acquisition alternatives, which include rental, leasing, purchase, or any hybrid arrangement the vendor may consider. Besides one-

time and on-going expenses, the vendors should supply all on-request service costs, such as special requests for maintenance and backup, which may be absorbed as part of the acquisition contract.

7. *Request for user-support requirements.* This contains items often forgotten—until it is too late. What are the environmental requirements for products and services that the user is responsible for? Who absorbs the costs and what assistance will the vendor supply? How much program conversion is necessary and how will the vendor assist? How much training is required and is provided by the vendor? These considerations are important because they can be time consuming and costly.

Joslin makes an excellent recommendation when he suggests that the RFP be replaced by a *solicitation document.* The same information is provided to vendors as on an RFP, and the same requests are made, but the solicitation document is a turnaround document. Each vendor need only supply the information requested in spaces made available, and return this document. This approach has many advantages. It eliminates the need to retype information and possibly adding errors. The mandatory requirements can be preceded by a paragraph stating that the following requirements must be met and, if they are met, requesting a signature as indication of such, and also requesting identification of sources to be referenced for verification that mandatory requirements are actually met and have not been misinterpreted. Although less critical, reference sources must also be requested for vendor responses to desirable requirements.

A final benefit is that a single document provides all the user statements and vendor responses, with all the vendors supplying their responses in the same format, making a comparison easy. An ideal situation is to receive vendor's approval to include the solicitation document as part of the final contract. Each vendor's opinion of this practice can be obtained by including on the solicitation document the question, Can this document be included as part of the final contract? Agreement to this practice will avoid promises and claims that are unrealistic or that a vendor had no intention of keeping, and will avoid omissions in the contract.

After the vendors have had adequate time to examine the solicitation document, clarification may be necessary, even if only to confirm the necessity of restrictions included or to explore possibilities not mentioned. By having all vendors present when additional information and guidelines are presented to any single vendor, all vendors hear the responses and thus no one had unfair advantage over the other vendors.

EVALUATING PROPOSALS

To properly evaluate proposals, many factors must be considered, and a large variety of questions must be answered. Some of the questions to be answered are:

Are all mandatory requirements met?
How well are desirable requirements satisfied?
How do costs compare?
Are there any special cost arrangements?
What training is needed?
Who performs the training and where?
How good is the documentation?
Can delivery and installation meet the deadline?
What is the MTBF (mean time between failures)?
What is the MTTR (mean time to repair)?
What preventive maintenance is recommended?
What maintenance is provided?
How financially sound is the company?
How do users rate equipment reliability and company service?

Answering these questions can be time consuming and is likely to provide an accumulation of vast documentation and personnel comments and notes. If a document such as the solicitation document is not used, the information provided is certain to be in different formats, using different terminology and measurements, and is certain to make comparison tedious and inefficient—and unsure. Thus, use of a standard format and insistance on adherence to specified terminology and measurements are strongly recommended. The intention is not to limit their initiative and creativity, but to make their ingenuity and the benefits of their proposals clearly apparent and compatible in format, terminology, and measurements to permit easy comparison. The proposal-evaluation procedure consists of three steps:

- Validate vendor claims
- Analyze proposed alternatives
- Question users of equipment and services

Validate Vendor Claims

Any vendor who states that one or more mandatory requirements cannot be met is automatically rejected. The remaining vendors have stated that they meet these requirements and have indicated references for verification. These claims must be verified, looking for adequate proof that the mandatory requirements were properly understood and are actually satisfied. Then the references supplied for the desirable requirements are verified. Instead of searching through large quantities of vendor-supplied manuals, other sources can be used to verify computer characteristics, such as the *Auerbach Computer Characteristics Digest.*

The last item to validate, and often the most time consuming, is each vendor's claim to process the workload within the time limits specified. In addition, it must also be determined as precisely as possible how much time will be consumed. This in many cases is the deciding factor in selecting one proposal over the others. Of the methods used for determining time consumption, three have gained the highest user acceptance: hand-timing, simulation, and benchmarking. Hand-timing requires estimating the number of processing and I/O operations a job will perform and then estimating the total running time for the job. This approach is unsatisfactory because it cannot account for the overhead of the system software and effect of overlapping operations, especially in a multiprogramming environment. Simulation requires the processing of selected input by a simulation software package (such as SCERT, CASE, and SAM), which simulates how the computer being evaluated will process the input, and generates reports on the computer's performance. Users of this technique have found it inaccurate, and some believe that an error of ±30 percent is possible. The remaining technique, benchmarking, is generally the most favored and will now be examined in some detail. Illustration 6–3 indicates how heated the conflict is between adherents to simulation and benchmarking.

The Federal Information Processing Standards (FIPS) Publication 42, *Guidelines for Benchmarking ADP Systems in the Competitive Procurement Environment,* states that benchmarking "consists of user-witnessed running of a group (mix) of programs representative of the user's predicted workload on a vendor's proposed computer system in order to validate system performance."[3] Benchmarking is also referred to as "benchmark mix demonstration" and live test demonstration (LTD). The FIPS definition stresses two points: (1) The actual running of the benchmark should be observed by the user. This provides several benefits, which include assuring adherence to procedures established for all vendors and making the results of the benchmark easier to interpret. (2) The programs selected for the benchmark should be representative of the actual workload. Thus, if 75 percent of the workload is I/O bound, of the programs selected, 75 percent of the selected programs should also be I/O bound.

Phillip C. Howard, Editor of *EDP Performance Review,* asks the question, "Why is it that for all the thousands of benchmarks that have been conducted so few have been documented in the literature?"[4] The reasons he gives consist of the following:

1. Vendors, especially the losers, are reluctant to admit the results.
2. Legal departments may be concerned about publicizing the results.
3. Trade magazines are reluctant to print material that may upset advertisers.
4. Magazines less dependent on advertisers, who are considered more academically oriented, may consider benchmarks crude.
5. Users who performed benchmarks may not be confident in their findings, and thus may not want to expose their approach and conclusions to their peers.[5]

It is Howard's conclusion that users will be less reluctant to release benchmark procedures and conclusions for publication, and magazines less reluctant to print these, "if the benchmark process were better defined, the objectives better stated, and the results less subject to erroneous interpretation."[6] The benchmarking procedure is rather straightforward; it consists of preparing for bench-

---

[3] *Guidelines for Benchmarking ADP Systems in Competitive Procurement Environment,* Federal Information Processing Standards Publication 42-1, National Bureau of Standards, U.S. Department of Commerce, May 15, 1977, p. 5.

[4] Phillip C. Howard, "Measuring System Performance with Benchmarks," *EDP Performance Review,* September 1973, p. 1.

[5] Ibid.

[6] Ibid.

The Benchmark/Simulation Controversy

Since the first "general purpose" computer simulation packages (SCERT, CASE, SAM) appeared on the market there has been an on-going controversy over which method is better for system selection, simulation or benchmarking. Needless to say, the major proponents of the simulation approach have been the vendors of simulation packages, although they have a reasonably strong following of apparently satisfied users.

One of the most outspoken individuals on the side of simulation has been Fred C. Ihrer, President of COMRESS, the originator of SCERT. In a November 1972 article in *Computers and Automation,* Mr. Ihrer stated his case against benchmarking in no uncertain terms. The article was primarily in response to a June 1972 decision by the GSA that benchmarking was to be "preferred" to simulation as a method for evaluating system performance. Specifically, the GSA ruling stated that (1) simulation input shall not be used as the only means of describing DP requirements in bid solicitations, (2) solicitation documents shall not require bidders to use a specific system simulator, and (3) bids will not be construed to be nonresponsive solely on the basis of simulation results.

Although Mr. Ihrer did not fault the GSA for these specific rulings, he naturally took the opposite view, namely that simulation was to be preferred to benchmarking for performance evaluation. His major arguments against benchmarking were that a benchmark doesn't tell a user why a program ran as long as it did, how long the rest of the workload will run, how long a program will run when combined with other runs; that it tells nothing about system utilization, reserve system capacity, queueing delays, turnaround, or bottlenecks; and that it yields no analysis of individual program execution, and provides no estimate of optimum blocking, file assignments, schedules, costs, etc. He states that the reason "benchmarking does none of these things is because it does not take into account the powers of third-generation computer systems." He finally draws a distinction between "measurement" and "analysis", categorizing benchmarking as a measurement tool and simulation as an analysis tool. He concludes:

"But benchmarking is one thing, and analysis is another. On the whole, as the answer to the evaluation of computer systems performance, benchmarking is outdated, simplistic, and hopelessly inadequate. It is clearly and unmistakably no substitute for simulation. These, we think, are inescapable conclusions."

As one would expect, not everyone agreed completely with Mr. Ihrer's portrayal of benchmarking. In rebuttal to his viewpoint, Norris S. Goff, a computer specialist with the U.S. Dept. of Agriculture, took the opposite view in a May 1973 article, also in *Computers and Automation.* He stated that Ihrer had failed to present the reasons for benchmarking and that his description of the benchmarking process was inadequate. He defines the most common elements of a benchmark to be (1) a mix of jobs, representative of the users' projected peak workload, to be completed within a limited time, (2) a demonstration of data storage equipment and techniques to aid in establishing configuration requirements, (3) computer programs designed to test specific required functions, and (4) the demonstration of other system features which do not lend themselves to testing by common computer programs. He goes on to describe in greater detail how the throughput job mix is constructed and makes the point that "system software has an overwhelming impact on performance of a large system." He expresses doubt at the ability of any simulator to adequately model the complexities of constantly changing software. He does admit that the modeling of hardware is somewhat more successful when software does not have a major impact on performance. His conclusion is stated in equally as strong terms as Mr. Ihrer's.

"It is my opinion that benchmarking is at present the only available means of evaluating large and complex ADP systems by a common standard. The diversity of computer hardware and techniques employed in large systems precludes their simulation by a common model. The complexity, diversity, and dynamic nature of system software also precludes their simulation by a common model."

Who is right in this controversy or is there even a clearcut, yes or no answer? It is our feeling that Mr. Ihrer tends to weaken his own case somewhat by overkill. Some of his arguments simply don't hold water for well-designed and well-run benchmarks. Mr. Goff, on the other hand, draws conclusions against simulation which are not particularly well supported by solid evidence.

The fact of the matter is that there is a place for both approaches. Benchmarks have their place in situations involving equipment upgrades and replacements where the performance of new equipment on existing and expanding workloads is the primary consideration. The use of sound human analysis of benchmark results does permit reasonably accurate projection of total workloads, system utilization, reserve capacity and other system characteristics which Mr. Ihrer claims to be impossible. Simulation is generally oriented more toward a total workload analysis and bypasses the need for human projections but is, of course, based on "artificial" representations of the programs to be run. Simulation may be preferable to benchmarks in cases where new application or processing approaches are involved, where the proposed hardware configurations are not available for benchmarking, or where the workload is unevenly distributed over time, resulting in major peaks and valleys of utilization.

There is also an element of human preference to be considered. Some individuals will feel more comfortable with the "real-world" connotation of a benchmark and the feeling that he has observed with his own eyes how well a system performs. He must, however, be confident that his benchmark is truly representative of his total workload. Another individual may prefer the broader evaluation provided by a simulation and the avoidance of problems associated with running benchmarks at many vendor locations. He may also wish to make use of simulation as a system design aid. Just as the individual running a benchmark must be confident that he has a representative set of programs, the simulation user must have confidence in his ability to define his workload and in the accuracy of the simulation.

ILLUSTRATION 6-3. The Conflict Between Proponents of Benchmarks and Simulation: *Source:* Phillip C. Howard, EDP Performance Review, Sept. 1973, p. 4.

marking, monitoring the benchmark procedure, and analyzing the results.

Preparing for Benchmarking. The first step in the procedure is assigning someone to the function of benchmark coordinator. This person is responsible for answering vendor questions, providing missing or defective benchmark material, and providing information that will support equal and fair opportunity for all vendors. Thus, besides technical knowledge, this person must be patient and diplomatic. Then estimates must be made of how much time is required to convert programs, if necessary, and to provide data, job-control information, and supporting documentation to vendors. When this has been estimated, on-site attendance at benchmarking demonstrations is scheduled.

The selection of representative programs requires insight into the characteristics of the total workload to be processed by the system to be selected. The time required to process the selected workload will be used to project the time required for the total workload. For this reason, it must represent a realistic mix of CPU-bound programs, I/O-bound programs, compiles, sorts, and other utilities. It is desirable to select a mix that requires from one to two hours of processing. The longer the run, the more accurate the results, minimizing the distortion, called "tailing," that occurs in a multiprogramming environment. Tailing occurs when all jobs selected for the benchmark are completed but one. This one job, if included as part of the timing, does not represent reality since, in actual processing, other programs will overlap with this program. If the time for this program is short, it can be ignored; if it is not short, however, only part of this additional time should be used.

Any program conversion necessary should conform to the organization's standards, not to conventions that conflict with these standards but are advantageous to a vendor, that is, uses his equipment more efficiently.

Before the benchmark should be considered ready for the vendors, it should be run on the data center's present computer. This dry run assures that all programs, data, job-control information, and supporting documentation are ready for vendor use.

Monitoring the Benchmark Procedure. The primary reason for observing the actual benchmark

processing at the vendor's site is to assure no variation from the defined procedure. The goal is to obtain fair and equal benchmark demonstrations from all vendors, not permitting short cuts that improve the performance of a vendor's equipment where the short cuts ignore processing requirements and data center standards.

Two other advantages are gained from monitoring the processing. First, it is possible to obtain clarification of reports produced and conclusions arrived at. By questioning vendor personnel about the meaning of report entries and the terminology used, later confusion is minimized when the results are interpreted and compared with those of other vendors. Another advantage of monitoring is the opportunity to observe the complexity and potential problems of the job control and the operating system and to become aware of useful features and output that the vendor may not have stressed or even mentioned.

It is advisable to prepare a checklist of information wanted, such as total elapsed time, CPU time, and core used, and to obtain confirmation of this information from vendor representatives. In addition, operational and procedural questions should also be listed. For example, what job-control statement changes are required from one run of a program to the next? How are error conditions indicated and where are these conditions explained? How well are these conditions explained? How will the computer system affect the tape library procedure, scheduling, and other procedures?

Analyzing the Results. Basically, this final step of validating vendor claims assures that all computer performance and related information has been obtained and is understood. Thus, the elapsed time for the benchmark should be projected for the total workload. Any areas difficult to compare should be noted. It may be possible to enter on a single sheet for each vendor the benchmark results, aiming to provide as easy a means as possible for comparing and analyzing the alternative proposals, the next step in the proposal evaluation procedure.

Analyze Proposed Alternatives

The benchmark demonstrations provide performance information, but other factors are involved in a full analysis of proposals. Proposals must also be judged for vendor service, maintenance provisions, and all the desired requirements entered on the solicitation document. Four techniques have received particular favor with various users; although the names used for these techniques vary, they are generally referred to as the weighted-scoring technique, the cost/effectiveness technique, the cost-value technique, and the requirements-costing technique. The last two techniques, requirements-costing and cost-value, are nearly identical evaluation techniques developed by Dr. Edward O. Joslin. Requirements-costing is his latest technique and is explained in detail.

The Weighted-Scoring Technique. All desired requirements and other factors to be used as criteria for evaluating each proposal are assigned a weight, that is, a value indicating the relative importance of each criterion. Then for each proposal a score is determined for each criterion, which is a value indicating the degree to which the criterion

is satisfied in that proposal. By multiplying each score for a criterion by the weight assigned to that criterion, a weighted score is obtained for that criterion for the proposal being considered. If, for example, the criterion "reliability" has a weight of 10 and the score for proposal *A* (considering a scale of 0 to 100) is 90, then the weighted score is 10 times 90, a weighted score of 900. This is the weighted score for a single criterion for proposal A. By adding the weighted scores for all criteria for proposal A, its total weighted score is obtained. This process is repeated for each proposal. The proposal with the highest total (the highest-ranking proposal) will be the chosen proposal if the final phase of proposal evaluation, questioning of users, does not cause adjustment of scores.

The form shown in Illustration 6–4 assists in performing the required calculations. The form is annotated to indicate where assigned and calculated values are entered. The weight for the first criterion is placed at *A*, the score for that criterion for the first proposal is placed at *B*, the weighted

ILLUSTRATION 6–4. Weighted-Scoring Analysis: This form is convenient for evaluating alternatives by the weight of importance assigned to each criterion, and by the score assigned to each criterion for each alternative.

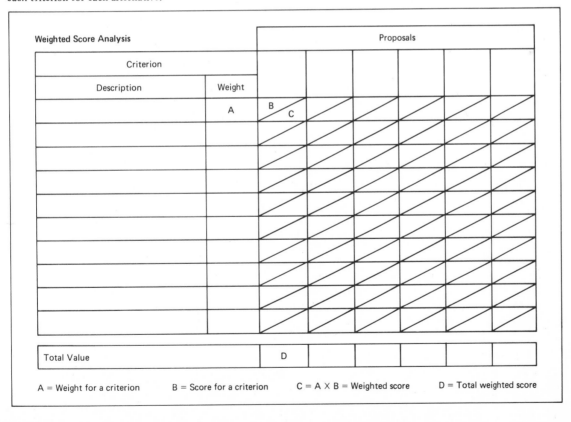

CHANGES REQUIRED	VALUE
None	$60,000
Less than 2%	30,000
Less than 4%	20,000
5%	10,000
6%	0
7–8%	–10,000
9–10%	–40,000
10–15%	Up to –$60,000

ILLUSTRATION 6-5. Value Template for Code Conversion: Dollar values are directly related to the time and cost required for COBOL code conversion, indicating cost benefits and penalties. *Source:* Edward O. Joslin, *Computer Selection* (Mass.: Addison-Wesley, 1968), p. 137.

score (*A* times *B*) is placed at *C,* and the total of all weighted scores for the first proposal is placed at *D.* A major criticism of this technique is that cost is not given adequate importance. Even if cost is included as a criterion, how can it be compared to performance or to any of the other criteria? Is cost as important as performance? Twice as important? Ten times as important? In other words, how much weight is assigned to cost?

The Cost/Effectiveness Technique. This technique takes the weighted-scoring technique one step further, attempting to minimize the deficiency of treating cost as a separate factor. The cost/effectiveness technique simply requires that the total system cost for each proposal be divided by the total weighted score for that proposal. The proposal with the lowest ratio is the chosen proposal. This ratio indicates the cost-to-effectiveness value; but as Joslin comments, this technique does not produce results that indicate a "meaningful relationship between cost and effectiveness."[7]

The Requirements-Costing Technique. The principle feature of this technique (as of the cost-value technique) is that for every criterion used, a dollar value is pre-established. This value is usually an estimation of the financial loss if the criterion cannot be satisfied, or can be satisfied at an excessive cost. Since it is generally more appropriate to assign a sequence of costs for criteria, a "value template," as Joslin phrases it, can be prepared for each criterion requiring more than one cost value. Two such value templates are shown in Illustrations

[7] Edward O. Joslin, "Requirements Costing: A Superior Computer Evaluation Methodology," in *Analysis, Design, and Selection of Computer Systems,* 2nd ed., ed. Edward O. Joslin (Clifton, Virginia: College Readings, 1974) p. 164.

6-5 and 6-6. The value template in Illustration 6-5 shows that $60,000 is subtracted from the bid if no program-coding changes are required; $0 is subtracted if 6 percent must be changed: –$40,000 is subtracted if 9 percent or 10 percent must be changed—in other words, $40,000 is actually added to the bid. The value template in Illustration 6-6 applies to equipment-delivery date, where early delivery financially benefits the data center and thus justifies subtracting a cost from the bid; however, late delivery creates additional data center expenses, making that proposal more expensive, and thus justifies adding to the cost of the bid. The proposals are then evaluated considering *all* costs (the vendor's bid plus the cost for each criterion). The proposal with the lowest life cost is selected. Joslin states that the costs added to the bid should include the life costs for all expenses related to the proposal, such as for the environment, personnel, and supplies, also considering bids in terms of the different financial acquisition means.[8] A simple analysis using the requirements-costing technique is shown in Illustration 6-7. Proposal *C* is chosen since it has the lowest total cost. However, observing the differences between the highest and lowest total values, the difference is only $35,000 for equipment costing over $1 million. This is less than 3 percent of the total cost. If all criteria have been included, the analysis can be accepted—but if the difference is small, as it is here, and if factors such as vendor rapport and cooperation have not been considered, these factors may justify considering another choice.

[8] Edward O. Joslin, "Requirements Costing."

ILLUSTRATION 6-6. Value Template for Deadline Date: Dollar values are directly related to the financial gains from early receipt of equipment, and to financial losses from late delivery. *Source:* Edward O. Joslin, *Computer Selection* (Mass: Addison-Wesley, 1968), p. 137.

DELIVERY DATE	VALUE
January 1969	$ 50,000
February 1969	25,000
March 1969	10,000
April 1969	0
May 1969	–10,000
June 1969	–30,000
July 1969	–60,000
August 1969	–100,000

Evaluation Items	Maximum Values	Vendor's Cost		
		A	B	C
Vendor Costs		$1,000,000	1,200,000	1,300,000
Other Costs		100,000	95,000	90,000
Assessments				
System Potential	$400,000	240,000	100,000	20,000
Technical Characteristics	200,000	60,000	35,000	10,000
Vendor Support	50,000	40,000	25,000	0
Total Cost		$1,440,000	1,455,000	1,420,000

ILLUSTRATION 6-7. Requirements-Costing Technique: All the costs incurred to obtain mandatory and desirable requirements are summed, and the lowest total is the alternative selected. *Source:* Edward O. Joslin, "Requirements Costing: A Superior Computer Evaluation Methodology," in *Analysis, Design and Selection of Computer Systems*, 2nd ed., ed. Edward O. Joslin (Virginia: College Readings, 1974), p. 164.

Joslin rightly believes that all criteria should have been stated and analyzed, and the results of the analysis should be accepted.

Question Users of Equipment and Services

The vendor may state that their equipment is reliable, and the benchmark demonstration may not have indicated any problems. The vendor may boast of 24-hour, 7-day service. There may be no reason to question any of these claims, but it is only necessary to read a few issues of *Computerworld* to realize that claims and promises have been made and not met. In most instances, intentions were sincere, but in some situations the impetus to be awarded the contract led to exaggerated statements. The results have been inefficiency, loss of competitive edge, financial loss, and time-consuming litigation. Thus, caution and a doubting attitude are wise.

The time spent visiting and questioning users of the equipment and services being considered is not a guarantee that difficulties will be avoided, but if a serious problem exists, it is likely to become apparent. Consider the situation where equipment is released to the market before it is ready. This, unfortunately, is not uncommon. Users who have become accustomed to standing around watching repairmen working on the latest equipment, while the old equipment is chugging along as reliably as ever, are sure to comment on the extensive downtime and lack of productivity. If problems are uncovered, the proposal chosen may be changed, or the acquisition may be delayed.

One warning: Do not question users recommended by the vendor. The vendor is obviously going to recommend only satisfied customers—and they may be one in a hundred. User opinions also can be obtained from surveys conducted by publishers such as Auerbach and Datapro.

The pros and cons for proposals can be presented with the same lack of real commitment used by a speaker at the Georgia Legislature to present facetiously the pros and cons of whiskey drinking:

> Gentlemen, I am willing to take a stand on any issue at any time even though it may be fraught with controversy. Now on the whiskey question—if when you say whiskey you mean the Devil's Brew, the Poison Scourge, the Demon Rum that defiles innocents, dethrones reason, creates misery and poverty, yea, literally takes bread out of the mouths of babes—then I am against it heart and soul!

> But Sires, if when you say whiskey you mean the oil of conversation, the philosophic elixir that is consumed when good fellows get together—if you mean Christmas cheer—that stimulating drink that puts spring in an old man's step on a frosty morning, the sale of which pours into our treasury untold millions of dollars which are used to provide tender care for our little crippled children, our blind, our deaf, our pitifully aged and infirm—then I am for it—100 percent.

> That is my stand. I shall not be swayed from it. I shall not compromise.[9]

This legislator was parodying the tendency to be noncommittal; a data center manager, however, cannot be noncommital. Choices must be made, and the techniques described make the process of choosing methodical, supporting careful compilation of factors affecting proposal selection and the assignment of values to these factors. The goal is to use the analytic tools available to arrive at a reasoned conclusion: not to be indecisive, accepting

[9] J. David Williamson, "Experience in a Multi-Vendor Shop," *Data Management*, September 1974, p. 38.

all choices and deciding on none; not to be impulsive, deciding intuitively on only a few factors and a few facts.

FINANCING THE ACQUISITION

Types of Acquisition Methods

The various means of acquiring equipment are part of the process of evaluating proposals. The requirements-costing technique includes these means as different cost bases, in effect, as alternative bids from a single vendor. There are basically three acquisition methods: rental, leasing, and purchase, with several variations for each.

Rental. This means of equipment acquisition refers to obtaining equipment from the vendor; it is also referred to as a *vendor lease.* Rental is usually a short-term lease, requiring periodic renewal and negotiation. Its primary advantages are that the user does not have to retain equipment for a long period of time when it has proved to be unsatisfactory or has become obsolete—although, as repeatedly mentioned, the tendency to obtain the latest unproven "advance" may lead to poor productivity and frustration because of error-prone equipment and software. Rental permits flexibility in equipment choice and configuration at each renewal period, and it also provides financial leverage. The primary disadvantages are that it is the most expensive of the equipment-acquisition methods, and additional charges are added if the user exceeds the number of operating hours per month agreed upon by user and vendor.

A variation of the rental agreement is the *lease with purchase option.* This option permits the user to purchase the equipment after a predetermined amount of rental has been paid. Thus, equipment that has been found to be satisfactory and will meet requirements for a reasonably long time period can be obtained at a reduced cost, instead of having to negotiate a separate agreement for an inevitably higher purchase price.

Leasing. This term is used when referring to third-party leases. A leasing company purchases the equipment from the vendor and then leases it to the user. Third-party leasing of computer equipment started in 1956 as a result of a court ruling

against IBM, which directed IBM to sell as well as rent their equipment.[10] This ruling permitted a third-party to purchase from IBM and lease to users. The advantages of leasing, where this term is understood to refer to third-party leasing, are greater flexibility in leasing arrangements, lower cost, and no additional charge for use of equipment beyond any fixed number of hours. As for disadvantages, the time period of the lease is usually longer, and there is uncertainty as to how much, if any, personnel and software support the vendor will supply. The three types of lease arrangements prevalent are:

1. *The operating lease.* This is also referred to as a *partial-payout lease,* since the lease is relatively short and does not cover the cost and expenses of the lessor for the purchase and other expenses, plus profit, of the equipment. The cost of this lease is the most expensive third-party lease arrangement because of its short duration and the risk to the lessor of not having another user for the equipment when the short-term lease has ended.

2. *The finance lease.* This lease is also referred to as a *full-payout lease,* since it is generally a long-term lease that provides a means of purchasing the equipment. At the end of each lease period, the user has the option of purchasing the equipment, so that the previously paid leasing amounts and the purchase amount cover the lessor's purchase and supplementary expenses, plus profit and the residual value for the equipment, where the residual value is the equipment's value at the time of the purchase decision.

3. *The lease-to-ownership plan.* Joslin indicates that this is a method increasingly used by the Navy; in his own words, with this approach "monthly lease payments are made until some given number (normally 60 payments) have been made or until some given amount (the purchase price of the system) has been paid, and then title of the computer passes to the lessee. Until that time, however, the lessee has no obligation beyond a normal lease plan. Further, these Lease-to-Ownership Plans, over the stated systems life, normally cost little more than straight Lease

---

[10]Jerome Kleinfield, "Lease vs. Purchase Considerations," *EDP Solutions* (Debron, N.J.: Datapro Research Corp., 1976), p. E80-450-101.

Plans, and in some cases cost less."[11] The economic significance of this acquisition method is indicated when Joslin comments, "Had these programs been available five to ten years earlier, the cost of computers in the federal government would be $40 million less each year than it presently is."[12]

Purchase. Outright purchase of equipment is financially advantageous if the equipment will be retained for a period of time exceeding the trade-off point for leasing the same equipment. This usually occurs at about eight years. But purchasing exposes the user to the serious disadvantages of possibly owning unsatisfactory or obsolete equipment. The large initial money outlay and the potential difficulty of obtaining vendor maintenance service add to these disadvantages. In spite of these shortcomings, it is generally agreed that for long-term use of proven equipment, purchasing is financially the best method, leasing from a third-party is second best, and renting from a vendor is the poorest choice.[13]

An alternative to purchasing, avoiding the immediate large outlay of money, is to finance the purchase with a bank loan, usually for up to three years. This approach, however, incurs several disadvantages, such as the additional expense of interest, and also restrictions on the organization's actions without the bank's approval. The bank may be able to restrict the selling of certain assets and may even restrict the restructuring of the organization. These restrictions may cause investment opportunities to be lost, opportunities that may far exceed the financial benefits obtained by having money available for investment.

Analysis of Acquisition Methods

Three techniques used for financially analyzing the rent-lease-purchase decision that are *not* recommended are:

1. *Rate of return.* The average annual cash flow for the life of the investment is divided by the initial investment, producing an annual percentage rate; the higher the rate the better the investment.
2. *Pay-back method.* This method determines the amount of time required to recover the initial financial outlay.
3. *Break-even analysis.* Curves are drawn on a graph to relate accumulated costs against time; the points at which the curves cross indicate at what time periods purchasing becomes more beneficial than renting and leasing.

These techniques are criticized for various reasons, but they all have a common deficiency: they do not consider the time value of money, the changing value of money for each year. Illustration 6–8 clarifies this concept. If the dollar depreciates at 6 percent each year, the present value of $1.00 spent one year from now is $0.94340; four years from now it is $0.79209. To scale these values up, the present value of $1000 spent one year from now is $943.40, and four years from now it is $792.09.

A technique that is recommended and that includes consideration of the changing value of money is *discounted cash flow.* This method, however, does have the shortcoming that the rate, once chosen, remains constant for all time periods. Ted Szatrowski, vice-president at Peoples National Bank in Seattle, has very effectively explained and illustrated this technique.[14] Illustration 6–9 includes his table of typical purchase and rental costs for a computer system. Illustrations 6–10, 6–11, 6–12, and 6–13 show the discounted cash-flow-analysis tables for four acquisition methods: rental, full-payout lease, partial-payout lease, and purchase with zero residual.

The four cash-flow-analysis tables provide the present value for each of eight years at rates of 6, 8, 10, and 12 percent. The accumulated present-value costs for all eight years is shown in the year-0 column for each method. The tables include the factors affecting the cash flow, such as maintenance, insurance, and the various taxes.

The effect of the various rates on the financial advantageousness of the different acquisition methods after eight years is apparent in Illustration 6–14. As shown, a full-payout lease is a better choice than purchasing when the rate is greater than approximately 6.5 percent, and a partial-

[11] Edward O. Joslin, *Analysis, Design, and Selection of Computer Systems*, p. 343.

[12] Ibid., p. 348.

[13] Dick H. Brandon, Arnold D. Palley, and A. Michael O'Reilly, *Data Processing Management: Methods and Standards* (New York: Macmillan, 1975), p. 498.

[14] Ted Szatrowski, "Rent, Lease, or Buy," *Datamation*, February 1976.

Year:	0	1	2	3	4	5	6	7	8
Present Value Factor @ 6%	1.0000	.94340	.89000	.83962	.79209	.74726	.70496	.66506	.62741
Present Value Factor @ 8%	1.0000	.92593	.85734	.79383	.73503	.68058	.63017	.58349	.54027
Present Value Factor @ 10%	1.0000	.90909	.82645	.75131	.68301	.62092	.56447	.51316	.46651
Present Value Factor @ 12%	1.0000	.89286	.79719	.71178	.63552	.56743	.50663	.45235	.40388

ILLUSTRATION 6-8. Present Value Factors: If the value of money descreases 6% each year, the present value of $1000 five years from now is only $747.26; at 12% yearly decrease, only $567.43. *Source:* Ted Szatrowski, "Rent, Lease, or Buy," *Datamation,* Feb. 1976, p. 61.

	COST				RATIO ANALYSIS
EQUIPMENT DESCRIPTION	Purchase	Rental/Monthly	Monthly Maintenance	True Rental (Less Maintenance)	Purchase ÷ True Rental
370/145 Central Processing Unit (256 K)	$715,125.00	$14,932.00	$1,161.00	$13,771.00	51.9
1403-N1 Printer	34,350.00	885.00	199.00	686.00	50.0
2821-1 Control Unit	40,190.00	1,060.00	49.00	1,011.00	39.7
1419 Reader Sorter	124,470.00	2,714.00	252.00	2,462.00	50.5
2540-1 Card Reader/Punch	32,930.00	710.00	124.00	586.00	56.2
2314-B1 Disc Storage Control	61,570.00	1,620.00	62.00	1,558.00	39.5
2319-B1 Disc Storage	38,250.00	1,000.00	210.00	790.00	48.4
3803-1 Tape Control Unit	34,430.00	900.00	106.00	794.00	43.4
3420-3 Tape Unit (3)	50,520.00	1,320.00	195.00	1,125.00	44.9
TOTAL	$1,131,835.00	$25,141.00	$2,358.00	$22,783.00	49.6

ILLUSTRATION 6-9. Typical Computer System Purchase and Rental Costs: The total values shown are used for the cash flow anlaysis tables in Illustrations 6-10, 6-11, 6-12, and 6-13; these tables are then used to prepare the graphs in Illustrations 6-14 and 6-15. *Source:* Ted Szatrowski, "Rent, Lease, or Buy," *Datamation,* Feb. 1976, p. 61.

Year:	0	1	2	3	4	5	6	7	8
Rental Payments	—	301,692	301,692	301,692	301,692	301,692	301,692	301,692	301,692
Tax Savings	(37,728)*	(144,812)	(144,812)	(144,812)	(144,812)	(144,812)	(144,812)	(144,812)	(144,812)
After-tax Cash Flow	(37,728)*	156,880	156,880	156,880	156,880	156,880	156,880	156,880	156,880
Present Value Cost @ 6%	965,680	152,439	143,810	135,670	127,990	120,745	113,911	107,463	101,380
Present Value Cost @ 8%	899,854	151,068	139,878	129,516	119,922	111,039	102,814	95,198	88,147
Present Value Cost @ 10%	841,050	149,748	136,134	123,758	112,506	102,279	92,981	84,528	76,844
Present Value Cost @ 12%	788,344	148,474	132,566	118,362	105,681	94,358	84,248	75,221	67,162

*Investment tax credit of 3⅓%

ILLUSTRATION 6-10. Discounted Cash Flow Analysis for Rental. *Source:* Ted Szatrowski, "Rent, Lease, or Buy," *Datamation,* Feb. 1976, p. 61.

Year:	0	1	2	3	4	5	6	7	8
Lease Payments	—	206,802	206,802	206,802	206,802	206,802	206,802	206,802	206,802
Insurance & Property Tax (1.2% of Value)	—	13,582	12,414	11,124	9,699	8,125	6,387	4,467	2,344
Maintenance	—	28,296	28,296	28,296	28,296	28,296	28,296	28,296	28,296
Pre-tax Cash Flow		248,680	247,512	246,222	244,797	243,223	241,485	239,565	237,442
Tax Savings	(113,184)*	(119,366)	(118,806)	(118,187)	(117,503)	(116,747)	(115,913)	(114,991)	(113,972)
After-tax Cash Flow	(113,184)*	129,314	128,706	128,035	127,294	126,476	125,572	124,573	123,469
Present Value Cost @ 6%	698,675	125,653	117,984	110,725	103,853	97,344	91,178	85,333	79,789
Present Value Cost @ 8%	645,889	124,523	114,758	105,703	97,306	89,519	82,296	75,594	69,374
Present Value Cost @ 10%	598,814	123,435	111,687	101,003	91,392	82,456	74,425	67,121	60,479
Present Value Cost @ 12%	556,406	122,385	108,759	96,600	85,751	76,071	67,435	59,731	52,858

*Investment tax credit of 10%

ILLUSTRATION 6-11. Discounted Cash Flow Analysis for Full-Payout Lease. *Source:* Ted Szatrowski, "Rent, Lease, or Buy," *Datamation,* Feb. 1976, p. 62.

Year:	0	1	2	3	4	5	6	7	8
Lease Payments	—	271,522	266,997	262,472	257,946	253,421	248,896	244,370	239,845
Tax Savings	(113,184)*	(130,331)	(128,159)	(125,987)	(123,814)	(121,642)	(119,470)	(117,298)	(115,126)
After-tax Cash Flow	(113,184)*	141,191	138,838	136,485	134,132	131,779	129,426	127,072	124,719
Present Value Cost @ 6%	741,789	137,195	127,274	118,033	109,431	101,426	93,976	87,045	80,593
Present Value Cost @ 8%	687,062	135,961	123,792	112,679	102,534	93,273	84,821	77,110	70,076
Present Value Cost @ 10%	638,114	134,773	120,479	107,670	96,193	85,915	76,709	68,468	61,091
Present Value Cost @ 12%	594,183	133,627	117,321	102,975	90,357	79,261	69,504	60,929	53,393

*Investment tax credit of 10%

ILLUSTRATION 6-12. Discounted Cash Flow Analysis for Partial-Payout Lease. *Source:* Ted Szatrowski, "Rent, Lease, or Buy," *Datamation,* Feb. 1976, p. 62.

Year:	0	1	2	3	4	5	6	7	8
Purchase Payment	1,131,835	—	—	—	—	—	—	—	—
Depreciation	—	251,518	220,078	188,639	157,200	125,760	94,320	62,880	31,440
Insurance & Property Tax (1.2% of Value)	—	13,582	10,563	7,922	5,659	3,772	2,263	1,131	377
Maintenance	—	28,296	28,296	28,296	28,296	28,296	28,296	28,296	28,296
Pre-tax Cash Flow	1,131,835	41,878	38,859	36,218	33,955	32,068	30,559	29,427	28,673
Tax Savings	(113,184)*	(140,830)	(124,290)	(107,931)	(91,754)	(75,757)	(59,942)	(44,307)	(28,854)
After-tax Cash Flow	1,018,651	(98,952)	(85,431)	(71,713)	(57,799)	(43,689)	(29,383)	(14,880)	(181)
Present Value Cost @ 6%	679,902	(93,351)	(76,033)	(60,212)	(45,782)	(32,647)	(20,714)	(9,896)	(114)
Present Value Cost @ 8%	697,343	(91,623)	(73,243)	(56,928)	(42,484)	(29,734)	(18,516)	(8,682)	(98)
Present Value Cost @ 10%	713,302	(89,956)	(70,604)	(53,879)	(39,477)	(27,127)	(16,586)	(7,636)	(84)
Present Value Cost @ 12%	727,940	(88,350)	(68,105)	(51,044)	(36,732)	(24,790)	(14,886)	(6,731)	(73)

*Investment tax credit of 10%

ILLUSTRATION 6-13. Discounted Cash Flow Analysis for Purchase. *Source:* Ted Szatrowski, "Rent, Lease, or Buy," *Datamation*, Feb. 1976, p. 64.

ILLUSTRATION 6-14. The Effect of Rate on Accumulated Cost: For the rates used, as the rate increases, the accumulated cost after eight years makes leasing the best choice, with renting being the poorest choice. *Source:* Ted Szatrowski, "Rent, Lease, or Buy," *Datamation*, Feb. 1976, p. 64.

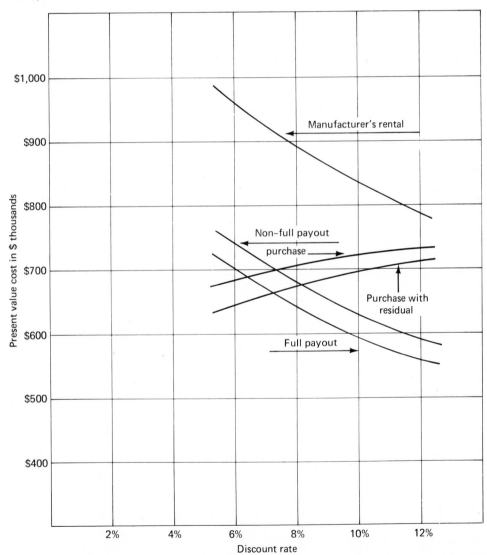

payout lease (here referred to as non-full-payout) is a better choice than purchasing when the rate is greater than approximately 7.5 percent. When the residual value of equipment is also considered, respectively, a full-payout lease is the best choice at approximately 7.2 percent and the partial-payout lease is the best at approximately 8.2 percent. Rental for all rates used is not financially attractive.

This graph reflects the effect of various rates on accumulated present value for eight years, but if the rate is held constant and the years are examined as the variable, the graph shown in Illustration 6-15 presents the results at 6 percent. If the equipment is retained less than 6 years, purchasing is the most expensive and leasing is the least expensive. If retained seven years, renting is the most expensive and leasing is still the least expensive. After 7.5 years, however, purchasing is the least expensive, and this does not consider the residual value of the equipment, which would cause purchasing to be advantageous over leasing at an earlier time. The graph shows that the accumulated cost for purchasing levels off, whereas those for renting

ILLUSTRATION 6-15. The Effect of Time on Cost: At a 6% rate, the accumulated cost for purchasing decreases, and increases for both leasing and renting. At approximately 6½ years, purchasing becomes less expensive than renting, and at approximately 7½ years, less expensive than leasing.

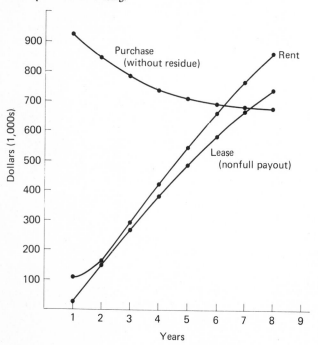

and leasing continue to rise, ever increasing the advantage of purchasing after 7.5 years.

NEGOTIATING THE CONTRACT

The purpose of a contract is succinctly stated by Richard L. Bernacchi and Gerald H. Larsen: "Ideally, a contract should clearly express the intentions of a buyer and seller and the responsibilities of each in the process of achieving these objectives."[15] The goal, thus, is to obtain a "fair contract," one that protects both the buyer and the seller. Several forces act against the buyer receiving a fair contract, and these are:

1. *Vendor-prepared contracts protect vendors.* As stated by Ken Brindle of International Computer Negotiations, "What the user has to understand is that the contract he is asked to sign was written to protect the vendor. It's up to him to equalize that agreement."[16] The buyer must protect himself or herself by understanding what is contained in the contract, by knowing what must be included in the contract and what should be negotiated, and by having a lawyer who is knowledgeable about computer contracts review the contract.

2. *Professional sellers versus amateur buyers.* Sellers are in the business of negotiating contracts on a daily basis, whereas data center managers examine contracts infrequently, and even then with limited time available and limited understanding. The approach recommended is for a lawyer to examine what is in the contract and to comment on what should be in it, using the checklist in Appendix E as a guide to evaluate the contract and to prepare for contract negotiations. The presence of a lawyer and the checklist will help the buyer to face the negotiating difficulties indicated by Brindle, when he states, "All too often we see users either not negotiating the contract, or negotiating for all the wrong things; asking the vendor to do things he really can't do, or not asking for the things he can do—things that may be done with little or no insistence from the user."[17]

3. *Absence of proposal claims and promises in the contract.* Too often the proposal is viewed by the vendor as a sales tool, not as claims and promises to be included in

[15] Richard L. Bernacchi and Gerald H. Larsen, *Data Processing Contracts and the Law* (Boston: Little, Brown, 1974), p. 15.
[16] Larry Lettieri, "Negotiating the Contract Maze," *Computer Decisions*, April 1977, p. 22.
[17] Ibid., p. 21.

the contract. The surest approach to avoid the absence of these committals in the contract is to include the solicitation document as part of the contract. Beforehand, the vendors should be informed that the solicitation document will be included in the contract in order to avoid later confusion and disagreement. If this agreement cannot be obtained, it will be necessary to verify all claims and promises contained in the solicitation document, as well as other agreements, to be assured that they have been included in the contract. The inclusion of all specifications, prices, and services must be verified.

4. *Misrepresentation by sales representatives.* Exaggerated and erroneous claims by sales representatives may not be intentional; in many cases these statements result from what the sales representatives were told, as they understood what they were told. They receive simplified statements about the product and services and are not aware of limits, restrictions, and exceptions. The only protection is to verify claims and to have claims included in the contract.

5. *Absence of penalties for contract violations.* The penalties necessary in a contract should vary in degree of severity in accordance with the severity of the violation. A severe problem such as the inability to produce the work as claimed should permit cancellation of the contract and reimbursement for expenses incurred and income lost. Less-severe violations, such as missing the installation and acceptance deadline, should consider only additional expenses and lost income.

6. *Vendor disclaimers of responsibility.* Penalties for such occurrences as missed deadlines are usually negated by vendors disclaiming responsibility under the phrase, "acts of God." A lawyer is definitely needed to patch that loophole. There are many disclaimers in the standard vendor contract, requiring the data center manager's scrutiny and caution. One such disclaimer that is nearly always present is called the "integration clause." A typical wording for this clause is, "This is a complete and exclusive statement of the agreement between the parties. It supersedes all proposals or prior agreements, oral or written, and each and every other communication between the parties relating in any way to the subject matter of this agreement." In other words, the vendor takes no responsibility for anything said or written if it is not in the contract—that is why it is necessary to verify that all claims and promises are included.

Contracts quite obviously cannot be treated causally. They would receive more attention if data center managers were more aware of the large number of litigations occurring. IBM, for example,

was sued by Catamore Enterprises on the basis of claims of fraud, negligence, and breach of contract and warranty; for similar reasons, Ross Perot's Electronic Data systems was sued by Schaefer Brewing Company.[18] In a $3.5 million suit, Investment Counseling Services sued Hewlett-Packard Co. because of claims including misrepresentation of products' performance capabilities, inefficient time-sharing and data-entry library systems, and terminal failures.[19] Contract protection cannot correct the inefficiencies, frustration, and loss of user trust experienced, but it can at least recover financial losses.

Categories of Potential Contract Problems

There is not an absolute classification of problems, but in their book *Data Processing Contracts and the Law*, Richard L. Bernacchi and Gerald H. Larsen segment potential contract problems into five useful categories:[20]

1. Matters of fact
2. Matters of law
3. Questions of risk
4. Questions of evidence
5. Questions of technology

1. *Matters of fact.* This includes all the specifics for the products and services the buyer expects to receive. Receipt of products and services that the buyer assumes are included may not be, and this may result in delays and additional costs. It is natural, for example, to assume that when equipment is ordered, cables are also included. This may not be true. And in this example, it is necessary to verify not only that the cost of cables is included, but also whether or not the seller is responsible for their installation.

2. *Matters of law.* The specifics included in the contract must be stated in terms that can be enforced in a court of law. A lawyer may not be able to verify the adequacy of specifics such as performance expectations, but he can verify that what has been agreed upon is stated in legally correct terms. In addition, matters of law include

[18] Ibid., p. 21.
[19] Brad Schultz, "Billing Service Firm Brings $3.5 Million HP Suit," *Computerworld*, September 4, 1978, p. 7.
[20] Richard L. Bernacchi and Gerald H. Larsen, *Data Processing Contracts and the Law*, pp. 15–16.

general provisions such as method of payment, confidentiality, and insurance requirements—to mention only a few.

3. *Questions of risk.* Both the seller and the buyer face risks. If the seller is a leasing company, it faces the risks of quick obsolescence and depreciation of equipment, possibly resulting in a loss in investment. The buyer's risks fall into four categories:

a. Direct risks associated with the failure of technology
b. Indirect risks associated with consequential events due to the failure of technology
c. Direct risks of nonperformance due to financial problems in the seller's organization
d. Direct risks of nonperformance or delayed performance due to management failures in the seller's organization[21]

4. *Questions of evidence.* The means must be stated for judging and proving the adequacy, or inadequacy, of the products and services identified under matters of fact. How will computer performance that is below acceptable levels be proved? How will lack of adherence to maintenance agreements be proved? Does downtime affect evaluation of production performance and penalty agreements?

5. *Questions of technology.* Many problems can arise because of the inadequacy of data-processing terminology. Many of the terms used are ambiguous, possibly having several gradations of meanings. When an organization wants a FORTRAN compiler, what is wanted? What is supplied? There are, for example, various versions of FORTRAN, with different features and complexities, with different diagnostics, and with different efficiencies.

Computer-Contract Checklist

The points to be considered by the data center manager and his lawyer when preparing to negotiate a contract or to review a contract should protect against the hindrances to a fair contract and the potential contract problems already mentioned and should attend to the items listed in the checklist in Appendix G. This checklist appeared in *Your Computer and the Law,* by Robert P. Bigelow and Susan H. Nycum. It considers the following aspects of a contract:

1. System design
2. Responsibilities

[21] Ibid, p. 230.

3. Basic system specifications
4. Site preparation
5. Personnel training
6. Delivery and acceptance
7. Finances
8. General operations
9. Maintenance
10. Modifications and terminations
11. Miscellaneous contract terms

The General Services Administration (GSA) has the buying power to force fair contracts on vendors, in fact, to force buyer-oriented contracts on vendors. Examining the contents of their contracts is an education, indicating what can be included, or at least used, for points for negotiation. The components for GSA's purchase and leasing contracts are shown in Appendix H.

Between the computer-contract checklist and the GSA contract components in Appendices G and H, the data center manager has good guidance in negotiating a contract. However, the multivendor shop requires special consideration. Two recommendations are made: first, approval should be obtained from vendors to attach the equipment of other vendors; second, to minimize delays in resolving problems in a multivendor shop and to avoid the costs for repairmen from the various vendors, the use of a single third-party maintenance firm should be considered.

SOFTWARE ACQUISITION

Most of the suggestions and precautions presented for hardware evaluation and acquisition also apply to software acquisition. But before considering the types of software available, the pros and cons of acquiring software packages, and the actual acquisition process, a peculiar phenomenon must be highlighted: the cobbler's-son-wears-unmended-shoes condition. The most sophisticated systems may be executed in a data center, but the running and control of the data center itself is primarily dependent on pen-and-parchment methods.

The quantity of software packages available for the data center increases each year, and their quality tends to improve each year. Yet, except for an occasional acquisition or the development of an in-house system, staff and management intuition and experience-by-error support and control data center activities. It is now time for the data center to mend its own shoes, to use the powerful computer resources not only to benefit other departments. The first recommendation to data center managers is that personnel should be assigned to keep abreast of software developments as they occur and to evaluate these developments in terms of the tradeoff between their cost and time overhead against the benefits they provide. And the benefits are many, as the summary of data center software will indicate.

Types of Data Center Software

A convenient summary of the software available appeared in *Computerworld* and is included in Appendix I. This summary includes software of concern to programmers and systems development personnel, as well as data center personnel. The categories shown were prepared by William B. Engle of Auerbach Publishers. It is not the only method of grouping software types, but it is adequate for obtaining a perspective of what is available. Two particularly important software types, however, are hidden in these groups and require some searching to uncover: software for job accounting and for job scheduling. Job-accounting software is listed under Tape/Disk Utilities, and job-scheduling software is listed under Performance Evaluators.

Putting aside generally available utilities in every data center, which includes sorts and compilers, the software often absent that should be considered for acquisition are:

Job Accounting. The primary function of job-accounting software is to indicate how much it costs to execute applications and the reasons for these costs. This information permits analysis of the worth of applications and consideration of their elimination or improvement.

Computer-performance Evaluators. The efficient use of computer resources is analyzed. Underutilization and overutilization of resources are examined for possible means of improving the distribution of the workload. Besides promoting efficient use of resources now, warnings are possible of inadequate resources in the near future,

permitting preparation for this occurrence before it becomes critical and affects data center service.

Job Scheduling. Sophisticated software is available to automatically sequence jobs and determine their job mix so that, while observing requirements for priority treatment and the meeting of deadlines, throughput and the use of resources is optimized. Without consideration of all significant factors, which a console operator or a simple scheduling program cannot do, the data center's ability to meet commitments to users is uncertain.

Tape Library Management. Manual control of tapes is cumbersome and error prone. A computer system, on the other hand, attends to releasing tapes for reassignment or cleaning or disposal with no fuss, and it provides a variety of useful reports. Some tape library systems are very elaborate and actually assign tapes to jobs, generate labels and job-control documents, and generate job-control statements to process jobs and produce all the resulting output.

Source-program Management. Control of adding, changing, and deleting source programs is necessary to avoid unauthorized access and to minimize updating errors. These systems also use storage space economically and provide backup files.

There are three frequently used sources for information on software products and their suppliers. These are Auerbach Publishers, Datapro Research Corp., and International Computer Programs (ICP). Each of these organizations provides important information, and it is definitely worthwhile to refer to all three. However, among all three, a comprehensive listing of all software packages available does *not* exist. Thus, it is necessary to be attentive to advertisements in data-processing magazines and newspapers.

The Pros and Cons of Software Packages

Any of the packages available from software suppliers can be developed in-house. The question is: Should these packages be developed in-house?

Consider the advantages of acquiring ready-to-use packages. An obvious advantage is the immediate availability of a package, which means that the benefits of the software can be obtained with minimum delay. This is particularly important if serious problems and inefficiencies can be lessened. To develop any of these packages in-house requires not only programming expertise but also insight into the factors involved and awareness of the complex logic often necessary. For example, few organizations have personnel with the knowledge needed to develop a scheduling system.

Even if in-house personnel could develop a system equivalent to what is available, putting aside that the delay is likely to be extensive, the cost is also likely to be much higher than the purchase of a software package. The software supplier spreads its development costs among its many users; the developer of an in-house system absorbs the entire cost. In addition, before any money is committed to acquisition of a package, its quality can be evaluated—something that cannot be done with systems developed in-house. Since software suppliers have to sell their packages, they tend to provide adequate documentation, whereas in-house personnel are notorious for their negative attitude toward documentation. Also, if the system is developed in-house, staff personnel must maintain the system, whereas packages can be obtained from software suppliers with maintenance agreements. Thus, the primary advantages of acquiring software packages are:

- Immediate availability
- Specialized knowledge
- Lower cost
- Quality can be evaluated
- Generally well documented
- Staff relieved of maintenance

The advantages of developing systems in-house actually center around the risks that exist in acquiring software packages:

1. *The varying quality of products.* Packages generally are efficient and error-free; however, some actually disrupt processing and incur excessive cost and time overhead. The best protection against this risk is to obtain evaluations from current users.

2. *The threat of vendor bankruptcy.* This is a real possibility because many software firms are small and have small capital resources. If a user has not received source coding, enhancement and maintenance of the software is dependent on the vendor. When the financial stability of a company is doubtful, this risk is eliminated by insisting upon a duplicate of the source coding.

3. *The threat of infringement.* If the seller does not have definite rights to the software, or to parts of it, a third party may involve the buyer in a lawsuit. Protection against this risk is to have the vendor state in the contract that he has clear title to the software and will defend against any infringement claims.

The pros and cons of software-package acquisition presented justify the preference of acquiring packages to in-house development, with the restrictions that the quality of the product be verified, that duplicate source coding be obtained if the financial stability of the vendor is doubtful, and that protection from third-party litigations be included in the contract.

When acquiring packages, the question arises, Should packages be obtained from hardware vendors or from independent software suppliers? Generally, software suppliers should be preferred. This view is based on user evaluations resulting from surveys performed by Datapro Research Corp. In one of their surveys, for example, hardware vendors represented 40 percent of what was being used, but according to user evaluations, only 8 percent were considered to be of superior quality.[22] Users commented that independents supplied software that was easier to install, had better installation support, provided better service, and exposed users to less risk of a defective product.

The Software-Acquisition Process

The process is similar to that for hardware acquisition, although less complex, with fewer uncertainties, and less time consumption. Many requirements for hardware acquisition are unnecessary, such as the preparation of solicitation documents, the assignment of costs to desirable features, and the variety of financing arrangements. A demonstration of a package provides certainty of what it can do, and quick verification with present users provides adequate confirmation. The end result is that the entire process can be performed relatively

[22] Ernest E. Keet, "Eliminating the Risks of Buying Software," *Infosystems,* February 1978, p. 60.

quickly. The process consists of seven steps:

1. Assign personnel
2. Prepare a checklist of requirements
3. Prepare requests for information
4. Evaluate alternatives
5. Contact users for confirmation
6. Decide whether to purchase or lease
7. Negotiate the contract

An additional step may be of value in some circumstances. Between steps 3 and 4, a demonstration of the candidate packages may be requested. This is done if the documentation is not clear as to exactly what is produced, if a comparison is needed of outputs resulting from the same input, and if there is uncertainty as to the storage, computer-processing, and manual-processing overhead. If only additional information is wanted, a vendor presentation may be adequate, or the buyer may prefer to attend vendor-given classes or seminars for the more complex software.

1. *Assign personnel.* As in the case of hardware acquisition, the recommended approach is to have a team of specialists, but since this is unlikely in most environments, the next best approach is to have at least one person who is a specialist in software evaluation. The worst, but most common, approach is to assign one or more persons who have no or little experience in software selection on an ad hoc basis.

2. *Prepare a checklist of requirements.* The mandatory requirements, those that must be met, must be separated from those that are desirable, that are useful but not necessary. The list should be comprehensive, and if there are many entries, the desirable requirements should be separated into high, medium, and low priority items.

3. *Prepare requests for information.* If the competing packages are few, the request should be for the information needed to arrive at a decision; if, however, there are many packages being considered, to reduce the number to a manageable size, only basic information is needed from each supplier. In the first case, each supplier should receive a complete copy of listed requirements. In the second case, it is only necessary to indicate intentions and mandatory requirements, such as the hardware and operating system with which the software must be compatible.

4. *Evaluate alternatives.* Appendix J contains a checklist for software evaluation. From this checklist and the checklist of requirements, the form in Illustration 6–4 can be used. In some cases, the short checklist in Illustration 6–

16 may be adequate. If packages are evaluated by systems-development personnel, a peculiar but common problem is likely to occur, especially if packages are being compared to the alternative of developing a similar system in-house. It is referred to as the NIH, or not-invented-here, syndrome. This attitude is avoided to a large extent when there are specialists assigned to software evaluation.

5. *Contact user for confirmation.* There is no better way to learn about software problems and deficiencies, and also about service problems and deficiencies, than by questioning present users. As recommended for hardware evaluation, the users recommended by software suppliers should be avoided; they are the satisfied customers, possibly the only satisfied customers. Warren H. Sargent, Jr. of University Computing Company recommends that current users should be asked the following questions:

> How easy was the package to install?
> How satisfied are you with the package now?
> Have you had any problems with the package?
> How responsive is the vendor to meeting your needs?
> Is the documentation thorough?
> Was the training adequate?
> Did you pay full price for the system?
> What would you change in the package?
> Does the system perform efficiently and in a reliable manner?[23]

6. *Decide whether to purchase or lease.* This decision depends on the costs for the expected life of the package. Such costs as those for installation and maintenance should also be considered. If a price is not guaranteed for a lease, the price is likely to increase for each renewal, and a percentage should be added for each renewal.

7. *Negotiate the contract.* Since it is impossible to state explicitly what the software should do under all conditions, the intentions of the buyer should be stated as a point of reference if a dispute arises over a point not explicitly stated. Ernest E. Keet, president of Turnkey Systems, Inc., provides a half-dozen excellent warnings:

1. Don't buy a software product that isn't warranted against program defects, at least for one year. The vendor's obligation to repair must be clearly stated.
2. Don't buy a product if the vendor won't accept financial liability, at least up to the monies paid for the product, in the event the product fails to perform as specified.

---

[23]Warren N. Sargent, Jr., "Evaluating Software is an Art," *Infosystems*, April 1976, p. 61.

Software Vendor Evaluation Checklist

	Rating (5 highest) Circle one

1. *Experience:* assign '1' for two years or less in software business, '2' for 2–4 years, '3' for 4–6 years, etc.

  1 2 3 4 5

2. *Organization size:* '1' for less than $1 million in sales, '2' for 1–2 million, 3' for 2–3 million, etc.

  1 2 3 4 5

3. *Scope of geographic coverage:* '1' if local, '2' if regional, '3' if North American, '4' if multi-national, '5' if world-wide.

  1 2 3 4 5

4. *Profitability:* '1' if financial information un-vailable or if unprofitable, '2' if vendor certifies profitability without audited state-ments, '3' if prior year profitability established via audited statements, '4' if three-year record of audited profitability available, '5' if five year record of audited profitability available.

  1 2 3 4 5

5. *Primary markets:* '1' if software sales are incidental, '2' if software sales are minor but separate line of business, '3' if software is significant element of business, '4' if soft-ware is major element of business, '5' if software is only line of business.

  1 2 3 4 5

6. *Local service competence:* '1' if local service specialist is responsible for more than ten software products, '2' for 6–10, '3' for 4–5, '4' for 2–3, and '5' if staff is dedicated.

  1 2 3 4 5

7. *Educational services:* '1' if no education, '2' if initial (installation time) training only, '3' if installation and scheduled training at vendor HQ site, '4' if installation and regional-ly scheduled training, '5' if installation, follow-up 'on-site' and regional courses available.

  1 2 3 4 5

8. *Emergency support services:* '1' if no such preplanned support, '2' if avaialble locally only, '3' if regional specialist, '4' if central 'hot line' available to customers, '5' if central 'hot line' *plus* dispatchable support specialist assigned to emergency support)

  1 2 3 4 5

9. *Vendor references:* '1' if in random sampling of five users only one would enthusiastically endorse vendor's integrity, product commit-ment, competence, and service; 2 if two, etc.

  1 2 3 4 5

10. *Standard contract terms:* '1' if vendor sells "as is," '2' if vendor unconditionally war-rants product, '3' if vendor also guarantees or conducts installation, '4' if vendor also accepts limited financial liability, '5' if vendor also accepts unlimited financial liability.

  1 2 3 4 5

11. *Customer base:* '1' if less than 10 reference-able clients, '2' if 10–50, '3' if 51–100. '4' if 101–200, '5' if over 200.

  1 2 3 4 5

How to interpret results

11–24	Caveat Emptor!	45–50	True professionals. No risk.
25–35	A strong contract is essential. Moderate risk.	50 +	The best. A blue chip soft-ware company. You can't do better.
36–44	A solid company. Minimum exposure.		

ILLUSTRATION 6-16. Software Vendor Evaluation Checklist. *Source:* Ernest E. Keet, "Eliminating the Risks of Buying Software," *Infosystems*, Feb. 1978, p. 61.

3. Don't sign a contract unless the vendor guarantees that he has clear title to the product and is willing to defend against any trade secret, patent, trademark, or copyright infringement claims.

4. Don't sign a contract without clearly establishing maintenance terms and cost: remember that "maintenance" is different from a warranty in that it covers enhancements and upgrades as well. Be sure to obtain the right to the latest version of the system for no more than the current system price less the price you pay.

5. Don't sign a contract without incorporating the vendor's literature, including sales brochures and proposals related to the product, into the agreement as referenced attachments. If verbal claims were made which aren't evidenced in the literature, make sure they are reduced to writing.

6. Don't commit to a software product without reducing installation responsibilities and acceptance procedures to writing.[24]

[24] Ernest E. Keet, "Eliminating the Risks of Buying Software," p. 62.

part two

DATA CENTER PROCESSING

7

DATA CENTER
STANDARDS AND
PROCEDURES

GOAL

To establish standards and procedures, with standards as yardsticks to judge performance, with procedures as guides to attain desired performance.

HIGHLIGHTS

Benefits of Standards and Procedures

The benefits include control of data center efficiency, service, and cost, while permitting smooth adaptation to technological and environmental changes.

Types of Standards and Procedures

Standards and procedures apply to all aspects of the data center and can be separated conveniently into four categories: administration, operating, contingency, and support services.

Development of Standards and Procedures

To assure attention to all developmental activities, the following seven-phase procedure is recommended:

- Project initiation
- Project preparation
- Draft preparation
- Draft review
- Revision for substance
- Revision for expression
- Printing and distribution

Enforcement of Standards and Procedures

Although good standards and procedures enforce themselves, external enforcement is also necessary; this consists of personnel education, random testing and "fire drills," and frequent monitoring.

"The only things that evolve by themselves in an organization are disorder, friction, and malperformance."[1] This statement succinctly states what can be expected when guidelines do not exist for directing and evaluating data center activities.

Consider an actual instance where things were permitted to evolve by themselves. At one installation no documentation existed at all to explain the manual and program sequence for any of the jobs processed, and no job-control language statements existed to help. The only person who could run these jobs was the head computer operator. If this person left the company, most jobs could not be executed—to state the situation bluntly and truthfully. This also applies to payroll and other critical systems. This data center's method of functioning evolved by itself over five years without any apparent awareness of its obvious deficiencies and its inherent potentialities for crippling the organization. In this situation, fortunately, a new manager of the data center quickly saw the dangers and insisted upon immediate documentation of the processing steps; this was completed in less than one month, and the serious deficiency was eliminated.

Most data centers are not permitted to evolve with such total lack of forethought. Data center managers are usually very alert and conscientious, and they devote attention to *some* aspects, aspects that are not permitted to evolve by themselves. The difficulty suggested by the phrase "some aspects" is simply that, although some aspects of the data center are attended to with great concern, others are ignored or treated, at best, casually. Some data centers, for example, closely monitor computer performance; others do not. Some stress data center security, as well as data and program security; others stress these to only a small degree. Some control input receipt and output distribution; others do not control them at all, or on some occasions but not on others. The simple but critical matter of conveying processing and status information from the operator on one shift to the operator on the next shift is frequently inadequate. Even where activities are clearly established, the adequacy of documentation and the means provided for updating this documentation vary for each data center—from excellent to barely visible. Even data centers with excellent documentation

are almost certain to cover only some aspects of data center activities, not treating other aspects at all. Unfortunately, some of these untreated aspects are likely to be critical. Many otherwise excellent data center manuals, for example, do not include access security procedures, data center disaster plans, or procedures for coordinating user-data center activities.

Each person in a data center can provide many other instances of inadequately defined and documented data center activities. A law that should govern each data center is: *Do not permit things to evolve by themselves.*

Several terms that are used loosely in every data-processing environment must be precisely defined. The terms relevant to the present discussion are *policy, standard,* and *procedure.* These terms provide a definite hierarchy of concepts. A *policy* is a statement that clearly defines an overall objective without stating the specific means of determining attainment or of stating how the objective should be attained. Upper management, for example, may simply state that definite levels of service must be provided that are acceptable to users, but do not incur unwarranted data center inefficiencies. True, this statement of policy does include indefinite phrases. What services are being referred to? What are the acceptable levels of service to users? What are the unwarranted inefficiencies? Furthermore, how will levels of service and inefficiencies be measured? A policy does not attend to these details; it merely indicates what the general objectives are, what the expected overall effects should be, and where emphasis should be placed. The end result is that management converts a requirement for detail decision-making to generic decision-making, leaving the detail decision-making and the definition of means to lower-level managers and technicians. Peter Drucker expresses this idea when he comments, "The effective executive does not make many decisions. He solves generic problems through policy."[2]

The meeting of policies, or the solving of specific problems, is a two-phase process, the statement of precisely what should be accomplished and the statement of precisely how it should be accomplished. *Standards* state what should be accomplished, and *procedures* state how they should be accomplished. Consider the policy of satisfying user service requirements. Standards are

[1] Peter Drucker, *MBA Communications*, October 1976, p. 61.

[2] Peter Drucker, *MBA Communications*, October 1976, p. 61.

expressed in terms that permit determination of accomplishment. The measurements used are likely to include the meeting of time constraints for scheduled and unscheduled jobs, the satisfying of response-time averages and limits. These standards may also include control of input-data receipt, job processing, and output distribution. Once standards are established, the procedures for attaining these standards can be examined and agreed upon. Procedures indicate the specific sequence of actions to be performed, by whom, and how.

A clear picture of the relationships between policy, standards, and procedures is obtained by considering the government policy on air pollution resulting from automobiles. The policy, in somewhat oversimplified terms, is that air pollu-

tion limits for automobiles should be made progressively more stringent. This is a fairly clear statement, but it is not very specific. That is where statements of standards become important. Specific, measurable limits are set for the various types of automobile exhaust emissions, and these limits are periodically evaluated and made more stringent. With these specific standards as guidelines, various groups must establish procedures to meet these requirements. Automobile manufacturers must satisfy design constraints to make these limits attainable with proper production control and user maintenance. The user must adhere to maintenance schedules to pass inspections. The inspection stations must have their procedures, and each automobile maintenance shop must have

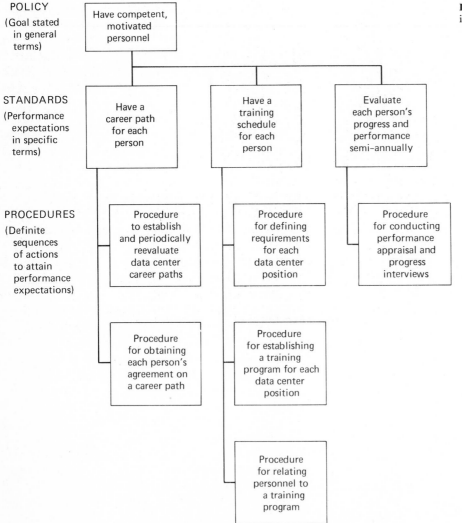

ILLUSTRATION 7–1. Hierarchy of Policy, Standards, and Procedures.

adequate procedures for checking pollution-control devices and for making any necessary corrections.

Illustration 7-1 defines policy, standards, and procedures and shows their hierarchy.

Policy considerations apply to the general objectives introduced throughout this book. This chapter focuses on only standards and procedures, and the topics to be considered are:

- Benefits of standards and procedures
- Types of standards and procedures
- Development of standards and procedures
- Enforcement of standards and procedures

BENEFITS OF STANDARDS AND PROCEDURES

Before considering the benefits resulting from adequate standards and procedures, two objections to them should be examined: their apparent inflexibility and the difficulty of maintaining them up-to-date. The criticism that they are inflexible, that they restrict actions and actually hinder processing, is justifiable if the standards are not reasonable, if the procedures have not considered the processing variations that may be necessary, or if the procedures have not been kept up-to-date to reflect technological and environmental changes. For example, if the procedure for processing batches of data states that all data must be available for computer processing before any data is processed it is unnecessarily restrictive if each batch can be processed separately. In this case the standards should be changed. It would be wrong to conclude that because these standards are unnecessarily restrictive, standards are undesirable; instead, the conclusion should be that unrealistic standards are undesirable. This brings us to the second objection: that standards and procedures are difficult to keep up-to-date. The solution to this situation is to update documentation before new standards and procedures are allowed to become effective.

These criticisms, however, do not state the staff's real reasons for criticizing and disregarding standards and procedures. All too often, many individuals object to being restricted, to not being permitted to deviate so as to expedite their tasks more quickly and with less personal attention. For example, personnel may not understand the benefits received from checking control counts and amounts,

making entries in logs, or preparing documentation. Therefore, they will resent these activities. Efforts to bypass these activities, or attempted "efficiencies," will actually lead to delays in many situations (long delays in some situations) and are likely to result in uncertain processing, sacrificing reliability, quality, and user service.

Instead of hindering processing, standards and procedures actually instill discipline from which reasonable variations and creative thinking is possible. They provide a sound groundwork from which improvements can be evaluated and, when justified, added. Without precisely defined standards and procedures, any new ideas implemented are likely to have unpredictable results; even if the results are satisfactory, only a few persons are likely to know about them. Thus, only a few persons will be able to adhere to them.

Five general categories of benefits result from having adequate standards and procedures in the data center:

- Control of processing activities
- Control of processing quality
- Control of time, costs, and resources
- Improvement of personnel morale
- Adaptability to changes

Control of Processing Activities

Clarification of standards, of expectations, permits the development of procedures to satisfy those expectations. These procedures, in turn, not only indicate the actions required, but also indicate when these actions are taken and by whom. Thus, if the standard for maintaining tape drives states that the tape heads must be cleaned at least once every four hours, procedures should be established to attend to this action and to monitor this procedure to assure adherence. Without this standard, tape-head cleaning may occur only once a day—or once every third, or fourth, or seventh day. Where standards are absent or vaguely defined, processing control becomes uncertain and unreliable.

Thus, standards support processing consistency and reliability. Processing consistency is supported by standards since any deviations from standards become apparent and receive corrective action. In many instances, when a deviation at the start of a process is not attended to, the following operations are wasted effort and must be repeated. This occurs, for example, when batch totals are not present or are not verified; the batches involved may be processed and reports may be produced and possibly even delivered to users, only to reveal discrepancies and to require rerunning.

With adequate standards and procedures it becomes possible to control processing activities, and it becomes possible to set schedules with confidence that they will be met. The meeting of schedules is one of the primary criteria for judging a data center's effectiveness and one of the most important means of instilling user confidence in the data center's ability to serve the user.

Control of Processing Quality

Processing quality definitely depends on the data center's ability to process all input received, to use the correct files, and to distribute the output properly. When these basic quality controls are absent, input is misplaced or only partially processed, the wrong files are used or possibly even destroyed, and outputs are improperly processed, incorrectly distributed, or even lost. These occurrences have been witnessed in most installations, with varying degrees of severity; in installations with few standards (and these undocumented) all may occur, and occur frequently. In one instance, at an installation with an absolute minimum of standards, a file containing information for check printing consisted of three reels—but only the first reel was used. The remaining two reels were used later only because an observant computer operator became suspicious just as they were about to be scratched—two weeks later.

Adequate standards and procedures also permit attention to controls built into application systems. With adequate verification procedures and processing documentation, data center personnel are able to assure that a job proceeds and terminates as expected. Control counts and amounts are verified, and console messages are properly understood and responded to. Such questionable practices as bypassing discrepancies in standard label processing are used cautiously, instead of automatically being used whenever they occur. Naturally, standards can only support those application-system controls that exist. Illustration 7-2 shows a simplified diagram of an actual system. This diagram represents an actual system that had no control counts at all. It was a typical occurrence to enter 1500 claims into the system and have 600 claims placed on tapes for payment, without any idea of what happened to the other claims, that is, whether they were rejected or "lost" in the system or whether the rejected claims were corrected and reentered or simply filed and forgotten, which in fact occurred for many claims. The filed claims were forgotten and no one knew the difference. As for the claims placed on tapes for check printing, no controls existed to verify that they were actually printed. This system and its associated

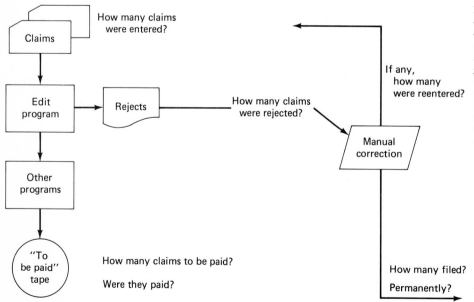

ILLUSTRATION 7-2. The Absence of Processing Controls: The absence of processing controls in the data center, as for the claims processing system shown, creates confusion and generates criticism, with uncertainty as to what has happened and what should be done. The system shown had no processing counts and, thus, could not answer any of the questions on the diagram, and many others.

"procedures" had no controls. The data center can only support and be responsible for those application-system controls that exist. Furthermore, not having adequate data center standards and procedures to provide this support can only add additional quality control problems to poorly controlled systems and also exposes the data center to criticism that is difficult or impossible to reveal as false.

Control of Time, Costs, and Resources

The efficiency and avoidance of wasted effort, which are benefits resulting from standards and procedures, save time, lessen the personnel and equipment resources required for a job, and thus reduce the cost for a job. The time and resources saved then become available for other jobs, and since resource usage is reduced, acquisition of hardware with increased capacity is delayed. This delay results in lower processing costs. Since efficient processing of jobs results in lower processing cost for jobs, jobs can be processed that otherwise may only marginally justify their cost for the benefits received.

Improvement of Personnel Morale

With procedures to guide their activities and with standards to judge their performance, data center personnel can proceed confidently and are more likely to assume responsibility for the results. Personnel are exposed to endless criticism and frequent errors when expectations are not documented, those not informed of these "secrets" are likely to make mistakes, to be criticized, and to become discontented. Documented standards and procedures have the opposite effects: expectations become known and personnel avoid mistakes and criticism, act confidently, and derive satisfaction from their work.

The relationships between data center personnel and users are also affected. By making all aware of what is expected from one another, conflicts can be avoided, or at least minimized. Properly defined procedures provide means for communicating job expectations and problems, and for coordinating activities. Data center personnel are likely to become sensitive to user problems and provide alternative procedures to meet these

problems. Data center personnel will also understand that user deadlines are meaningful and will be motivated to meet these deadlines. Users, on the other hand, will become aware of data center requirements to process their jobs properly and also to appreciate resource limitations. Although these benefits are idealistic, they can be attained to a large extent, but only upon a sound foundation of documented standards and procedures.

With increased efficiency and reliability, users will become more trustful of data center service. This trust is all too often missing. The presence of standards and procedures, therefore, supports personnel morale and stimulates user trust.

Adaptability to Changes

What happens when documented standards and procedures do not exist—and personnel leave? The new persons hired must learn from verbal instructions, no matter how incomplete and hurried they are, or by trial and error—not a very satisfactory situation. Documented standards and procedures make the difference. Since these documents guide actions and clarify expectations, avoiding most if not all mistakes, the detrimental effects of personnel turnover are minimized.

Other changes occur in a data center, and these also are adapted to much more easily than otherwise when standards and procedures exist. A basis is provided for modification instead of the task of total examination and definition. These other changes may be organizational, such as the addition of a management level or the addition of a control or support group. When this occurs, first the existing standards are reviewed for modification, and then the procedures are reviewed for any changes they require. The same is true, for example, when there are changes to equipment configurations or operating-systems software. Changes may be necessary because of the information reported, the method of gathering this information, or the assignment of responsibilities.

It is apparent that the existence of standards and procedures is not a trivial matter, a matter to be postponed until "some free time becomes available," which is not likely to occur. Standards and procedures are the foundation on which a stable, efficient, reliable data center depends. They provide the direction and control absolutely necessary in a data center.

TYPES OF STANDARDS AND PROCEDURES

Standards and procedures have been viewed and categorized from various viewpoints. In fact, standards and procedures have been defined as two types of standards. Dick Brandon, in *Management Standards for Data Processing*, does this and provides definitions consistent with those used earlier for "standards" and "procedures." His phrases and their definitions are:

- *Methods standards:* As guides, standards are used to establish uniform practices and common techniques.
- *Performance standards:* As yardsticks, standards are used to measure the performance of the data processing function.[3]

What Brandon defines as "performance standards" has been defined earlier as "standards," what should be accomplished, expectations by which satisfactory performance can be judged. And what is referred to as "methods standards" has been defined as "procedures," as the means to attain standards, the sequence of activities. This explains why the documented guidelines and yardsticks for a data center are sometimes referred to collectively as "standards and procedures." Although standards and procedures are usually documented together, it is preferable for clarification of their totally distinct functions to consider them separately, remembering that *performance standards, or simply standards, are yardsticks for evaluating performance, and methods standards, or procedures, are guides to attain performance standards.*

Since standards and procedures apply to all aspects of the data center, they apply to the entire contents of this book, as indicated in Illustration 7-3. As a result, standards and procedures attend to such questions as:

How will attainment of data center objectives be judged?

How will the data center be structured to meet these objectives?

How will adequacy of personnel career paths be judged?

How will adequate career paths be established?

[3]Dick H. Brandon, *Management Standards for Data Processing* (New York: D. Van Nostrand, 1963), p. 2.

How will effective budgeting be judged?

How will the budgeting be done?

These are only a few of the questions that must be considered when preparing data center standards and procedures. Naturally, at first, only the most important and urgent standards and procedures should be established, thus avoiding the delay that would result if full documentation were required before any documentation was released. The less-critical items can then be included over a period of time, possibly in several phases.

ILLUSTRATION 7-3. Data Center Standards and Procedures: All aspects of the data center are candidates for standards and procedures.

Organizational

    Classification of data center objectives and functions
    Classification of responsibilities and lines of authority
    Coordination and rapport between user and data center personnel

Personnel

    Establishing job requirements and career paths
    Preparation of training programs and schedules
    Job enrichment and other personnel motivation programs
    Personnel appraisals for attaining data center and personnel objectives

Finances

    Budgeting technique and variance control
    Chargeout or chargeback of data center expenses to users
    Cost-benefit analysis of data center expenses

Data Center Site

    Selection and preparation factors and procedure
    Safety and security precautions and contingency plans
    Data center relocation methodology

Hardware and Software

    Requesting proposals and making selections
    Evaluation of financial alternatives
    Contract negotiation and preparation

Standards and Procedures

    Establishing documentation needs and documentation standards
    Preparing a standards and procedures manual and stating how it is maintained
    Monitoring and enforcing standards and procedures

Processing Control

    Control of workflow and activities at each work station
    Scheduling data center resources for efficiency and service
    Control of on-line reliability and security
    Evaluation and improvement of computer and data center performance

Categories of Standards

Standards can be classified in many ways. Since detailed classification varies with each installation, standards will be classified here into four general categories: standards for administration, operations, contingencies, and support services.

Administration standards include activity and performance reporting requirements, budget control, and personnel appraisal and career path guidance. Some installations have clearly defined standards, as well as procedures, on such topics. Others have very vague standards, usually because of the day-to-day operating pressures, and these distractions are often the result of poor work stations and workflow standards and procedures. When emergency job rescheduling and emergency file recreation are necessary, management has little time available for the less urgent but no less important concerns of resource-usage efficiency and personnel guidance. Because of the low immediate urgency of these standards and procedures, and because of their high importance, they require special effort to have them defined, documented, and established.

Operations standards applies to work stations and workflow, which are obvious targets for standardization. The performance expected for batch and on-line processing, whether production or testing, must be known to data center personnel. How well these standards are met determines how efficiently and reliably the data center functions and how the users are served. Because of the extensiveness of these standards, they are discussed in Chapters 8 and 12; Chapter 8 discusses work station and workflow activities, and Chapter 12 discusses data center performance evaluation. Operations standards also include such topics as user billing algorithm and JCL requirements. When standards are normally discussed, often only operations standards are considered.

Contingency standards can be considered part of operations standards, but because they are not part of daily activities and occur only under emergency conditions, their documentation is kept separate, possibly even in a separate binder. Also because of the absence of immediate urgency, they are frequently ignored, as was mentioned for administrative standards. These standards attend to varying degrees of emergencies, from breakdown of several disk drives to destruction of the entire data center. Thus, several contingency plans are needed, including disaster plans for using backup programs and data at a backup site.

Support service standards, the last category of standards, includes data center relocation, equipment selection, computer performance evaluation, and documentation. These and other support services, with the exception of documentation, are discussed elsewhere in this book. Because documentation is central in obtaining adherence to standards and procedures, and because it is generally inadequate, it will now be discussed. After defining documentation types, documentation criteria and documentation control are explained.

Documentation types. The documentation in any data center can be segmented into four types: overall data center documentation, specific user application system documentation, vendor-supplied documentation, and user-data center coordination documentation.

1. *Overall data center documentation* is usually collected into a single binder and given a title such as *The Data Center Standards and Procedures Manual, Computer Center Handbook, or Operations Guidelines.* Whatever title is used, the functions and contents of the manual are basically the same for all installations. It should contain all four categories of standards and their associated procedures. Thus, this manual is the primary guide for all data center activities, but requires the other three types of documentation for total guidance of data center activities. Illustration 7-4 shows a typical table of contents. Included in this documentation must be samples and explanations of all forms and listings used in the data center. This avoids variations in what is entered on forms and how listings are interpreted; frequently because of confusion in this area, needed information is not entered on forms, and critical information on listings is ignored. In some organizations, considerable information is included on JCL requirements and on how to use cataloged procedures. All manuals should start with an organization chart, general career path information, a diagram of the hardware configuration, and a listing of the system software used. This provides the orientation data center personnel require. The specific topics that should be included in this manual are those already mentioned, topics discussed throughout this book, and any special topics relevant to the needs of a particular installation. Thus, tape library information must be present, and some installations should include standards and procedures

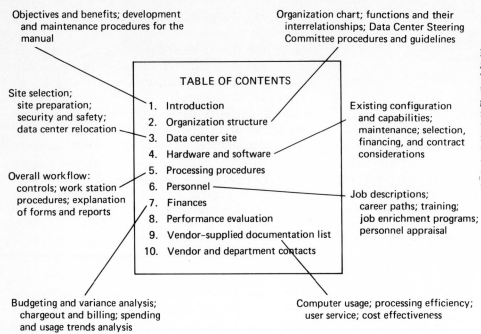

Objectives and benefits; development and maintenance procedures for the manual

Organization chart; functions and their interrelationships; Data Center Steering Committee procedures and guidelines

Site selection; site preparation; security and safety; data center relocation

Overall workflow: controls; work station procedures; explanation of forms and reports

TABLE OF CONTENTS

1. Introduction
2. Organization structure
3. Data center site
4. Hardware and software
5. Processing procedures
6. Personnel
7. Finances
8. Performance evaluation
9. Vendor-supplied documentation list
10. Vendor and department contacts

Existing configuration and capabilities; maintenance; selection, financing, and contract considerations

Job descriptions; career paths; training; job enrichment programs; personnel appraisal

Budgeting and variance analysis; chargeout and billing; spending and usage trends analysis

Computer usage; processing efficiency; user service; cost effectiveness

ILLUSTRATION 7-4. *Data Center Standards and Procedures* Manual Table of Contents: Each entry in the table of contents shown is stated in general terms, providing a section name for which there may be many topics. The recommended approach is to start each section with a detailed table of contents for the topics in that section. The annotations indicate some of the topics that can be included.

for computer output microfilm, page printers, and mass-storage systems.

2. *Application-systems documentation* for user jobs are kept either in separate folders or collected into large binders. Each organization has its own preference. Large binders are preferred by some to avoid misplacing job documentation; however, when a job may be executed on one of several machines, it is necessary either to have duplicate documentation for each machine or to use separate folders. Several organizations have placed application-systems run information on microfiche. This approach permits duplicate documentation at each console, in an on-site library, and at an off-site location. These documents, whether separated by system or collected together, are generally called *run books* or *operations manuals.* The information on each job step for a job is provided in detail, indicating the input needed, processing messages and restart procedures, the output generated, and their distribution. The documentation for the job steps should be preceded by a system flowchart, which for most systems will require more than one page. Besides clarifying job-step continuity, these documents state what manual processing and verification are required. Illustration 7-5 shows a cover sheet that should precede the documentation for each system or program. The table of contents shown applies to an on-line system; for batch systems, a table of contents would be needed for each major program; sort and other utility job steps do not require a table of contents. Carefully designed forms should be used for the various documents. Uniformity of documentation resulting from the use of forms will prevent many operator errors and permit

quick access to information. Typical forms are presented in the next chapter when computer-room procedures are discussed.

3. *Vendor-supplied documentation* is obtained from hardware and software vendors. The documentation provided tends to be comprehensive—and bulky. Being comprehensive, the documentation usually contains all the information needed; however, bulkiness tends to make the needed information difficult to locate. In these situations it is usually advisable to collate the frequently referenced information and store it near the computer consoles. In situations where even the collated information would contain extraneous information, possibly poorly organized and referenced, it may be necessary to rewrite and summarize the desired information. Since vendors are continually correcting and enhancing their products, the receipt and inclusion of updated documentation must be attended to in a timely manner. It is also advisable to maintain a listing of all vendor-supplied documentation. The form shown in Illustration 7-6 can be used.

4. *User data-center coordination documentation* provides users with insight into the functioning and the requirements of the data center. This insight permits coordination of activities and supports the development of rapport and trust between user and data center personnel. This documentation is called the *user/data center handbook,* or simply *user handbook.* Illustration 7-7 indicates a useful table of contents for the handbook. The handbook should start with a letter from upper management indicating support of the standards and procedures that follow. This will stress the seriousness that is associated with what is stated,

Application System Operator's Documentation Checklist		System ID
		System title

✓	Document	Comment
	1. Personnel contacts	
	2. System summary	
	3. System flowcharts	
//////	4. Preprocessing	//////////////
	4.1 Hardware requirements	
	4.2 Software requirements	
	4.3 Files required	
	4.4 Output produced	
	4.5 Scheduling requirements	
//////	5. Processing	//////////////
	5.1 Startup procedure	
	5.2 Processing controls	
	5.3 Master terminal messages	
	5.4 Master console messages	
//////	6. Postprocessing	//////////////
	6.1 Closedown procedure	
	6.2 Offline processing	
	7. Backup and restart procedures	

ILLUSTRATION 7–5. Operator's Documentation for an Application System: All possible documentation types that may be wanted are shown on a cover sheet checklist, such as the one shown for a datacommunication's system. A checkmark indicates that the document is supplied or not applicable. The comment area can indicate the date a document will be supplied, or it may simply state "not applicable."

ILLUSTRATION 7–6. Vendor-Supplied Documentation List.

Vendor Supplied Documentaiton				Date:
Document title	Reference number	Location	Frequently referenced topic	Page number

and thus will make enforcement much easier. Then the purpose and anticipated benefits are explained, stressing how the user benefits from compliance with procedures. After stating the data center's organization and facilities, user chargeout and performance-evaluation information is provided. Users can determine from this information how cost is associated with their demands on data center resources, thus accepting responsibility for the costs incurred; they also can determine the adequacy of data center service and efficiency by comparing stated performance standards against periodically reported performance. This places user evaluation of the data center on a quantitative basis, minimizing unfair criticism over factors beyond the control of data center management and staff. For example, if turnaround standards are not met, the periodic reports can state why these standards were not met, which may be ascribed

to late receipt of user data, equipment and power failures, or slow response of users to correction of rejects. The handbook can then explain the data center steering committee's functions and procedures. This committee can be a large factor in improving user-data center personnel rapport and cooperation. The next section for the handbook contains all the procedures that users must know to interact with the data center. The final section explains how the procedures will be monitored to assure adherence.

If these four types of data center documentation are properly prepared, it is possible to obtain consistent data center performance and service. Unfortunately, documentation is often not prepared properly, and that is what the next section examines. By stating the documentation criteria that should be satisfied, it is possible to guide documentation activities and to judge the results.

Documentation Criteria. Just as the functioning of a data center is uncertain without standards, the preparation of documentation will suffer from many ills if standards are not established to guide activities. The ills that can result fall into two general categories and are also the criteria for evaluating documentation: faults in content and faults in format. Typical content faults are inaccuracies, absence of necessary information, hazy or totally unclear explanations, and (when an attempt is made to provide complete documentation) bulky, hard-to-locate information. These faults lead to the isolation of the documentation criteria pertaining to content, which are accuracy, completeness, clarity, and conciseness.

The ills resulting from faults in format cause filing problems, difficulty in locating frequently referenced information, and frustration and mistakes in updating documentation. These faults result when documentation is more an exercise in creative scattergrams than in rational separation and location of critical information. It thus becomes apparent that the documentation format criteria are ease of reference, ease of use, and ease of maintenance. The four content criteria and three format criteria for documentation will now be considered in terms of how they can be made adequate.

1. *Accuracy.* The obvious means of obtaining accurate information is to obtain it from those who are most intimately involved with the details being documented. It is

ILLUSTRATION 7-7. *User-Data Center Handbook* Table of Contents: This handbook coordinates user and data center activities, and encourages rapport between user and data center personnel.

hard to believe, except by those who have witnessed this in most aspects of data processing, that this is infrequently done. For example, it is common to have persons develop or evaluate library systems, document procedures, and design forms for library systems without talking to the personnel in the library, except possibly for a few bits of scattered information. In one instance, documentation for an installation's library procedures, besides being incomplete (covering about one fifth of the procedures), was infested with inaccuracies and vague statements. The librarians would comment about the quick visit they had by the person preparing this documentation, and then they were able to show one error after another, at the same time commenting on omissions.

Besides going to the most authoritative sources for information, the information received should be reviewed and commented on by having others familiar with the details review it. It is not uncommon to discover that several persons all doing the same job have been doing the job differently. In these situations it is necessary to resolve these discrepancies and obtain agreement on which is the best approach, or possibly the only correct approach. Are these recommendations obvious? Maybe. But considering the great number of systems and the great number of procedures that have been poorly documented, these basic actions will continue to be bypassed if not considered important.

2. *Completeness.* If a job is supposed to be accepted for production only if it is accompanied by specific documentation, such as full data preparation, computer processing, and post-processing information, it should not be accepted unless complete. Too often a job is accepted with the understanding that documentation will be supplied soon. Five years later, documentation has not arrived, and during that time several emergencies have resulted from incorrect processing, and confusion has occurred in such activities as program restarts and distribution of output. It has been the experience of most computer operators to receive cryptic messages on their consoles, without the slightest hint in the documentation of what they mean or of what should be done. The equivalent occurs for procedures, where it is common to refer to forms and reports without supplying annotated copies. In some cases annotations may not be necessary, but in all cases samples should be supplied.

3. *Clarity.* Clarity depends on the structure of sentences, the relationship between sentences, and the choice of words. Sentence structure should be straightforward. Each statement should make clear what is being commented on and what is being said about that subject. The frequently made suggestion for paragraph clarity is to state a conclusion or generality about the subject, and then provide clarifying details and, when necessary, supporting evidence to justify the conclusion. Parenthetical comments and qualifications should be used sparingly within the same sentence that makes the basic statement. It is generally best to place a basic statement such as, "Users should sign for output upon receipt," in a separate sentence; comments and qualifications should be in the following sentences, which may include the comment, "This procedure provides control of output distribution and quickly resolves user complaints about not receiving output for which they signed." Paragraph coherence results when the information is presented in a definite sequence and with transitional words and phrases, such as thus, as a result, next, and however.

Sentence and paragraph structure may be clear, but the statements may still be unclear if word choice is poor. Any time words wander from observable details to general, abstract representations, their meaning becomes vague and may be interpreted differently by different persons. Data processing, in particular, is overloaded with high-level generalities and abstractions, which is made worse by the use of acronyms. For example, instead of stating "forward forms to the data center," state "forward claim applications to the data control clerk." And instead of stating "schedule some of the test jobs," state "schedule all test jobs requiring excessive computer resources" or, even more specifically, "schedule all test jobs requiring tapes, more than two CPU seconds, or operator intervention."

4. *Conciseness.* The goal of documentation is to guide activities, and if the documentation is bulky and cumbersome, its use becomes tedious and may be avoided. When forms and tables are used, information can be compressed, permitting quick and easy access. Attention to sentence phrasing can eliminate unnecessary verbiage. Instead of stating "backup tapes are used to avoid disruptions in processing and loss of time in recreating data," shorten the statement to "backup tapes avoid processing disruptions and time losses."

5. *Ease of reference.* How often has it been difficult to locate such information as deadlines or control numbers on documents? The frequent violation of this simple consideration indicates that the persons who designed these forms, or prepared documentation without forms, did not visualize their use. It becomes obvious, when reflected upon, that if the documentation is to be filed by job number, that number should be in a conspicuous location. The best location for most filing information is in the upper right corner of a document.

6. *Ease of use.* If a form is used by more than one person, instead of forcing each person to enter informa-

CRITERION	QUESTIONS
Accuracy	Has information been obtained from the most knowledgeable, and has it been reviewed and commented upon by the *most* and the *least* knowledgeable?
Completeness	Are all questions that are likely to occur answered—including the who, what, where, when, why, and how questions?
	Have procedures actually been followed, and have forms actually been completed?
Clarity	Do sentences progress logically and smoothly?
	Are sentences direct statements, with comments and qualifications clearly separated?
	Are the chosen words precise and, when necessary, defined?
Conciseness	Have unnecessary words, phrases, sentences, and paragraphs been eliminated?
	Are forms, tables, and graphs used whenever possible?
Ease-of-reference	Is reference information, such as control number or deadline, conspicuously located?
Ease-of-use	Is information segmented and sequenced according to who will use it and in what sequence it will be used?
Ease-of-maintenance	Is documentation prepared in small independent modules, permitting easy updating or even total replacement?

ILLUSTRATION 7-8. Documentation Criteria.

tion in various locations on the form, all the information relevant to each person should be grouped together. Furthermore, the information for each person should be sequenced to conform to how it will be entered or referenced, which avoids skipping back and forth. When the sequences for entering and referencing information are different, a choice or compromise must be decided on. If the information will be entered only once but referenced many times, then obviously the sequence that is best for referencing the information must be chosen.

7. *Ease of maintenance.* The secret of easy maintenance is modularity. Instead of having documents that continue for several pages, with new topics occurring at any time on any part of a page, each topic should be treated on one or a few pages, with continuation pages for those topics that may require them. This separation of documentation into small modules permits replacement of only the altered topics and does not affect any other topic. To ensure independence of topic documentation, cross-referencing should be avoided. Naturally, each topic must

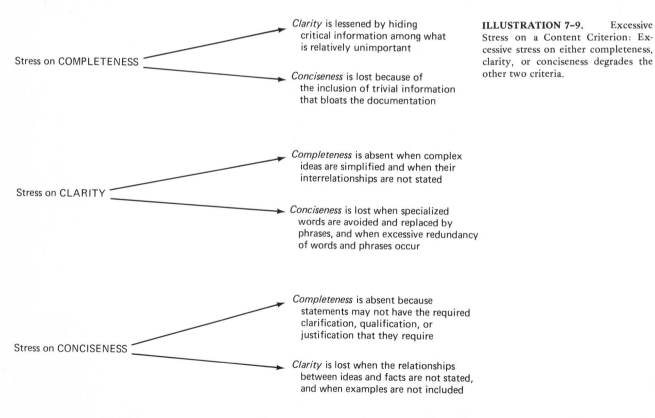

ILLUSTRATION 7-9. Excessive Stress on a Content Criterion: Excessive stress on either completeness, clarity, or conciseness degrades the other two criteria.

Stress on COMPLETENESS
- *Clarity* is lessened by hiding critical information among what is relatively unimportant
- *Conciseness* is lost because of the inclusion of trivial information that bloats the documentation

Stress on CLARITY
- *Completeness* is absent when complex ideas are simplified and when their interrelationships are not stated
- *Conciseness* is lost when specialized words are avoided and replaced by phrases, and when excessive redundancy of words and phrases occur

Stress on CONCISENESS
- *Completeness* is absent because statements may not have the required clarification, qualification, or justification that they require
- *Clarity* is lost when the relationships between ideas and facts are not stated, and when examples are not included

be assigned identification numbers for proper sequencing and for quick and easy location.

These seven documentation criteria and their basic questions are summarized in Illustration 7–8. Although completeness, clarity, and conciseness are criteria for documentation adequacy, they should be treated with approximately equal stress. Excessive stress on any one of these three criteria can degrade the documentation according to the other two criteria. Stress on completeness can result in cumbersome (not concise) material that includes trivial information (affecting clarity); stress on clarity may oversimplify complex ideas and relationships (lack of completeness) and produce unnecessary simple sentences and repeated definitions of words and phrases (reducing conciseness); and stress on conciseness may leave statements without adequate clarification and justification (affecting completeness) and may not show the relationship between topics and how techniques are applied (reducing clarity). The effects of stressing one of these criteria and affect-

ILLUSTRATION 7–10. Format Criteria Violations and Corrections.

Job Run Sheet

Job name
Job number

Job step name
Job step number

Files

Instructions

- *Ease-of-Reference* is ignored since the identification numbers for job and job step are poorly located

- *Ease-of-Use* is ignored since preparatory information is found after file processing information, and also the file information is not separated into input and output files

- *Ease-of-Maintenance* is ignored since different types of information occur on the same sheet, possibly requiring continuation sheets and thus requiring the updating of several sheets for a single change

Job Run Sheet

Job overview

Manual preparation

Other preparation

Job		
name		number
Job step		
name		number

Instead of using a single form, each type of information can be entered on a different form, such as the preparation for computer processing form shown; thus, *maintenance becomes easy.*

By sequencing the different forms according to how it is used, each of which has information sequenced according to how it is used, *use becomes easy.*

Since the identification numbers are located in the upper right-hand corner of each form, where it is easy to quickly locate, *reference becomes easy.*

ing the other two are summarized in Illustration 7-9.

To clarify the three format criteria, Illustration 7-10 compares a form that violates these three criteria with a corrected form. Once the corrected form is examined, it becomes apparent how documentation benefits from conspicuous location of reference information, proper segmenting and sequencing of information, and modularity of documentation for easy maintenance. Because of the importance of format, forms should be evaluated according to the three format criteria. A more extensive guide to evaluating or designing forms is provided by the forms analysis checklist in Illustration 7-11. Forms are important because they support a pattern of thinking and acting; they provide a checklist for gathering information; they initiate actions and show if they have been performed; they connect and coordinate activities; they lessen the amount of procedural documentation needed. In general, forms support data center procedures.

Documentation control. Documentation control starts with upper management support and may end if support is absent. Definition of what documentation is required is a wasted effort if these requirements are ignored. It is absolutely necessary to be able to retaliate against pressure from user managers to bypass documentation requirements—and this includes pressure from the systems development department. In some organizations, cooperation from user departments is possible only with upper management support. Upper management support, thus, is desirable in some organizations and necessary in others.

After receiving upper management support and publishing a standards and procedures manual, it is necessary to enforce these standards and procedures. This is done by not permitting exceptions, or at least by not casually permitting exceptions. Realistically, deadlines cannot be ignored, particularly legal deadlines that may result in fines or service deadlines that may result in loss of business. In these cases, it should be made clear that when an exception is approved, the situation is not considered acceptable and some error in planning or control exists. If the deviation from standards, for example, is putting a job into production without complete documentation, it must be made clear that the missing documentation will be supplied by a predetermined date. It should also be part of management reporting standards to report these deviations to management, thus bringing attention to those persons disregarding standards and procedures.

In addition, enforcement should include periodic, if not constant, monitoring of the adequacy of documentation, checking such factors as the updating of documentation for any changes and monitoring the adequacy of, and adherence to, documentation standards and procedures. In a large organization, one or more persons may be assigned full time to this and to other data center

ILLUSTRATION 7-11. Forms Analysis Checklist: This checklist guides forms analysis and design activities, and also assists in evaluating existing forms. *Source:* Howard Schaeffer, "Developing Operations Forms," *Data Center Operations Management* (N.J.: Auerbach Publishers, 1978), portfolio number 46-01-06, p. 5.

Forms Analysis Checklist

Form's Purpose

Has the form's purpose been precisely stated?
Will it initiate action and/or record or report performance of actions?
Is it really needed?
Can it serve additional purposes?
Can an existing form serve or be altered to serve?
Will it affect procedures or personnel?

Form's Information Requirements

What information is needed on the form?
What information is needed for controlling, routing, and filing?
What signatures and dates are needed?
Have users verified the identification of all needed information?

Form's Procedural Requirements

Who will initiate the form, enter information, and reference information?
In what sequence will personnel use the form?
How should information be grouped to correspond to this sequence?
How should information within each group be sequenced for each person?
Can procedural information be included in this form?

Form's Physical Requirements

Are titles, headings, and instructions precise and concise?
What information should instructions precede?
Where should control, routing, and filing information be located?
What constant information can be preprinted?
What is the maximum amount of space needed for each entry?
Is information typed or entered by hand?

monitoring activities, such as evaluation of the safety and security measures and of the adherence to these measures. These same persons should also evaluate computer and data center performance. In smaller organizations, part-time monitoring by a single person may be adequate. Whatever personnel assignments are decided on, the important point is that definite responsibilities must be assigned.

One final precaution must be taken: documentation must be protected. Just as data and programs should be copied and stored off-site, so should documentation. The documentation procedure should require duplication of documentation for off-site storage before its acceptance. And when documentation in the data center is updated, so should the documentation at the off-site location. The need for backup documentation is apparent when a computer room disaster is visualized, such as a fire in which the existing documentation is destroyed. If a disaster plan exists, it is almost certain that the plan includes location of backup files and programs off-site; but how many disaster plans include storing backup documentation off-site? If backup documentation is not available, the ability to process jobs at a backup site may depend totally on the memory of data center personnel. When stated in these blunt terms, it is obvious that this situation is not desirable.

Categories of Procedures

A similar situation exists for procedures as exists for standards: most of what can be termed procedures are spread throughout the entire book. This is true because, wherever standards state expectations, procedures generally follow stating how expectations can be met.

It is advantageous for each aspect of data center operations to be treated in specialized chapters for a coherent treatment. As in the case of standards, procedures are segmented into the same four categories. These categories provide perspective for the procedures presented throughout this book, and these categories are:

- Administrative procedures
- Operations procedures
- Contingency procedures
- Support service procedures

Administrative Procedures. Although they consist of clearly defined sequences of activities,

administrative procedures tend to be flexible and are often stated as guidelines. There should be definite procedures for developing budgets, analyzing variances, and appraising data center performance; but there can only be guidelines for developing rapport and cooperation, for motivating personnel through job-enrichment and career-path programs. These are only a few of the administrative procedures. As is the case for all procedures, administrative procedures and guidelines should be periodically reexamined for effectiveness. They should be examined not only in terms of completing the work efficiently and reliably, but also in terms of the rapport and motivation generated.

Operations Procedures. Each work station in the data center should have its procedures for processing jobs, including any exception processing that may be necessary. It should be clear what sequence of activities each person must adhere to, what forms must be prepared, and what logs must be completed. It must also be clear to each person when processing cannot continue for a job, and in these cases what should be done. Closely connected to work-station procedures is workflow control, which permits smooth, well-controlled transfer of data and jobs and output from one work station to another. Work-station procedures and workflow control are discussed in the next chapter.

Contingency Procedures. These procedures apply to emergency situations. Therefore, although they may never be used, they must always be well defined and capable of immediate implementation. The range of emergencies covers a wide range of seriousness. A minor emergency, for example, is to lose the use of a few data center resources, such as a few tape drives. This may make it impossible to process some jobs that have been scheduled. It is necessary in these cases to be able to reschedule jobs so that the available resources can be used to the full capacity available. Several scheduling packages are available that can do this with no difficulty at all. At the other extreme is the disaster situation, the situation where the data center is totally inoperative and a backup site must be used. A smooth transition to this backup site depends on planning and on the training of the data center personnel. The development of contingency procedures is a task that management is most likely to put off from day to day, and for which upper management and auditors are likely to be critical of data center management.

Support Service Procedures. These procedures indirectly affect how well jobs are processed; they attend to the monitoring, evaluation, and correction functions in the data center. Procedures should be established for monitoring and evaluating, and correcting when necessary, data center activities; this includes the adequacy of all standards and procedures and the adherence to these standards and procedures. If a processing checkpoint is being bypassed, or if it does not even exist, this deficiency should be detected and corrected. Another important aspect of the data center that should be monitored and evaluated is the performance of hardware and software. Many hardware- and software-monitoring aids are available. Also included as part of hardware and software evaluation is the actual choice of hardware and software to be used in the data center. These are specialized skills, and specialists should be trained to perform these activities. Whereas administrative skills are primarily the concern of management personnel, support service procedures are primarily the concern of technical specialists.

DEVELOPMENT OF STANDARDS AND PROCEDURES

The very first standards and procedures that must be developed and documented are those for establishing and documenting data center standards and procedures. This is best accomplished by defining the phases for developing the standards and procedures manual, and for each phase, stating the standards to be met—in other words, the results to be obtained for a phase before the next phase is started. Then the procedure for that phase is provided, stating actions to be taken and indicating precautions and recommendations. The entire process can be conveniently separated into seven phases:

1. Project initiation
2. Project preparation
3. Draft preparation
4. Draft review
5. Revision for substance
6. Revision for expression
7. Printing and distribution

Phase 1: Project Initiation

The data center manager is responsible for initiating this project. This is accomplished by selecting a title for the project, defining its scope, choosing a person to be the project controller, and choosing a person to be editor; the same person may be both project coordinator and editor. The title selected could be simply "Manual Preparation," or more fully it could be "Preparation of the Data Center Standards and Procedures Manual." In either case, the data center manager must also state, in somewhat general terms, what will be included. Will the manual include all aspects that it should contain, or will all aspects be assigned priorities and be prepared as several successive projects? The last approach is what is usually chosen. The most critical topics are prepared and released first, then the remaining important topics, and finally the remaining less-important topics. With the scope of the project defined, the next step is to choose the project controller. This person must have the managerial ability to direct and coordinate all activities and the technical knowledge to judge the reasonableness of the material prepared. If a documentation-support group exists, the ideal person to choose is someone from this group who has both editorial experience and technical knowledge. That person can also serve as the editor, the person responsible for revising the manual to achieve adequacy of expression and conformity with the organization's style standards. If the project controller does not have the editorial experience, another person will have to be chosen to be the editor.

Phase 2: Project Preparation

The project controller uses the data center manager's statement of project scope as a starting point in preparing an outline for the manual. Through discussions with others, additional topics may be added, subtopics may be suggested, and alternate topics and topic titles suggested. An outline results when a comprehensive list of topics and subtopics is obtained and when their relationships become apparent. The preparation of the manual's outline is a very critical step and can actually be considered the most important step in the entire process. The organization must be logical, easy to adjust for changing technology, and easy to relate to for quick location of information. Any mistakes made at this step may lead to a poorly organized manual that is difficult to use and difficult to update. In addition, when the manual is completed, restructuring may require extensive rewriting. Therefore, comments on structure should be obtained from those with insight into what it should contain and how it should be used, and their comments should be taken seriously. The outline is then shown to the data center manager for approval, being sure to mention any worthwhile comments made and any alternative arrangements and phraseology that are worth considering.

With agreement on the outline, the project controller selects the topics to be done (if not all topics are to be prepared before the manual is released), prepares a schedule, and determines who should prepare the various topics. Each schedule should be documented on a Gantt chart, and this chart should be accompanied by a document stating who is assigned to each topic. The data center manager is then asked to approve the schedule and the personnel assignments. After adjustments, if any, are made, the preparatory work for the project has been completed: an outline, a schedule, and personnel assignments have been completed and have been approved by the data center manager.

Phase 3: Draft Preparation

Each writer assigned to prepare material discusses with the project controller what is to be included for each topic, the manner of presentation, and the degree of detail. With these matters clarified, the writer is then ready to collect the material required, including samples of any forms and reports referred to. These writers must avoid a common pitfall at this point, and that is to confer only with the supervisors responsible for the various work areas, possibly questioning staff personnel only occasionally. Many supervisors may not actually know the details of what each staff member performs or, in other instances, may know the details but be more concerned with the overall effect, forgetting to supply details. Thus, each writer must have as a governing principle that most of the information gathered and verified should come from those working closely with this information, in other words, the clerks and assistants.

It is a frequent occurrence, for example, in the development of application systems, for the most

knowledgable persons in the user departments not to be questioned in any depth. The data center has been the victim of these hazardously designed systems, as have the end users. Consider an actual system developed by a team of systems analysts. These analysts frequently gathered around worktables brainstorming, preparing elaborate charts and tables. Some of these charts were fascinating, apparently representing a strange solar system in some far-off galaxy. Throughout their months of systems design and actual programming, only occasional visits were made to the user departments, and no visits were ever made to the persons working with the details of the operations that they hoped to automate. After the completion of the many complex programs and procedures, and just before the release of the system for production testing, a meeting with the users was held—to which a few clerks were invited who had no previous involvement in the project. The result was disaster. The analysts came from that meeting pale and suddenly silent. They had been told that some of their assumptions and many of their "facts" were wrong, that the system could not perform as needed, and the procedures were nearly totally meaningless. The redesign and reprogramming activities to make the system and procedures workable took several months, time that would have not been needed if only these clerical persons had been spoken to, or at least had been shown what was being developed.

The moral of this story is that the writers must work closely with those who are most knowledgable, with those who have the information needed. Besides gaining the information needed, a second significant benefit results from frequent meetings with the intended users of the manual. Acceptance of the standards and procedures is more likely, thus reducing difficulties in enforcing adherence. Personnel who are involved in the development activities, whose opinions and recommendations are considered, are more likely to accept requirements than those who learn of the requirements only when they are released.

As information is gathered, new relationships and requirements for topics are likely to become apparent. An updated outline should be prepared and approved by the project coordinator. After the information has been gathered, it is organized, and a first draft is written. The goal at this time is to produce a logically structured draft that clearly presents the information; the concern is *not* how well the information is expressed. Thus, the goal is to get the information on paper for review as to its accuracy and completeness, and only when this is accomplished and the content changes are made, should anyone consider the niceties of expression and the conformity with the organization's style standards.

Phase 4: Draft Review

The first draft has been prepared and it is now time to have its contents and organization reviewed and commented on. What is wanted are responses to the following questions:

- What information is inaccurate?
- What information is missing?
- What requires clarification?
- What restructuring is advisable?
- What charts and diagrams would be useful?

As in the case of gathering information, the best persons to review and make comments are those most knowledgeable of the topics presented. An excellent method to locate deficiencies is to simulate actual processing, to follow procedures and observe where confusion or problems may occur. When forms are referred to, they should be filled as instructed. It is even advisable to have the least-experienced persons in the data center try to follow the procedures presented. This practice is excellent because any missing instructions will not be automatically performed, but instead will cause processing to come to a halt, or at least cause processing to be performed inadequately. A novice to data center terminology will make apparent which terms and phrases must be defined. It must be remembered that procedures are not for historical record, or something to show auditors, but for guidance of data center personnel.

Phase 5: Revision for Substance

The writers now can include the worthwhile comments and recommendations in the first revision of the text. Obviously, before rejecting comments and recommendations, their rejection should be justified. If their worth is questionable, or if their meaning is not clear, a meeting should be called to clarify and to judge worth. Once it is decided what additions, changes, and possibly deletions should be made, it is the responsibility of the writers to make these changes. Although they will make changes to obvious expression weaknesses and errors, their primary responsibility is to revise for context and structure.

Phase 6: Revision for Expression

The written material, after revision for substance, becomes the responsibility of the editor, who, as mentioned earlier, may be and preferably should be the project controller. The editor revises for conformity to correct English usage and the organization's style standards, which should include such information as topic numbering, heading locations and capitalization, information on blocking and indenting, and exhibit identification and reference. For organizations without style standards, the editor must either select an existing manual to use as a model or personally establish the basic style standards. The editor will also revise to obtain clear and concise expression, while at the same time assuring the smooth flow of ideas and facts.

The editor's revisions are then typed as final copy for the manual, or, as some organizations prefer, the final copy is typeset. The editor reviews the final copy and makes any corrections necessary, and then checks that the corrections were made properly. Careful editing is necessary. A quick examination of published books and magazine articles will reveal many typesetting errors, including reversal of letters or words, omission of words, and frequently omission of entire sentences; in extreme cases, entire sentences may be swapped. This step is more difficult than it may appear. The editor's mind is likely to anticipate what is not present, and even though words are missing or repeated, it will be easy to proceed as if all were well. It takes a disciplined mind to ignore the content and to read what is actually on the page.

Phase 7: Printing and Distribution

After the manuals have been printed and the editor has checked that all pages have been printed and assembled correctly, it is advisable to have orientation seminars. At these seminars the significance and benefits expected from the standards and pro-

PHASE	RESPONSIBILITY	ACTIVITIES
1. Project initiation	Data center manager	1. Select a title for the project. 2. Define the project's scope. 3. Choose someone for project controller. 4. Choose someone for editor.
2. Project preparation	Project controller	5. Prepare an outline for the manual. 6. Obtain the data center manager's approval of the outline. 7. Prepare a schedule for the project. 8. Assign writers for the various topics. 9. Obtain the data center manager's approval of the schedule and the assignments.
3. Draft preparation	Writers	10. Discuss content and structure with the project controller. 11. Obtain information, comments, and recommendations. 12. If necessary, update the outline and obtain the project controller's approval. 13. Write the first draft, focusing attention on content and structure, not on manner of expression.
4. Draft review	Users	14. Obtain comments on content and structure from the most knowledgeable, and also from the least knowledgeable. 15. Test procedures and forms by actually using them.
5. Revision for substance	Writers	16. Discuss corrections, comments, and recommendations that require clarification or justification. 17. Revise content and structure.
6. Revise for expression	Editor	18. Revise for conformity with English usage and the organization's style standards. 19. Revise for clarity, conciseness, and smooth flow. 20. Have the draft corrected; review the revised draft and have necessary corrections made, if any.
7. Printing and distribution	Editor and project controller	21. Have the manual printed. 22. Review printing and manual assembly. 23. Conduct orientation seminars. 24. Distribute the manuals.

ILLUSTRATION 7–12. The 7-Phase Procedure for Developing Standards and Procedures.

cedures can be stressed, and the organization of the manual can be explained. The primary purpose of these seminars is to encourage acceptance and adherence and to explain how information can be assessed quickly. When the data center personnel are comfortable with the organization and contents of the manual, the manuals can be distributed. Illustration 7–12 summarizes the seven-phase development process, indicating personnel responsibilities and their primary activities.

Once the manual is in use, responsibility for its usefulness does not stop. One or more persons must be responsible for monitoring adherence to its contents and for verifying its accuracy. And when updating is necessary, the revisions must be made in a reasonably timely manner. Excessive delays lead to errors and confusion and destroy personnel's trust in the manual's content. Some

organizations update manuals once a month; other organizations update manuals once every three months, with additional updates for particularly critical changes or additions.

ENFORCEMENT OF STANDARDS AND PROCEDURES

"Good standards enforce themselves,"[4] comments Dick Brandon, using "standards" to refer to both standards and procedures. Deviations become apparent, whether the deviations are from performance expectations or procedural activities. Management reports highlight performance deviations,

[4] Dick H. Brandon, *Managerial Standards for Data Processing*, p. 2.

187

whereas data center control logs and other data center forms permit location of procedural deviations. In fact, the necessity of completing data center logs and forms forces adherence to procedures. The absence of information indicates an incompleted activity, possibly indicating information not really needed and thus initiating a revision of the form and the associated procedure. Whether forcing adherence or changes, standards and procedures are enforcing themselves.

Since the importance of forms as a control of data center activities is generally unappreciated, a few more words on this topic are justified. Consider that the existence of spaces for information and signatures makes the absence of entries obvious, and that the omissions must be either justified or corrected. This is the silent strength of forms. They are frequently treated with casual or annoyed attention, but they actually indicate how jobs are processed, how personnel act, and in fact how personnel think. If information is required on a form, someone must do whatever is necessary to supply that information. Thus, the form initiates action. If a form contains estimated arrival time for a job and a blank space is present for actual arrival time, personnel are forced to reflect and investigate what has happened to the job or data, whether the job can still meet its scheduled completion time or must be rescheduled. Many forms have built-in station-to-station processing checks, which may consist of a transaction total, a processing time, or merely a checkmark. Any of these will indicate whether or not processing was completed at a particular work station and whether the job is ready for further processing.

Besides self-enforcement inherent in standards and procedures, there is externally imposed enforcement, which consists of personnel education, standards and procedures testing, and standards and procedures monitoring.

Personnel Education. A basic means of enforcing standards and procedures is to make personnel aware of the significance of standards and procedures and of the benefits personnel receive. It can be easily conveyed and proven to personnel that standards and procedures make processing more efficient and reliable, but it may not be apparent to them that their confidence will improve, that confusion, frustration, and criticism will be minimized. This is what results and it should be conveyed. When personnel understand and believe in the value of standards and procedures, enforcement becomes relatively easy. If, however, personnel remain unconvinced, enforcement must be actively attended to, and it becomes a difficult rather than an easy task. Education is necessary to obtain the desired attitude. Personnel must be shown that standards and procedures are not inconsequential, but significant to their well-being and to the well-being of the data center, and not arbitrary, but the result of careful analysis and decision-making.

Standards and Procedures Testing. The more dramatic method is the actual testing of standards and procedures, sometimes referred to as "fire drills." This involves periodic disruption of processing (preferably without any warning) and requires personnel to follow alternate contingency plans. Fire drills permit observation of how personnel adjust to minor emergencies, such as equipment malfunction, and to disaster situations, such as a complete shutdown of the data center. Violations and inadequacies in the contingency plans may be observed. A milder form of testing involves the introduction of test jobs and the observation of how they are processed, noting where procedures are ignored—or "twisted a little." Another test of adherence to standards and procedures involves such actions as attempting to bypass access security. It is not unusual to find an installation with man-trap plus guard at the main entrance to a data center, and with an unlocked and unguarded door to a nearby utility area (such as a supply area), giving unhampered access to the data center.

Standards and Procedures Monitoring. The mildest form of standards and procedures testing, which consists of occasional random observations of processing, is inadequate and should be replaced by frequent monitoring. Thus, personnel will know that monitoring is, in effect, constant, and if for no other reason, they will adhere to standards and procedures. Responsibility for this monitoring may be assigned to one person, on a part-time basis in small installations, or to a team, which is definitely desirable in very large installations. This person or team submits a report to management on any deviations found; the report can actually be a form, making the results as comprehensive as desired, consistent in what is included, and easy to prepare and reference. When deviations are noted in the report, the causes and recommended corrections must also be included. The corrections may consist of additional education for personnel, stern condemnation, or reevaluation of the standards and procedures and how they are documented. When the violator is from the user department, it may be necessary to correct the situation through user management enforcement, possibly by the data center steering committee.

One final comment on performance standards: all performance standards are bases for stability and for setting higher standards. They are to be viewed not as static goals, but as goals, once attained (producing a stable data center), to be used as stepping stones to higher levels of performance. Thus, a dynamic situation arises, periodically alternating between stabilizing at levels of performance and breaking through to higher levels of performance. As Henry Ford stated it, "If you think of 'standardization' as the best that you know today, but which is to be improved tomorrow—you get somewhere."

DATA CENTER WORKFLOW

GOAL

To smoothly and efficiently control the flow of jobs and data through the data center.

HIGHLIGHTS

Overall Workflow

Several criteria are used to guide the development of a general workflow model for the control of jobs and data from receipt to distribution.

Data Center Work Stations

The workflow model consists of seven work stations:

- *Data control:* to control input receipt and output distribution
- *Data conversion:* to convert user-supplied information to machine-readable data
- *Job control:* to schedule jobs, assemble them for computer processing, and disassemble them for distribution
- *Data center library:* to control access to files, programs, and documentation, and to store backup material off-site
- *Computer processing:* to process jobs, monitor their progress, attend to problems, and perform preventive maintenance
- *Postcomputer processing:* to perform output processing, such as decollating and bursting
- *Data center supplies:* to control the levels of supplies, avoiding shortages and excesses

On-Line Job Control

Job-control logs can be replaced by an on-line job-control system that, besides providing job-status and job-delay information, permits job scheduling, rescheduling, or cancellation.

Whereas data center procedures refer to all the procedures in the data center, including those for budgeting and for hardware evaluation, processing procedures refer only to those procedures occurring at the various work stations in the data center. These processing procedures include control of work received and processed, with attention to deadlines and priorities; they conclude with the correction of rejected transactions and the distribution of output. Each work station, however, is not isolated or independent of the other work stations. The flow of data and jobs from one work station to another can be controlled and stable, or unreliable and erratic. This flow activity, controlled or not, is referred to as the data center's workflow. Data center workflow, naturally, applies to batch processing, and not to alternative processing methods such as remote job entry, distributed data processing, and interactive on-line processing. These alternative methods affect work-station processing when they require such activities as scheduling and output processing. Generally, the data center provides only support services for these alternatives, transferring responsibility for scheduling, input preparation, error correction, and output control to the user departments.

OVERALL WORKFLOW

The workflow for batch processing is basically the same for all data centers; in fact, it is impossible to imagine how it can vary to any significant degree. A job request must exist; input documents must be received, converted to machine-readable data, and assembled with required files before computer processing can occur; and computer processing must be completed before reports can be decollated, burst, and distributed. But in spite of forced constraints on the data center's workflow, the degree of processing efficiency and reliability varies considerably from one data center to another. To arrive at a workflow model for emulation, criteria must be defined to guide its development and to judge its adequacy.

An Army publication suggests the primary criteria for establishing and evaluating a data center's workflow when it states, "Measures must be taken to insure that processing proceeds in a planned orderly manner, i.e., by production control. This involves scheduling the various phases through which data flows, monitoring progress, and speeding up delaying areas."[1] The criteria for a workflow model are stated as those necessary for production control, which is natural because the data center is, in effect, a factory. Raw material arrives in the form of documents; it progresses through the data center's production line, and output eventually results. Just as the absence of adequate controls on an automobile production line has produced cars with poor-fitting and malfunctioning parts, this same lack in the data center has resulted in incomplete, inaccurate, and lost output. Rephrasing the Army's criteria for production control results in the following criteria:

1. Establishing activities and workflow
2. Scheduling work-station activities
3. Monitoring work-station activities
4. Expediting disrupted processing

Establishing Activities and Workflow. Without established and documented work-station and workflow procedures that are complete, processing variations are inevitable, causing varying degrees of efficiency and reliability. The absence of procedures is apparent at all work stations. For example, it is common to see documents in various in-baskets in the data-conversion area, and then to have keying operators snatch these documents without any regard for their deadlines or priority. Sometimes the guiding rule is that the first job in is the first job out; or the job on the top of the heap is the one processed—in other words, the most recent job in may be the first job out. Sometimes procedures are defined with too many restrictions; this occurs infrequently in private industry, but is more common in government agencies. It should not be necessary to delay processing because non-

[1]*Data Processing Installation Management Guide,* Department of the Army, no. 18–7, August 1971.

essential information is missing on a form. The presence of such unnecessary restrictions clog government procedures, making them slow and expensive; the absence of enough restrictions in private industry's procedures, on the other hand, makes work flow too quickly, with inadequate controls, and this results in incomplete transactions and inaccuracies. A balance is recommended. Procedures should be complete, but at the same time should indicate which actions are not critical and not permitted to delay processing.

One more precaution: overall effectiveness must take precedence over local efficiency. If the procedure in the data-conversion area optimizes that area's productivity, ignoring commitments to users, the data-conversion area's production statistics may be appealing, but the data center's service reliability suffers. This fault occurs when personnel are assigned to low-priority jobs that will delay processing of a high-priority job which will soon arrive. This is the old battle between processing efficiency and processing effectiveness. It sacrifices overall effectiveness to local efficiency.

Thus, considering the problems and inefficiencies that can occur, the establishment of procedures for work-station activities and workflow is basic to production control. Yet, how often is this left to the creative imagination of each staff member? Without definite procedures, the remaining production-control requirements for scheduling, monitoring, and expediting jobs become difficult, if not impossible, to obtain.

Scheduling Work-Station Activities. Most data centers attend to computer scheduling but totally ignore the scheduling of activities before and after computer processing. How can a job be scheduled for computer processing if a deadline is not set for receiving material for data conversion? What if a job that requires two hours of data conversion is scheduled to be executed at 3:00 P.M., and the material for data conversion arrives at 2:00 P.M.? Simply, the job will be run late, and because of other scheduling commitments, it may have to be scheduled for another shift, or even another day. The same reasoning applies to scheduling post-computer processing. Executing a 30-minute job at 3:00 P.M. does not mean that the job will be ready at 3:30 P.M. Reports may have been produced. They may have to be decollated, burst, and possibly bound. Thus, if postcomputer pro-

cessing is anticipated to take two hours and the user requires the output at 3:30 P.M., the job cannot be run later than 1:30 P.M. Therefore, it is apparent that all data center activities must be scheduled.

Based on a solid foundation of adequate procedures, scheduling sets into motion job processing that can be effective with proper monitoring and expediting of delayed jobs.

Monitoring Work-Station Activities. Monitoring provides awareness of job status, permitting responses to user inquiries and permitting control of delayed jobs. Many installations cannot even assure users that jobs have been received at the center, much less pinpoint their work-station locations. Putting aside the discomfort experienced by data center personnel because of this inability, just the time lost in attempting to respond can be considerable. When a user can receive a quick, confident response, the impression is that processing is under control, which may be true or at least have the potential to be true.

Knowing the status of jobs makes it possible to be alerted to delayed jobs—possibly before their delay becomes serious. By being aware that a job has been delayed, personnel can either give it special attention to keep it on schedule or at least inform the user of the delay and of the new anticipated completion time. Frequent monitoring also supplies trend information. If a user is negligent and indifferent to meeting input delivery commitments, but insists on unreasonable service, monitoring provides the documentation needed to justify the data center's inability to meet these unreasonable demands. In one case, a user frequently demanded, "Where is my job," and received the standard response from the data center manager, "Do we have the input?" The unbelievable answer was always, "No." To what can such foolish demands be attributed? Inability to think? Lack of effort to think? In this case, it was an attempt to monopolize the data center resources, accompanied by indifference to the needs of other users.

Monitoring, besides controlling delayed jobs and documenting unreasonable user demands, provides other benefits. Monitoring hampers and detects fraudulent activities, observes adherence to standards and procedures, and provides data for performance evaluation. Any one of these benefits is enough to justify constant monitoring. To stress these benefits, they are now listed:

- Control delayed jobs
- Document unreasonable user demands
- Hamper and detect fraudulent efforts
- Observe adherence to standards and procedures
- Provide data for performance evaluation

Expediting Disrupted Processing. Processing can be disrupted for a number of reasons. It can result from users supplying input later than scheduled, from a bug in an application program, from a bug in an operating system's program, from an operator error, from a hardware failure, or from a data center disaster such as a fire. Procedures must exist to reschedule jobs according to the jobs ready for processing, and in the case of equipment failure, according to the data center resources available. Any software failures should be quickly reported to the persons most capable of resolving the problems, particularly for the operating system, which can halt the processing of all application programs. As for operator errors, corrective and restart procedures must be available, and operators must be trained in their use. The point is that all possible problems that may disrupt processing must be anticipated and planned for. Disasters require even more thorough preparation. These situations may require the use of a backup site with backup data, programs, and documentation.

Besides the randomly occurring disruptions mentioned, there are "normal" disruptions. These include the rejects occurring for an application program that require correction and recycling through the processing cycle, disrupting the processing of other applications and threatening the meeting of deadlines. The first question that arises is, Who

corrects the rejects? The users? The data conversion personnel? When deciding on these issues, it is necessary to consider the effect of the extra workload and to balance expediency against location of the greatest expertise. It often happens that the most knowledgeable persons for user applications are those in the data-conversion area. In these situations it is natural for them to assume the responsibility for correction. If the errors are primarily keying errors that arose in the data-conversion area, again it should be the responsibility of that area to make corrections. This problem, however, is slowly vanishing from the data center because users are doing more and more of their own keying and making their own corrections, thus assuming total responsibility for the accuracy and the availability of input.

The Data Center Workflow Model

The four criteria to be satisfied, expressed in different terms, are (1) precisely defining the processing activities and their sequence, (2) scheduling these activities, (3) monitoring the status and the deviations of jobs as they progress through these activities, and (4) controlling jobs that deviate from schedules.

Illustration 8-1 shows a functional flowchart of the data center's workflow. The activities are segmented and sequenced logically, with the numbers indicating activity sequence. A few possible exceptions to this sequence are worth noting. It is not necessary for converted data to be returned to data control, but if on-line updating of job-status information is not available, and if the recommended basic job-processing control is

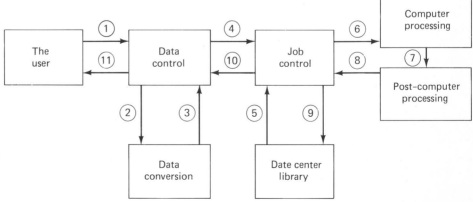

ILLUSTRATION 8-1. Data Center Workflow Model: The circled numbers indicate the normal flow of activities.

Production Control Log

Sheet ___ of ___   Date: _____

Job no.		Job name	Time			Turned over to shift			Comments
			Received	Completed	Pick-up	1	2	3	

ILLUSTRATION 8-2. Production Control Log. *Source:* Federal Reserve Bank of New York.

accepted as will be defined, it is necessary for data control to know that data conversion has been completed. Another variation is that job assembly does not have to wait for delivery of data to prepare control cards, assemble files, and any other preparatory work required; job assembly can be notifed to start job assembly as soon as data control receives a job. In many instances all the material needed for a scheduled job is already available, and it is only necessary for job assembly to assemble jobs according to the schedule. The final major deviation from this workflow is that the data center library can make files directly available to computer-room personnel and receive those files back from them; it is recommended as shown to provide another area for file-usage verification, and also to avoid supplying only part of jobs for pro-

cessing, either prior files without new data or new data without prior files. This workflow model defines the general activities and their sequence, the requirement of the first criterion.

The next criterion to be satisfied is scheduling these activities. Generally, this is thought to consist of scheduling only the jobs to be executed on the computer. In this case, scheduling would normally occur in the job-assembly work station. The scheduler would be solely concerned with obtaining data when needed and having all the files and other material ready. However, many of the scheduling problems occur because of delays that occur in converting data from processing and in preparing output for distribution, as already stated. Therefore, total data center scheduling is recommended. If this data center scheduling is done on-line, it is likely to be combined with job monitoring and to occur in the job-assembly area. But if it is not done on-line, it is likely to be combined with the data-control activities, since the data-control logs will be the single source of job-status information.

Having the data-control work station as the source of job-status and job-deviation information satisfies the third criterion for a data center workflow model, monitoring job status. Consider Illustration 8-2. This is a very useful log, supplying the primary status information needed for job monitoring and control. The log's capability can be increased since, as shown, it simply states that a job arrived at the data center, and whether or not it is ready for distribution and has been picked up. If a user were to inquire about a job that arrived at the data center but has not been com-

pleted, the only information that could be provided is that it is somewhere in the data center. The user would not know if the job was run but the reports have not been decollated, if the job is assembled for computer processing but not processed, or if the data for the job has not been converted. The job may require five minutes or five hours of processing, and the production-control log would not provide any hints. The log can be expanded to answer the following questions:

> Has the job been received?
> Is data conversion completed?
> Is computer processing completed?
> Will the job be rerun?
> Is the output ready for distribution?
> Has the output been picked up?

ILLUSTRATION 8-3. Job Monitoring Log.

| Job | | Receipt | | Data conv. completed | Computer Processing | | Job completion | | Pick-up signature |
Number	Name	Est.	Act.		W/Probs.	Acceptable	Deadline	Actual	

Job Monitoring Log Date:

These are the basic status questions. The expanded log, the job-monitoring log, shown in Illustration 8-3 can answer these questions. This log does create one communication problem. It is necessary for data control to become aware of the completion of computer processing and the results. This can be accomplished by periodic personal visits, by the receipt of special forms or lists, or, in the most sophisticated and the preferred method, by accessing a job-status data base from an on-line console. The last approach is discussed in the final section of this chapter. Putting the on-line-inquiry approach aside for now, the job-monitoring log is necessary and basic to answer job-status inquiries. A job's status is uncertain when, during computer processing, it abnormally terminates or when transactions are rejected and must be corrected and reentered before the output can be distributed to the user. In the first case, a programmer may be examining a program; in the second case, the data-conversion area or the user may be correcting the input. The log will indicate that computer processing was not completed satisfactorily. This, actually, is all that can be expected from a job-status log. If a user wants more information, it should be available from a log for processing problems or from a problem reporting sheet.

The remaining criterion is expediting delayed jobs, jobs deviating from anticipated progress through the data center. The cause, as already mentioned, can result from many problems, ranging from rejected transactions to a total data center disaster. Total disruption may require the implementation of a disaster plan and the use of a backup facility. The failure of some equipment is likely to cause some jobs to be canceled because of inadequate resources, and will require rescheduling of the remaining jobs; the scheduler must be ready to do this at a moment's notice. Job delays because of program bugs or rejected transactions are more common and should have predefined procedures for implementing their correction. For reject correction, it must be decided who will make the corrections, how they will be controlled, and how they will be reentered.

It may be necessary to expedite delayed jobs by having personnel work overtime or to pay for outside services. The availability of outside services should always be known and can be viewed as an inexpensive alternative to having excess resources—although many data center managers prefer to have the excess resources for emergencies and for easing scheduling difficulties. These policies and procedures must be established before the delays occur and eventually become critical. Unfortunately, the data centers that most need these policies and procedures are so enveloped in fire-fighting that no time is available for preventive measures.

DATA CENTER WORK STATIONS

Besides overall control of job processing through a job-monitoring log, each work station must have means of conducting and controlling its activities. The data-conversion area, for example, should have a record of how many jobs were received and completed and of how many remain to be completed. This policy provides local control and also permits isolation of a job-accountability problem between work stations and the entries on the job-monitoring log. Control logs should exist in the data-control, data-conversion, data center library, computer-processing, and possibly postcomputer-processing work stations; but it is not likely to exist for the job-assembly/disassembly work station. The control in this case is obtained by comparison of the data-control log entries for jobs delivered to job assembly against those received for computer processing.

For all work stations, forms guide activities, whether as logs or as individual job-control documents. It becomes apparent that forms are an important part of data center processing. An entire book can be devoted to samples of forms and recommendations as to variations—and such a book should be prepared. The increased use of on-line processing to record information and to control operations lessens dramatically the number of forms used, but actually replaces most of these forms with formatted displays to receive and present information. These displays require the same thought and insight when deciding what should be included, how much space is needed, the best sequence, and general formatting considerations. To avoid providing a book-length chapter showing many forms, only the most critical were chosen for inclusion.

The workflow model of the data center in Illustration 8-1 provides perspective and orientation of how each work station relates to the others, with the possible variations mentioned earlier. While examining the responsibilities of each work station, the relationships between work stations should be kept in mind.

Data Control

By initiating entries on the job-monitoring log and by entering processing information on each job as it proceeds through the data center, the data-control station does more than merely record this information, or at least has the potential of doing more. It can actually perform the following services:

1. Encourage timely receipt of input material
2. Review the completeness of input material
3. Control the receipt of all batches
4. Receive and control on-request jobs
5. Respond to job-status inquiries
6. Inform users about delayed jobs
7. Control the correction of rejected transactions
8. Control the distribution of output

Encourage Timely Receipt of Input Material. Prior to the start of each day, the scheduler should inform the data-control area of jobs to be run that require the receipt of input material. As the estimated receipt time gets closer, if the material has not arrived, the user is informed that it has not been received and that late receipt may require

rescheduling of the job. A policy should be set for when users are notified. For example, a warning notice one-half hour before the estimated receipt time may be considered appropriate. An added benefit of this practice is that it shows concern that users receive their output on schedule, creating an atmosphere of cooperation.

Review the Completeness of Input Material. By scanning the input material received, the absence of needed information can be located early, thus avoiding unnecessary processing before the absence becomes apparent. By this practice a small delay would replace a much longer delay, making the meeting of schedules more likely. This task, however, can be time consuming and should be reserved primarily for priority jobs. In most cases, verification will consist of only checking that information is present, not that the information appears reasonable. Reasonability verification should be part of the keying instructions in the data-conversion area, providing another early incorrect-input-detection area, and should definitely be part of the editing logic in the application system.

Control the Receipt of all Batches. Most jobs have the input material delivered in a single batch. For those jobs, the *routing ticket* in Illustration 8–4 is excellent. The routing ticket shown contains

ILLUSTRATION 8–4. Routing Ticket: The first part of this two-part form accompanies a job through the data center; the second part can be used instead of the Job Monitoring Log to record and report job status. *Source: Management Controls for Data Processing,* GF20–0006–1, IBM, p. 43.

Routing Ticket					
Job-source name:		Job-source no.:			Batch no.:
Last batch: ☐	No. in batch:			Priority:	
Operation	Date scheduled	Initials	Date completed	Initials	Remarks
Received					
Key transcription					
Key verification					
Job scheduling/staging					
Computer					
Report checked					
Report distributed					
Input data filed					

BATCH TICKET

Date _____

DESCRIPTION	TICKETS OR SHEETS	ENTRIES OR TRANS.	CARDS	TIME RECEIVED	
				CODING	K/P

	CODER	CHECKER	KEYPUNCHER	VERIFIER
Assigned To				
Time Assigned				
R/E				
Scheduled Completion				
Actual Completion				

Remarks & Special Instructions: _____

ILLUSTRATION 8-5. Batch Ticket.

only dates; it is desirable to also show time. This ticket can be used for multiple batches of input material for a job, as the existence of a batch number and check box for last batch indicate. Each separate batch of input transactions will arrive at data control with its own routing ticket. For example, if 20,000 transactions are separated into 20 batches of 1000 transactions each, each batch will have its own routing ticket. This ticket can be modified, as it is in many installations, to contain more control information than merely batch sequence number and the number of transactions in the batch. This additional control information may be various counts and dollar amounts. Counts can be for items in the transactions, or hash counts can be used for number not intended to be added, such as serial numbers and zip codes.

Many organizations prefer to use a *batch ticket* such as shown in Illustration 8-5. This form is helpful in locating inefficiencies and the causes of errors. However, this form should also include batch number and a means of indicating last batch.

The variations possible in a form's content and format are now apparent. Whatever ticket is used to accompany data, it is also advisable to maintain a control log, such as that shown in Illustration 8-6. Again, it is usually desirable to include both date and time information for receipt of batches. Without a batch-control log, it is almost certain to periodically "misplace" batches and to be embarrassed by being unable to answer inquiries as to what was received and what was processed.

Receive and Control On-Request Jobs. A form is needed for on-request jobs, one that provides all the preparation, computer processing, and post-computer processing information required for the job. The Request For Computer Services form shown in Illustration 8-7 is a form used at many data centers for a large company. It is likely that other companies, however, may want to provide space specially formatted for keying and report information. (The company using this request for computer services form has a separate form

		Input Data Log Sheet					

Job name: _____   Job no.: _____

		Document A		Document B		Document C	
		Name:		Name:		Name:	
		Source no.		Source no.		Source no.	
Day of month/ Day of week	Date	Batch no.	Volume	Batch no.	Volume	Batch no.	Volume
Total volume							
Expected volume							

ILLUSTRATION 8–6. Input Data Log Sheet. *Source: Management Controls for Data Processing*, GF20–0006–1, IBM, p. 42.

Request for Computer Services

Priority
☐ High ☐ Low
☐ Normal ☐ Economy

Punch job card ☐ Yes

Punch region on job card ☐ Yes

Job _____ of _____

| Charge number | Procedure ID | CPU Time (min) | User ID | Building | Room | Extension |

User surname

☐ IMS ☐ ICS ☐ TSO   System

Estimated running time (CPU–10) _____ (If more than 15 min.)

Call ☐ Punched output _____ Cards   Calcomp plotting _____ Plots

Card input _____ Boxes
(If over one box)

Estimated printout _____ Lines
(If over 50,000)

Run job concurrently with _____

Noncurrently on _____ the

Region _____ k

Tape set up

Volume serial (or scratch)	Library number	Multi volume input order	User supplied	Write (ring in)	Save	Tracks 9	Tracks 7	9 Track density 800	9 Track density 1600	Label SL	Label NL	External label description for saved tape volumes

Disk set up

Volser	Volser	Volser	Volser	Volser	Volser

Operations comments

User special instructions

Operations use only

Number _____   HASP Number _____   Tapes _____ Disks _____

Time in _____   Time out _____

Class _____   Priority override _____

System

ILLUSTRATION 8-7. Request for Computer Services.

for data-conversion services.) The service-request form accompanies the job, and is used to make entries on the job-monitoring log.

Respond to Job-Status Inquiries. As stated, the job-monitoring log permits the answering of status inquiries for both scheduled jobs and on-request jobs. It is necessary to decide if it is an acceptable policy to provide more detailed answers on job status. For example, is it adequate to state that a job was delivered to data conversion and has not been received back, or should it be required, possibly only for priority jobs, that the data-conversion area be asked what the status of the job is and then to inform the user. This policy can also apply to job assembly, computer processing, and postcomputer processing. Frequent responses to status inquires are likely to disrupt processing and delay jobs, ironically reducing service to users by attempting to provide more service.

Inform Users About Delayed Jobs. A job can be delayed for many reasons. Whatever the cause, the user should be informed of the delay and given an estimate of the new completion time. Failure to do this can only antagonize the users—not that conscientiously informing them will cause the news to be received with joy. Naturally, preparation for the possible causes of delays minimizes the amount of delay and may even eliminate the need to inform users of the occurrence of a problem. What is definitely wanted is to avoid surprising users with missed deadlines, particularly if it was apparent hours earlier that the deadline could not be met. If users are informed of delays, they may be able to alter their schedules to use output later than originally anticipated and, possibly, not seriously hamper their operations.

Control the Correction of Rejected Transactions. Many types of rejects can occur during computer processing. In the case of batches of data, dollar amounts, for example, could be entered with the data, and discrepancies may occur. Also, rejects may result from fields checked for type of data and for reasonability of data—but fields cannot be checked for accuracy; a computer program could not tell if a value of $24.50 should have been $42.50, as long as both values are reasonable, that is, within the permitted range of values. Rejects may occur because of inconsistency

between fields. For example, a person with a sex code of M, indicating male, is not likely to be eligible for maternity benefits. Whatever the cause of rejects, their correction and reentering into the system must be controlled. This control can occur by having an error-correction log in the data-control area, or by including this additional control information on the job-monitoring log, which, if there are multiple rejects, may be clumsy. It is probably best to indicate on the job-monitoring log that the job has not been run successfully, since space is already provided for this, and to have a separate error-correction log. The indication that a job has not been completed successfully will cause the error-correction log to be referenced.

Control the Distribution of Output. It is an unfortunate but frequent occurrence that users claim that they have not received output that they misplaced. Thus, what is needed is some form of record that they did receive the output. One method is to have a user person responsible for all output for a job, no matter how many reports and how many copies of each; this person would sign for the output in the space provided on the job-monitoring log. Another method is to keep a separate output-distribution control log. This log should have space for the receiver of each copy of a report to enter signature and date of pickup. This has been successful at many installations but may be cumbersome at large installations. A third method is to have a two-part computer-printed distribution-control slip, such as shown in Illustration 8–8. The receiver of a report signs and enters receipt date and time on this form, receiving one copy and leaving the second copy for the data center files in case of a disagreement. This is an excellent approach for an annoying problem. Naturally, the form should be redesigned to meet the particular needs and preferences of the installation. All the locations for signatures and dates shown, for example, may not be necessary.

Before leaving the data-control work station, an excellent method for becoming aware of potential job delays, although not for providing quick access to job-status information, is the use of a card file.[2] For each job scheduled, a job-status card is prepared and stored in a card box kept in

[2] Ronald Yearsley and Roger Graham, *Handbook of Computer Management* (Epping, Great Britain: Gower Press, 1973), pp. 157–159.

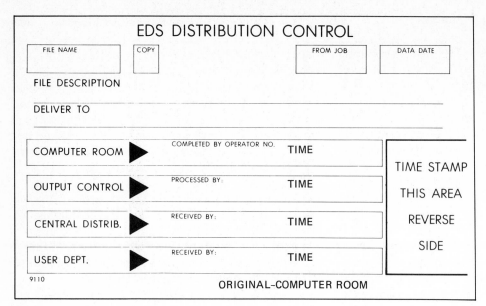

EDS DISTRIBUTION CONTROL

| FILE NAME | COPY | | FROM JOB | DATA DATE |

FILE DESCRIPTION

DELIVER TO

COMPUTER ROOM ▶	COMPLETED BY OPERATOR NO.	TIME
OUTPUT CONTROL ▶	PROCESSED BY:	TIME
CENTRAL DISTRIB. ▶	RECEIVED BY:	TIME
USER DEPT. ▶	RECEIVED BY:	TIME

TIME STAMP

THIS AREA

REVERSE

SIDE

9110

ORIGINAL—COMPUTER ROOM

ILLUSTRATION 8–8. Distribution Control Slip. *Source:* Federal Reserve Bank of New York.

the data-control area. Each card lists all work stations that will process the job, with start time for each station. Each of these cards is located behind a tab labeled for a time preceding the time the job is expected at the next work station, possibly one or two hours prior to the scheduled time. Thus, at the beginning of each time period, a data-control clerk examines the cards present and determines if a potential delay may occur, in which case the appropriate person is notified, whether a user or a work-station supervisor. When a job arrives at its scheduled work station, its card is relocated for its next status check.

Data Conversion

Input material arrives in the data-conversion area and is converted to punched cards or to magnetic formations on tape, disk, or drum. This area usually receives high workload demands and pressure for quantity production with a high level of accuracy. This often results in stress on productivity, not on the jobs themselves. Time is used to speed work through the area instead of deciding on which jobs should be processed first, except for those jobs with emergency status. In most cases, deadlines and priorities are ignored, and the accuracy of results is likely to be uncertain. Although stress is generally placed on the processing activities in the computer room, it is the data-conversion area, as well as the postcomputer-processing area, that accounts for many, if not most, bottlenecks. Thus, the functioning of this area requires more concern and regimentation than is customary. This requires

attention to three distinct aspects of the processing activities: control of preparation, correct preparation, and efficient preparation.

Control of Preparation. As is the case for the data-control area, a control log is the recommended tool for controlling data conversion. This data-conversion control log should include the estimated and actual dates and times for job receipt and completion. It should also include priority and quantity information. Using this information, the data-conversion supervisor can judge which jobs should be processed first and can report any jobs anticipated to miss deadlines. With prior notification of scheduled jobs and the data-conversion effort required, preferably several days in advance, the supervisor can predict when the demand will exceed the resources on hand. This permits scheduling modifications, the scheduling of overtime, and possibly the arrangement for outside assistance.

The log should also show who was assigned to each job, so that status inquiries can be answered quickly. This log therefore provides total control of data-conversion activities. Even a small data-conversion area with low demands benefits from the use of this log. The supervisor may be able to recall at the time of data conversion who is doing each job and its status, but if inquiries are made several days later as to what occurred, how many transactions were prepared, whether they were verified, and who did the work, a log is the only reliable means to provide this information. Furthermore, this information is more readily accepted, since it is documented and can be reviewed by anyone. The use and dependence on this log presents the image of a professionally run organization, not one based on "maybes" and "I think," which suggests an unmanaged environment.

Correct Preparation. A primary obstacle to correct preparation is the poor design of forms used to contain information for preparing data. The most blatant form-design errors are those involving how information is sequenced on the forms. It is customary for a keying operator to have to locate the first piece of information from the center of the form, the second from the upper part, the third from another location, and continuing in this fashion, hopping to various points on the form. A form designed with the keying operations in mind attempts to provide the information in the sequence that it will be keyed. Other form-design defects are inadequate space for entries and the use of ambiguous captions, causing the wrong information to be entered.

Another source of errors is the absence of data-conversion instructions, or when this information is available, it is sketchy and permits operators to key fields differently. Two formats that can be used for documenting data-conversion instructions are shown in Illustrations 8–9 and 8–10. These instructions provide basic reasonability checks and include keying instructions for data justification and zero fill. Thus, a field that will contain a name may be left-justified, with the remaining positions blank, and a field that will contain a dollar value may be right-justified, with the preceding positions filled with zeros instead of remaining blank. The adequacy of the instructions provided can be tested by having someone unfamiliar with the data follow the keying instructions, at the same time commenting on any doubts that may arise.

Although the data-conversion instructions should be able to guide keying operations without any other assistance, it is advisable to periodically provide orientation and education seminars, particularly for newly introduced applications. These seminars would explain the significance of the applications, the transactions, and the instructions provided. This would make the work more meaningful, and the existence of meaningless information apparent, as well as the absence of needed information. This insight also makes the work

more meaningful and interesting to the data-conversion personnel, lessening and possibly totally eliminating the boredom that results when keying activities are performed mechanically, without any awareness of how it relates to the needs of users.

Efficient Preparation. Efficiency can be improved by observing patterns in the data prepared and using drum cards for keypunch machines or their equivalents for key-to-tape and key-to-disk machines. This permits quick, automatic advancements of the media for entering data. The occurrence of duplicate data from one transaction to the next should also be considered and used to permit quick duplication of this information instead of repeatedly keying the same data.

Keypunching is not as efficient as key-to-tape and key-to-disk operations. These alternate keying methods, for example, permit quick correction of fields without having to duplicate prior fields, and also permit records longer than the 80-position limit for most punch cards. The efficiency of these alternatives is generally accepted and has been documented many times. These findings are summarized by the statement, "Users have reported that keyboard systems have increased throughputs by as much as 20% to 50% as compared to keypunching.[3] This increased efficiency contributes to the significant cost reductions that these alternative methods provide. Whereas 6000 to 9000 strokes per hour can be expected for keypunching, 12,000 strokes per hour can be expected for keyboards; and whereas the cost per 1000 strokes for keypunching is likely to be about $0.57, the cost for keyboards is likely to be about $0.27.[4]

An alternative to increasing the efficiency of the data-conversion process is to transfer the workload burden from the data-conversion area to the user area. This places the responsibility for meeting data-conversion deadlines and for correcting rejects on the users. Because of this trend, many data centers that had large keying staffs now have skeleton staffs for preparing control cards and for doing some data conversion. Staffs of over 150 persons have dwindled to less than 10.

[3] Alfonso F. Cardenas, "Data Entry: A Cost Giant," in *Computer Readings for Making it Count,* 2nd. ed., ed. Edward O. Joslin (Clifton, Virginia: College Readings, 1976), p. 58.
[4] Ibid., pp. 63–64.

Automated Services Division	Date released	Effective date	Number	
	Application		Section	Page
Arizona Highway Department				

System no. _____

DATA CONVERSION INSTRUCTIONS

System title

Date	Division name	Phone

Source document name	Number	Frequency

Volume	Card name	Card form number

Due in	Due out	Note: If the source document is obviously incomplete or incorrect, do not process.

Card columns	Verify	Field name	Field size	Alpha/num.	Zero fill	Justify	Required	Field description or special instructions

ILLUSTRATION 8-9. Data Conversion Instruction. *Source:* Arizona Highway Department.

Source Document / Header Information

SOURCE DOCUMENT ID (FORM NO.)	Receiving Inspection Report 1-74
SOURCE DATA PREPARED AT/BY	Receiving Dept.
FREQUENCY	Daily
VOLUME	233
PROGRAM NAME & NO.	P5010-Validate
OUTPUT FILE ID	TRANSF2
CARD ID NO. AND COLOR	2433 Pink
PREPARED BY	Jon Dough
DATE	10/10/75

Field layout reference (card columns):

Stock No. | Qty. Rec. | Date Rec. | Purch Order No. | Vend No. | Lot No.

Main Conversion / Validation Table

FIELD NO.	FIELD/DATA NAME	RECORD POS. FROM	TO	PICTURE	NUM	RNG	MIN.	MAX.	AND/OR RELATIONSHIP	SPECIAL INSTRUCTIONS
1	STOCK-NO	01	06	X99999						
2	QUAN	07	13	9(6)	✓	✓	60	5000		
3	REC-DATE	14	19	99999						MUST BE ≤ 7 DAYS PRIOR TO TODAYS DATE
4	P-O-NO	20	27	XX9(6)						
5	VENDOR	28	33	9(6)						MODULUS 9 CHECK DIGIT
6	LOT-NO	34	40	9(7)						
7	INSP-COD	41	41	X						MUST EQUAL CHAR 1 OF STOCK-NO
8	PART-CD	42	42	A						A = COMPLETE B = PART-CHECK = ERROR

Legend

PICTURE = Picture of the field as it will be stored on magnetic tape/disc (As seen on magnetic tape/disc)

AND/OR RELATIONSHIP = Name of other fields (Used with Range or independently)

** P B:
P = PACKED
B = BINARY

*P — PUNCH AS IS:
D = DUPLICATE
S = SKIP

LJ = LEFT JUSTIFY
RJ = RIGHT JUSTIFY
XC = OVERPUNCH IF CREDIT

SB = SKIP IF BLANK
ZB = ZERO FILL IF BLANK
LZ = LEFT ZERO

ILLUSTRATION 8-10. Data Conversion and Validation Instruction. *Source: Management Controls for Data Processing*, GF20-0006-1, IBM, p. 44.

Job Control

Whereas data control is responsible for reporting job status and reporting delays, job control's responsibilities are restricted to scheduling jobs and assembling and disassembling jobs. Thus, job control attends to some of the job-control activities, and data control attends to the remaining job-control activities. Necessarily, these two areas work closely together. In fact, it is recommended that they be located close to each other. Since work flows from data control to job control, this arrangement *almost* always occurs; where it does not occur, it is inevitable that work flow and coordination become awkward, and communication and efficiency suffer. This division of job-control responsibilities vanishes when the job-control area has on-line access to a job-status data base, as is explained later.

Job Scheduling. Job scheduling depends on access to scheduling information on production jobs, such as the information required on the data center schedule information sheet shown in Illustration 8–11. This information can be used to prepare a job-scheduling data base from which schedules will be computer-generated, although these systems will need more information than shown, particularly information on resource requirements. Besides information on computer resources, such as the number of tape and disk

ILLUSTRATION 8–11. Job Scheduling Information. *Source:* Post Office Department.

POST OFFICE DEPARTMENT

POSTAL DATA CENTER ADP SCHEDULE

PROJECT NO.	PROJECT TITLE	REFERENCES	DATE

TYPE OF JOB

☐ RECURRING–NEW REQUIREMENT ☐ SPECIAL–SEE FREQUENCY ☐ TEST RUN
☐ RECURRING–CHANGED REQUIREMENT ☐ RERUN–SEE REMARKS ☐ OTHER ________

FREQUENCY

☐ ONE TIME ☐ WEEKLY ☐ A/P ☐ POSTAL QTR. ☐ SEMI-ANNUAL ☐ AS REQUESTED BY ________
☐ DAILY ☐ PAY PERIOD ☐ MONTHLY ☐ CALENDAR QTR. ☐ ANNUAL ☐ OTHER ________

PROCESSING SEQUENCE

STEP NO.	ACTION UNIT	JOB NO.	DESCRIPTION	ESTIMATED PROCESS TIME (*Tenths*)							DUE OUT		SCHEDULE JOB		REPLACES THESE JOBS
				MAN	K.P.	083	519	085	557	1200	DAY	HOUR	BEFORE	AFTER	

REMARKS

TO(✓)	FROM ○	OFFICE	DATE	INITIAL
	9000	DIRECTOR, PDC		
	9010	ADMINISTRATIVE OFFICER		
	9100	DIRECTOR, PROCESSING & CONTROL DIVISION		
	9200	DIRECTOR, SYSTEMS & PLANNING DIVISION		
	9210	CHIEF, SYSTEMS BRANCH		
	9220	CHIEF, PRODUCTION SCHEDULING BRANCH		
	9300	DIRECTOR, DATA OPERATIONS DIVISION		
	9310	CHIEF, DATA PREPARATION BRANCH		
	9320	CHIEF, COMPUTER OPERATIONS BRANCH		

POD Form 846
Oct. 1967

POD, WASH., D. C.

drives needed, information is needed on expected data conversion and postcomputer time consumption. This resource information is also needed to manually schedule jobs, that is, if an attempt is going to be made to utilize resources as fully as possible.

Scheduling becomes increasingly difficult as the number of on-request jobs increases. One solution to the variety of job requests that may occur is to assign blocks of time to each type of request. Thus, blocks of time will be assigned to scheduled production jobs, unscheduled jobs, programmer compilations and tests, and maintenance. By alternating and balancing the amount of time allocated, it becomes possible to restrain one type of request to degenerate service provided to the other types. However, although these time periods should be adhered to, some flexibility should also be allowed. If a critical deadline must be met for a job, it is reasonable to move the time period for program testing, for example, one or two hours later. The primary purpose of scheduling is not to focus on scheduling technique but to attain results, to meet deadlines while using data center resources efficiently.

Thus, the job scheduler not only initiates a job schedule, but also has the responsibility for modifying this schedule, possibly even cancelling a job from one day's workload and putting it on another day. This is most likely to occur when hardware failures occur. It is these situations that make the benefits of computer-generated schedules apparent. It merely is necessary to indicate to the scheduling system what resources are available and to have it generate a new schedule. To do this manually in a multiprogramming environment requires examination of the resource requirements of all jobs scheduled and then to attempt to arrive at a reasonable job mix, that is, a balance of the types of jobs that should be run at the same time to efficiently use computer resources.

Job Assembly. It is necessary to assemble all the material needed to process each job before it is delivered to the computer room. This requires knowledge of the data and files required, the control or parameter cards required, as well as any other preparatory work required, such as sorting and collating, which is still performed at many installations on electronic accounting machines. This assembly information, as well as the computer-

processing information needed for scheduling, should be on job information sheets. By comparing the job requirements documented against what is provided, it is possible to locate and possibly to remedy any deficiency. In many installations it is not necessary to review this documentation, since the information is in a data base and a library system is used to print a job-stream report showing the material required.

The data center workflow model in Illustration 8–1 shows that the job-control area obtains files from the data center library and passes them with the jobs to the computer room. This is generally not done. It is suggested to provide an additional location for verifying files sent to the computer room and those received back, and to assure that jobs delivered for processing have the required files. But this procedure does require additional file handling, and many installations prefer to receive files directly from the data center library and to store them on racks in the computer room.

Job Disassembly. This is a straightforward two-step procedure. First, the output is verified for completeness and satisfactory completion. The number of reports and the copies of each are compared against the job specifications. Also, if any counts, dollar amounts, or sequence checks are used to verify data and processing accuracy, they are verified. The second step is to separate each job and deliver its components to their proper destinations. Thus, the files will be returned to the data center library, and usually the rest of the material will be forwarded to data control for distribution to the user. However, it is a general practice not to forward control cards and converted data to the user; these are usually retained in the data center.

Data Center Library

The tape librarian's duties are usually thought to consist of only supplying tape files and later receiving them back, either removing files from their racks or replacing them. Actually, the tape librarian's responsibilities are far more extensive; and when responsibility for controlling program tapes and documentation is added, the need for strict library control becomes apparent. These added responsibilities justify changing the tape librarian's job title to data center librarian, and changing the work station's name from tape library to data center library. Thus, the data center library consists of three libraries: the tape library, the program library, and the documentation library.

Tape Library. A basic decision necessary for establishing a tape library is how to sequence tapes on the racks: by application or by volume serial number (VSN). Since the disadvantages for one approach are the advantages for the other, only the advantages of each approach need be stated, and only the primary advantages are stated. Filing tapes by application permits quick setup and reduces the number of tapes needed in the scratch pool, reducing cost and storage requirements. Quick setup is obvious, since all the tapes for an application are in one location and extensive walking and searching are not required to pull tapes from the various racks. But the need for fewer scratch tapes is not as obvious. Consider a data center generating 50 tape files, with five generations of each tape. Thus, if these applications were executed each day, a total of 250 tapes would be needed. No additional scratch tapes are needed because, for each run, the oldest-generation tapes are used and they become the new-generation tapes. However, if applications were filed by VSN, 50 additional scratch tapes would be needed to create the 50 new-generation tapes. Thus, 20 percent more tapes are required, and 20 percent more storage space is needed—this becomes significant when the difference is between 100,000 tapes and 120,000 tapes.

The advantages of filing tapes by VSN are that the librarian is less likely to use a recent generation of a file for a scratch tape, and that file security is increased since an unauthorized person would find it difficult to locate the files for a specific application. In fact, some installations do not attach content-identifying labels to reels; labels are attached to these reels only to show VSN.

Most data centers have a computer-controlled library system. This permits the production of many control reports that simplify the librarian's activities. If a computer system is not used, it is necessary to use manually maintained control logs. The most basic report is a listing of all the tapes in the library, indicating their status, when a file has been created for what data set, and when it can be released. A sample of this type of report, which is

produced by a commercially available library system, is shown in Illustration 8–12. Other reports are usually produced to list tapes assigned in sequence by application, tapes to be released for reassignment, tapes to be cleaned and tested, and tapes to be stored off-site. Commercially available library systems may provide all of these reports.

Maintenance of the files containing tape information is generally a simple process, particularly for software systems developed by software vendors. The variety of forms used to add or delete tapes, or to change their status, are many; the form shown in Illustration 8–13 is a good example. The needs of each data center determine what information requested is unnecessary and what additional information should be requested.

Various documents can be produced from a library system to aid job assembly, computer processing, and postcomputer processing. The setup sheet printed from one library system's data base, which is shown in Illustration 8–14, guides all these areas. All the files needed for job processing are identified, making file gathering and verification an easy task. Another feature provided by some library systems is the printing of pressure-sensitive labels at the completion of the computer processing for each job. These labels are automatically produced, they are accurate, and they can be immediately attached. The amount of information that can be included on these labels is impressive, as is indicated in Illustration 8–15.

The critical nature of many files requires that backup copies be prepared and stored off-site. The librarian is responsible for assuring the preparation of backup tapes and for controlling their delivery to off-site storage locations. Those installations desiring extreme data-file security by indicating only VSNs on labels must enforce strict security on the tape library data base and any reports relating VSN to contents.

Program Library. Some installations may still receive programs as decks of punched cards, but most installations now store source and object modules on disks. Programs and cataloged procedures, that is, sets of job-control language statements, are used to make program additions, changes, deletions, assemblies, compiles, and other functions easy to perform. Commercially available software also provides storage efficiency by com-

FILE ID	SER #	VERS	VOL	FIL ID	OWNR ID	SYST ID	DAY	CYC	EXP DATE	CREATION DATE	TIME	PART	DRIVE	MODE	JOB	AS OF DATE	TAPE ERRORS
KGA-SLS EOM ADS	001234	2	1	A1	KG		0	3		06/17/77	13 37	F2	283		5440144		
HALL M/E FILE A	001235	7	1	M2	FH		0	8		06/06/77	18 48	BG	282		4500682		
HALL TEMP BACKUP	001236	SCRATCHED ON 07/16/77															
ADS LOAD LIB 2	001237	SCRATCHED ON 07/14/77															
KGA-MASTER FILES	001238	4	1	A7	KG		0	5		06/24/77	20 05	BG	281		5440144		
BHB-WKLY A/R	001240	3	1	B1	BH		0	6		07/13/77	16 20	BG	282		2000224		
QMA-SEMI WKLY	001241	3	1	A1	QM		0	3		07/11/77	21 12	BG	283		8150114		
HALL M/E FILE A	001242	3	1	M2	FH		0	8		07/02/77	14 50	F2	280		4500644	06/30/77	C
LAA-WKLY B/U	001243	2	1	A1	LA		0	6		07/06/77	04 54	BG	280		5700124		
KRI-HRLY TAPEIN	001244	SCRATCHED ON 07/14/77															
KRI-HRLY FILES	001245	8	1	I7	KR		0	12		07/03/77	17 06	F2	281		5440924		
CTA-E/M MASTER	001248	3	1	A5	CT		0	3		07/13/77	13 45	BG	282		3200121		
URA-G/L EOM B/U	001249	1	1	A2	UR		0	3		06/22/77	02 45	BG	282		8750144		
IRB-A/R WKLY B/U	001250	1	1	B1	IR		0	5		07/15/77	09 51	BG	281		5200224		
KGA-SLS AFT INVT	001251	SCRATCHED ON 07/15/77															
KGA-PROD WKLY	001254	SCRATCHED ON 07/16/77															
FCA-E/M MASTER	001257	3	1	A5	FC		0	3		07/06/77	06 03	F2	283		4000143		
WEA-CHATS EOM	001258	1	1	A1	WE		0	6		06/18/77	06 37	F2	282		9850144		
ADB-JOB COST B/U	001259	3	1	B1	AD		0	3		07/15/77	08 55	BG	281		1000214		
KGA-PROD EOM ADS	001260	2	1	A5	KG		0	3		06/13/77	07 57	BG	280		NO NAME		
CHK REGISTER	001262	1	1	M9	FH		0	3		07/16/77		AR			10003AA		
HALL DAILY FILE A	001263	1	1	D2	FH		0	5		07/16/77	02 19	F2	282		4500414	07/15/77	C
IBA-SEMI-MO B/U	001264	1	1	A1	IB		0	24		07/11/77	11 24	BG	280		5000134		
SGA-G/L WKLY	001265	1	1	A1	SG		0	6		07/14/77	06 12	F2	282		8550124		
AEA-AFTER A/P EOM	001267	1	1	A2	AE		0	3		07/12/77	16 45	F2	281		1300144		
WNA-G/L WKLY	001268	3	1	A1	WN		0	6		06/29/77	01 25	BG	282		9910124		
QMB-A/P EOM B/U	001269	2	1	B1	QM		0	3		06/09/77	02 56	F2	283		8150344		
WNC-POLICY MASTER	001270	SCRATCHED ON 07/16/77															
FH A/P CHANGES	001271	SCRATCHED ON 07/16/77															
IRA-WIP WKLY B/U	001274	1	1	A1	IR		0	6		07/12/77	21 04	F2	283		5200124		
GSA-A/P EOM B/U	001275	1	1	A2	GS		0	3		07/08/77	15 50	BG	282		NO NAME		
KGC-A/P EOM CUST	001276	1	1	C3	KG		0	3		07/07/77	22 00	F2	283		5440344		
PLA-EOM B/U	001277	6	1	A1	PL		0	8		06/01/77	21 57	F2	283		7550197		
ASA-WKLY B/U	001278	6	1	A3	AS		0	7		06/21/77	16 19	BG	281		1550197		
KGC-A/P EOM ADS	001279	1	1	C2	KG		0	3		07/07/77	21 57	F2	283		5440344		
IRA-WIP EOM B/U	001280	1	1	A2	IR		0	3		07/07/77	10 24	F2	282		5200144		
IRA-WIP WKLY B/U	001282	5	1	A1	IR		0	6		07/03/77	18 12	F2	281		5200124		
GSI-TYPE MASTER	001284	1	1	A2	GI		0	4		05/27/77		AR			10003AA		
ASA-EOM B/U	001286	2	1	A1	AS		0	7		06/18/77	06 28	BG	281		1550144		
GSA-A/P SEMI-MO	001287	3	1	A1	GS		0	3		07/08/77	14 18	BG	281		NO NAME		
AEA-M/M TAPE	001289	1	1	A7	AE		0	5		07/12/77	16 43	F2	283		1300144		
IRB-A/R PRELIM	001292	1	1	B2	IR		0	3		07/06/77	14 39	BG	281		5200244		
AEA-AFTER SLS EOM	001293	1	1	A1	AE		0	3		07/12/77	16 41	F2	282		1300144		
IRA-WIP WKLY B/U	001294	6	1	A1	IR		0	6		06/28/77	20 03	BG	283		5200124		
MCA-EOM B/U	001295	1	1	A1	MD		0	3		07/09/77	03 41	F2	281		6710144		
HALL M/E FILE	001296	7	1	M1	FH		0	8		06/06/77	18 45	BG	281		4500682		
PBD-DEB EOM B/U	001297	3	1	D1	PB		0	3		06/10/77	06 42	F2	283		7800244		
WNC-DEC WKLY	001299	6	1	C1	WN		0	6		06/27/77	18 15	BG	280		9910324		
HALL BRANCH B/UP	001300	2	1	A7	FH		PERM	3	12/31/99	07/12/77	02 19	F2	280		4500584	07/11/77	C
KXX-C/P A/R CUST	001301	2	1	X3	KX		0	3		06/08/77	02 28	BG	281		5441244		

ILLUSTRATION 8-12. Listing of All Tapes. *Source:* CA-DYNAM/T: *Automatic Tape Library Control System*, Trans-American Computer Associates, Inc., Jerico, N.Y., fig. 2.

pressing data; provides program protection against unauthorized access, copying, or deletion; provides audit trails of changes made; and provides backup and restart capabilities. The software packages available include PANVALET from Pansophic Systems, SOURCEGUARD from Datasonics, and PROCLIB from National Computing Industries. With respect to these software packages, the librarian's primary concern and responsibility are to control the storage of backup tapes off-site. Most data center managers, however, do not have backup tapes of programs stored off-site; therefore, if the in-house program files are destroyed, they expose themselves to embarrassment—or worse.

Documentation Library. As in the case of data and programs, it is necessary to store duplicate documentation at an off-site location. Installations will suffer to varying degrees if operating instructions are missing. Those installations not receiving automatically generated job-setup sheets, being dependent on operator run manuals, are dependent on the memories of operators, which is a precarious situation at best and an inoperable situation at worst. Other installations may suffer less, but they still will suffer. Job execution may not be a problem if jobstream is automatically established and executed, but such activities as responses to program messages and the ability to restart programs become difficult, if not impossible. The librarian's responsibility, as in the case for backup programs, is to control the storage of backup documentation. In addition, the librarian also controls the updating of backup documentation when the operating documentation is updated.

Tape Maintenance Request Form

Requester information
Please print

Name: _____ Date: _____

Location: _____ Room: _____ Ext: _____

Div./Sec: _____ User I.D. _____ Charge no.: _____

Signature: _____

Type of request			
OS		TMS	
Catalog	☐	Save	☐
Uncatalog	☐	Scratch	☐
Build index	☐	Tape removal	☐
Delete index	☐	Tape returned	☐
Other			☐

To be completed by librarian		
Action	Date	Initials
Received		
Completed		

Please print

Volume serial #	Index and/or dsname	Expdt or retpd	Out-of-area (user I.D.)	Tape inventory #

ILLUSTRATION 8-13. Tape Maintenance Request.

```
************************************************************
*                                                          *
*      VALU-LIB SET-UP SHEET FOR   RCHK0300   REGPROC    75210    *
*                                                          *
*  DATA SET NAME                          R/G VOLSER RL CR-DT   *
*                                                          *
*        **** INPUT DATA SETS ****                         *
*                                                          *
*  FPADLY.P102020.RCHKMSTR.G0449V00         1   402041 01 75210  *
*  FPADLY.P102020.RCHKMSTR.G0449V00         1   402042 02 75210  *
*  FPADLY.P102020.AUDIRCHK.G0118V00         1   402117 01 75207  *
*  FPADLY.P102020.RCHKJRNN.G0440V00         1   406019 01 75209  *
*  FPADLY.P102040.RCHKCVDR.G0096V00         1   402161 01 75200  *
*  FPAWKLY.P102020.RCHKTRNF.G0437V00        1   405101 01 75205  *
*  FPAWKLY.P102020.RCHKTRNF.G0437V00        1   405102 02 75205  *
*  FPAWKLY.P102020.RCHKTRNF.G0437V00        1   405103 03 75205  *
*  FPAWKLY.P102020.RCHKTRNF.G0437V00        1   405104 04 75205  *
*                                                          *
*        **** OUTPUT/CYCLE DATA SETS ****                  *
*                                                          *
*  FPADLY.P102020.RCHKMSTR.G0444V00         5   402050 01 75200  *
*  FPADLY.P102020.RCHKMSTR.G0444V00         5   402051 02 75200  *
*  FPADLY.P102020.AUDIRCHK.G0115V00         3   402114 01 75207  *
*  FPADLY.P102020.RCHKJRNN.G0030V00        10   402110 01 75199  *
*                                                          *
*        **** COMMENTS ****                                *
*                                                          *
*        **** REQUIRED MOUNTABLE PACKS ****                *
*                                                          *
*     VSN    TYPE   STORAGE LOCATION                       *
*                                                          *
*   RCHK01   3330      BIN  22                             *
*   RCHK02   3330      BIN  23                             *
*                                                          *
*        ***** OPERATORS *****                             *
*                                                          *
*  PLEASE PRINT ALL REPORTS ON STOCK WHITE UNTIL FURTHER NOTICE  *
*                                                          *
*  OUTPUT MUST BE GIVEN TO CONTROL BY 4:00 PM TUESDAY      *
*                                                          *
*        ***** CONTROL *****                               *
*                                                          *
*  DO NOT BURST REPORTS                                    *
*                 SEND TO PAYROLL AS IS                    *
************************************************************
```

ILLUSTRATION 8-14. Job Set-Up Sheet. *Source:* Valu-Lib II Systems Summary, Value Computing, Cherry Hill, N.J., p. 1–8.

ILLUSTRATION 8-15. Pressure Sensitive Label. *Source:* Tape Library Management System, Capex Corporation, Houston, Texas.

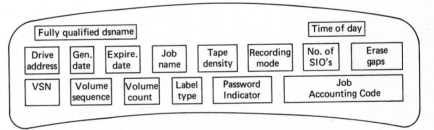

Do you hand-prepare or batch-prepare tape labels? If so, do they contain all of the fields that are shown above? This is the kind of label that is generated by TLMS in real time, as the data sets are written. Fourteen separate fields of information are completed.

```
WCHO. GCETWHP2                    0931

384 73008 73054 WDHOWHP2 1600    13672

H27131 3/ 3 S
```

```
RAPA.STKLOSS                      0933

480 73008 73040 PRHOCPY3 800 ET 9461 2

NLMOSH 1/1 N
```

Computer Processing

The presence of logs at various work stations has been seen to permit processing control. The same is true for the computer-processing work area. A form such as that shown in Illustration 8–16 is frequently used. It permits recording of any problems that occur and provides a record of what was accomplished. The primary documents that guide computer operators are the operating instructions for setting up a job, responding to program messages, and doing required postcomputer processing. Many formats have been used for these instructions. With the idea of keeping documentation modular, the use of separate documents for each type of processing information is recommended, such as the documents shown in Illustrations 8–17, 8–18, 8–19, 8–20, and 8–21. However, for small jobs that require relatively little information, a combined instruction sheet is preferred, such as the form shown in Illustration 8–22.

With these basic documents available, it is now possible to consider how operating activities can be made more reliable and efficient, and how software and hardware problems should be documented, resolved, and in the future avoided.

Reliability and Efficiency. The first necessity is to have an operations supervisor for computer processing. It is not usually satisfactory to have the lead operator perform these duties. The operations supervisor has a variety of tasks, which include monitoring adherence to standards and procedures for safety, security, and maintenance. These tasks are time consuming. It is difficult to imagine how a lead operator could operate a computer and attend to these other functions, particularly in an installation with several computers. Very likely, the monitoring tasks will be performed either infrequently or not at all. If, however, one or more persons are assigned to these monitoring tasks, it is possible for a lead operator to be responsible for supervising the computer operations. The environment determines whether or not this is an unacceptable practice.

The supervisor must be cautious, when reducing local cost, that overall cost is not actually increased. Consider the case where the number of operators assigned to a computer is reduced from two to one, thus saving the salary of one operator. Because the remaining operator is kept extra busy, processing may occasionally come to a halt, waiting for a response to a message or for a tape mount. The cost of such delays is likely to be much greater than one operator's salary, and there is a greater possibility of error because of the operator's hectic activity. Before cost or time savings are approved, their effect on overall operations should be examined.

Two data center activities that should be monitored but are often overlooked are unauthorized use of computers and performance of preventive maintenance. Many data center managers have been surprised to discover that computer operators have been using the data center resources for their own profit. In effect, these operators are in business for themselves. One method of protecting against unauthorized use is to review the console printout. To prevent unexplained missing console printout, a second copy can be produced that is immediately fed into a locked container. Another method is to write onto a data base all messages written on the console; this data base can be used to obtain a copy of console messages. Review of this printout makes it possible to locate, for example, unauthorized copying and selling of a mailing list, a frequent source of supplementary income.

Monitoring the performance of preventive maintenance is possible only if maintenance is precisely scheduled, which frequently is not possible. It may be specified that tape drive heads should be cleaned every four hours; but if a job is in progress, it may be cleaned in four and one-half hours or in five hours. One means of monitoring these activities is to have a sign-off sheet. To avoid a negative attitude toward the required maintenance and the sign-off sheets, the operators should be told the significance of the maintenance. It should be made clear that just as lack of attention to a broken motor mount in a car can lead to a major transmission repair, lack of attention to basic maintenance such as tape head cleaning can lead to unreliable and inefficient processing because of tape read errors, and possibly even to costly damage.

Turning from supervisory control to staff control of operations, there are several procedures they should perform. One that is generally treated casually is verification of control counts. These counts may be done merely to assure that the number of claims or employees or inventory items read are the same as the number processed. The control

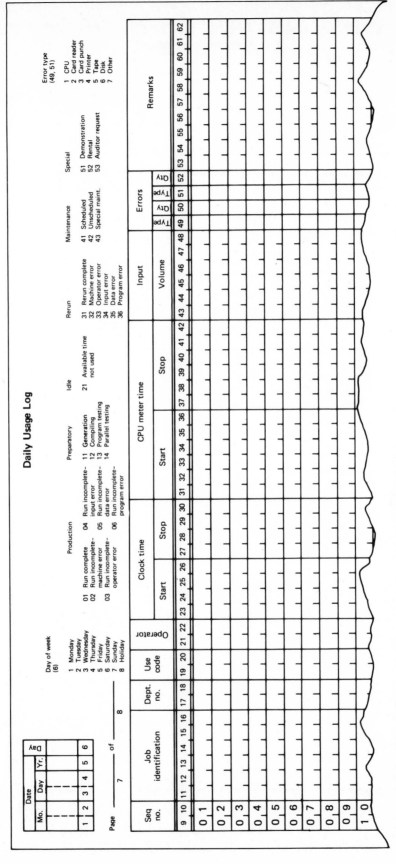

ILLUSTRATION 8-16. Dainly Usage Log. *Source:* IBM Data Processing Techniques: Management Planning Guide for a Manual of Data Processing Standards, GC20-1670-2, p. 62.

OPERATING INSTRUCTIONS FORM NO. 30
(TAPE/DISK)

System Name: _____ No. _____   Page _____ of _____

Date: _____

Program Name: _____ No. _____   Prepared by: _____

Disk Input/Output

File Name	File No.		Description of Input/Output File
		I / O	
		I / O	
		I / O	
		I / O	
		I / O	

Tape Input/Output

File Name	File No.		Description of Input/Output File
		I / O	
		I / O	
		I / O	
		I / O	
		I / O	
		I / O	
		I / O	

Sense Switch Settings

		Description of Condition
0 (A)	On / Off	Job Control will turn switch on when /* card is read.
1 (B)	On / Off	
2 (C)	On / Off	
3 (D)	On / Off	
4 (E)	On / Off	
5 (F)	On / Off	
6 (G)	On / Off	

ILLUSTRATION 8-17. Modular Operation Instructions for Tape/Disk. *Source:* Robert S. Kuehne, Herbert W. Lindberg, and William F. Baron, *Manual of Computer Documentation Standards with Forms* (Englewood Cliffs, N.J.: Prentice-Hall, 1972.)

OPERATING INSTRUCTIONS FORM NO. 31
(CARD/PRINTER)

System Name: No.   Page _____ of _____

                                          Date: _____

Program Name: No.   Prepared by:

CARD READER OUTPUT

Stacker	Input		Description of Output File
	1	Output	
	2	Output	

CARD PUNCH OUTPUT

Stacker	Output		Description of Output File
	1	Output	
	2	Output	

PRINTER OUTPUT

Form Name:

Form Number:

Number of Copies:

Carriage Tape Number & Name:

LINE SPACING:	6	8

Form Alignment Instructions:

SPECIAL RUN INSTRUCTIONS

ILLUSTRATION 8-18. Modular Operation Instructions for Card/Printer. *Source:* Robert S. Kuegne, Herbert W. Lindberg, and William F. Baron, *Manual of Computer Documentation Standards with Forms* (Englewood Cliffs, N.J.: Prentice-Hall, 1972).

OPERATING INSTRUCTIONS FORM NO. 32
(PARAMETER CARDS)

System Name: No.   Page _____ of _____

                                    Date: _____

Program Name: No.   Prepared by:

COLUMNS	DATA DESCRIPTION

ILLUSTRATION 8–19. Modular Operation Instructions for Parameter Cards. *Source:* Robert S. Kuehne, Herbert W. Lindberg, and William F. Baron, *Manual of Computer Documentation Standards with Forms* (Englewood Cliffs, N.J.: Prentice-Hall, 1972).

OPERATING INSTRUCTIONS FORM NO. 33
(JOB CONTROL CARDS)

System Name: *No.*   *Page* _____ *of* _____
Date: _____

Program Name: *No.*   *Prepared by:*
_____

Job Control Cards

Statement Name, Operation, and Operand:

Special Job Control Instructions:

ILLUSTRATION 8–20. Modular Operation Instructions for Job Control Cards. *Source:* Robert
S. Kuehne, Herbert W. Lindberg, and William F. Baron, *Manual of Computer Documentation
Standards with Forms* (Englewood Cliffs, N.J.: Prentice-Hall, 1972).

OPERATING INSTRUCTIONS (PROGRAM CONSOLE MESSAGES) FORM NO. 34

System Name: No.   Page _____ of _____
                                                   Date: _____
Program Name: No.   Prepared by:

_____

CONSOLE MESSAGE	HALT	CAUSE	ACTION

ILLUSTRATION 8–21. Modular Operation Instructions for Console Messages. *Source:* Robert S. Kuehne, Herbert W. Lindberg, and William F. Baron, *Manual of Computer Documentation Standards with Forms* (Englewood Cliffs, N.J.: Prentice-Hall, 1972).

360-Operations Guide

Page _____ of _____

Procedure I.D.	Application	Charge number
Schedule	No. of separate job steps	Region size	Estimated run time in minutes
Procedure description		CPU = _____
Remarks		I/O =

	Tapes	Disks	Other
Number of input			
Number of output			
Maximum utilization/step			
Remarks			

Device	I/O	Input source	L/N	Period	Description (complete DS name)	Cycles kept	Forward to

Output Identification

Form no.	Alias no.	No. parts	Carriage tapes	Burst	Dec.	Xerox	Remarks

Prime contact: Name _____ Phone _____

Operations acceptance by _____ Date _____

ILLUSTRATION 8-22. Single-Sheet Operating Instructions.

DATE	FROM	TO SHIFT			COMMENTS	Compl.
		1st	2nd	3rd		

SHIFT TURNOVER LOG — COMPUTER OPERATIONS DEPARTMENT

ILLUSTRATION 8-23. Shift Turnover Log. *Source:* Federal Reserve Bank of New York.

value may be a transaction count or a dollar amount on a batch control card; a computer program compares this value against what was actually processed and prints both expected and actual values. It is the operator's responsibility to check these values before proceeding to dependent job steps, which, if a discrepancy existed, would only waste computer resources and delay correction of the error.

Many operator errors occur when a job is in progress at the end of one shift and the operator of the next shift is not adequately informed of what has been done and what remains to be done. To avoid this difficulty, the operators should transmit job information to one another by using a shift-turnover log, such as the one shown in Illustration 8-23. This log permits communication of jobs that were delayed in prior shifts and must be run, providing any suggestions or precautions that may be of value.

Software and Hardware Problems. Software and hardware problems occur and should be expected. At any time, a user program or an operating-system error can disrupt or halt processing, or a hardware failure could occur and affect schedules. Without adequate procedures to expedite problem resolution, it is certain that confusion, frustration, and delays will occur. Consider how an application problem can be handled. The customary, informal approach is to contact a programmer who is familiar with the program. This approach may solve the problem quickly, but it is just as likely to require more time than necessary because of information and listings not supplied to the programmer. To avoid these delays and repeated requests for information and listings, a more formal approach is advisable, such as the completion of an official problem report. Illustration 8–24 shows a problem communication report that is particularly thorough; it is a two-sided, three-part form that permits some of the information to be keypunched for entry onto a problem control and reporting file. Simpler one-sided, one-part forms are more often used by installations, such as the form shown in Illustration 8–25.

Naturally, checkpoint and restart procedures should be used for all programs consuming a significant amount of time, which may be an expected run time of 30 minutes; each installation must establish a policy as to which jobs require checkpoints. It is a waste of data center resources to run a job for 30 minutes, encounter a processing disruption, eliminate the cause of the processing disruption, and then have to repeat the 30 minutes of processing already performed.

As for operating-system problems, the best approach is to have one or more resident system programmers who, besides resolving these problems, also analyze software deficiencies and consider means of enhancing system software. Although many organizations still prefer to have all software evaluations and enhancement performed in the programming department, an increasing number of data centers are accepting this responsibility. The system programmers are able to work more closely with operating personnel and to become aware of deficiencies that may otherwise go unnoticed and uncorrected. If a separate performance-evaluation group is not formed, these system programmers can be made responsible for this function, using software evaluators such as PPE for evaluating application performance, and using software monitors such as CUE for evaluating operating-system and hardware performance.

Hardware failures are the remaining problems that concern data center personnel. When such failures occur, the most satisfactory solution, if the problem cannot be resolved quickly, is to use backup hardware. But if backup hardware is not available, procedures should be defined to switch critical jobs to the hardware that is available. This will require job rescheduling, a difficult manual task, which further stresses the importance of a software-scheduling system. If serious hardware failures hamper execution of critical jobs, a backup facility reserved for these situations, as well as for disaster situations, should be used. The existence of adequate disaster plans permits quick and smooth transfer of jobs.

Many occurrences of hardware failures can be avoided with adequate preventive maintenance. The simpler maintenance, such as tape drive head cleaning, should be performed periodically without any need to interrupt processing. More extensive maintenance requires a significant amount of time and should be scheduled just as jobs are scheduled. The temptation to skip preventive maintenance, to devote the time "saved" for job processing, is likely to disrupt processing and waste more time than is saved. User pressure makes it difficult to adhere to convictions of proper data center management, but with documented policies and documented management support, it is possible to enforce these policies—unless upper management is doing the arm twisting. Fortunately, because of increased management enlightenment, this problem is occurring less often.

Hardware failures, however, will occur; and three questions must be answered:

> Is preventive maintenance adequate?
> Is corrective maintenance adequate?
> Is component failure rate excessive?

The first question requires analysis of the failures that have occurred and determination of the effect of additional preventive maintenance. To answer the last two questions requires documentation of the types of hardware failure, the amount of time taken to respond to each service call, and the amount of time used to correct each problem. Illustration 8–26 shows a form that provides this information. This log can be used to prepare a summary report, permitting evaluation of hardware reliability and repair service.

Postcomputer Processing

Activities such as report decollating and bursting usually occur in out-of-the-way corners in data centers. This occurs because of the relatively low significance given to these activities, which also

IF THIS PCR REQUIRES **URGENT** HANDLING, ENTER (X) ☐

PROBLEM COMMUNICATIONS REPORT No. 78887

GENERAL INFORMATION -- FOR INITIATOR USE ONLY
COMPLETE ALL APPLICABLE AREAS

JOB TITLE

PROGRAMMER NAME (IF TESTING)

REASON FOR INITIATING PCR

PERSON NOTIFIED

INITIATOR'S SIGNATURE

CHECKLIST (X)
☐ QUALITY CONTROL NOTIFIED ☐ TECH SECTION NOTIFIED ☐ MASTER CONSOLE SHEET
☐ ERRORS ☐ SEREP ☐ COREDUMP
☐ DEALLOCATION ☐ FILE DUMPS ☐ SYSOUT

JOB NUMBER	PREVIOUS PCR NO.	TODAY'S DATE MO. DAY YR.	TIME (24 HR.) HOUR MIN	SYSTEM	OPER. NO.	CONTROL NO.	WORK I.D.

ENVIRONMENT (X)
OS/VS DOS COS/30 EMUL COM GUP OCR OTHER S/U | ABEND CODE | DEVICE TYPE (2314, 2956, ETC.) | DEVICE ADDR. (OOC, OOE, ETC.) | DISK ONLY BANK MOD | DISK SERIAL NO. |

DAMAGE LOCATION CYL HEAD REC.	TAPE ONLY TAPE SERIAL NO.	DAMAGE LOC. (FEET)	CE NOTIFIED	CE ARRIVED	REPAIR TIME	RE-IPL (X)

PCR VERIFICATION -- FOR INITIATOR'S SUPERVISOR USE ONLY

PROBLEM CAN BE BEST CLASSIFIED AS: (ENTER AN 'X')
USER ☐ SOFTWARE ☐ PROGRAM ☐ HARDWARE ☐ JCL ERROR ☐ DOCUMENTATION ☐ DP GENERAL ☐ OTHER ☐

THE PCR IS AS COMPLETE AS POSSIBLE. ALL AVAILABLE DOCUMENTATION IS ATTACHED.

INITIATOR'S SUPERVISOR/QUALITY/CONTROL SIGNATURE

DATE

PROBLEM NOTIFICATION INFORMATION -- FOR QUALITY CONTROL USE ONLY

AREA	DATE NOTIFIED MO. DAY YR.	TIME NOTIFIED HR. MIN.	RESPONSE DATE MO. DAY YR.	RESPONSE TIME HR. MIN.	ON SITE REQ.(X)	PROBLEM SOLVER'S LAST NAME

ASSIGNMENT INFORMATION -- FOR QUALITY CONTROL USE ONLY
(COMPLETE FOR INITIAL PCR ASSIGNMENT

PCR ASSIGNED TO (LAST NAME)	AREA	SHIFT OR TEAM	OPER. NO.	DATE ASSIGNED MO. DAY YR.	QUALITY CONTROL SIGNATURE

TEMPORARY SOLUTION INFORMATION -- FOR PROBLEM SOLVER USE ONLY

WHAT WAS DONE TO INSURE THE COMPLETION OF THE JOB?

SIGNATURE TIME DATE

PERMANENT SOLUTION INFORMATION -- FOR FOLLOWUP SUPERVISOR'S USE ONLY

WHY DID THE PROBLEM OCCUR?

WHAT WAS DONE TO INSURE THAT THE PROBLEM WILL NOT OCCUR AGAIN?

SUPERVISOR'S SIGNATURE DATE

QUALITY CONTROL COPY

ILLUSTRATION 8-24a. A 3-Part Software Problem Reporting Form: The front of the first and third parts.

PROBLEM COMMUNICATIONS REPORT

C 78887

JOB NUMBER [ ][ ][ ][ ][ ][ ][ ][ ]
7-14

JOB DISPOSITION INFORMATION — FOR OPERATORS' USE ONLY

JOB COMPLETED NORMALLY (X)	JOB INCOMPLETE ENTER NEW PCR NO.	NEW PCR NO	SYSTEM	OPER NO	DATE RUN MO / DAY / YR	TIME RUN (24 HR) HR : MIN

HARDWARE / SOFTWARE PROBLEM INFORMATION

PSW/INSTRUCTION (8 BYTES) OS/DDS WAIT STATES/LOOPS
00 01 02 03 04 05 06 07

DOS WAIT STATE FIRST 4 BYTES OF STORAGE
00 01 02 03

CPU LIGHTS ON OR FLASHING (X)
SYS MAN WAIT TEST LOAD

LOOP INSTRUCTION ADDRESS (10 INSTRUCTIONS HEX)
1 2 3 4 5
6 7 8 9 10

TAPE DISK DISPOSITION INFORMATION — FOR TAPE LIBRARY USE ONLY

DISK DISPOSITION (X)	REPL / REINIT 15 16	TAPE DISPOSITION (X)	CLEAN REPL REINIT RECERT SCRAP NO PROB 17 18 19 20 21 22	TAPE, IF INPUT WAS ORIGINALLY CREATED ON	SYS 23 24	TAPE DR NO 25 27	DATE

TIME LOG-RECORD TIME SPENT RESOLVING PROBLEM

AREA	HRS	MINS	AREA	HRS	MINS	AREA	HRS	MINS	AREA	HRS	MINS	AREA	HRS	MINS
28 29	30 33		34 35	36 39		40 41	42 45		46 47	48 51		52 53	54 57	

PCR RESOLUTION INFORMATION — FOR QUALITY CONTROL USE ONLY

PROBLEM REASON CODE 58 61	AREA 62 63	TEAM OR SHIFT 64 65	OPER NO 66 67	SOLUTION CODE 68 69	DATE CLOSED MO / DAY / YR 70 75	INSUFF DOC 76	NOT PCR PROB 77	QUALITY CONTROL SIGNATURE

TS TECH. SECTION
QC QUALITY CONTROL
TL TAPE LIBRARY

PC PRODUCTION CONTROL
OP OPERATIONS
SP SYSTEMS PROGRAMMING

AREA CODES

SD SYSTEMS DEVELOMENT
SA SYSTEMS ASSURANCE
AP APPLICATIONS PROGRAMMING

US USER
MS MANAGEMENT SCIENCE

ADDITIONAL JOB INFORMATION — FOR QUALITY CONTROL USE ONLY

ALL JOBS INDICATED BELOW MUST BE RUN BEFORE GOING BACK TO JOB TICKET CONTROL NO.

EXP CODE	APPL	RUN NO	VAR	PROC REQ	AREA	OP. NO	SYS NO	SPECIAL INSTRUCTIONS

TASK / STATUS INFORMATION

TASK	INIT	DATE	TIME
STATUS	INIT	DATE	TIME
TASK	INIT	DATE	TIME
STATUS	INIT	DATE	TIME
TASK	INIT	DATE	TIME
STATUS	INIT	DATE	TIME
TASK	INIT	DATE	TIME
STATUS	INIT	DATE	TIME
TASK	INIT	DATE	TIME
STATUS	INIT	DATE	TIME

ADDITIONAL COPY REQUEST

NAME	DIVISION	BLDG.	FLOOR	FOR Q.C. USE ONLY

ILLUSTRATION 8–24b. A 3-Part Software Problem Reporting Form: The back of the first part.

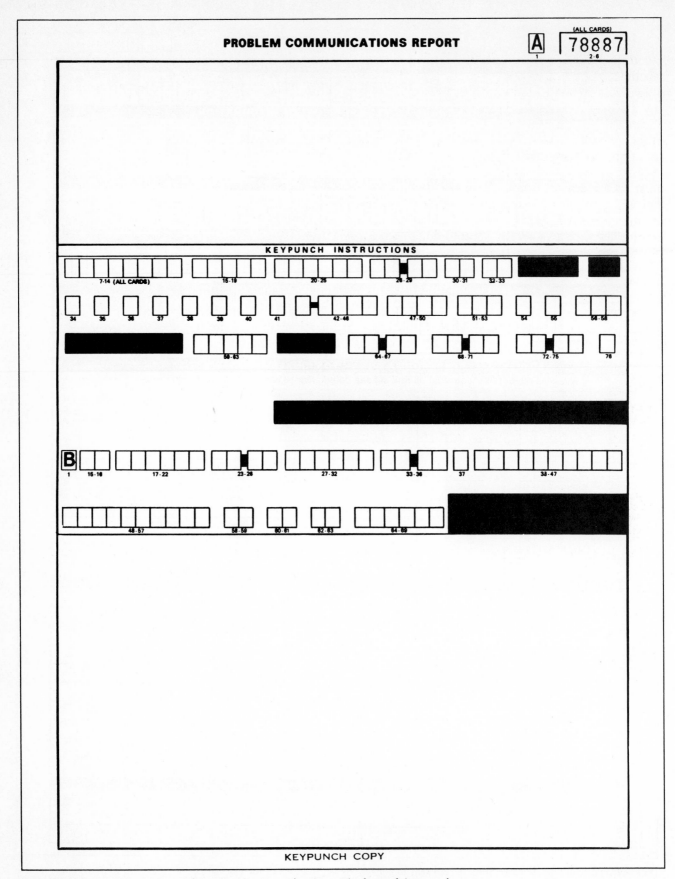

ILLUSTRATION 8-24c. A 3-Part Software Problem Reporting Form: The front of the second part.

accounts for why these activities are not usually scheduled. The end result is that peaks and valleys of workloads occur, without any forewarning or any attempt to level the workload. Sometimes the personnel in this area have nothing to do, and at other times reports are stacked on tables and on the floor, without any possibility of being processed to meet commitments. Thus, these activities must be included when forecasting job completion and when making commitments to users. Because of the low priority attached to these activities, another situation generally exists which degrades the service capability of this work station: inade-

quate work space and equipment. Small data centers use decollators that can separate only two-part reports. This means that a six-part report must be processed five times, an unfortunate and unnecessary waste of time. To make this situation worse, no backup decollator may be available. These false economies can nullify sophisticated computer processing and data center controls, and the malfunction of an inexpensive decollator can halt the flow of jobs out of the data center.

The larger data centers have several units and thus have automatic backup. Equipment failures therefore have less drastic effects. But, whether

ILLUSTRATION 8-25. A Single-Sheet Software Problem Reporting Form.

Software Problem		
Program name	Program ID	Problem number
Problem description:		
Reported by		Date
Causes of problem:		
Investigated by		Date completed
Actions taken:		
Performed by		Date completed

CONTINENTAL BANK
CONTINENTAL ILLINOIS NATIONAL BANK AND TRUST COMPANY OF CHICAGO

DATA PROCESSING DIVISION
COMPUTER TROUBLE LOG

PROBLEM INFORMATION			RESPONSE TIME						RERUN INFORMATION			IBM USE ONLY	
DATE / TIME	PCR NO. / OPER. NO.	DEVICE ADDRESS	DESCRIPTION OF PROBLEM	CE NOTIFIED (DATE / TIME)	RESPONSE REQUIRED (IMMED / DEF / UNTIL)	DISPATCH NOTIFIED (DATE / TIME)	CE ARRIVED (DATE / TIME)	TIME SPECIALIST ARRIVED (DATE / TIME)	PROBLEM REPAIRED (DATE / TIME)	ERROR ZONE	NON-BILLABLE TIME (ENDING / BEGINNING)	ELAPSED CPU TIME	CE METER READING (ENDING / BEGINNING)	CE'S INITIALS / CPU METER

IBM AUTHORIZED SIGNATURE _____ DATE _____

CUSTOMER AUTHORIZED SIGNATURE _____ DATE _____

RERUN HOURS _____ OTHER HOURS _____ TOTAL _____

ILLUSTRATION 8-26. Computer Trouble Log. *Source*: Continental Illinois National Bank and Trust Company of Chicago.

there are equipment failures or not, another problem generally exists. The machine operators are not likely to be aware of priorities, and they will process jobs in the sequence received, unaware of the jobs with critical deadlines. If a routing ticket accompanies each job, such as the one shown in Illustration 8-4, the machine operator should choose jobs according to comments in the Priority field. The machine operator should always contact the scheduler in case of serious equipment failures, thus permitting schedule adjustments and, if necessary, user notification of job delays. This is a matter of establishing procedures and training personnel to adhere to those procedures.

One other major problem occurs in postcomputer processing: output is stacked in unsecured areas. Even if there is security for access to the data center, there is almost always no security on the reports and checks generated and casually stacked. The number of personnel in a data center can vary from only a few (in some cases only one) to as many as 700 or more. It is impossible to guarantee that all these persons are honest, or at least that they would not be tempted. Considering the high occurrence of reported computer-related crimes, the likelihood is high that a crime will occur where output is not protected. In one situation, an analyst doing a study of printer speed for printing checks, considering alternative methods of printing checks, nonchalantly visited the computer room in a large installation, removed a box of printed checks to a secluded location, and counted print lines. Fortunately for this organization, the analyst was honest. This same analyst found secu-

rity problems in the delivery and storage of these checks. The carts used for the checks were occasionally left unattended in halls, and the user, after having these checks signed, left them in an unoccupied and unlocked room accessible to anyone.

Data Center Supplies

The primary concern of the personnel in the data center supply area is to have adequate supplies always available when needed. To do this it is necessary to know, for each inventory item, the reorder point (the minimum stock level that requires reordering), the reorder level (the amount to order at the reorder point, and the inventory-level status (how much is on hand).

Illustration 8-27 indicates the factors to be considered in determining the reorder point for each inventory item. This point depends on *safety stock* and *lead time.* The amount of safety stock required depends on the certainty of receiving an order when expected. If absolute certainty of receiving an order as expected exists, no allowance is needed for this extra inventory. As certainty diminishes, the more safety (or extra) stock is needed. Lead time refers to the amount of time anticipated to receive an order. Illustration 8-27 shows that the units of supply on hand continually lessen until the reorder point is reached, and then continue to lessen for the time span of the lead time, at the end of which the order is received just as the safety-stock level is reached. The diagram is an ideal representation. But it does stress the primary factors for determining reorder point.

ILLUSTRATION 8-27. Inventory Reordering Factors: As shown the reordering point is dependent on the lead time required to receive delivery and the safety stock required to protect against delayed delivery. *Source:* Charles T. Horngren, *Accounting for Management Control* (Englewood Cliffs, N.J.: Prentice-Hall, 1970), p. 547.

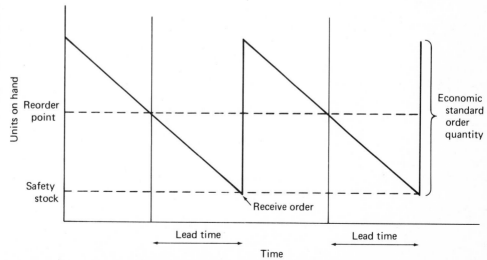

Stock Control		Stock title						Stock number			
Year		Estimated monthly usage				Reorder quantity		Reorder point			
Month	1	2	3	4	5	6	7	8	9	10	11	12
Usage												
On hand												

	Date	Vendor	Quantity	Dates	
				Ordered	Received
H					
i					
s					
t					
o					
r					
y					

ILLUSTRATION 8-28. Stock Control Card: Besides the indication stock on hand and reorder point to initiate an order, the information present permits analysis of trends, and as a result, guides updating of the reorder point and the quantity to be ordered.

ILLUSTRATION 8-29. The Primary Work Station Activities and Documents.

WORK STATION	PRIMARY ACTIVITIES	PRIMARY DOCUMENTS
Data control	1. Receive job requests and data. 2. Notify users of nonreceipt of jobs or data. 3. Control material delivered to and received from data conversion. 4. Deliver jobs and data to job control. 5. Receive job completion status after computer processing. 6. Distribute output.	Job Monitoring Log Request for Computer Services Routing Ticket Batch Control Log Distribution Control Slip
Data conversion	1. Prepare machine-readable data. 2. Verify converted data.	Data Conversion Control Log Data Conversion Instructions
Job control	1. Schedule jobs and inform data control of anticipated receipt of data. 2. Reschedule or cancel jobs. 3. Assemble jobs and deliver to computer processing. 4. Disassemble jobs received from post-computer processing and deliver to data control.	Job Scheduling Information Job Schedules
Data center library	1. Control delivery and receipt of files. 2. Control the release, cleaning, and testing of files. 3. Control the backup and off-site storage of files, programs, and documentation.	File Control Log Off-Site Storage Control Log "Listing of All Tapes" "Tapes To Be Released" "Tapes To Be Cleaned" Tape Maintenance Request Form
Computer processing	1. Execute jobs and record job processing information. 2. Respond to program messages. 3. Perform IPLs and program restarts. 4. Report software problems. 5. Record and control hardware problems.	Job Processing Log Shift Turnover Log Operating Instructions Software Problem Reporting Form Hardware Problem Recording Log
Postcomputer processing	1. Prepare reports for distribution—decollating, bursting, etc. 2. Prepare microfiche.	
Data center	1. Order supplies when their quantity is at the reorder-point. 2. Store supplies and make them available upon request.	Stock Record Cards

The reorder level is the amount to order at the reorder level. This is determined by vendor requirements for placing an order and by the financial advantage in ordering large enough quantities to obtain quantity-order discounts and to avoid charges for frequent ordering, but not too large a quantity, avoiding excessive overhead costs and storage problems. This is explained in Chapter 4. It is customary to determine the maximum stock level advisable, but supply availability can affect this. If paper is scarce, for example, as has happened, it may be necessary to overstock just to place an order and to obtain additional safety stock.

Basic to inventory control is awareness of inventory levels. The best approach is to use an inventory-control software system. These systems can print lists of supplies to be ordered, or actually print the orders. Putting aside software systems, one of the most successful approaches is to use stock-record cards, such as shown in Illustration 8–28. The particular card shown not only indicates ordering activity and stock balances, but also contains control and monthly-usage information. The usage information permits revaluation of reorder point, safety stock level, and reorder level. This information also permits forecasting of requirements and the preparation of supply-usage summary reports.

The primary activities and documents for each data center work station have been outlined. These are summarized in Illustration 8–29. The recommendations presented provide an opportunity to avoid various pitfalls and to improve data center efficiency and service.

ON-LINE JOB CONTROL

The recommended workflow controls presented are necessary for adequate processing control, but with the advent of on-line processing, they can be improved. A primary weakness of the controls recommended is the separation of job control between two work stations. The data-control work station reports on the status of job processing, whereas the job-control work station schedules jobs and controls their assembly and disassembly. With on-line processing, a single data base is maintained, and work stations enter job-status information in this data base. As shown in Illustration 8–30, the data base receives information that per-

mits answers to such questions as:

1. Has input arrived in the data center?
2. Has input been received in the data-conversion area?
3. Has job assembly received the data?
4. Has computer processing been started?
5. Has computer processing been completed?
6. Has postcomputer processing received the job?
7. Has job disassembly received the job?
8. Has the job been verified?
9. Is the output ready for the user?
10. Has the user received the output?

Thus job-control responsibility is no longer split between the data-control and the job-control areas. The data-control area can enter receipt and distribution information in the data base, and the job-control area is totally responsible for reporting job status, as well as for scheduling and, if necessary, rescheduling jobs. This also eliminates cumbersome communication that would otherwise be necessary between the computer-processing area and the data-control area about job completion. Without on-line processing, it would be necessary for someone, either through a document or verbal communication, to inform the data-control area of a job status, permitting data control to know when a job has been completed satisfactorily and has advanced to the postcomputer-processing area.

Besides centralizing responsibility and control, an on-line job-control system permits quick isolation of delayed jobs. In a manual system, it is necessary for data-control personnel to scan log entries for indication of delayed jobs; this may not be done because this task is time consuming, or it may be done inadequately because entries for delayed jobs may be missed. With an on-line system, it is only necessary to request a listing of delayed jobs, possibly limiting the search to only specific priority classes or to only those requiring specific resources. This capability, combined with the capability of immediately rescheduling jobs according to new priority and resource restriction information, makes job control thorough. That is why, when this total control exists in a data center, the job-control area can truly be considered the data center's nerve center.

"Nerve center" is a phrase that indicates the influence and energy radiating from the control area, but it does not suggest the pressure and

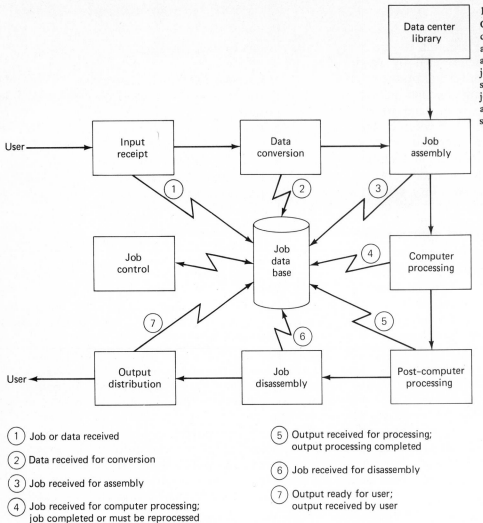

ILLUSTRATION 8-30. Online Job Control: Job status information is received from the various work stations as indicated by the circled numbers, and stored in a data base, which the job control area accesses to answer status inquiries and to locate delayed jobs for expediting. The job control area also controls job setup and job scheduling.

① Job or data received

② Data received for conversion

③ Job received for assembly

④ Job received for computer processing; job completed or must be reprocessed

⑤ Output received for processing; output processing completed

⑥ Job received for disassembly

⑦ Output ready for user; output received by user

tension placed on personnel. A phrase that suggests these conditions is "war room." This is particularly appropriate because the control area is usually in a separate room, and the activities resemble war tactics in deciding how to meet user demands while using data center resources efficiently.

The job-control area can also control actual jobstream submissions, a task usually performed in the computer room. To further increase the potential effectiveness of this area, job-performance monitoring can also be included. This is particularly important if resources are not being used close to their capacity, if on-line processing workload varies considerably, or if hardware, network, or power problems occur frequently.

In addition to day-to-day control of processing, the on-line job-control system provides other benefits. It permits user-service evaluation and resource-usage analysis. To do these tasks manually is time consuming, even if the information is available, which is not likely. With the on-line system, however, the information is waiting to be used and evaluated, limited only by the imagination of the data center personnel.

JOB SCHEDULING AND RESOURCE ALLOCATION

GOAL

To meet user commitments while allocating resources for maximum utilization and reduced costs.

HIGHLIGHTS

Scheduling Factors

Scheduling performance criteria are used to evaluate scheduling effectiveness, which depends on such factors as job requirements and data center capabilities, and on the choice of scheduling algorithm.

Scheduling Phases

After a scheduling methodology is developed and implemented, the scheduling process consists of three phases:

Forecasting to anticipate the overloading or underloading of data center resources.

Planning to schedule daily processing so that user commitments are met and data center resources are fully utilized.

Monitoring to report jobs status, to expedite delayed jobs, and to analyze and improve processing.

Scheduling Methods

Varying degrees of control and sophistication are available from the various scheduling methods, which can be classified as:

- Manual scheduling
- Operating-system schedulers
- Software scheduling packages

It is difficult to understand why the many aspects of scheduling do not receive adequate attention at many data centers. But this situation does exist, often with no attention given to how job sequencing affects resource utilization and the data center's ability to meet user deadlines. Larry Winkler of Crocker National Bank in California commented on this situation: "You would not attempt to set up an assembly line without proper scheduling of manpower, materials, and equipment. What makes a data-processing shop any different?"[1]

Possibly the reason little attention is given to scheduling is that the degenerative effects of inadequate scheduling are not adequately appreciated. Many analysts of computer utilization have commented on these degenerative effects: "Recent statistics in the U.S. and Europe show that the average large cpu to be only 30% active, many operating at 10% and below. . . . In general today's systems are poorly coordinated and wasteful, the cpu idle much of the time, with minimal cpu/peripherals overlap, and poor balance between overall hardware and software systems and the work they are performing."[2] A study conducted by A. T. Kearney and Company of 155 computer installations resulted in several interesting and, in some cases, somewhat shocking conclusions:

1. Only 48 percent of available time is used productively.
2. Computers are operated only 64% of available time.
3. Twenty-five percent of man-hours are wasted.
4. Large centers have the poorest performance in all categories of lost time.
5. Forty-two percent of the companies reporting do not maintain accurate records on computer performance.
6. Firms using multiprogramming achieve higher production.
7. Twenty-five percent of costs are wasted due to idleness, reruns, machine maintenance and downtime.[3]

[1] Larry Winkler, "Scheduling a Data Processing Center," *Data Management,* September 1975, p. 14.
[2] Vinod K. Sahney and James L. May, *Scheduling Computer Operations* (Norcross, Georgia: American Institute of Industrial Engineers, 1972), p. 2.
[3] Ibid., pp. 1–2.

It should be apparent to anyone living on a daily basis with computer processing that uncontrolled scheduling, or minimally controlled scheduling, results in alternating high- and low-workload periods, creating peak periods when job commitments cannot be met, and slack periods when data center resources rest idle. The data center alternates between poor service to users and expensive waste of data center resources. The data center should not be like a toll booth on a highway, where traffic demands cannot be controlled. At a toll booth during slack periods, attendants are forced to fidget about with little to do; however, during peak rush-hour demands, traffic jams occur, with long lines of cars crawling along. Data center managers should have better control of workload demands and should be able to level the demands made on data center resources, lessening the likelihood of alternating between poor service and poor resource utilization.

In spite of the above observations, a comment often heard is, "Our installation is different!" When pressed for justification of this statement, at least one of three reasons is given: any attempt to apply rigorous scheduling methods would fail because of (1) on-line processing, (2) programmer-submitted tests, or (3) unscheduled user requests. No doubt these processing demands are random and unpredictable, but they usually can be absorbed into a scheduling methodology, and many installations have done just that. These apparent roadblocks are discussed when scheduling factors are examined, and several solutions are suggested that have been implemented and have proved successful.

In spite of the importance of scheduling, if one or both of two conditions exist, scheduling need not be a primary concern, and possibly not a concern at all. What if a data center has few or no critical deadlines to meet, or if it has an abundance of resources that any demands made can be easily met? Obviously, no scheduling problem exists. These situations do not occur often. However, when they do, it indicates that the data center is wasting resources and incurring more expenses than it should. This is apparent in the situation of excess resources, but it may not be obvious in the situation where critical deadlines do not exist. In this case, resources are wasted because no attempt is made to level the workload, using only part of the capacity of the computer and the other data center resources.

The "other data center resources" referred to are the peripherals and the work stations preceding and following computer processing. These tend to be forgotten, since interest is generally centered only on the computer. Overloading or underloading these resources has the same effect as in the case of the computer; either user service deteriorates or data center resources are under-utilized. Even when a sincere attempt is made at rigorous scheduling, these other resources are often forgotten. In commenting on underutilization of resources, multiprogramming capability requires comment. Multiprogramming permits several programs to be executed at the same time; thus, if a job requires only 25 percent of the computer's real storage and only 3 of the 15 tape drives available, the remaining storage, tape drives, and other peripherals can be assigned to other programs, and all programs can be executed concurrently. The potential of multiprogramming is stimulating, but without careful scheduling, much of its capability is lost. Many ridiculous situations can occur. Several jobs can be executed at the same time, requiring the use of very few peripherals; thus, those resources are wasted. A low-priority job using many peripherals may not permit a high priority-job to be executed. Similarly, instead of using many peripherals, a low-priority job may require most of the real storage, thus blocking the loading of other jobs. The goal of multiprogramming, which cannot be attained through casual scheduling, is to determine the best *job mix,* the combination of jobs that will best use the resources available to meet job priority and deadline requirements.

The preceding comments on the problems and deficiencies that arise when scheduling is inadequate suggest some of the benefits to be expected when adequate scheduling is performed. There are, however, other benefits that may not be apparent. The potential benefits of scheduling are:

- Making users responsible for delivering input on schedule
- Meeting user deadlines
- Increasing user faith in data center service
- Leveling utilization of all data center resources
- Increasing data center throughput and turnaround
- Avoiding service degradation because of resource overloading
- Avoiding excessive cost because of resource underloading

- Making job delays apparent, permitting job expediting
- Allowing slack time for processing disruptions
- Providing schedules to improve communications with users
- Providing schedules to reduce data center confusion
- Utilizing multiprogramming potential
- Permitting evaluation of user cooperation
- Permitting evaluation of data center performance
- Predicting the effects of increased workload
- Predicting the need for more equipment and personnel

Some of the benefits listed are closely related, being either different viewpoints of the same results or one benefit leading to other benefits. The two benefits, "providing schedules to improve communications with users," and "permitting evaluation of user cooperation," are two viewpoints of having schedules for reference, since schedules aid communication and permit evaluation of deviations. As for the causal relationships of benefits to one another, consider the effect, for example, of "avoiding service degradation because of resource overloading." This benefit leads to "meeting user deadlines," which then leads to "increasing user faith in data center service." Some of the benefits listed may not be apparent. The benefit, "making users responsible for delivering input on schedule," is definitely desirable, but its relationship to data center scheduling may be obscure. This benefit can be anticipated if total data center scheduling is implemented, not only scheduling computer processing, but also scheduling precomputer and postcomputer processing—and precomputer scheduling includes the receipt of input. In this approach, when the user agrees to the date and time for computer scheduling, this data center commitment is made on the condition that input is received on schedule. It is understood that, if the input is not received as promised, the data center processing commitment is voided, although the data center is expected to cooperate and attempt to meet the user's deadline. The point is that users are made responsible for any missed deadlines for which they were the cause. To further increase user accountability for missed deadlines for which they are responsible, periodic reports should be prepared to document scheduling deviations and their causes.

SCHEDULING FACTORS

Scheduling factors can be classified as either job-related or data-center-related. After examining these factors and considering the primary scheduling difficulties that may occur, the various scheduling algorithms (rules guiding the sequencing of jobs) and the various scheduling performance criteria (criteria used for evaluating scheduling effectiveness) are defined and illustrated.

Job-Related Scheduling Factors

The most apparent factor is each job's resource requirements. These requirements vary widely from job to job. One job may require considerable real storage but only require a printer for output and no other peripheral. Another job may require little storage space but seven or eight tape drives, and possibly disk drives, a printer, and a card punch. But a job's resource requirements should not be viewed in these limited terms; all data center resource requirements should be considered. Thus, all data conversion, job setup, and postcomputer resources should be considered. Overloading of the data conversion work station can delay jobs, causing them to be assembled for computer processing later than scheduled. If the postcomputer-processing work station is overloaded, jobs may be executed and completed as scheduled; but they may then be delayed because reports have to be decollated, and possibly miss thier deadlines. In contrast, where overutilization of resources affects service, underutilization of any resources is wasteful and expensive.

Two other factors are closely related to resource usage requirements: computer processing time and input quantity. Computer processing time must be known to estimate how long a job will reside in real storage; processing time can only be estimated in a multiprogramming environment because job mix affects the overall processing time for a job. The input quantity affects the workload placed on data conversion and computer processing. Scheduling must consider these time-related factors as well as resource requirements.

Another job-related factor is job dependencies. A data center processes many single-program jobs, but many of the jobs processed consist of many programs, usually executed as separate job steps within a job or as separate jobs that must be processed in a definite sequence. Obviously, it is neces-

sary to know these job sequences; it would be ridiculous to attempt to execute a job that processes output from a job that had not been executed. Just as obviously, if a job is abnormally terminated, all dependent jobs must be cancelled and rescheduled, permitting time for the terminated job to be rerun. The importance of cancelling and rescheduling dependent jobs is easy to appreciate, but complex and difficult to perform. This is true when scheduling is done manually, but far less serious when done with one of the many excellent software scheduling packages available, as will be made clear soon. The remaining job factors affecting scheduling are priority and deadline. Some scheduling methods place primary importance on priority, selecting jobs for execution according to the highest-priority job that can be scheduled with the resources available. This scheduling rule is used by operating-system control programs, sometimes called *master schedulers,* that are supplied by mainframe vendors. Thus, the job-related factors are resource requirements, computer processing time, input quantity, job dependencies, job priority, and deadline.

Data-Center-Related Scheduling Factors

To prepare schedules, it is necessary to know the data center resources, capacities, and the workload demands. In fact, the scheduling goal of the data center can be stated as matching resource capacities to workload demands while satisfying user deadlines and priorities. This, however, is more easily said than done, easpecially when resource capacities vary, possibly because of hardware failure or personnel absenteeism, and when user demands are unpredictable. Thus, workload can exceed capacity, affecting service, or workload capacity can exceed workload, leaving resources unutilized. Workload demands on the data center resources must be leveled as much as possible and kept close to the maximum capacity of resources. This has been succinctly stated as follows: "The installation scheduling system must be so designed to avoid: overloading, which leads to a decline in service; underloading, which implies excess cost."[4]

[4] J. G. Rickerly, G. Mellor, and D. R. A. Coan, *Standards in Operations* (Manchester, Great Britain: National Computing Centre Publ., 1975), section 5.1, p. 3.

The preceding factors affect the preparation of schedules, but there are several factors that affect scheduling effectiveness. The foremost factor that disrupts schedules has already been mentioned, and that is late receipt of input from users. This results in hectic activity to meet original deadline commitments, possibly requiring job rescheduling and incurring user dissatisfaction and complaints. The users innocently do not realize that they are the cause of the delays. Several steps can be taken to minimize these occurrences.

1. Educate users as to the effects of late input delivery.
2. For all scheduled jobs, establish input receipt data and time.
3. Include slack time between scheduled receipt time and actual time it is required.
4. Remind users of data not received at a preestablished time before due time, possibly one hour in advance.
5. Use a chargeout or chargeback system to penalize users for late receipt of input.
6. Report scheduling deviations and their causes to management.

Another factor that affects scheduling effectiveness is the ability to reschedule quickly. This is necessary because delays occur, rejected transactions have to be reentered, special job requests may have to be included, and deadlines or priorities for scheduled jobs may change. The delays that are usually the most serious are those resulting from abnormally terminated jobs and hardware failures. Rejected transactions may not be a problem, since they are usually expected and thus the job should have been scheduled for one or more reruns. The submission of unscheduled job requests in some installations is excessive and does create a serious scheduling problem; possible solutions are mentioned in the next section on scheduling difficulties. Fortunately, changes in a job's deadline or priority are infrequent, requiring rescheduling, which, without adequate software support, can be troublesome. If inadequate slack is included in the schedule, rescheduling to execute these jobs sooner can seriously disrupt the schedule for other jobs.

One last factor should be considered under scheduling effectiveness, and that is the resolution of unrealistic scheduling demands from users, without any attempt to level their demand on data center resources. The only solution is to obtain user cooperation, and the means recommended is a data center steering committee. This committee consists of data center and user representatives who, with the support of upper management, have the authority to level the demands users make on data center resources. To function properly, resource forecasts must be prepared and examined at least one month in advance of intended scheduling. The members must understand the limitations of data center resources and be willing to use these resources effectively for all user requests, not for members to be concerned only about the departments they represent. Some installations have gone to the extreme of assigning total scheduling responsibility to a committee of user representatives, with weak or no data center representation; this places total responsibility for job scheduling on the users. Most data center managers, however, do not want this arrangement because it removes control of data center resources from the data center to the user departments. Would any other department permit other departments to dictate how its resources would be used?

Scheduling Difficulties

Assuming a static workload, with no jobs being added to the scheduled workload, even then actual job processing can soon be expected to deviate from the schedule. The reasons are the uncertainty about job processing time and disrupted processing. A job that usually requires 10 minutes of processing time because of a large increase in the input may require 15 minutes, thus delaying all the following jobs by 5 minutes. This is to be expected. The same is true for disrupted processing, whether it occurs because of a hardware failure or a software problem. Either the job cannot be executed and must be rescheduled or, in the case of a hardware failure where substitute equipment can be used, it can be restarted; but this restart causes the job to finish later than scheduled, delaying the following jobs. The only way to avoid delays, or at least minimize the effects of these delays, is to include slack time in the schedule. A safety factor of 10 percent, for example, can be added to the expected processing time. In the example given where processing increased from 10 to 15 minutes, 10 percent slack would be inadequate. Since the following jobs would also have slack time built into their scheduled processing time, the job overrun is likely not to be critical.

But workload does not remain constant; so the varying workload resulting from unscheduled job requests, programmer test submissions, and random teleprocessing submissions can make scheduling difficult and unreliable. Many data center managers dismiss rigorous job scheduling because of unpredictable workloads. This situation is not as bad as it appears. Installations have found several solutions to these apparently disabling situations. One solution in multicomputer environments is to assign one computer to these random jobs. Several installations, in fact, have assigned a single computer only for programmer-submitted tests. A similar and less drastic solution is to assign a partition or a maximum amount of real storage to these random requests. Thus, four fifths of real storage may be scheduled, with the remaining storage used for teleprocessing, which usually includes test submissions. Tests requiring additional resources may have to be scheduled as if they were production jobs. Unscheduled job requests can either be meshed in with the production jobs or be scheduled, with the requirement that they be submitted only after prior notification has been given, possibly 24 hours. Another method for accepting test jobs and unscheduled job requests is to actually schedule blocks of time for them. For example, two hours could be scheduled for each shift. Thus, it is clear that it is not necessary to consider these situations insoluble and reject rigorous scheduling as useless, thus continuing to waste data center resources, miss deadlines, and operate an unnecessarily expensive installation.

The final scheduling difficulty to be considered applies to multiprogramming environments. The challenge here, as indicated earlier, is to combine jobs so that resources are used to their maximum. In a nonmultiprogramming environment there is no problem; resources are underutilized and that must be accepted. This results from having all resources dedicated to a computer, even if they are not needed for a job. If a job needs only 25 percent of the real storage, the remaining storage is not used. What could be simpler? If two tape drives are needed and there are eight, six remain idle. The potential of multiprogramming is that by executing several jobs at the same time, more of the resources are used at any time. Thus, if one program is using 25 percent of real storage, the remaining storage

is available for other jobs, and the same is true if only two tape drives are used. The difficulty is obtaining a job mix that uses the most resources. The disappointment of not receiving the benefits expected from multiprogramming has been poetically expressed: "The grand promises have faded like dew in the morning sunshine."[5] Illustration 9–1 indicates how core and peripheral resources can remain unused as a result of job mix. It is difficult to imagine how optimum job mix can be obtained through manual scheduling; the solution to obtaining maximum advantage of multiprogramming is through some of the sophisticated scheduling software available.

Scheduling Algorithms

A scheduling algorithm is a rule used for scheduling; for example, the job with the earliest deadline is scheduled first, and for jobs with the same deadline, the job with the shortest processing time is scheduled first. This is a scheduling algorithm that considers two factors, deadline and processing time. Some scheduling algorithms consider only a single factor; this occurs primarily for manual scheduling methods. The sophisticated software packages available have much more complex scheduling algorithms, considering several factors and thus more realistically representing the complex nature of scheduling in a data center. Factors have been combined in various ways, and varying degrees of importance have been assigned to these factors. This results in many potentially useful algorithms for scheduling jobs. For the purpose of this chapter, only five scheduling algorithms are defined, four of which consist of only one factor and one of which consists of two factors.

First Come, First Served. In effect, no scheduling is actually performed. Jobs are processed in the sequence in which they arrive. If 20 trivial jobs arrive before a critical job, the critical job waits. The results of this scheduling algorithm are hazardous and usually extremely poor. However, it is the basic guideline for many data centers and is modified, fortunately, by occasionally attending to deadlines and priorities.

[5] "Rethinking Computer Operations—Part III: On-Line Scheduling by Computer," *Data Processing Manual* (Pennsauken, N.J.: Auerbach Publ., 1974), p. 1.

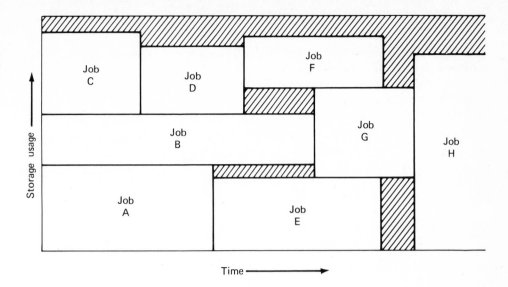

ILLUSTRATION 9-1. Multiprogramming Utilization of Resources: Storage and peripheral usage depends on job mix, which results from micro-scheduling.

Shortest Processing Time First. Adherence to this rule results in jobs being scheduled in ascending sequence according to processing time. Thus, a job requiring one minute to process would occur before a job requiring ten minutes, which would be scheduled before a job requiring five hours. This rule is usually included as one of the factors in every multifactor scheduling algorithm, since it provides several benefits. It is likely to maximize throughput, which is the number of jobs processed within a time period, and it is also likely to maximize the turnaround of jobs requiring a short processing time, which is the quick return of these jobs to users. This rule, however, does sacrifice the turnaround of jobs requiring a long processing time, and when used alone, it ignores deadlines and priorities.

Least Slack Time First. Slack time is the amount of time a job can be delayed and still meet its deadline; to express it another way, slack time is equal to a job's deadline minus its processing time. Deadline, also referred to as due time or comple-

tion time, is here restricted to computer processing completion time, assuming for illustrative purposes that precomputer and postcomputer processing times are zero, which is somewhat unrealistic. This rule tends to result in the fewest jobs being late, but does ignore priorities.

Earliest Due Time First. This rule sequences jobs according to their deadlines, with the job due first scheduled first. Although the rule ignores throughput and turnaround, it does minimize the occurrence of excessively late jobs. More jobs will be late than in the least-slack-time-first rule, but the latest job would be completed sooner. This rule also ignores priorities.

Lowest Weighted Processing Time First. This scheduling algorithm, involves two factors: processing time and priority. When priority value increases with a job's increased priority, this rule sequences jobs in ascending sequence according to weighted processing time, which is determined by dividing the processing time (in minutes) for a job by the priority value assigned to it. Thus, a job having a processing time of 10 minutes and a priority value of 2 would have a weighted processing time of 5; a job having a processing time of 10 minutes and a priority value of 5 (a higher priority value) would have a weighted processing time of 2. Note that the job with the highest priority value has the lowest weighted processing time; therefore, the second job is scheduled first. This example illustrates that this rule schedules high-priority jobs first when the processing time is the same. This rule also schedules the shortest processing time first when priority values are the same. A job that requires 10 minutes and has a priority value of 2 has a weighted processing time of 5; a job that requires 8 minutes and has a priority value of 2 has a weighted processing time of 4; thus, the job with the shortest processing time is scheduled first when priority values are the same.

In defining these scheduling algorithms, several comments on their advantages and disadvantages have indicated that there are criteria for evaluating their worth. These are called scheduling performance criteria and they will now be outlined in a more systematic manner.

Scheduling Performance Criteria

The criteria used to evaluate the worth and effectiveness of scheduling algorithms can be categorized as either user-oriented or data-center-oriented. Each installation must decide which of these criteria are of primary interest and which are to be used for establishing a scheduling algorithm and for judging its effectiveness. Often, the data center manager is required to satisfy the dual goal of maximum service at minimum cost. This type of statement places the data center manager in a very uneasy situation. When stress is placed on providing maximum service, inefficiencies result, costs rise, and the data center operations are criticized for these reasons; when stress is placed on obtaining minimum cost, service is sacrificed for optimum use of data center resources, and again the data center operations are criticized. What is required, therefore, is not only agreement on what criteria will be used but also agreement on the relative importance of each criterion.

User-oriented criteria. Since cost is usually not affected by scheduling, and since the user is not

concerned about resource utilization or data center efficiency, the user's evaluation of job-processing performance focuses on service received from the data center. The only time users are usually concerned about expensive underutilization of resources is when they are charged for these inefficiencies. This is one of the major justifications for a chargeout or chargeback system. Three of the most frequently used criteria for evaluating service are:

1. *Minimum mean job lateness.* This is obtained by averaging for all jobs their lateness, which, for each job, is completion time minus due time. Jobs completed late would have a positive late value, and those completed early would have a negative value. It is merely necessary to divide the total lateness value for all jobs by the number of jobs to obtain mean job lateness.

2. *Minimum mean job throughtime.* Throughtime is the amount of time a job remains in the data center; thus, throughtime is job completion time minus job arrival time. By dividing the total throughtime for all jobs by the number of jobs, the mean job throughtime is obtained.

3. *Maximum mean earliness.* Earliness is the amount of time a job is completed before its deadline, with jobs completed after their deadlines having a value of zero. It is only necessary to average the earliness values for all jobs to arrive at the mean earliness.

Data-Center-Oriented Criteria. The concern of the data center manager is to do as much work as possible, using resources efficiently at the lowest cost. Naturally, the data center manager is also concerned about user service. The data center manager usually follows the policy of utilizing resources as efficiently and inexpensively as possible—without sacrificing commitments to users. But the policy at data centers varies, with some stressing the best user service possible at any cost to the data center. Four data center criteria are often used to evaluate data center scheduling performance:

1. *Maximum mean throughput.* Simply, this is the number of jobs processed in a fixed time period. The more jobs processed in this period, the more effective the data center.

2. *Minimum number of jobs in the data center.* This is very similar to the concept of throughput.

ILLUSTRATION 9–2. Job Information for Sample Jobs: This information is used to examine five scheduling algorithms and three scheduling performance criteria.

Job	Defined			Calculated	
	Processing time (P)	Due time	Priority weight (W)	Slack time	Weighted processing time (P/W)
A	30	1110	1	$1\frac{4}{6}$	30
B	20	0940	1	$\frac{2}{6}$	20
C	10	1000	4	$\frac{5}{6}$	2.5
D	40	1040	4	$\frac{3}{6}$	10
E	20	0950	5	$\frac{1}{6}$	4

Whereas throughput stresses the number of jobs processed, this criterion stresses the number of jobs waiting to be processed.

3. *Maximum percentage of resource utilization.* Obviously, idle and unused resources are undesirable. It is a natural goal to use resources as much of the time as possible. As shown in Illustration 9-1, the amount of storage space used varies for different time periods, and the number of peripherals used also varies. Often, peripherals are utilized for only a small percentage of the available time.

4. *Minimum total processing cost.* The more efficiently resources are utilized, the fewer resources are needed and the lower the total processing cost. A cost that should also be included, although sometimes difficult to assign a dollar value, is the cost to users of missed deadlines, which may result in lost accounts or the incurring of fines.

The application of three of the scheduling performance criteria to the five scheduling algorithms is demonstrated in Illustrations 9-2 through 9-7. Illustration 9-2 provides the job information needed to apply the scheduling algorithms for five jobs. Illustration 9-3 shows the job sequences that result from these five scheduling algorithms. Illustrations 9-4, 9-5, and 9-6 show the results of applying three scheduling performance criteria: minimum mean job lateness, minimum mean job throughtime, and maximum mean job throughput. Finally, Illustration 9-7 summarizes the results of applying these three scheduling performance criteria to the five scheduling algorithms for the jobs defined. The results can be expected to vary for

ILLUSTRATION 9–3. Job Sequences for Five Scheduling Algorithms.

Time	First come, first served	Shortest processing time first	Least slack time first	Earliest due time first	Lowest weighted processing time first
0900	A	C	E	B	C
0910	A	B	E	B	E
0920	A	B	E	E	E
0930	B	E	B	E	D
0940	B	E	B	E	D
0950	C	A	D	C	D
1000	D	A	D	D	D
1010	D	A	D	D	B
1020	D	D	D	D	B
1030	D	D	C	D	A
1040	E	D	A	A	A
1050	E	D	A	A	A
1100					

JOB SEQUENCE	FIRST COME, FIRST SERVED	SHORTEST PROCESS TIME FIRST	LEAST SLACK TIME FIRST	EARLIEST DUE DATE FIRST	LOWEST WEIGHTED PROCESSING TIME FIRST
1	−60	−50	−30	−20	−50
2	10	−10	0	−10	−20
3	0	0	10	−10	0
4	20	−10	30	−10	50
5	70	40	−10	−10	−10
Total	40	−30	0	−60	−30
Average	8	−6	0	−12	−6

ILLUSTRATION 9-4. Scheduling Performance Criterion "Minimum Mean Job Lateness."

JOB SEQUENCE	FIRST COME, FIRST SERVED	SHORTEST PROCESSING TIME FIRST	LEAST SLACK TIME FIRST	EARLIEST DUE DATE FIRST	LOWEST WEIGHTED PROCESSING TIME FIRST
1	30	10	20	20	10
2	50	30	40	40	30
3	60	50	80	50	70
4	100	80	90	90	90
5	120	120	120	120	120
Total	360	290	350	320	320
Average	72	58	70	64	64

ILLUSTRATION 9-5. Scheduling Performance Criterion "Minimum Mean Job Throughtime."

TIME	FIRST COME, FIRST SERVED	SHORTEST PROCESSING TIME FIRST	LEAST SLACK TIME FIRST	EARLIEST DUE DATE FIRST	LOWEST WEIGHTED PROCESSING TIME FIRST
0915	0	1	0	0	1
0930	1	2	1	1	2
0945	1	2	2	2	2
1000	3	3	2	3	2
1015	3	3	2	3	3
1030	3	4	4	4	4
1045	4	4	4	4	4
1100	5	5	5	5	5
Total	20	24	20	22	23
Average	$2\frac{4}{8}$	3	$2\frac{4}{8}$	$2\frac{6}{8}$	$2\frac{7}{8}$

ILLUSTRATION 9-6. Scheduling Performance Criterion "Maximum Mean Job Throughput."

different groups of jobs. The findings agree with the viewpoints of most, if not all, scheduling experts: the first-come, first-served rule is the worst, and the shortest-processing-time-first rule should be included in any scheduling algorithm used. The shortest-processing-time-first rule should not be used alone, however, since it ignores job deadlines and priorities.

SCHEDULING CRITERIA	FIRST COME, FIRST SERVED	SHORTEST PROCESSING TIME FIRST	LEAST SLACK TIME FIRST	EARLIEST DUE DATE FIRST	LOWEST WEIGHTED PROCESSING TIME FIRST
Minimum mean job lateness	WORST			BEST	
Minimum mean job throughtime	WORST	BEST			
Maximum mean job throughput	WORST	BEST	WORST		

ILLUSTRATION 9-7. Evaluation of Scheduling Algorithms: Although only a small sample of jobs was used and only three scheduling performance criteria were applied, the conclusions agree with those of writers on scheduling: the worst algorithm is definitely "first come, first served"; the most promising algorithm is "shortest processing time first."

SCHEDULING PHASES

With appreciation of the benefits of scheduling and knowledge of the scheduling factors, it is now possible to establish procedures for the scheduling phases, which are forecasting workload demands, planning resource allocation, and monitoring job processing. But before doing this, the first task is to develop a job-scheduling methodology, that is, to provide the organizational framework for scheduling, define objectives, and select and implement the scheduling method. This is an apparently easy task, but many installations have stressed some of the steps that are recommended and have ignored others that are also recommended. An eight-step scheduling methodology is presented below, with the warning that the elimination of any of these steps should be done cautiously and should be justified.

1. Obtain management support
2. Form a data center steering committee
3. Establish scheduling performance criteria
4. Select a scheduling method
5. Establish and document scheduling procedures
6. Educate user and data center personnel
7. Implement the scheduling procedures
8. Evaluate scheduling performance criteria, method, and procedures

The purpose of most of these steps is clear and requires very little commentary. Step 1, obtain management support, is always a first requirement when establishing new standards and procedures and is a must for a complex, interdepartment process such as scheduling. Without this support, violations cannot be controlled, and, in effect, the scheduling standards and procedures can be easily ignored. To obtain management support, it is necessary to convey the benefits anticipated. Management is definitely not resistant to improved user service, improved use of resources, and reduced operating costs. At the same time, the data center manager must be prepared for such objections as "It cannot be done in our environment." Objections should be responded to in a logical, friendly, and diplomatic manner.

The advantages of forming a data center steering committee (step 2) have already been stated several times. With respect to job scheduling, this committee provides a means for the data center personnel to understand the needs and the problems of the users, and for the users to understand the resource potential and limitations of the data center. The insight gained enables data center personnel to cooperate on how best to schedule jobs to provide optimum user service and resource utilization. Without this committee, it would be difficult, if not impossible, to receive user agreement on transferring jobs from peak demand time periods to slack periods. The expectations for this committee are idealistic, but with careful selection of members and a leader, and with precise guidelines for conducting meetings, these ideals can be approached—if not attained.

Step 3, establishing scheduling performance criteria, is necessary for evaluating scheduling performance according to agreed-upon criteria. The stress on user-oriented or data-center-oriented criteria must be established to avoid later conflicts. Very likely, the agreement will be on a balance of these two types of criteria. Without these criteria, not only is evaluation difficult and hazy, but also improvements in scheduling are hampered. For example, improving turnaround of jobs is uncertain if turnaround is not defined as a performance criteria, if a turnaround performance level is not set, and if actual performance is not compared to anticipated performance levels.

Before selecting a scheduling method (step 4), it is necessary to know the scheduling methods available. These methods are discussed later in this chapter. After selecting a scheduling method, it is necessary to establish and document the procedures needed for the three phases of job scheduling; This is step 5 in the scheduling methodology. When analyzing procedural requirements and approaches, both supervisory and staff personnel should be included. They may uncover difficulties that are apparent only to persons living with scheduling on a day-to-day basis. It is also likely that their suggestions and ideas will improve the final procedures. Another benefit from their involvement in this process is their improved receptivity, acceptance, and adherence to the final procedures.

Step 6, educate user and data center personnel, is often forgotten. Without personnel understanding of the scheduling method and supporting procedures, lack of interest and errors are likely to result, leading to criticism and condemnation of the scheduling method and procedures. Personnel should also appreciate the benefits anticipated and how performance will be evaluated.

Only steps 7 and 8 now remain: step 7 for implementing the scheduling procedures, and step 8 for periodically evaluating scheduling performance criteria, method, and procedures. That is the eight-step scheduling methodology recommended. The three scheduling phases are now examined.

Forecasting Workload Demands

Effort to determine user demands and their effects on data center resources should not occur the week before the jobs are to be scheduled. Workload demands should be known at least one month in advance, and a rough estimate should be prepared one year in advance (actually, at least two months before the start of a new year). By having these workload demands early, more time is available to determine when excessive demands and inadequate demands are made on resources. Time is needed to obtain user approval to transfer jobs from peak demand periods to slack periods, striving to attain

the goal of leveled demands on resources. Illustration 9-8 shows the input needed to prepare a preliminary workload report for the upcoming year.

By preparing this report two months or more before the start of a new year, it becomes possible to analyze the distribution of workload and, if any peak and slack periods are apparent, to avoid assigning jobs to the peak periods while attempting to assign jobs to the slack periods. Early forecasts of workloads become increasingly important with the increase in the number of long-duration jobs, since these jobs have a greater effect on resource loading, especially if they cannot be transferred to a different time period. On the other hand, the advantage of the preliminary workload report diminishes as the number of unscheduled jobs increases at an installation. Some installations are predominantly involved with unscheduled jobs, which drastically reduces the value of monthly and weekly planning. This is not the situation for most installations, and these preliminary efforts are

ILLUSTRATION 9-8. Forecasting Workload Demand.

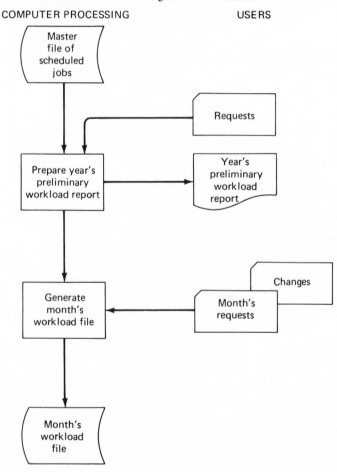

significant; in fact, users are self-motivated to submit job scheduling requests early to assure execution of their jobs at the preferred times.

As shown in Illustration 9–8, a file of scheduled jobs and additional job requests is used to prepare the preliminary workload report. The file consists of all recurring jobs, thus not requiring individual requests for each execution, and also consists of previously requested one-time job executions. The additional requests are received from user and programming departments. Programming personnel should be required to submit requests for any extensive testing anticipated for systems being developed or modified. These reports, besides indicating the month and day preferred, also indicate the due-in and due-out times, which depend on the desired completion time and on the amount of time required for precomputer, computer, and postcomputer processing.

Each month, at least one month in advance, user and programming-department requests and changes are submitted, and an updated file of scheduled jobs is generated. The changes may reflect attempts to transfer jobs to slack periods as well as reflect changes in deadlines, priorities, and anticipated total data center processing time.

Planning Resource Allocation

The updated file of scheduled jobs is used to prepare tentative monthly schedules, which, as shown in Illustration 9–9, are forwarded to the user and programming departments. The user and programming personnel can then judge if the schedule is satisfactory, if any changes are required, and if any adjustments can be made to relieve overloaded time periods. They then submit changes and any new requests at least one week before the end of the month, and a final monthly schedule is printed and distributed. This schedule is the last schedule user and programming personnel will receive. Any additional requests will be submitted as unscheduled jobs.

To prepare the tentative and the final monthly schedules, two levels of scheduling should occur: macroscheduling for all data center processing and microscheduling for only the computer and its resources. Macroscheduling thus attends to establishing due-in time for input, receipt and completion time for all data center work stations

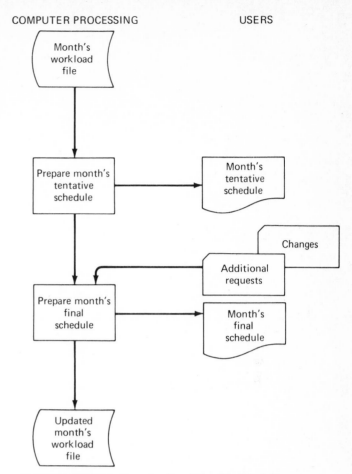

ILLUSTRATION 9–9. Preparing Users' Monthly Schedules.

(including the computer area), and due-out time for distributing the output. It is necessary to coordinate all data center activities to adhere to these schedules. Macroscheduling focuses on meeting user commitments and allocating resources so that all data center resources are neither overloaded or underloaded.

Microscheduling focuses on optimizing utilization of computer resources. Since, in a nonmultiprogramming environment, all computer resources are dedicated to a job when it is being executed, job mix has no meaning and microscheduling does not apply. Multiprogramming, however, permits many combinations of jobs to be executed at the same time. Each combination makes different demands on computer resources; some result in poor resource utilization and others result in excellent resource utilization.

The final phases of resource allocation are the detailed weekly and daily schedules prepared for each work station, as shown in Illustration 9–10. Instead of showing each job's due-in and due-out

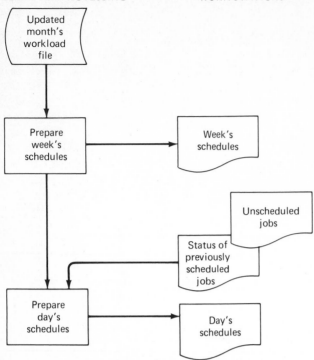

ILLUSTRATION 9-10. Preparing Data Center Schedules.

dates and times for the data center, these schedules show the due-in and due-out dates and times appropriate for each work station's schedule. Slack is built into these time requirements to minimize missed deadlines and permit job completion sooner than scheduled. A job that is expected to require 10 minutes of processing in the data-conversion area, for example, may be scheduled for 15 minutes. This slack allows for delays and disruptions and also permits the inclusion of unscheduled jobs.

The purpose of the weekly reports is to permit each work station to compare the workload against the resources available and, if necessary, plan for more resources or for use of unused resources. If the work station has inadequate resources for the workload, overtime or outside services may be necessary. This is expensive and, if it occurs often, indicates a scheduling problem. On the other hand, if resources are underutilized, it may be possible to sell the use of these resources to outside organizations, or possibly to charge their use to other divisions of the organization. The effect of selling the use of underutilized resources is to reduce the overall costs of the data center. However, frequent underloading, as in the case of overloading, indicates a scheduling problem. These conditions can occur, and they may be difficult to resolve when

they result from legal requirements or organization policies.

Monitoring Job Processing

Job monitoring provides two general categories of benefits: control of job processing and evaluation of the adequacy of job scheduling. Control starts with the existence of schedules, is sustained through awareness of job status and deviations, and is completed when deviations from the schedules can be corrected. Implementation of the scheduling methodology provides the schedules. Thus, the first condition is satisfied. Several means are available for knowing the status of jobs and the occurrence of deviations. The brute-force method of doing this is to assign someone to the task of visiting the various work stations and reviewing the status of jobs. This is a very inefficient and error-prone method, even in a small installation. A better method is to use control logs at the critical work stations, namely, at data-control, data-conversion, computer-processing, and postcomputer-processing work stations. With this method, each of these work stations can inform the scheduler of delayed jobs or disrupted processing.

The use of work-station schedules instead of control logs to locate delayed jobs is even more effective. To use logs, it is necessary to hand-enter scheduled start and completion times. Computer-generated work-station schedules avoid this tedious task. These schedules also indicate the amount of time estimated for processing and the amount of slack time provided. The best method for knowing job status and deviations is on-line access to scheduling information. This method is being used by an increasing number of data centers. It is only necessary for each work station to have at least one terminal to display the upcoming jobs, and if desired, a hard copy can be printed. The scheduler can respond quickly to job-status inquiries and can display delayed jobs, if desired, by work stations at which the jobs are delayed.

The remaining requirement for job-scheduling control is the procedure for expediting delayed jobs and, if necessary, notifying users of delays.

The second benefit of monitoring job processing is the ability to evaluate the adequacy of job scheduling. How would it be possible to know if any attempt is being made to adhere to schedules if job processing were not monitored? Without monitoring, user or programming personnel may place pressure on data center personnel to modify schedules because of their "really important" jobs, ignoring the effort and thought given to the schedules prepared. Although data center personnel hate to admit it, it often is true that the squeaky wheel is the wheel that receives attention—and many users are expert at being squeaky!

Besides monitoring adherence to schedules, it is also possible to observe deficiencies in how jobs are scheduled. The following five situations indicate that a job-scheduling deficiency exists:

1. The data center frequently has to purchase outside computer time, although there are other periods when equipment is idle.
2. Some computers are in constant use while others have periods of no work.
3. There is a wide variance in the lateness of jobs. Some are quite early and others, quite late.
4. A low percentage of utilization of peripherals may indicate a poor job mix in the case of multiprogrammed computers.
5. The number of jobs waiting to be processed remains relatively the same while the average throughput time increases.
6. There are jobs in the data center, but they are not ready for the computer and the computer is idle.[6]

SCHEDULING METHODS

When considering the various scheduling methods available, it is generally best to choose the method that is most economical and most easy to live with. However, it may be necessary to accept the extra cost and complexity of a more sophisticated scheduling method if the environment requires it. The overriding single factor demanding a more sophisticated method is scarcity of resources. As mentioned previously, if no resource scarcity exists at all, a scheduling method may not be necessary; but as resources become more scarce, the more significant is the contribution of a scheduling method and the more critical is its selection.

Available resource capacity is not the only factor in judging the need for a sophisticated method. Two other factors are significant, and these are complexity of applications and predict-

ability of workload demands. Applications having complex job dependencies place an unrealistic demand on simple methods, particularly on manual scheduling methods. Even if job dependencies can be considered in setting up a schedule manually, the complex manipulations required if one of the jobs is abnormally terminated create difficulties in cancelling all dependent jobs, adjusting the schedule for the remaining jobs (which may not have their input ready for processing), and rescheduling the cancelled jobs. Sophisticated software packages are designed to accept this challenge with ease.

As for predictability of workload demands, this may be less critical if the unpredictable job requests (unscheduled job requests and test submissions) are assigned separate resources, such as a separate machine, a separate partition of memory, a maximum real-storage allocation, or several blocks of time during the day. If none of these approaches are accepted, installations with an unpredictable workload can anticipate scheduling problems, and any scheduling method, sophisticated or simple, is likely to lose most of its effectiveness.

Scheduling methods can be separated into three convenient categories: manual scheduling, operating-system schedulers, and software scheduling packages.

Manual Scheduling

The first question to be answered is, Who does the scheduling? Some installations attempt to have computer operators perform this function. This is fated to be a bad decision, with the possible exception of a small installation where the staff is small and the workload is small enough for the computer operator to maintain an overall perspective of commitments to users. In general, it is far better to have at least one person assigned solely to scheduling, with a backup person when needed.

The three types of manual scheduling have been referred to as job-sequence loading, control-period loading, and block booking.[7]

Job-sequence loading. Jobs are sequenced and assigned a specific date and time, with the start and completion times indicated. The form shown in

---

[6]Sahney, *Scheduling Computer Operations*, p. 36.

[7]Rickerly, *Standards in Operations*, section 5.4, p. 2.

Illustration 9–11 can be used for this purpose. Jobs are sequenced on this form, and their loading on precomputer, computer, postcomputer work stations is indicated. Thus, this form helps to level resource demands throughout the data center. The "earliest/latest" columns indicate the variation permitted for starting and finishing each job. Depending on the number of jobs to be scheduled, the period that this schedule represents can be an eight-hour shift with four-, two-, or one-hour time periods. If a separate sheet is prepared for two-hour periods, an eight-hour shift would require four sheets. Job-sequence loading is useful when workload is predictable, and unscheduled jobs can be easily assimilated.

Control-period loading. The stress with this method is not on determining job sequence but on relating workload to resource capacities. The form in Illustration 9–12 is useful for this purpose. By looking at entries on this form, it is possible to see which resources are close to full capacity utilization and which still can be assigned to jobs. This method is particularly effective in an environment with an unpredictable workload. When a job request arrives, it is only necessary to see when the resources needed will be available. Although not intended primarily for this purpose, the information entered on this form can also be used to analyze resource usage and adequacy.

Block booking. The amount of time needed for each job can be indicated by the amount of space allocated to it on a form such as that shown in Illustration 9–13; thus, the start and completion times are indicated by the lines drawn to contain either job name or job number. It is possible to prepare this schedule not only for computer processing, but also for other work stations, primarily for data conversion and output processing. The form shown permits scheduling one machine for

ILLUSTRATION 9–11. Manual Scheduling—Job Sequence Loading.

Schedule														Machine	Shift	Date

Priority	Start		Precomputer		Computer				Postcomputer			Finish		Comment
	Earliest	Latest	Conv	EAM	Time	Core	Disc	Tape	Proc*	Decol	Burst	Earliest	Latest	
High														
Medium														
Low														

*Processing may be off-line printing, COM, etc.

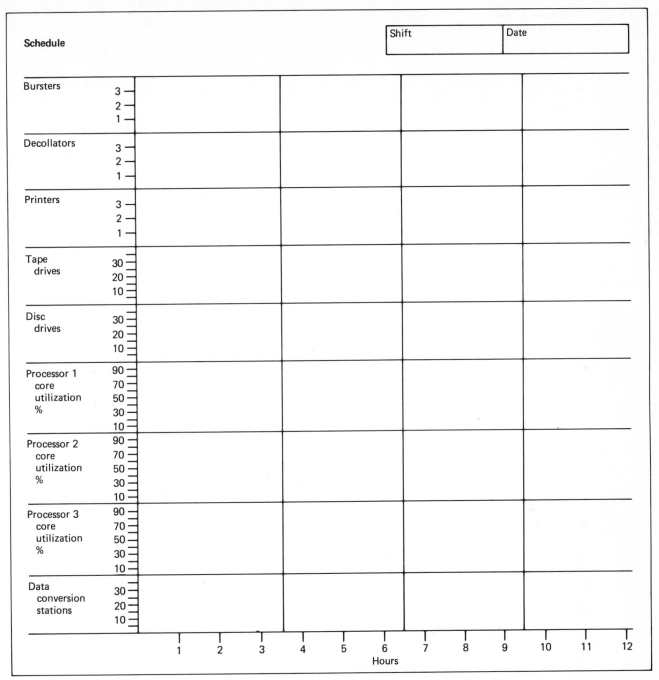

ILLUSTRATION 9-12. Manual Scheduling—Control Period Loading.

each day. In the data-conversion area, each "machine" can actually represent a group of machines, thus avoiding the need to schedule each machine separately. This reduces the scheduling effort and the cumbersomeness of the process. The same is true for output processing; however, since there are usually fewer machines, the schedules for three machines may actually represent three machines.

This form can be used differently. Instead of scheduling the individual jobs, blocks of time can be assigned for different work types. Thus, time (possibly in two-hour periods) can be assigned to production jobs, on-request jobs, tests from programmers, and maintenance. This approach is acceptable if the distribution of work is reasonably constant, possibly requiring periodic but infrequent adjustments as the distribution of requirements changes.

Schedule				Machine		Week ending	

Hours	Mon	Tue	Wed	Thu	Fri
0000					
0100					
0200					
0300					
0400					
0500					
0600					
0700					
0800					
0900					
1000					
1100					
1200					
1300					
1400					
1500					
1600					
1700					
1800					
1900					
2000					
2100					
2200					
2300					
2400					

ILLUSTRATION 9–13. Manual Scheduling—Block Booking.

There are alternatives to using forms. One is the use of cards inserted in a scheduling board, as shown in Illustration 9-14. The tops of these cards project above the pockets containing them, making their identifying name or number visible; instead of job ticket number, as shown in the illustration, a control number, job name or number, or procedure name or number can be used. Some of the commercially available card inserts are T-shaped, making the projecting tops of the cards more obvious and easier to grasp. An alternative to forms and card inserts is a scheduling board on which magnetic tags can be attached, as shown in Illustration 9-15. These tags are easier to move about the board than card inserts. The magnetic tags are generally preferred to card inserts, although they are more expensive. The magnetic tags and the card inserts can be obtained in various colors; this permits color coding of scheduled jobs, possibly by priority or by user department.

In a complex environment with a heavy workload, manual scheduling is likely to be disastrous. The experience of the data center personnel at the Crocker National Bank in San Francisco, California may be adequate forewarning. They tried and decided against the use of magnetic boards because, "To schedule 15 percent of the data processing center's workload, the system required 10 full time people. In addition, the projected annual budget for full implementation was placed at approximately $1/2 million."[8]

Operating-System Schedulers

Many organizations have rejected the manual method of scheduling and have turned to the operating-system schedulers supplied by mainframe vendors. These schedulers may be called control

[8] Winkler, "Scheduling a Data Processing Center," p. 15.

248

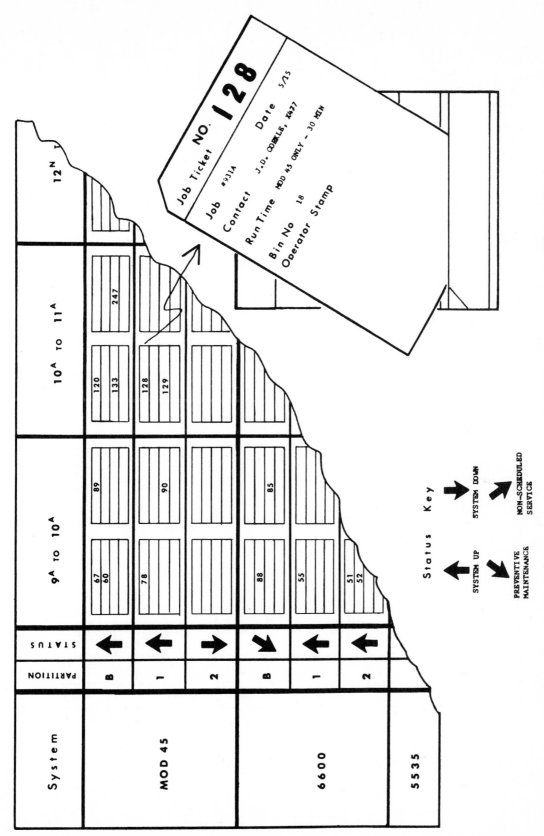

ILLUSTRATION 9-14. Scheduling Board With Card Inserts.
Source: Leonard I. Krauss, *Administering and Controlling the Company Data Processing Function* (Englewood Cliffs, N.J.: Prentice-Hall, 1969), p. 201.

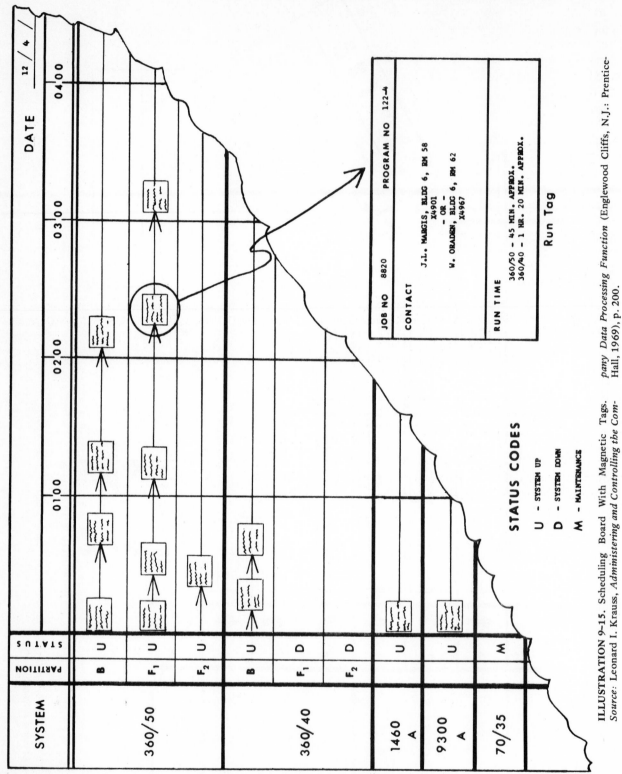

ILLUSTRATION 9–15. Scheduling Board With Magnetic Tags. *Source:* Leonard I. Krauss, *Administering and Controlling the Com-* *pany Data Processing Function* (Englewood Cliffs, N.J.: Prentice-Hall, 1969), p. 200.

250

programs or master schedulers. It would be difficult to find a bigger misnomer in all of data processing than the phrase "master scheduler." These master schedulers are more like fumbling novices. In fact, although for convenience they will still be referred to as schedulers, they are actually totally blind to deadlines and merely allocate resources. As expressed by Value Computing, a company that provides software packages for data centers, these schedulers actually "allocate the resources of the computer once the jobs have been scheduled onto the machine."[9] The "scheduling onto the machine" is, by necessity, done manually.

This criticism becomes clear when the functions these schedulers perform are examined. They are dependent on priority and resource-class information. The basic logic of these schedulers is to start with the highest-priority jobs in a queue awaiting execution and examine the resource requirements for these jobs, which are indicated by resource-class codes. The highest-priority job that has adequate resources available is "scheduled" as the next job. But what happens if a high-priority job requires five tape drives and only four are available? Obviously, it is bypassed and another job is chosen, possibly with a very low priority. It is possible that immediately after this low-priority job is assigned, another job is completed, releasing several tape drives that could have been held for the high-priority job. The high priority job waits, and waits, and waits, until five tape drives are free at the same time. This job may have a very long wait. The scheduler does not look ahead and anticipate the release of the extra tape drive needed: it functions like a poor chess player who evaluates the effect of the immediate move, ignoring the fact that the second move, as a result, will be disastrous. If this is not enough justification for criticizing these schedulers, consider the fact that no attention is given to deadlines. These schedulers are not oriented to meet user commitment, even though priority codes are included in their scheduling algorithm; they are oriented primarily to maximizing utilization of computer resources.

The next and most recent step in the development of operating-system schedulers is an extension of the operating system, such as Attached Support Processor (ASP), Local Attached Support

Processor (LASP), and Job Entry Subsystem 3 (JES 3). These schedulers—and they can now legitimately be called schedulers, although in a restricted sense—do consider deadlines. They include deadlines as a scheduling factor by increasing the priority code as the deadline becomes critical. But, still, their main concern is allocation of resources, not the meeting of deadlines. Their ability to allocate resources includes efficient spooling and the ability to assign jobs among several processors. Even if these schedulers do a good job of scheduling jobs, they still do not schedule processing outside the computer room; thus, jobs may be processed later than they should be because they are detained in the data-conversion area, or jobs may be executed but cannot be distributed on schedule because the decollators are overloaded. The main deficiencies of these operating-system schedulers are:

- They do not provide monthly or yearly workload forecasts, preventing location and resolution of overloaded and underloaded resources.
- They do not provide weekly work-station schedules, preventing preparation for overloaded or underloaded resources.
- They do not provide daily work-station schedules, preventing control of input for computer processing or control of output for distribution.
- They stress computer resource allocation and not computer scheduling, placing data center efficiency above user service in importance.
- They do not provide reports on user service or usage, thus, not assisting evaluation of processing effectiveness.

Software Scheduling Packages

Several software vendors quickly appreciated the importance of computer scheduling and, in a few cases, of data center scheduling. As a result, the data center manager has several excellent scheduling packages to choose from. Listings of these packages and their vendors can be found in Auerbach, Datapro, and ICP publications. A few of the packages available are:

Computer Scheduling and Control System (Value Computing Inc.)

Operations Scheduling and Reporting System (Computer Concepts Corp.)

[9] *Computer Job & Data Center Scheduling Systems Summary*, Value Computing, Inc., Cherry Hill, N.J., p. 6.

Computer Scheduling System (P.C. & Associates)

Operations Control System (Brandon Applied Systems)

Streamline (Tesdata Systems Corp.)

The disadvantages already given for manual and operating-system scheduling methods have suggested the advantages to be expected from scheduling packages. But unless a considerable amount of personal investigation is given to this topic, it is unlikely that the many advantages will be apparent. Therefore, to further stress the importance of scheduling and the use of software packages, these advantages are now listed:

1. *Jobs are not forgotten.* A job data base contains job scheduling information; thus, all recurring jobs can be automatically scheduled and are not dependent on the recollection of schedulers or computer operators. Also, complex scheduling requirements are handled easily, such as jobs to be scheduled on the third week of every other month or jobs to be scheduled every other Thursday.

2. *Overloading and underloading are forecasted.* Yearly and monthly reports can be generated of scheduled workloads, and overloaded and underloaded time periods become apparent and can be corrected leisurely. The same is true for the weekly schedules prepared for work stations; these reports are received far enough in advance to prepare for obtaining additional resources, in the case of overloading, or for making surplus resources available to others, in the case of underloading.

3. *Deadlines and priorities are attended to.* Deadlines and priorities, as well as resource allocations, are important. Thus, commitments to users are not sacrificed to equipment efficiency, which may be a major concern of hardware vendors, but should not be the major concern of data center personnel. In fact, it is likely that the scheduling algorithm chosen by most data centers would willingly sacrifice resource utilization to user service.

4. *Level allocation of all data center resources is attempted.* Even if user service is of paramount importance, proper loading of *all data center resources* is important, despite some sacrifice because of emphasis on user service. The phrase "all data center resources" is stressed to emphasize the need to consider precomputer and postcomputer processing as well as computer processing. The end result of efficient use of resources is lower data center costs.

5. *Support documents can be prepared for operators.* With the information available, it is possible to automatically prepare setup sheets, tape-pulling lists, and disk-mount lists for all jobs. It is only necessary to watch data center personnel for a short time as they enter volume serial numbers and other information on setup sheets or flowcharts for jobs to quickly appreciate the advantages of the automatically generated setup sheets.

6. *Rescheduling can be done quickly.* If anything is predictable in the data center it is that adherence to schedules is unlikely. Hardware fails, input is late, programs abort. Deadlines and priorities change. And then there is always the addition to the day's workload of new jobs, some of which may have critical deadlines. This requires rescheduling. In fact, rescheduling may be required several times a day, and it must be done quickly. Scheduling packages can do this.

7. *Jobstream can be executed automatically.* From the scheduling information available, the job control-language statements needed can be generated and then automatically executed. This can be done and is being done. One such system is that developed by Value Computing, called APOLLO.

8. *Delayed jobs can be reported.* Since the due-in and due-out dates and times for each scheduled job are available, it is possible to scan schedules to locate and expedite delayed jobs. For environments with on-line access to scheduling files, it is only necessary to request the display or printing of delayed jobs. It is possible to display or print delayed jobs in sequence by their priority, department, work station, or degree of lateness. Displays or listings sequenced by degree of lateness can sequence jobs with the latest job first.

9. *Dependence on computer operators is lessened.* Because of automatic scheduling, jobstream execution, delayed job reporting, and rescheduling, operator intervention is required infrequently. The lessening of operator intervention reduces the number of human errors likely to occur—the less done, the less likely to be done wrong. Reduced dependence on computer operators lessens the threat of computer operator unionization, which, if it were to occur in a dependent installation, would threaten the shutdown of the data center, and possibly the entire organization.

10. *What if? questions can be answered.* A data center manager wants the ability to forecast the effects of various actions or occurrences. It is necessary to anticipate problems and to judge the effects of actions. Answers may be wanted to such questions as: What if the quantity of transactions drastically increases for a job? What if a new system being developed were added to the workload? What would be the effects of various hardware failures? What if hardware were changed?

11. *Processing effectiveness can be analyzed for improvements.* The availability of processing-time and resource-utilization information permits analysis of scheduling and processing effectiveness. Such analysis permits isolation of problem areas and the correction of deficiencies. This information also permits comparison of actual performance against performance criteria previously defined. And these comparisons can be printed and distributed to users, indicating an open, honest attitude toward managing the data center.

Thus, the benefits of software scheduling packages are impressive—but, although these potential benefits may stimulate immediate acceptance, expectations should be moderated. These benefits are real, but it takes time to obtain them. Impatience is rewarded with discontent and dissatisfaction, which would not occur if adequate time were allocated for adapting the scheduling package chosen to the structure and policies of the organization. Personnel must be well trained, and they should appreciate the significance of the information received; they must become comfortable with the package. As stated in the promotional material of one software vendor, "Using these tools the chaos will not end overnight, but without techniques and systems such as we describe here, that chaos may never end."[10]

Software packages all depend on a data base for job-scheduling information; from that point they vary considerably, although having many features in common and producing reports that are similar. The degree of manual intervention varies from one to the next. Some software packages require none, except to enter the initial job information into the data base; others require submission of parameter cards for all jobs to be executed. Some are simple and straightforward, providing few sophisticated features; others provide many control and analytic reports, which may be printed as hard copy or displayed on a terminal. To compare these packages requires close examination of the material supplied by the vendors, review of comments in publications on software packages, consideration of actual user critiques, and attendance at demonstrations of these packages. For now, it will be of value to look at some of the reports that are produced. They have been separated into three categories: for

[10] *Computer Scheduling System,* Value Computing, Inc., Cherry Hill, N.J., p. 31.

scheduling personnel, for work-station personnel, and for data center managers.

Reports for Scheduling Personnel. The most basic report is one that shows the scheduled dates and times for starting and ending each job, and also showing the present status of these jobs. The report shown in Illustration 9–16 accomplishes these purposes. The second column in this report indicates the work station for which the report was prepared; each work station would receive its own schedule and status report, with scheduling personnel receiving a report on all jobs. The job-status code appears in the fourth column, where "C" indicates job completion. For display on terminals, an abbreviated format of this report is used, such as that in Illustration 9–17.

The scheduling personnel may want detailed information on how computer resources are allocated, on how data center resources are allocated, and on the workflow schedule for a specific job. Illustration 9–18 shows the jobs being executed at the same time and the resources allocated, including core storage. Illustration 9–19 is a fascinating summary report on data center resource allocation by work stations, indicating overloading and underloading situations. It is divided according to three work shifts and makes apparent how work can be transferred to other shifts to level the utilization of resources. Illustration 9–20 shows the workflow schedule for a specific job.

Reports for Work-Station Personnel. Besides the detailed schedule shown in Illustration 9–16, work stations may receive special assistance reports, such as the automatically prepared setup sheet in Illustration 9–21, the tape-pulling list in Illustration 9–22, and the disk-mounting list in Illustration 9–23. The advantages of automatically generating these reports are obvious; these reports eliminate the manual effort usually required and are error-free.

Since the work-station reports are particularly important for the operating effectiveness and for adherence to schedules, two other formats are shown for these in Illustrations 9–24 and 9–25. Illustration 9–24 provides some interesting information for the data-conversion work station. This includes task codes and priority codes. Illustration 9–25 gives a different viewpoint of work-station activity. It stresses the overlapping of

VCI STATUS AND REVISION REPORT - RUN ON FRIDAY   01/30/79   AT   8.02.   WORK CENTER # 02   . REL 01.00 VER 00   PAGE   11

** DETAILED REPORT **

Status Indicator:
R = Job is executing
A = Job abended
C = Job completed
E = Job is eligible to run
P = Job is awaiting predecessors

ILLUSTRATION 9-16. Detailed Job Schedule and Status Report. *Source:* Status and Revision Subsystem, Value Computing Inc., Cherry Hill, N.J., p. 18.

STR-015	JOB-NAME	WC	S T T	SCHED START TIME	ACTL START TIME	SCHED END TIME	ACTL END TIME	ACTL END DATE	COMP CODE	P R D	C-FLAG
STR-015	DC78	02	C	16:00	11:12	16:10	11:13	11/18		0	******
STR-015	DC74	02	A	16:00	11:12	16:10	13:01	11/18	S806	0	
STR-015	DC76	02	A	16:00	11:13	16:10	11:14	11/18	S806	0	
STR-015	DC88	02	C	16:00	11:14	16:10	11:14	11/18		0	******
STR-015	ADAMMIB	02	C	16:00	11:14	16:10	11:15	11/18		0	******
STR-015	ADMIB	02	A	16:00	11:14	16:10	11:15	11/18	S806	0	
STR-015	CSAV4PRT	02	A	16:10	11:10	17:30	12:34	11/18	S806	0	
STR-015	DC90	02	A	16:10	11:15	16:20	13:01	11/18	S806	0	
STR-015	GLDG0040	02	E		17:50					0	
STR-015	DPTYPREP	02	E	16:10		16:20				0	
STR-015	DD50	02	C	16:10	11:15	17:40	11:16	11/18		0	******
STR-015	DC80	02	A	16:10	11:16	16:20	13:01	11/18	S806	0	
STR-015	DD53	02	E	16:20		16:30				0	
STR-015	DD54	02	E	16:20		16:40				0	
STR-015	DC86	02	E	16:20		16:30				0	
STR-015	DC34	02	E	16:30		16:40				0	
STR-015	DD56	02	E	16:40		16:50				0	
STR-015	DPS1DLY	02	E	16:40		17:00				0	
STR-015	DD40	02	E	16:50		17:00				0	
STR-015	DC40	02	E	16:50		17:00				0	
STR-015	DC41	02	E	17:00		17:10				0	
STR-015	GR1099MO	02	E	17:00		17:30				0	
STR-015	DD41	02	E	17:00		17:10				0	
STR-015	DPTAPRAF	02	E	17:10		17:30				0	
STR-015	DD42	02	E	17:10		17:20					
STR-015	DD43	02	E	17:20		17:30				0	
STR-015	DD50	02	E	17:30		19:00				0	
STR-015	DA11	02	E	17:40		18:10				0	
STR-015	DPDYLMNT	02	E	17:50		18:00				0	
STR-015	OPER0360	02	E	18:00		19:30				0	
STR-015	DA12	02	P	18:10		18:20				1	
STR-015	PVJOB	02	E	18:10		18:20				0	
STR-015	CORP8PRT	02	A	18:10	11:08	19:30	11:09	11/18	S806	0	
STR-015	DA13	02	P	18:20		18:30				3	
STR-015	DC32	02	E	18:20		19:30				0	
STR-015	DA16	02	P	18:30		18:40				3	
STR-015	DA17	02	P	18:40		18:50				3	

VCI STATUS AND REVISION REPORT—RUN ON THURSDAY 11/18/76 AT 12:55. WORK CENTER = ALL. REL02.00 VER 00
WORK CENTER REPORT

WC	NUMBER SCHED JOBS	NUMBER COMPL JOBS	NUMBER INCMPL JOBS	NUMBER N/S JOBS	SCHED RUN TIME	ACTUAL RUN TIME	N/S RUN TIME	DEVIA-TION	PERCNT DEVIA-TION	PERCNT JOBS SCHED	PERCNT TIME SCHED
02	64	5	59	248	3:20	0:03	35:17	3:17	98	20	8
ALL	64	5	59	248	3:20	0:03	35:17	3:17	98	20	8

WORK CENTER 02
FOR ALL WORK CENTERS

ILLUSTRATION 9-17. Abbreviated Job Schedule and Status Display. *Source:* Status and Revision Subsystem, Value Computing Inc., Cherry Hill, N.J., p. 19.

SYSTEM III SCHEDULER   VALUE COMPUTING INC.

TIME	CLASS_A	CLASS_B	CLASS_C	CLASS_D	CLASS_F	CLASS_J	COR	UTL	TAP	7TR	PRT
08.00	IDA90108	IDA26001	IDA90111				438	70	4	3	2
08.05	I	I					474	80	5	3	3
08.10	I	I					474	80	5	3	3
08.15	I	I					474	80	5	3	3
08.20	IDA30003	IDA30002	IDA261				364	70		4	4
08.25	I	I					402	80		4	4
08.30	I	I					402	80		4	4
08.35	I	I					402	80		4	4
08.40	I	IDA30001					402	80		4	4
08.45		IDA36001	IDA36002				418	70		4	4
08.50	IDA35502	IDA35501	IDA40002	IDA36003			320	60			4
08.55	I	I	I	IDA357			290	60			4
09.00	I	IDA390	IDA40001	IDA356	IDA35002		356	50		1	4
09.05	I	MI968301	IDA34002				454	70	8	1	4
09.10	MC200301	I	IDA34001				494	70	10	2	2
09.15	I	I	I				494	70	10	2	2
09.20	I	MI968302	IDA90109				504	70	11	2	1
09.25	MC365301	I	TR101101				534	70	11	1	2
09.30	I	I	I				534	70	11	1	2
09.35	I	I	I				534	70	11	1	2
09.40	I	I	I				534	70	11	1	2
09.45	MC397201	MI968303	TR101012				534	70	11	1	4
09.50	I	MI968304	I				534	70	11	1	4
09.55	I	I	I				534	70	11	1	4
10.00	I	I	I				534	70	11	1	4
10.05	I	MI968305	I				534	70	11	1	4
10.10	I	I	I				546	70	11	1	4
10.15	I	I	I				546	70	11	1	4
10.20	I	I	I				546	70	11	1	4
10.25	I	I	I				546	70	11	1	4
10.30	I	I	I				546	70	11	1	4
10.35	I	I	I				546	70	11	1	4
10.40	I	MI968306	I				546	70	11	1	4
10.45	I	I	I				536	70	11	1	4
10.50	I	IDA35001	I				536	70	11	1	4
10.55	I	IDA34003	I				522	70	9	2	4
11.00	I	I	I				518	70	9	2	4
11.05	I		I				518	70	9	2	4
11.10			I				562	80	11	2	4
11.15			I				600	90	11	3	4
11.20			I				600	90	11	3	4
11.25			I				600	90	11	3	4
11.30			I				600	90	11	3	4
11.35			I				600	90	11	3	4
11.40			I				600	90	11	3	4
11.45			I				600	90	11	3	4
11.50			I				600	90	11	3	4
11.55			I				600	90	11	3	4

ILLUSTRATION 9–18. Schedule Showing Allocation of Resources. *Source:* Value Computer Scheduling System, Value Computing Inc., Cherry Hill, N.J., p. 10.

ILLUSTRATION 9–19. Data Center Workload Forecast: This report forecasts peak and slack workload periods, permitting workload leveling or adjustment in resources available. *Source:* Automated Schedule, Western Airlines.

WORKLOAD FORECAST

DP 300

04/23/80

	00.01--08.00			08.01--1600			16.01--24.00			TOTAL	
	PROC TIME	AVAILA TIME	OVER LOAD	PROC TIME	AVAILA TIME	OVER LOAD	PROC TIME	AVAILA TIME	OVER LOAD	PROC TIME	OVER LOAD
INPUT CNT	.00	.00	.00	.13	7.17	.00	.45	.15	.00	.58	.00
SET-UP	.00	.00	.00	1.38	12.22	.00	2.35	1.25	.00	4.13	.00
EAM	.00	.00	.00	.25	6.35	.00	.00	.00	.00	.25	.00
KEY PUNCH	.00	.00	.00	64.40	12.20	.00	85.15	.00	8.15	149.55	8.15
COMPUTER	3.10	12.50	.00	3.01	12.59	.00	6.13	9.47	.00	12.24	.00
RUN-CONTR	.00	.00	.00	1.50	5.10	.00	1.10	.00	.10	3.00	.10
OUTPUT CT	.00	.00	.00	3.05	3.55	.00	1.35	.00	.35	4.40	.35

```
DP 3007-A                    D A I L Y   T A S K   F L O W
                                    04/24/80
SYSTEM NAME  OS SOURCE LIBRARY                                        BOOK NUMBER 050

STREAM NAME DPO5010-OS SOURCE LIBRARY                                 STREAM NUMBER 10

      STATION        TASK DESCRIPTION        TASK #    DUE IN     EST. TIME    DATE OUT

      SYS CONTR      SETUP CTL CD & RUNSHEET   001      14.00      00.15       04/24/80
      COMPUTER       DP05010-OS SOURCE LIBRARY 005      14.30      00.20       04/24/80
      SYS CONTR      CK SEL MEMB, TRNS, SCR&PSL 010     15.20      00.05       04/24/80

      TOTAL OF TASKS 3
      TOTAL PROCESS TIME    0.40 HRS.
```

ILLUSTRATION 9–20. Workflow Schedule for a Job. *Source:* Automated Schedule, Western Airlines.

ILLUSTRATION 9–21. Job Set-Up Sheet. *Source:* Computer Job and Data Center Scheduling Systems Summary, Value Computing Inc., Cherry Hill, N.J., p. 64.

```
*********************************************************
*      VALU-LIB SET-UP SHEET FOR   RCHK0300   REGPROC     75210  *
*                                                               *
*  DATA SET NAME                          R/G VOLSER RL CR-DT   *
*                                                               *
*      **** INPUT DATA SETS ****                                *
*                                                               *
*  FPADLY.P102020.RCHKMSTR.G0449V00         1   402041 01 75210 *
*  FPADLY.P102020.RCHKMSTR.G0449V00         1   402042 02 75210 *
*  FPADLY.P102020.AUDIRCHK.G0118V00         1   402117 01 75207 *
*  FPADLY.P102020.RCHKJRNN.G0440V00         1   406019 01 75209 *
*  FPADLY.P102040.RCHKOVDR.G0096V00         1   402161 01 75200 *
*  FPAWKLY.P102020.RCHKTRNF.G0437V00        1   405101 01 75205 *
*  FPAWKLY.P102020.RCHKTRNF.G0437V00        1   405102 02 75205 *
*  FPAWKLY.P102020.RCHKTRNF.G0437V00        1   405103 03 75205 *
*  FPAWKLY.P102020.RCHKTRNF.G0437V00        1   405104 04 75205 *
*                                                               *
*      **** OUTPUT/CYCLE DATA SETS ****                         *
*                                                               *
*  FPADLY.P102020.RCHKMSTR.G0444V00         5   402050 01 75200 *
*  FPADLY.P102020.RCHKMSTR.G0444V00         5   402051 02 75200 *
*  FPADLY.P102020.AUDIRCHK.G0115V00         3   402114 01 75207 *
*  FPADLY.P102020.RCHKJRNN.G0030V00        10   402110 01 75199 *
*                                                               *
*      **** COMMENTS ****                                       *
*                                                               *
*  **** REQUIRED MOUNTABLE PACKS ****                           *
*                                                               *
*   VSN     TYPE    STORAGE LOCATION                            *
*                                                               *
*  RCHK01   3330       BIN  22                                  *
*  RCHK02   3330       BIN  23                                  *
*                                                               *
*      ***** OPERATORS *****                                    *
*                                                               *
*  PLEASE PRINT ALL REPORTS ON STOCK WHITE UNTIL FURTHER NOTICE *
*                                                               *
*  OUTPUT MUST BE GIVEN TO CONTROL BY 4:00 PM TUESDAY           *
*                                                               *
*      ***** CONTROL *****                                      *
*                                                               *
*  DO NOT BURST REPORTS                                         *
*              SEND TO PAYROLL AS IS                            *
*********************************************************
```

TAPE PULLING LIST

JOB NAME MINOR APPL	DATA SET NAME	DATA SET DESCRIPTION	VOLUME SER NO	RELL #	CREATE DATE	TIME
IVNBCM01 1013300128	IVNBCT.FPI22.MASTER.G0002V00	MASTER	201515		74267	09.44
	IVNBCT.FPI22.MASTER.G0003V00	MASTER	102448		74298	
	IVNBCT.FPI22.MASTER.G0004V00	MASTER	101653		74326	15.47
	IVNBCT.FPI23.TMASTER.G0002V00	TMASTER	101818		74267	09.48
	IVNBCT.FPI23.TMASTER.G0003V00	TMASTER	102441		74298	10.12
	IVNBCT.FPI22.TMASTER.G0004V00		101246		74326	
MACMCR02 2072210735	MACMCT.PMI12.MASTER.G0182V00	MASTER	101504		74337	21.11
	XSGNLT.IEBGENER.TRANBKUP.G0042V00	TRANBKUP	102292		74339	19.32
	CONBCT.ACO14.TRANS.G0041V00	TRANS	102537		74322	17.07
PLGNLD01 3072202040	PLGNLT.LGL12.MASTER		102233		74338	
PRWEND01 2072212938	PRWENT.NSA22.MASTEXTR.G0036V00	OUTPUT TRAN	102902		74338	10.57
PRWENWA7 2072292938	PRWENT.GAI20.GAIMASTR.G0034V00	GAIMASTER	102181		74338	16.27
PRWENW01 2072212938	PRWENT.NSA20.NOSAVPWM.G0032V00	OUTPUT TRAN	102496		74330	
	PRWENT.WFA13.PATMASTP.G0030V00		101009		74340	
	PRWENT.NSA20.NOSAVPWM.G0033V00	OUTPUT TRAN	102379	0001	74338	10.31
			102540	0002		
	PRWENT.NSA20.NOSAVPWM.G0032V00	OUTPUT TRAN	102496		74330	

ILLUSTRATION 9-22. Tape Pulling List. *Source:* Computer Job and Data Center Scheduling Systems Summary, Value Computing Inc., Cherry Hill, N.J., p. 63.

DATE-06/30/80   (REVISION)   SYSTEM III SCHEDULER

DIRECT ACCESS MOUNTS LIST   DIRECT ACCESS MOUNTS LIST

TIME	JOB NAME	CFG	MOUNT	VOL SER	DISP	DATA SET NAME
20.05	LFFPREST	1	MOUNT	LF0003	OLD	LF.LFFPMSTR
			MOUNT	LF0003	OLD	LF.LFFPLNVL
20.05	PNSPCRPT	1	MOUNT	333333	OLD	PN.PDFILE
20.10	DPGOBOLX	1	MOUNT	333333	SHR	DP.LOGCATLG
20.15	ADSPLREG	1				** NONE **
20.15	ADUWARPT	1				** NONE **
20.15	DPANALYS	1				** NONE **
20.15	GCASODLY	1	MOUNT	GR0002	OLD	GC.ASOCNTL
20.15	INIT3	1				** NONE **
20.15	LFEMMNT	1	MOUNT	FM7070	OLD	FL.RCARDS
20.20	FDFILFSA	1	MOUNT	FD3330	SHR	FD.FDMAXI
			MOUNT	GOR001	SHR	FD.FDMINI
			MOUNT	TP2301	SHR	FD.FDCLAIMS
			MOUNT	FD3330	SHR	FD.FDNAMFLE
			MOUNT	TP2302	SHR	FD.FDALPHAX
			MOUNT	TP2302	SHR	FD.FDPOLINX
			MOUNT	TP2302	SHR	FD.FDPOLEXT
			MOUNT	TP2302	SHR	FD.FDJCL
			MOUNT	FD0001	OLD	FD.FDJCLDD
			MOUNT	TP2302	SHR	FD.FDPGMJCL
			MOUNT	FD0002	OLD	FD.FDPGMDD
20.30	PLAMAIN2	1	MOUNT	CD0003	SHR	PL.PLAPPFIL
			MOUNT	CD0003	SHR	PF.PLTPAPP
20.35	DPRMAINT	1				** NONE **
20.50	GREM0020	1				** NONE **
20.50	GROCR	1	MOUNT	333333	SHR	CR.OCRTPFLE
21.00	GRPEPPLN	1	MOUNT	GR0009	OLD	GR.GRPPDET
			MOUNT	GR0010	OLD	GR.GRPPDET
			MOUNT	GR0009	OLD	GR.GRPPMAS
			MOUNT	LF0004	SHR	AX.CVFINDER
			MOUNT	LF0004	SHR	AX.CSVALUES
			MOUNT	GR0002	OLD	GR.GRTAB0001
			MOUNT	GR0002	OLD	GR.PPMAINT
			MOUNT	GR0009	OLD	GR.CNTROL01
			MOUNT	GR0002	OLD	GR.PPBILL
			MOUNT	GR0001	OLD	GR.HOBIXMAS
			MOUNT	GR0007	OLD	GR.HOBIXMAS
			MOUNT	GR0002	OLD	GR.CNTROL02
21.00	SDUPDTE	1				** NONE **
21.20	GRHOBBL2	1	MOUNT	GR3330	OLD	GR.HOBDETAL
			MOUNT	GR3331	OLD	GR.HOBDETAL
			MOUNT	GR0002	OLD	GR.CNTROL02
			MOUNT	GR0001	OLD	GR.HOBIXMAS
			MOUNT	GR0007	OLD	GR.HOBIXMAS
21.20	GRPPBKUP	1	MOUNT	GR0009	OLD	GR.GRPPDET
			MOUNT	GR0010	OLD	GR.GRPPDET
			MOUNT	GR0009	OLD	GR.CNTROL01
			MOUNT	GR0009	OLD	GR.GRPPMAS
21.30	GR1099M0	1				** NONE **
21.35	LFCHGLOG	1	MOUNT	333333	SHR	LF.CNTROLT

ILLUSTRATION 9-23. Disk Mounting List *Source:* Value Computer Scheduling System, Value Computing Inc., Cherry Hill, N.J., p. 15.

STATION WORKSHEET

STATION   KEY PUNCH   DATE 04/24/80

BOOK	STRM	TASK	PRTY	SYSTEM DESCRIPTION	TASK DESCRIPTION	DUE IN TIME	PROCESS TIME	DUE OUT TIME	DUE OUT DATE
34	5	1	6	A/C FLYING TIME	KEY OP0002-0 FLT TIMES	4.00	.30	5.00	04/24/80
79	1	5	5	FLIGHT PAY	KEY FP5013-0	4.15	5.00	8.00	04/24/80
34	10	1	6	A/C FLYING TIME	PUNCH CORRECTION CARDS	5.45	.30	7.00	04/24/80
26	1	5	5	TAPE LIBRARY CNTL.	PCH DAILY TRANS IN CTL	6.00	2.00	8.30	04/24/80
33	1	5	5	ADDITIONAL COMP	PUNCH ADD COMP CARDS	8.05	1.00	10.05	04/24/80
18	1	5	5	INTERLINE BILLING	KEY RCPT TICKETS TA PE	8.15	35.00	16.00	04/24/80
36	1	5	5	ACT VS SCH FLY TIM	KEY SP0105-0 (OPTIONAL)	8.15	.30	9.00	04/24/80
38	1	5	6	DAILY A/C MAINT	PUNCH ENGINE UPDATE CARDS	9.05	.30	9.30	04/24/80
86	1	5	6	ON REQ E/D TEARDWN	PCH EC-ON1267,1283A&B CDS	9.15	.10	9.30	04/24/80
20	5	5	5	FLT STATS TAX RPTS	KEY FS4230-0 TAPE	12.15	.30	13.00	04/24/80
17	1	6	5	AREA SETTLEMNT PLN	KEY 1/3 FINAL CUT OFF TAP	13.15	68.45	23.30	04/24/80
16	30	5	5	SPAIN Y	KEY BLK SCHED CORR TAPE	16.15	2.00	19.00	04/24/80
74	45	2	5	A/F TRANS MANIFEST	KEY AF3092-0 TAPE	16.15	2.00	18.30	04/24/80
84	1	5	5	WAL LOC & OCCUP	PUNCH TRANSACTION CARDS	16.15	1.00	17.30	04/24/80
94	1	3	5	VOUCHERS	PUNCH VOUCHER ACCTG CARDS	16.15	.30	17.00	04/24/80
104	5	5	5	FLIGHT STATISTICS	KEY FS1105-0	16.15	2.00	18.50	04/24/80
119	1	5	5	MAILING SERVICES	PUNCH PARAMETER CARDS	16.15	.05	17.30	04/24/80
124	1	5	5	LIQUOR CONTROL	KEY LC1000-0 TAPE DAILY	16.15	8.00	8.00	04/25/80
133	1	5	5	P D I	PUNCH DATA FROM/TO PDI'S	16.15	.10	18.00	04/24/80
27	1	5	6	SHOP PAYROLL	PUNCH PAIDOUT CARDS	16.15	1.00	18.50	04/24/80
74	60	5	5	AIR FREIGHT	KEY AIRBILLS TO AF8000-0	16.30	15.00	8.00	04/24/80
3	1	25	5	GOVERNMENT BILLING	KP GTRS INTO GOV BILL CDS	17.00	3.00	21.00	04/24/80
41	1	1	5	KEYPUNCH ANALYSIS	KEY DP1101-0 TAPE	17.00	1.00	22.00	04/24/80

TOTAL TASK = 23

TOTAL HOURS = 149.55

ILLUSTRATION 9–24. Work Station Schedule Sequenced by Job Due-In Time. *Source:* Automated Schedule, Western Airlines.

BURS-DLV   DATE – PRESCD#1   DATA CENTER SCHEDULER   VALUE COMPUTING INC.

TIME	DELEAVER1	DELEAVER2	BURSTER1	BURSTER2	BURSTER3	BURSTER4
06.00		I	I			
06.05		I	I	BVRD25		
06.10		I	I	I		
06.15	ZXC417	I		I		
06.20		I	BXC417			
06.25		I				
06.30		I				
06.35					BXP110P	
06.40	ZXP164				I	
06.45	I				I	
06.50	ZXP190		BLD462	BXP164	I	BLD602
06.55	I		I	I	I	I
07.00	I				I	I
07.05			BXP190		I	I
07.10	ZRS02	ZRS03	I		I	I
07.15	I	I	I		I	I
07.20			BRS02	BRS03	I	
07.25			I	I	I	
07.30			I	I	I	
07.35			I	I		
07.40	ZXP110Q					

ILLUSTRATION 9–25. Work Station Schedule Showing Machine Assignment and Overlap. *Source:* Value Computer Scheduling System, Value Computing Inc., Cherry Hill, N.J., p. 25.

activities, the allocation of jobs to the various deleavers and bursters in the postcomputer-processing work station. It immediately indicates what jobs are affected by the breakdown of one of these machines, permitting selection and transferring of critical jobs by the operators.

Reports for Data Center Managers. Data center managers are interested in a detailed listing of all jobs executed (Illustration 9–26) and in a report that compares actual and scheduled processing times (Illustration 9–27). The detailed listing of all completed jobs provides an audit trail and, with the addition of initial program loading (IPL) information, calls attention to a potential problem situation if the number of IPLs is excessive. The same is true for the report that compares actual and scheduled processing time. This report also may indicate potential problems. These two reports focus on job processing time.

Data center managers also want reports that focus on resource utilization and resource problems. Illustration 9–28 shows a report consisting of several graphs that indicate resource utilization. It

VALUE COMPUTING INC.
SUMMARY OF RUNS FOR 11/15/78   CONFIG NO. 2, 158   PAGE 15

N NAME	MINOR REMARKS	START END EXEC	ELAPS EXEC	CPU MMM.MM	REQ USED	PI PO	ABND	CARDS IN CDS PCH	LINES 4/8 3270 TER	TAP4 IO	DISK IO STR HRMN	TAP8 IO 4TAP 800	CLS PRTY PROG	Q ON TIM END SOUT	3350 IO 1K HR.MN
I03PCR	0003	10.06 10.10	.04	.17	256	33		154	1975	277	79		P 13	7.30	
		10.06	.02		252	13							PAY ECR	10.17	4.12
P56TRIAL	W056	10.08 10.10	.02	.27	192	30			6235				L 12	10.06	
		10.09	.02		188							6062	TRIAL PR	12.23	6.16
P56NOTES	W056	10.11 10.12	.02	.26	192	7			5982				L 12	10.10	
		10.11	.02		188							5913	NITICES	12.28	6.16
P56ZBI	W056	10.13 10.13	.00	.02	192	1			564				L 13	10.11	
		10.13	.00		188							495	ZBI	10.16	3.08
P563X5	W056	10.14 10.16	.02	.45	192				10380				L 12	10.14	
		10.14	.02		188							10163	O?K	12.36	6.16
I41TWIC2	M041	10.01 10.16	.15	.28	192	28						753	M 05	10.00	
		10.01	.14		188	20			1694			.12	DEMAND.C	10.19	43.52
034DEL	1801	10.21 10.21	.00	.00	192								M 05	10.21	
		10.21	.00		188				95				VARY.DEV	10.21	3.08
I34OFF	0034	10.23 10.23	.00	.00	640				79				I 09	10.22	
		10.23	.00		636								OFFLINE	10.24	10.36
I78DCOPY	0078	10.19 10.23	.04	.11	256	26			155	1186	1036		P 09	10.19	
		10.20 IPL 10.39	.03		252	2							INTERFAC	10.24	16.48
E31BLCR1	0031	10.53 10.58	.05	.26	256	10			2131				B 05	10.53	
		10.57	.01		252	1						5351	BLUE.CRO	12.28	4.12
I30SMFPT	1751	10.53 10.59	.06	.30	256	9		182	858		387		S 13	6.47	
		10.54	.05		256	2							LARRY YO	12.21	17.04
I809PBLD	1751	10.59 11.02	.03	.02	256	7		2	50		589		S 13	7.57	
		11.01	.01		256	3							LARRY YO	12.21	4.16
034UCTLG	0034	11.01 11.02	.01	.03	640	3		20	120				I 13	11.01	
		11.01	.01		34								UNCATALO	12.22	.34
I30DSDAC	0030	10.54 11.03	.09	.26	192	8		100	2643		365		L 14	6.46	
		10.57	.04		192	2							R.MCNAME	12.23	12.44
I30PSYSD	0030	11.04 11.05	.01	.01	192	11		4	66		1		L 13	11.04	
		11.05	.00		192								PRINT.SY	12.28	3.12
034SUP58	0034	11.06 11.07	.01	.15	320	23	S222	27	106		203		D 13	11.04	
		11.06	.01		316	1							SUPER.SC	12.28	5.16
030TS002	0030	10.53 11.10	.17	1.61	640	289	SOC5	219	12445	581	7866		S 13	7.50	
		10.53	.15		640	52							B.BARSTO	12.26	85.04
034BK58C	0034	11.05 11.11	.06	.37	192	14			1011	78	2781		L 13	11.04	
		11.05	.06		34	10							RES158.C	12.29	3.24
E71DLUX2	0087	11.17 11.24	.07	.12	320	1			73	145	1475		D 09	11.17	
		11.17	.07		316								DELUX	12.28	36.52
034DITTO	1701	11.27 11.31	.04	.01	640	4 0300			84	96			I 11	11.27	
		11.27	.04		636							96	DITTO	11.53	42.24
034SUP58	0034	11.10 11.36	.26	2.27	640	10	S222	27	15782		8498		O 13	11.07	
		11.10	.15		636	11							SUPER.SC	12.31	95.24
034DITTO	1701	11.32 11.40	.08	.03	640	9	S222		101	130			I 12	11.27	
		11.32	.08		636	7						129	DITTO	11.53	84.48
I08MMINE	1761	11.02 11.40	.38	5.13	256	51			202	57071			S 06	8.31	
		11.02	.35		252	22							CIF.MTLY	12.28	75.36
034DTPBK	0034	11.11 11.53	.42	5.13	192	24		1	95	60484	29870		L 13	11.05	
		11.11	.42		50	7							TP0001.B	12.26	35.00
I86UCOPY	0086	11.52 11.53	.01	.02	384	1			72	182	181		P 13	11.51	
		11.52	.01		380								FMS.DDA.	12.26	6.20
T03PUD	P023	11.36 11.54	.18	.51	640	16			2266	1250	600		8 04	4.41	
		11.37	.11		636	6		89				117	BRAVO	13.36	42.24
I32SRRP2	0032	11.56 12.14	.18	.07	256				167	410	6		R 13	6.41	
		11.56	.04		252								FOMAS RR	12.29	16.48
034CPYSH	0034	12.18 12.19	.01	.05	256	9		5	130		1065		D 13	12.17	
		12.18	.01		256	2							COPY SHR	12.27	4.16
034CUOPT	1751	12.20 12.23	.03	.10	256	21		2	79		2652		D 13	12.20	
		12.20	.03		256	2							MAINTENA	12.27	12.48
034BKTPC	0034	11.53 12.26	.33	3.14	192	1			8478	1072	26578		L 12	11.05	
		11.53	.33		28	8							TP0001.B	12.30	15.24
*034TLFLK	0030	12.26 12.26	.00	.05	192	9		2	78		1420		L 13	12.25	
		12.26	.00		192								MAINT	12.28	3.12
E87DLUX3	0087	12.00 12.30	.30	2.21	384	80		5	3305	54544	6085		Y 12	11.59	
		12.00	.17		380	17							DELUXE	12.31	57.00
034TPMNT	0030	12.28 12.34	.06	.13	192	55			331		152		L 13	12.28	24
		12.29	.04		188	2							B.BARSTO	12.34	9.24

ILLUSTRATION 9–26. Listing of All Executed Jobs. *Source:* Value Computer Scheduling System, Value Computing Inc., Cherry Hill, N.J., p. 16.

DAILY ACTUAL VERSUS SCHEDULE REPORT   RLSE 7.01   01/30/79   CONFIG = 158   SCHEDULE - 5   PAGE 02

JOB NAME	MINOR-APPL	ACTUAL TIMES START	END	ELAPS	SCHEDULED TIMES START	END	ELAPS	F	ACT SCD CORE	F	ACT SCD UTIL	F	DUE OUT	F	ABND CODE	COMMENTS
RA40J600 R 00000		8.54	10.18	1.24	7.06	8.10	1.10		512 512		17 13	*			----	CLS 04 DEV DIFF ACT 3 SCD 4
IU05J350 R 04000		7.19	10.18	2.59											S224	DSN RECS2 D30025 MCS1.MA21D101
KA10J100 R 01000		7.24	10.21	2.59											S222	
JM05J717 J 08000		10.25	10.27	.02												
NW50J900 N 08060		10.22	10.28	.06												
AA04J100 N 00000		10.27	10.30	.03	11.00	11.05	.05		512 512		4 5	*				
NP02J900 N 03000		10.27	10.30	.03												
CA35J100 N 00000		10.30	10.31	.01												
NM35J700 N 00000		10.33	10.35	.02												
CD10J13A N 00000		10.35	10.37	.02											S813	
CA05J991 C 00000		10.37	10.39	.02												
NW50J120 N 00000		10.39	10.40	.01												
DU50J100 N 00000		10.40	10.43	.03												
KE05J111 K 04000		10.40	10.45	.05	11.40	11.45	.05		512 512		3 3				SOC7	DSN RECS2 D30021 MCS1.LIVE.AA0
AA05J111 A 00000		10.40	10.46	.06												
NW20J900 N 06000		10.40	10.46	.06												
AL00J737 N 00000		10.46	10.47	.01												
NW30J995 N 08000		10.52	10.53	.01												
CA04J100 C 00000		10.41	10.59	.18	15.20	15.35	.15		512 512		12 12					DSN ADDED D00001 SYS1.NWB1D050 DSN ADDED D00001 SYS1.CYLINDEX
NW50J900 N 03000		10.55	11.00	.05												
AT05J50A N 07000		10.06	11.10	1.04											S222	
DG05J317 C 02000		10.59	11.14	.15	11.45	12.10	.25		512 512		10 7	*			S222	
CA15J100 C 00000		11.04	11.30	.26	23.10	2.00	2.50	*	512 512		10 14	*				
NW30J100 N 00000		11.34	11.38	.04												
AA00J103 A 03000		11.11	11.42	.31	11.40	11.40	.30		512 512		9 8	*				
NW50J900 N 08000		11.15	11.44	.29												
NW30J995 N 08000		11.35	11.45	.07												
KE05J444 K 06000		11.26	12.03	.05												DSN RECS2 D30023 MCS1.LIVE.AA0
NP20J970 N 12000		11.27	12.07	.22	10.00	10.10	.10		512 512		3 4	**				DSN RECS2 D30022 MCS1.LIVE.AA0
CA15J100 C 00000		11.20	12.11	.11	15.00	15.05	.05		512 512		3 5	**				
CA15J900 C 00000		12.23	12.25	.02	15.00	15.05	.05		512 512							
CA35J900 C 00000		12.24	12.26	.02												
CA05J900 C 00000		12.26	12.27	.01												
CA05J991 C 00000		12.07	12.30	.23												
TWTRA TW00000		12.04	12.34	.30												
NL70J970 N 06000		12.27	12.35	.01												
TWTRA TW00000		12.27	12.42	.08												
EA30J001 E 08000		12.27	12.45	.18												
NW50J900 N 05000		12.47	12.53	.06												
CA70J123 C 03000		12.45	12.55	.10												

ILLUSTRATION 9–27. Report Comparing Scheduled and Actual Processing Times. *Source:* Value Computer Scheduling System, Value Computing Inc., Cherry Hill, N.J., p. 21.

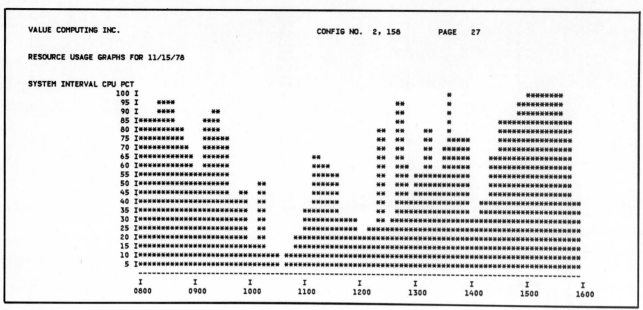

ILLUSTRATION 9-28a. Resource Utilization Graph. *Source:* Value Computer Scheduling System, Value Computing Inc., Cherry Hill, N.J., p. 17.

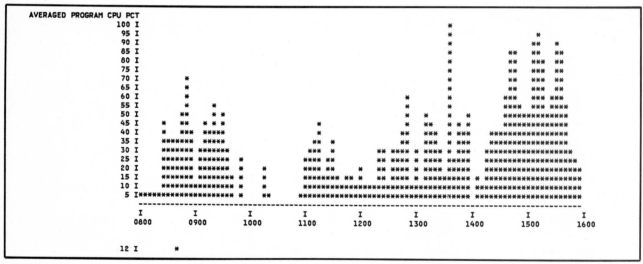

ILLUSTRATION 9-28b. Resource Utilization Graph. *Source:* Value Computer Scheduling System, Value Computing Inc., Cherry Hill, N.J., p. 17.

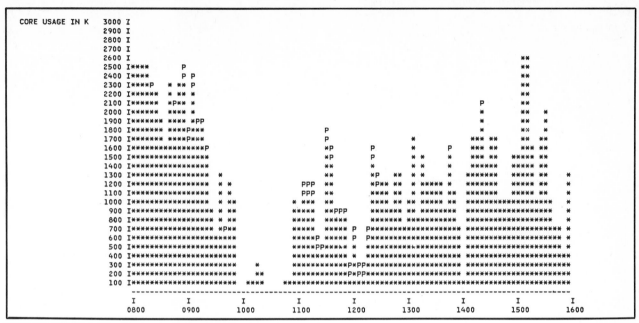

ILLUSTRATION 9-28c. Resource Utilization Graph. *Source:* Value Computer Scheduling System, Value Computing Inc., Cherry Hill, N.J., p. 17.

ILLUSTRATION 9-28d. Resource Utilization Graph. *Source:* Value Computer Scheduling System, Value Computing Inc., Cherry Hill, N.J., p. 17.

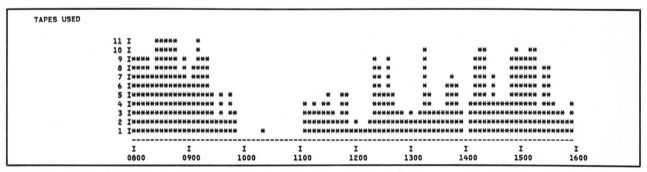

ILLUSTRATION 9-28e. Resource Utilization Graph. *Source:* Value Computer Scheduling System, Value Computing Inc., Cherry Hill, N.J., p. 17.

```
                    DEVICE UTILIZATION AND MALFUNCTION REPORT
                               FOR 11/15/78

            DEVICE        DEV   TOTAL   PCT   DEVICE     DOWN  NO  PCT
            DESCRIPTION    MN   ALLOC  UTIL  EXCP COUNT  TIME  DN  DOWN
            -------------  ----  -----  -----  ----------  -----  --  -----
            SYS RDR        RDR    .57    4.0     17080
            3505 READER    00C    .00    0.0
            3505 READER 8TH 01E   .00    0.0
            WITHERSPOON RDR 30C   .00    0.0
            SYS WTR        WTR  32.07  136.1   4811035
            3800 PRINTER   40B    .00    0.0
            3211 PRINTER   41D    .00    0.0
            4TH WTR        00E    .00    0.0
            WITHERSPOON WTR 30E   .00    0.0
            3800 PRINTER   40E    .00    0.0
            3211 PRINTER   01A    .00    0.0
            SYS PCH        PCH    .04    0.2       862
            PUNCH          00D    .00    0.0
            3420 TAPE      370   2.14    9.4     33883
            3420 TAPE      371    .35    2.4      8330
            3420 TAPE      372    .29    2.0      1622
            3420 TAPE      373   1.08    4.8     21997
            3420 TAPE      374   3.17   13.9     43337
            3420 TAPE      375   6.41   28.3     77570
            3420 TAPE      376  12.01   50.9    142590
            3420 TAPE      377  13.37   57.7    228029
            3420 TAPE      378  16.35   70.3    278767
            3420 TAPE      379  16.11   68.6    121865
            3420 TAPE      37A  15.43   66.6    329846
            3420 TAPE      37B  12.48   54.2     88025
            3420 TAPE      37C  13.41   58.0    137903
            3420 TAPE      37D  11.39   49.3    140270
            3420 TAPE      37E   8.38   36.6     87664
            3420 TAPE      37F   9.51   41.7    174330
            3330 DISK      130    .52    3.6      1914
            3330 DISK      131  12.55   54.7     93528
            3330 DISK      132  20.11   85.5     21838
            3330 DISK      133  20.04   85.0    237675
            3330 DISK      150    .22    1.5      3525
            3330 DISK      151   9.22   39.7     61274
            3330 DISK      152   8.59   38.0     48475
            3330 DISK      153   5.06   21.6     62131
            3330 DISK      154    .00    0.0
            3330 DISK      155    .00    0.0
            3330 DISK      156    .00    0.0
            3330 DISK      157    .00    0.0
            3330 DISK      240   5.30   23.3     12015
            3330 DISK      241  19.52   84.2    184939
            3330 DISK      242  17.33   74.4     77741
            3330 DISK      243  20.21   86.2    236571
            3330 DISK      244  14.22   60.9     99040
            3330 DISK      245  18.14   77.3    223686
            3330 DISK      246  13.50   58.6     88693
            3330 DISK      247   2.36   11.0     26757
```

ILLUSTRATION 9–29. Device Utilization and Malfunction Report. *Source:* Value Computer Scheduling System, Value Computing Inc., Cherry Hill, N.J., p. 20.

shows CPU, core, and peripheral utilization. These graphs immediately make apparent where over-utilization and underutilization occur. The remaining type of report data center managers want are those showing individual device utilization and malfunction, such as the report shown in Illustration 9–29. These reports indicate which devices may not be serviced correctly or are unreliable and should be replaced.

Acceptance of the value of a good scheduling method is not enough. Good intentions must be put into practice; the data center manager cannot benefit from a scheduling methodology by just reading about it—it must be implemented. As Larry Winkler comments, "The potential gains to be derived from a scheduling system are limited only by the extent to which you—as progressive and professional data processing managers—are willing to utilize it."[11]

[11] Winkler, "Scheduling a Data Processing Center," p. 18.

GOAL

To set a sound foundation of concepts and techniques for managing the data communications environment.

HIGHLIGHTS

Processing Types

Flexibility results from awareness and appreciation of the processing types available which are:

- Off-line processing
- On-line batch processing
- Data gathering
- Inquiry-response processing
- Real-time processing

Planning Aspects

Planning consists of establishing policies, standards, and procedures for modifying organization structure, implementing the data communications system, and controlling its operation.

Data Communications Elements

Design and operating guidelines can be applied effectively only through insight into the functions of and relationships between hardware units, communication links, and software support.

Design and Operating Guidelines

These guidelines can be conveniently segmented into five categories:

- Data integrity
- Data security
- Network availability
- Network service
- Network adaptability

What is data communications? What, specifically, does that phrase mean? It is only necessary to eavesdrop on the conversation of persons working daily with data communications to realize that ambiguity exists. As part of the author's research and visits to many data centers, personnel were casually asked, How do you define and relate the phrases "data communications," "real-time processing," "on-line processing," and "teleceommunications?" The intention was to determine how these phrases were interpreted and related by persons designing, monitoring, and modifying data communication systems. Illustration 10–1 suggests the array of phrases often used, sometimes interchangeably, without any feeling of how they are related.

The desire for precise distinctions is not academic. Lack of precision in the use of these phrases leads to communication difficulties. Frequently the phrases "on-line processing" and "data communications" are used interchangeably, totally ignoring that data communications also includes off-line processing. Besides clouding discussions about these systems and the technical aspects related to these discussions, alternative methods of processing are ignored, such as the possibility of off-line processing as a positive and beneficial alternative to on-line processing.

Thus, the first goal of this chapter is to define

ILLUSTRATION 10–1. Vaguely Related Datacom Phrases: These phrases are often used interchangeably, resulting in confusion and in limited consideration of design alternatives.

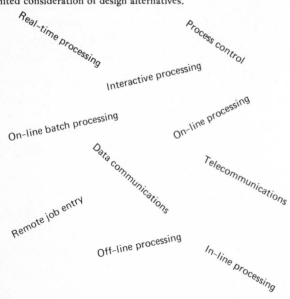

precisely the primary data communications phrases and to show their relationships. The chapter continues with a discussion of the managerial and design aspects required to plan for a data communications system; the discussion then turns to the elements in a data communications system and to the guidelines for designing and operating it.

First, the use of the word "system" in "data communications system" should be clarified. Whereas "data communications network" refers to hardware and communication links (to be defined soon), "data communications system" includes the software used for data communications, including the application systems, and sometimes is understood to include the data-base-management system. In this chapter, "data communications system" is used in its most general sense: it includes all software connected with processing a data communications application and therefore also includes the data-base-management system.

PROCESSING TYPES

As a result of discussing the phrases shown in Illustration 10–1 and examining the many books and dictionaries defining these phrases (sometimes containing startling and glaring inconsistencies), the following phrases were identified as the most critical and are now defined:

Telecommunications. Transmission and receipt of signals, which may or may not be data.

Data communications. Transmission and receipt of digital data that are converted to analog signals for transmission and back to digital data upon receipt.

Off-line processing. Transmitted data are not under the control of the computer that will eventually process the data. Data after receipt must still be submitted for processing.

On-line processing. Transmitted data are under the control of the computer that will process the data. Data are immediately queued for processing.

On-line batch processing. For input, all data are accumulated at a remote site before being transmitted for execution; for output, a job is executed and completed before the output is transmitted to the remote site. This manner of processing is also called remote job entry (RJE).

In-line processing. Transmitting and receiving, and possibly processing, each transaction as it becomes available.

Data gathering. Accumulation of transmitted transactions as they become available, without performing any data-base updating.

Interactive processing. Conversational-type processing that alternates between the receipt and transmission of messages.

Inquiry-response processing. Alternating transmission and receipt of messages that do not affect the activities being monitored and do not modify a data base.

Real-time processing. Alternating transmission and receipt of messages that do affect the activities being monitored or do modify one or more data bases.

Illustration 10–2 indicates the hierarchical relationships of these transmission activities. It becomes

clear that many of these phrases are categories that include more than one type of specific processing, such as in-line processing, including data gathering and interactive processing. But since interactive processing is itself a category consisting of inquiry-response and real-time processing, it is advisable to refer to specific types of processing instead of categories when discussing any particular data communications system. Thus, as annotated in Illustration 10–2, there are actually only five types of data communications processing:

- Off-line processing
- On-line batch processing
- Data gathering
- Inquiry-response processing
- Real-time processing

ILLUSTRATION 10–2. Hierarchy of Datacom Categories and Processing Types.

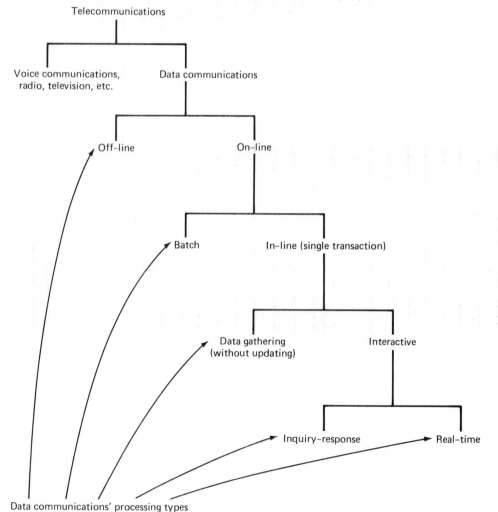

These are considered below. Frequently, for expediency, the phrase "data communications" is written as data-communications, datacommunications, or simply datacom; for the remainder of this chapter, the term *datacom* is used.

Off-line Processing

This type of processing is, without doubt, the simplest form of datacom. It is the ideal means for an organization initially becoming involved with datacom, instead of plunging in and having regrets, and possibly poisoning everyone's attitude toward datacom for quite a while. Off-line processing is simple because data transmission is kept totally separate from the processing of the data. Data stored on cards, paper tape, or magnetic tape are transmitted from one site to another, where they are copied onto magnetic tape. One or both ends of the transmission may be under the control of a computer, primarily to format and possibly to edit the data—but this is still referred to as off-line processing, since the actual processing of the data does not occur. Such activities as data-base updating and output preparation do not occur at the time of transmission.

The most widespread application of off-line processing occurs in processor-controlled data entry. In these applications a minicomputer or a microprocessor edits, formats, and pools input from several data-entry stations and places the input onto tape, disk, or drum. The off-line-processed data are submitted at a later time for processing. Actually, this simple form of datacom provides the feeling of real-time processing, even though the actual processing for the transactions does not occur. The appearance of real-time processing occurs because of the interaction between the work-station operators and the editing program. Field and interfield errors displayed on the operator's terminal can be easily corrected. Actual processing for the transactions, however, does not occur until these pooled transactions are submitted for application processing. The limitation of off-line editing becomes clear when it is realized that consistency checking of transactions against application data bases is not possible.

Off-line processing becomes a natural choice when the execution of the data can be delayed a day or longer. Consider the requirement for pro-

cessing Medicare claims, where the Social Security Administration (SSA) must be queried if a claimant's records show that the $50 deductible amount has not been reduced to zero. This is necessary because a second insurance company may have reduced or eliminated the claimant's deductible balance, and only the SSA would have the most up-to-date status. The method often used for this purpose is off-line processing, where accumulated status inquiries are transmitted from a tape unit at the insurance company to the SSA location in Baltimore, Maryland.

Off-line processing, besides being simpler than other types of datacom, is also less costly and lessens the workload on the datacom system during peak activity periods. These benefits should be apparent: (1) cost is reduced because there is less hardware and software overhead; and (2) workload is lessened during peak periods because files prepared off-line can be processed at any time, such as during the third shift. All in all, this method of datacom should be considered and used instead of other datacom methods when possible. The benefits of simplicity, low cost, and low effect on high-priority critical datacom systems are significant.

On-line Batch Processing

Whereas off-line processing involves transmitting data that are accumulated at the site where processing is scheduled, on-line batch processing accumulates the data for jobs before transmission and immediate queueing for execution. This provides faster processing of jobs than in off-line processing since the jobs are immediately placed in a queue, to be executed according to their priorities and resource requirements. Thus, if a delay of a day or more for processing cannot be tolerated but immediate processing is not necessary, this method is ideal. Next to off-line processing, it is the simplest, least expensive, and least demanding on network and computer resources.

On-line batch processing is ideal for transmitting data for such applications as payroll, accounts receivable, accounts payable, inventory control, and student applications. Student applications, for example, usually require minimal resources and are executed quickly—particularly because of the high percentage of compiles-only and abnormal terminations. These jobs, with their data, can be accumulated and periodically transmitted. One difficulty that often occurs for low-priority on-line batch jobs, such as those from students, is that they have been known to linger in a queue for days while jobs with higher priority push ahead of them.

Many organizations use on-line batch processing as the preferred alternative to hand-delivering jobs and data to a data center. In fact, many sophisticated datacom systems include on-line batch processing in a somewhat disguised form. It is common practice for a branch office to do local processing on a small or medium-size computer and, at the end of the day, to transmit summary data as an on-line batch job to a large computer at a central location.

Illustration 10–3 shows how three departments process their daily sales and perform their credit checking, and at the end of the day transmit data for batch processing, permitting updating of sales, inventory, and credit files. This approach has the distinct advantage of making each department's processing operations independent of degraded or disrupted processing at the central site during the day. It also reduces the workload on the central computer during peak processing time periods. However, it also has the deficiency of permitting a person to use the full credit limit shown on the local files at each of the three stores—and this

improper activity becomes apparent only after the evening processing at the central site.

Data Gathering

By transmitting data as they become available, it is possible to edit and correct and have data ready for immediate execution at any time desired. This is in contrast to on-line batch processing, which transmits data for execution only when all the data have been accumulated. This may require considerable correction of rejected data, thus delaying completion of the job. Some applications permit execution with the data available, not requiring transmission of all the data for an application. Data-base updating for inventory control and accounts receivable are such applications. Payroll, on the other hand, cannot be executed until all data have been received, but even then data gathering is still advantageous because of the error corrections that can be performed.

Data gathering is frequently used for recording scientific and process data. These data are gathered from various measuring devices, transmitted, and stored for later analysis. Measurements for a process may include temperature, humidity, and ingredient percentages. However, if the data

ILLUSTRATION 10–3. Online Batch Processing: Realtime processing is used at the local locations to check credit ratings and to record sales made. Once a day, sales information is transmitted in batch to a central location for updating credit, sales, and stock files. *Source:* John E. Bingham and Garth W. P. Davies, Planning for Data Communications (New York: John Wiley, 1977), p. 35. By permission of Macmillian, London and Basingstoke.

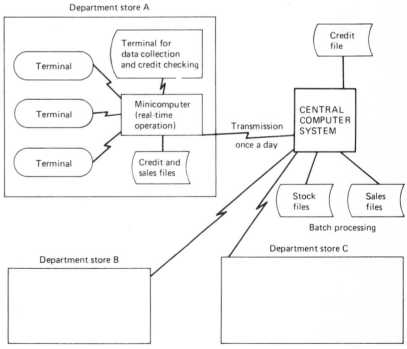

gathered are intended to control the processes occurring, data gathering as an in-line but noninteractive process is totally useless. It is apparent that, if immediate control of a process is required, by definition, real-time processing is the only approach. Data gathering limits itself to transmitting data for accumulation, but does not update a data base or affect an application's operations.

Inquiry-Response Processing

Although this processing consists of interaction between operator and computer, there is no interaction between data and what the data refer to. In other words, the data do not affect the data base or any action, except possibly that of prompting the operator.

This datacom method applies to a large variety of applications. Banks use this method to answer an inquiry about a checking-account balance; insurance companies use it to answer an inquiry about a claim's status; and educational institutions use it to determine a student's registration and financial status. There are many more complex applications. Student programmed-instruction is one. Another application is location of qualified personnel; the qualifications for a job are matched against a data base of personnel available, and the names of the qualified personnel are displayed or listed. Similarly, a real-estate office can isolate potential houses for a buyer by matching the buyer's requirements with a data base of houses available.

This processing is distinguished from real-time processing because no operation is affected. The next inquiry is not affected by a previous response—except after a significant time span, and in the last two examples, only after a person has been hired or a house has been purchased.

Real-time Processing

This datacom method of processing is the most complex, the most costly, and the most exposed to processing disruptions. The hardware and software used and the control required demand the highest levels of system designing expertise. This is particularly true for processing that cannot tolerate extensive disruptions, and in some cases, no disruptions at all. An airline-reservation system could tolerate some disruption, but a process-control system cannot. A process-control system continually monitors activities and automatically adjusts these activities, whether they are temperature, mixtures, or any of the many parameters that can be measured. Even a short disruption can result in the production of many defective products that may have to be scrapped—a costly disruption.

Airline reservation and process control represent the two types of real-time systems: people-dependent and machine-dependent systems. An airline-reservation system requires that an operator request information, and if a reservation is placed, changed, or cancelled, the system updates a data base. In contrast, a process-control system obtains information and modifies the processing automatically, without human intervention. There is another characteristic of these two types of real-time systems that distinguishes them: an airline-reservation system depends on a centralized data base, whereas a process-control system uses a local data base, usually transmitting summary information as an on-line batch job to a central location.

The distributing of data processing among several locations that are in some way connected is referred to as distributed data processing (DDP). A DDP system is often considered to be another name for a real-time system. This is not correct. Illustration 10–3 shows that, in a DDP system, various types of datacom processing may occur, such as real-time processing and on-line batch processing. The flexibility of DDP is further stressed in Illustration 10–4. Here it is possible that all five types of datacom processing are present, from the simplest off-line processing to the most complex real-time processing. The data-collection activity shown at the upper left can be either off-line data gathering or on-line data gathering, where the minicomputer performs the function of collecting and forwarding transactions as they become available. Although not indicated in the illustration, the data-collection activity may even involve on-line batch transmissions, where the minicomputer may perform preliminary processing. At the lower left of the illustration is an example of real-time processing, since data-base updating is performed; if updating were not performed, inquiry-response processing would occur. Similarly, the time-sharing processing shown at the upper right can be either real-time or inquiry-response processing. On-line batch processing with three alternate routes for

ILLUSTRATION 10-4. Distributed Data Processing: Processing is distributed among separate but interconnected locations, where one location collects data before transmissions, and other locations have data collected for transmission to other sites, possibly to computers at the same site. *Source:* John E. Bingham and Garth W. P. Davies, *Planning for Data Communications* (New York: John Wiley, 1977, p. 37. By permission of Macmillian, London and Basingstoke.

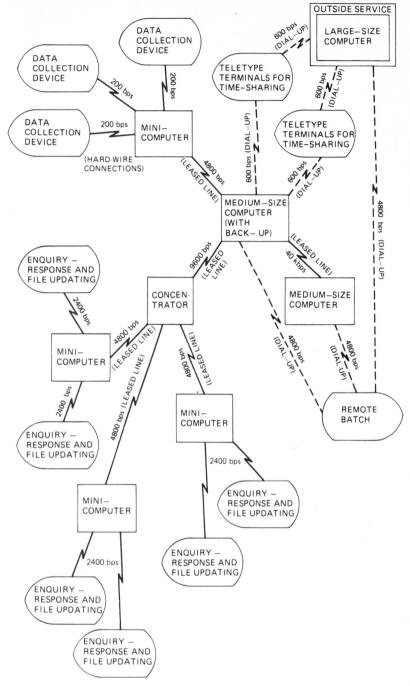

transmissions is shown at the lower right of the illustration.

A complex DDP network is IBM's Corporate Consolidated Data Network (CCDN). In 1977 this network consisted of a dozen large computers and over 4000 terminals, and IBM's intentions were to double the network's size.[1] Although there has been considerable disagreement on a precise and

all-inclusive definition of distributed data processing, there is general agreement about its basic functions and benefits; consider the following comments:

Fundamentally, distributed processing involves *offloading*—the transfer of certain functions to local or regional processing sites.[2]

[1] Howard L. Giles, "Management Strategy for Controlling Network Operations," *Data Communications*, August 1977, p. 42.

[2] Felix Kaufman, *Distributed Processing*, Coopers & Lybrand, Newark, N.J., 1977, p. 4.

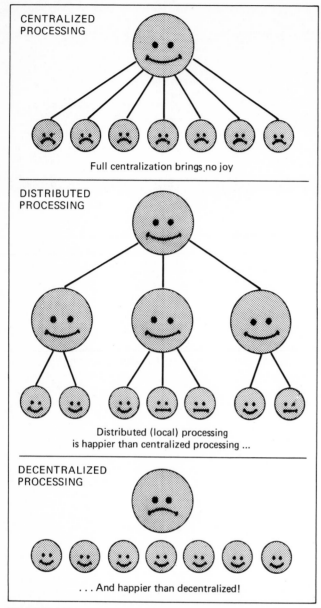

CENTRALIZED
PROCESSING

Full centralization brings no joy

DISTRIBUTED
PROCESSING

Distributed (local) processing
is happier than centralized processing ...

DECENTRALIZED
PROCESSING

. . . And happier than decentralized!

ILLUSTRATION 10-5. User "Happiness Factor": The highest level of general satisfaction is anticipated when processing and its control is distributed between central and remote sites. *Source:* Felix Kaufman, *Distributed Processing,* prepared for Coopers and Lybrand, 1977, p. 14.

Distributed processing offers the advantages of local control and participation without losing the advantages of centralized coordination and integration.[3]

There is now a presumption in favor of coordinated small dedicated units in place of large systems that must handle varied and demanding workloads.[4]

[3] Ibid., p. 4.
[4] Ibid., p. 11.

Distributed data processing is compared to centralized and decentralized processing in terms of user satisfaction, "the happiness factor" in Illustration 10-5. Centralized processing generally creates user dissatisfaction because it gives users an overall feeling of impotency and inability to schedule their applications. Decentralized processing with no exchange of information provides user independence and creates user satisfaction, but also creates upper management dissatisfaction at the central site because of the absence of the information needed to control activities and to plan for the future. Distributed processing, in contrast, gives local sites autonomy and also gives the central site control, a generally more satisfying arrangement. The resulting stable but dynamic environment accounts for the strong interest in distributed data processing.

PLANNING ASPECTS

EDP trade literature abounds with grandiloquent statements by hardware and software vendors who not only extol the virtues of their own on-line products, but also explain how easy it is to install an on-line system.[5]

Salvatore Catania of Coopers & Lybrand hopes to bring a rational and mature attitude to expectations from datacom processing. Instead of uncritical belief in the claims and promises of vendors, and blind acceptance of the hopes of data center personnel, what is needed is a healthy respect for the complexity and potential problems of datacom processing, as well as an appreciation of its potential benefits. Optimism is healthy, but overoptimism is unrealistic and is bound to lead to frustration and to general distrust of future datacom processing.

One of the benefits that can be expected is a drastic reduction in the clutter of reports produced. As more uses for computers became apparent in the past, more pounds of paper were printed, distributed, stored, and disposed of. Datacom can be expected to dramatically reduce this expensive aspect of data processing. Consider Illustration 10-6. This graph indicates the typical occurrences

[5] Salvatore C. Catania, *Going On-Line: Guidelines for Designing an Efficient System,* Coopers & Lybrand, Newark, N.J., pp. 3-4.

ILLUSTRATION 10-6. Datacom's Effect on Report Preparation: Computer time consumption increases as interactive processing is added to the workload; but eventually the information displayed at terminals permit elimination of reports, thus ultimately consumming less computer time than what was consumed before the addition on interactive processing. *Source:* John E. Bingham and Garth W. P. Davies, *Planning for Data Communications* (New York: John Wiley, 1977), p. 26. By permission of Macmillian, London and Basingstoke.

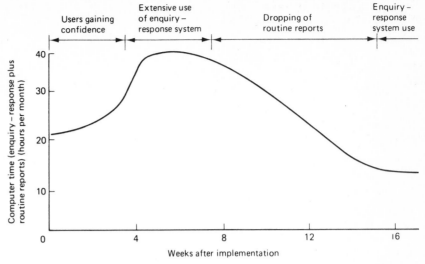

when datacom processing is added. As the information gained from inquiry-response systems increases, the overall computer processing time required for these systems and the off-line batch system used to prepare routine reports increases. And then the overall computer processing time dramatically drops as routine reports are discontinued.

Datacom systems, in general, are more user-oriented than data center-oriented. Whereas a multiprogramming batch-processing environment attempts to optimize the utilization of computer resources, datacom random-demand processing caters to the wishes of users, sacrificing efficient use of computer resources. The data center personnel have little control of full or even moderate utilization of peripheral equipment; they also have little control in leveling user demands on resources. To make this situation even worse, users become even more demanding than they were for batch processing. They become intolerant to short disruptions of service (longer than accustomed response time) and to slowness in adjusting to their processing requirements. Thus, the data center personnel become caught in the middle of the users' paradoxical demands for stable, reliable operations and for flexible adjustment to their changing processing workloads and requirements. To provide satisfactory service and to maintain an efficient and effective data center, planning is necessary—planning that attends to organization structure, network design, and operating control.

Before considering these three aspects of planning, the significance of planning for a datacom system should be stressed. Errol Gold of Computer Automation, Inc., in California, comments

that the importance assigned to planning in comparison to implementation and follow-up is different for a datacom system.[6] For an off-line batch system, the "40-20-40" formula is appropriate as a guide, allocating 40 percent of the resources to planning, 20 percent to implementation, and 40 percent to follow-up. But because of the complexity of a datacom system and the need to anticipate a variety of problems and future user demands, the recommended resource allocation formula is 60-20-20. The more thought given to planning, the more likely the system is to have adequate management control, datacom system design, operation control, and user satisfaction.

Organization Structure

Most organizations include a datacom support group as part of the data center organization structure, but the tendency in large organizations is to form a datacom department separate from the data center. When this is done, coordination becomes critical between the datacom department and the systems development department and the user departments, as well as with the data center. This department is sometimes referred to as the communications department or network department. Basically, the functions of this new department or support group are:

1. Review user requests for datacom services, considering immediate and future effects.

[6] Errol Gold, "Management Entering Age of Master Planning," *Computerworld*, November 27, 1978, p. S/34.

2. Analyze current applications for discontinuance, modification for improved efficiency, and conversion to less-demanding types of processing, such as on-line batch processing, off-line processing, and even non-datacom batch processing.

3. Analyze resource utilization, transmission reliability and security, cost-effectiveness, and other performance criteria.

4. Be aware of technological changes and opportunities for improvements, in addition to changes in tariff regulations.

5. Monitor datacom processing and isolate and correct datacom problems.

6. Recruit and train personnel for datacom processing.

7. Train and assist user personnel in efficient and effective use of terminals.

8. Establish policies, standards, and procedures for datacom processing and datacom documentation.

With competent managers and technicians in the datacom department or support group, these functions, although challenging, can be performed well. Awareness of user requirements and the adequacy of production applications, however, is particularly difficult. The only way to attain these objectives is by developing rapport with the users, and this can be accomplished only by showing concern for their needs and problems. To do this, communication channels must be established through such means as the data center steering committee and a data center newsletter. The committee provides opportunities for data center and user personnel to become aware of each other's intentions and needs. The newsletter provides a means of informing users of changes in the data center organization, hardware, and systems, and also enables users to compare actual datacom performance against anticipated performance. The end result of these two communication channels is that data center personnel can be informed of intended workload and system changes, and users can be informed of data center activities and suspected wastes of datacom resources. It is surprising how once an application is put into production, it continues unquestioned. This is a serious error. Consider the following anecdote:

> While there are plenty of examples to show how effective data communications systems can be, there are also, unfortunately, many where the system is of

very doubtful value indeed. One example known to the authors involved the continuous transmission of high-speed lines of production data from a manufacturing plant to a computer centre located 100 km away. After some simple but costly processing (mainly sorting) the data were then transmitted back to the plant. When asked what they did with the computer-generated information, the employees at the plant said they "checked it." It emerged that they used a manual system (which produced a more sophisticated analysis of the basic data, more quickly and at lower cost) and checked their results against the computer results! If there was a discrepancy, they corrected the *computer data* and sent in the appropriate correction sheets to the computer center! The information stored at the computer centre was never used for any other purpose.[7]

Fortunately, not many applications are such total wastes. However, many applications are likely to be of marginal value, with potential for streamlining to eliminate useless output, or at least to produce more selective output. To rephrase Parkinson's law: user applications tend to be added to consume the available datacom capability.

Network Design

For those organizations considering the use of datacom for the first time, prior to actually designing datacom systems it is necessary to decide upon the overall strategy for introducing these systems into the organization. Should the basic components (hardware and software and communications links) be installed and used for on-site systems development? Or should an off-site installation be used? Since the installation of resources on-site would result in their low utilization and high cost, an off-site installation is usually desirable—if the resources needed are available.

Alltrans International Group chose the off-site development approach; they determined the capabilities and facilities they needed and then searched for a time-sharing service that could serve them.[8] They decided on National CSS. As their first and most basic datacom system they designed and im-

[7]John E. Bingham and Garth W. P. Davies, *Planning for Data Communications* (New York: John Wiley, 1977), pp. 3–4.

[8]F. Pack, P. Spool, and G. Cokorinos, "Thinking Ahead Keeps Shipping Service Net from Foundering," *Data Communications*, August 1978, pp. 57–58.

plemented a general data-gathering subsystem. This subsystem was used as the basis for five applications. These applications were functional in less than one year. Since Alltrans believed that their preference in terminals was likely to change by the time they transferred the systems to their own installation, they decided to use dumb, inexpensive terminals instead of the more expensive intelligent terminals. To assist in isolating problems and determining user usage errors, hard-copy DEC Decwriters were used instead of CRT (cathode-ray tube) terminals. The printers were rented on a monthly basis and consisted of IBM 3775s and 3776s, which print 120 and 300 lines per minute respectively.

Since the cost of time-sharing services is expensive, it was desirable to transfer the applications to in-house operations as soon as possible. This required attention to be transferred from datacom applications to datacom network design. The time-sharing service made the design requirements and complexity of the network transparent to its users. Thus, by first developing several functioning datacom applications and then designing the in-house network to support them as two distinct and separate phases, the problems and complexities of these two types of considerations were kept separate, lessening discouragement and avoiding unnecessary expenses. And after testing the network and transferring the proven applications, thus adequately utilizing the datacom network, additional applications can be added as the next phase. This multiphase implementation of datacom processing is generally recommended.

The actual procedure used for designing a datacom network varies from one organization to another, sometimes ignoring several critical factors. The following listing of steps to be taken should be used as a framework and modified according to policies, organization structure, and resources available—and the resulting procedure should agree with or be used to develop adequate documentation and reporting standards:

1. Assign personnel to datacom network analysis and design, and prepare a schedule.
2. Collect information on anticipated distribution of traffic and on operating requirements.
3. Identify potential benefits, such as cost reduction, revenue increase, quicker turnaround, greater processing flexibility, and reduced paper usage.
4. Agree on performance criteria and standards, such as availability, response time, access security, data integrity, and ability to meet changing user needs, technology, and tariffs.
5. Collect information on hardware, software, and communication links.
6. Define alternatives that meet user requirements and are likely to satisfy performance standards.
7. Perform cost-benefit analysis, considering direct costs such as equipment and personnel and indirect costs such as training and support services.
8. Select an approach considering immediate and future benefits, particularly overall reliability and general adaptability.
9. Establish policies, standards, and procedures for implementing, documenting, and operating the datacom network.
10. Assign personnel to implement and operate the datacom network, and prepare a schedule.

Most of the specifics required to follow this procedure can be provided by either management or technical staff members, but one glaring deficiency often occurs: inflexibility. The word "flexibility" is used in its most general sense, not restricted only to the ability to modify the network to meet user needs; "flexibility" requires inclusion of the component and link redundancy needed to improve system availability, and to include vendor-independency to permit cost reduction and increased range of components to choose from. The flexibility required to permit network modifications and adequate redundancy are responsibilities of the datacom network designer; policy about vendor-independence is a management responsibility. Many organizations intentionally remain single-vendor-dependent, stressing their desires to keep all components compatible. Considering the modularity and interchangeability of components, this excessive cautionary attitude seems unnecessary. Opposing this attitude is the position for vendor-independence upheld by Home Federal of San Diego; as stated by Bob Finley, "Our philosophy is to be as self-sufficient as possible."[9] In fact, they even felt it was necessary to obtain custom-designed components, although they then found it necessary to have their own maintenance staff.

[9] "The Homemade System: A Vision of Associations' Data Processing Future?," *Savings & Loan News*, February 1977.

Operating Control

Establishing a rational organization structure with effective policies and management practices, and implementing an excellently designed network, does not assure that the actual processing will proceed smoothly and under adequate control. It is only necessary to visit several data centers with datacom processing to witness that in most, if not all, lack of coordination, processing disruptions for extensive periods of time, and a general atmosphere of confusion and frustration are accepted as normal. Although these situations probably cannot be totally eliminated, they can be drastically reduced, and with firm resolution, possibly to the point where all disruptions have been anticipated and planned for. The end result desired is to replace hectic and frantic activity with controlled, efficient alleviation of difficulties. Three types of activities are of primary importance to control operating activities:

- Supporting operating competency
- Monitoring processing activities
- Assisting user personnel

Supporting Operating Competency. Nondatacom processing permits operator errors and operator uncertainties because an application can be restarted and restarted again until done properly and because users are usually not aware of delays. Datacom processing, in contrast, requires quick, efficient action, especially since users usually become immediately aware of processing disruptions. Thus, operators must be well trained in restart and emergency procedures. The importance of alert, well-trained operators cannot be underestimated. More than the common affirmative head-nodding and affirmative verbal statements of an operator's worth is needed; their competency and preparation must be actively promoted. As expressed by Salvatore Catania, "New and improved levels of disciplined performance and competence are required for the operating staff. The demand is two-pronged: The staff must react immediately to equipment failures, and they must know how to isolate the source of the breakdown and react appropriately.[10] In addition, as technology and procedures change, operators must be trained in their use.

[10] Catania, *Going On-Line: Guidelines for Designing an Efficient System*, p. 6.

Even the most competent and the most conscientiously trained operators cannot function reliably in a void of poor system controls and inadequate documentation. All the system controls, such as automatic file-usage controls and adequate error-message generation, should be present. Standards in this area are available and generally adhered to, but documentation is often the weakest link, often a missing link. A good guide to the documentation required for datacom application systems is indicated by the table of contents shown in Illustration 10–7. This documentation provides the material for the operator's manual, guiding all operating activities, including startup, restart, and shutdown. The introductory material provides the operators with insight into each application, permitting intelligent instead of blind processing.

Monitoring Processing Activities. Just as batch processing should have a control area for scheduling jobs and monitoring their progress, datacom processing should have a control area for monitoring datacom processing. For large installations a separate room is frequently used for this purpose, with several persons assigned to it full time. The establishment of a network control center provides various types of control; it permits:

1. Centralized problem identification, isolation, reporting, resolution, and control.
2. Centralized analysis of service provided and of service degradation, and prediction and avoidance of failures.
3. Centralized network-performance evaluation and centralized analysis of trends.
4. Analysis and simulation of network changes considering such factors as service, security, and cost-effectiveness.
5. Management of backup and restart activities, including user notification about anticipated delays.
6. Communication and coordination between in-house specialists and outside personnel, and controlling and reporting on service received.

The network control center contains equipment for continual or periodic monitoring and testing. The personnel in this area may be responsible for operating the patching and switching equipment that permits transfer to backup components. Sometimes these personnel will only

√	Document	Comment
	1. Personnel contacts	
	2. System summary	
	3. System flowcharts	
////	4. Preprocessing	////////////////
	4.1 Hardware requirements	
	4.2 Software requirements	
	4.3 Files required	
	4.4 Output produced	
	4.5 Scheduling requirements	
////	5. Processing	////////////////
	5.1 Startup procedure	
	5.2 Processing controls	
	5.3 Master terminal messages	
	5.4 Master console messages	
////	6. Postprocessing	////////////////
	6.1 Closedown procedure	
	6.2 Offline processing	
	7. Backup and restart procedures	

Application System
Operator's Documentation
Checklist

System ID

System title

ILLUSTRATION 10–7. Operator's Manual: This table of contents suggests the information that may be needed for a datacom system. The comment entries may contain the phrase "not applicable," or it may contain due dates for the receipt of documentation, although it is a poor policy to permit systems to be released for production use without complete documentation.

inform the operators of what transfers are needed, and the operators will perform the actual transfers. The trend, however, is to centralize all datacom network control activities.

Assisting User Personnel. Whereas the data center steering committee and the distribution of data center newsletters support the spread of information and the coordination of general activities, a means is needed for users to obtain immediate assistance when they encounter problems at their terminals: A "hotline" is needed. The area in the data center responding to this hotline is often referred to as the "help desk." When a user is having difficulties at the terminal, the help desk is telephoned. The person at the help desk then observes at a terminal what the user is doing. If the user requires procedural assistance, the user is informed what was done incorrectly, how it should be done, and where this procedure is documented. Without

the help desk, users would be embarrassed to ask their peers in their department for assistance, possibly exposing themselves to ridicule. Thus they would avoid using the terminal and may criticize its worth. The result: poor press for datacom processing.

DATA COMMUNICATIONS ELEMENTS

To design and control a datacom system, besides making a clear distinction between datacom processing types and having a sound framework for implementing a datacom network, it is also necessary to understand the basic terminology of datacom elements and their relationships. Most data center personnel have a vague and partial (possibly erroneous) understanding of these terms and their relationships. The basic datacom elements to be

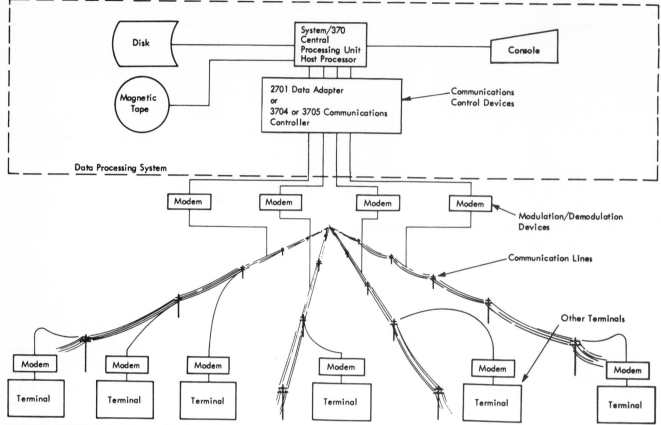

ILLUSTRATION 10-8. Datacom Hardware Elements: The basic datacom hardware elements are terminals, modems, and communications controllers. *Source: Introduction to IBM Data Processing Systems,* IBM Student Text #GC20-1684, p. 6-2.

examined are shown in Illustration 10–8 and consists of hardware units, communication links, and software support.

Hardware Units

As shown in Illustration 10–8, the primary hardware units are terminals, modems, and communications controllers. In addition, several other units will be introduced which are included in the network to increase flexibility, efficiency, and cost-effectiveness.

Terminals. Nearly everyone is accustomed to seeing these devices in a data center. Although some of these devices may be dedicated to only entering or receiving information, most are used for both entering and receiving information. Except when hard copy is wanted, CRT display units are generally used. It is only necessary to stress two features available that many data center personnel are not aware of. First, terminals are available with

a queued transaction handling (QTH) feature. This feature permits entry of data into local storage, and if the host or the communications link fails, the stored data can be transmitted as soon as the failure has been corrected. This feature permits the operator to batch transactions for transmission, in effect, permitting the terminal to function as a remote batch-entry station. This feature thus provides fewer interruptions of processing and, with batch transmissions, can provide less-costly processing.

The second feature is local format storage (LFS) which greatly reduces the quantity of display data transmitted. It may be difficult to believe, but approximately 80 percent of the network's capacity is used to transmit formatting information.[11] By using terminals with the LFS feature, most of the format information is stored in the terminal, and the load on the network is dramatically reduced, as shown in Illustration 10–9. In fact,

[11] Anthony J. Alcorn, "Distributed DP Can Upgrade Centralized Nets," *Computerworld,* November 28, 1977, p. S/6.

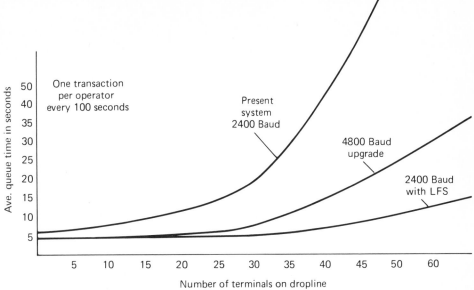

ILLUSTRATION 10-9. Terminals with LFS: LFS (local format storage) is a feature available on terminals that avoids transmitting format information, resulting in faster transmission speeds than result from upgrading to double the existing transmission line's speed. *Source:* Anthony J. Alcorn, "Distributed DP Can Upgrade Centralized Nets," Computerworld, Nov. 28, 1977, p. S/6.

LFS is less expensive than upgrading the network, for example, from 2400 to 4800 baud; and, as shown in Illustration 10-9, it is also more effective.

Modems. The term "modem" is a contraction of this unit's two functions: *mo*dulation and *dem*odulation. Illustration 10-10 clarifies the functions of a modem. Digital data enters a modem and is transformed to an analog signal for transmission by modulating the carrier signal. At the receiving end of the transmission, the analog signal is received by another modem, which transforms the signal to digital data, that is, the signal is demodulated.

ILLUSTRATION 10-10. Data Conversion for Transmission: Before transmission, serial characters are converted to serial bits, and then to analog signals that modulate a carrier signal; upon reception, the modulated analog signals are converted back to characters. *Source: Introduction to IBM Data Processing Systems,* IBM Student Text #GC20-1684, p. 6-3.

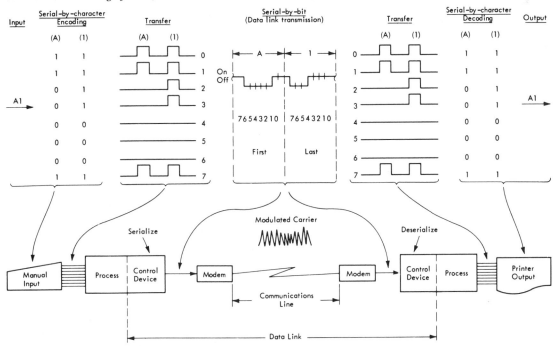

Modems are defined according to whether they are half-duplex or full-duplex, whether they are synchronous or asynchronous, and whether they operate at slow, medium, or high speed. *Half-duplex* means that data transmission can occur in one direction or the other, but not in both directions at the same time; *full-duplex,* in contrast, means that data transmission can occur in both directions at the same time. *Synchronous* and *asynchronous* refer to the means of timing transmissions and their receipt: The former involves fixed time periods, and the transmission of timing information, and the latter involves varied time periods and the transmission of start and stop characters for units of transmission. As for modem transmission speeds, a slow-speed modem transmits at 1200 baud per second (usually bits per second), a medium-speed modem at 1800 to 2400 bits per second, and a high-speed modem at 4800 bits per second or more. Some modems have a low-speed fallback mode, permitting slower-than-normal speed for sending, receiving, or both. The advantage of this feature is that it permits transmissions when degraded line quality would otherwise force transmissions to be discontinued.

Communications Controllers. These units refer to a control device that is external to and interfaces with a modem and a computer or a terminal, as shown in Illustration 10–10. Besides serializing and deserializing data, these control devices synchronize transmissions, identify sender and receiver, delimit the beginning and ending of data, and perform error detection and recovery. When these devices are internal units, they are generally referred to as data adapters.

Because of high overhead for computers to monitor and control transmission activities of many transmissions, minicomputers frequently replace these control devices. These minicomputers are referred to as front-end processors (FEP). Illustration 10–11 indicates how a hierarchy of minicomputers can be introduced into a network to function not only as communications controllers, but also as relay nodes for determining transmission paths and as processors for performing local processing. The IBM 3790 Systems shown are minicomputers used for distributed data processing, and the IBM 3276 units are control-unit display stations that are microprocessors for controlling other terminals.

Other Units. Instead of having a separate communication link to connect each pair of modems, various devices are available to collect data and transmit the collected data over a single communication link. These devices are classified as either multiplexers or concentrators. Whereas a multiplexer permits transmission of several transmissions at the same time over a single link, a concentrator collects data for transmission and transmits the collected data as units. Concentrators are the more flexible, since they can accept data at different speeds and according to different transmitting procedures, known as protocols. Often multiplexers or concentrators are used as nodes in a network for gathering, routing, and spreading data.

Just as multiplexers and concentrators lessen the number of communication links needed, devices are available to lessen the number of local lines needed, the lines between modems and terminals or between modems and computers, specifically, the computer ports that send or receive data. Instead of having lines connecting each terminal to a separate modem, a modem-sharing unit (MSU) is connected to a single modem and the terminals are connected to the MSU. This significantly reduces cost for local lines and additional modems.[12] In a similar manner, a port-sharing unit (PSU) permits attachment of several modems to a single computer port. This unit also reduces costs.[13]

Another device, which may or may not reduce costs, is the biplexer. This unit permits two voice-grade lines to perform as a single high-speed line. This device is often used to transmit concentrated signals between a concentrator and the computer. Its cost-effectiveness depends on the cost of voice-grade lines as compared to high-speed lines. In the past, the biplexer has resulted in significant savings, and sometimes dramatic savings.

Communication Links

Confusion generally exists between the phrases "communication link," "communication channel," and "communication line." These phrases are often used interchangeably, leading to lack of precision in verbal and written communication.

---

[12]Patrick McGregor, "Effective Use of Data Communications Hardware," *Auerbach Computer Technology Reports* (Pennsauken, N.J.: Auerbach Publishers, 1976), portfolio no. 050.0000.920, p. 6.

[13]Ibid., p. 12.

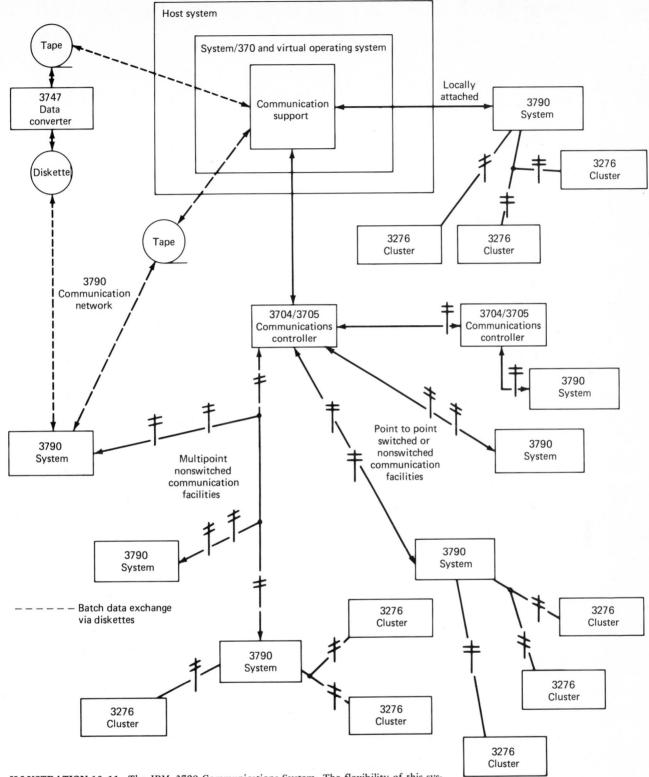

ILLUSTRATION 10-11. The IBM 3790 Communications System: The flexibility of this system for distributed processing is suggested by the interface between communication support and offline processing, an IBM 3790 minicomputer, and an IBM Communications Controller, which in turn coordinates processing from minicomputers on multipoint and point-to-point communication links. *Source: An Introduction to the IBM 3790 Communication System,* IBM manual #GA27-2807-2, p. 1-2.

The most precise phrase for the means used to transfer data from one modem to another is "communication channel." Datacom design experts may prefer this phrase, but the term "channel" tends to cause some confusion with the function of "I/O channels," and for this reason it is usually avoided. Whereas "communication channel" refers to all means of transferring data, whether by physical lines or microwave radio signals, the often-used phrase "communication lines" casually excludes microwave radio transmissions—an unacceptable situation. Thus, the phrase used to this point in the chapter and that will continue to be used is "communication link," which includes all means of transferring data. This phrase avoids confusion with I/O channels and also provides a solid feeling of the linking process used between modems or between whatever intermediate relay nodes may occur in the network.

The primary characteristics used to describe a communication link are whether it is half-duplex or full-duplex, point-to-point or multipoint, and switched or nonswitched.

Half-duplex or Full-duplex. Simply, as explained for modems, half-duplex links permit transmissions in either direction, but not at the same time; full-duplex links permit transmission in both directions at the same time. Whereas a full-duplex link would be used between computers, possibly between computers and multiplexers or concentrators, half-duplex would be used between a user station, whether a terminal or a batch-processing station, and the rest of the network. The term "full-duplex" is often replaced by the term "duplex."

Point-to-Point or Multipoint. Illustration 10–11 shows both types of links. Point-to-point links refer to a single link between units, for example, between a communications controller and an IBM 3790 System or between an IBM 3790 System and an IBM 3276 Cluster. In contrast, a multipoint link is a single link connecting one unit to two or more units. In the illustration three IBM 3790 Systems are connected to a single communication controller, and two IBM 3276 Clusters are connected to a single IBM 3790 System. Multipoint links are also referred to as "multidrop links."

Switched or Nonswitched. A switched link is also referred to as a "dial-up link," indicating that

a dialing action is necessary to obtain a connection. A nonswitched link, also referred to as a "dedicated link," is always connected and does not require dialing to obtain a connection. As suggested in Illustration 10–11, a multipoint link can be only a switched link, but a point-to-point link can be either switched or nonswitched. Another characteristic of switched and nonswitched links is that a common carrier must be used for switched links, but a nonswitched link can be either a leased link provided by a common carrier or a private link installed by the organization and for its own use. As a final distinction between switched and nonswitched links, all switched links are half-duplex, and thus nonswitched links are required for full-duplex transmissions.

Software Support

Stepping from the clearly defined topic of communication links to the vaguely defined topic of datacom software support moves us from objective facts to subjective opinions, and sometimes very heated differences of opinions. For example, a dispute has existed for some time between large network services and network control equipment vendors concerning the amount of software functions that can be supported by microprocessors.[14] Both Boeing Computer Services and General Electric Information Service comment that they have written their own software support but believe that 90 percent of the software support can be provided by microprocessors. Whether or not software support functions are transferred to microprocessors, it is important to know the functions involved and to have software-selection guidelines.

Illustration 10–12 provides a generalized diagram of the software that can be involved in datacom processing. As shown, the operating system is central for controlling and coordinating all application processing, data accessing, and telecommunication activities. Typical operating systems are IBM's Operating System (OS) and IBM's Disk Operating System (DOS). The trend has been to transfer functions, previously the responsibility of the operating system, to supplementary software, which may or may not have been supplied by the vendor for the operating system. Scheduling

[14]Glenn Hartwig, "Network Control: Managing the Data Environment," *Data Communications*, December 1977, p. 42.

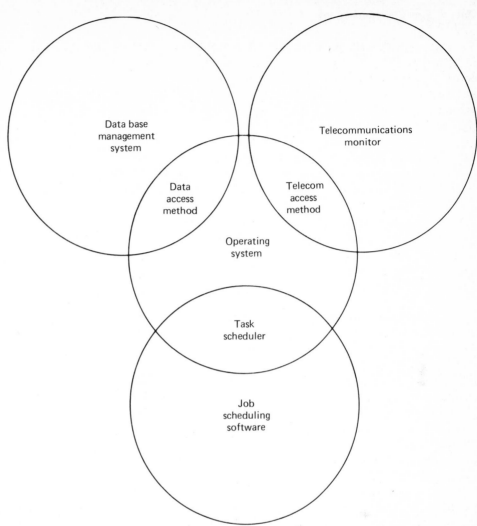

Data base management system

Telecommunications monitor

Data access method

Telecom access method

Operating system

Task scheduler

Job scheduling software

systems have replaced some of the functions of the task schedulers, data-base-management systems have replaced some of the functions of the data-access methods, and telecommunication monitors have replaced some of the functions of the tele-communications-access methods.

Often the data- and telecommunications-access methods for an operating system are confused. To lessen this confusion for IBM access methods, consider that data-access methods include (SAM) (sequential-access method), ISAM (indexed sequential-access method), and DAM (direct-access method). An operating system supporting telecommunications also has a tele-communications-access method, and these include BTAM (basic telecommunications-access method), QTAM (queued telecommunications-access method), TCAM (telecommunications-access method), and VTAM (virtual telecommunications-access

method). Some of the data-access functions are often transferred to data-base-management systems such as Total, IMS, and ADABAS; and some of the telecommunications-access functions are often performed by telecommunications monitors such as CICS, Environ/T, and Intercomm. Telecommunication functions that can be transferred to a monitor and the selection of a telecommunication monitor are our primary concerns.

How a telecommunications monitor performs its functions is complex, but its basic functions are easy to comprehend; a telecommunication monitor can:

- Initiate network activity
- Assemble or disassemble messages
- Adhere to predefined protocols
- Detect errors and failures
- Support startup and recovery

These functions are easy to comprehend—except, possibly, for what is meant by "protocols." A protocol, also called a "line discipline," is a set of rules for transferring data from one location to another in an orderly manner. A protocol must provide:

- Procedures for determining which network will transmit and which will receive at any given time
- Procedures for surrounding actual data with sufficient control information (data framing) to insure proper recognition and reception
- Procedures for indicating whether previous data transmissions were error-free and for requesting retransmission of incorrect information.[15]

With insight into the functions of a telecommunications monitor, the obvious question is, What telecommunication monitor should be chosen? To assist in answering this question, all that can be done is to provide one warning and several criteria to guide selection. The editors of *Data Communications* magazine provide this warning: "While it might seem trite to say that the best monitor is the one which best fits a user's needs, that consideration is often forgotten by technical personnel dazzled by the technical sophistication provided by some systems."[16] Too often, as in the situation of having the latest multicolored, light-flashing hardware "enhancement," features of questionable value may entice technicians to recommend one monitor over another, although another monitor may be simpler, less error-prone, less costly, and more efficient and useful. The editors continue their survey of telecommunication monitors by recommending several criteria to guide selection:[17]

- *Throughput,* usually measured by traffic rate, the number of messages in a time period
- *Peak level,* the maximum workload anticipated, as well as the length of time the peak load may occur

- *Response time,* the time from initiation of a transmission to receipt of the first character for a response
- *Unit processing level,* work required for each message, which includes overhead for communications, I/O units and operations, CPU, and queue waits

The definitions and explanations provided here have been basic and brief, but they should satisfy their purpose of providing definitions and explanations of the basic datacom elements, and also provide a perspective of how these elements are related.

DESIGN AND OPERATING GUIDELINES

In effect, all that has been presented so far sets the basis for an effectively functioning datacom system, but far from assures its successful operation. Management and staff personnel may have insight into the types of datacom processing, the elements of a datacom system, and the overall strategy for planning and implementing a datacom network, but what criteria should guide its design and its control? And what means are available to satisfy these criteria—or at least come close to satisfying them?

The complexity of networks and their immediate effect on users in case of processing disruptions make the answers to these questions critical. Often, it is only necessary for a single modem, a single communication link, a single application program to fail to cause long-term processing halts, possibly for many or all users. In some large organizations it is not uncommon for a voice to come over the intercom system stating, "TSO will be down for 15 minutes," repeated once or twice every hour for several hours. Usually, only the personnel in the data center and the system development departments are recipients of this information; user department personnel merely stare at the unresponsive terminals. All personnel find extended processing disruptions intolerable, since they are likely to cause work to be hampered and commitments to be missed.

Various criteria are used for guiding the design of a datacom system and assuring its acceptable

---

[15] "Design of Data Communications Software," *Auerbach Computer Technology Reports* (Pennsauken, N.J.: Auerbach Publishers, 1975), portfolio no. 050.0000.810, p. 3.

[16] "Telecommunications Monitors Can Improve Throughput," *Data Communications,* August 1978, p. 49.

[17] Ibid., pp. 49 and 51.

operation. It is often surprising how a few criteria are stressed and others are totally ignored. To be comprehensive, design and operating guidelines must include the following criteria:

- Data integrity
- Data security
- Network availability
- Network service
- Network adaptability

These criteria will now be examined, starting with narrow consideration of data integrity and security, the protection of data from modification or loss or unauthorized access; then continuing with the wider consideration of network availability and the service provided when available; and concluding with the consideration of the network's ability to adapt to changing needs.

Data Integrity

As already stated, data integrity actually refers to protecting data from modification or loss. Both of these threats are examined in terms of their primary causes, their detection, and their control.

Data Modification. It is unlikely that this problem will ever be totally eliminated. Once a signal is transmitted, it can be interrupted, distorted, or adulterated. Signal interruption may cause either total signal discontinuance or signal fading, and this may fluctuate or occur for a long period of time. The types of signal distortion are many—to pun, signal distortion comes in many shapes. For example, distortion can result from the proximity of a high-power radar transmitter or high-voltage power line to the communication link. Enthusiasts of high-fidelity equipment are familiar with multipath distortion, which results from signal reflections off such obstructions as buildings and mountains. This also occurs for television transmissions, resulting in ghosts, and it occurs for microwave radio transmission of data. Other types of distortions result in modification of signal strength, amplitude, and phase. Signal adulteration is the addition of extraneous signals to the transmitted signal and is also referred to as "noise." These extraneous signals not only modify the signal, but also cause signal loss and loss of transmis-

sion synchronization. The possible sources of noise are many and include atmospheric conditions, power fluctuations, electronic switching, equipment failures, and channel crosstalk.

The relationship that can be expected to occur between transmission speed and error rate for all data-transmission modifications are shown in Illustration 10-13. As the transmission speed increases, it is likely that the error rate also increases. That is why some modems have the low-speed fallback mode, a feature permitting transmissions that would otherwise have to be discontinued because of a high error rate.

Detection of data modification is accomplished by either program verification of data received or hardware comparison of signals it transmits and then receives back. Program verification includes examination of transmission control characters, counts, and formats, and also examination of application content validity, including interfield consistency of critical fields that were duplicated. The means used for verifying the transmission and receipt of signals independent of applications is to have test equipment transmit a test pattern, to have the signal transmitted back, and to compare these two sets of signals. This test equipment should function constantly, testing all paths in the network.

Two measurements often used for error rates are bit error rate (BER) and block error rate (BKER). These two measurements result from the formulas:

$$BER = \frac{\text{number of erroneous bits received}}{\text{total number of bits received}}$$

$$BKER = \frac{\begin{array}{c}\text{number of blocks received}\\\text{with at least one bit error}\end{array}}{\text{total number of blocks received}}$$

The "blocks" referred to are those used in the test pattern transmitted by test equipment. Whereas BER indicates the general quality of the link, BKER indicates the distribution of errors in time. If, for example, 500 errors occur in 500 seconds, they may all occur in a very short period of time or they may be spread throughout the entire 500 seconds. The BER would be the same, but in the first case, the BKER would be low and the throughput would be only slightly affected, and in the second case, the BKER would be very

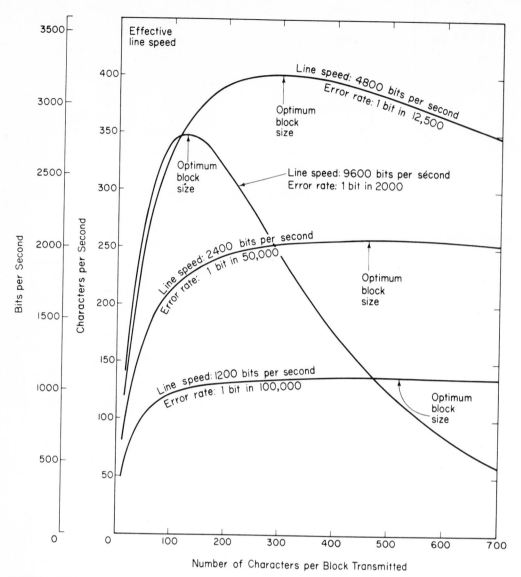

ILLUSTRATION 10-13. Effect of Line Speed on Error Rate: As shown, as line speed increases, error rate also increases. *Source:* James Martin, *Systems Analysis for Data Transmission* (Englewood Cliffs, N.J.: Prentice-Hall, 1972), p. 549.

high, very likely totally destroying the entire transmission. Thus, it is clear that BER indicates general link quality and BKER indicates effect on throughput.

Having identified the causes and the means for detecting data modifications or loss, the means for controlling this situation can be considered. The most direct approach is to correct or eliminate the sources of the problems. If this cannot be done, the only means of controlling any serious consequence of these problems is to be able to restore any data base affected. Three techniques are often used to restore a data base to the condition existing before its integrity became question-

able: dual data-base updating, periodic data-base copying, and transaction logging.

1. *Dual data-base updating.* As one data base is being created or updated, a second is at the same time generated. Thus, a duplicate data base is automatically available for backup. This technique is generally unsatisfactory. Its major deficiency is that it provides data-base protection if only one data base loses integrity, such as the occurrence of an internal parity error or external physical damage (for example, a head crash). But what happens if both data bases lose their integrity at the same time? This can occur because of a program error that alters the content of both data bases, or because of such incidents as a power failure

or the transmission of distorted or adulterated data. Not only is this technique generally ineffective in protecting data-base integrity, it also consumes considerable data-storage resources and drastically increases I/O activity.

2. *Periodic data-base copying.* Many organizations use this technique, particularly time-sharing services. Periodically, data bases are copied onto tape, usually once a day. The major fault with this technique is that an entire day's transactions can be lost, requiring their retransmission. Some organizations try to minimize this deficiency by "dumping" data bases several times a day. This lessens the number of transactions lost, but it does not resolve the problem. Another difficulty encountered is that data-base dumping and restoring is time consuming. To lessen the seriousness of this difficulty, only the critical data bases may be dumped, and to increase the speed of the dumping process, physical instead of logical dumps should be used. Since data-base integrity may become questionable several days or months later, a set of backup tapes must be kept, permitting restoration of the data base to the last time it was reliable. Edward Yourdon recommends the following procedure to obtain seven *daily* tapes, four *weekly* tapes, twelve *monthly* tapes, and one *yearly* tape:

1. A disk dump is taken each day.
2. At the end of each week, the most-recent daily dump tape replaces the oldest weekly dump tape.
3. At the end of each month, the most-recent weekly dump tape replaces the oldest monthly tape.
4. At the end of each year, the most-recent monthly tape becomes a yearly tape, which is saved forever.[18]

3. *Transaction logging.* The deficiency of having to retransmit transactions from the time a data base loses integrity for the previous technique (the periodic data-base copying technique) is avoided by recording on tape all transactions received. Thus, it would be necessary *only* to restore the last reliable data-base copy and to process all the transactions received since the copy was made. "Only" is an understatement. This technique is cumbersome if the data base is large, if many transactions have accumulated, or if failures occur frequently. However, it can be streamlined and made much more efficient by including on the transaction tape either a copy of each data-base record before updating, or a copy of this record before and after updating. Illustration 10–14 shows the content for these three types of transaction-logging tapes.

[18]Edward Yourdon, *Design of On-Line Computer Systems* (Englewood Cliffs, N.J.: Prentice-Hall, Inc., 1972), pp. 344–345.

The first format, as already stated, requires processing of all transactions since a data base lost integrity. The second format shows the presence of a copy of each data-base record before updating, and it is only necessary to locate the last transaction not processed, to restore the data-base records affected to their status before updating, and to continue transaction processing from that point. The data base does not have to be reloaded. This technique is effective if the situation that occurred was merely a disruption of transaction processing, not one that destroyed the data base. If, however, the data base was destroyed, it is necessary to reload the data base; fortunately, this situation occurs less frequently than transaction disruption.

The third format shows the presence of the data-base record before and after updating. This technique greatly lessens the time consumed for restoring the status of a destroyed data base. Instead of having to process all transactions, it is necessary only to reload the data base and alter only those data-base records updated with the copy of the updated records on the transaction logging tape. Thus, this format uses the "before record" for the more-frequent occurrences of disrupted processing and uses the "after record" for the less-frequent occurrences of data base destruction. Obviously, this is the most flexible technique for effectively and efficiently maintaining data integrity.

Data Loss. Data are lost when they are transmitted but either not received or not processed. The solution is for the sender to require acknowledgment of receipt and of processing. If processing is disrupted, the sender must know whether or not to retransmit the transaction. Not knowing when to retransmit a transaction can result in nonprocessing of transactions, duplicate processing of transactions, or occurrences of both.

James Martin's solution to this problem is shown in Illustration 10–15, and is explained in the following procedure:

1. The terminal operator sends the message.
2. It is received in the transmission-control computer. This computer adds a unique number to it and stores the transaction and its number in a table.
3. The items are checked, edited, and then queued in the transmission-control computer. The main

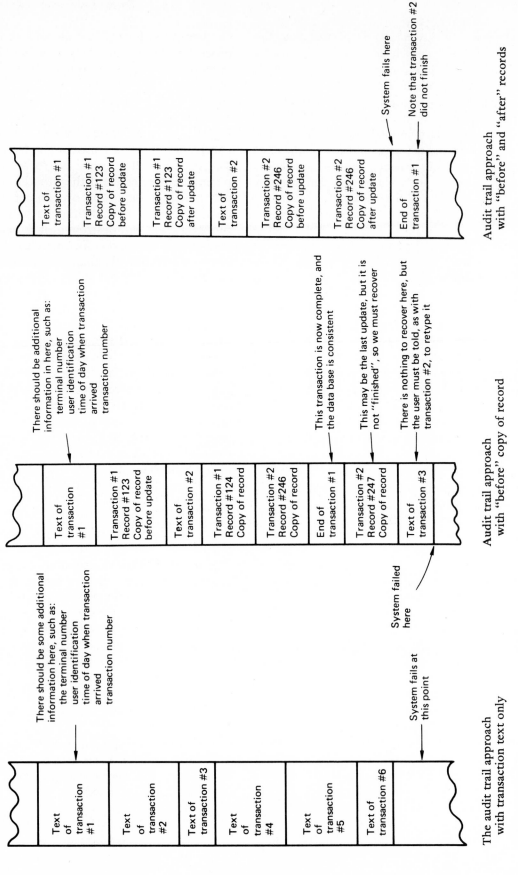

There should be some additional
information here, such as:
the terminal number
user identification
time of day when transaction
arrived
transaction number

There should be additional
information in here, such as:
terminal number
user identification
time of day when transaction
arrived
transaction number

Text
of
transaction
#1

Text
of
transaction
#2

Text of
transaction #3

Text of
transaction #4

Text
of
transaction
#5

Text of
transaction #6

System fails at
this point

The audit trail approach
with transaction text only

Text of
transaction
#1

Transaction #1
Record #123
Copy of record
before update

Text of
transaction #2

Transaction #1
Record #124
Copy of record

Transaction #2
Record #246
Copy of record

End of
transaction #1

Transaction #2
Record #247
Copy of record

Text of
transaction #3

System failed
here

Audit trail approach
with "before" copy of record

This transaction is now complete, and
the data base is consistent

This may be the last update, but it is
not "finished", so we must recover

There is nothing to recover here, but
the user must be told, as with
transaction #2, to retype it

Text of
transaction #1

Transaction #1
Record #123
Copy of record
before update

Transaction #1
Record #123
Copy of record
after update

Text of
transaction #2

Transaction #2
Record #246
Copy of record
before update

Transaction #2
Record #246
Copy of record
after update

End of
transaction #1

System fails here

Note that transaction #2
did not finish

Audit trail approach
with "before" and "after" records

ILLUSTRATION 10-14. Transaction Logging: Transaction data
and transaction activity information can be stored to avoid loss of
data, to avoid duplicate transmission of data, and to permit after
a processing interruption quick restoration of data bases and

quick restart of processing. *Source:* Edward Yourdon, *Design of
On-Line Computer Systems* (Englewood Cliffs, N.J.: Prentice-Hall,
1972), pp. 346, 348, 350.

computer reads them one at a time from the transmission-control computer.

4. The main computer stores the transaction with its number in a table or message-reference block.

5. As soon as the transmission-control computer receives confirmation that the main computer has received the transaction correctly, it sends the transaction number to the terminal operator.

6. The main computer processes the transaction and prepares to update the files.

7. The unique transaction number is written on each file record as it is updated and remains there until the file record is again updated by another different transaction.

8. The main computer composes the reply.

9. The transmission-control computer transmits the reply and notes this in its transaction table.

10. When the hardware signals that the terminal has correctly received the answer-back, the transmission number is deleted in the transmission-control computer's table, and the message is deleted from the core of the main computer.[19]

The operator's response to computer failure depends on whether or not the transmission-control computer also failed and on what messages

[19] James Martin, *Design of Man-Computer Dialogues* (Englewood Cliffs, N.J.: Prentice-Hall, Inc., 1973), p. 470.

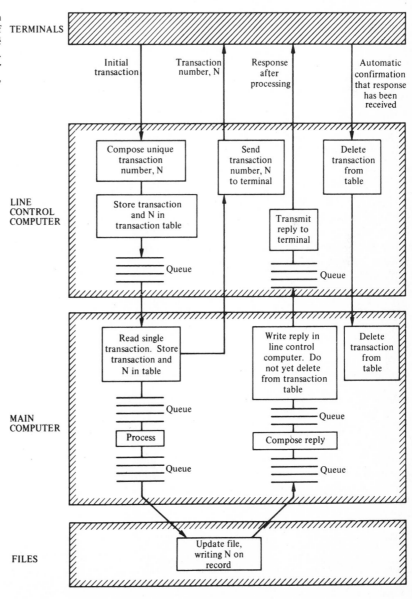

ILLUSTRATION 10–15. Transaction Transmission Control: This procedure assures retransmission of all transactions not processed and, at the same time avoids duplicate processing of transactions. *Source:* James Martin, *Design of Man-Computer Dialogues* (Englewood Cliffs, N.J.: Prentice-Hall, 1973), p. 469.

were received. If the main computer failed but the transmission-control computer did not fail, and if the transaction number was received, even partially, the transaction should not be retransmitted; if the transaction number was not received, the transaction must be retransmitted. If the transmission-control computer also fails, and if the answer-back was received, the transaction should not be retransmitted; if the answer-back was not received, the transaction must be retransmitted. When an operator follows these rules, the data center can recover those transactions in one of the queues and can avoid skipping or duplicating data-base updating.

This procedure can be combined with transaction logging to provide total data-integrity control. Instead of being stored in a transaction table, transactions can be written onto a transaction-logging tape, and this tape can also contain the data-base records before and after updating was performed.

Data Security

The number of reported cases of unauthorized access to programs and data in a datacom network has been well publicized. It requires little reflection to suspect that only a small percentage of violations have come to management's attention, and of these, only a small number have been publicly admitted. Since a large number of violations have been detected and publicized, but represent a small percentage of what occurs, considerable concern is justified. The initiative and skill shown by violators indicate that a casual attitude is dangerous and that careless security measures cannot be condoned. Consider the following example:

> An enterprising young thief managed to gain access to a utility company's computer by buying used telephone equipment, and by retrieving computer listings and operational documents from trash bins. Armed with this simple equipment, he caused several hundred thousand dollars worth of the utility company's equipment to be delivered to him at various addresses. When the delivery arrived, he simply reloaded the equipment onto a legally purchased second-hand company van and drove off. He then sold the equipment— sometimes back to the company from which it was stolen—at an enormous profit.[20]

[20]Hal B. Becker, "Network Security in Distributed Data Processing," *Data Communications,* August 1977, p. 33.

Security for a datacom system is much more complex and challenging than for a batch-processing environment. Considering the difficulty data centers have in securing their batch-processing environment, the situation for datacom processing is somewhat overwhelming. Not only must the data center site be protected from unauthorized access, but so must the communication links (including units such as multiplexers and switching panels) and the terminals. The primary protection for these three areas of vulnerability—the data center site, the communication links, and the terminals—are now considered.

The Data Center Site. What already has been stated for data center security in Chapter 5 applies to site security for datacom processing. However, one additional security weakness is added to a datacom system when transaction logging is performed. Besides the existence of copies of records on the transaction tape, there is the existence of transactions in queues and buffers, which are exposed to access. If transactions are written on a tape as soon as received, without any queuing or buffering, this problem is greatly reduced, although processing efficiency is also reduced because records are not blocked.

The Communication Links. Whereas non-switched lines (private or public) are difficult to be made secure, switched lines (dial-up lines) are impossible. Anyone with a terminal, whether in an office or in a home, has access to the line. Thus,

ILLUSTRATION 10-16. Exposure to Internal Wiretapping: Switching centers and distribution panels are located in unprotected, sometimes unlocked, closets in infrequently used hallways, *Source:* David J. Sykes, "Practical Approaches to Network Security," in Computer Security Manual, ed. Peter S. Browne (Mass.: Computer Security Institute, 1976), p. 4.73.

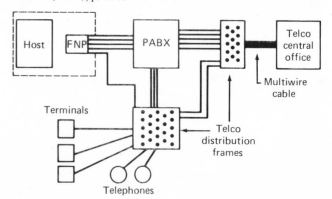

switched lines should be avoided for critical data that must be protected. Unauthorized access to nonswitched lines is more difficult, but many locations are exposed to wiretapping. Illustration 10–16 shows a few of the internal locations, often forgotten, where wiretapping is possible. The switching center—private automatic branch exchange (PABX) or private branch exchange (PBX)—or the many telephone distribution panels are easy to tap. Often, these switching centers and distribution panels are located in unlocked closets in secluded sections of hallways. The distribution panels are frequently clearly marked to indicate transmission sources; this is definitely an aid to quick maintenance, but it also is an aid to quick wiretapping.

On-premises and off-premises links, multiplexers, concentrators, and front-end computers can also be tapped and, as far as possible, should be secured. This is easier to say than to do. Access, for example, to cables on telephone poles or underground is not difficult. This is also true for datacom units. Protection against physical access is necessary.

The next means of protection is to disguise the transmissions. This can be accomplished by multiplexing the signals, using alternate transmission paths, and encrypting data. Illustration 10–17 shows the use of a key at the sending and receiving modems to alter data for transmission and to return it to its former configuration when received. The illustration shows the hoped-for astonishment that a wiretapper may experience. The key used establishes a bit pattern for encrypting the data. Encryption does not, however, hamper access to data but does make it difficult to understand; it does not provide total protection from those with the proper expertise. One way to protect data even from the experts is to frequently change the key. However, this solution creates another problem: how to transmit the key to remote sites. One potential solution to this new problem is to code the key and transmit it so that only one or two persons at the remote sites can decode the key. But can this code be protected? Can the persons who can decode the key be trusted—now and in the future?

There is one method of detecting wiretapping that is effective in an environment with little line interference. This involves line monitoring. When a device is attached to a communication line, the synchronization of transmissions is affected and

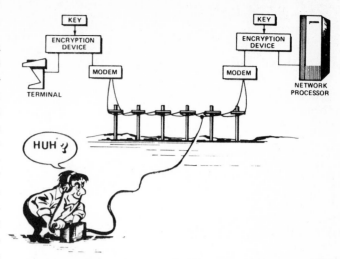

ILLUSTRATION 10–17. Data Encryption: Generally, it is true that persons intercepting encoded data cannot understand what is being transmitted; however, knowledgeable persons can use techniques to overcome this difficulty, particularly if the key is not frequently changed. *Source:* David J. Sykes, "Practical Approaches to Network Security," in Computer Security Manual, ed. Peter S. Browne (Mass.: Computer Security Institute, 1976). p. 4.74.

errors are introduced. The occurrence of these problems then indicates that investigation is necessary to determine if the cause is from wiretapping or from line interference.

The Terminals. First, there is physical security. This can be accomplished by having terminals in secured locations, using key locks on the terminals when not in use, and using magnetically coded or hole-punched cards to identify users. Next, there is the use of passwords. Passwords and user IDs should identify who has access to specific data bases. To protect passwords from becoming generally known, they should not be displayed on terminals and they should be changed periodically, at least once a month. Often, someone would sign-on and walk away from a terminal for a short period of time, leaving the terminal unattended and available for anyone's use. To avoid this situation, to some degree, some installations have a maximum wait period between transmissions from a terminal, and when that time expires, the terminal is automatically disconnected. This is usually set for five minutes—still allowing enough time for an unauthorized person to do considerable damage.

A record should be kept automatically of every sign-on and attempted sign-on. These records can be kept on a tape that is examined for unsuccessful attempts to sign-on and for excessive activity for a user or a location, even though the sign-on was acceptable.

291

There are no easy solutions to security problems. Often, the measures taken are adequate, but lack of personnel adherence to the required procedures nullify all the analysis and planning performed. Therefore, after security measures have been agreed upon, they must be well documented, they must be explained to personnel, and then they must be strictly enforced.

Network Availability

Many datacom systems seem to be very accident prone. Users never know when the system will be available, or if available, when it will suddenly fail. A datacom system, instead of suddenly failing, may provide fluctuating or degrading service. A single user may be affected, as in the case of a mechanical or electrical failure at a terminal; an entire link may fail, as in the case of a failure in a modem, multiplexer, relay, or a communication link itself; the entire network may fail, as in the case of a software, hardware, power, or environmental failure for a host or front-end computer. The possibilities and extents of failures are numerous.

Failures should be expected to occur, possibly often, with immediate impact on users; but the frequency and seriousness of failure can be greatly reduced by taking adequate precaution and by planning for the occurrences of failures. These views are also expressed in the following comments:

> For proper planning, it is *absolutely imperative* that the system specifier makes the assumption that every component in the system will eventually fail; if he does not make this assumption, he will be in for some nasty surprises.[21]

> Unlike cars or TV sets, which fail only occasionally, most on-line systems have failure rates that can be counted in failures *per day*.[22]

> Because of the system's intimate contact with the user world, reliability, on a minute-to-minute basis, becomes a vital design issue.[23]

[21] Edward Yourdon, "The Causes of System Failures," *Modern Data*, February 1972, p. 51.

[22] Salvatore C. Catania, *Going On-Line: Guidelines for Designing an Efficient System*, Coopers & Lybrand, Newark, N.J., 1976, p. 5.

[23] Walter A. Levy, "Real-Time System Design," *The Information Systems Handbook*, ed. F. Warren McFarlan and Richard L. Nolan (Homewood, Illinois: Dow Jones-Irwin, Inc., 1975), p. 632.

Many of the standard precautions tend to assume greater importance in such an environment because of the greater impact on the system of *any* failure.[24]

Users—whether they be time-sharing subscribers or EDP managers—must recognize that system failures are not events that just "happen," but can and should be planned for. Once failures are accepted as part of the natural machine condition, downtime occurrences can be reduced, downtime periods can be shortened, and downtime costs can be minimized.[25]

Before identifying the types of failures that can occur, their prevention and detection, and recovery from them, the terms "availability" and "reliability," which are often used as synonyms, should be defined precisely. Reliability should be viewed as the probability of a component failing, such as a terminal, modem, or a multiplexer. Availability, in contrast, should be used when referring to the existence of service, whether or not one or more components have failed. Thus, if a modem fails but a backup modem does not permit service to be affected, the modem's reliability may be very low while the network's availability may be very high. The conclusion that can be derived from this distinction is that, although component reliability is important and is dependent on careful choice of components, the goal of the network administrator and technicians is to provide a high level of network availability. And network availability is directly related to the care and thoroughness given to network planning—to the awareness of the types of failures that can occur and to the means for preventing failures, quickly becoming aware of existing or impending failures, and quickly recovering from failures.

Types of Failures. Edward Yourdon identifies eleven types of datacom system failures in his book *Design of On-Line Computer Systems*.[26] Since he has done an excellent and comprehensive job of identifying datacom failures (as he has for other topics related to practical datacom design and processing), it is merely necessary to list and

[24] John E. Bingham and Garth W. P. Davies, *Planning for Data Communications*, (New York: John Wiley, 1977), p. 148.

[25] Edward Yourdon, "Different Concepts of Reliability," *Modern Data*, January 1972, p. 36.

[26] Edward Yourdon, *Design of On-Line Computer Systems*, pp. 518–532.

comment on his eleven categories:

1. *Processor errors.* Errors such as dropping bits or incorrect performance of an operation are rare, but when they do occur, they can be catastrophic, not only disrupting service but also corrupting data. Fortunately, these errors do not occur often. It is easy to visualize how arithmetic instruction operations, although not disrupting processing in most instances, result in gibberish being stored or displayed. When these errors do occur, user application programs are often incorrectly blamed, causing considerable disagreement between users and data center personnel. Periodic execution of a diagnostic program is likely to uncover processor errors.

2. *Memory parity errors.* A parity bit is generated whenever data are stored, and this bit is checked whenever data are read. Parity errors, as in the case of processor errors, are rare, and can be catastrophic. To circumvent these failures it is necessary for programs using the defective memory locations to be cancelled and for these defective memory locations to be bypassed. The cancelled programs can be restarted using good memory locations, while the defective memory is repaired. Most operating systems, however, do not support this process. In this case, it is necessary either for a field engineer to bypass these memory modules by setting switches or for the operator to modify memory allocation tables to indicate which memory modules should not be used.

3. *Failures in the communication network.* These failures can result from a terminal's failure, a modem's failure at the terminal or at the computer, or a failure at any component or communication link between. Since backup generally exists for terminals and modems, the primary areas of concern are the communication links, multiplexers, concentrators, and front-end processors that do not have backup.

4. *Failures in the peripheral devices.* Tape drives, disk drives, drum units, and mass-storage units involve considerable mechanical activity and thus are likely sources of failures. Since most of these problems are transient, the automatic retry logic associated with these devices usually avoids serious processing disruptions—although processing efficiency suffers. These failures do become serious, however, when data are degraded or when control directories are modified.

5. *Operator errors.* The basic means to protect against these errors, although not protecting against operator carelessness and lack of concern, are well-documented operating and contingency procedures, careful choice of operators, and thorough operator training, with periodic training to introduce new procedures and to assure ad-

herence to existing procedures. Operator activity varies from passive monitoring for sophisticated real-time systems, to hectic tape mounting, paper changing for printers, and constant telephone calling for RJE processing. The more dependent processing is on satisfactory operator actions, the more likely it is that errors will occur. The details and complexity of procedures for startup, restart, and shutdown can be greatly simplified through the use of cataloged procedures. However, protection from carelessness is impossible. Operators have been known to disrupt processing by casually leaning on switches, and to make a unit inoperative by carelessly spilling coffee on it.

6. *Program bugs.* The only control that data center personnel have over program bugs is to obtain proof that programs adhere to programming standards and that they have been thoroughly tested. This also applies to all program corrections and enhancements. Techniques such as modular programming and structured programming greatly reduce the likelihood of bugs and greatly help in the quick location and correction of those bugs that do occur. Software packages such as MetaCOBOL assure adherence to many coding standards.

7. *Power failures.* Devices can be added to the power lines to control power fluctuations and interference. Various types of backup power are available, ranging from stored power (permitting a quick and somewhat graceful shutdown) to generated power for uninterrupted processing. The critical nature of the processing performed must determine how much an organization is willing to spend for the various levels of power protection. This is discussed in Chapter 5.

8. *Environmental failures.* These failures include such threats as fire, explosions, and flooding, whether caused intentionally or not. Besides preventive measures, adequate contingency plans and insurance are necessary. This is discussed in Chapter 5.

9. *Gradual erosion of the data base.* This can result from the hardware and software failures already mentioned. To become aware of data-base erosion before it becomes extensive and difficult to correct, seriously affecting processing, it is possible to use a diagnostic program. This program would check the reasonability of the data stored. If, for example, critical data are loaded to tape once a day, the load program can include the diagnostic logic needed to check the reasonability of individual field values and interfield values.

10. *Saturation.* If the software is not designed to handle overloaded resources, a total system failure may occur. The means to avoid a system failure because of saturation, besides adequate software to handle overloads, is predictive software. Such software indicates when an

overload condition is likely to occur, permitting action to be taken to reduce the workload or to increase the resources available before the condition becomes critical.

11. *Unexplained failures.* Often the cause of a failure cannot be identified. The major reasons for most unidentified failures are inadequate documentation of the information needed for analysis, and inadequate personnel time spent on the analysis of the information that is available. As part of the failure-identification procedure, it is usually necessary to have memory dumps and supplementary information. Without adequate information and personnel time available for failure analysis, the unidentified failure of today is likely to become the failure of tomorrow—and tomorrow—and tomorrow.

Prevention of Failures. The initial attack against hardware failure is the presence of backup components. This could include backup for links, modems, line-control elements, preprocessors, front-end processors, concentrators, multiplexers, message-switching systems, file-management systems, physical-storage elements, application processors, power, air conditioning, local loop and house cabling, terminal controllers, and terminals. Not a small request, but the failure of any one of these elements can cause a processing disruption.

The next attack against hardware failures is adequate preventive maintenance, and this should be supported by quick corrective maintenance and

the availability of spare parts. As for operator-caused errors, as stated earlier, the best protections are automatic procedures where possible, adequately documented procedures, and thorough training.

These preventive measures are well known, but there is one idea that is not familiar to many and thus has not been implemented as often as it should. Monitoring of a network should not be restricted to passive waiting for a failure; it should also include active monitoring to predict failures. By establishing activity standards, for example, of the types of transactions received from various locations and their quantity, it is possible to monitor activity and observe an abnormality that may indicate the oncoming or the existence of a problem. An abnormality may indicate the beginning of service degradation that may lead to a service disruption. A sudden decline in activity may indicate transmission difficulties, whether because of a component or because of a link problem. As for a sudden increase in activity, this may indicate that the user is retransmitting transactions because of a software problem. In any case, it is forewarning that the system may become overloaded, leading to service degradation or failure.

Data gathering and analysis for predictive measurements can be complex and can result in excessive processing overhead. To avoid this situation,

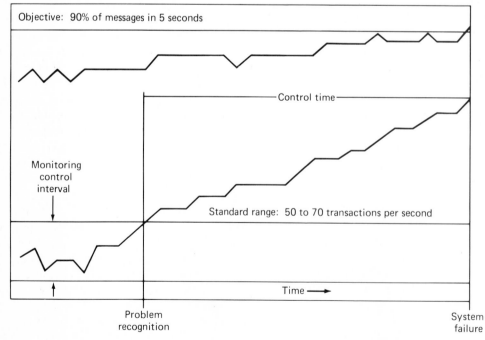

ILLUSTRATION 10-18. Traffic Rate as a Predictive Standard: Since changing traffic rate provides earlier warning of potentially degrading service than is provided by changing response time, traffic rate should be monitored to predict service degradation, while response time should be used at a later time to evaluate performance. *Source:* Howard L. Giles, "Successful Network Management Hinges on Control," *Data Communications,* Aug. 1978, p. 38.

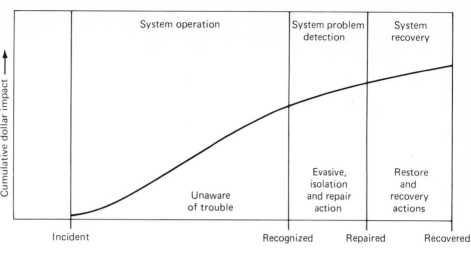

ILLUSTRATION 10-19. Problem Life Cycle: The obvious goals are, first, to detect problems as early as possible, and second, to resolve these problems as quickly as possible, thus minimizing the extent of system degradation and downtime. *Source:* Howard L. Giles, "Successful Network Management Hinges on Control," *Data Communications*, Aug. 1978, p. 37.

predictive standards should be chosen carefully, and only when deviations occur should it be necessary to collect additional data. Howard Giles of IBM provides guidance in selecting predictive measures: "The most widely used variables include traffic ratio (by system and line), inquiry type distribution by locations, line errors by line, database or I/O calls by inquiry, interface calls, and traffic calls."[27]

The absence of response time as a predictive standard from this list may be apparent. The reason for this is that response time is actually an evaluation standard for judging performance, not for predicting service degradation or system failure. Traffic rate, the number of input or output transactions occurring per time period, is a predictive standard, since it provides early indication of an abnormal condition. Illustration 10-18 shows how these two standards function. Traffic rate has a control interval assigned to it, and as shown in the illustration, when this control interval is exceeded, a time duration, called the *control time*, exists from when a problem is recognized to when a failure will occur; the traffic rate standards provide early notification and thus a long control interval. Response time, in contrast, fluctuates, has a less-steep change in value, and is generally judged by the highest degree of degradation permitted; thus, response time provides late notification and almost no control time to avoid a system failure.

Another predictive standard closely related to traffic rate is buffer utilization. For example, it can be stated that buffer utilization should not exceed 80 percent.

[27]Howard L. Giles, "Management Strategy for Controlling Network Operations," p. 46.

Detection of Failures. Illustration 10-18 shows the desirability of a long control time to avoid a system failure. The life cycle of a problem is shown in Illustration 10-19. The evasive activity shown may be use of a backup unit for the failing unit or it may be the substitution of another processing means until repairs have been made. This illustration also indicates, in a general manner, the increasing accumulated cost associated with the duration of a problem. Therefore, the conclusion is to become aware of the problem as soon as possible and to correct it quickly.

Waiting to receive a telephone call that a user is not being served, and may not have been served for a long period of time, is definitely not the recommended method for detecting failures. It is likely that, while discovering that the user's terminal is down, it will be discovered that his or her temper is up. What is needed is monitoring equipment. Monitoring equipment ranges in complexity from a CRT display screen and data-collection tape to computer monitoring and automatic control of network problems. These sophisticated computer control systems automatically switch to backup units. At this time, this method is not used extensively. One reason is cost; another reason is general disinterest in monitoring. Gary Angell of Codex Corporation comments on this indifference; "Most users will accept marginal performance right up to the point of failure."[28]

It would probably be easy to justify the cost of monitoring equipment if the network downtime for one year were assigned a cost value and related to how much would be saved if downtime were

[28]Hartwig, "Network Control: Managing the Data Environment," p. 52.

lessened because of quicker problem detection, isolation, and resolution. When the increase in user service and satisfaction is added to this cost picture, an overwhelming argument exists.

Digital tests are used to isolate the datacom element that failed. This is performed by loopback tests that involve sending a signal and receiving it back; in this way, the problem is isolated to the modem at one end of a link, at the other end of a link, or in the link itself. When the problem is not in the link, additional digital tests can be performed. But if the problem is in the link, analog tests are necessary, and this is best left to the telephone company, unless the equipment and specially trained personnel are available in-house. Many large organizations are prepared to perform analog tests and line-problem analysis; few small or medium-size organizations would consider this.

Problems should be documented, preferably on a form such as that in Illustration 10–20. This comprehensive form permits technicians to observe trends and assists in problem resolution. It is also advisable to log problems by datacom element. This log permits the grouping of problems by datacom element; thus, several problems affecting an element can be corrected at the same time. This procedure also avoids the inevitable situation where one fix negates one or more other fixes.

Recovering from failures. Of the various methods of categorizing approaches to recovering from system failures, the categories provided by Edward Yourdon are particularly useful:[29]

1. *Bring the system to a complete halt.* With adequate planning, an orderly shutdown is possible, including notification to users of the temporary shutdown. The operator should have the documentation of the recovery procedures to follow and should receive all the information needed to follow the procedures. The shutdown procedures should occur automatically for failures such as memory parity errors; occurrences such as fires and flooding usually require operator action.

2. *Stop processing the terminal for the user or task that caused the error.* A local problem usually requires only a local action. Some users may consider partial service termination a crude approach, but if another approach is not possible, this one is better than a total system shutdown.

3. *Fall back to a less efficient mode of operation.* Instead of terminating processing for all or part of the net-

[29] Yourdon, *Design of On-Line Computer Systems,* pp. 534–542.

work, it is usually preferable to still provide service to all users, but with less efficiency. For example, if a memory parity error is detected, the defective modules can be bypassed; this will result in less memory being available, increasing paging activity and thus slowing processing and response activities. If the processor fails, transactions can be accumulated off-line. In the case of a high-speed-printer failure, data can be stored on tape for later printing.

4. *Switch to a standby subsystem.* This is possible when backup units are included in the datacom network. It is common practice to have a dial-up line as backup for a nonswitched line. Patching and switching panels are used to transfer transmissions from one or more faulty units to backup units. Automatic patching and switching equipment is available, some requiring operator approval, and others notifying the operator after transferring control. Operator approval is advantageous when the condition is often transitory and transfer of control would be unnecessary. Notification after transfer of control is necessary for real-time systems that cannot tolerate disruptions.

5. *Switch to a standby system.* Only real-time systems that must be kept operable, or small real-time systems where the cost would not be prohibitive, could have total system backup. One New York City bank has a high-priority real-time application to which an IBM 370/168 is dedicated—and there are three other IBM 370/168s as potential backup systems. Naturally, these three systems are utilized when not needed for backup; but when needed, one is immediately made available.

The matrix in Illustration 10–21 relates the alternative recovery approaches that may be taken for the various types of failures. Each organization may want to modify this matrix according to its policies and recovery-approach preferences.

Network Service

Data may be protected from modification or unauthorized access, and the network may be available for adequate periods of time, but service to users still may be poor. It is only necessary to visualize a manager waiting for critical information, a clerk whose activities are halted until a response is received for a request, or a customer waiting for credit approval to understand that a network can be functioning, but if responses are delayed for 30 seconds, 2 minutes, or longer, dissatisfaction is inevitable.

Thus, putting aside all the other factors already discussed which affect user satisfaction, it is apparent that the overriding criterion commonly used

Communications Trouble Report

1

Otr no. ___/___/___	Reported to telecom.
Date	Name _____
Time	Time _____

Items 1–3
To be completed by GCD personnel
Items 4–9
To be completed by telecom. personnel

S/370 operator _____
Remote station operator _____

2 Console information

A. HASP line(s)/device address(es) _____

B. Memorex/S 370 system configuration _____

C. CRT and/or printer console message(es): ☐ Yes ☐ No
   Record or attach to CRT _____

D. Display status of line(s) to HASP, TCAM, BTAM, and OS via console printer. Circle each response and attach printout to CTR. (D, U, TP, online; $DRM: $DU).

E. Symptoms(s) and remarks: _____

3 Remote station information (Record for one station only)

A. Line _____

B. Name of job _____

C. Circumstance under which problem occurred:
   1. ☐ Terminal 1 PL: ☐ Successful ☐ Unsuccessful
   2. ☐ Entering console command: Name of command _____
   3. ☐ Loading job
   4. ☐ Printing/punching/executing job—enter in remarks.
   5. ☐ Other (i.e.; station idle, but online)—enter in remarks
   6. ☐ Console message(s): _____
   7. Remarks: _____

ILLUSTRATION 10-20a. Communications Trouble Report. *Source:* Federal Reserve Bank of New York, New York City.

4 Memorex information

Complete roliers and indicator status.
Fill out form for each trouble line.

5 Datascope information

6 Lines(s) and modems status

7 Other diagnostic information and results

8 Corrective action taken/results/date and time

9 Problem resolved by _____

Day/time _____

Remarks: _____

ILLUSTRATION 10-20b. Communications Trouble Report.

Failure Type	Approaches				
	A. Bring the system to a halt.	B. Stop processing terminal for user or task that caused the failure.	C. Fall back to a less efficient mode of operation.	D. Switch to a stand-by subsystem.	E. Switch to a stand-by system.
1. Processor	✓				✓
2. Memory parity	✓		✓		
3. Communications network		✓		✓	
4. Peripheral devices		✓	✓	✓	
5. Operator					
6. Program		✓			
7. Power failure	✓			✓	
8. Environmental	✓				✓
9. Erosion of the data base		✓			
10. Saturation			✓		
11. Unexplained					

ILLUSTRATION 10–21. Matrix Relating Failure Types to Recovery Methods.

to judge datacom service is response time. Response time is explored in some detail in Chapter 12; at this time, it is useful to consider how response time can degrade and how degraded service can be made tolerable or how it can be avoided. As shown in Illustration 10–22, as the number of users increases for a network (increasing the workload to be serviced), the response time, as is to be expected, increases. If, as in the case of the illustration, an acceptable level for response time is set at four seconds, the threshold for the number of users is 55. The response time degrades at an increasing rate as more users add their workload to the network. Users may have been informed that for 90 percent of the time the response time will be four seconds or less. But when users must wait longer, they can be expected to become impatient. One nonremedial but placating approach to this situation is the following. Monitor network workload and response time and, when it is possible to predict excessively long response time, notify users at their terminals that the response time will be longer than they may find acceptable; If they wish, they can sign off and use the network at a later time. Users should also be informed of anticipated response time at time of log-on, possibly also indicating the number of users already logged-on. This approach definitely signifies to users that the data center personnel are concerned about the service provided and are doing their best to serve.

Network monitoring to observe and inform users of degraded service has another benefit. If a user complains, "I'm always waiting a long time for responses—it seems like minutes," it is possible to provide statistics on what percentage of the time response has been below 4 seconds, between 4 seconds and 30 seconds, and over 30 seconds. This would avoid a lot of haggling.

Several remedial approaches are available for controlling excessive response time. Howard Giles categorizes these as design, operational, and economic controls.[30] Design controls involve actual changes to the network to change its capacity and the distribution of its resources. For example, unused backup links can be used for the surplus transactions, or transactions can be rerouted to use less heavily used parts of the network. Operational control applies to controlling user access to the network, restricting access according to priority, agreed-upon maximum workloads, or by location, user, or transaction type. The final control method, economic control, uses such means as chargeback of network expenses, with increased rates to those who exceed predetermined limits. Economic control also includes making available network resources at discounted costs on "off-hours." Thus, users can expect to pay premium rates at peak-activity time periods and bargain rates for lunch hours and second and third shifts. This approach helps to level the demands made on the network.

Naturally, such design changes as using increased transmission rates, faster modems, or additional links reduce response time—but they also increase the cost of processing. A balance between performance and cost must be chosen carefully, on one hand, to provide adequate service, and on the other hand, to avoid unnecessary costs.

If service degrades seriously and the user cannot obtain good service, the user may want to use

[30] Giles, "Management Strategy for Controlling Network Operations," p. 46.

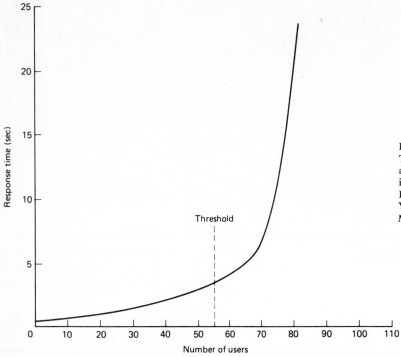

ILLUSTRATION 10–22. Degradation of Response Time: Response time degenerates not proportionately but at an increasing rate as the number of users increase. *Source:* John E. Bingham and Garth W. P. Davies, *Planning for Data Communications* (New York: John Wiley, 1977), p. 27. By permission of Macmillian, London and Basingstoke.

alternate processing approaches. This can be simply batch processing, either on-site or off-site, or it can be a processing approach such as performing data gathering and later submitting the job as an on-line or off-line batch job. As a last fallback approach, there can be manual procedures—this is particularly important if there is a total system failure and an alternate site is not available.

Network Adaptability

Too often, only the present system needs and workloads are considered, totally ignoring the changes that are likely to occur for existing systems, the addition of new systems, and the ever-present threat of suddenly increased workloads. Two comments are particularly relevant here:

> These systems are constantly changing through their useful life cycles, and the ability to accept changing load gracefully, however difficult to provide, is vital.[31]

> The communications systems that grow and adapt survive and those which are immobile become a severe liability and, sometimes, contribute to organization failure.[32]

[31] Levy, "Real-Time System Design," p. 633.
[32] Giles, "Management Strategy for Controlling Network Operations," p. 42.

This design factor, therefore, is extremely important. How a network is made adaptable depends on the imagination and effort of the network designer. Adaptability depends on such considerations as the ability to change the network's configuration and capacity, and to quickly make these changes. The ability to change input and output devices, such as adding hard-copy terminals, is one type of adaptability; the ability to restrict access by location, transaction type, user and data base or portions of data bases is a second type of adaptability.

All discussions of datacom processing types, datacom planning, and datacom elements had as their end goals (goals by which datacom processing performance is evaluated) examination of the design and operating criteria; data integrity, data security, network availability, network service, and network adaptability. All of these criteria are important—the datacom system is as strong as the criteria receiving the least attention. Ignoring any criteria weakens the entire datacom system.

part three

DATA CENTER PERFORMANCE

GOAL

To acquire adequate, but not excessive, resource capacities and to utilize resources efficiently and effectively.

HIGHLIGHTS

The Goals and Benefits of CPE

The direct benefits of CPE are to control, tune, and forecast performance; the indirect benefits are just as impressive—to reduce operating costs, speed user service, and strengthen users' image of management control and effectiveness.

The CPE Program Proposal

The method recommended to obtain upper-management enthusiasm and approval of a CPE program is to prepare a proposal that management can relate to, stressing control, service, and cost benefits.

The CPE Process

Thorough, controlled computer-performance improvements result from a six-step process:

- Define performance criteria
- Establish monitoring methodology
- Produce performance reports
- Analyze performance data
- Document conclusions and recommendations
- Implement improvements

Computer-performance evaluation (CPE) confines itself to the performance of the computer and closely related resources, such as channels and peripherals. CPE is the subject of this chapter, but as in the case of scheduling, where computer scheduling is referred to as microscheduling and data center scheduling is referred to as macroscheduling, CPE can be considered microevaluation, and total data center evaluation, as macroevaluation. Evaluation of data center performance is the subject matter of the next chapter. Illustration 11-1 suggests the factors in these two categories of performance evaluation. After stating the goals and benefits of CPE, guidelines are presented for estab-

lishing a CPE program and for performing the CPE process.

THE GOALS AND BENEFITS OF CPE

The phrase "computer-performance evaluation" can be misleading. Some performance analysts prefer phrases such as "computer-performance monitoring" or "computer-performance management." Each of these phrases focuses on a different aspect of the process to be performed. Computer-performance evaluation, however, is the most generally accepted phrase, and no problem results as long as it is kept in mind that CPE involves all the activities suggested by these various phrases, and that CPE activities include performance monitoring, evaluating, improving, and managing.

In its most comprehensive usage, CPE refers to five goals, of which the first two do not apply to the subject of this chapter, since they do not apply to the performance of an existing computer system. The five goals are:

1. *Hardware and software selection.* Competing hardware and software are evaluated and compared before an acquisition choice is made. This process is explained in the chapter on hardware and software acquisition. The evaluation technique recommended is the use of benchmarking, although some performance analysts argue for the use of simulation.

2. *New system performance projection.* It is desirable and sometimes necessary to know what effect a new system will have on the data center's workload and ability to meet existing commitments. Most data centers have experienced service degradation when a large system was released for production without any projection of its effects. In fact, in many instances the data center management may not even have known of the new system's existence. The only satisfactory tool for projecting performance of a nonexisting system is simulation.

3. *Performance control.* This is the first and most basic goal of CPE for existing systems. Performance limits are set and actual performance is compared against these limits. Control consists of keeping performance within these limits. For example, data center management may make a commitment to users that on-line processing response time will be five seconds or less for at least 90% of the time. If this commitment is not met and nothing is done to correct this situation, performance control has been lost.

ILLUSTRATION 11-1. Micro and Macro Performance Evaluation.

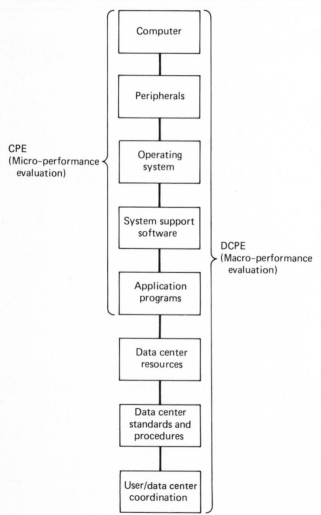

4. *Performance tuning.* Controlling performance is fine and admirable, but a stagnant environment can result, and that is not acceptable. After performance has been controlled, means should be sought to tune the system for better than acceptable performance. This goal adds another dimension to merely maintaining performance levels; it focuses on breaking through to higher levels of performance.

5. *Performance forecasting.* This aspect of CPE requires anticipating how workload and technological changes will affect resource capacity and the resulting performance. The effects of workload increases can be serious. It is not a comfortable situation to be surprised when an increase in transactions for a system, although an apparently minor increase, has a dramatic effect on performance. A 25 percent increase in transactions has been known to greatly degenerate performance and to cause frantic searches for additional resources that may not have been needed if early analysis and modifications were performed in a calm, logical manner.

Thus, the goals of CPE as they affect the existing computer system are to control, tune, and forecast performance. Some of the benefits of CPE are already apparent, since they are inherent in the goals defined. It is apparent, for example, that serious service degradation and resource wastes are less likely to occur, but the list of benefits is longer and may be surprising. The direct benefits of CPE are that management and staff

1. become aware of degrading performance;
2. use a rational basis for improvement decisions;
3. minimize ineffective "improvements";
4. utilize resources more fully;
5. eliminate waste because of underutilized resources;
6. eliminate bottlenecks because of overutilized resources;
7. make efficiently utilized resources available for new applications and increased workloads;
8. defer equipment upgrading;
9. organize data storage more efficiently;
10. make application programs in production more efficient;
11. make application programs being developed more efficient; and
12. reduce personnel overtime, possibly an entire shift.

These are the direct benefits of CPE. The indirect benefits are even more impressive, par-

ticularly from the users' viewpoint. Controlled, efficient, accountable utilization of resources reduces operating cost, speeds user service, and strengthens users' image of management control and effectiveness. Costs are reduced when unneeded resources are eliminated and when expensive, improperly utilized resources are replaced by less expensive, properly utilized resources. When jobs are processed more efficiently, more jobs are processed in a fixed time period; thus, jobs are returned to users more quickly, accounting for improved user service. The third indirect benefit of CPE, the users' image of management control and effectiveness, results from the ability of data center personnel to publish their performance standards, and to insure periodic reports on how well these standards are met. Management control and effectiveness are also demonstrated through management's ability to identify trends and to permit planning to meet those trends.

Many instances of successful CPE are available. Unfortunately, when resources are apparently fully utilized, many organizations do not perform any analysis, but merely do the obvious—obtain resources with greater capacity, and pay more. One company that intended to replace the existing computer with a larger, more expensive computer fortunately decided to analyze present resource utilization.[1] The findings were enlightening. One finding was that one selector channel was used less than one percent of the time; a second finding was that another selector channel was not needed at all. Action was taken—and it did not include upgrading the computer. By returning one selector channel to the vendor and making several changes, a savings of approximately $45,000 resulted each year. Instead of incurring the additional cost of the more powerful computer, the operating expenses were actually reduced.

The amount saved because of CPE has been even more impressive at other installations. One government agency monitored performance, and as a result invested $60,000, a one-time expense, in performance optimization.[2] The yearly savings is dramatic. Each year this agency saves $433,000. Putting aside all the other benefits of CPE, just the

[1]Louis J. Desiderio, Dennis Saloky, and Arnold Wasserman, *Measuring Computer Performance for Improvement & Savings,* Coopers & Lybrand, Newark, N.J., 1974, p.5.

[2]"Why Use Hardware Monitoring," *Data Processing Manual* (Pennsauken, N.J.: Auerbach Publishers, 1973), portfolio no. 5-03-01, pp. 2-3.

potential dollar savings should be enough to justify the relatively low cost of conducting CPE.

Sometimes just a small change can result in tremendous savings. In an analysis of an operating system at a utility company, a surprising discovery was made.[3] It was found that 40 percent of all system CPU activity was consumed by a redundant operating-system module. A simple branch was patched into the operating system to bypass the unneeded instructions. This simple action extended the life of the system two years, saving an estimated $2 million dollars. When programmers are made aware of the efficiency and savings possible through efficiency-conscious coding, better programs are certain to be released into production. As Robert Tykal of Motorola's Software Service Group comments, "Our development people look at the total cost of a job and attempt to minimize the cost."[4] Rapport between data center and systems development personnel can stimulate this attitude.

Even with the apparent usefulness of CPE, even with the continual changes and increased complexity of user applications and technology, and even with escalating costs and increased demand for management accountability, the degree of indifference shown to CPE is surprising. Many times, lip service is given to the worth of CPE, but it is not implemented; often when implemented, it is done so casually and with a low level of effort. Criticism of this lack of enthusiasm and effort has been expressed by many persons. Joe Leisher of Clark Equipment Company, a Michigan-based company, comments, "If we were to rely on the procedures we used in the past, we'd be making decisions by the seat of our pants. . . . We *never* want to be in that situation again, and the only way we can insure this is by constantly monitoring and tuning our system."[5]

The need for CPE was stated even more succinctly by the manager of a large installation for a bank in New York City: "How can a manager manage resources without knowing how the resources are being used?"

[3]Ibid., p. 3.
[4]"Improving Cost Conscious Program Development," *Booleanworld*, Spring 1977, p. 1.
[5]"Heavy Equipment Manufacturer Plans to Avoid Performance Problems Pushing Them Against the Wall," *Booleanworld*, Summer 1978, p. 13.

THE CPE PROGRAM PROPOSAL

The possibilities for improvements are apparent to data center technical, operating, and managerial personnel, but these improvements are not likely to be apparent to upper management. Because of this situation, the establishment of a CPE program meets its first, and most likely its biggest obstacle: the need to convince upper management of the value of a CPE program. The tool for selling management on this program, and for guiding the implementation of it, is the *CPE program proposal*. For this proposal to be thorough and convincing, it must consist of three sections: benefits anticipated, financial analysis, and implementation plan. Less than these sections would detract from the effectiveness of the presentation and leave questions unanswered; more than this would make it unnecessarily cumbersome and complex.

Benefits Anticipated

Benefits must be expressed in terms meaningful to management. To state that 1500 jobs instead of 1000 jobs will be processed in a specified time period is likely to be received with obvious lack of interest, and enthusiastic declaration of expected increase in the multiprogramming factor is almost sure to lead to undisguised dozing.

The CPE program must be seen from management's point of view. They are interested, primarily, in reducing expenses and improving service. These benefits must be stressed. They can appreciate the value of increased efficiency and operating control, but these improvements should be presented as causes for lessened expenses and improved service. Although it is unlikely that the means for improving performance are certain at this time, comments can be made on the experience of others having an active CPE program, and several possible areas for improvement can be indicated. It is possible, for example, to mention the elimination of unneeded resources, such as underutilized channels. It is also possible to indicate the savings that will result from delaying the upgrading of the present equipment and from avoiding the need for personnel overtime.

Then, after commenting on the dollar savings anticipated, the benefits to users can be suggested. These would include greater certainty in meeting scheduling commitments, faster turnaround for batch jobs, and quicker response time for on-line jobs. Improved reliability is also likely. Not only would processing activities be better controlled, but also unnecessary activities would be avoided, such as frequent equipment upgrading that often disrupts processing.

Financial Analysis

Management obviously wants to know what the "true savings" are, that is, the savings anticipated minus the cost of the CPE program. The anticipated savings have already been stated in general terms under "benefits anticipated." In this part of the proposal, the anticipated savings should be justified. Savings and costs must be stated precisely, preferably in tables that permit easy comprehension. The costs to be expected include the means used to measure performance, whether software or hardware; the personnel required, both staff and management, and possibly outside consultants; and finally the equipment costs, including those used for input preparation and output processing, as well as for computer processing.

Illustration 11-2 is a table of typical savings and costs projections. This simplified method of presenting financial information is helpful for comprehension and for assisting discussion. To justify the entries in this table, however, the entries should be annotated and comments should be included to explain why the amounts shown are reasonable. The table in the illustration, projects the savings and costs over four years, with adjustments made for the present value of money at whatever percentage was chosen as appropriate. (Present value and its use is explained in the chapter on hardware and software acquisition.)

The table also shows the *payback ratio.* This is the ratio of the savings to the cost. Some companies may want to establish a minimum payback ratio for acceptance of the CPE program. This, for example, can be set at 2. But this practice seems somewhat arbitrary. What if the ratio is 1, but the other benefits received are considerable? In fact, what if there is a loss, but the other benefits, such as resolving a serious operating problem, cannot be ignored? Therefore, this ratio is useful only if the other benefits are not considered significant. And this is not likely.

ILLUSTRATION 11-2. Financial Analysis for a CPE Project. *Source:* "Cost Justifying Performance Evaluation Projects," *EDP Performance Review,* July 1975, p. 3.

	YEARS			
	1	2	3	4
PROJECTED SAVINGS ($000)				
Equipment Reduction	40			
Postponed Purchases		100		
Reduced Overtime	30	50	40	30
Annual Savings	70	150	40	30
Present Value Factor (@ 15%)	1.0	.870	.756	.658
P.V. of Annual Savings	70	131	30	20
P.V. of Total Savings = $251,000				
PROJECTED COSTS ($000)				
Outside purchases	30			
Manpower	40	10	10	10
Computer Time	20	5	5	5
Annual Cost	90	15	15	15
Present Value Factor (15%)	1.0	.870	.756	658
P.V. of Annual Cost	90	13	11	10
P.V. of Total Cost = $124,000				
Net Present Value = $251,000 – $124,000 = $127,000				
Payback = $251,000/$124,000 = 2.02				

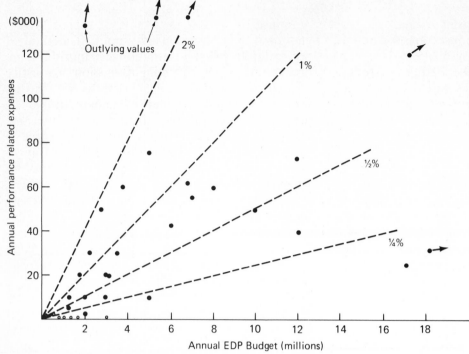

ILLUSTRATION 11–3. Expenditures for CPE: Although considerable variations exist, a survey of actual expenditures indicate that most CPE-conscious installations spend between ½% to 2% of the annual EDP budget on CPE. *Source:* "Survey Data on CPE Expenditures, Usage Statistics," *EDP Performance Review,* June 1978, p. 3.

Besides considering the program's justification in terms of benefits received for money spent, it is customary to relate the program's cost against the total data-processing budget for the year. In a small-scale survey performed by the editors of the *EDP Performance Review* newsletter, the trend suggested, although inconclusive, is shown in Illustration 11–3. This scatter diagram represents the response of only 35 organizations with CPE programs. The results are definitely not conclusive, but they do suggest that the generally stated guideline of spending 5 percent of the total data-processing budget for the year is excessive. It appears that the amount spent should be closer to 1 percent. As shown in the diagram, smaller installations tended to spend less than 0.25 percent of their budget, while larger installations spent about 1 percent. However, a few small installations spent more than 2 percent, and a few large installations spent less than 0.25 percent. The deviations from the 1-percent norm are considerable and suggest different levels of enthusiasm about, and commitment to, CPE.

Implementation Plan

The concluding part of the proposal is concerned with how the CPE program would be implemented if approved. Management would want to know the schedule for implementing the CPE program, the personnel required to conduct the CPE process once the program is implemented, and the means for management to control and verify attainment of the anticipated benefits.

Implementation Schedule. The schedule would indicate how much time will be allocated for defining and documenting the CPE process to be followed, the phases of CPE implementation, and the personnel needed for each implementation phase. It is likely that the defining and documenting of the CPE program will be a one-person operation. The first phase for implementation of the program is also likely to require only one person. This person will establish the framework for the CPE process and judge the adequacy of detail, exception, and summary reporting. With a satisfactory framework of procedures and supporting reports, other phases of the program can be implemented, each gathering more data and permitting more-detailed analysis, and likely requiring more personnel. Where the first phase would attend to overall CPU and channel utilization, for example, the later phases will consider disk-storage and application-program efficiencies. Also as part of the schedule, deadlines should be stated for when management reports will be prepared and distributed and for when the first positive results from the program can be anticipated.

Personnel Requirements. In response to the survey by *EDP Performance Review,* less than 10 percent of the respondents had no one assigned to CPE, less than 10 percent had more than six persons assigned, and the greatest number had one person assigned part time.[6] Since these responses came from only 72 organizations, the results can only indicate what is being done, and, for that matter, only for those organizations with obvious interest in CPE. The results of this survey are summarized in Illustration 11–4. Besides having the number of performance analysts required, it is also necessary to have competent analysts. The

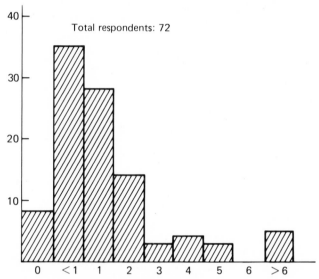

ILLUSTRATION 11-4. Personnel Assigned to CPE: The trend indicated in a survey is that most installations have only one person assigned to CPE, and that more likely than not only part-time. Some installations, approximately 8%, had no one assigned to CPE, while nearly as many installations had more than six persons assigned. *Source:* "Survey Data on CPE Expenditures, Usage Statistics," *EDP Performance Review,* June 1978, p. 4.

requirements for performance analysts are demanding. They must be able to interpret large masses of details, to reason from this data, and to communicate conclusions and recommendations. Performance analysts use these abilities as doctors use similar abilities—to cure, to prevent, and to improve. Whereas a doctor cures or prevents an illness, a performance analyst eliminates or prevents a deficiency; and both attempt to improve health, one for patients and the other for computer systems.

[6] "Survey Data on CPE Expenditures, Usage Statistics," *EDP Performance Review,* June 1978, p. 4.

Management Control. It is necessary to remember that the proposal for a CPE program is directed to upper management for their approval. Thus, it is their concern, and therefore the concern of those preparing the proposal, that upper management is told how performance expectations and actual performance are communicated. Therefore, the proposal must clearly state when management will receive reports and what they will contain. The common arrangement is to provide reports for each month's performance. As for the manner of presentation, the goal should be to provide only the basic information useful to management, supported where necessary by additional documents. Thus, the monthly report may consist of a single summary sheet, a few required detailed information sheets, and several optional sheets when needed to support statements on the summary sheet. It is definitely advisable that all of these sheets be carefully formatted to present information in consistent and easy-to-comprehend formats. Carefully designed forms would be ideal. Several of these types of reports and forms are presented throughout this and the next chapter.

THE CPE PROCESS

Although the process about to be presented applies primarily to a periodically repeated ongoing process of performance evaluation, it also applies to project-type performance evaluations, where special problems are to be solved or specific deficiencies are to be eliminated. These two types of activities are similar to periodic visits to a doctor to control a person's health, and emergency visits to a doctor, that can occur at any time, to attend to an illness or injury. Other analogies can be used for these two types of performance-evaluation activities; for example, a mechanic performs periodic tune-ups to control a car's performance and also performs on-demand repair to correct a deficiency or failure.

The CPE process centers on alerting personnel to both actual and potential problems. Performance analysts, as well as doctors and car mechanics, if competent, do not restrict analysis and improvements to only existing deficiencies and problems, but extend analysis to deficiencies that may become serious at a later time. For an analyst to comment that on-line response time and batch

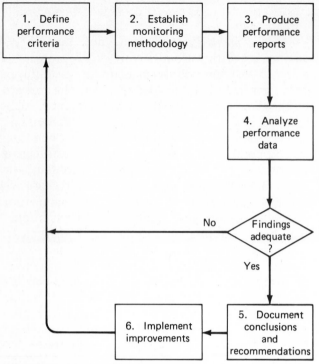

ILLUSTRATION 11-5. The CPE Process.

The CPE process itself consists of six phases, as shown in Illustration 11-5:

1. Define performance criteria
2. Establish monitoring methodology
3. Produce performance reports
4. Analyze performance data
5. Document conclusions and recommendations
6. Implement improvements

The first two phases are reviewed for each cycle of the process, and if advisable, the criteria, the methodology, or both are modified. The third and fourth phases, producing performance reports and analyzing the data in those reports, are the basic and necessary activities for every cycle of the process. These two phases are repeated until reliable conclusions result and definite recommendations can be prepared. The last two phases are performed only when these conclusions and recommendations are ready for documentation, approval, and implementation. Now to consider each of the six phases.

Phase 1: Define Performance Criteria

Many criteria are used for judging performance, and these criteria are usually presented as many unconnected items to be examined in any sequence, with only vague relationships to one another. To remedy this state of confusion, all performance criteria are segmented into three cate-

turnaround time meet the standards set, without commenting that the trends for these two criteria indicate impending service degradations, indicates inadequate performance analysis. This inadequacy may result from lack of knowledge of what should be done, or it may result from an individual's lack of concern and initiative. Precise and thorough definition of information to be reported would make these analysis deficiencies apparent and would permit their elimination. This control of analytic activity becomes an automatic feature of a correctly established CPE process.

Some organizations have computer performance monitored continually, but because of the software and personnel overhead costs incurred, this approach can waste more resources than it saves. How often performance is monitored depends on the seriousness of the deficiencies present. Generally, it is adequate to monitor one day's activities each week. This provides performance information without incurring overhead for each day. If the pattern and quantity of demands vary significantly from one day of the week to the next, a different day can be monitored each week. Each organization must decide on the frequency of performance evaluations, and as part of the performance evaluation process, this decision should be reevaluated.

ILLUSTRATION 11-6. Categories of Performance Criteria.

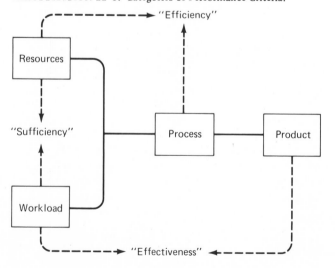

310

gories, those related to "sufficiency," "efficiency," and "effectiveness." As the quotation marks indicate, these terms can be defined various ways and therefore require clear distinction. These three terms are related to a computer's resources, workload, process, and product, as presented in Illustration 11-6.

Sufficiency. As shown, the term "sufficiency" relates resources to workload. Two basic questions must be asked and answered. The first question is: "Are resource capacities for the various computer resources adequate for the workload?" The second, closely related question is: "Are resource capacities for the various computer resources excessive for the workload?" The concept of sufficiency is very easy to visualize. The capacity of the CPU, for example, can be compared to the capacity of a container. Consider a 10-gallon gasoline container. If, at any time, the largest quantity of gasoline stored in this container is only 4 gallons (which can be related to computer workload), the container is never more than 40 percent full. A 5-gallon container would be adequate. The same is true for a computer, but a much more extravagant waste. What if, in contrast, 14 gallons were to be stored? The container would not be adequate. The same is true for computer capacity. If the workload exceeded computer capacity, insufficient resources would cause degraded service. The overcapacity and undercapacity of resources can be referred to as the "adequacy" criterion.

A closely related criterion, and the only other criterion in the sufficiency category, is "availability." Resources may appear inadequate for the workload, where in reality they would be adequate if resources were available for productive work more than they are. Several questions should be asked: Are resources available only two shifts? Should they be available for three shifts? When resources are available, what part of that time is used for productive work? For testing? For maintenance, scheduled and unscheduled? For what part of the time are resources idle? These are all important questions and are directly related to meeting workload commitments. Thus, the two criteria in this category are resource adequacy and resource availability.

Efficiency. This category of criteria centers on the process itself and on how resources are utilized.

It is totally indifferent to the workload and the resulting product; there is no concern about the quantity of work to be done or the priority and deadlines associated with jobs. What is done is irrelevant; how well it is done, however, is an efficiency consideration. Focus is on resource utilization, processing wastefulness, and application wastefulness.

1. *Resource utilization.* The most expensive and thus the most significant resource is the CPU. Whereas resource sufficiency focuses on the need to eliminate or acquire resource capacity, resource utilization focuses on how well existing resources are utilized. Poor resource utilization can give the appearance of inadequate capacity. For example, if idle time is excessive, computer availability for productive work is less, and the capacity may appear inadequate. If paging activity is excessive, productive activity will appear greater than actually exists, and again capacity may appear inadequate. Resource utilization can be divided into two subcategories: resource activity and resource allocation. The primary resource activity criteria are:

    a. Idle time
    b. CPU supervisory/program state ratio
    c. paging rate
    d. traffic rate

All of these activities must be kept under control and lessened when possible. Naturally, paging rate applies only to virtual-memory operating systems, and traffic rate applies only to datacom processing.

The primary resource allocation criteria are:

    a. CPU, memory, channel, and device usage
    b. multiprogramming factor
    c. degree of CPU/channel overlap
    d. organization of data on disk
    e. configuration's adaptability to changes

The significance of some of these criteria are made obvious when phase 4 of the CPE process, performance data analysis, is considered. It is apparent that resource utilization consists of many criteria and accounts for much of the performance analyst's activities.

2. *Processing wastefulness.* It is not enough to fully use resources if this full utilization results because it is necessary to rerun jobs. Thus, this is an important measurement of processing efficiency. Two other closely related measures of wasteful activity are the number of IPLs (initial program loadings) that must be performed and the operator error rate, that is, the number of operator errors. Besides these three sources of processing wastefulness, there

are also measures related to equipment failures. They are mean time between failures (MTBF) and mean time to repair (MTTR). Poor performance for MTBF indicates poor-quality servicing, and for MTTR, poor servicing response. Thus, the five criteria in the processing wastefulness category are:

    a. number of reruns
    b. number of IPLs
    c. operator error rate
    d. MTBF
    e. MTTR

3. *Application wastefulness.* Simply, this criterion refers to application programs that are inefficient and disrupt processing. It is the questionable industry standard to release programs for production without considering program efficiency, thus wasting resources and processing time. Not only is it almost always possible to streamline programs so that they will perform their processing quicker, but it is also usually possible to greatly reduce if not eliminate program errors and processing delays. It is not uncommon to have programs that require frequent rerunning to obtain a satisfactory completion—often without the users or the systems-development personnel being aware of these wastes. Many programs still include second-generation programming concepts, such as issuing a message to the computer operator and halting the program until a response occurs; often the information requested could be supplied on input control cards. Furthermore, if the operator is busy with the other duties, or if the information needed is not readily available, delays can be extensive.

Effectiveness. In contrast to efficiency, effectiveness is concerned not with how well resources are used, but with how well the results of processing (the product) satisfy the workload demands made by users. Effectiveness is concerned with what is accomplished, not how it is accomplished. Although improved processing efficiency improves effectiveness, and although degraded processing degrades effectiveness, efficiency can be satisfactory while effectiveness is poor, and efficiency can be poor while effectiveness is satisfactory. Resources, for example, can be efficiently and fully utilized, but because of a heavy workload, service can be poor. In contrast, because of a light workload, resources may not be fully utilized, but service can be excellent. Effectiveness consists of three criteria familiar to all data center personnel: throughput, turnaround, and response time.

Throughput means the number of jobs processed in a fixed time period. For example, one university processes about 1000 jobs in an eight-hour day, which includes many student jobs that are compiled or executed for only a very short period of time. Since the concern at this time is restricted to computer processing, and not to overall processing in the data center, this is a measure of the number of jobs completed by the computer in a specified time period, and not of the number of jobs completed and ready for users. In other words, no consideration at this time is given to the time required for precomputer processing, such as data conversion and type pulling, or for postcomputer processing, such as decollating and bursting.

Turnaround and response time are closely related. Whereas *turnaround* refers to batch processing, *response time* refers to on-line processing. Turnaround, in terms of computer, not data center, processing, is measured as the amount of time consumed from the loading of a job for execution to its computer-processing completion. Response time is similar. It is the time required for the first character of a response to appear at a terminal after the "enter" key is pressed at the terminal.

Thus, the three categories of criteria and their stresses are:

    sufficiency—relates workload to resource capacities
    efficiency—focuses on how resources are utilized
    effectiveness—focuses on meeting workload demands

Phase 2: Establish Monitoring Methodology

Before deciding on the method for monitoring performance, it is necessary to consider what information must be gathered to evaluate performance according to the performance criteria selected. Considerable data must be gathered from various components of the computer configuration. An interesting and useful method of segmenting the computer configuration into functional components, each of which has its associated performance criteria, is suggested in an IBM performance study at the Management Information Division of the State of Illinois.[7] Their graphical representation of

[7]"Volume 3 Part 2; Study Results: State of Illinois," *Data Security and Data Processing,* IBM Manual no. G320–1373–0, June 1974.

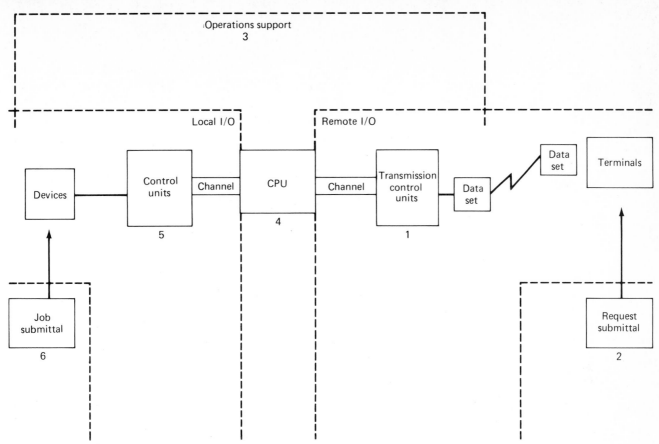

ILLUSTRATION 11-7. Performance Measurement Subsystems. *Source:* "Volume 3 Part 2: Study Results: State of Illinois," *Data Security and Data Processing,* IBM manual #G320-1373-0, June 1974, p. 206.

the six subsystems is shown in Illustration 11-7. Their table, shown in Illustration 11-8, relates performance criteria to the six subsystems, referring to performance criteria as "indicators." These criteria include some of the efficiency and effectiveness criteria previously listed, but they do not include the sufficiency criteria, which are general, overall issues that can be analyzed separately. The six subsystems and some of their associated criteria are:

1. *Remote I/O.* Here the stress is totally on resource utilization efficiency, such as channel utilization, stored-data organization, and traffic rate.

2. *Remote requests.* The stress changes to processing effectiveness, to considerations such as response time.

3. *Operations support.* Although an entry is not shown for a performance criterion in the table, this subsystem actually is judged primarily by resource wastefulness due to operator delays and errrors.

4. *CPU utilization.* Efficiency is the main concern here; attention is focused on adequate CPU activity, as compared to idle time, and adequate real-storage utilization, considering also multi-programming factor and paging activity.

5. *Local I/O.* As in the case of remote I/O, this subsystem focuses on efficient utilization of resources, examining channel and device utilization.

6. *Local requests.* Again, as in the case of remote requests, this subsystem focuses on processing effectiveness, considering throughput and turn-around.

The segmentation of the total computer configuration into a few, easy-to-relate-to components provides at least two benefits. It increases the likelihood of thorough and logical data gathering; it suggests a convenient method for analyzing performance and for reporting conclusions. The table in Illustration 11-8 also suggests some of the variable factors for each subsystem. These factors fall

Sub-system	Indicators	Variables		
		Controllable	Uncontrollable	Catastrophic

1. Remote I/O	• Channel utilization	• Terminals/line
		• Terminal types
		• # Lines
		• Line types
		• # Transmission
		  control units
			• Terminal down
			• Line or modem down
			• Line quality
				• Channel down
				• Transmission
				  control
				  unit down

2. Remote Req.	• Response time
	• # Transactions/
	  time unit
	• Time last request
	  processed
			• Monthly fluctuations
			• Weekly fluctuations
			• Daily fluctuations
			• Hourly fluctuations
			• Programmer
			  attendance
			• Software status
				• Agency conditions

3. Operations support			• Request time delay • # Operator errors • # Operators	• Operator error

4. CPU	• CPU utilization
	• Avg. time
	  transactions
	  in queue
	• Avg. # transactions
	  in queue
		• SYSGEN Options
		• PARMLIB Options
		• # Initiators
		• Same sub-system
		  tasks
		• Same core
		  allocation
			• Operator actions	• CPU down

5. Local I/O	• EXCP count
	• Channel utilization
		• Hardware
		  configuration
		• Volume
		  configuration
		• Library placement
			• Devices unavailable
			• Sharing devices
			• Error recovery
				• Hardware failure

6. Job submittal
   (Batch/RJE)
	• Turnaround time
	• Thruput
	• Backlog size
	• Job queue
	  averages
			• Monthly fluctuations
			• Weekly fluctuations
			• Daily fluctuations
			• Hourly fluctuations
			• Programmer
			  attendance
			• Software status
				• Agency conditions

ILLUSTRATION 11–8. Subsystems, Criteria, and Variables. *Source:* "Volume 3 Part 2: Study Results: State of Illinois," *Data Security and Data Processing,* IBM manual #G320-1373-0, June 1974, p. 207.

into three categories: controllable, uncontrollable, and catastrophic. For the installation used in this study, the factors may be correctly categorized, but for many installations some of the factors may occur in the other categories shown. For example, some of the factors shown as uncontrollable may actually be controllable, such as workload fluctuations, the number of operators available, and device sharing.

Now the question arises: Knowing what performance criteria to use for evaluating performance, and knowing what information to gather to apply these criteria, how should this data be gathered? One of the most thorough listings of methods for gathering data, whether the data are actual, estimated, or calculated, occurs in an article by Henry C. Lucas, Jr. in ACM's journal, *Computing Surveys.*[8] The eight methods identified are shown in Illustration 11-9. Lucas examines the acceptability of the various methods for selecting hardware, for predicting the performance of new application systems, and for controlling and improving the performance of the existing system configuration—of which only the performance of the existing system configuration is the subject of this chapter. A short

[8]Henry C. Lucas, Jr., "Performance Evaluation and Monitoring," *Computing Surveys*, September 1971.

definition of these methods follows, although only the last method, monitors, is recommended and explained in some detail.

1. *Timings.* This method has no relevancy for evaluating operating performance, since it mainly considers comparison of a CPU's cycle and add times—and is not even adequate for comparing computers for selection, as the evaluations in Illustration 11-9 indicate.

2. *Mixes.* The attempt here is to be more realistic than in the use of timings and to consider the likely mix of instructions that will occur in an operational situation. This method is totally inadequate, because it still ignores actual computer performance and its relationships to all other operating factors.

3. *Kernels.* A kernel is a "typical" program, if there is such a thing, but without I/O considerations; it is used to predict performance as changes are made. This method also ignores interaction between the various operating factors, as well as not being able to accurately represent complex I/O activity.

4. *Models.* A model of a system is a mathematical representation of the characteristics and interrelationships between factors. Preparing a model is a complex, time-consuming, and tedious activity. Some analysts, however, put considerable faith in this method; from the table in Illustration 11-9 it is apparent that Lucas does not. It is unlikely that a model can reliably represent a complex

ILLUSTRATION 11-9. Suitability of Methodologies for Performance Evaluation. *Source:* Henry C. Lucas, Jr., "Performance Evaluation and Monitoring," *Computing Surveys*, Sept. 1971, p. 81.

Evaluation Technique	Selection Evaluation (System Exists Elsewhere)		Performance Projection (System Does Not Yet Exist)		Performance Monitoring (System in Operation)	
	New Hardware	New Software	Design New Hardware	Design New Software	Reconfigure Hardware	Change Software

—. Technique not applicable
1. Has been used but is inadequate
2. Provides some assistance but is insufficient; should be used in conjunction with other techniques
3. Satisfactory

Evaluation Technique	New Hardware	New Software	Design New Hardware	Design New Software	Reconfigure Hardware	Change Software
Timings	1	—	1	—	—	—
Mixes	1	—	1	—	—	—
Kernels	2	1	2	1	—	1
Models	2	1	2	1	2	—
Benchmarks	3	3	—	2	2	2
Synthetic programs	3	3	2	2	2	2
Simulation	3	3	3	3	3	3
Monitor (hardware and software)	2	2	2	2	3	3

configuration and its high degree of random activity, and any simplification of a model can be depended upon to greatly lessen the model's value.

5. *Benchmarks.* The execution of a hopefully typical set of programs on various computers can definitely assist computer selection, but it is of limited value for performance evaluation. First of all, the selected applications may not represent the typical workload, and second, benchmarking does not reflect the changing demands made upon the system—it does, however, permit comparison of before and after performance for system changes.

6. *Synthetic programs.* These programs are like kernels, but with much more comprehensive consideration of I/O activities, and they are used as benchmarks would be used. Although synthetic programs are more flexible in their definition of characteristics than a benchmark consisting of actual programs, they have the same limitations as benchmarks.

7. *Simulation.* Instead of describing a system in mathematical terms as in a model, a software model of the system is prepared and executed. The results are analyzed and changes are made and also analyzed. This method has been criticized because of its development and operating costs and because of the time consumed. Considering the costs and time consumption associated with software and hardware monitoring, this criticism may not be as justified as some believe. This requires cost analysis. But the main reason for discrediting this method is its high degree of unreliability in providing accurate performance information.

8. *Monitors.* Simply stated, monitors, whether hardware or software, collect performance data from the actual system configuration as the system executes its workload. Thus, it does not guess or calculate performance statistics; it obtains the true performance data as activities actually occur—within the limitations imposed on a monitor to assess data. This limitation applies mainly to software monitors that cannot truly monitor the operating system's supervisory activity, since the operating system has a higher priority than the monitor. Hardware and software monitors are now discussed in more detail.

Liba Svobodova, of Massachusetts Institute of Technology, has identified five structural elements of monitors, whether the monitors are hardware or software.[9] These are listed in Illustration 11-10 along with a short statement of each element's purpose and use in hardware and software monitors. The elements are (1) instrumentation to assess data, (2) selector to choose only the assessed data of interest, (3) processing to relate and summarize selected data, (4) recording to retain processed data, and (5) interpreter to interpret recorded data for further analysis.

We will consider hardware monitors first. Hardware monitors obtain data through electrical probes that are attached to computer signal points. This is a somewhat delicate operation and incorrect connections can easily occur. The delicate nature of these attachments is made clear when the probe attachments in Illustration 11-11 are considered. Through these probes it is possible to measure the duration of events or the number of events. The second and third elements of a hardware monitor, selecting and processing, result from logical hardware or software processing, such as using a logical AND function for CPU and channel activities to determine their overlap. Where the probes are attached, naturally, determine what information is

[9] Liba Svobodova, *Computer Performance and Evaluation Methods: Analysis and Applications* (New York: Elsevier North-Holland, 1976), pp. 80–87.

ILLUSTRATION 11-10. Structural Elements of Monitors.

STRUCTURAL ELEMENT	ELEMENT'S PURPOSE	HARDWARE MONITOR	SOFTWARE MONITOR
Instrumentation	Access to system activities	Electronic probes	Traps or sampling
Selector	Chose activities of interest	Logical plugboard or software	Software
Processing	Relates and summarizes data	Logical plugboard or software	Software
Recording	Stores or displays processed data	Counters or secondary storage	Main or secondary storage
Interpretation	Interprets data to permit further analysis	Displays real-time or postprocessing software	Real-time or postprocessing software

ILLUSTRATION 11–11. Hardware Monitor Probes. *Source:* Computer Performance Evaluation Service: Hardware Monitoring, from Ernst & Whinney (formerly Ernst & Ernst), 1977.

collected. This may sound simpler than it actually is. Of the tens of thousands of signal points that can be used, vendors supply documentation on the location of only a small number, possibly only 100. Experimentation is required to locate the points wanted. Generally, the processed data are stored on tape and later interpreted by software, which generates reports for analysis.

A very rational evaluation of hardware monitors is given by Ron Gallagher, of Bendix Corporation, who comments on his experience with hardware monitors and shares his conclusions

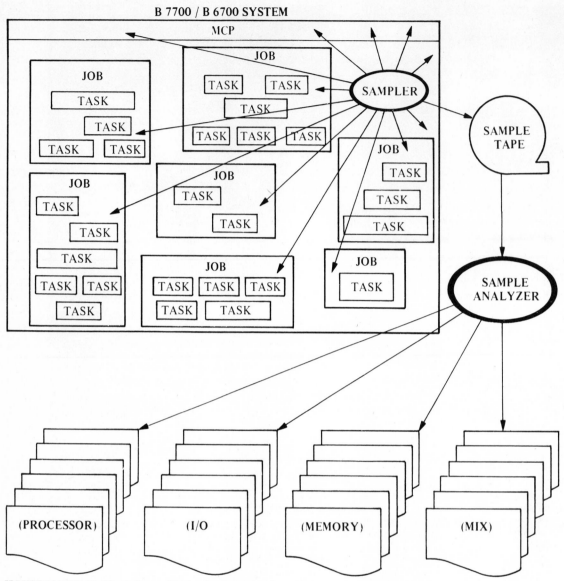

ILLUSTRATION 11–12. Software Monitoring-Reporting Process. *Source:* "SPARK: Sampler and Sampleranalyzer," *B 7700/B 6700 User's Manual,* Burroughs, manual #5001357, p. 1–2.

in the statement: "It gives very accurate information, but it's difficult and time-consuming to install. In addition, it takes much longer to verify and analyze the data than we would like. So we were willing to give up 1 percent or 2 percent of accuracy for a tool which was more easily usable by a non-hardware technician. We still use the hardware monitor occasionally, but with our limited staff, the software monitor is the better choice."[10]

Now we turn our attention to software monitors. Basically, software monitors are programs

[10] "CPE Effort Eases Manufacturer's DP Functions," *Computerworld,* November 27, 1978, p. 31.

that are loaded into a computer's real storage and that obtain data either by accessing data as specific events occur or by sampling whatever is occurring periodically. Whichever method is used, it is obvious that storage and computer time are consumed by the software monitors themselves, which is not the case for hardware monitors. This collecting activity—and the later recording and interpreting and reporting activities—is clearly presented in Illustration 11–12, an overview of Burrough's software-performance system, called SPARK (Systems Performance Analysis Review Kit). Monitors often use information gathered and made available by the computer's operating system. IBM has data collected by their System Management Facility (SMF), and CDC, as another example, has their facility, called SCOPE. The reliability of SMF, however, has been criticized as misleading and inaccurate.[11] The information collected and how it is interpreted and presented are usually determined by indicating the options to be used at time of execution.

There are several comments on software monitors that are of interest:

We have found management very receptive to our proposals since we began collecting real information and presenting it in a professional manner.[12]

Without a monitor such as CUE, we would have to rely on experience and intuition. Frankly, the days of tolerating this type of "seat-of-the-pants" judgment have long since passed—at least with our man-

agement. I should add it has also made us much more certain of the recommendations we make to management.[13]

When money is tight, as it is at the present time, facts are a lot easier to present than "gut feel." We've been able to and will continue to show management that we are allies, not adversaries.[14]

There are various levels of software monitors. First, there are what may be called entry-level packages, which are actually job-accounting packages. These packages are primarily intended for chargeout and chargeback purposes, but they do provide considerable performance information and thus are often used by those entering the performance-evaluation arena and want to do it cautiously. The next level contains the general software monitors that provide considerable information about the overall computer configuration performance, such as Boole & Babbage's CUE

[11] Aso Tavitian, "SMF Data Valid for Billings but Bad for Measurement," *Computerworld*, December 17, 1975, p. 16.
[12] "Hard Facts for Management Provided by Monitor Use," *Computerworld*, January 15, 1975, p. 15.

[13] Ibid., p. 15.
[14] Ibid., p. 15.

ILLUSTRATION 11-13. Comparison of Software and Hardware Monitors.

APPROACH	ADVANTAGES	DISADVANTAGES
Software monitors	Low purchase or lease cost.	Significant overhead for CPU activity and storage.
	Easy to obtain information on application program activities, file activities, data organization, and paging activities.	Does not truly represent supervisory activity since supervisory activity has a higher priority than the monitor.
	Flexibility, permitting quick change of options as to what is collected and analyzed, and how the results are presented.	Must be updated for each operating system update since it is operating system dependent.
	Moderate level of personnel skill required.	Simultaneous measurements cannot be obtained.
Hardware monitors	No CPU or storage overhead.	High purchase or lease cost.
	Any CPU or I/O activity can be measured.	Does not measure activities for individual application programs or individual operating system modules.
	Accurate measurement of short duration activities.	High level of skill is needed to attach probes.
	Measures activities simultaneously.	Long setup time consumption.
	Can be attached to any computer.	Possibility of incorrect probe attachments and thus providing incorrect results.
		A limited number of probes can be attached.
		Probes can be accidentally disconnected.
		Accidental pressure on probes may damage equipment.

(Configuration Utilization Evaluator). And the final level in software monitors includes those designed for very specialized purposes, such as for analyzing the paging activity for a multiprogramming operating system, the organization of data stored on direct-access devices, or the distribution of application-program activity. All of these monitors are valuable and should be considered for adoption into the CPE program.

The advantages and disadvantages of hardware and software monitors were suggested several times during the preceding discussion, but many significant pros and cons have not been mentioned and are summarized in the table shown in Illustration 11–13. The survey performed by the editors of *EDP Performance Review*, which was already referred to and indicated as not decisive, states that according to the responses received hardware monitor use decreased from 39 percent in 1974 to 29 percent in 1977, and software monitor use increased from 46 percent in 1974 to 83 percent in 1977; the use of job-accounting packages remained about the same, rising from 80 percent in 1974 to 87 percent in 1977.[15]

Phase 3: Produce Performance Reports

A number of fascinating performance reports are available, and it requires considerable restraint not to dedicate many pages to displaying and commenting on them. Reason requires this restraint. Before considering the data contained in these reports, we consider the various methods of presenting the data.

[15]"Survey Data on CPE Expenditures, Usage Statistics," pp. 2–3.

ILLUSTRATION 11–14. Daily Shift Report. *Source: Value Computer Scheduling System,* from Value Computing Inc., 1974, p. 18.

```
VALUE COMPUTING INC.                        CONFIG NO.  2, 158       PAGE   34

              *****************************************************
              *                                                   *
              *            DAILY SHIFT REPORT FOR 11/15/78         *
              *                                                   *
              *****************************************************

DESCRIPTION          0000 - 1200     1200 - 0000           -- TOTALS --   PRIOR WEEK AVG   PRIOR MONTH AVG
-------------------  -----------     -----------           ------------   --------------   ---------------
AVAILABLE TIME          12.00           12.00                 24.00
PROCESSOR ACTIVE        11.35           12.00                 23.35          12.41            20.18

EXECUTION TIME          59.04           37.57                 97.01          25.00            93.26
THROUGHPUT              77.57           65.52                143.49          25.54           122.58
INITIATION RATIO         0.75            0.57                  0.67           0.96             0.75

MULTIPROGRAM FACTOR      6.72            5.48                  6.09           2.04             6.05

NUMBER OF IPLS              1               0                     1              1                0

NUMBER OF RUNS            247             130                   377             63              286

PROB PROG CPU TIME       3.23            6.34                  9.57           2.42             9.14
SYSTEM CPU TIME          4.09            3.03                  7.12           1.08             5.10
SYSTEM WAIT TIME         4.03            2.23                  6.26           8.51             5.54
PCT CPU TIME            65.03           80.13                 72.72          30.22            70.93

SYSTEM PAGES / MIN     289.40          138.19                212.46

TSO LOGONS                  0               0                     0
TSO CONNECT TIME         0.00            0.00                  0.00

PCT OF THROUGHPUT       54.20           45.79
```

```
DESCRIPTION      NO   TIME  PCT   NO   TIME  PCT       NO   TIME   PCT   NO   TIME  PCT   NO   TIME   PCT
---------------  --   ----  ---   --   ----  ---       ---  ------ ---   --   ----- ---   ---  ------ ---
4TH FL PROD     132  48.48   33  129  53.43   37      261  102.31  71   56  13.33  52  199  100.28  81
4TH FL PRT       17   1.44    1    1    .09    0       18    1.53   1              .00   0   16    2.33   2

SUB TOTAL       149  50.32   35  130  53.52   37      279  104.24  72   56  13.33  52  215  103.01  83

CLASS M & E      89  22.43   15                        89   22.43  15    7  12.21  47   64   17.02  13
PROGRAMMING       8   3.22    2                         8    3.22   2              .00   0    4    1.30   1
FINE SORT JOBS                                                     .00   0         .00   0         .00   0

ALL PARTIAL       1   1.20    0         12.00    8      1   13.20   9              .00   0         1.24   1

SUB TOTAL        98  27.25   19         12.00    8     98   39.25  27   63  25.54 100  283  122.57  99

TOTAL           247  77.57   54  130  65.52   45      377  143.49 100   63  25.54 100  286  122.58 100
```

All reports fall into two general categories: those in tabular format and those in graphical format. A tabular format presents specific numeric values in columns and rows. This manner of presentation therefore contains precise and specific values, and not approximate values. Naturally, the actual accuracy of the values depends on how carefully data are collected and processed. In contrast, a graphical format only approximates the actual values, indicating the values by the positions of lines or other value indicators with respect to the axes. Despite this loss of precision, these graphs are extremely important. At a glance they indicate what is occurring, that is, trends and either adherence to or deviation from performance standards. Often, precision is added to graphs by indicating actual values at critical locations within the graph, such as at the end of bar lines for a bar graph.

To provide order for the data contained in the large number of reports available, the reports are introduced according to their primary stress on category of criteria. Thus we introduce first reports stressing resource sufficiency, then reports stressing processing efficiency, and finally reports stressing processing effectiveness.

Reports Stressing Resource Sufficiency. The first question usually asked is, How much of the available computer time was used? The next question asked is, How was that time used? The daily shift report in Illustration 11-14 answers these questions. The annotations shown indicate some of the insight this summary-type report can provide. It indicates what is being done right and what is being done wrong. By comparing the reports of several months, trends become apparent, and the beginning of a problem may be observed before it becomes serious. This report stresses resource availability, and what is needed now is a report that stresses the other criteria for sufficiency, a report that indicates the adequacy of resources to satisfy workload demands, without those resources being excessive. The report shown in Illustration 11-15 satisfies this need. These graphs show at a glance the daily resource usage for various resources—in the case of the illustration shown, for CPU activity, the number of tape drives used, real storage usage, the memory partitions used, and disk usage. One comment is necessary to clarify the Ps and dots shown for core usage; the Ps

indicate space allocated for partitions, whether the space was used or not, and the dots indicate the space actually used.

Reports Stressing Processing Efficiency. The number of reports in this category is by far the largest. For convenience, they are presented as related to supervisory overhead, resource usage, disk organization, paging activity, and application program activity.

1. *Supervisory overhead.* Illustration 11-16 shows a graph of CPU time usage, where O indicates operating system overhead, * indicates TSO user time, and – indicates batch jobs. The report shown is from LOOK, an on-line performance monitor. The information shown is basic and necessary. The ratio of the time consumed by the operating system and the time for productive application processing is critical. One of the goals of a performance analyst is to lessen supervisory overhead.

2. *Resource usage.* Some resource-usage information has already been shown in Illustration 11-15. What is not shown in that illustration is the overlap of CPU and channel activities; typical information of this type is shown in Illustration 11-17. Observe that the percentage of the total time for "CPU busy" is 37.22 percent and that for "CPU wait and any channel busy" is almost as high, 36.43 percent. More overlap of CPU and channel should be obtained.

3. *Disk organization.* Among the reports available is the analysis of disk-arm movements shown in Illustration 11-18. These reports guide data-set reorganization to lessen the time required to locate data. Some specialized data-set-organization software monitors actually analyze inefficiencies and provide remedies.

4. *Paging activity.* Paging activity is directly related to real-storage space allocated to programs. Paging rate decreases when more space is allocated, but the multiprogramming factor, the number of programs executed at the same time, is reduced. If less real-storage space is allocated, the multiprogramming factor increases, but unfortunately so does the paging rate, which may waste a considerable amount of time for paging. The optimum space allocation is called the "working set size" for a program. Therefore, what is needed is a report that isolates those programs that apparently have incorrect space allocations. The report shown in Illustration 11-19 shows paging activity and paging rates for various programs, isolating those programs that may gain the most from space-allocation optimization.

5. *Application-program activity.* One of the most basic goals when analyzing program efficiency is to determine which instructions account for the greatest amount of

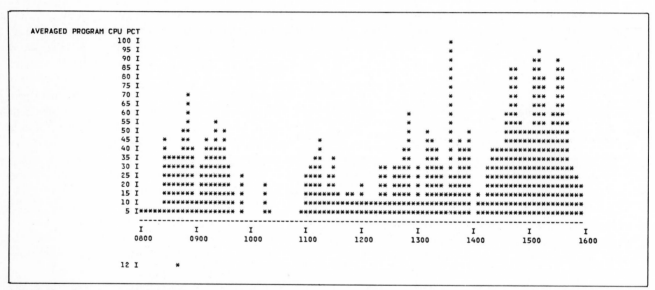

ILLUSTRATION 11-15. Daily Resource Usage Graphs. *Source: Value Computer Scheduling System*, from Value Computing Inc., 1974, p. 17.

```
CORE USAGE IN K   3000 I
                  2900 I
                  2800 I
                  2700 I
                  2600 I                                                                              **
                  2500 I****        P                                                                 **
                  2400 I****          P P                                                             **
                  2300 I****P   *  ** P                                                               **
                  2200 I******    *  ** *                                                             **
                  2100 I******   *P** *                                                    P          **
                  2000 I******   **** *                                                    *          **      *
                  1900 I*******  **** *PP                                                   *          **    *
                  1800 I*******  ****P***                    P                              *          *  *  *
                  1700 I*******  ****P***                    P                    *         ***  **    **  **
                  1600 I***************P                     *P        *          *    P    ***  **    *** **
                  1500 I***************                      *P        P          *  *   *  ***  **    ***** **
                  1400 I***************                      **        *          *  *   *  ******    ***** **
                  1300 I***************   *                  **    *P  **  *   *   *  ******   ****** ***** **        *
                  1200 I****************  * *                PPP **   *P** ** * ***** * *******   ***** **         *
                  1100 I****************  * *                PPP **   **** **  * ***** **  *******   ***** **       *
                  1000 I*****************  * **              * *** **   **** ** ** ** ** ********************      *
                   900 I******************* * **            ***** **PPP *******  ** ******** ******************    *
                   800 I******************* * **            *****  *****   ******* *********** *****************   *
                   700 I******************* *P** P          *****   ***** P P*********************************** *
                   600 I********************** P     ****** P  P*********************** ************************* *
                   500 I**********************      *****PP***** * ***************************************** *
                   400 I**********************      **********  * ****************************************** *
                   300 I**********************      *     *    *********P*PP*********** ************************
                   200 I**********************         **     ***********P*PP*********** ************************
                   100 I**********************    ****      ****************************************************
                       ------------------------------------------------------------------------------------------
                       I          I          I          I          I          I          I          I          I
                      0800       0900       1000       1100       1200       1300       1400       1500       1600
```

```
PARTITION MAP    12 IXXXXX      X
                 11 IXXXXXXXXXX    XXXXXX         X       XXXXXXXXXXXXXXXXXXXX   XXXXXXXX              XX
                 10 IXXXXXXXXXXXXX     X XX        XXXXXXXXXXXX          X             XXXXXXX    X
                  9 IXXXXXXXXXXXX   XXX XX           X                                 XXXXXXXXX
                  8 IXXXXXXXXXXXXX          XXXXXXXXX    XXX X      XXX   XXXXXXXXXXXXXXXXXX
                  7 IXXXXXX XXXXXXXXXX    XX   X   X             XX       XX
                  6 IXXXXXXXXXXXXXXXXXXX
                  5 IXXXXXXXXXXXXXX
                  4 IXXXXXXXX    XXXX                          XXX   XXXXXXXX     XXXXXXXXXXXXXXXXXXXXXXXX
                  3 IXXXXXXXXXXX    XXX   XXX          XXXXXX         XX  XXX
                  2 IXXXXXXXX   XXXXXXX XXX   XXX              XX       XX   XXXXXXXX   XXXXXX
                  1 I          XXX                   XX      XXXXXXXXXXXXXXXX  XXXXXXX   XXXXXX
                  0 I                     XXXXXXXXXXXXXXXXXXXXXXXXXXXXXXXXXXXXXXXXXXXXXXXXXXXXX
                    ------------------------------------------------------------------------------------------
                    I          I          I          I          I          I          I          I          I
                   0800       0900       1000       1100       1200       1300       1400       1500       1600
```

```
TAPES USED
                 11 I     *****     *
                 10 I     *****     *                                    *            **      *  **
                  9 I**** *****  *  ***                        *  *      *            ***    ******
                  8 I**** **** * ****                          ** *      *            ***    ****** **
                  7 I*************  ****                        ** *      *     *      *** *  ****** **
                  6 I******************                                 ** *    *  *** *** *  ****** **
                  5 I****************** * *                    *  **     ***** ** *** *** *  ****** **
                  4 I****************** * *            * * **  **  *****   ** *** *************** *** *      *
                  3 I****************** * **           ****** **  ******* * ********* ********************** *
                  2 I******************              ********* * *********************** *******************
                  1 I******************        *       ***************************** **********************
                    ------------------------------------------------------------------------------------------
                    I          I          I          I          I          I          I          I          I
                   0800       0900       1000       1100       1200       1300       1400       1500       1600
```

ILLUSTRATION 11-15. (cont)

323

```
    0       Identifies operating system CPU time
    *       Identifies TSO users CPU time
    -       Identifies batch jobs CPU time
```

```
               0         20        40        60        80       100
               +.........+.........+.........+.........+.........+
00:00:00       .0------- .         .         .         .         .
01:00:00       .00------ .         .         .         .         .
02:00:00       .00----- .          .         .         .         .
03:00:00       .0--     .          .         .         .         .
04:00:00       .0---    .          .         .         .         .
05:00:00       .0--     .          .         .         .         .
06:00:00       .-       .          .         .         .         .
07:00:00       .000----- .         .         .         .         .
08:00:00       .000*********--------- .        .         .
09:00:00       .0000****************--------------- .          .
10:00:00       .0000***********************-------------------- .
11:00:00       .000000****************************------------------
12:00:00       .0000****************-------------------------
13:00:00       .0000*********************--------------
14:00:00       .00000***************************-------------  .
15:00:00       .0000*****************************-------------- .
16:00:00       .00000*********************-------------------  .
17:00:00       .0000*********--------------------------  .       .
18:00:00       .0------------------------- .         .         .
19:00:00       .0------------------------ .          .         .
20:00:00       .00------------------------ .         .         .
21:00:00       .00------------------ .      .         .         .
22:00:00       .00------------- --- .       .         .         .
23:00:00       .0------------------- .      .         .         .
               +.........+.........+.........+.........+.........+
```

ILLUSTRATION 11-16. CPU Usage Graph. *Source: Proceedings of the First LOOK User Group Meeting,* Applied Data Reserach, Oct. 17–18, 1977, p. 11.

ILLUSTRATION 11-17. CPU and Channel Activity. *Source:* Kenneth W. Kolence, "A Software View of Measurement Tools," *Datamation,* Jan. 1, 1971, p. 36.

Equipment sampled	Amount of time	Percentage of total time
CPU busy	2679.84 sec	37.22
CPU busy in supervisor mode	303.84 sec	4.22
CPU wait and no device busy	578.88 sec	8.04
Any channel busy	3060.72 sec	57.46
CPU busy and any channel busy	1514.16 sec	21.03
CPU busy and no channel busy	1355.96 sec	18.82
CPU wait and any channel busy	2622.96 sec	36.43
CPU wait and only channel 1 busy	1779.84 sec	24.71
CPU wait and only channel 2 busy	275.04 sec	3.82
CPU wait and only channel 3 busy	180.72 sec	2.51
CPU wait and channel 1 busy	1844.64 sec	25.62
CPU wait and channel 2 busy	611.28 sec	8.49
CPU wait and channel 3 busy	317.52 sec	4.41
Correlation coefficient of channel busy and CPU in wait state:		
Channel 1 0.72		
Channel 2 0.14		

execution-time consumption. Software monitors are available to produce reports such as that shown in Illustration 11–20. The graph shows the percentage of run time consumed for the various program storage locations. It is only necessary for a programmer to examine the most time-consuming storage locations to locate the most time-consuming instructions. This makes the best use of a programmer's time and provides the greatest benefit for the least amount of programmer time.

Because of the complexity of computer processing and the associated efficiency reporting, many complex and interesting reports have been created. Since the performance analysts and managers reviewing these reports can appreciate any assistance that clever summarizing and formatting of information can provide, a few of the many clever reports generated by Burroughs' software performance package SPARK are now shown.

Illustration 11–21 is one method of showing distribution of a resource among various usages.

This illustration shows three categories of space-usage allocation, indicated by slashes, Ss, and blanks. The space available but unused is indicated by As. Illustration 11–22 is a report displaying two factors against time, thus providing considerable information on a single sheet. Illustration 11–23 goes even further by relating three factors against time. As a final extension of the last two reports, Illustration 11–24 shows how, besides by relating three factors to time, three accumulative graphs can also be included. In addition to the many graphs available, tabular reports can be generated that contain detailed entries, summaries of details, or only exception data requiring attention.

Reports Stressing Processing Effectiveness. These reports may not indicate the data center's resource sufficiency or its processing efficiency, but they do determine the users' image of the data center and its personnel.

Consider the very simple summary report

ILLUSTRATION 11–18. Data Base Arm Movement Analysis. *Source:* "The Operation of Hardware Monitors," *Data Processing Manual* (N.J.: Auerbach Publishers, 1973), portfolio #5–03–02, p. 11.

		Data base arm movement analysis all cylinders Monitoring period 9 24 52 to 16 08 25 10/1/71			
Cyl no.	No. seeks with arm movement	Total cyls moved to get to this cyl	No seeks without arm movement	Avg. seek with arm movement	Avg. seek incl. zero arm movement
00	7125	350707	6310	49 2	26 1
01	14720	746770	27130	52 3	18 0
02	2371	126007	1946	53 1	29 2
03	1571	85348	1457	54 3	28 2
04	1508	79677	1490	52 8	26 6
05	1610	75234	1371	46 7	25 2
06	1260	52303	1395	41 2	19 6
07	1588	74610	1211	47 6	26 8
08	1987	109217	1810	55 0	33 1
09	1974	104877	1067	53 1	34 5
0A	1699	95888	1054	56 4	34 8
0B	1418	72317	1219	51 0	27 5
0C	1259	68648	958	52 9	30 1
0D	1085	49977	936	46 1	24 7
0E	1048	53900	942	51 4	27 1
0F	1047	52004	1090	48 3	24 2
10	1000	46996	914	47 0	24 5
11	817	43280	864	52 9	26 7
12	551	29203	774	53 0	22 0
13	744	38317	597	51 5	23 6
14	675	34255	438	50 7	30 8
15	508	25231	506	50 0	25 0
16	582	35093	588	60 3	30 0
17	471	21672	617	46 0	19 9
18	678	28536	744	56 8	27 1
19	506	29252	543	55 4	27 3
1A	88	1814	58	48 9	17 7
1B	40	1903	42	49 6	24 2

PRODUCED BY APOWKLD(1.0)

REPORT PERIOD FROM 28 APR 76 AT 21.47.04 TO 30 APR 76 AT 02.33.19   REPORT DATE 28 MAY 76

SORT KEY IS: PROGRAM USAGE BY TOTAL PAGING

TOTAL PAGING	PROGRAM NAME	TOTAL RUNS	TOTAL TIME ELAPSED HHHH.MM.SS	TOTAL CPU TIME HH.MM.SS	AVERAGE CORE USED	TOTAL EXCPS	TOTAL PAGE INS	TOTAL PAGE OUTS	TOTAL PAGING	PAGING RATE (PAGING/ELAPSED)
1,425,995	TAPMGETC	214	30.16.51	02.26.00	415K	932,260	719,494	706,501	1,425,995	13.39
262,977	IELOAA	290	13.17.46	02.31.10	191K	210,005	158,115	104,862	262,977	7.21
167,620	BLCDRWV8	16	04.04.29	01.02.29	512K	10,724	92,038	75,582	167,620	11.62
151,414	GO	20	07.57.57	05.12.37	149K	17,320	84,011	67,403	151,414	5.30
140,886	IEKAA00	86	03.59.17	00.23.41	250K	7,035	84,875	56,011	140,886	12.39
106,953	DTLCPL	7	02.32.20	00.24.35	448K	23,051	77,592	29,361	106,953	11.77
97,898	DTLCP	12	01.46.15	00.12.50	448K	19,824	69,838	28,060	97,898	15.63
95,250	CSIOLB	29	03.18.28	01.23.39	188K	41,297	64,664	30,586	95,250	8.34
93,012	IEWL	316	03.49.20	00.15.05	124K	76,562	72,004	21,008	93,012	9.90
77,666	BBEDIT	5	01.19.25	00.12.47	198K	15,960	40,184	37,482	77,666	16.55
70,468	BLCSYSMR	85	04.50.04	02.11.43	232K	110,803	48,033	22,435	70,468	4.39
69,282	PBMCL	1	01.15.34	00.09.35	176K	6,250	49,503	19,779	69,282	15.30
58,960	BBACTG	14	01.47.26	00.07.31	170K	77,442	35,427	23,533	58,960	9.63
54,084	IEBGENER	380	08.58.56	00.31.35	49K	286,352	47,841	6,243	54,084	1.83
52,215	IFOX00	115	03.38.24	00.46.10	173K	60,591	36,857	15,358	52,215	4.80
51,149	PSLIST	6	02.25.25	00.10.49	181K	200,539	32,104	19,045	51,149	5.88
50,347	MC1050V1	13	02.18.52	00.24.04	208K	129,310	27,036	23,311	50,347	6.17
45,763	XSCDVRSS	11	05.22.15	02.52.38	240K	10,242	31,319	14,444	45,763	2.41
45,060	FEDRAWTC	9	01.11.31	00.17.58	448K	13,694	28,130	16,930	45,060	10.98
44,438	LCVAL	7	05.42.12	03.29.17	168K	1,885	20,736	23,702	44,438	2.17
43,758	JMPRN2MR	28	03.03.59	01.39.51	176K	40,280	29,322	14,436	43,758	4.05
41,422	PSUPDMR	66	03.00.02	00.52.09	182K	12,977	25,967	15,455	41,422	4.09
35,802	ALDFLMHS	122	05.09.21	03.01.08	116K	89,037	24,815	10,987	35,802	2.01
33,637	FETRY2RH	17	01.59.38	00.47.49	448K	34,285	22,728	10,909	33,637	4.83
33,129	TGSCH2SS	48	00.51.07	00.15.14	249K	11,834	23,197	9,932	33,129	12.61
31,783	ACMPRS	2	00.57.11	00.04.13	100K	7,606	23,552	8,231	31,783	9.33
31,362	BLFUP	4	00.53.49	00.03.37	96K	1,735	23,741	7,621	31,362	9.99

ILLUSTRATION 11–19. Paging Activity. *Source: APO: The Automatic Paging Optimizer,* from Boole & Babbage, p. 6.

E. CODE EXECUTION FREQUENCY FOR EACH INTERVAL

STARTING LOCATION	ENDING LOCATION	INTERVAL PERCENT	CUMULATIVE PERCENT	HISTOGRAM – PERCENT OF RUN TIME (EACH * = 0.1 PERCENT)
				.0 1.0 2.0 3.0 4.0 5.0
0386E0	0386FF	0.52	14.29	-*****
038700	03871F	0.36	14.66	-****
.038720	03875F	0.0	14.66	-
038760	03877F	0.29	14.94	-***
038780	03879F	0.13	15.08	-*
0387A0	0387BF	0.52	15.59	-*****
0387C0	0387DF	0.13	15.73	-*
0387E0	0387FF	0.13	15.86	-*
038800	03881F	0.23	16.09	-**
.038820	03887F	0.0	16.09	-
038880	03889F	0.25	16.34	-**
.0388A0	0388DF	0.0	16.34	-
0388E0	0388FF	2.78	19.12	-***************************
038900	03891F	0.17	19.29	-**
038920	03893F	2.11	21.40	-*********************
038940	03895F	0.21	21.61	-**
038960	03897F	0.0	21.61	-
038980	03899F	0.10	21.70	-*
0389A0	0389BF	0.11	21.82	-*
0389C0	0389DF	0.46	22.28	-*****
0389E0	0389FF	0.25	22.53	-**

NOTE PPA031 – EACH '.' INDICATES A COMBINED INTERVAL.

ILLUSTRATION 11–20. Application Program Activity. *Source: TSA/PPE,* from Boole & Babbage, p. 7.

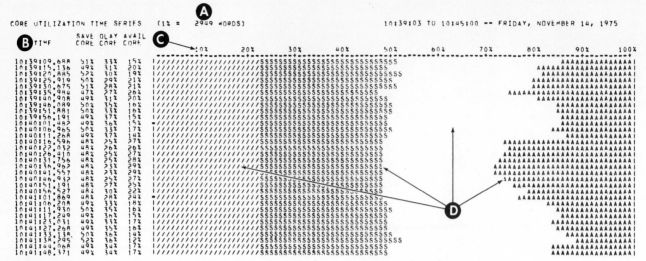

ILLUSTRATION 11–21. Time Series Data on Memory Usage. *Source:* "SPARK: Sampler and Sampleranalyzer," *B 7700/B 6700 User's Manual,* Burroughs, manual #5001357, p. 3–2.

ILLUSTRATION 11–22. Two Factors Displayed Against Time. *Source:* "SPARK: Sampler and Sampleranalyzer," *B 7700/B 6700 User's Manual,* Burroughs, manual #5001357, p. 3–8.

ILLUSTRATION 11-23. Three Factors Displayed Against Time. *Source:* "SPARK: Sampler and Sampleranalyzer," *B 7700/B 6700 User's Manual,* Burroughs, manual #5001357, p. 6-15.

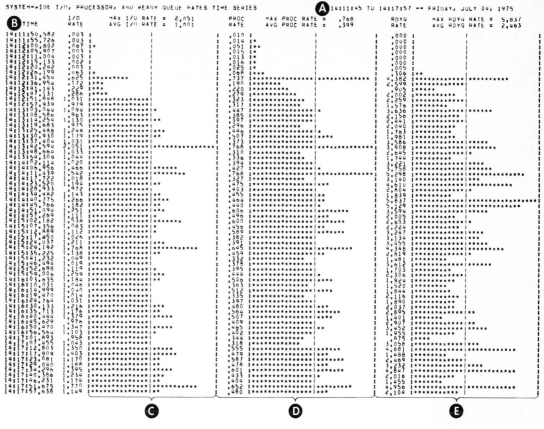

ILLUSTRATION 11-24. Three Factors and Accumulated Results Displayed Against Time. *Source:* "SPARK: Sampler and Sampleranalyzer," *B 7700/B 6700 User's Manual,* Burroughs, manual #5001357, p. 7-3.

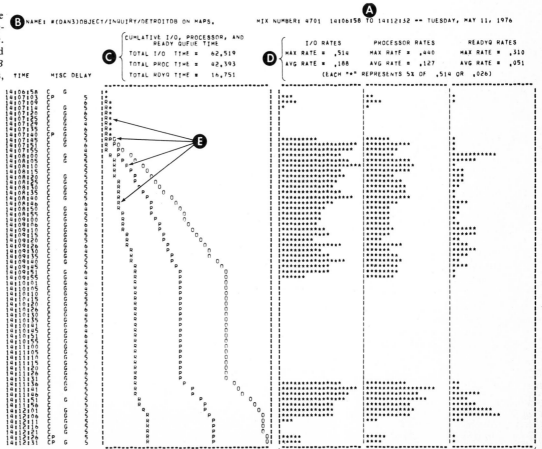

shown in Illustration 11-25. It indicates response time (actually, turnaround time for batch jobs and response time for IMS-type processing and on-line processing) and throughput for all three types of processing workloads. However, if this report were distributed to users, it would be misleading for batch processing, since it indicates turnaround and throughput only for computer processing, not for noncomputer processing within the data center. Precomputer processing and postcomputer processing can greatly delay the return of jobs to users. But for the microperformance effectiveness considerations of this chapter, this report is ideal.

All of these reports on sufficiency, efficiency, and effectiveness indicate the data that can be collected. To show what data are collected by installations interested in performance evaluation, the editors of *EDP Performance Review* prepared from two surveys the table in Illustration 11-26. This table shows the high, low, and average usage values for various performance measurements for three computer sizes: IBM 370/168, IBM 370/158, and IBM 370/145. The number of responses received during *Performance Review* survey for each measurement is indicated by the N value. The entries for Capex are from an independent Capex survey. Since the number of responses was small, the values should be used only for comparative purposes, and not as guidelines or standards. The values shown merely indicate the performance ranges and averages for a small sample.

Phase 4: Analyze Performance Data

With the mass of data provided in the various reports, it is necessary to define some guidelines for conducting a performance analysis and to segment potential improvements into the areas affected. Analysts involved in performance evaluation soon become aware of some of the guidelines useful for efficient performance analysis. They evolve a few personal discoveries, some less comprehensive than others and some emphasizing the trivial instead of the significant. Because of the absence of documented guidelines, each analyst must, in effect, rediscover the wheel. And because the discovered guidelines are not formally stated, they are often forgotten—or simply not applied. Performance analysts, experienced or novice, should find the following guidelines useful:

1. *Study only improvements that can be implemented.* It is obviously wasteful to consider improvements that will not be financed, that will not have personnel allocated to them, and that are certain of management's rejection.
2. *Collect only useful data.* No matter how interesting data may be, if they cannot aid performance analysis, they should not clutter and hide the worthwhile data and waste the resources used to gather and present them.
3. *Do the obvious first.* All too often, the challenging, complex, and subtle problems and solutions command an analyst's attention while clearly defined problems exist and obvious solutions wait to be implemented.
4. *Set priorities.* Attend to the most significant activities by applying the 20/80 rule. Generally, it can be expected that 20 percent of the activities will provide 80 percent of the benefits, and that 80 percent of the activities will provide only 20 percent of the benefits. Therefore, the few activities providing the most benefits should be identified and performed. These activities are often referred to as the "vital few."
5. *Consider interrelationships between criteria.* When one criterion is being optimized, it is pos-

```
                    BASIC EXAMPLE

*** PRINCIPAL RESULTS ***

WORKLOAD                  RESPONSE TIME          THROUGHPUT       % CPU

  1 BATCH PROCESSING       133.98 SEC             102. PER HOUR    36.9 %
  2 DATA BASE TRANS          3.17 SEC            4000. PER HOUR    22.8 %
  3 TIME SHARING USERS       3.31 SEC            3815. PER HOUR    33.9 %
                                       TOTAL CPU UTILIZATION =     93.6 %


BEST/1>
```

ILLUSTRATION 11-25. Service Effectiveness Summary (when 4000 data base transactions are processed per hour). *Source: Best/1: Computer System Capacity Planning, Release 4.0,* from BGS Systems, manual #BE77-010-2, p. 22.

ILLUSTRATION 11–26. Performance Measurements Actually Collected By Installations.

	IBM 370/168				IBM 370/158					IBM 370/145				
	N	Avg	Hi	Lo	N	Avg	Hi	Lo	Capex	N	Avg	Hi	Lo	Capex
Hours of operation (monthly avg)														
Total manned hours	24	652	720	520	23	648	720	400	523	12	620	720	400	445
Active hours (at least 1 job exec)	16	590	691	472	18	592	720	380		12	575	720	350	
Idle hours	14	85	374	8	16	41	212	0	29%	12	33	84	0	38%
Down (lost) hours	17	17	56	3	17	12	70	0		12	13	75	1	
Job activity (monthly avg)														
Total jobs completed	24	28,388	60,000	10,580	24	13,120	40,000	3,785	11,000	11	10,034	18,400	4,500	5,600
Jobs abended	13	1,798	3,680	500	23	1,100	5,000	115	10%	5	319	700	130	11%
Jobs cancelled	7	938	3,490	28	17	361	1,500	64	7%	5	169	420	18	12%
Jobs rerun	7	368	910	30	8	359	1,500	10		9	213	980	27	
Average core/program	12	272	512	100	12	176	398	70	92	11	85	280	20	128
Multiprogramming factor	15	9.7	16	5	17	6.9	16	2.5	3.5	9	3.7	5	1.6	2.2
Jobs/hr (calculated)		48				22			21		17			13
CPU activity (average)														
Percent CPU busy	24	64	100	31	23	70	97	33	58	11	66	88	40	59
Percent problem program state	20	37	58	19	16	34	65	15	29	4	42	62	25	32
Percent system state	20	29	58	12	15	36	55	17	28	4	24	31	13	26
Percent wait time	21	36	69	8	21	33	66	3	43	5	22	40	12	42
I/O activity (average)														
Paging rate/CPU second	17	8	25	1	14	15	35	2	9.3	9	4.3	10	.5	6.3
Disk excp rate/CPU second	17	133	400	32	13	71	135	20	80	9	42	140	1	43
Tape excp rate/CPU second	16	90	320	30	12	30	86	6	67	6	41	150	1	31
Queue times (average)														
Job queue (min)	15	48	130	9	8	33	120	4	43					88
Initiation (sec)	12	51	82	14	5	41	109	1	75					12
Execution (min)	14	10	16	4	12	14	52	2	14					46
Turnaround (min)	17	114	255	29	11	110	234	25	68					
									N = 30					N = 10

Source: "Survey Data on CPE Expenditures, Usage Statistics," *EDP Performance Review*, June 1978, p. 5.

sible that one or more other criteria may be worsened. For example, if less real storage is allocated to application programs, the multiprogramming factor increases, but so does the paging rate and the response time, which are definitely not desirable.

6. *Observe performance trends.* It is necessary to step back from all the mass of details collected for each day and to observe the changes from one day to the next, and from one month to the next. By this process, gradual performance degradation becomes apparent, and performance deficiencies are observed and corrected before they become problems.

With these guidelines for conducting a performance analysis, it is now appropriate to consider potential performance improvements. These improvements occur in five distinct areas: hardware configuration, system software, applications programs, data-set organization, and operating procedures. Although only a few of the possible improvements are mentioned, those mentioned do indicate what can be done.

Hardware Configuration. Reconfiguration of hardware could be extensive and expensive, but it can also be simple and inexpensive and still be effective. One case study presented by Saul Stimler of Stimler Associates illustrates the analysis used to guide hardware reconfiguration.[16] His presentation is now simplified and presented in terms of the

[16] Saul Stimler, *Data Processing Systems: Their Performance, Evaluation, Measurement, and Improvement* (N.J.: Motivational Learning Programs, 1974), pp. 62–75.

ILLUSTRATION 11-27. Hardware Configuration (before analysis). *Source:* Saul Stimler, *Data Processing Systems: Their Performance, Evaluation, Measurement, and Improvement* (N.J.: Motivational Learning Programs, 1974), p. 63.

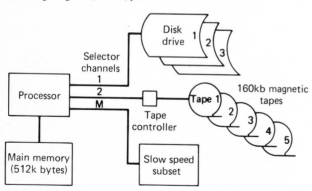

problems present, the solutions implemented, and the results obtained. The problem was that the workload was approaching the capacity of the hardware and expensive hardware upgrading was being considered. The analyst's objective was to obtain as much overall performance improvement in a short period of time, specifically, to reduce throughput rate by at least 20 percent and to accomplish this in only four weeks. It was decided to investigate the efficiency of a major system that each day consumed from 6 to 14 hours to update a master file. Illustration 11–27 shows the existing hardware configuration, and Illustration 11–28 shows CPU and channel data in a system profile chart; this chart immediately makes it apparent that CPU activity, channel activity, and CPU/channel overlap are poor.

It was decided to overlap input-tape reading and output-tape writing. To accomplish this, it was actually decided to use slower tape drives, but those connected to a two-port controller, permitting input and output overlap. It was also decided to lessen the idle time resulting from CPU inactivity while a computer operator mounted tapes. To accomplish this, two tape drives were assigned to input tapes and two were assigned to output tapes. Since the master file consisted of 11 tapes, considerable idle time was thus eliminated.

The new hardware configuration is shown in Illustration 11–29, and the resulting system profile chart is shown in Illustration 11–30. Even at a quick glance it is apparent that considerable improvements have resulted. The specific results are:

1. Reduced total run time, from 23,116 seconds to 15,574 seconds, that is, from 6.4 hours to 4.3 hours.
2. Reduced idle time, from 4153 seconds to 363 seconds; thus, from 17.9 percent of the total run time to only 2.3 percent.
3. Increased CPU/channel overlap time, from 1388 seconds to 4176 seconds, that is, from 6 percent of the total run time to 26.8 percent.
4. Increased channel-1/channel-2 overlap from 0 seconds to 3420 seconds, that is, from 0 percent of the potential overlap time to 94.6 percent.

The end result is that hardware upgrading and increased cost were avoided. The problems stated for this case study were solved. In fact, the use of slower tape drives actually reduced hardware costs.

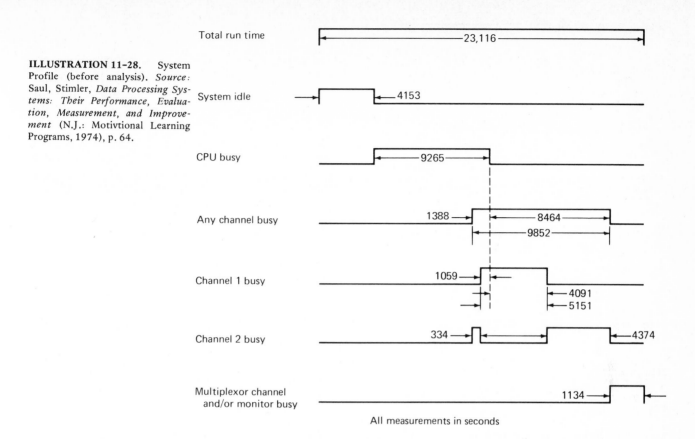

Total run time |←————— 23,116 —————→|

ILLUSTRATION 11–28. System Profile (before analysis). *Source:* Saul, Stimler, *Data Processing Systems: Their Performance, Evaluation, Measurement, and Improvement* (N.J.: Motivtional Learning Programs, 1974), p. 64.

System idle — 4153

CPU busy ← 9265

Any channel busy 1388 — 8464 / 9852

Channel 1 busy 1059 — / 4091 / 5151

Channel 2 busy 334 — / 4374

Multiplexor channel and/or monitor busy 1134 —

All measurements in seconds

System Software. Often, more efficient software is available than that supplied by the mainframe vendor. This is particularly true for utility and support software, such as sorts and data-base-management systems. An even more direct approach has already been mentioned: the elimination of unneeded or redundant system modules. In the situation referred to earlier, about 40 percent of the system CPU activity was consumed by a redundant, unneeded module. This type of improvement includes elimination of all options not used. Even if these options may not consume CPU time, they do consume space.

Application Programs. Program efficiency is usually outside the control of data center personnel, but controls should be installed to assure that programming personnel are attempting to produce efficient programs. The two major tools the data center and programming personnel have for isolating inefficient programs are reports on paging activity and on instruction activity, such as the reports already referred to in Illustrations 11–19 and 11–20. Paging activity is dependent on the amount of real storage allocated to a program and on how the program is segmented. If more space is allocated, more pages can be retained at any time, thus reducing the paging rate. As for program segmentation, programmers should attempt to segment programs so that when pages are loaded into real-storage page frames, they are used as fully as possible to avoid repeated reloading.

Whether or not paging activity is optimized, the instruction activity should be analyzed, particularly for the high-usage programs. Illustration 11–20 shows that two storage areas for instructions account for high processing activity. These areas are from hexadecimal location 0388EO to 0388FF,

ILLUSTRATION 11–29. Hardware Configuration (after analysis). *Source:* Saul Stimler, *Data Processing Systems: Their Performance, Evaluation, Measurement, and Improvement* (N.J.: Motivational Learning Programs, 1974), p. 63.

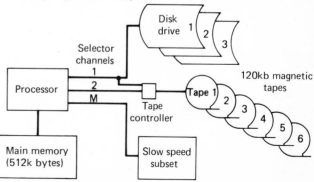

333

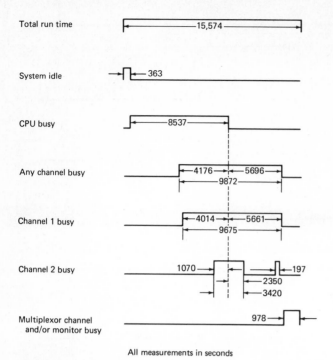

Total run time |—————— 15,574 ——————|

System idle →□—363

CPU busy |————— 8537 —————|

Any channel busy |← 4176 →|← 5696 →|
|————— 9872 —————|

Channel 1 busy |← 4014 →|← 5661 →|
|————— 9675 —————|

Channel 2 busy 1070 →| |← 197
|← 2350 →|
|← 3420 →|

Multiplexor channel and/or monitor busy 978 →□←

All measurements in seconds

ILLUSTRATION 11-30. System Profile (after analysis). *Source:* Saul Stimler, *Data Processing Systems: Their Performance, Evaluation, Measurement, and Improvement* (N.J.: Motivational Learning Programs, 1974), p. 71.

and from 038920 to 03893F. It remains for a programmer to examine the instructions stored at these locations and, if possible, make the instructions more efficient. By isolating the instructions that have the greatest effect on processing time, programmer's time is used efficiently, avoiding any attempt to optimize the instructions in the entire program. Illustration 11-31 shows one bank's experience with program optimization.

Data-set Organization. The goals here are to minimize head movement and disk contention.

When data sets are well organized for an application, head movement is kept to a minimum; however, to minimize head movement requires careful analysis. When two programs are attempting to access a disk drive, disk contention and delays result. Separation of data sets among disk drives permits overlap of data-accessing activities. The trend at most organizations is to store data on disks whenever possible; and the more disks storage is used, the more important is optimization of data-set organization.

Operating Procedures. Performance analysts are accustomed to thinking in terms of paging rates and disk rotation speeds; but they often ignore the more mundane aspects of operating procedures, and these can account for considerable waste. Often, procedures do not exist for assuring readiness of jobs for processing, such as having tapes mounted before a message is issued. CPU time is wasted while the operator mounts the tapes, and wasted time can be considerable if an operator is not immediately available. Time may also be wasted because backup procedures are not defined at all or are poorly defined. Some form of instruction usually exists for preventive maintenance in the hope of lessening downtime, and just as often the instructions are only partly adhered to. It is also likely that none of the above instructions are documented, which increases the probability of operator errors. One final aspect of operating procedures often ignored is the effect poor room layout has on smooth, efficient workflow. Poor workflow causes time to be lost because of excessive walking and excessive cross-traffic. Poor loca-

ILLUSTRATION 11-31. Improvement of Application Programs Resulting from Analysis. *Source:* Louis J. Desiderio, Dennis Saloky, and Arnold Wasserman, *Measuring Computer Performance* for Improvement and Savings, for Coopers & Lybrand, 1974, p. 7.

| | CENTRAL PROCESSING UNIT RUNNING TIME (MINUTES) | | | |
PROGRAM	ORIGINAL	AFTER ANALYSIS	TIME SAVED (MINUTES)	PERCENTAGE IMPROVEMENT FROM ORIGINAL
A	126	72	54	43
B	99	67	32	32
C	148	93	55	37
D	66	32	34	52
E	55	23	32	58
F	57	42	15	26
G	32	21	11	34

WORKLOAD	RESPONSE TIME	THROUGHPUT	% CPU
1 BATCH PROCESSING	151.31 SEC	90. PER HOUR	32.6 %
2 DATA BASE TRANS	22.96 SEC	5500. PER HOUR	31.3 %
3 TIME SHARING USERS	3.82 SEC	3747. PER HOUR	33.3 %
		TOTAL CPU UTILIZATION =	97.3 %

ILLUSTRATION 11-32. Service Effectiveness Summary (when 5500 data base transactions are processed per hour). *Source: Best/1: Computer System Capacity Planning, Release 4.0,* from BGS Systems, manual #BE77-010-2, p. 39.

tion of work tables and storage units such as tape racks results in lost time because of misplaced or inconveniently located materials. One bank discovered that the primary causes of the low (15 percent) CPU activity were excessive I/O setup activity and poor equipment layout.

Before leaving this discussion of performance analysis, it is necessary to realize that analysis is not restricted to improving present performance; it is also used to anticipating degradation of future performance. Changes in technology and workload should be expected, and some means is necessary to predict how performance will be affected. Modeling software such as BGS System's BEST/1 permit these forecasts, and modeling software also permits analysis of these predictions. Thus, it

is possible to obtain answers to two very important types of questions: "What if?" questions and "Why?" questions.

Consider the report in Illustration 11-25. It results from actual processing, where the arrival rate for data-base transactions is 4000 per hour and the resulting average response time for a transaction is 3.17 seconds. The performance analyst may have been informed that a new application will soon be released for production and that the arrival rate is expected to increase to 5500 per hour. The increase does not appear to be threatening performance to a significant degree—but modeling proves this impression false. The analyst uses BEST/1 to answer the question, What if the data-base transaction rate is 5500 per hour? The report

RESPONSE TIME PROFILE (IN MSEC) BY WORKLOAD

	WKL 1	WKL 2	WKL 3
MEMORY QUEUE	**********	838.8	221.5
TOTAL IN SYSTEM TIME	133978.6	2329.3	3090.6
TOTAL RESPONSE TIME	133978.6	3168.1	3312.1

SERVER

	WKL 1	WKL 2	WKL 3
1 CPU - 370/168	65681.8	1159.8	1873.1
2 DRUM 1	1410.7	107.0	119.4
3 DRUM 2	3244.4	242.0	292.4
4 TAPE	397.3	0.0	0.0
5 TAPE	500.2	0.0	0.0
6 3350 BATCH	757.8	0.0	0.0
7 3350 BATCH	204.3	0.0	0.0
8 3350 SYSTEM PACK	5865.0	17.1	105.6
9 3350/JESQ	17052.6	0.0	0.0
10 3350/JESQ	17054.4	0.0	0.0
11 3350 SCRATCH	3004.9	79.5	52.3
12 3350 SCRATCH	3012.5	77.2	57.4
13 3350 SWAP	4675.4	231.8	156.4
14 PAGE PACK	4677.1	231.8	156.4
15 3350 USER PACK	1477.6	37.3	277.6
16 3350 USER PACK	1137.0	31.4	0.0
17 3350 USER PACK	1909.0	55.4	0.0
18 3350 USER PACK	1916.5	59.0	0.0

BEST/1>

ILLUSTRATION 11-33. Response Time Profile (when 4000 data base transactions are processed per hour). *Source: Best/1: Computer System Capacity Planning, Release 4.0,* from BGS Systems, manual #BE77-010-2, p. 24.

received is shown in Illustration 11-32. A problem becomes apparent. For the increased rate, the response time can be expected to increase from 3.17 to 22.96 seconds. The next question that must be answered is, Why is response increased so dramatically? The reports in Illustrations 11-33 and 11-34 show the wait time in the various queues for the arrival rates of 4000 and 5500 transactions per hour, as well as for the other workloads. It becomes apparent that the cause of the increased response time is the increased memory wait time. One of the solutions is to allocate more memory to data-base transactions. Various allocations can be simulated, and the optimum chosen.

At the end of the analysis phase of the CPE process, the performance analyst must decide if the findings are adequate to justify conclusions and to permit preparation of recommendations for improvements. If additional analysis is advisable, the first two phases, defining performance criteria and establishing monitoring methodology, are reviewed for adequacy; then phases 3 and 4,

producing performance reports and analyzing performance data, are repeated. If additional analysis is not necessary, the next phase of the CPE process is performed, the documenting of conclusions and recommendations.

Phase 5. Document Conclusions and Recommendations

It is customary for management to receive performance-analysis results once a month, and sometimes each week. It is also definitely recommended that standardized formats be used, in fact, that all performance information, conclusions, and recommendations be entered on forms. The forms should be grouped and introduced by a cover letter, and this cover letter should indicate the main points to be stressed, particularly any existing or potential problems. The method of actually presenting the information in this report is now separated according to the three categories of performance criteria: resource sufficiency, processing efficiency, and processing effectiveness.

```
                RESPONSE TIME PROFILE (IN MSEC) BY WORKLOAD


                               WKL   1      WKL   2     WKL   3

MEMORY QUEUE                 **********    20438.5      327.2
TOTAL IN SYSTEM TIME          151313.1      2523.4     3492.8

TOTAL RESPONSE TIME           151313.1     22961.8     3820.1

SERVER

   1 CPU - 370/168            82442.4       1325.4     2248.3
   2 DRUM 1                    1481.0        108.5      121.2
   3 DRUM 2                    3579.6        252.8      310.5
   4 TAPE                       399.9          0.0        0.0
   5 TAPE                       503.2          0.0        0.0
   6 3350 BATCH                 761.9          0.0        0.0
   7 3350 BATCH                 205.7          0.0        0.0
   8 3350 SYSTEM PACK          5835.9         16.8      101.4
   9 3350/JESQ                16514.5          0.0        0.0
  10 3350/JESQ                16516.2          0.0        0.0
  11 3350 SCRATCH              3109.2         79.7       52.4
  12 3350 SCRATCH              3113.1         77.4       57.4
  13 3350 SWAP                 5131.7        240.0      165.8
  14 PAGE PACK                 5133.5        240.0      165.8
  15 3350 USER PACK            1488.8         37.3      270.0
  16 3350 USER PACK            1159.0         31.2        0.0
  17 3350 USER PACK            1963.4         55.3        0.0
  18 3350 USER PACK            1974.3         59.0        0.0
BEST/1>
```

ILLUSTRATION 11-34. Response Time Profile (when 5500 data base transactions are processed per hour). *Source: manual #BE77-010-2,* p. 39.

| Computer Utilization | | | | | | | | | | | System 1 ID | System 2 ID | Date |

		Week ending										Monthly totals	
Productive (meter hrs.)		System 1	System 2	System 1	System 2	System 1	System 2	System 1	System 2	System 1	System 2	System 1	System 2
Applications	Scheduled												
	Non-scheduled												
Testing	Applications												
	Data center												
Other													
	Total hrs.												
Non-prod. non-controllable (clock hrs.)													
Misplaced jobs													
Source data errors													
Data preparation errors													
Program errors													
Operator errors													
Other													
	Total hrs.												
Non-prod. controllable (clock hrs.)													
Hardware failures													
System softwares errors													
Power failures													
Enviornment (fires, etc.)													
Maintenance	Scheduled												
	Non-scheduled												
Other													
	Total hrs.												
Total (prod. and non-prod.)													

ILLUSTRATION 11-35. Detailed Computer Utilization Report.

Resource-sufficiency Information. Consider the criterion of availability. Management wants to know the length of time the computer was available and for what part of that time it was used for production. Management also wants to know how unproductive time was consumed. A report such as that shown in Illustration 11-35 satisfies these needs. This report permits weekly summary information for two systems and also provides for a monthly summary. It may be adequate as shown, but naturally it must be modified if only one system exists or if more than two systems exist. It must also be modified if daily entries are wanted instead of weekly entries. Although considerable information can be contained on a report of this type, the trend of actual usage is not likely to be apparent. Therefore, for the purpose of stressing usage trends, a form such as the one shown in Illustration 11-36 is useful. The trend for the available hours used productively becomes immediately apparent. The chart can show reasonably constant good or poor productive values, or it can show improving or degrading performance. Other plots can be drawn on this chart, such as those for the available time used for program testing and for maintenance.

The second criterion for resource sufficiency is adequacy of CPU capacity. Illustration 11-37 is an excellent method of relating actual and projected workload demands to current capacity and planned capacity upgrading. The two curves indicate projected high and low workload demands. The horizontal "current capacity" line indicates that toward the middle of 1979 the current capac-

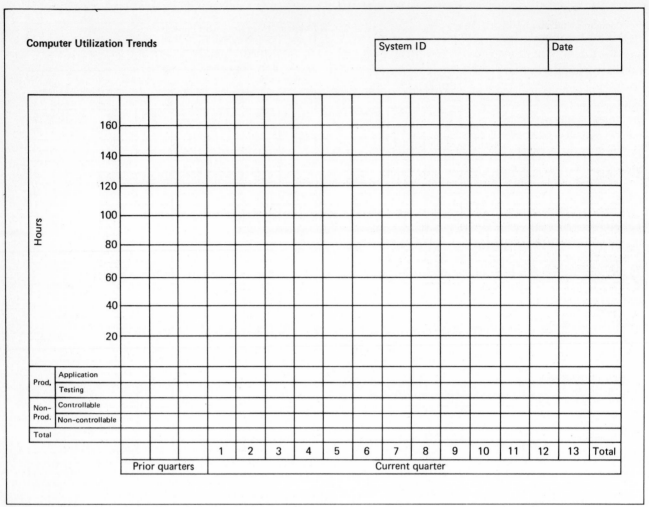

Computer Utilization Trends

System ID

Date

Hours						1	2	3	4	5	6	7	8	9	10	11	12	13	Total
160																			
140																			
120																			
100																			
80																			
60																			
40																			
20																			

Prod.	Application			
	Testing			
Non-Prod.	Controllable			
	Non-controllable			
Total				

Prior quarters Current quarter

ILLUSTRATION 11-36. Trend-Oriented Computer Utilization Report.

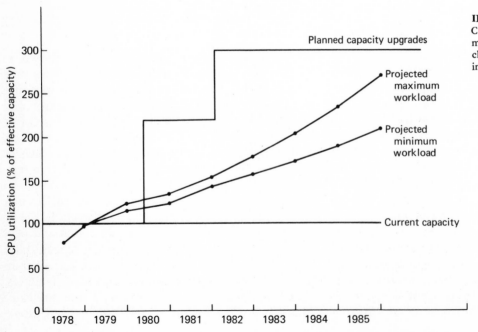

Planned capacity upgrades

Projected maximum workload

Projected minimum workload

Current capacity

CPU utilization (% of effective capacity)

1978 1979 1980 1981 1982 1983 1984 1985

ILLUSTRATION 11-37. Workload/Capacity Chart: Anticipated minimum and maximum workloads are charted, and so are the planned increments for CPU capacity.

ity will be exceeded by the workload demands, and that inadequate capacity will exist until the middle of 1980, when the system will be upgraded. To avoid future capacity inadequacy, another upgrade is planned for the beginning of 1982. This chart presents a considerable amount of information in a form that is extremely clear and that supports management's discussions and decision-making.

Processing-efficiency Information. Various schemes have been used to present the rather technical information associated with this category. But most of it is of little use to management, particularly in the tedious manner usually presented. The most successful method of presenting some of this information is through the use of what has become known as *Kiviat graphs.* Four Kiviat graphs are shown in Illustration 11–38. Once management and staff become accustomed to these graphs,

ILLUSTRATION 11-38. Kiviat Graphs: These graphs quickly present performance information; they permit visual identification of performance characteristics and permit quick comparison with previous performance graphs. *Source:* Copyright 1973 CW Communications/Inc., Framingham, MA 01701. Reprinted from Computerworld, October 3, 1973.

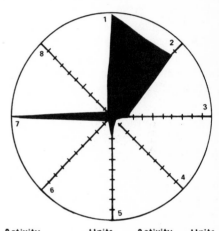

Activity	Units (%)	Activity	Units (%)
1 CPU Active	91	2 CPU Only	6
3 CPU/Chan O'lap	85	4 Chan Only	7
5 Any Chan Busy	92	6 CPU Wait	7
7 Problem State	78	8 Sup. State	13

Figure 1. A "Fedsim Star"

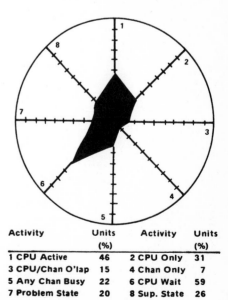

Activity	Units (%)	Activity	Units (%)
1 CPU Active	98	2 CPU Only	84
3 CPU/Chan O'lap	14	4 Chan Only	2
5 Any Chan Busy	16	6 CPU Wait	2
7 Problem State	97	8 Sup. State	1

Figure 2. The CPU Sailboat

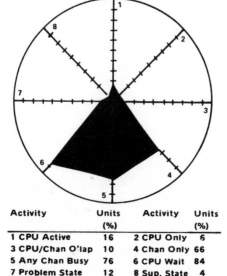

Activity	Units (%)	Activity	Units (%)
1 CPU Active	16	2 CPU Only	6
3 CPU/Chan O'lap	10	4 Chan Only	66
5 Any Chan Busy	76	6 CPU Wait	84
7 Problem State	12	8 Sup. State	4

Figure 3. The I/O Wedge

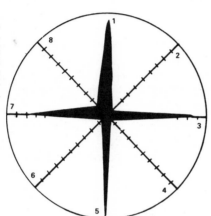

Activity	Units (%)	Activity	Units (%)
1 CPU Active	46	2 CPU Only	31
3 CPU/Chan O'lap	15	4 Chan Only	7
5 Any Chan Busy	22	6 CPU Wait	59
7 Problem State	20	8 Sup. State	26

Figure 4. The Wait Leg

variations from what is the customary performance pattern become apparent at a glance. Undesirable and desirable performance patterns can be quickly identified. The first graph, "Fedsim Star," is an ideal performance pattern. It shows high CPU and program activity and high CPU/channel overlap. The second graph, "CPU Sailboat," indicates high CPU and program activity, but extremely low channel activity—in other words a CPU-bound system. In contrast, the third graph, "I/O Wedge," indicates an I/O-bound system, with high channel activity and high CPU waiting. The last graph, "Wait Leg," shows excessive CPU waiting and low CPU and channel activity.

Kiviat graphs are excellent for presenting the information shown, but it is likely that a performance analyst will have to supplement this graph with additional information. Management may want to judge performance by examining such criteria as multiprogramming factor, paging rate, the number of reruns, the number if IPLs, the number of operator errors, and the amount of delay because of program errors and inefficiencies. It may be necessary to prepare a special form for the additional information wanted by management—in fact, as already enthusiastically recommended, a form should always be used.

Processing-effectiveness Information. This is the information that management is most often concerned about, especially if the data center receives complaints about excessive response time or poor off-line batch-processing turnaround. Poor turnaround may have led to missed deadlines and possibly to fines or lost business. Therefore, management will definitely look closely at the throughput, turnaround, and response-time information provided. The form in Illustration 11–39 provides this information for three shifts. It is necessary to recall that CPE considers throughput and turnaround information only for processing in the computer room, and not for processing in the data center. Data center effectiveness information is considered in the next chapter, which will focus

ILLUSTRATION 11–39. Summary Report of Computer Service Effectiveness.

		Throughput			Turnaround			Response time								
Month	Week							< 3			≥ 3 and ≤ 8			> 8		
		Shift 1	Shift 2	Shift 3	S 1	S 2	S 3	S 1	S 2	S 3	S 1	S 2	S 3	S 1	S 2	S 3
	1															
	2															
	3															
	4															
	5															
	1															
	2															
	3															
	4															
	5															
	1															
	2															
	3															
	4															
	5															
Quarterly averages																

Computer Service Effectiveness Report

on the meeting of schedules and on the turnaround of unscheduled jobs through the data center. With all the information presented to management, most of the performance analyst's conclusions may be obvious to management, but still they have to be stated.

As in the case of obtaining approval for the CPE program, recommendations must be viewed from the perspective of management. It is necessary to be able to provide data to justify conclusions and recommendations, but it is also necessary to state these conclusions and the results of implementing or not implementing the recommendations in terms that they can relate to, specifically, in terms of dollar savings and service improvements. Merely stating that efficiencies will result is not adequate. This type of presentation, although consisting of considerable amounts of details, can be expected to appear abstract and distantly related to the welfare of the data center and its users.

In presenting recommendations, the best, but infrequently used, approach is similar to that used for zero-base budgeting. This approach consists of stating the alternative approaches, and stating for each alternative the costs to implement, the results if not implemented, and the benefits if implemented; finally, the alternative approaches are ranked, with the recommended approach ranked first. This information should be expressed clearly, directly, and succinctly, leaving no doubts as to what is being recommended and why. Too often, the heavy underbrush of verbiage disguises an otherwise excellent recommendation; and when this occurs, management may put the recommendation aside until it can be translated into intelligible terms—which may never happen.

Phase 6: Implement Improvements

It now remains to implement the recommended improvements—once they have been accepted and officially approved. Actual implementation is usually straightforward, since the changes required usually involve adding, modifying, or removing equipment; thus implementation is not a long-term activity requiring project planning and control.

What must be considered, however, are the effects implementation of recommendations will have on the criteria used, the methodology followed, and the reports prepared. The criteria may be affected because they may have to be modified, possibly by deleting or adding new criteria. For example, the original criteria may not have included close attention to the number of reruns and their causes. But analysis may have shown that reruns are causing a significant waste of resources. Thus, it will be necessary to add this criterion to those already existing. It is also possible that implemented performance improvements are expected to permit more stringent standards for performance criteria. This is true, for example, if it is anticipated that response time may be reduced (possibly for 90 percent of the responses) from 6 seconds to 4 seconds.

Changes in criteria often require changes in methodology. It is necessary to modify methodology to collect data for any new criteria. In the past, operators may not have been required to comment on the cause of reruns, for example, even if only to state that the cause has not been identified. But if improvements include minimizing the number of reruns, close attention to these incidents requires procedural changes to gather the new information. Another change required in methodology is the ability to verify the occurrence of the improvements anticipated; if these improvements do not occur, means must be available to isolate the causes of these failures.

Closely related to changes in methodology are changes in reporting. It is usually necessary to change the content and format of computer-generated reports and manually prepared forms to display the information required because of changes to the criteria or the methodology. Some information may be added, some may be deleted, and other information may be presented in a different manner. For example, instead of presenting information in abstract-appearing tables, it may be desirable to present actual performance as percentages of deviations from goals, or to present this information in graphs, making deviations and trends more apparent.

GOAL

To be aware of all data center activities, and to control data center performance.

HIGHLIGHTS

Micro- and Macroperformance Evaluation

Microperformance evaluation, like micro-scheduling, is restricted to computer processing; macroperformance evaluation, like macro-scheduling, extends to include all data center activities.

Information on All Activities

The information gathered should include the information related to:

- Organization structure
- Management
- Personnel
- Finances
- Site
- Security and safety
- Hardware and software acquisition
- Standards and procedures
- Workflow
- Scheduling and resource allocation
- Data communications
- User relationships
- Vendor relationships

Information for Management

Although sometimes interested in detailed reports, data center and user managers are primarily interested in summary and exception reports on:

- Resources sufficiency
- User service
- Cost control

This is the most important chapter in this book. All of the other chapters recommend policies, guidelines, and techniques. This chapter is concerned with all that has been recommended, with the performance of all aspects of the data center. Data-center-performance evaluation (DCPE) should make apparent any deficiencies in the data center and should highlight any aspects not receiving adequate attention. Some data centers, for example, give considerable thought to security, but none to personnel career paths or to chargeback of data center expenses to users. In other words, some aspects of the data center receive considerable attention, some receive minimal attention, and the rest receive no attention. The proportions vary from one installation to the next. In this respect, each data center has its own personality of admirable virtues and embarrassing vices.

A data center manager who does not see the actual data center activities, who receives inadequate information about data center performance, is like a person separated from reality by a solid, obstructing brick wall. As an increasing amount of activity and performance information becomes available, however, it is as if a hole in that brick wall is being widened, until the time when a DCPE program has been implemented and is adequate, and the brick wall no longer exists. Vision becomes unhampered, attainment of standards becomes possible, and progressive breakthroughs to higher levels of performance can be controlled. The sad fact is that a brick wall does not physically exist, and hindered perception and insight is often ignored.

Another analogy will further clarify the situation in many data centers. If the health of a data center is compared to that of a human being, monitoring will probably uncover various illnesses, possibly some requiring intensive care. Serious deficiencies, possibly requiring intensive care, include waste of data center resources, degradation of user service, and unnecessary data center costs. Other serious deficiencies are excessive downtime, poor data security, and high personnel turnover. It is likely that some of these and other deficiencies can justify continual activity and performance monitoring, similar to that used for patients in a hospital's intensive care ward. Once the deficiencies are corrected and operations are under control,

less-frequent and less-intensive monitoring will be adequate.

With adequate monitoring and control, it is possible to restore a data center's health. Without any monitoring and control, a data center's health is not a matter of luck—it is certain to become and remain ill.

The obvious benefits of data processing to an organization, and the enthusiasm that results, paradoxically, have been detrimental to data center efficiency and effectiveness. A statement that concisely states this situation is:

> In many cases, the initial benefits have been impressive and the cost savings clearly identifiable. Early successes provided additional momentum to the rapid growth in EDP usage. Unfortunately, this rapid growth has frequently been accompanied by a decline in efficiency, cost effectiveness, and responsiveness to the users of data processing systems.[1]

The concern about data center deficiencies is widespread. As would be expected, the United States government, one of the biggest users of data processing, is very concerned. The government has examined and reported on the effectiveness of its data-processing operations. In a GAO (General Accounting Office) report entitled "Computer Auditing in the Executive Departments: Not Enough is Being Done," costly wastes resulting from inadequate monitoring are mentioned. In an article commenting on some of these inadequacies, the concluding remark is, "In summary, too little, too casual, and if we don't get some action, it will be too late."[2] With an adequate DCPE program, action will not be too little or too casual—and hopefully not too late.

MICRO- AND MACROPERFORMANCE EVALUATION

Attention is often centered on processing in the computer room, with data center personnel considering the processing that occurs before and after

---

[1] Joe E. Kasparek and Richard C. LaVelle, "Evaluating EDP Operations Performance," *The Arthur Anderson Chronicle*, April 1976, p. 63.

[2] Walter L. Anderson, "The General Accounting Office's Recent Work on Federal ADP Policies," *Computers and People*, May 1978, p. 21.

relatively unimportant. The unacceptability of this view becomes particularly apparent when job-turnaround objectives are set, and then actual performance is measured. In an industrial engineer's study of one data center, which is representative of most data centers, it was concluded that the average turnaround for a job was 14.8 hours, which conflicted with the agreed-upon maximum turnaround of 6 hours.[3] The activities accounting for the 14.8-hour average, stated in approximate percentages of the total time, are:

    20% in input
     3% in spool-in
     1% in the CPU
     3% in spool-out
    73% in delivery

Illustration 12-1 portrays this distribution of time consumption. Obviously, postprocessing is the primary bottleneck and preprocessing is the secondary bottleneck. Without this analysis of time consumption for the average job, the conclusion might be, as it often is, to upgrade the computer. But as the analysis shows, the real problem is a production problem of moving jobs into and out of the data center. The solution may be as simple as ob-

[3] Jim Garrett, "Data Center Schedulers," *Guide 46 Proceedings,* Florida, May 21–26, 1978, p. 336.

ILLUSTRATION 12-1. Distribution of a Job's Time Consumption: Most of a batch job's time is often consumed in pre-computer and post-computer processing. *Source:* Jim Garrett, "Data Center Schedulers," *Guide 46 Proceedings,* Florida, May 21–26, 1978, p. 344.

WORK FLOW ANALYSIS

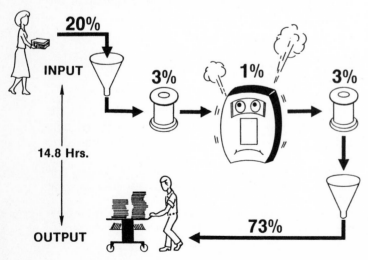

taining more delivery carts, or not much more difficult, to obtain more personnel and to improve receipt and delivery procedures.

This example makes it apparent that interest should not be restricted to the computer room, but must include all data center activities. Microperformance optimization of computer processing is ineffective when macroperformance optimization of data center processing is ignored.

Performance criteria for computer processing are segmented in the previous chapter into three categories: sufficiency, efficiency, and effectiveness. These three categories can also be applied to performance criteria for data center evaluation. Illustration 12-2 lists the primary criteria in these three categories for both computer and data center evaluation. Whereas resource availability and resource adequacy are limited to computer-room resources for CPE, all precomputer and postcomputer resources are included in DCPE. Thus, the adequacy, for example, of data-entry and report-bursting equipment and personnel are considered, including the occurrences of peak-activity and slack-activity time periods. It is therefore clear how the category of sufficiency is easily extended to apply the availability and adequacy criteria to data center performance. In a similar manner, turnaround time, which is a resource-efficiency criterion, is extended to include all data center processing; that is, the total processing time for a job includes all activities from job receipt to job pickup or distribution. As for effective use of resources, where, for example, application wastefulness for CPE was limited to program-coding problems that caused processing inefficiency, errors, and delays, DCPE also considers such factors as input format, from which the data can be prepared either haltingly or speedily, with numerous errors or with few. DCPE also evaluates output usage; it considers whether output can be reduced or eliminated, whether copies can be eliminated, and whether microfilm or microfiche can be used.

Illustration 12-2 shows that several critical criteria are added to the categories of efficiency and effectiveness. These include analysis of how data center expenses are allocated and the use of a chargeback system to recover expenses from users. The effectiveness criteria added are data accuracy, data security, error detection, and coordination between the user and data center personnel. It is necessary to evaluate the ability of

	SUFFICIENCY (Resources vs. workload)	EFFICIENCY (Use of resources)	EFFECTIVENESS (Production of results)
CPE (computer performance evaluation)	Availability Adequacy	Resource utilization Processing wastefulness Application wastefulness (coding inefficiencies, errors, and delays)	Throughput Turnaround Response time
DCPE (data center performance evaluation)	Availability Adequacy	Resource utilization Costs Application wastefulness (input format and output usage)	Meeting scheduled deadlines Turnaround for unscheduled jobs Response time for online jobs Data security Data accuracy Error detection User/data center coordination

ILLUSTRATION 12–2. CPE and DCPE Criteria.

data center personnel to detect errors and to locate the sources of these errors. It is also the obligation of data center personnel to do what is within their power to protect the users' data and to coordinate activities with users. Opportunities for coordination have already been mentioned; they include the existence of a data center steering committee, a user help desk, and a data center newsletter.

The DCPE process, as is to be expected, is identical with that presented for CPE. However, three serious questions do arise. How can personnel be found to adequately evaluate the entire data center? How can objective evaluation be obtained? How can user acceptance of performance standards be obtained?

Overall Knowledgeability

To obtain personnel with the varied background needed to obtain dependable evaluations on all data center criteria and activities, it is often necessary to hire outside consultants who have specialized in evaluation of data center performance. Since DCPEs do not have to be done as often as CPEs, this policy is acceptable and the cost can be justified. In fact, the cost may be less than when using in-house personnel, because a specialist is likely to be more efficient. But the important point is that the evaluation will have considerably more credibility.

One approach to in-house evaluation of data

center activities and performance has been effective. A team of knowledgeable persons is formed from one or more divisions to evaluate another division's data center. The team often consists of three persons. Obviously, this can be done only by an organization with several divisions and with knowledgeable persons at these divisions who can evaluate the entire data center.

Objectivity of Judgment.

The solution for obtaining objectivity of judgment is the same as for obtaining overall knowledgeability: use either outside consultants or use a team formed of personnel from other divisions in the organization. If a staff person working in a data center evaluates that data center's activities and recommends changes, there is always concern about "making waves" and sacrificing promotions, possibly even resulting in loss of the performance analyst's job. There should never be fear of this. The goal of the analysis and the resulting evaluation is not to criticize and place blame, but to focus on the positive aspects of recommending improvements, not to be a threat to anyone. This is another reason for using an independent team or hiring an outside consultant. They are trained to bolster the egos and to improve procedures of data center personnel. They seek means to improve without creating new problems.

If, however, it is decided to use in-house personnel, they should be trained to locate deficiencies and to focus on corrective measures, not on condemning anyone. In addition to being trained in the basics of performance evaluation, they should keep well informed of the latest thinking in the performance-evaluation field. To accomplish this, they should read the reports of (or actually be members of) ACM's SIGMETRICS and the government's CPEUG (Computer Performance Evaluation Users Group). A basic publication that should be received (which has been already mentioned several times) is the *EDP Performance Review* newsletter.

User Acceptance of Standards

If data center personnel state the user-related performance standards without prior discussions with user department representatives, user dissatisfaction is almost certain. Without these discussions, users will not understand the thinking that led to the standards, and they may consider the standards unnecessarily conservative. But if they are involved in establishing and later evaluating these standards, they will not have a feeling of impotency, and they will realize that data center personnel are concerned about meeting reasonable standards.

There are several hindrances to conducting an evaluation or to implementing improvements:

1. *Threat of adverse evaluation.* Data center personnel will be reluctant to cooperate if they believe that they will be blamed or will suffer from an evaluation. Supervisors may believe that procedural and operating problems may reflect on their ability to direct, coordinate, and control. They should be assured that the objectives are to uncover deficiencies for improvement and to discover opportunities for improvements even if performance is satisfactory. In a similar manner, staff should be asked to cooperate in improving performance as well as their work conditions and data center activities in general. The stress must always be on seeking improvements, not on condemning individuals.

2. *Problems ignored until they become critical.* There is a tendency to ignore minor problems, even though they have the potential of becoming serious. Just as ignored low oil pressure in a car's engine can lead to expensive repairs and a long period of downtime, so can ignored data center problems. For example, the absence of sufficient documentation for processing applications may require some guessing and careful attention from computer opera-

tors who are familiar with the applications. But if these experienced operators are not available, it may be impossible to execute some or most of the jobs, and those that are executed may be executed improperly, possibly even destroying or corrupting data files. The moral is that minor deficiencies, especially those that can become disruptive or expensive, should not be casually ignored.

3. *Optimizing one criterion may degrade others.* As shown in Illustration 12-3, increase in production goals (throughput) or implementation of cost-reduction strategies is likely to deteriorate quality or to increase the number of errors made and the number of delays that result. On the other hand, the addition of quality-checking functions inevitably improves quality, but it also increases processing costs and processing time. Another example may be useful. Illustration 12-4 indicates the tradeoff between resource utilization and user service. As resource utilization increases, the cost per unit of utilization decreases—and so does user service. The chart indicates that there is a point where user service remains excellent while resource utilization is fairly good, although in this chart it does appear lower than acceptable. So if an analyst focuses on optimizing resource utilization, forgetting user service, service may become merely acceptable or even unacceptable. If, instead, attention is focused on service, resources will be underutilized and the data center expenses will be unnecessarily high.

4. *Local optimizing may degrade overall performance.* Performance improvement is the goal, but performance in one part of a data center may lessen the overall performance of the data center. This fault occurs most frequently with efficiency improvements in computer processing. Often, in an effort to process as many jobs as possible in a time period (to optimize throughput), job priorities and deadlines are partially ignored and output accumulates for postcomputer processing; this accumulated work tends to be processed according to its proximity to equipment and personnel and not according to its priorities and deadlines. The result is that, although computer throughput may be impressive, user service suffers.

5. *Blind adherence to the KISS rule.* Any time complexity exists, it should be investigated. This is the essence of the KISS (Keep It Simple, Stupid) rule. But sometimes complexity is necessary and must be accepted. In these situations attempts to simplify may lead to uncertain performance and confusion, and ultimately to reduced user service. For example, a complex procedure may be necessary for accepting and putting into production a new application system. This is a procedure that is often kept too simple, with inadequate safeguards, resulting in excessive mistakes and disagreements between data center and

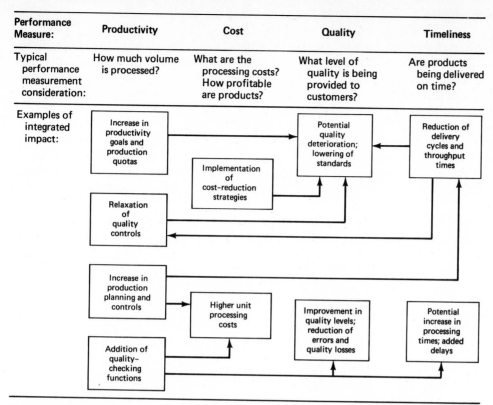

Performance Measure:	Productivity	Cost	Quality	Timeliness
Typical performance measurement consideration:	How much volume is processed?	What are the processing costs? How profitable are products?	What level of quality is being provided to customers?	Are products being delivered on time?

ILLUSTRATION 12–3. The Interrelationship of Criteria: Improvement of one criterion can deteriorate other criteria. *Source:* Roger G. Langevin, *Quality Control in the Service* Industries (N.Y.: Amacom, 1977), p. 33. © 1977 by AMACOM, a division of American Management Associations. All rights reserved.

ILLUSTRATION 12–4. Utilization-Service Tradeoff: As utilization of resources increase, cost per unit of utilization decreases and service degenerates. *Source:* Joe E. Kasparek and Richard C. LaVelle, "Evaluating EDP Operations Performance," *The Arthur Anderson Chronicle,* April 1976, p. 65.

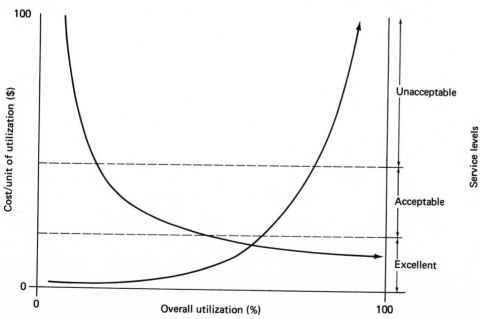

systems-development personnel. No matter how complex a procedure may have to be, it can always be segmented into several simple segments, and this is what should be done instead of obtaining a single simple procedure.

6. *No funding for "subtle" improvements.* Often a performance analyst can only comment that improvements can be expected if, for example, a software package is obtained and applied. It may be a package to analyze disk-arm movement, paging activity, or data-entry productivity. In other instances, time and money expenditures may be necessary to obtain expected long-term benefits. The only reasonable attitude that management can take is that if the recommendation results from sound analysis, and if it does not merely involve an interesting technique, faith should be placed in the analyst.

INFORMATION ON ALL ACTIVITIES

In addition to evaluating performance, it is also necessary to consider the adequacy of all data center activities. In effect, this means considering all aspects discussed in the preceding chapters. Briefly, some of the activities to be judged are:

- *Organization structure.* Are its objectives clearly stated? Does it function with adequate direction, coordination, and control?
- *Management.* Is a stimulating, goal-oriented environment provided? Is there trust and rapport between management and staff?
- *Personnel.* Do job descriptions and career paths exist? Are there procedures for personnel recruiting, preparation of training programs, personal motivation, and personnel-performance evaluation? Are these documented?
- *Finances.* Is budgetary control adequate? Has a chargeback system been considered? Have financial alternatives been analyzed?
- *Site.* Have criteria been identified for a satisfactory site? Is it adequately prepared?
- *Security and safety.* Have preventative and detection precautions been taken? Is there adequate insurance? Are there contingency plans?
- *Hardware and software.* Is there a comprehensive proposal-evaluation procedure? Are thorough financial analyses performed? Is contract negotiation performed with adequate care?
- *Standards and procedures.* Are standards and procedures complete, clear, and concise? Are they documented?

- *Workflow.* Can the status of all jobs be reported in a timely manner? Are all jobs controlled?
- *Scheduling and resource allocation.* Are all data center activities scheduled? Are peak and slack periods minimized?
- *Data communications.* Is it monitored adequately? Is there adequate backup? Is access to links secured?
- *Computer-performance evaluation.* Are sufficient data collected and analyzed? Are the analyses acted upon?
- *User relationships.* Do user and data personnel understand and appreciate one another's problems? Is there satisfactory coordination and rapport?
- *Vendor relationships.* Do vendors cooperate in resolving problems? Do they respond quickly to service calls? Is their service satisfactory?

The preceding considerations are only a few of the highlights from the various chapters. More thorough checklists can be tailored for each installation. The data center evaluation checklist in Appendix L can be tailored to the particular needs at an installation. Each section of this checklist corresponds to a chapter in this book. Since this checklist includes evaluation of all data center activities, a more encompassing phrase than "data-center-performance evaluation" may therefore be appropriate, such as "data center auditing" or "data center appraisal."

Rapport with users requires some more comment. If user satisfaction is not actively evaluated, the only time the data center manager will become aware of dissatisfaction is when user complaints have reached a critical point. The damage is done. Complaints are made, and rapport is lost. A data center manager should be concerned about user satisfaction and rapport not only to fulfill service obligations, but also for self-protection. Users have been known not to communicate their discontent, but instead to silently collect damaging statistics. Sometimes these secretive activities result from deep concern, and sometimes from personal insecurity or maliciousness. The best self-protection is awareness of user service problems, the maintenance of communication with users, and the development of rapport.

The best means for stimulating rapport between user departments and the data center is for the data center manager to periodically visit the user departments. Many data center managers have been shocked when their devotion to data center activities was interpreted as indifference to user problems.

Some organizations assure awareness of user attitudes towards the data center by periodically submitting a questionnaire to each user department. The responses to this questionnaire confirm or disprove what data center management believes their attitudes to be, and just as important, they call attention to problems that may not have been apparent or may not have appeared significant. The questionnaire need not be complex. It can merely require checkmarks for various statements in several categories, where a checkmark can be entered to indicate ratings such as excellent, above average, average, below average, and poor. The categories for the statements requiring responses can include those for timeliness, reliability, availability, competency, cost-effectiveness, coordination and communication, and responsiveness. Some of the statements that should be present are:

- Awareness of data-processing costs
- Control over your expenses
- Explanation received of data center services
- Types of services provided
- Understanding of data center structure
- Accuracy of reports
- Accuracy of reports one year ago
- Timely receipt of reports
- Assistance from data center personnel
- Knowledgeability of data center personnel
- Responsiveness of data center personnel
- General satisfaction

One of the major concerns is how to eliminate wasteful reports. What reports are not needed as often as received? What reports are not needed at all? Can copies of reports be eliminated? Data center managers suspect, and systems analysts know, that reports are frequently received by the pound by personnel who merely store them away; personnel often receive reports because of an old, obsolete procedure and sometimes receive reports for prestige. A means must be found to uncover these wastes of data center resources and time. Report-usage questionnaires such as the one in Illustration 12-5 are valuable. This questionnaire is particularly comprehensive, but simpler ones can be prepared. If a report and a number of copies are needed, an attempt should be made to substitute summary and exception reports for

detailed reports, and to substitute microfiche for paper. It is always interesting to trace reports to departments and to observe how they are used—or not used. It is sometimes discovered that the reports have been delivered to the wrong department and that this has been occurring for a long time. Some installations discontinue delivery of reports to uncover who is actually waiting for them. Unfortunately, many individuals wait for a report even though they have no practical use for it, except to put it in a binder or to file it away.

Another interesting questionnaire is one that requests user forecasts of their workloads. Illustration 12-6 shows such a questionnaire, which also includes space for users to indicate the performance standards desired for service criteria. The information users supply may be reasonable or unreasonable, but in either case it provides a basis for discussion. Furthermore, the data center manager's interest in discussing these issues should convince users of sincere concern in satisfying user requirements. Instead of opponents differing on what can be done, the atmosphere becomes one of user and data center personnel working side by side in providing the best service possible within the limits of the available resources or the resources to be obtained.

INFORMATION FOR MANAGEMENT

Data center managers are naturally interested in information on the adequacy of, and adherence to, data center policies and procedures. As stated earlier, this would require information on a diverse number of activities, such as personnel career paths, data center workflow, and job scheduling. However, there is information of interest to both data center and user managers. Just as data center managers are interested in resource utilization, so are users. Users want to know if resources are adequate for their workload, and they also want to know if waste of resources is affecting service. More directly, users are concerned about the actual service received. They are concerned about meeting deadlines for scheduled jobs, receiving reasonably quick turnaround for unscheduled jobs, obtaining satisfactory response time for on-line jobs, and receiving error-free output. Finally, users should be as concerned as data center managers about the cost of data center processing. They are likely to

PDC REPORT USER QUESTIONNAIRE

SEE INSTRUCTIONS ON REVERSE PRIOR TO COMPLETION

POSTAL DATA CENTER - *Complete Items 1 through 9)*

1 *a.* REPORT TITLE

b. COPY NO.

2. PDC PREPARING

3. REPORT NO. AT PDC

4. PROGRAM NO.

5. RUN NO.

6. DATE DUE OUT

7. ATLANTA PDC STUDY SYSTEMS DOCUMENTATION "PROCESS" NO.

8. TIME MANAGEMENT SYSTEM "WORK ASSIGNMENT" CODE *(If known)*

9. FREQUENCY *(A/P, Monthly, etc.)*

RECIPIENTS OF PDC REPORTS – *(Complete Items 10 through 24)*

10. BY WHAT OTHER TITLES *(If any)* IS THIS REPORT KNOWN

11. IS IT RECEIVED ON TIME
- ☐ ALWAYS
- ☐ USUALLY
- ☐ SELDOM

12. TRANSMITTAL USED
- ☐ ROUTE SLIP
- ☐ MEMO
- ☐ OTHER *(Specify)*

13. HOW IS THIS REPORT USED

14. IS THE INFORMATION CURRENT ENOUGH FOR THIS PURPOSE
- ☐ YES
- ☐ NO

15. *a.* WOULD ANOTHER FREQUENCY FOR THIS REPORT BE PREFERABLE *(If "Yes," Specify)*[1] ☐ YES ☐ NO

15 *b.* SHOULD IT BE ISSUED ON AN "EXCEPTION" BASIS *(If "Yes," State basis)* ☐ YES ☐ NO

16. IS THE AMOUNT OF THE INFORMATION
- ☐ ADEQUATE
- ☐ INADEQUATE
- ☐ MORE THAN ADEQUATE

17. WHAT DATA ELEMENTS SHOULD BE ADDED TO IMPROVE THIS REPORT[2]

18. WHAT DATA ELEMENTS SHOULD BE REMOVED

19. WHAT DATA ELEMENTS IN THIS REPORT ARE DUPLICATED IN OTHER REPORTS

a. DATA ELEMENTS

b. REPORTS

20. IS THERE DISAGREEMENT OR CONFUSION ABOUT THE MEANING OF ANY OF THE DATA ELEMENTS *(If "Yes," identify elements and explain)*
- ☐ YES
- ☐ NO

21. HOW LONG DO YOU KEEP THIS COPY

22. LIST BELOW OTHER REPORTS PREPARED FROM THIS REPORT COPY

TITLE	REPORT NO. *(If any)*	FREQUENCY	REFERENCE TO DIRECTIVE	
			ESTABLISHING REPORT	WITH PREPARATION INSTRUCTIONS

23. OTHER USERS OF THIS COPY *(Name, Title, Organization and City)*

24. PREPARED BY *(Printed Name & Title)*

ORGANIZATION

CITY

[1] *If you are recommending another frequency, distinguish between such periods as calendar year, fiscal year and postal fiscal year. If this report should be issued only when some event occurs, or some limits are exceeded, describe the event or circumstances that should trigger the issuance.*

[2] *A data element is defined by the Bureau of the Budget as "a grouping of informational units which has a unique meaning based on a natural or assigned relationship and subcategories (data items) of distinct units or values." For example, "month" is a data element whose data items are "January," "February," etc.*

ILLUSTRATION 12–5a. Report Usage Questionnaire (front of form). *Source:* U.S. Post Office.

INSTRUCTIONS

In an effort to improve the usefulness of reports produced by the Data Centers, a study of current reports and users' requirements is being conducted. This questionnaire is intended to give every user of reports from PDC's an opportunity to comment on their content, format, frequency, other characteristics and to suggest improvements. In addition, some users will be contacted personally concerning certain reports. PDC's should complete items 1 through 9 and recipients of PDC reports should complete the balance and return this form to their PDC. If additional space is required continue in the Remarks item.

RETURN TO:

ILLUSTRATION 12-5b. Report Usage Questionnaire (back of form).

User Workload Forecast Worksheet

Application _____ Forecast units _____ Charge no. _____

Function / Volume	Jan	Feb	Mar	Apr	May	Jun	Jul	Aug	Sep	Oct	Nov	Dec	Total
Input handling													
Data preparation													
Machine services													
Output handling													

Time per unit

Forecast unit found in

Job name _____ Step name _____ Dataset name _____

Service level requirements

Timeliness

Prime shift

Turnaround time		
High	Norm	O'night

Response time	
TSO	IMS

Schedule	
In	Out

Accuracy

Must this application be corrected whenever problems occur? If so, is documentation available to operations

☐ Yes ☐ No

Provide a telephone contact for 24-hour problems resolution if needed

_____

_____

Reliability

Are there any unusual requirements for:

System availability

_____

Backup in case of system failure

_____

Variability in processing times

_____

_____

Cost

How should this application be billed

☐ Fixed fee

☐ Per unit

☐ Resource used

ILLUSTRATION 12–6. User Workload Forecast Worksheet. *Source:* Barry A. Stevens, "CPE Measurement Activities for Data Processing," *EDP Performance Review,* May 1976, p. 3.

be concerned, however, only if a chargeback system exists and they feel the results of inefficiencies and unwarranted user requests.

Illustration 12-7 graphically indicates the three factors that are the basis for users' judgment of a data center. An effective data center is directly dependent on controlled resource sufficiency, controlled user service, and controlled data center costs. The information collected and reported to managers permits these controls, or at least permits awareness of deficiencies so that they can be corrected and then controlled. An effective data center depends on the existence of all three controls. The absence of any one of these controls can greatly reduce, if not cripple, a data center's functioning.

Data center management activities can be effectively viewed as a cycle consisting of planning, processing, and performance evaluation. When these three types of activities are related to the three types of performance criteria, the relationships between the reports received for performance evaluation and the preceding planning and processing activities become clear. For example, forecasts of the adequacy of data-entry equipment are made,

ILLUSTRATION 12-7. Factors of an Effective Data Center.

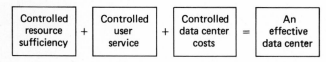

Controlled resource sufficiency + Controlled user service + Controlled data center costs = An effective data center

but monitoring of actual usage may indicate either underutilization or overutilization. Detailed reports are used by the technical staff to prepare summary and exception reports for management. The technical staff also uses the detailed reports to prepare improvement proposals and, if requested, to justify all reports and proposals submitted to management. Thus, the adequacy of data-entry equipment proceeds through all three of the management activities, from forecasting, to monitoring, to evaluating. Illustration 12–8 provides a simplified matrix of data center management activities and user-related performance criteria.

When managers are presented with performance information (particularly user managers), they should receive it in a simplified form and they should receive only that information useful to them. Thus, long tables of data should be avoided; instead, graphs and ratios should be stressed, using tables of data only when they are short. If managers receive too much data, the truly significant

data may not receive adequate attention—in fact, it may not be found. Many managers, however, are accustomed to receiving bulky listings each day. Their devotion and endurance are to be commended, but this policy indicates that little or no analysis of computer-generated data is performed by staff members and it definitely indicates that valuable time is being wasted. In most cases, it is possible to use summary or exception reports.

As for the information provided, it should be measurable, specific information. It is unlikely that managers (even data center managers) want information on paging activity and channel overlap, at least not when managers want to evaluate the overall health of the data center. Users definitely have no interest in, and no understanding of, the significance or meaning of these measurements. In fact, it is likely that data center managers in a data center with competent performance analysts will not want to see this information. It is the analyst's job to optimize these performance mea-

ILLUSTRATION 12–8.
Data Center Management-Performance Matrix.

DATA CENTER MANAGEMENT ACTIVITY	PERFORMANCE CRITERIA		
	RESOURCE SUFFICIENCY	USER SERVICE	DATA CENTER COSTS
Resource planning	Forecast adequacy of resources	Review priorities	Identify obsolete hardware and software
	Anticipate resource potentials	Review new services and identify obsolete services	Identify inefficient procedures
	Forecast personnel needs	Review new systems and increased workload	Identify cost-effective innovations
Daily processing	Define acceptable usage levels	Define service levels	Identify data center costs
	Identify overutilized and underutilized resources	Monitor and control services provided	Identify data center trends
	Improve resource utilization—adding, modifying, or deleting resources	Improve services provided	Consider chargeout or chargeback of costs
Performance evaluation	Provide detailed reports to technical staff	Provide detailed reports to data center management	Provide detailed reports to data center management
	Provide summary and exception reports to data center management	Provide summary and exception reports to user management	Provide summary and exception reports to user management
	Provide improvement proposals to data center management	Provide user-data center coordination through a committee	Provide financial analysis reports to upper management

surements, and it is the data center manager's job to feel the pulse of the data center's health. It now remains to consider the information that managers should receive on resource sufficiency, user service, and data center costs.

Resource Sufficiency

An extremely useful chart, shown in Chapter 11, is the chart relating workload to computer capacity; it is shown again in Illustration 12-9. This chart immediately indicates when capacity must be changed to meet changing workloads. Instead of anticipating increased workloads, as illustrated, reduced workloads may actually be anticipated. The increased use of distributed data processing, for example, is likely to reduce workload and transfer it to one or more other sites. In this case, the capacity can be lessened, the excess capacity can be sold, or the surplus capacity can be retained for contingencies such as a failure at one of the other data centers. If the surplus capacity is retained, and if a chargeback system exists, the users should expect to benefit from any extra revenues received; if extra revenue is not received, they should expect to pay for the extra capacity, since it is retained to serve them in case of an emergency.

Resource sufficiency is not limited to the computer room. It is also necessary to know the adequacy of personnel and equipment in the precomputer processing and the postcomputer processing areas. It often happens that workload is excessive for the data-entry personnel available, but this situation is ignored. The result is overtime expenses, overworked personnel, discontent, and absenteeism, which make the situation even worse; there may also be a high rate of resignations. Therefore, data entry cannot be ignored. The trend in data-entry workload, however, has gone to the other extreme. Instead of needing more people, many installations are reducing their staffs. This trend results from the substitution of on-line processing for batch processing, and the preparation of input in the user departments instead of in the data center. At one installation in New Jersey, the number of data-entry personnel dropped from over 200 people to only 12, and these 12 people are primarily involved in preparing JCL and control cards.

Another useful form introduced in the last chapter is the one showing the trend of computer availability and utilization; this form is shown again in Illustration 12-10. The form permits graphing the available time used for production for each week of a quarter. Similar charts can be prepared for other data center equipment. For example, usage of the humble decollator can be observed. These simple devices are probably as responsible as any other piece of equipment for delays. Decollators are often chosen as a means to economize. Many data centers, because of the

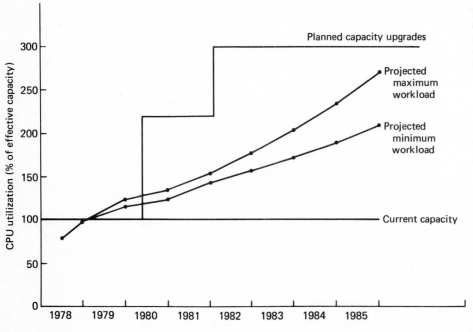

ILLUSTRATION 12-9. Workload/Capacity Chart: Anticipated minimum and maximum workloads are charted, and so are the planned increments for CPU capacity.

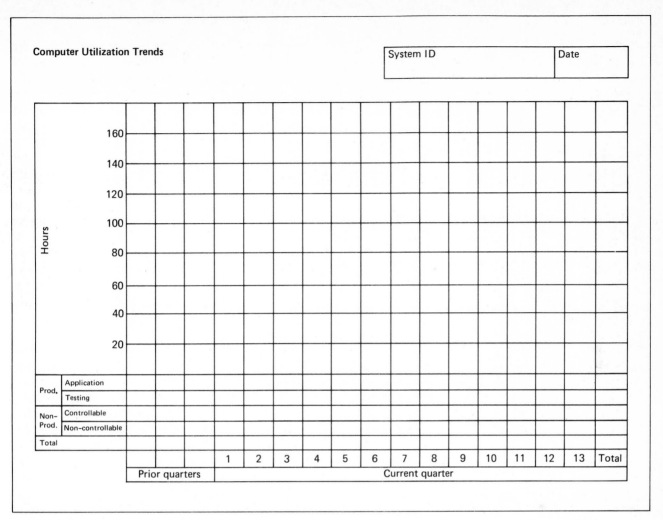

ILLUSTRATION 12-10. Trend-Oriented Computer Utilization Report.

policy to skimp on decollators, present a weird picture to visitors. In one area, data-entry personnel are working hard and pushing material into the computer room. The personnel in the computer room are quickly completing one job after another. Now it is only necessary to glance at the decollators—or decollator—if they can be seen behind the high piles of computer printout waiting to be processed.

An important addition to resource availability and utilization information is the comparison of expectations not only against average resource usage, but also against peak resource usage. Illustration 12-11 shows such a graph for monthly estimates and actual results for an entire year. As can be seen, not showing peak usage information can be misleading. It suggests that the average-usage information indicates that performance is well within acceptable limits, although in this illustra-

tion peak usage exceeds acceptable limits toward the end of the year. If similar charts are prepared for weekly and daily average and peak usage, and possibly slack usage, trends will become apparent when usage is erratic. It is likely that activity is consistently high on certain days of the week and low on other days. It is typical for Mondays and Fridays to be high-activity days. The same is true for weekly activity within each month. It is likely that the first and last weeks are the high-activity weeks, while the middle weeks are low. With this information documented, it is possible to discuss with users means for leveling the demands on the data center resources so that resources will not sit idle for some time periods and be unable to meet the demands for other time periods.

There is a problem with the word "availability." It would be wrong, for example, to believe that 16 hours are available because two 8-hour

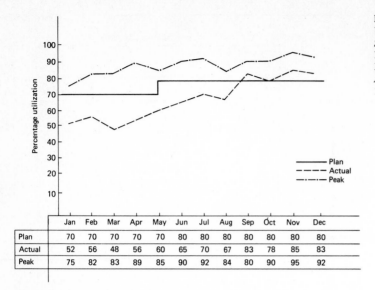

ILLUSTRATION 12-11. Resource Utilization with Peak Activity. *Source:* Joe E. Kasparek and Richard C. LaVelle, "Evaluating EDP Operations Performance," *The Arthur Anderson Chronicle,* April 1976, p. 71.

	Jan	Feb	Mar	Apr	May	Jun	Jul	Aug	Sep	Oct	Nov	Dec
Plan	70	70	70	70	70	80	80	80	80	80	80	80
Actual	52	56	48	56	60	65	70	67	83	78	85	83
Peak	75	82	83	89	85	90	92	84	80	90	95	92

ILLUSTRATION 12-12. "Availability" Time: Data center and user managers tend to define "availability" differently. Users consider an entire 8-hour shift as available time for their applications, ignoring the time needed for preventative maintenance and systems development. Users also differ with data center managers by defining startup and shutdown as non-productive activities. *Source:* David F. Stevens, "Obfuscatory Measurement," *Computer Performance Evaluation: Proceedings of the 1977 SIGMETRICS/CMG VIII Conference on Computer Performance: Modeling, Measurement, and Management,* Washington, D.C., Nov. 29-Dec. 2, 1977, p. 35. Copyright 1977, Association for Computing Machinery, Inc., and Computer Measurement Group, Inc., reprinted by permission.

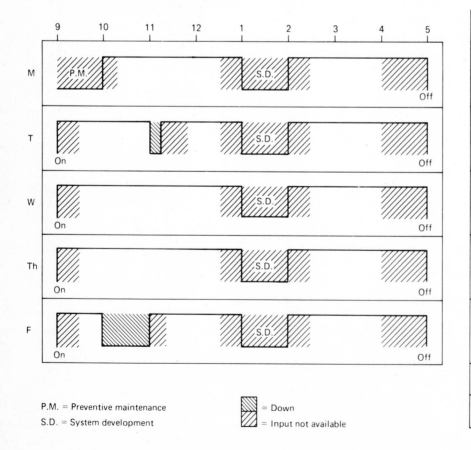

shifts exist in the data center. Users tend to consider availability from this viewpoint. But data center personnel view availability as uptime, in other words, the 16 hours potentially available minus startup and shutdown, minus time for maintenance and time lost because of failures. Other time-consuming activities must be subtracted from potential available time. These include tests for systems development and time for data center personnel to modify hardware configuration or to upgrade software.

Illustration 12–12 stresses the difference between potential availability time for application processing and actual availability time. The following time was lost from potential availability time for the week shown:

1. 5 hours for system development; 1 hour per day.
2. 1 hour for preventive maintenance on Monday.
3. 5 hours for "rundowns" when input is not accepted; this occurs for 0.5 hour each day at 12:30 P.M. and 4:00 P.M.
4. 8.5 hours for startups and shutdowns, where startups occur at the start of each day, after each system failure, and after system development activity; shutdowns occur the last half-hour each day.
5. 1.25 hours because of downtime.

Data center personnel and user personnel tend to view these activities differently. Data center personnel, as the table in Illustration 12–12 shows, do not consider preventive maintenance and system development time as potential user application time; users do. Data center personnel do not consider startup, rundown, and shutdown time as unproductive time; users do. The result is that data center personnel obtain 32.75 productive hours from 34 potential hours; thus, 96 percent of the potential time was used for user applications. But the users would comment that of the 40 hours potentially available, only 19.25 hours were actually used to process their application—the result being that only 48 percent of the potential time was actually used for application processing. The point is that when data center and user personnel communicate and examine reports, it must be clear as to how "availability" is being defined and how it will be used by all involved.

User Service

Users are primarily concerned about getting their work done within reasonable time limits—anyway, reasonable users are concerned about reasonable time limits. Fearful, aggressive users are a problem to data center personnel, but they can only be controlled by strong upper management or a strong data center steering committee. Unthreatened and emotionally stable user managers will be assumed for this discussion. These users are concerned about meeting deadlines for scheduled jobs, receiving quick service for unscheduled jobs, fast response time for on-line jobs, and reliable service, where reliable service is service plagued with few disruptions, and where those disruptions that do occur are of short duration. The means for reporting performance in these four service areas are now considered.

Reporting on Scheduled Jobs. It is customary to report on the percentage of jobs that meet the scheduled deadlines. This is important. But only too often this minimal reporting leaves more questions unanswered than answered. What percentage of the late jobs were only a half-hour or less late? How many were less than two hours late? Were the causes for missed deadlines primarily in operations? Were deadlines missed because of program-coding or system-design errors, or because of the users? Did users supply input late? How late? A half-hour? More than two hours? To permit improvement of service, it must be possible to answer these questions.

Several organizations have prepared clever forms to answer at least some of these questions. One of the most inspired forms is that used at Manufacturers Hanover Trust in New York City. This form, with typical entries, is shown in Illustration 12–13. The entries are for one of the smaller data centers at MHT. Observe that in January, 10 jobs were late, half of them by one-half hour or less. If documentation were inadequate, some criticism might occur; but since this form reports that the users provided the input late for 51 jobs, the report, instead, indicates commendable performance.

These reports can be made even more complex (not a goal but possibly a necessity) by indicating performance by job priorities. That is, percentages

Specialized Job Processing Center
Performance Reports—Scheduled Jobs

Dept. no. _____

Dept. name _____

Week _____

Month _____

	Item	Week 1	Week 2	Week 3	Week 4	Week 5	Total
W E E K L Y	No. of jobs						
	No. of jobs on time						
	No. of jobs late						
	On time %						
	INPUT < ½ Hr						
	INPUT > ½ Hr < 1 Hr						
	INPUT > 1 Hr < 2 Hr						
	INPUT > 2 Hr						
	OUTPUT < ½ Hr						
	OUTPUT > ½ Hr < 1 Hr						
	OUTPUT > 1 Hr < 2 Hr						
	OUTPUT > 2 Hr						
	OUTPUT Return items						
	OUTPUT Misroutes						
	Operations						
	Programming						
	System						
	User						

	Item	Jan	Feb	Mar	Apr	May	Jun	Jul	Aug	Sep	Oct	Nov	Dec	Total
M O N T H L Y	No. of jobs													
	No. of jobs on time													
	No. of jobs late													
	On time %													
	INPUT < ½ Hr													
	INPUT > ½ Hr < 1 Hr													
	INPUT > 1 Hr < 2 Hr													
	INPUT > 2 Hr													
	OUTPUT < ½ Hr													
	OUTPUT > ½ Hr < 1 Hr													
	OUTPUT > 1 Hr < 2 Hr													
	OUTPUT > 2 Hr													
	OUTPUT Return items													
	OUTPUT Misroutes													
	Operations													
	Programmings													
	System													
	User													

ILLUSTRATION 12–13. Performance Report for Scheduled Jobs. *Source:* Manufacturers Hanover Bank.

of jobs meeting and missing deadlines can be separated by high-, normal-, and low-priority job categories. When this is done, it is possible to state as standards that deadlines will be met for 100 percent of high-priority jobs, 95 percent of normal-priority jobs, and 90 percent of low-priority jobs. It is possible that an installation may also have remote batch processing, and a similar report would be wanted for these jobs.

Reporting on Unscheduled Jobs. A report like the one for scheduled jobs can be prepared for unscheduled jobs; however, instead of meeting deadlines, the criterion for performance is how quickly jobs are completed and returned to users, in other words, the turnaround for jobs. Another manner of presenting turnaround information that would quickly distinguish it visually is to use a graph such as that in Illustration 12–14. If the standard is that 80 percent of unscheduled jobs should be returned within 24 hours, the graph shows that this criterion is met for every month except October. However, since the objectives shown in the upper-right corner indicate that the standard is even less demanding, performance is more than adequate. Many data centers have more stringent objectives. It is not unusual to require that 80 percent of the jobs be returned within four hours and that the remaining jobs be returned within eight hours.

The tabular information below the graph states exactly how many jobs were submitted and how many were processed within the various performance categories. Again, it may be desirable to separate jobs by priority categories and to assign different performance standards for each category. Another factor that affects the ability to meet performance standards is resource requirements. It is common to classify jobs according to their resource requirements and to require that high-resource-demanding jobs be executed during the second or third shift. This factor complicates reporting and may be of little value to management; since it is primarily of value for scheduling, it may

ILLUSTRATION 12-14. Performance Report for Unscheduled Jobs.

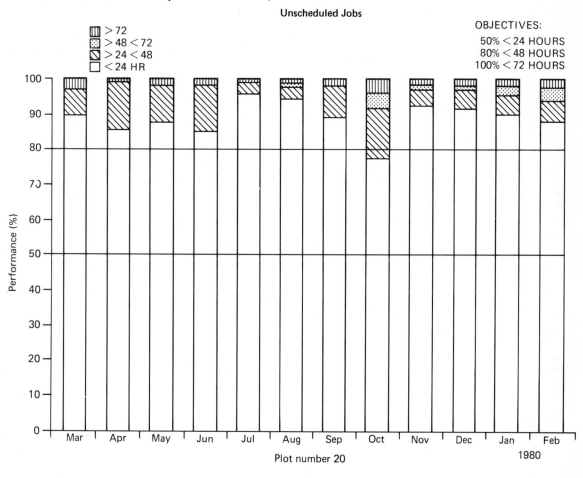

	Item	Mar	Apr	May	Jun	Jul	Aug	Sep	Oct	Nov	Dec	Jan	Feb
	No. of Jobs	427	423	430	575	553	517	569	597	792	783	946	1073
O U T P U T	# < 24 hr	385	364	379	491	444	490	509	463	735	721	856	949
	# > 24 < 48	29	57	40	77	87	17	54	88	37	50	56	64
	# > 48 < 72	2	2	4	3	20	5	4	24	10	9	18	37
	# > 72	11	0	7	4	2	5	2	22	10	3	16	23
	Returned items	9	12	14	41	15	10	12	9	14	27	16	7

Online Processing
Performance Report

Cumulative Percentages

15
14
13
12
11
10
9
8
7
6
5
4
3
2
1
0

Jan Feb Mar Apr May Jun Jul Aug Sep Oct Nov Dec

Objective = 97.0%

```
——— *    *Total downtime
— — +    +System-caused downtime
```

Date prepared _February 1979_

Prepared by _A.C. Benson_

Application _All online jobs_

	Start-ups		Late (hrs.)				Transactions	Number		Response times (sec.)								Systems disruptions	Hours				System summary	Downtime (min.)						
Month	Number Total	Time Total	<0.5	≥0.5<1	≥1<2	≥2	Total	Loc. A	Loc. B	Avg.	<3 #	<3 %	≥3<10 #	≥3<10 %	≥10<30 #	≥10<30 %	≥30 #	≥30 %	No.	<0.5	≥0.5<1	≥1<2	≥2	Time requested	System Late	System Disr	External Term	External Line	No. term	% Sys. down	% Total down
Jan	660	630	17	2	7	4	26360	3885	22475	1.8	2056	78	5577	21	170	1	52	0	416	142	57	15	2	515822	1984	6740	1450	721		1.6	2.1
Feb	661	650	6	1	2	2	26495	3587	22908	1.7	2074	78	5591	21	120	0	41	0	22	575	33	12	2	520429	559	6302	1233	824		1.3	1.7
Mar																															
Apr																															
May																															
Jun																															
Jul																															
Aug																															
Sep																															
Oct																															
Nov																															
Dec																															
Ytd tot																								1036251	2543	13042	2683	1545		1.5	1.9
Jan																															

ILLUSTRATION 12–15. Performance Report for On-line Processing.

appropriately be excluded from management reports. It is easy to complicate reports. The goal in management reporting is to provide only the information needed to make decisions and to control data center operations.

Reporting on On-line Jobs. Response time, as well as startup and disruption information, can be shown on a form such as that in Illustration 12–15. This form provides considerable tabular information, as well as a simple graph for response-time performance. In the case of the illustration, the objective is to have response time for 97 percent of the transmissions within three seconds. As shown, this objective is easily met—although the work involved to meet this objective may not have been too easy. Some organizations prepare separate forms of this type for each major application.

It may be desirable to combine the performance information for scheduled, unscheduled, and on-line jobs on a single form. To suggest another idea while combining this information, it is possible to show the performance for these processing types according to processing shifts.

This will permit isolation of performance problems according to shifts. The form in Illustration 12–16 is suitable for this purpose. Illustration 12–17, instead of stressing information on shifts, stresses local and remote processing according to priorities. Obviously, considerable flexibility is possible in what information is presented and how it is presented. The suggestions presented can be modified and combined according to an installation's particular needs.

Reporting in Reliability. Managers are concerned about the number and length of processing interruptions. Many data center managers express pride that processing interruptions are nearly nonexistent. And rightfully so. Some of these installations have about 99 percent computer uptime. Users at these installations have confidence that their work will be done. Other installations are not so fortunate, but with adequate reporting, a high level of reliability is possible. The factors that determine reliability have been commented on several times throughout this book. They include the establishment of good standards (includ-

ILLUSTRATION 12–16. Performance According to Job Types and Processing Shifts.

		Scheduled jobs (% meeting deadlines)			Unscheduled jobs (% meeting stds.)			Online processing (response time)								
								< 3			≥ 3 and ≤ 8			> 8		
Month	Week	Shift 1	Shift 2	Shift 3	S 1	S 2	S 3	S 1	S 2	S 3	S 1	S 2	S 3	S 1	S 2	S 3
	1															
	2															
	3															
	4															
	5															
	1															
	2															
	3															
	4															
	5															
	1															
	2															
	3															
	4															
	5															
Quarterly averages																

User Service Summary Report

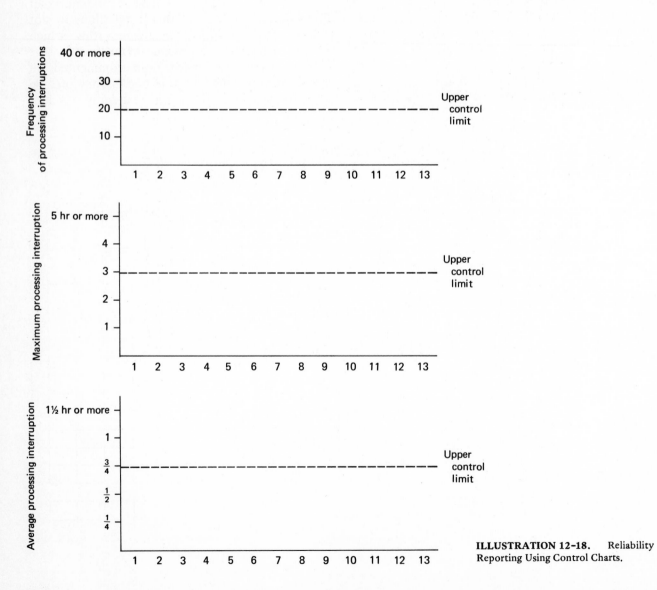

Processing type		Job priorities								
		High			Normal			Low		
		Goal	Act.	Dev.	Goal	Act.	Dev.	Goal	Act.	Dev.
Batch	Local scheduled									
	Local on–demand									
	Remote scheduled									
	Remote on–demand									
Online	Local TSO									
	Local IMS									
	Remote TSO									
	Remote IMS									

ILLUSTRATION 12-17. Performance According to Job Types and Priorities.

ILLUSTRATION 12-18. Reliability Reporting Using Control Charts.

362

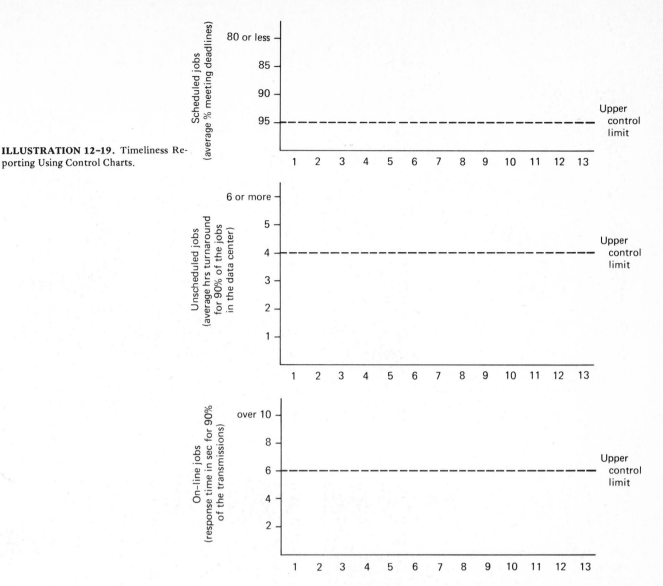

ILLUSTRATION 12-19. Timeliness Reporting Using Control Charts.

ing those for backup) and adherence to those standards.

A satisfactory and attractive means for presenting reliability performance information is shown in Illustration 12-18. The dotted lines indicate the upper limits of acceptable performance. The limits shown are not acceptable in many installations, since they are very lenient. In any case, these graphs permit quick verification of performance and observation of trends. This manner of presentation can be adapted for reporting processing timeliness for scheduled, unscheduled, and on-line jobs, as shown in Illustration 12-19.

Cost Control

The data center manager must receive information on expenses and how they compare with the amounts budgeted. The user, however, may have little interest in expenses—unless there is a charge-back system. In either case, expense information and expense trends must be presented. This permits the data center manager (whether or not users are involved) to thoroughly analyze cost trends, which then permits justification of requests for additional money and also permits consideration of alternatives for the data center. For example, if personnel costs are rapidly rising while equipment costs are also as quickly dropping, as are the trends, means should be sought for stressing equipment acquisition over increases in personnel. The form in Illustration 12-20 permits observation of cost trends. It may be desirable to further break down some of the cost categories shown, such as separating personnel costs according to computer operations, other operating functions, administrative staff, and management.

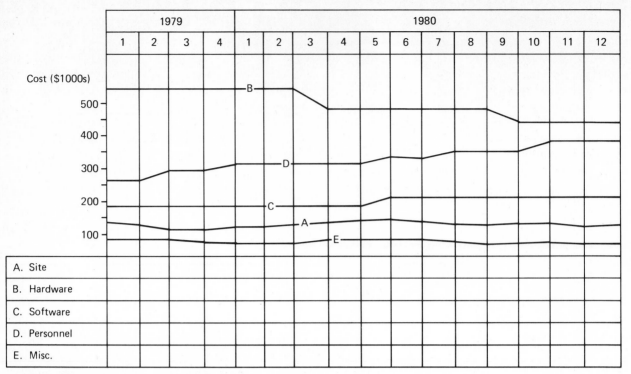

ILLUSTRATION 12-20. Data Cost Trend Reporting.

An entire chapter in this book is devoted to cost control, to budgeting, chargeback, and financial analysis. The techniques, forms, and reports included there provide the basis for management's control of cost.

Probably the biggest cause of unnecessary costs, and usually of poor resource utilization and poor user service, is inadequate thought given to alternatives. Some installations are totally dedicated to the hardware of a single vendor, totally ignoring compatible, less-expensive, and possibly faster and more-reliable hardware from other vendors. Other installations tolerate, for example, the use of a high-powered, expensive computer to be devoted to check printing—for several sequential days each month. This simple printing activity can be done as quickly on less-expensive equipment. The absence of adequate consideration of alternatives, of course, also occurs in systems development. Referring again to the check-printing example, systems actually exist where simple forms-design changes can reduce printing time to one fourth of the original printing time—that is, from three days to less than one day. (In a feasibility study performed by the author, in a situation of this type, printing was reduced to approximately 20 percent of the original processing time, and all the post-

processing delays, security risks, and manual handling were almost totally eliminated.)

These comments indicate the importance of evaluating computer hardware alternatives, but not limiting evaluation to computer hardware; even greater benefits can be expected by evaluating all data center activites and user applications.

Further Comments

It may be desirable to present performance information in a newsletter instead of in formal reports. One large organization provides to users each month the information shown in Illustration 12-21. However, this information consists almost entirely of user service information, with a line given on computer availability. It does not comment on resource sufficiency or data center costs. This organization does have a sophisticated chargeback system, and they use other means to report on these expenses. If, however, it is desirable to provide processing cost in the newsletter, the form in Illustration 12-22 may be useful. This form permits reporting on local and remote processing for batch and on-line jobs. It permits comparison of actual performance against standards, with indication of deviations. It is possible, if desired, to include priority classifications and location classifications for remote sites, as done in the newsletter in Illustration 12-21. The options are there; it is for each installation to decide what is useful for its purposes.

There is another fascinating method of presenting performance information, and it is based on the Kiviat graph introduced in Chapter 11. Illustration 12-23 shows one of the methods of using this graph to summarize performance data and to compare performance to standards. This single graph can quickly indicate deviations from standards and permits quick comparison with previously received graph patterns. Comparison of a previous graph and a recent graph immediately indicates improv-

ILLUSTRATION 12-21. Service Summary Provided in a Newsletter for Users.

November Performance Statistics

(Bold figures are objectives; plain figures are actual.)

Batch turnaround in minutes for unscheduled work submitted between 8 am and 5 pm eastern time

		Local					Remote				
		Normal		Low		High		Normal		Low	
X	20	13.9	30	32.9	60	113.3	40	15.8	60	11.2	180	44.9
A	35	34.5	60	44.0	180	98.4	50	12.3	90	18.5	200	53.6
B	50	70.3	120	123.6	300	264.7	60	99.0	160	157.9	400	269.9
O	60	39.5	140	498.5	360	152.1	90	—	400	—	500	—

IMS					TSO				
Availability (%)			Response		Availability (%)		Resp. (sec):	Local	remote
Loc. A	97.5	97.7	Response index	2.1 1.9	Loc. A 96	95.2	Logon com. 20	13.3	14.3
Loc. B	96.1	96.4					Logoff 15	5.8	11.2
Loc. C	96.3	97.0					Trivial com. 2	1.2	1.4
							DS access 15	6.9	9.3
							Compile 30	11.0	24.9
Computer system availability (%)	**98.5**	96.2					Start exec. 15	4.3	6.2

December Performance Statistics

(Bold figures are objectives; plain figures are actual.)

Batch turnaround in minutes for unscheduled work submitted between 8 am and 5 pm eastern time

		Local					Remote				
		High		Normal		Low		High		Normal		Low
X	20	10.6	30	25.9	60	82.7	40	39.5	60	80.3	180	190.3
A	35	25.8	60	31.0	180	63.5	50	7.6	90	14.1	200	65.4
B	50	68.9	120	121.4	300	234.9	60	75.2	160	202.8	400	335.2
O	60	152.4	140	137.2	360	366.0	90	—	400	—	500	—

IMS					TSO				
Availability (%)			Response		Availability (%)		Resp. (Sec)		
Loc. A	97.5	99.1	Response index	2.1 2.0	Loc. A 96	93.2	Logon com.	20	14.1
Loc. B	96.1	97.7					Logoff	15	6.6
Loc. C	96.3	97.8					Trivial com.	2	2.4
							DS access	15	9.1
							Compile	30	20.6
Computer system availability (%)	**98.5**	96.1					Start exec.	15	5.8

ing or worsening conditions. This graph actually provides a profile of data center performance.

There is one further aid in evaluating performance: the use of performance ratios, also called performance indices. Several of the most useful are:

$$\text{Availability index} = \frac{\text{actual availability}}{\text{potential availability}}$$

$$\text{Scheduling index} = \frac{\text{jobs late}}{\text{jobs scheduled}}$$

$$\text{Quality index} = \frac{\text{jobs rerun}}{\text{jobs executed}}$$

$$\text{Personnel index} = \frac{\text{number of persons}}{\text{number of work hours}}$$

$$\text{Personnel cost index} = \frac{\text{personnel cost}}{\text{total data center cost}}$$

$$\text{Personnel overtime index} = \frac{\text{overtime hours}}{\text{total personnel hours}}$$

$$\text{Hardware cost index} = \frac{\text{hardware cost}}{\text{total data center cost}}$$

$$\text{Software cost index} = \frac{\text{software cost}}{\text{total data center cost}}$$

Managers may want to collect and present more information than may seem necessary and then later decide which information has proved to be of significant value. Without making the collecting-presenting-reviewing process too cumbersome, it is better to have too much information than too little. Just as information is important to the end users, information on data center activity and performance is important to data center staff and management.

ILLUSTRATION 12-22. Service and Cost Report.

Processing type		Criteria	Upper control limit	Actual performance	Deviation
Batch	Local	Turnaround (ave.hrs)			
		Late reports (%)			
		Reruns (number)			
		Cost/Run (dollars)			
	Remote	Turnaround (ave. hrs)			
		Reruns (number)			
		Cost/Run (dollars)			
		Unavailability (%)			
On-line	Local	Response time (sec)			
		Cost/Trans. (dollars)			
		Unavailability (%)			
	Remote	Response time (sec)			
		Cost/Trans. (dollars)			
		Unavailability (%)			

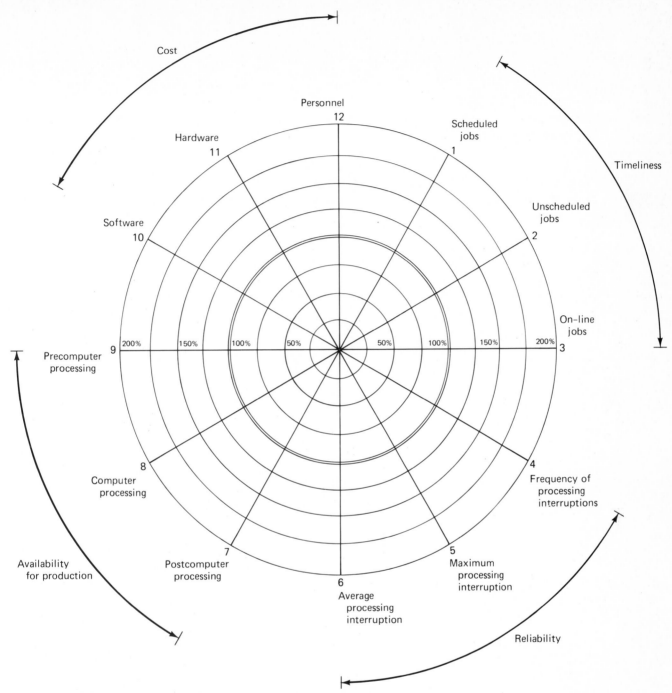

ILLUSTRATION 12-23. Data Center Profile.

A PERSONNEL NEED FULFILLMENT

SOURCE:

M. D. Wadsworth, *The Human Side of Data Processing Management* (Englewood Cliffs, N.J.: Prentice-Hall, Inc., 1973).

BACKGROUND AND BEHAVIOR INDICATIVE OF PEOPLE TRYING TO FULFILL PHYSIOLOGICAL AND SECURITY NEEDS

Background

By reviewing the information in personnel records and by obtaining information during interviews and discussions, you will be able to detect certain individuals whose backgrounds indicate that they are probably striving to fulfill physiological or security needs. You should take special note of people who:

1. Provide sole support for parents, relatives or children; especially:
   a. Unwed, divorced, or widowed mothers.
   b. Single males and females from minority groups who reside with their families in substandard areas.
   c. Parents of large families as the children begin to complete high school.
2. Have a history of severe medical problems within their family group. Of special concern are extensive hospitalizations and/or expensive treatments.
3. Are nearing retirement and have probably not made allowances for their retirement. Note especially anyone who must support others on his retirement income.
4. Are in areas that may be reorganized and/or eliminated by improved procedures and/or automation.
5. Have past histories of debt problems and/or salary garnishees.

Behavior

Observe certain types of behavior which indicate that the person is probably striving to fulfill physiological or security needs. Be especially attentive to people who:

1. Complain consistently or are extemely emotional about:
   a. The amount of their salary and raises (but tend to agree with their performance appraisal.
   b. The company's hospitalization and insurance benefits or specific portions of the benefit program.
   c. Retirement plans, profit sharing, and other company benefits.
   d. Their general inability to "make a decent living."
2. Continually spend more than they make and therefore:
   a. Borrow frequently from their co-workers.
   b. Rush to the bank as soon as they are paid.
   c. Receive frequent private phone calls at work and/or frequently request time off for personal reasons.
   d. Moonlight at other jobs.
3. Indicate that they fear the loss of their jobs by:
   a. Openly discussing the problem.
   b. Obstructing changes and hoarding knowledge of the job.
   c. Become very nervous and agitated when questioned about their work.
   d. Continually investigate openings within and outside the company but do not follow up on possible opportunities.
   e. Refuse to undertake new responsibilities.
   f. Are continually indecisive or always agree with all decisions of their peers and superiors.

BACKGROUND AND BEHAVIOR INDICATIVE OF PEOPLE PRIMARILY TRYING TO FULFILL SOCIAL NEEDS

Background

By reviewing the information in the personnel records and by obtaining information during interviews and discussions, you will be able to detect certain individuals whose backgrounds indicate that they are probably striving to fulfill social needs. You should take special note of people who:

1. Lack fulfillment in their home environment. This can be indicated by:
   a. Previous divorces; especially multiple or recent divorces.
   b. Single people, over thirty, who live by themselves or with their parents.

c. Widows or widowers; especially those who do not have children and/or were married for a number of years.

2. Exhibit few outside interests. These people will not:

a. Belong to any religious, political, fraternal, or professional societies.

b. Be members of any outside club or social organization.

c. Participate in company-sponsored activities such as sports, picnics, or clubs.

d. Be interested in any hobby or skill which requires participation by other people.

3. Exhibit excessive outside interests. These people usually:

a. Continually join new religious, political, fraternal, and professional societies, and are members of numerous clubs and social organizations.

b. Participate in almost all company-sponsored organizations.

c. Tend to develop socially centered skills such as public speaking, bridge, or dancing.

d. Attend a wide variety of courses, conventions, and seminars on widely divergent topics.

4. Are operating in new environments. These people will have recently:

a. Joined the company.

b. Been transferred to your department or area.

c. Been promoted to a new position.

Behavior

In addition to the individual's background, you can observe certain types of behavior which indicate that he is probably striving to fulfill social needs. You should be especially attentive to people who:

1. Do not handle their responsibilities in the manner of which they are capable because they socialize too frequently. These people:

a. Spend a great deal of time in non-work-related conversation.

b. Are absent from their work stations for unexplained or non-work-related reasons.

c. Disturb others who are trying to work.

d. Appear to be continually tired because of outside activities.

2. Are "loners" or are extremely introverted. These people:

a. Rarely engage in non-work-related discussions.

b. Never or almost never discuss their lives off the job.

c. Absent themselves from all office parties and social gatherings.

3. Exhibit symptoms of deep frustration by:

a. Openly destroying company property and/or their work.

b. Assaulting or threatening to assault other personnel.

c. Audibly conversing with themselves, sometimes obscenely.

4. Attempt to make social contact through extreme methods. Some methods include:

a. Adapting the appearance, clothing, and language of fringe groups during working hours.

b. Constantly attempting to lead groups or "be the life of the party" without success.

c. Continually attempting to enlist other personnel in professional, political, or religious organizations.

d. Continually creating betting pools and organizing social events.

e. Attempting to induce others to become involved in illegal sexual or drug-related practices.

BACKGROUND AND BEHAVIOR INDICATIVE OF PEOPLE PRIMARILY TRYING TO FULFILL ESTEEM NEEDS

Background

By reviewing the information in personnel records and by obtaining information during interviews and discussions, you will be able to detect certain individuals whose backgrounds indicate that they are probably striving to fulfill esteem needs. You should take special note of people who:

1. Believe that they have lost or been deprived of esteem within the company. This would be evidenced by backgrounds which include:

a. Demotions to jobs of lesser responsibility.

b. Numerous lateral or downward transfers.

c. Frozen (maximum) salaries for considerable periods of time.

d. Extremely rapid rise or growth followed by average or less than average growth.

2. Have encountered problems outside of work that, they believe, tend to diminish their esteem. These problems can include:
   a. Divorces and/or separations.
   b. Unwed Parentage.
   c. Bachelorhood or spinsterhood.
   d. Known family problems (i.e., alcoholism, drug habits, arrest records).
   e. Membership in racial or religious minorities.
   f. Overspending on material items to keep with or outdo their friends and neighbors.
3. Satisfy their esteem needs primarily through interests outside of work. These interests can include:
   a. Membership, participation, and leadership in social, fraternal, religious, political, and professional organizations.
   b. Moonlighting at jobs that require special training or expertise.
   c. Avid participation in sports, hobbies, and recreational pursuits that require special skills, knowledge, or expertise (i.e. golf, tennis, hunting, bowling, carpentry, art, music, drama, bridge, chess, etc.)

Behavior

In addition to the individual's background, you can observe certain types of behavior which indicate that he is probably striving to fulfill esteem needs. You should be especially attentive to people who:

1. Require continual recognition for their efforts. These people:
   a. Constantly solicit favorable opinions about their work. This can be done openly or disguised as feigned concern over their work and their ability to accomplish it.
   b. Become extremely emotional when criticized for poor performance.
   c. Are reluctant to undertake new responsibilities unless total success is assured.
   d. Are more concerned with the raises they get than with your evaluation of their performance.
   e. Are more interested in what others think of their work than in improving it.
   f. Constantly attempt to undertake tasks and responsibilities which they are not capable of handling, without being requested to do so.

2. Try to improve their esteem by:
   a. Openly and actively criticizing the company management and "the system" which have not allowed them to perform to the extent of their capabilities.
   b. Flaunting company rules to demonstrate their superiority to the rules.
   c. Developing and participating in intra-company political alliances.
   d. Degrading the work of others.
3. Try to become leaders in the area by:
   a. Monopolizing all conversations by talking continually and loudly even when they are not well informed.
   b. Continually relating anecdotes which indicate their expertise and abilities when such anecdotes are not appropriate to the conversation.
   c. Trying to organize parties, outings, betting pools, and other events which they can lead.
   c. Affecting abnormal dress or behavior to attract attention.

BACKGROUND AND BEHAVIOR INDICATIVE OF PEOPLE WHO ARE PRIMARILY TRYING TO FULFILL ACCOMPLISHMENT NEEDS

Background

By reviewing the information in personnel records and by obtaining information during interviews and discussions, you will be able to detect certain individuals whose backgrounds indicate that they are probably striving to fulfill accomplishment needs. You should take special note of people who:

1. Do not have backgrounds which would place them at another level of need (Tables One-Three).
2. Have grown and risen in the company at a faster than normal rate or who have a steady pattern of past successes.
3. Have stable home lives and are active, but not overactive, outside of work.

Behavior

In addition to the individual's background, you can observe certain types of behavior which indicate that he is probably striving to fulfill accomplishment needs. You should be especially attentive to people who:

1. Do not exhibit behavior that would place them at another level of need.
2. Continually work with you to establish short-term and long-range goals for their future growth. These goals may be:
   a. Realistic.
   b. Beneath their capabilities.
   c. Beyond their capabilitites.
3. Accept established goals as commitments to perform. These people:
   a. Express confidence in their ability to achieve the established goals.
   b. Put forth the effort necessary to achieve the goals, even when exceptional efforts are required.
   c. Can accept reverses beyond their control and can re-establish new goals.
4. Display a definite interest in their profession, the company, and the industry. Many times this interest will be typified by:
   a. Controlled or uncontrolled competitiveness and/or aggressive behavior.
   b. Logical or unplanned inquiry into the basis for all procedures and company activities.
   c. Continuous unsolicited recommendations for change.

B

SUGGESTED ORGANIZATION OF A CHART OF ACCOUNTS

SOURCE:

"Guidelines for Cost Accounting Practices for Data Processing," *Data Base,* Winter 1977 Supplement.

CHART OF ACCOUNTS

The chart of accounts represented herein is intended as a guide to be followed in establishing standard accounts and their meaning for the systems and data processing activities within the company. Obviously, these accounts must comply with one's own company accounting system and no intention is being made to design a structured numbering system, although a structured approach is used to illustrate the concept. The chart of accounts depicted herein is intended as a guide and should not be construed as being the complete set of accounts for any given company. Some may be added, others deleted. Refer to Chart 2.

Descriptions

The following descriptions pertain to individual accounts within the chart of accounts structure. They represent a classification system intended to identify types of costs incurred to satisfy regulatory and economic decision making requirements.

Detail Accounts and Their Decisions

I. *Salaried and Related* (See Chart B–1)
  a. Base Wages:
    That compensation periodically paid to an individual for regular work or service.
    1. Management
    2. Nonmanagement
  b. Part-Time Wages:
    That compensation paid to an individual for work or services not considered full-time employment.
  c. Overtime:
    That compensation paid for hours worked beyond the base hours which are normally compensated for by base wages.
  d. Premium:
    That compensation paid as premium incentive for special hours (nights) or incentives for increased productivity.
  e. Benefits:
    Those costs incurred in providing the associate with company-paid benefits such as medical and life insurance, retirement plans and so on.
  f. Taxes:
    Those costs incurred in payment to city, state and federal agencies which have been assessed on the associate's wages but paid for by the employer, i.e. state and federal unemployment taxes.
  g. Training:
    This account includes the costs incurred in

Chart B-1 of accounts	Systems and programming — Study, program and installation maintenance									Technical support					Data processing operations — Administration	Control					Off-line				Computer operations — Processing				Computer operations — Peripheral									
	Administration	Systems analysis	Systems design	Program design	Applic prog	Systems testing	Systems install.	Systems maint.	Postinstallation audit	Administration	Standards	Software	Hardware	Assistance and training	Administration	Data collection	Data control	Data distribution	Quality control	Production control	Data entry	Tabulating	Teletype	Microfilm	Local batch	Remote batch	On-line	Time sharing	Printing	Card reading	Card punching	Scanning	Paper tape	Plotter	Ticket conversion	Telecomm	Analog digital	Perm storage
1. Salaries and related																																						
(a) Base wages																																						
(1) Management	D	D	D	D	D	D	D	D	D	D	D	D	D		D	I	I	I	I	I	I	I	I	I	I	I	I	I	I	I	I	I	I	I	I	I	I	I
(2) Nonmanagement	D	D	D	D	D	D	D	D	D	D	D	D	D		D	D	D	D	D	D	D	D	D	D	I	I	I	I	I	I	I	I	I	I	I	I	I	I
(b) Part-time wages	D	D	D	D	D	D	D	D	D	D	D	D	D		D	D	D	D	D	D	D	D	D	D	I	I	I	I	I	I	I	I	I	I	I	I	I	I
(c) Overtime	D	D	D	D	D	D	D	D	D	D	D	D	D		D	D	D	D	D	D	D	D	D	D	I	I	I	I	I	I	I	I	I	I	I	I	I	I
(d) Premium	D	D	D	D	D	D	D	D	D	D	D	D	D		D	D	D	D	D	D	D	D	D	D	I	I	I	I	I	I	I	I	I	I	I	I	I	I
(e) Benefits	D									D					D																							
(f) Taxes	D									D					D																							
(g) Training	D									D					D																							
(h) Travel	D									D					D																							
(i) Employment cost	D									D					D																							
(j) Moving expense	D									D					D																							
(k) Other	D									D					D																							

approved courses, both company-sponsored and private.

h. Travel:

This account shall include the cost of transportation of employees while engaged in activities authorized as company business. This would include costs of meals, lodging, transportation and other incidental expenses incurred.

i. Employment Expenses:

This account shall include those costs incurred in recruiting associates for either full- or part-time employment. This would include media advertising, testing, identification, searches and agency fees.

j. Moving Expenses:

This account shall include those expenses incurred by the associate and family in connection with a transfer. This would include transportation, meals, lodging, moving and storing of household and other personal property and any other costs associated with relocation.

II. *Occupancy and Related Expenses* (See Chart B-2)

a. Rent:

This account shall include rents paid or payable for the use of space in buildings occupied as a whole or in part by the company and may be an allocation from a corporate charge.

b. Utilities:

This account shall include costs of all utilities supplied to the company for use in company-occupied buildings and for which the company is liable for payments. It may be an allocation from a corporate charge.

1. Electrical

This account shall include the costs for electrical power supplied the company by outside sources.

2. Heat

This account shall include the cost of heat, or gas to generate same, supplied the company by outside sources.

3. Water

This account shall include the costs for water supplied the company by outside sources.

c. Taxes:

This account shall include tax amounts payable on real estate or personal property owned by the company. This includes taxes assessed which are levied by virtue of state-wide statutes affecting the company's property in common with the property of others. This includes such taxes on property involved which are levied for the support of

Chart B-2 of accounts	Systems and programming: Study, program and installation maintenance — Administration	Technical support — Administration	Data processing operations: Control — Administration
2. Occupancy and related			
(a) Rent	O	O	O
(b) Light	O	O	O
(c) Heat	O	O	O
(d) Water	O	O	O
(e) Taxes	O	O	O
(f) Depreciation	O	O	O
(g) Building improvements	D	D	D
(h) Maintenance and repair	D	D	D
(i) Insurance	D	D	D
(j) Security service	D	D	D
(k) Environmental		D	D
(l) Other	D	D	D

Additional column headers (all unmarked for these rows): Systems and programming — Systems analysis, Systems design, Program design, Applic prog, Systems testing, Systems install., Systems maint., Postinstallation audit; Technical support — Standards, Software, Hardware, Assistance and training; Data processing operations — Control (Data collection, Data control, Data distribution, Quality control, Production control), Off-line (Data entry, Tabulating, Teletype, Microfilm), Computer operations: Processing (Local batch, Remote batch, On-line, Timesharing), Peripheral (Printing, Card reading, Card punching, Scanning, Paper tape, Plotter, Ticket conversion, Telecomm, Analog digital, Perm storage).

state, county, city or other government agencies.

d. Depreciation:

This account shall include the amounts reserved for depreciation based upon investments in buildings owned by the company.

e. Housekeeping:

This account shall include the expense involved in routine building cleaning and related services.

f. Maintenance and Repair:

This account shall include expenses in connection with regular upkeep repair and maintenance costs in company-owned and occupied buildings.

g. Insurance:

This account shall include the costs of insurance reserves or premiums purchased or provided for protection against losses to company-occupied buildings due to fire, weather damage, theft and so on.

h. Security Service:

This account shall include the costs incurred to furnish security guard service at company-occupied buildings.

i. Environmental Control:

This account shall include the costs to provide various control devices to regulate the environment within company-occupied buildings as well as the control of emissions from within buildings.

j. Other Company and Related:

This account shall include all expenses incurred in connection with occupancy and related items not specifically covered by accounts or subaccounts in the series.

III. *Equipment and Related* (See Chart B–3)

This account shall include charges for rental or lease and other operations-related expense of EAM and EDP equipment.

a. Computer Hardware:

This account shall include charges for rental or lease and other operations-related expense of EDP equipment.

1. Rental—Computers

This account shall include charges for rental expense of EDP equipment.

2. Lease—Computers

This account shall include charges for lease equipment of EDP equipment.

3. Depreciation—Computers

This account shall include reserves estab-

Chart B-3 of accounts	Systems and Programming — Study, program and installation maintenance			Technical support	Data processing operations — Administration	Data processing operations — Control	Data processing operations — Off-line	Data processing operations — Computer operations — Processing	Data processing operations — Computer operations — Peripheral
	Administration	Systems analysis / Systems design	Program design / Applic prog / Systems testing / Systems install / Systems maint	Postinstallation audit // Administration / Standards / Software / Hardware / Assistance and training	Administration	Data collection / Data control / Data distribution / Quality control / Production control	Data entry / Tabulating / Teletype / Microfilm	Local batch / Remote batch / On-line / Timesharing	Printing / Card reading / Card punching / Scanning / Paper tape / Plotter / Ticket conversion / Telecomm / Analog digital / Perm storage
3. Equipment and related									
(a) Computer hardware									
(1) Rent							D D		
(2) Lease							D D		
(3) Depreciation							D D		
(4) Extra use rental							D D		
(5) Maintenance							D D		
(b) Office machines							D D		
(1) Rent						D D D D D	D D		
(2) Lease						D D D D D	D D		
(3) Depreciation						D D D D D	D D		
(4) Extra use rental						D D D D D	D D		
(5) Maintenance						D D D D D	D D		
(c) Hardware related software						D D D D D	D D		
(1) Rent							D	| | | |	| | | | | | | | | |
(2) Lease							D	| | | |	| | | | | | | | | |
(3) Depreciation							D	| | | |	| | | | | | | | | |
(4) Maintenance							D	| | | |	| | | | | | | | | |
(d) Insurance					O				
(e) Property tax							D D D D	D D D D	D D D D D D D D D

lished for the depreciation of company-owned EDP equipment.

4. Extra-Use Rental—Computers
This account shall include amounts charged and payable for use of EDP equipment above the standard monthly base hours and/or outside the established prime shift usage.

5. Maintenance—Computers
This account shall include the maintenance charges of owned EDP equipment.

b. Office and EAM Machines
This account shall include charges for rental or lease and other operations-related expenses of office and EAM machines.

1. Rental—Office and EAM Machines
This account shall include charges for rental expenses of office and EAM machines.

2. Lease—Office and EAM Machines
This account shall include charges for lease agreements of office and EAM machines.

3. Depreciation—Office and EAM Machines
This account shall include reserves established for the depreciation of company-owned office and EAM machines.

4. Extra-Use Rentals—Office and EAM Machines
This account shall include amounts charged and payable for use of office and EAM machines above the standard monthly base hours and/or outside the established prime shift usage.

5. Maintenance—Office and EAM Machines
This account shall include the maintenance charges of owned office and EAM machines.

c. Hardware Related Software
This account shall include the expense in connection with the rental, lease or ownership of software packages for use with EDP equipment.

1. Rent—Hardware Related Software
This account shall include the expense in connection with the rental of software packages for use with EDP equipment.

2. Lease—Hardware Related Software
This account shall include the expense in connection with the lease agreements of software packages for use with EDP equipment.

3. Depreciation—Hardware Related Software
This account shall include the reserves established for the depreciation of company-owned packages for use with EDP equipment.

4. Maintenance—Hardware Related Software
This account shall include the maintenance expense charged for support of company-owned software for use with EDP equipment.

d. Insurance
This account shall include the costs of reserves or premiums purchased to provide for protection against losses of software packages and EDP equipment due to accidental or deliberate destruction.

e. Property Tax
This account shall include tax amounts payable on company-owned hardware and related software that is classified as personal property.

f. Other
This account shall include all expenses incurred in connection with the rent, lease or other operating-related expenses not specifically covered by accounts or subaccounts in the series.

IV. *Communications and Related* (See Chart B-4)

a. Communication Interface Hardware:
This account shall include the costs in connection with providing terminal hardware devices for intra- and/or interoffice communication or data transmission, excluding facilities provided by telephone companies.

1. Rent
This account shall include the rental costs associated with providing terminal hardware devices for intra- and/or interoffice communications or data transmission, excluding regular voice communication facilities provided by telephone companies.

2. Lease
This account shall include the lease agreement cost associated with providing terminal hardware devices for intra- and/or interoffice communications or data transmission, excluding regular voice communications facilities provided by telephone companies.

3. Depreciation

Chart B-4 of accounts

Data processing activities	Systems and programming: Study, program and installation maintenance				Technical support					Data processing operations	Control					Off-line				Computer operations: Processing				Computer operations: Peripheral									
	Administration	Systems analysis / Systems design	Program design / Applic prog / Systems testing / Systems install / Systems maint	Postinstallation audit	Administration	Standards	Software	Hardware	Assistance and training	Administration	Data collection	Data control	Data distribution	Quality control	Production control	Data entry	Tabulating	Teletype	Microfilm	Local batch	Remote batch	On-line	Timesharing	Printing	Card reading	Card punching	Scanning	Paper tape	Plotter	Ticket conversion	Telecomm	Analog digital	Perm storage
4. Communications and related																																	
(a) Communications Hardware																																	
(1) Rent																D				D	D										D		
(2) Lease																D				D	D										D		
(3) Depreciation																D				D	D	D									D		
(4) Maintenance																D				D	C	D									D		
(b) Communication lines																D				—	—	D									—		
(c) Property tax																D				D	D	D									D		
(d) Other																D				D	D	D									D		

This account shall include the reserves established for the depreciation of company-owned terminal hardware devices for intra- and/or interoffice communication or data transmission.

4. Maintenance

This account shall include the maintenance of charges of company-owned terminal hardware devices for intra- and/or interoffice communication of data transmission.

d. Data Communication Lines:

This account shall include the costs in connection with the providing of intra- and/or interoffice private lines for voice communication or data transmission.

c. Property Tax:

This account shall include tax amounts payable on company-owned hardware devices for intra- and/or interoffice communication or data transmission.

d. Other Communications and Related:

This account shall include all expenses incurred in connection with the providing of intra and/or interoffice communication or data transmission (excluding regular voice communication facilities provided by telephone companies) that are not specifically covered by accounts or subaccounts in this series.

V. *Supplies:* (See Chart B-5)

a. Tape:

Chart B-5 of accounts

Data processing activities	Systems and programming: Study, program and installation maintenance				Technical support					Data processing operations	Control					Off-line				Computer operations: Processing				Computer operations: Peripheral									
	Administration	Systems analysis / Systems design	Program design / Applic prog / Systems testing / Systems install / Systems maint	Postinstallation audit	Administration	Standards	Software	Hardware	Assistance and training	Administration	Data collection	Data control	Data distribution	Quality control	Production control	Data entry	Tabulating	Teletype	Microfilm	Local batch	Remote batch	On-line	Time sharing	Printing	Card reading	Card punching	Scanning	Paper tape	Plotter	Ticket conversion	Telecomm	Analog digital	Perm storage
5. Supplies																																	
(a) Tape																D				D	D	D	D										
(b) Disc																D																	D
(c) Cards											D	D														D							
(d) Ribbons																D								D					D				
(e) Continuous forms												D	D											D					D				
(f) Film																		D															
(g) Chemicals																		D															
(h) Packaging															D			D															
(i) Binding															D																		
(j) Other	D				D					D																							

This account shall include the costs of purchase and maintenance of magnetic tape.

b. Disk Packs:

This account shall include the costs of purchase and maintenance of disk packs.

c. Cards: (Stock)

This account shall include the costs of providing stock cards to be used in the operation of the data-processing facility.

d. Ribbons:

This account shall include the costs of ribbons to be used in connection with the operation of EAM and EDP equipment.

e. Continuous Forms (Stock):

This account shall include the costs of providing stock continuous forms to be used in the operation of the data-processing facility.

f. Film:

This account shall include the costs of providing film used for the microfilming operation within the data-processing facility.

g. Chemicals:

This account shall include the costs of providing film-developing chemicals used for the microfilming operation within the data-processing facility.

h. Packaging Materials:

This account shall include the costs of providing packaging materials used in connection with the output media distribution within the data-processing facility.

i. Other Supply Expenses:

This account shall include all expenses incurred in connection with providing and maintaining minor items and supplies not specifically included under other accounts and used initially by the data-processing facility.

VI. *Other Operating Expenses* (See Chart B-6)

a. Freight:

This account shall include expense of freight shipment.

b. Subscriptions and Manuals:

This account shall include the costs of purchase and/or subscription to all magazines, periodicals, newspapers and technical manuals published by outside companies.

c. Stationery and Office Supplies:

This account shall include the costs of miscellaneous office supplies such as pencils, paper tablets, erasers, paper clips, ink, lead, route slips and so on.

d. Telephone and Telegraph:

This account shall include the costs of

Chart B-6 of accounts	Systems and programming — Study, program and installation maintenance: Administration	Systems analysis / Systems design	Program design / Applic prog / Systems testing / Systems install / Systems maint	Postinstallation audit	Technical support: Administration / Standards / Software / Hardware / Assistance and training	Data processing operations — Administration	Control: Data collection / Data control / Data distribution / Quality control / Production control	Off-line: Data entry / Tabulating / Teletype / Microfilm	Computer operations — Processing: Local batch / Remote batch / On-line / Time sharing	Computer operations — Peripheral: Printing / Card heading / Card punching / Scanning / Paper tape / Plotter / Ticket conversion / Telecomm / Analog digital / Perm storage
6. Other operating expenses										
(a) Freight	D				D	D				
(b) Subscriptions and manuals	D				D	D				
(c) Stationery and office supplies	D				D	D				
(d) Telephone and telegraph	D				D	D				
(e) Postage	D				D	D		D	D D D	
(f) Outside services	D				D	D				
(g) Consulting services	D				D	D				
(h) Printing and reproduction	D				D	D				
(i) Audio/visual services	D				D	D	D D			
(j) Messenger services	D				D	D				
(k) Dues	D				D	D				
(l) Entertainment	D				D	D				
(m) Miscellaneous	D				D	D				

services provided by telephone and telegraph companies. This account excludes that equipment and service covered by account series IV, Communications and Related Expense.

e. Postage:

This account shall include the expense of purchasing postage used for mailing material and data and where the expense of same is not covered under other accounts.

f. Outside Services:

This account shall include the expense of purchasing the services of outside companies for providing service functions not normally considered a part of the regular operations of the business.

g. Consulting:

This account shall include the expense of hiring outside consultants.

h. Audiovisual

This account shall include the expense incurred in connection with the development and presentation of audiovisual programs.

i. Messenger:

This account shall include the expense involved in connection with using messenger or delivery service.

j. Maintenance:

This account shall include the cost of providing maintenance services for buildings and equipment through hiring outside companies.

k. Printing and Reproduction:

This account shall include the expense of hiring outside service companies to provide printing and reproduction services.

l. Other Miscellaneous Expenses:

This account shall include those operating expenses incurred in connection with hiring outside companies to provide service functions not normally considered a part of the regular operations of the business and not specifically provided for under this account series.

VII. Allocated Expenses (See Chart B–7)

a. Headquarters:

This account shall include those costs incurred at headquarters on behalf of a lower entity and later spread back to said lower entities; this is commonly known as corporate or central office overhead.

b. Marketing:

This account shall include those costs incurred in connection with sales advertising and merchandising for the company's products and later spread back to lower entity levels.

c. Other Allocated Expenses:

This account shall include those expenses incurred at a centralized point and later spread to lower level entities where those expenses are not specifically covered under other accounts in this series.

VIII. *Unallocated Expenses (Minus):*

a. Subsidies:

This account shall include those costs incurred by the data-processing facility that are the responsibilities of the performing organization; therefore, no allocation is to be made to a benefiting entity.

1. Experimental/Development:

This account shall include the costs in-

Chart B-7 of accounts	Systems and programming: Study program and installation maintenance — Administration	Systems analysis / Systems design	Program design / Applic prog / Systems testing / Systems install / Systems maint	Postinstallation audit	Technical support — Administration	Standards / Software / Hardware / Assistance and training	Data processing operations — Administration	Control: Data collection / Data control / Data distribution / Quality control / Production control	Off-line: Data entry / Tabulating / Teletype / Microfilm	Computer operations — Processing: Local batch / Remote batch / On-line / Time sharing	Peripheral: Printing / Card reading / Card punching / Scanning / Paper tape / Plotter / Ticket conversion / Telecomm / Analog digital / Perm storage
7. Allocated expenses (a) Central office overhead	O				O		O				
(b) Marketing	O				O		O				
(c) Charges from other departments	O				O		O				

curred by the data-processing facility in connection with experimental/developmental operations.

2. Conversion:

This account shall include the costs incurred by the data-processing facility in connection with hardware and/or software conversions that benefit all functions served.

3. Reserve Capacities:

This account shall include the costs incurred by the data-processing facility in connection with providing excess or reserve hardware and/or software that benefit all functions served.

b. Other Unallocated Expenses:

This account shall include costs or income generated within the data-processing facility that is not specifically provided for in the above.

RISK CONTROL CHECKLIST

SOURCE:

Peter S. Browne [unpublished manuscript, May 1972].

TAXONOMY OF SECURITY AND INTEGRITY

A. General.

1. Security protection should safeguard against the following threats:
   a. Accidental.
      (1) User error.
      (2) System error.
   b. Passive infiltration.
      (1) Tapping of communications lines.
      (2) Emanations pickup.
   c. Active infiltration.
      (1) Browsing through files via an on-line terminal.
      (2) Masquerading as a legitimate user.
      (3) Physical acquisition of files (cards, tapes, listings).
      (4) Exploiting the system (through dumps, "trapdoors" in the executive, etc.).
2. The first step is to analyze the entire system. Then, design safeguards. Perform the following:
   a. Description of the environment in which the system is intended to operate.
   b. Identification of protection features that are needed (see following pages for a "menu").
   c. Determination of the presence or absence of such features in the given system.
   d. Documentation as to how these features are applied or should be applied.
   e. Ordering of these safeguards into a framework showing the manner or degree that they are applied.
   f. Determination as to whether the features actually meet the requirements of "b" above.
   g. Examination and attempted subversion of all system security features for the purposes of testing.
   h. Evaluation of test results to determine whether adequate protection can and will be provided in accordance with established requirements.
3. The security system should support separate identification for the following objects:
   a. Individual users.
   b. Terminals/stations/areas by location.
   c. Individual programs (jobs) by name and function.
   d. Data—down to element or record level if necessary.
4. Access restrictions should be constrained in any or all of the following manners:
   a. By hierarchical classification (Top Secret, Confidential, etc.).
   b. By category or compartments (codeword data, accounting department, etc.).
   c. By listing specific constraints and applying them to specific objects (Browne can read the personnel, accounting and inventory files, but can write the inventory file only; terminal "A" can only access Secret or below data; terminal "B" only can access payroll data).
   d. By the content of data (all salaries over $20,000).
   e. By constraints based on the context of data (logistics data in conjunction with performance data).
   f. Through user supplied procedures or formularies that apply only to special situations.
5. Users or programs should be restricted to any or all of the following privileges:
   a. Read.
   b. Write.
      (1) Modify—(increment, decrement, change, set to zero).
      (2) Append—(elements, entries, records, files).
      (3) Insert—(elements, entries, records, files).
   c. Delete (or set to null).
6. The ultimate goal of a secure system is to insure that all data movement is identified, authorized, receipted, and recorded.

B. Administrative and Organizational

1. Administrative.
   a. Limit unescorted access to the central computer facility (use visitor's logs).
   b. Control the authority to modify critical systems software.
   c. Test and verify changes to systems software and security routines.
   d. Develop administrative cross-checks between system, operations, and security controls.
   e. Limit personnel privileges as much as possible.
   f. Control all input and output. Classify all data as to sensitivity and value.
   g. Analyze audit and performance data for security impact. Monitor operations, meter hours vs. schedules, downtime, distribution of output, etc.

h. Maintain manual audit records for access to the system, changes to systems software, maintenance and system faults or restarts.

i. Insure personnel competence and integrity—background checks, cross-training, changing of jobs, continuing education, identification of disgruntled employees, and immediate release of those who are laid off or fired.

2. Organizational.

a. Develop a consistent security policy throughout the entire organization.

b. Appoint a full-time system security officer and give him authority as well as responsibility.

c. Make an individual responsible for security at each terminal location.

d. Secure the tape and disk libraries and insure that a full-time librarian is on duty at all times.

e. Separate the responsibilities and authority of those individuals who are critical to system security.

f. Select key personnel on the basis of integrity and competence.

g. Control vendor and contract maintenance personnel as strictly as in-house employees.

h. Form a computer security committee that crosses organizational boundaries.

3. Procedural.

a. Set up written procedures for:
   (1) Start up of the system.
   (2) Shut down of the system.
   (3) Restarts (reboot or IPL).
   (4) Control of tapes, disks, cards, listings.
   (5) Identification of users to the system.
   (6) Control of access to the central facility and to terminals.
   (7) Software changes—application as well as systems software.
   (8) Changes to security parameters.
   (9) Maintenance.
   (10) Control of jobs and job flow.
   (11) Certification and system tests.

b. Devise and practice procedures for disaster recovery to include an implementation plan for back-up facilities. Test them periodically.

c. Train for bomb threats and other civil disturbances.

d. Devise restrictive policies regarding:
   (1) Visits to the computer areas.
   (2) Publicity regarding EDP operations.

e. Insure that stored tapes and disks are periodically cleaned, sampled for dropouts, stored in appropriate containers and certified.

f. Maintain documentation according to predetermined standards. Review this documentation on a periodic basis.

g. Document retention cycles for each data and program application area. Coordinate with the standards effort.

h. Develop internal audit controls over computer usage, data input, output distribution, program changes, error reporting, quality control, program testing, and backup.

i. For commercial installations, buy adequate insurance protection.

C. Physical, Hardware, Communications

1. Physical.

a. Implement "closed shop" access control—use guards, badge readers, closed circuit TV, limited entry points, central monitoring, etc.

b. Control access to terminals and remote entry stations in accordance with the protection needs for input and output designated for that station.

c. Insure that the facility is protected against exposure from fire, flooding, and natural elements—by means of construction, proper drainage, protected location, fire/smoke detectors, noncombustible furniture, etc.

d. Protect against utility unreliability by protection and backup of sources of power and air conditioning. Use dual feeds, redundant equipment, etc.

e. Demand good housekeeping; prevent accumulations of trash, dispose of waste materials, prohibit smoking in EDP rooms, and clean on a regular basis.

f. Lock critical software and documentation in a secured area.

g. Provide for backup files of programs and data at a secondary location. Keep current inventories of all software, data files and documentation.

h. Control access to vital areas for custodial and maintenance personnel.

i. Implement a two-man policy for all physical areas involved with data processing.

j. Implement controls on entry to sensitive areas by visitors, vendors, and programmers. Badge readers, guards, man-traps, or other variants of controlled access systems can be used for this purpose. Non-controlled exits should be alarmed.

2. Hardware.

The computer hardware should come equipped with the following features. The first six should be required, the last five are optional.

a. Two modes—privileged and user (or master/slave).

b. Boundary control registers, permission registers, memory protect keys or a base addressing scheme for core limits protection.

c. Every operations code should have a known response. Any non-legal instruction or bit pattern will result in an interrupt and abort.

d. Both read and write protect (fetch and store).

e. Positive hardware identification of terminals and peripherals.

f. Detection and notification of errors, failures and attempts to utilize unauthorized devices. All such interrupts should be trapped by the security or authorization software.

g. Key switches or lockouts of peripherals, clocks, terminals, and other devices.

h. Hardware registers that allow cross-checks for actual versus presumed contents.

i. Access control to be implemented in microcode.

j. Hardware erase features.

k. Consoles that are wired for update only or access only.

3. Communications.

a. All terminals and peripherals should be protected by tamper-free or cryptographically secure lines that are proofed against physical and/or emanations intrusion.

b. All messages should be numbered and dated.

c. The communications subsystem should include horizontal and vertical parity checking of messages.

d. There should be closed loop verification of message traffic (ACK/NAK, echoing of message, etc.).

e. The technical control or switching area should be protected against misconnection of lines and terminals by means of color coding, different plug sizes or other methods.

f. Telephones and intercoms should be protected against leakage of background or sensitive information by means of push-to-talk features or disconnects.

g. Circuit switched systems need special protection by means of stringent access control requirements and positive identification of terminals.

h. If line dropout occurs, the system must be able to recover or invalidate traffic in progress.

i. A highly desirable feature would be for the hardware to validate formats and protocol through microprogramming.

D. Software

1. Access control.

a. Security objects such as individuals, terminals, programs, and data must be explicitly identified to the system. For individuals, the following approaches may be used:
   (1) Passwords—and/or account numbers.
   (2) Credit cards, badges, magnetically inscribed objects.
   (3) Identification based on personal characteristics such as voiceprint or fingerprints.

b. Further authentication may be made by use of passwords or challenge and reply procedures.

c. If passwords are used, they should:
   (1) Be randomly generated and of sufficient length to avoid compromise.
   (2) Be changed periodically, preferably every time used.
   (3) Be protected at least in accordance with the level of data they safeguard.

d. The access control system should be sufficiently flexible to support a variety of constraints and mixes of objects. Users could be checked against terminals, programs, or data. An access list could be attached to any or all of the above depending on the needs of a particular installation.

e. Every access to a given file or device must be capable of being trapped through the access control system in order to give the capability for additional authorization or identification checks.

2. Data security.

a. Data objects should be labeled with identification and security information. It is preferable to place this adjacent to the data rather than in a directory or index that is physically separated. The system should check these labels.

b. All input and output should be labeled with security identification.

c. Code words (lock words) can be placed within files to prevent reading of sensitive information. This type of access control, called gating, can allow a lock to be associated with given data.

d. Data could be ordered or chained by classification level or structure. Sensitive data could be physically separate from public information.

e. A history of data use could be declared in order to alleviate the problem of inference.

f. Restricted data fields can be deleted or set to null on output.

g. Data should always be accessed through indirect referencing—e.g., through a user directory to an owner's catalog to the data itself.

h. Data and programs can be internally transformed (encrypted).

3. Data integrity.

This includes prevention against damage, update conflict, or the processing of incorrect data.

a. System, data and program backups must be taken periodically for purposes of recovery.

b. Data transfers should be validity checked. Recall of parts of a file should prohibit accidental retrieval of any other part of the file.

c. The data itself could be validated by a series of crosschecks, reasonableness checks, consistency checks, range checks, and sequence-of-event checks.

d. Loading of programs and data should be assured through check-sum totals or equivalent.

e. Program development should be controlled by means of automated procedures that bookkeep all changes. It should be possible to retain an audit trail of all program modules, their status and their use in production jobs.

f. If data is to be modified, a lockout or queuing mechanism should protect against contention or access to invalid information. Lockout should occur as late as possible and at as low a level as possible. On-line updates should be limited with all changes verified.

4. System control and integrity.

a. All unauthorized accesses and I/O requests must result in termination of job, sounding of an alarm, purging of queues and refusal of service to the offending terminal.

b. All operations associated with memory allocation, system interrupt, and the mode of an operation must be controlled.

c. All user programs should be coded so that access to data is made through system calls that pass through the authorization mechanism.

d. Addresses passed between users and the system should be logical in nature. Real (physical) addresses are not acceptable. A virtual memory system is inherently safer than standard addressing.

e. Entrance points to the supervisor should be well defined with expected conditions enumerated. The supervisor (O/S) must be well documented.

f. Software should check security of output messages against routing indicators and the transmission lines.

g. There should be a mechanism for automatic determination of access rights for newly created data and programs.

h. Memory and peripherals should be cleared of residue between jobs.

i. If results of computations are unpredictable, operations should be curtailed and defaulted to more secure situations.

j. Restarts after "crashes" would include the loading of a fresh copy of the supervisor and a check of the consistency of system files.

k. Shutdown should be orderly with "graceful degradation."

5. Protection of the security system.

a. Do not give out information on denials.

b. Set a limit, generally one to three, for allowing repeated attempts to access the system after an invalid log-on.

c. The operating system should run in the user state insofar as possible.

d. Debugging must be through a certified interpreter and protection against dumping of system security information is essential.

e. Do not suspend security for system degradation or for testing purposes.

f. Contents of security files must be protected at the highest levels.

g. Assembly language programming should be limited or curtailed, especially at terminals. Attempt to restrict remote use to parameter driven interpreters.

h. No changing of security tables must be allowed except at a designated facility or console.

E. Audit, Testing, and Certification

1. System auditing.
   a. The ideal security situation is to have all data movement recorded. The system should at least log the events listed below under "threat monitoring."
   b. A complete historical record must be capable of being reconstructed if the need arises.
   c. Retention of program status and environmental conditions is necessary.
   d. A program to analyze and evaluate audit statistics is needed. It probably should be written in-house.
2. Testing.
   a. A subverter program to generate false addresses, unauthorized attempts to access data, simulated failures, and other probes should be an essential part of testing the security system.
   b. The supervisor (O/S) must be checked and verified.
   c. Procedures, especially the little-used ones, are candidates for analysis.
   d. Security test programs should be written and run immediately after violations or system maintenance, program load, or restart.
   e. Control the testing and debugging of all applications programs.

f. Validate security tables and access routines.
g. Validate output for correctness and consistency.
3. Threat monitoring.
   a. The following events should be logged on a journal that is protected against modification by any user program:
      (1) Jobs on and off, to include user/terminal/program identification, date, and time.
      (2) Data requested.
      (3) Files accessed, to include type, number of accesses, and access keys.
      (4) Disposition of data (number of records output or displayed, program status information, etc.).
      (5) Unauthorized log-ons.
      (6) Response to random queries.
      (7) Any special use of the system.
      (8) All descriptor changes.
      (9) Configuration changes.
      (10) Changes to security tables and the supervisor.
      (11) Restarts and machine faults.
      (12) Attempted violations of memory.
      (13) Aborts and parity errors.
   b. Use the data developed above to:
      (1) Make a real time (or near real time) analysis of security problems.
      (2) Develop patterns to close potential or actual loopholes.

CARE OF MAGNETIC MEDIA AND EQUIPMENT

SOURCE:

Memorex Corporation, Santa Clara, California.

D-1

D-3

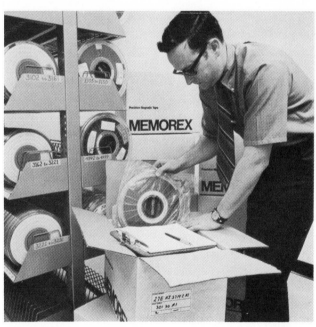

D-2

D-4

ILLUSTRATION D-1. Initial Inspection: Proper care and handling begins with the receipt of the tape products from the manufacturer. Make a careful inspection for external damage to the shipping carton.

ILLUSTRATION D-2. Thorough Inspection: If damage is detected, make an immediate inspection of each reel and canister and report any visual damage to the carrier.

ILLUSTRATION D-3. Environment is Important: Precision magnetic tape should be stored within the following environmental range: 60° to 90°F, 20 to 80% RH. Preferable environment is 70°F, 50% RH.

ILLUSTRATION D-4. Tape Acclimation: When at all possible allow tape to acclimate in the shipping cartons. This will insure against any rapid temperature changes.

D-5

D-7

D-6

D-8

ILLUSTRATION D-5. Tape Storage: Store tape upright in its protective canister. This practice not only protects the tape from airborne contamination but also properly supports the reel by its hub.

ILLUSTRATION D-6. Proper Labeling Procedures: Labels should be made out prior to placing them on the reels. When labeling the reel, care must be taken not to exert any pressure on the flanges.

ILLUSTRATION D-7. Maintain Proper Records: Each reel of tape should be promptly logged in by your librarian. Memorex records show that 80% of all damaged tape does not have a proper library record.

ILLUSTRATION D-8. Proper Cleaning Procedures: The tape transport should be cleaned with a solvent recommended by the transport manufacturer.

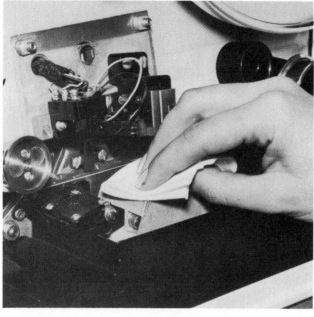

D-9

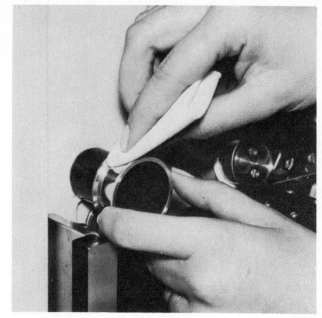

D-11

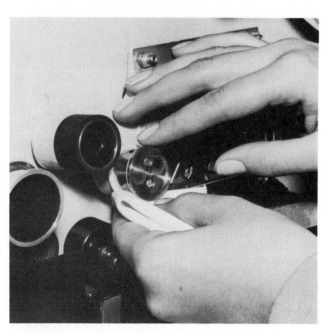

D-10

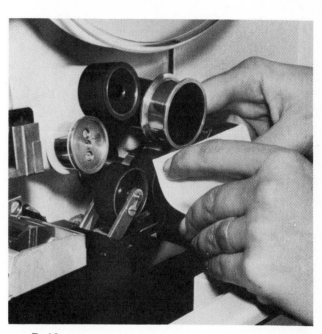

D-12

ILLUSTRATION D-9. Cleaning the Head Area: Care should be taken to remove any contamination on the head area. The correct cleaning motion on the head is the same direction as the tape path.

ILLUSTRATION D-10. Spring Guides: Special attention should be given to insure no build-up that may cause edge damage to the tape.

ILLUSTRATION D-11. Rewind Idler: Although such idlers rotate with the tape movement, they still can collect contamination.

ILLUSTRATION D-12. Rubber Capstans: Rubber parts such as capstans and pinch rollers generally come in direct contact with the oxide surface. To prevent tape contamination cleaning rubber parts is a must.

D-13

D-15

D-14

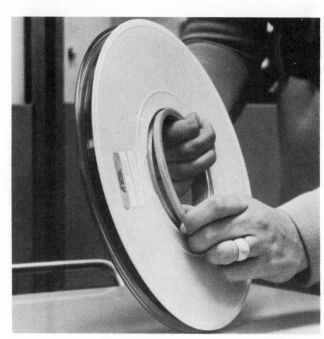

D-16

ILLUSTRATION D-13. Loop Columns and Vacuum Chamber: To insure error-free operation, it is essential to clean the entire tape path. The most frequently overlooked are the loop columns and vacuum chambers.

ILLUSTRATION D-14. Handling the Canister: Always place the canister lid with the handle side facing upward.

ILLUSTRATION D-15. Proper Tape Handling: Care should be taken not to compress the flanges when removing tape from the canister.

ILLUSTRATION D-16. Write Enable Ring: If the "write" mode is to be used, place a write enable ring in the slot provided on the reel. Be sure that the ring is seated correctly.

D-33

D-35

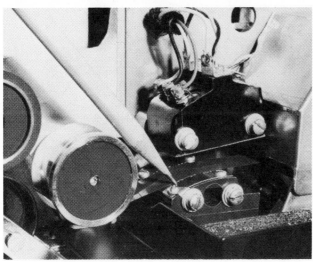

D-34

D-36

ILLUSTRATION D-33. Head: A common fault: is a worn area caused by tape wear creating improper head to tape contact. The Result: is signal instability and low output resulting in loss of data.

ILLUSTRATION D-34. Cleaning Plate: Worn or channeled cleaning plate may result in edge damage and contamination.

ILLUSTRATION D-35. Rewind Idler: A common fault: is the edges of the idler become worn or contaminated, causing damage to tape edge. Contamination may be wound into the reel.

ILLUSTRATION D-36. Spring Loaded Guide: A common fault: is the spring guide can become contaminated and cause tape to skew across the head. The Result: is edge damage and loss of data.

The entire tape drive should be cleaned after every use. The smallest particle of debris can generate a chain reaction that will result in contamination creating dropouts and serious loss of information.

Good housekeeping really pays off in the maintenance of your computer drives. We might mention general computer room cleanliness. Don't use a broom on your floors. Instead provide for a vacuum cleaner with a long hose attachment so that the power unit and exhaust bag can remain outside the room.

Use a cleaning mechanism that won't redistribute the contaminants in the room.

CARE AND HANDLING OF YOUR MEMOREX DISC PACK

Preuse Checking

Freight carriers can damage even well-packaged disk packs. Before using your new disk pack, visually examine each carton for evidence of damage. If no obvious damage can be seen, proceed with the following method of checking before installing the pack on a disk drive:

1. Remove bottom cover.
2. Make sure you have a firm and steady grip on the cover handle, then turn the pack upside down and level it so it can be spun freely inside the cover.

IMPORTANT: Apply spinning force to the center of the pack only. Do not touch the bottom disk as this may affect alignment.

ILLUSTRATION D-37. Hold pack cover tightly.

3. As the pack is spinning, visually inspect it for excessive up and down motion of any individual recording disk. Noticeable separation between the sector disk and the recording disk adjacent to it indicates the pack has been damaged and should not be used.

Labeling

Only Memorex bezel labels are recommended for labeling Memorex disk packs. They are made of contamination-free material, and are designed to maintain proper pack balance. Memorex labels come in 9 colors for rapid identification, and are easily removed or replaced. Since the top disk is an integral part of the pack, labels should never be applied there. This would upset critical pack balance. Use only inner area of bezel shield for labeling.

WARNING: When attaching a new label, always remove old label first. A thickness of three or more labels will not allow the cover to properly engage and lock on pack. Additional space for labeling is also provided on Memorex cover sets.

ILLUSTRATION D-38. Use Memorex labels only, centered inside bezel shield.

Environmental Acclimation

It is important that new disk packs be allowed to rest in their new environment for at least 24 hours. This will assure proper track registration. Accelerated acclimation can be accomplished by mounting the pack on an available drive and allowing it to rotate for at least one hour. This procedure should be used in emergency cases.

Loading

A disk pack is a precise, delicate mechanism, manufactured to exacting tolerances. It is most vulnerable to damage during the loading and unloading operations. Extreme care in handling should be taken at all times to assure long life and proper functioning.

IMPORTANT: To maintain fine tolerances, never handle disk pack unless top cover and/or bottom cover is in place. The surface of a disk should never be touched with your fingers or other objects, such as paper, pencils, etc. This exposes the pack to unnecessary contamination.

1. Remove bottom cover.
2. Hold the pack by the top cover handle and lower it carefully into the drawer, perpendicular to the cone.

    IMPORTANT: Avoid any contact between disk pack and drive housing as this could result in permanent disk pack damage.

3. Turn the handle clockwise until it comes to a complete stop.
4. Remove the top cover carefully, making sure it does not contact the disks.
5. Always reassemble empty top and bottom covers to keep the inside dust free.

Unloading

1. IMPORTANT: Allow pack to stop spinning by itself. Never stop it by pressing on the top disk or inside bezel shield. This may affect critical alignment.

2. Carefully replace top cover over pack. Again, take extreme care not to allow the cover to contact edges of the disks.

ILLUSTRATION D–39. Never stop pack by touching.

3. Turn the cover counterclockwise until you hear one distinct click. This secures the cover and allows it and the pack to be removed as a unit from the drive spindle.

ILLUSTRATION D–41.

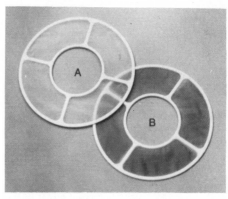

ILLUSTRATION D–41. Have dirty air filters replaced. "A" is clean filter, "B" is dirty filter.

4. Attach the bottom cover to the pack. Disk pack air filters should be visually checked after each use. Replacement is indicated when filters are discolored. For best operation, try to keep filters as close to white in color as possible. WARNING: Never try to clean dirty filters. They are available free-of-charge from Memorex.

Storage

1. Short-Term Storage: Ideally disk packs should be stored in temperatures no lower than 60° and no higher than 90°F. Relative humidity should range between 8 and 80%. Do not store in direct sunlight or near strong magnetic fields.
2. Always store flat, right-side-up, resting on bottom cover. Storing the packs on their edge could result in a disk misalignment.

3. Long-Term Storage: Replace disk pack in shipping container. Long-term storage temperatures can range from –40° to 150°F.

Additional Tips for Proper Handling

1. Vacuum clean pack covers regularly, inside and out, to prevent dust build-up.
2. Keep drive covers or file drawers closed at all times, except when loading or removing a pack.
3. Vacuum pack file cabinets regularly to remove dust particles.
4. Never put notes or foreign objects of any kind inside the cover set or pack.
5. Use only 91% isopropyl alcohol for cleaning (9% distilled water).
6. If a pack is a suspect damaged pack, don't put it into use until it has been inspected by Memorex.

ILLUSTRATION D–42. The Memorex customer engineer's maintenance kit.

Maintenance of your disk pack is provided by a Memorex customer engineer. He's an expert in disk pack operation. If you have any questions, just call. He's prepared to give you full service assistance.

TAPE REPLACEMENT WORKSHEET

SOURCE:

Data Devices International, Woodland Hills, California.

TAPE REPLACEMENT WORKSHEET

The object of the tape replacement worksheet is to determine at which point an old tape should be removed from the library of active tapes and replaced by a new tape.

I.   **Summary of Cost Factors:**

A tape replacement decision should be based on economic factors such as the cost of new tape and the cost of computer time. These factors can be properly combined to determine when a tape should be replaced. The following information is required:

		Example
1.	Cost of a new reel of tape	$11.00
2.	Cost per error of computer time, (example: If monthly rental is $30,000, cost per error is 3.8¢. See Table I).	3.8¢
3.	Number of reels in tape library	2,000
4.	Number of tape reels mounted per day.	150

Table I

Actual Cost Of Write Check Error

ACTUAL COST OF WRITE CHECK ERROR

MONTHLY CPM RENTAL	CPU* COST PER SECOND	COST** OF ERROR
$ 5 K	.008¢	.6¢
$10 K	.016¢	1.3¢
$20 K	.032¢	2.5¢
$30 K	.048¢	3.8¢
$40 K	.064¢	5.1¢
$50 K	.080¢	6.3¢
$60 K	.096¢	7.6¢
$70 K	.112¢	8.8¢
$80 K	.128¢	10.1¢
$100 K	.160¢	13.0¢

*Computation based on 22 working days per month, one 8 hour shift operation.
**This cost defined as the time lost when the computer is in a wait state while the tape unit attempts to write a record on a defined area of tape. Computation for a standard tape unit with 10 automatic retries before skip command.

These cost factors can be examined one at a time to develop a systematic tape management program. The first information required is how many times a year an average tape is used. This is equal to the number of tapes used per day times the number of days per year divided by the number of active tapes in the library.

EXAMPLE:

1. 150 tapes mounted per day x 5 days per week x 52 weeks per year = 39,000 tape mounts per year.

2. $\dfrac{39,000 \text{ mounts}}{2,000 \text{ reels}} = \begin{array}{l} 19.5 \text{ mounts per year} \\ \text{for the average tape} \end{array}$

Next, the yearly cost of one error on each tape must be determined and compared with the cost of new tape to establish a replacement criteria.

EXAMPLE:

1. 19.5 mounts x 3.8¢ cost for each error = 74.1¢ is yearly cost of one error

2. $\dfrac{\$11.00 \text{ cost of new tape}}{\$\ 0.741 \text{ cost per error}} = \begin{array}{l} 15 \text{ errors per tape} \\ \text{(replacement point)} \end{array}$

Every tape with 15 or more errors costs $11.11 per year to use - more than the new tape cost of $11.00. This information permits us to develop an organized and systematic magnetic tape maintenance program:

This systematic approach is outlined in the chart attached. Tapes with more than **x** errors should be repaired or discarded and tapes with less than **x** errors should be returned to active use or reviewed for repair.

Each Data Processing Center requires maximum efficiency. Tapes with less than **x** errors should be divided into two categories:

1. For use in critical applications (file tapes) or

2. Normal work tape applications (production tapes)

It is recommended that tapes with less than ½ **x** errors be reserved for critical applications - payroll, financial information, etc. Tapes with more than ½ **x** errors but less than **x** errors can be used for all normal work tape applications.

This systematic control of tape use will maximize computer efficiency and reduce computer tape cost to an absolute minimum.

TAPE REPLACEMENT WORKSHEET

ACTUAL COST OF WRITE CHECK ERROR

MONTHLY CPM RENTAL	CPU* COST PER SECOND	COST** OF ERROR
$ 5 K	.008¢	.6 ¢
$10 K	.016¢	1.3 ¢
$20 K	.032¢	2.5 ¢
$30 K	.048¢	3.8 ¢
$40 K	.064¢	5.1 ¢
$50 K	.080¢	6.3 ¢
$60 K	.096¢	7.6 ¢
$70 K	.112¢	8.8 ¢
$80 K	.128¢	10.1 ¢
$100 K	.160¢	13.0 ¢

*Computation based on 22 working days per month, one 8 hour shift operation.

**This cost defined as the time lost when the computer is in a wait state while the tape unit attempts to write a record on a defined area of tape. Computation for a standard tape unit with 10 automatic retries before skip command.

	EXAMPLE	FILL IN YOUR FIGURES HERE
1. Determine the average number of tapes mounted on drives each day.	150 tapes/day	_____ tapes/day
2. Determine the number of tapes mounted on drives each week — (Multiply by number of schedule work days per week).	150 × 5 = 750 tapes/week	_____ X _____ _____ tapes/week
3. Determine the number of tapes mounted on drives each year. (Multiply x 52 weeks).	750 × 52 = 39,000 tapes/year	____ X 52 = _____ tapes/year
4. Determine the number of active reels of tape in library.	2,000 reels	_____ reels
5. Determine the average number of times each reel of tape is used per year by dividing Line 3 by Line 4.	$\frac{39,000}{2000} = 19.5$ times/year	_____ = _____ times/year
6. Determine the yearly cost of one error on each tape. Refer to the chart to determine the cost of each error. Multiply the number of times a tape is used on Line 5 by the cost per each error determined from the chart.	19.5 × 3.8¢ = 74.1¢ yearly cost per error	____ X ____ ¢ = _____ yearly cost per error
7. Determine the number of errors required per tape to justify replacement. Divide the cost of a new reel of tape by the cost per error determined on Line 6.	$\frac{\$11.00}{\$.741} = 15$ errors per tape	$ _____ = ____ $ errors per tape

SUMMARY:

Each tape should be repaired or discarded whenever it has 15 or more errors.

REQUEST FOR PROPOSAL RFP

SOURCE:

Edward O. Joslin, *Computer Selection,* augmented edition (Fairfax Station, Va.: The Technology Press Inc., 1977), pp. 179–203.

The following pages contain a fictitious (and slightly condensed) Request for System Proposals, preceded by a sample of a letter that might accompany such a Request for System Proposals. This RFSP not only gives a brief case history; it also introduces the selection criteria to be used later in the example.

THE USER CORPORATION

Racine, Wisconsin

Mr. A Vendor
Proposal Manager
4th Generation Computer Company
Kansas City, Kansas

April 10,198x

Dear Mr. Vendor:

In previous correspondence you have expressed an interest in proposing a system to fulfill our computer requirements. Attached are three copies of our Request for System Proposals (RFSP). This RFSP consists of three sections. The first contains a statement of the ground rules under which the system proposals are requested. The second section contains three subsections, the first of which describes the system requirements in general terms and then provides an example of an equipment configuration which would be considered to be responsive to the system requirements. The second subsection lists the mandatory conditions which must be met by any system proposed and then describes additional features or capabilities desired from the system or its support, and describes the values established for inclusion of additional features. The third subsection contains a brief description of each of the application benchmark programs to be run (a detailed listing of these programs is provided in the appendixes to this RFSP) and then briefly describes how these programs are to be used to determine systems timing. The third section of the RFSP contains instructions specifying the desired makeup of proposals to be submitted.

If, after reading the attached material, you are still interested in submitting a proposal, please contact this office so that we will keep you on our mailing list for changes or explanations as the need for them arises.

Yours truly,

I. L. Pick
Selection Manager

SECTION 1: STATEMENT OF GROUND RULES

1. The purpose of this RFSP is to solicit proposals for a computer system to replace our present system (leased) with one of greater compatibility, in order to support our increased workload (present and projected). A description of this workload is contained in the second part of this RFSP.

2. All inquiries concerning this RFSP should be addressed to:

Mr. I. L. Pick
Selection Manager
USER Corporation
Racine, Wisconsin

All questions should be submitted in writing, citing the particular RFSP part and paragraph number. Answers to all questions of a substantive nature (as well as copies of the questions) will be given to all vendors being solicited unless the question is of such nature that it is proprietary to the asking vendor. The closing date for the asking of questions, and other pertinent dates, are given in the next paragraph.

3. The dates pertinent to this selection are as follows:

a)	Release of RFSP	April 10, 1968
b)	Vendors' briefing	May 1, 1968
c)	Closing date for inquiries	June 30, 1968
d)	Benchmark demonstrations	May 1 to June 30, 1968
e)	Submission of proposals	July 10, 1968
f)	Vendors' presentation	July 17, 1968
g)	Contract award and debriefing	September 10, 1968
h)	Desired installation	April 10, 1969

4. Benchmark demonstrations will be conducted at a date mutually satisfactory to both the vendor and the selection manager. Vendors are urged to demonstrate the capabilities of their computer systems at the earliest possible time in order to ensure that they will have ample time for a rescheduled demonstration in case of some mishap or failure of equipment on their first attempt. If a vendor, after he has successfully demonstrated, should be able to substantially improve the operation of his system before the closing date for demonstrations (June 30), he will be permitted to redemonstrate.

5. Your proposal must be submitted, in triplicate, to Mr. Pick's office before the close of the work day (5 P.M.) of July 10, 1968. In fairness to all vendors, we must state that proposals received after that date will not be considered in the selection.

6. Vendors are encouraged to supplement their written proposals with oral presentations. These presentations provide the vendor with an opportunity to clarify any unusual equipment characteristics or to call to our attention other significant elements.

7. The systems proposed in response to this RFSP should be available for lease or purchase either by USER corporation or by a third party, a leasing company. This stipulation should apply not only to the entire system but also to the individual components of the equipment, so that split acquisition will be one possibility of procurement.

8. The costs incurred in running the benchmark programs, in preparing the proposals, or incurred in any other manner by the vendor in responding to this RFSP may not be charged to USER corporation.

9. The content of the proposal of the successful bidder will be considered as contractual obligations. Failure to meet these obligations may result in cancellation of the contract.

10. USER Corporation reserves the right to reject any and all proposals received in response to this request if some other manner of negotiation better serves the interests of USER Corporation. USER Corporation does not necessarily intend to award the contract solely on the basis of this request, or otherwise pay for the information solicited or obtained. However, unless we announce otherwise, we shall select the winning proposal on the basis of its total cost (including cost of supporting personnel and of conversion) minus the cost-values awarded for desirable capabilities proposed.

11. As changes to the RFSP are required, or as pertinent answers to the questions raised by vendors are prepared, these will be sent to all interested vendors.

12. If at any time your company decides not to bid in response to this RFSP, please inform the selection manager of your decision.

SECTION II: SYSTEM REQUIREMENTS

1. Equipment requirements

A. This new system is being acquired to replace our present leased 1410 computer system. The following table shows the major components and their present and projected usage in hours per month.

Quantity	Components	Present Usage	Projected Usage At Replacement*
1	Processor and 40,000 cores	425	510
7	729 IV tape drives	175	225
1	1403 Printer	400	600
1	1402 card reader/card punch	375	400
1	1301 28 million IAS	425	510

*Operational use time per component.

Within the next five years the workload is expected to double. The workload consists, in essence, of programs like those shown in the appendix (omitted in this example).

B. We feel that a computer system with approximately 64,000 words of main memory, 10 high-speed tape drives, 50,000,000 words of random-access capability, a 1000-line-per-minute printer, a 500-card-per-minute reader, and a 250-card-per-minute punch, and with sufficient processing capability to handle in six hours the mix of programs given, would prove satisfactory for this application.

2. Mandatory and Desirable Requirements

A. The mandatory requirements for this selection are summarized below. Any system not possessing the minimal capabilities or otherwise failing to meet the requirements stated below will not be considered in this selection.

(1) Capability of handling existing COBOL problems.
(2) Capability of handling projected workload increases to 200% of workload at time of 1410 replacement.
(3) Capability of processing the five application benchmarks to the satisfaction of the computer-evaluation personnel.
(4) Submission of complete proposal by 10 July 1968.

B. The desired capabilities for this application are stated below.

(1) Software packages: sort/merge, automatic debug, and PERT.
(2) Workload expansion capability: it would be desirable if the system were able to handle the 200% expansion in from 350 to 400 hours a month or less.

(3) Equipment capability: it would be desirable if the system were such that an optical document scanner could be tied on which would handle "turn-around" documents at the rate of approximately 100 per minute. If this capability is available, and if an optical scanner is to be proposed, then an additional benchmark test employing the scanner will have to be run in order to determine timing.
(4) Vendor support (desirable to have):
   a. On-site maintenance
   b. 250 hours of program test time
   c. Three program-support personnel for six months
(5) Less than 6% hand changes required for existing COBOL programs.
(6) Equipment delivery: delivery before 10 April 1969 is desired.
(7) Space available: desirable that system fit within the existing 45-by-20-foot room.
(8) Cost: lease cost, $10,000–20,000 per month.

C. The presence of these desired capabilities in a vendor's proposal will be rewarded as shown in the following paragraphs and evaluation templates.

(1) *Software packages*
   (a) Sort/merge: The value of having a sort/merge package proposed is about equal to the cost of writing, or having written, such a package. A package of this sort has been calculated to cost approximately $100,000.
   (b) Automatic debug: The value of having an automatic debug package proposed is about equal to the cost of writing, or having written, such a program. A program of the type desired would cost approximately $60,000. This worth can be cross-checked by interpreting this $60,000 as six man-years of debug time. The organization has 12 programmers, probably salaried at $10,000 a year on the average. If the automatic debug package would save 10% of the programmers' time by avoiding the extra debugging, the organization would save $12,000 a year. Over the five-year life of the system, this would amount to $60,000. Hence this figure is reasonable.
   (c) PERT: The value of having a PERT package proposed is considered to be worth only about $20,000, because of its limited use, it spite of the fact that it would cost about

$75,000 to obtain such a program from a software consultant.

(2) *Workload expansion capabilities.* Assuming that cost of the equipment for the stated five-year life of a minimal system will be about $500,000, we have established the following value figures for system life (workload expandability) in excess of this stated life. (These values will be used only in the event that the system is purchased, since if the system is leased it would probably be advisable to lease a larger system to obtain the desired expansion capability.)

Additional Life	Expansion Over Fifth Year, %	Hours Required To Process Fifth-Year Stated Workload	Value Assigned
0	20	520	$ 0
1	25	462	70,000
2	60	400	110,000
3 or more	100	346	140,000

(3) *Equipment capability.* The value of being able to tie an optical scanner into this system is measured by the fact that it would save an additional expenditure of approximately $150,000 for a special-purpose optical-scanning system. Thus a system which contains an optical scanner and which is capable of performing the scanning benchmark test will receive an additional cost-value of as much as $150,000.

(4) *Vendor support of system*

   (a) On-site maintenance. It is assumed that, in any given month, there will be approximately seven occasions calling for unscheduled action by the maintenance engineer. If his presence saves an hour (valued at $100) each time, this is a $700 a month or approximately $40,000 over the life of the system.

   (b) Program test time. The maximum number of hours of program test time to be made available by the vendor is 250. Every hour of predelivery program test time made available (up to 250 hours) is considered to have a value of $100 an hour. Every hour of postdelivery test time (the number of postdelivery hours must not exceed 250 *minus the number of predelivery hours used*) is considered to be worth $50 dollars an hour.

The maximum value of program testing by the vendor is to be no more than $25,000.

   (c) Program-support personnel. One and a half man-years of program support is considered desirable; if the vendor supplies this, it should be worth $40,000 at a maximum.

(5) *Hand changes to COBOL.* The cost-value is naturally greatest if no changes in coding are required. Conversely, if more than 15% of the program needs changing, the trouble and expense incurred in making these changes by hand makes COBOL almost useless for existing programs.

Changes Required	Value
None	$60,000
Less than 2%	30,000
Less than 4%	20,000
5%	10,000
6%	0
7–8%	–10,000
9–10%	–40,000
10–15%	Up to –$60,000

(6) *Equipment delivery.* The cost-value of early delivery is determined by projecting the amount it would cost to lease additional facilities to process the expanding workload, plus estimating the dollar value of the inconvenience this would cause.

Value template

Delivery Date	Value
January 1969	$ 50,000
February 1969	25,000
March 1969	10,000
April 1969	0
May 1969	–10,000
June 1969	–30,000
July 1969	–60,000
August 1969	–100,000

(7) *Space available.* If the proposed system should be of such size that it will not fit within the 900 square feet available, an immediate charge of $2,000 will be made for the necessary removal of the adjacent wall, plus an additional charge of $50 a square foot for each additional square foot of floor space needed by the proposed system.

Table 1

(1) If the vendor does not propose an optical scanner, the following problems must be run:

Problem	Processing Compile	Execute	I/O
A	3	1	Full
B	–	2	Full input only once Full output both times
C	4	5	Full I/O on compile twice, input only on other two Execution output to tape
D	2	2	Full
E	8	1	Full

(2) If the vendor does propose an optical scanner, the following problems must be run:

Problem	Processing Compile	Execute	I/O
A-E	As above		
F	–	2	Full

(8) *Cost.* Costs will be figured on a straight additive basis over the estimated life of the system, considering both one-time and continuing costs. The system which costs least will naturally be the most desirable. The cost items that will be used in making the comparison are as follows:
(a) Equipment cost, based on projected duration of usage*
(b) Cost of operating personnel, based on projected duration of usage*
(c) Maintenance cost, based on projected duration of usage*
(d) Vendor support of system
(e) Site preparation
(f) Equipment installation
(g) Equipment transportation
(h) Any other differentiating cost items*

3. Benchmark Programs

A. Five benchmark programs have been selected to represent the entire existing workload to be handled by the new computer system. A sixth benchmark program represents the type of workload which would be added by the capability to handle an optical scanner. These six programs are described below:

(1) Benchmark *A*: Payroll
(2) Benchmark *B*: Sales forecasting
(3) Benchmark *C*: Application summaries
(4) Benchmark *D*: Market research
(5) Benchmark *E*: Inventory control
(6) Benchmark *F*: Document scanner

B. The system proposed will have to be capable of handling the thruput of the following mix (depending on whether or not a scanner is proposed). The system must handle this thruput in twelve hours to be considered responsive to the first year's requirements and in six hours in order to be considered still responsive in the fifth year of life of the system. (The order of running the programs within the mix may be optimized, if possible.) (*See* Table 1.)

SECTION III: PROPOSAL INSTRUCTIONS

The proposal instructions consist of two basic parts and can be outlined as follows:

1. Format instructions
   A. Purpose
   B. Proposal format
   C. Tables and instructions
2. Tables and timing information
   A. Questionnaire
   B. Benchmark problem instructions
   C. Timing and cost tables

1. Format Instructions

A. PURPOSE
(1) These instructions prescribe the format of proposals and describe the approach which should be used for the development and presentation of proposal data.
(2) These instructions are designed to ensure the submission of information essential to the understanding and comprehensive evaluation of equipment proposals. The instructions are not intended to limit the contents of proposals. The instructions do permit the

*This system is estimated to have a life of five years. Thus five years is the period of time which we shall use as a basis for continuing cost.

inclusion of any additional data or information a vendor deems pertinent.

B. PROPOSAL FORMAT

(1) Each proposal is to be submitted in two parts, each separately bound, preferably in loose-leaf binders. Part I should contain the system proposal and Part II should contain the technical data.

PART I. SYSTEM PROPOSAL

Section 1. Introduction

1-1 Covering letter. Letter of transmittal.

1-2 Summary. Should contain a brief statement of the salient features of the proposal, including conclusions and generalized recommendations.

Section 2. Requirements

Administrative, contractual, and other mandatory requirements. In this section of his proposal, the vendor must provide a positive statement concerning his position with respect to each mandatory requirement and each desired capability, and state the degree to which his system is capable of satisfying each mandatory or desired requirement.

Section 3. System Processing

3-1 System concept and description. The vendor should explain the conceptual approach he used in solving the problems presented by the system, and should furnish a statement indicating whether or not the system as proposed in the RFSP was used. He should explain any variation he has made in system processing in terms of concept, and give detailed backup information.

3-2 Workload processing capabilities. The vendor should describe or explain the capabilities of the proposed configuration(s) to process the total workload within the required operational use hours. Summary totals abstracted from the timing tables, with suitable explanation of terms and data, will suffice. He should also express his system's capability in terms of future planned applications, with regard to the additional equipment requirements such expansion will necessitate.

3-3 Timing tables. Timing tables are to be completed in accordance with the instructions furnished with them.

Section 4. Cost Data

4-1 Cost tables. Cost tables are to be completed in accordance with instructions furnished.

4-2 Cost questionnaire. The cost questionnaire is to be completed in accordance with instructions furnished therewith and in the RFSP. The vendor should include a positive statement as to the guaranteed price period involved for any service, hardware, or software proposed. All questions must be answered. Additional appendices may be submitted to augment specific replies.

4-3 Special cost elements. The vendor should describe any special discounts (equipment, training, education, etc.) or price/cost concessions which may or may not appear elsewhere in the proposal, but which are deemed sufficiently advantageous to USER Corporation to warrant special notice or emphasis.

Section 5. Contract Provisions

5-1 Certificate of cost. To assist in the preparation of any procurement documents resulting from this RFSP, the vendor should submit in quadruplicate, a certificate of cost, signed by a corporate official.

5-2 Procurement plans. The vendor should state and explain each of the procurement plans that his company offers, insofar as they relate to this proposal.

Section 6. Proposed Data-Processing Facility

The vendor should state the housing requirements necessary for the proposed configuration. This section should specify the requirements for space, power, air conditioning and humidity control, engineering maintenance area, raised flooring, etc.; where applicable, these specifications should be given for individual components. Also, if certain components will be necessary for future expansion, the vendor should specify the additional space, power, etc., requirements necessary to integrate them.

Section 7. Detailed Questions Regarding System Proposal

The questionnaire is to be completed in accordance with the instructions furnished. All questions must be answered. Additional appendices may be submitted to augment specific replies.

Section 8. Vendor's Addendum (optional)

This section is provided so that the vendor may submit any additional data on his system which he has not included elsewhere, and which he considers to be pertinent to this proposal.

PART II. TECHNICAL DATA

Section 1. Technical Literature

The vendor is to submit all appropriate technical literature regarding both hardware and software characteristics of the proposed configuration(s). The literature is to be submitted as additional, separately bound volumes accompanying Part II of this proposal. A list of the literature to be submitted is to be provided in Section 1 of Part II.

Section 2. Equipment Characteristics and Software

2–1 Equipment configuration charts and exhibits.

A detailed description of the technical characteristics of each major component of the proposed equipment configuration(s) is to be provided. The information is to relate only to the equipment proposed, and should depict in tabular form all the equipment proposed, indicating the designation, types, and model number of each major component. These data should be identical to the equipment configuration(s) reported in the cost table.

2–2 Schematic diagram

a) The vendor should provide a functional schematic drawing showing all devices proposed. This drawing should also identify the devices needed to meet the expandability requirements, and the interconnections between the equipment proposed for the present needs and the equipment proposed for future expansion.

b) In order to reveal the maximum expandability possible within the limitations of equipment comprising the proposed configuration, the vendor should furnish an additional schematic chart, reflecting the maximum possible add-on equipment (specifying categories and numbers) which the proposed configuration is capable of accepting without excessive downtime, without the replacement of the computer system or a major component thereof, and without extensive reprogramming of existing operations.

c) On a component-by-component basis, the vendor should translate the maximum capability made available by subparagraph (b), above, into benefits to the system, specifying the kind and amount of benefit and the estimated amount to be derived. (For example, the percentage reduction in time needed to accomplish the workload, over that reflected in the timing tables.)

2–3 Software. The vendor should list each software package which is being proposed with the equipment configuration, stating when the software classified as mandatory will be operationally available (i.e., whether it has been field tested). He should also state whether the other-than-mandatory software packages being proposed are now operationally available; if they are not now available, he should include a date by which they will become operational. He should briefly describe the function of each operationally available package (and should include technical literature), and indicate its storage requirements. For each of the program packages recommended for the proposed installation, procedures and plans for maintenance and future development should be indicated.

2–4 Software equipment requirements. For each software package to be furnished with the proposal, the minimum equipment configuration needed to use each such package should be specified, component by component. A table similar to the following may be used.

Name of Program	Core	Magnetic Tapes	Disk *	Card Reader	Device A†	Feature B†
Assembly	4,000	2	10	Model "X"	X	
COBOL	12,000	4	20		X	
PERT	8,000	3	15		X	X
Debug	2,000					
Sort						

*Whenever appropriate defince capacity.
†Identify kind and model number, if appropriate.

Section 3. Vendor Support of System

3-1 Training. The vendor should define his capability to meet the training requirements, i.e., to train programmers, operators, etc., and should describe any teaching aids to be used, qualifications of instructors, and any other information he may consider significant with regard to his training capacity.

3-2 Personnel Support. The vendor should specify the type and number of people he will provide to support the computer facility. He should list titles, types of positions, and functions, and give a description of the responsibilities of each position. "Supporting personnel" includes personnel for installation, programming, training, and maintenance.

3-3 Maintenance. The vendor should discuss the time required for preventive maintenance, as well as type of maintenance recommended. He should discuss also the solution of such problems as transportation, communication, etc., as they relate to the maintenance environment.

Section 4. Detailed Questions Regarding Technical Data

The questionnaire is to be completed in accordance with the instructions furnished. All questions must be answered.

Section 5. Vendor's Addendum (Optional)

This section is provided so that the vendor may submit any additional technical data which he has not included elsewhere and which he considers is pertinent to this proposal.

C. Tables and Instructions. Specific timing and cost data required for evaluation of system proposals are to be included in tabular form, in accordance with the proposal format outlined in Sections 3 and 4 above. Deviations from the prescribed format are not permitted. If an element is not applicable, this fact should be stated.

    (1) *Timing tables*
        (a) If more than one system is proposed—for example, a primary system with one or

more satellite systems—separate tables should be prepared for each system.
        (b) All timing entries are to be expressed in minutes and hundredths of minutes.
    (2) *Cost tables*
        (a) Supplementary written explanations necessary to expand on entries should be included where required.
        (b) If special or additional features must be attached to a given component to complete the processing requirements, the features and their prices should be listed beneath the component.
        (c) In addition, the vendor should furnish a statement, by component, of lease/purchase options and maintenance charges for purchased equipment.
        (d) All costs figures are to reflect any relevant discounts.

2. Tables and Timing Information

A. Questionnaire. The vendor should discuss each of the following items and list detailed references where additional or supporting information may be obtained.

    (1) *System proposed*
        (a) Compatibility with other systems
        (b) Advantages over competitive systems
        (c) Sites at which a configuration similar to the proposed one is currently operational
    (2) *System components*
        (a) Central processor
            (i) Speed: formulas for computing arithmetic operations; transfer, conversion, and logic operations
            (ii) Capacity: address structure (fixed or variable), length of words, binary or decimal storage, reserved storage
            (iii) Hardware features: index register, indirect addressing, buffers, etc.
        (b) Auxiliary storage (for each type)
            (i) Speed: formulas for determination of speed; transfer times, speed of loading unit, etc.
            (ii) Capacity: bit structures, density gaps, addressable record sizes, head arrangement, etc.
        (c) Peripheral devices and control
            (i) Input/output channels: number, operation, restrictions

(ii) Input/output buffers: location, operation, restrictions

(iii) Controllers: functions

(iv) Card read/punch: speed, capacity, restrictions, clutch points, conversion, data verification, testable conditions

(v) Printer: speed, number of copies, print positions, testable conditions, character sets available

(vi) Other peripherals (with particular attention to remote terminals)

(d) Real-time interfaces (detailed specifications)

For the system, as proposed, and for each component of the system, explain any simultaneity that exists and how this simultaneity can be increased.

(4) *Checking features*

(a) Error detection. For each device proposed (i.e., central processor, card reader, remote, etc.), the vendor should fully explain the error-detecting features it contains.

(b) Error correction. For each device proposed, the vendor should explain any automatic error-correcting techniques proposed.

(5) *Operating software*

For each of the operating systems packages the vendor proposes (schedulers, input/output control systems, memory allocators, memory protect, etc.), he should enumerate the purposes and advantages, and discuss the package's influence on system timing (overhead) with respect to the entire system; he should also discuss the package's flexibility.

(6) *Software packages*

For each software package proposed, the vendor should discuss the following items in detail.

(a) Highlights of the package: its advantages over other types of handling, over competitive packages, etc.

(b) Ease of use: method of inserting changes, amount of operator intervention possible or required, recommended length of training for programmers and operators, etc.

(c) Efficiency: how the package compares with machine coded instructions, in speed of operation and capacity requirements

(d) Flexibility

(7) *Vendor support*

Describe the type of support to be furnished in the following categories.

(a) Training: courses offered, duration of courses, etc.

(b) Program testing: hours to be made available to complete tests (prior to and after delivery), test configuration, location at which tests will be run, etc.

(c) On-site programming and conversion assistance: personnel, programs, etc.

(d) Backup facilities: location and configuration

(e) Maintenance offered: on-site or on-call; hours, spare parts, test equipment, etc.

(f) Programs offered: conversion, application, control, etc.

(g) Documentation: types, amounts, etc.

(h) Other support: explanation of any additional support available

(8) *Equipment requirements*

(a) Space

(b) Air conditioning

(c) Power

(d) Other requirements

(9) *Cost data*

The following cost data should be supplied.

(a) Equipment cost (for each component)
   (i) Lease (basic and extra)
   (ii) Purchase and maintenance
   (iii) Other plans

(b) One-time cost
   (i) Transportation
   (ii) Installation
   (iii) Other

(c) Vendor's support of system
   (i) Personnel
   (ii) Test time
   (iii) Documentation
   (iv) Test equipment
   (v) Other

(d) Supplies (all major supplies)

(e) Conversion

(f) Other costs (these should be listed and defined)

B. Benchmark Problem Instructions

(1) Each vendor will be required to perform a live demonstration of the mix of benchmark problems designed to demonstrate the capabilities of the equipment and the software which he proposes for the processing of current applications (including optical scanner if proposed), and which he proposes to meet the require-

ments for future expansion. The demonstration will be considered as being the validation of the timing estimates included in proposals. Sample and live test data will be supplied by this office.

(2) The appendix, with its exhibits, contains the test problems and necessary documentation so that vendors may analyze the requirements for the benchmark exercise. The sample test data have been withheld. Each participating vendor will signify his intention to perform the benchmark exercise in a formal letter, at which time the sample test data will be released to him. If we do not receive such a letter from the vendor, this will signify that the vendor does not desire to remain in the competition for the contract to be awarded for this computer system.

(3) The live test demonstration will require:

    (a) Processing the representative mix of benchmark problems presented in the appendix.

    (b) Demonstration of any concurrent multiprogramming and/or multiprocessing capabilities claimed in proposals.

    (c) Demonstration of the system's COBOL capabilities.

(4) The mix of problems to be run is shown in the following tables:

C. Timing and Cost Tables. The timing and cost tables which the vendor should complete are presented in Exhibits 1 through 5 (see pages 198–203). These tables are as follows.

    (1) A detailed timing table (Exhibit 1) is to be completed for every program timed.

    (2) One mix timing summary table (Exhibit 2) should be completed. The vendor should justify any simultaneity of functions claimed in preparing this table by means of written material attached to this table.

    (3) One monthly timing summary table (Exhibit 3) should be completed.

    (4) A separate table setting forth costs of a leased system (Exhibit 4) is to be made up for each year of system life.

    (5) One table summarizing costs of a purchased system (Exhibit 5) should be prepared.

The appendix, containing program listings, has been omitted from this condensed version of an RFSP, since including these listings would serve little purpose.

---

a) If the vendor does not propose an optical scanner, the following problems must be run:

| Problem | Processing | | I/O |
	Compile	Execute	
A	3	1	Full
B	–	2	Full input only once
			Full output both times
C	4	5	Full I/O on compile twice,
			input only on other two
			Execution output to tape
D	2	2	Full
E	8	1	Full

b) If the vendor does propose an optical scanner, the following problems must be run:

| Problem | Processing | | I/O |
	Compile	Execute	
A-E	As above		
F	–	2	Full

Exhibit 1 Detailed Timing Table (Time Expressed in Minutes and Hundredths of Minutes.)

Program number _____
A. Input/output requirements: (sample)

								Frequency in mix		
Files	Number Reports	Record Size	Block Factors	Number Of Reels/packs	I/O Media	Channel Assignment	Component Time	Time (Component) Shared	Chargeable Time	Total Time
Program load time	12	10,000	1	1	MT-04	1	1.76	All against	1.76	1.76
In-Pr master file	2,500	576	1	2	MT-01	4	2.08	Pr-01	123.97	
Transaction file	1,200	69	1	1	MT-02	3	.32		123.97	
Out-Pr master file	2,500	576	1	2	MT-03	2	2.08		123.97	
Report No. 1	2,500	28 lines			PR-01	1	123.97	0	123.97	125.73

B. Central processor requirements: (sample)

Functional Areas	Memory Utilized
Fixed-overhead locations	12
Fixed-overhead routines	540
Semifixed-overhead routines	1870
I/O routines	327
Read/write areas	2682
Program main path	5100
Program subpaths	1250
Others (specify): work areas, etc.	8625
Totals	20,406

C. Setup requirements: (sample)

	Component Times	Time (Component) Shared	Net Operator Time
Chargeable functions			
Multiple reels/packs changes	8.00	2.00(MT-01)	6.00
Rewinds	1.00	—	1.00
Nonchargeable functions			
Set up/take down	4.00	—	4.00

D. Total chargeable time   132.73
E. Total elapsed time   136.73

Exhibit 2

Program description	Set-up	Components																	Elapsed time
		Card reader		MT 1		MT 2		Ptr 1		Ptr 2		Card punch		IAS unit 1		IAS unit 2		CPU		
		CT	CA	CT	CA	CT	CA	CT	CA	CT	CA	CT	CA	CT	CA	CT	CA	CT	MR	
Total, min																				
Total, hr																				

CT = Changeable time
CA = Channel assignment
MR = Memory requirement
MT = Magnetic tape

Exhibit 3

Description of monthly utilization	Set-up	Component							Elapsed time
		Card reader	MT 1	MT 2	Ptr 1	Ptr 2	Card punch	IAS unit 1	IAS unit 2	CPU	
Total mix time											
Total extrapolated monthly requirements											
1st year											
2nd year											
3rd year											
4th year											
5th year											
6th year											
7th year											
8th year											

Exhibit 4

Equipment			Use rates		Chargeable time		Extra cost		Total cost		
					Hr/month		Extra shift	Extra maint.	Basic	Extra	Total use
Model no.	Description	Quantity	Basic	Extra	Basic	Extra					

Exhibit 5

Equipment		Purchase unit price	Total price	Maintenance					5-year total price	Month to break even
Model	Quantity			1st year	2nd year	3rd year	4th year	5th year		

COMPUTER
CONTRACT
CHECKLIST

SOURCE:

Robert P. Bigelow and Susan H. Nycum, *Your Computer and the Law* (Englewood Cliffs, N.J.: Prentice-Hall, Inc., 1975), pp. 213–231.

This is a checklist of items which the data processing manager and his attorney should consider from a contractual viewpoint when a system is installed or expanded.

1 SYSTEM DESIGN

Before you start contractual negotiations, a feasibility study should be made. The applications which the proposed system is to handle should be specified in as complete detail as possible both for internal use and for delivery to possible suppliers of hardware, software, and other services.

The critical factors in each application should be clearly identified. These include:

a. Accuracy standards—can any error be tolerated?
b. Permissible limits—e.g., man-hours, dollars.
c. Job scheduling—how long until project completed?
d. Outside factors affecting the application. (One example might be a very complicated collective bargaining agreement specifying pay rates; this would have a considerable effect on a payroll application.)

The assumptions that are made should also be specified in detail. These might include:

a. The volume of input expected for each job (e.g., weekly payroll) both at normal levels and at peak load.
b. Personnel availability, including operators, programmers, and management.

2 RESPONSIBILITIES

Management should give detailed study to the various people whose work will need to be coordinated in preparing, installing, and operating the proposed data-processing system. These include:

a. The user.
b. The consultant, if any.
c. The hardware manufacturers, both of central processing units and of each peripheral unit.
d. The hardware owner, such as a leasing company.
e. The company(ies) that will supply communications (telephone, telegraph).
f. Suppliers of forms, furniture, etc.

g. Service bureaus for parts of the application, overflow, or backup.
h. Designers of special software.
i. Suppliers of prepared software packages.
j. The contractor who will handle the construction work necessary for site preparation and all his subcontractors, such as carpenters and electricians.
k. The movers of equipment, both hardware and furniture.
l. The landlord.
m. Insurance agents.

The individual or individuals who are going to coordinate all of the above people, the individual who has the final decision in each area, and the individual who makes the final determination on any dispute should be decided upon at the very beginning.

3 BASIC SYSTEM SPECIFICATIONS

In designing the system, certain specifications should be nailed down completely and should be covered in proposals received by the company. These will include:

3.1. Hardware

a. Performance specifications for each unit; for example 900 cards per minute. The greater the detail in specification the less likelihood of dispute at a later date. For example, even the address assignment methods in operating systems can differ and two systems which appear the same on the surface—but have different methods—may be incompatible.
b. Manufacturers' specifications for accessories such as cards, ribbons, etc. should be determined in as complete detail as possible.
c. Operating manuals should be specified.
d. The communications equipment required should be clearly defined.
e. Whenever it is possible, the system specification should call for standard items rather than for items particularly designed for the user. Not only do they cause less trouble, but they can be replaced more easily and are much less liable to be the cause of argument as to what is included within the description.
f. In secondhand sales, the equipment is usually

FOB Seller. Title aspects and insurance coverages should be checked, see ¶8.3; a buyer should also be sure that the equipment has been properly maintained, and should obtain a written commitment for maintenance from the manufacturer or from a maintenance company before executing a purchase agreement. See ¶9.3.

3.2. Software

In specifying software, several matters should be considered, including:

a. Utility routines and diagnostics.
b. Assemblers, compilers, and generators.
c. Application packages, including (1) those developed by the manufacturer, (2) those developed by an independent programming service, and (3) those developed jointly by the manufacturer and the user, or by the programming house and the user.
d. For each type of program, the following items should be clearly determined: (1) the ownership rights in the program, (2) any limitations on use, such as the number of times the program can be run, whether it can be run at all installations the user has, whether the user has the right to copy for internal use, for external use, etc., (3) personalization costs of packages, (4) provision for updates, error corrections, and error reports, (5) where corrections will be made, vendor site or user's site, and (6) who pays for travel and personnel time for corrections.
e. Documentation requirements should be clearly set forth, including (1) by whom the documentation is to be done, (2) in what detail it is to be done, and (3) who is responsible for updating and modifying documentation when there are changes in the programs. The reference and operator manuals to be supplied should be listed.
f. The performance specifications in the software should be clearly detailed.

The system should specify that both hardware and software suppliers will indemnify the user against claims for infringement of patents, copyrights, or other proprietary legal protection.

The user's attorney should also review the software specifications to ensure that the programs proposed do not contemplate activities that would violate regulatory laws. A too obvious example is a program that would divide the market in violation of the laws; the documentation required to support the program could prove the opposition's case.

4 SITE PREPARATION

4.1. Suppliers, particularly hardware manufacturers, must supply specifications in sufficient time to permit the user to construct the necessary facilities. These time requirements must be clearly stated in the contract.

4.2. Operating and environmental requirements. Contractual documents should clearly specify site requirements for:

a. Air conditioning, both regular and emergency.
b. Power and light, both regular and emergency.
c. Floor-load limits.
d. Fire protection.
e. Communications wiring.

4.3. Space requirements. The following items should also be clearly spelled out:

a. Equipment layout, including (1) the air space around each hardware unit and (2) the maintenance access requirement for each unit.
b. Service areas and storage.
c. Libraries, including (1) vault space, (2), fire protection, and (3) temperature and humidity controls.
d. Management and operations offices.
e. Offices for the programming staff.
f. Power rooms.
g. User protection or pickup area.

4.4 Security Requirements

The user should also review its proposed security arrangements, including:

a. Fire protection.
b. Library check-in and check-out procedures.
c. Limitations on access to the computer room.
d. System security.

5 PERSONNEL TRAINING

Considerable attention should be given to the problem of personnel training, including who gets the training, such as:

    a. Programmers.
    b. Systems analysts.
    c. Operators.
    d. Management.

What preliminary training do the students need before they attend the training courses? How long is each course? When are the courses given, such as:

    a. Pre-installation.
    b. During installation test periods.
    c. After acceptance.
    d. When modifications are made to the system.

Who gives each course:

    a. The supplier.
    b. The user.
    c. A consultant.

Who pays for instruction; travel and living expenses? Where are the courses given?

    a. At supplier's facility.
    b. On site.
    c. At an education institution.

6 DELIVERY AND ACCEPTANCE

6.1. Delivery Dates Should be Specified in Considerable Detail.

    a. Software. Software should be delivered to the user before the hardware is delivered so that the user may train his personnel to become familiar with the software. The user should also be sure that the necessary equipment and the proper configuration is specified and will be available when the software is ready. One point should be clearly covered—who pays the cost involved in this training and familiarization period, including equipment rental and travel?

    b. Hardware. The contract should specify (1) in what order the units will arrive, and (2) who pays for storage if the equipment arrives before the site is ready. See ¶7.6.

    c. Remedies for supplier's failure to meet his delivery dates should be clearly set forth. See ¶7.7.

6.2. Installation

Certain problems can arise in the installation itself and should be considered well beforehand. They include:

    a. Getting the necessary permits to block the street if a crane is necessary to install the equipment.

    b. Coordination of the transportation of equipment.

    c. Determining who pays if the equipment is damaged in the course of transport. This usually depends on whose fault it is. Sec ¶8.3.

    d. Investigating union requirements. In Honeywell, 1 CLSR 807, the manufacturer had to use union electricians, even though it ordinarily used its own personnel, and the government was not compelled to pay for the additional cost. See also ¶7.6d.

6.3. Testing

The testing stage is very important and should be considered in detail. Items to be considered and set forth in the contract include:

    a. An initial checkout before beginning operating tests.

    b. The test period schedule. This should cover all phases of the operation, including normal downtime. At least a month is needed to check on the time between failures and on the time needed to bring the system up to full operating speed again.

    c. Benchmark tests, including (1) diagnostic routines, (2) tests using actual proven data, and (3) tests using specially prepared test data. The contract should specify who will prepare the tests, who will validate them, how long before the tests the software should be ready, and who will determine whether the tests have been met.

    d. The performance levels required should be spelled out in detail, including (1) maximum downtime in a period (week, month), (2) maximum length of a continuous period of downtime, (3) maximum time allowed to get the system restarted and operating again, (4) the average downtime per month, or similar period, (5) the average time to restore failure (mean time to repair), and (6) mean time to failure.

6.4. The rent should not start, nor the first purchase or lease payment be due, until the sys-

tem has met the tests. Some contracts provide that payment becomes due when the manufacturer certifies the equipment as ready. See National Cash Register Co. v. Marshall Savings and Loan Ass'n, 2 CLSR 332.

7 FINANCES

This paragraph covers quite a few items which might perhaps be expected to appear elsewhere, but since they all relate to money, they have been grouped here.

7.1. Rental arrangements. All of the following items should be covered, or at least considered, in preparing a contract for rental of hardware or software:

    a. Is the equipment rental based on a specified number of hours per month? On shifts?

    b. How is the chargeable time defined? Does it include set-up time, reruns? Is it charged on the central processor only, or on each piece of equipment, including each peripheral individually?

    c. Are there shift differentials?

    d. What is the amount of up time which has been guaranteed by the supplier and what are the adjustments for failure to meet this guarantee?

    e. What credits are given for downtime? This can be particularly important when the computer system includes equipment from several companies, and other lessor's equipment is rendered inoperable by one lessor's failure. See ¶10.5d.

    f. Does the rent include maintenance?

    g. Does the rent include supplies?

    h. If software is rented, how are the charges determined—is there a rate per use, a rate per month, or what?

    i. What is the rental period?

    j. What records are to be maintained by the user, and what rights does the user have, if any, to inspect the supplier's records?

    k. What use discounts are available?

7.2. Purchase of equipment and software. Among other points, the contract should cover:

    a. Options to buy, including (1) when the option may be exercised, and (2) whether the user can assign the option to a third party.

    b. Whether payments made as rent will be applied toward the purchase price.

    c. The payment arrangement upon exercise of an option and, specifically, whether the payments can be made in installments. Is there a "balloon" payment (big lump sum payment) at the end?

    d. The seller's security that installments will be made.

    e. The buyer's right to use the equipment when he is in default in his payment schedule.

    f. The time when the ownership and title to the property passes from the seller to the buyer.

    g. Particularly with respect to software, the buyer's right to resell or otherwise dispose of the property.

7.3. If the user is a nonprofit institution, it may be able to get a special discount from the supplier.

7.4. If the buyer has sufficient muscle, it may be able to get a special discount from the supplier—or a "most favored supplier"clause—in which case the supplier agrees that if it later gives anyone else—including the government—a better deal, it will change the contract to give the same deal to this user.

7.5. The question of taxes should be discussed with the user's accountants before the contract is signed, and the contract should cover, to the extent possible, these items:

    a. Investment credit.

    b. Depreciation policy.

    c. Sales and use taxes.

    d. Personal and real property taxes; particularly with respect to equipment.

7.6. Site preparation, shipping, and installation charges should be covered contractually.

    a. The user usually pays site preparation costs, but the supplier may assist, particularly if the installation is an experimental one.

    b. In commercial situations, the cost of transporting both hardware and the media of software is usually paid by the supplier, but this should be clearly spelled out.

    c. There should be agreement on who is paying the cost of the supplier's personnel during the installation and training period. Frequently these costs have been charged to the user, who has found to his regret that the individuals in question live in the best hotels and enjoy their creature comforts to the fullest.

    d. If the people who do the installation, checkout,

and other work prior to acceptance are not part of the user's staff, must they be union personnel? If this is not considered, the user may have labor-management problems. See ¶6.2d.

e. The cost of warehousing, if equipment is delivered before the site is ready, will probably depend upon why the site is not ready. The user should be sure that his construction contract includes these costs in the event that the delay is caused by the contractor.

7.7. Consideration should be given to the penalties for nonperformance or late performance. These are becoming much more frequent and, in some cases, up to one thousand dollars per day can be negotiated.

7.8. The person handling the contract should also review the paragraphs on:

   a. When the liability for rent or purchase price commences ¶6.4.
   b. Personnel training ¶5.
   c. Maintenance ¶8.3.
   d. Site preparation ¶4.

8 GENERAL OPERATIONS

Many items which will affect operations should be covered contractually when you deal with suppliers. Even if these items are not covered in the contract, they will affect the form it takes.

8.1. Environment Specifications

The user must know, and the supplier must tell him, the limits on:

   a. Permissible temperature and humidity, both high and low for (1) hardware, unit by unit, and (2) the tape library.
   b. Permissible power-range limits for (1) voltage, (2) frequency, and (3) waveform.

8.2. Personnel Problems

   a. The personnel requirements for (1) operators, (2) librarians, (3) programmers, and (4) management, should be determined as early as possible.
   b. The problem of unionization should be covered.

There have recently been quite a few cases involving the unionization of console personnel as well as programmers. Collective bargaining agreements should be reviewed with counsel during the planning stage.

   c. The training of new personnel should be reviewed. See ¶5.
   d. User's counsel should review the provisions of manufacturers' contracts for support by systems and field engineering personnel and should discuss with management the problems likely to be encountered, for example, confidentiality of the user's data.

8.3. The Contract

The contract should cover loss of, or injury to, equipment or software and injury to personnel, and it should clearly set forth who pays for the injury in each possible case. The user should also examine his insurance coverages, not only those relating to the data-processing installation, but also to general liability and workmen's compensation. Reviewing insurance coverage is particularly important in the sale or purchase of used hardware, since the contractual documents may be minimal.

9 MAINTENANCE

The maintenance of the hardware and software is a very important aspect of any data-processing installation and should be given considerable attention not only in the planning stage, but throughout the life of the installation. The contractual aspects of this should be specified as clearly as possible and as far in advance as possible.

9.1. Particularly with equipment, the supplier should give guarantees of reliability, including:

   a. Minimum hours of usable time per day.
   b. Mean time between failures.
   c. Maximum time to repair.

9.2. Backup equipment. Management must consider where it can get backup equipment in a compatible configuration for use when there is a breakdown.

   a. This might be supplied by the manufacturer or might be an installation of another user.

b. Management should arrange for continuing information on other installations that have compatible configurations.

c. Consideration should be given to the cost of arranging for backup equipment on a standby basis, and also for the actual usage of it. The method of determining these costs should be specified. Management should also check insurance coverage on the data-processing installation to determine whether their policy covers all or part of these costs.

9.3. In routine maintenance there are several factors to be considered. These include:

a. The source of supply, which can be either the supplier of the hardware or software, or an independent maintenance service.

b. The costs of the various types of maintenance. These include (1) a service contract or payment on a one-job basis, (2) travel and other expenses, and (3) how much notice does user get before rate change becomes effective. Upon occasion computer manufacturers have delayed maintenance costs because companies which had bought their equipment and leased it to users were frozen into their maintenance contracts.

c. What personnel will be supplied? Will they be full time or part time? Will they be regular supplier personnel or moonlighters? Should such personnel be unionized to avoid labor-management problems for the user?

d. What kinds of maintenance personnel are supplied: engineers, installers, programmers, mechanics?

e. When will in-house work be done—(1) during established downtimes, (2) maintenance during the operating cycle, (3) prime shift, (4) second or third shift?

f. What response time will be guaranteed by the supplier of maintenance, particularly as to (1) off-premises repairs, and (2) emergencies? This is particularly important, since even the standard computer system may have numerous unexpected interruptions, and suppliers of small peripheral equipment may not have large service forces.

g. What space requirements are needed for maintenance and maintenance personnel? Review ¶4.3.

h. Will maintenance personnel be on site or on call?

i. What is the effect of modifications of equipment or software on the maintenance problem? See ¶10.2.

10 MODIFICATION AND TERMINATION

No data-processing installation is static and modifications will take place in both hardware and software. It is also possible that the contract will be terminated with one supplier and a new system brought in or, in extreme cases, the data-processing department will be dispensed with entirely. This is particularly likely when the company is absorbed by a larger company which already has its own data-processing system. Management should consider the following, both from the management and contractual points of view.

10.1 Improvement by Suppliers

These can be both hardware and software, and consideration should be given to the following aspects:

a. If reliability is improved, the supplier should usually bear the cost.

b. If the capabilities of the equipment or the software package are improved or upgraded, the cost is usually borne by the user. However, under certain contracts the supplier will agree to furnish these improvements without additional charge.

c. The supplier should be required to inform the user of bugs discovered in hardware and software and of any changes or improvements which will assist the user in improving and operating his installation.

d. The user should be sure to get full documentation of any changes made in either hardware or software, to help him with later changes.

e. The user should have the option to refuse changes that he feels will not be useful to him.

10.2 Modifications by User

The user's rights to modify equipment or programs, particularly when rented, should be clearly spelled out. Among the items to be considered are:

a. What notice the user must give the supplier before the modification is started.

b. What effect these modifications may have on the maintenance contracts.

c. What ownership rights will the user and the sup-

GSA CONTRACT COMPONENTS

SOURCE:

Richard L. Bernacchi and Gerald H. Larsen, *Data Processing Contracts and the Law* (Boston: Little, Brown, 1974), pp. 651–674.

428

Throughout this book we have discussed the technical and contractual aspects of data processing procurements. The contract clauses that were analyzed in Chapters V through XIII were excerpted from standard contracts used in the private sector of the economy. Since these contracts were prepared by manufacturers and vendors, they obviously contain provisions which, if not completely favorable to the vendor, at least substantially limit the vendor's responsibilities. Naturally, the manufacturer or vendor isn't going to assume any greater burden than he feels is necessary to conclude the procurement.

As you might expect, a contract would be substantially different if it were drafted by a buyer or user of data processing equipment with bargaining power at least equal to that of the manufacturer or vendor. The classic example of this is the contract proposed by the United States government General Services Administration (GSA). The United States government is the single largest buyer of data processing equipment and services in the world. GSA is charged with the responsibility of developing standard procurement practices for many government agencies. GSA defines these procurement practices in an annual series of contracts and related clauses which are submitted to all interested manufacturers who wish to do business with the United States government. Substantially utilizing these contract clauses promulgated by GSA, each manufacturer is then expected to propose a standard agreement between himself and GSA which forms the basis for negotiations with GSA to reach a mutually agreeable final contract for any given GSA procurement. While there is room for negotiation, GSA has the obvious negotiating strength to remain relatively firm in its demands for contract terms and conditions. Manufacturers recognize the phenomenal buying power of the United States government and, with few exceptions, offer very little resistance to the GSA terms and conditions. The GSA contract is one of very few written primarily from the customer's point of view. Furthermore, each of the specific terms and conditions has evolved over a period of years, since each year GSA has sought additional or better contract clauses to protect the government's interests. Like other "standard" contracts, the GSA contract provisions have their limitations. However, in many respects the terms in the GSA contracts offer the government outstanding benefits (or lack thereof) found in most commercial data processing contracts. As you review each of the clauses in the prototype GSA contract, you will find obvious areas in which manufacturers could and should offer comparable protection to their commercial customers.

Our constant assumption has been that a contract between two parties is a negotiated document which fits the peculiar needs of the parties and the circumstances surrounding each procurement. Our comments with regard to the GSA contracts should not be interpreted as suggesting that we are departing from that notion. GSA, in its negotiations, has the objective of making one contract cover all situations for the sake of simplicity and standardization. But, as we have pointed out, individual customers who are negotiating contracts for the procurement of data processing equipment or services often have unique problems that require special considerations in drafting the contract. Nonetheless, the GSA contract clauses do provide a good reference point for the customer who is unwilling to accept the manufacturer's standard commercial contract. The GSA contract offers a number of distinct advantages that should logically be available to commercial customers.

For example, Section 1 ("General") of the GSA clauses contains a rather broad reference to any written commitment made by the contractor, whether or not it is incorporated into a purchase order. This, coupled with the fact that the government secures extensive written proposals and commitments from the vendors with whom it deals, goes a long way towards achieving the objective of including in the contract very detailed specifications for the equipment, services, or other products being procured. Needless to say, more specific references to the buyer's requirements and the vendor's response thereto should be included to insure that there is no uncertainty with respect to the documents which set forth the vendor's commitments.

Note also that in Section 2 ("Installation and Delivery Dates") the fact that the equipment is "installed, ready for use" does not trigger the government's obligation to start paying for the product. Instead, it merely signals the beginning of a formal acceptance period (covered in Section 4, "Standard of Performance and Acceptance of Equipment") during which the product must meet the performance criteria established by the government. As we saw in Chapter III G, most commercial contracts provide for a different effect, i.e., the customer begins paying when the product is "installed, ready for use," and no provision is made for acceptance testing.

As we discussed in Chapter III H, the GSA contract contains a liquidated damages clause (Section 3), a clause that is rarely found in commercial data processing contracts. But as we noted in that chapter, the GSA approach places a value on nondelivered or nonacceptable items which is directly proportional to their price in the contract. This is not always a realistic approach, since the failure to deliver one item may have financial or operational consequences far beyond the value of that individual item. This illustrates the need for evaluating each of the GSA contract clauses in light of the buyer's unique requirements.

For purposes of illustrating the GSA clauses, we have combined the rental and purchase clauses from the 1971 GSA schedule into a single set. Because to a large extent both kinds of clauses are identical, our arrangement eliminates considerable redundancy. Specific contract terms which apply only to purchase or only to rental are so indicated in brackets after the heading of the clause. With these exceptions, all terms and conditions in the GSA clauses are identical for both purchase and rental. We have included only the GSA clauses for automatic data processing equipment to serve as our illustration, although GSA schedules cover other product and service areas as well. If, after studying the main text of this book, you still feel that a cookbook approach to data processing contracts is what you want, here is the Larousse Gastronomique of the EDP world—a GSA schedule.

1. *GENERAL*

    a. *Period of Rental.* [Rental Only] —The contractor shall honor orders for periods of one year or less. After the contractor receives written notice from the Government, the Government may discontinue use and rental thirty (30) days thereafter or on shorter notice when agreed to by the contractor. However, the Government may extend the original discontinuance date upon written notice to the contractor provided such notice is furnished at least 10 days prior to the original discontinuance date.

    b. *Contractor Commitments, Warranties and Representations.* Any written commitment by a contractor within the scope of this contract shall be binding upon the contractor whether or not incorporated into a purchase order. Failure of the contractor to fulfill any such commitment shall render the contractor liable for liquidated or other damages due the Government under the terms of this contract.

For the purpose of this contract a commitment by a contractor includes (1) prices and options committed to remain in force over a specified period(s) of time (provided that in any fiscal year covered by the commitment the Government may, at its option, order the equipment under the contractor's Federal Supply Schedule contract for that fiscal year. Such order shall not operate as a waiver of the original commitment for any subsequent fiscal year.), (2) any warranty or representation made by the contractor in a proposal as to hardware or software performance, total systems performance, any other physical, design or functional characteristics of a machine, software package or system, (3) any warranty or representation made by a contractor concerning the characteristics or items described in (2) above made in any literature, descriptions, drawings or specifications accompanying or referred to in a proposal, (4) any modification of or affirmation or representation as to the above which is made by a contractor in or during the course of negotiations whether or not incorporated into a formal amendment to the proposal in question, and (5) any representation by a contractor in a proposal, supporting documents or negotiations subsequent thereto as to training to be provided, services to be performed, prices and options committed to remain in force over a fixed period of time, or any other similar matter regardless of the fact that the duration of such commitment may exceed the duration of this contract.

When orders are accepted which include commitments as to prices, options, etc., to endure beyond the period specified on the face of this contract, the contractor agrees to either amend the contract accordingly or to provide the Contracting Officer with a copy of the order, within ten (10) days of acceptance by the contractor.

2. *INSTALLATION AND DELIVERY DATES.*

a. *Equipment (Hardware).*

(1) The contractor shall install equipment, ready for use, before an installation date (day, month, year) agreed to by the contractor and the Government in writing. At the time of such agreement the contractor shall also specify a period of time within which the order must be received by the contractor and beyond which the agreed to installation date will no longer be binding. In the event the purchase order is received after the period of time provided for that purpose and the contractor refuses to accept the order, a new agreed to installation date and purchase order receipt date may be established.

(2) The agreed to installation date shall be written into an order and forwarded to the contractor by certified mail.

(3) Any changes by the Government to an order, or any part thereof, may require the establishment of a new and/or additional mutually agreed to installation date. The Government may delay the installation date by notifying the contractor at least 30 days before the installation date previously established.

(4) The equipment shall not be considered ready for use until the contractor provides the Government with the documentation of successful system audit performed at the site which demonstrates that the equipment meets minimum design capabilities and after review of the documentation the Government agrees that the equipment is ready to begin the acceptance test. The diagnostics used for this purpose shall be those provided under Paragraph 2b(1) below.

(5) If the equipment is certified to be ready for use on a day prior to the installation date, the Government, at its option, may elect to use the equipment and change the installation date accordingly. In this event, the order shall be so amended by the Government.

(6) The Government agrees to have the site prepared in accordance with the contractor's written site specifications at least thirty (30) days before the installation date.

(7) The Government shall provide the contractor access to the site for the purpose of installing the equipment prior to the installation date. The contractor shall specify in writing the time required to install the equipment.

b. *Programming Aids (Software).*

(1) The contractor shall provide programming aids, including programs, routines, subroutines, translation compilers, a complete set of diagnostic routines used for system maintenance and audit, and related items, which it has announced for general use with the type of equipment ordered, without additional charge on a delivery date agreed to by the contractor and the Government in writing. At the time of such agreement the contractor shall also specify a period of time within which the order must be received by the contractor and beyond which the agreed to date of delivery will no longer be binding. In the event the purchase order is received after the period of time provided for that purpose and the contractor refuses to accept the order, a new agreed to delivery date and purchase order receipt date may be established. The programming aids shall perform in accordance with the contractor's technical specifications and data requirements. The programming aids required and the date of delivery shall be written into the same purchase order with the hardware. These terms shall apply to any other programs which the contractor has agreed to develop and deliver.

(2) Any changes by the Government to an order or any part thereof may require the establishment of a new and/or additional agreed to delivery date. The Government may delay the delivery date by notifying the contractor at least 30 days before the delivery date previously established.

(3) In the event the contractor fails to deliver the programming aids by the date specified in the order and the delay is more than thirty (30) calendar days, then by written notice of default to the contractor the

Government may:

(a) Prior to installation, immediately terminate the right of the contractor to install the equipment, or,

(b) If such delay occurs after installation but prior to the completion of a successful performance period, require the removal of the equipment immediately, or,

(c) [Rental Only] If such delay occurs after the completion of a successful performance period, discontinue the use and rental of the equipment immediately.

(4) When requested by the Government the contractor shall furnish a copy of his technical specifications for COBOL, ALGOL, FORTRAN, etc. The specifications furnished shall be recognized as the "Standard" for the purpose of measuring performance.

(5) When requested by the Government the contractor shall furnish without additional charge to the Government any programs, compilers, routines, sub-routines, etc., which it has or may develop at a future date for general use with the type of equipment ordered.

c. Nothing in this Paragraph 2 shall be construed so as to relieve the contractor from any commitment concerning installation and delivery dates which is made in a proposal.

3. *LIQUIDATED DAMAGES.*—(Note: In addition, when applicable, the default provisions of Standard Form 32 shall also apply.)

a. *Equipment.*

(1) If the contractor does not install all the equipment (designated by the contractor's type and model numbers), including the special features and accessories included on the same order with the equipment, ready for use as defined in Paragraph 2a(4), before the installation date, the contractor shall pay to the Government, as fixed and agreed liquidated damages for each machine whether or not installed, for each calendar day's delay beginning with the installation date, but not for more than 180 calendar days, $100 or 1/30th of the basic monthly rental and maintenance charges, whichever is greater.

(2) If some, but not all of the machines on an order are installed, ready for use during a period of time when liquidated damages are applicable, and the Government uses any such installed machines, liquidated damages shall not accrue against the machines used for any calendar day the machines are used.

(3) If the delay is more than thirty (30) calendar days, then by written notice to the contractor, the Government may terminate the right of the contractor to install, and may obtain substitute equipment. In this event, the contractor shall be liable for liquidated damages until substitute equipment is installed, ready for use, or for 180 days from the installation date, whichever occurs first.

(4) If the Government is unable to use the equipment because the contractor failed to furnish programming aids on or before the delivery date or furnished programming aids which do not perform in accordance with Paragraph 2b(1), liquidated damages as specified in Paragraph 3a(1) shall apply in addition to the liquidated damages as specified in Paragraph 3b(1).

b. *Programming Aids (Software).*

(1) If the contractor does not deliver the programming aids identified in the order for the equipment or their equivalent ready to perform as prescribed in Paragraph 2b(1) on or before the delivery date specified on the order, the contractor shall pay to the Government as fixed and agreed liquidated damages $100 for each calendar day's delay for each programming aid not delivered as prescribed in Paragraph 2b(1) and for any other programming aids not usable as a result thereof or for each calendar day an amount equal to 1/30th of the basic monthly rental and maintenance charges for the equipment, whichever is greater, but not for more than 180 calendar days.

(2) In the event the provisions of Paragraph 3a(3) are applicable and substitute equipment is installed, the contractor shall be liable for liquidated damages for the period of time between the delivery date specified in the order until the programming aids for the substitute equipment are delivered,

ready for use, or for 180 days from the delivery date, whichever occurs first.

c. *Exception.*

Except with respect to defaults of subcontractors, the contractor shall not be liable for liquidated damages when delays arise out of causes beyond the control and without the fault or negligence of the contractor. Such causes may include, but are not restricted to, Acts of God or of the public enemy, acts of the Government in either its sovereign or contractual capacity, fires, floods, epidemics, quarantine restrictions, strikes, freight embargoes, and unusually severe weather; but in every case the delays must be beyond the control and without the fault or negligence of the contractor. If the delays are caused by the default of a subcontractor, and if such default arises out of causes beyond the control of both the contractor and subcontractor, and without the fault or negligence of either of them, the contractor shall not be liable for liquidated damages for delays, unless the supplies or services to be furnished by the subcontractor were obtainable from other sources in sufficient time to permit the contractor to meet the required performance schedule.

4. *STANDARD OF PERFORMANCE AND ACCEPTANCE OF EQUIPMENT.*

a. This Paragraph 4 establishes a standard of performance which must be met before any equipment listed on a purchase order is ac-accepted by the government.

This also includes replacement, substitute machines and machines which are added, or field modified, after a system has completed a successful performance period.

b. The performance period shall begin on the Installation Date and shall end when the equipment has met the standard of performance for a period of 30 consecutive days by operating in conformance with the contractor's technical specifications or as quoted in any proposal at an effectiveness level of 95% or more.

c. In the event the equipment does not meet the standard of performance during the initial 30 consecutive days the standard of performance test shall continue on a day-by-day basis until the standard of performance is met for a total of 30 consecutive days.

d. If the equipment fails to meet the standard of performance after 90 calendar days, from the

installation date, the Government may at its option request a replacement or terminate the order in accordance with the provisions of Paragraph 11 entitled Default, Standard Form 32, incorporated by reference.

e. [Rental Only]—Rental and Maintenance charges shall apply beginning on the first day of the successful performance period.

f. The effectiveness level for a system is computed by dividing the operational use time by the sum of that time plus system failure downtime.

g. The effectiveness level for an added, field modified, substitute, or replacement machine is a percentage figure determined by dividing the operational use time of the machine by the sum of that time plus downtime resulting from equipment failure of the machine being tested and therefore the hours prescribed in Paragraph 4-n are not applicable.

h. Operational use time for performance testing for a system is defined as the accumulated time during which the Central Processing Unit is in actual operation including any interval of time between the start and stop of the Central Processing Unit.

i. Operational use time for performance testing for a machine added, field modified, substitute or replacement machine is defined as the accumulated time during which the machine is in actual use.

j. System failure downtime is that period of time when any machine in the system is inoperable due to equipment failure.

k. During periods of system downtime, the Government may use operable equipment when such action does not interfere with maintenance of the inoperable equipment. The entire system will be considered down during such periods of use.

l. Machine failure downtime for added, field modified, substitute, or replacement machines after the system has completed a successful performance period is that period of time when such machines are inoperable due to their failure.

m. Downtime for each incident shall start from the time the Government makes a bona fide attempt to contact the contractor's designated representative at the prearranged contact point until the system or machine(s) is returned to the Government in proper operating condition, exclusive of actual travel time required by the contractor's maintenance personnel but not in excess of one hour on the day such services were requested.

n. During the performance period for a system a minimum of 100 hours of operational use time with productive or simulated work will be required as a basis for computation of the effectiveness level. However, in computing the effectiveness level the actual number of operational use hours shall be used when in excess of the minimum of 100 hours.

o. The Government shall maintain appropriate daily records to satisfy the requirements of Paragraph 4 and shall notify the contractor in writing of the date of the first day of the successful performance period.

p. Equipment shall not be accepted and no charges shall be paid until the standard of performance is met. [Purchase Only]—The date of acceptance shall be the first day of the successful performance period.

q. Operational use time and downtime shall be measured in hours and whole minutes.

r. Should it be necessary, the Government may delay the start of the performance period, but such delay shall not exceed 30 consecutive days; therefore, the performance period must start not later than the 31st day after the Installation Date.

4. *GUARANTEE.* [Purchase Only]

a. The contractor will furnish all maintenance and parts for a period of 90 days beginning on the first day of acceptance. If rented equipment is purchased in accordance with Paragraph 14, a guarantee period of 90 days shall apply from the date of purchase.

b. All replaced parts during the guarantee period shall become the property of the contractor.

c. Prior to the expiration of the guarantee period, whenever equipment is shipped for mechanical replacement purposes, the contractor shall bear all costs, including, but not limited to, costs of packing, transportation, rigging, drayage and insurance. This guarantee shall apply to the replacement machine beginning on the first day of its acceptance.

5. *TERMS OF USE.* [Rental Only]—(Note: There are three optional use arrangements. An offer on Option C will not be considered unless accompanied with an offer on Option A or B or both.)

a. *Option A—Unlimited Use (Total System).*

(1) The basic monthly rental shall entitle the Government to unlimited use of all equipment and to operate all equipment at any time and for any period of time at the convenience of the Government (exclusive of the time required for preventive and remedial maintenance) and shall not be restricted to consecutive hours, length of personnel shifts, or for any other reason.

(2) The basic monthly rental and maintenance charges for fractions of a calendar month shall be computed at the rate of 1/30th of the basic monthly rental and maintenance charges for each day the equipment was installed.

b. *Option B—Unlimited Use (Peripherals)—200 Hours (CPU).*

(1) The basic monthly rental shall entitle the Government to operate all equipment at any time and for any period of time at the convenience of the Government (exclusive of the time required for preventive and remedial maintenance) and shall not be restricted to consecutive hours, length of personnel shifts, or for any other reason.

(2) The basic monthly rental shall entitle the Government to unlimited use of all equipment except the Central Processing Unit (CPU).

(3) The basic monthly rental shall entitle the Government to a maximum of 200 hours of operational use time for the CPU during each full calendar month and for less than a full calendar month 1/30th of 200 hours for each day the equipment is installed. Any unused portion of the 200 hours shall not be carried over into subsequent months.

(4) The basic monthly rental and maintenance charges for a machine initially installed for fractions of a calendar month shall be computed at the rate of 1/30th of the basic monthly rental and maintenance charges for each day in the period beginning with the Installation Date through the last calendar day of the month. A machine discontinued at other than the end of a calendar month shall be billed for its basic monthly rental and maintenance charges less 1/30th of

the Basic Monthly Rental and Maintenance Charges for each calendar day in that month following the date of discontinuance.

(5) Measurement of operational use time.

    (a) Operational use time shall be recorded on a CPU metering device installed and maintained by the contractor. This meter will record time only when the CPU is in actual operation and will not record time during halt operations.

    (b) Operational use time on the CPU shall not accrue for rental purposes for:

      (1) Time required for preventive or remedial maintenance;

      (2) Time required to test contractor-provided programming aids;

      (3) Rerun time due to equipment failure or failure of Government equipment in the same system with rented equipment both of which are maintained by the same contractor or rerun time due to failure of contractor-provided software;

      (4) Set-up time;

      (5) Idle time, i.e., when not actually processing data even though the executive program may be in waiting loop status;

      (6) Where there is more than one CPU of the same type in a Government installation and under the jurisdiction of the same Government agency the maximum operational use time shall be the product of 200 hours multiplied by the number of like CPUs. In such case, even though an individual CPU is used more than 200 hours, no extra use charges shall be multiplied by the number of like CPUs installed for the entire month. When extra use charges are payable, they shall be computed at the average basic monthly rental rate of all like CPUs.

      (7) Extra use charges.

        (a) Operational use time for the CPU in excess of the 200 hours per month entitlement for the basic monthly rental shall be paid for at the extra hourly use rate shown in the pricelist.

        (b) Extra use charges shall be computed to the next lower full half hour.

c. *Option C—Limited Period(s) of Operation.*

    (1) The basic monthly rental(s) as shown in the pricelist shall entitle the Government to use the equipment during a Principal Period of Operation (PPO) except for remedial maintenance. The Principal Period of Operation is any eight (8) consecutive hours per day plus an official meal period not to exceed one hour per day for 5, 6, and 7 consecutive days per week.

    (2) Additional period of operation hourly rate charge.

      (a) The Government may operate the equipment outside the Principal Period of Operation at the additional hourly rate charge shown in the pricelist.

      (b) The total additional hourly rate charges shall be computed to the next lower full half hour.

d. *Use and Discount Options, and Rental Reductions.*

    (1) The Government requests basic discounts from established price lists and for the following:

      (a) Reduced rental charges which will entitle the Government to use the equipment less than 200 hours a month based on a decreased percentage scale(s) of the basic monthly rental charges.

      (b) *Monthly Rental Credits for Extended Rental Periods.* Offerors should state various lengths of extended rental periods in months and monthly rental credits therefor. The rental credits for extended rental periods will be applied to the final months of the extended rental period(s) by reducing or eliminating rental charges. Regular rental charges will prevail during the preceding months.

      (c) Reduced rental options to allow for percentage discounts of the basic monthly rental charges under the following conditions:

(1) For multiple data processing systems installed in
  (a) same Government installation
  (b) different Government installation.

(2) For multiple data processing systems proposing the application of at least one standard or common program to be applied to all systems installed in the same Government agency.

(3) For qualified Government school and training institutions when primary application of the data processing system is for educational and training purposes.

(4) For equipment no longer in production and for outmoded systems when new models of comparable class and size are announced with increased speed and capability.

(5) Whenever the contractor reduces the purchase price for any equipment, comparable reductions shall be made in the monthly rental charges.

(6) Whenever the total rentals paid equal the purchase price, the contractor shall provide reduction in monthly rental charges on a descending scale.

(2) Discount to Government hospitals.

(3) Prompt payment discount.

(4) Other discounts and allowances not specified above.

e. *Government Records.* The Government shall maintain an appropriate record of use for Option B of each CPU during the calendar month and for Option C, the number of additional hours of operation.

f. *Invoices and Payments.*

(1) Subject to the provisions of Paragraph 4, of this contract, rental and maintenance charges shall begin on the installation date.

(2) The contractor shall render invoices (5 copies) for basic monthly charges in the month following the month for which the charges accrue and are payable when billed. Invoices shall provide as a minimum: (a) Type and description of equipment; (b) Serial number; (c) Basic monthly charge for each machine and feature; and (d) Total charges.

(3) In case of extra use or additional hourly rate charges, the Government shall furnish the contractor monthly with an authorization to bill which shall list the following information for each type of machine: Number of extra hours; extra or additional rate applied; and total extra charges for the month.

(4) Invoices for extra or additional charges are payable when billed.

(5) Any credits due the Government may be applied against contractor's invoices with appropriate information attached.

(6) Invoices for vendor prepaid transportation charges must be accompanied by a bill of lading.

6. *MAINTENANCE OF EQUIPMENT.* [Rental Only] (1. Note: Either "On-Site" or "On-Call" Maintenance or both may be offered). (2. Note: The basic monthly rental rate shall not include charges for the maintenance of equipment outlined in Paragraph 6. Monthly maintenance charges for rented equipment shall be listed separately. In the space provided below and in addition to quantity discounts offerors should submit discounts from their basic maintenance charges for each item of rented equipment for installations within a 50-mile radius of their service locations provided more than one installation including both Government and commercial are being maintained by the offeror. _____%. This condition applies to both Government and commercial owned and/or rented equipment.)

a. *General Provisions.* (Applicable to Both "On-Call" And "On-Site" Maintenance)

(1) The contractor shall keep the equipment in good operating condition and, subject to security regulations, the Government shall provide the contractor access to the equipment to perform maintenance service.

(2) *Preventive Maintenance.* Preventive (scheduled) maintenance shall be performed at a time other than during the Government's working hours unless otherwise specified by the Government. The contractor shall specify in the pricelist the number of hours of preventive maintenance required for

each machine, per month, which shall be consistent with the contractor's established standards for preventive maintenance. The contractor shall also specify in writing the frequency and duration of the preventive maintenance required for the equipment listed on the order and the Government shall specify the schedule for the performance of the preventive maintenance. This schedule may be modified by mutual agreement.

(3) *Remedial Maintenance.* Remedial maintenance shall be performed after notification that the equipment is inoperative. The contractor shall provide the Government with a designated point of contact and shall make arrangements to enable his maintenance representative to receive such notification.

(4) *Service Calls.* For "on-call" service, the contractor's maintenance personnel shall arrive at the Government's installation site within one hour after notification by the Government that service is required. Except for causes beyond the control of the contractor, if the maintenance personnel fail to arrive at the Government's installation site within one hour, the contractor shall grant a credit to the Government in the amount of 1/200th thereof (prorated) beginning with the time of notification and ending with the time or arrival.

(5) *Malfunction Reports.* The contractor shall furnish a malfunction incident report to the installation upon completion of each maintenance call. The report shall include, as a minimum, the following:

    (a) Date and time notified;
    (b) Date and time of arrival;
    (c) Type and Model Number(s) of machine(s);
    (d) Time spent for repair;
    (e) Description of malfunction;
    (f) List of parts replaced;
    (g) Additional charges, if applicable.

(6) *Replacement Parts.*
    (a) There shall be no additional charges for replacement parts.

(7) *Maintenance Credit for Equipment Malfunction.*

(a) If a machine remains inoperative due to a malfunction through no fault or negligence of the Government for a total of 12 hours or more during any 24-hour period, the contractor shall grant a credit to the Government for each such hour in the amount of 1/200th of the basic monthly rental and maintenance charges for the inoperative machine plus 1/200th of the basic monthly rental and maintenance charges for any machine (including machines under rental from other vendor(s)) not usable as a result of the breakdown. Downtime for each incident shall start from the time the Government makes a bona fide attempt to contact the contractor's designated representative at the pre-arranged contact point until the machine is returned in good operating condition. When maintenance credit is due the total number of creditable hours shall be accumulated for the month and adjusted to the nearest half hour. Time required to reconstruct data stored on disk files, on drums, tapes, memories, etc. shall be considered as downtime.

For equipment rented by the Government under a plan which provides less than 200 hours of monthly use the maintenance credits specified in this paragraph shall be adjusted proportionately with the monthly hours of use plan under which the equipment is being rented.

(b) When maintenance credit is due under the provisions of Paragraph 6a(7)(a) and Government-owned equipment is not usable as a result of the breakdown of the contractor's rented equipment, the contractor shall grant a credit to the Government for each such Government-owned machine not usable for each hour, including all re-run time, in an amount equal to .5 percent of its monthly maintenance charges.

(c) Exclusive of the provisions of Paragraph 6a(7)(a) above, the contractor shall grant a credit to the Government for any machine which fails to perform at an effectiveness level of 90% during any month. The effectiveness level for a machine is computed by dividing the operational use time by the sum of that time plus machine failure downtime. The credit shall be a reduction of the total monthly rental and maintenance charges by the percentage figure determined by subtracting the actual effectiveness level percentage from 100%. For example, if the effectiveness level for a machine is 82%, the credit would be 18%. Any downtime for which credit was granted in accordance with Paragraph 6a(7)(a) above shall not be included in the effectiveness level computation.

(d) In the event that a machine is inoperative, due to machine failure, and the total number of hours of downtime exceeds ten percent (10%) of the total operational use time for three consecutive calendar months, the Government reserves the right to require the contractor to replace the machine. The purchase option and/or age depreciation credits for the replacement machine shall not be less than the credits accrued from the date of installation of the original machine, regardless of whether the replacement is made at the request of the Government or for the convenience of the contractor.

(8) *Maintenance Facilities.* The Government shall provide adequate storage space for spare parts and adequate working space including heat, light, ventilation, electric current and outlets for the use of the contractor's maintenance personnel. These facilities shall be within a reasonable distance of the equipment to be serviced and shall be provided at no charge to the contractor.

(9) A separate Principal Period of Maintenance may be specified for each system when there are two or more systems of the same vendor at the same installation. The PPM's shall be determined by the Government and may be changed upon seven (7) days written notice to the contractor.

(10) There shall be no additional maintenance charges for:

(a) Preventive maintenance, regardless of when performed.

(b) Remedial maintenance which was begun during the principal period of maintenance or extension thereof or when the contractor was notified during the principal period of maintenance or extension thereof of the need for remedial maintenance.

(c) Remedial maintenance required within a 48-hour period due to a recurrence of the same malfunction.

(d) Time spent by maintenance personnel after arrival at the site awaiting the arrival of additional maintenance personnel and/or delivery of parts, etc., after a service call has commenced.

(e) Remedial maintenance required when the scheduled preventive maintenance preceding the malfunction had not been performed.

b. *"On-Site" Maintenance.*

(1) The basic monthly maintenance charges set forth in the pricelist shall entitle the Government to maintenance personnel in attendance during the entire time of a principal period of maintenance.

(2) The Government, by giving seven (7) days written notice to the contractor, may extend the principal period of maintenance in the time increments, and for the charges as follows: (Specify)

(3) The minimum number of maintenance personnel in attendance during the principal period of maintenance or extension thereof shall be agreed to by the Government and the contractor. A credit in the monthly charges shall be taken by the Government due to any absence of contractor's maintenance personnel during such periods. Such credit shall be 1/200th of the basic monthly maintenance charges (Item 132-11) for each hour of absence.

(4) The principal period of maintenance or extension thereof may be changed by the Government upon seven (7) days written notice to the contractor. The Government may use the equipment whether or not the contractor is able to provide maintenance personnel in attendance.

(5) Should the Government require maintenance service outside the designated principal period of maintenance or extension thereof on an on-call basis, charges for such additional maintenance service shall be at an hourly rate of _____. The maximum charge for any one occurrence shall be _____. Only one maintenance man shall respond to a request for maintenance unless it is mutually agreed that more than one man is required.

c. *"On-Call" Maintenance.*

(1) The basic monthly maintenance charges set forth in the pricelist shall entitle the Government to maintenance service during a principal period of maintenance.

(2) The Government, by giving seven (7) days written notice to the contractor, may extend the principal period of maintenance in the time increments, and for the charges as follows: (Specify)

(3) The principal period of maintenance or extension thereof may be changed by the Government upon seven (7) days written notice to the contractor.

(4) Should the Government require maintenance service outside the designated principal period of maintenance or extension thereof on an on-call basis, charges for such additional maintenance service shall be at an hourly rate of _____. The maximum charge for any one occurrence shall be _____. Only one maintenance man shall respond to a request for maintenance unless it is mutually agreed that more than one man is required.

d. *Government Maintenance.*

(1) When it is determined to be in the best interests of the Government, e.g., due to security or operational necessity, the Government at its option, after 60 days' written notice to the contractor, may perform all or part of the maintenance service, in accordance with the following terms and conditions:

(a) The contractor shall train an adequate number of Government personnel, including the initial complement and normal replacements to perform the maintenance service for those systems for which the Government elects to exercise this option.

(b) The Government's maintenance personnel shall perform preventive and remedial maintenance and exercise due care in the performance of the service so as to maintain the equipment in good operating condition except for normal wear and tear. At the Government's request the contractor shall make periodic inspections and shall assist the Government's maintenance personnel in particularly difficult repair situations. The contractor may also make periodic inspections upon notification to the Government.

(c) The contractor shall provide an adequate on-site inventory of parts, maintenance manual schematic diagrams and amendments, tools and test equipment sufficient to maintain the machines in good operating condition. In the event the on-site inventory does not contain the part(s) required to correct a malfunction, the provisions of Paragraph 6a(7) shall apply. Title to these items shall remain with the contractor and the equipment shall be used by the Government only for maintenance of the system for which provided.

(d) The contractor shall grant a credit to the government to be applied to the basic monthly rental and maintenance and extra use charges for each such Government maintained/rented machine an amount equal to _____ percent of the contractor's basic and additional monthly maintenance charges which would have been payable if the contractor provided separate maintenance for Government-owned equipment.

(e) The Government at its option may elect to perform the maintenance service in conjunction with the contractor's maintenance personnel. In the event such split maintenance teams are utilized mutually agreeable arrangements shall be made with respect to the composition of the team and the percentage of maintenance credit allowed.

(f) The Government may, upon 60 days

written notice, elect to change the maintenance responsibility back to the contractor or to change between total and split maintenance service arrangements. In the event total maintenance responsibility is returned to the contractor or upon discontinuance of rental of the system or machines, the Government shall return all unused parts, tools, and test equipment to the contractor in good condition.

e. *Replacement Parts.*

The contractor shall furnish in his pricelist opposite each model, type, or feature the number of years all replacement parts will be available beginning with July 1, 1972. After the expiration of the period during which his replacements will be available the contractor when requested by the Government must furnish all necessary data which will enable the Government to have such parts manufactured elsewhere.

7. *SUBSTITUTIONS AND ADDITIONS.* [Rental Only]

a. *Substitutions.*

The Government, or its authorized agent(s) may replace any equipment components of a system or subsystem with substitute equipment which is similar or identical to the equipment being replaced, whether or not the substitute equipment is obtained from or manufactured by the system (or sub-system) supplier. Equipment being replaced by substitutions shall be discontinued in accordance with the provisions of the contract under which it is rented.

(2) When equipment substitutions are made by the Government or its agents: (i) The Government shall be responsible for damage caused to the system or sub-system contractor's equipment provided the damage results solely and directly from the use of substitute equipment obtained from another supplier. (ii) The system or sub-system contractor shall be relieved of the obligation (s), if any, specified elsewhere in this Item 132-1, to provide credits to the Government for equipment malfunctions, provided the downtime condition which would otherwise have resulted in credits was caused by or resulted solely

and directly from the use of substitute equipment obtained from a different supplier. (iii) The system or sub-system contractor shall not be held responsible for defects in software if such defects are caused by or result solely and directly from the use of substitute machines obtained from a different supplier.

b. *Additions.*

(1) The Government or its authorized agent(s) may add equipment (such as additional memory, tape drives, etc.) to systems (or sub-systems), whether or not the additions are obtained from or manufactured by the supplier of the system or sub-system.

(2) When additions are made by the Government or its agent(s) (i) The Government shall be responsible for damage caused to the system or sub-system contractor's equipment provided the damage results solely and directly from use of additional equipment obtained from another supplier. (ii) The system or sub-system contractor shall be relieved of the obligation(s), if any, specified elsewhere in this Item 132-1, to provide credits to the Government for equipment malfunctions, provided the downtime conditions which would otherwise have resulted in credits were caused by or resulted directly and solely from use of additional equipment obtained from another supplier, (iii) The system or sub-system contractor shall not be held responsible for defects in software, provided such defects are caused by or result solely and directly from the use of additional equipment obtained from another supplier.

c. The system or sub-system contractor agrees to provide the Government, or its authorized agent(s), with any detailed technical information that may be requested by the Government or its agent(s), to ensure that the contemplated equipment additions and/or substitutions can be installed and used safely and efficiently, without jeopardy to personnel, equipment or operational missions of the installation.

8. *NEED FOR EQUIPMENT DUE TO EMERGENCY OR CONVERSION.* [Rental Only]

a. *Emergency.*

(1) The contractor shall make every effort to

assist the Government in procuring use of equipment compatible with that used by the Government to meet emergencies such as a major breakdown, unforeseen peak loads, etc.

    (2) The Government, at its option, may accept or reject the offer of use of emergency equipment. If accepted, the charge for such use, if any, shall be a separate arrangement between the ordering agency and the Government agency or the commercial concern providing the machine time.

  b. *Conversion.*

    (1) When substituting one contractor's machine(s) or system for another contractor's machine(s) or system, an equipment conversion period of up to thirty (30) days shall be established.

    (2) This period shall commence on the installation date.

    (3) A credit, not to exceed 30 calendar days of rental and maintenance charges of the replaced machine(s) or system, shall be applied against the rental and maintenance charges of the machine(s) or system being installed.

9. *MAJOR FIELD MODIFICATIONS.* [Rental Only]

  a. The contractor may provide for the on-site field modifications of equipment. These modifications may be based upon a Government request or engineering changes sponsored by the contractor.

  b. Rental and maintenance charges will be discontinued on the equipment being modified and for equipment not usable during the modification period on the day the equipment is turned over to the contractor for modification. Rental and maintenance charges will commence on the equipment on the day following the day the contractor certified in writing that the modified equipment is installed and ready for use. The modified equipment is subject to the provisions of Paragraph 4.

10. *ALTERATIONS AND ATTACHMENTS.* [Rental Only]

  a. The Government or its authorized agent(s) may make alterations or install attachments to the equipment. The contractor will be notified of any such alterations or attachments.

  b. If the Government agrees that such changes substantially increase the cost of maintenance,

mutually agreeable arrangements for additional maintenance charges shall be made on an individual installation basis, outside the scope of this contract.

  c. Such alterations or attachments shall be removed and the equipment restored to the prior configuration at Government expense after discontinuance of rental of the equipment, but before it is returned to the contractor if not the property of the contractor.

11. *PROGRAM TESTING AND COMPILING TIME.*

  a. The contractor's proposals solicited for planned installations shall, upon request, include a statement of the total program testing and compiling time required for each program application area specified by the Government to permit the Government to use the equipment productively immediately following the installation date.

  b. The program testing and compiling time specified above shall be provided without additional charge on equipment identical in configuration with that on order or mutually agreed to as adequate at the contractor's facilities or by mutual agreement at another installation or at the Government's option on site prior to and/or after the installation date or a combination of the above.

  c. The contractor shall provide without charge the necessary translation compilers and machine time to permit the conversion from source programs written in the Common Business Oriented Language (also known as COBOL), FORTRAN, ALGOL, etc., to programs of the particular data processing systems covered by this contract.

  d. In those instances where programs are to be developed at a single installation for use by multiple installations, the total time which accrues for all installations may be utilized at the option of the Government at a single installation.

11. *NEED FOR EQUIPMENT DUE TO EMERGENCY.* [Purchase Only]

  a. The contractor shall make every effort to assist the Government in procuring use of equipment compatible with that used by the Government to meet emergencies such as major breakdowns, unforeseen peak loads, etc.

  b. The Government, at its option, may accept or reject the offer of use of emergency equipment.

If accepted, the charge for such use, if any, shall be a separate arrangement between the ordering agency and the Government agency or the commercial concern providing the machine time.

12. *TRAINING AND TECHNICAL SERVICES.*

  a. *Training.* The contractor, without additional charge to the Government, shall train an adequate number of operating and programming personnel, including the initial staff and replacements, at the contractor's training location, or if mutually agreed to, at a Government location.

  b. *Technical Services.* The contractor's technical personnel shall be available to assist the Government in implementation, review, and improvement of existing data processing systems and in programming, development, and implementation of new systems involving the contractor's equipment.

13. *SITE PREPARATION.*

  a. Site preparation specifications shall be furnished in writing by the contractor as a part of the equipment proposal. These specifications shall be in such detail as to ensure that the equipment to be installed shall operate efficiently from the point of view of environment.

  b. The Government shall prepare the site at its own expense and in accordance with the specifications furnished by the contractor.

  c. The contractor shall inspect the site. The contractor shall report to the Government in writing the dates of the inspection, any rejections, the reasons therefor and the final inspection and acceptance.

  d. Any alterations or modifications in site preparation which are attributable to incomplete or erroneous specifications provided by the contractor which would involve additional expenses to the Government, shall be made at the expense of the contractor.

  e. Any such site alterations or modifications as specified in Subparagraph d above which cause a delay in the installation date will also result in liquidated damages for equipment as specified under Paragraph 3.

13. *PURCHASE DISCOUNTS.* [Purchase Only]

  The Government requests basic discounts from established pricelists and for the following:

  a. For multiple data processing systems installed in:

  (1) same Government installations.
  (2) different Government installations.

  b. For multiple data processing systems proposing the application of at least one standard or common program to be applied to all systems installed in the same Government agency.

  c. For outmoded systems when new models of comparable class and size are announced with increased speed and capability.

  d. For qualified Government schools and training institutions when primary application of the data processing system is for educational and training purposes.

  e. For Government hospitals.

  f. Prompt payment discount.

  g. Other discounts not specified above.

14. *TRANSPORTATION, INSTALLATION, RELOCATION, AND RETURN OF EQUIPMENT.*

  a. *Transportation.*

  (1) Shipments to and from the installation site shall be made at Government expense by padded van or air freight either on a Government Bill of Lading or a Commercial Bill of Lading for conversion to a Government Bill of Lading at destination, or the contractor shall prepay the transportation charges and invoice such charges for payment by the Government.

  (2) Authorization for the method of transportation shall be furnished to the contractor prior to shipment.

  (3) Transportation charges for the shipment of empty packing cases shall be paid by the contractor except when equipment is moved from one Government location to another.

  (4) Transportation charges, regardless of point of origin or destination of the equipment, shall not exceed the cost of shipment between the Government's location and the location of the contractor's nearest plant of manufacture.

  (5) The contractor shall bear the cost of transportation whenever the equipment is shipped for mechanical replacement purposes unless the replacement was due to the fault or negligence of the Government.

  (6) The Government shall pay only those rigging and drayage costs incurred at the Government's location except that the contractor shall pay all rigging and dray-

age costs when the equipment is moved for mechanical replacement purposes.

b. *Installation.*

    (1) The Government shall furnish such labor as may be necessary for packing, unpacking, and placement of equipment when in the possession of the Government.

    (2) Supervision of packing, unpacking, and placement of equipment shall be furnished by the contractor without charge to the Government.

c. *Relocation.*

    (1) Except in an emergency, equipment shall not be moved from the general location in which installed, unless the contractor has been notified that a move is to be made.

    (2) Upon written notification to the contractor, equipment may be transferred from one Government location to another without rental and maintenance charges during the period of transfer not to exceed thirty (30) calendar days.

    (3) The contractor shall supervise packing, unpacking, relocation of equipment, and install in good operating condition without charge to the Government.

d. *Return of Equipment.*

    (1) Within thirty (30) days after the date of the discontinuance of rental, the contractor shall cause the equipment to be made ready for shipment and shall provide the Government with shipping instructions.

    (2) Within thirty (30) days after receipt of the shipping instructions or the date of discontinuance, whichever is later, the Government shall cause the equipment to be shipped.

14. *PURCHASE OF INSTALLED RENTED EQUIPMENT.* [Purchase Only]

a. The Purchase Price will be governed by the provisions of Paragraph 20, Item 132-1.

b. All applicable provisions of this Item 132-6 will apply.

c. Provided that the documented system audit run performed by the contractor on the last day of rental clearly demonstrates that the system is in good operating condition, the effective date of purchase shall be either:

    (1) The day following receipt by the contractor of a notice to purchase, or

    (2) an earlier date when mutually agreed to, or

    (3) a later date if so specified on the order.

d. Title to each machine will be transferred to the Government when the purchase price is paid. Title to a special feature installed on a machine and for which only a single use charge was paid under Special Item 132-1, shall pass to the Government at no additional charge, together with title to the machine on which it is installed.

15. *RISK OF LOSS OR DAMAGE.* The Government is relieved from all risks of loss or damage to the equipment during periods of transportation, installation, and during the entire time the equipment is in possession of the Government, except when loss or damage is due to the fault or negligence of the Government.

15. [Purchase Only] The contractor, if requested, shall furnish maintenance service in accordance with Item 132-11.

16. *CONTRACTOR'S LIABILITY FOR INJURY TO PERSONS AND/OR DAMAGE TO PROPERTY.* The contractor shall be liable for damages arising out of injury to the person and/or damage to the property of the Government, employees of the Government, persons designated by the Government for training, or any other person(s) designated by the Government for any purpose, other than agents or employees of the contractor, prior to or subsequent to acceptance, delivery, installation and use of the equipment either at the contractor's site or at the Government's place of business, provided that the injury or damage was caused by the fault or negligence of the contractor or caused by the contractor's equipment.

17. *SUPPLIES* [Rental Only] Rental and maintenance charges do not include supplies.

17. *REPLACEMENT PARTS AVAILABILITY.* [Purchase Only] The contractor shall furnish in his pricelist opposite each model, type or feature the number of years all replacement parts will be available beginning with July 1, 1972. After the expiration of the period during which replacement parts will be available the contractor, when requested by the Government, must furnish all necessary data which will enable the Government to have such parts manufactured elsewhere.

18. *STATE AND LOCAL TAXES.* Notwithstanding the provisions of Article 27 of the Supplemental Provisions (GSA Form 1424), the contract price excludes all state and local taxes levied on or measured by the contract or sales price of the services or completed supplies furnished under

this contract except state and local taxes based upon the contractor's or the Government's use of the equipment or its components. Taxes excluded from the contract price pursuant to the preceding sentence shall be separately stated on the contractor's invoices and the Government agrees either to pay to the contractor amounts covering such taxes or to provide evidence necessary to sustain an exemption therefrom.

18. *SCHEMATIC DIAGRAMS.* [Purchase Only] in addition to the diagnostic routines provided under Paragraph 1b. (2) (a), the contractor shall provide the schematic diagrams which are required for the proper maintenance of the equipment purchased by the Government.

19. *TITLE.* [Rental Only]
   a. Clear title to equipment, accessories, and devices rented under this contract shall be available for transfer to the Government upon exercise of the purchase option. During the term of this contract and any renewals or extensions thereof, no action by the contractor shall impair the Government's rights to exclusive possession and use of rented equipment without interruption.
   b. All devices and accessories furnished by the contractor, except those purchased by the Government, shall accompany the equipment when returned to the contractor.
   c. Upon mutual agreement between the contractor and the Government, the Government may exchange its title of Government-owned equipment for that of similar equipment under rental at another location.

20. *PURCHASE OPTION.* [Rental Only]
   a. The Government may, at any time, following acceptance of the equipment, purchase any or all machines. At the request of the Government, the contractor shall furnish the date of manufacture, and, if applicable, the date of the last major refurbishing for the machines which may be purchased by the Government.
   b. The price the Government shall pay will be the purchase price prevailing at the time such equipment was initially ordered for rental or the purchase price prevailing at the time of purchase, whichever is the lesser, less _____% for each month of age from capitalization date, and in addition, less an amount equal to _____% of rental and maintenance paid during the period(s) that the equipment to be purchased

was on rental within the various Government agencies.
   (1) The contractor agrees that the General Services Administration shall have the right to apply any purchase option credits which have accrued to the Government as a whole, towards the purchase of installed equipment on rental at any Government installation, provided that the total amount of such accrued purchase option credits are, in each instance, applied only towards the purchase of the same type and model of equipment that earned the purchase option credits.
   c. The equipment shall be discontinued from rental and maintenance on the day immediately preceding the effective date of purchase.
   d. Upon exercise of the purchase option, the contractor, if requested, shall furnish maintenance service in accordance with Item 132-11.
   e. The Government shall have the right to transfer its purchase option credits to a third party.

21. *OVERSEAS INSTALLATIONS.* The terms and conditions of this contract shall apply to all orders for installation of equipment in areas listed in the pricelist outside the 48 contiguous states and the District of Columbia except for the following modifications:
   a. In place of an Installation Date for equipment, a shipping date shall be specified on the order. Liquidated Damages in accordance with Paragraph 3 based on noncompliance for installation of equipment applicable to an Installation Date shall be applicable to the Shipping Date.
   b. The Government agrees to have the site prepared in accordance with the contractor's written site specifications before the Shipping Date.
   c. The contractor agrees to install promptly all equipment ready for use. In the event that equipment is not installed within 30 calendar days after it reaches the Government installation, Liquidated Damages in accordance with Paragraph 3 shall apply beginning on the 31st day.
   d. Subject to the provisions of Paragraph 4, rental and maintenance charges for the equipment shall begin on an Installation Date which shall be established as the first workday following the day on which it is installed and certified ready for use.

e. Upon request of the contractor, the Government, on a reimbursable basis, may provide logistics support, as available, in overseas areas in accordance with all applicable Government regulations, to the contractor's technical personnel whose services are exclusively required for the fulfillment of the terms and conditions of this contract.

f. The contractor shall maintain back-up engineers with clearance for immediate entry into foreign countries.

g. Upon request of the Government, the contractor shall modify equipment so that it will operate on 50 or 60 cycle current without additional charge.

SUMMARY OF SOFTWARE PACKAGES

SOURCE:

Brad Schultz, "Systems and Utility Software," *Computerworld,* July 31, 1978, pp. S/4–5.

DATA BASE MANAGEMENT SYSTEMS (DBMS) ($3,000 to $120,000)

While some users may find it necessary to design their own DBMS, most should be able to satisfy their needs with one of the many excellent data base management systems commercially available. These systems cost only a fraction of what would normally be expended to design a custom package, have proven to be totally reliable and cost effective and are supported by competent software professionals.

INFORMATION STORAGE AND RETRIEVAL (IS&R) ($4,000 to $140,000)

The objective of IS&R software is to facilitate the retrieval of documents or text extracted from documents. Documentation retrieval includes helping the user locate the document, outputting textual documentation summaries (e.g., abstracts, extracts) and amplifying information (e.g., bibliographical citations containing title, author and publisher) and providing entire documents. Some types of IS&R systems retrieve formatted data that is not part of the documents or text.

DATA COMMUNICATIONS MONITOR ($6,000 to $75,000)

These monitors manage critical system resources such as memory and processor time and provide access for other components to a variety of services and physical facilities. Functions which must be provided are task scheduling, interrupt handling, I/O management, mass storage space management and operator interfacing.

SOURCE PROGRAM MANAGEMENT ($1,250 to $11,000)

- Has advantages of OS for DOS installations
- Has authorization and security controls to prevent wrong library from being updated and to prohibit unauthorized updates

- Offers highly compressed mode that allows substantial disk savings
- Lets entire modules be inserted, deleted or replaced
- Stores JCL statement sets and test data
- Provides backup and recovery to as many as 15 prior levels
- Provides paired functions of linkage editing and library maintenance
- Generates job streams automatically
- Scans for updating based on various conditions, makes data string and substring substitutions
- Allows temporary addition of statements to a member in a job stream without change to master
- Provides error checking in modifications
- Automatically reuses space when deleting
- Controls simultaneous updating
- Provides call interface for user-written programs
- Offers unlimited storage of temporary updates for program development
- Provides comprehensive reports detailing library status and changes

TAPE LIBRARY MANAGEMENT ($5,000 to $11,000)

- Has complete control over installation's tape library
- Rejects wrong tape mounts and prevents inadvertent overwriting
- Automatically maintains list of scratch tapes based on expired retention dates
- Allows tape drives to be shared across DOS partitions
- Pinpoints correct historical masters for recovery situations
- Traces a data set through previous generation even though data set name has changed

PROGRAM AND DATA GENERATORS, CODE OPTIMIZERS ($4,500 to $27,000)

- Give drastic reduction in program preparation and execute times
- Eliminate much Cobol verbiage through macros, with reductions in code of as much as 60%
- Reduce size of OS or OS/VS Cobol object modules

- Produce machine-efficient and documented Cobol programs from problem-oriented specifications
- Offer runtime debugging and program performance monitoring
- Aid in development of data gathering, inquiry and conversational Cobol applications
- Provide decision table analysis
- Facilitate semi-automatic programming for generating structured programs
- Generate Cobol programs from simple statements prepared by nonprogrammers
- Permit data definitions and 77-level entries in procedure division

PROGRAM TEST/DEBUG ($4,000 to $15,000)

- Measures execution characteristics of Cobol programs
- Debugs, tests and optimizes Cobol source code
- Generates data files to test programs written in any language
- Debugs, times and analyzes Fortran source code
- Generates highly flexible test data for Cobol programs
- Reports execution activity by the user's symbolic procedure names
- Provides flexibility that makes programmers want to use the test facilities
- Rapidly checks output files and documents errors as they occur
- Allows uncoverted DOS programs to run on OS and OS/VS systems
- Effects up to 50% reduction in paging

PROGRAM TRANSLATORS ($3,000 to $10,000)

Various packages are available for translating programs from a language no longer used to a currently used language, including Autocoder to Cobol, 1400 to Cobol, BAL to Cobol, Easycoder to Cobol, PL/I to Cobol, RPG/RPG-II to Cobol, Autocoder to PL/I, Burroughs Corp. to IBM and Honeywell Information Systems, Inc. to IBM.

REPORT GENERATORS ($2,500 to $20,000)

This has become a very generalized category of software that is basically characterized by the ability to provide formatted outputs from computer files through the use of simplified parametric inputs prepared by nonprogrammers. Services range from simple report formatting to fairly complex file creation and manipulation, including interfaces with data base systems for sophisticated information retrieval capabilities. Several packages were specifically designed to meet the needs of organizational auditing staffs.

SPOOLERS ($350 to $10,000)

- Significant throughput increase
- Peripheral, pooling; automatic allocation/deallocation
- Partition balancing, device equates, job accounting, JCL procedure libraries
- Ability to expand to utilize unused core; significant reduction in core requirements
- Shared use by multiple CPUs

DATA HANDLERS ($595 to $36,000)

- Provide significantly more efficient and faster access methods
- Supplement OS job management functions for very significant throughput improvement
- Provide on-line access to system data sets
- Offer reduced channel and control unit time to read sequential data from disks
- Offer virtual access method for MVT
- Offer IBM 370 functions for 360 systems
- Provide significant augmentation of IBM OS/360 job management
- Provide comprehensive multistep job restarting
- Execute complete job streams without handling JCL
- Create JCL procedure library in any partitioned data set
- Process DOS job stream on any partition without JCL change
- Offer very flexible dump and copy facility

PARTITION BALANCERS
($2,000 to $3,000)

- Has optimum CPU and I/O processing balance
- Provides throughput increase as high as 30%
- Offers significant channel usage time reductions
- Ensures that CPU-bound jobs will not freeze out others
- Sets priorities by analyzing general operating characteristics of jobs

SORT/MERGE UTILITIES
($350 to $7,000)

- As much as 30% reduction in sort time
- Most appropriate optimization modes (i.e., I/O time, CPU time, I/O accesses) user-selectable
- Disk space used efficiently without JCL changes
- Sort exits writable in Cobol
- Secondary sort space automatically obtained
- Parameters alterable from invoking program without necessity to recompile the program
- Best executing mode dynamically determined in on-line systems

TAPE/DISK UTILITIES
($175 to $15,000)

- Benefit of Vsam for nonvirtual shops
- OS-like disk management for DOS systems
- Isam, Vsam replaced for significant improvement in efficiency
- Disk files compressed 30% to 60%
- System libraries built, reorganized and condensed

- Tape read errors reduced 30% to 50%
- Disk loading/unloading to tape done quickly, saving disk resources and minimizing pack changing
- Vtoc analysis and reporting improves disk utilization
- Disk housekeeping functions with automatic release of unused areas
- File and library backup with automatic Isam reorganization
- Workspace automatically assigned to application programs
- Jobs scheduled to complement each other, make better use of CPU time

PERFORMANCE EVALUATORS
($1,000 to $60,000)

- Measure how well your software is using your hardware for a given job mix
- Especially useful with MVS where user has unprecedented control over how jobs are processed and the amount of resources they can use
- Detect (some resolve) queuing conflicts, reserve lockouts, job looping or hanging in wait state, CPU thrashing, core fragmentation
- Automatically reorganize system data sets
- Provide comprehensive job billing as auxiliary function
- Have real-time analysis and outputs
- Show jobs in memory awaiting CPU or jobs with peripherals assigned awaiting memory
- Simplified reports need less skilled analyst for interpretation

SOFTWARE EVALUATION CHECKLIST

SOURCE:

Robert V. Head, *A Guide to Packaged Systems* (New York: Wiley-Interscience, 1971), pp. 38–9.

PACKAGE EVALUATION CHECKLIST

Cost

What services are provided as part of the basic purchase price?

Installation

Training

Maintenance

Are both lease and purchase options available?

Are there special costs of conversion from existing systems?

Are modifications in the system required?

Is there a surcharge for multi-installation usage?

What are the recurring costs of production running?

Availability

What is the operational history of the system?

Has the system been installed in multiple locations?

Will the supplier warrant error-free performance of the system?

Can references be contacted to determine operational status?

Equipment Configuration

What is the *minimum* configuration required for system operation?

What is the *optimum* configuration, i.e., that on which the system was designed to operate most efficiently?

Can the system be readily modified to work on other configurations?

Can peripherals be used interchangeably, e.g., disks for tapes?

Software Environment

Are purchaser's programmers familiar with the programming language used in the system?

Is the operating system employed the same as that used by the purchaser?

Are there special software features not typically found in user installations, e.g., special data management techniques?

Quality of System Design

Was the system originally designed as a generalized package or merely retrofitted from a custom design?

Does the system possess sufficient modularity to permit easy adaptation to purchaser's particular requirements?

Does the system offer useful options to the user, e.g., in input media, data management?

Can the system be readily expanded to accommodate increases in processing volume?

Is throughput performance comparable to that of custom designed systems?

Documentation

Is there a general information manual describing the system in over-all terms?

Is there adequate system level and program level documentation?

Are there instructions for computer operations and for source data preparation?

Are "source decks" needed for an understanding of the system and is the supplier willing to provide them?

Does the documentation provided measure up to purchaser's in-house standards?

Installation Support

How much on-site installation assistance is required for package installation?

Is installation support included in system purchase price?

Does supplier provide a pre-installation assistance "kit" to aid in system conversion?

Is training in system usage provided as part of installation support?

Maintenance

Is the supplier willing to commit to post-installation maintenance support?

What is the cost of system maintenance service?

Enhancement

Does the supplier plan further enhancements to the system?

What is the cost basis for providing future system enhancements?

Integrity of Supplier

Does the supplier have the personnel and financial resources to provide adequate on-going system support?

Is the supplier committed to future maintenance and enhancements of the system?

K

DATACOM SECURITY AND RELIABILITY CHECKLIST

SOURCE:

Gerald I. Isaacson, "Security and Reliability Checklist," *Auerbach Computer Technology Reports* (Pennsauken, N.J.: Auerbach Publishers Inc., 1976), portfolio no. 050.0000.970, pp. 3–11.

DESIGN CONSIDERATIONS

I. System Planning Requirements to Consider

A. Prevention of Physical Access to the System Environment

1. Is entry to the operating area restricted to authorized personnel or to only those who have a need to be there?
2. Are all persons who are permitted entry to the operating area positively identified and required to continuously display current identification?
3. Is a list of authorized personnel maintained and kept up to date?
4. Are unauthorized persons challenged when they attempt to enter the area?
5. Are persons not assigned to the area required to sign in and out?
6. Is the entrance to the area housing terminals and message preparation equipment physically separated from the administrative and other working areas by means of partitions?
7. Does the main entrance to the computer switch area open into an administrative area?
8. Is the administrative area physically separated from the computer switch and supervisory terminal control sections by floor-to-ceiling partitions?
9. Are all exterior entrances, i.e., windows and doors, secured to prevent intrusion?
10. Is the computer switch area locked at the end of the day?
11. Are maintenance and security personnel permitted in the switch area when employees assigned to the area are not present?
12. Is the number of people who have access to the system, as well as the number of occasions for system intervention, kept to a minimum?

B. Prevention of Operational Access to the System

1. Does the communications system software verify the sending user with the input station address of the inputting terminal?
2. Are type code restrictions placed on messages input from different operating areas?
3. Are the supervisory control terminals restricted to entering control-type and broadcast messages?
4. Can accounting or other applications programs be altered by computer operators?
5. Can executive or supervisory programs be altered by computer operators?
6. Does the computer switch assign sequence numbers to all requests for transfers from on-line users?
7. Does the actual message copy include the sequence/control number assigned to the transfer request?

C. Protection from Unauthorized Monitoring of Data Transmission

1. Has message (data) encryption been considered in the design of the system?
2. Are multiplexed transmission facilities contemplated?
3. Does the communications protocol utilize synchronous transmission?
4. Are alternate routing paths to be utilized?
5. Are communications lines to be be shielded—routed through secure conduits with all service access points, terminal rooms, and such physically secured, including access control to these areas?

II. Component Design Considerations

A. Computer Facilities

1. In selecting the location, have the following been taken into consideration?
   a. Topography (flooding potential, bad weather accessibility, strong electrical or electromagnetic fields, etc.).
   b. Access to communications and power facilities.
   c. Accessibility to unauthorized personnel.
   d. Proximity to sources of radio frequency interference.
2. In the course of physical construction and site planning, have the following questions been considered?
   a. Are fireproofing and fire-fighting facilities integrated into the construction?
   b. Is entry access limited?
   c. Is vulnerability (windows, etc.) reduced?
   d. Are air conditioning and power available from primary and backup sources?

e. Is a combination of effective alarms and response or guard force planned?

f. Does the installation conform to national and local codes (building, fire, electrical, etc.)?

3. Have the following equipment reliability questions been answered?

a. Is alternative hardware available for critical units?

b. Are emergency power and air conditioning available?

c. Are fall-back communications being considered?

d. Has maintenance time been allocated in the planned operation?

e. Has equipment reliability at other installations been considered during the equipment selection process?

f. Are spare parts available on site when required, or is there a local spare-parts depot?

g. Is diagnostic test equipment available on site?

h. Have plans been made for full on-site maintenance coverage by qualified engineers?

4. Have the following architectural design questions been considered?

a. Has the system been configured for redundant critical peripherals and mainframe computers?

b. Is the architecture selected for recovery of the shared load type or "Hot" standby type?

c. Are duplicate data storage facilities provided both on- and off-site?

d. Is historical data to be encrypted?

e. Are stringent terminal sign-on protocols designed into the system?

B. Network Facilities

1. Has transmission facility planning included consideration of the following items from a security and reliability aspect?

a. Selection of ownership of the communication lines and equipment (public, private, etc.).

b. Type and conditioning (wire, microwave, etc.).

c. Line philosophy (dedicated lines, switched lines).

d. Contingency circuits and alternate routing paths.

e. Error monitoring and correction.

f. Format medium (analog, digital).

2. Has communications system design included consideration of the security aspects of the following?

a. Message or block transmission.

b. Error-handling requirements.

c. Transmission speeds.

d. Transmission code and level (5-level, 8-level, etc.).

e. Basic system philosophy (store-and-forward, etc.).

f. Use of concentrators and multiplexers.

g. Use of encryption devices.

C. Terminal Facilities

1. Have the following types of equipment been considered?

a. Telegraphic.

b. Programmable.

c. Computer.

d. Encryption devices.

2. Has reliability of the following been considered?

a. Contingency equipment.

b. Maintenance and spares.

c. Alternate power supplies.

d. Software requirements.

3. Has physical protection of the terminal been considered, in regard to the following items?

a. Location.

b. Access.

c. Control mechanisms.

III. Message (Data) Planning Considerations

A. Does Message Authorization Include the Following Checks?

1. Validation of the originating terminal as to ownership, correct station for the line, etc.

2. Verification that the station is authorized to transmit at the particular time of the day or week.

3. Confirmation of the operator sign-on.

4. Validation of message format.

5. Verification of the authority of the operator (station) to transmit the type of message.

6. Validation of the message numbering sequence.

7. Test for correct authorization codes embedded in the message.

8. Are there procedures for processing messages that fail these checks?

B. Is the Message Validation Composed of at Least the Following?

1. Positional edits for correct control characters, address and data fields, line and format constraints.
2. Data validation for routing numbers, addresses, type codes, currency amount and type, and specific handling instructions.
3. Authorization checks for coded data, test words, and other security-type tests, such as multiple identical dollar or quantity fields.

C. Are the Following Checks Made to Confirm and Verify Message Delivery?

1. That the destination is a valid point in the network.
2. That the destination is authorized to receive the type of traffic involved.
3. That a positive connection is made with the station and validated before and after message transmission.
4. That positive acceptance of the message is received from the terminal upon delivery, with terminal identification included in the acknowledgment.
5. That unbroken, sequential output numbers are transmitted as part of the message.
6. That a historical log is kept of all messages transmitted.
7. That queuing and routing algorithms provide for efficient processing of traffic to prevent undue delay of messages in transmit.
8. Are any means employed to anticipate the number of messages to be received at a destination?

D. Is Message Protection Enhanced Through the Use of the Following Techniques?

1. Encryption devices and processes at various points in the system.
2. Code words in the message to reduce the chances of unauthorized modification of messages.
3. Multiplexing messages with others to increase the difficulty of monitoring.

E. Have the Following Questions Been Considered in Order to Ensure Message Accountability?

1. Is every message safely stored on a permanent device from which it can be retrieved and restored to the active system when required?
2. Are multiple copies of messages placed in storage to ensure accountability if a device fails?
3. Are internal system controls in the form of numbering systems or other internal addressing mechanisms designed to permit retrieval of message data as required?
4. Are internal controls stored with each message? Do these controls contain audit trail data including at least the following?
   a. A system reference number unique to the message.
   b. Identification of the input station and line.
   c. Time of input and date.
   d. Data on any significant errors.
   e. Message size (in number of characters).
5. When the message is delivered, is the following data added to the controls prior to placing the message and its controls in historical storage?
   a. Output station and line identification.
   b. Delivery data and time.
   c. Number of copies delivered.
6. Does the system design require positive acceptance or rejection of all messages, with this notice being returned to the originator?
7. Are all deliveries acknowledged automatically by the receiving station?
8. Does the station provide confirmation of identification prior to and after a message is delivered?
9. At least once in every 24-hour period, are the switching system files checked for the previous day's traffic?
10. Does the system design accommodate file-aging mechanisms?
11. Are the system recovery programs designed to account for all in-transit messages after a failure?
12. Are retrieval programs designed to permit only authorized parties to gain access to delivered messages?
13. Are retrievals clearly identified as not being originals, and are they independent of any accounting or settlement processes?
14. Does the design of the message trace system permit following a message both within and outside the system?
15. Are off-line programs designed to permit a complete analysis of message logs? This would involve edited dumps, message search programs, etc.

F. Are Settlement and Accounting Programs Designed with the Following Capabilities to Facilitate Communications Control?

1. System reference numbers in accounting reports and statements.
2. Line and station identification data included.
3. Accounting and settlement errors generate rapid automatic notifications to operator personnel.

OPERATIONAL CONSIDERATIONS

I. Physical Requirements

A. The Following Security-related Aspects Must be Verified.

1. Are security measures used so that unauthorized persons, such as outside employees, may be safely admitted to the communications control areas?
2. In this regard, does each area supply the security group with a list of outside employees who are required to visit the areas regularly, such as vendor personnel?
3. Are visitors permitted to proceed to these areas without authorization from the area?
4. Does each area give written authorization to those employees who will be in the areas outside of normal working hours?
5. Is each area regularly patrolled, and is the patrol verified by a time punch?
6. Is the security group familiar with the layout of the terminal rooms in each operating area, as well as with the layout of the computer switch area?
7. Is access to the terminals and message preparation equipment strictly controlled?
8. Is the operation of terminals and message preparation equipment restricted to certain personnel?
9. Do dual-control conditions exist in the two areas after normal system operating hours?
10. Do dual-control conditions exist during testing?
11. Is entrance to the computer switch and supervisory terminal control areas restricted to authorized personnel?
12. Is a list of authorized personnel maintained?
13. Are all persons not assigned to the organization operating the switch required to sign in and out of the area?
14. If backup equipment is maintained in the operating area, is it disabled when not in use?
15. Is backup equipment tested periodically?
16. Are terminals assigned an out-of-service status at the end of operations?
17. Does the supervisory staff maintain a current log of operating and non-operating equipment during the day?
18. Do one or two people close up at the end of the day, inspecting the switch area to ensure that all terminals are shut down and all documents, etc., are locked away?
19. Is there a retention schedule for documents relating to transactions?
20. Are the documents retained in a secure place and visibly identified as to level of sensitivity?
21. Is refuse collected at the end of the day, retained for a period of time to ensure that no sensitive data has been inadvertently discarded, and subsequently shredded or burned?
22. Are documents and manuals relating to the operation of terminal and message preparation equipment stored in a lockable receptacle?
23. Is there off-site backup of tapes, discs, and/or cards containing vital programs and program changes?
24. Are production copies of programs and changes stored in fire-resistant cabinets when not in use?
25. Are program source listings maintained in off-site storage?
26. Is CRT, teletype, and computer equipment shut down after normal working hours?
27. In the case of supervisory control terminals, is an unbroken monitor copy of all messages maintained throughout the day, representing an audit trail of interventions in system operations?
28. Are logs of all down-time and the reasons for it maintained for all equipment?
29. Is access to the electrical supply closely controlled?
30. Are test word and authorized signature lists, start-up procedures, and forms secured at the end of the day or when not in use?
31. Is the risk of fire minimized?
32. Is the ventilation system automatically shut down by the fire alarm system?
33. Are there fire/smoke detectors and automatic fire extinguishers under the raised floor or in the ceiling?
34. Are master emergency switches positioned near the exit?

35. Is the computer switch area protected against damage from water and fire in neighboring areas?
36. Is there a fire prevention and evacuation plan for the computer switch area and for the terminal areas?
37. Is a responsible person in charge of these plans?
38. Are employees trained in using fire-fighting equipment, shutting down electrical equipment, reporting fires, and evacuating personnel?
39. Is the computer switch area kept clean and free from excess combustibles and refuse?
40. Besides having fire-detection and -fighting equipment, is the computer switch area checked regularly by an expert in fire prevention? By the local fire department?
41. Is the air-conditioning system sufficiently protected against failure, and is backup equipment available?
42. Is the air-conditioning equipment checked regularly, even during periods outside normal working hours?
43. Is the computer system completely powered from a single electrical source? If so, is backup electrical power available?

B. Reliability as a Factor in Providing a Secure System Can be Evaluated on the Basis of the Following Questions.

1. Is there a scheduled, periodic maintenance program for the equipment?
2. Is the on-site spare-parts inventory adequate?
3. Are spare units available for critical pieces of equipment?
4. Are maintenance personnel available when required?
5. Is sufficient diagnostic test equipment available?
6. Are constant checks made on performance and reliability?

II. System Considerations in an Operational Environment

A. Examination of Operating Procedures and Control of the Traffic.

1. Are there dual-control and separation of duties in the control and processing of message requests?
2. If a sequence/control number is to be assigned to a message request, does the employee accepting the request assign the number?
3. Is the original request compared to the actual message copy made at the time of transmission?
4. Does the terminal operator verify input and output sequence numbers at the terminal?
5. Are logs provided for this check?
6. Are intercepted messages processed and controlled?
7. Are messages received too late for processing logged and strictly controlled until they can be processed?
8. Are rejected messages and all relevant information examined to discover the reasons for rejection?
9. Are there procedures to reprepare and successfully transmit rejected messages?
10. Is an unbroken monitor copy of all messages that have been sent or received maintained on the terminal?
11. Are employees permitted to prepare messages without producing hardcopy?
12. Is the number of messages delivered to or received from on-line terminals reconciled daily?
13. Is the total number of requests verified with the requester?
14. Are the source documents attached or referenced to copies of the message transmitted?
15. Are the two documents compared for accuracy?
16. Are requests for adjustments strictly controlled and only granted for specific reasons?
17. Are adjustments reviewed by management?
18. Are "open" or unreconciled items for all users promptly investigated and reconciled?
19. Are adjustments made on the basis of written authorization?
20. Have procedures been developed for all situations and committed to writing?
21. Are all employees, especially supervisory personnel, familiar with these procedures?
22. Are supervisory employees aware of the potential security vulnerability of the communications system?
23. Is the supervisor or his designated equivalent always present in the terminal and message preparation area?
24. Are supervisors responsible for the opening and closing of the communications network pertaining to their functions?
25. Does the supervisory staff review terminal and message copy more than once a day?

26. Are separation of duties, dual controls, and individual responsibilities clearly defined and their importance impressed upon all employees?

27. Are all exceptions to standard procedures promptly investigated and corrective measures taken?

28. Is an audit trail available for any message introduced into the system?

29. Does this audit trail also track illegal or erroneous attempts to enter a message?

B. Software Considerations

1. Are adequate levels of authority required to review and approve system changes?

2. Are software changes fully documented, tested, reviewed, and approved before implementation?

3. Do test plans include attempts to enter invalid messages to determine if error-checking routines are working?

4. Does the system software comply with all edit and validity checks specified in operational procedure manuals?

5. Is the software recoverable within the time designated in the functional specification?

6. Does full documentation, including flowcharts, exist for all system programs?

7. Are all changes to system software fully documented?

8. Is a historical record of all changes to the system software maintained on an up-to-date basis?

9. Is the system documentation modified to reflect any changes, including flowcharts if applicable?

L

CHECKLIST FOR DATA CENTER EVALUATION

This checklist permits an evaluation of the data center according to some of the factors discussed in this book. The ten sections of the checklist correspond to chapters 2 thru 11. This checklist helps:

- Locate and eliminate current deficiencies
- Locate and avoid potential problems
- Locate opportunities for improving performance

The questions shown are basic to the evaluation of any data center. It is likely, however, that additional questions may need to be added, concerning those aspects in a data center that have been troublesome. For this reason, space for additional questions has been included in the checklist, permitting the checklist to be tailored to the needs of each data center.

The question remains: Who will actually perform the evaluation? The options are to have the evaluation performed by a data center supervisor, a staff member, in-house group assigned to performance evaluation, or an outside consultant. An outside consultant may be the choice for occasional evaluations, providing the benefits of an objective judgement, a fresh perspective, and the contribution of varied experiences. It is advisable, however, that these consulting services supplement, not replace, more frequent evaluations performed by in-house personnel.

The summary below can be used to show the total number of "yes" and "no" responses for each of the ten categories of questions, with a "no" response indicating a possible problem area. Space is also provided for comments concerning corrective action taken or recommended.

Data Center Evaluation Summary

TOPIC	NUMBER OF		COMMENT
	YES	NO	
Organization Structure and Management Control			
Personnel Recruitment, Advancement, and Appraisal			
Budgeting, Chargeout, and Financial Analysis			
Site Selection and Preparation, and Data Center Relocation			
Hardware and Software Acquisition			
Data Center Standards and Procedures			
Data Center Workflow			
Job Scheduling and Resource Allocation			
Data Communications			
Computer Performance Evaluation			

Organization Structure and Management Control (Chapter 2)

QUESTION	YES	NO
1. Are all data center objectives defined, and are they documented in measurable terms?		
2. Are all necessary specialized support functions present in the organization?		
3. Are responsibilities for all functions assigned and are they accompanied by sufficient authority?		
4. Are management levels kept to a minimum, and are spans of control appropriate?		
5. Is the existing centralization, decentralization, or mixture of both satisfactory?		
6. Is there satisfactory rapport between management, staff, and users?		
7. Are there sufficient management reports (but not too many), a data center steering committee, and a user handbook?		
8.		
9.		
10.		

Personnel Recruitment, Advancement, and Appraisal (Chapter 3)

QUESTION	YES	NO
1. Besides a person's technical knowledge and skills, does the recruitment procedure consider motivation and compatibility with others?		
2. Are potential employees evaluated according to their ability to fit future positions?		
3. Is an adequate career path program present, with attention given to personnel needs and to assurance of backup personnel for critical positions?		
4. Are personnel reference documents adequate, including the use of career ladders, job/skills matrices, skill narratives, job/pay charts, and job descriptions?		
5. Are motivational techniques, such as management-by-group-objectives and job enrichment, in actual use?		
6. Are personnel appraised periodically, and is there agreement on individual and data center goals and activities for the next time period?		
7. Do appraisal interviews reaffirm each person's career path intentions and the training to be provided?		
8.		
9.		
10.		

Budgeting, Chargeout, and Financial Analysis (Chapter 4)

QUESTION	YES	NO
1. Are budgeted expenses justified instead of being automatically incremented?		
2. Are expenses providing long-term benefits fairly considered in spite of insufficient short-term benefits?		
3. Is a chargeout or chargeback system needed to make users aware of (and possibly control) data center costs?		
4. Is it likely that a chargeout or chargeback system will eliminate wasteful applications?		
5. Are cost trends, such as rising personnel costs, used to guide methodology decisions?		
6. Are application programs analyzed for efficiencies, and are application systems analyzed for alternative approaches?		
7.		
8.		
9.		
10.		

Site Selection and Preparation, and Data Center Relocation (Chapter 5)

QUESTION	YES	NO
1. In selecting a site, were the factors involved carefully chosen—including factors such as reliable electrical power and the availability of backup facilities?		
2. Was layout examined for efficient work flow, adequate storage, and flexibility to accomodate replacement or additional equipment?		
3. Are the precautions for safety and security adequate, including the monitoring of adherence to procedures?		
4. Are there contingency plans for the various types of processing disruptions, which may require operating with fewer resources or at another site?		
5. Are personnel trained in the contingency procedures, and are there periodic drills?		
6. Is insurance adequate in the case of hardware loss, software loss, or data loss?		
7. If relocation is being considered, are the many factors and activities being studied by a relocation committee?		
8.		
9.		
10.		

Hardware and Software Acquisition (Chapter 6)

QUESTION	YES	NO
1. Are necessary and desirable criteria identified and precisely stated?		
2. Are vendor proposals objectively compared to these criteria—avoiding unjustified preference for a one-vendor shop?		
3. Are products tested, or at least observed in action, using benchmarks when possible?		
4. Are customers for the vendors asked about reliability, performance, and vendor service?		
5. Are financial alternatives for acquisition evaluated?		
6. Are contract terms carefully examined and negotiated?		
7.		
8.		
9.		
10.		

Data Center Standards and Procedures (Chapter 7)

QUESTION	YES	NO
1. Are there performance standards for each work area?		
2. Are these standards in measurable terms that permit easy evaluation?		
3. Are these standards clearly documented?		
4. Are there procedures to support these standards?		
5. Are these procedures documented, preferably in a form such as "Playscript"?		
6. Is documentation easy to use and maintain—and is it actually kept up-to-date?		
7. Are documentation standards clearly defined, comprehensive, and concise—and documented?		
8. Are duplicates of critical data, programs, and documentation stored off-site?		
9.		
10.		

Data Center Workflow (Chapter 8)

QUESTION	YES	NO
1. Is a method available, through logs or on-line access, to record receipt of jobs in the data center, and their movements and eventual distribution?		
2. Using this method, is it easy to locate jobs that are delayed, and can requests about job status be easily answered?		
3. Are there adequate forms for job receipt, batch control, keying instructions, and all other needs in the data center?		
4. Are the tape library system and accompanying procedures satisfactory?		
5. Is the correction of rejected transactions carefully controlled?		
6. Are control totals for jobs checked?		
7.		
8.		
9.		
10.		

Job Scheduling and Resource Allocation (Chapter 9)

QUESTION	YES	NO
1. Are statistics available for computer and other data center resource capacities, and for actual usages?		
2. Are the resources being utilized adequately?		
3. Are resource capacities likely to be adequate in one year and in five years?		
4. Is user delivery of input data within standards established for their timely receipt?		
5. Is data center service to users within performance standards for scheduled jobs, unscheduled jobs, and on-line jobs?		
6. Is computer scheduling adequate, attending to priority and deadline constraints?		
7. Are precomputer and postcomputer activities scheduled?		
8. Do users help in leveling demands on resources?		
9.		
10.		

Data Communications (Chapter 10)

QUESTION	YES	NO
1. Are all persons associated with datacom familiar with its basic concepts and terminology?		
2. Are specialists always available to monitor and assure reliable and protected datacom processing?		
3. Are users notified of delays, and are attempts made to level demands on resources?		
4. Are redundancies of hardware present, and are alternative processing methods available?		
5. Are provisions adequate to protect against unauthorized access to computers, programs, and data?		
6. Are data reconstruction procedures defined and documented?		
7. Are personnel trained in all critical procedures, and are these procedures periodically tested for adequacy?		
8.		
9.		
10.		

Computer Performance Evaluation (Chapter 11)

QUESTION	YES	NO
1. Has a CPE program been implemented?		
2. Is the CPE procedure documented, and is at least one trained person assigned, even if only part-time?		
3. Are all the significant performance criteria measured, including capacities of resources for workloads, effectiveness in serving users, and efficiency in utilizing resources?		
4. Are computer-produced reports and the analyses performed by the performance analysts adequate?		
5. Are actions taken upon the conclusions of the performance analysts?		
6. Is management informed of the analyses, the actions taken, and the effects of these actions?		
7.		
8.		
9.		
10.		

BIBLIOGRAPHY

Overview of Data Center Operations

The Information Systems Handbook.
edited by F. Warren McFarlan and Richard L. Nolan, Homewood, Ill.: Dow Jones-Irwin, Inc., 1975.

Besides many introductory articles relevant to data center operations, there are excellent introductory articles on the numerous topics related to other aspects of data processing.

Organization Structure and Management Control

Administrative Action. (2nd ed.),
William H. Newman, Englewood Cliffs, N.J.: Prentice-Hall, Inc., 1963.

Provided is a clear description of, as well as practical guidance for performing such managerial functions as planning, organizing, staffing, directing, and controlling.

Managerial Breakthrough.
J. M. Juran, New York: McGraw-Hill Co., 1964.

A stimulating and detailed examination of management control to attain predetermined performance standards, and of management breakthrough to attain higher levels of performance.

Personnel Recruitment, Advancement, and Appraisal

Successful Management by Objectives.
Karl Albrecht, Englewood Cliffs, N.J.: Prentice-Hall, Inc., 1978.

A down-to-earth treatment of MBO, presenting it as a way of thinking and acting instead of as a cumbersome, complex system of paperwork.

The Human Side of Data Processing Management.
M. D. Wadsworth, Englewood Cliffs, N.J.: Prentice-Hall, Inc., 1973.

A practical procedure is presented for applying Maslow's theory of the hierarchy of needs to the motivation of personnel and the resolution of "people problems."

Budgeting, Chargeout, and Financial Analysis

Zero-Base Budgeting Comes of Age.
Logan M. Cheek, N.Y.: Amacom, 1977.

Besides providing insight into the purposes and the procedure of ZBB, Cheek presents various techniques, ideas, and a large variety of formats for decision package forms and ranking forms.

EDP Job Costs and Charges.
Kenneth W. Kolence and Robert A. James, Calif.: Institute for Software Engineering, Inc., 1976.

This book examines the bases and the means for charging out data center expenses and, at the same time, relates resource usage to resource capacity and to performance evaluation.

Data Processing Technology and Economics.
Montgomery Phister, Jr., Santa Monica, Calif.: Digital Press and The Santa Monica Publ. Co., 1979.

Graphs are used extensively to present financial and resource utilization trends, thus providing insight into these trends, which in turn aids planning and decision making.

Site Selection and Preparation, and Data Center Relocation

Guidelines for Automatic Data Processing Security and Risk Management.
(Federal Information Processing Standards Publication, FIPS PUB 31, National Bureau of Standards, June 1974)

This is one of many excellent FIPS publications: this manual provides a perceptive introduction to data center security and safety.

SAFE: Security Audit and Field Evaluation for Computer Facilities and Information Systems.
Leonard I. Krauss, N.Y.: Amacom, 1972.

This is a comprehensive checklist for periodic appraisal of data center security and safety.

| Hardware and Software Acquisition | *Computer Selection,* (augmented edition), Edward O. Joslin, Va.: The Technology Press, Inc., 1977. |

A sound approach is recommended for evaluating hardware acquisition, while explaining several alternate approaches and considering various financial acquisition methods.

Your Computer and the Law.
Robert P. Bigelow and Susan H. Nycum, N.J.: Prentice-Hall, Inc., 1975.

A good, if not necessary, companion for each data center manager to provide awareness of legal aspects and potential problems.

Data Processing Contracts and the Law.
Richard L. Bernacchi and Gerald H. Larsen, Boston: Little, Brown and Co., 1974.

A thorough treatment of the factors involved in negotiating a contract for hardware or software acquisition. This is an excellent book, but more of a companion to a lawyer.

| Data Center Workflow | *Management Controls for Data Processing.* by Price Waterhouse & Co., International Business Machines, manual no. GF20–0006–1, April, 1976. |

A basic introduction to workflow and processing controls, and their effects on auditability, for both batch and on-line processing.

Data Processing Control Practices Report.
researched by Susan Higley Russell, Tom S. Eason, and J. M. Fitzgerald of Stanford Research Institute; prepared for the Institute of Internal Auditors, Inc. International Business Machines, 1977.

A thorough and logical segmentation of overall data-processing activities, their major considerations, and many ideas for incorporating controls.

| Data Communications | *Design of On-Line Computer Systems.* Edward Yourdon, Englewood Cliffs, N.J.: Prentice-Hall, Inc., 1972. |

Besides providing a good introduction to many data communications concepts, it is a practical guide for maintaining reliable, well-controlled data communications systems.

Security, Accuracy, and Privacy in Computer Systems.
James Martin, Englewood Cliffs, N.J.: Prentice-Hall, Inc., 1973.

Among Martin's excellent books on data communications, this book should be of particular interest to data center personnel; as the title states, besides the question of privacy, the book focuses on accuracy and security—two major concerns of data center personnel.

Computer Performance Evaluation

Computer Performance Measurement and Evaluation Methods: Analysis and Applications.
Liba Svobodova, New York: American Elsevier Publ. Co., Inc., 1976.

A good introduction to CPE; it considers various system models and workload models, as well as simulation for CPE and the use of software and hardware measurement tools.

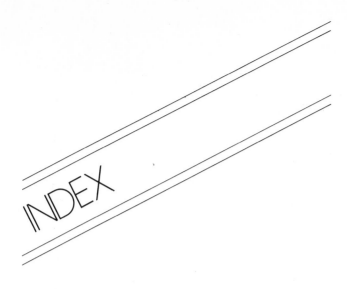

INDEX

the book of the pekingese

FROM PALACE DOG TO THE PRESENT DAY

by

Anna Katherine Nicholas

and

Joan McDonald Brearley

A History of the Lion Dog of Peking,
with many hundreds of photographs,
a large quantity dating from the
Turn of the Century.

Cover:
The magnificent Ch. Dagbury of Calartha, photographed in January, 1973 when he celebrated his six Best in Show wins and 42 Toy Group Firsts. Dagbury is co-owned by Mrs Walter M. Jeffords, Jr., and Michael Wolf of New York.

Back cover:
Show scenes. . . these photos appear in the color sections of this book, where they are individually captioned.

ISBN 0-87666-348-X

Distributed in the U.S.A. by T.F.H. Publications, Inc., 211 West Sylvania Avenue, P.O. Box 27, Neptune City, N.J. 07753; in England by T.F.H. (Gt. Britain) Ltd., 13 Nutley Lane, Reigate, Surrey; in Canada to the book store and library trade by Clarke, Irwin & Company, Clarwin House, 791 St. Clair Avenue West, Toronto 10, Ontario; in Canada to the pet trade by Rolf C. Hagen Ltd., 3225 Sartelon Street, Montreal 382, Quebec; in Southeast Asia by Y.W. Ong, 9 Lorong 36 Geylang, Singapore 14; in Australia and the south Pacific by Pet Imports Pty. Ltd., P.O. Box 149, Brookvale 2100, N.S.W., Australia. Published by T.F.H. Publications Inc. Ltd., The British Crown Colony of Hong Kong.

This book is dedicated
to the Pekingese we have
known and loved
in the past,
and to those we shall love
in the future.

ACKNOWLEDGEMENTS

The authors greatly appreciate the material contributed towards the compilation of this book. They are grateful to Iris de la Torre Bueno for show records and photographs; to Pekingese News for advance publicity; to Robert R. Shomer, VMD., for expert counsel; to Stephen McDonald for additional research information; and to all the proud owners whose treasured photographs of the little lion dogs have helped to make this book a special tribute to a magnificent and ancient breed.

CONTENTS

ANNA KATHERINE NICHOLAS

Anna Katherine Nicholas finds it difficult to recall a time when dogs did not play a major role in her life. Down through the years, from the much loved pets of childhood, which included a Boston Terrier, an Airedale, German Shepherds, a little white dog which strongly resembled a Bichon, and of course the Pekingese with which she most frequently has been associated, until the present day, when a dearly loved small adopted Terrier mix who was a stray and a beautiful champion Beagle share her home, dogs have been of interest and importance to her.

The first of her Pekingese, a gift when she was seven years old, led to an interest in dog shows. Her interest has not been as an exhibitor, as she has not cared to show her pets, but as a writer about dogs and a judge of them. In both fields she has met with significant success, as the record proves.

Miss Nicholas' first published article was a column about Pekingese, in *Dog News* magazine in the early thirties. This was followed by the famous breed column, PEEKING AT THE PEKINGESE, for many years featured in *Dogdom* magazine, and later in *Popular Dogs*. She has been Boxer columnist for the *American Kennel Gazette* and has written an Eastern column for *Boxer Briefs,* both during the forties. More recently she has had numerous articles of general interest to the Fancy published in the *Gazette and Pure Bred Dogs*. Her column "It Seems To Me" was a feature of *Popular Dogs* from the mid-sixties until just recently; at present she is a feature staff writer for *Kennel Review*. Late in the thirties her first book, *The Pekingese,* was published; it was later revised and sold out both editions under the Judy Publishing Company banner. Then came *The Skye Terrier Book,* published by the Skye Terrier Club of America, also a sell-out and now a collector's item bringing high prices whenever a copy can be located and re-sold. Her latest offering, prior to this volume, was the award-winning (Dog Writers Association of America Best Technical Book 1970) Howell Book House publication *The Nicholas Guide to Dog Judging,* which has met with wide acclaim throughout the dog show world. And her part in *This Is The Bichon Frise* was brought about by an overwhelming admiration for the breed which began in 1968, when her first meeting with a Bichon led her to want to learn all about these dogs. Two articles on Bichons, written by Miss Nicholas and published in *Popular Dogs,* one in 1969 and the other in 1971, created much favorable comment and helped to spread knowledge of the breed. She has also

About the Authors

just collaborated with Joan Brearley on *This is the Skye Terrier.* For the past three years, Miss Nicholas has been a nominee for the *Kennel Review* Journalism Award.

As a judge, Miss Nicholas officiated at her first dog show in 1934. She is now approved for all Hound, Toy and Non-Sporting breeds, most of the Terrier breeds, and Pointers, Boxers and Dobermans. Her services are constantly in demand for important assignments, including many National Specialty Shows. She is only the third woman in history to have judged Best in Show at the prestigious Westminster Kennel Club event, which honor befell her at the Club's 1970 show at Madison Square Garden in New York City.

Miss Nicholas has been a hard-working member of numerous dog clubs through the years. She is a former President of the Progressive Dog Club, the New York Boxer Club, and the American Pomeranian Club. She was founder and president for ten years of the Interstate Kennel Association and has held office in the Skye Terrier Club of America, the Pekingese Club of America, and the American Boxer Club, to list just a few. Presently she is an Honorary Member of the American Pomeranian Club and of the Queensboro Kennel Club.

7

JOAN McDONALD BREARLEY

Joan Brearley has loved animals ever since she was old enough to know what they were . . . .

Over the years·there has been a constant succession of dogs, cats, birds, fish, rabbits, snakes, turtles, alligators, squirrels, lizards, etc., for her own personal menagerie. Through these same years she has owned over twenty different breeds of pure-bred dogs, as well as countless mixtures, since the door was never closed to a needy or homeless animal.

A graduate of the American Academy of Dramatic Arts, Joan started her career as a writer for movie magazines and as an actress and dancer. She also studied journalism at Columbia University and has been a radio scriptwriter, copywriter for some of the major New York City advertising agencies, and a producer-director in radio and television for a major New York City network.

Her accomplishments in the dog fancy include being an American Kennel Club approved judge, a breeder-exhibitor of top show dogs (and cats!), a writer for the *American Kennel Club Gazette,* and author of *This Is the Afghan Hound, The Samoyeds* and co-author of *This Is the Bichon Frise, This is the Saint Bernard,* and *This is the Skye Terrier,* regarded as the "Bibles" for the breed. From August, 1967 through March, 1972 she was Executive Vice President of Popular Dogs Publishing Company and Editor of *Popular Dogs Magazine.* Joan Brearley is as active in the cat world, and in almost as many capacities, as she is in the dog world, particularly in the area of legislation.

She is an avid crusader and speaker for humane causes and legislation for animals. She is well known as a speaker before kennel clubs and humane organizations on this subject and has received many awards and citations for her work on behalf of the good and welfare of all animals.

At present Joan Brearley lives in a penthouse apartment in New York overlooking the East River and all Manhattan with an Afghan Hound, a Shih Tzu, a Cavalier King Charles Spaniel, and a dozen or more cats, all of which are Best In Show winners and have been professional models for television and magazines. Joan has the rare distinction of having bred a Westminster Kennel Club group winner in her very first litter of Afghan Hounds, Champion Sahadi (her kennel prefix) Shikari, the top-winning Afghan Hound in the history of the breed.

In addition to her activities in the world of animals, Joan Brearley spends much time at the art and auction galleries, the theatre, creating needlepoint (for which she has also won awards), dancing, the typewriter,—and the zoo!

CHAPTER 1

ORIGIN OF THE PEKINGESE

It was in the year 1860 that British troops stormed the Imperial Palace in Peking, finding the five Lion Dogs or Pekingese, which were to become the founders of the breed in England. Before this date, these small and courageous animals were sacred dogs of China, guarded by special attendants whose duty it was to look after them on the penalty of death should harm befall one of their royal charges.

Just when or how the Pekingese came into being is a question to which we have no definite answer. The popular ancient legend relates that he is the offspring of a lion and a marmoset, the former of which sacrificed his size and strength but not his brave heart for love of the diminutive charmer.

But undoubtedly the breed is of the most ancient origin. Through the centuries we find reference to these little Lion Dogs in early Chinese literature, and they often appear in Chinese paintings or porcelain.

The last ruler of the old Chinese Empire, the Dowager Empress Tzu Hsi, loved these small dogs, and they were honored residents in the Imperial Palace.
While the Chinese did not keep written pedigrees, they were selective in the breeding of their dogs, and possessed remarkable ability to remember the ancestors of every dog for several generations.

Of the dog now called the Pekingese, Empress Tzu Hsi said: "Let the Lion Dog be small; let it wear the swelling cape of dignity around its neck; let it display the billowing standard of pomp above its back. Let its face be black; let its forefront be shaggy; let its forehead be straight and low, like unto the brow of an Imperial harmony boxer. Let its eyes be large and luminous; let its ears be set like the sails of a war junk; let its nose be like that of the monkey god of the Hindus. Let its forelegs be bent, so that it shall not desire to wander far, or leave the Imperial Palace.

"Let its body be shaped like that of a hunting lion spying for its prey. Let its feet be tufted with plentiful hair that its footfall may be soundless; and for its standard of pomp, let it rival the whisk of the Tibetan Yak, which is flourished to protect the Imperial litter from the attacks of flying insects. Let it be lively, that it may afford entertainment by its gambols; let it be timid that it may not involve itself in dangers; let it be domestic in its habits that it may live in amity with the other beasts, fishes, or birds that find protection at the Imperial Palace.

"And for its color, let it be that of the lion—a golden sable to be carried in the sleeve of a yellow robe, or the color of a red bear, or a black or a white bear, or striped like a dragon, so that there may be dogs appropriate to every costume in the Imperial wardrobe. Let it venerate its ancestors and deposit offerings in the canine cemetery of the Forbidden City on each new moon. Let it comport itself with dignity; let it learn to bite the foreign devils instantly.

"Let it be dainty in its food that it shall be known for an Imperial dog by its fastidiousness. Sharks' fins, curlews' livers, and the breasts of quails, on these it may be fed; and for drink, give it the tea that is brewed from the spring buds of the shrub that groweth in the province of Hankow, or the milk of the antelope that pasture in the Imperial parks.

"Thus shall it preserve its integrity and self-respect; and for the day of sickness let it be anointed with the clarified fat of the leg of a sacred leopard, and give it to drink a throstle's eggshell full of the juice of the custard apple in which has been dissolved three pinches of shredded rhinoceros horn, and apply to it piebald leeches. So shall it remain—but if it die, remember thou, too, art mortal."

The ancient Pekingese were bred to vary in size, as they are today, and ranged from the tiny sleeve dogs popular with the ladies, to the larger and more sturdy type. Pure white Pekingese were not popular, since they were regarded as the embodiment of the spirit of some great man now deceased. The Empress loved color, and the bright shadings of the Lion Dogs were especially pleasing to her.

Ch. Nanking Noel, owned by John Royce of Massachusetts and photographed in the nineteen thirties.

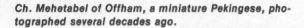

Ch. Mehetabel of Offham, a miniature Pekingese, photographed several decades ago.

Champion Clamarlow Pung Toi, a winner and obviously liking it. Owned by the Misses Lowther, Clamarlow Kennels, Riverside, Connecticut.

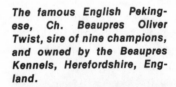

The famous English Pekingese, Ch. Beaupres Oliver Twist, sire of nine champions, and owned by the Beaupres Kennels, Herefordshire, England.

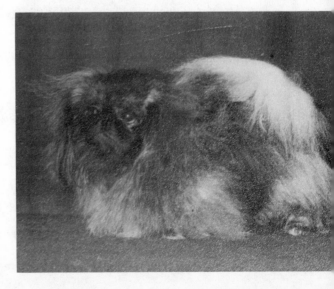

CHAPTER 2

HISTORY & DEVELOPMENT OF THE PEKINGESE IN ENGLAND

There were four females and one male of the five Pekingese brought from China to England in 1860.

The red-brindle dog, Schlorff, who lived to be eighteen years old and the black and white bitch, Hytien, were brought back by Admiral Lord John Hay. He presented Hytien to his sister, the Duchess of Wellington. Two other bitches were given to the Duchess of Richmond and Gordon by a cousin, these two becoming the founders of the world-famous Goodwood strain, carried on with notable success by the Duchess and later for more than thirty years by her sister, Lady Algernon Gordon-Lennox. The fifth of the original Pekingese in England was the fawn-and-white parti-colored bitch, Looty, a gift to Queen Victoria by General Dunne. These five Pekingese were all small in size, as were the majority of those since imported from China.

In 1893, Loftus Allen was commanding a ship in the Chinese trade and purchased the grey brindle Pekin Peter from a taxidermist in Shanghai, bringing it home as a gift for his wife. Shown at Chester the following year in the "Any Variety Not Exceeding 90 Pounds" Class, Pekin Peter was the first Pekingese to be exhibited in England. He won the class, defeating a Chow, a Samoyed, and a Skye Terrier. Mrs Loftus Allen later sold Pekin Peter to Mrs H. Kingston, and when bred to a Goodwood bitch he eventually became the grandsire of the second Pekingese champion, Goodwood Chun.

Ch. Booker Tee, home-bred Pekingese owned by Etta Hodnette.

English Ch. Bon Dah of Kingswere, owned by Mrs. H. Gambier, of England, and photographed by Thomas Fall, London.

Drama of Dah Lyn, pictured at three months of age, bred and owned by John B. Royce. Drama was sired by Jai Bee of Dah Lyn ex Changa of Dah Lyn.

Two years after Pekin Peter's arrival, Mrs Loftus Allen received two blacks, Pekin Prince, weighing eight pounds, and the six pound bitch, Pekin Princess. Shortly after reaching England, the latter whelped four puppies, one of which was the noted Pekin Pretty.

In 1896 that famous pair, Ah Cum and Mimosa, were purchased by Mrs Douglas Murray from an official attached to the Royal Palace. These two, both reds, were less than a year old at the time. A number of the Goodwood matrons were bred to Ah Cum, one of them producing the first Champion Pekingese, Goodwood Lo.

Mr George Brown, for many years a Vice-Consul in China, brought several dogs and bitches back to England. Other importations of the time include Li Tzu, owned by Mrs Carnegie and exhibited in 1907, Lara, and the pure white Zin, wedding gifts in 1876 to Lord and Lady John Hay; the black-and-tan Foo, sent to replace Zin after the latter's untimely death; and two dogs exported from China in 1885 by Admiral Sir William Dowell.

The well-known parti-colored bitch, Fantails, was bred by George Brown out of his Palace-raised Mu Kwa. Fantails came to England in 1889, a gift from Commander Gamble to Mrs Browning, and with her Mrs Browning founded the Brackley strain, which was the first in England to produce short faces.

The famous Minister Li Hung Chang presented a dog, Chang, and a bitch, Lady Li, to Major Heuston in 1898. These became the founders of the Greystones Kennel, from which came numerous English and American Champions.

The year 1900 saw the arrival of the dark red dog, Glenbrane Boxer, and the bitch, Quama, both imported by Major Gwynne. These were the last two of the Palace dogs to come to England.

About 1897 the Manchu Kennel was started, followed shortly by Alderbourne and Broadoak. Of these three, Alderbourne still remains in existence some 75 years later, carried on by Miss Cynthia Ashton Cross, daughter of the founder.

Top: Gertrude, the Lady Decies, noted English sportswoman and Pekingese fancier, pictured in 1910 with two of her famous dogs, Pearl and Manchu Cheng-Tu.

Left: English Ch. Yu Fuh of Alderbourne, owned by Miss Marjorie Ashton Cross. Thomas Fall photograph taken several decades ago.

The Kennel Club recognized the breed in 1898, and a Standard of Points was drawn up by the Japanese Spaniel Club. In 1904, the inaugural meeting was held of the Pekingese Club, Mrs Loftus Allen having proposed that the Japanese Spaniel and Pekingese Clubs should become independent organizations.

Mrs Ashton Cross, with the support of Lady Algernon Gordon Lennox, founded the Pekin Palace Dog Association, which stipulated ten pounds as the weight limit.

In 1898, the Ladies Kennel Association provided special classes for Pekingese at its show; the breed had previously been relegated to the Any Variety Class. Pekin Pretty and her

The Aquarium Show in 1898 provided eleven classes for Pekingese, but had only one entry, Pekin Pretty. At Crufts' in 1900, the first year this event honored the Pekingese with their own classification, Pekin Yen, owned by the Edgar Boehms, was the single dog to enter.

The Sutherland Avenue Kennels came into being in 1904, when Mrs Frances Mary Weaver purchased from Mrs MacEwan the

sire, Pekin Prince, were first and second respectively in the Open Class; Ah Cum and Mimosa were placed first and second in Novice Class. Prior to this, Pekin Prince and Pekin Princess were exhibited at the Pet Dog Show and Ladies Kennel Association in 1896. Joss, the property of Lady Algernon Gordon Lennox, was shown in 1897.

Top: Chen Tiao Kismet of Valhalla, bred by Miss Ashton-Croft and owned by Miss Theodora Wilbour, and Wingerworth Chu-Chu. Photo by Aime Dupont.

Middle: Mrs Paul A. Sorg's team of champion Pekingese photographed in the very early 1900's.

Right: All-Celia's Hop A Long, photographed in 1919, and owned by Mrs C. de la Torre Bueno of New Rochelle, New York.

13

The famous English Champion from the early 1900's Ch. Ko-Tza of Burderof, winner of 20 championships, the record number for a Pekingese.

A parti-colored English Pekingese exhibited before the 1920's and photographed by the famous English photographer Thomas Fall.

Antique English postcard featuring a Pekingese and entitled "Bother the clock!"

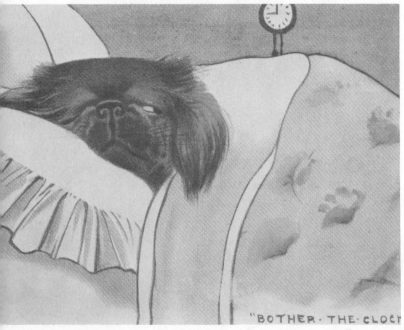

bitch, Manchu Wei Wei (by Ch. Manchu Cheng Tu ex Ch. Palace Shi), in whelp to Manchu Tao Tai (Ch. Goodwood Chun ex C. Gia Gia), producing in the ensuing litter five puppies, including Champion Chu Erh of Alderbourne, and Sutherland Ouen Teu Tang, two of the greatest studs this breed has ever known. Chu Erh, along with a litter sister, went to Mrs Ashton Cross; while Mrs Weaver, who had already decided that she did not care to become an exhibitor, kept Ouen Teu Tang, considering him a better stud prospect than Chu Erh, who was a topflight quality show dog.

Another distinguished early Pekingese was Lady Hunloke's champion, Wingerworth Chin Chin, the first sleeve Pekingese to gain titular honors in England.

Other unforgettably great names in English Pekingese history are those of the black-and-tan bitch, Champion Kin Wha, and her famous son, Champion Broadoak Beetle, also black-and-tan, both owned by Mrs Sealy Clarke. Kin Wha was a daughter of Champion Pekin Peri, while Beetle's sire was the winner of many Challenge Certificates Roydom Ah Sahi, grandson of Champion Goodwood Lo and Pekin Paul. Beetle was a magnificently headed dog, possessing a broad flat topskull, lovely large eyes, and the desirable wide nostrils. He is said to have been equally outstanding in soundness, body conformation, and balance. His record shows him outstanding as a show dog and particularly as a stud, he having been the sire of the marvelous Ch. Kotzu of Burderop, the winner of twenty or more Challenge Certificates. We believe that Kotzu was the first of his breed ever to attain such consistent honors. Ch. Lyncroft Chops was another worthy Beetle son.

Ch. Kotzu of Burderop sired the great Tsan Pam of Chinatown, the latter's dam being China Confucia, by Toto of Noke from Lady Portlington. A few of Tsan Pam's best-known progeny were Champion Ouen Chu Tsan of Thorpe, out of an Ouen Teu Tang bitch; Ch. Yuan of Hartlebury; Fun Yeng Shang, and Champion Wun Dah of Chinatown, from a Champion Nanking Wenti bitch out of a daughter of Champion Chuty of Alderbourne. He was the outstanding sire of his day, and like Champion Chu Erh and Ouen Teu Tang, is to be found behind the pedigree of practically every modern winning Pekingese.

The breeding of Champion Chu Erh of Alderbourne and of Sutherland Ouen Teu Tang has already been discussed. Their illustrious offspring form a formidable list. Champion Chu Erh was a successful campaigner at the shows, and stamped the Alderbourne

strain with his style, perfect body, showmanship, and the excellent carriage of his tail. He was a red dog with profuse coat, short bowed legs, and the true Pekingese rolling action. His nose was short, broad, and well placed, his head large and square.

Oeun Teu Tang was more masculine in type, also excelling in the proportions of his head with the ideal strong, broad and level underjaw. Large dark eyes were another desirable feature which Ouen passed along to his descendants.

Champion Chinky Chog was campaigned at the shows at the same time as Ch. Kotzu of Burderop, these two splendid dogs providing exciting competition at many events. It is interesting that Chinky Chog was bred in India from imported Chinese stock. He was a large grey brindle dog, outstanding in forequarters and correct in coat texture. Numerous knowledgeable fanciers considered him most typical of all the early Pekingese, and being used as an outcross for the already established strains, he had tremendous beneficial influence on the breed in England.

Still other names unforgettable to Pekingese historians are those of Champion Nanking Wen Chu, Champion Chuty of Alderbourne, Champion Brackley Biondina, Champion Choo Tai of Egham, Champion Chu Erh Tu of Alderbourne, and Champion Yen Chu of Newnham.

Mrs Herbert Cowell's homebred Champion Tai Yang of Newnham was whelped in 1920. Sired by Champion Tai Choo of Alderbourne from a daughter of Champion Chuty of Alderbourne (ex a Champion Yen Chu of Newnham bitch) Tai Yang had to his credit the amazing record of winning forty Challenge Certificates. He was a perfect showman, a sire par excellence, and a Pekingese difficult to fault in any way.

English Ch. Marvel of Kyratown, owned by Mr W. Hindley Taylor.

English Ch. Sandboy of Sherhill, winner of nine challenge certificates and owned by Miss M.S. Allen of Spencer's Wood, England. Photograph taken in the late twenties.

Int. Ch. Whitwort Michael, owned by Mrs Richardson Strathy.

Ch. Kann Doo, owned by Mrs Richardson Strathy.

Ch. Caversham Black Queen of Orchardhouse, Bettina Belmont Ward, owner. Sire: Kinbourne Morning Glory of Chyanchy; Dam: Helenes Black Sprite of Orchardhouse.

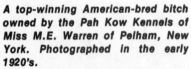

A top-winning American-bred bitch owned by the Pah Kow Kennels of Miss M.E. Warren of Pelham, New York. Photographed in the early 1920's.

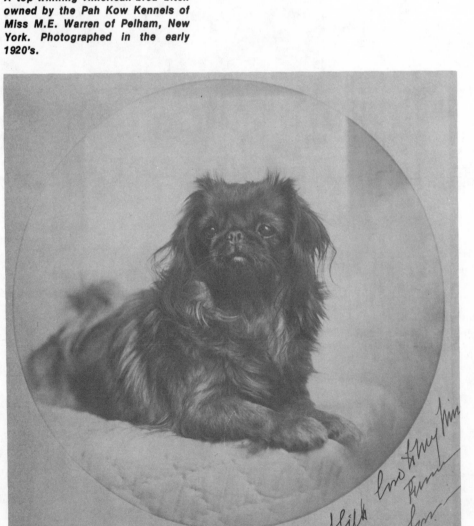

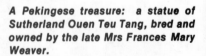

A Pekingese treasure: a statue of Sutherland Ouen Teu Tang, bred and owned by the late Mrs Frances Mary Weaver.

16

CHAPTER 3

HISTORY & DEVELOPMENT OF THE PEKINGESE IN AMERICA

The Empress Tzu Hsi of China was well disposed towards Americans, and presented a number of her cherished Lion Dogs to visitors from this country. Most noted of these was Dr Mary H. Cotton's black Chaou Ching Ur, which later became America's first Pekingese champion bitch. J. Pierpont Morgan was the recipient of a handsome brace of parti-colors; other gifts were a black dog to Mrs Alice Roosevelt Longworth, puppies to Mrs Conger and Mrs Uchida, and the golden-and-white parti-color Melah to Miss Carl, the artist who visited the Summer Palace while painting a portrait of the Empress. But these Palace exports were not bred from extensively, English stock having been used almost entirely for the establishment of the breed in America.

The first American Pekingese exhibitors were Mrs Eva Guyer and A. J. S. Edwards, both of Philadelphia.

Peking 1, a Chinese importation we are told, was shown at the Philadelphia event in 1901, where he was second in the Miscellaneous Class under 25 Pounds. Mr Edwards' homebred, Wu Ting Fang, a son of Chutney, was a first prize winner at Wissahickon in 1904 under Charles G. Hopton.

During late 1900, Harry R. Kendall and his father brought back two dogs from Manchuria but both of them met with untimely deaths.

The first Pekingese to be seen at shows in the New York area were Pekin Chang and Pekin Pu Taiy, bred by Lady Gooch and exhibted by Mrs Benjamin Guinness in the Miscellaneous Class at the Westminster Kennel Club Dog Show. Shortly after, Mrs Morris Mandy brought out the team on which the Downshire Kennels were founded. At Cedarhurst, in 1905, Tsang of Downshire, owned by Mrs Mandy, made his debut. Tsang became America's first champion Pekingese. He was a splendid small son of Hai Tung, by Goodwood Put Singh from Mi Chou of Downshire, and excelled in type and quality. There was a close resemblance between Tsang and the Palace import mentioned previously, Dr Cotton's Chaou Ching Ur. The latter completed her title in 1908.

Mrs A.M. Hunter, the popular secretary of the Pekingese Club, with two of her noted Arden Kennel winners. Ho Hang Ti of Downshire was a winner and best sire. This photograph dates back to the turn of the century.

Ch. Pekin-Shi, a lovely red bitch and mother of Vic Thara. Photographed in the early nineteen hundreds.

Mrs A. Goodson with her two noted dark chestnut red stud dogs, Ai-Gee-Toddie (left) and Ch. Ai-Gee-Chummie. A turn of the century photograph.

Mrs M.E. Harby with the famous Pekingese Ch. Chu-Jen of Toddington, Best of Breed and winner for Best Dog in Variety (the way they referred to the Groups at the time) and Nanking Peo-Kwei, a class winner at the Greenwich Show. Photo owned by Charles Hopton: from the early nineteen hundreds.

Ch. Tsang of Downshire's best puppy was Ch. Ki of Downshire, her dam having been Sueng Pao Ki of Alderbourne. Champion Ki had only one litter, which included Miss Lydia Hopkins' undefeated Champion Huhi.

Mr. Edwards' Tai Tai II, also destined for championship, made his initial bow in the puppy classes during 1905. The same year saw the first special classes for Pekingese at Westminster. There were seven members of the breed in competition; six from Mrs Benjamin Guinness' kennel, and one, Hsia Li, owned by Miss Helen Brice. A little later, J. P. Morgan joined the ranks of active fanciers by purchasing Cragston Sing and several others.

In 1910, Mr and Mrs Alfred Goodson founded their Ai Gee Kennels. They imported Broadoak Fatima from Mrs. Sealy Clark, later selling her to Mrs Paul Sorg for whom she became a champion. Ai Gee was also the home of Champion Tai Pam, purchased from her importer, Mrs Olivia Cedar.

Mrs Richard McGrann, Mrs M. E. Harby, and Mrs A. McClure Halley were also among the owners of the earliest kennels. Credit for having introduced the truly short-faced Pekingese to America goes to Mrs Halley: she had lived in China for many years and had been the owner of a famous Japanese Spaniel kennel before transferring her affections to the Pekingese. During a trip to England in 1911, she bought Sun of Llenrud, who was the first flat-faced Pekingese to be seen in America, and created a sensation on his arrival. This feature, combined with other characteristics of a short body, and well sprung ribs, was passed down through several generations of Sun's descendants.

The Pekingese Club of America was founded in April 1909 by Dr Mary Cotton, Mr and Mrs Morris Mandy, Mrs Benjamin Guinness, Miss Anna Sands, and Mrs Philip Lydig. Their inaugural show was held in 1911; Mrs Guinness,

Top: Ch. Toydom Man-Zee Tu, the property of Mrs A.C. Williams of Yorkshire, England. Circa nineteen thirties.

Linda of Frere, whelped on January 23rd, 1913. This lovely black and tan was winner of many first prizes and an Eideris championship.

Tchak of Arcady, imported to the United States by Mrs H.A. Baxter of Great Neck, New York. This little stud dog was acknowledged to be the best parti-color Pekingese in America at the time. Early nineteen hundreds.

at the time the club president, judged the 94 entries. Tsang of Downshire took Winners Dog and Broadoak Fatima was Winners Bitch. At the second show, Mrs McGrann officiated, Fatima again being Winners Bitch and the purple for dogs being won by Mrs Harby's Ch. Nowata Minchi.

One hundred and sixty-eight entries were assembled at the third show for the opinion of the English judge, Mrs Sealy Clark, who pronounced the famous Ch. Nowata Chun of Egham Winners Dog and Mrs Louis de Lancy Ward's Ch. Sheng Dai Winners Bitch.

Spurred on by the success of this show, the Club decided to have an English judge again the following year, 1914, this time Mrs Herbert from London. Winners Dog was Mrs Harby's Chu Jen of Toddington and Winners Bitch was Miss Theodora Wilbuour's Chin Hua of Moor Park.

One hundred and fifty-five entries were judged by Miss Lydia Hopkins at the next show. Miss Margaret Van Buren Mason's Hop Ting of Downshire took the purple in dogs and Mrs Harby's Nowata Mochoktin in bitches. In 1916 Mrs Herbert judged the Specialty for the second time, placing Mrs Michael M. Van Beuren's Prince Kung of Alderbourne and Mrs A. L. Holland's Ch. Cairnwhin Tinto first in their respective sexes.

It was at the third Specialty of the Pekingese Club of America that breeders were first given the chance to compete for two of the most coveted and beautiful trophies of the dog show world: The J. P. Morgan Trophy for Best in Show and the James Gordon Bennett Trophy for Best in the American-bred Classes, sired in America. Both were to be won five times for permanent possession, and both strangely enough were retired in the year 1937, the Morgan Trophy being finally won by Mrs Richard S. Quigley, and the Bennett Trophy by the Misses Clara and Margaretta Lowther.

Of the earliest American Pekingese kennels, Sherwood, owned by Miss Lydia Hopkins,

Top: William Torren's Goodwood Chun, photographed in the early nineteen hundreds.

Co-author Anna Katherine Nicholas and her first Pekingese dog photographed in 1929. Whitworth Cherie on the left, and Ming Toi.

Bottom: Ch. Nowata Min-Chi originally imported to the States by Charles Hopton of New York City, and sold to Mrs M.E. Harby.

was one of the most successful. Miss Hopkins' first Pekingese, Champion Huhi, was a gift from his breeder, Margaret Barron, and was a son of Shepton Li Li (one of the first Pekingese imported from England to America) who was a grandson of Ch. Goodwood Lo from a daughter of Glanbrane Boxer. Ch. Ah Moy of Downshire, by Toddie of Ai Gee ex Ch. Mihu, was purchased from Mrs Morris Mandy as a mate for Huhi. These two, with Ch. Ming of Downshire, by a son of Ah Cum, formed the foundation stock on which Miss Hopkins' strain was established. Ch. Sherwood Su Wang was her first homebred dog to gain the title. Miss Hopkins purchased the parti-colored bitch, Hollywood Fatima, renamed Sherwood San Loy, in whelp to Wong Ti of Alderbourne, who, in his turn, was the son of Ch. Chu Erh. This gave her three champions in Sherwood Wing, Sherwood Nan Nui, and Sherwood Maku. The next purchase was Yuan Shi Kai of Braywick, while another valuable outcross was Sherwood Choggy of Winkfield, by Ch. Chinky Chog ex a Ch. Broadoak Beetle bitch. In 1917 Miss Hopkins closed her kennel temporarily, reopening in 1923 with Sherwood Michu.

Nowata and Llenrud were extremely successful kennels which left a strong mark on the Pekingese through several decades. Mrs Harby founded Nowata with two American-bred bitches. One, mated to Tim Chong of Downshire, became the grand-dam of Ch. Sheng Dai. Ch. Nowata Min Chi, by Sutherland Ouen Teu Tang; Ch. Nowata Chun of Egham, grandson of Ch. Broadoak Beetle; and Ch. Chu Jen of Toddington, by Prince Tuan of Toddington, were three of Mrs. Harby's better-known winners.

Mrs. McClure Halley's first Pekingese was one of the long-nosed type which she bought from Frank Sternberg. But she became really known as the pioneer of the short-faced dog in America with her import in 1912 of Sun of Llendrud. He had a tremendous influence not only on Mrs Halley's own kennel but on the breed generally. He was sired by Sun Yi, a son

Top: Mrs Edward Jackson Holmes with Chin Lu and Sut Ba, an albino Pekingese, photographed in 1914.

Ch. Ouen Fei, winner of 11 championships. A lovely red Pekingese bitch which won over 300 prizes during her show ring career.

Bottom: Mrs Edward Jackson Holmes with her Pekingese Chin Lu. The photo was taken in 1911: courtesy of Mary Lagercrantz.

of Lim Ko ex Glanbrane Fai Yen, out of Roydom Cum Si by Roydom Ah Sahi ex Cottesmore Fi Fi. Another of Mrs Halley's importations was Sadie Weaver of Llenrud which, bred to Sun, produced Ch. Ouena of Llenrud and Sun's Ouen of Llenrud, the latter the sire of Ch. Sun Flash and Sun Star of Llenrud. Mrs Halley also brought over a number of black dogs, chief among them being Fo of Llenrud. Unquestionably the finest Pekingese to have left England prior to World War I was Nanking Mei of Llenrud; Mr Halley made a special trip to purchase him in England after Mei had defeated all the other top English winners. The superb little dog continued his winning ways by defeating all comers in America too, but unfortunately died suddenly of a heart attack only four months after his arrival.

Nowata Sam Son of Meridale was the first of Mrs F. C. McAllister's champions. Purchased from Mrs Harby as a puppy, Sam Son was by Nowata Chun II and was a grandson of Chu Jen of Toddington, the first Pekingese Club champion.

The famous Glen Iris kennel was begun in 1917 and was owned by Mrs Sydney Franc, founder of the Progressive Dog Club. Her first champion was Iyo Jen, followed by numerous others including the mighty Ch. Glen Iris Dai Dream, so vastly admired by all who saw him.

Mrs Thomas Hastings, owner of Bagatelle Kennels, was another of the breed's most loyal early fanciers and did much to further the Peke's popularity in America. Bagatelle was founded on the Goodwood strain.

The famous Sut Ba, an albino Pekingese, owned by the Edward Jackson Holmes, cousins of the J.P. Morgans who also owned Pekes. Sut Ba was the Boston Red Cross' mascot and chief fund raiser during World War I. He is pictured here at less than a year of age, but in adulthood was known for his terrific coat. Photo courtesy of Mrs Eric Lagercrantz, niece of Mrs Holmes.

A Pekingese photograph of the early nineteen hundreds owned by Mrs C. de la Torre Bueno.

St. Aubrey Dodo of Tzumiao, one of Mrs Nathan Wise's imports from England. He is pictured here winning Best in Show at Knoxville, Tennessee, with Mrs Tom Eaglin handling for the owner. Judge was Mrs W.C. Edmiston. The dog was a Best in Show winner in England and the United States.

BEST
DOG

Mrs Harry L. Sears, photographed in the nineteen thirties with her famous black dog, Tri-International Ch. Roger of Hesketh and some of his magnificent trophies.

Sutherland Avenue Tzu-Eh, sire of the prominent Tri-International Champion Pierrot, and whelped in February, 1926. Bred by Mrs Hazelton of England and later the property of the late Mrs Richard S. Quigley of Lock Haven, Pennsylvania.

Wei Kung Choo of Walthman, imported from England by Mrs W.C. Edmiston.

Lassock of Ashcroft, a Toy Group winner in 1934, owned by John B. Royce.

Ch. Sun-Su of Clamarlow, owned by the Lowthers of Riverside, Connecticut.

One of Lottie Hall's American-bred champion bitches shown several decades ago.

Sister Sue, photographed in the early 1920's.

CHAPTER 4

FAMOUS ENGLISH PEKINGESE THROUGH WORLD WAR II

The most long-lived of England's famous Pekingese kennels is Alderbourne, founded three-quarters of a century ago by Mrs Ashton Cross. Following their mother's death during the forties, the Misses Cynthia and Marjorie Ashton Cross continued breeding and showing their dogs. And though Marjorie passed away a few years ago, Cynthia's enthusiasm for her magnificent Pekingese has not waned.

From the turn of the century, when Chu Erh flashed into prominence, Alderbourne has held its own against all challengers as the premier Pekingese kennel. Chu Erh, himself a champion of champions, sired such famous champions as Chu Erh Tu, grandsire of Champion Bumble Bee (the dam of Champion Humming-bee); Chuty, sire of Champion Choo Tai of Egham; Yen Chu of Newnham, etc. Champion Tai Yang of Newnham was by Alderbourne's Champion Tai Choo, a grandson of Chuty. Later, Tai Yang was bred to Anderson Manor's Chuty Pet (Champion Chuty Too of Alderbourne, ex Peg Su of Alderbourne), from which litter came one of the most strikingly beautiful Pekingese of all time, Champion Yu Chuan of Alderbourne. The death of this glorious dog when only a few years old is one of the tragedies of Pekingese history. In his all too brief lifetime he not only chalked up a formidable list of show ring victories, but he was a sire par excellence. Among his best-known progeny were Ti Fuh of Sherhill, Ch. Sutherland Avenue Avenue Han Shih, Ch. Chuanne of Alderbourne, and Fan Yue of Alderbourne, the latter the dam of Champions Yu Fu and Fo Yu of Alderbourne. One of the most beautiful models made of a Pekingese—a depiction of perfection in the breed—is of Yu Chuan. It was, regrettably, a limited edition, the only one I know of in America being owned by Miss Clara Lowther who brought it back from England during the late thirties. May Alderbourne continue long to flourish! Its good influence on the Pekingese breed has earned it a unique place in the world of pure-bred dogs.

Yu Tuo of Alderbourne, pictured at one year of age, and weighing 6½ pounds. Yu Tuo was the winner of 25 first prizes at all the principal shows of 1939 and winner of his junior warrant at 9½ months of age, accomplished in six weeks time. This was a record for the breed in England. He was owned by Miss Marjorie Ashton Cross of Ascot, England. Fall photograph.

The Yu Chuan son, Ti Fuh of Sherhill, owned by the Misses Allen, was the sire of Champions Fuh Chuan of Sherhill, Yu Fuh of Alderbourne, Ku Rai of Remenham, Fuh Anna of Sherhill, and Chee Kee Wun of Hartlebury. Fuh Chuan in turn sired Champions Chu Fuan of Sherhill, Ti Fuh of Caversham, etc. Han Shih, a tower of strength at Mrs Quigley's Orchard Hill, numbered among his American champions such dogs as Ch. Han Chuan of Orchard Hill, Japeke Han Shih's Domino, and Han Chee of Chu Jai, while another son, Han's Kho Yan of Orchard Hill, had to his credit Ch. Han's Khoo Hansi of Merricka and Ch. Han's Khoo Yankee of Orchard Hill and the bitch, Han's Khoo Jas Min of Orchard Hill who is to be found in the pedigree of the mighty American Champion Jai Son Fu of Orchard Hill.

Shan Ling Wendy when bred to Chu Erh Tsun produced Pung Chow of Alderbourne, sire of many winners. Bumble Bee when bred

Chuan Tu of Alderbourne photographed at 11 months of age and owned by the Alderbourne Kennels in England. This special dog was shown in the nineteen thirties.

Manstone Yu-Pung, fawn son of Ch. Pung-Chow of Alderbourne ex Manstone Yu-Chu. This dog was winner of many first prizes, cups and specials in England. Photographed in 1931 by Thomas Fall for owner Mrs D.M. Stains, Kent, England.

to a Chuty grandson, gave the exquisite miniature, Ch. Humming Bee of Alderbourne, sire of Ch. Princess Picotte of Orchard Hill, Ch. Fang Sheng of Willowtoun, Ch. Li of Silbir, and Ch. Meng of Alderbourne. Among the post World War II champions that helped Alderbourne kennel continue setting new records were Yu Tong, Yula, Lin Yuan, Pandora, and Tong Tuo.

Alderbourne supplied foundation stock for a tremendous number of leading kennels. Even today there are probably few if any winning Pekingese whose pedigrees may not eventually be traced back to this kennel. Ch. Chuty of Alderbourne was the predominant sire in the early Sherhill winners, this kennel having been one of the best in England. Owned by the Misses Allen, its first champion, brought out in 1922 and the winner of 23 Challenge Certificates was Tu Tzu. Ch. Sandboy of Sherhill, son of Bambino of Hartlebury, was from Tu Tzu's younger half-sister. Champion Fuh Chuan of Sherhill, winner of 21 Challenge Certificates, Best Pekingese on 36 occasions (in the days when this was a tremendous record) was one of the world's most famous and admired show dogs.

Then who of those who have studied the Pekingese has not come to have a healthy respect for the Caveishams, which are also primarily descended from Alderbourne?

Founded by Miss I. M. de Pledge, later owned by her in partnership with Mrs Lunham —now Mrs Warner Hill—Caversham has carved an unforgettable niche in Pekingese history. Of the early Caveishams, Champion Tarsa was by Headmaster of Shantung from a Pung Chow of Alderbourne daughter. Hei Chu Tzu brought in the Sutherland outcross, he having been a son of Ch. Tzu Eh ex a Champion Bon Ton of Ashcroft daughter. Hei Chu Tzu quickly took his place as a sire par excellence, among his progeny having been Champion Hei Tsun of Caversham-Clamarlow and Champion Remenham Fo. Latto Tsun of Caversham sired Champions Tai Chang and Sha Sha of Caversham, the latter the dam of the great little miniature, Tai Choo of Caversham. "Robin," as Tai Choo was called, died suddenly at an early age, an inestimable loss to the breed. The outstanding American champion, Che Le of Matsons-Catawba—the Pekingese that made American Best in Show judges really aware of Pekingese quality—was a son of Tai Choo. Other noted winners by him included Ch. Arellian Choo Leen of Catawba, Ch. Rosette of Sherhill, Ch. Gold Dust of Hartlebury, Ch. Tung Bee of Caversham, and Yung Tai Choo of Caversham, whose promising show career was cut short by World War II. A post-war English "star" from Caversham was the phenomenal Ch. Ku Chi, sired by Puffball of Changking ex Marigold of Elfann, combining Alderbourne, Caversham and Yu Sen breeding. And then came Ch. Chik Tsun of Caversham, America's record-holding Best in Show winner of any breed.

Mrs Frances Mary Weaver's Sutherlands kennel was founded at the same time as Alderbourne and continued until 1930. Although Mrs Weaver never exhibited her dogs, others who purchased them did so with marked success. When disbanded, the kennel included such "greats" as Sutherland Avenue Han Shih, Tzu Eh, Tou Tseng, Chi Sun, Tou Wang, etc. It was Mrs Richard S. Quigley who had the good judgment and foresight to purchase the majority of Mrs Weaver's dogs when they became available, the results of which will be discussed in the next chapter.

Miss M. L. Heuston, owner of the Greystones Pekingese, did much to perpetuate the Sutherlands as well as to earn acclaim for the quality of her own Greystones strain, the forebears of which came directly from the Chinese Imperial Palace. The gorgeous Ameri-

Ch. Fang Hou of Luebon, a very famous English sire, owned by Mrs C. Ashton Cross of England.

Alderbourne Cream Puff of Tongland, winner of nine first prizes at championship shows in England and 1st prize and C.A.C. in Paris in May 1948. Thomas Fall photo, for owners the Misses Ashton Cross.

Chuo of Alderbourne, owned and bred by Mrs Ashton Cross of England. Chuo was born in August 1938; he was sired by Yu Tuo of Alderbourne and his dam was Samette of Alderbourne. Fall photograph.

Alderbourne Lin Yutang photographed in post war England. This lovely Peke was owned by the Misses Ashton Cross.

Alderbourne Cream Puff of Tongland, owned by the Misses Ashton Cross and photographed by Thomas Fall, England.

Wee Yula of Alderbourne, 7½ pounds and pictured at nine months old. Photograph by Thomas Fall.

A group of English champions and big show winners from many decades ago... Ch. Pearl, winner of 16 certificates and many times Best in Show; Diamond, also winner of many prizes and a championship; Ch. Manchu, a Best in Show winner; Ch. Chi-Li, winner of many prizes and championships and Ch. Pekin Thi, another big winner. Thomas Fall photograph.

Best in Show at the Pekingese Club of America 1944 Specialty Show was Ch. Jai Son Fu of Orchard Hill. Owner, Mrs R.S. Quigley, and the judge, Mrs W.T. Quick.

The house presented to Sir Francis Drake by Queen Elizabeth called Little Shardeloes, in Bucks, England. For many years this was the home of the famous Alderbourne Kennels.

Mrs Philip Hunloke of Derbyshire, England, photographed in 1920 with her Ch. Wingerworth Chiu Chiu.

Top: Tai-Choo of Caversham photographed in 1936 with Her Royal Highness' Princess Victoria's Jubilee Trophy. Owned by Mary de Pledge, this magnificent dog is behind many of the Caversham Pekingese. Photo by Fall.

Above: Ch. Ku-Chi of Caversham. This great English champion was a dominant sire owned by Mrs Tunham and Miss de Pledge.

English Ch. Chu-Fuan of Sherhill, owned by Miss M. Allen and a winner in the late thirties.

Sutherland Avenue Ouen-Sha, whelped in 1932. Bred by Miss Heuston, he was the property of Mrs Frances Mary Weaver of London, England.

The great English Champion Fuh Chuan of Sherhill, owned by Miss M. Allen in the nineteen thirties.

English Ch. Fuh-Anna of Sherhill, photographed at eight months of age in the nineteen thirties. Miss M. Allen, owner.

Ch. Sutherland Avenue Han Shih, imported by Mrs R.S. Quigley of the Orchard Hill Kennels, Lock Haven, Pennsylvania. Fall photograph.

Sutherland Av. T'ou Tseng, whelped May 14th, 1928, and bred by Mrs Frances Mary Weaver, photographed when he was just one year old. He was the property of Mrs Richard Quigley of Lock Haven, Pennsylvania.

A line of future champions from the Iwade Pekingese Kennels, photographed at Moraths, in Liverpool, England.

Mrs Foster Burgess, well-known proprietress of the equally well-known Iwade Kennels in Liverpool, England. Later Mrs Stowell Brown, is pictured with several of her top winning Iwade champions of the thirties.

Ch. Yu Chuanne of Iwade, owned by Mrs Stowell Brown, the former Mrs Foster Burgess, of England.

Left: A trio of white puppies from the Appledore Kennel of Mrs Adams in England.

Right: Sanell Wen, whelped January 5th, 1935, and owned by Mrs Hugh Duberly.

can Champion King Pippin of Greystones, came from this kennel. He was purchased by Mrs Christian Hager of Braddock, Pennsylvania, and was a favorite of the author's during her early years as a Pekingese enthusiast.

Dr and Mrs John A. Vlasto were owners of the world famous Remenhams, founded on Ch. Brackley Biondina. Names that Pekingese historians will recall from this kennel include Ku Su, Kotzina, Remenham Mitzu, Peggoty, See Mee, Remenham Dimple and Shana of Greystones. Then followed Ku Rai of Remenham, with her champion title in England while still a puppy and which afterwards became an American champion for Mrs Quigley.

Top: A lovely Peke from Scotland! Mrs Bessie B. Douglas's Jennifer Jane of Broughty pictured at nine months of age. She is by Dominic of Broughty ex Mercy of Broughty. A big winner at all leading shows in 1933.

Middle: Another of Mrs Hugh Duberly's darling Pekingese puppies... this one is the four month old dog Sanell Chong, whelped July 4th, 1937.

Bottom: Mrs Hugh Duberly's Sanelle Hsi, born in April, 1939.

Ch. Remenham Fo was an especially successful stud dog and the grandsire of Tri-Int. Ch. Remenham Derrie of Orchard Hill. Soon after the start of World War II, Mrs Vlasto exported to Mrs Quigley a number of her best dogs, including Remenham Tombo, Knut of Remenham, Remenham Pipsy, Wang of Remenham (son of Tang Hou of Luebon) and some half-a-dozen others.

Chinatown, owned by Mr and Mrs Weil, was another famous English kennel, Tsan Pam of Chinatown and Ch. Wun Dah of Chinatown having left their mark on descendants through many generations. It was a son of Tsan Pam, Fun Yeng Shang, the extremely influential sire, who figured strongly in the development of Mr and Mrs Hugo Ainscough's Hesketh Pekingese, whence came the fabulous Tri-Int. Ch. Rajah of Hesketh Wu Kee, Ch. Grey Spider, and many others that figured notably in the Pekingese world of the late twenties and the thirties.

Another sensational English kennel was Iwade, owned by Mrs H. Stowell Brown (at that time Mrs Foster Burgess), which blazed a trail of show-ring glory with Ch. Feisal, Ch. Yu Feisal, and Ch. Redd Boi in England, and with Ch. Sand Boi, imported to America by F. L. Maytag (of washing-machine fame) and eventually purchased by Mrs Stanley Ferguson.

The fantastic show winner, Ch. Redd Boi of Iwade with a few of his sterling silver trophies. This photograph taken in December, 1936.

Ch. Tula of Ifield, bred and owned by Mrs S. Whitehead of Sussex, England. Tula was famous for her full title of champion at three consecutive shows, won in March, April and May of 1935.

Sanell Sha-Na, owned by Mrs Hugh Duberly, and whelped on the fourth of July, 1937.

Kyratown, owned by Mr Hindley Taylor, became a legend in the Pekingese world. Who could ever forget Champions Marvel, Chinaman, Rosette, Lovely Maid, Fairy, and all those that came later to bring added laurels to this strain? Mr Taylor's recent death was a sad loss to the Pekingese world, for he was known and respected as a breeder, a judge (officiating at least twice at Pekingese Club of America Specialty Shows, with expertise and aplomb), and as an author of an excellent book about this breed.

Other breeders and kennels that AKN recalls with admiration from a 1936 visit to England, include Mrs Hugh Duberly of Sanell, and Lady Holder of Hartlebury.

At the close of World War II, the Yusens flashed into prominence under the guidance of owner, Miss S. A. Higgs. Headliner at this kennel, was English Ch. Yusen Yu Toi, who died tragically in a plane in 1947 en route to American purchaser, Mrs Quigley. Yu Toi, sired by Yusen Yu Chuo, was the winner of ten Challenge Certificates during his short career in England, and was the sire of Int. Ch. Bonraye Fo Yu of Orchard Hill, subsequently sold to Mrs Quigley by Mr Joe Higgs.

The post-war Pekingese kennels in England were many and successful. Some that were going strong early in the sixties include the Coughton Kennels, owned by Lady Isabel Throckmorton. Champion Ping Yang of Coughton, whelped in 1958, by Patrician of Perryacre ex Mimosa of Coughton, was a glamorous figure at the shows, and by 1963 had won no less than ten Challenge Certificates, including those at Crufts, for three consecutive years. Two of his much admired sons are Coughton Franchard Pen Tsun Tu, and Ping Gable of Coughton. Another lovely dog at this kennel during the sixties, Ogle of Coughton, was sired by the great Champion Goofus le Grisbie.

Craigfoss Kennels also had a lovely son of Le Grisbie, in Gussie of Alderbourne. And owner J. Sloane-Stanley had a marvelous-looking white, in Ivory Knight of Craigfoss, bred from white parents.

Isti Pekingese, who belonged to Mrs I. Staveley Taylor, included The Leprechaun of Isti, an eight pound dog, double line bred from le Grisbie. Pendarvis was just making a comeback following owner Mrs Kinnersley's unfortunate period of poor health.

By 1963, W. Hindley Taylor's Kyratowns could boast winning two hundred and thirty-seven post-war Challenge Certificates. What a formidable number that list must have reached before Mr Taylor's recent death! We shall not

Above: Ch. Alderbourne Lin Yutang at nine months of age —a beautiful Pekingese bred by the Misses Ashton Cross of England during the post-war period.

Below: English Ch. Lu-Tong Of Kyratown, photographed in 1954 and owned by W. Hindley Taylor of England.

Kopi of Kyratown, an important English dog owned by the late H. Hindley Taylor, of England.

Sha-Fuh of Ifield, a famous stud dog from the Ifield Kennels of Mrs Sybil Whitehead of England.

A lovely head study of Mrs F.C. McAllister's Pekingese, photographed in the early thirties.

Candee of Ifield, bred and owned by Mrs Sybil Whitehead, and photographed by Thomas Fall, London, at the age of 11 months.

The saucy Alderbourne Lin Yutang pictured here at seven months of age. Winner of 13 first prizes at three shows, and he was also three times Best of any age bred by exhibitor. He earned his Championship and Best of Breed in victories over other champions.

English Ch. Mignonette of Rosterloy, one of Britains most famous Pekingese in the 1950's. Owned by the late W. Hindley Taylor of the Kyratown Kennels in England.

Puscon of Ifield, son of the famous Lai-Fah, who was unbeaten in the classes at 18 months of age and winner of a Reserve Championship. He was the property of Mrs Sybil Whitehead of England.

soon forget the beauty of the pictures we saw in the early sixties of Champion O'Sand Boi of Kyratown and his sons San Ying and San Pier of Kyratown.

Mrs Hoynck had a lovely show and stud dog in Kumeh of Mathena. Mrs Pownall's Linsowns were active. Mrs Mitchell's Micklee dogs and the Alderbournes also figured prominently.

The Alderbourne Pekingese of this period were breathtaking. Champion Goofus le Grisbie retired in 1963 after winning Best in Show, his Challenge Certificates numbering twelve. His son, Alderbourne Li Fu of Rem-

Tinee Tim of Ifield, a rare grey brindle born in September 1928. Tim was the propery of Mrs Sybil Whitehead of Sussex, England.

Ch. Tula of Ifield, bred and owned by Mrs. S. Whitehead of Sussex, England. Tula was famous for her full title of "champion" at three consecutive shows, won in March, April and May of 1935.

37

Cho-Lin of Ifield, born August 6th, 1934, who weighed just seven pounds at the time he was winning. This darling Peke was owned by Mrs Sybil Whitehead of England.

English Ch. Wee Pung.

English Ch. Lai Fah of Ifield, owned by Mrs Sybil Whitehead and photographed in November 1936. Lai Fah was the winner of many Bests of Breed and Best Toy Dog in Show.

ward, was then just coming out and starting off with a Challenge Certificate, a Best Toy, and a Best in Show, which were prophetic of things to come. Champion Tul Tuo, whelped in the mid-fifties, was one of the most important post-war Alderbourne dogs. And Champion Yu Tong of Alderbourne, his son Champion Tong Tuo of Alderbourne, and Tong Tuo's son, Champion Alderbourne Lin Yutang, have all made great records in the ring. As this book is written we have lately learned that Alderbourne dogs have sired more than two hundred and fifty champions, and that their dogs have won more than forty-five thousand prizes.

Chintoi Pekingese, belonging to Miss E. A. Page, had a glamorous pair of littermates, Twee Jin of Chintoi and Cheryl of Chintoi, by Champion Twee Choo of Caversham ex Cherokee of Chintoi, the eighth generation of Chintoi breeding on their dam's side. Mrs Shipley's Champion Margo of Kettlemere was an outstanding homebred winning bitch. The late Mrs Rae's Perryacres bred many champions, including Champion Franchard Penanne of Perryacre, Champion Piersyl of Perryacre, Champion Black Wing of Wanstrow, Champion Pu Chi of Perryacre of Orchard Hill, and her dogs also sired many champions for other breeders. Mrs Eileen Stewart's Cheranganis have made good records, as have Mrs Holman's Etives. Miss Mayhew's Mingshangs is one of the long-established British kennels and noted for exceptional quality; in the sixties, Champion Minshang Starla and her sire, Champion Twee Choo of Caversham, were both gaining honors in the show ring.

Mrs Drake's Champion Tarka of Drakehurst was a splendid dog. Mrs Stains' Manstones, another kennel well remembered from pre-war days, had the outstanding Manstone Ku Yu of Mafasaga, an extremely worthy champion. And Mrs Chandler's Ifields, which Anna Katherine Nicholas so greatly admired when she attended English dog shows in the thirties, were still going strong. Mrs Helen Bruce's Champion Wellion Lari, a le Grisbie grandson was an eye-catcher. (Notice how frequently that name le Grisbie appears during this period; his influence on post-war English Pekingese was tremendous.)

The Copplestones were very much in evidence. As for the Cavershams, then as always they were superlative. Mary de Pledge was a very competent breeder and the present day record as well as earlier history of this breed abounds with the names and accomplishments of these dogs.

CHAPTER 5

FAMOUS AMERICAN PEKINGESE
FROM THE THIRTIES THROUGH THE SIXTIES

Throughout the years, there has been great kinship between England and America so far as Pekingese are concerned. No one could possibly deny the fact that we owe gratitude to the English breeders who have exported to us the dogs from which our fanciers have worked so well in producing those American-breds in which we now take such justifiable pride.

Unquestionably America's greatest breeding kennel of Pekingese was Orchard Hill, founded about 1930 by Mrs Richard S. Quigley and surviving until her death in 1970. Mrs Quigley often remarked that she had never been interested in anything without getting to the top, and this definitely proved to be the case where her activities in the Pekingese world were concerned. A strong-minded, purposeful and intelligent person, Mrs Quigley proved to have a touch of magic where raising Pekingese was concerned. Many years ago Orchard Hill produced its 100th champion. We daresay that when the complete record is tabulated (Orchard Hill dogs are still being shown and winning) the number will be closer to twice that. Ch. Grey Spider of Hesketh was the first big winner which Mrs Quigley campaigned. Among other leaders from her kennel have been Ch. Khoo Yas Min; Tri-Int. Ch. Cha Ming Yin Hsing (the first and possibly only Pekingese bitch to have gained titular honors in France, Spain, and the United States); Int. Ch. Sandee of Hesketh (grandsire of the Frank Downings' Ch. Wun Dah of Holly Lodge, first American-bred Pekingese to win Best in Show all breeds); Cha Ming Ayee, (whose brilliant career was unfortunately terminated by an early death); Ch. Sutherland Avenue Han Shih; Champions Princess Picotte and Butterfly of Pechelee; Ch. Kim's Tzu Shan

Ch. Jai Son Fu of Orchard Hill with the Halley Memorial Trophy at the Pekingese Club of America Specialty. Owner, Mrs R.S. Quigley of Lock Haven, Pennsylvania.

The late Dorothy S. Quigley, owner of the Orchard Hill Kennels in Lock Haven, Pennsylvania. Mrs Quigley was one of the most consistent winners for many years in the breed, and imported many, many fine Pekingese to this country.

Above: A typical Pekingese puppy, Yung Kai Choo of Dah Lyn at 2½ months. Owned by John B. Royce, Brookline, Massachussetts.

Above: The noted international winning Pekingese, Tim Yee Kung of Alderbourne, owned by the Yankibourne kennel, New York City. Early nineteen hundreds.

Below: From the thirties, Sutherland Avenue Chi-Sun, owned by Mrs Richard S. Quigley of Lock Haven, Pennsylvania.

Below: Ch. Orchid Lanes Ku Lee, Best in Show winner owned by Mrs Richard Quigley of Lock Haven, Pennsylvania.

Tri-International Champion Pierrot Hartlebury, 7½ pound red brindle Pekingese and a very famous dog in his time. Sire was Ch. Sutherland Av. Tzu-eh ex Sutherland Av. Tou Yu. Property of Mrs Richard S. Quigley.

The first Amer-
ican champion Pekingese
. . . Ch. T'Sang of Down-
shire.

"Ch Tsang of Downshire"

Above: Ch. Yu Go Han of
Orchard Hill, owned by Mrs
Copp's Spring Island
Kennels. This dog was a
famous winner several
decades ago.

Below: Ch. Han Chuan of
Orchard Hill, the first
Quigley home-bred
champion.

Cham. Ouen Fei

Above: Ch. Ouen Fei, in a
photograph by Everill taken
in the early nineteen
hundreds.

CHAMPION HAN CHUAN OF ORCHARD HILL

41

Mrs Richard S. Quigley's Ch. Kim's Tzu Shan of Orchard Hill, a winner in the thirties. Percy Jones photograph.

The English Ch. Ku-Rai of Remenham of Orchard Hill, photographed in 1931. This dog was imported by Mrs Richard S. Quigley of the Orchard Hill Kennels in Lock Haven, Pennsylvania.

Mrs Richard Quigley with Tri-International Ch. Remenham Derrie of Orchard Hill, who was pictured just as he got off the boat from England in the 1940's.

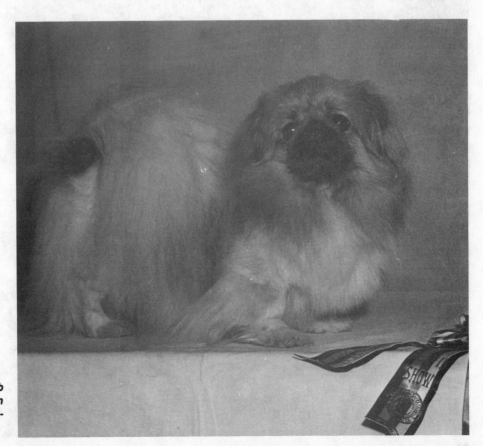

Winner of the 1941 Pekingese Club of America was Ch. Kims Tzu Shan of Orchard Hill, owned by Mrs Richard S. Quigley, Lock Haven.

Right: American and Canadian Ch. Ku Chi Noela of Orchard Hill, owned by Ronald N. Rella of Union, New Jersey. William P. Gilbert photograph.

Below: A lovely portrait study of Ch. Nia-Jai-Niki of Orchard Hill, another of the Orchard Hill Kennel dogs owned by Mrs Richard Quigley of Lock Haven.

Ch. Kai Lung of Orchard Hill, owned by Mrs Richard S. Quigley. Brown photo.

Ch. San-Dee of Hesketh, an Orchard Hill Kennel import, is the grandson of Mrs Downings Ch. Wun Dah of Holly Lodge, the first American-bred Best in Show Pekingese. Famous in the thirties.

Another beautiful Pekingese photographed in 1939 from the Orchard Hill Kennels. Delos L. Glossner, photographer.

Above: Best in Show at the Pekingese Club of America in 1943 was Ch. Jai Son Fu of Orchard Hill, owned by Mrs Richard Quigley, pictured above with judge William Brennan.

Top left: Orchid Lane's KuLee with her handler, Betty Johnstonbaugh. Owner, Mrs. Dorothy Quigley of Lock Haven, Pennsylvania. Frasie photo.

Bottom left: Best of Breed at the Pekingese Club of America Specialty show in 1953 was Kai Lung of Vinedeans of Orchard Hill, imported by Mrs Richard Quigley of Lock Haven, Pennsylvania. Mrs Warner Hays was the judge at this event. Shafer photo.

Above: From the early forties Mrs Richard S. Quigley's Tri-International Ch. Remenham Derrie of Orchard Hill. Derrie was sired by Diamond of Ashcroft ex Remenham Marigold.

Top left: An important Peke of yesteryear, Mrs Richard S. Quigley's Pier Buzz of Orchard Hill.

Best Toy at the Fairfield County Kennel Club Show in 1944 was Mrs Quigley's Ch. Jai Son Fu of Orchard Hill, under judge Anna Katherine Nicholas.

Devon Dog Show Best in Show winner in 1954 was Ch. Kai Lung of Orchard Hill owned by Mrs Richard S. Quigley. Left to right, Mrs Priscilla St. George Ryan, judge, Mrs Quigley, Mrs John A. LaFore, Jr., president of the Club and Mrs Betty Johastonbaugh, handler.

Ch. Nia Jai Niki of Orchard Hill, Best of Breed winner at the Pekingese Club of America show in March of 1964 under judge Anna Katherine Nicholas. Nia Jai was owned and shown by Mrs Richard S. Quigley. Shafer photo.

Anna Katherine Nicholas awards Best Toy to Mrs Quigley's Ch. Jai Son Fu of Orchard Hill as Dr Samuel Milbank looks on.

Nia Bon Tia of Orchard Hill, pictured winning the Pekingese Club of America Specialty in 1959. Judge Mrs M.M. Shoemaker, Mrs Johnstonbaugh, handler for owner Mrs Richard Quigley. The Club president Dr E.R. Blamey presents the trophy.

Ch. Sanell Sudi, whelped in October 1932, and photographed here in 1935. Her sire was Dee Dee of Lue-bon ex Sanell Tzu Eh. Owner Mrs Hugh Duberly, Staughton Manor, Huntingdonshire, England.

Below: Ch. Bonraye Yu Fei of Orchard Hill, owned by Mrs Richard Quigley of Lock Haven, Pennsylvania.

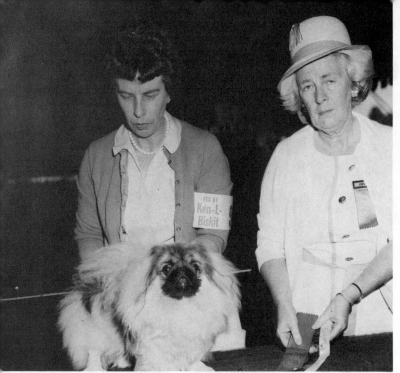

Winner of the Toy Group at the Huntingdon Valley Kennel Club show in June, 1961 was Ch. Nia-Jai-Niki of Orchard Hill—owned by Mrs Richard S. Quigley and handled for owner by Betty Johnstonbaugh. Mrs Fortune Roberts, judge.

Best in the Toy Group at National Capital Kennel Club was Ch. Kai Lung of Vinedeans of Orchard Hill. Mrs Johnstonbaugh handling for owner Mrs Richard Quigley. Mrs C.F. Dowe, judge.

Best of Breed at the 1960 Pekingese Club of America was Ch. Orchid Lane's Ku Lee, owned by Mrs Richard S. Quigley. Mrs Henry E. Longacre, judge and Dr E.R. Blamey, Club president presenting the trophy. Handler, Betty Johnstonbaugh.

Tri-International Ch. Bonray Fo Yu of Orchard Hill, pictured winning at Pawling, New York, in 1951, under judge Anna Katherine Nicholas. Betty Johnstonbaugh handling for the owner, Mrs R.S. Quigley, Orchard Hill Kennels.

Mrs Dorothy Dwyer Hanson of Mt. Sinai, New York, holding her Han's Chuty Wun of Mt. Curve, on the right, and Mrs Lansdowne's Ch. Han's Udgee of Orchard Hill. Photograph taken at the Morris and Essex Dog show in 1941. Both dogs were double line-bred from Tri-International Ch. Sutherland Avenue Han Shih.

Best in Show at Bald Eagle Kennel Club event in 1952 was Mrs Richard Quigley's Ch. Bonraye Fo Yu of Orchard Hill. Dr Mitten, judge.

51

Left: Mrs Richard
Quigley's Cha Ming Agee
of Orchard Hill, one of the
greats from the thirties.

Right: Ch. St. Aubrey Judy
of Calartha of Orchard Hill,
owned by Mrs Richard S.
Quigley

Below: Ch. Jai Son Fu of
Orchard Hill, photographed
in 1942. Owned by Mrs
Richard S. Quigley, of Lock
Haven, Pennsylvania.

International Ch. Bonraye Fo Yu of Orchard Hill, owned by Mrs Richard S. Quigley of Lock Haven, Pennsylvania. Photographed by Thomas Fall in London before being exported to Mrs Quigley.

Tri-International Ch. Remenham Derrie of Orchard Hill, imported by Mrs Richard S. Quigley after a fantastic European show ring career.

Butterfly of Pechelar of Orchard Hill, owned by Mrs Richard S. Quigley of Lock Haven, Pennsylvania and photographed in 1934.

A charming informal study of Mrs James M. Austin and five generations of Pekingese. . . Lamdah of Catawba, Cynthia of Catawba, Ladina of Catawba, Tinga of Toytown, and Ch. Dahna of Chinatown.

From the early forties, Mrs James Austin's Ch. Che Le of Matsons-Catawba, the first consistent Pekingese Best in Show winner.

Below: The Progressive Dog Club show in 1939. Anna Katherine Nicholas, president, with James W. Trullinger, judge, and Mrs James M. Austin with her Best in Show winner, Ch. Che Le of Matsons-Catawba.

of Orchard Hill; Int. Ch. Ku Rai of Remenham; Tri. Int. Ch. Pierrot of Hartlebury; Ch. Han Chuan (the first Orchard Hill homebred to gain the title): Champions Pier Jai Fo, Jai Fo Son, Van's Panzee, and the ultimate achievement, Ch. Jai Son Fu of Orchard Hill. The redoubtable Jai Son for years was considered the finest Pekingese to have been bred in the United States. Sound, sturdy, well balanced, he excelled in head features, body shape, front and rear, and was truly a dog in which all American Peke fanciers can take pride.

By 1950 Orchard Hill dogs represented nine or more generations, all setting the type for which it was noted. Although she never missed an opportunity to import an outstanding dog for show and breeding, Mrs Quigley was primarily interested in her homebreds, and used these importations thoughtfully and judiciously for the improvement of her own breeding program. Tri-Int. Ch. Pierrot of Hartlebury was the predominant stud dog, he and his sons being found somewhere in the pedigree of practically every Orchard Hill homebred winner. Jai Son Fu, by Ch. Jai Fo Son from Ch. Van's Panzee, proved a great sire as well as show dog. His accomplishments include being the only dog to have five times won the Pekingese Club of America Specialty Show, also Best Toy at both Westminster and Morris and Essex. Ch. Bonraye Fo Yu became a big time Toy Group and Best in Show winner and had a strong influence on the later winners from this kennel, of which more in a following chapter.

The most celebrated Pekingese to appear in America prior to the late forties was Ch. Che Le of Matsons-Catawba, a trail-blazer for the breed in that he broke through to become the first consistent Best in Show Pekingese, and amassed a Best in Show record that was one of the finest of any American show dog of any breed of his day. Until the arrival of "The Duck," as Che Le was affectionately known to his host of friends, Best in Show honors for Pekingese or any of the Toys were infrequent, to say the least. But when Che Le flashed upon the scene, all that changed. Who could ever forget the picture of that small, sturdy, well-balanced little figure wearing so proudly his bright red coat with sparking white bib sailing around the ring under the expert guidance of Ruth Burnette Sayres? He had to his credit approximately 30 Bests in Show, in a period when it was not usual to campaign one's winners as extensively as is now the custom. Che Le was seldom defeated in his breed or in his group. He was truly a superlative Pekingese.

A typical Pekingese from the famous Catawba Pekingese Kennels.

Below: English and American Ch. Che Le of Matsons-Catawba, owned by Mrs James M. Austin and photographed in 1939.

Left: English and American Ch. Tang-Hao of Caversham-Catawba, Pekingese imported by Mrs James M. Austin of Old Westbury.

Mrs James M. Austin of Old Westbury, New York winning the Toy Group at an Interstate Kennel Association show in the forties, with a home-bred Catawba Pekingese. Judge was Jack Royce. Club president Anna Katherine Nicholas completes the picture.

Left: Tang's Tuadore Glory owned by Mrs James M. Austin and dating back to the thirties.

Above: Ch. Deermont Kayo, owned by Mrs James M. Austin, and a winner during the 1930's.

Above: Mrs James M. Austin's International Ch. Liebling of Huntington.

Below: Ch. Tang-Hao of Caversham-Catawba, imported in the thirties by Mrs James M. Austin.

Below: English and American Ch. Tang-Hao of Caversham-Catawba, owned by Mrs James M. Austin and campaigned in the nineteen thirties.

Above: Mrs James M. Austin with her great Best in Show winner, Ch. Che Le of Matsons-Catawba. William Brown photograph.

Below: Ch. Che Le of Matsons-Catawba, winning the first of his many Best in Show victories, at the Long Shore Kennel Club in 1939. Mrs Austin receiving the trophy from Mrs Herbert Neal, the judge.

Above: Yung Kai Choo of Dah Lyn, sired by Triple Ch. Kai-Choo of Dah Lyn, a rich red and white parti-color. Bred and owned by John B. Royce, Brookline, Massachusetts.

Below: Mrs James M. Austin with Rah Lai of Merricka [left] and Ch. Tang's Tuadore Glory, two of her big winners during the early forties. This photograph taken in 1942 by William Brown.

Above: Ch. Che Le of Matsons-Catawba, owned by Mrs James M. Austin, wins Best in Show at the 1941 Lackawanna Kennel Club Show in Mount Pocono, Pennsylvania. Mrs A.M. Lewis, presenting the trophies, was the judge. Percy Jones photograph.

Below: Mrs James M. Austin's Ch. Che Le of Matsons-Catawba winning at the Buffalo show in 1941 with Ruth Sayres handling. Anna Katherine Nicholas was the judge at this show.

Below: Miss Ruth Burnette receiving cup for a Best in Show win for Ch. Che Le of Matsons-Catawba, owned by Mrs James M. Austin.

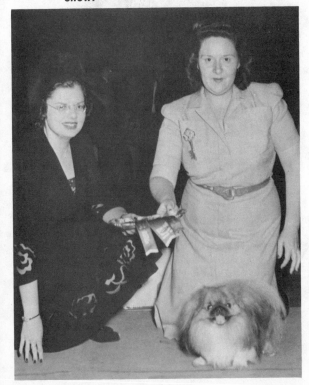

Left: Jai Bee of Dah Lyn, bred and owned by John Royce, photographed at the Pekingese Club of America Specialty Show after having won Best in Show at just eight months of age, in January 1942.

Below: Best in Show at the Pekingese Club of America Specialty several years ago was the 8½ month old puppy dog, Jai Bee of Dah Lyn, owned by Mr John B. Royce. Mrs Richard Quigley was the judge.

The importation of Che Le, who was a son of Tai Choo of Caversham from Fuchsia of Matsons, came several years after Mrs Austin had returned to the showing of the breed. During earlier years she had owned some splendid Pekingese, and her fellow fanciers were thus delighted when she resumed exhibiting in 1937. During January of that year she received from England the young red champion, Tang Hao of Caversham, a son of Ch. Tang Hou of Luebon, to bring out at Westminster. He went through to first in the Toy Group there, and completed his championship his third time shown, going on to annex Pekingese Club championship at the Summer Specialty (Morris and Essex), and later becoming a Canadian Champion as well. Other top winners owned by Mrs Austin include Tri-Int. Ch. Liebling of Huntington, Int. Ch. Wu Foo of Kingswere, Ch. Cherie of Huntington, Ch. Deermont Kayo, Ch. Dahna of Chinatown, Int. Ch. Posy of Caversham, Ch. Tang's Tuadore Glory (the latter two being Tang Hao daughters), and numerous others, both imported and homebred.

To John B. Royce goes credit for having owned America's greatest winning Pekingese bitch of her day, Champion Kai Lo of Dah Lyn. Kai Lo was twice Best in Show and three times Best American-bred in Show, in addition to 49 times Best Toy. Although Mr Royce was not actually the breeder of Kai Lo, she was entirely from his stock and was sired by his imported Ch. Kai Lung of Remenham, son of Billie Bee of Remenham. The Dah Lyn Kennels were founded in 1925 by Mr Royce and his sister Mrs Paul Anderson, the former Carolyn Royce. Many famous Pekingese were owned and personally handled to splendid records by Mr Royce, who was one of the breed's most loyal devotees. Among his best-known winners were Ch. Lassock of Ashcroft, Ch. Kai Lung of Remenham, Tri-Ch. Kai Choo of Dah Lyn, Ch. Chusan of Ifield, the

Top: Philadelphus Antonio of Dah Lyn, a half brother to the Best Toy Dog winner at Crufts in 1953. Imported and owned by John B. Royce of Brookline, Massachusetts.

Middle: Lassock of Ashcroft, the dam of the sensational Bondina of Dah Lyn. She was bred and owned by John B. Royce of Brookline, and photographed here in 1932.

Bottom: Lassock of Ashcroft, owned by John B. Royce of the Dah Lyn Kennels in Massachusetts and taken in 1934.

Mrs Carolyn Royce Anderson with Ch. Kai Fo of Dah Lyn, winner of Best of Breed at Morris and Essex show, and owned by her brother, John B. Royce.

John B. Royce of Brookline, Massachusetts, with Chang Tai and Tri-Ch. Kai-Choo of Dah Lyn. Photographed in the nineteen forties by Percy Jones.

Below: Ch. Dah Lyn Kai Jin of Caversham, owned and handled by John B. Royce. This dog was a Best in Show winner of the 1940's.

John B. Royce's Int. Ch. Nanking Noel of Dah Lyn, a famous winner in the late thirties and forties. Noel won an early Best in Show all-breed at Alexandria.

Kai-Choo of Dah Lyn, bred and owned by John B. Royce, and whelped in January, 1942. Photographed for owner by Tauskey.

Two adorable Pekingese puppies from the Dah Lyn Kennels of John B. Royce.

Above: 6½ month old puppy, later Ch. Tim's Posy of Pekestone Dah Lyn, owned by Mr. John B. Royce, Brookline, Massachusetts.

Below: Kai Lo of Dah Lyn, sired by the well-known Kai Lung of Remenham, both owned by John Royce. He is pictured here at 18 months of age on December 5, 1937.

Left: A Group Winner in the late forties. . . Ch. Dah Lyn Priority of Ascot Acres, owned by John B. Royce. Weight 10½ pounds, and sired by Tri-Ch. Kai-Chao of Dah Lyn.

Below: John B. Royce's famous bitch of the 1930's, Ch. Kai Lo of Dah Lyn. From a painting by Mrs Herbert Mapes.

Above: Ch. Monarque of Dah Lyn, Best in Show at the New York Pekingese Club of America Specialty Show in 1946.

Ch. Nanking Noel, 8½ pound red brindle, whelped December 25th, 1935. Noel was bred and owned by John B. Royce of the Dah Lyn Kennels, Massachusetts.

Kai-Choo of Dah Lyn, bred and owned by John B. Royce, Dah Lyn Kennels, Brookline, Massachusetts. Whelped January 6th, 1942, Kai-Choo was sired by Ch. Kai Lung of Remenham ex Griselda of Caversham. She was a brilliant golden red and white and weighed 6½ pounds. Percy Jones photograph.

Ch. Monarque of Dah Lyn, Best of Winners at Westminster for four points in 1945, Best of Breed at the Progressive Toy Dog Show in 1944. Owned by John B. Royce of Brookline.

Left: Ch. Greenwich Bennie, owned by Mrs F.Y. Mathis of Greenwich, Connecticut. Bennie was a winning dog in the forties.

Left: In Albany, New York in November 1949 judge Anna Katherine Nicholas gives Best in Show to Jack Royce and his Kai Jin. Otto Dube presenting trophy; Brown photograph.

Below: Ch. Monarque of Dah Lyn winning Best in Show at Corpus Christi, Texas. Mr. Forest Hall was the judge, owner-handler Jack R. Watts. The year was 1948.

noted International Ch. Nanking Noel, and the glorious puppy Jai Bee of Dah Lyn that accomplished the considerable feat of going from first in the Futurity Stakes to Best in Show at the Pekingese Club of America Specialty when only eight months old. Champion Jai Bee was just gaining recognition as a sire when Mr Royce's kennel was wiped out by distemper, and Jai Bee was among the many fine Pekes lost.

Dah Lyn came back stronger than ever after this heartbreaking occurrence, however, winning well with Ch. Monarque, who was Best in Show at the 1946 Specialty, had a fine Group record, and was eventually sold to Jack Watts. Ch. Yung Kai Choo of Dah Lyn, Kai Choo Bee of Dah Lyn, and Priority of Ascot Acres all made their presence felt under Mr Royce's ownership. And then there was the mighty Ch. Kai Jin of Caversham, a superb Pekingese that made a fine Best in Show career for himself and was widely admired.

Another breeder back in the 1920's was Mrs F. Y. Mathis. Her Greenwich strain was founded on much the same lines as Bagatelle. It was Mrs Mathis who selected Dan of Toddington for Mrs Hastings, and he later came to live at Greenwich. Dan had 7 champion offspring and they produced another 5 champions. In England during 1925, Mrs Mathis purchased two three-month-old bitches, Cha Ming Princess Confucia and Khoo Yas Min. Both became famous champions, and Yas Min the dam of Ch. Greenwich Ringo Soy, who was by Ch. Greenwich Cha Ming Prince Confucious.

Another great son of Confucious was Champion Greenwich Prince Chong Yow. Prince Confucious was by Champion Wundah of Chinatown from Paula of Hesketh. Champion Cha Ming Dah Wun Dah and Champion Cha Ming Ku Dah were among Mrs Mathis'

Top: From the early thirties, Ch. Greenwich Chong Yow, owned by Mrs F.Y. Mathis of Greenwich, Connecticut.

A classic candid study of Mrs F.Y. Mathis with Mrs Margaret Gude's Ch. Pay Ching Wo San, photographed many years ago.

Also from the early thirties, one of the most typical Peke puppy pictures of the time. Sired by Ch. Benjamin of Toddington. Both father and son owned by Mrs F.Y. Mathis of Greenwich.

Bottom: Ch. Cha Ming Ku Dah, photographed in the nineteen thirties and owned by Mrs F. Mathis.

Top left: Ch. Rajah's Tangku of Wu-Kee, owned by Mrs Thomas R. Fay of Port Washington, New York. A popular winner in the thirties.

Ming Wu Wu Kee of the Terrace, owned by Anna Katherine Nicholas. This dog was noted for his lovely head. Wu-Kee was whelped in 1932.

Bottom left: Ch. Clamarlow Princess Silver Dust, owned by Clara and Margaretta Lowther.

Top right: Clamarlow Tom Moo, owned by the Misses Lowther of the Clamarlow Kennels in Riverside, Connecticut.

From the nineteen twenties comes this photograph of Mrs F. Mathis' famous Pekingese, Bagatelle Dan of Tade.

Bottom right: Ming Wu-Wu Kee of the Terrace, owned by Anna Katherine Nicholas. Wu-Kee is pictured here at three years of age. He was bred by Mrs Harry L. Sears and weighed between seven and eight pounds.

famous winners, as were the renowned Champion Benjamin of Toddington (a marvelous red Champion Pung Chow of Alderbourne son that was a brilliant winner) and Champion Pekoe of Luebon (a small Champion Yu Fuh of Alderbourne son three times inbred from Champion Yu Chuan). The last of Mrs Mathis' top dogs was Champion Greenwich Bennie, a magnificent dog sired by Champion Jai Son Fu of Orchard Hill.

Queenie Chang Jen Chu was the first of Mrs Harry L. Sears' Wu-Kees. Bred to her sire, Wung Lung, she produced three bitches that Mrs Sears mated to outstanding representatives of Llenrud, Minoru, Hydegree, and Chinatown. Chin Pao of Wu Kee became Mrs Sears' first homebred champion. He was by Wang Ching of Wu Kee from Champion Woo Sung of Wu Kee.

It was in 1929 that Mrs Sears made history in the Pekingese world with the importation of four dogs whose names became familiar to Pekingese fanciers everywhere. These were English Champion Rajah of Hesketh Wu Kee (who quickly added American and Canadian titles to become the first and for many years only Toy Tri-International Champion), International Champion Sunset of Chynah Wu Kee, Champion Gem of Hesketh and Champion Tallulah of Hesketh, followed shortly by Champion Domino and Romano of Hesketh.

The mighty Rajah was one of history's unforgettable Pekingese. Rather on the large side, he was a massive dog of tremendous substance, black and tan in color, sound, abundantly coated, with a very wide, strong face. Many were the Sunday afternoons Anna Katherine Nicholas spent sitting on the Sears' living room floor with Rajah stretched out beside her enjoying a good rub. In temperament, conformation, and show ring presence, Rajah was a supreme dog.

Early in the thirties, Mrs Sears added Cha Ming bloodlines to her kennel, combining them with her Hesketh strain. From this came some of her loveliest homebred champions. Rajah's four champion sons were Che Mah, Rajah's Fox, and Rajah's Tong Ku, all of Wu Kee, and Prince Tang of Clitheroe. His most gorgeous and best known grandson was Anna Katherine Nicholas' Ming Wu Wu Kee of the Terrace, by Rajah's Fox from Shansi of Wu Kee, she by Champion Cha Ming Pung Chow Tsun.

At the start of World War II, during which Mrs Sears did excellent work for defense, the Wu Kee dogs became the property of Mrs Clarence Hale.

The Misses Clara and Margaretta Lowther held a personal record in having about twenty-five champions at their Clamarlow

One of the leading breeders of yesteryear, Mrs Harry L. Sears with her friend Mrs Fay's Ch. Rajah's Tangku of Wu-Kee.

Miss Clara G. Lowther with Ch. Clamarlow Yangtse Yen, photographed in the nineteen thirties.

Above: Ch. Clamarlow Tsan Wee Boi, photographed with one of his magnificent trophies in the forties. Owned by the Misses C. and M. Lowther.

Top left: A lovely charcoal drawing of Ch. Clamarlow Silver Star owned by Margaretta and Clara Lowther.

left: Ch. Mingshang Toni T'sun of Clamarlow, also owned by the Misses Lowther. Toni was an import and a winner.

The Misses C. and M. Lowther's Ch. Belinda of Hartlebury-Clamarlow, a fine winning bitch from the past. The Clamarlow Kennels were located in Riverside, Connecticut.

Kennels, one of the breed's most influential during the thirties and into the fifties. Their foundation stock consisted of two bitches and a dog, these having been Sutherland Avenue Gia Gia, by Nanking Wenti; Christine; and the miniature male, Tchip of Arcady. Gia Gia was bred to Tchip and produced Sun Su and Ta Su of Clamarlow, the first two American-bred Pekingese littermates to become champions.

An especially dominant stud was Clamarlow Pung Chow, a son of Champion Yu Yen of Frere-Clamarlow (by Champion Pung Chow of Alderbourne) from Clamarlow Nan Shen of Chinatown. Pung Chow sired Champions Clamarlow Pung Yen and Pung Toi among others.

The Lowthers' most famous winner was the beloved Champion Hei Tsun of Caversham-Clamarlow. This dog holds an unforgettable place in the breed's history, and in the East was its leading winner at one period.

Other Pekingese that brought fame to this kennel were Champion Clamarlow Tsan Wee Boi, the imported Champion Belinda of Hartlebury, Champion Whitworth Fond Hope, Champion Clamarlow Po Li An, Champion Clamarlow Yangtse Yen, Champion Mingshang Toni Tsun of Clamarlow, and Champion Silver Dust. Miss Margaretta Lowther passed away some years ago; since then her sister Clara (a former President of the Pekingese Club of America) has withdrawn from active participation in the Pekingese world though she still keeps the beautiful home on Long Island Sound at Riverside, Connecticut, and many recall with respectful admiration the sportsmanship and quality for which Clamarlow was famous.

The Dah Wong Pekingese of Miss Sara F. Hodges and Mlle A. Perret also earned a niche in the history of Pekingese development in America. The foundation for this kennel came from two bitches, a daughter of Champion Greenwich Choggy Koo bred to Champion Glen Iris Dai Dream, and a daughter of Champion Iyo Jen that was bred to one of the famous Gerry Snow importations from Alderbourne. Dah Wong of Dah Wong was from such mating and was the dominant factor in the establishment of the Dah Wong Kennels. Champion Yo Ling of Dah Wong, Champion Lotus Blossom of Dah Wong, Champion Wu Tsi Tu of Dah Wong, Champion Lee Ya Ching of Dah Wong, and Champion Sho Shan of Dah Wong were big winners from this kennel. The top winner, however, was the lovely Champion Tai Chuo Tsun of Dah Wong, a Best in Show winner that also won the Pekingese Club of America Specialty on several occasions.

Miss Clara G. Lowther, with one of the many home-bred champions from her Clamarlow Kennels. This photograph was taken in the late thirties or early forties.

Below: Miss Anna Katherine Nicholas holds a puppy donated by the Misses C. and M. Lowther to be raffled off for Dogs For Defense benefit at the Pekingese Club Show in 1943. Seated is Mrs Wellington Koo, wife of the Chinese ambassador to Great Britain [and formerly to U.S.A.] holding two Pekes owned by Dah-Lyn Kennels.

Winner of the 1950 Specialty show under judge Iris de la Torre Bueno was Ch. Tai Chuo's Son of Dah Wong, owned by Misses S.F. Hodges and Mlle. A. Perret.

Left: A consistent winning Peke of the fifties . . . Ch. Tai Chuo of Dali Wong, bred, owned and handled by Sara F. Hodges, Wilton, Connecticut, pictured here winning under judge Anna Katherine Nicholas at the Suffolk County Kennel Club Show in September, 1951.

Miss Sara F. Hodges winning Best of Breed at the Pekingese Club of America Specialty Show in 1953 with Ch. Tai Chuo Son of Dali Wong. Betty Johnstonbaugh handles Mrs Quigley's bitch to Best of Opposite Sex. Judge, Anna Katherine Nicholas.

Ch. Hei T'sun of Caversham-Catawba, owned by the Misses Lowther. This dog was the star of their Clamarlow Kennels and a big winner of the thirties, winning at all the important Eastern shows. J.O. Henschel photograph.

Left: Ch. Tien Fah of Dah Wong, owned by Mr Jack R. Watts, photographed several years ago.

Ch. Silver Dust, owned by C.M. Lowther and photographed by Percy T. Jones.

Ch. Kohgnae Chula pictured winning at the
Elm City Kennel Club Show in August, 1965,
under judge Delphine McIntyre. The sire is
Ch. Goofus Buggati ex Kohgnae Ginette and
he is bred, owned and handled by Mrs Everett
M. Clark of Pound Ridge, New York.

Ch. Wu's Crown Jewel of Miralac, bred and
owned by Mrs Everett M. Clark of Pound
Ridge, New York. Jewel is pictured winning at
the 1969 Rhode Island Kennel Club Show under judge Mrs Grybinski, and is handled by
Mrs Hermine Cleaver. Jewel's sire was Ch.
Merry Lee's Mr Wu of Miralac ex Chula's Si Si
of Miralac.

Ch. Merry Lee's Mr Wu of Miralac, pictured
with his handler, Hermine Cleaver, winning at
the 1968 Pekingese Club show under the late
judge Clara M. Alford. His sire was Ch. Monte
Verde Ricky Tick and the dam was Ch. Miralac
Merry Lee. Bred and owned by Mrs Everett M.
Clark of Pound Ridge, New York.

Ch. Bu-Ku of Kaytochand Miralae is shown
here winning the Toy Group in 1958 at the
Queensboro Kennel Club Show under judge
Anna Katherine Nicholas. Handled and owned
by Mrs E.M. Clark of Pound Ridge, New York.

Mrs Herbert L. Mapes' Whitworth Pekingese were founded in 1913 with the Nanking and Alderbourne bloodlines predominating. Later, Chinatown was introduced through Champion Wun Dah's progeny and Caversham through Boltonio Choo Tai's offspring. The Caversham line was strengthened in the forties when Mrs Mapes bred several of her top bitches to Champion Arellian Choo Leen of Catawba. Another stud used successfully was Champion Pagan Chieftain O'Palart, owned by the late Mrs Bertha Hanson. Among the champions for which Mrs Mapes' was noted were Chieftain's Wee Chu II, Fu Dah of Chinatown, Whitworth Ponchee, International Champion Whitworth Michael, Whitworth Beau Michael, Whitworth Fond Hope, Whitworth China Clipper, Whitworth Debutante, Whitworth Chieftain, Whitworth Knickerbocker, Gold Dust of Hartlebury, Razzle of Willowtoun, Whitworth Peterkin, Whitworth Manzee, and Whitworth Peer. Both Mrs Mapes and her husband contributed tremendously to the progress of Pekingese in America: Mr Mapes as a judge of the highest knowledge and integrity and also as a respected columnist, Mrs Mapes as an artist who portrayed some of the finest Pekingese of the thirties and forties on canvas, her portraits of American champions being accurate and exquisite. Mrs Mapes' niece, Mrs Fortune Roberts, carries on the family interest in Pekingese, as will be discussed in a later chapter.

Miralac Kennels began when Mrs Everett M. Clark purchased a bitch puppy from Mrs Mapes. While establishing her own strain, Mrs Clark used as studs Mrs Jarvis' Chung of Lamar and one of the Clamarlow champions. The former line remained strong at Miralac for many years, and was later combined with Whitworth, Hesketh, Hartlebury, and Remenham. One of Mrs Clark's early Pekingese

The famous Pekingese, Zat-Tu of Palart, owned by Mrs Bertha Hanson of Little Falls, New Jersey.

sensations was Teenah of Miralac, weighing all of three pounds which was outstanding even in competition against the larger Pekes. The purchase from Mrs Sears of Da Zeng of Miralac, a very beautiful son of Champion Che Mah of Wu Kee, was an important one for Mrs Clark as he sired two champions: Major Mite and Totsu of Miralac. Major Mite sired Champion Ho Yan of Miralac and was later sold to Mrs Nathan Wise and then sired the famous Best in Show winner, Champion Major Mite of Ho Nan. Mrs Clark's interest in Pekingese has remained constant through the years, and during the past decade she has continued to breed winning Pekingese and to import some excellent examples.

With the death of Mrs Bertha Hanson and of Mrs Richardson Strathy during the forties, there came to an end two kennels which had figured high in Pekingese competition in the East, namely Palart and Hidden Garden.

Ch. Fang Sheng of Willowtown O'Palart, photographed in the thirties. Owner is Mrs Berta Hanson of Little Falls, New Jersey.

A Tauskey photograph of a Mardale Kennels Pekingese taken in 1930.

Mo Chu of Earlsberry of Tien Hia, a reserve championship winner in England, left undefeated when he was imported by Mrs Murray Brooks of San Antonio, Texas.

Tombo's Tang How of Tien Hia with his new owner Jack Watts of New Orleans, Louisiana, photographed in April of 1946. Tien Hia was a Group Winner in the forties.

The former was noted for Champions Yu Yen of Frere-Clamarlow, Clamarlow Tai Tu, Zat of Lavrock, Fang Shen of Willowtoun, Razzle of Willowtoun, Chee Kee Wun of Hartlebury, Gold Dust of Hartlebury, and Pagan Chieftain O'Palart. All the aforementioned champions were of excellent type and quality and contributed much to the future of the breed.

Mrs Strathy's Hidden Garden Kennels were housed in the charming Washington Square section of New York and time was divided between her spacious apartment and the walled in, very private little garden that she rented across the courtyard from her building. Her lovely little dogs included International Champion Whitworth Michael, the homebred Champion Kann Doo (with as excellent a Pekingese head as can be recalled), Kann Doo's son, Champion Whitworth China Clipper, and Champion Whitworth Knicker-bocker, by Mrs Austin's imported Champion Arellian Choo Leen of Catawba.

In Buffalo, New York, Mrs Martha Mosher raised some outstanding dogs under the Pekestone affix. Her top stud dog was Pepper of Pekestone, descended from the English Moonland strain, and through his daughter Champion Shang's Sallie of Orchard Hill, he is to be found behind some worthy winners.

In 1932 Miss Helen E. Samuel, at the time of the thirty-fifth wedding anniversary of her parents, Mr and Mrs Thomas Samuel, acquired the foundation stock for some truly gorgeous Pekingese of the next two decades. Her first purchases were Fan Kewi of Tien Hia, a granddaughter of Tsan Pam of China-town and Champion Remus of Ashcroft; Ching Suey, by Wong Ti of Walmsley, a granddaughter of Champion Wun Dah of Chinatown; Whitworth Me Me, by Mighty Mite of Whitworth, granddaughter of Bol-tonio Choo Tai and Champion Fu Dah of Chinatown; and the wonderful imported male, The Squire of Walmsley, a great grandson of Champion Chu Erh Tsun of Alderbourne. Squire's daughter, Whitworth Coquette, was also bought by Miss Samuel and was the last Peke she purchased. The Squire line through Little Boy Blue (who weighed exactly four pounds) and Champion Squirette (sixth generation of Miss Samuel's own breeding) produced Champion Little Boy Blue's Ace, Champion Ace's Little Ace, Champion Tippy Tin's Honey, Champion Squirette's Ming Pi Zillah, and other typey Pekingese.

In Macon, Georgia, were the Pint O'Pekes Kennels belonging to Mrs W. Allen Chappell, who became Mrs Joseph Shaw after Mr Chappell's death. This fancier became a highly

From the nineteen thirties, the famous breeder Mrs Bertha Hanson with Ch. Chee Kee Wun of Hartlebury O'Palart, her imported winner.

Mrs Richardson Strathy's Ch. Whitworth China Clipper photographed several decades ago by Brown.

Patti of Winkfield and her family, owned by H.C. Jennings of West End Avenue, New York and photographed many years ago.

Mrs Murray Brook, with one of her Pekingese, Tien Hia, sired by International Ch. Remus of Ashcroft. Photograph circa early nineteen hundreds.

Ch. Kuku's Sun Flash of Tien Hia was the sire of Ch. Annabelle of Tien Hia pictured above; her dam was Silver Princess of Tien Hia. Annabelle finished for her championship in 1972 undefeated in the breed. She is owned by Mrs Murray Brooks of San Antonio, Texas.

Mrs Philip M. Schaffner of Merrick, Long Island, New York, photographed several decades ago with two of her famous Pekingese.

78

respected judge and officiated at least once at the Pekingese Club of America Specialties. Her kennel, founded in 1931, was based on several lovely Hesketh bitches and the imported dog, Dream Boi of Wango. The best known of the Pekingese produced here was Champion Sun Set Soon of Pint O'Pekes, by Dream Boi from Han's Picotee of Orchard Hill. Sunny finished his championship without a defeat in the breed and won at least thirteen Toy Groups, which in those days was considered an exciting record.

Orchid Lane Kennels, owned by Jack R. Watts, was an active and busy enterprise over a number of years, and I think it very likely that this highly respected judge must still have at least a few members of the breed even though he no longer maintains a kennel. Chief among his show dogs were the Best in Show winning Champion Monarque of Dah Lyn, purchased from John R. Royce, and the exquisite small Champion Orchid Lane's Ku Lee with which he won well and which continued making records after being sold to Mrs Quigley.

As you read the kennel histories which appear later in this book, you will note the numerous occasions on which credit is given to the Tien Hia Pekingese as having supplied foundation stock for breeders that are now important. Tien Hia must without a doubt be the oldest existing Pekingese kennel in America, since it was founded in 1921, and continues steadily active. Its charming owner, Mrs Murray Brooks, is still breeding, showing, and judging, and the kennel has earned a special niche in Pekingese history for the quality of its dogs and their inestimable accomplishments.

Top right: Hans Chuty Wun of Mount Curve and his son, Runnymede, owned by Dorothy Dwyer Hanson of Mount Sinai, New York. This photograph was taken several decades ago.

A big winner in the 1930's, an All-Celia Pekingese poses with some of his trophies. Courtesy of Iris de la Bueno.

Bottom: An informal portrait of Mrs Brooks Chik's Ku Ku of Tien Hia.

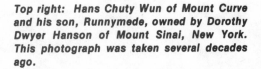

79

Champion Robinta of Kyra-town, owned by Mr. W. Hindley Taylor. Photo by C. M. Cooke.

Eng. Ch. Charterway Ung T'Sun, Mrs E.B. Partridge, owner. This beautiful dog is the only black champion in England.

Champion Fee-Bee of Kyra-town, owned by Mr W. Hindley Taylor. Photo by C. M. Cooke.

80

Lola Brooks' first champion was Wah Hoo Sam, sire of Champion Ming Tong of Tien Hia. A few years later International Champion Lo Hai Chi came to Tien Hia. Bred by Mrs McClure Halley, Lo Hai Chi was a son of the noted Sun Star of Llenrud. He was an American, Canadian, and Pekingese Club Champion, and was one of the leading studs of his day. Champion Remus of Ashcroft and Champion Sundah of Chinatown were early importations that proved to be great assets. Sundah's show record is truly a standout: he gained his championship by taking Best in Show five times and was undefeated by any dog of any breed en route to the title.

During the forties, Mrs Brooks added Orchard Hill breeding, her big winner from there having been Champion Shan's Shadow, son of Champion Kim's Tzu Shan of Orchard Hill. Champion War Admiral of Tien Hia, Champion Duskie Princess of Tien Hia, Champion Prince Charming, Champion Remenham Tombo of Orchard Hill (one of the Remenhams imported by Mrs Quigley from the Vlastos—a gorgeous parti-color that Mrs Brooks purchased soon after his arrival in America), and Tombo's sons, Champion Tombo Star and Champion Tombo Diamond are among the dogs that carried the Tien Hia banner to victory prior to the fifties. Tien Hia winners of that period combined Chinatown, Ashcroft, Alderbourne, Hartlebury, Sherhill, Earlesfery, and Remenham breeding.

There have been many additional Tien Hia champions since 1950, some American-bred and some imported. You will see them referred to and illustrated with frequency in the later pages of this book.

Many students of pedigrees will find that there are Cha Ming Pekingese behind their dogs. This kennel was established during 1922 in London when Mrs Charmian Lansdowne acquired two pets, the female of which she bred to Sutherland Avenue Sha Tzu. Shortly thereafter Sutherland Avenue Shazina (by Remenham Patse) was purchased, eventually producing Cha Ming Don Tzu by Sutherland Avenue She Tzu. This dog became Mrs Lansdowne's first stud.

Sutherland Avenue Chu Hsieh next joined the kennel, followed by the famous Winkle of Parkfield. Winkle sired three American champions. Cha Ming Yuan Dah joined the kennel in 1927, as did Cha Ming Pung Chow Tsun in 1929.

An American branch of the Cha Ming Kennel was opened on Long Island in 1930, and the following year Mrs Lansdowne moved to Southern California, where she has since

Above: Tea party at Pekeland. . . Owner, Gladys Butler of Saratoga, California.

Left: 2½ month old Pekeland's Moy Lan, owned by Mrs Gladys Butler of Saratoga, California.

Right: Cha-Ming Pung Chow T'Sun, born in 1928, and registered with both the English and American Kennel Clubs. Owned by Mrs Charmain Lansdowne.

Below: Cha-Ming Yuan Dah, whelped in December, 1924, and bred by Mrs H. Taylor. Yuan was sold to Mrs Charmain Lansdowne, of Bellmore, Long Island, New York.

81

American and Canadian Ch. Nia-Jai-Mi-Tu of Orchard Hill, pictured winning the Toy Group at the Middlesex Kennel Club show in June 1972 under judge Joseph Gregory. Handled by Lynn Olson, this was the last Pekingese bred by the late Mrs Richard S. Quigley to attain its championship. Owners, Ol'Seville Pekingese, Brunswick, Maine; Shafer photo.

been located and where she became a noted portrait photographer. She also wrote a very fine book about Pekingese which has long since been out of print.

Cha Ming Pung Chow Tsun, Cha Ming Lacquer Lady, King San Fu of Wu Kee, and Cha Ming Shen Hung were Mrs Lansdowne's first champions to gain their titles on the Pacific Coast, and were followed by a whole series of Cha Ming champions either bred by her or from her stock. The Cha Mings were sound and massive little dogs with fine heads and beautifully grotesque expressions. Wishing an outcross in 1939, Mrs Lansdowne imported two dogs from the Toydom Kennel in England, and during 1944 she came East and persuaded Mrs Quigley to sell her Champion Han's Pudgee of Orchard Hill. A famous winner and among the last that Mrs Lansdowne campaigned was Champion Cha Ming Tang Wu of Kel Lee.

In California, Mrs Gladys Butler owned the Pekelands dogs, which were beautiful and successful. Empress Ming Lee, dominant in the Chinatown strain, was foundation bitch here. In the only litter she produced was Mrs Butler's first homebred champion, the well-known Wong Sing of Ly. A matron from Tri-International Champion Pierrot of Hartlebury and Champion Sutherland Avenue Han Shih bloodlines was selected for breeding to Wong, which proved a wise choice as this combination produced Champion Wong Sing of Loy Junior, the six pounder that won well and in turn sired Champion Pekelands Pung Tzu and other winners.

Mrs Butler strengthened her Orchard Hill line and acquired a Champion Cherub of Theldon daughter that gave her some lovely homebreds. Two of her biggest winners were Champion Pekeland's Pung Tzu (twenty-five times Best of Breed) and Champion Pekeland's Wong Loy.

Above right: Four home-bred Pekeland Kennels champions owned by Gladys Butler and photographed in the early forties: Pung Tzu, Wong Sing of Loy Junior, Wong Sing of Loy and Mr Wu.

Pekeland's Nan Ling, eight pounds, and Pekeland's Miss Wong Sing, seven pounds. Both are also owned by Gladys Butler, Pekeland Kennels, Saratoga, California.

Bottom: Pekeland Pung Tzu White Star and Pekeland Pung Tzu's White Sun—otherwise known as Snowie and Frostie—at six weeks of age. Pekeland Kennels are owned by Gladys Butler of Saratoga, California.

83

Above: Ruinaito's Chummie Boy, Man Chun, So Big and Joi of Balcroft, photographed in the early nineteen hundreds at the White Studio in Rochester, New York.

Above: Ch. Chin-Liu, sired by Ch. Pekin Peri ex Cinders. Photographed in the early nineteen hundreds.

Below: Peke postcard entitled "Bunty's Toilet," from the collection of Anna Katherine Nicholas.

Below: Canadian Ch. Sing Lee of Jalna, owned by Mrs Zara Smith of the state of Washington; photo taken in the 1940's.

Mrs Samuel Lightner Hyman of San Francisco is also remembered. She owned Champion Tung Bee of Caversham, Gracious of Caversham, and their lovely son, Champion Yung Tung Bee.

Mrs Zara Smith, original owner of the Jalna Pekingese, earned renown in the Pacific Northwest and in Canada. She bought her first Pekingese in 1934, prior to that time never having attended a dog show. Her first Canadian champion, Hao K'on Shia Kin, was homebred from the Ashcroft and Alderbourne bloodlines. His dam was Canadian Champion Chee Lee Kee of Yun Nan. From that time until her death during the fifties, Mrs Smith piloted numerous dogs to high show honors. Included were Canadian Champion Sing Lee of Jalna, Champion H'in San of Car-O-Del, International Champion Wee Ster Lett of Jalna, International Champion Shia Wee Toi, International Champion Cha Ming Jing She, Canadian Champion Shia Chin See of Yun Nan, Champion Po Ling's Tanya, etc. During 1946 Mrs Smith completed no less than five championships for her kennel, and several more soon gained titular honors. By the fifties, Jalna consisted primarily of Cha Ming and Orchard Hill bloodlines.

Other prominent names in the Pekingese world during the first half of this century include the Sunnyfields Farm Kennels owned by Mrs Michael M. van Beuren of Newport, Rhode Island. This great lady of the Fancy was a most capable President of the Pekingese Club of America over a whole series of years, and her own Pekingese represented excellent quality. The last of her winners, in the late forties, was Champion Pier Wanli of Orchard Hill.

Mrs Marie Plankers, from Minnesota, made the Chu Jai Pekingese well known. She was herself a breeder, and also at one period managed and handled the Orchard Hill dogs for Mrs Quigley. If we recall correctly, it was she who met and flew Champion Sutherland Avenue Han Shih to his American debut when Mrs Quigley imported him, thus earning for him the designation of "the airplane dog." For although it is routine custom nowadays, dogs were not in the habit of travelling by plane back in the early thirties. Mrs Plankers herself owned several widely admired champions.

Mrs. Florence Morehead's Dovershams did well at California events. Mrs Ethyle Ferguson's Sun Tu's included such glorious dogs as Roi of Iwade, International Champion Sand Boi of Iwade (originally imported by F. L. Maytag for his Ceylon Court Kennels which Mrs Ferguson managed at one time). Mrs Nathan

A most gracious lady of the early Pekingese world, Mrs Michael M. van Beuren, President of the Pekingese Club of America, with two Pekes from her Sunnyfields Farm Kennels at Newport, Rhode Island.

A beautifully headed winning Pekingese, owned by Mrs Carrie Sass, a long-time breeder of the twenties and thirties.

Four charming daughters of Canadian Ch. Sing-Lee of Jalna ex Charming Dusky Duchess. The late Zara Smith of Seattle, Washington was breeder and owner.

Above: Fong Soy, owned by Mrs H. Bohnet of New Orleans. A winner in the thirties. Krause Studio photograph.

Left: Mrs F.Y. Mathis of Greenwich, Connecticut, a famous cat and dog judge, exhibitor and club woman in the thirties.

Below: Mrs Richardson Stratley's Ch. Whitworth Michael photographed in October, 1931. Mrs Stratley was from New York city.

S. Wise chalked up impressive records with Champion Major Mite of Ho Nan, Champion Bond Hill Belinda, and others at her kennel in Ohio. Mrs William C. Smith's Chin Clair Kennel at Stratford, Connecticut, was small but maintained high quality Pekes. Mrs Thomas R. Fay had some fine Pekes of Wu Kee strain. Sisters Miss Dorothy P. Lathrop and Miss Gertrude Lathrop won sensationally with good Pekingese (and are still actively making champions); they provided the Peke fancy with one of its most exciting Westminsters when their lovely bitch, Champion Beh Tang, handled by her novice owner swept through to Best Toy there.

Another Pekingese fancier from the pre-fifties was Mrs Allerton Cushman who made considerable impact when she imported the very fine Champion Fu Chow Paladin of Alderbourne just in time for one year's Westminster, and arranged to have him brought over and shown by Miss Marjorie Ashton Cross.

Then there was Mary Eleanor Boalt (Mrs Ralph G. Boalt at that time) from Winona, Minnesota, who later became Mrs E. R. Thoenen. This charming young lady decided that she wanted some show Pekingese and arranged to take Mrs Sadie Edmiston the noted all-breed judge who was a professional handler in those days to do some Pekingese shopping with her in England. They brought back English Champion Wu Foo of Kingswere and English Champion Liebling of Huntington, both of which quickly became American and eventually Tri-International Champions.

Judith Connell had many importations at her Toytown Kennels in the thirties. Mrs Philip M. Schaffner owned the Merricka Kennels on Long Island, home of several champions. Mrs Frank Downing, mother of the popular all-breed judge Melbourne Downing, had Champion Wundah of Holly Lodge that was the first American-bred Pekingese to win Best in Show.

Top right: Lillian Tiffany, a famous breeder, judge, and an even more famous painter of dogs. This photograph was taken of Mrs Tiffany in the thirties with two of her Pekingese.

Photographed in 1931, Mrs M.G. Carke's Ashton-More Wen-Chu-Mo. English import.

Bottom: A lovely grey brindle bitch from the thirties sired by Marvlus of Moonland ex Bonnee of Moonland.

Miss Theodora Wilbur's Chin Hua of Moor Park. Winners Bitch at the 4th Pekingese Club show many years ago.

Mrs Justin Herold pictured winning with a lovely puppy at the Pekingese Club of America Specialty Show in 1953 under judge Anna Katherine Nicholas.

At the 1971 Westbury Kennel Club show judge Beatrice Godsol awards Best of Breed to Int. Ch. Copplestone Mr. Pinkcoat. Owner-handled by Betty Shoemaker, Cumlaude Kennels, Bridgeton, New Jersey. Shafer photo.

Han H'Sing of Forlands, photographed for the 1933 Westminster catalogue. Owner: Mrs Edgar Miller of Riverton, New Jersey.

St. Aubrey Kai Lo of Raymeade of Bond Hill, imported by Mrs Nathan S. Wise of Cincinnati, Ohio, for her Bond Hill Kennels. Kai is pictured here winning Best in Show in October, 1955 under judge Mrs Grace Bonney at the Progressive Dog Club of Wayne County. Frasie photograph.

Mrs Nathan Wise and her Pekeclan Tao Wu of Green Pine, winning Best of Winners at the Pekingese Club of America Specialty Show in September, 1950. Judge Jack Watts awards Winners Bitch to Miss M. Lowther's Clamarlow Black Dust. Shafer photo.

Ch. Chunking Tiuo, owned by Mrs Saunders
Meade. Ruth Sayres, handler. Mrs Fred
Hamm and Slim Secor present trophies at this
Queensboro Kennel Club Show in November,
1955 under judge Anna Katherine Nicholas.
Brown photo.

Right: Int. Ch. St. Aubrey Kai Lo of Ray-
meade wins Best in the Toy Group at the 1957
Leamington, Ontario show. This dog won 12
out of 13 consecutive Toy Groups in the
U.S.A. and Canada for owner Mrs Nathan S.
Wise of Bond Hill Kennels, Cincinnati, Ohio.
Norton of Kent photo.

Whitworth Knickerbocker, owned by Mrs
Richardson Stratley of the Hidden Garden
Kennels, Washington Square, New York City.
This photograph was taken in the nineteen
thirties.

Above, top: International Ch. Wu Foo of Kingswere, imported by Mrs Ralph Boalt, and later owned by Mrs J.M. Austin.

One of the famous Toy Town Pekingese owned by Mrs E.W. Connell and Miss Judith Connell.

Top right: Mrs Ralph G. Boalt and her Tri-Ch. Liebling of Huntington and Int. Ch. Wu Foo of Kingswere. Photographed in the thirties.

Middle right: Whelped in May, 1936, Ch. Japeke Han Shiho was owned by Mrs Pearl Cassla.

Bottom right: The exquisite Pekingese bitch, Ch. Beh Tang, bred and owned by Miss Dorothy P. Lathrop. This little bitch scored a smashing Best Toy victory at the Westminster Kennel Club Show in the early forties. She was by Ch. Jai Son Fu of Orchard Hill ex Cheetah of Dah-Lyn and was whelped in 1941. Odell photograph.

Adorable son of Whitworth Peterkin, owned and bred by Mildred K. Gates.

Ch. Honey of Toy Town, a winner in 1939, owned by the Toy Town Kennels.

Below: Ch. Wei Tiko of Pekeboro, Best In Show-winning Pekingese, owned and handled by Rose Marie Katz of Syracuse, New York, pictured here winning Best of Breed at the Progressive Dog Club Show in 1954 under judge Anna Katherine Nicholas. Brown photo.

It was during the fifties that Mrs Rose Marie Katz flashed into prominence with her Roh Kai Kennels at Syracuse, New York, and it is a matter of profound regret that illness cut short her association with the dog show world just as she was taking her merited place as one of America's most distinguished and talented Pekingese breeders. Mrs Katz was probably proudest of her homebred Champion Roh Kai Tom Mi, a sound, typey, perfectly-balanced little dog that was enough to make any breeder's dream come true. The chief mainstay of her kennel, however, was the splendid multiple Best in Show winner Champion Wei Tiko of Pekeboro that sired many champions for her.

Mrs Agnes Nourse, too, was devoted to Pekingese and the breed lost a loyal supporter when she passed away. Several of her pets were champions, and she was herself a Director and Vice-President of the Pekingese Club of America.

The Richard Bells from Oradell, New Jersey, were devoted to Pekingese and were hard working members of the Pekingese Club, of which Mrs Bell was a Director. Both are missed today. Among others recalled in looking toward the past are the following. Mrs William Copp was briefly active and purchased from Mrs Quigley the lovely dog Champion Yu Go Han of Orchard Hill. Mrs Vega especially loved white Pekingese and was at one time a Pekingese Club of America Director. Mrs Alice Waldo of the Morsemeres possessed dogs that were among the earliest

Top right: Ch. Wei Tiko of Pekeboro, owned by Mrs Katz of Syracuse, New York. Her Best in Show winner is a top stud force at her Roh Kai Kennels.

Middle: The Ox Ridge Kennel Club Show in 1956 saw judge Anna Katherine Nicholas award Best of Breed to Mrs Marie Katz' dog, Ch. Wei Tiko of Pekeboro.

Bottom: Ch. Mao-Ling of Dah Wong II, a foundation bitch in the fifties and dam of five champions at Rose Marie Katz' Roh Kai Kennels in Syracuse, New York.

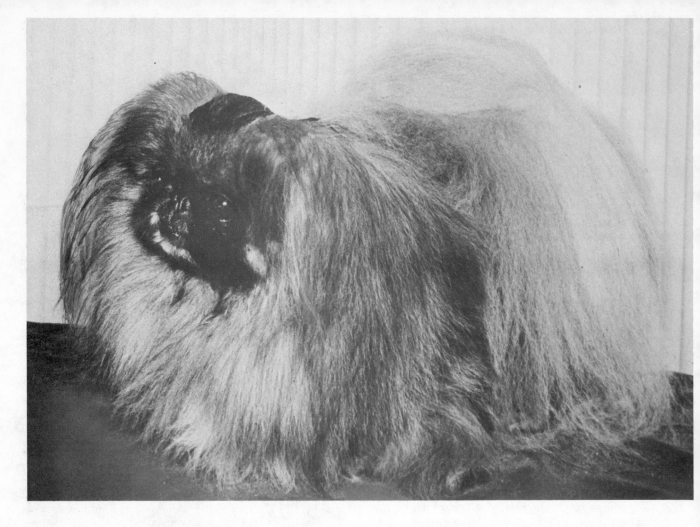

Above left: Ch. Wei Tiko of Pekeboro and Roh Kai was the sire of 21 champions including many Best in Show and group winners. He won 11 Bests in Show and 64 Toy Groups—a record at the time. Tiko was owned and handled by Rose Marie Katz of Syracuse, New York. Frasie photo.

Below left: A charming father-daughter portrait of Ch. Wei Tiko of Pekeboro and his daughter Roh Kai Tikette, just 12 weeks old. Owned by Rose Marie Katz, Roh Kai Kennels. Photograph taken in 1955.

Above: Ch. Wei Tiko of Pekeboro's first litter of three females, pictured at three months of age. All are owned by Rose Marie Katz of the Roh Kai Kennels in Syracuse, New York.

Below: Five-month-old puppies bred by Rose Marie Katz of Syracuse, New York, owner of the Roh Kai Kennels.

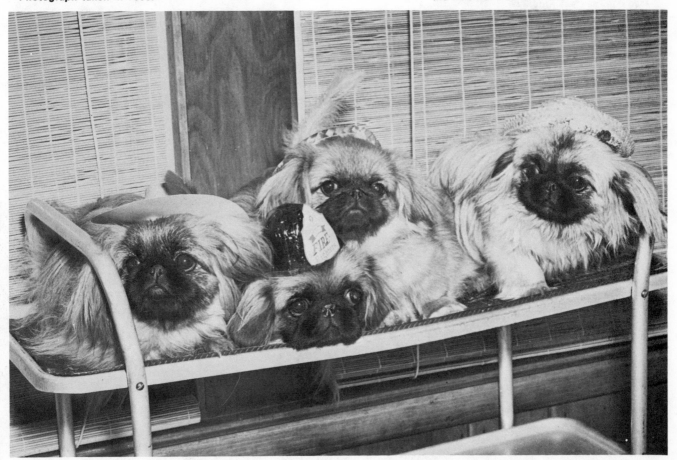

At the Progressive Dog Club Show in October, 1959 judge Anna Katherine Nicholas chose Bettina Belmont Ward's Pekingese Bettina's Kow Kow Best for Best in Show and Dr Vincent Calverisi's Ch. Musi of Villa Malta, Maltese dog, as Best American Bred. Mrs Edwin R. Blamey presented the trophy. Shafer photograph.

A portrait study of the magnificent Ch. Roh Kai Tom-Mi, sired by Ch. Wei Tiko of Pekeboro, and bred by Rose Marie Katz of Syracuse, New York.

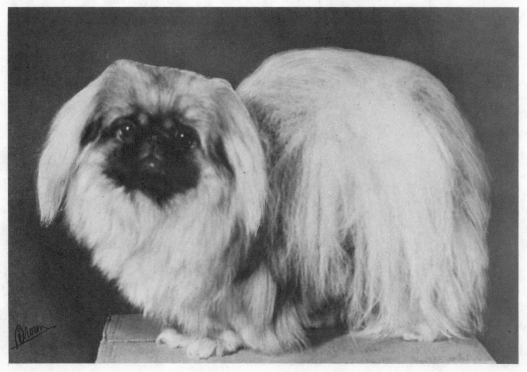

to carry the correct, unbroken wrinkle in the days when this feature was a rarity. The New York City penthouse garden of Mrs Warner Hays was always graced by at least one Peke among her champion Japanese Spaniels. Mrs Helen Nelson Drake of Minnesota had several estimable winners. Reverend George Bindley Davidson was author of a book on Pekingese, a popular judge, and a breeder. Mrs Christian Hager owned the great imported Champion King Pippin of Greystones that was a favorite of Anna Katherine Nicholas in the thirties. Mrs Saunders Meade (of the mighty Seafren Poodles) owned Champion Caversham Ko Ko of Shanruss and Champion Chungking Tino, both Best in Show winners that died tragically during a kennel fire.

One bit of excitement which is missing from the Pekingese fancy nowadays is that of the ''from boat to show ring'' importation! How breathlessly we would all wait, back before Westminster demanded the qualification in the dogs entered having had wins in the U.S. previous to closing date, and before the Pekingese Club of America Specialty was limited for the important winter show, to American-breds! At that time top fanciers vied with one another, it seemed, to have the latest dog here from England for these events! And the suspense was often breathtaking—for these shows in January (the P.C.A. date then) and February (Westminster) were at the time of year when weather often delayed the schedule arrival of the big liners bringing the

Miss Helen E. Samuel winning Best in the Toy Group at the National Capital Kennel Club Show in 1943 with her home-bred Ch. Ace's Little Ace. Anna Katherine Nicholas, the judge, presents the trophy. Photo by William Brown.

Best in Show at the 1957 Western Pennsylvania Kennel Association show went to Ch. Wei Tiko of Pekeboro, owned by Mrs Rose Marie Katz of Syracuse, New York. The judge was Frank Foster Davis. William Rodgers, the club president, is presenting the trophy.

97

Tish Foo Ling waits with his handler to go into the ring at the Bermuda Kennel Club show. His owner is Louis Tavares of Harrington Hundreds, Smith's Parish, Bermuda. Bermuda News Bureau photo.

Right:
Benjamin of Toddington, an English dog owned by Mrs F. Mathis.

At the 1945 Mexican Kennel Club show the winner was Blak, owned by Senora Dolores Chavez de Lozano. Photo by Ricardo Ayluardo.

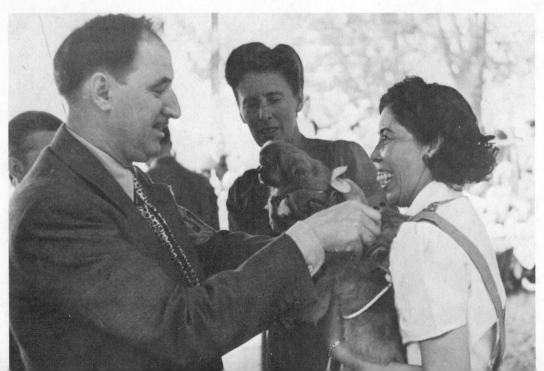

Top right: Three female Pekingese puppies owned by Rose Marie Katz of Syracuse, New York, pictured at seven weeks of age.

Bottom right: Ch. St. Aubrey Wee Yen of Church Road Farm, winning at the Kennel Club of Northern New Jersey in March, 1965. Owner, Mrs Arthur B. Gowie of Troy, New York. Shafer photograph.

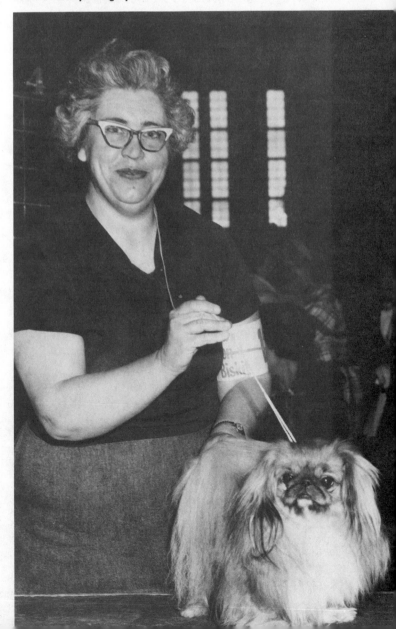

prized acquisitions, sometimes within a matter of hours before judging. At times the widely heralded new arrivals had barely a chance to get their land legs before being rushed into the ring. All this was, of course, accompanied by considerable publicity; it was hotly resented, we might remark, by the other exhibitors who felt that their dogs were thus placed at a disadvantage.

As a preface to the kennel stories which follow, we think it would be interesting to comment on what has happened in Pekingese at Westminster during the past quarter century. This is America's most prestigious dog show, and an insight into what has happened here gives a quite accurate picture of the Pekingese fancy during this period.

Among the fanciers who showed at Westminster during the fifties, we find many of those already mentioned. Additionally, there were Dr and Mrs Cohenour; Irene Miles Herring, of the Ir Ma Mi Kennels; Mrs Kate McBroom, who came down with some of her Pekes from Canada; R. E. Mort; Mrs J. Lento with Orchard Hill stock; and Mrs J. B. Harp, from the South who has bred and shown some lovely Pekingese and who is a highly esteemed judge. Others include Geraldine Pearce, from New England, very active at that time as both a breeder and as an exhibitor, working primarily with Dah Lyn strain; L. O. Lamb; Mary Brewster, whose big kennel of several Toy breeds included some splendid Pekingese, among them importations from the leading English kennels; L. E. Fitzgerald; E. L. Harper; A. Smithson; Bettina Belmont Ward, well known as the owner of the many times Best in Show winner, Champion Bettina's Kow Kow. (It is interesting that even though Kow Kow was born right here in Mrs Ward's bedroom, he was officially an import, as the breeding that produced him took place in England prior to his dam, the exquisite Champion Caversham Black Queen, being shipped to her new home.)

Top: Amazing trio of Pekingese belonging to Ms Cathleen Ertle of Ossining, New York. Left to right, Ch. Presleen Sammie Yong, with littermates Ca-La-Ma Tai Ling and Ch. Ca-La-Ma Wei Tian, at two years of age.

Far left: Ch. Palaceguard Hai Tor pictured winning at a recent show under the late judge Alva Rosenberg. Hai Tor is owned by the William Blairs of Connecticut.

Bottom right: Ch. Palaceguard Maximillian winning at the 1969 Somerset Hills Kennel Club show. Hermine Cleaver handles for owners, the William Blairs of Connecticut.

BEST of BREED
(Variety)

BREED
iety)

Alert and inquisitive Pekingese puppies at 10 weeks of age. Owned by Roh Kai Pekingese.

Top right: Ch. Dan Lee Dragonseed pictured winning Best in Show over 2,581 entries at the 1969 Boardwalk Kennel Club Show in Atlantic City. The judge was Ted E. Gundersen. John Berry, club president, is presenting the trophy. Michael Wolf is owner-handler.

Pekingese owner and breeder, Cathleen Ertle of Ossining, New York, with Ca-La-Ma Kin Tsae and her son Ca-La-Ma Harree, first in 9-12 month class and Futurity Winners Dog. Tsae was Veteran Bitch winner at the 1972 Winter Pekingese Show.

Mrs Quigley won Best of Breed at Westminster in 1953 with Champion St. Aubrey Judy of Calartha, the first of the scores of famous Pekingese brought to America by Nigel Aubrey Jones. A winner in 1954 was Jack Royce with his eye-catching pale cream Champion Philadelphus Antonio of Dah Lyn. In 1956 the future champion, Caversham Ko Ko of Shanruss, came through from the classes to Best of Breed and was third in a hotly contested Toy Group. Mrs Katz' Champion Wei Tiko of Pekeboro was twice a Westminster Best of Breed winner, once under Anna Katherine Nicholas and once under Sara F. Hodges. On the latter occasion, Miss Hodges placed him over Champion Chik Tsun of Caversham. A great furore was created in the Toy Group the following day (under the highly respected late Richard Kerns) when a protest was made by other fanciers against this dog, claiming that his coat showed powder. All was for naught, however, as the American Kennel Club vindicated Tiko and his placement was allowed to stand.

The Venables had a clean sweep in 1957 when Chik Tsun with his kennel mate, Champion Venable's Beautiful Star, scored both Best of Breed and Best of Opposite Sex under Herbert L. Mapes. Then there was also the unforgettable triumph for both Chik Tsun and for Pekingese in 1960 when Chik Tsun was Best of Breed under Mrs Herold, best in the Toy Group under Dr Calvaresi, and Best in Show, the first time ever for a Pekingese at Westminister, under that marvelous, knowledgeable gentleman, George Hartman. With this, Chik Tsun retired, holding the all-time record as America's leading Best in Show winner. There was much happiness that night for the late Clara Alford, Chik Tsun's handler, and for the Pekingese fancy who were wholeheartedly supporting him.

Left: Ch. Wei Tiko of Peke-boro pictured winning Best of Breed at the Ox Ridge Kennel Club show in 1956 under judge Anna Katherine Nicholas. Owner and handler is Rose Marie Katz of Syracuse, New York. Shafer photograph.

Below: Palaceguard Pu Gee, owned by the William Blairs of Connecticut.

Palaceguard Pat-Ti pictured winning at the 1964 North Shore Kennel Club show under judge Iris de la Torre Bueno. Pat-Ti is handled by Jane Forsyth for owners Mr and Mrs William Blair of Connecticut.

1971 Futurity Winner at the Winter Specialty Show under judge Mrs. Fortune Roberts was Ca-L-Ma Kwan Foo, handled by Barbara Partridge for owner Cathleen Ertle of Ossining, New York. Unfortunately, Kwan Foo died just before her second birthday, but had won 8 points and 1 major toward her championship.

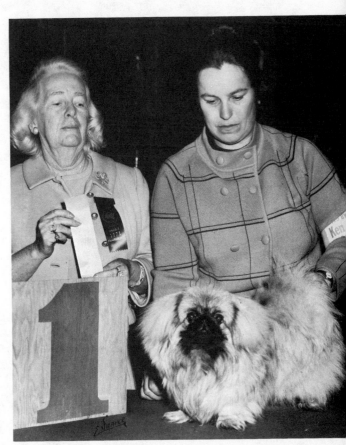

St. Aubrey Mi-Wun of Jehol, Best of Winners at the 1969 Wallkill Kennel Club show. Handled by Hermine Cleaver for owners Mr and Mrs William Blair of Connecticut.

Tang Sing, Tang Sangu and Tang Chu, born March 6th, 1936.

Below: Alderbourne Franklin Junior. Bred by Miss E. Evana of England, and whelped in March, 1943.

Three puppies belonging to the Ca-La-Ma Pekingese Kennels of Cathleen Ertle of Ossining, New York. They are a son and daughters of Ch. Presleen Sammie Yong.

In the sixties, the Westminster entry lists brought forth some new names: Miss Louise Ruddell with her purchases from Jack Royce, most notably the lovely Tuppence of Dah Lyn; Mrs C. Hendershott; D. H. Mehl; Mrs L. S. Greenleaf, Jr. with an Alderbourne importation; W. J. Gordon; Mrs D. Morris; J. C. Walker; D. C. West; V. S. Lee; Mrs P. Alexander; Frank Jones; Mrs Binaco; and Mrs Vera F. Crofton, the California lady who during the past two decades has built up a spectacular breeding and showing kennel in California; Mrs R. O'Daniel with her Kentucky Colonel dogs; Bill Blair in partnership with Lew Prince; Mrs D. Morris, and the Ertles who consistently breed correct, typey Pekes, must be included along with Mrs H. Cleaver, well-known both as a breeder and as an expert professional handler who has made a fine credit list with Pekingese champions; Dolores Scharff; C. J. Hollands (St. Aubrey Maribeau of Elsdon); Mr and Mrs V. A. Hearne from Canada; Mrs W. A. Bailey, who has bred beautiful champions, including the lovely dog with which Bettina Ward won the Pekingese Club of America Specialty the year Hazelle Ferguson judged; K. L. Winters; Richard Del Grosso, owner of admirable Pekes and the capable breed columnist for *Popular Dogs*. Then there were Dr Harold

Huggins and his wife, one of our most popular judging teams of many breeds; Mr and Mrs F. Engstrom; Charleen Prescott; Mike Leynor; the Russomannos; John Brown, that gifted young man from California whom all of us associate with those outstanding Pekingese, Champion Dan Lee Dragonseed and Champion Dan Lor Dragonfire; Ed Jenner, who has owned fine dogs of many breeds, and Catherine Eadie Adams, also owner of lovely Pekes.

In 1961 Champion Bettina's Kow Kow added a Westminster Best of Breed and a Group Fourth to his record and in 1962 Mrs Crofton had the Best of Breed in Champion St. Aubrey Seminole of Wanstrow. In 1964 it was Mrs Quigley's Ku Lee Tul Tuo of Orchard Hill that came through from the classes over nine specials. And here it seems pertinent to comment that from the early thirties when she started exhibiting, Mrs Quigley's dogs have undoubtedly been Best of Breed more times at Westminster than the Pekingese of any other exhibitor.

In 1965 Mrs Ruschaupt made her only Westminster trip to date and won the breed. In 1966 the winner was Mrs Crofton (again in partnership with Nigel Jones and Bill Taylor) with that lovely Champion Goofus Buggati. In 1967 the American-bred Champion Bettina's Kettle Drum owned by Bettina Ward and J. B. Binaco was victor. John Brown came East in 1968 with Dragonseed (that had just been sold to Mike Wolf) to gain an easy Best of Breed under Anna Katherine Nicholas and first in the Toy Group under Virginia Sivori.

Rounding out the sixties, Edna Voyles brought Ed Jenner's spectacular import, Champion Golden Jasper O'Dene Shay, to sail right through from the classes to Best of Breed under Melbourne Downing and a Group placement.

Mrs Shuman's handsome Champion Beaupres Tomsjoy Lea Chim, beautifully presented by Frank Sabella, started off the seventies by winning the breed, then the Toy Group under Mrs Van Court, and being very seriously considered in the finals for Best in Show by Anna Katherine Nicholas.

Ch. Bey Li Kish Mi KuKu owned by the William Blairs of Connecticut.

Ch. Sunstar Saton of Se-Je, bred by Mrs Jack Garrison and owned by Roy and Beverly Mooneyham of the Beverlyhill Pekes, Houston, Texas. Saton is a multiple Best in Show winner. Photograph by Twomey.

Ch. Sha Yen Montae of Beverlyhill, bred by Mr and Mrs Leslie Hardt and owned by Roy and Beverly Mooneyham, Beverlyhill Pekes, Houston, Texas. Photograph by Twomey.

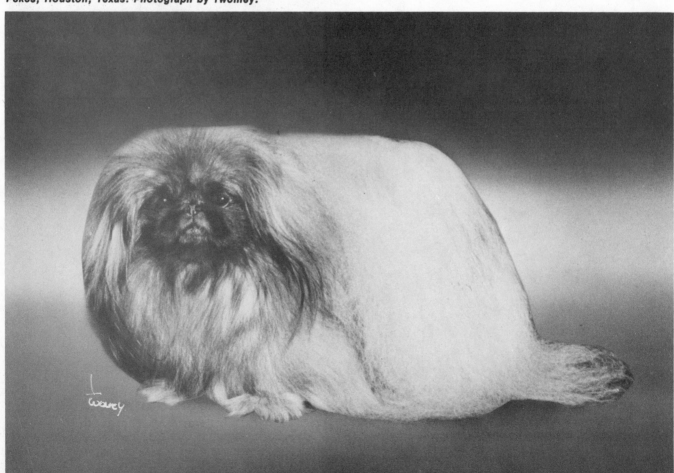

Ch. Sha Yen Bit O'Fortune, bred by W. and Mildred Haines, and owned by Roy and Beverly Mooneyham of Houston, Texas. Sire: Ch. Sha Yen Silver Fortune, dam; Nia-Tul-Dot of Orchard Hill. Photography by Twomey.

Ch. Buddha's Mr Pres of Beverlyhill, sired by Silver Buddha of Chinalion out of Beverlyhill Mar-Chin Rebecca. Mr Pres was bred and is owned by Roy and Beverly Mooneyham of Houston, Texas.

Ch. Beverlyhill Knight's Sass-Cee was Best of Winners and Best of Opposite Sex under Percy Roberts at the 1972 Louisiana Kennel Club show. Handled by Mrs Sandy Tremenot and bred by Mary McEachin, Sass-Cee is owned by Roy and Beverly Mooneyham of the Beverlyhill Pekes, Houston, Texas.

Ch. Cinnaman of Ho Tai is Winners Dog at the 1971 San Antonio Kennel Club show under judge Joseph Faigal. Bred by Karen Mahler, Cinnaman is owned by Beverlyhill Pekes, Houston, Texas and is shown by Roy Mooneyham.

CHAPTER 6

NOTED AMERICAN KENNELS OF THE SEVENTIES

Even though the Pekingese has always been one of the most popular of the purebred dogs, we are well aware that entries at dog shows, obedience trials, and registrations with the American Kennel Club are increasing at an amazing rate.

The growing appreciation of this breed can be credited to the reputable breeders who are devoted to raising good, healthy puppies from worthy stock to insure the future of the Pekingese. We also owe a debt of gratitude to the majority of owners who have one or two dogs and, presenting the breed at its best, contribute in their own way to its popularity.

The successes and accomplishments of these dogs have been recorded over the years in the show catalogues, stud files, magazines and books, and are a part of history. But the future of the breed lies in the hands of the kennels and breeders of today. We present now in alphabetical order a few of the most prominent breeders and kennels of the seventies whose influence on the breed today is undeniable and in whose hands lies the future of the Pekingese.

Beverlyhill

Pekingese entered the lives of Roy and Beverly Mooneyham of Houston, Texas, after a fascination with the breed which began even prior to their marriage some ten years ago. After they acquired a puppy and fell in love with all the special breed characteristics it epitomized, they decided to obtain still another Pekingese, possibly a better example, suitable for showing. And so came about the beginning of the Beverlyhill Kennels. This was also the beginning of years filled with happiness of the very special sort that Pekingese bring to their owners. There followed deep involvement in related activities, such as Roy Mooneyham's Presidency of the Pekingese Club of Houston and his work as columnist for the breed magazine, *Pekingese Parade*.

Beverlyhill's initial acquisition of show stock was made from Mrs Murray Brooks, whose Tien Hia Pekingese have been justly renowned for many decades now. The Mooneyhams bought all the bitches she had available at the time, which were Gloriana of Tien Hia,

Future champion Jason of Lisret at six months of age. Jason was bred by Mrs P. Finch and is owned by Mrs C.W. Reasons of Miami, Florida.

Beverlyhill Jai's China Jewel, pictured winning Winners Bitch and Best of Opposite Sex for a 3-point major under judge Winifred Heckmann at the Beaumont Kennel Club show, in April, 1973. Jewel is bred and owned by Roy and Beverly Mooneyham of the Beverlyhill Pekingese in Houston, Texas.

Silver Queen of Tien Hia, and Ping's Silva Sonnet of Tien Hia. Then Tien Hia related stock was purchased from Mrs Mary McEachin's Mar Chin Kennel in Houston (the grand matrons Beverlyhill's Knight's Sass Cee and Beverlyhill's Mar Chin Rebecca came from here); from Mrs Austin in Dallas, were purchased three daughters of Champion Gemini of Tien Hia, these including Austin's Gem of Beverlyhill and Gemini's Vicki of Beverlyhill. All of these bitches were strongly descended from Champion Caversham Khi Ku of Pendarvis, Champion Chik Tsun of Tien Hia, and Champion Pollyanna of Tien Hia.

The Mooneyhams wisely believed in using outside studs for their early breeding, carefully selecting for their excellent bitches some of the brightest stars of the Pekingese world, especially those dominant in Alderbourne and Caversham. The success of this system speaks for itself.

Although the Mooneyhams' other activities necessitate that they keep their kennel small, they have personally finished at least a couple of champions during each of the past several years. Others have been finished by purchasers of their stock. These breeders take pleasure in selling promising puppies to future exhibitors, and have done so with frequency, sharing their good dogs and at the same time encouraging the interest of others in the breed.

Among the better known bitches either bred, owned, or sold by the Mooneyhams are Champion She Yen Montae of Beverlyhill, Champion Ping's Silva Sonnet of Tien Hia, and Champion Beverlyhill's Knight's Sass Cee; among the dogs have been Champion Buddha's Mr Pres of Beverlyhill and Champion Cinnamon of Ho Tai. It is interesting that Pekingese from Beverlyhill Kennels have been the only ones to date that have walked away with Winners Dog, Best of Winners, and Best of

Top left: Dol-Shar-Jay-Jade, the pride and joy of the late Philip Panelli. Jade needed only one major to finish for his championship but died on June 19, 1969—the same day as Mr. Panelli—from no apparent cause. He had three Bests in Match to his credit before starting his ring career for championship.

Bottom left: Radiance of Alderbourne, bred by Cynthia Ashton Cross of England and imported by Betty Shoemaker of Bridgeton, New Jersey. Radiance is just six months old in this photograph, and her sire was Limelight of Alderbourne ex Alderbourne Miss Chintz.

Breed awards at both of the top Southern Specialties, the Delta Pekingese Club and the Pekingese Club of Texas. These honors were gained during 1971 and 1972 by Champion Buddha's Mr Pres of Beverlyhill and Champion Sunstar Saton of Sa Je.

Owning so many outstanding bitches, Beverlyhill then set out over two years ago to buy a really grand special dog to use in establishing their own particular ideal strain. Such a dog was found in Champion Sunstar Saton of Se Je, a lovely young winner which they bought from Mrs Sina Garriston of Fort Worth, Texas. Saton has been the kennel's most outstanding Pekingese to date, and its most valuable acquisition. Champion Saton's show victories include two all breed Bests in Show, six Specialties, twenty-two Best Toy wins, and over fifty other Toy Group placements, with a total of over eighty Bests of Breed. These have placed him among the Nation's Top Five Pekingese for several years.

The Mooneyhams take particular pride in the success of their Pekingese on their appearances at Westminster in 1972 and 1973. In 1972 Champion She Yen Bit O'Fortune, owned and shown to the title by Beverlyhill Kennels and currently owned by Phil Cross, was Best of Opposite Sex under the late Mrs Clara Alford. The following year Champion Sunstar Saton won the nod from Edd Biven for Best of Breed over a breathtaking array of the nation's finest Pekes. This kennel also had winning representation at the Pekingese Club of America Summer Specialty in 1972.

Current future hopefuls at Beverlyhill are an eleven-month-old bitch, Beverlyhill Jai's China Jewel, that already boasts ten points including a major, and six-month-old Beverlyhill Saton's Shanahan, representing three generations of homebreds.

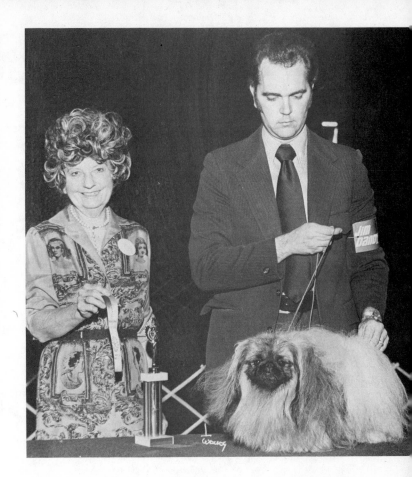

Top right: Ch. Sunstar Saton of Se-Je wins Best of Breed at the 1973 Austin Kennel Club show under Judge Dorothy Bonner. Owner-handler is Roy A. Mooneyham, Beverlyhill Pekes, Houston, Texas.

Bottom right: Pekes are popular in Japan also! Several color covers of the leading dog magazine INU NO SAKI features the little Lion Dogs. This one was the cover of the August, 1970, issue.

A darling Pekingese puppy from the Lakshmi Kennels of Mrs C.W. Reasons of Miami, Florida.

Above: Ch. Caccia's Angelique, shown winning Best In Show at the Pekingese Club of America Specialty Show in 1972 under judge Peggy Carr. She was sired by Ch. Welion Cynthar Lara Mee ex C. Welion Rina. She was bred, and is owned and handled by Norman J. Cacciatore of Bessemer, Alabama.

Left: Ch. Welion Selman, first champion to be finished at Norman Cacciatore's Caccia Pekingese Kennels in Bessemer, Alabama. He is a sire of champions and was bred and exported by Mrs Helen Bruce of the Welion Kennels. He is pictured here winning Best of Breed under judge Anthony Stamm at the Birmingham, Alabama Kennel Club Show in 1965.

112

Caccia

Two successful Pekingese Kennels have come into existence because two young men frequently passed the Hallmark Kennels whenever they returned home from college. Never did they do so without admiring the beautiful little dogs to be seen in the yard there. Subsequently Norman Cacciatore and Vincent Agro each purchased an excellent bitch puppy from Gary and Eston Hallmark.

There were many noted winners at Hallmark, but the dog the two friends considered most intriguing was the glorious International Champion Chik Tu of Peperstiche. They found him fascinating for his obvious quality, and also because Mr Hallmark valued this dog so highly that he purchased a full fare ticket on the plane from Europe, enabling him to ride back as a passenger and share the seat with his master.

Above: Ch. Caccia's Marco Polo pictured winning the Best in Show rosette at the 1971 Pekingese Club of America Specialty Show under breeder-judge Mrs Fortune Roberts. His first Best in Show was in 1970 under the late, and great, Pekingese fancier, Mr W. Hindley Taylor. Marco Polo was bred and is owned and handled by Norman J. Cacciatore, Caccia Pekingese, Bessemer, Alabama.

Ch. Caccia's Rina's Replica, outstanding seven pound bitch, completed her championship in three shows with three five point majors. She has also gone on to Best of Opposite Sex at four Specialty Shows. Rina was bred, and is owned and handled by Norman J. Cacciatore of Bessemer, Alabama, who is pictured with her winning under judge R. Gilliland on the way toward her championship.

Caccia Kennels was established by Mr Cacciatore in the summer of 1963 and is located at Bessemer, Alabama. It came to the attention of the Pekingese world in a big way through the great little Champion Caccia's Marco Polo, that gave his owner the thrill of a lifetime at the Pekingese Club of America Specialty in New York. As judged by Hindley Taylor, owner of the famous Kyratowns, who had come from England for the assignment, Marco Polo won Best of Breed and impressed Mr Taylor so highly that glowing praise of his quality appeared in Mr Taylor's statement to the *New York Times* and the English *Dog World*. One of Mr Cacciatore's treasured possessions is the letter in praise of the dog he received from Mr Taylor after his return to England.

When Marco Polo won the Winter Specialty the following year, this time under Mrs Fortune Roberts, and won again in 1974, retaining several famous trophies, Mr Cacciatore's elation was boundless, and his enthusiasm continues to grow steadily.

Mr Agro, meanwhile, has established the Ven Cen Kennels and is also breeding lovely Pekes. Little did they realize when they purchased their two little bitch puppies that each would found a kennel and become an owner of champions.

Ch. Cedarwood Amah, Winners Bitch and Best of Opposite Sex at the 1969 Eastern Dog Club show, under judge Virginia Sivori. Amah is owned, bred and handled by Emily-Jean Hennessey of Hanson, Massachusetts.

Above: Cedarwood Tam Mee Ku, winner of Parade magazine's First Annual Bitch Award in 1970 for producing the most champions. Her breeder and owner is Emily-Jean Hennessey of the Cedarwood Pekingese in Hanson, Massachusetts.

Bottom left: Artist Robert Hickey captures the great beauty of Ch. Cedarwood Chikee Ling, bred and owned by Emily-Jean Hennessee of Hanson, Massachusetts.

Below: Ch. Cedarwood Ku Chik resting on some of his "laurels" in the form of his winning ribbons. He was bred and owned by Emily-Jean Hennessey of Hanson, Massachusetts. Photo taken by the owner.

Cedarwood

Cedarwood Kennels, owned by Emily-Jean Hennessey at Hanson, Massachusetts, truly represents a "labor of love." Each dog has individual accommodations, and there are eight big, shady, fenced-in runs where they can exercise and enjoy their toys.

Miss Hennessey started with Pekingese in 1954 when she acquired a pet named Rowdy. In 1957 he was joined by Foo Jin Pamela of Hanson. With the advice and guidance of Marilyn Allen (owner of Coronation, another prominent New England kennel), Pammy was bred. In her second litter, by Coronation Ku Ling Ku, Pammy produced Cedarwood Tam Mee Ku—to become a top-producing bitch with four champion offspring, five pointed, and one on the way to a companion dog title

Pammy's first champion daughter, Cedarwood Ku Chik, finished with three four-point majors among her wins, including Winners Bitch and Best of Opposite Sex at the Blue Hills Pekingese Club Specialty. Four years later, having been out of the ring and not even on a lead during that time, Ku Chik re-entered competition in what might be called a blaze of glory by taking Best of Opposite Sex at the Pekingese Club of America Summer Specialty under Anna Katherine Nicholas.

The next Cedarwood champion did not find the going quite so easy. Cedarwood Chikee Ling had gained her first major as a puppy prior to an outbreak of distemper in the kennel, from which one bitch and five puppies of the nineteen dogs there did not pull through. Chikee Ling herself was practically given up by the veterinarian, but she did recover under her owner's loving care and eventually completed her title. Then, after resting on her laurels for awhile, she re-appeared as a special when an eight-and-a-half-year-old, going Best of Breed in a major entry and six months later taking Best of Opposite Sex at the Eastern Dog Club in Boston.

Cedarwood lost more than a year of showing because of this distemper but the dogs were finally brought back to full bloom and ready to start resuming their ring careers. Cedarwood Robin Rob Bob gained his title easily, as did Cedarwood Amah the following year.

Miss Hennessey calls the Eastern her lucky dog show, for in the past eight years her Pekes have been Best of Opposite Sex there on six occasions.

Marilyn Allen's death was a sad blow to Miss Hennessey, but the latter continues to work along the lines of the breeding program which Mrs Allen had worked out for Cedarwood and which is progressing well. A steady succession of future winners from this kennel may be expected.

Cedarwood Pixie Joi Toyi pictured here winning Winners Bitch and Best Opposite Sex from the Puppy Bitch Class at eight months of age under judge Mrs S.J. Fishman, at the Ladies Dog Club show in 1969. Owner is Emily-Jean Hennessey of Hanson, Massachusetts.

Ch. Cedarwood Ku Chik, pictured here winning Best of Opposite Sex at the 1969 Summer Specialty of the Pekingese Club of America, held in conjunction with the Westchester Kennel Club. The judge was Anna Katherine Nicholas. Breeder and owner is Emily-Jean Hennessey of Hanson, Massachusetts.

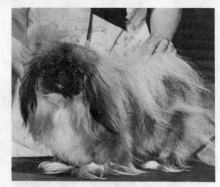

Above: Best of Breed at the 1970 Carroll County Kennel Club show—under judge Iris de la Torre Bueno—was Emily-Jean Hennessey's Cedarwood Kam Mee Ki Ku.

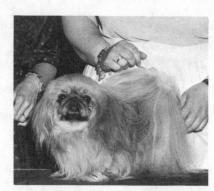

Above: Ch. Cedarwood Chikee Ling, Winners Bitch and Best of Opposite Sex under judge Anna Katherine Nicholas at the 1967 Springfield Kennel Club show. She is another champion bred and owned by Emily-Jean Hennessey.

Below: Cedarwood Tam O'Jin photographed after winning at the Pekingese Club of America Specialty show in 1973 under judge Winifred L. Heckmann. Breeder-owner is Emily-Jean Hennessey of the Cedarwood Pekingese Kennels in Hanson, Massachusetts.

Below: Ch. Cedarwood Robin Rob Bob was one of Emily-Jean Hennessey's winning Pekingese in 1968. This photograph shows Robin winning Best of Winners and Best of Breed under judge Maurice L. Baker at the Ladies Dog Club Show. His sire was Hong Kong of Coronation ex Cedarwood Tam Mee Ku.

Above: Cedarwood Buddha T'Sun—Best of Winners under judge Marianne Grybinski at the Springfield Kennel Club show in 1972. Breeder, owner is Emily-Jean Hennessey of Massachusetts.

Char-Min

Char-Min Pekingese began on 6 July 1968, when Minnie Wisdom of Poplar Bluff, Missouri, whelped a litter of five belonging to her sister, Anna L. Brown. In appreciation of the nerve-wracking four hours she had gone through, Mrs Wisdom was presented with the gift of a male puppy.

This little Peke, Jo Dee, immediately won his owner's heart and she began thinking of a bitch for him and a name for her future kennel. Her husband, Charles, solved the latter with the suggestion of Char-Min from the first letters of their two names. The bitch puppy was found and purchased from Mc-J. J. Kennels, and has proved to be a great asset by bearing lovely puppies. She is Tonya Star of Char-Min. Bred to Mrs. Ruby Dudley's Champion Dud-Lee's Little Joe, she became the dam of Little Joe's Natika of Char-Min, Reserve Winners Bitch her first time in the show ring when only seven months old. Mrs Wisdom hopes that Natika will become her first homebred champion.

There are two sons of Champion Ku Chi Tom Mi of Seng Kay at Char-Min and Mrs Wisdom takes great pride in this. They are Ku Chin Tom Mi Joe of Dud-Lee's and Tom Mi's I'm A Dandy of Dud-Lee's, both contributing tremendously to the establishment of this kennel.

Mrs Wisdom was excited over a litter born in December 1972 by a daughter of Tom Mi Joe bred to Dandy, thus intensively linebred to the great Champion Ku Chi Tom Mi of Seng Kye. One puppy, named Mia Tribute To Tom Mi of Char-Min, is especially promising and would seem to have a bright future.

Mrs Wisdom also has brought several fine Pekingese from Mary Davis of Bel Mar; her kennel is established on a sound foundation and should become well-known in the Pekingese world.

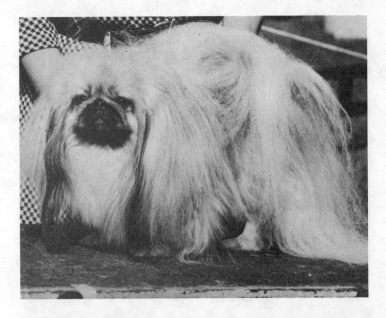

Ch. Ku-Coon of Caversham, owned by Mrs I. de Pledge. Cooke photo.

Ch. Belknap Buck of Jamestown, imported from England by owner Mrs Kay B. Cooke of Margate, New Jersey. Bred by Mrs T.W. Horn, his sire is English Ch. Yu Yang of Jamestown ex Belknap Volksmana Kiki Dee. He is shown exclusively by Mrs Ernie Panelli of Atco, New Jersey.

Bottom: Ch. Jason of Lisret, pictured at 14 months of age, was Best of Winners at the Pekingese Club of Alabama Specialty Show in December, 1971. His sire was Nathaniel of Wongoille ex Ch. Sunshen Fan T'An. He was whelped in February, 1970 and is owned by Mrs C.W. Reasons of Miami, Florida. Lionel Young photograph.

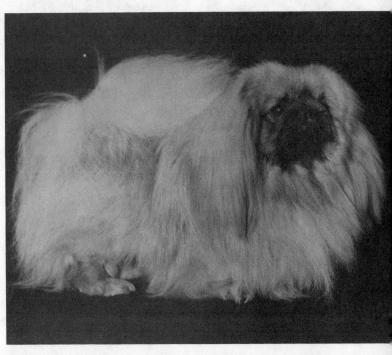

Prince's Tiger Eye of Claymore, bred and owned by Mrs Robert I. Ballinger, Jr. of the Claymore Pekingese, Villanova, Pennsylvania. Tiger is pictured here winning at the Pekingese Club of America Specialty show in March 1973, under judge Winifred Heckmann. Whelped in May, 1972, his sire is Ch. Fairy Prince of Kanghe ex Tiger Mist of Claymore. He is handled by Mrs Ballinger.

Claymore

Claymore Pekingese are owned by Mrs Robert I. Ballinger, Jr., at Villanova, Pennsylvania.

This is a small kennel (numbering usually about ten Pekingese) that has been in existence for less than three years. Mrs Ballinger thoroughly enjoys her dogs, which are purely a hobby, and her ambition is to own and show truly top quality members of the breed. She is off to a good start in this direction.

Claymore Pekingese at present include American and Bermudian Champion Pasha of West Winds, sired by Linsown Ku Chello, a grandson of English Champion Linsown Ku Che Pet. There is also Dorodea Yu Sam Tsun, by English Champion Yu Yang of Jamestown, only just starting out, with a five point major. Volksmana Mi Queen, by Chungking My Wong (which in turn is by International Champion Fu Yong of Jamestown) is a bitch that had gained thirteen points towards her title before her show career was interrupted for maternal duties. A puppy which Mrs Ballinger describes as her "first really good homebred," is Prince's Tiger Eye of Claymore (by Champion Fairy Prince of Kanghe). At nine months of age he took Reserve Winners Dog at the March 1973 Pekingese Club of America Specialty.

Above: Paweja's Willen Barkus, a young hopeful owned by Paul W. Ausman of Birmingham, Alabama, and named after a character in Dicken's David Copperfield. His sire was Ch. Yung Yu of Jenntora ex Paweja's Chynette; photograph taken in 1973.

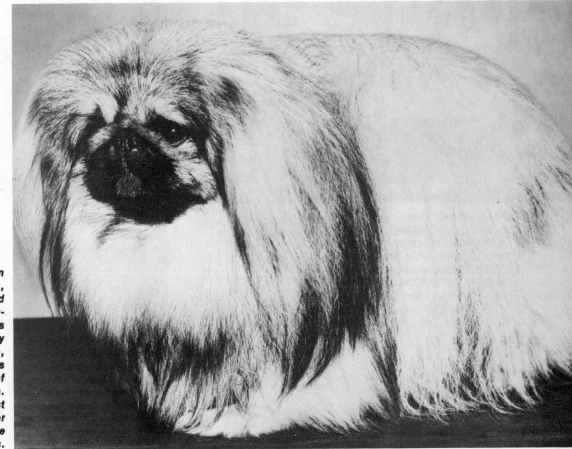

American and Bermudian Ch. Pasha of West Winds, whelped in July, 1970 and sired by Ch. Linsown Ku-Chello out of Tom-Mi's Jubilee Sing Lee. Bred by Mrs Horace H. Wilson, Pasha is owned by Mrs Robert I. Ballinger, Jr., of Villanova, Pennsylvania. Pasha was the first champion Pekingese for the Ballinger's Claymore Kennels.

119

Volksmana Mi Queen, or Ondine as she is called by her owner, Mrs Robert I. Ballinger, Jr., Claymore Kennels, Villanova, Pennsylvania. Bred by Mrs B.M. Acott, Ondine was sired by Chungking Mi-Yong ex Volksmana Solitaire, and was whelped in May of 1971.

Dai Lee

Dai Lee's Pekingese, in New Orleans, Louisiana, are owned by Mrs Althea Daily, who takes particular pride in her lovely bitch, Champion Annabelle of Tien Hia, a daughter of Champion Pin Tsun of Craigfoss ex Silver Princess of Tien Hia. Annabelle was bred by Mrs Murray Brooks, and on the first day she was campaigned (handled by Mrs Edna Voyles) she placed Winners Bitch and Best of Opposite Sex, and went on directly to complete her title.

Mrs Daily also owns Champion Paweja Ku Jon, that finished with five majors and two Toy Group seconds in two consecutive week-ends. Ku Jon is a son of the noted Champion Paweja's Ku Kan Jin (a puppy champion and winner of five Toy Groups and a Best in Show) and his dam was Champion Paweja's Wee Roc-N-Rohll. All of his grandparents hold titles, and he has a total of twenty-two champions in five generations behind him.

The other top stud at Dai Lee Kennels is a son of Champion Christopher of Tien Hia (Toy Group winner) ex Champion Simba Tar Baby of Orchard Hill (that finished with four majors). He is Dai Lee's Khan Temyin. A litter sister to this dog, Dai Lee's Lil Simba Tar Baby, won points as a puppy.

The Pekingese at Dai Lee Kennels include imports from England's Ralsham Kennel. A granddaughter of Champion Ku Lee of Orchard Hill is there too. The splendid bitch, Ralsham's Fanella Ku, producer of champions, was sold recently by Mrs Daily to Richard Cullen.

Mrs Althea Daily with a five point major winner at the 1971 Delta Pekingese Club show. On her left, the British import, Ralsham's Fenella Ku; on her right is the America-bred bitch winner, Joanna of Tien Hia. Mrs Daily's Dai Lee Kennels are located in New Orleans, Louisiana.

Left: Handler Edna Voyles and owner Mrs Althea Daily pose with winning Joanna of Tien Hia. Joanna won three days in succession at the Lexington, Louisville, and Hodgenville Kentucky shows in September 1972. Mrs Daily's Dai Lee Kennels are in New Orleans, Louisiana.

Right: Canadian and American Ch. Annabelle of Tien Hia, a beautiful bitch whelped in 1967, bred by Mrs Brooks, is pictured winning under judge Earle T. Adair in 1972 at an Indiana show. Her owners are Althea and Wallace Daily of the Dai Lee Kennels, New Orleans, Louisiana.

Above: Joanna of Tien Hia, bred by Mrs Murray B. Brooks, and owned by Wallace and Althea Daily of Louisiana. She is pictured here winning at a show under judge Robert Waters.

Above: Ch. Simba Tar Baby of Orchard Hill, beautiful black female Pekingese bred by E. Gatewood of Pennsylvania, and owned by Wallace and Althea Daily of the Dai Lee Kennels. Tar was whelped in 1967 and was sired by Westering Snow Bunting ex Shai Maing.

Below: Presleen Whisperina, bred by Miss Prescott and owned by Mrs Althea D. Daily of New Orleans, Louisiana.

Right: Lady Isbell of Seng Kye, whelped in 1968 and bred by Harry W. Aldrich. Owners, Althea and Wallace P. Daily of the Dai Lee Kennels.

Above: Top winning female Champion in England in 1972 and now an American champion with four major wins in six consecutive shows is English and American Ch. Ralsham's Lovely Lady, owned by Mrs Althea Daily of New Orleans. Lady was Best of Opposite Sex as well at the 1973 Westminster Kennel Club Show at Madison Square Garden in New York City.

Below: King Emperor T, magnificent Pekingese owned by Mrs Althea Daily of the Dai Lee Kennels in New Orleans, Louisiana.

Above: Mrs Althea Daily's Ch. Paweja's Ku Jon, whelped in 1967, and pictured winning at a recent show with his handler, Edna Voyles. He was bred by P.W. Ausman, and has Group Placings to his credit, including two Group Seconds from the classes.

Del Vila

The kennel name Del Vila of Scarsdale, New York, was registered in 1929 by Mrs Justin Herold and her sister, Miss Delphine J. McEntyre. Fine dogs of several breeds, Welsh Terriers, Cocker Spaniels, and Scottish Terriers in addition to Pekingese have been housed there. But always, with both Delphine and Vila (from whose first names the kennel prefix was derived) Pekingese have had a special place.

Some of us will recall the handsome dog, Del Vila Kong Moon, that was widely admired several decades back. And that beautiful little champion of the thirties, Champion Wee Jock of Hesketh, was a valuable addition to the kennel and represented England's fine Hesketh strain.

Among the most famous of the Del Vila dogs, one thinks immediately of the excellent Champion Del Vila Debonaire, a consistent winner during the sixties. By Champion Calartha Yen Lo of Suelane, he had Champion Rikki of Calartha and Champion Calartha Mandarin of Jehol ancestry on his sire's side, while his dam was strong in Champion Caversham Ko Ko of Shanruss and Alderbourne.

Then Champion Del Vila Chi Tu completed his title in twenty-eight days. A home-bred like Debonaire, he represents Caversham and Alderbourne strains. Ku Chi Tu's homebred son, Champion Del Vila Toney Pandy, is another that has done well at the shows. Del Vila Glamor Girl and Del Vila Bikini are two exquisite homebred bitches that were close to titles when they were withdrawn from the ring for maternity.

Right top: Del-Vila Tai-Lo, owned and bred by Mrs Justin Herold and Delphine J. McEntyre, and winner of the 1953 Futurity Puppy award at the Pekingese Club of America Specialty Show under judge Anna K. Nicholas. The sire was Ch. Fei Jai Son of Orchard Hill. Del-Vila Kennels are in Scarsdale, New York.

Right bottom: Pekingese Club of America Futurity winners, Del-Vila Wee San-Pan and Del-Vila Tai Yu S'Tien, also owned and bred by Delphine J. McEntyre and Mrs Justin Herold.

Above: At the 1964 Progressive Dog
Club, Ch. Del-Vila Debonaire won Winners Dog under judge Edwin S. Pickhardt. Breeders and co-owners were the
late Delphine J. McEntyre and, handling, Mrs Justin Herold.

Below: Ch. Del-Vila Toney Pandy emer-
ged as Best of Breed at the 1968 Wallkill
Kennel Club Show under judge Mrs
Horace Wilson. Owned and bred by the
late Delphine J. McEntyre and Mrs Jus-
tin Herold. Mrs Herold handling.
Pandy's sire was Ch. Del-Vila Ku-Chi-
Tu ex Del-Vila Fantessa. Shafer photo.

Because of their owners' popularity as judges, the Del Vila dogs have not been campaigned as widely as many others. Both Mrs Herold and Miss McEntyre have for years been in demand for important assignments, and although they judged in California and in England, they really preferred the shows nearer home. This, of course, did raise a conflict with exhibiting. Both appeared frequently on the Westminster panel, and at all the leading shows in the Eastern area.

Mrs Herold discontinued all breeding and kennel activity temporarily in 1970 following the death of Miss McEntyre. However, litters are again being planned and reared at Del Vila, and so more quality champions can be expected in the future. We understand that there are several exciting puppies coming along at this time, and Mrs Herold has also imported from England a beautiful grand-daughter of Champion St. Aubrey Carnival Music of Eastfield.

Mrs Herold is a former President of the Pekingese Club of America and was a governor of this club for many years. She and her sister were founders of the Saw Mill River Kennel Club in White Plains, New York, and Mrs Herold is still an active Committee Member.

Above: Del-Vila Glamor Girl, winning a five-point major as a puppy under judge James Trullinger at the Kennel Club of Northern New Jersey Show in 1962. Her sire was Ch. St. Aubrey Jin T'Sun of Holmvallee ex Del-Vila Flower Drum Song. Owned and handled by Mrs Justin Herold.

Below: Ch. Cho Sen Kan Venture, bred, owned and handled by Edna Voyles of Louisville, Kentucky, is pictured finishing at the 1965 Chicago International Show. Kan Venture is a producer of champions at Mrs Voyles' Cho Sen Kennels.

Below: Ch. Cho Sen Brite Mischief, top winning Pekingese for 1964 and number three Toy. He has six Bests in Show to his credit and over 21 Group Firsts. He was sired by a Best in Show winner, Ch. Cho Sen Brite Future. Owners G.W. and Edna Voyles of Louisville, Kentucky.

127

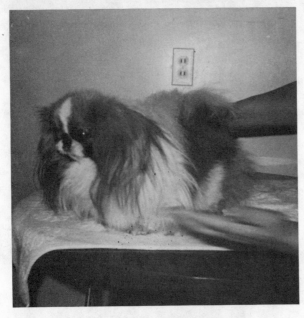

Left: Fancy Pants of Dragonhai, exquisite sire of three champions to date. He is a miniature parti-color Pekingese of exceptional quality and is owned by Harold Fraser and Allen Williams of the Dragonhai Pekingese, Aquasco, Maryland.

Below: Ch. Dragonhai Kristal Bukay winning at 6½ months of age under judge Edwin Pickhardt at the Sara Bay Kennel Club show in 1967. Breeders, Dragonhai Kennels, Aquasco, Maryland.

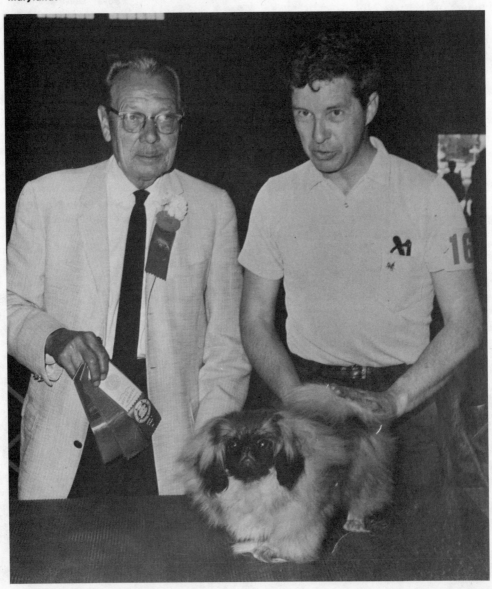

Dragonhai

Dragonhai Pekingese, at Aquasco, Maryland, came into existence as the result of a double project of the cousins and business partners Allen Williams and Harold Fraser, each to surprise the other with a puppy as a birthday gift. Hal had frequently mentioned his affection for a pair of Pekingese belonging to a childhood friend, and Allen acknowledged having been completely won away from his Toy Poodle interest when he saw a friend's lovely pale biscuit Pekingese, son of Champion Dorrister's Wu Bee. So what, each thought, could make a more perfect gift for the other than a Pekingese?

Hal's birthday came first, and on it he received a card bearing the picture of a red Pekingese puppy and the notation "This is an I.O.U. Your present hasn't quite been born yet." Two weeks later the foundation bitch of the Dragonhai Pekingese came into the world and was named Fuji Mum of Banyan, which was their original kennel name in honor of the Florida mansion where they lived at the time. Fuji's sire combined Champion Dream Boi of Pekeholme and the bitch line of Mr and Mrs Mapes' famous Whitworths. Her dam was by Champion Thomas Quong Kee's Ho Ying, from a daughter of Champion Alderbourne Cream Puff of Tongland.

As Fuji grew and flourished, so did her owner's interest in the breed, and it was soon decided that Fuji should have a litter. The stud selected was Chin Choo's Loo Chen, closely bred to the El Acre strain. This mating resulted in the June 1960 whelping of Champion Fan Tan of Banyan. She became their first

Top right: *Ch. Dragonhai Chota Benji, the winner at the 1968 Harrisburg Kennel Club show under judge Mrs Maxner. Benji's sire was Ch. St. Aubrey Wee Yen of Church Road Farm, ex Shan Gri La of Dragonhai. Co-owners Hal Fraser and Allen Willaims of Aquasco, Maryland.*

Ch. West Winds Fan Gee, grandson of Ch. Caversham KuKu of Yam, and out of Goofus Allouetta. Fan Gee's sire was Ch. Bettina's Kow Kow. Fan Gee finished with a four point major as Best of Winners at a Progressive Dog Club show under judge Anna Katherine Nicholas. Fan gee was bred by Mrs Horace H. Wilson and is owned by Dorothy P. Lathrop of Falls Village, Connecticut.

Bottom: *Lute Song of Dragonhai wins at the 1967 Pekingese Club of America show under judge William Bergum. Owned by Hal Fraser and Allen Willaims of Aquasco, Maryland; Mr. Willaims handling.*

Left: Ch. Cho Sen's Futurama, Best of Breed at the Atlanta Pekingese Specialty Show with breeder, owner and handler Edna Voyles. On the right is Cho Sen's Gay Venturouse, Best of Winners, and finished for the title. Venturouse, Best of Winners, and finished for the title. Venturouse is the dam of Ch. Cho Sen's Brite N Gay, owned by Cleda Olsen of the Shady Acres Kennels.

A fabulous English Pekingese of the thirties. . . English Ch. Yu Chuan of Alderbourne, winner of 20 Challenge Certificates in three years; owned by Miss Marjorie Ashton Cross. He is pictured here at just 9 months of age.

Left: Ch. Jamestown Kan-Jin of Caversham, owned by Mrs G.W. Voyles of Louisville, Kentucky. Photo by Frasie.

homebred puppy, the mother of their first homebred champion, and herself their second champion bred at home.

After several unsuccessful attempts to purchase quality foundation stock in America, Mr Fraser and Mr Williams answered an advertisement by Orchidell Kennels of Northern Ireland. Chi La Tu of Orchidell, tracing back to Puffball (the fountainhead here, through Caversham, Alderbourne, Perryacre, and Mathena stock), was imported and became an American champion. She has exerted a profound influence on the Dragonhai line.

Enthusiasm for the Caversham strain then induced them to write to Miss I. M. de Pledge of their ambition for an outstanding kennel and asking if she had a dog for sale. This resulted in the purchase of a six-month-old puppy (sired by Champion Ku Jin of Caversham from Champion Caversham Chik-Ita of Swanbury) that grew up to become American Champion Shan Jin of Caversham. In addition to his excellent type and quality, Shan Jin brought with him balance, posture, show attitude, and that undefinable star-quality that sets a dog apart. Both partners have frequently stated that without him there probably never would have been a Dragonhai.

It was at this period that the partners decided to leave Florida for the Washington area, and since early 1962 they have been settled in rural Maryland. The present name of Dragonhai was adopted upon relocation of the kennel.

Shantung Fan of Dragonhai captures Winners Bitch at the Pekingese Club of America Specialty Show in March 1964. Shafer photograph.

Canadian Ch. Hi-Winds Ju-Li Treasure, bred by Mrs Benjamin Sugden of British Columbia, Canada, and is owned by Dr Tad Pfister, of Nogales, Arizona. The sire was Canadian Ch. Ravenswood Dubonnet and the dam Ku Zinnia of Farnsworth, two imports.

Below: Lin Gow Tro Jin Merry Man, bred by Mrs Arthur B. Gowie and owned by Dorothy P. Lathrop of Falls Village, Connecticut. Lin Gow is finishing toward his championship at the time this book is being written [1973]—he already has a Toy Group placing to his credit and lacks only one major to finish. His sire is Ch. Calartha Mandarin of Jehol ex Ch. St. Aubrey Marianne of Elsdon.

English import Miladdo of Pendarris was an English Junior Warrant Winner in England and had 7 points including a 4-point major in America before an injury cut short his show ring career. Bred by Lydia Kinnersley and sired by Jin Tong of Pendarris ex Sharon of Ingford, he is owned by Pat O'Shea of Sioux Falls, South Dakota.

Left: Canadian Ch. Ravenswood Dubonnet, import, bred by Mrs I. Young of England, and owned by Mrs Benjamin Sugden of B.C., Canada. Dubonnet is shown going Best of Winners under the late judge Vic Williams of Vancouver, B.C., Canada, at the Kamloops and District Kennel Club Show in June, 1971. Sire was Silverdjinn Whisky Mac ex Ravenswood Janine.

In 1965 Dragonhai came to its first Pekingese Club of America Specialty Show, again on Hal's birthday, with three of their Pekes. Anna Katherine Nicholas was judging and she was so impressed with the quality of these Pekingese that all three entries were declared winners in their classes. Future Champion Shantung Fan of Dragonhai (the first born daughter of Champion Shan Jin of Caversham and Champion Fan Tan of Banyan) went from the Bred by Exhibitor Class to Winners Bitch and Best of Winners her first time in the ring, and Gimmi Kissi of Dragonhai won Best Puppy in Show.

The following year another Fan Tan daughter, Champion Charme of Dragonhai, was Best Futurity Puppy and Reserve Winners Bitch at the tender age of seven-and-a-half months. With one daughter finished and another on the way, Fan Tan made Dragonhai's first trip to Westminster, where she captured a four point major by taking Winners Bitch.

Dragonhai has never been a "Specials" kennel, preferring to concentrate on consistent winning with many dogs rather than big winning with one. They have not shown a "special" more than half a dozen times, but take pride in the fact that in ten years of showing they have made twenty champions, fifteen of them homebred and the other five carefully selected imports.

Among these champions are Shantung Fan of Dragonhai, Shan Jingle of Dragonhai, Shan Sonnet of Dragonhai, Shansun Ra of Dragonhai, Shan Osiris of Dragonhai, Shan Isis of Dragonhai, Shana Jindi of Dragonhai, Meadowbrook Jingle Merrily, and Radiance of Dragonhai. The above champions were all sired by Champion Shan Jin of Caversham. Other prized possessions include Champion Dragonhai Chota Benji by Champion St. Aubrey Wee Yen of Church Road Farm from a Shan Jin daughter, and from Champion Chi La Tu of Orchidell came Champions Ginian of

Dragonhai, Dragonhai Kristal Bukay, and her daughter Champion Candanham Kris An The Mum.

Dud-Lee's

Dud-Lee's Pekingese, owned by Mr and Mrs W. L. Dudley, was begun in 1959 when Ruby and Bill Dudley thought that they were buying a Pomeranian for their daughter Rita's twelfth birthday. But this turned out to be a Pekingese-Pomeranian cross: to make things right, the breeder gave the Dudleys the best Pekingese bitch she had. Goldie was far from a top show specimen, but she had all the charms with which Pekes so quickly endear themselves to those who know them.

Several years later Ruby Dudley determined to breed Pekingese of which she could be really proud. She bought a good bitch from Mrs Quigley, Nia Le Txu of Orchard Hill; it refused to show so was bred to a son of Champion Bey Li Purple Passion. One daughter was retained from this litter, and in turn was mated to the Dudleys' first champion, Zodiac Joe. Two of her grandchildren are still in the kennel.

Champion Zodiac Joe attracted Mrs Dudley's attention at a show in 1965. Thinking him the most beautiful Pekingese she ever had seen, she persuaded owner Pat Cole to sell him to her. Joe was bred by Penny D. Macklin, sired by Champion Mr Peepers of Brown's Den, from the great producing bitch Monte Verde Kioko. The first week-end Mrs Dudley had him out, Clara Alford asked if she might take him to campaign. Joe was started out with Mrs Alford in April 1965, after a winter for growing coat and promptly became a champion by placing in the Toy Group several times from the classes. That Fall Mrs Dudley herself showed Joe, and he became a Toy Group winner and on the Top Ten Pekingese list.

Top right: Zodiac Joe's Luv-Li of Dud-Lee's, bred and owned by Mrs Ruby Dudley of Creston, Iowa.

Ch. Dud-Lee's Little Joe, sired by Ch. Zodiac Joe ex Presleen Featherstep, is owned, bred and handled by Mrs W.L. Dudley of Creston, Iowa.

Bottom: Ch. Khi-Lyn's Tometta of Dud-Lee's, winner of the North Central Illinois Pekingese Specialty Show Sweepstakes over ane entry of 15 at the January 1973 show. Tometta was just seven months old at the time this photo was taken, and she has since finished for her title in May, 1973 with three majors, under judge Gus Wolf, at 11 months old. The judge of the Sweepstakes was Ruth Ludvigson. Owned and shown by Mrs Ruby Dudley of Dud-Lee's Kennels, Creston, Iowa.

133

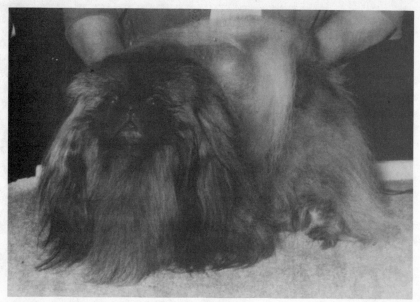

Above: Ch. Ku Chin Tom-Mi of Seng Kye, taken shortly before his death on December 11, 1972 at ten years of age. Mrs Ruby Dudley of Creston, Iowa in August, 1969, from Mrs A. Ruschhaupt.

Right: Ch. Beh Tang, bred and owned by Dorothy P. Lathrop of Falls Village, Connecticut. This bitch made her championship in three shows with five point major wins. She also won a Toy Group at Westminster. Her sire is Ch. Jai Son Fu of Orchard Hill ex Ch. Cheetah of Dah-Lyn.

Below: Ch. Zodiac Joe's Buffy of Dud-Lee's, finished to his title with a four point major at the Egyptian Kennel Club Show in April, 1969. He is owned and shown by Mrs Ruby Dudley.

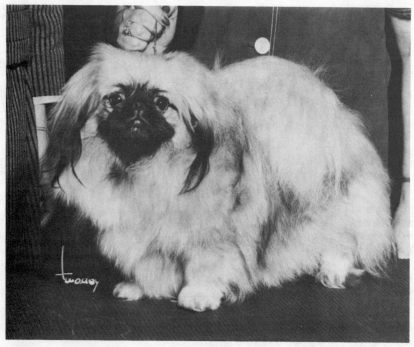

134

Much of the success at Dud-Lee's Kennels is credited to Champion Zodiac Joe. He provided foundation for the kennel and is behind the majority of the fourteen Dud-Lee's champions; he is sire of Champion Zodiac Joe's Buffy of Dud-Lee's and of Champion Dud-Lee's Little Joe. The former was made a champion under Lorraine Heichel's handling, the latter under that of Mrs Dudley. It was this that gave Mrs Dudley the confidence to handle her own dogs as she has done almost without exception since that time. Champion Dud-Lee's Little Joe is the grandsire of Champion Simon's Dragon of Dud-Lee's and Champion Masterpiece Zodiac of Dud-Lee's.

In the summer of 1969 a lovely granddaughter of Champion Zodiac Joe was bred to Champion St. Aubrey Manikin of Elsdon. From this mating came Champion Manikins' Simon of Dud-Lee's (owned by the Dudleys) and Champion Simon's Manikin of Dud-Lee's (owned and shown by Vance and Dorothy Tyndall). Champion Manikin's Simon of Dud-Lee's sired Champion Simon's Dragon of Dud-Lee's, from a daughter of Duane Doll's Champion Dud-Lee's Little Joe.

During the eventful year of 1969 Mrs Dudley purchased the marvelous American-bred Best in Show winner and great producer, International Champion Ku Chin Tom Mi of Seng Kye from Irene Ruschaupt. Tom Mi was bred by Amy Aldrich in California and won four all breed Bests in Show, nine Specialties, thirty-nine Toy Groups, and twenty Toy Group seconds. He has been Best of Breed at Westminster in 1965 over an impressive array of famous champions; in 1967 he was Fourth Toy and Second Pekingese in the nation, and was also top Western Toy. He was Top Sire in 1971, and the first Pekingese named by *Kennel Review* as a top producer.

Tom Mi died in December 1972 when only ten years old. His influence will be felt for many generations as he was truly an excellent, dominant sire. Fifteen of his progeny are champions, with several others headed toward titles.

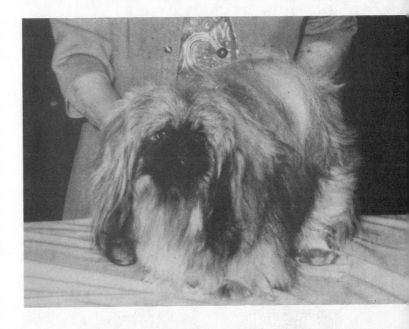

Top right: The famous Ch. Zodiac Joe, stud force at the Pekingese Kennels of Mrs Ruby Dudley of Creston, Iowa.

English Ch. Linsown Ku-Che-Tu, winner of three Challenge Certificates and sire of numerous winners, including the famous American Ch. Merellen Manikin. He won the Toy Group and C.C. at the Manchester, England show at just 10 months of age. Owned and bred by Mrs Pownall of Grove Lodge, Essex, England.

Bottom: Ch. Tom-Mi Masterpiece Sing-Lee, bred by Mrs A.A. Ruschhaupt and owned by Mrs W.L. Dudley.

Tom Mi offspring owned by the Dudleys include Champion Tom Mi's Yuh Chin of Dud-Lee's, Champion Tom Mi's Khi Lyn Ette of Dud-Lee's, Champion Khi Lyn's Tometta of Dud-Lee's, Champion Dud-Lee's Khi Lyn Etta, and Champion Tom Mi's Ho Tai of Dud-Lee's. Champion Yuh Chin finished in six shows with four majors. Lyn Ette, Tomsetta, and Khi Lyn Etta are full sisters, their dam being Mrs Dudley's beloved producer, Champion Khi Yu-Ki Ku's Khi Lyn of Dud-Lee's, that won eight consecutive shows out of nine to finish in the Spring of 1970. She is sired by a pointed son of Champion Khi Kuki Ku of Wei Toi that was purchased from Fourwinds Kennels ex a granddaughter of Sunshen Yen Chu.

In January 1971, the Dudleys again went to Sing Lee for an addition to their kennel. This time they purchased one of Tom Mi's best sons, Champion Tom Mi Masterpiece Sing Lee. That this was a wise selection has already been proved; he is sire of the exquisite little bitch, Champion Masterpiece Naomi of Dud-Lee's, from a double Champion Podiac Joe granddaughter, and also of the magnificent young Toy Group winner, Champion Masterpiece Zodiac of Dud-Lee's, from a daughter of Champion Dud-Lee's Little Joe.

Mrs Dudley considers Champion Masterpiece Zodiac the best Pekingese yet produced in her kennel, and the consensus of those who have judged him is that he has an exciting future in the show ring. At eighteen months of age, he has been Best of Breed twenty-eight times, has won two Specialty Shows, two Toy Groups, and several seconds; he was handled on all occasions by Mrs Dudley.

Another little dog the Dudleys are proud to own is Champion Ku Chin Timothy of Tom Thumb, purchased from his breeder, Maida L. Sutton. Timothy is a grandson and a great-grandson of International Champion Ku Chin Tom Mi of Seng Kai, being sired by Champion Isaiah Sing Lee of Tom Thumb ex Panelli's Tashma of Tom Thumb.

Five Dud-Lee's homebred champions gained their titles in 1972, and five others produced in this kennel finished during the first six months of 1973.

Fourwinds

The first Pekingese at Fourwinds Farm in Seneca, Illinois, was purchased as a pet. But after one dog show, owners Mary Ann and Bob Jackson decided to establish a kennel with top quality show stock. Mr Jackson's experience in raising and showing champion Dorset sheep and Angus cattle was extremely helpful, as they realized from the start the importance of bloodlines and genetics.

With breeding in mind, their early purchases were from Orchard Hill, Dah Lyn, and Langridge. From the former came a male, Feisal Lui, and a bitch, Mi Jai Naneen. Bred to one another they produced the first champion whelped at Fourwinds Kennels. This was Lu Jai Me Too and she got off to a flying start when just six months old by going Best Puppy and Reserve Winners Bitch under Mrs Sadie Edmiston at the Chicago Pekingese Club Specialty.

From Dah Lyn came Ku Tong of Dah Lyn, the male that won several points and was also the sire and grandsire of champions. Wee Yula of Dah Lyn was bred to Lui and she produced the Jacksons' second homebred champion, Lu Tong Tu of Fourwinds.

When Mrs Amy Smith's Langridge Kennel was offered for sale after her death, three bitches of entirely English bloodlines were purchased by Fourwinds. These included an imported daughter of the famous English Champion Ku Chi of Caversham and a daughter of hers sired by English Champion Tong Tuo of Alderbourne. The daughter, Ku Tong Ku of Langridge, quickly made her championship and was a marvelous bitch, going Best of Breed over Specials en route to her title.

About the same time, brother and sister puppies were purchased from Mrs Stella Solecki, well-known handler and Pekingese personality of that era. These were of Orchard Hill bloodlines, and the male (Royal Mon of Park Manor), delighted his new owner by going Best Puppy and on to Winners Dog and Best of Winners at the Chicago Pekingese Specialty when eight months old and appearing for the first time in the ring. His title was gained shortly thereafter.

All of the above took place during the fifties, and the Jacksons have since that time been fortunate in owning some of the top sires in the breed.

Champion Hi Oasis of Brown's Den, purchased as a youngster from his breeder, Mrs Cora W. Brown, won his title with all majors

Mandarina of Fourwinds, owned and shown by Mrs Robert Jackson of Seneca, Illinois.

Ch. Galaxys Adonis, pictured winning Best of Winners at the 1973 Pekingese Club of America Winter Specialty Show in New York City. The judge was Mrs Winifred Heckmann. Adonis has won majors at three different specialties: Delta Pekingese Club in New Orleans in 1972, N.C. Illinois Pekingese Club in 1973 and this winter specialty. Shown and owned by Robert Jackson, Fourwinds Pekingese, Seneca, Illinois. Evelyn Shafer photograph.

Left: Ch. Khi Yu Lee Sa of Fourwinds winning Best of Winners and finishing for her championship under judge Clara Alford at the 1968 Pekingese Club of America Specialty. Owned by Mr and Mrs Robert Jackson of Seneca, Illinois, and handled by Mr Jackson.

Below: The 1970 Wheaton, Illinois Kennel Club show found Mani Chips of Fourwinds Best of Winners from puppy class. He is handled by Mrs Robert Jackson, while his grandsire, Ch. Merellen Manikin won Best of Breed and was handled by Robert Jackson. The judge was Clara Alford. Photo by Ritter.

Right: Ch. Khi Ku's Kin of Fourwinds, pictured winning Best of Breed at the Lake Shore Kennel Club show under judge Percy Roberts. He is the sire of five champions. Handled here by Robert Jackson who co-owns with Mrs Jackson.

Below: The 1970 Lake Shore Kennel Club show saw Best of Breed win go to Ch. Merellen Manikin, while on the left Ray Mel's Mi-T-Manikin was Winners Dog and Best of Winners for five points from the puppy class; on the right, Lindy's Dream Valley of Loring was Winners Bitch from puppy class for five points. Bother was sired by Manikin. Handlers are Richard Cotton, Lorraine Heichel, and Robert Jackson.

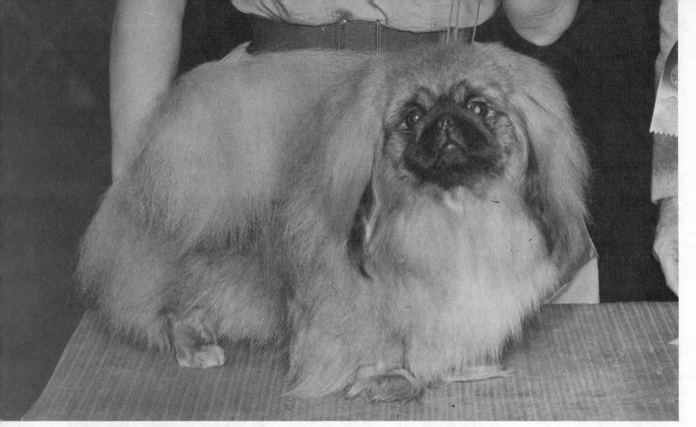

Ch. Khi Yuki Ku of Wei-Toi, sire of seven champions. He is a grandson of the famous English Ch. Caversham KuKu of Yam. Owners are Mr and Mrs Robert M. Jackson of Seneca, Illinois.

Ch. Hi-O-Flame of Fourwinds, 14th champion sired by the Robert Jackson's Ch. Hi-Oasis of Brown's Den, shown here winning his class at the 1968 Pekingese Club of America Winter Specialty Show, under the late judge Alva Rosenberg. He is handled by owner Robert Jackson. Flame has since been purchased by Althea Adams.

and Bests of Breed over specials. But his true fame was to come as a sire. Three of his first litter won majors and two finished as puppies. He was a very dominant sire, stamping his type on all his offspring from bitches of various bloodlines. In different years he was the top Pekingese sire of champions; from him came a total of fourteen champions and many second generation offspring who also became champions. This dog was entirely American-bred for four generations.

Watching the Pekingese judging at Chicago International one year, the Jacksons' attention quickly focused on a young, bright red dog as he went from the American-bred Class to Best of Winners for five points. Later that year they succeeded in buying for their kennel this Champion Khi Tuki Ku. He was a son of Champion Caversham Khi Ku of Pendarvis, who sired numerous champions and was, in turn, a son of English Champion Caversham Ku Ku of Yam.

A complete outcross, Champion Yuki's bloodlines agreed perfectly with Hi Oasis daughters and he sired seven champions. He twice won the Stud Dog Class at the Pekingese Club of America Specialty, and was a great favorite of his owners.

The best known of his sons is Champion Khi Ku's Kin of Fourwinds, whose dam was Hi Oasis Merri of Fourwinds, a Champion Hi Oasis of Brown's Den daughter. He sired five champions and is grandsire of a dozen others.

Perhaps the best purchase thus far made by Fourwinds was that of Merellen Manikin from an English breeder, Mrs P. E. Gomer. His handler was Lorraine Heichel and the first time in the ring together he went Best in Show at Atlanta, Georgia, under Louis Murr. Next day he won the Pekingese Club of Georgia Specialty under Mrs Harp over other Best in Show dogs. He gained all of his championship points with Group victories; by the time he was fifteen months old he was on the list of Top Ten Toys in America and had two Bests in Show and eight Toy Groups.

Manikin now has a total of fifteen champions to his credit; the first puppy he sired won her title, and numerous others have earned points and there are many second generation champions. He was the leading Pekingese sire of 1972, five of his progeny having finished during that year. He retired from the ring with 23 Toy Groups in addition to three Specialty Bests of Breed and his all-breed Best in Show.

Fourty-four Pekingese owned or sold by Mr and Mrs Jackson have thus far become champions, and there are a goodly number sired by Fourwinds dogs that have similarly distinguished themselves.

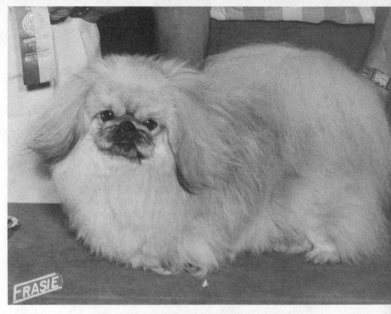

Ch. Hi-Oasis of Brown's Den, sire of 15 champions, and owned by Mr and Mrs Robert Jackson of Seneca, Illinois. Photo by Frasie.

A magnificent puppy which grew up to be a Best in Show winner—Ch. Merellen Manikin, also owned by the Robert Jacksons.

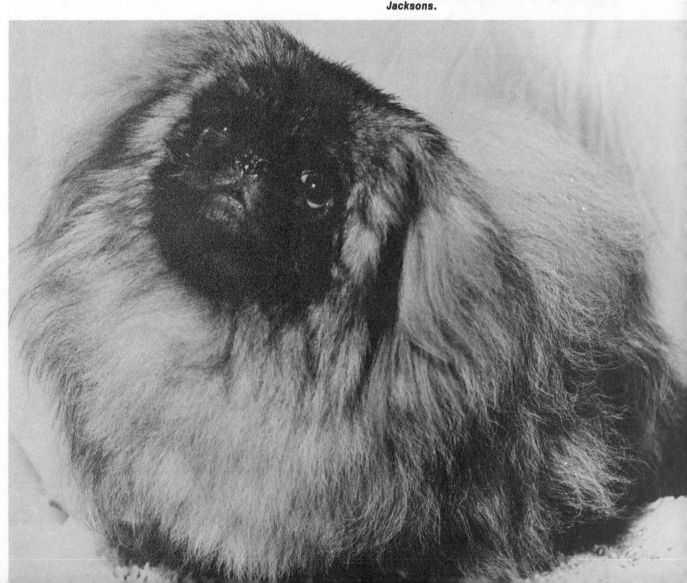

Freelands

Mrs Mildred T. Imrie's interest in Pekingese started as long ago as 1912, and there have since then always been one or more dogs of this breed in her life—even though until fairly recently her Freelands Kennel at Lahaska, Pennsylvania, has been more closely associated with Cocker Spaniels at first and then with Miniature Poodles. Freelands produced over forty Cockers that gained championships in less than a decade; after World War II, Poodles predominated and won an array of championships and other awards. During the past few years however, Pekingese have taken over. Mrs Imrie employs a kennel-man, but she enjoys training, grooming, and showing her dogs personally and is having great fun with them.

It was in the mid-fifties that Mrs Imrie brought a Pekingese bitch home with her from an English visit. From this came the lovely dog, Vee of Freelands, that had all but two points for his title when illness terminated his career.

Mrs Imrie then purchased a bitch (Livingston's Shen Moo of Womer), from Mrs Livingston of California and made her a champion. Next St. Aubrey Marina of Elsdon was shown to her title, followed by Ko Ko's Samee of Baildiff, handled for her by Tom Gately.

Enthusiasm increased; and when Mrs Imrie saw St. Aubrey Goofus Brescia, she promptly fell in love with him and with Mrs Nathan Allen (who had also owned noted Poodles) decided that they would like to co-own him. He has been shown rather infrequently, among his wins are several Specialty Shows, important Bests of Breed, and Toy Group victories. Ruth Burnette Sayrres handles this excellent dog.

Champion Mar B Lorraine of St. Aubrey was purchased by Mrs Imrie and bred to Brescia, from which came Champion Su Zee of Freeland. In 1972 she was the first bitch to go Best of Breed at the Pekingese Club of America Specialty Show in thirty-three years. Her litter brother, Chin Kee of Freeland, lacks but one point for his championship. He was victim of an unfortunate accident that held him back from competition for a year, but he recently gained his two majors.

St. Aubrey Goofus Monza was purchased by Mrs Imrie and became a champion, placing in Toy Groups in four shows. He is shown only occasionally as he dislikes hot weather. Monza has also sired quality youngsters, and for one daughter in particular Mrs Imrie has high hopes.

The Freelands stud force also includes Champion Yendis Bugle Boy, a dog that Mrs Imrie saw in England as a puppy and showed here to his championship. Singlewell Battling is a fabulous black boy that has not yet started to campaign, beyond winning his class at the Pekingese Club of Southern New Jersey Specialty in 1972. A splendid year-old son of his will also soon be in competition. With

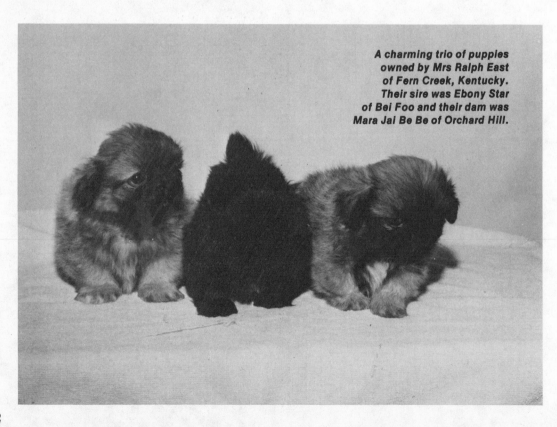

A charming trio of puppies owned by Mrs Ralph East of Fern Creek, Kentucky. Their sire was Ebony Star of Bei Foo and their dam was Mara Jai Be Be of Orchard Hill.

William Blair, Mrs Imrie also co-owns Champion St. Aubrey Goofus Diablo, a full sister to Brescia.

Ho Dynasty

Mrs G. Blauvelt-Moss is pleased with the good fortune by which her Ho Dynasty strain of Pekingese will be carried on even after she is gone. Instead of being allowed to die out as has so often happened with important kennels, hers will continue because a nine-year-old girl named Jennifer had stopped to admire three little Ho Dynasty littermates at a dog show. She was joined by her parents, Melvin and Joanne Goble, who explained that Jennifer had been promised a small dog to show, and it was Jennifer's decision that this must be a Ho Dynasty Pekingese.

Shortly thereafter a partnership was formed and all of Mrs Blauvelt-Moss' Pekingese were put in joint ownership with the Gobles. Legal papers were drawn up willing all of her rights and obligations in connection with Ho Dynasty to Mr and Mrs Goble, who will honor them. The authors congratulate Mrs Blauvelt-Moss on her foresight and concern for the future of her dogs, and on having taken such positive action. For anyone owning even one pet this is important to do, and especially so where an excellent strain of show stock is concerned and can be perpetuated by a little careful planning.

A six-week-old puppy was originally responsible for the love affair between Gilma Blauvelt-Moss and Pekingese that was to last a lifetime. The invaluable teachings of Jack Royce, access to his fabulous library, and the opportunity to study his superb collection of English pedigrees are gratefully acknowledged by Mrs Blauvelt-Moss.

Mrs Blauvelt-Moss wrote to Alderbourne and Caversham requesting the best bitches available. These she purchased in whelp to leading English studs. She also purchased through an English advertisement the last son and daughter of the famous Puffball of Chungking. They were from the same dam that bore Mrs Quigley's Champion Kai Lung of Vinedeans.

Unfortunately the kennel had to be temporarily disbanded, except for two thirteen- and fourteen-year-old "youngsters." But after several years of absence from the dog show world, Mrs Blauvelt-Moss again became active, starting out with a visit to Orchard Hill. There she saw the three-month-old future champion, Nia Ku Tulyar, which she was told was not for sale. Also seen was another lovely dog that was to become Champion Ku Chi's Kris of Orchard Hill. Believing that she

PCA Ch. Ho Dynasty's T'Su Hsi photographed as an adult. This lovely dog has a Group First and several Group Placings to his credit as well as many Bests of Breed over male Specials. Owned by Mrs Gilma Blauvelt-Moss of Hohokus, New Jersey and Mr Fred D'Amato.

Progressive Dog Club Show in 1957 shows judge Anna Katherine Nicholas awarding Winners Dog to Mrs Mary Brewster. William Brown photograph.

Right: Ch. Zin Ru of Micklee pictured as a puppy while making his mark in England before he was imported to America by Mrs Gilma Blauvelt-Moss, Ho Dynasty Pekingese, Hohokus, New Jersey. He is now co-owned by Mrs Blauvelt-Moss and the Melvin Gobles.

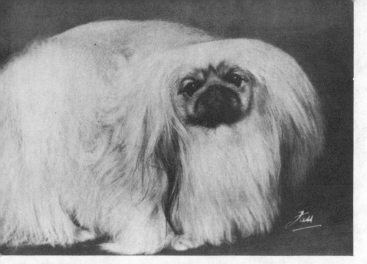

Above: English and American Ch. Mathilda of Kettlemere, imported by Mrs Gilma Blauvelt-Moss of Hohokus, New Jersey, owner of the Ho Dynasty Pekingese. Mathilda has passed on her regal glamour and refinement to five generations of Ho Dynasty Pekingese.

Above: Ho Dynasty's Castinet, pictured winning the Puppy Toy Group at the Kennel Club of Northern New Jersey Match show in 1969, handled by her breeder Gila Blauvelt-Moss who co-owns Castinet with Terrence Childs. She is now pointed and on the way to her championship.

Below: Mrs Gilma Blauvelt-Moss with Mary Poppins, Best Senior Puppy in the Toy Group at the 1966 Ramapo Kennel Club Match Show. Bushman photograph.

Above: American and Canadian Ch. Ku Chi's Kris of Orchard Hill, owned by Joan Sisco and Gilma Blauvelt-Moss of New Jersey. Kris was Winners Dog from the Bred by Exhibitor Class at a Westminster Kennel Club show under judge Anna Katherine Nicholas.

145

Above: Ho Dynasty's Zin Buddha and Go-Go photographed at three months of age. Buddha is owned by Joan Sisco and Gilma Blauvelt-Moss and Go-Go is now owned by Mrs Gerald Fitzgerald of Amsterdam, New York, and Florida. Their dam is Ho Dynasty's Ch. Coppleston Pu Zin Zee.

Below: Ch. Ho Dynasty's Desperado, photographed at just one year of age. This magnificent show winner is owned by Karen and Emidio Franzoso of South Bound Brook, New Jersey, and photographed for them by William P. Gilbert.

could not have Tulyar, Mrs Blauvelt-Moss returned home with Kris. But Tulyar was not forgotten, and eventually Mrs Quigley was persuaded to sell him too.

The breeding of Pekingese soon became the entire interest of Mrs Blauvelt-Moss. Of primary importance to a future breeder was of course the acquisition of the best bitch she could purchase from a top producing line. Thus she chose Copplestone Pu Zin Zee, by Tri-International Champion Copplestone Pu Zin, whose sire, Pu Zee, had at the time produced more champions than any other Pekingese in England.

American, Bermudian, and Canadian Champion Nia Ku Tulyar of Orchard Hill finished his American title during his first year. American and Canadian Champion Ku Chi's Kris of Orchard Hill gained his Canadian title the same year. Champion Copplestone Pu Zin Zee was Winners Bitch and Best of Opposite Sex at Westminster her first year, completing her title in time to be mated to Kris. This produced Ho Dynasty's Go Go that won the Pekingese Club of America Futurity when only five days over six months old. Ho Dynasty's Buddha went to Winners Dog from the Bred-by-Exhibitor Class at Westminster under Anna Katherine Nicholas.

From Tulyar's first litter, Ho Dynasty had a record-breaking Pekingese Club of America Champion Ho Dynasty's Tsu Hsi. Shown entirely from the Puppy Class and taking Winners Bitch when eight months old at the Pekingese Club of America Summer Specialty under the eminent English breeder-judge Mrs Warner Hill, (who co-owned the Cavershams during their latter years with Mary de Pledge), she finished with a Best Toy award at only ten months under the late Alva Rosenberg. There was also a lovely, successful sister from the litter Champion Ho Dynasty's Mary Poppins.

Top right: Ho Dynasty's Sunny Jim pictured at 10 months of age winning Winners Dog under judge Tom Stevenson at the Kennel Club of Pasadena Show on the way to his championship. Jim is co-owned by Gloria L. Wallis and Kay Crow, pictured handling him. His sire was Ch. Ho Dynasty's Intrepid and his dam Ch. Ho Dynasty's Fuji, bred by Mrs G. Blauvelt-Moss. Joan Ludwig photograph.

Bottom right: Ho Dynasty's Bit O'Breshia, winner of the sweepstakes at the Pekingese Club of Southern New Jersey under judge Harry Aldrich. She has several Bests of Breed and other wins to her credit while on the way to her championship. She is owned by Mrs Nathan Allen.

Ho Dynasty's Renel's Toya Gin, pictured winning Best of Breed at the 1972 Saw Mill River Kennel Club Show. Sired by American Bermudian and Canadian Ch. Nia Ku Tulyar of O.H. ex American and Canadian Ch. Ho Dynasty's Tallulah. She is co-owned by Gilma Blauvelt-Moss and Terrence Childs. She is being shown by Mr Childs.

Below: Ch. Ho Dynasty's Darin Yung Man pictured winning Winners Dog at nine months of age at the Trenton Kennel Club Show under judge Grybinski. He was sired by the American, Bermudian, and Canadian Ch. Nia Ku Tulyar of O.H. ex Ch. Roma of St. Aubrey-Elsdon. At the time this photograph was taken he needed only a few points to finish to championship. Handled by Richard Bauer for co-owners Gilma Blauvelt-Moss and the Gobles.

Below: Ho Dynasty's Chub-Bie Checkers shown here winning Best of Winners under the late judge John Murphy. Chub-Bie has two Bests of Breed to his credit while on the way to his championship. He is co-owned by Melvin Goble and Gilma Blauvelt-Moss; Mr Goble is handling.

For another top producing line, Mrs Blauvelt-Moss purchased from St. Aubrey Kennels a champion daughter of Champion Calartha Mandarin of Jehol, a champion daughter of Champion St. Aubrey Mario of Elsdon, and a second daughter of Mario which she later made a champion. Every litter from each of these three bitches produced at least two champions. Of these, Champion Ho Dynasty's Fuji finished with seventeen points in four shows, thirteen of them in three days, and American and Canadian Champion Ho Dynasty's Intrepid took Best Brace in Show with his sire, Tulyar, in keen all-breed competition.

It was a 2 a.m. telephone call from the owners of St. Aubrey Kennels that finally settled the question of "who gets Mathilda," for several fanciers had been making tempting offers in their anxiety to own this magnificent bitch. The decision that Mrs Blauvelt-Moss was to have her, came as a tribute to St. Aubrey's respect for her as a breeder, and they had the satisfaction of seeing their opinion upheld when Champion Mathilda of Kettlemere made her final appearance at Westminster, taking Best of Opposite Sex. More exciting however, was the fact that though she took the prize herself, she was surrounded

Top right: Best in Show at the 1973 Pekingese Club of America Specialty Show under judge Winifred Heckmann, was Ch. Ho Dynasty's Desperado. Desperado is owned by Emidio and Karen Franzoso of South Bound Brook, New Jersey.

Ch. Zin Ru of Micklee, winner of two CCs and several reserve CCs in England. The beautiful English dog is sire of American and Bermudian Ch. Ho Dynasty's Ru-Lette, owned by Mrs Gilma Blauvelt-Moss and Joanne Goble.

Bottom: Ch. Ho Dynasty's Fuji Yama taking a four point major win at just nine months of age from the Bred by Exhibitor class. His sire was American and Canadian Ch. Ho Dynasty's Intrepid ex Ch. Ho Dynasty's Fuji.

He is owned by Mrs Janice L. Magee of North Carolina.

in the ring that day by four generations of her champion descendants.

Ho Dynasty is called with good reason by many "the home of famous bitches," for Mrs Blauvelt-Moss believes that excellent bitches are basic in any breeding program. With such foundation, one can breed to proved producers of desired qualities.

The policy at Ho Dynasty is to sell the best available young males to people who are interested in breeding and showing. But Mrs Blauvelt-Moss laments the fact that, while generally this works out well, the purchaser sometimes goes back on a promise of this sort and a splendid show and stud prospect is lost to the future of the strain and of the breed.

Mrs Blauvelt-Moss feels strongly that no Pekingese with a hereditary fault should ever be bred, but that they should be spayed or altered and kept only as pets. She believes that it is the responsibility of breeders to discourage the mating of inferior bitches to their studs and thus help to cut down the whelping of surplus puppies as well as maintaining the breed standard. Ho Dynasty is proud of the consistent quality produced in the kennel.

149

Top left: Ch. Bandit of Westwinds, son of Ch. Dah-Lyn Yen Chu Tu and Ch. Morning Glory of Westwinds, finished at this 1970 show and is the sire of champions. Bandit went to Canada after this victory and took Best of Breed three times, plus a Group First, and died tragically on the way back. Owned and handled by owner Herbert E. Jacques, Jr. of Ja-Lar Pekingese, Charlestown, Rhode Island. Gilbert photograph.

Above: At the 1972 Rhode Island Kennel Club show, judge Irene Khatoonian chose as winners two Ja-Lar Pekingese. On the left is Ch. Ja-Lar's Yen Chu, and on the right is Ch. Lee's Mee Tu's Dar-Lin. Both won majors from the classes and went on to win Best of Breed and Best of Opposite Sex. Owner-handler, Herbert E. Jacques of Ja-Lar Pekingese.

Left: Ch. Cooke's Chu Yen of Dah-Lyn is Heywood Hartley's choice at the Eastern Dog Club Show. Sire of champions, this lovely clear red is owned and shown by Herbert E. Jacques, Jr. of Ja-Lar Pekingese, Charlestown, Rhode Island. Shafer photo.

Ja Lar

Ja Lar Pekingese at Charlestown, Rhode Island, are the property of Herbert E. Jacques, Jr. This kennel has made a good start both in the show ring and in its breeding program. Mr Jacques has selected some excellent stock on which he hopes to establish an outstanding line of winning homebreds. That he is off on the right foot would seem evident when one considers that Champion Ja Lar's Yen Chu is a third-generation homebred.

Other noted early winners at Ja Lar include Champion Bandit of Westwinds, Champion Lo Jinx of Westwinds, Champion Cooke's Chu Yen of Dah Lyn, and Champion Lee's Mae Tu's Dar Lin.

Right: Ch. Lo Jinx of Westwinds, pictured winning Best of Breed under judge Geraldine Hess at the 1970 South Shore Kennel Club show. Jinx went on from this second major to win Group Third. Owned and handled by Herbert Jacques, Jr. of Ja-Lar Pekingese, Charlestown, Rhode Island.

Left: Linsown Yung Ku-Che of Devana, bred by Mrs Manning of Cambridge, England. Winner of one CC and sire of many other winners. Sire was Ch. Linsown Ku-Che-Tu ex Copplestone Puchanne. Owned by Mrs Pownall of Grove Lodge, Essex, England.

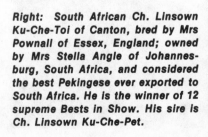

Right: South African Ch. Linsown Ku-Che-Toi of Canton, bred by Mrs Pownall of Essex, England; owned by Mrs Stella Angle of Johannesburg, South Africa, and considered the best Pekingese ever exported to South Africa. He is the winner of 12 supreme Bests in Show. His sire is Ch. Linsown Ku-Che-Pet.

151

Left: Peek-A-Boo Princess pictured winning under judge Derek Rayne at the Evergreen State Pekingese Specialty show in 1965. Bred by Gale Green, the owner is Anne L. Samek, Jalna Pekingese, Bainbridge Island, Washington.

Below: Jalnas's Robin Hood and Jalna's June Valentine, two Jalna Pekingese puppies that grew up to be champions. Owned by Anne L. Samek of Bainbridge Island, Washington.

Jalna

The Jalna Pekingese at Bainbridge Island, Washington, were founded by Zara Smith as mentioned earlier. The kennel is now owned by Anne L. Samek.

In 1955 the foundation bitch at Jalna, International Champion Wee Star-Lett, received the Canine Award of Distinction for her show record and the production of eight champions. Many of these were Toy Group and Best in Show winners in addition to being fine producers.

The Sameks bought their first Pekingese, Yu Fo Shan T'Sun (Champion Jalna's Fo Shan Yu ex Ieka's Yu Lan) from Zara Smith in 1956. The following Spring they purchased two Jalna bitches. With these and a black, Sin Dee Lee of Dahlia, they started their Melana Kennel. Zara Smith and Mrs Samek jointly purchased Langridge Wee Gem from Irene Francisco at about this time.

When Zara Smith became ill in May 1955, she sent some of her Pekingese to be cared for by the Sameks. That Fall she made Mrs Samek co-owner of those dogs. The next year these two ladies formed a partnership, combining their two kennels under the Jalna prefix. For several years prior to Mrs Smith's death all but a few of her Pekes lived with the Sameks on their island.

Above: Ch. June Valentine, bred and owned by the late Zara Smith of the state of Washington. Valentine's sire was Alderbourne Chuty Tuo of Kam-Tin and the dam was Jalna's Star-Ling.

Below: Jalna's Quick Silver pictured winning at the Pekingese Club of America 1971 show under judge Mrs Fortune Roberts. Breeder-owners— Anne L. and Melvin H. Samek of Jalna Pekingese, Bainbridge Island, Washington. Quick Silver's sire was American and Canadian Ch. Jalna's Ho Hum ex Jalna's Bam Boo.

Right: Ch. Jalna's Justa Toi, owned by the late Zara Smith of the state of Washington.

Right: Jalna's Tyna, shown going Best Puppy at the Rose City Pekingese Specialty Show under judge Irene Khatoonian. Bred and owned by Anne and Melvin Samek, Jalna Pekingese.

Below: Ch. Peek-A-Boo Princess, Best of Breed, Ch. Coomes Calypso, Best of Opposite Sex, and Jalna's Starfire, Best Puppy at the Evergreen State Pekingese Specialty Show in 1965 under judge Derek Rayne. Owners and handlers are Anne L. and Melvin H. Samek, Bainbridge, Washington.

Among her outstanding sires and show dogs, Mrs Samek speaks particularly of the quite magnificent Champion Melana's Calypso (Champion Langridge Wee Gem ex Sin-Dee-Lee), and his loss when only two and a half years old was a sad blow indeed. During his brief lifetime, he sired three champions, and he was just hitting his stride as a show dog, having won the Toy Group on his final two ring appearances.

The Sameks have continued the type-breeding program which has always characterized Jalna Pekingese. They consider good bitches of the utmost importance, thus point with pride to the fine examples from their kennel. These include Champion Jalna's Pandora (Champion Langridge Wee Gem ex Han Lin's Wee Sin Dee Lee); Champion Jalna's Peek A Boo Princess (Champion Melana's Calypso ex Shia Wee Toi Tu); Champion Jalna's Tyna (Dominic of Tom Thumb ex Jalna's Starfire), and Champion Jalna's Quick Silver (Champion Jalna's Ho Hum ex Jalna's Bam Boo).

The latest top winner in the Samek kennel is American and Canadian Champion Jalna's Ho Hum (Champion Dan Lee Dragonseed ex Jalna's Chu Kara). He is a Group winner in both the United States and Canada. Others with numerous breed and group wins include Champion Jalna's Firefly of Melana, Champion Coomes' Calypso, Champion Langridge Wee Gem, Champion Jalna's Fan Fare, Champion Jalna's War Lord, and Champion Jalna's Calypso.

Above: Ch. Jalna's War Lord pictured winning Best of Winners at the Golden Gate Specialty on the way to his championship, under judge Keith Browne. His sire was Jalna's Jigg T'Sun ex Jalna's Red Robin. Handled by John Brown for owners Anne and Melvin Samek of Bainbridge Island, Washington.

Below: Ch. Jalna's Calypso, owned by Anne and Melvin Samek of Bainbridge Island, Washington.

Below: The lovely Ch. Japeke Stormy's Di-Nah II, bred, owned and shown by Marjory Nye White, Japeke Kennels, in Los Angeles, California. This photograph was taken when Di-Nah was ten months old.

Right: From the nineteen forties, Ch. Japeke Nebraska, bred, owned and shown by Marjory Nye White of the Japeke Kennels, Los Angeles, California. The sire was Japeke Omaha and the dam Japeke Rajah's Brownie.

Below: Japeke Han Shih's Domino, owned by Mrs Faye D. Morrison of St. Paul, Minnesota.

Below right: An adorable and very typey two-month-old Pekingese puppy from the Japeke Kennels of Marjory Nye White in Los Angeles. Her name is Japeke Mid-nite Angel. Her sire was the imported Langridge Farnsworth KuKi and the dam Japeke Duskee Duchess.

Ch. Japeke Ruf-i-Ann and a little friend, sired by Ch. Tang Yu's Pia-Boi ex Pai-Ti-Li of Hollywood, bred by Marjory Nye White and co-owned by Mrs White and Vivian Longacre.

Japeke Stormy Weather, bred and owned by Marjory Nye White in the forties, was sired by Japeke Fla Go Han, Junior ex Japeke Rajah's Brownie.

Japeke

The first of the Japeke Pekingese was registered in 1929 by Miss Marjory E. Nye of Omaha, Nebraska. In October 1934, Miss Nye became Mrs Robert Phulps and with her husband and forty-three dogs moved in two cars and two trailers to California. Mr Phulps passed on and in 1963 she became Mrs Charles F. White. Steadily through the years, although more recently as a judge rather than as a breeder, Mrs White has maintained her keen interest in Pekingese.

Anna Katherine Nicholas recalls that in the early thirties when she was first writing her "Peeking at the Pekingese" columns, she and Marjory Nye carried on a lively correspondence, for Japeke was a busy kennel and its owner a successful breeder.

Marjory Nye had a special fondness for solid black Pekingese, which were seldom seen in those days although black and tan or black and fawn coloring was fairly common. Thus she determined to endeavor to breed some blacks good enough to gain titular honors. Her success in this venture is made manifest when one considers that Champion Japeke Han Shih's Domino (the result of introducing the Champion Sutherland Avenue

Han Shih line—Han Shih himself was a striking blond—into her earlier strain) became the first American-bred jet-black Pekingese champion. Some two decades later, Champion Japeke Stormy Di Nah II became the first American bred jet-black champion bitch.

Other splendid winners owned by Mrs White have included Champion Japeke All Black Paul, Champion Japeke Nebraska, Champion Japeke Lee Pu (a parti-color), and Champion Japeke Ji-Shih. Mrs White also owned part interest in Champion Chia Lee's Tiny Tim of Han Lin, by whom some excellent young stock was sired. Present young hopefuls at Japeke include a lovely litter sired by Champion Mar Pat Pied Piper's Piccolo, and another promising one by the imported Ku Ki of Farnsworth.

Since 1957 Mrs White has been active in the Order of the Eastern Star, and she and Mr White also devote much time to the Order of the White Shrine of Jerusalem. Thus the dogs have gradually been moved into second place, but they remain very much in evidence in Mrs White's affections and we are sure that the day will never come when she will not have at least a few Pekingese.

Left: Ch. Japeke Han Shih's Domino, photographed in December, 1937; owned by Mrs Pearl R. Cassler of Sharon Hill, Pennsylvania.

Right: Believed by Marjory Nye White to be the most beautiful black she ever bred, Japeke Tiny Tim's Keu Tee was unfortunately never shown. Her sire was Coomes See Mee Tu and the dam Japeke Tiny Tim's Fi-Na-Lee.

Left: Ch. Japeke Zi Tso, bred by Marjory Nye White, owner of the Japeke Kennels in California, and owned by Emily Hunt. Tso's sire was Japeke Tse Ho Ming, ex Japeke Zi Tseng.

Right: Ch. Japeke Han Shih's Domino, the first American-bred jet black champion in the United States. Bred by Marjory Nye White and owned by Faye D. Morrison, the sire was the very famous Ch. Sutherland Avenue Han Shih and the dam was Japeke Dixiana. Circa early nineteen thirties.

158

Lagercrantz

Mrs Erik G. Lagercrantz, of Dobbs Ferry, New York, was destined from early childhood to become a Pekingese fancier, as her introduction to the breed when three-and-a-half-years old had considerable impact. To go back a bit further, her father's oldest sister married Edward F. Holmes of Boston, the only grandchild of Dr. Oliver Wendell Holmes, and his first cousin married J. P. Morgan, Jr., whose family was noted for interest in Pekingese.

Kuei Kuan Cricket of Dah-Lyn pictured at nine weeks of age in the arms of her owner, Mrs Lagercrantz.

Ch. St. Aubrey Craigfoss Cheryl, bred by J. Sloane-Stanley and Miss Bella Piggott in March of 1971, is pictured finishing for her championship under Ronald Rella at the Rockland County Kennel Club show in September, 1972. R. Stephen Shaw handling for owner Mrs Eric G. Lagercrantz of Dobbs Ferry, New York.

Aunt Mary (Mrs Holmes) was coerced by Aunt Jessie (Mrs Morgan) into securing a Pekingese and became so charmed with the breed that Chin Lo (which was either a son or grandson of the famed Broadoak Beetle) entered as the first of a series of Pekes in the family.

The meeting between the present Mrs Lagercrantz and Chin Lo was eventful. Mary's father had Airedales, which until the day of a large family funeral were about the only breed of dog with which little Mary was acquainted. Both she and Chin Lo, with nurse and maid, had been sent to a small cottage on the farm during the funeral. Leaping before she looked, Mary reached for Chin Lo—and was promptly bitten! However, she and Chin Lo became fast friends after this incident, Mary impressed by the fact that the little dog had bitten her, and Chin Lo by her having ignored it. From this time, the breed has had Mary's undying love and admiration.

Mary Lagercrantz acquired her own first Pekingese in 1950, again because of the interest of her aunts in the breed. Aunt Mary was suddenly widowed and had suffered a slight stroke; as she had not had a Pekingese for some time, the family felt that she again would enjoy one. Thus Aunt Mary and Mrs Lagercrantz went to look at a litter of three at Jack Royce's Dah Lyn Kennel. On this occasion Mrs Lagercrantz bought the chun red-and-white for herself, while Aunt Mary took the two black-and-tans. These were royally bred from Champion Kai Lung of Remenham and International Champion Nanking Noel bloodlines. Aunt Mary's pair turned out to be excellent show quality; Mary's choice did not, but was soon ruler of the family, having enslaved Erik Lagercrantz by taking off after a huge Belgian hare four times her size when only seven weeks old. This was Wan Chi.

When Isabel Benjamin heard that her friend Mary Lagercrantz had become owner of a

Pekingese, Miss Benjamin promptly came to call and brought a copy of her charming book "Letters From A Pekingese" and an urgent invitation to Mrs Lagercrantz to join the Pekingese Club of America. She did join and became a Governor.

Mrs Lagercrantz is not a large-scale breeder, and has raised only a few litters. She has to date owned three champions, the first of which was the beautiful Copplestone Yusen Carmelita.

The Sleeves are Mrs Lagercrantz' particular favorites, and she feels that there is an inclination for our present day Pekes to be too large. Probably her most loved Peke was her tiny Champion Chik Tsun of Caversham daughter, Papoose, sadly lost at quite an early age. Her two present champions, both bitches, have made fine records en route to their titles.

Above: Mandralyn Hair, littermate of Ch. Mandralyn Oh! Calcutta!, is shown winning under judge Betty Shoemaker at the North Central Illinois Pekingese Match in October, 1972. Owners are W. Timothy Dyer and Richard Kruger.

Ch. Mandralyn Oh! Calcutta! pictured winning Winners Dog for a five point major over 33 class males under judge Mrs Yan Paul at the North Central Illinois Pekingese Club's Winter Specialty. He was bred and is owned by William Timothy Dyer and Richard F. Kruger of Peoria, Illinois.

BEST OF
OPPOSITE
SEX

Photo by Ritter

1. *Ch. Bel-Mar O'Jay's Thumbelina, bred, owned and handled by Mary Davis of Borger, Texas and shown to this 1971 win at the Southern Colorado Kennel Club show under judge Glenn Fancy for a 3-point major as Best of Winners. Sire was Quilin Kim Toi's Jai Son Tu ex Bel-Mar O'Jay's Jin Jah.*

2. *Ch. Paweja's Ku Jon, bred by the Paul Ausmans and owned by Mrs. W.P. Daily. Handled by Edna Voyles. The judge of this Peoria Kennel Club show was Edward Klein.*

3. *Talkabout Yung T'Sun Pepper, owned by Catherine Schell of Louisville, Kentucky.*

4. *Ch. Dud-Lee's Khi-Lyn-Etta is shown here winning at the Stone City Kennel Club show in 1973 under judge Dorothy Bonner. This show was the North Central Illinois Pekingese Specialty spring show. Etta was bred, shown and is owned by Mrs Ruby Dudley of Creston, Iowa.*

5. *Laparata Gay Martine, bred by Lilian Snook and pictured winning at a recent show with her owner, Mrs. E.H. Gatewood of Burlington, New Jersey. The sire was Laparata Gay Sir ex Yu Peach of Devanna.*

6. *Ch. MC-JJ Man O'War of Mo-Kai, sired by Ch. Monte Verde Robin of St. Aubrey ex Mogene's Ballerina of Cho-San. Man O'War is handled and owned by Mary Schmierback of Belleville, Illinois and was bred by Mogene Kennels and Betty Kavanaugh.*

7. *Hazelle Phaleta Ferguson, pictured at the age of 25 with her first Pekingese. This black and white parti-color was named Sun Toi Kaye. Mrs. Ferguson's Phaleta Kennels are still active in California today.*

8. *Ch. Milota's Go Big Red by Chanson pictured winning Best of Breed under judge Mrs Harold Hardin. Bred and owned by Julia A. Milota of Papillion, Nebraska.*

9. *The 6-pound miniature, or sleeve, Pekingese, Japeke Ji-Shih's Tiny Tim, bred and owned by the Japeke Kennels in Los Angeles. Inset shows length of ear fringes on this dog, which was known for his fabulous coat. His sire was Ch. Japeke Ji-Shih and his dam Japeke Tiny Tim's Keu Tii.*

10. *At a Chicago International Kennel Club, show judge Joseph Faigel awards a 4-point major to Copplestone Miss Pinkcoat, owned by Betty Shoemaker, Cumlaude Kennels, Bridgeton, New Jersey. Photo by Ritter.*

11. *Japeke Black Tux-E-Do, photographed as a puppy. His sire was Japeke Black Sha-Dow of Ir-Ma-Mi ex Japeke Su Kee Ji Shih. Bred and owned by Mrs Marjory Nye White of Los Angeles, California.*

12. *Ch. Mani Genie of Fourwinds, pictured above finishing at the Stone City Kennel Club show in 1972 at 12 months of age under judge Mrs Mildred Heald. Genie won three majors and Best of Opposite Sex over champion bitches twice from the Puppy Class. Handled by Robert Jackson for owner Mrs Robert Jackson of Senca, Illinois.*

13. **Ch. Mar-B-Hi-O-Samantha** pictured winning a major on her way to her championship at the Grand River Kennel Club Show in July, 1970 under judge Mrs David Crouse. Bred by Maria Bjerk, she is owned by Anna and Robert Park of Callydon Pekingese, Ferndale, Michigan and handled by Mrs Park.

14. **Tyneen Mirabelle,** pictured winning at the Terry-All Kennel Club show in 1973 under judge Mrs G.W. Dow. Mirabelle is handled by her owner, Mrs Sam R. Magun of Albuquerque, New Mexico. Mirabelle was bred by Mrs H. Ross-Watt of Scotland, sired by Fyre Fly of Tyneen out of Caversham Annette.

15. **Presleen Dimity** pictured winning Best of Winners and Best of Opposite Sex at the Central Ohio Kennel Club show in 1970, under judge Clara Alford. Owner is Ruth S. Kennedy of Chesterland, Ohio. Norton of Kent photograph.

16. **Chi-Lyn's Ku-Chin Tom-Mi of Dud-Lee's,** Best of Winners and Best of Breed under judge Isidore Shoenberg at a recent show. He is owned by Mrs W.L. Dudley of Creston, Iowa.

17. **Ch. Ho Dynasty's Jasmin,** owned by Karen and Emidio Franzoso of South Bound Brook, New Jersey, is pictured winning the Winners Bitch award from the 9-12 month old Puppy Class for a 5-point major under judge Harry Aldrich at the 1969 Pekingese Club of Southern New Jersey Specialty Show. Jasmin was also Winners Bitch at Westminster in 1970 and went Best of Opposite Sex over 7 champions at the Specialty Show as well.

18. **Kenmor's Ding Ho** is pictured winning under judge Jane Kay at the 1973 Rockingham County Kennel Club show. Bred by Frances Kukla and Frances McDade, Ding Ho is owned by Patricia and Charles Farley and Ken Falconi. He is handled by Charles Farley. His sire was Tinker of Westwinds ex Ding Ho's Soso.

19. Ch. Dragonhai Radiance, pictured winning Best of Winners at the Pekingese Club of America Specialty show held in conjunction with the 1973 Old Dominion Kennel Club show under judge Mrs S. Rowe. Co-owners of Radiance are Hal Fraser and Allen Williams, Dragonhai Kennels, Aquasco, Maryland.

20. The Gorgeous Gobi Dragon of Teakwood pictured winning under judge Henderson Bratcher at a Match Show before owner Margaret Carey of Pasadena, California, started his show ring career in 1973. Photograph by Missy Yuhl.

21. Ch. St. Aubrey Goofus Monza, bred by Miss G. Redwood and owned by Mrs Matthew H. Imrie, is pictured here winning a Best of Breed at the Longshore Southport Kennel Club show in 1972 with handler Ruth Sayres. Monza went on to Group Second under judge Ramona Van Court. William Gilbert photograph.

22. Ch. Raylmar Maximus of Neesoow winning Best of Breed under judge Iris de la Torre Bueno at the Cedar Rapids Kennel Club Show in 1972. Handler Tim Dyer. Co-owned by William Timothy Dyer and Richard F. Kruger of Peoria, Illinois. Breeders E. and D.A. Gilbert.

23. Rujim Mai Lei, handled by Evelyn M. Schaefer for breeder-owner Ruth S. Kennedy of Chesterland, Ohio. She is pictured winning a 3-point major as Winners Bitch and Best of Opposite Sex at the 1971 Ravenna Kennel Club Show under judge Ramona Van Court. Norton of Kent photograph.

24. Ch. St. Aubrey Marbeau of Elsdon completing his championship at a New Hampshire show with his handler R. Stephen Shaw. The sire was Ch. Goofus Bugatti ex St. Aubrey Pekeheus Polka, and was born June 1, 1971. Owner, Mrs Fortune Roberts.

B.O.W.
photo by Ashbey

B.O.B.
photo by Gilbert

CEDAR RAPIDS K.A
BEST OF BREED
JUNE 24, 1972
OLSON PHOTO

BEST OF
WINNERS
PHOTO BY Tatham

25. *Chyanchy Wellbarn Jin-Chi, imported from England by Mrs Mary E. Spicer of Pittsford, New York. He is pictured here starting his show career in America with his handler, Hermine Cleaver. His sire was Ch. Chyanchy Ah Yang of Jamestown and his dam is Chyanchy Wellbarn Jenny.*

26. *Canadian Ch. Toccata's Shadow of Geodan, Winners Bitch and Best of Opposite Sex at the Sandusky Kennel Club show under judge Ruth Turner, winning on the way toward his American championship. Owner-handled by Jean Carrol of Euclid, Ohio.*

27. *Dawoo Blackhall Hey Ho, an English import bred by Mrs K.M. Aitken and owned by Mrs E.H. Gatewood of Burlington, New Jersey. The judge is William Kendrick and the handler is Joan Sisco. Hey Ho's sire was Alderbourne China Maniken and his dam Linsown Ho-ping.*

28. *American and Canadian Ch. Half Note's Toccata of Su-Con, Best of Breed at a recent Sandusky Kennel Club show under judge Virginia Keckler. Toccata won the Canadian title at 10 months of age and the American championship under two years of age. Breeder-owned and handled by Jean Carroll, Su-Con Pekingese, Euclid, Ohio.*

29. *Rujim Music Man, C.D., wins Best of Winners at the 1970 Chagrin Valley Kennel Club Show under judge Isidore Shoenberg. Sired by Presleen Fu Song ex Joanna of West Winds, he is handled by Evelyn Schaefer for breeder-owner Ruth S. Kennedy of Chesterland, Ohio. Photo by Ritter.*

30. Ch. Ku-Chin Timothy of Tom Thumb finished for title at the 1969 Heart of America Kennel Club show under judge Emil Klinkhardt. Bred by Naida I. Sutton, Timothy is owned and shown by Ruby Dudley of Creston, Iowa.

31. Ch. Khi Yu Ki-Ku's Khi-Lyn of Dud-Lee's was judge Vincent Perry's choice for a 3-point major win at the 1970 Dubuque Kennel Club Show. Bred, owned and handled by Ruby Dudley, Creston, Iowa.

32. Ch. Masterpiece Naomi of Dud-Lee's winning a 4-point major under judge Edward Biven at the 1973 Ozark Kennel Club show. Bred, owned and handled by Mrs Ruby Dudley, Creston, Iowa.

33. Ch. Manikin's Simon of Dud-Lee's finished for his title at the 1972 Council Bluffs Kennel Club show under judge Beulah Hatch. Sire of Ch. Simon's Dragon of Dud-Lee's, he himself was sired by Triple Ch. St. Aubrey Manikin of Elsdon ex Impie's Rosemary of Dud-Lee's and is owned and shown and bred by Mrs W.L. Dudley of Creston, Iowa.

34. Judge Charles C. Venable awarded a 3-point major to Ch. Tom-Mi's Yuh-Chin of Dud-Lee's at the 1971 Heart of America Kennel Club show. Yuh-Chin finished for her title in six shows with 4 majors. Handled, bred and owned by Mrs Ruby Dudley of Creston, Iowa.

35. Tom-Mi's Ho-Tai of Dud-Lee's pictured winning a 3-point major under judge Erica Dixon Huggins at the 1973 Egyptian Kennel Club show on the way to his championship. He finished with 3 majors. Bred, owned and handled by Mrs W.L. Dudley of Creston, Iowa.

36. *Ch. Mar-Pat's Lilliput winning the Pekingese Club of Southern New Jersey Specialty Show in 1970 under judge Henry Stoecker. Owner-handled by Michael Wolf of New York.*

37. *Singlewell King Zin, an English dog imported and handled by new owner Mae Jordan of Charlotte, North Carolina. He is shown here taking Winners Dog at a North Carolina show. His sire is English Ch. Belgran Kings Ransom; his dam is Singlewell Rainbow. Earl Graham photograph.*

38. *Chun-Chu-Fu's Destiny's Pharoh Tu, photographed winning at 9 months of age under judge Margaret M. Shoemaker at the Pacific Coast Pekingese Specialty Show in Beverley Hills, California. Sired by Canadian, Mexican and U.S. Ch. Chun-Chu-Fu's Destiny of Norlee ex Chun-Chu-Fu's Cleopatra. Owned and handled by Shirley Stone of Burbank, California.*

39. *Ch. Ho Dynasty's Sand Man scoring a good win under judge Ackerman at a Ramapo Kennel Club show in 1970.*

40. *Judge Anna Katherine Nicholas giving Winners Dog to the Pekingese owned by Mrs G. Blauvelt-Moss at the Westminster Kennel Club Show in 1968. William P. Gilbert photograph.*

41. *Ch. Candanham Fu, Winners Dog and Best of Opposite Sex at the Peking-ese Club of America 1972 winter show, pictured winning at another 1972 summer show with his handler, Hermione Cleaver. His sire was English, Canadian and American Ch. Alderbourne Lifu of Remward ex Mokai Alderbourne Ky Twiggee. Breeders and owners are the Herbert McCalls of Stafford, Virginia.*

42. *Obedience winner! Windemere's Fu Wings-O-Glory, C.D. Glory has her Companion Dog title in both Canada and the U.S.A. She is pictured above being awarded a trophy as High-Scoring Dog In The Class for the second time in a row. This completed her Canadian C.D. title, at the Northern Interior Kennel Club, Prince George, British Columbia, Canada. Bred by Joy Strickler, she is owned, trained, and handled by Mary Jane Callaway of Portland, Oregon.*

43. *Chu Lai's Little Sissi Su (on the left) and her son Ch. Chu Lai's Dan Dee Ting win Winners Bitch and Best Opposite Sex as well as Best of Breed under judge Virginia Keckler at the 1973 Merrimack Valley Kennel Club show. Handling are the breeder-owners, Patricia A. and Charles W. Farley of Norton, Massachusetts.*

44. *American and Bermudian Ch. Ho Dynasty's Ballad, shown here finishing for his American championship title under judge Bergum. The following weekend he won his Bermuda title and Best Visiting Dog In Show. He is co-owned by Joanne Goble and Gilma Blauvelt-Moss. Handled by Melvin Goble.*

45. *Chun-Chu-Fu's Comet's Czarina, bred, owned and handled by Shirley Stone of California. She is pictured here winning at the 1973 Lancaster, California Kennel Club show under judge Mrs Harold Hardin. Her sire is Canadian, Mexican and U.S. Ch. Chun-Chu-Fu's Monarque's Rajah ex Ch. Chun-Chi-Fu's Comet Chan Tu.*

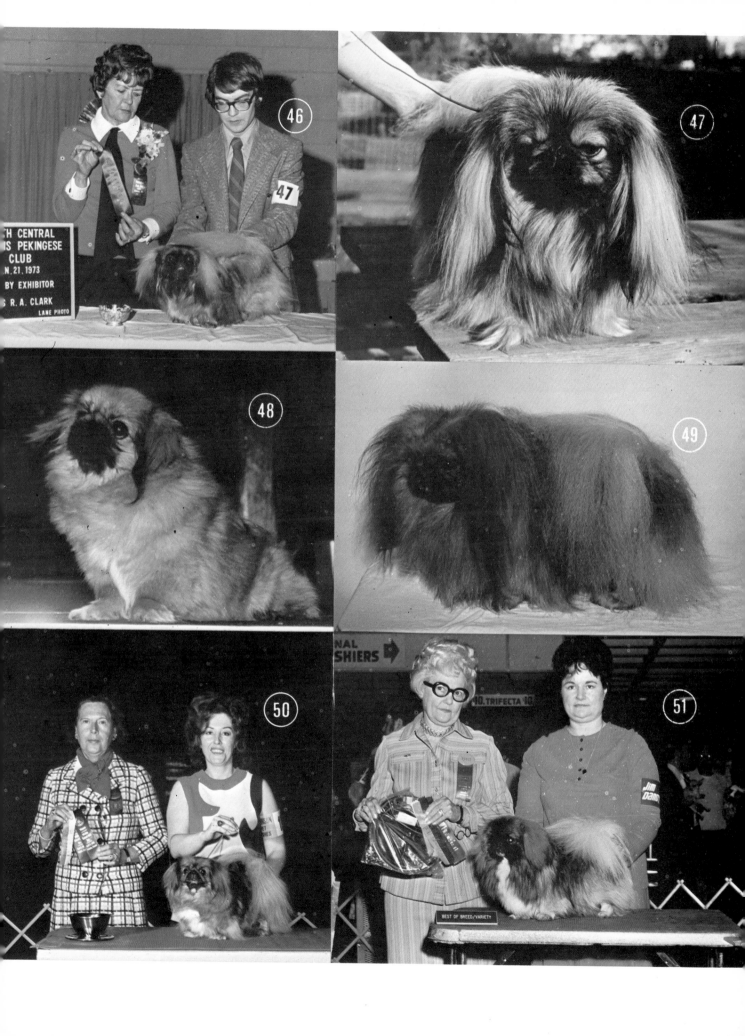

GH CENTRAL
IS PEKINGESE
CLUB
N. 21, 1973
BY EXHIBITOR
S R. A. CLARK
LANE PHOTO

BEST OF BREED/VARIETY

46. *Mandralyn Lady Maxine, pictured winning at 11 months of age at the North Central Illinois Pekingese Club show in 1972 under judge Mrs R.A. Clark. Handler is co-owner Timothy Dyer who bred Maxine with Richard Kruger, both of Peoria, Illinois.*

47. *Ch. June Valentin, bred and owned by the late Zara Smith of the State of Washington. Valentin's sire was Alderbourne Chuty Tuo of Kam-Tin and the dam was Jalna's Star-Ling.*

48. *Swallowdale Bumblebee, a gorgeous red sitting pretty at a recent dog show, waiting for owner Mrs E.H. Gatewood of Burlington, New Jersey. Bred by Lt. Col. and Mrs D.L. Swallow. The sire is Dawoo Prince Orsil* ex *Swallowdale Mittens. Stephen Klein photograph.*

49. *Ch. Mara-Bon-Tuo of Orchard Hill, owned by Mrs Ralph East of Fern Creek, Kentucky, a beautiful 9-pound red sable which combines the Orchard Hill and English St. Aubrey-Elsdon bloodlines.*

50. *Ch. Raylmar Brabanta Su-Yang, English import sired by Ch. Yu-Yang of Jamestown* ex *Brabanta Sweet Su, pictured winning under judge Ramona Van Court. Owned by Pat O'Shea of Sioux Falls, South Dakota.*

51. *Callydon Sam-Son Select, pictured winning Best of Breed from the Puppy Class at the Livonia Kennel Club Show in September, 1971 under judge Dorothy Nickles. Handled by Anna Park and owned by Anna and Robert Park, Callydon Pekingese, Ferndale, Michigan. The sire was Ch. Merellen Manikin* ex *Ch. Mar-B-Hi-O Samantha.*

52. *Panelli's Raven of TeeLing started his show career as Best Puppy and Best Sweepstakes Puppy at the Pekingese Club of Southern New Jersey Specialty Show. An unfortunate accident has prevented him from finishing his show career, but he continues as a stud dog at the Panellis' Kennel in Atco, New Jersey. Whelped in 1970, he was handled here by his owner, Mrs Ernie Panelli.*

53. *Lor-Jo-Al Ricky T'Sun finishing with his fourth major win under judge Dr William Field. Ricky was bred by Mrs Arthur B. Gowie, is owned by Joan E. Stetson and handled by Joan Sisco. Ricky is sired by the late Ch. Monte Verde Ricky Tick ex a Ku Jin of Caversham daughter, Fu Tu of Shenfue.*

54. *Wongville Olympia, a beautiful rich red bitch owned by Mary Hilton, Wongville Kennels, Dorset, England.*

55. *American and Bermudian Ch. Ho Dynasty's Ru-Lette, lovely 7-pound bitch is pictured winning at the 1972 Union County Kennel Club Show under the late judge John Murphy. Ru-Lette is the top winning bitch in the U.S.A. and has many Group Placings. Her sire is Ch. Zin Ru of Micklee ex PCA Ch. Ho Dynasty's T'Su Hsi. Owner, Mrs Gilma Blauvelt-Moss of Hohokus, New Jersey.*

56. *The lovely Jellison's Ku Chen, bred by the late John Royce and whelped in March, 1967, is pictured winning Best of Breed for his first major at the Framingham District Kennel Club Show in June, 1972. The judge was Mr Hayden Martin. His sire is Dah-Lyn Sunboi Tu ex Bettina's Yvonne, the dam of 3 champions. An unfortunate accident has prevented Ku Chen from finishing to championship. He is owned by Wallace Swett Jr. and Kenneth E. Oberg of the Mordor Kennels and Aviary, Easy Weymouth, Massachusetts, and was handled by Hermine W. Cleaver.*

W.D.

photo by Gilbert

B.O.B.

photo by Gilbert

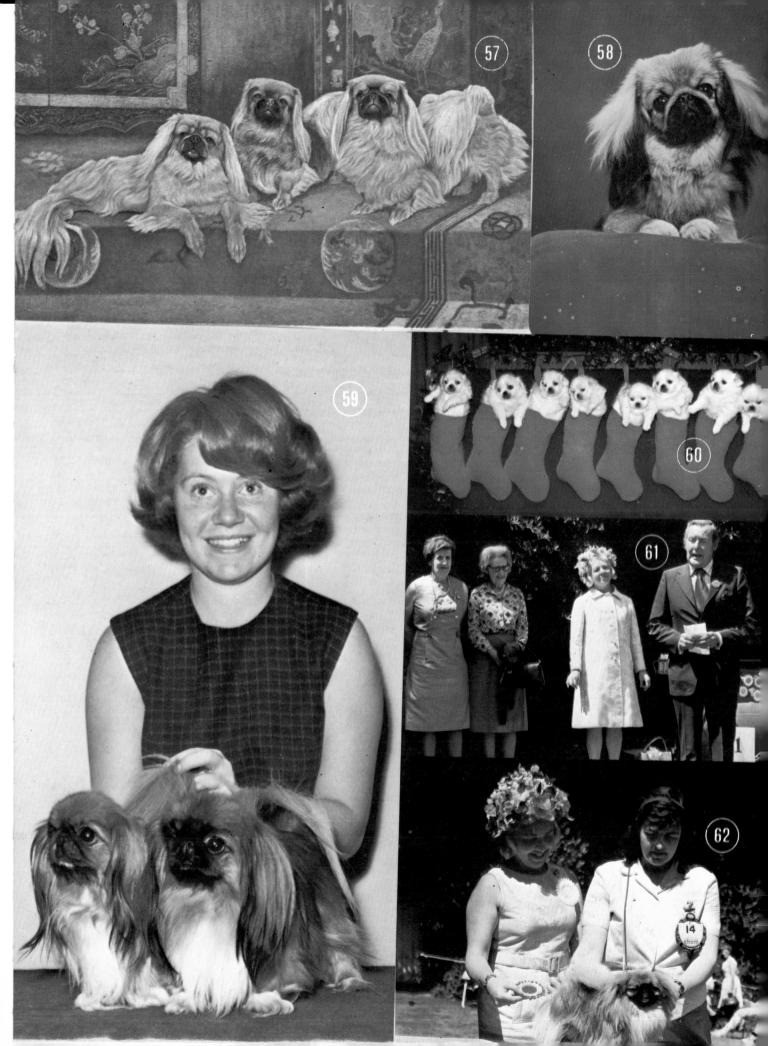

NORTH CENTRAL
ILLINOIS PEKINGESE
CLUB
JAN 21, 1973

BEST OF BREED
JUDGE MS R. A. CLARK
LAKE PHOTO

BEST OF
BREED

B.O.S.
photo by Gilbert

63

64

65

66

67

68

69

PEKINGESE CLUB
SOUTHERN NEW JERSEY
3RD. SPECIALTY SHOW
NOV. 21, 1971

BEST OF BREED
OR VARIETY

70

71

72

73

PEKINGESE CLUB
SOUTHERN NEW JERSEY
3RD. SPECIALTY SHOW
NOV. 21, 1971

BEST OF
OPPOSITE SEX

68. At the 1972 Lima, Ohio show, judge Mrs Byron Hofmann awarded Winners Bitch and Best of Opposite Sex to Talkabout Yu Yang Amanda Lee; Best of Winners and Best of Breed went to Talkabout Yung Yu T'Sun Pepper. Pepper, litter brother to Amanda, went on to win Group Fourth at this show. Bred, owned and handled by Catherine Schell of Louisville, Kentucky.

69. Ch. Ho Dynasty's Desperado winning the coveted Best of Breed rosette at the Pekingese Club of Southern New Jersey show in 1971 under judge Mrs Yan Paul. This lovely dog is owned by Emidio and Karen Franzoso of South Bound Brook, New Jersey, and is handled by Mrs Franzoso. Stephen Klein photograph.

70. Ch. Rujim Happy Charlie wins Winners Dog and Best of Winners for a 4-point major win under judge Geraldine Hess at the 1972 Western Reserve Kennel Club Show, on the way to championship. Breeder-owner-handler is Ruth S. Kennedy of Chesterland, Ohio. This show completed his championship. His sire was Ch. Presleen Tul Yen Hih, C.D., ex Rujim Charmaine.

71. Ch. Simon's Dragon of Dud-Lee's (on the left) and Ch. Tom-Mi's Khi Lyn-Ette of Dud-Lee's pictured winning at a 1972 Hutchison Kennel Club show under judge Roy M. Cowan. Simon's Dragon is owned and handled by Duane C. Doll; Ette was bred and is owned and handled by Mrs Ruby Dudley of Creston, Iowa.

72. Ferry-Lands Man Chu Dragon being campaigned to championship in 1973 by owner Margaret Carey of Pasadena, California. Man Chu has both majors and is pictured winning a 4-point major under judge Gladys Groskin at the Kennel Club of Beverley Hills Show in June, 1972. He was sired by Ch. Dragonseed's Fu Tai Yin. Bill Francis photograph.

73. Ch. Lee's Mee Tu's Darlin, photographed here winning Winners Bitch and Best of Opposite Sex at the Pekingese Club of Southern New Jersey Specialty Show in 1971 over 21 bitches. Mickey went on to finish for her championship with five majors. Owned by Herbert E. Jacques, Jr., Ja-Lar Pekingese, Charlestown, Rhode Island.

74. *Judge Cowrie gives Copplestone Mr. Pinkcoat his first point on the way to his American championship. Owned and handled by Betty Shoemaker of Bridgeton, New Jersey. Photo by Ritter.*

75. *American and Canadian Ch. Fu Song's Half Note of Su-Con, pictured winning Best of Breed over four Specials at the Chagrin Valley Kennel Club show under judge Mrs Doris Glover. Owned, bred and handled by Jean Carroll, Su-Con Pekingese, Euclid, Ohio.*

76. *Mrs Matthew H. Imrie showed her beautiful black Singlewell Batling to first place in the Open Dog Class at the 1972 Pekingese Club of Southern New Jersey Specialty Show. The judge for this occasion was Edward Jenner. The dog was bred by Mrs P.M. Edmond. Bushman photograph.*

77. *Ch. Raylmar Satchmo of Royceland, handled by John Milota, and Ch. Mi'lotas Angel Lace by Satchmo, handled by Julia A. Milota, pictured winning under judge Mrs Harold Hardin at the Nebraska Kennel Club show. Satchmo was Best of Breed and Angel was Winners Bitch for a 3-point major and Best of Opposite Sex. The Milotas are from Papillion, Nebraska.*

78. *Ch. Niftee's Jewel of Wegner, sired by Copplestone Puzinate ex Ch. Fan't T'zee's Jewel of Wegner's, pictured winning at the Harrisburg Kennel Club show under judge William Kendricks. Handled by Mike Smith for owner Mrs E.H. Gatewood of Burlington, New Jersey.*

79. *American and Canadian Ch. Ho Dynasty's Tallulah, a Toy Group winner, pictured here winning her first two Canadian championship points under judge Edith Nash Hellerman in 1971. She was undefeated in class bitch competition, and is a granddaughter of Ch. Copplestone Pu Zin and Ch. Nia-Ku-Tulyar of Orchard Hill. Owned by Timothy Dyer and Richard Kruger of Peoria, Illinois, and handled by Mr Dyer.*

80. *Ch. Dittos Gee-Whiz Sing Lee, pictured winning Best of Winners at the 1973 Arizona Pekingese Club Specialty Show under judge Charles Venable. Owned and bred by Mrs Adolph R. Rauschhaupt of the Sing Lee Kennels, Fresno, California. Photo by Schley.*

81. *The Central Florida Kennel Club Show in Orlando in January, 1973 saw judge Betty Young place Betty Shoemaker's Int. Ch. Copplestone Mr. Pinkcoat Best of Breed. The Shoemakers' Cumlaude Kennels are in Bridgeton, New Jersey. Earl Graham photo.*

82. *Judge Betty Shoemaker from the USA presents her Cumlaude Challenge cup to Teijon Hei Jetta, darling little black and tan Sleeve Pekingese and her owner Mrs T. Brickwood. The cup is in memory of Mrs Shoemakers Copplestone Miss Pinkcoat and reads: "In memory of Bonnie, world renowned for her beauty, excellence and charm." Presented at the first Sleeve Pekingese show in England.*

83. *Mandolin's Fu Wing Adventurer was Reserve Winners Dog for three days in a row at the Northern Interior Kennel Club in British Columbia, Canada. Just six months old, he is pictured above winning under judge Forest Hall. Bred by Joy Strickler and Mary Jane Callaway, he is owned and trained by Mary Jane Callaway of Portland, Oregon.*

84. *Minuet Marlo of Callydon, bred by Maye Gimbel and owned by the Robert Parks, Callydon Pekingese, Ferndale, Michigan. This photograph taken at Grand River Kennel Club show in July, 1972 with an important win under judge Emma Stevens on the way to championship.*

85. *East Winds Nancy, 4 pounds, pictured winning first in the 6-9 months class in the Sweepstakes at the Pekingese Club of Southern New Jersey show in 1971 under breeder-judge Jerry Hess. Nancy went on to win Best of Opposite Sex in the Sweepstakes and first in Open under-6 pounds class also. Owned by Philas Cooke of Chelsea, Massachusetts, and handled by Mrs Cooke. Klein photo.*

86. *Ch. Gwynne's Treasured Truffle pictured on the way to her championship as Winners Bitch under judge Ruth Turner for a 4-point major win at the 1973 Wilmington Kennel Club show. Owner Betty Shoemaker, Cumlaude Kennels, Bridgeton, New Jersey.*

87. *Ch. Mar Pat That's Mi Boi of Glory K, pictured winning at 16 months of age at the Cheyenne, Wyoming show on the way to his championship. Handled by John Brown for co-owners Gloria L. Wallis and Kay Crow of Huntington Beach, California.*

88. *Ch. Ho Dynasty's Fuji pictured winning Best of Opposite Sex at the second annual Pekingese Club of Southern New Jersey Specialty Show in November, 1970 under judge Henry Stoecker. Stephen Shaw handles for the late Mrs Gilma Blauvelt-Moss of Hohokus, New Jersey.*

83

84

Reserve
Winners

Hodges

BEST OF
WINNERS

85

SE CLUB OF
MERN NEW JERSEY
SPECIALTY SHOW
NOV. 21, 1971
1ST.

86

W.B.
photo by Gilbert

87

88

PEKINGESE CLUB OF
SOTHERN NEW JERSEY
SPECIALTY SHOW
JUDGE = MR. STOECKER
NOV. 15, 1970

Mandralyn

The Mandralyn Kennel of Pekingese is owned by Tim Dyer and Richard Kruger of Peoria, Illinois, and was started in the late sixties when they acquired a delightful puppy called Georgy Girl. She was shown only three times, managing to win a single point from puppy class. However, what she did accomplish was to motivate her owners to begin an exhaustive study of her breed.

Mandralyn's first brood bitch came from the Jacksons' Fourwinds Kennels. This was Fu Sal Chu of Whitewalls, a granddaughter of International Champion Fu Yong of Jamestown with two lines also to the noted producer, Champion Hi Oasis of Brown's Den. Sally produced a splendid bitch, Mandralyn's Marmalade, that was recently sold to Janet and Martha Saunders of Lexington, North Carolina, where it is hoped she will do well. Marmalade is line-bred to Champion Fu Yong of Jamestown through his son, American and Canadian Champion Floray's Petersham.

The first show quality Pekingese owned by Mr Dyer and Mr Kruger was Su Lan Sung's American Cousin, a grandson of Champion St. Aubrey Mario of Elsdon, which they purchased with three others from Susan's Pekingese in Canada. Unfortunately, this lovely dog died of heat prostration with just two points towards his championship.

Later Mandralyn acquired American and Canadian Champion Ho Dynasty's Tallulah and Champion Beaupres Lady Jane of Ecila, both of which went Reserve Winners Bitch at Pekingese Club of America Specialties from

Ch. Mandralyn Oh! Calcutta! with co-breeder-owner William Timothy Dyer. Calcutta finished his championship in December, 1972, handled exclusively by Mr Dyer. Co-owner is Richard F. Kruger, Peoria, Illinois.

the six-to-nine month Puppy Class. Tallulah did so under Alva Rosenberg, who on a later occasion awarded her a Toy Group; Lady Jane won under Iris Bueno. In June 1971 Mr Dyer took Tallulah to Canada, where she attained her title undefeated in the bitch classes at eight consecutive shows. She was Best of Winners at four of them and twice defeated 1970's top Canadian Toy.

The most outstanding litter to date at Mandralyn was sired by Peggy Carr's Champion Langridge Fargo's Lariat ex Gidget of Tien Hia, she a daughter of International Champion St. Aubrey Manikin of Elsdon ex Champion Pollyanna of Tien Hia. Mandralyn Hair and Mandralyn Oh! Calcutta were kept from this litter, Calcutta becoming the kennel's first homebred champion when he finished with four majors, including five points at the North Central Illinois Pekingese Club's first Winter Specialty.

Bracewell Agostini, known as William to his breeder, Mrs Hazel Lancaster, and his owners Tim Dyer and Richard Kruger. William is seen here at three months in a Percy Clegg photograph.

Champion Raylmar Maximus of Neesown, an under eight-pound son of English Champion Mr Redcoat of Kanghe, holds first place in his owners' affections. Mr Dyer showed him to Best Toy from the classes at their hometown show in Peoria under Joseph Faigel, then finished him for the title two days later.

The eleven Pekingese now at Mandralyn include four champions and two others with points that are on the way. One of these is Bracewell Agostini, a two year old clear orange grandson of the famous Beaupres Oliver Twist and Robert of Pekespan, purchased from Michael Wolf. This one has seven points including a major, and twice has gone Best of Breed over Specials.

Mandralyn Lady Maxine, by Champion Raylmar Maximus ex Champion Beaupres Lady Jane, is considered by her owners to be their finest homebred. A more recent acquisition at the kennel is Mandralyn Rubilee of Dud-Lee's, by Champion Tom Mi Masterpiece Sing Lee ex Champion Tom Mi's Yuh Chin of Dud-Lee's, bred by Mrs W. L. Dudley.

An outstanding puppy picture! Mandralyn Hair pictured winning at a puppy match. Owned and bred by Timothy Dyer and RichardKruger of Illinois, and handled by Mr Dyer.

Left: Ch. Bel-Mar Ku Loo San winning a three point major as Best of Winners at the Lawton-Fort Sill Kennel Club show under judge Henry Stoecker in 1972. Bred, owned and handled by Mary E. Davis, Borger, Texas.

Mandolin's Beau Dancer, photographed for the first time at just eight weeks of age. Bred and owned by Mary Jane Callaway of Portland, Oregon. The sire was Beaupres Leander, an English import, and the dam Windermere's Pu Yong Dancer.

Hi-Princess of Brown's Den, pictured at 17 months of age, photographed in 1954. Her owner was Mrs Cora W. Brown of Rivera, California.

A typical Pekingese shown in the 1920's. Picture from the personal collection of Iris de la Torre Bueno.

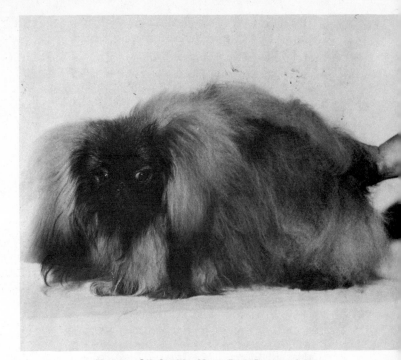

Above: Ol' Seville Mara Bon Deno, photographed as a puppy and to be campaigned in the 1970's by owner Mrs Ralph East of Fern Creek, Kentucky. The sire was Ch. Mara-Bon-Tuo of Orchard Hill ex Ch. Ka-Jin Ju-Dee of Mei Foo.

Mei Foo

Mei Foo Pekingese Kennels at Louisville, Kentucky, were founded in 1952 when Ralph and Mary East acquired their first Pekingese while he was in the Marine Corps. This little Peke was line-bred to Tri-International Champion Remenham Derrie of Orchard Hill. When five months old he weighed just thirteen ounces and a veterinarian informed the Easts that he would never live out his first year. However, he survived and happily proved the vet mistaken by living to the age of thirteen years, then being put to sleep because of various illnesses.

A Pekingese champion from the Dale-Wong Kennels.

Since Orchard Hill was behind this dog, the Easts came to know Mrs Quigley through correspondence and visits to her marvelous kennel at Lock Haven, Pennsylvania, and eventually became interested in breeding and exhibiting.

When the Easts acquired their first Pekingese, Ralph was stationed at Albany, Georgia, and assigned limited accommodation. But when the Marine Corps service ended, the Easts moved to Louisville. This is in one of the country's busiest show-giving areas; soon they became further interested in exhibiting, and then having ample space, they added more Orchard Hill dogs and were off to the hard work, heartbreak, and fun of the Pekingese world.

They do their own handling in the show ring and house now about thirty Pekes. Among these are the old dogs that have been retired and are living out their lives in comfort. To quote Mrs East: "They have given to us and now we give to them." This is an attitude the authors admire and agree with.

The Easts thoroughly enjoy their Pekingese, and cannot imagine anyone who has owned a Peke ever choosing another breed. In addition to their kennel, they are presently involved in the formation of a new Pekingese Specialty Club in their area.

Millrose

It would be difficult to find two persons more devoted to a breed than are Dr. and Mrs Edwin Reginald Blamey to the Pekingese. Mrs Blamey owns the Millrose Kennels at New York City and at Mount Sinai, New York, while Dr. Blamey is one of the most highly regarded veterinarians in the United States.

Dr. Blamey was born in London, England. From 1894 to 1906 he lived about five miles from Englefield Green, where Mrs Ashton Cross, Mrs McEwen, and Mrs Murray owned Pekingese. Dr. Blamey became familiar with the breed by working with the family of veterinarians who took care of these dogs. In 1906 he came to the United States and worked with Dr. Sherwood, who also admired the breed. Shortly he became acquainted with Mrs M. E. Harby, who introduced him to all the local breeders in her capacity as Club Secretary. For many years he served the Pekingese Club of America as Official Veterinarian at the Annual Shows. Having always admired the courage and forthrightness of the Pekingese, Dr. Blamey was delighted when his wife decided to raise an occasional litter of them. From the very beginning, Millrose Kennel was as now a "home project." The well-known Champion Millrose Hornet and the great show bitch Champion Millrose Ballerina were house pets and constant companions. Ballerina made a spectacular record as a Best of Breed and Toy Group winner and was widely admired by our most knowledgeable judges.

Mrs Blamey's winning Pekingese were all homebred. Hornet and Ballerina's dam, that also garnered some wins, were littermates. Ballerina was a fine example of the fact that bitches can and do win at the Shows when of sufficiently excellent quality. Mrs Blamey also had a truly magnificent dog, a son of Hornet. He attracted much attention by his striking beauty, but did not care for dog shows so was retired to enjoy just being a family dog.

Through the years both Dr. and Mrs Blamey have given very generously of their time and effort in furthering the interests of Toy dogs in general and Pekingese in particular. Dr Blamey is a long-time President of the Pekingese Club of America and its former delegate to the American Kennel Club. For more than a decade Mrs Blamey has done an outstanding job as President of the Progressive Dog Club, which is devoted to the Toy breeds. Dr and Mrs Blamey are both Directors of these two clubs.

Mike-Mar

Mrs Walter M. Jeffords, Jr., of New York attended the Bronx County Kennel Club Show in March 1971 and was much impressed as she saw the recently imported Dagbury of Calartha making his debut. Michael Wolf, owner of Mike-Mar and of Dagbury, piloted this latest arrival at his Long Island kennel through to Best of Breed over a strong field of Specials from the classes under Anna Katherine Nicholas, then to first in a quality Toy Group under Nancy Phelps Buckley. These victories were repeated next day at Teaneck, and Mrs Jeffords was hardly able to take her eyes off this little dog. No offer

Below: The first Pekingese owned by N.E. Toothaker and H.R. Norris, and the foundation of their Watonga Kennels in Dallas, Texas. Ch. St. Aubrey Hun-Nee Bun of Elsdon was bred by Nigel Aubrey-Jones and R. William Taylor and is the dam of champions. Her sire was Goofus Fangio Tu and her dam Ch. Stu Aubrey Ku-Ella of Elsdon.

Right: Ch. Caversham Ku-Ku of Yam, owned by Mrs I. de Pledge and Mrs H. Lunham. Photo by C.M. Cooke.

Above: Ch. Dan Lee Dragonseed winning the Pekingese Club of America Specialty Show under judge Anna Katherine Nicholas in 1969. Owner-handler Michael Wolf of Babylon, Long Island, New York.

to buy him tempted Mr Wolf in the least, however; but the happy thought came to both parties of Mrs Jeffords becoming Dag's co-owner. So well did this work out that Mrs Jeffords and Mike Wolf formed a partnership by which her Boston Terriers and Pekingese and Mr Wolf's Pekingese, Maltese, Standard Poodles, and various other canine "stars" are now under joint ownership of these two fanciers, and, the Mike-Mar Kennel seems destined for even greater achievements when one considers the lovely youngsters and the importations which it will be presenting in the future.

Michael Wolf showed an Italian Greyhound under Anna Katherine Nicholas at Elm City's Summer Show during the late sixties. This was when she first met him and became aware of his dedicated enthusiasm for fine show dogs. During the next few years, the principal breed at Mike-Mar was the Maltese, and Mr Wolf owned and has bred consistent Toy Group and Best in Show winners. Then he purchased from John Brown that mightiest of all American-bred Pekingese, Champion Dan Lee Dragonseed. Mr Brown had been sweeping the boards with him in the Group

and Best in Show rings at California's leading shows, and this acquisition by Mike-Mar began a Pekingese trend with an impact that will be felt far into the future. Both Michael Wolf and Mrs Jeffords dearly love the breed, and both of them have unerring instinct in selecting good examples of it as is being repeatedly proved.

Dragonseed had already piled up an enviable list of victories before coming East, and there were those who felt that perhaps his best winning days might be behind him. The fallacy of that idea became clear when he proceeded to win the Westminster Toy Group his first time out after Mr Wolf had purchased him; two of the Pekingese Club of America Summer Specialty Shows—the open shows, where competition is always especially keen; a long procession of Toy Groups; and, to cap it all, five consecutive Bests in Show at the East's largest and most prestigious Autumn fixtures. He was truly a super Pekingese. Our American breeders can well be proud of him, and Dragon is keeping everyone reminded of his greatness through the quality of his sons. They include Champion Jalna's Ho Hum and Champion Dan Lee Dragonfluff, the latter being the sire of the present Pacific Coast sensation and Best in Show multiple winner, Champion Don Lor's Dragonfire.

Michael Wolf also brought from California Champion Mar Pat Solo's Lilliput, that won many Groups and is also a Best in Show dog. Lilliput is the sire of the widely admired Champion Rickshaw Renaissance, a young dog just starting his career and already a Group winner.

Champion Hi Swinger of Brown's Den won a recent Pekingese Club of America Winter Specialty under Alva Rosenberg, and has been widely admired. He is proving an especially fine sire, among his "get" being the Group-winning Champion Soo Hoo Twister and some of the finest of the young puppies now at Mike-Mar.

Mrs Jeffords, prior to formation of the partnership with Mr Wolf, imported and campaigned the handsome English winner, Beau of Kyratown, which had been called to her attention by Mr Rayl. Under Mrs Edna Voyles' handling, Beau quickly gained his American title plus some worthy honors in the ring.

The owners of Mike-Mar make frequent trips to England, selecting Pekingese to show and for their future breeding program. Among some half-dozen really top flight prospects that have been obtained are Changte Silver Bon Bon and The Honorable Mr Twee

of Kanghe, English Best in Show winners. Another is Tweeson of Micklee (a lovely little dog that is off to a good start here), and perhaps the most exciting of all, King's Music of Calartha—like Dagbury, from Mr Sam North's justly famous kennel.

With so much going for them, it seems inevitable that Mrs Jeffords and Mr Wolf have many exciting events in their Pekingese future, especially from the homebreds which are now coming along.

Mordor

Mordor Pekingese were founded at East Weymouth, Massachusetts, in June 1967 by K. Oberg and W. Swett, Jr.

Jellison Ku Chen (bred by the late John B. Royce), is the lovely top dog here, and one in which the owners take particular pride. Ku Chen was one of Jack Royce's last homebreds, and is the little dog that Marilyn Allen smuggled into the hospital during Jack's final illness so that he might have the pleasure of seeing him.

Following Mr Royce's death, Ku Chen was sold to Mary Jellison and belonged to her for four years. In 1971 he was purchased by Mr Oberg and Mr Swett. Ku Chen enjoyed only a brief career as a show dog; he quickly gained ten points, but an accident terminated his career. He is, however, at six-and-a-half-years looking his glamourous self and siring exceptional puppies with which his owners plan to carry on the line in tribute to his breeder.

Although Mordor is not yet a famous kennel, Mr Oberg and Mr Swett look forward to the day when it will be well known. They have set a high standard for themselves and hope to produce Pekingese of excellence through the years.

Muh Lin

Mrs James M. Mullendorf has established a fine small kennel known as Muh Lin Pekingese at Charlottesville, Virginia. The stock is based on Hi Lo, Jamestown, and Caversham bloodlines, and averages about a dozen dogs.

The manner in which this kennel was started is interesting—that of beginning with a beautiful older champion no longer needed by its former owner, a method which Anna Katherine Nicholas frequently advocates. As a newlywed, Mrs Mullendorf did not feel that she could afford the young show-type Pekingese she wanted. Rather than settle for less, she purchased every book on the breed and related subjects that she could find, studied them, corresponded with breeders on differences in type, and committed countless pedigrees to memory. When she felt that she had learned enough to begin, she selected a gorgeous retired champion bitch to give her a good home and to learn still further about Pekingese from her. This was Champion Jinnetta of He Lo: she patiently (though enjoying every moment of the attention) allowed Mrs Mullendorf to work with her to perfect the technique of grooming, show ring technique, etc. In her every move she taught Mrs Mullendorf to cherish true class in a Pekingese and Mrs Mullendorf continues to this day in striving to reproduce this bitch's quality.

Champion Black Bandit of Hi Lo, Black Gem of London (co-owned with Candy McCall), and the excellent young grandson of Champion Tux-Ce-Do, Top Hat's Confetti of He Lo are the studs at Muh Lin Kennel, and some splendid young homebreds will be coming out about the time of this book's publication.

Left top: Best in Show at the 1972 Longshore-Southport Kennel Club show went to Ch. Dagbury of Calartha, co-owned by Mrs Walter M. Jeffords, Jr., and Michael Wolf. Mr Wolf handling.

Left opposite: Mrs Walter M. Jeffords, Jr, and four Pekingese co-owned by her and Michael Wolf. Left to right are Changkim Moon Raker, bred by Mrs Irene Pearson of England; Ch. Rickshaw Renaissance, bred by Ronald Rella; Mistypoint Yong-Ee, bred by Miss Jeanne Kennedy of England and Mistypoint Pasha, litter brother to Yong-Ee and bred by Miss Kennedy.

Right: Ch. Calartha Wee Bo Bo of Ecila, owned by Mr S. North. Photo by C.M. Cooke.

Pan-Zee

Pan-Zee Pekingese at Tacoma, Washington, are owned by Lloyd Stacy. He takes special pleasure in locating and importing excellent dogs from England then campaigning them to American and Canadian championships; he has been extremely successful, having finished an average of one champion annually since starting on this venture. Several of these have died through the years, but presently Pan-Zee houses eight champions, and Mr Stacy is proud of the fact that four of his title holders have each won two or more Bests in Show.

Having always had a Pekingese as a pet and being well acquainted with the charms of the breed, Mr Stacy naturally chose Pekingese when he wanted to start out as an exhibitor. Mrs Rose Marie Katz was doing conspicuously well with her fine dogs at the time and Mr Stacy communicated with her to purchase a winner to campaign in his area. Mrs Katz invited him to come to Syracuse to see her dogs and discuss the matter. As a result of this visit he purchased his first champion, the lovely Roh Kai Genie's Ching Jen, and also a little female called Rosie. Starting to campaign Ching Jen, Mr Stacy was thrilled to have him win Best in Show his third time out. And needless to say, from that day forward he was even more enthusiastic. Ching Jen went on to make a big record, and Mr Stacy went all-out to assemble the finest possible collection of outstanding show dogs.

Becoming acquainted with Miss Cynthia Ashton Cross of the famed Alderbourne Pekingese in England, Mr Stacy explained to

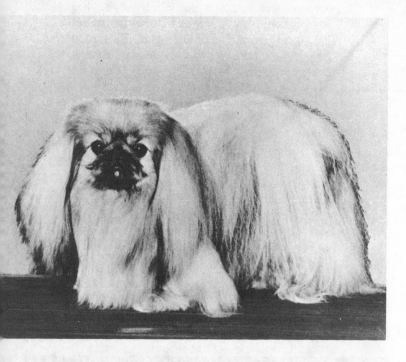

Top: American and Canadian Ch. St. Aubrey Ribena M'Lord, bred by Mrs E.J. Armstrong, and owned by Lloyd Stacy, of Tacoma, Washington. The sire was Rabena Belgran Bimbo ex Rabena SunshenErica. Photo by Fall.

American and Canadian Ch. St. Aubrey Perri of Elsdon, bred by Albert Lapointe, and also owned by Lloyd Stacy. The sire was Ch. St. Aubrey Seminole of Wanstrow ex St. Aubrey Rigilda of Elsdon.

Bottom: Another Lloyd Stacy champion: American and Canadian Ch. Alderbourne Hei Yen of Remward, bred by Dr and Mrs C.S. Drawmer. Sire, Goofus Le Grisbie ex Tui Mei Mei of Alderbourne.

her his ambitions for his dogs, stating that he was interested only in the very best. Over the years, she has sent him some excellent dogs, two of which came here as English Champions. One was famous Alderbourne Lifu of Remward; the other, International Champion Penang Kum Kwa, presently being shown with striking success. Another of Mr Stacy's dogs to make a big name for himself is Champion St. Aubrey Perri of Elsdon. Before being retired, he had been Best of Breed seventy-three times, Best Toy forty-three times, and Best in Show six times.

Pekehaven

Pekehaven Kennels are well-known in our modern Pekingese world. Their owner, Mrs Frank S. Hess of Huntington, Long Island, is on officer of the Pekingese Club of America and of the Progressive Dog Club. She recalls as a little girl that the first of the breed in her family arrived in 1918, from the Greenwich Kennels of Mrs F. Y. Mathis. His name was Lord Row Din but he was called, more appropriately, Rowdy. Mrs Hess smiles as she recalls how she and her sister used to dress him in doll clothes and how cute he looked with his small black wrinkled face peering out of a bonnet. (Such reminiscing serves to point out how patient a Pekingese can be with

children he loves.) From that time, there has always been a Peke in the family, but only as house pets, as the future Mrs Hess and her father were engrossed in the raising and showing of Sealyham Terriers.

It was in 1957 that Jerry Hess entered the world of Pekingese exhibitors with a dark red sable bitch puppy that she had purchased from Mrs Horace Wilson's West Winds Kennel. There were others during the following happy years, but this Bridget was the foundation bitch of the Pekehaven Kennels.

Bridget was bred to Mrs Wilson's Champion Sun T's Imp Sing Lee. Her daughter and granddaughter, Tabitha Tuo of Pekehaven and Tillena Ku of Pekehaven, were both bred back into the West Winds line, to Champions Ko Ko of West Winds and Champion Tuki of West Winds respectively. Among others produced was Tuki Su of Pekehaven that was well known with her mother in the Brace Class. These two won Best Brace on many occasions and were so nearly identical that even their owner sometimes mistook one for the other.

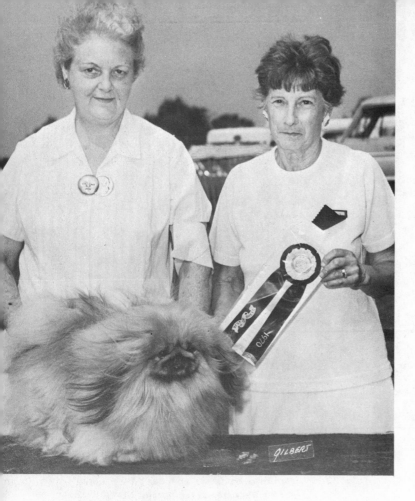

Tillena Ku of Pekehaven became the first champion Pekingese owned by Mrs Hess. Always shown in the Bred-by-Exhibitor Class, she also became a Pekingese Club of America Champion, which requires all fifteen points to be in major wins, and at least one of these to have been won at a Pekingese Club of America Specialty. She was then retired and was bred to International Champion Calartha Mandarin of Jehol at the St. Aubrey Kennels in Canada. From this mating came Champion Vanessa, and with her that line ended, as Mrs Hess felt that she was too small to be safely bred.

Meanwhile Mrs Hess had the great good fortune to acquire, also from Mrs Wilson, a dog puppy by Mrs Wilson's Champion Dah Lyn Yen Chu Tu out of Champion White Jade of West Winds. This was Jade's Buccaneer of Pekehaven, that was destined to become the outstanding member of the Pekehavens. At seven months and his first time out he went second in the Toy Group. At ten months he went Best of Breed over five champions, then third in the Group at the Progressive. He finished his title at fourteen months, followed the next week (while awaiting confirmation) by five points and Best of Winners at the Pekingese Club of America Winter Specialty.

Buccaneer continued a brilliant two-year career as a special, winning many Toy Group placements under a wide variety of judges. He died a few months ago.

Because of trouble with her back, Mrs Hess has had to give up showing and breeding for the present. Meanwhile she is building up an excellent reputation as a talented judge, which occupation she finds "utterly fascinating."

Top: The beautiful Ch. Jade's Buccaneer of Pekehaven, pictured winning Best of Breed at the Putnam Kennel Club Show in 1970 under judge Mrs David Crouse. Butch was two years and seven months old at this time, and is owned and shown by Jerry Hess, Pekehaven Kennels, Huntington, Long Island, New York.

Su-Con Stocking Stuffer... a three month old Pekingese puppy anyone would love to find by their Christmas tree! Owned and bred by Jean Carroll of Euclid, Ohio.

Bottom: Three generations of Pekehaven breeding—left to right: Tuki Su, great grandaughter, six months old; Ch. Tillena Ku, daughter, two years; and Bridget, seven years old. Owned by Jerry Hess of Huntington, Long Island, New York.

Pekingese House

Pekingese House owned by Mr and Mrs Charles L. Jordon, of Charlotte, North Carolina, is the home of fourteen champions, many of them homebred and almost without exception handled to their splendid ring records by Mae Jordon herself.

Included among the foundation of this kennel are the following: International Champion Tai Chuo of Charterway (Tai Yiang of Charterway ex Missie Yu Tong of Daiden), an English import that is a Best in Show and Group winner; Champion St. Aubrey Lin Yuanne of Elsdon, a silver daughter of Champion Lin Fu Chu of Hayreed of Elsdon

Above: Mrs Charles L. [Mae] Jordan of Charlotte, North Carolina, with Venable's Crystal Doll and Li Chik Song of Chette, sired by International Ch. Chik T'Sun of Caversham.

Below: Best of Breed winner at the Georgia Pekingese Club Specialty show in 1965 was Mrs Charles L. Jordan's Ch. Mae's Silver Sheenah. Handled by his owner, under judge Mrs J.B. Harp. Sheenah's sire was Ch. Chik T'Sun of Caversham ex Ch. Bettina's Kow Slip. Bill Evans photo.

171

Above: Ch. Luv Li Ta-Ho, pictured winning Best of Breed under judge Edith Nash Hellerman at the 1965 Charleston Kennel Club show. Luv Li was also reserve winner at the Westminster Kennel Club show the third time she was shown. Handled and owned by Mrs Charles L. Jordan of Charlotte, North Carolina.

Below: The Best in Show winning Pekingese, Ch. Mae's Woo Pe Kwo Choo, owned, bred and handled by Mrs Mae Jordan of Charlotte, North Carolina. This coveted win under judge Frank Foster Davis. Alexander photo.

ex Breakhouse Black Velvet; Champion Bettina's Kow Slip, litter sister to Champion Bettina's Kow Kow, by English Champion Caversham Ku Ku of Yam ex Champion Black Queen of Orchard House. A Toy Group winner that was the only bitch listed in the 1963 Top Ten Pekingese in the nation, Kow Slip is the dam of three champions; English import, Champion Don Hung Chin of the Dell (Champion Don Wong Ti of the Dell ex Do Peta of the Dell); Champion Loo Loo's Wi Wun Tai (International Champion Tai Chuo of Charterways ex Loo Loo Ming Toi); Champion Chuo's Ku Ku Tuh Kow Slip (International Champion Tai Chuo of Charterway ex Champion Bettina's Kow Slip), and Champion Hung Chin's Ying Hwa (Champion Don Hung Chik of the Dell ex Mekong Empress of Chette).

Other outstanding Pekes of this kennel are Champion Mae's Wu Pe'Kwo'Choo (Champion Chik Tsun of Caversham ex Champion Bettina's Kow Slip), a best in Show winner that completed his title with four majors, won the Georgia Pekingese Specialty under Alva Rosenberg, Best of Opposite Sex at Westchester (the Pekingese Club of America Summer Specialty) under Mrs Fortune Roberts, and an all breed Best in Show under Frank Foster Davis. He is retired from the ring because of an injury.

Champion Mae's Silver Sheenah, litter sister to the above, also made her presence

Below: Ch. Hung Chin's Ying Hwa, lovely Pekingese bitch who won a four point major her first time in the show ring. Handled, bred, and owned by Mae Jordan of North Carolina.

strongly felt at the shows, was a Toy Group winner, Best of Breed at the Georgia Specialty under Mrs J. B. Harp, and Best of Opposite Sex two years consecutively at the Pekingese Club of America Winter Specialty.

Champion Glenn's Chik O'Li (International Champion Tai Chuo of Charterways-Mae's Kwan Yin), Champion Mae's Little Girl Ku (International Champion Tai Chuo of Charterways-Mai's Ku-Ti-Pai), and Champion Luv Li Ta Ho (Champion Alderbourne Tulyar of Marvonne-Luv Li Feathers), and Champion Mae's Golden Slipper (Champion Luv Li Ta Ho ex Mae's Ku-Ti-Pai) are among others that have contributed to the success at Pekingese House.

Expected to have a bright future is Champion Raylmar Van Royal of Elbin (Royal Sovereign ex Dorodea's Cindy of Elbin), an importation with many Best of Breed wins, including the 1973 Georgia Pekingese Specialty under Mr Venable. Also with bright prospects is the Jordon's latest acquisition from abroad, Singlewell King Pin, by Champion Belgran King's Ransom ex Singlewell Rainbow. He is already well started towards his title. Then too, a six-month-old homebred puppy, Mae's Par-Ti Girl, is considered to be especially promising.

Mrs Jordon is a teacher and thus has limited time for breeding and showing, deserving all the more credit for the magnificent job she has done with her little Orientals.

Above: Ch. Ralymar Van Royal of Ellru, winning under English judge Stanley Dangerfield at the 1971 Spartenburg Kennel Club Show; he also won Best of Breed at the Georgia Pekingese Club Specialty Show in 1973. Sire: Royal Sovereign of Dorodea ex Cindy Lu of Ellru. Owner and handler Mrs Chalres L. Jordan of Charlotte, North Carolina.

Below: Ch. Mae's Golden Slipper, bred, owned, handled and finished by Mrs Charles L. Jordan of Charlotte, North Carolina. Earl Graham photograph.

Below: Eight month old future champion, Ber-Gum's Topaz Lin, bred and owned by Mrs Elaine Bergum of Ventura, California.

Right: Ch. Mae's Little Girl Ku, bred, finished to championship, and owned by Mrs Charles L. Jordan of North Carolina. Photo by Glen Mills.

Below: At the Pekingese Club of America Specialty Show in March, 1965, Best of Breed went to Mrs Quigley's Ch. Nia Jai Niki of Orchard Hill, and on the right, Best of Opposite Sex to Mae Jordan's Ch. Mae's Silver Sheenah. Shafer photo.

Phaleta

Phaleta Pekingese are owned by Hazelle Ferguson of Hollywood, California whose first Peke, Sun Toi Kayo, was a black-and-white parti-color purchased in a pet shop for thirty-five dollars. He was a big coated dog with a grand short body and a world of personality, but with a bit of nose. His sire was a champion that Miss Ferguson later went to see and found to be a beautiful solid black. Sun Toi Kayo sired only one litter, but among the offspring was the exquisite black Champion Phaleta's Sun Toi.

By the time Sun Toi Kayo, the kennel's original Peke, was a year old, Miss Ferguson had learned a great deal about the breed. As a librarian with access to any book she wished, she began studying and stored up much useful information for the future. She had decided that what she wanted were show dogs. As is often the case, none were immediately available for sale.

But eventually she had the good fortune to locate a fine bitch that she could take for one breeding. Miss Ferguson lost no time in availing herself of this opportunity and when the time came, selected the best stud she could locate—Champion Cha Ming Pierrot owned by Kay Francis of Altadena. This mating produced four bitches and one male. Miss Ferguson kept one bitch, Phaleta's Empress, and the male, Phaleta's Lacquer La Mu Tan Chu. These two were the foundation of all the Phaleta champions that have followed.

Empress was line bred to her sire's side and a very fine, typey bitch, Linda T'se an Mei Ling, was kept. With the mating of Lacquer and Linda, Phaleta was really on its way. Their first litter was of six puppies and five of them became champions, as did both of the second litter puppies.

Miss Ferguson's first two champions were littermates, Champion Phaleta's Gay Tune and Champion Phaleta's She Lan. It is interesting

Top right: Hazelle Ferguson of California with three of her Pekingese puppies, all of which went on to become American and/or Mexican champions. Photo by Joan Ludwig.

Right: Ch. Gaye Tune, Hazelle Ferguson's first champion at her Phaleta's Pekingese kennel in California.

175

Right: Mexican, American and Canadian Ch. Phaleta's Buddah, bred by Rose C. LeVoy, and handled in the show ring by her owner Hazelle Ferguson of California. Sire was Mexican and American Ch. Phaleta's Lu T'Sing ex Mei Ling's Fu Jin China Empress. Joan Ludwig photograph.

Below: Ch. Shelan Phaleta, bred by Anna E. Anderson and owned by Hazelle Ferguson of California. Shelan's sire was Lacquer La Mu Tan Chu ex Linda T'Se An Mei Ling. This bitch is the dam of Mrs Ferguson's beautiful black Ch. Phaleta's Sun Toi.

to note that Gay Tune and Irene Ruschaupt's first champion finished on the same day at San Diego, making that show one of true significance to the Pekingese fancy.

Miss Ferguson's breeding pattern is to make her bitches champions first and then to breed each of them for two litters only. In this way the dams stay youthful and pretty over a longer period. Phaleta puppies are never advertised and are seldom available for sale. There are many calls for stud service, but only a few are accepted. Miss Ferguson's Pekingese are raised solely to keep her supplied with something to enjoy showing.

The Phaleta Pekingese are quite small in size, mostly under nine pounds. Six of the champions have been miniatures, or sleeves, tipping the scales at less than six pounds!

Through the years since that first litter of Lacquer and Linda's only two litters have failed to produce at least one champion. A proud record, in which any breeder must take satisfaction.

Among current young hopefuls are two from Champion Go Go and Champion Reward of Wanstrow. The bitch is exceptional. Another is a red male by King's Court the Makado from a sister to Champion Cadet that looks outstandingly promising, and there are three others, which were all Futurity Puppies for the Pacific Coast Pekingese Club 1973 Specialty.

Ch. Phaleta's Sun-Toi, pictured at 11 years of age winning at the Pacific Coast Pekingese Club under judge Essie Love Jones. Owner, breeder and handler is Hazelle Ferguson of California. Her sire was Phaleta's Sun-Toi Kayo ex Ch. Shelan Phaleta.

Below: Mexican and American Ch. Phaleta's Lu T'Sing winning at Richmond, California under judge Lou Starkey. Breeder, owner and handler is Hazelle Ferguson.

Below: Hazelle Phaleta Ferguson of California with three of her early Pekingese: Ch. Phelan, 6½ pounds, Ch. Gay-Tune, 6½ pounds, and Wei Tune, a Sleeve Peke weighing 4 pounds.

Right: Mexican Ch. Phaleta's Four Star General. Bred, owned and handled by Hazelle Ferguson, he is pictured winning at the Club Canofile De Baja, California. The General's sire was Mexican and American Ch. Phaleta's Cadet ex Phaleta's Lulu. Photograph by Joan Ludwig.

Below: Mexican and American Ch. Phaleta's Wei Doll, pictured winning at the Silver Bay Kennel Club Show at San Diego, California. Breeder, owner and handler is Hazelle Ferguson of California. Wei Doll's sire was Ch. Copplestone Pulle ex Ch. Phaleta's Linda Ann. Photo by Joan Ludwig.

Left: Mexican and American Ch. Phaleta's Sug-Ar Ku-Kee wins Best of Breed at the Eden Kennel Club Show. This six pound Sleeve Pekingese was bred by Mrs Adolph A. Ruschhaupt and is owned by Hazelle Ferguson of California. Photo by Joan Ludwig.

Below: Ch. Wong Loy, many times a Group winner and also with two Bests in Show to his credit. Owner is Hazelle Phaleta Ferguson of California.

Presleen

Miss Charleen Prescott, owner of the Presleen Kennels in Ohio, came to love Pekingese as a child, her mother, Mrs Brayton Prescott, having purchased one as a pet for her youngsters who were growing up.

When Miss Prescott decided that she would like to breed Pekingese, it must have been prophetic that the only one she could find available was a white, for she has developed a strong interest in the dogs of this color.

By going to dog shows, the Prescotts soon added to their knowledge of the breed. Becoming acquainted with Nigel Aubrey-Jones and R. William Taylor led to the acquisition of their first two champions. They were also Toy Group winners. The second of these, Champion St. Aubrey Jin Tsun, became their main stud dog and founder of the Presleen line.

Shortly afterwards, Nigel Jones, knowing that Miss Prescott was fond of the whites, brought her a three-month-old paper-white puppy bitch sired by England's only white champion, Silberdjinn Splash, from the kennels of Mrs McFarlane. This highly perfected strain represented years of endeavor to breed whites that could rival in quality the best of the colors. Splashette is the founding dam, and another English import, Champion Langridge Alderbourne Top Notch, is the sire of the Presleen white line. Notch is a grandson of the great English Champion Ku Jin of Caversham.

One of the two outstanding achievements of Miss Prescott in the Pekingese world was showing Top Notch to Best of Winners at the Pekingese Club of America Specialty in conjunction with Westchester 1964. The other was the acquisition of the fabulous little English Champion Fu Yong of Jamestown for her kennel. Fu Yong quickly won a host of admirers here, to the extent that during his first eighteen months in America he serviced forty-three bitches and had to be refused to many more.

Miss Prescott is semi-retired from breeding, and now raises only a few litters annually. She is specializing in the whites, both because the latter are in constant demand and because her line is such a fine one. Presleen whites seem to carry none of the distressing faults which have often plagued Pekingese of this color. They are of good substance, broad-chested, sound in legs and topline, cobby, and free of eye discharge.

Above: Presleen Tul Yen Hih wins Best of Winners under the late judge Alva Rosenberg, at the 1966 Shawnee Kennel Club Show. His sire was Ch. St. Aubrey Ku Mandy ex Presleen Tul Kiki. Owned and shown by Ruth S. Kennedy of Chesterland, Ohio.

Right: Ch. Fu Young of Jamestown pictured winning Best of Breed at the Greenwich Kennel Club Show under judge Anna Katherine Nicholas. Fu Yong went on to Group Four in this same show. He is shown by Catherine Headershot and owned by Charleen Prescott of Ohio. Shafer photograph.

Roberts

As Mrs Fortune Roberts looks back through the years to the little parti-color Pekingese puppy that was a Christmas gift when she was eight years old, she realizes what real joy this hobby has brought to her. When a child, she devoured every book and magazine article she could find about Pekes, and she looked forward to spending vacations with her aunt and uncle, Mr and Mrs Herbert L. Mapes, owners of the Whitworth Pekingese. She especially enjoyed helping to wean the puppies, to lead-train them, and introduce them to ring procedure. Best of all was when she could skip school and go off to the Specialty, which in those days was held during January at the Grand Ballroom of the Plaza Hotel in New York City.

Mary Lou Roberts was given the lovely puppy Whitworth Pyxie as a wedding gift, and she did very well in the ring, even at the famed Morris and Essex. Pyxie was bred to a fine English import, but the arrival of the litter was somewhat harrowing as the Roberts were then living on the Naval Base at Hampton Roads, Virginia and no competent veterinarian was available.

The next tour of duty was in California. Mrs Roberts had a fine young dog, Whitworth Wicked, that had been Best Junior Puppy at the Pekingese Club of America. She entered him at San Diego and he won five points under an all-rounder. Wicked was a cobby little dog weighing just over eight pounds, and made his competitors that day look large and rangy by comparison. Mrs Roberts comments: "It is a challenge to win with a smaller dog, but if you are convinced that the ideal Pekingese is a compact dog, you will stick to breeding and buying the correct type. The satisfaction of having an outstanding Pekingese to improve the breed gives more pleasure than making records."

Mrs Roberts has never had a kennel. Her Pekingese are part of her family and share her home. When she goes away, she travels with them, on ships, trains in the old days, and mostly in the car. She finds them very adaptable and quiet, so they are welcome in the most particular places. Through the years she has made some very special friends who also are Pekingese buffs and who share her other interests of gardening, music, antiques, and art.

In 1972 Mrs Roberts enjoyed judging at Three Counties in England, where 175 Pekingese were shown.

Mrs Roberts has two lovely imports, both under eight pounds, that have finished in good company. St. Aubrey Manstone Annabelle, took a major at Westchester and another the following week at the Summer Specialty while under a year old. She finished a few weeks later, with a Best of Breed. As a special she went Best of Opposite Sex at the Pekingese Club of Southern New Jersey and also at Philadelphia. The young male, St. Aubrey Marbeau of Elsdon, finished recently. He took Best of Winners for five points at the Southern New Jersey Specialty. It is hoped that these two will produce some quality show dogs.

A darling Peke puppy from the Presleen Pekingese Kennels of Charleen Prescott.

Presleen Sweet Dream, a famous white Peke belonging to Charlene Prescott, Presleen Pekingese, Cleveland, Ohio.

A photograph for a Christmas card from the Presleen Pekingese Kennels of Charlene Prescott of Cleveland, Ohio. Pure white with black points.

Rosedowns

Rosedowns Pekingese, owned by Mrs Evelyn Ortega of Wilton, Connecticut, has been prominent in the Eastern part of the United States for a considerable period of time, and is noted for Pekingese of excellence. Mrs Ortega, a longtime former director of the Pekingese Club of America, has imported, purchased in the United States, and bred many famous winners. It is currently reported that she is contemplating the purchase of at least one promising campaigner for the future.

Recently, she has completed a novel, "Her Husband's Brother," in which a little Pekingese named Fifi makes an interesting addition to the story.

The first Pekingese owned by Mrs Ortega was an actor and a model, having appeared in three plays and on a magazine cover. One of the plays was "Some Girl" in summer stock, and he almost ended his theatrical career by biting the director. But he was forgiven. . . . Then came "Baby Cyclone", a Broadway presentation in which the Pekingese played the title role. He also played with Mrs Ortega in "The Legacy," starring Florence Reed and Louis Calhern. Though a successful French play, it had a lamentably short run here. Mrs Ortega adds that Florence Reed loved dogs, owned a pair of Yorkshires, and it was she who wanted Tsen Tsen in the play.

Ch. Yung Tony of Dah-Lyn, owned by Evelyn Ortega of the Rosedowns Kennels in Norwalk, Connecticut.

Champion Mingshang Lindy Loo of Harborough and Rosedowns, photographed by the Famous London dog photographer, Thomas Fall, before being exported to the United States where she became a top show winner for her new owner Mrs Evelyn Ortega of Norwalk, Connecticut.

Above: Lin Tong of Rosedowns, 10 month old son of Int. Ch. Ting Tong Son of Marvonne and Rosedowns, owned by Evelyn Ortega of Connecticut.

Right: Ch. Hai Hwang of Rosedowns photographed at six months of age. Breeder and owner— Evelyn Ortega, Rosedowns Kennels, Connecticut.

182

Above: Jade Song of Rosedowns, photographed by famous dog photographer Percy Jones in April, 1945 for breeder and owner, Evelyn Ortega of Rosedowns Kennels, Norwalk, Connecticut.

Above: Baby sitter. . . Jai Minx and Jai Chu Pao of Rosedowns. Puppy by Ch. Jai Son Fu of Orchard Hill ex Star Ruby of Rosedowns. Bred and owned by Evelyn Ortega of Norwalk, Connecticut.

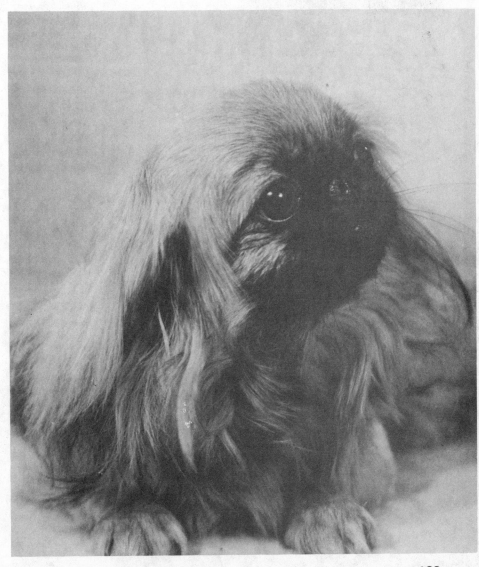

Right: A typical Rosedowns Kennels puppy. . .

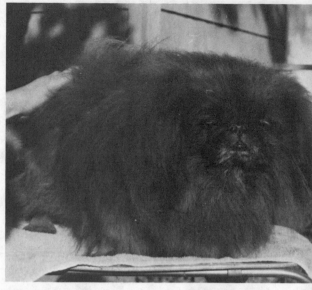

Left: Int. Ch. Jai T'Sun Jin Tong of Seng Kye, bred by Harry W. Aldrich, pictured winning at the March 1967 Pekingese Club of America Specialty show under judge William Bergum. Handled by J.P. Goode for owners Vic and Mimi Russomanno.

Directly above: Ku Chik's Ku Chi of Seng Kye photographed at almost 11 years of age. Bred and owned by Harry W. Aldrich, Seng Kye Kennels, Chico, California. This dog was the sire of Mr Aldrich's famous Tom-Mi dog.

Left: Suo Tu Yang of Seng Kye, bred by Harry W. Aldrich and owned by Doris Nagel. Mr. Aldrich's Seng Kye Kennels are located in Chico, California.

Bottom left: Twee Jai Nena of Seng Kye pictured winning Winners Bitch for a three point major at the Del Monte Kennel Club Show under judge Hazelle Ferguson. Bred and owned by Harry W. Aldrich and handled at this show by Mr. Aldrich.

Directly below: Ch. Ku Chi Jai-Mi of Orchard Hill, bred by Mrs R.A. Quigley and owned by Harry W. Aldrich of the Seng Kye Kennels, Chico, California. This was Mr. Aldrich's first champion.

3

Seng Kye

Seng Kye Kennels, at Chico, California, was begun in 1962 when Harry Aldrich bought three Pekingese to start as a breeder and exhibitor.

His success in the breed was almost immediate, and it was outstanding. In less than ten years, until the time that his wife's illness necessitated termination of the kennel, Seng Kye produced at least twenty champions. These included Specialty and all breed Best in Show winners, and Seng Kye dogs were noted from coast to coast. Mr Aldrich's stock has done well at such prestigious events as Westminster, International, Beverly Hills, Del Monte, San Francisco, the Pekingese Club of America Specialty in the United States, and at important shows in Mexico and Canada.

A believer in selective line-breeding with an occasional well-planned outcross, Mr Aldrich has raised Pekingese which are to be found behind many fine young winners. Additionally, he is a popular judge of the breed, and has written many excellent and thought-provoking articles about Pekes.

Above: Ch. Chi Chen Sin of Seng Kye, pictured winning a five point major at the Westchester Kennel Club Show in September, 1968 under judge Iris de la Torre Bueno. Bred by Harry W. Aldrich, and owned by Mimi Russomanno.

Below: Ku Chik's Kuchi of Seng Kye photographed at 10 years of age in March of 1972. Bred and owned by Harry W. Aldrich of Chico, California.

Above: Mrs Adolph R. Ruschhaupt of Fresno, California, with her first three Sing Lee Pekingese champions... Ch. Wong Sing Lee, Ch. Lee Sing Lee and Ch. Starlett Sing Lee.

Below: Ch. Ku-Chello Ditto Sing Lee pictured in March, 1972. Another top winning Pekingese from the Sing Lee Kennels of Mrs Adolph R. Ruschhaupt of Fresno, California.

Sing Lee

How fortunate it is for our American Pekingese fancy that Mrs Adolph Ruschaupt, whose Sing Lee Kennels at Fresno, California, are among the world's best known for the breed, was not the kind of exhibitor to become discouraged by less than instant success! We note this fact as an inspiration to future owners who may tend, as many do, to lose heart unless they step immediately into the magic of the winners' circle.

It was in 1934 that Mrs Ruschaupt selected Sing Lee (which she later learned was Chinese for "victory") as the family name for her dogs, and embarked on her breeding and showing program. There were twelve years of "always coming in second" before 1947 and 1948 and finally making her first champions. During those two years she finished three: Champion Wong Sing Lee, Champion Lee Sing Lee, and Champion Star Lett Sing Lee. The list of champions for Sing Lee Pekingese now exceeds seventy four. These include Specialty Show Best of Breed winners, all-breed Best in Show winners, and Toy Group winners. Quite a bit of history has been made since Toy Sing Lee, weighing less than four pounds, became the first of this now very illustrious canine family.

Mrs Ruschaupt speaks with justifiable pride of the Champions, International Champions, and Tri-International Champions that she has bred. Among them is Champion Sun T'Yung

Namise

Wong Sing Lee, sire of twenty-three champions, and thus the top producing American-bred Pekingese of record. There were also American and Canadian Champion Shanling Sing Lee, the first California member of his breed to win Top Pekingese in the Nation (under the Phillips System), whose total wins include four Bests in Show, six Specialty Bests of Breed, and forty-nine Toy Groups. And American and Mexican Champion Ku Chin Tom Mi of Seng Key won the Kennel Review Award for Best Western Toy in 1966, as well as second Pekingese and fourth Toy in the nation under the Phillips System. Other honors won by her dogs have included Best Toy Owned in California, awarded to a homebred.

Mrs Ruschaupt has only twice found it possible to come to Eastern events. But when she did come, she made her presence felt, winning Best of Breed and a Toy Group placement on the occasion of her Westminster visit, and Best of Breed over one hundred and five Pekingese the year she attended the Pekingese Club of America Specialty.

Sing Lee Pekingese are noted for their excellence of type, their truly correct, massive heads, and their soundness. America can take pride in the quality produced at this kennel. But best of all from the Ruschaupts' point of view is the pleasure the dogs have brought them, working with their Pekes having truly become a way of life and a very happy one.

Above: Ch. Chu Lee Sing Lee, Best of Breed at the Pekingese Club of Central California Specialty Show in 1953, under judge Iris de la Torre Bueno. Owner, Mrs Adolph Ruschhaupt; Joan Ludwig photo.

Right: Ch. Linsown Ku-Chello, an English import and top show winner in this country after his arrival. Owner Mrs Adolph R. Ruschhaupt of Fresno, California, owner of the Sing Lee Pekingese kennels.

Left: A Pekingese class of winners on the Arizona circuit during the early seventies. Ch. Ku Kai Wong of San Sun, Best of Breed; Ditto's Gee-Whiz Sing Lee, Best of Winners; and Ditto's Jas-Min Sing Lee, Winners Bitch and Best of Opposite Sex—bred and/or owned by Mrs Adolph R. Ruschhaupt of Fresno, California. Joan Ludwig photograph.

187

Above: Ch. Ku Kai Wong of San Su pictured winning under judge James Trullinger at the 1973 Superstition Kennel Club Show. Ku Kai was Best of Breed and won the Toy Group. Owner-handled by Mrs A. Ruschhaupt of Fresno, California.

Left: Ch. Ku-Chellos Ko-Ket Sing Lee. This dog was sired by the famous Ch. Linsown Ku-Chello, the top winning English import, owned by Mrs Adolph R. Ruschhaupt of Fresno, California.

Below: Hai Style Sing Lee, pictured winning Best of Breed at the 1965 Santa Ana California show under judge Iris de la Torre Bueno. Shown by Mr A.A. Ruschhaupt, and owned by Mrs Ruschhaupt, Hai Style went on to win Group Second at this show.

Talkabout

A small kennel of high caliber show-winning Pekingese is Talkabout, at Louisville, Kentucky, which is owned by Catherine and John Schell.

This couple's interest in the breed began while they were stationed in England with the United States Air Force, and it was there that the foundation bitch was purchased. This was Oscar's Hope of Coughton (from Lady Isabel Throckmorton's famous Coughton strain) and she is to be found in the pedigree of all the current Talkabout winners.

Among them are Champion Talkabout Pepper's Missy Yang, line-bred Coughton sired by the late Champion Saint Aubrey Pepper of Elsdon; Champion Talkabout Yu Yang Amanda Lee (Coughton-Jamestown breeding) sired by Champion Yung Yu of Jenntora ex Champion Talkabout Pepper's Missy Yang; her litter mate, Talkabout Yung Yu Tsun Pepper, pointed and Best of Breed wins to his credit; Talkabout Yu Yang Mi Fan T Zee (from a repeat of the same breeding that produced the above two) with both majors before ten months old, and Talkabout Fu Yong Manchu Idol, son of Champion Mandragora Gowd (deceased) ex Champion Talkabout Pepper's Missy Yang (now owned by Reverend Edwin Yonkers and Reverend Paul Leake in Albuquerque, New Mexico).

From the above, it is apparent that Missy Yang deserves tremendous credit as an excellent producer as well as a show bitch, for her contribution has been considerable to the success at Talkabout.

The Schells breed on a limited scale, and point with pride to the fact that all of the Pekingese they have ever shown have been in the ribbons. Serious illness has several times during the past few years temporarily reduced Mrs Schell's activity with the dogs, but Mr Schell is equally enthusiastic about them and gladly takes over in emergencies.

Talkabout Yu Yang Amanda Lee pictured winning at the Mid-Kentucky Kennel Club Show in 1972 under judge Melbourne Downing. This show was a four point major. Breeder, owner and handler, Catherine Schell, Talkabout Pekingese, Louisville, Kentucky. Earl Graham photograph.

Left: Mrs Horace H. Wilson, West Winds Kennels, Wilton, Connecticut, photographed with eight month old Kung Fu Tsu of West Winds. He is a son of Mrs Wilson's famous Ch. Dah-Lyn Yen Chu.

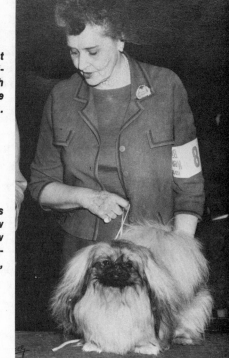

Right: Ch. Little Sun of West Winds wins Best of Breed at the 1964 Saw Mill River Kennel Club Show in New York. Peanuts is owned by his handler, Mrs Horace H. Wilson of Wilton, Connecticut.

Below: Ch. Dah-Lyn Yen Chu Tu, bred by John B. Royce and owned by Mrs Horace H. Wilson, West Winds Kennel, Wilton, Connecticut. Unretouched photograph by William M. Anderson.

West Winds

The West Winds Kennels, owned by Mrs Horace H. Wilson at Wilton, Connecticut, were started with two little Pekingese given her by her husband as a Valentine.

These unrelated dogs were a small male and a bitch of normal size. It took almost no time at all for Mrs Wilson to begin thinking what fun it would be to have a litter. She had previously raised Wire Haired Fox Terriers, Briards, and English Setters so anticipated no problems. Soon the two were bred, and in due course five healthy puppies arrived.

The next big step at West Winds was the purchase soon after World War II of the splendid English Champion Tong Tuo of Pekeboro. This was the first post-war Pekingese champion to come to the United States. He was a son of the great Champion Tong Tuo of Alderbourne ex a Caversham bitch, so represented England's finest bloodlines and proved a real asset. With a Wethersfield bitch purchased from Miss Miller in England, and a Sing Lee dog purchased from Mrs Ruschaupt in California, Mrs Wilson then had a solid foundation on which to build her kennel.

Tuo started his career in American shows by winning the Toy Group under Jack Royce his first time in the ring. There has since followed a succession of West Winds champions at the rate of one or two each year.

Following Jack Royce's death a few years ago, Mrs Wilson bought from Mrs Marion Haven the young dog of which he was most proud, Dah Lyn Yen Chu Tu, feeling that he closely resembled Tong Tuo. At fourteen months Yen Chu Tu completed his title, then took over as top stud at West Winds. To date he has sired five champions in the home kennel and several for other breeders.

While Mrs Wilson feels that the time seems to have arrived for her to give up breeding, she will always have several of these beloved Orientals in the family, including at least one of them for the shows to keep her in touch with her Pekingese friends.

In 1964 Mrs Wilson was granted judging approval, and high spots for her as a judge have included officiating at the San Francisco, Arizona, and Pekingese Club of America Specialties, and Westminster. But probably the most exciting and challenging event was the Windsor Championship Show in England, where over three hundred Pekingese were assembled for her appraisal.

Above: Volsmana Mr. Sunshine of Chungking pictured winning Winners Dog and Best of Winners at the Pekingese Club of America Summer specialty in 1971 under judge Mrs Martha Amos-Ollivier. This show was a five point major win. Owner and handler is Mrs Horace H. Wilson, West Winds Pekingese, Wilton, Connecticut.

Right: Ch. Ko Ko of West Winds photographed by Brown at two years of age. Owner and breeder, Mrs Horace H. Wilson of Wilton, Connecticut. His sire: Int. Ch. Tong Tuo of Pekeboro ex Ko Ket of West Winds, a daughter of famous Int. Ch. Caversham Ko Ko of Shanruss.

Above: International Ch. Tong Tuo of Peke-
boro with his owner Mrs Horace H. Wilson of
Wilton, Connecticut, owner of the West
Winds Kennels.

Above: Tong Tuo of Pekeboro, owned by Mrs
Horace H. Wilson of Wilton, Connecticut. Tuo
is a champion in England as well, finishing
before Mrs Wilson imported him for a show
career in this country.

Below: Ch. Dah-Lyn Yen Chu Tu pictured
center winning the Stud Dog Class at the Pekingese Club of America Winter Specialty
Show in 1969 with two of his sons, Ch. Buck-
aneer of Pekehaven and Adam of West Winds.
Owner of Yen Chu Tu is Mrs Horace Wilson of
Wilton, Connecticut.

Micklee Munji, the Pekingese with whom Mrs Louise Carwithen Snyder fell in love while in England. Munji was bred by Mr and Mrs Jack Mitchell, and was whelped on December 30th, 1970. He has one CC, six Reserve CC's and a junior warrant in England. He was sired by American Ch. Micklee Zin Rodi of Holmvalle ex Soo Yuka of Micklee. Mrs Snyder and her Windtryst Pekingese are located in Malvern, Pennsylvania.

Windtryst

Stately Louise Carwithen Snyder started showing Pekingese before World War I. Louise spent her childhood in Merion, Pennsylvania, and grew up in a family that loved animals of all kinds. Her great-grandmother showed Pekingese in 1917 through 1919.

It was in 1931 that a friend brought home a Peke from Monte Carlo and Louise fell madly in love with the dog and decided to import Ivory Tien Ku from the Ivory Kennels in Monaco for herself. At her first show two years later, Louise and Tinny took second place and Louise was "hooked" on dog shows. That was the beginning of a long and illustrious career of showing both beautiful Pekingese and a fine line of Afghan Hounds.

Louise's mother died in 1961; she was president of the Pennsylvania Women's S.P.C.A., and had a private shelter as well on her Glomar Farm. This was known as the Carwithen Foundation, and when she died there were 136 stray or abandoned animals which Louise and her sister maintained until every animal died a natural death.

Louise is married to George Snyder, an engineer, and has a son, Ward M. French, and a daughter, Louise French Gehret, by her first marriage. She also has two grandsons and a granddaughter, children of Ward and Janis French.

The Snyders keep an assortment of Pekingese, mongrels, cats, birds, and horses at Windtryst, which was a registered kennel from 1947. It is one of the few in the country to have a permanent registration. Another of Louise's occupations is The Crop Shop, a charming shop which specializes in English Saddlery.

Her memberships and positions in kennel clubs are almost too numerous to mention, but she is a member of the Board of Governors of the Pekingese Club of America.

Of all her dogs Louise admits to a few favorites. She says that each has given a little of him or herself, but she thinks Fairy Prince of Kanghe and Me Mo Te of Pickering Forge have the biggest claims to a place in her heart. She says that one of the biggest thrills of her life was when she saw Chik Tsun of Caversham win Best in Show at the Garden. In her opinion, he is THE greatest of all time.

When her beloved Prince died unexpectedly in 1973, Didi Ballinger offered Louise his only American-bred daughter, Fairymist of Claymore. Her first show was a Pekingese Fun Match in Mount Holly, New Jersey, in 1973 and she delighted Louise by going Best of Opposite Sex.

Recently Louise returned from England and brought home with her a splendid male she had fallen in love with. His name is Micklee Munji: he was bred by Mr and Mrs Jack Mitchell and was whelped in December of 1970. While in England he won 1 CC, 6 Reserve CC's, and a Junior Warrant. Great things are expected of him here.

We share Louise's philosophy for having fun in the dog fancy: "Don't ever take yourself, your wins, or your losses too seriously." Such a viewpoint indicates why Louise is so highly respected and admired in the sport she loves so much.

We feel it worthwhile to mention the contribution being made to Pekingese by Mollie and Gene Dudgeon through their magnificent publication, *The Pekingese News*.

Micklee Munji and Fairy Mist of Claymore owned by Louise Snyder, Windtryst Kennels. Munji is a recent import, bred by Mr and Mrs Jack Mitchell of England; Fairy Mist was bred by Mrs Robert Ballinger, Jr., and is a daughter of Mrs Snyder's American and Bermudian Ch. Fairy Prince of Kanghe.

CHAPTER 7

BRITISH KENNELS IMPORTANT TODAY

Alderbourne

There have been frequent references to the Alderbourne Pekingese earlier in this book. A kennel of such stature deserves very special coverage, and the authors seriously doubt that anywhere in the entire world of pure-bred dogs is there one to exceed, if even equal, the duration and accomplishments of this remarkable kennel of Pekingese.

Founded by Mrs Ashton Cross at the turn of the century and still going strong today under the ownership of her daughter, Miss Cynthia Ashton Cross, Alderbourne has been responsible for literally hundreds of magnificent champion Pekingese in all sections of the world.

Anna Katherine Nicholas warmly recalls her visit to Miss Ashton Cross, her mother and sisters Aimee and Marjorie during a trip to England about 1936. At that time the family was living at Little Shardeloes, at Amersham, in a very charming house which had been presented by Queen Elizabeth I to Sir Francis Drake. (A ghost was also believed to be in residence.) A more beautiful home, more ideal kennels, and more estimable dogs cannot well be imagined. Not long thereafter, the move to the present lovely location at Ascot was made, and it is there that Cynthia Ashton Cross still lives, with an invalid brother, and where about twenty-five to thirty of the superb Alderbourne Pekingese are kept, along with some lovely pure-bred cats. The remainder of the dogs are boarded out with a lady who has thus accommodated the Ashton Crosses during the past forty years.

Cynthia Ashton Cross wishes that she could do more showing than is possible for her to manage nowadays, but an ailing back limits her activities in this regard. She says, however, that she enjoys breeding future champions for other fanciers to show; certainly quality remains supreme.

Top star of the present is the bright young hopeful, Alderbourne Princely Gift. He is indeed well named to judge by his pictures, and is line-bred to the famous Champion Chinaman of Alderbourne. The latter was the wonderful son of Champion China Doll of Alderbourne that tragically died of an unidentified malady when only two-and-one-half years old, so Miss Ashton Cross is especially happy at having this excellent descendant. Chinaman's dam, Champion China Doll, was a special favorite of Miss Ashton Cross, who says of her "I think her the best bitch ever bred. Not only marvelous to look at, but the loveliest character. Ideal in every way, and such an eye-catcher. Her son, Chinaman was perfection, a dream come true."

Champion Tul Tuo of Alderbourne was the sire of Champion Goofus le Grisbie, purchased by the Ashton Crosses from Mrs Ogle. Grisbie's progeny seemed to "nick" just right with those by Chinaman, with the result that they are behind innumerable winners and champions.

Miss Ashton Cross points out that the fabulous post-war Ca021bbreeding. Which is hardly surprising, for a warm friendship and admiration for one another's dogs quite obviously existed between the ladies of Alderbourne and Mary de Pledge even back in the days when Anna Katherine Nicholas became friends with them all. And the pre-war Cavershams, too, as mentioned in the historical chapter, were based on the early Alderbourne dogs.

Champion Yu Tong of Alderbourne and his son, Champion Tong Tuo of Alderbourne, are responsible for half the champions in England, largely through Champion Ku Chi of Caversham and Champion Caversham Ku Ku of Yam. Champion Ku Chi of Caversham was an Alderbourne grandson on both sides, his dam having been bred and sold by the Ashton Crosses. His son, Champion Caversham Ku Ku of Yam, was out of a Champion Tong Tuo of Alderbourne daughter ex a daughter of Grey Toi of Alderbourne, and "remarkably like Tong Tuo." It is almost overwhelming to contemplate the contribution these four dogs, Yu Tong, Tong Tuo, Ku Chi, and Ku Ku have made to the breed!

Above: Ch. Alderbourne China Doll, grand-daughter of champions Tong Tuo of Alderbourne and Don Wongti of the Dell. Bred and owned by the Misses Ashton Cross of England.

Right: The great Tulyar of Alderbourne, one of the most famous of all sires. Sire of Ch. Tul Tuo and many, many other champions and show winners. Bred and owned by the Misses Ashton Cross of The Wilderness, Berks, England. Photograph by Thomas Fall, London.

Below: Prince Fong of Alderbourne, a half-brother to the famous Princely Gift of Alderbourne, both bred and owned by the Misses Ashton Cross of England.

Then there was Champion Tul Tuo of Alderbourne, son of the mighty Champion Tulyar of Alderbourne, the latter by Tong Tuo. Tulyar was also the sire of a special favorite, Champion Tul Yuling of Alderbourne, that was never used for breeding as she was almost a sleeve. The aforementioned Champion China Doll of Alderbourne was a granddaughter of Champion Tong Tuo. And among Tong Tuo's history-making progeny was also Champion Alderbourne Lin Yutang (from Champion Lin Yuan of Alderbourne) that became a full champion before he was a year old. Lin Yutang, in turn, sired the glorious bitch, Champion Tang Yua of Alderbourne.

Another remarkable bitch was Champion Yula of Alderbourne. She was not only a superb winner, but was dam of many winners, including two daughters, Wee Yula and Tong Yula, and a beautiful son, Wee Tulo. He was a great sire, one of his daughters being the dam of Champion Copplestone Pu Zee.

In England now, the famous white dog, Limelight of Alderbourne, is gaining tremendous prestige as a sire, giving magnificent puppies of all colors. Everyone wants to use him, and he is getting more white than colored mates. There are dozens of winners to his credit, at least several of which would seem to be certain future champions. Miss Ashton Cross has a beautiful red daughter of his with black mask, and a grey son with black mask. These are Golden Light of Alderbourne and Shining Light of Alderbourne. There are also two pure whites. The demand for his pups is so tremendous that she has difficulty keeping any of them for herself.

For details on the earliest Alderbournes, we refer you to the chapter on History and Development of the Breed in England, and also to the comment in the section on post World War II period.

Top right: Three generations of champions from the famous Alderbourne Kennels in England. Ch. Yu Tong on the bottom step, his son Ch. Tong Tuo on the middle step, and his son, Ch. Ling Yu Fang on top! Owner—Miss Ashton Cross.

Alderbourne Chinese Prince, son of the famous Ch. Tul Tuo, and sire of Alderbourne Princely Gift and Prince Fong. Owner, Miss Ashton Cross of The Wilderness, Berks, England.

Bottom: Chinamen of Alderbourne at one year of age. Owned by the Misses Ashton Cross, England.

Left: Ch. Meng of Alder-bourne and Ch. Chuanne of Alderbourne with a friend. Owned by the Misses Ashton Cross.

Left: The beautiful white, Limelight of Alderbourne, a great show winner and an outstanding sire at the Alder-bourne Kennels of Miss Ashton Cross in England.

Left: A corner of the Alder-bourne Trophy Room. All these trophies were won outright, including the bowl for champion of all breeds, at the famous Crufts show—the world's largest dog show. Alder-bourne is owned by the Misses Ashton Cross of The Wilderness, Berks, England.

A lovely headstudy of Alderbourne Princely Gift, owned by the Misses Ashton Cross of England.

Right: Champion Antoinette of Loo-foo, featured on her owner's Christmas calendar in 1952. Owned by Mrs R. Jones, Keepers Cottage Farm, in England.

Below: Princely Gift of Alderbourne, pictured at five months of age. Bred and owned by the Misses Ashton Cross of The Wilderness, Berks, England.

Right: Alderbourne Chinese Princess, a big show winner and a superb brood bitch from the English kennels of the Misses Ashton Cross in Berks, England.

199

Left: Ch. Alderbourne Lin Yutang, whelped August, 1948, bred and owned by the Misses Ashton Cross, The Wilderness, Berks, England. Lin Yutang was the youngest champion ever—under nine months of age when he gained his title.

Right: Ch. Chu-anne of Alderbourne photographed in the early thirties. She is by Ch. Yu Chuan of Alderbourne. The Alderbourne Kennels are located in England.

Right: Ch. Tong Tuo of Alderbourne, bred by Mrs Ronald Silcock and owned by the Misses Ashton Cross, The Wilderness, Berks, England. Tong was whelped in September 1946, and was the sire of the famous Ch. Lifu of Alderbourne.

Beaupres

The Beaupres Pekingese are owned by Mrs Elizabeth Mirylees and Miss Fiona Mirylees at How Caple, Herefordshire, England.

Mrs Mirylees was born in 1920 and her first husband, Lt. Col. Garnons Williams, was killed in action during World War II. Subsequently she married Major J. S. Mirylees, now a noted authority and judge of cattle and sheep

Below: Ch. Kefof Silber, winner of 158 prizes at open and championship shows in England. Property of Mrs A.L. Beart, Walton on Thames, England.

and also District Commissioner of the Pony Club. They had five daughters and a son who died when only eight months old.

Mrs Mirylees describes her interest in Pekingese as "almost an obsession," and the depth of this interest is reflected in the success and quality of her dogs. Although she sometimes feels neglectful of her family, she says "my marriage has lasted for twenty-seven years, so I cannot have been too blatant."

Mrs Mirylees likes most dog breeds, but after Pekes, likes especially Borzois (of which she once owned a champion), Chihuahuas, and Yorkshires. A Persian cat and a Whippet also share what remains of her home after the Pekingese have finished with it. Also she loves her garden and floral arrangements, and is "houseproud to the point of lunacy." None of these are helped by keeping dogs, so Mrs

Mirylees says that she lives in a state of split personality, alternately switching from "House Beautiful" to "Dog's Life."

No one else is entrusted with the care of the Beaupres Pekingese except Miss Mirylees. All breeding, whelping, grooming, training, and the handling are done personally by mother and daughter. Mrs Mirylees has been British correspondent for "Pekingese Parade" for five years, and has written many articles for other publications.

Daughter Dawn Braham was the original partner in Beaupres and helped her mother handle International Champion Beaupres Lovely Star of Grimston to many of his splendid wins. Dawn is now a Director of Market Research in London, and her eight-year-old daughter is already being schooled by grandmother in the art of becoming a breeder of show Pekingese.

Fiona is the second daughter and Mrs Mirylees' "indispensable right hand." It is Fiona who now handles the Pekingese in the ring; she has the distinction of being Britain's youngest International Champion show judge of Pekingese. Daughters Clementina, Jackie, and Jean are the "horse branch" of the family, following a passion that their mother can no longer pursue.

Mrs. Mirylees owned her first Pekingese when she was aged three, and has never since been without at least one only except the barren eleven years following the war when her husband was a District Officer in Germany. Immediately upon return to England she began breeding Pekingese seriously. About ten years ago, an export of hers became the first from her kennel to win an American championship. This was American Champion Beaupres Kan Jin of Jamestown, and as Dawn was in America at the time, she helped handle him to his title.

English Champions owned by Beaupres have included previously-mentioned famous International Champion Beaupres Lovely Star of Grimstoy (by Champion Ping Yang of Coughton) and his dam, Champion Ku Nanette of Grimstoy, that won the "Pekingese Parade" trophy for the bitch producing the most champions. Nanny died in 1972, having spent a happy old age (she was fourteen) with her breeder, Dorothy Williamson, who also bred Lovely Star.

Champion Toydom Sunshen Chu Tsun was also a great favorite at Beaupres. Bred by Mrs Colomb, he was purchased by Mrs Mirylees from Mrs A. C. Williams, owner of the Toydom Kennels. Mrs Mirylees credits him with putting coat and big round eyes into her strain.

Then there was Champion Sheraton Toydom Contessa, bred by Mrs Brown, that produced in her very last litter Champion Beaupres Harlequin Lad of Laughton Brook, sire of many winners for Michael Hughes Halls in South Africa. Mr Halls also owns Champion Beaupres Berserk that has already sired two African champions.

White Pekingese are favorites at Beaupres, and some good ones are being bred. Both of the white studs are championship show winners, and their puppies look lovely.

Of all her many dogs, the one that shines brightest in Mrs Mirylees' heart and in the Beaupres strain is Oliver Twist. She purchased his dam from Miss Hilton of the Wongvilles, a small black bitch mated to Oliver of Wongville. The resulting litter consisted of just the one puppy—"the ugliest, most miserable thing I ever saw. Only his personality saved him from the scrap heap." However, by the time he was a year old he was looking quite nice and had proved himself as a sire. Before his first litter was born, Mrs Mirylees had promised him to Fred Schultz in Canada, so off he went. To Mrs Mirylees' surprise, this

Top left: Ch. Beaupres Oliver Two-Tone, bred by Mr and Mrs D.G. Thomas and owned by Julia A. Milota of Papillion, Nebraska. Oliver is shown here winning Best in Show under judge Henry Stoecker at the 1968 Michiana Kennel Club show. Handled for his owner by Judy Slaughter. E.H. Frank photograph.

Left: Ch. Cho Sen Master Khan, shown with owner and handler Mrs J.A. Riney, Jr. Master Khan was bred by the G.W. Voyles of Louisville, Kentucky, and is the sire of many champions.

Below: English Ch. Toydom Sunshen Chu T'Sun, owned by Mrs E. Mirylees and Miss F. Mirylees, of the Beaupres Kennels in Herefordshire, England. Frances Pilgrim photograph.

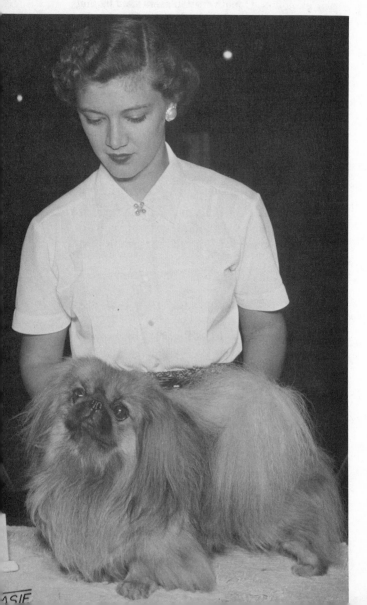

litter contained the exquisite parti-color American Champion Beaupres Oliver Two Tone that won his Junior Warrant before being sent to America to do some marvelous Toy Group and Best in Show winning under the handling of Judy Slaughter. Also in the litter was a gorgeous bitch, Beaupres Miss Oliver Twist, that also won her Junior Warrant and Reserve Challenge Certificate. Fred Schultz very kindly allowed Mrs Mirylees to repurchase Oliver. This little dog weighed seven pounds, carried a huge coat and was excellent in body and legs, but could not be shown because of a marked eye. However, he sired winner after winner, including nine champions of which Mrs Mirylees is certain, three Reserve Challenge Certificate winning daughters, four Junior Warrant winners, and numerous other excellent offspring. Oliver died in 1972, but his influence on Beaupres Pekingese will continue through succeeding generations.

Probably the most exciting export to America for Mrs Mirylees has been Champion Beaupres Lea Chim, a grandson of Beaupres Robert of Pekespan. Lea Chim quickly became an American champion, has piled up a formidable array of top awards, and gave Mrs Mirylees her greatest thrill when she heard that he had been Best Toy and seriously considered for Best in Show at Westminster 1969.

As the Best in Show judge there that year, Anna Katherine Nicholas confirms the fact that this lovely Pekingese was pressing extremely hard for the top honors. The Beaupres overseas champions have been legion, and Mrs Mirylees follows their careers with ardent interest.

Champion Oakmere The Baron is another export to America in which Mrs Mirylees takes pride, for it is she who directed him to Mrs Painter. Champion Beaupres Wonderful Prisca was later sold to Mrs Painter, and is already the sire of three American winners in addition to doing well himself in the ring.

Beaupres keeps only twenty adult Pekingese, never using one for breeding unless it is good enough to win at championship shows. This policy has paid off, as the kennel qualified seven dogs and bitches for Crufts 1973, and three other Beaupres Pekingese qualified for their owners. Mrs Mirylees believes that no other kennel can beat that record.

203

Donhead Hall, in Dorset, England, the estate of Mrs Horn, hostess for the Sleeve Pekingese Club of England's first show. Here the show committee and exhibitors gather to welcome American judge Betty Shoemaker of Bridgetown, New Jersey, at a buffet luncheon before the judging.

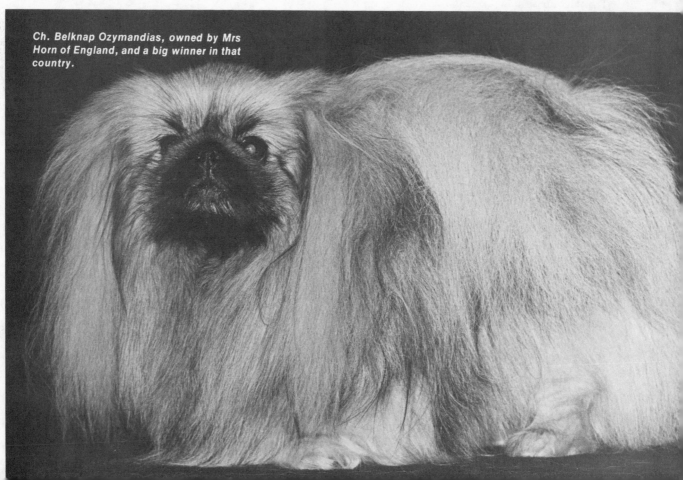

Ch. Belknap Ozymandias, owned by Mrs Horn of England, and a big winner in that country.

Belknap

The Belknap Pekingese are owned by Mrs T. W. Horn of Dorset, England, who founded them entirely on descendants of Champion Caversham Ku Ku of Yam.

Champion Suzie Wong of Jamestown, Belknap Jin Song of Jamestown, and Belknap Jinella of Caversham are the Pekingese to which Mrs Horn credits her success, for these were her original stock. Suzie Wong, a famous winner in her own right, will go down in history as the dam of English, American, and Canadian Champion Fu Yong of Jamestown. Jin Song has numerous high awards to his credit, including Reserve Challenge Certificate. And Jinella, bred to Champion Ping Yang of Coughton, produced Belknap Beau that has won three Reserve Challenge Certificates and sired two champions.

Champion Belknap Ozymandias, one of Beau's sons from Belknap Volksmana Kiki Dee, the latter a full sister to Champion Chunking Yong Tisun, has done especially well for Mrs Horn, having taken the 1973 Reserve Challenge Certificate at Crufts after beating seven other champions in the Open Class and also having gained the 1972 Pekingese Club Gold Medal.

Belknap Solitaire is a daughter of Champion Suzie Wong and was sired by Champion Ku Jin of Caversham. She has thus far won a Challenge Certificate and a Reserve Challenge Certificate; Belknap Ilya, grandson of Suzie Wong, has a Reserve Challenge Certificate. Champion Belknap Sugar Plum is by Belknap Beau from Belknap Faygold Sugar, the latter a daughter of Belknap Jin Song of Jamestown.

There are also Belknap Boy Blue and Belknap King Bee, both sons of Champion Yu Yang of Jamestown from a Champion Ku Ku of Yam descended parti-color Reserve Challenge Certificate winning bitch. Both of these dogs also have Reserve Challenge Certificate wins to their credit.

All the Pekingese at Belknap live in the house, many with the family always, the others by turns. Mrs Horn finds breeding and showing an utterly fascinating occupation and a thoroughly rewarding hobby.

Belknap Jin Song of Jamestown, photographed in superb condition at 11 years of age. Another great winning dog owned by Mrs Horn of England.

Ch. Suzie Wong of Jamestown, with her daughter Belknap Solitaire, owned by Mrs Horn of England.

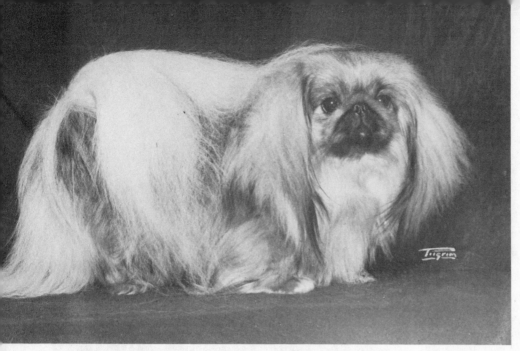

Belknap Solitaire,
owned by Mrs Horn of
England.

Belknap King Bee, photographed
by Pilgrim of England for the owner, Mrs
Horn.

Mrs Horn's Belknap
Beau, photographed by
Pilgrim in England when he
was 18 months of age.

Ch. Belknap Sugar
Plum, owned by Mrs Horn
of England and photo-
graphed by Pilgrim.

Changte

The Changte Pekingese, located at Wakefield, England, are owned by Mrs Pauline Bull, a devotee of this breed since childhood.

Mrs Bull's first bitch was of the Chinatown strain. When her puppies were due, the young owner though only thirteen years of age at the time, whelped the litter personally and selected a bitch puppy to keep. Such a good choice did she make that this little one took Best Puppy in Show her very first day in the ring.

Approving of her daughter's hobby, Mrs Bull's mother bought her two more Chinatown bitches, then several from the Parkfield Kennel. One of these was named Bonzette of Changte; and, since she was of similar bloodlines, she was mated to Champion Bon Dah of Kingswere and thus became the bitch on which the Changte Kennel was founded.

In 1937 a fawn brindle male called Cho Dah of Changte was added, he being a grandson of Champion Yu Dah of Chinatown. This dog won numerous Best of Breed and Best in Show awards and is behind all of the present Changte stock.

Mrs Bull's first champion was Storm Chief of Changte, by Sunstorm of Changte. He distinguished himself by winning thirty-five Best in Show awards. His grandson, Dorian, sired three champions, including the noted Champion Do Do of Changte. Another Champion Storm Cloud son, Champion Yung Chief of Changte, was the first post war champion in Australia and sire of many Royal Show winners.

Mr and Mrs Bull were married in 1939. Happily, Mr Bull shares his wife's enthusiasm for Pekingese. In fact, love of Pekingese seems to run in the family, as their daughter, Lyndal (born in 1947), has been going to dog shows since she was six months old, and is now a well-known judge.

Champion Crown Prince of Changte is described by his owner as having been one of her most valued producers, having truly left his mark on the breed. He won his third Challenge Certificate and thereby became a champion at the Pekingese Reform Show in London in April 1962, where he was also Best of Breed. There were thirteen top-flight champions entered at this show.

Meeko of Changte, a beautiful orange-red of fine type and grandeur, won the Challenge Certificate and Best of Breed at Leicester in 1959. He sired three champions, including Champion Crystal Crown of Changte that has five Challenge Certificates. She in turn has produced several winners, including Champion Kybourne Crystal Coral of Changte that

English Ch. Tudor Treasure of Changte, winner of four CC's including Crufts and several Best in Show awards. She has her name on the Crufts Lady Betty Cup and also won her Junior Warrants in record time. . . within 13 days at two shows, Crufts and Pekin Palace. Owner is Pauline Bull, Changte Pekes of Wakefield, England.

won Challenge Certificates at Crufts and the Pekingese Club among his current total of five. Her litter brother is the International Champion Chuffy's Crown of Changte that won Best in Show at an all breed championship show in Brazil during 1973.

Another of Mrs Bull's outstanding sires has been Tudor Prince of Changte, a chun red miniature with a fabulous coat and ear fringes that touched the ground. He won well as a puppy, but, unfortunately, a marked eye ended his show career. He sired Champion Tudor Beau, Champion Tudor Queen (with fifteen Challenge Certificates), Champion Tudor Treasure (four Challenge Certificates including one at Crufts under Mrs Rae) and Tudor Gem, who has one Challenge Certificate and two reserves.

Champion Tudor Treasure of Changte and Tudor Gem of Changte both have their names engraved on the Crufts Lady Betty Cup. (For those who do not remember, "Lady Betty" was Miss L. C. Smythe who for years wrote the Pekingese column in one of England's leading dog magazines.) Both won their Junior Warrants in record time, within thirteen days at two shows only, Crufts and the Pekin Palace Specialty. The Changte affix is also the first to appear on the Rosalind Becket Trophy presented by the Pekingese

Above: Changte Chuffy's Laurel, pictured at 10 months of age, a beautiful home-bred owned by Pauline Bull in England. Whelped in 1972, she was sired by Ch. Chuffy's Charm.

Above: English Ch. Crown - Prince of Changte, the magnificent grandsire of the top winning male and the top winning female in Britain today. Owned by Pauline Bull of the Changte Pekingese, Wakefield, England.

Reform Club. Royal Crown, litter brother to Champion Crystal Crown, won the J. E. Parker Memorial Trophy presented for the first time to the winner of the Toy Group in 1964. Champion Chuffy's Charm won the President's Trophy on offer for the first time for Best in Show at the Pekingese Club Championship Show in 1970 and the Kyratown Cup on offer for the first time at the Invicta Championship Show in 1971.

Probably the most exciting dog show Mrs Bull can recall as an exhibitor was Birmingham 1970, where Crystal Coral won the bitch Challenge Certificate and Chuffy's Charm won the dog Challenge Certificate and Best of

Breed under Lady Isobel Throckmorton, the Toy Group under Mr J. Bradden, and on the second day won the Best Dog or Bitch in the Toy Group under Herr Olaf Roig.

Mrs Bull takes pride in the fact that she has built up a strain which is producing not just one outstanding dog but a succession of good dogs. In 1966 she mated Champion Tudor Treasure to Champion Crown Prince, from which came Prince Chuffy of Changte. In his short life, this beautiful dog won six Bests in Show, and in less than two years at stud, he sired three champions: Champion Crystal Coral of Changte, International Champion Chuffy's Crown of Changte, and the top winning homebred Pekingese, Champion Chuffy's Charm of Changte—who represents Changte strain for seventeen generations.

Below: English Ch. Chuffy's Charm, winner of the Presidents Trophy for Best in Show at the Pekingese Club Championship Show in 1970 and winner of the Kyratown Cup offered for the first time at the Invicta Championship Show in 1971. Owned by Pauline Bull, Changte Pekingese, England.

Below: Changte Silver Charm, Reserve CC winner and owned by Mrs Pauline Bull of the Changte Pekingese, Wakefield, England.

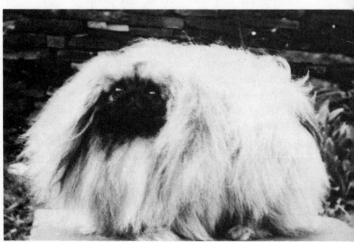

Kinwong

Mrs G. A. G. Williams, owner of the Kinwong Kennels at Bushy Heath, Herts, England, made her first Pekingese championship during 1931 in the country now known as Sri Lanka. This was Ceylon Champion Tai Moo of Alderbourne.

A homebred daughter of Champion Goofus le Grisbie that became Canadian Champion Tondelayo of Kinwong, was her second to gain the title. This was in 1961, during her husband's two year diplomatic appointment at Ottawa.

Mated to American and Canadian Champion St. Aubrey Mario of Elsdon, Tondelayo produced five puppies, among which were Canadian Champion Frederick The Great and two lovely bitches, Kinwong's Princess Pretty Girl and Kinwong's Little Tania, both imported back to England with Tondy. Pretty Girl became the dam of American Champion Romana of Kinwong.

Champion Tondelayo's descendants have produced a number of overseas champions since then, and also Mrs Williams' exciting young future hopeful, Kinwong Moon Shadow, by Mrs Holman's English and American Champion Etive Copplestone Pu Zin, Jr., which was bred by Mrs Williams.

An unfortunate accident cut short the show career of a beautiful parti-color, Dawn of Kinwong, by Champion Lawrence of Wongville, who had already won two Challenge Certificates and thus needed but one more for her title. She has, however, produced two excellent parti-color daughters, Kinwong Morning Star and Kinwong Snowflower. The latter has given Mrs Williams Kinwong Flavia, by Limelight of Alderbourne, as yet too young for the shows, but a promising well-marked parti-color.

Top right: Dawn of Kinwong at just nine months of age. This lovely little parti-color has won two challenge certificates, one Reserve C.C., and a Junior Warrant. Bred by Mrs Betty Williams of England and owned by Mrs Rees.

Nordic Champion Moonman of Kinwong, photographed at six months of age in January, 1969. He was sired by Ch. Sunshen Fan Tan ex Kinwong Peakette of Pendarvis, is owned by Mrs Lundquist of Sweden, and bred by Mrs Betty Williams of England.

Bottom: Kinwong's Princess Pretty Girl, sired by American and Canadian Ch. St. Aubrey Mario of Elsdon ex Canadian Ch. Tondelayo of Kinwong. Owned and bred by Mrs G.A.G. Williams of England.

Canadian Ch. Tondelayo of Kinwong, sired by Goofus Le Grisbie ex Kinwong Snowflower of Alderbourne. Owned and bred by Mrs G.A.G. Williams of Herts, England.

Below: A six-week-old litter by Canadian Ch. Tondelayo of Kinwong, sired by American and Canadian Ch. St. Aubrey Mario of Elsdon, and bred by Mrs G.A.G. Williams while she resided in Canada. The center puppy was bought by the late Mrs Mosely of Orchardhous prefix and became Canadian Ch. Frederick the Great.

Lotusgrange

Lotusgrange Pekingese are owned by Mrs Mary Robertshaw, who bought her first Peke in 1952. However, it was her second purchase made shortly after that really started the development of the strain from which all her present winners are descended.

This important bitch was named Betee Meng of Lotusgrange, whose mother's line was based on the Yen Chow Pekingese famous in England for several descades. Mrs Robertshaw lived near Miss Coleman, who owned the Yen Chows. They became friends and she was permitted to breed her bitch to Miss Coleman's beautiful Yen Chow Chi Su. From this mating came Mrs Robertshaw's first winner, Yeng Sing of Lotusgrange, to be found in the pedigree of nearly every Lotusgrange show Pekingese since that time.

The magnificent Champion Jina of Lotusgrange was from Mrs Robertshaw's third purchase. Jina started her show career at the age of seven-and-a-half months, at the Pekingese Reform Association Championship Show in April 1962, under Mrs Helen Bruce on her first day of championship judging. Jina won Special Puppy Bitch, and she was never thereafter beaten in her classes until she became a champion at fourteen months old. At only one championship show during her short life was she placed below first, and this was at the British Pekingese Club Championship Show one week after she had finished her title.

Jina was in the ring again in January 1963 at the Pekingese Club Championship Show in London, winning Open Bitch and taking the Reserve Challenge Certificate to Miss Pilgrim's lovely Champion Cheryl of Chintoi. At only eighteen months of age she went to Crufts 1963, and under that great authority, Miss Cynthia Ashton Cross, she was judged

Above: Flavia of Kinwong, whelped 1972 and sired by Limelight of Alderbourne ex Kinwong Snowflower. Breeder and owner Mrs G.A.G. Williams, Herts, England.

Jina of Lotusgrange arrives at her first dog show! Just seven months old, future Ch. Jina of Lotusgrange was carried to the Pekingese Reform Association Championship Show at Seymour Hall in London. She is owned by Mrs M. Robertshaw of Yorkshire, England.

Fair N' Square of Lotusgrange, a lovely cream dog owned by Mrs M. Robertshaw, Lotusgrange Pekingese, Yorkshire, England.

Best of Breed. At the time of writing she is the last Pekingese bitch to gain Best of Breed at Crufts.

One month later she was dead, a heart-breaking loss to her owner and to her breed. Mrs Robertshaw picked up, however, and continued breeding from Jina's half-sister, Choola of Lotusgrange, and has since continued to produce a long string of top class winners, many of which have become champions abroad.

Top dog presently in Mrs Robertshaw's kennel is World Venture of Lotusgrange, winner to date of a Challenge Certificate, and sire of some fine youngsters now coming out with good success. World Venture's older full-brother is Dutch Champion Fu Yang of Lotusgrange, whose progeny are gaining Challenge Certificates for his Dutch owner, Mrs Oosterhof of Utrecht. Before leaving

An oil painting of Ch. Jina of Lotusgrange, with the Douglas Murray Challenge Trophy which she won at Crufts in 1963 as Best of Breed. The artist was Margaret Redfern Smith. Jina's sire was Bracewell Jen Yuan of Caversham and her dam Lotusgrange Titian Girl of Telota. Owner is Mrs M. Robertshaw of Yorkshire, England.

England, Fu Yang sired a lovely bitch, Only A Wish of Lotusgrange (now owned by Mrs C. Sterling), that had three Reserve Challenge Certificates and should gain her title.

Fair N Square of Lotusgrange is a splendid show dog and producer for Mrs Robertshaw. On his dam's side he goes straight back to her Yeng Sing line, his sire being mostly of the Silverdjinn strain for which Mrs McFarlane is famous. This excellent dog seems to make a perfect stud for Mrs Robertshaw's other line, which is from bitches that were sired by Jamestown dogs. Latest litter at the kennel is by World Venture of Lotusgrange ex a Fu Yang daughter, and it is hoped that one of these puppies may follow in Jina's illustrious pawprints.

Oakmere

One of England's fine, and very successful, Pekingese kennels is Oakmere, belonging to Mrs O. M. Clay at Stafford.

1957 was the year in which Mrs Clay's foundation female was purchased from Queensmere Pekingese. After breeding two litters of pet puppies from her, Mrs Clay decided that she would prefer to concentrate on show stock so took her bitch to the late W. Hindley Taylor's kennel where she was mated to Champion Oberon of Kyratown. From this came a very lovely parti-color bitch that was named Maid Marion of Oakmere. She in turn was mated to Yung Tong Loo of Kanghe, owned by Miss L. M. Mould. The result was two male puppies, one of which Mrs Clay sold to a friend. The other had not especially interested Mrs Clay until Miss Mould asked if he were for sale, at the early age of seven weeks. From which inquiry Mrs Clay assumed that he must have been more promising than she had realized, and she decided to keep him.

This dog matured into a truly beautiful Pekingese. He loved the shows, thus always did his best in the ring. Very seldom was he not winner of an award, and Mrs Clay's greatest thrill with him was at Crufts in 1963 when he was selected for the Challenge Certificate by that very knowledgeable judge, Miss Cynthia Ashton Cross. As do all show dogs, he had his ups and downs, but in due time he gained his other two Challenge Certificates under Mrs Drake and Mrs Strachan, becoming Champion Sandiacre of Oakmere. Mrs Clay received numerous tempting offers from the United States for this dog.

Sadly, Sandiacre only reached the age of seven years. But he left a heritage of many excellent first and second generation offspring, and Mrs Clay is still showing and winning with his descendants. The most popular of these is the outstanding Dolly Daydream, an exquisite miniature weighing a mere four-and-one-half pounds. This charming parti-color has tremendous character and is dearly loved by fanciers, both of Pekingese and of other breeds. Mrs Clay speaks of her as being the top-winning miniature of the present time.

Another handsome Oakmere homebred was the famous American Champion Oakmere the Baron, owned by Ruthe and Irving Painter, so successfully campaigned by his handler, Elaine Rigden.

There are many lovely show specimens at Oakmere as this is written, all of them winners at the championship shows. Some also have gone to other countries, where they have done well for their new owners.

At present Mrs Clay has high hopes for two youngsters of exceptional promise; Oakmere the Count and Oakmere the Countess.

The strikingly beautiful Oakmere Dolly Day Dream of Upcot, owned by Olive Clay, Staffordshire, England.

International Ch. Oakmere Ku-Zin-Zee, bred by Olive Clay of Staffordshire, England. Owned by Irene and Herbert Hess of West Germany.

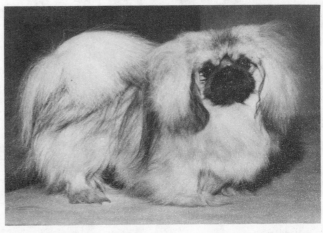

213

Left: Oakmere Clover of Kanghe, magnificent Pekingese photographed by Pilgrim for breeder Olive Clay of Staffordshire, England, and now the property of Mrs and Miss Mirylees.

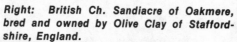

Right: British Ch. Sandiacre of Oakmere, bred and owned by Olive Clay of Staffordshire, England.

Left: Patrick of Oakmere, the lovely Pekingese owned by Mrs Olive Clay of the Oakmere Kennels in Staffordshire, England and photographed for her by Thomas Fall.

Right: Manstone Ku-Chi of Oakmere, the property of Mrs Olive Clay of England.

Wongville

Wongville Pekingese were founded in 1960 by Miss M. Hilton of Clarendon, near Salisbury in Wiltshire. This is a small kennel of highest show type Pekingese and never houses more than eight adults at a time.

Miss Hilton made her first champion after only three years as an exhibitor. This was Lawrence of Wongville, that besides winning nine Challenge Certificates, four Reserves, Junior Warrant, etc., gained Supreme Champion All Breeds at England's second largest indoor show, the Ladies Kennel Association, and was reserve for the honor at Chester Championship Show when he was only sixteen months of age. Lawrence additionally was the Top Toy Dog in Great Britain for 1964. His sire was International Champion Wongville Tio Pepe of Shirleymoore, his dam Wongville Gay Wun of Dromeden. She also produced Oliver of Wongville that besides winning Junior Warrant, Reserve Challenge Certificate, and Best in Show was even better known as a superlative sire.

Oliver's progeny include Champion Humphrey of Wongville, Olivia of Wongville, and other well-known winners. Olivia, a Reserve Challenge Certificate winner, became dam of of the beautiful Barnaby of Wongville that, with another of Oliver's daughters, Olwyn of Wongville, produced the "fabulous twins" International Champion Nathanial of Wongville and Wongville Dream of Olwyn that has won a Challenge Certificate, two Reserves, Junior Warrant, Best in Show, and other honors.

Champion Nathanial sired the lovely Wongville Kinwong Nathanial, Reserve Challenge Certificate and Junior Warrant winner before going to the States. Nathanial also sired other champions before he was exported to Switzerland.

Another son of Oliver of Wongville is the handsome Obediah of Wongville, perhaps the most beautiful of them all. Already a Best in Show winner, he is considered to be a future champion. Obediah's first daughter in the ring is Wongville Olympia and already a first prize winner.

The Wongvilles are very carefully line-bred and are all house pets, having delightful personality and manners. Only about three litters are produced here annually, which makes Miss Hilton doubly proud of their record as compared to those of far larger kennels. Truly, Wongville stands for quality rather than quantity.

Oliver of Wongville, another handsome Peke owned by Miss Mary Hilton.

Ch. Lawrence of Wongville, a familiar winner in Britain, owned by Miss Mary Hilton of Dorset, England.

Olwyn of Wongville, a British winner owned by Miss M. Hilton of Dorset, England. Photo by Pearce.

Below: Ch. Chun-Vhu-Fu's Monarque's Pasha bred and owned by Shirley Stone of Burbank, California, is shown winning at the 1966 Greater Miami Dog Club show. Handled for owner by Leota Vandeventor.

Above: Olivia of Wongville, fawn brindle bitch owned by Mary Hilton of the Wongville Pekingese, Dorset, England. Diane Pearce photograph.

Below: Chinky Sing's fifth birthday party on December 19th, 1936. Photograph from the collection of Iris de la Torre Bueno.

CHAPTER 8

PEKINGESE IN OTHER COUNTRIES

Pekingese in Canada

Pekingese interest in Canada has been consistently strong through the years. The most widely-known kennels there are undoubtedly those owned by Mr Nigel Aubrey-Jones and Mr R. William Taylor but there are many others of excellence.

Mrs A. R. Caruso started breeding in 1928 with an English importation and later added other importations from the Chinatown line, eventually developing her own strain. Three homebred, pre-fifties champions from this kennel were Champion Chief Fee Tee, International Champion Sou Chow of Orchid (sold to Mrs Bradley of Detroit during the late forties), and Champion Moley.

Mrs Winifred M. King also did well with Chinatown stock, her first brood matron having come from that English kennel in 1929. This importation was mated to Champion Chipps of Chinatown (owned by the late Archie Semple, whose Pekingese kennel was one of the largest in Western Canada during the twenties and who had a worthy list of champions to his credit, a goodly number of them homebred). His first litter produced Champion Kingwin Kao Shing and Cactus Yan Yan for Mrs King. Yan Yan in turn sired Champion Cactus Ku Chi, the grandsire of Champion Straven My-ka-lon. Champion Kingwin Ted Dee among others that made their presence felt at the shows. The Kingwin Kennel was a small one, with never more than three matrons at a time, making Mrs King's percentage of winners more noteworthy.

Mrs Gladys Creasey's name is also familiar to Pekingese fanciers who remember events of a few years ago. Her foundation stock was based on the Cha Ming San Fu line (Champion King San Fu of We Kee-Champion Cha Ming Wee Tykee II), going back to both Mrs Lansdowne's and Mrs Sears' excellent dogs, and an Ashcroft outcross through descendants of Champion Regent's and Champion Monarque's. The quality of Mrs Creasey's Pekingese is obvious when one reads back to recall that from April 1944 to May 1945 they won five Bests in Show and twelve Toy Groups, and important breed victories in both Canada and the United States. They added considerably to these honors during following years.

The Hill Ridge Kennels of Mrs Hilda M. Brint were based on foundation stock from Orchard Hill, Whitworth, Toytown, Willowtoun, and Ashcroft. Mrs Brint had little time to spend in showing, and sold the majority of her finest puppies, usually keeping not more than twenty Pekingese in the home kennel for breeding. Champion Romeo Tu of Orchard Hill, by Pierson of Orchard Hill (Tri-International Champion Pierrot of Hartlebury of Orchard Hill ex Hula of Chinatown of Orchard Hill) from a Champion Han Chuan of Orchard Hill (by the mighty Champion Sutherland Avenue Han Shih) daughter was purchased by Mrs Brint from Mrs Quigley and become a tremendous asset as the sire of winners.

The Wu San Kennels were started by Mrs Germaine Mattice during the forties and she owned some beautiful Pekes. Mrs Mattice,

The beautiful Canadian Ch. H'In San's Tinker Toi.

Above: Ch. Chop Chop of Elmore, bred by Pius Sullivan, Jr., and owned by Mrs David Mabon of Canada. Chop Chop is pictured winning Best In Show at Amherst, Nova Scotia in May, 1965 under judge Louis Murr. Handler is Mrs Mabon.

Below: Canadian Ch. Kyratown Red Robin of Kofu, Group First at the New Brunswick Kennel Club Show in Saint John, N.B., Canada. Judge for this show was Melbourne Downing. Robin was bred by Mrs E. Ball and was sired by English Ch. Puz Puz of Kyratown ex Li Sel of Kofu. Owners are Mr and Mrs David H. Mabon, Montague, P.E.I., Canada.

Bottom: Canadian Ch. Puz Althaea of Kyratown wins Best In Show at the Abegwett Kennel Club's all-breed show in June, 1971. Bred by Mr W. Hindley Taylor, Puz is owned by Mr and Mrs David Mabon of Canada and handled by Mrs Mabon. His sire was Int. Ch. Puz Kin of Ardpriory ex English Ch. Althaea DoDo of Kyratown.

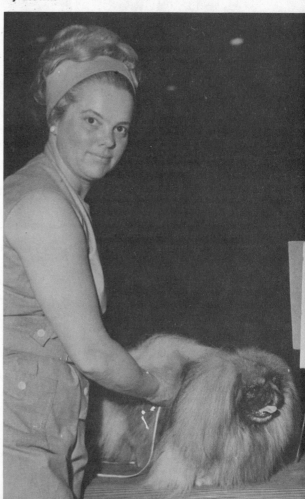

who formerly lived in Montreal, moved to the country in 1941 to have more space for the Pekingese kennel she had always wanted. There she started to assemble a fine foundation stock. From a visit to Jack Royce's, she brought back two bitches, Desteena of Dah Lyn and Noel's San San (by International Champion Nanking Noel). Several months later she added Chang Wu of Dah Lyn (son of Champion Pier Simba of Orchard Hill) and Noel's Zara of Dah Lyn. Wu San Kennel also owned Belinda of Dah Lyn, which was of double Champion Kai Lung of Remenham breeding on her sire's side and of double International Champion Nanking Noel's on her dam's. Chee Kee of Dah Lyn, by Champion Pagan Chieftain O'Palart, and Shen Tung, by Champion Cha Ming Shen Hung were also there.

One of the most popular of toy judges is Mrs Yan Paul; she is also a long-time Canadian Pekingese breeder, having based her kennel on Ashcroft, Rowantree, and Wu Kee dogs.

Mrs Kate McBroom was a faithful exhibitor and breeder of Pekes in the fifties, making many visits to Westminster and other American shows as well as to those in Canada. Among her Pekingese were Daisy's Ying of Acol, Poppy's May Quay, Daisy Wu San, Jasmine of Ciffnock, and Poppy's Toy Sun.

In the sixties, Mr and Mrs V. A. Hearne started making their presence felt both here and in Canada. One of their best-known campaigners was the exquisite bitch, Champion St. Aubrey Marie Dee of Elsdon. They also had Peter of Mingulay, Champion St. Aubrey Eloise of Elsdon, and a number of other quality Pekes with them on their rather frequent visits to the United States shows.

Data follows on two of Canada's most successful Pekingese kennels of the present. There are of course others, but this introduction will give some idea of who and what are currently in the Canadian limelight.

Sanpan Pekingese are owned by Mrs David H. Mabon, who has recently moved to Montague on Prince Edward Island in Canada, and is presently occupied with getting a new kennel constructed and ready for increased activity with the dogs now she has retired from business.

Mrs Mabon's first Pekingese was purchased in 1959, and she has been a breeder since 1963. Her first Best in Show was won in 1965 by Champion Chop Chop of Elmore under Louis Murr. This happy event, however, soon became a sad memory as Chop Chop came to an untimely death less than two weeks later.

Canadian Ch. Sanpan's Perry Puz-Kin, bred and owned by the David Mabons of Canada. Puz-Kin was Best Canadian-bred in Show at the 1972 show at Moncton, New Brunswick, Canada. The judge was Mr Harvey Grafton. Handler is Mrs Mabon.

Canadian Ch. Sanpan's Yung Mario, pictured winning Best In Show at the New Brunswick, Canada, Kennel Club Show in Saint John, in November of 1967. The judge was George Kane. Mario was handled by David Mabon, his breeder and joint owner with Mrs Mabon.

CAN. & AM. CH. ST. AUBREY
MARIO OF ELSDON

ENG. & AM. CH. CALARTHA
YEN LO OF SUALANE

ENG., CAN. & AM. CH. CALARTHA
WEE BO BO OF ECILA

CAN. & AM. CH. ST. AUBREY
NO NA OF ECILA

CAN. & AM. CH. ST. AUBREY
MARIGOLD OF ELSDON

AM. CH. TEMPLE BELLS OF
BLOSSOMLEA

CAN. & AM. CH. ST. AUBREY
MARIETTA OF ELSDON

ST. AUBREY ROSEBUD OF
WANSTROW

ST. AUBREY TINKABELLE
OF ELSDON

ST. AUBREY-ELSDON

Above: *A reproduction of the December, 1961 issue of Dogs in Canada, featuring nine of the world-famous St. Aubrey-Elsdon Pekingese which were owned or handled by Nigel Aubrey-Jones and R. William Taylor of Canada. Many of these dogs were later sold to others who campaigned them in the show ring of Canada and America.*

Below: International Ch. St. Aubrey Argus of Wellplace, top-winning show Pekingese bearing the kennel prefix of Nigel Aubrey-Jones of Canada.

Ch. Gwynne's Fran-Kee, photographed in November, 1969 and bred and owned by Mrs Florence Gwynne, Vincentown, New Jersey. The sire was St Aubrey's Etive Chipples ex Stack's Holly Sun.

220

Int. Ch. Chik T'Sun of Caversham, bred by Miss I.M. de Pledge and Mrs H. Lunham. He was imported by Nigel Aubrey-Jones and R. William Taylor and owned by Mr and Mrs C.C. Venable. Throughout his brilliant and record-breaking show ring career he was handled by the late Clara Alford.

St. Aubrey Eloise of Elsdon, winner of the Toy Group at the 1963 Windham County Kennel Club Show under judge Edwin Pickhardt. Co-owned by Nigel Aubrey-Jones and R. William Taylor of Canada.

In 1968 Mrs Mabon imported from W. Hindley Taylor what she considers to be her first truly great dog, Champion Puz Althaea of Kyratown. Champion Sanpan Penelope was bred to this dog and from that mating came Champion Sanpan Perry Puz Kin. This youngster has followed in the manner of his sire and his dam by becoming a Best in Show winner in May 1972 when eighteen months old.

Since then there has been a lull in activity at Sanpan while the Mabons were moving from St. John, Nova Scotia, to their new home. Mrs Mabon now feels that Sanpan is about to embark on its finest era, as she will now have the time that she could not spare before in which to do considerably more breeding and showing of her dogs. First step towards this will be getting a litter from an exquisite imported bitch, Puz Melody of Kyratown, sired by Champion Sanpan Perry Puz Kin.

The St. Aubrey-Elsdon Pekingese are located at Red Roofs, the charming home of Nigel Aubrey Jones and R. William Taylor at Ste. Therese, Quebec. These two Pekingese enthusiasts were pen-pals exchanging ideas on their mutual interest in the breed when Mr Taylor lived in Canada and Mr Jones in Wales. Bill Taylor went to England for two years; when he returned home, Nigel Jones came with him to settle in Canada. The combined talents of these two men brought them phenomenal success and their importations and their opinions have had a vast influence on our modern Pekingese world. In addition to their imports, they are outstanding breeders and have produced many exquisite and widely acclaimed homebreds in their kennel.

At one time, Mr Jones was asked to name the most important of his importations. The

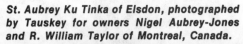

St. Aubrey Ku Tinka of Elsdon, photographed by Tauskey for owners Nigel Aubrey-Jones and R. William Taylor of Montreal, Canada.

English, American and Canadian Ch. Caversham Ko Ko of Shanruss. Imported by Nigel Aubrey-Jones and R. William Taylor, Ko Ko was Best In Show at Westchester in 1956 and eventually was owned by Mrs Saunders Meade.

English Ch. St. Aubrey Fairy Ku of Craigfoss, bred by Miss B. Piggott of England, and owned by Nigel Aubrey-Jones and R. William Taylor of Canada.

Canadian Ch. St. Aubrey Debonaire of Elsdon wins Best in Show at the United Kennel Club in Montreal, under American judge Percy Roberts. Debonaire had five Groups and three Bests In Show on the five occasions she was shown in Canada before she was 16 months of age. Club president Mrs Sylvia Dempster appears in this 1965 photograph with handler Nigel Aubrey-Jones who co-owns Debonaire.

answer was "English, Canadian, and American Champion Caversham Ko Ko of Shranruss, Best in Show at Westchester in 1956 over two thousand dogs." Ko Ko was later sold to Mrs Saunders Meade, handled by Ruth Burnette Sayres, and his death before he had the opportunity to attain his potential as a show and stud dog was a tragic loss.

Mr Jones felt that Ko Ko's spectacular success at Westchester really paved the way for another of his importations, the magnificent Champion Chik Tsun of Caversham, which was sold to Mr and Mrs Charles Venable and piloted by Clara Alford to become America's numerically leading Best in Show winner of all breeds with one hundred and twenty-five top awards.

Among the Best in Show winning Pekingese brought to America by Nigel Aubrey Jones are English, Canadian, and American Champion Calartha Mandarin of Jehol (sire of more than twenty champions), Champion Rikki of Calartha, St. Aubrey Mario of Elsdon, and St. Aubrey Seminole of Wanstrow, all of which were sold to Mrs Vera F. Crofton and all were sires of Best in Show winners.

English, Canadian, and American Champion Bingo of Elsdon; Champion St. Aubrey Debonaire of Elsdon; English and American Champion Mathilde of Kettlemere; English, American and Canadian Champion Goofus Buggati; Champion St. Aubrey Tinkabelle of Elsdon, and scores of other widely known winners are owned by Mr Jones and Mr Taylor or have found their way to new owners through them.

Above: American and Canadian Ch. St. Aubrey Goofus Brescia, bred by Roberta Ogle, and imported by Nigel Aubrey-Jones and R. William Taylor. Brescia is owned by Mrs Nathan Allan and is pictured here winning at the Kennel Club of Philadelphia show in December, 1967, under judge Ramona Van Court; handled by Nigel Aubrey-Jones.

Right: English, American and Canadian Ch. Calartha Yen Lo of Sualane, imported by Nigel Aubrey-Jones and R. William Taylo of Canada. Yen Lo is owned by Mrs G. Livingston.

International Champion St. Aubrey Tinkabelle of Elsdon, Best In Show winning Pekingese owned by Nigel Aubrey-Jones and R. William Taylor of Canada. Photographed for the owners by Evelyn M. Shafer.

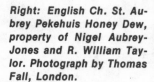

Right: English Ch. St. Aubrey Pekehuis Honey Dew, property of Nigel Aubrey-Jones and R. William Taylor. Photograph by Thomas Fall, London.

American and Canadian Ch. St. Aubrey Marietta of Elsdon, bred and owned by Nigel Aubrey-Jones and R. William Taylor of Canada. Marietta was photographed in 1961.

Right: Two St. Aubrey-Elsdon puppies sired by the famous Tri-International Ch. Goofus Bugatti; owned by Nigel Aubrey-Jones and R. William Taylor.

Ch. Bingo of Elsdon, co-owned by Nigel Aubrey-Jones and R. William Taylor of Canada. He won Best of Breed at the Specialty Show of the Pekingese Club of America held in 1958 under the late judge Alva Rosenberg.

Right: Ch. Calartha Mandarin of Jehol pictured winning at the Baltimore County Kennel Club Show in April of 1959. Mandarin was owned and handled at this time by Nigel Aubrey-Jones who captured this win under judge Anna Katherine Nicholas. The dog was later sold to Mrs Vera Crofton of California. Shafer photograph.

225

Left: Ch. Smoki-Wyncote, C.D., and Ch. Lundilu's Honeymoon, top dogs at Fran and Ray Alcock's Pekingese Kennels in North Bay, Ontario, Canada. This lovely black and tan male is top stud dog at their Canadian kennel.

Left: Ch. Smoki-Wyncote, C.D. photographed in this magnificent portrait for owners Fran and Ray Alcock of North Bay, Ontario, Canada.

Pekingese in New Zealand

At Christchuch, New Zealand, the Montresor Kennels owned by Mrs Hazel Ridgen have been at the center of the Pekingese world since 1937 when Mrs Ridgen imported her first Peke from England.

This was the very typical eight-pound dog, Toydom Pung Kee, that quickly gained his championship and won many Best in Show awards. Mated with imported bitches (that also easily became champions), he was an immediate success as a sire in his new home, a number of his offspring attaining championship and Best in Show honors.

The records list Champion Toydom Pung Kee offspring as Best Pekingese at twenty championship shows and Best Pekingese Puppy at twenty-four shows during 1940. To him also goes the credit for having brought the previously much needed flat face to New Zealand's Pekingese.

Pung Kee was the sire of Mrs Ridgen's first homebred Best in Show winner (Champion Man Zee of Montresor) and also of Champion Moonflower of Montresor, the first of Mrs Ridgen's Pekingese to gain its title while still a puppy. His most famous daughter was Champion Mittens of Montresor who produced whole litters of champions and Best in Show winners. The number of outstanding champions whelped at this time made Montresor the kennel to win most often in New Zealand, but then the war put a curb on breeding and showing.

To maintain the continuity of the splendid line that had been established, it was necessary to keep on importing dogs from England each year. Over a period of some thirty years Mrs Ridgen brought in some fifty Pekingese representing England's leading champions and stud forces, a total unapproached by any other kennel in New Zealand. After the war, one of the first Montresor importations was the very valuable Champion Ching Wu of Sherhill which had a wonderful career in New Zealand, during which she was undefeated for Best in Group and was many times Best in Show at some of New Zealand's largest championship events. A son of Ching Wu, Champion Timothy of Montresor, won the star puppy attraction at the Dominion, the Canterbury one hundred pound Puppy Stakes (an award which has come to Montresor on various other occasions as well) and other important honors.

Following the war there was naturally what amounted to a stampede for good stock in England, and as the availability of first-rate Pekingese was consequently quite limited, Mrs Ridgen decided to open kennels in London under the control of her sister, Mrs Irene Tennant. In this way it was possible to use the best and most expensive stud dogs in England and bring out only the cream of their stock to New Zealand, Mrs Tennant buying and mating the Pekingese selected mainly on pedigree by Mrs Ridgen. Using this method, Mrs Ridgen found it possible to achieve more within five years than she could possibly have hoped for had she continued simply sending for importations from time to time. On the best bitches procurable, world famous sires were used. Among these were English Champion Yu Tong of Alderbourne, English Champion Ku Chi of Caversham, English Champion Yusen Yu Toi, Yung Tai Choo of Caversham, Tai Yun of Shangtoi, and the noted Puffball of Chungking that sired such an outstanding number of English champions.

In addition to various Pekingese that had been sent out previously, Mrs Tennant left London for New Zealand in 1950 bringing along eighteen of the best ever to leave England in a group. Included were such excellent bitches and Best of Show winners as Champion Araminta of Montresor and Champion Tong's Lien Tzu of Montresor (a grand-

Left: A happy Betty Shoemaker of Bridgeton, New Jersey, posed for this Philadelphia Inquirer photograph after winning the first of three (to date) Best Brace in Show awards with her Sleeve Pekingese, at the Pekingese Club of Southern New Jersey show.

La Baronesse de Bondeli with her famous team of Pekingese, which were all winners at the continental shows. This photograph was taken in Paris, France, in 1913.

daughter of Champion Yusen Yu Toi), and Champion Puffball of Montresor that won high acclaim as a sire in New Zealand.

With all the magnificent bitches in the kennel, an outcross was needed for the splendid youngsters being bred from them. Two fine dogs were selected; Kelpie of Sherhill, son of English Champion (and later American Champion) Caversham Ko Ko of Shanruss, and Ku Tuo of Pendarvis, son of English Champion Caversham Ku Ku of Yam. Both dogs proved to be valuable sires, and a daughter of Kelpie, Champion Ko Yula of Montresor, made history by winning the Canterbury One Hundred Pound Stakes at the age of five and one half months.

In 1956 Mrs Tennant visited England again and brought back three more bitches, the most successful of which was Champion Fu Shen of Leeway that became a Best in Show winner in New Zealand.

Famous winners of the early sixties at the Ridgen kennel were Champion Ko Tong of Montresor, winner of many successive Bests in Show, and Champion Red Emperor of Montresor, a dog that won Best in Show six times and Reserve Best in Show three times in his last ten showings.

In 1962 Mrs Ridgen visited Miss de Pledge in England and was fortunate in being able to secure a beautiful young dog, Jin Tuo of Caversham, a small but heavy eight-and-a-half-pound Peke, inundated with coat and fringes. He fulfilled Mrs Ridgen's hopes for him by transmitting his splendid coat and type to his descendants. His progeny included Champion Bacchus of Montresor, that had the remarkable distinction of winning Best of Group every time shown during 1968, 1969, and 1970. Another litter by him contained American Champion Jin Choo of Montresor owned by Mr and Mrs J. R. Henderson of Colorado, and the outstanding Best in Show winning bitch Champion Jinta of Montresor.

On still another visit to England, in 1969, Mrs Ridgen purchased the Championship Show winning puppy, Simona of Loofoo, from Mrs Jones. Simona finished her championship quickly upon her arrival in New Zealand, and when mated to a son of Champion Etive China Boi of Alderbourne, purchased earlier from Miss Ashton Cross, she produce dthe stunning fawn dog, Champion Dandino of Montresor. After a number of Best in Show wins during 1972, Dandino went on to win the award of Best in Show all breeds at championship events no fewer than seven times during the first four months in 1973, becoming a leading contender for New Zealand's "Dog of the Year" for all breeds.

In selecting her Pekingese, Mrs Ridgen feels that it has been a tremendous advantage that she has frequently visited Britain while on round-the-world judging tours. Mrs Ridgen is on the New Zealand Kennel Club's Judges Panel for all breeds, and has judged in some twenty countries. Her judging assignments seem almost invariably to include Pekingese, thereby giving her the pleasure of evaluating the breed at such prestigious events as Westchester (the Pekingese Club of America Summer Specialty) in the United States, International Championship events in Sweden, Finland, Switzerland, etc. In 1971 Mrs Ridgen became the only woman in the world living outside the British Isles to be on the English Kennel Club's "A" list for the judging of Pekingese at Championship shows.

It is generally said that the Montresor Pekingese are bright, intelligent, and very human. Which may be attributed to the fact that they have never been treated as kennel dogs but are all house pets and have the constant companionship of human beings in a home managed with the comfort of the dogs of prime concern.

Left: Miss Virginia Brittingham awards Best of Breed to Mrs Quigley's Pier Chi Son of Orchard Hill at the Pekingese Sleeve Dog Association show on September 13th, 1935.

Below: Miss Virginia Brittingham judging the Winners Bitch Class at the Pekingese Sleeve Dog show on September 13, 1935. Exhibitors from left to right, are: Miss Hodges, Miss Samuel, Mrs Mathis, Mrs Schaffeur, Mrs Quigley and Mrs Austin, all prominent Pekingese owners and breeders of the thirties.

CHAPTER 9

THE SLEEVE PEKINGESE

For a considerable period of time, little attention has been paid the to smallest members of the Pekingese family, popularly known as the Sleeves, yet these were perhaps the most popular and desired of all during the breed's development in China. We should not forget that the Chinese empress said of them "Let the Lion Dog be small, and for its color, let it be that of the lion—a golden sable to be *carried in the sleeve* of a yellow robe, or the color of the red bear, or a black or a white bear, or striped like a dragon, so that there may be dogs appropriate *to every costume in the imperial wardrobe*," which would mean that such a Pekingese would indeed need to be within the six-pound weight limit which designates the sleeve dog.

The five original Pekingese which were taken from China to England in 1860 are described as having been small, and we have heard it said that Looty, the parti-color presented to Queen Victoria, was actually a Sleeve.

Here in the United States, Sleeve Pekingese were so appreciated four or five decades ago to the extent that a Pekingese Sleeve Dog Association of America was formed, and held an Annual Specialty open only to Pekingese weighing less than six pounds. Anna Katherine Nicholas was Show Secretary for the event held by this Association on September 13, 1935, at the estate of its President, Mrs James M. Austin, Catawba Farm, Old Westbury, Long Island.

Other officers of the Association at that time were Vice-Presidents Mrs M. E. Harby of Huntington, Long Island, and Mrs Michael M. Van Beuren of Gray Craig, Newport, Rhode Island, and Secretary-Treasurer Mrs F. Y. Mathis of Greenwich, Connecticut.

The event was judged by Miss Virginia Brittingham of Scarsdale, New York, and there were twenty-seven dogs in thirty-six entries.

Exhibitors were Mrs Richard S. Quigley, Lock Haven, Pennsylvania, with eight dogs; Miss Helen E. Samuel, Arlington, Virginia, with three; two each from Mrs Everett M. Clark, Schroon Lake, New York, the Misses S. F. Hodges and A. Perret, Ridgefield,

Connecticut, Mrs H. B. Kerner, St. Albans, Long Island, and John B. Royce, Gloucester, Massachusetts. Single entries were owned by Mrs Austin, Mrs Mathis, Mrs Carrie Sass of Rockville Centre, Mrs Philip M. Schaffner of Merrick, Miss Camilla Muller of Brooklyn, and Mrs Marian Walters of Cold Spring Harbor the latter all New York State.

Puppy Dog Class, 6-9 months

Mrs Clark's Dee Dee of Miralac (Da Zeng of Miralac–Loakai of Roblips: December 21st 1934. Breeder, Mrs A. Spilbor).

Mrs Quigley's Pier Yu Go of Orchard Hill (Pier Son of Orchard Hill–Hula of Chinatown O'Orchard Hill: February 21st 1935. Breeder, owner).

Two entries

Puppy Dog Class, 9-12 months

Mrs Kerner's Sambo (Ker's Romeo of Mi-K–Ken Lu Go Go. Breeder, owner).

One entry

Novice Dogs

Mrs Sass' San Toy (Chang Kai Sung–Mi Fu: September 4th 1934. Breeder, owner).

One entry

American-bred Dogs

Miss Samuel's Little Boy Blue (The Squire of Walmsley–Me Me II: May 1st 1933. Breeder, owner).

Mrs Quigley's Pier Chi Son of Orchard Hill (Pierre Pont of Orchard Hill–Chi Malita of Orchard Hill: June 10th 1934. Breeder, owner).

Mrs Clark's Dee Dee of Miralac (Particulars above).

Three entries

Limit Dogs

The Misses Hodges and Perret's Shokin of Dah Wong (Chin Clair Sun Star–Majang Adaer: no date of birth. Breeder, Mrs Salmanson).

One entry

Open Dogs, red or sable

Miss Quin's Ming Toy Boy II (Ski Sik of Fu Jay–Wee Wee of Sunny Ning Po: October 29th 1932. Breeder, Mrs Minnie Nelson).

One entry

Open Dogs, any other color

Mrs Clark's Dee Dee of Miralac (Particulars above).

One entry

Open Dogs, black or black and tan

Mrs Kerner's Sambo (Particulars above).

One entry

Puppy Bitch Class, 6-9 months

Mrs Clark's Totsu of Miralac (Da Zeng of Miralac–Lokai of Roblips: December 21st 1934. Breeder, Mrs A. Spilbor).

Mrs Quigley's Han's Chuty Pet of Orchard Hill (Champion Han Chuan of Orchard Hill–Maizee of Huntington Orchard Hill: January 18th 1935. Breeder, owner).

Mrs Mathis' Greenwich Bar Bee (Champion Pierrot of Hartlebury–Barbara of Toddington: December 25th 1934. Breeders: Miss Carolyn and John B. Royce).

Mrs Quigley's Pyxie Tu of Orchard Hill (Vanity of Pechelee of Orchard Hill–Pyxie San of Orchard Hill: March 12th 1935).

Mrs Quigley's Pier Janina of Orchard Hill (Pier Son of Orchard Hill–Ceedah of Chinatown: March 11th 1935. Breeder, owner).

Five entries

Puppy Bitch Class, 9-12 months

Miss Samuel's Little Bo Peke (Fu Chin Hai Tzu–Ching Nuitzu: October 10th 1934. Breeder, owner).

Mrs Kerner's Gond De Moun of Mi K (Ker's Romeo of Mi K–Ken Lu Go Go. Breeder, owner).

Two entries

Novice Bitches

Mrs Quigley's Pier Gran Nee of Orchard Hill (Pier Jai Foo of Orchard Hill–Chi Malita of Orchard Hill: January 29th 1935. Breeder, owner).

Mrs Quigley's Tzu Chu Tai of Orchard Hill (Champion Sutherland Avenue Tzu Eh–Champion Ku Rai of Remenham O'Orchard Hill: January 15th 1935. Breeder, owner).

Mrs Mathis' Greenwich Bar Bee (Particulars above).

Three entries

American-bred Bitches

Mrs Samuel's Little Miss Muffet (The Squire of Walmsley–Me Me II: May 1st 1933. Breeder, owner).

Mr Royce's Simba of Dah Lyn (Champion Pierrot of Hartlebury–Barbara of Toddington: December 25th 1934. Breeder, Miss Carolyn and John B. Royce).

Mrs Quigley's Tzu Bi Jou of Orchard Hill (Champion Sutherland Avenue Tzu Eh–Champion Ku Rai of Remenham O'Orchard Hill: January 15th 1935. Breeder, owner).

Mrs Austin's Chin Clair Trinket of Catawba (Sam Lo of Meridale–Chin Clair Pee Chee: September 5th 1930. Breeder, Chin Clair Kennels).

Mrs Walters' Clearwater Mai Mai (Clearwater Nowata Jim-Mi–Clearwater Nowata Sis-Tr: July 13th 1930. Breeder, owner).

Mrs Clark's Totsu of Miralac. (Particulars above).

Six entries

Limit Bitches

Miss Muller's Kewpie Doll of Rellum (Ieu Ieu–Chinkey B.M.: December 28th 1931. Breeder, Mrs Ava Curtis).

One entry

Open Bitches, red or sable

Mrs Schaffner's Tweedle Dum of Ashcroft of Merricak (Rufus of Ashcroft–Bon Nee of Ashcroft: August 29th 1933. Breeder, Mrs H. Weaver).

Mrs Austin's Chin Clair Trinket of Catawba (Particulars above).

Two entries

Open Bitches, any other color

Mr Royce's Delilah of Dah Lyn (Champion Pierrot of Hartlebury–Barbara of Toddington December 25th 1934. Breeders, Miss Carolyn and John B. Royce).

Mrs Clark's Totsu of Miralac (Particulars above).

Two entries

Open Bitches, parti-color

Miss Quin's Tzu Eh Lin (Sutherland Avenue Chi Sun–Sutherland Avenue Tzu Lin: March 10th 1932. Breeder, owner).

Misses Hodges and Perret's Tatsu of Dah Wong (Dah Wong of Dah Wong–Hsuan No of Dah Wong: April 30th 1934. Breeders, owners).

Two entries

Mrs Clark had an entry in the Brace Class. And Miss Muller's Kewpie Doll was entered in Special American-bred Dogs and Bitches.

We think it interesting to note that three of the entries, those bred by Carolyn and Jack Royce, were from the same litter, and all very small—as also the number from Mrs Quigley's strain.

Of the Sleeve Pekingese that Anna Katherine Nicholas remembers with particular admiration through the years, three stand out especially. These are Mrs Quigley's fabulous Champion Pier Simba of Orchard Hill, Mrs Everett M. Clark's Teenah of Miralac, and Miss

Helen E. Samuel's Little Boy Blue. These were tiny Pekingese of noted excellence. Simba made his title in very keen competition, attracting tremendous praise for his big, "doggy," excellently proportioned head, his beautiful body, and his soundness. He was truly a miniature edition of what one looks for in a Pekingese. Teenah was an absolute doll, smaller than Simba at only about two-and-three-quarter pounds, while Simba, if memory serves correctly, weighed about five pounds. Teenah's appearance in the show ring invariably created a sensation, and it must be certain that Mrs Clark refused many tempting offers from those of the fancy who would have loved to own her. Sadly she died while very young. Little Boy Blue was also a handsome little dog of true quality, and was sire and grandsire of many of Miss Samuel's winning Pekes. Most of his descendants were larger than he was.

The Tri-International Champion Pierrot of Hartlebury of Orchard Hill and his descendants were behind a goodly number of the small Pekes of the thirties and forties, as will be noted from particulars of those entered at the 1935 Sleeve Dog Show. Although not himself a Sleeve, Pierrot was a small dog and transmitted this quality to his progeny.

England has had some outstanding Sleeve Pekingese. Champion Humming Bee of Alderbourne is among the more notable of the thirties; his progeny included Champions Princess Picotte of Orchard Hill, Champion Fang Sheng of Willowtoun, English Champion Li of Silbir (for whom the equivalent of fifteen thousand dollars is said to have been refused at one period), and English Champion Meng of Alderbourne. All of them were larger than their sire.

At New Brunswick Kennel Club another Best In Show win for Betty Shoemaker and her Sleeve Pekingese: Mi Toi and Int. Ch. Mai Toi.

English Ch. Humming Bee of Alderbourne, photographed by Thomas Fall of London, for owner Mrs C. Ashton Cross.

There was also the winning Miniature, Tai Choo of Caversham, Miss de Pledge's dearly loved Robin, who through his own excellence as a sire and the producing qualities of his descendants had a tremendous influence on the breed. Robin was a son of the noted bitch, Champion Sha Sha of Caversham, and among his progeny was Champion Che Le of Matsons-Catawba.

The English Kennel Club has recently recognized the Sleeve Pekingese Club of Great Britain, which held its first Specialty Show in 1971 and drew the fantastic entry of one hundred and seventy-nine for the scrutiny of Mrs Betty M. A. Shoemaker. This American judge is doing a great deal to help gain respect and appreciation for the Sleeve Pekingese in the United States. Mrs Shoemaker owns the Cumlaude Pekingese at Bridgeton, New Jersey, which we believe to be the only kennel in the United States devoted to the breeding and exhibiting of top quality Sleeves. She is doing a splendid job and has made many judges and fanciers "Sleeve conscious" during the past few years, a tribute to the quality and presentation of her tiny Pekes.

Mrs Shoemaker's love of Sleeve Pekingese came about through an act of kindness. One morning she received a telephone call from a lady whom she had only met once; she was

Eight-week-old Gwynne's Tobias Parvus Bubo, which means Little Olive. Bred by Florence E. Gwynne of Vincentown, New Jersey and owned by Betty Shoemaker of the Cumlaude in Bridgeton, New Jersey.

about to enter hospital for major surgery and could not afford to provide care for her dogs. One of these was a dam with puppies and Mr and Mrs Shoemaker agreed to accept temporary responsibility. At the kennel, they found that fifteen pure-bred Poodles and Pekingese were to be put to sleep because no provision had been made for their care. Mrs Shoemaker could not allow this and brought all the dogs home and cared for them for three months until their owner's recovery. Included in the group were a matched pair of Sleeve Pekingese bitches. The breeder told her that Sleeves did not win championships, and that she was not yet strong enough to give these tiny mites any special care so would have them put to sleep. She suggested that perhaps in the circumstances Mrs Shoemaker might like to keep them as there had been no payment for looking after the dogs during the breeder's illness. This offer was promptly accepted.

A Peke breeder realized their potential and encouraged Mrs Shoemaker to enter them at

Below: At the Progressive Dog Club Show in October 1971, judge and breeder Mrs Frank Hess awards Best of Winners and Best of Breed to Copplestone Mr Pinkcoat, Betty Shoemaker's import which became the International Champion Copplestone Mr. Pinkcoat.

Right: Half a dozen of the wonderful little Iwades Pekingese, owned by Mrs H.S. Brown of England.

the Pekingese Club of America Specialty. There at eleven months of age they won Best Brace and created a considerable and admiring commotion. They won on their own natural beauty and showmanship, for Mrs Shoemaker at that time had no ring experience. These little dogs won the Brace competition every year they were shown at the Specialty. Their career record stands at seventeen times Best Brace in Show and Best Toy Brace at Boston, Chicago International, Pittsburgh, and Bermuda in addition to wins at many smaller shows along the way. One of these bitches, Mai Toi II, became a champion in the United States and in Bermuda. At four-and-a-half pounds each, red with white chest and feet, they have done a tremendous job to arouse renewed interest in Sleeve Pekes; they have certainly proved by the rigorous schedule of shows and travel that such tiny mites are not lacking in stamina. They have shown and won on uneven ground, among long grass, in conditions of scorching heat, and have traveled thousands of miles in the unpressurised part of planes.

The famous English brother and sister Sleeves, Copplestone Miss Pinkcoat (Bonnie) and Copplestone Mr Pinkcoat (Clyde) were

Left: Another Best Brace in the Toy Group win for Betty Shoemaker's Sleeve Pekingese, Ti Toi and Int. Ch. Mai Toi II. This win took place at the International Kennel Club of Chicago show in April 1970.

Below: Dog Show Week in Bermuda found four of Betty Shoemaker's Pekes on hand for the competition. Left to right, Ch. Copplestone Mr. Pinkcoat, Krypto of Knostro, Radiance of Alderbourne, and Ti Toi. Home is the Cumlaude Kennels, in Bridgeton, New Jersey. Bermuda News Bureau photo.

Above: Second prize at the Sleeve Dog Show in England in the mid-thirties was the Alderbourne entry.

Below: Six-month-old Alderbourne Queen of Sheba, bred by Cynthia Ashton Cross in England, and imported by Betty Shoemaker, Cumlaude Kennels, Bridgeton, New Jersey. Sheba's sire was Prince Tong of Alderbourne and her dam Sheba of Alderbourne.

imported by Mr Shoemaker as a gift for his wife. The former was truly one of the finest Sleeves yet produced, and was Best of Opposite Sex in Chicago over "Specials" bitches for four points, then took four points in Pittsburgh for a total of eight points in one weekend. Her early demise was mourned as a great loss to the breed. Clyde came here as an Irish Champion and went along undaunted to gain his American title as well. At the Progressive in New York, he went from the classes to Best of Breed over a fine assortment of larger Pekes, and has been Best of Breed frequently since then.

At Cumlaude Kennels the aim is not to make champion after champion, but rather to promote the good Sleeve to its rightful importance. The Shoemakers also own a splendid nine-pound winner, International Champion Linsown Ku Chello, now semi-retired and being shown only occasionally. He has to his credit thirty-one Bests of Breed and twenty-seven Group Placements. He was third Top Pekingese in 1969. But it is in the Sleeves that Mrs Shoemaker takes her greatest pleasure.

The Rittenhouse Square Dog Show in Philadelphia is an event of long tradition and thanks to Mrs Shoemaker's efforts has been the scene of some enchanting presentations of the Sleeve Pekingese. One year she made a stunning display of the Sleeves wearing tiny Chinese kimonos and riding in an eight-foot Oriental sedan chair. On another occasion they wore straw coolie hats and rode in a Chinese junk; in 1972 Mrs Shoemaker commemorated the fact of the Pekingese coming to Great Britain in 1860, by wearing a dress of that period while the dogs rode in an antique English pram.

Betty Johnstonbaugh is another fancier who owns an especially splendid little Sleeve, one of Orchard Hill breeding and having a nice record of wins.

In judging Sleeve Pekingese, it is well to remember the importance of balance and of everything being a matter of proportion. Bone and substance entirely adequate to the size of a four pound dog would look light and out of place on a bigger one; likewise a tiny dog with a larger dog's bone structure would look deformed. A Sleeve Pekingese should have bone heavy for his size, a proportionately large head, and an Oriental expression. But everything should be scaled to the dog as a whole for that all-important balance. Sleeves usually carry heavy fringes, and are now being seen with better texture and quantity of body coat. Sleeve Pekingese are definitely not runts; they are the result of careful breeding to strains which produce small specimens. A Miniature painting is a delicate work of art in its own right: an attractive Sleeve qualifies for similar consideration.

A portrait study of the Best In Show winning Brace owned by Betty Shoemaker. . . left, Ti Toi and on the right, Int. Ch. Mai Toi II.

Best Brace in Show at the Queensboro Kennel Club Show in 1972 under judge Schuman was Betty Shoemaker and her Sleeve Pekingese, Mi Toi and International Ch. Mai Toi. William Gilbert photograph.

Two Sleeve Pekes form a rickshaw team at the Sleeve Dog Show in England many years ago. Ch. Humming Bee and Ki-loo-loo of Alderbourne win the prize for this remarkable turnout in the costume competition.

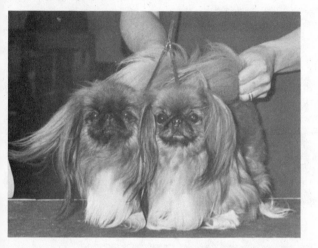

This charming photograph of J. Peter Shoemaker and his wife Betty was taken at their Cumlaude Kennels in Bridgeton, New Jersey in 1972. Peter Shoemaker holds Krypto of Knostro, Betty holds Alderbourne Queen of Sheba and left to right are Int. Ch. Mai Toi II, Ti Toi, Gywnne's Treasured Truffle, Jeros Angel Dream, Int. Ch. Copplestone Mr. Pinkcoat, and Int. Ch. Linsown Ku-Chello.

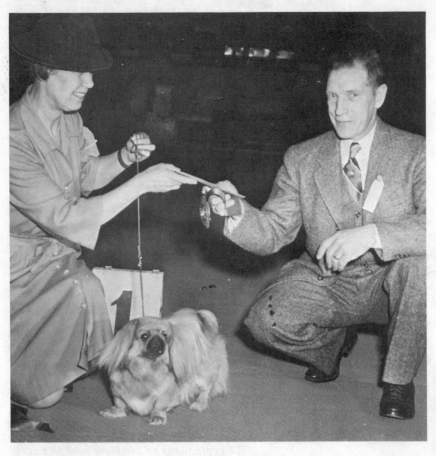

Left: At the 67th annual dog show of the West-minster Kennel Club show in February 1943, Best in the Toy Group was Dorothy P. Lath-rop's Pekingese Beh Tang. Mr Frank Downing was the judge.

Below: An informal "at home" photograph of Betty Shoemaker at her Cumlaude Kennels in Bridgeton, New Jersey. On the fireside bench are Int. Ch. Mai Toi II and Ti Toi; Mrs Shoemaker holding Int. Ch. Linsown Ku-Chello, and from left to right: Ch. Mani Kin of Fourwinds, Copplestone Miss Pinkcoat, Pekchins Cola [2½ pounds!], Krypto of Knostro and Int. Ch. Copplestone Mr. Pinkcoat.

CHAPTER 10

THE PEKINGESE CLUB OF AMERICA

On March 4th 1973, the Pekingese Club of America held its one hundred and eleventh Specialty Show. This is a proud record, and one which is quite outstanding in our Fancy. The Club's first Specialty Shows, with the winners, have already been mentioned in the chapter on the early history of the American Pekingese. Its subsequent history follows.

The Inaugural Show of the Pekingese Club of America in 1911 was judged by Mrs Benjamin Guinness. The actual number of dogs was ninety-five, but some were entered in several classes and brought the total entry listing to two hundred. This is a custom seldom practised nowadays, probably because of the high entry fees. Some years ago, however, many fanciers took pleasure in winning class ribbons and awards rather than concentrating mainly on the points, and it was not at all unusual to find a dog entered in every class for which he or she was eligible. Sometimes this created problems for judges, lest they should reverse themselves in placing these multiple class entries.

Mrs Benjamin Guinness judged the Inaugural Show. The Specialty following was also held during 1911 and was judged by Mrs Richard P. McGrann, for whom one hundred and eleven Pekingese created a total entry of two hundred and forty-four. The year after, one hundred and sixty-six dogs in three hundred and thirty-three entries appeared for the judging of Mrs Sealy Clark. In 1913 there were one hundred and sixty in three hundred and twenty-eight entries for judging by Mrs W. H. Herbert; one hundred and fifty-five dogs in two hundred and eighty nine entries were judged by Miss Lydia Hopkins in 1914.

No Specialty was held in 1915, but next year there were one hundred and sixty-seven dogs in two hundred and ninety-five entries judged by Mrs C. Herbert. And in 1917 there were two shows, the first drawing two hundred and thirty-six dogs in three hundred and eighty-five entries for judging by Mr Lefroy Dean and Mrs Haley Fiske: and the summer Specialty had one hundred and twenty-nine dogs in one hundred and eighty-four entries

for judging by Mrs Frederick Edey with Mr E. G. Snow, Jr., acting as referee. (Mrs Edey is a former President of the Pekingese Club of America and was also President of the Girl Scouts of America.)

In 1918 Mrs Haley Fiske (whose husband, a prominent attorney, had been instrumental in drawing up the Constitution and By-Laws of the Pekingese Club) and Mrs Frank T. Clarke judged one hundred and ninety-one dogs in three hundred and two entries, with Mrs A. McClure Halley serving as referee. Referees no longer appear in dog show rings, but it was common in those days and the referee made the final decision in situations wherein a difference of opinion arose between judges.

In 1919 Mrs Halley, alone and unaided, performed the somewhat staggering task of judging the splendid turnout of two hundred and forty-eight dogs in four hundred and three entries. At the Summer Specialty that year, Mrs Michael M. Van Beuren had one hundred and fifteen dogs in one hundred and ninety-three entries.

The largest Pekingese Club of America Specialty held thus far was the Winter Specialty of 1920 wherein Mrs Philip Hunloke performed the gigantic job of judging two hundred and sixty-three dogs in four hundred and fifty-two entries. At the 1920 Summer Specialty, Mrs Alfred Goodson had one hundred and twenty-five in one hundred and ninety-five entries.

The Specialties through the twenties were judged by Mrs M. E. Harby, Mrs Michael M. Van Beuren (twice), Mrs Charles G. West, Jr. (who became Mrs James M. Austin), Mrs M. H. Ehlerman, Mrs A. McClure Halley, Mrs Charles E. Engel, Mrs F. C. McAllister, Mrs F. Y. Mathis, Mrs Edward H. Whitman, Mrs Howell Woolley (twice), Mr W. H. Weil, Miss Marie Alice Stovell, and Mrs Pearl Zellen. The numbers of dogs ranged from eighty-five at one of the Summer Specialties to the two hundred and six judged by Mrs Mathis in 1925. (The largest number of entries —315—for these events was also made by Mrs Mathis.)

Miss Jean G. Hinkle judged the 1930 Specialty wherein appeared one hundred and fifty-five dogs in two hundred and twenty entries. Mr. George Hatcher appraised one hundred and fifty-two dogs in two hundred entries in 1931, and Alva Rosenberg judged one hundred and sixty-three dogs in two hundred and thirty-five entries in 1932. Miss Hinkle officiated again in 1933 and one hundred and twenty-one dogs in one hundred and fifty-nine entries were presented for her judgement.

Later in 1933, the Summer Specialty was held in conjunction with the Morris and Essex Kennel Club Dog Show and Enno Meyer judged seventy-nine dogs in ninety-four entries.

Chin Clair Sun Star, owned by Mrs William C. Smith of Stratford, Connecticut, and the first American-bred winner of the Pekingese Club of America Specialty show on January 13, 1936.

Frank Downing judged one hundred and twenty-two dogs in one hundred and fifty-three entries in 1934, and Mrs Mathis evaluated one hundred in one hundred and nineteen entries in the Summer Specialty at Morris and Essex.

Jack Royce judged one hundred and eleven dogs in one hundred and twenty-seven entries in 1935. This was the final Pekingese Club of America Winter Specialty held as an open show, as a decision reached by the Club was that the Winter Specialty would henceforth be limited to American-breds to encourage production of more and better homebred Pekingese—while the Summer Specialty would continue to remain open to imports as well.

This caused quite a flurry at the time but the wisdom of the decision is reflected in the increasing quality of American-bred Pekingese which has followed, and which by now has reached the point where they can hold their own against competition from all parts of the world.

The first of the American-bred Specialties was held in 1936, with Mrs James M. Austin judging. It was won by Champion Chin Clair Sun Star, owned by the Chin Clair Kennels of Mrs William C. Smith. Since then, Mrs Quigley has won the American-bred Specialties more times (19) than any other exhibitor: in 1937, 1940, and 1941 with Champion Kim's Tzu Shan of Orchard Hill, in 1943, 1944, 1945, and 1948 with Champion Jai Son Fu of Orchard Hill, in 1950 and 1951 with Champion Fei Jai Son of Orchard Hill, in 1954 with Champion Bon Ray Yu Toi of Orchard Hill, in 1956 and 1957 with Champion Tulo Yu Chuo of Orchard Hill, in 1959 with Nia Bon Tia of Orchard Hill, in 1960 and 1962 with Champion Orchid Lane's Ku Lee, and in 1963, 1964 and 1965 with Champion Nia Jai Niki of Orchard Hill.

John B. Royce follows with record wins. He has five Best of Breed wins at the American-bred Specialties: in 1942 with Champion Jai Bee of Dah Lyn, in 1946 and 1947 with Champion Monarque of Dah Lyn, in 1955 with Champion Fabulous of Dah Lyn, and in 1958 with Champion Sing Hi's Sun Tu. The Misses Hodges and Perret won on two occasions, in 1952 and 1953 with Champion Tai Chuo's Sun of Dah Wong. Norman J. Cacciatore has also won in 1970, 1971 and 1973 with Champion Caccia's Marco Polo.

Single time winners have been Judith Connell in 1939 with Champion Honey of Toytown, Mrs Nathan S. Wise in 1949 with Champion Major Mite of Honan, Mrs A. A. Ruschaupt in 1966 with Champion Ku Chin Tom Mi of Seng Kye, Mr J. P. Goode in 1967 with Champion Jai Tsun Jin Tong of Seng Kye, Mrs G. Blauvelt-Moss in 1968 with Champion Nia Tulyar of Orchard Hill, and Mr Michael Wolf in 1969 with Champion Hi Swinger of Brown's Den.

The Pekingese Club of America is one of the few holding both a Winter Specialty and a Summer Specialty each year. In the early days, these Summer Specialties were held as separate shows, but have more recently been held in conjunction with Morris and Essex, North Westchester, and the Westchester Kennel Club. The Ox Ridge Kennel Club is at the present time the host to these shows.

The only interruption in the annual Winter Specialty Shows was in 1915. All plans had been formulated, including the acceptance of an English judge, but cancellation was forced by World War I.

One of the most famous trophies in the dog show world is the splendid Lasca McClure Halley Sterling Silver Challenge Cup (a perpetual trophy in memory of Mrs Halley) open to all and offered only at the Winter Specialty Shows of the Pekingese Club of America. The name of each winner is engraved on the cup and the owner of the winner gains possession of it for one year. A sterling silver picture frame is also presented by the Club to commemorate the win.

It is interesting, too, that Miss Isabel Benjamin, a long-time member and also Governor of the Pekingese Club of America, willed a sum of money to the Club for use in providing special prizes.

Members of the Pekingese Club of America have some forty beautiful and valuable trophies for which they alone are entitled to compete at the Winter Specialty Shows. These must usually be won from three to five times to gain possession, and almost without exception are in memory and honor of famous people and well-known dogs that have figured prominently in the history of the breed.

The Pekingese Club of America medals are highly prized trophies. These (for award only to members of the Pekingese Club of America) are available upon request for first prize in the Bred-by-Exhibitor Classes at all Pekingese Specialty Shows. In fourteen carat gold, they are also offered, open to all, for Winners Dog and Winners Bitch at the Winter Specialty Shows and for Best of Breed at the Summer Specialty Shows.

In conjunction with the Winter Specialty, the Pekingese Club of America holds a Futurity Stakes that deserves greater popularity than it presently enjoys. This certainly should make an ideal showcase for the puppies. It is divided into four classes for each sex, and nomination of the bitch is only five dollars in addition to the usual entry fee for each competing puppy. These monies and fifty dollars added by the Club are divided among the winners on a graduated scale.

Mrs Benjamin Guinness was the first President of the Pekingese Club of America. Mrs Michael M. Van Beuren held the office for several decades, the longest tenure thus far. Dr. Edwin R. Blamey is the current President. Others who have held this office since the thirties are Mrs James M. Austin, Miss Clara Lowther, and Mrs Justin Herold. Miss Iris de la Torre Bueno has been Club Secretary since the early thirties. Miss Bueno is the Show Secretary as well and is doing an outstanding

One of the many famous stage and screen personalities who favor Pekes... Tallulah Bankhead is pictured returning from a European vacation aboard the S.S. Europa with two of her Pekes. Miss Bankhead owned several Pekingese which she purchased from the Mapes.

job. As no superintendent is employed, the work includes all of the tasks involved with the Winter Specialty Show, truly a great responsibility.

Vice-Presidents currently serving are Mrs Fortune Roberts, Mrs Frank S. Hess, and Mr William Blair. The Board of Governors consists of all the Officers plus Mrs G. Blauvelt-Moss, Mrs Florence Gwynne, Mrs Nathan Allen, Mrs E. R. Blamey, Mrs Everett M. Clark, Mrs Eric Lagerkrantz, Mrs Mildred Imrie, Mrs L. J. Ertle, Mrs Betty Shoemaker, Mrs Barbara L. Fallass, and Mrs George Snyder.

The Pekingese Club of America is, to our knowledge, the only Specialty Club which offers a Club Championship, and though it has fallen into disuse recently, the following is part of the Bye-Laws:

The Pekingese Club of America's highly coveted perpetual sterling silver trophy open to all for Best In Show at the national specialty show each year. This trophy was donated by MCClure Halley.

At a meeting of the Board of Governors held on October 15th 1913, there were discussed the conditions of the American Kennel Club rules pursuant to which the title "Champion" is conferred. It was pointed out that these rules provided only that a fixed number of dogs be exhibited at a show to entitle that show to claim a definite number of points, that no provision is made for positive competition in any one breed as a condition precedent to the title of "Champion" in such breed and that one Pekingese could earn said title under said rules although exhibited only at shows in the South and West where there are few, if any Pekingese with which to compete. Accordingly a resolution was adopted providing in effect for the creation of the title "Pekingese Club Champion," and that to earn the right to said title a Pekingese must not only have been a champion under the American Kennel Club rules but it must have been the best in the winner's class, or have been the best Pekingese, at shows of not less than three points each with a total rating of at least fifteen points and there must have been exhibited at each of said shows at least fifteen Pekingese.

RESOLVED, that the Pekingese owned by a member of the Pekingese Club of America that will have been awarded 15 points in the winner's class under three different judges at shows, each of which shall be accorded by the American Kennel Club a rating of not less than three points, and provided that there will have been exhibited at each of said shows not less than 15 Pekingese, shall thereby be entitled to be called "Pekingese Club Champion" and shall be entitled to a championship certificate to be issued by this Club properly reciting the conditions and compliance therewith provided for in this resolution and on payment of $30.00 shall receive the Club's gold medal whereon shall be engraved the name of such winner and the words "Pekingese Club Champion."

RESOLVED FURTHER, that the Club shall issue such certificate and deliver such medal when application shall have been made therefor, provided that the records of the American Kennel Club shall show that the above conditions have been complied with.

RESOLVED FURTHER, that one of the wins necessary for a Pekingese to become eligible to the Pekingese Club of America Championship must have been made at a Pekingese Club of America show.

The passage of time, and the improvement in the American Kennel Club's requirements for championship rating, have made this Pekingese Club of America championship almost obsolete. Now that the amount and quality of competition in every section of the country is improved and the American Kennel Club demands for conferring of the title are at least as stringent as demanded in the past for award of the Club title, such award is no longer unique. But some may well remember the pride with which exhibitors boasted of their Club Championship several decades back, and how dogged they were in their determination to earn it, often bringing a finished A.K.C. champion back into the classes to collect that major win which was necessary—to the

Above: Burma-Lita, a Pekingese winner in the 1940's owned by Jetty Remy.

Above: Whitworth Peterkin, winner of the Pekingese Club of America show and Best of Breed at Westminster in 1944.

Right: A darling four-pound Sleeve Peke, the little bitch bred by Rubye Turner Williams and owned by Mrs H. David Holmes of Houston, Texas, is named Quilkin Knight's Firefly. Her sire is Etive Happy Knight ex Etive Ku Tina.

extreme annoyance of rival exhibitors who felt that they were being unfairly deprived of important points by the re-appearance of a champion in the classes.

The Pekingese Club of America is the parent specialty club for the breed. It and the Pacific Coast Pekingese Club are the only two for the Pekingese which are member clubs of the American Kennel Club. The Pekingese Club of America does not have affiliated clubs. However, any and all other Specialty Clubs formulated in the United States for this breed must have the parent specialty club's approval before being granted recognition by the American Kennel Club.

At the present time, there are ten other Pekingese Clubs holding Specialties in various sections of the Country. These are the Rose City Pekingese Club, the Pekingese Club of Georgia, the Evergreen State Pekingese Club, the Pekingese Club of Alabama, the Arizona Pekingese Club, the Delta Pekingese Club, the Pekingese Club of Texas, the Pekingese Club of Central California, the Pekingese Club of North Central Illinois, and the Pekingese Club of Southern New Jersey.

Should one be asked what year has been the most important in the history of the Pekingese Club of America, we are quite certain that the answer would be 1915. That was the year in which several quite dedicated people became members: Mrs Cecelia V. de la Torre Bueno (owner of All-Celia Kennels active in breeding Pekingese as well as Brussels Griffons in earlier days, and mother of Miss Iris de la Torre Bueno) was a devoted member of the Club until her death in the late sixties. The Misses Clara and Margaretta Lowther, owners

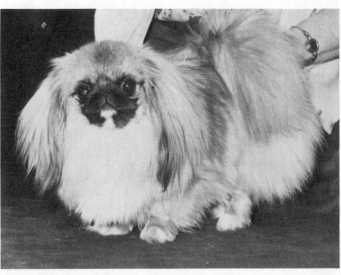

Ch. Gleymoor's Pedlo of Pickway, Winners Bitch and Best of Opposite Sex at the Southern Oregon Kennel Club Show in September, 1967, under judge L.E. Piper. She is sired by Ch. Mar-Pat Tom the Piper's Son ex Empress Sunna of Pickway. Owner-handled by Mrs Bessie V. Pickens, of Portland, Oregon.

of Clamarlow, also became Pekingese Club members during 1915, as did Mrs Herbert L. Mapes of Whitworth Pekingese, Mrs F. Y. Mathis of Greenwich Pekingese, and Mrs Charles G. West, the future Mrs James M. Austin, of the great Catawba Kennels.

Mrs Michael M. Van Beuren was an even earlier member, having joined in 1910, and Miss Isabel Benjamin became a member in 1911. It is also noteworthy that all of these ladies (with the exception of Miss Clara Lowther who withdrew from her Pekingese activities after the loss of her sister in the fifties) remained members throughout the rest of their lives.

CHAPTER 11

THE AKC STANDARD

EXPRESSION—Must suggest the Chinese origin of the Pekingese in its quaintness and individuality, resemblance to the lion in directions and independence, and should imply courage, boldness, self-esteem and combativeness rather than prettiness, daintiness or delicacy.

SKULL—Massive, broad, wide and flat between the ears (not dome-shaped), wide between the eyes. *Nose*—Black, broad, very short and flat. *Eyes*—Large, dark, prominent, round, lustrous. *Stop*—Deep. *Ears*—Heart-shaped, not set too high, leather never long enough to come below the muzzle, nor carried erect, but rather drooping, long feather. *Muzzle*—Wrinkled, very short and broad, not overshot nor pointed. Strong, broad underjaw, teeth not to show.

SHAPE OF BODY—Heavy in front, well-sprung ribs, broad chest, falling away lighter behind, lionlike. Back level. Not too long in body; allowance made for longer body in bitch. *Legs*—Short forelegs, bones of forearm bowed, firm at shoulder; hind legs lighter but firm and well shaped. *Feet*—Flat, toes turned out, not round, should stand well up on feet, not on ankles.

ACTION—Fearless, free and strong, with slight roll.

COAT, FEATHER AND CONDITION—Long, with thick undercoat, straight and flat, not curly nor wavy, rather coarse, but soft; feather on thighs, legs, tail and toes long and profuse. *Mane*—Profuse, extending beyond the shoulder blades, forming ruff or frill round the neck.

COLOR—All colors are allowable. Red, fawn, black, black and tan, sable, brindle, white and parti-color well defined: back masks and spectacles around the eyes, with lines to ears are desirable. *Definition of a Parti-Color Pekingese*—The coloring of a parti-color dog must be broken on the body. No large portion of any one color should exist. White should be shown on the saddle. A dog of any solid color with white feet and chest is *not* a parti-color.

TAIL—Set high; lying well over the back to either side; long, profuse, straight feather.

SIZE—Being a toy dog, medium size preferred, providing type and points are not sacrificed; extreme limit, 14 pounds.

Scale of Points

Expression	5
Skull	10
Nose	5
Eyes	5
Stop	5
Ears	5
Muzzle	5
Shape of body	15
Legs and feet	15
Coat, feather and condition	15
Tail	5
Action	10
Total	100

Penalizations—Protruding tongue, badly blemished eye, overshot, wry mouth.

Disqualifications

Weight—over 14 pounds; Dudley nose.

Ch. Chu Lai's Dan Dee Ting winning Best of Breed at the 1973 Rhode Island Kennel Club show under judge Mrs. Carl B. Cass. Ting is bred and owned by Patricia and Charles W. Farley and handled by Mr. Farley. His sire was Greenbrier's Nikko Toro ex Chu Lai's Little Sissi Su.

BEST
OF
BREED
SHAFER PHOTO

Left: Best In Show at the Pekingese Club of America Specialty Show in New York City in 1940 was Ch. Kim's Tzu Shan of Orchard Hill, owned by Mrs Richard S. Quigley of Lock Haven, Pennsylvania.

Below: Judging one of the bitch classes at the 47th Specialty Show of the Pekingese Club of America in January 1941. Competing in the class is Mrs Philip Schaffner's Hu-Shi of Merricka; the Misses Lowther's Clamarlow Po-Li-Ann; Mrs Richard Quigley's Wee Ray Pyx of Orchard Hill; the Misses Lowther's Clamarlow Yen T'Sing; Mrs Richard Quigley's Pier Kwai Wha of Orchard Hill; Mrs Herbert Mapes' Whitworth Dreamer, and Mrs Marshall Sewall's Shanette of Dah Wong.

CHAPTER 12

PEKINGESE CHARACTER AND TYPE

Nowhere in the canine world is there to be found a more interesting or fascinating breed of dog than the Pekingese. Proud and aloof, but loyal and devoted, he makes an unequalled companion whether you live in city, suburbs, country, apartment, bungalow, or mansion.

The adaptability of the Pekingese is one of his greatest charms. He will stay quietly for hours napping at your side, yet be ready on a second's notice to romp, play, or go walking with you.

As a watchdog, the Pekingese is constantly on duty and cannot be surpassed; his alertness to any unusual sound and the promptness with which he barks a warning have been proved on many occasions. You may perhaps feel that a small dog is of little value for this purpose, but the authors disagree. Remember that a prowler or burglar fears most of all any noise that will call attention to his presence and activities. This the Pekingese can and does provide. And since he is small enough to readily elude the prowler, barking furiously meanwhile, his nuisance value is considerable. His vocal tones also demand respect, for he has an unusually deep bark and growl for a Toy dog and gives the impression that he is of greater size. He does not make as easy a target as a bigger dog, and most Pekingese are also difficult to bait with food, being somewhat fastidious in their eating habits. There is added recommendation in that they are not "yappers" inclined to bark for no reason, and you can therefore be sure that when one of them gives voice, there is good cause.

Serious injustice has been done to Pekingese in two respects and we wish to correct both errors.

First, they are *not* "snappy," and not given to biting, as people unfamiliar with the breed seem to think. Dogs of most breeds will bite when under stress, and to this the Pekingese is not an exception. They are basically dogs of good disposition, and unless teased, tormented, or hurt, there is very little chance of your being bitten by one.

Secondly, the false impression created by misguided cartoonists and others who have delighted in portraying Pekingese as useless, foolish little creatures reclining on satin cushions or being squeezed and coddled by a doting mistress, is refuted as directly contrary to the true Pekingese character. Actually, these dogs have great aversion to such treatment and respond to the indignity of being hugged or kissed by drawing back with pained expressions on their faces while struggling to get free at the earliest possible moment. People knowledgeable in Pekingese personality delight in the aloofness of these dogs, for the Pekingese is in actuality a snob. Bred from countless generations of palace dogs, he seems never for a moment to forget his ancestry, but brings with him a surrounding aura of all the pride and dignity of the ancient Chinese Empire.

Pekingese are not likely to fawn over strangers, they more usually show restraint until their friendship has been earned. Never rush at or grab for a Pekingese. Extend the back of your hand, speaking pleasantly, and allow him to make the advances or your relationship may be set back considerably, if not permanently. Once he knows and has accepted you, the Pekingese will be your friend for life. For he seems never to forget those he likes— nor those he dislikes.

Two things the Pekingese hate are being laughed at and being bullied. They may sulk for hours with the feeling that your laughter has been directed at them. While they are basically obedient and enjoy pleasing those they love, harsh or domineering treatment will gain nothing. Remember that an Oriental must never lose face: a Pekingese expects the same consideration.

The Pekingese is not destructive; he does not chew or scratch furniture nor tear rugs, bedspreads, or draperies. He is always fastidiously clean, being almost like a cat in this respect and his intelligence is outstanding. He is known for his fearlessness, being downright belligerent towards dogs and in situations which are far beyond his actual capacities.

We have sometimes been asked whether the Pekingese is delicate in constitution. No, he is not. Pekingese are at least as hardy as any other dogs of their size, and given adequate care, they will live to an age of twelve to sixteen years.

Pekingese are bright and intelligent, and will be found very quick to learn. Simple tricks, such as sitting up, seem to be almost second nature to them, and it is not unusual to see even three- or four-month-old puppies rise up and beg in a very appealing manner. Some years ago in England the breed was rather extensively taught to perform, and the Pekin Palace Dog Assocation Shows before World War II featured special classes in which various turnouts drawn and driven by Pekingese competed against one another for prizes. There were obedience tests too, with straight and steeplechase races, contestants refusing food upon command, and other feats perhaps amazing to any onlooker who underestimated the intelligence and ability of these small dogs.

His distinctive beauty, intelligence, loyalty, courage, and many endearing traits, his "dogginess" combined with diminutive size, and the fact that he is a completely delightful little animal add up to account for the popularity of the Pekingese. Even though he is officially considered a Toy, he has all the attributes of dogs many times his size; he is indeed a lion-hearted, gallant small dog that well deserves his position as one of the world's most popular breeds.

The Pekingese as an Obedience Dog

Mary Jane Callaway of Portland, Oregon, is an obedience enthusiast who has found Pekingese to be well suited for this work.

For while some might imagine that a dog of the haughty attitude and strong character of a Pekingese might prove difficult to train, the Pekingese in actuality has the extreme intelligence to make him excel at learning.

Obedience titles are discussed under *Obedience Trials* later in the book, but a dog must pass a prescribed set of tests under three different judges to earn any degree. He must not score less than 170 total points, and should be awarded at least half the points allowed in each of the individual exercises. Miss Callaway notes that several Pekingese hold the distinction of having earned perfect scores of 200 points in these trials.

The title to be gained first is Companion Dog, which one might liken to a high school diploma. Next comes Companion Dog Excellent, comparable to a college degree, while the title Utility Dog is considered the obedience Ph.D. of Dogdom.

Training your Pekingese for obedience competition is an enriching experience. You will enjoy a rapport with your dog not otherwise felt, and your dog will become a far more pleasant companion. Imagine *your* dog coming every time you call, and at the *first* call! The three bywords to remember to attain success in training are love, patience, and perseverance.

Breed Character or Pekingese Type

Previously we have discussed Pekingese *characteristics* as the word is generally accepted by the layman. To the enthusiast for pure-bred dogs, however, the expressions *characteristics* or *breed character* take on a considerably wider meaning. In dog-show language, breed character is synonymous with "type," and by "type" is meant the physical appearance of the dog in addition to traits of personality, talents, and disposition.

When a breeder of pure-bred dogs, or a fancier or a judge of them, speaks of "type," the reference is to the composite features making that particular breed of dog distinctive, as setting it apart from all other breeds and making it easily recognizable. To be strong in breed character or of good type, a dog must adhere not only in personality but in conformation as well to what is considered ideal for his breed. This "ideal" is described in the Standard of Points, which outlines the perfection which breeders seek to attain.

Such a standard of perfection is the guide for those wishing to produce show quality dogs, and is the tool by which they are judged. The dog it describes is the one constantly in judges' minds as they evaluate members of the breed.

The Pekingese Club Ch. Kai Lo of Dah Lyn, photographed on January 19th, 1939, at the Pekingese Club of America Specialty Show. Kai Lo was America's leading Toy Dog in 1938 and was owned by John B. Royce of Brookline, Massachusetts.

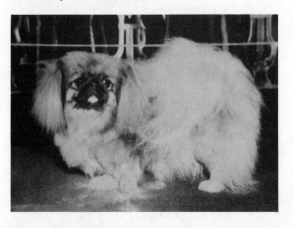

A darling puppy from the Callydon Pekingese Kennels of Anna and Robert Park of Ferndale, Michigan. Her name: Callydon Highland Queen.

This Standard is the result of long and dedicated work on the part of knowledgeable members of each breed's parent Specialty club. The American Kennel Club as governing body of the pure bred dog world in the United States must approve such a Standard before it becomes effective. The average breed Standard is based upon deep study of the history of the breed, earlier Standards in the countries where it was previously known, and the goals for which the breed was developed. All of these points must be carefully weighed in laying down an ideal for modern representatives of the breed.

In the case of the Pekingese, present Standards have obviously been adapted from the Empress Tzu Hsi's immortal words that appear in the opening chapter of this book, as the Pekingese today is quite clearly as he was then. There is now more attention paid to detail and fuller descriptions in some cases, but the Pekingese is still the original "Lion Dog."

In appearance the Pekingese is one of the world's most distinctive breeds of dog. He is truly "one of a kind," and for this reason a special knowledge of this breed is essential if one is to evaluate it correctly. In judging, a general knowledge of dog structure and anatomy is not sufficient; the breed is unique and shares essentials with no other.

The head of the Pekingese is one of the breed's most important features, and must always be large and massive in proportion to the size of the dog. On handling the head, one finds it big and bony to the touch, with the topskull broad and absolutely flat from ear to ear. Heads can be groomed to appear fairly level in skull, and a tight lead pulled up close around the neck is sometimes helpful in creating an illusion of a flatness which does not exist in reality. On the other hand, heavily coated dogs often have unusually thick fur on their heads, and this can give a skull which is actually flat an appearance of roundness. If there is any question, one must handle before passing an opinion. To examine a Pekingese head correctly, smooth the fur on top and pull the ears gently forward and down; a proper skull then appears flat.

From the front, the Pekingese face must be broad and short with nose set directly between well-spaced eyes and giving a smoothly finished appearance to the whole. Crowded faces, with the features set close together giving a pinched aspect are not correct. Foreheads should be low, the stop deep, and the muzzle well padded, the latter appearing as broad, or nearly so, as the topskull. The truly typical face must give the impression of squareness, possibly just a hair's breadth shorter from top to bottom than in width. Twenty years ago, the tendency was toward heads that were deep and narrow. Then the pendulum swung to the other extreme, and the aim was toward heads so wide and shallow that they appeared anything but massive and made the dog seem poorly balanced, almost to the point of deformity. More recently, the tendency has been away from both extremes and the massive head, square in appearance is the form for which breeders strive as correct and typical for the Pekingese.

The ideal underjaw is broad, short and level, with lips meeting firmly and evenly. Weak, receding underjaws are unattractive and are considered by many, including the authors, to be a serious fault. The teeth of the Pekingese should not be level; when they are, one often finds the jaw slightly overshot. The upper row should meet just behind the lower teeth for a perfect effect when the mouth is closed. However, teeth do not count in the actual rating of the Pekingese; Pekingese authorities feel that if the mouth, lips, and the closed jaws appear correct, it should be assumed that they conform to acceptable standards and no examination of them should be made by judges. If, of course, there is some question as to wryness of mouth or other deformity, the judge must investigate.

Lips should be short and even, neatly circling the underjaw on top and sides but never hanging even a tiny bit below. In profile the face must be absolutely flat and tipped slightly back from underjaw to topskull. The bone structure of the face is not only short but upturned, which in the correct face, leaves the deep stop required by the Standard easily discernible behind the nose leather when the skin of the forehead is pulled gently back. The deeper the stop the better.

Above: Mogene's Danseur, photographed at 2½ years of age, and sired by Ch. St. Aubrey Ku Kuan of Jehol ex Mogene Ballerina. Owners, Gene and Mollie Dudgeon, Mogene Kennels, Terre Haute, Indiana.

The expression should be bold, Oriental, and grotesque. A black mask is attractive on a red or fawn dog, although many fanciers prefer a black muzzle only as an entire mask of this color tends to obliterate the detail of face, sometimes to the point of making the dog appear expressionless. A dog with no black markings at all on the face usually lacks expression also.

Black spectacles, eyes rimmed with black, and black shadings on the face and forehead are extremely typical and a decided addition to the beauty of the Pekingese. In the black-and-tan and the black-and-fawn colorings, the small, red or fawn spots above the eyes appear like punctuation marks and bring expression to the face.

One of the most individual features of the Pekingese is his unbroken wrinkle. When many dog-fanciers first became interested in the breed a few decades ago, this type of wrinkle was a rarity which caused high excitement and was dearly prized. Now, however, it has become "standard equipment" on the Pekingese, and seldom if ever do we see a member of the breed without it. However, all manifestations are not the correct unbroken wrinkle. While one form is an attractive addition to the well-finished, typical face, the other (usually a huge roll lying heavily on the stop, protruding over the nose, and covering part of the eye) is an abomination.

The perfect unbroken wrinkle is fitted in appearance, lying slightly above the stop, and therefore not accompanied by low nose placement as is usually the case with the other type. The wrinkle should be only full enough to fit neatly around the nose leather and should never protrude in profile. Some wrinkles in-

correctly go over the nose, ending about halfway down on either side of the muzzle; the wrinkle properly extends to the lower part of the muzzle, broadening as it reaches the lowest point, and thus adds to the desirable broad and well-padded appearance.

The size, color, and position of the eyes are of utmost importance in Pekingese. They have tremendous influence on the expression, making it either typical or incorrect. In color, the eyes should be dark brown, appearing almost black in any but the strongest sunlight. Some years ago light eyes were fairly common, but there has been improvement recently and this fault has become far less apparent. Light eyes appear most frequently in red dogs descended from red stock, and the tendency is corrected by an outcross breeding with black, fawn, or fawn-brindle stock having definitely dark eyes for two generations. According to the Standard, eye-color counts exactly one point in rating. But light eyes mar the beauty and spoil the expression of the loveliest Pekingese face, which is why they are considered an objectionable fault.

Size is also essential when considering the correctness of eyes. Small eyes are decidedly untypical, and are in our opinion even less attractive than typically large ones a trifle off in color. Eyes should be widely-spaced to bring out the desired appearance of general breadth of face. However, they should never be so far apart as to appear on the sides of the head rather than on the face. They should be luminous and expressive, and the whites should not show. A slightly marked eye, while of course penalized, is no longer a disqualification. However, a blind or partially blind dog cannot be shown under American Kennel Club rules, and a badly scarred or disfigured eye may be reason for disqualification and at least counts heavily against the dog.

The correct placing of the ears is another point of major importance. Ears should be set well on the far corners of the topskull, hanging close to the sides of the face to form an attractive frame. If set too low, the ears take away from the desired squareness of the skull, and are inclined to fly when the dog is in action. If they are too high, the fault is called prick ears. The leather itself should be heart shaped with the ideal length bringing the tip to the bottom of the muzzle. They should hang close to the cheeks, but must never have the droopy look characteristic of Spaniels; Pekingese ears are light in weight and should be carried slightly erect at the base. Fringes should be profuse, the ears of a well-coated Pekingese being covered with soft, long fur, with lengthy black strands close to the face often adding to the dog's attractiveness. Small tufts of fur standing up and out at the base of the ear are typical and grotesque. It will be found that puppies of eight to ten weeks which mature into heavily fringed animals generally have tight, round curls bordering their ear leather.

The ideal nose placement of a Pekingese is for the leather to be exactly between the eyes so that a line drawn across the centers of the eyes would go directly through it. The nose should be short and with no bridge showing when viewed in profile. The leather should be tilted in and upward at the top, fitting in with the general upturn of the face, and it must be black.

Correctly, the Pekingese nostrils should be large, wide, and well open. It is a cause for alarm among Pekingese devotees to note a sharp increase in the number of small, pinched nostrils buried in overly heavy wrinkles that has been appearing recently. This is a serious fault and can be a weakening one, since it causes laborious breathing and places undue strain upon the unfortunate dog. Breeders should remember that this type of nose is not in keeping with the Standard, that it spoils the expression, of which the wide, well-open nostrils are an important part, and that it is harmful to the well-being of the breed. It should be avoided in breeding and penalized by judges in the ring.

Medium-short and shapely, with well-sprung ribs tapering to a clearly defined waist-line, is the ideal Pekingese body, often described as "pear-shaped" or "lion-like." Balance is of utmost importance in Pekingese and the length of the body is to be in proportion to the size of head (which must appear massive) and to the length of leg—which must be short. Too short a body is not typical of a Pekingese, as it interferes with his extremely important rolling action. But neither should he be excessively long, although a trifle more body-length is acceptable in bitches than in dogs. The ribs should be rounded, prominent, and well-sprung; the brisket or chest should be deep and broad, and the back perfectly level and strong, as the unattractive hump of the roach-back. The downward slope of the swayback are signs of structural weakness and unsoundness. The body of a Pekingese in show condition will be sturdy and solid to handle, with bones well-covered with flesh but not fat.

The tail must be set high, lying flat over the back with the tip curling slightly to either side. It should be heavily fringed with long feathering. If set too low at the base, the tail cannot be carried correctly, as it is then impossible for the plume to lie flat, and a tail carried at half-mast is an especially unattractive fault.

The correct foreleg of a Pekingese is short and thick, heavy in bone, and well-bowed. This bow extends the entire length of the fore-arm, the leg arching outwards for about a third of its length, the wrists coming closer together, and the feet turning just moderately outwards. The forefeet are round and neat in appearance. The dog should stand well up on his toes, never back on the wrist or pastern, which should be firm and upright. The dog should be firm at the shoulders and elbows. The bow comes from correct structure of the foreleg, which is in keeping with very short-legged heavily-chested dogs, not from unsoundness in the shoulder or elbow assemblage. To examine for a correct front, place the Pekingese on a skid-proof table; raise his front with your hand under his chest until his feet are several inches above the table, then let his front down easily until he is again firmly on his feet. Any looseness of shoulder or elbow joints will become immediately apparent, as the dog will not come down standing correctly if he is unsound in either respect.

Hindquarters should be lighter in bone and longer than forequarters if the dog's back is to be level. The hind legs should be firm, set close together, with feet pointing straight ahead, and with plenty of muscle in the upper thigh. They must be well let down in hocks and it is especially important that they be absolutely straight when viewed from behind. Both cow hocks (when knees come together) and bandy legs (the opposite) are incorrect.

Below: Mogene's Diminuendo, photographed at 2½ years of age. Bred by Gene and Mollie Dudgeon, Mogene Pekingese. Diminuendo was co-owned by the Dudgeon's and Mrs Al James of the Wi-Ja Pekingese. The sire is St. Aubrey Ku Juan ex Mogene Ballerina.

Pekingese action, a smooth, rhythmic roll, is one of the most distinctive, and sometimes misunderstood, characteristics of the breed. It is not to be confused with the loose shuffling action caused by unsound shoulders, nor the mincing trot which results from excessively short bodies, lack of bone, or a narrow-chested straight front. A Pekingese should be moved at a moderate pace for an accurate evalution of his action and for appreciation of the really correct roll which results from a combination of the perfect front, moderate body length, and strong nicely flexing hindquarters.

Featherings on the toes of the Pekingese are attractive in moderation, like many things. But they should not be allowed to grow excessively long. A sound Pekingese with ample opportunity to exercise seldom becomes hampered with over-abundant toe featherings, but should be trimmed with scissors if necessary. Excess feathering will only accentuate any weakness that may appear in the pastern; and even the soundest dog will have trouble travelling if every step he takes must be over a wad of long fur.

Technically speaking, the Pekingese has two coats. The under coat is quite soft, short and slightly "crimpy," giving a spring to the whole; the outer coat is long, straight, and harsh to the touch. The coat must be absolutely free of silkiness, and must show no inclination to wave. A "wooly" coat is also incorrect, as is one which lies flat to the body.

The coat consists of a long, straight, stand-off ruff, so typical of the lion, with shorter fur over the waist and hips, in keeping with the desired tapering appearance. While this is not perhaps a generally shared opinion, the authors believe that too much coat is as undesirable as too little. A dog smothered in a mop of fur appears shapeless and incongruous; therefore, stripping out excess fur must be resorted to occasionally. An insufficiency of coat is also unflattering, and in many cases makes a dog appear long, lanky, and high on leg. There is no truer saying than that a correct coat can cover a multitude of sins.

Fringes should be plentiful and the tail plume long and luxuriant, sometimes completely covering the top of the head when the dog is posed. Ear fringes, too, should be long and heavy, as should the breeches. The forelegs should have long "cuffs" ranging from wrist to just above the elbow.

Practically any coloration except liver color is permissible in a Pekingese. (Liver color is generally accompanied by light eyes and matching nose.) Red and fawn are the most popular colors, the former ranging from the deep chun red named for Champion Good-

wood Chun to clear, bright shades, while the latter includes a clear, grayish beige and a taupe shade sometimes referred to as biscuit. There are also both red and fawn brindles, as well as gray brindles. These colors are a combination of red, fawn, or gray with black hairs intermixed in the outer coat. Black muzzle and tippings usually accompany these colors. Black-and-tan and black-and-fawn Pekingese are becoming increasingly popular, and they are of tremendous importance in breeding if we are to keep dark eyes, good pigmentation and facial markings. These dogs are solid black except for red or fawn markings on chest, legs, feet and face (the latter a small dot of the color over each eye), and usually light fringes on tail and breeches. Coal-black and pure-white Pekingese are also increasing in popularity.

The following is the Pekingese Club of America definition of a parti-color Pekingese:

The coloring of a parti-colored dog must be broken on the body. No large portion of any color should exist. White should be shown on the saddle. A dog of any solid color with white feet and chest is NOT a parti-color.

Although any shade may be combined with white to make the parti-color, the most frequent combination is of red and white. It is important that the markings on head and face be evenly divided, with a white blaze on the forehead.

As the Pekingese Club's definition points out, a dog is simply red-and-white, fawn-and-white, brindle-and-white, and so on as the case may be, but *not* a parti-color unless the color is evenly divided. The black-and-white parti-color is quite rare, and though it is greatly admired by some, other Pekingese fanciers object to this combination and contend that it is more typical of a Japanese Spaniel than of a Pekingese. From early prints and other examples of ancient Chinese art, it would appear parti-colors were favored in those days, at least sharing honors to a considerable extent with the more lion-like colors.

It is well to remember in judging Pekingese, however, that all colors mentioned above are equally acceptable and that personal preferences have no place in the ring.

It is difficult to judge the weight of a Pekingese by its size. Many large dogs are lacking substance ("shelly" in build) and may thus look enormous but actually tip the scales within the fourteen pound limit. A Pekingese should always be decidedly heavier than his appearance leads one to believe. The ideal size in the view of most authorities is a dog that

The most serious faults in Pekingese are, of course, those listed in the Standard as disqualifications and penalizations. In the event that any of our newer fanciers are unfamiliar with one of these conditions, we should explain that a Dudley Nose is liver colored, flesh colored, or sometimes spotted, and is usually accompanied by light eyes. With very young puppies, such noses are inconsequential as they usually change to the correct black before the end of the first month.

An undershot appearance is brought about by lack of sufficient underjaw, such a face looking weak with the muzzle seeming to hang over a barely visible underjaw. One of the first essentials of a correct Pekingese face is its upturn and it is easy to see why such a fault is particularly objectionable.

Wry mouths are equally undesirable. This condition is one of crookedness, sometimes confined to the underjaw, but often affecting the entire face. It is far from attractive in all forms. Wry mouth and protruding tongue do not necessarily occur together, though they often do. It is when this condition is suspected that a judge should open and examine the mouth of a Pekingese or request that the handler do so.

Special Puppy Characteristics

Pekingese puppies—like those of other breeds—have a way of appearing wholly outstanding at six weeks or two months of age, then going decidedly wrong between the ages of three and seven or eight months, but sometimes coming back to fulfill original promise.

A high-placed nose with a good upward tilt can usually be depended upon to remain correct, as can a square, massive head that is large in proportion to the puppy's body. Ears sometimes fly during teething, then settle back to the correct carriage. It is important during teething to see that the baby teeth are well out of the way when the second set starts growing, lest the former force the second teeth out of place to spoil a mouth which might otherwise have been perfect.

Broad, black nose leather, dark eyes, well-sprung ribs, and heavy chest can be judged at an early age, and can be counted on to remain. Future soundness and body length, however, are unpredictable in youngsters.

A well-placed tail is usually retained, and a slightly incorrect tail-carriage in a puppy is often improved when the heavy coat and fringes appear at maturity.

Champion Lor-Jo-Al Ricky T'Son with owner Mrs Joan E. Stetson and his six month old daughter, Lor-Jo-Al Ricky's Venus, of Mount Holly, New Jersey. Philadelphia Bulletin *photograph.*

appears to be of about seven or eight pounds but which actually weighs in at about nine pounds. Such a dog will have good substance while appearing of medium size.

The "sleeve-type" miniatures have been making great strides recently. In America, they must weigh less than six pounds; in the past this has meant that they were lacking in bone and were somewhat "weedy" in appearance. During recent years, however, there has been some good breeding, and the result is that championships are being won and enthusiasm increasing both here and in England.

Above: Best In Show at the 1950 Roanoke Kennel Club was Ch. Cah Lyn Kai Jin of Caversham, owned and handled by John B. Royce. The judge was Dr Arthur Mitten. A.R. Minton, Mayor of Roanoke, Virginia presents the trophy; Dr Howard D. Sackett, Club President, completes the picture. Shafer photograph.

Winner of the Pekingese Club of America Specialty Show in 1957 was Ch. Tulo Yu Chuo of Orchard Hill, owned by Mrs Richard S. Quigley. Mrs Fortune Roberts was the judge.

Below: A West Winds Kennel Pekingese learns to eat. Owner, Mrs Horace H. Wilson, Wilton, Connecticut.

CHAPTER 13

BUYING YOUR PEKINGESE PUPPY

There are several trails that will lead you to a litter of puppies where you can find the particular puppy of your choice. Write to the parent club and ask for the names and addresses of members who have puppies for sale. The addresses of the breed clubs can be secured by writing the American Kennel Club, 51 Madison Avenue, New York, N.Y. 10010. They keep an accurate, up-to-date list of reputable breeders where you can seek information on obtaining a good, healthy puppy. You might also check listings in the classified ads of major newspapers. The various dog magazines also carry listings; for example, POPULAR DOGS magazine carries a column on the breed every month.

In England, lists of breeders and the names and addresses of the dog clubs are available from the Kennel Club at 1 Clarges Street, London, W.1.

It is to your advantage to attend a few dog shows in the area where many purebred dogs of just about every breed are being exhibited in the show ring. Even if you do not wish to buy a show dog, you should be familiar with what the better specimens look like so that you may get at least a worthy specimen for your money. You will learn a lot by observing the dogs in action in the show ring, or in a public place where their personalities come to the fore. The dog show catalogue will list the dogs and their owners with local kennel names and breeders which you can visit to see the types they are breeding and winning with at the shows. Exhibitors at these shows are usually delighted to talk to people about their dogs and the specific characteristics of particular breeds.

Once you have selected the Pekingese as your choice of the breeds because you admire its exceptional beauty, intelligence, and personality, and because you feel that the Pekingese will fit in with your family's way of life, it is wise to do a little research on breed.

The American Kennel Club library, your local library, bookshops, and the breed club can usually supply you with a list of written material on the breed, past and present. When you have drenched yourself in your breed's illustrious history and have definitely decided that this is the dog for you, it is time to start writing letters and making phone calls to set up appointments to see litters of puppies.

A word of caution here: don't let your choice of a kennel be determined by its nearness to your home, and your buy be the first "cute" puppy that races up to you or licks the end of your nose. All puppies are attractive, and naturally you will have a preference among those you see. But don't let preferences sway you into making a wrong decision.

If you are buying your dog as a family pet, a preference might not be a serious offense. But if you had, say, a preference of color since you first considered this breed, you would be wise to stick to it: the color is extremely important because you will want your dog to be pleasing to the eye as well. And if you are buying a show dog, an accepted coat is essential according to the Standard laid down for the breed. In considering your purchase you must think clearly, choose carefully, and make the very best possible choice. You will, of course, learn to love your *own* dog, whichever one you finally decided upon, but a case of "love at first sight" can be disappointing and expensive later on if a show career was your primary objective.

To get the broadest possible concept of what is for sale and the current market prices, it is recommended that you visit as many kennels and private breeders as possible. With today's reasonably safe, inexpensive, and rapid flights on major airlines, it is possible to secure dogs from far-off places at additional costs that are not excessive. This will allow you to buy the valuable bloodline of your choice if you have thoughts toward a breeding program in the future.

While it is always safest actually to *see* the dog you are buying, there are enough reputable breeders and kennels for you to buy a dog with minimum risk once you have made up your mind what you want and have decided whether you will buy in this country or import to satisfy your concept of the breed Standard. If you are going to breed dogs, breeding Standard type is a moral obligation, and your concern should be with buying the very best bloodlines and individual animals obtainable, in spite of cost or distance.

Ch. Tai Yang of Newnham with a few of his many trophies and cups, photographed at 18 months after winning his first championship. This dog is behind many, many champions in both this country and England.

It is customary for the purchaser to pay the shipping charges, and the airlines are very willing to supply information and prices upon request. Rental on the shipping crate, if the owner does not provide one for the dog, is nominal. While unfortunate instances have occurred on the airlines in the transporting of animals, the major airlines are making improvements on safety measures and have reached a point of reasonable safety and cost. Barring unforeseen circumstances, the safe arrival of a dog you buy can be pretty well assured if both seller and purchaser are meticulous about all details of the shipment.

The Puppy You Buy

Let us assume that you want to enjoy all the antics of a young puppy and decide to buy a six- to eight-week-old pup. This is about the age at which a puppy is weaned, wormed, and ready to go out into the world under the care of a responsible new owner. It is not advisable to buy a puppy under six weeks of age as it is not yet ready to be separated from its mother. At eight to twelve weeks of age a puppy's appearance and behavior can be more critically noted. Puppies as they are remembered in our fondest childhood memories, are gay and active and bouncy, as well they should be! The normal puppy should be interested, alert, and curious, especially about a stranger. If a puppy appears a bit reserved or distant however, this need not be misconstrued as shyness or fear. It merely indicates that he hasn't made up his mind as to whether or not he likes you. But he should not be fearful or terrified in the presence of a stranger, and especially should show no fear of his owner.

In direct contrast, the puppy should not be ridiculously over-active either. The puppy that frantically bounds around the room and is never still is not particularly desirable. And beware of "spinners!" Spinners are puppies or dogs that have become neurotic because of having been kept in cramped quarters or in crates and behave in such emotionally unstable manner upon being loosed in a spacious area. Upon release they run about in circles and seemingly go wild. Puppies with this sort of traumatic background seldom regain full composure or ever adjust to the big outside world. The puppy that has had the proper exercise and appropriate living quarters will have a normal, though spirited outlook on life and will do his utmost to win you over without going into a tailspin.

If the general behavior and appearance of the dog thus far appeals to you, it is time for you to observe him more closely for additional physical requirements. First of all, you cannot expect to find in the puppy all the coat he will bear at maturity, thanks to the good foods and the many grooming aids to be found today. Of course, the healthy puppy's coat should have a nice shine to it, and the more dense it is at this age, the better the coat will be when the dog finally reaches adulthood.

Look for clear, sparkling eyes, free of discharge. Dark eye rims and lids are indications of the good pigmentation which is important in a breeding program, and even for generally pleasing good looks. From the time that the puppy first opens his eyes until he is about three months old, however, it must be remembered that the eyes have a slight bluish cast. The older the puppy, the darker the eyes, so always ascertain the age of the puppy in considering the degree of darkness of eyes at the particular time of life.

When the time comes to select your first puppy, take an experienced breeder along if possible. Otherwise, have the breed Standard at hand. You are then prepared to interpret the Standard as best you can by making comparisons between the puppies you see.

Check the bite carefully. While the first set of teeth can be misleading, their placement, even at such young age, can be a fairly accurate indication of what the bite will be in maturity. The gums should be a good healthful pink in color and the teeth should be clear, clean, and white. Any brown cast to the teeth could indicate a past case of distemper, and would assuredly count against the dog in the show ring, or against the dog's general appearance when grown.

Puppies take anything and everything into their mouths to chew upon while they are teething, and many infectious diseases are introduced in this way. The fore-mentioned distemper is one, and the brown teeth resulting from this disease never clear. The puppy's breath should not be sour, nor unpleasant or strong. Any acrid odor could indicate a poor food mixture or low quality meat, especially if it is being fed raw. Many breeders have compared the breath of a healthy puppy to the smell of fresh toast—or vaguely like garlic. At any rate, a puppy should never be fed just table scraps, but should have a well-balanced diet containing a good dry puppy chew, and a good grade of fresh meat. Poor meat, too much cereal, or fillers, tend to make the puppy too fat. We like puppies to be in good flesh, but not fat from the wrong kind of food.

Of course we want to find clean puppies. The breeder or owner who shows you a dirty puppy is one to avoid. Look closely at the skin. Rub the fur the wrong way or against the grain; make sure that it is not spotted with insect bites or red, blotchy sores or dry scales. Around the tail and vent area there should be no evidence of diarrhea or inflammation. The puppy's fur should also not be matted from dry excrement nor smell of urine.

True enough, you can wipe dirty eyes, clean dirty ears, and give the puppy a bath when you get it home, but the need to do such things gives indication that the puppy did not have the best of care during the important

and formative first months of its life and its future health and development may have been vitally influenced. There are many reputable breeders raising healthy puppies in clean and otherwise suitable establishments so there is no need to risk a series of veterinary bills and a dog of questionable constitution.

Male or Female

The choice of sex of your puppy is also something that must be given serious thought before you shop. For the pet owner, the sex of a dog is not of paramount importance. But for the breeder or exhibitor there are factors needing consideration. If you are looking for a stud to establish a kennel, it is essential that you select a dog with both testicles evident, even at an early age, and verified by a veterinarian before a purchase is agreed upon.

Being a monorchid (having but one testicle) automatically disqualifies a dog from the show ring and from a breeding program. Monorchids are capable of siring, and they frequently produce offspring with the same deficiency; to introduce this trait into a bloodline knowingly is against an unwritten law in the dog fancy. A monorchid can also sire cryptorchids, dogs that have no testicles and are sterile.

If you desire a dog to be a member of the family, the best selection would probably be a female. You can always go out for stud service if you should decide to breed. You can choose the bloodlines producing the most winners because they should be bred true to type, and you will not have to foot the bill for financing a show career. You can always keep a male from your first litter that will bear your own "kennel name" should you decide to proceed in the kennel business.

As additional considerations in the male versus female decision for the private owner there might be the problem of leg-lifting with a male, and with females there is the inconvenience when they are in season. However, this need not be the problem it used to be; pet shops now sell "pants" for both sexes, which aid in controlling the situation at home.

The Planned Parenthood Behind Your Puppy

Never hesitate to ask pertinent questions about the puppy, as well as about the sire and dam. Feel free to ask the breeder if you may see the dam, not only to establish that she is in good health but to ascertain that her appearance is representative of the breed. Ask also to see the sire if he belongs to the kennel.

Ask what the puppy has been fed or should be fed after weaning. Ask to see the pedigree and inquire as to whether the litter or the individual puppies have been registered with the American Kennel Club. Find out how many of the temporary and/or permanent inoculations the puppy has had, when or if the puppy has been wormed, and if it has had any illness, disease, or infection.

You need not ask if the puppy is house-broken; it won't mean much. He may have got hold of an idea of where "the place" is at his present home, but he will need new training to learn where "the place" is in his new home. You cannot expect too much control from a puppy this young anyway, and housebreaking is entirely up to the new owner. It is known that puppies always eliminate after eating, so it is up to you to take the dog out immediately after each meal. Puppies also eliminate when they awaken and sometimes dribble when they become excited. If friends or relatives are coming over to see the new puppy, make sure that he is walked before he greets them at the front door; this will help.

With puppies of about three months of age, two to three hours between eliminations is normal. So as the time draws near, take the puppy out or indicate the newspapers spread for the purpose. Housebreaking is never easy, but anticipation is about 90 per cent of solving the problem. The schools that offer to house-break your dog are virtually useless; he will learn the location of "the place" at the school but will require retraining upon returning home.

A reputable breeder will welcome any and all questions you may ask and will voluntarily offer additional information, if only to boast about the tedious and loving care he has given the litter. He will also sell a puppy on a 24-hour veterinary approval. This means that you have a full day to get the puppy to a veterinarian of your choice to obtain his opinion regarding the general health of the puppy before you make a final decision. There should also be veterinary certificates and full particulars on dates and types of inoculations that have been given.

Puppies and Worms

Not a very pleasant subject, but worms must be brought to your attention. Generally, almost all puppies come in contact with worms even though reared in clean quarters. They can be passed from the mother before birth or picked up by early contacts with the earth or flooring of quarters. But to say that you must not buy a puppy because of the presence of worms is nonsensical. You might thus pass up a fine quality animal that can be freed of worms in a single treatment. But it is also true that a heavy infestation of any kind of worms is dangerous and debilitating.

The extent of infestation can be readily determined by a veterinarian and he can advise you as to whether or not the future health and conformation of the dog has been damaged. He can also supply the medication and prescribe the dosage at that time, and you will already have one of your problems solved. The kinds and varieties of worms and how to detect their presence is discussed in detail elsewhere; it is therefore advised that you check the matter out further if any doubt remains in your mind regarding the problem of worms in dogs.

Veterinary Inspection

While your veterinarian is going over the puppy you have selected for your purchase, you might just as well ask for his opinion of it as a specimen of the breed as well as the facts about its health. While few veterinarians can claim to be experts in breed standards, they usually have a good eye for a fine specimen and can advise you where to go for further information. Perhaps he can also recommend other breeders to consult for an opinion. The vet can point out structural faults or organic problems that affect all breeds and can usually judge whether or not an animal has been abused or mishandled and if it is over- or undersized.

We would like to emphasize here that it is only through this sort of close cooperation between owners and veterinarians that we can expect to reap the harvest of modern research and be enabled to advance. Most reputable veterinarians are more than eager to learn about various purebred dogs, and we in turn must acknowledge and apply what they have proved through research and experience in their field. We can perhaps buy and breed the best dogs in the world, but when disease strikes we are safe only as our veterinarians are capable—so let's keep them informed breed by breed and dog by dog. The veterinarian often represents the difference between life and death!

CHAPTER 14

BREEDING YOUR PEKINGESE

Let us assume the time has come for your dog to be bred, and you have decided you are in a position to enjoy producing a litter of puppies that you hope will make a contribution to the breed. The bitch you purchased is sound, her temperament is excellent and she is a most worthy representative of the breed.

You have taken a calendar and counted off the ten days since the first day of red staining and have in this way determined the tenth to fourteenth day which will be the best days for the actual mating. You have additionally counted off 59 to 63 days before the puppies are due to be born to make sure that everything necessary for their arrival will be in good order by that time.

From the moment the idea of having a litter occurred to you, your thoughts should have been given to the selection of a proper stud. Here again the novice would do well to seek advice on analyzing pedigrees and tracing bloodlines for the best breedings. As soon as the bitch is in season and you see color or staining and a swelling of the vulva, it is time to notify the owner of the stud you have selected and make an appointment for the breeding. There are several pertinent questions you will want to ask stud owners after having decided upon the pedigree.

The Health of the Breeding Stock

Some of your first questions should be: Has this adult male ever sired a litter? Has his sperm count been checked? Has he been X-rayed for Hip Dysplasia and found to be clear? Does he have two normal-sized testicles? Do not be impressed with the owner's romantic tales of his "Romeo" behavior. You can hear just as many stories about the amorous male that thinks he's a stud, but has never yet made a successful tie. Ask if he needs human assistance to complete a breeding and what his score is on the number of breedings that have produced a litter. Is he a lazy or aggressive stud; in other words, does he give up easily if the bitch does not cooperate?

When considering your bitch for this mating, you must take into consideration a few important points that lead to a successful breeding. Has she had normal heat cycles? Four months may be normal for some, but six or nine months is normal for most. Has she ever been bred before and what were the results? Did she have normal puppies? Too many runts—mis-marks, brown noses, etc? Has she ever had a vaginal infection? Did she have a normal delivery and did the pregnancy go its full term? Did she have to have one or more Caesarean sections? Was she a good mother, and did she have a lot of milk, or none at all? Did she allow assistance during delivery? Did the puppies all survive or did you lose several from the litter shortly after birth?

Don't buy a bitch that has problem heats and never a litter. And don't be afraid to buy a healthy maiden bitch, since chances are, if she is healthy and from good stock, she will be a healthy producer for you. Don't buy a monorchid male, or one with a low sperm count. Any veterinarian can give you a count and you will do well to require one, especially if it is to be the stud dog for a kennel. Older dogs that have been good producers and are for sale are usually not too hard to find at good established kennels. If they are not too old and have sired show quality puppies, they can give you some excellent litters from which to establish your breeding stock from solid bloodlines.

The Day of the Mating

Now that you have decided upon the proper male and female combination to produce what you hope will be—according to the pedigrees—a fine litter of puppies, it is time to set the date. You have selected the two days (with a one day lapse in between) that you feel are best for the breeding, and you call the owner of the stud. The bitch always goes to the stud, unless, of course, there are extenuating circumstances and the stud then goes to the female. You set the date and the time and arrive with the bitch and the MONEY.

Standard procedure is payment of a stud fee at the time of the first breeding, if there is a tie. For the stud fee, you are entitled to two breedings with ties. Contracts may be written up with specific conditions on breeding terms, of course, but this is general procedure. Often a breeder will take the pick of a litter to protect and maintain his bloodlines. This can be especially desirable if he needs an outcross for his breeding program, or if he wishes to continue his own bloodlines if he sold you the bitch to start with, and this mating will continue his line-breeding program. This should all be worked out ahead of time and written and signed before the two dogs are bred together. Remember that the payment of the stud fee is for the services of the stud—not for a guarantee of a litter of puppies. This is why it is so important to make sure you are using a proven stud. Bear in mind also, that the American Kennel Club will not register a litter of puppies sired by a male that is under eight months of age. In the case of an older dog, they will not register a litter sired by a dog over 12 years of age, without a witness to the breeding in the form of a veterinarian or other responsible person.

Many studs over 12 years of age are still fertile and capable of producing puppies, but if you do not witness the breeding there is always the danger of a "substitute" stud being used to produce a litter. This brings up the subject of sending your bitch away to be bred, if you cannot accompany her.

The disadvantages of sending a bitch away to be bred are numerous. First of all, she will not be herself in a strange place and be difficult to handle. Transportation if she goes by air—while reasonably safe, is still a traumatic experience and there is the danger of her being put off at the wrong airport, not being fed or watered properly, etc. Some bitches get so upset that they go out of season and the trip, which may prove expensive, especially on top of a substantial stud fee, will have been for nothing.

If at all possible, accompany your bitch so that the experience is as comfortable for her as it can be. In other words, make sure before setting this kind of schedule for a breeding that there is no stud in the area that might be as good for her as the one that is far away. We do not wish to have you sacrifice the proper breeding for convenience, since bloodlines are so important, but we do put the safety of the bitch above all else. There is always a risk in traveling, since dogs are considered cargo on a plane.

How Much Is the Stud Fee?

The stud fee will vary considerably—the better the bloodlines, the more winning the dog does at shows, the higher the fee. A top winning dog could run up to $500. Here again, there may be exceptions. Some breeders will take part cash and then, say, third pick of the litter. The fee can be arranged by a private contract, rather than the traditional procedure we have described.

It is obviously wise to get the details of the payment of the stud fee in writing to avoid trouble.

**Sanell Wenti,
born August 27th, 1935,
and owned by Mrs
Hugh Duberly.**

The Actual Mating

It is always advisable to muzzle the bitch. A terrified bitch can even in fear bite one of the people involved, and may snap or attack the stud, to the point where he will become discouraged and lose interest in the breeding. Muzzling can be done with a lady's stocking tied around the muzzle with a half knot, crossed under the chin and knotted at the back of the neck. There is enough "give" in the stocking for her to breathe or salivate freely and yet not open her jaws far enough to bite. The owner holds onto her collar and talks to her and calms her as much as possible.

If the male will not mount on his own initiative, it may be necessary for the owner to assist in lifting him onto the bitch, perhaps even guide him to the proper place. But usually, once he gets the idea, the tie is accomplished. The owner should remain close at hand however, to make sure the tie is not broken and before an adequate breeding has been completed. After a while the stud may get bored and try to break away. This could prove injurious. It may be necessary to hold him in place until the tie is complete.

We must stress at this point, that while some bitches carry on physically and vocally during the tie, there is no real way the bitch can be hurt. However, a stud can be seriously or even permanently damaged by a bad breeding. Therefore, the owner of the bitch must be reminded that she must not be alarmed by any commotion. All concentration should be devoted to the stud and a successful and properly executed service.

Many people believe that breeding dogs is simply a matter of placing two dogs, a male and a female, in close proximity, and letting

Above: Booker Tee, whelped January 10th, 1934, bred and exhibited by Etta F. Hodnette of Denver, Colorado. His sire was Han Shih ex *Pee-O-Nee.*

nature take its course. While often this is true, you cannot count on it. Sometimes it is hard work, and in the case of valuable stock it is essential to supervise to be sure of the safety factor. Especially if one or both of the dogs are inexperienced. If the owners are also inexperienced it may not take place at all!

Artificial Insemination

Breeding by means of artificial insemination is usually unsuccessful, unless under a veterinarian's supervision, and can lead to an infection for the bitch and discomfort for the dog. The American Kennel Club requires a veterinarian's certificate to register puppies from such a breeding. Although the practice has been used for over two decades, it now offers new promise since research has been conducted to make it a more feasible procedure for the future.

Great dogs may eventually look forward to reproducing themselves years after they have left this earth. There now exists a frozen semen concept that has been tested and works. The study, headed by Dr. Stephen W. J. Seager, M.V.B., instructor at the University of Oregon Medical School, has the financial support of the American Kennel Club, indicating that organization's interest in the work. The study is being monitored by the Morris Animal Foundation, Denver, Colorado.

Dr. Seager announced in 1970 he had been able to preserve dog semen and to produce litters with the stored semen. The possibilities of selective, world-wide breedings by this method are exciting. Imagine simply mailing a vial of semen to the bitch! The perfection of line-breeding by storing semen without the threat of death interrupting the breeding program is exciting.

As it stands today, the technique for artificial insemination requires the depositing of semen (taken directly from the dog) into the bitch's vagina, past the cervix and into the uterus by syringe. The correct temperature of the semen is vital, and there is no guarantee of success.

The storage method, if adopted, will open a new era in the field of purebred dogs.

The Gestation Period

Once the breeding has taken place successfully, the seemingly endless waiting period of 63 days begins. For the first ten days after the breeding, you do absolutely nothing for the bitch—just spin dreams about the delights you will share with the family when the puppies arrive.

Around the tenth day it is time to begin supplementing the diet of the bitch with vitamins and calcium. We strongly recommend that you take her to your veterinarian for a list of the proper or perhaps necessary supplements and the correct amounts of each for your particular bitch. Guesses, which may lead to excesses or insufficiencies, can ruin a litter. For the price of a visit to your veterinarian, you will be confident that you are feeding properly.

The bitch should be free of worms, of course, and if there is any doubt in your mind, she should be wormed now, before the third week of pregnancy. Your veterinarian will advise you on the necessity of this and proper dosage as well.

Probing for Puppies

Far too many breeders are over-anxious about whether the breeding "took" and are inclined to feel for puppies or persuade a veterinarian to radiograph or X-ray their bitches to confirm it. Unless there is reason to doubt the normalcy of a pregnancy, this is risky. Certainly 63 days are not too long to wait, and why risk endangering the litter by probing with your inexperienced hands? Few bitches give no evidence of being in whelp, and there is no need to prove it for yourself by trying to count puppies.

Alerting Your Veterinarian

At least a week before the puppies are due, you should telephone your veterinarian and notify him that you expect the litter and give him the date. This way he can make sure that there will be someone available to help, should there be any problems during the whelping. Most veterinarians today have answering services and alternate vets on call when they are not available themselves. Some veterinarians suggest that you call them when the bitch starts labor so that they may further plan their time, should they be needed. Discuss this matter with him when you first take the bitch to him for her diet instructions, etc., and establish the method which will best fit in with this schedule.

Do You Need a Veterinarian in Attendance?

Even if this is your first litter, we would advise that you go through the experience of whelping without panicking and calling desperately for the veterinarian. Most animal births are accomplished without complications, and you should call for assistance only if you run into trouble.

When having her puppies your bitch will appreciate as little interference and as few strangers around as possible. A quiet place, with her nest, a single familiar face and her own instincts are all that is necessary for nature to take its course. An audience of curious children squealing and questioning, other family pets nosing around, or strange adults should be avoided. Many a bitch which has been distracted in this way has been known to devour her young. This can be the horrible result of intrusion of the bitch's privacy. There are other ways of teaching children the miracle of birth, and there will be plenty of time later for the whole family to enjoy the puppies. Let them be born under proper and considerate circumstances.

Labor

Some litters—many first litters—do not run for the full term of 63 days. So, at least a week before the puppies are actually due, and at the time you alert your veterinarian as to their arrival, start observing the bitch for

signs of commencement of labor. This will manifest itself in the form of ripples running down the sides of her body, which will come as a revelation to her as well. It is most noticeable when she is lying on her side—and she will be sleeping a great deal as the arrival date comes closer. If she is sitting or walking about, she will perhaps sit down quickly or squat peculiarly. When you notice this for the first time, your vigil has begun. As the ripples become more frequent, birth time is drawing near and you will be wise not to leave her. Usually within 24 hours before whelping, she will stop eating, and as much as a week before, she will begin digging a nest. The bitch should be given something resembling a whelping box with layers of newspapers (black and white only) to make her nest. She will dig more and more as birth approaches and this is the time to begin making your promise to stop interfering unless your help is specifically required. Some bitches whimper, others are silent, but whimpering does not necessarily indicate trouble.

The Arrival of the Puppies

The sudden gush of green fluid from the bitch indicates that the water or fluid surrounding the puppies has "broken" and they are about to start down the canal and come into the world. When the water breaks, birth of the first puppy is imminent. The first puppies are usually born within minutes to a half hour of each other, but a couple of hours between the later ones is not uncommon. If you notice the bitch straining constantly without producing a puppy, or if a puppy remains partially in and partially out for too long, it is cause for concern. Breach births (puppies born feet first instead of head first) can often cause delay or hold things up, and this is often a problem which requires veterinarian assistance.

Below: Japeke Tiny Tim's Fi-Na-Lee [bitch] and Japeke Tiny Tim's Han Shih [dog] pictured as young puppies. Bred and owned by Marjory Nye White of the Japeke Kennels in Los Angeles, California.

Feeding the Bitch Between Births

Usually the bitch will not be interested in food for about 24 hours before the arrival of the puppies, and perhaps as long as two or three days after their arrival. The placenta which she cleans up after each puppy is high in food value and will be more than ample to sustain her. This is nature's way of allowing the mother to feed herself and her babies without having to leave the nest and hunt for food during the first crucial days. The mother always cleans up all traces of birth in the wilds so as not to attract other animals to her new-born babies.

However, there are those of us who believe in making food available, should the mother feel the need to restore her strength during or after delivery—especially if she whelps a large litter. Raw chop-meat, beef bouillon, and milk are all acceptable and may be placed near the whelping box during the first two or three days. After that, the mother will begin to put the babies on a sort of schedule. She will leave the whelping box at frequent intervals, take longer exercise periods, and begin to take interest in other things. This is where the fun begins for you. Now the babies are no longer soggy, little, pinkish blobs. They begin to crawl around and squeal and grow before your very eyes!

It is at this time, if all has gone normally, that the family can be introduced gradually and great praise and affection given to the mother.

Breech Births

Puppies normally are delivered head first. However, some are presented feet first, or in other abnormal positions, and this is referred to as a "breech birth." Assistance is often necessary to get the puppy out of the canal, and great care must be taken not to injure the puppy or the dam.

Aid can be given by grasping the puppy with a piece of turkish toweling and pulling gently during the dam's contractions. Be careful not to squeeze the puppy too hard, merely try to ease it out by moving it gently back and forth. Because even this much delay in delivery may mean the puppy is drowning, do not wait for the bitch to remove the sac. Do it yourself by tearing the sac open to expose the face and head. Then cut the cord anywhere from one-half to three-quarters of an inch away from the navel. If the cord bleeds excessively, pinch the end of it with your fingers and count five. Repeat if necessary. Then pry open the mouth with your finger and hold the puppy upside down for a moment to drain any fluids from the lungs. Next, rub the puppy briskly with turkish or

paper toweling. You should get wriggling and whimpering by this time.

If the litter is large, this assistance will help conserve the strength of the bitch and will probably be welcomed by her. However, it is best to allow her to take care of at least the first few herself to preserve the natural instinct, and to provide the nutritive values obtained by her consumption of the after-births.

Dry Births

Occasionally, the sac will break before the delivery of a puppy and will be expelled while the puppy remains inside, thereby depriving the dam of the necessary lubrication to expel the puppy normally. Inserting vaseline or mineral oil via your finger will help the puppy pass down the birth canal. This is why it is essential that you be present during the whelping so that you can count puppies and afterbirths and determine when and if assistance is needed.

The Twenty-four-hour Checkup

It is wise to have a veterinarian check the mother and her puppies within 24 hours after the last puppy is born. The vet can check for cleft palates or umbilical hernia and may wish to give the dam—particularly if she is a show dog—an injection of Pituitin to make sure of the expulsion of all afterbirths and to tighten up the uterus. This can prevent a sagging belly after the puppies are weaned and the bitch is being readied for the show ring.

False Pregnancy

The disappointment of a false pregnancy is almost as bad for the owner as it is for the bitch. She goes through the entire 63 days

International Ch. Beaupres Lovely Star of Grimstoy pictured winning under judge McFarlane in 1965. Dawn Braham, daughter of owner Mrs E. Mirylees, handling and pictured on the right. Dog on the left is Ch. Cheryl of Chuitei. Lovely Star is owned by the Beaupres Kennels, Herefordshire, England. C.M. Cooke photo.

with all the symptoms—swollen stomach, increased appetite, swollen nipples—even makes a nest when the time comes. You may even take an oath that you noticed the ripples on her body from the labor pains. Then, just as suddenly as you made up your mind that she was definitely going to have puppies, you will know that she definitely is not! She may walk around carrying a toy as if it were a puppy for a few days, but she will soon be back to normal and acting just as if nothing happened—and nothing did!

Caesarean Section

Should the whelping reach the point where there is a complication, such as the bitch not being capable of whelping the puppies herself, the "moment of truth" is upon you and a Caesarean section may be necessary. The bitch may be too small or too immature to expel the puppies herself; or her cervix may fail to dilate enough to allow the young to come down the birth canal; or there may be torsion of the uterus, a dead or monster puppy, a sideways puppy blocking the canal, or perhaps toxemia. A Caesarean section will be the only solution. No matter what the cause, get the bitch to the veterinarian immediately to insure your chances of saving the mother and/or puppies.

The Caesarean section operation (the name derived from the legend that Julius Caesar was delivered into the world by this method) involves the removal of the unborn young from the uterus of the dam by surgical incision into the walls through the abdomen. The operation is performed when it has been determined that for some reason the puppies cannot be delivered normally. While modern surgical methods have made the operation itself reasonably safe, with the dam being perfectly capable of nursing the puppies shortly after the completion of the surgery, the chief danger lies in the necessity to spark life into the puppies immediately upon their removal from the womb. If the mother dies, the time element is even more important in saving the young, since the oxygen supply ceases upon the death of the dam, and the difference between life and death is measured in seconds.

After surgery when the bitch is home in her whelping box with the babies, she will probably nurse the young without distress. You must be sure that the sutures are kept clean and that no redness or swelling or ooze appears in the wound. Healing will take place naturally and no salves or ointments should be applied unless prescribed by the veterinarian, for fear the puppies will get it into their systems. Check the bitch for fever if there is any doubt, restlessness (other than the natural concern for her young), or a lack of appetite, but do not anticipate trouble.

Episiotomy

Used rather frequently in human deliveries, episiotomy (pronounced A-PEASE-E-OTT-O-ME) is the cutting of the membrane between the rear opening of the vagina back almost to the opening of the anus. After delivery it is stitched together, and barring complications, heals easily, presenting no problem in future births.

Socializing Your Puppy

The need for puppies to get out among people and other animals cannot be stressed enough. Kennel-reared dogs are subject to all sorts of idiosyncrasies and seldom make good house dogs or normal members of the world around them when they grow up.

The crucial age, which determines the personality and general behavior patterns which will predominate the rest of the dog's life are formed between the ages of three to ten weeks. This is particularly true during the 21st to 28th day. It is essential that the puppy be socialized during this time by bringing him into the family life as much as possible. Floor surfaces, indoor and outdoor, should be experienced; handling by all members of the family and visitors is important, preliminary grooming (use a toothbrush gently on small breeds) gets him used to a lifelong necessity; light training, such as setting him up on tables and cleaning teeth and ears and cutting nails, etc., has to be started early if he is to become a show dog. The puppy should be exposed to car riding, shopping tours, a leash around its neck, children—your own and others—and in all possible ways relationships developed with humans.

It is up to the breeder, of course, to protect the puppy from harm or injury during this initiation into the outside world. The benefits reaped from proper attention will pay off in the long run with a well-behaved, well-adjusted grown dog capable of becoming an integral part of a happy family.

CHAPTER 15

THE POWER OF PEDIGREES

An old dog philosopher once remarked, the definition of a show prospect puppy is one third the pedigree, one third what you see, and one third what you *hope* it will be! Well, no matter how you break down the qualifying percentages, we all agree that good breeding is essential if you have any plans at all for a show career for your dog! Many breeders will buy on pedigree alone, counting largely on what they can do for the puppy themselves by way of feeding, conditioning and training. But needless to say, that important piece of paper, commonly referred to as "the pedigree" is very reassuring to a breeder or buyer when they are new at the game, or when they have a breeding program in mind and are trying to establish their own bloodline.

One of the most fascinating aspects of tracing pedigrees is the way the names of the really great dogs of the past keep appearing in the pedigrees of the great dogs of today. This is proof positive of the strong influence of heredity, and bears witness to a great deal of truth in the statement that great dogs frequently reproduce themselves, though not necessarily in appearance only. A pedigree represents something of value when one is dedicated to breeding better dogs.

To the novice buyer, or one who is perhaps merely switching to another breed, and see only a frolicking, leggy, squirming bundle of energy in a fur coat, a pedigree can mean *everything!* To those of us who understand the working of heredity, a pedigree is more like an insurance policy. . . .

We have gathered in this chapter several pedigrees from the past and present which have strongly influenced the breed. We hope you will find the lineage of these great dogs as interesting to follow as we did.

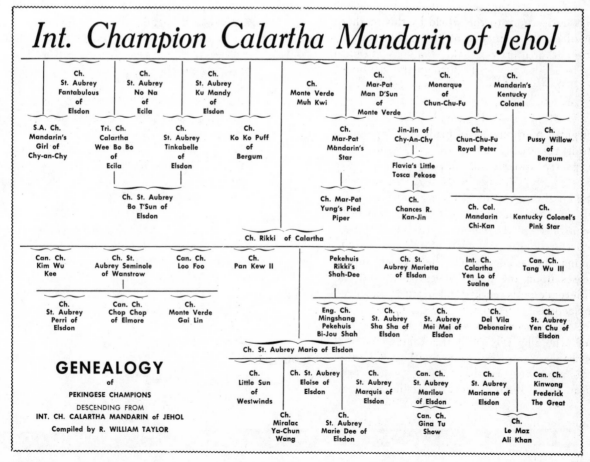

Int. Champion Calartha Mandarin of Jehol

GENEALOGY
of
PEKINGESE CHAMPIONS
DESCENDING FROM
INT. CH. CALARTHA MANDARIN of JEHOL
Compiled by R. WILLIAM TAYLOR

CERTIFIED PEDIGREE

REGISTERED NAME... CHIK T'SUN OF CAVERSHAM   BREED... PEKINGESE   SEX... Male

DATE WHELPED... REGISTERED NUMBER... BREEDER... V. AUBREY JONES & W TAYLOR   ADDRESS...

COLOUR, MARKINGS, AND GENERAL DESCRIPTION... BRILLIANT RED WITH BLACK MASK

				SIRE
			SIRE CH. KU-CHI OF CAVERSHAM	
		SIRE CH. CAVERSHAM KU-KU OF YAM		DAM
				SIRE
			DAM REGINA DE YAM	
SIRE KU-CHIK OF CAVERSHAM				DAM
REGISTERED NUMBER...				SIRE
			SIRE CH. CAVERSHAM KO-KO OF SHAN RUSS	
	DAM KO-LEE OF CAVERSHAM			DAM
				SIRE
			DAM MO-LEE OF CAVERSHAM	
				DAM
				SIRE
			SIRE PUFF BALL OF CHUNGKING	
		SIRE CH. KU-CHI OF CAVERSHAM		DAM
				SIRE
			DAM MARIGOLD OF ELFAUN	
DAM NAXOS KU-CHI FILLE OF CAVERSHAM				DAM
REGISTERED NUMBER...				SIRE
			SIRE WINALO OF SHERIDE HAM	
	DAM PSYCHE OF NAXOS			DAM
				SIRE
			DAM RENA OF IFIELD	
				DAM

CERTIFIED PEDIGREE

REGISTERED NAME... Int: Ch: TANG HAO OF CAVERSHAM-CATAWBA   BREED... PEKINGESE   SEX...

DATE WHELPED... REGISTERED NUMBER... BREEDER... Miss I.M. de PLEDGE   ADDRESS...

COLOUR, MARKINGS, AND GENERAL DESCRIPTION...

				SIRE
			SIRE YUKO OF CAVERSHAM	
		SIRE MISTER VVU OF LUEBON		DAM
				SIRE
			DAM PINK PONG OF LUEBON	
SIRE Engl: Ch: TANG HOU OF LUEBON				DAM
REGISTERED NUMBER...				SIRE
			SIRE Am: Ch: SUTHERLAND AVENUE TZU EH	
	DAM POOH PAY OF LUEBON			DAM
				SIRE
			DAM GOURMOND	
				DAM
				SIRE
			SIRE Ch: BON TON OF ASHCROFT	
		SIRE PICKWICK OF LUEBON		DAM
				SIRE
			DAM GOURMOND	
DAM SOUCHONG OF CAVERSHAM				DAM
REGISTERED NUMBER...				SIRE
			SIRE Ch: PUNG CHOW OF ALDERBOURNE	
	DAM PING PONG OF LUEBON			DAM
				SIRE
			DAM LUE LUE OF LUEBON	
				DAM

CERTIFICATE OF PEDIGREE

REGISTERED NAME...PIERROT DE HAETLEBURY...BREED..........SEX.........

DATE WHELPED................REGISTERED NUMBER..........BREEDER..........ADDRESS..........

COLOUR, MARKINGS, AND GENERAL DESCRIPTION ....

			SIRE...........
		SIRE...NEA SHAZA	
	SIRE SUTHERLAND AVENUE SHA TZU		DAM...........
		DAM CH. FARALINE WENTZU	SIRE...........
SIRE CH. SUTHERLAND AVENUE TZU EH			DAM...........
REGISTERED NUMBER..............		SIRE SUTHERLAND AVENUE HSIEN LO	SIRE...........
	DAM CHACKMORE WANG		DAM...........
		DAM CHACKMORE TANGO	SIRE...........
			DAM...........
		SIRE ASHTON MORE WEN LO	SIRE...........
	SIRE SUTHERLAND AVENUE TOUEN		DAM...........
		DAM MATZU	SIRE...........
DAM SUTHERLAND AVENUE TOU YU			DAM...........
REGISTERED NUMBER..............		SIRE BOOFLESS OF BRYN-Y-MOR	SIRE...........
	DAM SUTHERLAND AVENUE YU EH		DAM...........
		DAM BIDDIE OF BRYN-Y-MOR	SIRE...........
			DAM...........

CERTIFIED PEDIGREE

REGISTERED NAME...WU FOO OF KINGSWERE...BREED..PEKINGESE...SEX.........

DATE WHELPED................REGISTERED NUMBER..........BREEDER..........ADDRESS..........

COLOUR, MARKINGS, AND GENERAL DESCRIPTION ....

			SIRE...........
		SIRE BONZODAH OF PARKFIELD	
	SIRE CH. BON DAH OF KINGSWERE		DAM...........
		DAM DOLLY OF CHELDON	SIRE...........
SIRE BONZO-ET OF KINGSWERE			DAM...........
REGISTERED NUMBER..............		SIRE CH. YU CHUAN OF ALDERBOURNE	SIRE...........
	DAM CHU-TZU OF KINGSWERE		DAM...........
		DAM SUTHERLAND AVENUE TAN TZU	SIRE...........
			DAM...........
		SIRE BONZODAH OF PARKFIELD	SIRE...........
	SIRE BONZODAH TSUN OF CHELDON		DAM...........
		DAM ANDERSON MANOR KAI	SIRE...........
DAM LANDAH OF CHELDON			DAM...........
REGISTERED NUMBER..............		SIRE FARALINE THADI TSUN	SIRE...........
	DAM DOLLY OF CHELDON		DAM...........
		DAM BABSIE OF CHELDON	SIRE...........
			DAM...........

CERTIFICATE OF PEDIGREE

REGISTERED NAME .... Ch: KAI LUNG OF REMENHAM .... BREED .... PEKINGESE .... SEX ....

DATE WHELPED .... REGISTERED NUMBER .... BREEDER .... ADDRESS ....

COLOUR, MARKINGS, AND GENERAL DESCRIPTION ....

		SIRE Ch: HUMMING BEE OF ALDERBOURNE	SIRE ....
	SIRE Ch: MENG OF ALDERBOURNE		DAM ....
		DAM SUKI OF HARBOROUGH	SIRE ....
SIRE BILLIE BEE OF REMENHAM			DAM ....
REGISTERED NUMBER		SIRE CUM LI RALLY	SIRE ....
	DAM REMENHAM MOPSIE		DAM ....
		DAM REMENHAM FLORA	SIRE ....
			DAM ....
		SIRE Ch: YU CHUAN OF ALDERBOURNE	SIRE ....
	SIRE NANKING YU WEN		DAM ....
		DAM NANKING WEN TSAN	SIRE ....
DAM REMENHAM NANETTE			DAM ....
REGISTERED NUMBER		SIRE NANKING WEN TZU	SIRE ....
	DAM NANKING TSE AN		DAM ....
		DAM NANKING KOSI	SIRE ....
			DAM ....

CERTIFIED PEDIGREE

REGISTERED NAME .. BEAUPRES KOBERT OF PEKESPAN .. BREED PEKINGESE .. SEX ....

DATE WHELPED .... REGISTERED NUMBER .... BREEDER .... ADDRESS ENGLAND ......

COLOUR, MARKINGS, AND GENERAL DESCRIPTION ....

		SIRE FINN.CH. KU-JI. OF CAVERSHAM	SIRE CH. KU. JIN. OF. CAVERSHAM
	SIRE SUNSHEN YEN CHU		DAM CH. KU. LOON. OF. CAVERSHAM
		DAM SUNSHEN YEN	SIRE WANSTROW SNOW BALL
SIRE CH. TOY DOM. SUNSHEN CHU T'SUN			DAM SUNSHEN CHEN YING
REGISTERED NUMBER		SIRE INT. CH. COPPLESTONE PAI PHU	SIRE CH. CAVERSHAM KU KU. OF YOH
	DAM SUNSHEN PEONY		DAM COPPLESTONE PETAL
		DAM SUNSHEN KU'S KISS	SIRE SUNSHEN KU. T'ZU
			DAM MEI MEI OF NEKOCHE
		SIRE TOY DOM. ZAR KU	SIRE TONGLAND PAI FOO OF LOO FOO
	SIRE PAI FOO OF PEKESPAN		DAM RICHARD MIGNONETTE
		DAM SAYEE OF PEKESPAN	SIRE PEI WEI OF PEKESPAN
DAM WEI TUR OF PEKESPAN			DAM KOER OF KYRATOWN
REGISTERED NUMBER		SIRE CH. TOY DOM T.S. ZEE	SIRE PHILADELPHUS CAVALIER OF ALDERBOURNE
	DAM WHITE HYACINTH OF PEKESPAN		DAM EDWINA OF IQUHIDE
		DAM WHITE HYACINTH OF ELOC	SIRE ELOC BLANCO OF CHUNG-KING
			DAM QUEENIE LOO OF ELOC

270

CERTIFIED PEDIGREE

REGISTERED NAME MING WU WU KEE OF THE TERRACE   BREED ....   SEX ....

DATE WHELPED ....   REGISTERED NUMBER ....   BREEDER ....   ADDRESS ....

COLOUR, MARKINGS, AND GENERAL DESCRIPTION ....

			SIRE MON. CHINK OF HESKETH	SIRE MONKEY OF MONKEY TOWN
				DAM PEGGY
	SIRE INT. CH. RAJAH OF HESKETH WU KEE			
			DAM FUN HEOW PANNIE	SIRE GUMBALA TAO TAI
				DAM CHUT TERH
SIRE CH. RAJAH'S FOX OF WU KEE REGISTERED NUMBER				
			SIRE CH. GUMBALA HESHAS	SIRE MON CHINK OF HESKETH
				DAM MIMSA SHANG
	DAM GREY FOX OF HESKETH WU KEE			
			DAM LUMBALA LO TZU	SIRE BALAVODDAN LI KU DAH
				DAM LO TSU OF KUEN LAN
			SIRE CH. PUNG CHOW OF ALDERBOURNE	SIRE CHU ERH TSUN OF ALDERBOURNE
				DAM WENDY OF SHAN LINE
	SIRE CHA MLOE PUNG CHOW TSUN			
			DAM ROCHARD HAI HAI	SIRE PUKKA SHAZADA
				DAM ROCHARD TSU TSING
DAM SHANSI OF WU KEE REGISTERED NUMBER				
			SIRE CHA MING YUAN DAH	SIRE CH. WUN DAH OF CHINATOWN
				DAM BOLTONIA CHONGETTA
	DAM CHA MING YUANETTA			
			DAM NISHIETA	SIRE PEKECLAN WU
				DAM WOLPAT SUKISU

Note the strong linebreeding here on the sire's side to Mon
Chink of Hesketh.

CERTIFIED PEDIGREE

REGISTERED NAME WHITWORTH MICHAEL   BREED PEKINGESE   SEX ....

DATE WHELPED ....   REGISTERED NUMBER ....   BREEDER MRS. H. L. MAPES   ADDRESS ....

COLOUR, MARKINGS, AND GENERAL DESCRIPTION ....

			SIRE HA PAH CUTNEY	SIRE ....
				DAM ....
	SIRE BOLTONIA CHOO TAI			
			DAM SHU YEN OF CAVERSHAM	SIRE ....
				DAM ....
SIRE CHOO TAI OF WALMESLEY REGISTERED NUMBER				
			SIRE WIZARD OF WALMSLEY	SIRE ....
				DAM ....
	DAM AINSTAR NANETTE			
			DAM YIN OF KUENLUN	SIRE ....
				DAM ....
			SIRE CH. WUN DAH OF CHINATOWN	SIRE ....
				DAM ....
	SIRE CH. FU DAH OF CHINATOWN			
			DAM PRI OF CHINATOWN	SIRE ....
				DAM ....
DAM RUFFLES RED GIRL REGISTERED NUMBER				
			SIRE DING TI OF WALMSLEY	SIRE ....
				DAM ....
	DAM WHITWORTH TREDSEE			
			DAM JANE OF WALMESLEY	SIRE ....
				DAM ....

CERTIFIED PEDIGREE

REGISTERED NAME YU GO HAN OF ORCHARD HILL   BREED PEKINGESE   SEX

DATE WHELPED ....   REGISTERED NUMBER ....   BREEDER MRS. R. S. QUIGLEY   ADDRESS ....

COLOUR, MARKINGS, AND GENERAL DESCRIPTION ....

		SIRE INT. CH. PIERROT OF HARTLEBURY
	SIRE PIERSON OF ORCHARD HILL	
		DAM HULA OF CHINATOWN O'ORCHARD HILL
SIRE CH. PIER YU GO OF ORCHARD HILL		
REGISTERED NUMBER		SIRE HOY'S GOI OF HEDLS
	DAM HULA OF CHINATOWN O'ORCHARD HILL	
		DAM BLOSSOM DE CROTTON
		SIRE CH. YU CHURN OF ALDEABOUENE
	SIRE CH. SUTHERLAND AVENUE HAN SHIH	
		DAM SUTHERLAND AVENUE CHI SI
DAM HAN'S H'OULA OF ORCHARD HILL		
REGISTERED NUMBER		SIRE CH. NANKING CHU JAI
	DAM CHU JAI'S OULA OF ORCHARD HILL	
		DAM DONAGH OF REMENHAM

CERTIFICATE OF PEDIGREE

REGISTERED NAME BEAUPRES RORA OF JENNTORA   BREED PEKINGESE   SEX

DATE WHELPED ....   REGISTERED NUMBER ....   BREEDER   ADDRESS ENGLAND

COLOUR, MARKINGS, AND GENERAL DESCRIPTION ....

		SIRE CH. CAVERSHAM KU KU OF YAM
	SIRE FRANCHARD PENNJINN	
		DAM CAVERSHAM JIN JIN OF WETHERSFIELD
		SIRE ACRE ACRE PATRICIAN
	DAM CH. FRANCHARD PERRYACRE PENANNE	
		DAM PERRYACRE PENELLA
SIRE CH. CHERANGANI CHIPS		
REGISTERED NUMBER		SIRE CH. CAVERSHAM KU KU OF YAM
	SIRE CH. GOOFUS LE GRISBIE	
		DAM GOOFUS PAINTED LADY
	DAM CHERANGANI CHA-CHA	
		SIRE SHERATON ROYALIST
	DAM SHERATON MERRILY	
		DAM SHERATON LARKS
		SIRE CH. CAVERSHAM KU KU OF YAM
	SIRE CH. KU JIN OF CAVERSHAM	
		DAM CAVERSHAM JIN JIN OF WETHERSFIELD
	SIRE TRI-CH. FU WONG OF JAMESTOWN	
		SIRE JAMESTOWN JIN CHI DE CAVERSHAM
	DAM CH. SUSIE WONK OF JAMESTOWN	
		DAM JAMESTOWN ALOUETTE OF TILDOCK
DAM HATIE OF JENNTORA		
REGISTERED NUMBER		SIRE CH. KWALA OF IFIELD
	SIRE SERAPH OF IFIELD	
		DAM IFIELD CREAMCRACKER OF POETHORE
	DAM SERENA OF JENNTORA	
		SIRE KU CHIK OF CAVERSHAM
	DAM BABY SHAM OF JENNTORA	
		DAM LINBOURNE TUL ANNA

Ch. Tuppence of Dah-Lyn, John B. Royce,
owner. Sire: Ch. Philadelphus Antonio of
Dah-Lyn, dam: Millie of Dah-Lyn.

Below: Ch. Greenwich Ringo Soy, sired by
Ch. Prince Confucious ex Ch. Khoo Yos Miu,
and owned by Mrs C. Neilson of Bywood,
Pennsylvania. Another Pekingese of the thirties.

Tom Tit of Kingswere, whelped November
2nd, 1935, and owned by Mrs H. Gambier.
Photographed by Thomas Fall of London.

Below: Champion Wei Bella-Twee of Kyratown, owned by Mr W. Hindley Taylor. Photo
by C.M. Cooke.

Betty Shoemaker pictured in front of her home with International Champion Ti Toi and Mai Toi in the carriage. She is holding International Champion Copplestone Mr. Pinkcoat in her arm. Photo by Connelly-Moy.

CHAPTER 16

GENETICS

No one can guarantee nature! But, with facts and theories at your command you can at least, on paper, plan a litter of puppies that should fulfill your fondest expectations. Since the ultimate purpose of breeding is to try to improve the breed, this planning, no matter how uncertain, should be earnestly attempted.

There are a few terms you should be familiar with to help you understand the breeding procedure and the structure of genetics. The first thing that comes to mind is the Mendelian Law—or The Laws of Mendelian Inheritance. Who was Mendel? Gregor Mendel was an Austrian clergyman and botanist born in Brunn, Moravia. He developed his basic theories on heredity while working with peas. Not realizing the full import of his work, he published a paper on his experiments in a scientific journal in the year 1866. That paper went unnoticed for many years, but the laws and theories put forth in it have been tried and proven. Today they are accepted by scientists as well as dog breeders.

To help understand the Mendelian Law as it applies to breeding dogs, we must acquaint ourselves with certain scientific terms and procedures. First of all, dogs possess glands of reproduction which are called gonads. The gonads of the male are in the testicles which produce sperm, or spermatozoa. The gonads of the female are the ovaries and produce eggs. The bitch is born with these eggs and, when she is old enough to reproduce, she comes into heat. The eggs descend from the ovaries via the Fallopian tubes to the two horns of the uterus. There they either pass on out during the heat cycle or are fertilized by the male sperm in the semen deposited during a mating.

In dog mating, there is what we refer to as a tie, which is a time period during which the male pumps about 600 million spermatozoa into the female to fertilize the ripened eggs. When the sperm and the ripe eggs meet, zygoates are created and the little one-celled future puppies descend from the Fallopian tubes into the uterus where they attach themselves to the walls of the uterus and begin to develop. With all inherited characteristics determined as the zygote was formed, the dam now must only assume her role as incubator for her babies, which are now organisms in their own right. The bitch has been bred and is now in whelp!

Let us take a closer look at what is happening during the breeding phenomenon. We know that while the male deposits as many as 600 million sperm into the female, the number of ripe eggs she releases will determine the number of puppies in the litter. Therefore, those breeders who advertise their stud as "producer of large litters" do not know the facts. The bitch determines the size of the litter; the male the sex of the puppies. It takes only one sperm of the 600 million to produce a puppy.

Each dog and bitch possesses 39 pairs of chromosomes in each reproductive germ cell. The chromosomes carry the genes, like peas in a pod, and there are approximately 150,000 genes in each chromosome. These chromosomes split apart and unite with half the chromosomes from the other parent and the puppy's looks and temperament are created.

To understand the procedure more thoroughly, we must understand that there are two kinds of genes—dominant and recessive. A dominant gene is one of a pair whose influence is expressed to the exclusion of the effects of the other. A recessive gene is one of a pair whose influence is subdued by the effects of the other. Most of the important qualities we wish to perpetuate in our breeding programs are carried on by the dominant genes. It is the successful breeder who becomes expert at eliminating recessive or undesirable genes and building up the dominant or desirable genes. This principle holds true in every phase of breeding—inside and outside the dog!

There are many excellent books available which will take you deeper into the fascintaing subject of canine genetics. You can learn about your chances of getting so many black, so

many white, and so many black and white puppies, etc. Avail yourself of this information before your next—or hopefully, first—breeding. We have, merely touched upon genetics here to point out the importance of planned parenthood. Any librarian can help you find further information, or books may be purchased offering the very latest findings in canine genetics. It is a fascinating and rewarding program toward creating better dogs.

Above: The English import Ch. Changkim Fire Storm, bred by Mrs Irene Pearson is pictured winning under judge Erica Huggins at the 1970 Mid-Continent Kennel Club show. Owners are N.E. Toothaker and H.R. Norris of the Watonga Kennels, Dallas, Texas. Handler is H.R. Norris.

Above: Ch. San Kow Gargoyle Tien Hia, owned by Mrs F. Henry Brooks, Wah Bagin Kennels, Framingham, Massachusetts. Another popular Peke of the nineteen thirties.

Left: Ch. Quilkin Te Amo Jai Sonya, judge Maurice Baker's choice for the Best of Opposite Sex win at the 1969 San Antonio Kennel Club Show. "Bill" Norris handled for owner H. David Holmes of Houston, Texas.

276

CHAPTER 17

FEEDING AND NUTRITION

Feeding Puppies

There are very many diets available today for young puppies, including all sorts of products on the market for feeding the newborn, for supplementing the feeding of the young and for adding this or that to diets, depending on what is lacking in the way of a complete diet.

When weaning puppies, it is necessary to put them on four meals a day, even while you are tapering off with the mother's milk. Six in the morning, twelve noon, six in the evening and midnight is about the best schedule since it fits in tolerably well with most human eating plans. Meals for the puppies can be prepared immediately before or after your own meals, without too much of a change in your schedule.

The 6 a.m. Meal

Two meat and two milk meals are best and should, of course, be served alternately. Assuming the 6 a.m. feeding is a milk meal, its contents should be based on goat's milk if possible. This is the very best milk to feed puppies, but it is expensive and usually available only at drug stores—unless you live in farm country where it may be readily available fresh and still less expensive. If goat's milk cannot be obtained, use evaporated milk (which can be changed to powdered milk later on) diluted to two parts evaporated milk and one part water, along with raw egg yolk, honey or Karo syrup, sprinkled with a high-protein baby cereal and some wheat germ. As the puppies mature, cottage cheese may be added or can be substituted for the cereal at one of the two milk meals.

The Noon Meal

A puppy chow which has been soaked in warm water or beef broth according to the time specified on the wrapper should be mixed with raw or simmered chop meat in equal proportions with a vitamin powder added.

The 6 p.m. Meal

Repeat the milk meal—perhaps varying the type of cereal from wheat to oats, or corn or rice.

The Midnight Meal

Repeat the meat meal. If raw meat was fed at noon the evening meal might be perhaps simmered.

Please note that specific quantities are not given in this suggested diet. Each serving will depend entirely upon the size of the litter and will increase proportionally with their rate of growth. However, it is safe to say that the most important ingredients are the milk and cereal and the meat and puppy chow since these form the basis of the diet. Your veterinarian can advise on the sizes of portion if there is any doubt in your mind as to how much to use.

If you notice that the puppies are "cleaning their plates," it is possible you are not feeding them enough to keep up with their rate of growth. Increase the amount at the next feeding. Observe them closely; puppies should each "have their fill" because growth is so rapid at this age. If they have not satisfied themselves, increase the amount so that they do not have to fight for the last morsel. They will not overeat if they know there is enough food available. Instinct will usually let them eat to suit their normal capacity.

If there is any doubt in your mind as to any ingredient you are feeding, ask yourself, "Would I give it to my own baby?" If the answer is No, then don't give it to your puppies. At this age, the comparison between puppies and human babies is not fanciful and can be a good guide.

If there is any doubt in your mind, we repeat that you should ask your veterinarian to be sure.

Many puppies will regurgitate their food, perhaps a couple of times, before they manage to retain it. If they do bring up their food, allow them to eat it again, rather than clean it away. Sometimes additional saliva is necessary for them to digest it, and you do not want them to miss a meal because it is an unpleasant sight for you to observe.

This same regurgitation process sometimes holds true for the bitch, who may every now and then bring up her own food for her puppies. This is a natural instinct on her part, stemming from the days when dogs gave birth in the wilds. The only food the mother could then provide at weaning time was too rough and indigestible for her puppies. She therefore, took it upon herself to pre-digest the food until it could be taken and retained by her young. Bitches will sometimes resort to this today, especially those which love having litters and have a strong maternal instinct. Some dams will help you wean their litters, and even give up feeding entirely once they see you are taking over.

Weaning the Puppies

When weaning the puppies, the mother is kept away from the little ones for longer and longer periods of time. This is done over a period of several days. At first she is separated from the puppies for several hours, then all day, leaving her with them only at night for comfort and warmth. This gradual separation aids in helping the mother's milk disappear gradually and she suffers less distress after feeding a litter.

If the mother continues to carry a great deal of milk with no signs of it tapering off, consult your veterinarian before she gets too uncomfortable. If she is uncomfortable she may cut the puppies off from her supply of milk too abruptly and before they should be completely on their own.

There are many opinions on the proper age to start weaning puppies. If you plan to start selling them between six and eight weeks, weaning should begin between two and three weeks of age. Here again, each bitch will pose a different situation. The size and weight of the litter should help determine the time; your veterinarian will form an opinion as he determines the burden the bitch is carrying by the size of the litter and her general condition. If she is being pulled down by feeding a large litter, he may suggest that you start at two weeks. If she is glorying in her motherhood without any apparent taxing of her strength, he may suggest three to four weeks. You and he will be the best judges. But remember there is no substitute that is as perfect as mother's milk—and the longer the puppies benefit from it, the better. Other food yes, but mother's milk first and foremost for the healthiest puppies!

Feeding the Adult Dog

The puppies' schedule of four meals a day should drop to three by 6 months and then to two by 9 months. By the time the dog reaches one year of age, it should be eating only one meal a day.

The time when you feed the dog each day can be a matter of the dog's preference or your convenience, so long as once in every 24 hours the dog receives a meal that provides him with a complete, balanced diet. In addition fresh clean water should, of course, be available at all times.

There are many brands of dry food, kibbles and biscuits on the market which are all of good quality. There are also many varieties of canned dog food which are of good quality and provide a balanced diet for your dog. But, for those breeders and exhibitors who show their dogs, additional care is given to providing a few "extras" which enhance the good health and good appearance of show dogs.

A good meal or kibble mixed with water or beef broth and raw meat is perhaps the best ration to provide. In cold weather many breeders add suet or corn oil (even olive or cooking oil) to the mixture and others make use of the bacon fat from breakfast by pouring it over the dogs' food.

Salting a dog's food in the summer helps replace the salt he pants away in the heat. Many breeders sprinkle the food with garlic powder to sweeten the dog's breath and prevent gas, especially in breeds that gulp or wolf their food and swallow a lot of air. We prefer garlic powder, the salt is too weak and the clove is too strong.

Sister Sue, photographed in the early 1920's.

There are those, of course, who cook very elaborately for their dogs, which is not necessary if a good meal and meat mixture is provided. Many prefer to add vegetables, rice, tomatoes, etc., in with everything else they feed. As long as the extras do not affect the nutritional balance, there is little harm, but no one thing should be fed to excess. Occasionally liver should be given. Fish, which most veterinarians no longer recommend even for cats, is fed to puppies, but should not be given more than once a week. Always remember that no single thing should be given as a total diet: balance is most important—steak or 100 per cent meat can even kill a dog.

In March of 1971, the National Research Council investigated the great stir in the dog fancy over the controversy on feeding dogs an all-meat diet. It was established that meat and meat products constitute a complete balanced diet for dogs *only* when they are further enriched with vitamins and minerals.

Therefore, a good dog chow or meal mixed with meat provides the perfect combination for a dog's diet. While the dry food is a complete diet in itself, the fresh meat additionally satisfies the dog's appetite which is anatomically and physiologically oriented to meat. While dogs are actually carnivores, it must be remembered that when they fed themselves in the wilds they ate almost the entire animal they captured—including its stomach contents, which provided some of the vitamins and minerals we must now add to the diet.

The standards for diets which claim to be "complete and balanced" are set by the Sub-committee on Canine Nutrition of the National Research Council (NRC) of the National Academy of Sciences. This is the official agency for establishing the nutritional requirements of dog foods. Most foods sold for dogs and cats meet these requirements and manufacturers are happy to say so on their labels, so look for this when you buy. Pet food labels must be approved by the Association of American Feed Control Officials, Pet Foods Committee. Both the Food and Drug Administration and the Federal Trade Commission of the AAFCO define the word "balanced" when referring to dog food as: ". . . a term which may be applied to pet food having all known, required nutrients in a proper amount and proportion based upon the recommendations of a recognized authority (The National Research Council is one) in the field of animal nutrition, for a given set of physiological animal requirements."

With this much care given to your dog's diet, there can be little reason for not having happy well-fed dogs in proper weight and proportions for the show ring.

Obesity

As we have just mentioned, there are many "perfect" diets for your dogs on the market today, that when fed in proper proportions should keep your dogs in the best of form. However, there are those owners who more often than not indulge their own appetites and are inclined to overfeed their dogs as well. A study in Great Britain in the early 1970's found a major percentage of obese people also had obese dogs.

Obesity in dogs is a direct result of the animal being fed more food than he can properly burn up over a period of time, so it is stored as fat or fatty tissue in the body. Pet dogs are more inclined to become obese than show dogs or working dogs, but obesity also is a factor to be considered with the older dog since his exercise is curtailed.

A lack of "tuck up" on a dog, or not being able to feel the ribs, or great folds of fat which hang from the underside of the dog can all be considered as obesity. Genetic factors may enter into the picture, but usually the owner is at fault.

The life span of the obese dog is decreased on several counts. Excess weight puts undue stress on the heart as well as the joints. The dog becomes a poor anesthetic risk and has less resistance to viral or bacterial infections. Treatment is seldom easy or completely effective, so emphasis should be placed on not letting your dog get FAT in the first place!

Orphan Puppies

The ideal solution to feeding orphaned puppies is to be able to put them with another nursing dam who will take them on as her own. If this is not possible within your own kennel, or a kennel that you know of, it is up to you to care for and feed the puppies. Survival is possible but requires a great deal of time and effort on your part.

One of Lottie Hall's American-bred champion bitches shown several decades ago.

Your substitute milk formula must be precisely prepared, always served heated to body temperature and refrigerated when not being fed. Esbilac, a vacuum-packed powder, with complete feeding instructions on the can, is excellent and about as close to mother's milk as you can get. If you can't obtain Esbilac, or until you do so, there are two alternative formulas that you might use.

Mix one part boiled water with five parts of evaporated milk and add one teaspoonful of di-calcium phosphate per quart of formula. Di-calcium phosphate can be secured at any drug store. If they have it in tablet form only, you can powder the tablets with the back part of a tablespoon. The other formula for newborn puppies is a combination of eight ounces of homogenized milk mixed well with two egg yolks.

You will need baby bottles with the three-hole nipples. Sometimes doll bottles can be used for the newborn puppies, which should be fed at six-hour intervals. If they are consuming sufficient amounts, their stomachs should look full, or slightly enlarged, though never distended. Amount of formula to be fed is proportionate to size and age and growth and weight of puppy, and is indicated on the can of Esbilac or on the advice of your veterinarian. Many breeders like to keep a baby scale nearby to check the weight of the puppies to be sure they are thriving on the formula.

At two to three weeks you can start adding Pablum or some other high protein baby cereal to the formula. Also, baby beef can be licked from your finger at this age, or added to the formula. At four weeks the surviving puppies should be taken off the diet of Esbilac and put on a more substantial diet, such as wet puppy meal or chopped beef. However, Esbilac powder can' still be mixed in with the food for additional nutrition. The baby foods of pureed meats make for a smooth change over also and can be blended into the diet.

How to Feed Newborn Puppies

When the puppy is a newborn, remember that it is vitally important to keep the feeding procedure as close to the routine of the natural mother as possible. The newborn puppy should be held by hand in your lap in an almost upright position with the bottle at an angle to allow the entire nipple area to be full. Do not hold the bottle upright so the puppy's head has to reach straight up toward the ceiling; do not let the puppy nurse too quickly or take in too much air and possibly get the colic. Once in a while, take the bottle away and let it rest for a moment and swallow several times. Before feeding, always test the nipple to see that the fluid does not come out too quickly, or by the same token, too slowly so that the puppy gets tired of feeding before he has had enough to eat.

When the puppy is a little older, you can place him on his stomach on a towel to eat, and even allow him to hold on to the bottle or to "come and get it" on his own. Most puppies enjoy eating and this will be a good indication of how strong an appetite he has and his ability to consume the contents of the bottle.

It will be necessary to "burp" the puppy. Place a towel on your shoulder and hold the puppy on your shoulder as if it were a human baby, patting and rubbing it gently. This will also encourage the puppy to defecate. At this time, you should observe for diarrhoea or other intestinal disorders. The puppy should eliminate after each feeding with occasional eliminations between times as well. If the puppies do not eliminate on their own after each meal, massage their stomachs and under their tails gently until they do.

You must keep the puppies clean. If there is diarrhea or if they bring up a little formula the puppy should be washed and dried off. Under no circumstances should fecal matter be allowed to collect on their skin or fur.

All this—plus your determination and perseverance—might save an entire litter of puppies that would otherwise have died without their real mother.

Gastric Torsion

Gastric torsion, or bloat, sometimes referred to simply as "twisted stomach" has become more and more prevalent. Many dogs that in the past had been thought to die of blockage of the stomach or intestines because they had swallowed toys or other foreign objects are now suspected of having been the victims of gastric torsion and the bloat that followed.

Though life can be saved by immediate surgery to untwist the organ, the rate of fatality is high. Symptoms of gastric torsion are unusual restlessness, excessive salivation, attempts to vomit, rapid respiration, pain and the eventual bloating of the abdominal region.

The cause of gastric torsion can be attributed to overeating, excess gas formation in the stomach, poor function of the stomach or intestine, blockage to entrances or exits of the stomach or intestine, or general lack of exercise. As the food ferments in the stomach, gases form which may twist the stomach in a clockwise direction so that the gas is unable to escape. Surgery, where the stomach is untwisted counter clockwise, is the safest and most successful way to correct the situation.

The condition itself is not limited to size of breed of dog, so to avoid the threat of gastric torsion, it is wise to keep your dog well exercised to be sure the body is functioning normally. Make sure that food and water are available for the dog at all times, thereby reducing the tendency to overeat. With self-service, dry feeding, where the dog is able to eat intermittently during the day, there is not the urge to gobble a lot at one time.

If you notice any of the symptoms of gastric torsion, call your veterinarian immediately! Death can result within a matter of hours.

CHAPTER 18

TRAINING YOUR PEKINGESE

There are few things in the world a dog would rather do than please his master. Therefore, obedience training, or even the initial basic training, will be a pleasure for your dog, if taught correctly, and will make him a much nicer animal to live with for the rest of his life.

When to Start Training

The most frequently asked .question by those who consider training their dog is, naturally, "What is the best age to begin training?" The answer is, "not before six months." A dog simply cannot be sufficiently or permanently trained before this age and be expected to retain all he has been taught. If too much is expected of him, he can become frustrated and it may ruin him completely for any serious training later on, or even jeopardize his disposition. Most things a puppy learns and repeats before he is six months of age should be considered habit rather than training.

The Reward Method

The only proper and acceptable kind of training is the kindness and reward method which will build a strong bond between dog and owner. A dog must have confidence in and respect for his teacher. The most important thing to remember in training any dog is that the quickest way to teach, especially the young dog, is through repetition. Praise him when he does well, and scold him when he does wrong. This will suffice. There is no need or excuse for swinging at a dog with rolled up newspapers or flailing hands, which will only tend to make the dog hand shy the rest of his life. Also, make every word count. Do not give a command unless you intend to see it through. Pronounce distinctly with the fewest possible words, and use the same words for the same command every time.

Include the dog's name every time to make sure you have his undivided attention at the beginning of each command. Do not go on to another command until he has successfully completed the previous one and is praised for

it. Of course, you should not mix play with the serious training time. Make sure the dog knows the difference between the two.

In the beginning, it is best to train without any distractions whatsoever. After he has learned to concentrate and is older and more proficient, he should perform the exercises with interference, so that the dog learns absolute obedience in the face of all distractions. Needless to say, whatever the distractions, you never lose control. You must be in command at all times to earn the respect and attention of your dog.

How long should the lessons be?

The lessons should be brief with a young dog, starting at five minutes, and as the dog ages and becomes adept in the first lessons, increase the time all the way up to one-half hour. Public training classes are usually set for one hour, and this is acceptable since the full hour of concentration is not placed on your dog alone. Working under these conditions with other dogs, you will find that he will not be as intent as he would be with a private lesson where the commands are directed to him alone for the entire thirty minutes.

If you should notice that your dog is not doing well, or not keeping up with the class, consider putting off training for awhile. Animals, like children, are not always ready for schooling at exactly the same age. It would be a shame to ruin a good obedience dog because you insist on starting his training at six months rather than at, say, nine months, when he would be more apt to be receptive both physically and mentally. If he has particular difficulty in learning one exercise, you might do well to skip to a different one and come back to it again at another session. There are no set rules in this basic training, except, "don't push"!

What You Need to Start Training

From three to six months of age, use the soft nylon show leads, which are the best and safest. When you get ready for the basic training at six months of age, you will require one of the special metal-link choke chains sold for exactly this purpose. Do not let the word "choke" scare you. It is a soft, smooth chain and should be held slack whenever you are not actually using it to correct the dog. This chain should be put over the dog's head so that the lead can be attached over the dog's neck rather than underneath against his throat. It is wise when you buy your choke collar to ask the sales person to show you how it is to be put on. Those of you who will be taking your dog to a training class will have an instructor who can show you.

To avoid undue stress on the dog, use both hands on the lead. The dog will be taught to obey commands at your left side, and therefore, your left hand will guide the dog close to this collar on a six-foot training lead. The balance of the lead will be held in your right hand. Learn at the very beginning to handle your choke collar and lead correctly. It is as important in training a dog as is the proper equipment for riding a horse.

What to Teach First

The first training actually should be to teach the dog to know his name. This, of course, he can learn at an earlier age than six months, just as he can learn to walk nicely on a leash or lead. Many puppies will at first probably want to walk around with the leash in their mouths. There is no objection to this if the dog will walk while doing it. Rather than cultivating this as a habit, you will find that if you don't make an issue of it, the dog will soon realize that carrying the lead in his mouth is not rewarding and he'll let it fall to his side where it belongs.

We also let the puppy walk around by himself for a while with the lead around his neck. If he wishes to chew on it a little, that's all right too. In other words, let it be something he recognizes and associates with at first. Do not let the lead start out being a harness.

If the dog is at all bright, chances are he has learned to come on command when you call him by name. This is relatively simple with sweet talk and a reward. On lead, without a reward, and on command without a lead is something else again. If there has been, or is now, a problem, the best way to correct it is to put on the choke collar and the six-foot lead. Then walk away from the dog, and call him, "Pirate, come!" and gently start reeling him in until the dog is front of you. Give him a pat on the head and/or a reward.

Walking, or heeling, next to you is also one of the first and most important things for him to learn. With the soft lead training starting very early, he should soon take up your pace at your left side. At the command to "heel" he should start off with you and continue alongside until you stop. Give the command, "Pirate, sit!" This is taught by leaning over and pushing down on his hindquarters until he sits next to you, while pulling up gently on the collar. When you have this down pat on the straight away, then start practising it in circles, with turns and figure eights. When he is an advanced student, you can look forward to the heels and sits being done neatly, spontaneously, and off lead as well.

The "Down" Command

One of the most valuable lessons or commands you can teach your dog is to lie down on command. Some say it may save his life: it is invaluable when traveling with a dog or visiting, if behavior and manners are required even beyond obedience. While repeating the words, "Pirate, down!" lower the dog from a sitting position in front of you by gently pulling his front legs out in front of him. Place your full hand on him while repeating the command, "Pirate, down!" and hold him down to let him know you want him to *stay* down. After he gets the general idea, this can be done from a short distance away on lead along with the command, by pulling the lead down to the floor. Or perhaps, you can slip the lead under your shoe (between the heel and the sole) and pull it directly to the floor. As the dog progresses in training, a hand signal with or without verbal command, or with or without lead, can be given from a considerable distance by raising your arm and extending the hand palm down.

The "Stay" Command

The stay command eventually can be taught from both a sit and a down position. Start with the sit. With your dog on your left side in the sitting position give the command, "Pirate, stay!" Reach down with the left hand open and palm side to the dog and sweep it in close to his nose. Then walk a short distance away and face him. He will at first, having learned to heel immediately as you start off, more than likely start off with you. The trick in teaching this is to make sure he hears "stay" before you start off. It will take practice. If he breaks, sit him down again, stand next to him, and give the command all over again. As he masters the command, let the distance between you and your dog increase while the dog remains seated. Once the command is learned, advance to the stay command from the down position.

The Stand for Examination

If you have any intention of going on to advanced training in obedience with your dog, or if you have a show dog which you feel you will enjoy showing yourself, a most important command which should be mastered at six months of age, is the stand command. This is essential for a show dog since it is the position used when the show judge goes over your dog. This is taught in the same manner as the stay command, but this time with the dog remaining up on all four feet. He should learn to stand still, without moving his feet and without flinching or breaking when approached by either you or strangers. The hand with palm open wide and facing him should be firmly placed in front of his nose with the command, "Pirate, stand!" After he learns the basic rules and knows the difference between stand and stay, ask friends, relatives, and strangers to assist you with this exercise by walking up to the dog and going over him. He should not react physically to their touch. A dog posing in this stance should show all the beauty and pride of being a sterling example of his breed.

Formal School Training

We mentioned previously about the various training schools and classes given for dogs. Your local kennel club, newspaper, or the yellow pages of the telephone book will put you in touch with organizations in your area where this service is performed. You and your dog will learn a great deal from these classes. Not only do they offer formal train-

Ch. Whitworth Knickerbocker, owned by Mrs Richardson Strathy.

ing, but the experience for you and your dog in public, with other dogs of approximately the same age and with the same purpose in mind is invaluable. If you intend to show your dog, this training is valuable ring experience for later on. If you are having difficulty with the training, remember, it is either too soon to start—or YOU are doing something wrong!

Advanced Training and Obedience Trials

The AKC obedience trials are divided into three classes: Novice, Open and Utility.

In the Novice Class, the dog will be judged on the following basis:

TEST	MAXIMUM SCORE
Heel on lead	35
Stand for examination	30
Heel free—on lead	45
Recall (come on command)	30
One-minute sit (handler in ring)	30
Three-minute down (handler in ring)	30
Maximum total score	200

If the dog "qualifies" in three shows by earning at least 50% of the points for each test, with a total of at least 170 for the trial, he has earned the Companion Dog degree and the letters C.D. (Companion Dog) are entered after his name in the AKC records.

After the dog has qualified as a C.D., he is eligible to enter the Open Class competition, where he will be judged on this basis:

TEST	MAXIMUM SCORE
Heel free	40
Drop on Recall	30
Retrieve (wooden dumbbell) on flat	25
Retrieve over obstacle (hurdle)	35
Broad Jump	20
Three-minute sit (handler out of ring)	25
Five-minute down (handler out of ring)	25
Maximum total score	200

Again he must qualify in three shows for the C.D.X. (Companion Dog Excellent) title and then is eligible for the Utility Class, where he can earn the Utility Dog (U.D.) degree in these rugged tests:

TEST	MAXIMUM SCORE
Scent discrimination (picking up article handled by master from group) Article 1	20
Scent discrimination Article 2	20
Scent discrimination Article 3	20
Seek back (picking up an article dropped by handler)	30
Signal exercise (heeling, etc., on hand signal)	35
Directed jumping (over hurdle and bar jump)	40
Group examination	35
Maximum total score	200

For more complete information about these obedience trials, write for the American Kennel Club's *Regulations and Standards for Obedience Trials.* Dogs that are disqualified from breed shows because of alteration or physical defects are eligible to compete in these trials.

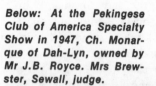

Left: Jack Watts and his Orchid Lanes Yung Pan photographed in 1952 when Yung was eight months old.

Above: Ch. Oakmere the Baron, pictured winning under judge Virginia Sivori, with handler Elaine Rigden, and his owner Mrs Ruth Painter of Pennsylvania.

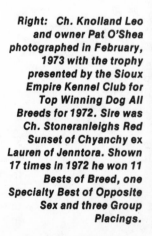

Right: Ch. Knolland Leo and owner Pat O'Shea photographed in February, 1973 with the trophy presented by the Sioux Empire Kennel Club for Top Winning Dog All Breeds for 1972. Sire was Ch. Stoneranleighs Red Sunset of Chyanchy ex Lauren of Jenntora. Shown 17 times in 1972 he won 11 Bests of Breed, one Specialty Best of Opposite Sex and three Group Placings.

CHAPTER 19

SHOWING YOUR PEKINGESE

Let us assume that after only a few months of loving care, you realize your dog is developing beyond your wildest expectations and that the dog you selected is very definitely a show dog! Of course, every owner is prejudiced. But if you are sincerely interested in going to dog shows with your dog and making a champion of him, now is the time to start casting a critical eye on him from a judge's point of view.

Ch. Mon Chink Too of Dah-Lyn, owned by Carolyn Royce.

There is no such thing as a perfect dog. Every dog has some faults, perhaps even a few serious ones. The best way to appraise your dog's degree of perfection is to compare him with the Standard for the breed, or before a judge in a show ring.

Match Shows

For the beginner there are "mock" dog shows, called Match Shows, where you and your dog go through many of the procedures of a regular dog show, but do not gain points toward championship. These shows are usually held by kennel clubs, annually or semi-annually, and much ring poise and experience can be gained there. The age limit is reduced to two months at match shows to give puppies four months of training before they compete at the regular shows when they reach six months of age. Classes range from two to four months; four to six months; six to nine months; and nine to twelve months. Puppies compete with others of their own age for comparative purposes. Many breeders evaluate their litters in this manner, choosing which is the most outgoing, which is the most poised, the best showman, etc.

For those seriously interested in showing their dog to full championship, these match shows provide important experience for both the dog and the owner. Class categories may vary slightly, according to number of entries, but basically include all the classes that are included at a regular point show. There is a nominal entry fee, and, of course, ribbons and usually trophies are given for your efforts as well. Unlike the point shows, entries can be made on the day of the show right on the show grounds. They are unbenched and provide an informal, usually congenial atmosphere for the amateur, which helps to make the ordeal of one's first adventures in the show ring a little less nerve-wracking.

The Point Shows

It is not possible to show a puppy at an American Kennel Club sanctioned point show before the age of six months. When your dog reaches this eligible age, your local kennel club can provide you with the names and addresses of the show-giving superintendents in your area who will be staging the club's dog show for them, and where you must write for an entry form. A sample entry form is included in this book.

The forms are mailed in a pamphlet called a premium list. This also includes the names of the judges for each breed, a list of the prizes and trophies, the name and address of the show-giving club and where the show will be held, as well as rules and regulations set up by the American Kennel Club which must be abided by if you are to enter.

A booklet containing the complete set of show rules and regulations may be obtained by writing to the American Kennel Club, Inc., 51 Madison Avenue, New York, N.Y., 10010.

When you write to the Dog Show Superintendent, request not only your premium list for this particular show, but ask that your name be added to their mailing list so that you will automatically receive all premium lists in the future. List your breed or breeds and they will see to it that you receive premium lists for Specialty shows as well.

Unlike the match shows where your dog will be judged on ring behavior, at the point shows he will be judged on conformation to the breed Standard. In addition to being at least six months of age (on the day of the show) he must be a thoroughbred for a point show. This means both of his parents and he are registered with the American Kennel Club. There must be no alterations or falsifications regarding his appearance. Females cannot have been spayed and males must have both testicles in evidence. No dyes or powders may be used to enhance the appearance, and any lameness or deformity or major deviation from the Standard for the breed constitutes a disqualification.

With all these things in mind, groom your dog to the best of your ability in the specified area for this purpose in the show hall and walk into the show ring with great pride of ownership and ready for an appraisal of your dog by the judge.

The presiding judge on that day will allow each and every dog a certain amount of time and consideration before making his decisions. It is never permissible to consult the judge regarding either your dog or his decision while you are in the ring. An exhibitor never speaks unless spoken to, and then only to answer such questions as the judge may ask— the age of the dog, to see the dog's bite, or to ask you to move your dog around the ring once again.

However, before you reach the point where you are actually in the ring awaiting the final decisions of the judge, you will have had to decide on which of the five classes in each sex your dog should compete.

Point Show Classes

The regular classes of the AKC are: Puppy, Novice, Bred-by-Exhibitor, American-Bred, Open; if your dog is undefeated in any of the regular classes (divided by sex) in which it is entered, he or she is REQUIRED to enter the Winners Class. If your dog is placed second in the class to the dog which won Winners Dog or Winners Bitch, hold the dog or bitch in readiness as the judge must consider it for Reserve Winners.

Puppy Classes shall be for dogs which are six months of age and over but under twelve months, which were whelped in the U.S.A. or Canada, and which are not champions. Classes are often divided 6 and under 9, 9 and under 12 months. The age of a dog shall be calculated up to and inclusive of the first day of a show. For example, a dog whelped on Jan. 1st is eligible to compete in a puppy class on July 1st, and may continue to compete up to and including Dec. 31st of the same year, but is not eligible to compete Jan. 1st of the following year.

The Novice Class shall be for dogs six months of age or over, whelped in the U.S.A. or Canada which have not, prior to the closing of entries, won three first prizes in the Novice Class, a first prize in Bred-by-Exhibitor, American-Bred or Open Class, nor one or more points toward a championship title.

The Bred-by-Exhibitor Class shall be for dogs whelped in the U.S.A. which are six months of age and over, which are not champions, and which are owned wholly or in part by the person or by the spouse of the person who was the breeder or one of the breeders of record. Dogs entered in the BBE Class must be handled by an owner or by a member of the immediate family of an owner, i.e., the husband, wife, father, mother, son, daughter, brother or sister.

The American-Bred Class shall be for all dogs (except champions) six months of age or over, whelped in the U.S.A. by reason of a mating that took place in the U.S.A.

The Open Class is for any dog six months of age or over, except in a member speciality club show held for only American-Bred dogs, in which case the class is for American-Bred dogs only.

Winners Dogs and **Winners Bitches:** After the above male classes have been judged, the first-place winners are then REQUIRED to compete in the ring. The dog judged "Winners Dog" is awarded the points toward his championship title.

Reserve Winners are selected immediately after the Winners Dog. In case of a disqualification of a win by the AKC, the Reserve Dog moves up to "Winners" and receives the points. After all male classes are judged, the bitch classes are called.

Best of Breed or Best of Variety Competition is limited to Champions of Record or dogs (with newly acquired points, for a 90-day period prior to AKC confirmation) which have completed championship requirements, and Winners Dog and Winners Bitch (or the dog awarded Winners if only one Winners prize has been awarded), together with any undefeated dogs which have been shown only in non-regular classes, all compete for Best of Breed or Best of Variety (if the breed is divided by size, color, texture or length of coat hair, etc.).

Best of Winners: If the WD or WB earns BOB or BOV, it automatically becomes BOW; otherwise they will be judged together for BOW (following BOB or BOV judging).

Best of Opposite Sex is selected from the remaining dogs of the opposite sex to Best of Breed or Best of Variety.

Other Classes may be approved by the AKC: **Stud Dogs, Brood Bitches, Brace Class, Team Class:** classes consisting of local dogs and bitches may also be included in a show if approval by the AKC (special rules are included in the AKC Rule Book).

The **Miscellaneous Class** shall be for purebred dogs of such breeds as may be designated by the AKC. No dog shall be eligible for entry in this class unless the owner has been granted an Indefinite Listing Privilege (ILP) and unless the ILP number is given on the entry form. Application for an ILP shall be made on a form provided by the AKC and when submitted must be accompanied by a fee set by the Board of Directors.

All Miscellaneous Breeds shall be shown together in a single class except that the class may be divided by sex if so specified in the premium list. There shall be **no** further competition for dogs entered in this class. Ribbons for 1st, 2nd, 3rd and 4th shall be Rose, Brown, Light Green and Gray, respectively. This class is open to the following Miscellaneous Breeds: Australian Cattle Dogs, Australian Kelpies, Border Collies, Cavalier King Charles Spaniels, Ibizan Hounds, Miniature Bull Terriers and Spinoni Italiani.

If Your Dog Wins a Class . . .

Study the classes to make certain your dog is entered in a proper class for his or her qualifications. If your dog wins his class, the rule states: *You are required* to enter classes for Winners, Best of Breed and Best of Winners (no additional entry fees). The rule states, "No eligible dog may be withheld from competition." It is not mandatory that you stay for group-judging. *If your dog wins a group, however, you must stay for Best-in-Show competition.*

The Prize Ribbons & What They Stand For

No matter how many entries there are in each class at a dog show, if you place first through fourth position you will receive a ribbon. These ribbons commemorate your win and can be impressive when collected and displayed to prospective buyers when and if you have puppies for sale, or if you intend to use your dog at public stud.

All ribbons from the American Kennel Club licensed dog shows will bear the American Kennel Club seal, the name of the show, the date and the placement. In the classes the colors are blue for first, red for second, yellow for third, and white for fourth. Winners Dog or Winners Bitch ribbons are purple, while Reserve Dog and Reserve Bitch ribbons are purple and white. Best of Winners ribbons are blue and white; Best of Breed, purple and gold; and Best of Opposite Sex ribbons are red and white.

In the six groups, first prize is a blue rosette or ribbon, second placement is red, third yellow, and fourth white. The Best In Show rosette is either red, white and blue, or incorporates the colors used in the show-giving club's emblem.

Qualifying for Championship

Championship points are given for Winners Dog and Winners Bitch in accordance with a scale of points established by the American Kennel Club based on the popularity of the breed in entries, and the number of dogs competing in the classes. This scale of points varies in different sections of the country, but

Below: Ch. Japeke All Black Paul, bred in 1939 by Mrs Marjory Nye White at her Japeke Kennels in Los Angeles, California. His sire was Paul IV and his dam Japeke Rajah's Black Shadow.

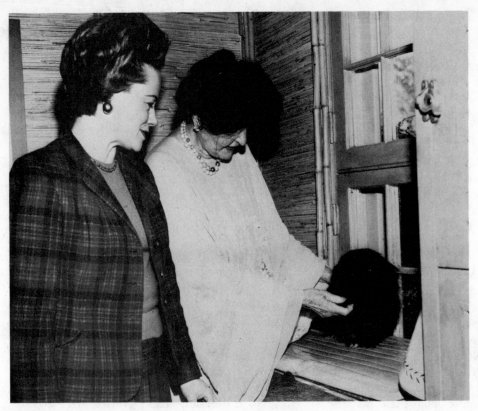

Co-author Joan Brearley admires a black Pekingese bred by Barbara Lowe Fall-ass during an interview she was writing in 1970 for a Toy Group issue of Popular Dogs magazine.

the scale is published in the front of each dog show catalog. These points may differ between the dogs and the bitches at the same show. You may, however, win additional points by winning Best of Winners, if there are fewer dogs than bitches entered, or vice versa. Points never exceed five at any one show, and a total of fifteen points must be won to constitute a championship. These fifteen points must be won under at least three different judges, and you must acquire at least two major wins. Anything from a three to five point win is a major, while one and two point wins are minor wins. Two major wins must be won under two different judges to meet championship requirements.

Obedience Trials

Some shows also offer Obedience Trials which are considered as separate events. They give the dogs a chance to compete and score on performing a prescribed set of exercises intended to display their training in doing useful work.

There are three obedience titles for which they may compete. First, the Companion Dog or CD title; second the Companion Dog Excellent or CDX; and third, the Utility Dog or UD. Detailed information on these degrees is contained in a booklet entitled Official Obedience Regulations and may be obtained by writing to the American Kennel Club.

Junior Showmanship Competition

Junior Showmanship Competition is for boys and girls in different age groups handling their own dog or one owned by their immediate family. There are four divisions: Novice A, for the ten to 12 year olds; Novice B, for those 13 to 16 years of age, with no previous junior showmanship wins; Open C for ten to 12 year olds; and Open D, for 13 to 16 year olds who have earned one or more JS awards.

As Junior Showmanship at the dog shows increased in popularity, certain changes and improvements had to be made. As of April 1, 1971, the American Kennel Club issued a new booklet containing the Regulations for Junior Showmanship which may be obtained by writing to the AKC at 51 Madison Avenue, New York, N.Y. 10010.

Dog Show Photographers

Every show has at least one official photographer who will be more than happy to take a photograph of your dog with the judge, ribbons and trophies, along with you or your handler. These make marvelous remembrances of your top show wins and are frequently framed along with the ribbons for display purposes. Photographers can be paged at the show over the public address system. if you wish to obtain this service. Prices vary, but you will probably find it costs little to capture these happy moments, and the photos can always be used in the various dog magazines to advertise your dog's wins.

Two Types of Dog Shows

There are two types of dog shows licensed by the American Kennel Club. One is the all-breed show which includes classes for all the recognized breeds, and groups of breeds; i.e., all terriers, all toys, etc. Then there are the Specialty shows for one particular breed which also offer championship points.

Benched or Unbenched Dog Shows

The show-giving clubs determine, usually on the basis of what facilities are offered by their chosen show site, whether their show will be benched or unbenched. A benched show is one where the dog show super-intendent supplies benches (cages for toy dogs). Each bench is numbered and its corresponding number appears on your entry identification slip which is sent to you prior to the show date. The number also appears in the show catalog. Upon entering the show you should take your dog to the bench where he should remain until it is time to groom him before entering the ring to be judged. After judging, he must be returned to the bench, until the official time of dismissal from the show. At an unbenched show the club makes no provision whatsoever for your dog other than an enormous tent (if an outdoor show) or an area in a show hall where all crates and grooming equipment must be kept.

Benched or unbenched, the moment you enter the show grounds you are expected to look after your dog and have it under complete control at all times. This means short leads in crowded aisles or getting out of cars. In the case of a benched show, a bench chain is needed. It should allow the dog to move around, but not get down off the bench. It is also not considered "cute" to have small tots leading enormous dogs around a dog show where the child might be dragged into the middle of a dog fight.

Professional Handlers

If you are new in the fancy and do not know how to handle your dog to his best advantage, or if you are too nervous or physically unable to show your dog, you can hire a licensed professional handler who will do it for you for a specified fee. The more successful or well-known handlers charge slightly higher rates, but generally speaking there is a pretty uniform charge for this service. As the dog progresses with his wins in the show ring, the fee increases proportionately. Included in this service is professional advice on when and where to show your dog, grooming, a statement of your wins at each show, and all trophies and ribbons that the dog accumulates. Any cash award is kept by the handler as a sort of "bonus".

When engaging a handler, it is advisable to select one who does not take more dogs to a show than he can properly and comfortably handle. You want your dog to receive his individual attention and not be rushed into

The 1950 Pekingese Club of America Specialty Show winner was Ch. Fei Jaison of Orchard Hill, owned by Mrs Richard Quigley of Pennsylvania. Mrs Warner Hayes was the judge. Evelyn Shafer photograph.

the ring at the last moment, because the handler has been busy with too many other dogs in other rings. Some handlers require that you deliver the dog to their establishment a few days ahead of the show so they have ample time to groom and train him. Others will accept well-behaved and previously trained and groomed dogs at ringside, if they are familiar with the dog and the owner. This should be determined well in advance of the show date. NEVER expect a handler to accept a dog at ringside that is not groomed to perfection!

There are several sources for locating a professional handler. Dog magazines carry their classified advertising; a note or telephone call to the American Kennel Club will put you in touch with several in your area. Usually, you will be billed after the day of the show.

Do You Really Need a Handler?

The answer to the above question is sometimes yes! However the answer most exhibitors give is, "But I can't *afford* a professional handler!" or, "I want to show my dog myself. Does that mean my dog will never do any big winning?"

Do you *really* need a handler to win? If you are mishandling a good dog that should be winning and isn't, because it is made to look simply terrible in the ring by its owner, the answer is yes. If you don't know how to handle a dog properly, why make your dog look bad when a handler could show it to its best advantage?

Some owners simply cannot handle a dog well and still wonder why their dogs aren't winning in the ring, no matter how hard they try. Others are nervous and this nervousness travels down the leash to the dog and the dog behaves accordingly. Some people are extroverts by nature, and these are the people who usually make excellent handlers. Of course, the biggest winning dogs at the shows usually have a lot of "show off" in their nature too, and this helps a great deal.

The Cost of Campaigning a Dog With a Handler

Some Pekingese champions are shown as many as 25 times before completing a championship. In entry fees at today's prices,

that adds up to about $200. This does not include the owner's motel bills, traveling expenses, or food. There have been champions finished in fewer shows, say five to ten shows, but this is the exception rather than the rule. When and where to show should be thought out carefully so that you can perhaps save money on entries. Here is one of the services a professional handler provides that can mean a considerable saving. Hiring a handler can save money in the long run if you just wish to make a champion. If your dog has been winning reserves and not taking the points and a handler can finish him in five to ten shows, you would be ahead financially. If your dog is not really top quality, the length of time it takes even a handler to finish it (depending upon competition in the area) could add up to a large amount of money.

Campaigning a show specimen that not only captures the wins in his breed but wins group and Best in Show awards gets up into the big money. To cover the nation's major shows and rack up a record as one of the top dogs in the nation usually costs an owner between ten and fifteen thousand dollars a year. This includes not only the professional handler's fees for taking the dog into the ring, but the cost of conditioning and grooming, board, advertising in the dog magazines, photographs, etc.

There is great satisfaction in winning with your own dog, especially if you have trained and cared for it yourself. With today's enormous entries at the dog shows and so many worthy dogs competing for top wins, many owners who said, "I'd rather do it myself!" and meant it, became discouraged and eventually hired a handler anyway.

However, if you really are in it just for the sport, you can and should handle your own dog if you want to. You can learn the tricks by attending training classes, and you can learn a lot by carefully observing the more successful professional handlers as they perform in the ring. Model yourself after the ones that command respect as being the leaders in their profession. But, if you find you'd really rather be at ringside looking on, then do get a handler so that your worthy dog gets his deserved recognition in the ring. To own a good dog and win with it is a thrill, so good luck, no matter how you do it.

CHAPTER 20

GENERAL CARE AND MANAGEMENT

Tattooing—Ninety per cent success has been reported on the return of stolen or lost dogs that have been tattooed. More and more this simple, painless, inexpensive method of positive identification for dogs is being reported all over the United States. Long popular in Canada, along with nose prints, the idea gained interest in this country when dognapping started to soar as unscrupulous people began stealing dogs for resale to research laboratories. Pet dogs that wander off and lost hunting dogs have always been a problem. The success of tattooing has been significant.

Tattooing can be done by the veterinarian for a minor fee. There are several dog "registries" that will record your dog's number and help you locate it should it be lost or stolen. The number of the dog's American Kennel Club registration is most often used on thoroughbred dogs, or the owner's Social Security number in the case of mixed breeds. The best place for the tattoo is the groin. Some prefer the inside of an ear, and the American Kennel Club has ruled that the judges officiating at the AKC dog shows not penalize the dog for the tattoo mark.

The tattoo mark serves not only to identify your dog should it be lost or stolen, but offers positive identification in large kennels where several litters of the same approximate age are on the premises. It is a safety measure against unscrupulous breeders "switching" puppies. Any age is a proper age to tattoo, but for safety's sake, the sooner the better.

The buzz of the needle might cause your dog to be apprehensive, but the pricking of the needle is virtually painless. The risk of infection is negligible when done properly, and the return of your beloved pet may be the reward for taking the time to insure positive identification for your dog. Your local Kennel Club will know of a dog registry in your area.

Outdoor Housebreaking

If you are particular about your dog's behaviour in the house, where you expect him to be clean and respectful of the carpets and furniture, you should also want him to have proper manners outdoors. Just because the property belongs to you doesn't necessarily mean he should be allowed to empty himself any place he chooses. Before long the entire yard will be fouled and odorous and the dog will be completely irresponsible on other people's property as well. Dogs seldom recognize property lines.

If your dog does not have his own yard fenced in, he should be walked on leash before being allowed to run free and before being penned up in his own yard. He will appreciate his own run being kept clean. You will find that if he has learned his manners outside, his manners inside will be better. Good manners in "toilet training" are especially important with big dogs!

Other Important Outdoor Manners

Excessive barking is perhaps the most objectionable habit a dog indulges in out of doors. It annoys neighbors and makes for a noisy dog in the house as well. A sharp jerk on the leash will stop a dog from excessive

The first American-bred Champion dog in America, and California's first Pekingese champion, the undefeated Champion Huhl, owned by Miss Lydia Hopkins of the Sherwood Hall Kennels in California.

barking while walking; trees and shrubs around a dog run will cut down on barking if a dog is in his own run. However, it is unfair to block off his view entirely. Give him some view—preferably of his own home—to keep his interest. Needless to say, do not leave a dog that barks excessively out all night.

You will want your dog to bark at strangers, so allow him this privilege. Then after a few "alerting" barks tell the dog to be quiet (with the same word command each time). If he doesn't get the idea, put him on leash and let him greet callers with you at the door until he does get the idea.

Do not let your dog jump on visitors either. Leash training may be necessary to break this habit as well. As the dog jumps in the air,

Ch. Sun-Su of Clarmarlow, owned by the Lowther's of Riverside, Connecticut.

pull back on the lead so that the dog is returned to the floor abruptly. If he attempts to jump on up you, carefully raise your knee and push him away by leaning against his chest.

Do not let your dog roam free in the neighborhood no matter how well he knows his way home. Especially do not let your dog roam free to empty himself on the neighbor's property or gardens!

A positive invitation to danger is to allow your dog to chase cars or bicycles. Throwing tin cans or chains out of car windows at them has been suggested as a cure, but can also be dangerous if they hit the dog instead of the street. Streams of water from a garden hose or water pistol are the least dangerous, but

leash control is still the most scientific and most effective.

If neighbors report that your dog barks or howls or runs from window to window while you are away, crate training or room training for short periods of time may be indicated. If you expect to be away for longer periods of time, put the dog in the basement or a single room where he can do the least damage. The best solution of all is to buy him another dog or cat for companionship. Let them enjoy each other while you are away and have them both welcome you home!

Geriatrics

If you originally purchased good healthy stock and cared for your dog throughout his life, there is no reason why you cannot expect your dog to live to a ripe old age. With research and the remarkable foods produced for dogs, especially this past decade or so, his chances of longevity have increased considerably. If you have cared for him well, your dog will be a sheer delight in his old age, just as he was while in his prime.

We can assume you have fed him properly, if he is not too fat. Have you ever noticed how fat people usually have fat dogs because they indulge their dogs' appetite as they do their own? If there has been no great illness, then you will find that very little additional care and attention are needed to keep him well. Exercise is still essential, as is proper food, booster shots, and tender care.

Even if a heart condition develops, there is still no reason to believe your dog cannot live to an old age. A diet may be necessary, along with medication, and limited exercise, to keep the condition under control. In the case of deafness, or partial blindness, additional care must be taken to protect the dog, but neither infirmity will in any way shorten his life. Prolonged exposure to temperature variances, overeating, excessive exercise, lack of sleep, or being housed with younger, more active dogs may take an unnecessary toll on the dog's energies and introduce serious trouble. Good judgment, periodic veterinary checkups and individual attention will keep your dog with you for many added years.

When discussing geriatrics, the question of when a dog becomes old or aged usually is asked. We have all heard the old saying that one year of a dog's life is equal to seven years in a human. This theory is strictly a matter of opinion, and must remain so, since so many outside factors enter into how quickly each individual dog "ages". Recently, a new chart was devised which is more realistically equivalent:

DOG	MAN
6 months	10 years
1 year	15 years
2 years	24 years
3 years	28 years
4 years	32 years
5 years	36 years
6 years	40 years
7 years	44 years
8 years	48 years
9 years	52 years
10 years	56 years
15 years	76 years
21 years	100 years

It must be remembered that such things as serious illnesses, poor food and housing, general neglect and poor beginnings as puppies will all take their toll on a dog's general health and age him more quickly than a dog that has led a normal, healthy life.

While good care should prolong your dog's life, there are several "old age" disorders to be on the lookout for no matter how well he may be doing. The tendency toward obesity is the most common, but constipation is another. Aging teeth and a slowing down of the digestive processes may hinder digestion and cause constipation, just as any major change in diet can bring on diarrhea. There is also the possibility of loss or impairment of hearing or eyesight which will also tend to make the dog wary and distrustful. Other behavioral changes may result as well, such as crankiness, loss of patience and lack of interest; these are the most obvious changes. Other ailments may manifest themselves in the form of rheumatism, arthritis, tumors and warts, heart disease, kidney infections, male prostatism and female disorders. Of course, all of these require a veterinarian's checking the degree of seriousness and proper treatment.

Take care to avoid infectious diseases. When these hit the older dog, they can debilitate him to an alarming degree, leaving him open to more serious complications and a shorter life.

Dog Insurance

Much has been said for and against canine insurance, and much more will be said before this kind of protection for a dog becomes universal and/or practical. There has been talk of establishing a Blue Cross-type plan similar to that now existing for humans. However, the best insurance for your dog is You! Nothing compensates for tender, loving care. Like the insurance policies for humans, there will be a lot of fine print in the contracts revealing that the dog is not covered after all. These limited conditions usually make the acquisition of dog insurance expensive and virtually worthless.

Blanket coverage policies for kennels or establishments which board or groom dogs can be an advantage, especially in transporting dogs to and from their premises. For the one dog owner, however, whose dog is a constant companion, the cost for limited coverage is not necessary.

Ho Dynasty's Bit O'Brescia, pictured winning at the Pekingese Club of Southern New Jersey Specialty Show. She is pictured with Mrs Gilma Blauvelt-Moss of Hohokus, New Jersey who co-owns with the Gobles of Maryland.

The High Cost of Burial

Pet cemeteries are mushrooming across the nation. Here, as with humans, the sky can be the limit for those who wish to bury their pets ceremoniously. The costs of satin-lined caskets, grave stones, flowers, etc. run the gamut of prices to match the emotions and means of the owner. This is strictly a matter of what the bereaved owner wishes to do.

In the Event of Your Death . . .

This is a morbid thought perhaps, but ask yourself the question, "If death were to strike at this moment, what would become of my loved dogs?"

Perhaps you are fortunate enough to have a relative, friend or spouse who could take over immediately, if only on a temporary basis. Perhaps you have already left instructions in your last will and testament for your pet's dispensation, as well as a stipend for their perpetual care.

Provide definite instructions before a disaster occurs and your dogs are carted off to the pound, or stolen by commercially minded neighbors with "resale" in mind. It is a simple thing to instruct your lawyer about your wishes in the event of sickness or death. Leave instructions as to feeding, etc., posted on your kennel room or kitchen bulletin board, or wherever your kennel records are kept. Also, tell several people what you are doing and why. If you prefer to keep such instructions private, merely place

Above: Teijon Hei-Jetta. Lovely black and tan Sleeve Pekingese owned by Mrs T. Brickwood of England.

The Sherwood Kennels stud force photographed in 1917. Left to right: Ch. Sherwood Su Wang, Sherwood Choggy of Winkfield, Sherwood Yuan Shi Kai of Braywick, Sherwood Peter of Braywick and Sherwood Shun Shi. All owned by Miss Lydia Hopkins of California.

them in sealed envelopes in a known place with directions that they are to be opened only in the event of your demise. Eliminate the danger of your animals suffering in the event of an emergency that prevents your personal care of them.

Keeping Records

Whether you have one dog, or a kennel full of them, it is wise to keep written records. It takes only a few moments to record dates of inoculations, trips to the vet, tests for worms, etc. It can avoid confusion or mistakes, or having your dog not covered with immunization if too much time elapses between shots.

Make the effort to keep all dates in writing rather than trying to commit them to memory. A rabies injection date can be a problem if you have to recall that "Fido had the shot the day Aunt Mary got back from her trip abroad, and, let's see, I guess that was around the end of June".

In an emergency, these records may prove their value if your veterinarian cannot be reached and you have to use another, or if you move and have no case history on your dog for the new veterinarian. In emergencies, you do not always think clearly or accurately, and if dates, and types of serums used, etc., are a matter of record, the veterinarian can act more quickly and with more confidence.

CHAPTER 21

YOUR DOG, YOUR VETERINARIAN, AND YOU

The purpose of this chapter is to explain why you should never attempt to be your own veterinarian. Quite the contrary, we urge emphatically that you establish good liaison with a reputable veterinarian who will help you maintain happy, healthy dogs. Our purpose is to bring you up to date on the discoveries made in modern canine medicine and to help you work with your veterinarian by applying these new developments to your own animals.

We have provided here "thumbnail" histories of many of the most common types of diseases your dog is apt to come in contact with during his lifetime. We feel that if you know a little something about the diseases and how to recognize their symptoms, your chances of catching them in the preliminary stages will help you and your veterinarian effect a cure before a serious condition develops.

Today's dog owner is a realistic, intelligent person who learns more and more about his dog—inside and out—so that he can care for and enjoy the animal to the fullest. He uses technical terms for parts of the anatomy, has a fleeting knowledge of the miracles of surgery and is fully prepared to administer clinical care for his animals at home. This chapter is designed for study and/or reference and we hope you will use it to full advantage.

We repeat, we do *not* advocate your "playing doctor." This includes administering medication without veterinary supervision, or even doing your own inoculations. General knowledge of diseases, their symptoms and side effects will assist you in diagnosing diseases for your veterinarian. He does not expect you to be an expert, but will appreciate your efforts in getting a sick dog to him before it is too late and he cannot save its life.

Aspirin: No Panacea

There is a common joke about doctors telling their patients, when they telephone with a complaint, to take an aspirin, go to bed and let him know how things are in the morning! Unfortunately, that is exactly the way it turns out with a lot of dog owners who think aspirins are cure-alls and give them to their dogs indiscriminately. Then they call the veterinarian when the dog has an unfavourable reaction.

Aspirin are not panaceas for everything—certainly not for every dog. In an experiment, fatalities in cats treated with aspirin in one laboratory alone numbered ten out of 13 within a two-week period. Dogs' tolerance was somewhat better, as far as actual fatalities, but there was considerable evidence of ulceration in varying degrees on the stomach linings when necropsy was performed.

The famous Pekingese, Ch. Ku-Rai of Remenham, owned by the Remenham Kennels, England.

Aspirin has been held in the past to be almost as effective for dogs as for people when given for many of the everyday aches and pains. The fact remains, however, that medication of any kind should be administered only after veterinary consultation and a specific dosage suitable to the condition is recommended.

While aspirin is chiefly effective in reducing fever, relieving minor pains and cutting down in inflammation, the acid has been proved harmful to the stomach when given in strong doses. Only your veterinarian is qualified to determine what that dosage is, or whether it should be administered to your particular dog at all.

What the Thermometer Can Tell You

You will notice in reading this chapter dealing with the diseases of dogs, that practically everything a dog might contract in the way of sickness has basically the same set of symptoms. Loss of appetite, diarrhea, dull eyes, dull coat, warm and/or runny nose, and FEVER!

Therefore, it is most advisable to have a thermometer on hand for checking temperature. There are several inexpensive metal rectal-type thermometers that are accurate and safer than the glass variety which can be broken. This may happen either by dropping, or perhaps even breaking off in the dog because of improper insertion or an aggravated condition with the dog that makes him violently resist the injection of the thermometer. Either kind should be lubricated with vaseline to make the insertion as easy as possible, after it has been sterilized with alcohol.

The normal temperature for a dog is 101.5° Fahrenheit, as compared to the human 98.6°. Excitement, as well as illness can cause this to vary a degree or two, but any sudden or extensive rise in body temperature must be considered as cause for alarm. Your first indication will be that your dog feels unduly "warm" and this is the time to take the temperature, not when the dog becomes very ill or manifests additional serious symptoms. With a thermometer on hand, you can check temperatures quickly and perhaps prevent some illness from becoming serious.

Coprophagy

Perhaps the most unpleasant of all phases of dog breeding is to come up with a dog that takes to eating stool. This practice, which is referred to politely as coprophagy, is one of the unsolved mysteries in the dog world. There simply is no explanation to why some dogs do it.

However, there are several theories, any of which may be correct. Some say nutritional deficiencies are the cause; another says that dogs inclined to gulp their food (which passes through them not entirely digested) find it still partially palatable. There is another theory that the preservatives used in some meat are responsible for an appealing odor that remains through the digestive process. Then again poor quality meat can be so tough and unchewable, the dog swallows it whole and it passes through him in large undigested chunks.

There are others who believe the habit is strictly psychological, the result of a nervous condition or insecurity. Others believe the dog cleans up after itself, because it is afraid

of being punished as it was when it made a mistake on the carpet as a puppy. Others claim boredom is the reason, or even spite. Others will tell you a dog does not want its personal odor on the premises for fear of attracting other hostile animals to itself or its home.

The most logical of all explanations and the one most veterinarians are inclined to accept is that it is a deficiency of dietary enzimes. Too much dry food can be bad and many veterinarians suggest trying meat tenderizers, monosodium glutamate, or garlic powder which gives the stool a bad odor and discourages the dog. Yeast or certain vitamins, or a complete change of diet are even more often suggested. By the time you try each of the above you will probably discover that the dog has outgrown the habit anyway. However, the condition cannot be ignored if you are to enjoy your dog to the fullest.

There is no set length of time that the problem persists, and the only real cure is to walk the dog on leash, morning and night and after every meal. In other words, set up a definite eating and exercising schedule before coprophagy can become an established pattern.

Masturbation

A source of embarrassment to many dog owners, masturbation can be eliminated with a minimum of training.

The dog which is constantly breeding anything and everything, including the leg of the piano or perhaps the leg of your favorite guest, can be broken of the habit by stopping its cause.

The over-sexed dog—if truly that is what he is—which will never be used for breeding can be castrated. The kennel stud dog can be broken of the habit by removing any furniture from his quarters or keeping him on leash and on verbal command when he is around people, or in the house where he might be tempted to breed pillows, people, etc.

Hormone imbalance may be another cause and your veterinarian may advise injections. Exercise can be of tremendous help. Keeping the dog's mind occupied by physical play when he is around people will also help relieve the situation.

Females might indulge in sexual abnormalities like masturbation during their heat cycle, or again, because of a hormone imbalance. But if they behave this way because of a more serious problem, a hysterectomy may be indicated.

A sharp "no!" command when you can anticipate the act, or a sharp "no!" when caught in the act will deter most dogs if you are consistent in your correction. Hitting or other physical abuse will only confuse a dog.

Rabies

The greatest fear in the dog fancy today is still the great fear it has always been—rabies!

What has always held true about this dreadful disease still holds true today. The only way rabies can be contracted is through the saliva of a rabid dog entering the bloodstream of another animal or person. There is, of course, the Pasteur treatment for rabies which is very effective. There was of late the incident of a little boy bitten by a rabid bat having survived the disease. However, the Pasteur treatment is administered immediately, if there is any question of exposure. Even more than dogs being found to be rabid, we now know that the biggest carriers are bats, skunks, foxes, rabbits and other warm-blooded animals, which pass it from one to another, since they do not have the benefit of inoculation. Dogs that run free should be inoculated for protection against these animals. For city or house dogs that never leave their owner's side, it may not be as necessary.

For many years, Great Britain, because it is an island and because of the country's strictly enforced six-month quarantine, was entirely free of rabies. But in 1969, a British officer brought back his dog from foreign duty and the dog was found to have the disease soon after being released from quarantine. There was a great uproar about it, with Britain killing off wild and domestic animals in a great scare campaign, but the quarantine is once again down to six months and things seem to have returned to a normal, sensible attitude.

Health departments in rural towns usually provide rabies inoculations free of charge. If your dog is outdoors a great deal, or exposed to other animals that are, you might wish to call the town hall and get information on the program in your area. One cannot be too cautious about this dread disease. While the number of cases diminishes each year, there are still thousands being reported and there is still the constant threat of an outbreak where animals roam free. And never forget, there is no cure.

Rabies is caused by a neurotropic virus which can be found in the saliva, brain and sometimes the blood of the warm-blooded animal afflicted. The incubation period is usually two weeks or as long as six months, which means you can be exposed to it without any visible symptoms. As we have said, while there is still no known cure, it can be

controlled. It is up to every individual to help effect this control by reporting animal bites, educating the public to the dangers and symptoms and prevention of it, so that we may reduce the fatalities.

There are two kinds of rabies: one form is called "furious," and the other is referred to as "dumb." The mad dog goes through several stages of the disease. His disposition and behavior change radically and suddenly; he becomes irritable and vicious; the eating habits alter, and he rejects food for things like

Sutherland Avenue Tzu-Eh, sire of the prominent Tri-International Champion Pierrot, and whelped in February, 1926. Bred by Mrs. Hazelton of England and later the property of the late Mrs. Richard S. Quigley of Lock Haven, Pennsylvania.

stones and sticks; he becomes exhausted and drools saliva out of his mouth almost constantly. He may hide in corners, look glassy eyed and suspicious, bite at the air as he races around snarling and attacking with his tongue hanging out. At this point paralysis sets in, starting at the throat so that he can no longer drink water though he desires it desperately; hence, the term hydrophobia is given. He begins to stagger and eventually convulse and death is imminent.

In "dumb" rabies paralysis is swift, the dog seeks dark, sheltered places and is abnormally quiet. Paralysis starts with the jaws, spreads down the body and death is quick. Contact by humans or other animals with the drool from either of these types of rabies on open skin can produce the fatal disease, so extreme haste and proper diagnosis is essential. In other words, you do not have to be bitten by a rabid dog to have the virus enter your system. An open wound or cut that comes in touch with the saliva is all that is needed.

The incubation and degree of infection can vary. You usually contract the disease faster if the wound is near the head, since the virus travels to the brain through the spinal cord.

The deeper the wound, the more saliva is injected into the body, the more serious the infection. So, if bitten by a dog under any circumstances—or any warm-blooded animal for that matter—immediately wash out the wound with soap and water, bleed it profusely, and see your doctor as soon as possible.

Also, be sure to keep track of the animal that bit, if at all possible. When rabies is suspected the public health officer will need to send the animal's head away to be analyzed. If it is found to be rabies free, you will not need to undergo treatment. Otherwise, your doctor may advise that you have the Pasteur treatment, which is extremely painful. It is rather simple, however, to have the veterinarian examine a dog for rabies without having the dog sent away for positive diagnosis of the disease. A ten-day quarantine is usually all that is necessary for everyone's peace of mind.

Rabies is no respecter of age, sex or geographical location. It is found all over the world from North pole to South pole, and has nothing to do with the old wives' tales of dogs going mad in the hot summer months. True, there is an increase in cases reported during summer, but only because that is the time of the year for animals to roam free in good weather and during the mating season when the battle of the sexes is taking place. Inoculation and a keen eye for symptoms and bites on our dogs and other pets will help control the disease until the cure is found.

Vaccinations

If you are to raise a puppy, or a litter of puppies, successfully, you must adhere to a realistic and strict schedule of vaccination. Many puppyhood diseases can be fatal—all of them are debilitating. According to the latest statistics, 98 per cent of all puppies are being inoculated after 12 weeks of age against the dread distemper, hepatitis, and leptospirosis and manage to escape these horrible infections. Orphaned puppies should be vaccinated every two weeks until the age of 12 weeks. Distemper and hepatitis live-virus vaccine should be used, since they are not protected with the colostrum normally supplied to them through the mother's milk. Puppies weaned at six to seven weeks should also be inoculated repeatedly because they will no longer be receiving mother's milk. While not all will receive protection from the serum at this early age, it should be given and they should be vaccinated once again at both nine and 12 weeks of age.

Leptospirosis vaccination should be given at four months of age with thought given to booster shots if the disease is known in the area, or in the case of show dogs which are exposed on a regular basis to many dogs from far and wide. While annual boosters are in order for distemper and hepatitis, every two or three years is sufficient for leptospirosis, unless there is an outbreak in your immediate area. The one exception should be the pregnant bitch since there is reason to believe that inoculation might cause damage to the fetus.

Strict observance of such a vaccination schedule will not only keep your dog free of these debilitating diseases, but will prevent an epidemic in your kennel, or in your locality, or to the dogs which are competing at the shows.

Snakebite

As field trials and hunts and the like become more and more popular with dog enthusiasts, the incidence of snakebite becomes more of a possibility. Dogs that are kept outdoors in runs or dogs that work the fields and roam on large estates are also likely victims.

Most veterinarians carry snakebite serum, and snakebite kits are sold to dog owners for just such purpose. To catch a snakebite in time might mean the difference between life and death, and whether your area is populated with snakes or not, it behooves you to know what to do in case it happens to you or your dog.

Your primary concern should be to get to a doctor or veterinarian immediately. The victim should be kept as quiet as possible (excitement or activity spreads the venom through the body more quickly) and if possible the wound should be bled enough to clean it out before applying a tourniquet, if the bite is severe.

First of all, it must be determined if the bite is from a poisonous or non-poisonous snake. If the bite carries two horseshoe shaped pinpoints of a double row of teeth, the bite can be assumed to be non-poisonous. If the bite leaves two punctures or holes—the result of the two fangs carrying venom—the bite is very definitely poisonous and time is of the essence.

Recently, physicians have come up with an added help in the case of snakebite. A first aid treatment referred to as Hypothermia, which is the application of ice to the wounds to lower body temperature to a point where the venom spreads less quickly, minimizes swelling, helps prevent infection and has some influence on numbing the pain. If fresh water ice is not readily available, the bite may be soaked in ice cold water. But even more urgent is the need to get the victim to a hospital or a veterinarian for additional treatment.

Emergencies

No matter how well you run your kennel or keep an eye on an individual dog, there will almost invariably be some emergency at some time that will require quick treatment until you get the animal to the veterinarian. The first and most important thing to remember is to keep calm! You will think more clearly and your animal will need to know he can depend on you to take care of him. However, he will be frightened and you must beware of fear biting. Therefore, do not shower him with kisses and endearments at this time, no matter how sympathetic you feel. Comfort him reassuringly, but keep your wits about you. Before getting him to the veterinarian try to alleviate the pain and shock.

If you can take even a minor step in this direction it will be a help toward the final cure. Listed here are a few of the emergencies which might occur and what you can do AFTER you have called the vet and told him you are coming.

Burns—If you have been so foolish as not to turn your pot handles toward the back of the stove—for your children's sake as well as your dogs—and the dog is burned, apply vaseline or butter and treat for shock. The covering will help prevent secondary infection if the burns are severe. Electrical or chemical burns are treated the same; but with an acid or alkali burn, use, respectively, a bicarbonate of soda or vinegar solution. Then apply vaseline. Check this with the veterinarian when you call him.

Drowning—Most animals love the water, but sometimes get in "over their heads." Should your dog take in too much water, hold him upside down and open his mouth so that water can empty from the lungs, then apply artificial respiration, or mouth-to-mouth resuscitation. Then treat for shock by covering him with a blanket, administering a stimulant such as coffee with sugar, and soothing him with voice and hand.

Fits and Convulsions—Prevent the dog from thrashing about and injuring himself, cover with a blanket and hold down until you can get him to the veterinarian.

Frostbite—There is no excuse for an animal getting frostbite if you are alert and care for the animal. However, should frostbite set in, thaw out the affected area slowly with a circulatory motion and stimulation. Use vaseline to help keep the skin from peeling off and/or drying out.

Heart Attack—Be sure the animal keeps breathing by applying artificial respiration. A mild stimulant may be used and give him plenty of air. Treat for shock as well, and get to the veterinarian quickly.

Suffocation—Artificial respiration and treat for shock with plenty of air.

Sun Stroke—Cooling the dog off immediately is essential. Ice packs, submersion in ice water, and plenty of cool air are needed.

Wounds—Open wounds or cuts which produce bleeding must be treated with hydrogen peroxide and tourniquets should be used if bleeding is excessive. Also, shock treatment must be given and the dog kept warm.

The First Aid Kit

It would be sheer folly to try to operate a kennel or to keep a dog without providing for certain emergencies that are bound to crop up when there are active dogs around. Just as you would provide a first aid kit for people, you should provide a first aid kit for the animals on the premises.

The first aid kit should contain the following items:

BFI or other medicated powder
jar of vaseline
Q-tips
bandage—1 inch gauze
adhesive tape
Bandaids
cotton
boric acid powder

A trip to your veterinarian is always safest, but there are certain preliminaries for cuts and bruises of a minor nature that you can care for yourself.

Cuts, for instance, should be washed out and medicated powder or vaseline applied with a bandage. The lighter the bandage the better so that the most air possible can reach the wound. Q-tips can be used for removing debris from the eyes, after which a mild solution of boric acid wash can be applied. Burns can be assuaged by an application of vaseline. As for sores, use dry powder on wet sores, and vaseline on dry sores. Use cotton for washing out wounds and drying them.

A particular caution must be given here on bandaging. Make sure that the bandage is not too tight to hamper the dog's circulation. Also, make sure the bandage is made correctly so that the dog does not bite at it trying to get it off. A great deal of damage can be done to a wound by a dog tearing at a bandage to get it off. If you notice the dog is starting to bite at it, do it over or put something on the bandage that smells and tastes bad to him. Make sure, however, that the solution does not soak through the bandage and enter the wound. Sometimes, if it is a leg wound, a sock or stocking slipped on the dog's leg will cover the bandage edges and will also keep it clean.

How Not to Poison Your Dog

Ever since the appearance of Rachel Carson's book, SILENT SPRING, people have been asking, "Just how dangerous are chemicals?" In the animal world where disinfectants, room deodorants, parasitic sprays, solutions and aerosols are so widely used, the question has taken on even more meaning. Veterinarians are beginning to ask, "What kind of disinfectant do you use?" or "Have you any fruit trees that have been sprayed recently?" when animals are brought in to their offices in a toxic condition. For unexplained death, or when entire litters of puppies die mysteriously, there is good reason to ask such questions.

Ch. Monte Verde Ricky Tick, owned by Mrs Fortune Roberts of Bronxville, New York.

The popular practice of protecting animals against parasites has given way to their being exposed to an alarming number of commercial products, some of which are dangerous to their very lives. Even flea collars can be dangerous, especially if they get wet or somehow touch the genital regions or eyes. While some products are a great deal more poisonous than others, great care must be taken that they be applied in proportion to the size of the dog and the area to be covered. Many a dog has been taken to the vet with an unusual skin problem that was a direct result of having been bathed with a detergent rather than a proper shampoo. Certain products that are safe for dogs can be fatal for cats. Extreme care must be taken to read all ingredients and instructions carefully before use on any animal.

Sam Tou of Meridale, an important stud force and show winner from the Meridale Kennels of Mrs F.C. McAllister, Great Neck, New York.

The same caution must be given to outdoor chemicals. Dog owners must question the use of fertilizers on their lawns. Lime, for instance, can be harmful to a dog's feet. The unleashed dog that covers the neighborhood on his daily rounds is open to all sorts of tree and lawn sprays and insecticides that may prove harmful to him, if not as a poison, as a producer of an allergy. Many puppy fatalities are reported when they consume mothballs.

There are various products found around the house which can be lethal, such as rat poison, boric acid, hand soap, detergents, and insecticides. The garage too may provide dangers: Antifreeze for the car, lawn, garden and tree sprays, paints, etc., are all available for tipping over and consuming. All poisons should be placed on high shelves for the sake of your children as well as your animals.

Perhaps the most readily available of all household poisons are plants. Household plants are almost all poisonous, even if taken in small quantities. Some of the most dangerous are the Elephant Ear, the Narcissus bulb, any kind of ivy leaves, Burning Bush leaves, the Jimson weed, the Dumb Cane weed, Mock Orange fruit, Castor Beans, Scotch Broom seeds, the root or seed of the plant called Four O'clock, Cyclamen, Pimpernel, Lily of the Valley, the stem of the Sweet Pea, Rhododendrons of any kind, Spider Lily bulbs, Bayonet root, Foxglove leaves, Tulip bulbs, Monkshood roots, Azalea, Wisteria, Poinsettia leaves, Mistletoe, Hemlock, Locoweed and Arrowglove. In all, there are over 500 poisonous plants in the United States. Peach, elderberry and cherry trees can cause cyanide poisoning if the bark is consumed. Rhubarb leaves either raw or cooked can cause death or violent convulsions. Check out your closets, fields, and grounds around your home to see what might be of danger to your pets.

Symptoms of Poisoning

Be on the lookout for vomiting, hard or labored breathing, whimpering, stomach cramps, and trembling as a prelude to the convulsions. Any delay in a visit to your veterinarian can mean death. Take along the bottle or package or a sample of the plant you suspect to be the cause to help the veterinarian determine the correct antidote.

The most common type of poisoning which accounts for nearly one-fourth of all animal victims is staphylococcic-infected food. Salmonella ranks third. These can be avoided by serving fresh food and not letting it lie around in hot weather.

There are also many insect poisonings caused by animals eating cockroaches, spiders, flies, butterflies, etc. Toads and some frogs give off a fluid which can make a dog foam at the mouth—and even kill him—if he bites just a little too hard!

Some misguided dog owners think it is "cute" to let their dogs enjoy a cocktail with them before dinner. There can be serious effects resulting from encouraging a dog to drink—sneezing fits, injuries as a result of intoxication, and heart-stoppage are just a few. Whisky for medicinal purposes, or beer for brood bitches should be administered only on the advice of your veterinarian.

There have been cases of severe damage and death when dogs emptied ash trays and consumed cigarettes, resulting in nicotine poisoning. Leaving a dog alone all day in a house where there are cigarettes available on a coffee table is asking for trouble. Needless to say, the same applies to marijuana. The narcotic addict who takes his dog along with him on a "trip" does not deserve to have a dog. All the ghastly side effects are as possible for the dog as for the addict, and for a person to submit an animal to this indignity is indeed despicable. Don't think it doesn't happen. Ask the veterinarians that practice near some of your major hippie havens! Unfortunately, in all our major cities the practice is becoming more and more a problem for the veterinarian.

Be on the alert and remember that in the case of any type of poisoning, the best treatment is prevention.

The Curse of Allergy

The heartbreak of a child being forced to give up a beloved pet because he is suddenly found to be allergic to it is a sad but true story. Many families claim to be unable to have dogs at all; others seem to be able only to enjoy them on a restricted basis. Many children know animals only through occasional visits to a friend's house or the zoo.

Ch. Whitworth Beau Michael, owned by Mrs Murray Brooks, and a winner several decades ago.

While modern veterinary science has produced some brilliant allergists, such as Dr. Edward Baker of New Jersey, the field is still working on a solution for those who suffer from exposure to their pets. There is no permanent cure as yet.

Over the last quarter of a century there have been many attempts at a permanent cure, but none has proven successful, because the treatment was needed too frequently, or was too expensive to maintain over extended periods of time.

However, we find that most people who are allergic to their animals are also allergic to a variety of other things as well. By eliminating the other irritants, and by taking medication given for the control of allergies in general, many are able to keep pets on a restricted

basis. This may necessitate the dog's living outside the house, being groomed at a professional grooming parlor instead of by the owner, or merely being kept out of the bedroom at night. A discussion of this "balance" factor with your medical and veterinary doctors may give new hope to those willing to try.

A paper presented by Mathilde M. Gould, M.D., a New York allergist, before the American Academy of Allergists in the 1960's, and reported in the September-October 1964 issue of the National Humane Review magazine, offered new hope to those who are allergic by a method referred to as hyposensitization. You may wish to write to the magazine and request the article for discussion with your medical and veterinary doctors on your individual problem.

Do All Dogs Chew?

All young dogs chew! Chewing is the best possible method of cutting teeth and exercising gums. Every puppy goes through this teething process. True, it can be destructive if not watched carefully, and it is really the responsibility of every owner to prevent the damage before it occurs.

When you see a puppy pick up an object to chew, immediately remove it from his mouth with a sharp "No!" and replace the object with a toy or a rawhide bone which should be provided for him to do his serious chewing. Puppies take anything and everything into their mouths, so they should be provided with proper toys which they cannot chew up and swallow.

Bones

There are many opinions on the kind of bones a dog should have. Anyone who has lost a puppy or dog because of a bone chip puncturing the stomach or intestinal wall will say "no bones" except for the Nylon or rawhide kind you buy in pet shops. There are those who say shank or knuckle bones are permissible. Use your own judgment, but when there are adequate processed bones which you know to be safe, why risk a valuable animal? Cooked bones, soft enough to be pulverized and put in the food can be fed if they are reduced almost to a powder. If you have the patience for this sort of thing, okay. Otherwise, stick to the commercial products.

As for dogs and puppies chewing furniture, shoes, etc., replace the object with something allowable and safe and put yourself on record as remembering to close closet doors. Keep the puppy in the same room with you so you can stand guard over the furniture.

Electrical cords and sockets, or wires of any kind, present a dangerous threat to chewers. Glass dishes which can be broken are hazardous if not picked up right after feeding.

Chewing can also be a form of frustration or nervousness. Dogs sometimes chew for spite, if owners leave them alone too long or too often. Bitches will sometimes chew if their puppies are taken away from them too soon; insecure puppies often chew, thinking they're nursing. Puppies which chew wool or blankets or carpet corners or certain types of materials may have a nutritional deficiency or something lacking in their diet, such as craving the starch that might be left in material after washing. Perhaps the articles have been near something that tastes good and they retain the odor.

The act of chewing has no connection with particular breeds or ages, any more than there is a logical reason for dogs to dig holes outdoors or dig on wooden floors indoors.

So we repeat, it is up to you to be on guard at all times until the need—or habit—passes.

Hip Dysplasia

Hip Dysplasia, or HD, is one of the most widely discussed of all animal afflictions, since it has appeared in varying degrees, in just about every breed of dog. True, the larger breeds seem most susceptible, but it has hit the small breeds and is beginning to be recognized in cats as well.

While HD in man has been recorded as far back as 370 B.C. HD in dogs was more than likely referred to as rheumatism until veterinary research came into the picture. In 1935, Dr. Otto Schales, at Angell Memorial Hospital in Boston, wrote a paper on Hip Dysplasia and classified the four degrees of dysplasia of the hip joint as follows:

Grade 1—slight (poor fit between ball and socket)

Grade 2—moderate (moderate but obvious shallowness of the socket)

Grade 3—severe (socket quite flat)

Grade 4—very severe (complete displacement of head of femur at early age)

HD is an incurable, hereditary, though not congenital disease of the hip sockets. It is transmitted as a dominant trait with irregular manifestations. Puppies appear normal at birth but the constant wearing away of the socket means the animal moves more and more on muscle, thereby presenting a lameness, a difficulty in getting up and severe pain in advanced cases.

The degree of severity can be determined around six months of age, but its presence can be noticed from two months of age. The problem is determined by X-ray, and if pain is present it can be relieved temporarily by medication. Exercise should be avoided since motion encourages the wearing away of the bone surfaces.

Dogs with HD should not be shown or bred, if quality in the breed is to be maintained. It is essential to check a pedigree for dogs known to be dysplastic before breeding, since this disease can be dormant for many generations.

Elbow Dysplasia

The same condition can also affect the elbow joints and is known as Elbow Dysplasia. This also causes lameness, and dogs so affected should not be used for breeding.

Patella Dysplasia

Some of the smaller breeds of dogs also suffer from Patella Dysplasia, or dislocation of the knee. This can be treated surgically, but the surgery by no means abolishes the hereditary factor. Therefore, these dogs should not be used for breeding.

All dogs—in any breed—should be X-rayed before being used for breeding. The X-ray should be read by a competent veterinarian, and the dog declared free and clear.

HD Program in Great Britain

The British Veterinary Association (BVA) has made an attempt to control the spread of HD by appointing a panel of members of their profession who have made a special study of the disease, to read X-rays. Dogs over one year of age may be X-rayed and certified as free. Forms are completed in triplicate to verify the tests. One copy remains with the panel, one copy is for the owner's veterinarian, and one for the owner. A record is also sent to the British Kennel Club for those wishing to check on a particular dog for breeding purposes.

The United States Registry

In the United States we have a central Hip Dysplasia Foundation, known as the OFA (Orthopedic Foundation for Animals). This HD control registry was formed in 1966. X-rays are sent for expert evaluation by qualified radiologists.

All you need do for complete information on getting an X-ray for your dog is to write to the Orthopedic Foundation for Animals at 817 Virginia Ave., Columbia, Mo., 65201 and request their Dysplasia packet. There is no charge for this kit. It contains an envelope

Top: The thirties, and the era of Wee Wo San of Toddington—photographed in London by J. Henschel.

The English Pekingese Piersyl of Perryacre, owned by the late Hindley Taylor, owner of the Kyratown Kennels in England.

large enough to hold your X-ray film (which you will have taken by your own veterinarian), and a drawing showing how to position the dog properly for X-ray. There is also an application card for proper identification of the dog. Then, we hope, your dog will be certified "normal." You will be given a registry number which you can put on his pedigree, use in your advertising, and rest assured your breeding program is in good order.

All X-rays should be sent to the address above. Any other information you might wish to have may be requested from Mrs. Robert Bower, OFA, Route 1, Constantine, Mo., 49042.

We cannot urge strongly enough the importance of doing this. While it involves time and effort, the reward in the long run will more than pay for your trouble. To see the heartbreak of parents and children when their beloved dog has to be put to sleep because of severe Hip Dysplasia as the result of bad breeding is a sad experience. Don't let this happen to you or to those who will purchase your puppies!

Additionally, we should mention that there is a method of palpation to determine the extent of affliction. This can be painful if the animal is not properly prepared for the examination. There have also been attempts to replace the animal's femur and socket. This is not only expensive, but the percentage of success is small.

For those who refuse to put their dog down, there is a new surgical technique which can relieve pain, but in no way constitutes a cure. This technique involves the severing of the pectinius muscle, which for some unknown reason brings relief from pain over a period of many months—even up to two years. Two veterinary colleges in the United States are performing this operation at the present time. However, the owner must also give permission to "de-sex" the dogs at the time of the muscle severance. This is a safety measure to help stamp out Hip Dysplasia, since obviously the condition itself remains and can be passed on.

CHAPTER 22

THE BLIGHT OF PARASITES

Anyone who has ever spent hours peering intently at their dog's warm, pink stomach waiting for a flea to appear will readily understand why we call this chapter the "blight of parasites." For it is the onslaught of the pesky flea that carries and aids worms and heralds their subsequent arrival.

If you have seen even one flea scoot across that vulnerable expanse of skin you can be sure there are more lurking on other areas of your dog. They seldom travel alone. So it is now an established fact that *la puce*, as the French refer to the flea, has set up housekeeping on your dog; it is going to demand a great deal of your time before you manage to evict them—probably just temporarily—no matter which species your dog is harboring.

Fleas are not always choosy about their host, but chances are your dog has what is commonly known as *Ctenocephalides canis*, the dog flea. If you are a lover of cats also, your dog might even be playing host to a few *Ctenocephalides felis*, the cat flea, or vice versa! The only thing you can be really sure of is that your dog is supporting an entire community of them, all hungry and sexually oriented, and you are going to have to be persistent in your campaign to get rid of them.

One of the chief reasons they are so difficult to catch is that what they lack in beauty and eyesight (they are blind at birth, throughout infancy, and see very poorly if at all during adulthood) they make up for in their fantastic ability to jump and scurry about.

While this remarkable ability to jump—some say 150 times the length of their bodies—stands them in good stead with circus entrepreneurs and has given them claim to fame as chariot pullers and acrobats in side show attractions, the dog owner can be reduced to tears at the very thought of the onset of fleas.

Modern research has provided a panacea in the form of flea sprays, dips, collars and tags which can be successful in varying degrees. But there are those who swear by the good old-fashioned methods of removing them by hand, which can be a challenge to your sanity as well as your dexterity.

Since the fleas' conformation (they are built like envelopes, long and flat) with their spiny skeletal system on the outside of their bodies, is specifically provided for slithering through forests of hair, they are given a distinct advantage to start with. Two antennae on the head select the best spot for digging and then two mandibles penetrate the skin and hit a blood vessel. It is also at this moment that the flea brings into play his spiny contours to prop himself against surrounding hairs and avoid being scratched off as he puts the bite on your dog. A small projecting tube is then lowered into the hole to draw out blood and another pumps saliva into the wound; this prevents the blood from clotting and allows the flea to drink freely. Simultaneously your dog jumps into the air and gets one of those back legs into action—scratching endlessly and in vain.

Now while you may catch an itinerant flea as he mistakenly shortcuts across your dog's stomach, the best hunting grounds are usually in the deep fur all along the dog's back from neck to tail. However the flea, like every other creature on earth, must have water, so several times during its residency it will make its way to the moister areas of your dogs such as the corners of the mouth, the eyes or the genital parts. This is when the flea collars and tags are useful. Their fumes prevent fleas from passing the neck to get to the head of your dog.

East Winds Miss Pinto, a Sleeve Peke bitch puppy at rest. This darling little black and white is owned by Philas Cooke of Chelsea, Massachusetts.

Your dog can usually support several generations of fleas, if he doesn't scratch himself to death or go out of his mind with the itching in the interim. The population of the flea is insured by the strong mating instinct and the well-judged decision of the female flea as to the best time to deposit her eggs. She has the unique capacity to store semen until the time is right to lay the eggs after some previous brief encounter with a member of the opposite sex.

When that time comes for her to lay, she does so without so much as a backward glance and moves on. The dog shakes the eggs off during a normal day's wandering, and there they remain until hatched and the baby fleas are ready to jump back on a dog. If any of the eggs remain on the dog, chances are the scratching of your dog will help them emerge from their shells.

Above: Mrs Howland's Ch. Yenny of Ashcroft, photographed several years ago.

Right: Ch. Dream of Ashcroft, owned by Mrs W.A. Martel of Los Angeles. From the nineteen thirties.

Left: Li of Sil-Bir, Pekingese Club Gold Medalist in 1933 in England. Fifteen thousand dollars is said to have been refused for the purchase of this dog in the 1930's. Bred and owned by Mrs A.L. Beart of Surrey, England.

Larval fleas are small and resemble grains of salt; they begin their lives eating their own egg shells until your dog comes along and offers the return to the world of adult fleas, whose excrement provides the predigested blood pellets they must have to thrive. They cannot survive on fresh blood, nor are they capable at this tender age of digging for it themselves.

After a couple of weeks of this free loading, the baby flea makes his own cocoon and becomes a pupa. This stage lasts long enough for the larval flea to grow legs, mandibles, and sharp spines and to flatten out and in general become identifiable as the commonly known and obnoxious *Ctenocephalides canis*. The process can take several weeks or several months, depending on weather conditions, heat, moisture, etc., but generally three

weeks is all that is required to enable the flea to start gnawing your dog in its own right.

And so the life-cycle of the flea is begun again, and if you don't have plans to stem the tide, you will certainly see a population explosion that will make the human one resemble an endangered species. Getting rid of fleas can be accomplished by the afore-mentioned spraying of the dog, or the flea collars and tags, but air, sunshine and a good shaking out of beds, bedding, carpets, cushions, etc., *must* be undertaken to get rid of the eggs or larvae lying around the premises.

However, if you love the thrill of the chase, and have the inclination for it, you can still try to catch them on safari across your dog's stomach. Your dog will love the attention—that is, if you don't keep pinching a bit of skin instead of that little blackish critter. Chances are great you will come up with skin rather than the flea and your dog will lose patience.

Should you be lucky enough to get hold of one, you must either squeeze it to death (which isn't easy to do) or break it in two with a sharp, strong fingernail (which also isn't easy to do) or you must release it *underwater* in the toilet bowl and flush immediately. This prospect is only slightly more likely. We strongly suggest that you shape up, clean up, shake out and spray—on a regular basis.

There are those people, however, who are much more philosophical about the flea, since, like the cockroach, it has been around since the beginning of the world. For instance, that old-time philosopher, David Harum, has been much quoted with his remark, "A reasonable amount of fleas is good for the dog. They keep him from broodin' on bein' a dog." We would rather agree with John Donne who in his *Devotions* reveals that "The flea, though he kill none, he does all the harm he can." This is especially true if your dog is a show dog! If the scratching doesn't ruin the coat, the inevitable infestations of the parasites the fleas inject into your dog will do it!

So we readily see that dogs can be afflicted by both internal and external parasites. The external parasites are the aforementioned fleas, plus ticks and lice. And while all of these are bothersome, they can be treated. However, infestations of the internal parasites, worms of various kinds, are usually deeply-seated before discovery and require more radical means of ridding the dog of them.

Internal Parasites

The most common worms are the round type. These, like many other worms, are carried and spread by the flea and go through a cycle within the dog host. They are excreted in egg or larval form and passed on to other dogs in this manner.

Worm medicine should be prescribed by a veterinarian. Dogs should be checked for worms at least twice a year, or every three months if there is an epidemic known in your area, and during the summer months when fleas are plentiful.

Major types of worms are hookworms, whipworms, tapeworms (the only non-round worms in this list), ascarids (the "typical" round worms), heartworms, kidney and lung worms. Each can be peculiar to a part of the country or may be carried by a dog from one area to another. Kidney and lung worms are fortunately quite rare. The others are not. Some symptoms for worms are vomiting intermittently, eating grass, lack of pep, bloated stomach, rubbing the tail along the ground, loss of weight, dull coat, anemia and pale gums, eye discharge, or unexplained nervousness and irritability. A dog with worms will usually eat twice as much as he normally would.

Never worm a sick dog, or a pregnant bitch after the first two weeks she has been bred, and never worm a constipated dog . . . It will retain the strong medicine within the body for too long a time.

The best and safest way to determine the presence of worms is to test for them before they do excessive damage. Worms alone can kill your dog if the infestation is severe enough. Even light infestations of worms can debilitate to the point where a

Above: Ch. Mingshang Toni T'Sun of Clamarlow, owned by the Misses C. and M. Lowther. A famous dog in his time.

English Ch. Feisal of Iwade, owned by Mrs S. Brown, and photographed in the nineteen thirties.

Tikuo Chuo-Le-Chips of Ri-Lee pictured winning at a February, 1969 show. Bred by Alice Riley, Chips is owned by Pat O'Shea of Sioux Falls, South Dakota.

Agnes Baker Nourse with some of her Pekingese, three of them home-bred champions.

dog becomes more susceptibe to serious diseases which can kill.

Today's medication for worming is relatively safe and mild, and worming is no longer the traumatic experience for either dog or owner that it used to be. Great care must be given, however, to the proper administration of the drugs. Correct dosage is a "must" and it is essential to maintain clean quarters to rid your kennel of these parasites. It is almost impossible to find an animal that is completely free of parasites; so we must consider worming as a necessary evil.

However mild today's medicines may be, it is inadvisable to worm a dog unnecessarily. There are simple tests to determine the presence of worms and this chapter is designed to help you learn how to make these tests yourself. Veterinarians charge a nominal fee for this service, if it is not part of their regular office examination. It is a simple matter to prepare fecal slides that you can check yourself on a periodic basis. Over the years it will save you much time and money, especially if you have more than one dog or a large kennel.

All that is needed by way of equipment is a microscope with 10x power. These can be purchased in the toy department in a department or regular toy store for a few dollars, depending on what else you want to get with it; but the basic, least expensive sets come with the necessary glass slides and attachments. Good results may also be achieved with a quality hand-glass of 10x or 12x power.

After the dog has defecated, take an applicator stick, a toothpick with a flat end and or even a wooden matchstick, and gouge off a piece of the stool about the size of a small pea. Have one of the glass slides ready with a large drop of water on it. Mix the two together until you have a cloudy film over a large area of the slide. This smear should be covered with another slide or a cover slip—though it is possible to obtain readings with just the open slide. Place your slide under the microscope and prepare to focus in on it. To read the slide you will find that your eye should follow a certain pattern. Start at the top and read from left to right, then right back to the left side and then left over to the right side once again until you have looked at every portion of the slide from the top left to the bottom right side.

Make sure that your smear is not too thick or the reading will be too dark to make proper identification; if it is too watery it will be confused.

If you would rather not make your own examinations, but would prefer to have the veterinarian do it, the proper way to present a segment of the stool for him to examine is as follows:

After the dog has defecated, a portion of the stool, say a square inch from different sections of it, should be placed in a glass jar or plastic container, and labeled with the dog's name and the address of the owner. If the sample cannot be examined within three to four hours after passage, it should be refrigerated. Your opinion as to what variety of worms you suspect is sometimes helpful to the veterinarian and may be noted on the label of the jar you submit to him for the examination.

Checking for worms on a regular basis is advisable not only for the welfare of the dog but for the protection of your family, since most worms are transmissible, under certain circumstances, to humans.

Right top: Canadian Ch. Mar-Gold's Oliver Twist, bred by Mrs E. Mirylees, of England, and owned by Mrs Benjamin Sugden of British Columbia, Canada. Oliver is pictured going Best Toy in Show and Best Canadian Bred at the Vernon District Kennel Club in Vernon, B.C., Canada, with her handler Donald Walker. This win was under judge Vincent Perry of California.

Canadian Ch. Floray's Twee Deedle Dum is pictured winning under American judge Louis Murr at the Calgary Kennel Club show in Alberta, Canada. Bred by Mr and Mrs James McDonald, the dog is owned by Mrs Benjamin Sugden of B.C., Canada, and handled by Mrs Sugden. The sire is the imported Ch. Etive Helenes Twee Jin ex Ch. Firebird's Foo Jin of Floray.

Left: English and American Ch. Suki of Lavrock O'Chuchow, property of Mrs C. Hager of Braddock, Pennsylvania. Suki is the dam of another famous Pekingese of the era, Ch. Zat of Lavrock of Palart.

Magnificent headstudy taken of future Ch. Mi Te Alexander, while just a puppy. Owner is Vincent Agro of the Ven Cen Pekingese, Fairfield, Alabama. Photograph by Twomey.

CHAPTER 23

NAMING YOUR PEKINGESE

Ai Jen	Beloved One	Hsiao Cho	Clown
Ai Tse	Favorite Son	Hsiao Guer	Major Mite
Baiy Er	Companion	Hsiao Hair	Baby
Bing	Soldier	Hsiao Heng	Mighty Mite
Cha Hua	Tea Blossom	Hsiao Mei	Little Sister
Chang Chia	Great Singer	Hsiao Tien Shih	Cherub
Chang Mao Go	Longhaired Dog	Hsiao Tse	Wee Child
Chi Go	Wonder Dog	Hsiung Ti	Brother
Chi Ping	Cavalcade	Hsuan Shang	Chosen
Chi Shih	Miracle	Hsueh	Snow
Chi Tsien Tsao	Marigold	Hsiung	Bear
Chia Yang	Reared at Home	Hu Po	Amber
Chia Pao	Pride of the House	Hu Tieh	Butterfly
Chiao	Pepper	Huan Lo	Merry
Chiao Lo	Pride and Joy	Huang Ho	Empress
Chih Shih Chieh	Intellectual Person	Huang Shang	Emperor
Chin Kang Shih	Diamond	Huang Ti	Reigning Monarch
Chin Se	Golden	Huei Hu	Grey Fox
Chin Tse	Gold	Huei Pai	Grey-and-White
Ching	Surprise	Huei Woo	Grey Mist
Ching Kuan	Mandarin	Hun Heng	Pugnacious
Ching Ting	Dragonfly	Hung Hsuing	Robin
Ching Tsu	Light on Feet	Hung Pao Shih	Ruby
Chu Chi	Marvel	Je Er	Sun Boy
Chu Jen	Master	Je Go	Sun Dog
Chu Pao	Jewel	Kan Chueh	Sensation
Chuan Hey	All Black	Kow Teng	Highest Rank
Da Chiao	Big Feet	Ku Er	Orphan
Di Yee	Ace of Spades	Kuai Tse	Chopsticks
Dian Shan	Lightning	Kung Chu	Princess
Fei Hing Chia	Flyer	Lai Yuen	Thundercloud
Hai Chun Ta Chen	War Admiral	Lan	Orchid
Han Sin	Mimosa	Lang	Wolf
Hey Chu	Black Pearl	Lee Hai	Mighty Atom
Hey Lien	Black Face	Lei	Thunder
Hey Pai	Black-and-White	Li Woo	Gift
Hey Yen	Dark Eyes	Lien Hua	Lotus
Hing	Star	Lo Er	Happy Boy
Hing Chen	Star Dust	Lo Tse	Bit of Joy
Hoong	Red	Lung	Dragon
Hoong Er	Red Boy	Ma	Mother
Hoong Hu	Red Fox	Mao	Feathers
Hoong Pai	Red-and-White	Mee Nan	Honey Boy
Hsiao Boo Dear	Tiny Mite	Ming Hsing	Bright Star

Above: Early or supplementary feeding is sometimes necessary. Notice correct angle of puppy's head and the nipple filled with formula so that puppy does not gulp air.

Above: Blak Sytan of N-Yueh Chia, owned by Howard and Frieda Reef of Ft. Collins, Colorado.

Below: Lassock of Ashcroft, a Toy Group winner in 1934, and owned by John B. Royce.

Wei Kung Choo of Waithman, imported from England by Mrs. W.C. Edmiston.

Ming Hua	Bright Flower
Ming Yuin	Bright Cloud
Mo Shui	Ink
Mung Nan	Dream Boy
Nan Er	Boy
Nee Au Er	Bird
Ngo Hsiang	Idol
Nu Er	Girl
Nung Tso	Can Do
Pa Pa	Father
Pai Chin	Platinum
Pai Hsiang	White Chest
Pai Hu	White Fox
Pao Bei	Gem
Pao Wu	Treasure
Ping Chuan	Man of War
Po Tung Go	Popular Dog
Sai Chi	Contender
Sha Er	Sand Boy
Sha Lo	Idiot's Delight
Shan	Flash
Sheng Chia	Victor
Shih Go	Lion Dog
Shou Ling	Leader
Tai Tze	Prince
Tai Yen Chier	Bespectacled
Tsao Chen	Dawn
Tso Tse	Dwarf
Tu Feng	Humming Bee
Tu Sheng	Only Child
Tuan Hei	Short Back
Tung Kuai	Merry
Wan Tui	Bowlegs
Wan Woo	Plaything
Wan Wu Hua	Toy Blossom
Wu Bee	Without Nose
Wu Tso	Perfection
Yang Hua	Pansy
Yang Tan Koo	Cream Puff
Yee Tui	Replica
Yeh	Night
Yeh Mao	Little Owl
Yin Hu	Silver Fox
Ying Hsuing	Hero
Ying Tao	Cherry
Yung Tsin	Brave Heart
Yung Hu	Gallant Fox

CHAPTER 24

PURSUING A CAREER WITH DOGS

One of the biggest joys for those of us who love dogs is to see a friend or member of the family grow up in the fancy and then go on to enjoy the sport dogs offer. Many dog lovers make provisions in their wills setting up veterinary scholarships for deserving youngsters who wish to make a profession out of association with dogs.

Unfortunately, many children who have this earnest desire are not always able to afford the expense of an education that will take them through veterinary school, and they are not eligible for scholarships. In recent years however, we have had an innovation in this field: a college course for those interested in earning an Animal Science degree, which costs less than half that of a complete veterinary course. A number of colleges are now offering the program.

Anyone who has visited veterinary offices during the past decade will readily agree that the waiting rooms become more crowded with each passing year. Demands on the doctors for research, consultation, surgery, and treatment are consuming more and more time after regular office hours. No relief of this situation appears likely; in fact, the steadily increasing number of pets indicates conditions will probably get worse.

Until recently, most veterinary help consisted of kennel men or women who were restricted to performing services more properly classified as office maintenance than as actual veterinary assistance. Their function in the operation of a veterinary office is obviously essential and appreciated; however, many veterinarians find it necessary to carry out tasks that could be handled by properly trained semi-professionals.

Two-Year Course in Animal Science

With exactly this additional service in mind, many colleges are now offering two-year courses in Animal Science for the training of such semi-professionals and are thereby opening an entire new field for animal technologists. The time saved through the assistance of such trained staff will relieve veterinarians of the more mechanical chores and allow them more time for diagnoses and general care for their clients.

The State University Agricultural and Technical College at Delhi, New York, has already graduated several classes of these technologists, and many other institutions of learning are offering comparable two-year courses at the college level. Entrance requirements are usually that each applicant must be a graduate of an approved high school or take the State University Admissions Examinations. In addition, each applicant for Animal Science Technology program must have some previous credits in mathematics and science, with chemistry an important part of the science background.

The program at Delhi Tech was a new educational venture for training of competent technicians for employment in the biochemical field and had been generously supported by a five-year grant designated as a "Pilot Development Program in Animal Science." Delhi is a unit of the State University of New York and is accredited by the Middle States Association of Colleges and Secondary Schools. Their campus provides offices, laboratories, and animal quarters, and they are equipped with modern instruments to train their technicians in laboratory animal care, physiology, pathology, microbiology, anaesthesia, X-ray, and germ-free techniques. Sizeable animal colonies are maintained in air-conditioned quarters, and include mice, rats, hamsters, guinea-pigs, gerbils, and rabbits, as well as dogs and cats.

First year students are given such courses as livestock production, dairy food science, general, organic, and biological Chemistry, mammalian anatomy, histology, and physiology, pathogenic microbiology, and quantitative and instrumental analysis.

Second year students study general pathology, animal parasitology, animal care and anaesthesia, introductory psychology, animal breeding, animal nutrition, hemotology and urinanalysis, radiology, genetics, food sanitation and meat inspection, histological tech-

Above: Three daughters and three Pekingese belonging to the famous Elizabeth Mirylees of the English Beaupres Kennels. Daughters Jean, Clementina and Jacqueline and their prized puppies.

niques, animal laboratory practices, and other techniques. These, of course, may be supplemented by electives that prepare the student for contact with the public in the administration of future duties. Recommended electives include public speaking, botany, animal reproduction, and related subjects.

In addition to Delhi and the colleges that began presentation of these courses, more and more universities are offering training for animal technologists. Students at the State University of Maine, for instance, receive part of their practical training at the Animal Medical Center in New York City, and after this experience they can carry out professional duties as soon as they take up employment with a veterinarian. Under direct veterinary supervision, they are able to perform all of the following procedures as a semi-professional:

Recording of vital information relative to a case,

Preparation of animals for surgery,

Preparation of equipment and medicaments to be used in surgery,

Preparation of medicaments for dispensing to clients on prescription of the attending veterinarian,

Administration and application of certain medicines,

Performing colonic irrigations,

Application and changing of wound dressings,

Preparation of food and the feeding of patients,

Instructing clients on how to handle and restrain their pets; explaining the needs for exercise, methods of house training, and elementary obedience training,

Performing first-aid treatment for hemorrhage, application of tourniquets,

Preservation of blood, urine, and pathologic material for the purpose of sending them to a laboratory,

Providing general care and supervision of the hospital or clinic patients to insure comfort, and

Trimming nails and grooming of patients.

High school graduates with a sincere regard for animals and a desire to work with veterinarians in performing such clinical duties will find that they can fit in especially well. Women can be particularly useful; their strong maternal instincts stand them in good stead in caring for sick or injured animals, and they will find that most of the duties are well within their physical capabilities. This is because a majority of the positions will be in the small animal field, and for the same reason their dexterity will also be invaluable. Students with financial restrictions that preclude their getting sufficient education to be licensed as full-fledged veterinarians can in this way pursue careers in the field of their interest. Assistance in the pharmaceutical field, wherein drug firms deal with laboratory animals, offers another wide area for trained assistants. The opportunities for careers are varied; job openings are to be found in many medical centers, research institutions, and government health agencies; the demand for graduates far exceeds the current supply of trained personnel.

Ch. Orchid Lanes Ku Lee, imported by Mr and Mrs Richard S. Quigley of Pennsylvania.

314

The starting salaries are estimated to average $5,000 annually. Basic college education expenses, range from about $1,800 to $2,200 per year for out-of-state residents, and include tuition, room and board, college fees, essential text-books, and limited personal expenses.

Personal and certain other expenses will, of course, vary with individual students. Preparational costs, it will be noted, are about half those involved in becoming a full-fledged veterinarian.

In England, there are part-time courses and one full-time course for those who want to help veterinarians. The part-time courses are organized by local education authorities and generally take place in the afternoons, sometimes the evenings. They are available at various centers over all the country. At the time of writing there are 15 part-time courses in England and one in Belfast: an up-to-date list is available from the Royal College of Veterinary Surgeons in London.

A full-time course may be taken at the Berkshire College of Agriculture. These courses are residential and last for six or three months—but students cannot be accepted for them until they have completed some training at the part-time courses mentioned above.

When training at these centers is completed the student may take the qualifying examinations and become a Registered Animal Nursing Auxiliary. This licence entitles him or her to use the initials RANA after his name and is universally recognised as a qualification.

An alternative course is offered in England by the Institute of Animal Technicians. The Institute does not require any academic qualifications for those taking the preliminary examination, but eighteen months' experience in an approved establishment is necessary before the Intermediate examination. This period can be shortened to nine months under certain circumstances. Part-time training courses for the Institute's examinations are organized by Local Education Authorities in many centers throughout the country; these usually start in September and are of one or two years' duration. Full information can be obtained from the Institute's Public Relations Officer at Geigy Ltd., Altrincham Road, Wilmslow, Cheshire.

Above: Ch. Black Bandit's Rascal of He'Lo, bred by Rubye Turner Williams and owned by Mrs E.H. Gatewood of Burlington, New Jersey. Rascal is pictured winning under judge Mary Brewster at the 1970 Delaware County Kennel Club Show with her owner and handler. Rascal's sire was Ch. Black Bandit of He'Lo ex Storymey's Gingham Girl.

Right: Ch. Bel-Mar Ku Loo San, bred, owned and handled by Mary E. Davis of Borger, Texas, is photographed here winning Best of Winners for a three point major under judge Joe Faigel at the 1971 Town and Country Kennel Club Show in Oklahoma. Petrulis photo.

Kennel Work

Another rewarding vocation for those who would like to work with animals is kennel work. Youngsters, whether or not planning to become veterinarians or animal technicians, can get valuable experience and earn some money by working part-time after school and week-ends, or full-time during summer vacations in a veterinarian's office. The exposure to animals and office procedures will be time well spent in any case, and the experience might lead to a decision regarding career.

Another great help to veterinarians has been the housewife who loves animals and wishes to put in some time at a job away from the home. This is a field open especially to those whose children are grown or are away at college. Such a job would be attractive to the owner of a new, and still small kennel; if she can clean up in her own kennel, she can certainly clean up in a veterinarian's establishment and she will learn much about handling and caring for her own animals while she is making some extra money.

Kennel help is also an area that is wide open for retired men. They are able to help in many areas where they can earn, learn, and stay active, and most of the work allows them to set their own pace. The gentleness that age and experience brings is appreciated also by the animals they will deal with, and they will find great reward in their contribution to animals while keeping the possibility of remaining active in the business world as well. Younger men might choose working for a large kennel as a vocation, with the variety of duties dependent upon the overall activities of the kennel.

Professional Handlers

For those who wish to participate in the sport of dogs and whose interests or abilities do not center around the clinical aspects of the fancy, there is yet another avenue of involvement.

Those who excel in the show ring, who enjoy being in the limelight and putting their dogs through their paces, might find much satisfaction in a career in professional handling. Handling may be limited to week-end showings of few dogs for special clients, or it may be a full-time career and possibly include boarding, training, conditioning, breeding, and showing of dogs for several clients.

Depending on how deeply one's interest runs, the issue can be simplified by careful preliminary consideration before it becomes necessary to make a decision. A first move might well be to have a long talk with a successful professional handler to learn the pros and cons of such a profession. Watching handlers in action from the ringside as they perform their duties could also be revealing. A visit to some of their kennels for down-to-earth revelations of the behind-the-scenes responsibilities is essential. Working with a handler full or part-time for a short while would be the best means of resolving any doubts one might have.

Professional handling is not all "glamour of the show ring." There is plenty of hard work behind the scenes 24 hours of every day. One must have the necessary ability and patience for this work, as well as the ability and patience to deal with the *clients*—the dog owners who value their animals above almost anything else and expect a great deal in the way of care and handling. And the 64-dollar question one must ask first of all is does one *really* love dogs enough to handle them.

Dog Training

Like the professional handler, the professional dog trainer has a very responsible job. He must not only be thoroughly familiar with the correct and successful methods of

Above: Japanese Champion Chun-Chu-Fu's Chuck-a-Luck photographed at 10 months of age. He was Best Futurity male at the 1960 Pekin Peke Club Show in Los Angeles, and was sold on March 31, 1961, to Paul Yoshida of the Golden Gate Kennels in Tokyo, Japan. He completed his Japanese championship in three straight shows. Bred by Shirley Stone and Irene Francisco.

Ch. Coomes Toi Boi, obviously voicing an opinion. Owned by Mrs E.N. Coomes of Phoenix, Arizona.

Ch. Redd Boi of Iwade, owned by Mrs Stowell Brown.

training a dog, but must also have the unique ability to communicate with them. It is very rewarding work, but training for the show ring, for obedience trials, or for guard dog work must be carried out exactly right for the successful results essential to build and maintain a reputation.

Training schools are very much the vogue nowadays, with all of them claiming success. A careful investigation should be made of a school before enrolling a dog, and even more careful investigation should be made of methods and of actual successes before becoming associated with one.

Ch. Sun'T Yung Wong Sing Lee, top producing Pekingese of all times pictured retiring the Atherstone Challenge Trophy by winning Best of Breed under judge Percy Roberts. Joan Ludwig photograph.

The late Mrs Nathan S. Wise of the Bond Hill Kennels, Cincinnati, Ohio with Ch. Langridge Yu Lin. Westlake photo.

Grooming Parlors

If one does not wish the 24-hour a day job which is required of a professional handler or professional trainer, but still loves working with and caring for dogs, there is always the very profitable grooming business. Poodles started the ball rolling for the plush grooming establishments that spring up all over like mushrooms in major cities; and all of them seem to do well! Here again, the proper handling of dogs and the public as well as skill in the actual grooming of the dogs of all breeds, is necessary for a successful operation.

While shops flourish in the cities, some of the suburban areas now have mobile units that will visit your home by appointment with a completely equipped shop on wheels and will groom your dog right in your own driveway. The operation of such a unit might also be attractive as a vocation.

The Pet Shop

Part-time or full-time work in a pet shop can help one decide rather quickly as to whether one is fitted to operate a shop of one's own. For those who love animals and are concerned with their care and feeding, the pet shop can be a profitable and satisfying association. Supplies which are available for sale in these shops are almost limitless and a comfortable living can be earned selling pet supplies if the location of the shop is carefully chosen.

Dog Judging

There are show judges whose profession or age or health prevent them from owning or breeding or showing dogs, and there are others who turn to judging at dog shows after their active years in the show ring are over. Breeder-judges make a valuable contribution to the fancy by their judgements from the benefit of their years of experience, and the assignments are enjoyable.

Miscellaneous

Besides the vocational and recreational activities discussed, there are others that can be of interest (some of them profitable) to people who are much interested in dogs. Those skilled in photography or artistically talented may devote themselves to dog photography and portrait painting; those with a talent for writing may direct their pens towards books, magazine articles, or club newsletters and the like. Other club activities are enjoyable and interesting. Making dog coats, typing pedigrees and other records, or just walking dogs can be of service and a source of satisfaction. Those who involve themselves in any such activity contribute to the sport and are sincerely appreciated by all in the fancy.

DICTIONARY OF DOG DISEASES

Abortion: When a pregnancy is not right the embryos may be prematurely expelled from the uterus. Usually, the bitch makes a rapid recovery. Abortion can also be the result of an injury or accident which can cause complications. If part of a fetus is left in the uterus, serious infection may occur. The first indication of this will be high fever, dry nose and lethargy. The immediate services of a veterinarian are necessary.

Abscess: A skin eruption characterized by a localized collection of pus formed as a result of disintegrating tissues of the body. Abscesses may be acute or chronic. An acute abscess forms rapidly and will more than likely burst within a week. It is accompanied by pain, redness, heat and swelling, and may cause a rise in temperature. An abscess is usually the result of infection of a bacterial nature. Treatment consists of medication in the form of antibiotics and salves, ointments, powders or a poultice designed to bring it to a head. A chronic abscess is a slow-developing headless lump surrounded by gathering tissue. This infection is usually of internal origin, and painless unless found in a sensitive area of the body. The same antibiotics and medications are used. Because abscesses of this nature are slow in developing, they are generally slow in dissolving.

Acarus: One of the parasitic mites which cause mange.

Achondroplasia: A disease which results in the stunting of growth, or dwarfing of the limbs before birth.

Adenoma: A non-inflammatory growth or benign tumor found in a prominent gland; most commonly found in the mammary gland of the bitch.

Agalactia: A contagious, viral disease resulting in lowered or no production of milk by a nursing bitch. It usually occurs in warm weather, and is accompanied by fever and loss of appetite. Abscesses may also form. In chronic cases the mammary gland itself may atrophy.

Alariasis: An infection caused by flukes (*Alaria arisaemoides*), which are ingested by the dog. They pass on to the bronchial tract and into the small intestine where they grow to maturity and feed on intestinal contents.

Allergy: Dogs can be allergic as well as people to outdoor or indoor surroundings, such as carpet fuzz, pillow stuffings, food, pollen, etc. Recent experiments in hyposensitization have proved effective in many cases when injections are given with follow-up "boosters." Sneezing, coughing, nasal discharges, runny, watery eyes, etc., are all symptomatic.

Alopecia: A bare spot, or lack of full growth of hair on a portion of the body; another name for baldness and can be the end result of a skin condition.

Amaurosis: Sometimes called "glass eye." A condition that may occur during a case of distemper if the nervous system has been affected, or head injuries sustained. It is characterized by the animal bumping into things or by a lack of coordination. The condition is incurable and sooner or later the optic nerve becomes completely paralyzed.

Analgesia: Loss of ability to feel pain with the loss of consciousness or the power to move a part of the body. The condition may be induced by drugs which act on the brain or central nervous system.

Anal Sac Obstruction: The sacs on either side of the rectum, just inside the anus, at times may become clogged. If the condition persists, it is necessary for the animal to be assisted in their opening, so that they do not become infected and/or abscess. Pressure is applied by the veterinarian and the glands release a thick, horrible-smelling excretion. Antibiotics or a "flushing" of the glands if infected is the usual treatment, but at the first sign of discomfort in the dog's eliminating, or a "sliding along" the floor, it is wise to check for clogged anal glands.

Anasarca: Dropsy of the connective tissues of the skin. It is occasionally encountered in fetuses and makes whelping difficult.

Anemia: A decrease of red blood cells which are the cells that carry oxygen to the body tissues. Causes are usually severe infestation of parasites, bad diet, or blood disease. Transfusions and medications can be given to replace red blood cells, but the disease is sometimes fatal.

Aneurysm: A rupture or dilation of a major blood vessel, causing a bulge or swelling of the affected part. Blood gathers in the tissues forming a swelling. It may be caused by strain, injury, or when arteries are weakened by debilitating disease or old age. Surgery is needed to remove the clot.

Anestrous: When a female does not come into heat.

Antiperistalsis: A term given to the reverse action of the normal procedures of the stomach or intestine, which brings their contents closer to the mouth.

Antipyretics: Drugs or methods used to reduce temperature during fevers. These may take the form of cold baths, purgatives, etc.

Antispasmodics: Medications which reduce spasms of the muscular tissues and soothe the nerves and muscles involved.

Antisialics: Term applied to substances used to reduce excessive salivation.

Arsenic Poisoning: Dogs are particularly susceptible to this type of poisoning. There is nausea, vomiting, stomach pains and convulsions, even death in severe cases. An emetic may save the animal in some cases. Salt or dry mustard (1 tablespoon mixed with 1 teaspoonful of water) can be effective in causing vomiting until the veterinarian is reached.

Arthritis: A painful condition of the joints which results in irritation and inflammation. A disease which generally confines itself to older dogs, especially in the larger breeds. Limping, irritability and pain are symptomatic. Anti-inflammatory drugs are effective after X-ray determines the severity. Heat and rest are helpful.

Ascites: A collection of serous fluid in the abdominal cavity, causing swelling. It may be a result of heavy parasitic infestation or a symptom of liver, kidney, tuberculosis or heart diseases.

Aspergillosis: A disease contracted from poultry and often mistaken for tuberculosis since symptoms are quite similar. It attacks the nervous system and sometimes has disastrous effects on the respiratory system. This fungus growth in the body tissue spreads quickly and is accompanied by convulsions. The dog rubs his nose and there is a bloody discharge.

Asthma: Acute distress in breathing. Attacks may occur suddenly at irregular intervals and last as long as half an hour. The condition may be hereditary or due to allergy or heart condition. Antihistamines are effective in minor attacks.

Ataxia: Muscular incoordination or lack of movement causing an inhibited gait, although the necessary organs and muscle power are coherent. The dog may have a tendency to stagger.

Atopy: Manifestations of atopy in the dog are a persistent scratching of the eyes and nose. Onsets are usually seasonal—the dog allergic to, say, ragweed will develop the condition when ragweed is in season, or, say, house dust all year round. Most dogs afflicted with atopy are multi-sensitive and are affected by something several months out of the year. Treatment is by antihistamines or systemic corticosteroids, or both.

Babesia Gibsoni (or Babesiosis): A parasitic disease of the tropics, reasonably rare in the U.S.A. to date. Blood tests can reveal its presence and like other parasitic infections the symptoms are loss of appetite, no pep, anemia and elevations in temperature as the disease advances; enlarged spleen and liver are sometimes evident.

Balanitis: The medical term for a constant discharge of pus from the penis which causes spotting of clothing or quarters or causes the dog to clean itself constantly. When bacteria gather at the end of the sheath, this causes irritations in the tissue and pus. If the condition becomes serious, the dog may be cauterized or ointment applied.

Blastomycosis: A rare infectious disease involving the kidneys and liver. The animal loses its appetite and vomits. Laboratory examination is necessary to determine presence.

Bradycardia: Abnormal slowness of the heartbeat and pulse.

Bronchitis: Inflammation of the mucus lining in the respiratory tract, the windpipe or trachea, and lungs. Dampness and cold are usually responsible and the symptoms usually follow a chill, or may be present with cases of pneumonia or distemper. Symptoms are a nagging dry cough, fever, quickened pulse rate, runny nose, perhaps vomiting, and congested nasal passages which must be kept open. Old dogs are particularly affected. It is a highly transmissible disease and isolation from other animals is important. Antibiotics are given.

Brucella Canis: An infectious disease associated with abortion in bitches in the last quarter of gestation, also sterility or stillbirths. Testicle trouble in male dogs is comparable. It is highly contagious and can be diagnosed through blood tests; animals having the infection should be isolated.

Cancer (tumors, neoplasia, etc.): A growth of cells which serve no purpose is referred to as a cancer. The growth may be malignant or benign. Malignancy is the spreading type growth and may invade the entire body. Treatment, if the condition is diagnosed and caught in time, may be successful by surgical methods, drugs, or radioactive therapy. Haste in consulting your veterinarian cannot be urged too strongly.

Canker (Otitis): A bacterial infection of the ear where the ear may drain, have a very unpleasant odor, and ooze a dark brown substance all the way out to the ear flap. Cause of canker can be from mites, dirt, excessive hair growth in the ear canal, wax, etc. A daily cleaning and administering of anti-fungal ointment or powder are in order until the condition is cured. Symptoms are the dog shaking his head, scratching his ear and holding the head to the side.

Caries: A pathologic change causing destruction of the enamel on teeth and subsequent invasion of the dentine; in other words, a cavity in a tooth. This may result in bad breath, toothache, digestive disorders, etc., depending upon the severity. Cavities in dogs are rare, though we hear more and more of false teeth being made for dogs and occasionally even root canal work for show dogs.

Castration: Surgical removal of the male gonads or sex organs. An anesthesia is necessary and the animal must be watched for at least a week to see that hemorrhage does not occur. It is best performed at an early age—anywhere from three to nine months. Older dogs suffering from a hormonal imbalance or cancer of the gonads are castrated.

Cataract: An opaque growth covering the lens of the eye. Surgical removal is the only treatment. Cataract may be a result of an injury to the eye or in some cases may be an inherited trait.

Cellulitis: Inflammation of the loose subcutaneous tissue of the body. A condition which can be symptomatic of several other diseases.

Cheilitis: Inflammation of the lips.

Cholecystitis: A condition affecting the gall bladder. The onset is usually during the time an animal is suffering from infectious canine hepatitis. Removal of the gall bladder, which thickens and becomes highly vascular, can effect a complete cure.

Chorea: Brain damage as a result of distemper which has been severe is characterized by convulsive movements of the legs. It is progressive and if it affects the facial muscles, salivating or difficulty in eating or moving the jaws may be evident. Sedatives may bring relief, but this disease is incurable.

Choroiditis: Inflammation of the choroid coat of the eye which is to be regarded as serious. Immediate veterinary inspection is required.

Coccidiosis: An intestinal disease of parasitic nature and origin. Microscopic organisms reproduce on the walls of the intestinal tract and destroy tissue. Bloody diarrhea, loss of weight and appetite and general lethargy result. Presence of parasites is determined by fecal examination. Sulfur drugs are administered and a complete clean up of the premises is in order since the parasite is passed from one dog to another through floor surfaces or eating utensils.

Colostrum: A secretion of the mammary glands for the first day or so after the bitch gives birth. It acts as a purgative for the young, and contains antibodies against distemper, hepatitis and other bacteria.

Conjunctivitis: Inflammation of the conjunctiva of the eye.

Convulsions: A fit, or violent involuntary contractions of groups of muscles, accompanied by unconsciousness. They are in themselves a symptom of another disease, especially traceable to one affecting the brain; i.e., rabies, or an attack of encephalitis or distemper. It may also be the result of a heavy infestation of parasites or toxic poisonings. Care must be taken that the animal does not injure itself and a veterinarian must be consulted to determine and eliminate the cause.

Cryptorchid: A male animal in which neither testicle is present or descended. This condition automatically bars a dog from the show ring.

Cyanosis: A definite blueness seen in and around the mucous membranes of the face; i.e. tongue, lips and eyes. It is usually synonymous with a circulatory obstruction or heart condition.

Cystitis: A disease of the urinary tract which is characterized by inflammation and/or infection in the bladder. Symptoms are straining, frequent urination with little results or with traces of blood, and perhaps a fever. Antibiotics, usually in the sulfur category, as well as antiseptics are administered. This is a condition which is of great discomfort to the animal and is of lengthy duration. Relief must be given by a veterinarian, who will empty bladder by means of catheter or medication to relax the bladder so that the urine may be passed.

Demodectic Mange: A skin condition caused by a parasitic mite, *Demodex*, living in hair follicles. This is a difficult condition to get rid of and is treated internally as well as externally. It requires diligent care to free the animal of it entirely.

Dermatitis: There are many forms of skin irritations and eruptions but perhaps the most common is "contact dermatitis." Redness and itching are present. The irritation is due to something the animal has been exposed to and to which it is allergic. The irritant must be identified and removed. Anti-histamines and anti-inflammatory drugs are administered, and in severe cases sedatives or tranquilizers are prescribed to lessen the dog's scratching.

Diabetes (Insipidus): A deficiency of anti-diuretic hormone produced by the posterior pituitary gland. It occurs in older animals and is characterized by the animal's drinking excessive amounts of water and voiding frequently. Treatment is by periodic injection of antidiuretic drug for the rest of the animal's life.

Diabetes (Mellitus): Sometimes referred to as sugar diabetes, this is a disorder of the metabolism of carbohydrates caused by lack of insulin production by the cells of the pancreas. Symptoms are the same as in the *insipidus* type, and in severe cases loss of weight, vomiting or coma may occur. Blood and urine analysis confirm its presence. It is treated by low carbohydrate diet, oral medication and/or insulin injections.

Digitoxin: A medication given to a dog with congestive heart failure. Dosage is, of course, adjusted to severeness of condition and size of the individual animal.

Disc Abnormalities (Intervertebral): Between each bone in the spine is a connecting structure called an intervertebral disc. When the disc between two vertebrae becomes irritated and protrudes into the spinal canal it forms lesions and is painful. (This is a disease which particularly affects the Dachshund because of its long back in comparison to length of legs.) Paralysis of the legs, reluctance to move, and loss of control of body functions may be symptoms. X-ray and physical examination will determine extent of the condition. Massage helps circulation and pain relievers may be prescribed. Surgery is sometimes successful and portable two-wheel carts which support the hindquarters help.

Distemper: Highly transmissable disease of viral origin which spreads through secretions of nose, eyes or direct oral contact. May be fatal in puppies under 12 weeks. Symptoms of this disease are alternate high and low fevers, runny eyes and nose, loss of appetite and general lassitude, diarrhea and loss of weight. This disease sometimes goes into pneumonia or convulsions if the virus reaches the brain. Chorea may remain if infection has been severe or neglected. Antibiotics are administered and fluids and sedation may be advised by your veterinarian. If the dog has been inoculated, the disease may remain a light case, BUT it is not to be treated lightly. Warmth and rest are also indicated.

Dropsy: Abnormal accumulation of fluid in the tissues or body cavities. Also referred to as edema when accumulations manifest themselves below the skin. In the stomach region it is called ascites. Lack of exercise or poor circulation, particularly in older dogs, may be the cause. While the swellings are painless, excess accumulations in the stomach can cause digestive distress or heart disturbances, and may be associated with diabetes. Occasional diarrhea, lack of appetite, loss of weight, exhaustion, emaciation and death may occur in the condition is not treated.

Dysgerminoma: A malignant ovarian tumor. Symptoms are fever, vaginal discharge, vomiting and diarrhea. Tumors vary in size, though more commonly are on the large size and from reports to date, the right ovary is more commonly affected. Radiotherapy may be successful; if not, surgery is required.

Ear Mange: Otodectic mange, or parasitic otitis externa. Ear mites suck lymph fluids through the walls of the ear canal. Infections are high where mites are present and a brownish, horrible smelling ooze is present deep down in the canal all the way out to the flap where the secretion has a granular texture. The dog shakes his head, rubs and scrapes. In extreme cases convulsions or brain damage may result. The ear must be cleaned daily and drugs of an antibiotic and anti-inflammatory nature must be given.

Eclampsia: A toxemia of pregnancy. Shortly before the time a bitch whelps her puppies,

her milk may go bad. She will pant as a result of high fever, and go into convulsions. The puppies must be taken away from the mother immediately. This is usually the result of an extreme lack of calcium during pregnancy. Also known as milk fever.

Ectropion: All breeders of dogs with drooping eyelids or exaggerated haws will be familiar with this condition, where the lower eyelid turns out. It can be a result of an injury, as well as hereditary in some breeds, but can be corrected surgically.

Eczema: Eczema is another form of skin irritation which may confine itself to redness and itching, or go all the way to a scaly skin surface or open wet sores. This is sometimes referred to as "hot spots." A hormone imbalance or actual diet deficiency may prevail. Find the cause and remove it. Medicinal baths and ointments usually provide a cure, but cure is a lengthy process and the condition frequently reoccurs.

Edema: Abnormal collection of fluids in the tissues of the body.

Elbow Dysplasia: Term applied to a developmental abnormality of the elbow joints. It is hereditary.

Emphysema: Labored breathing caused by distended or ruptured lungs. May be acute or chronic and is not uncommon.

Empyema: Accumulation of pus or purulent fluid, in a body cavity, resembling an abscess. Another term for pleurisy.

Encephalitis: Brain fever associated with meningitis. An inflammation of the brain caused by a virus, rabies or perhaps tuberculosis. It may also be caused by poisonous plants, bad food or lead poisoning. Dogs "go wild," running in circles, falling over, etc. Paralysis and death frequently result. Cure depends on extent of infection and speed with which it is diagnosed and treated.

Endocarditis: Inflammation and bacterial infection of the smooth membrane that lines the inside of the heart.

Enteritis: Intestinal inflammation of serious import. It can be massive or confine itself to one spot. Symptoms are diarrhea, bloody at times, vomiting, and general discomfort. Antibiotics are prescribed and fluids, if the diarrhea and vomiting have been excessive. Causes are varied; may follow distemper or other infections or bacterial infection through intestinal worms.

Entropion: A turning in of the margin of the eyelids. As a result, the eyelashes rub on the eyeball and cause irritation resulting in a discharge from the eye. Here again it is a condition peculiar to certain breeds—particularly Chow Chows—or may be the result of an injury which failed to heal properly. Infection may result as the dog will rub his eyes and cause a swelling. It is painful, but can be cured surgically.

Enterotoxemia: A result of toxins and gases in the intestine. As bacteria increase in

the intestine, intermittent diarrhea and/or constipation results from maldigestion. If the infection reaches the kidney through the circulatory system, nephritis results. The digestive system must be cleaned out by use of castor oil or colonic irrigation, and outwardly by antibiotics.

Eosinophilic Myositis: Inflammation of the muscles dogs use for chewing. Persistent attacks usually lasting one or more weeks. They come and go over long periods of time, coming closer and closer together. Difficulty in swallowing, swelling of the face, or even the dog holding his mouth open will indicate the onset of an attack. Anti-inflammatory drugs are the only known treatment. Cause unknown, outlook grave.

Epilepsy: The brain is the area affected and fits and/or convulsions may occur early or late in life. It cannot be cured; however, it can be controlled with medication. Said to be hereditary. Convulsions may be of short duration or the dog may just appear to be dazed. It is rarely fatal. Care must be taken to see that the dog does not injure itself during an attack.

Epiphora: A constant shedding of tears which stains the face and fur of dogs. It is a bothersome condition which is not easily remedied either with outside medication or by surgical tear duct removal. There has been some success in certain cases reported from a liquid medication given with the food and prescribed by veterinarians. This condition may be caused by any one or more of a number of corneal irritations, such as nasal malfunction or the presence of foreign matter in the superficial gland of the third eyelid. After complete examination as to the specific cause, a veterinarian can decide whether surgery is indicated.

Esophageal Diverticulum: Inflammation or sac-like protrusions on the walls of the esophagus resembling small hernias. It is uncommon in dogs, but operable, and characterized by gagging, listlessness, temperature and vomiting in some cases.

False Pregnancy (or pseudo-pregnancy): All the signs of the real thing are present in this heart-breaking and frustrating condition. The bitch may even go into false labor near the end of the 63-day cycle and build a nest for her hoped-for puppies. It may be confirmed by X-ray or a gentle feeling for them through the stomach area. Hormones can be injected to relieve the symptoms.

Frostbite: Dead tissue as a result of extreme cold. The tissues become red, swollen and painful, and may peel away later, causing open lesions. Ointments and protective coverings should be administered until irritation is alleviated.

Fusospirochetal Disease: Bad breath is the first and most formidable symptom of this disease of the mouth affecting the gums. Bloody saliva and gingivitis or ulcers in the mouth may also be present, and the dog may be listless due to lack of desire to eat. Cleaning the teeth and gums daily with hydrogen peroxide in prescribed dosage by

321

the veterinarian is required. Further diagnosis of the disease can be confirmed by microscopic examination of smears, though these fusiform bacteria might be present in the mouth of a dog which never becomes infected. Attempts to culture these anaerobes have been unsuccessful.

Gastric Dilation: This is an abnormal swelling of the abdomen due to gas or overeating. Consumption of large amounts of food (especially if dry foods are eaten) and then large quantities of water make the dog "swell." The stomach twists so that both ends are locked off. Vomiting is impossible, breathing is hampered and the dog suffers pain until the food is expelled. Dogs that gulp their food and swallow air with it are most susceptible. Immediate surgery may be required to prevent the stomach from bursting. Commonly known as bloat.

Gastritis: Inflammation of the stomach caused by many things—spoiled food which tends to turn to gas, overeating, eating foreign bodies, chemicals or even worms. Vomiting is usually the first symptom though the animal will usually drink great quantities of water which more often than not it throws back up. A 24-hour fast which eliminates the cause is the first step toward cure. If vomiting persists, chunks of ice cubes put down the throat may help. Or better, the dog will lick them himself. Keep the dog on a liquid diet for another 24 hours before resuming his regular meals.

Gastro-Enteritis: Inflammation of the stomach and intestines. There is bleeding and ulceration in the stomach and this serious condition calls for immediate veterinary help.

Gastroduodenitis: Inflammation of the stomach and duodenum.

Gingivitis or gum infection: Badly tartared teeth are usually the cause of this gum infection characterized by swelling, redness at the gum line, bleeding and bloody saliva. Bad breath also. Improper diet may be a cause of it. Feeding of only soft foods as a steady diet allows the tartar to form and to irritate the gums. To effect a cure, clean the teeth and perhaps the veterinarian will also recommend antibiotics.

Glaucoma: Pressure inside the eyeball builds up, the eyeball becomes hard and bulgy and a cloudiness of the entire corneal area occurs. The pupil is dilated and the eye is extremely sensitive. Blindness is inevitable unless treatment is prompt at the onset of the disease. Cold applications as well as medical prescriptions are required with also the possibility of surgery, though with no guarantee of success.

Glossitis: Inflammation of the tongue.

Goiter: Enlargement of the thyroid gland, sometimes requiring surgery. In minor cases, medication—usually containing iodine—is administered.

Harelip: A malformation of the upper lip characterized by a cleft palate. Difficulty in nursing in exaggerated cases can result in starvation or puny development. Operations can be performed late in life.

Heart Disease: Heart failure is rare in young dogs, but older dogs which show an unusual heavy breathing after exercise or are easily tired may be victims of heart trouble, and an examination is in order. As it grows worse, wheezing, coughing or gasping may be noticed. Other symptoms indicating faulty circulation may manifest themselves as the animal retains more body fluids as the circulation slows down. Rest, less exercise, and non-fattening diets are advised and medication to remove excess fluids from the body are prescribed. In many cases, doses of digitalis may be recommended.

Heartworm (*Dirofilaria immitis*): This condition does not necessarily debilitate a working dog or a dog that is extremely active. It is diagnosed by a blood test and a microscopic examination to determine the extent of the microfilariae. If positive, further differentials are made for comparison with other microfilariae. Treatment consists of considerable attention to the state of nutrition, and liver and kidney functions are watched closely in older dogs. Medication is usually treatment other than surgery and consists of dithiazine iodine therapy over a period of two weeks. Anorexia and/or fever may occur and supplemental vitamins and minerals may be indicated. Dogs with heavy infestations are observed for possible foreign protein reaction from dying and decomposing worms, and are watched for at least three months.

Heatstroke: Rapid breathing, dazed condition, vomiting, temperature, and collapse in hot weather indicate heat-stroke. It seems to strike older dogs especially if they are overweight or have indulged in excessive activity. Reduce body temperature immediately by submerging dog in cold water, apply ice packs, cold enemas, etc. Keep dog cool and quiet for at least 24 hours.

Hematoma: A pocket of blood that may collect in the ear as a result of an injury or the dog's scratching. Surgery is required to remove the fluid and return skin to cartilage by stitching.

Hemophilia: Excessive bleeding on the slightest provocation. Only male subjects are susceptible and it is a hereditary disease passed on by females. Blood coagulants are now successfully used in certain cases.

Hepatitis, Infectious canine: This disease of viral nature enters the body through the mouth and attacks primarily the liver. Puppies are the most susceptible to this disease and run a fever and drink excessive amounts of water. Runny eyes, nose, vomiting, and general discomfort are symptoms. In some cases blood builders or even blood transfusions are administered since the virus has a tendency to thin the blood. This depletion of the blood often leaves the dog open to other types of infection and complete recovery is a lengthy process. Antibiotics are usually given and supplemental diet and blood builders are a help. Vaccination for young puppies is essential.

Hernia (diaphragmatic): An injury is usually responsible for this separation or break in the wall of diaphragm. Symptoms depend on severity; breathing may become difficult, there is some general discomfort or vomiting. X-rays can determine the extent of damage and the only cure is surgery.

Hernia (umbilical): Caused by a portion of the abdominal viscera protruding through a weak spot near the navel. Tendency toward hernia is said to be largely hereditary.

Hip Dysplasia or **HD** is a wearing away of the ball and socket of the hip joint. It is a hereditary disease. The symptoms of this bone abnormality are a limp and an awkwardness in raising or lowering the body. X-ray will establish severity and it is wise in buying or selling a dog of any breed to insist on a radiograph to prove the animal is HD clear. The condition can be detected as early as three months and if proven the dog should have as little exercise as possible. There is no cure for this condition. Only pain relievers can be given for the more severe cases. No animal with HD should be used for breeding.

Hookworm: Hookworms lodge in the small intestines and suck blood from the intestinal wall. Anemia results from loss of blood. Loss of weight, pale gums, and general weakness are symptoms. Microscopic examination of the feces will determine presence. Emphasis on diet improvement and supplements to build up the blood is necessary and, of course, medication for the eradication of the hookworms. This can be either oral or by veterinary injection.

Hydrocephalus: A condition also known as "water head" since a large amount of fluid collects in the brain cavity, usually before birth. This may result in a difficult birth and the young are usually born dead or die shortly thereafter. Euthanasia is recommended on those that do survive since intelligence is absent and violence to themselves or to others is liable to occur.

Hydronephrosis: Due to a cystic obstruction the kidney collects urine which cannot be passed through the ureter into the bladder, causing the kidney to swell (sometimes to five times its normal size) and giving pain in the lumbar region. The kidney may atrophy, if the condition goes untreated.

Ichthyosis: A skin condition over elbows and hocks. Scaliness and cracked skin cover the area, particularly that which comes in contact with hard surfaces. Lubricating oils well rubbed into the skin and keeping the animal on soft surfaces are solutions.

Impetigo: Skin disease seen in puppies infested by worms, distemper, or teething problems. Little soft pimples cover the surface of the skin. Sulfur ointments and ridding the puppy of the worms are usually sufficient cure.

Interdigital Cysts: Growths usually found in the legs. They are painful and cause the dog to favor the paw or not walk on it at all. Surgery is the only cure and antibiotic ointments to keep dirt and infection out are necessary.

Above: Ch. Chun-Chu-Fu's Comet Chan Tu at seven months of age. Bred and owned by Shirley Stone of Burbank, California. Best Futurity Puppy at the Pekin Peke Club show in Los Angeles. His sire was Langridge Wee Lin ex Al-za's Kung Chu-Taza.

Below: Best Brace in Show at the 1966 Pekingese Club of America show was Jerry Hess's Ch. Tillena Ku of Pekehaven and her daughter, Tuki Su of Pekehaven.

THE PEKINGESE CLUB OF AMERICA, INC.
MARCH 6, 1966
BEST BRACE
JUDGE MRS. C.W. AUSTIN
LOCONTE PHOTO

Intestinal Obstructions: When a foreign object becomes lodged in the intestines and prevents passage of stool, constipation results from the blockage. Hernia is another cause of obstruction or stoppage. Pain, vomiting, loss of appetites are symptoms. Fluids, laxatives or enemas should be given to remove blockage. Surgery may be necessary after X-ray determines cause. Action must be taken since death may result from long delay or stoppage.

Iritis: Inflammation of the iris or colored part of the eye. May be caused by the invasion of foreign bodies or other irritants.

Jaundice: A yellow discoloration of the skin. Liver malfunction causes damage by bile seeping into the circulatory system and being dispensed into the body tissue, causing discoloration of the skin. It may be caused by round worms, liver flukes or gall stones. It may be either acute or chronic and the animal loses ambition, convulses or vomits, sometimes to excess. It may be cured once the cause has been eliminated. Neglect can lead to death.

Keratitis: Infection of the cornea of the eye. Distemper or hepatitis may be a cause. Sensitivity to light, watery discharge and pain are symptomatic. Treatment depends on whether the lesion is surface irritation or a puncture of the cornea. Warm compresses may help until the veterinarian prescribes the final treatment. Sedatives or tranquilizers may be prescribed to aid in preventing the dog from rubbing the eye.

Kidney Worm: The giant worm that attacks the kidney and kidney tissue. It can reach a yard in length. The eggs of this rare species of worm are passed in the dog's urine rather than the feces. These worms are found in raw fish. It is almost impossible to detect them until at least one of the kidneys is completely destroyed or an autopsy reveals its presence. There is no known cure at this point and, therefore, the only alternative is not to feed raw fish.

Lead Poisoning: Ingestion of lead-based paints or products such as linoleum containing lead is serious. Symptoms are vomiting, behavior changes and/or hysteria or even convulsions in severe cases. It can be cured by medication if caught early enough. Serious damage can be done to the central nervous system. Blood samples are usually taken to determine amount in the blood. Emetics may be required if heavy intake is determined.

Leptospirosis: This viral infection is dangerous and bothersome because it affects many organs of the body before lodging itself in the kidneys. Incubation is about two weeks after exposure to the urine of another affected dog. Temperature, or sub-temperature, pain and stiffness in the hindquarters are not uncommon, nor is vomiting. Booster shots after proper vaccination at a young age are usually preventative, but once afflicted, antibiotics are essential to cure.

Lockjaw (tetanus): Death rate is very high in this bacterial disease. Puncture wounds may frequently develop into lockjaw. Symptoms are severe. As the disease progresses, high fever and stiffness in the limbs become serious though the dog does not lose consciousness. Sedatives must be given to help relax the muscles and dispel the spasms. When the stiffness affects the muscles of the face, intravenous feeding must be provided. If a cure is effected, it is a long drawn-out affair. Lockjaw bacteria are found in soil and in the feces of animals and humans.

Lymphoma (Hodgkins disease): Malignant lymphoma most frequently is found in dogs under four years of age, affects the lymph glands, liver and spleen. Anorexia and noticeable loss of weight are apparent as well as diarrhea. Depending on area and organ, discharge may be present. The actual neoplasm or tumorous growth may be surrounded by nodules or neoplastic tissue which should be surgically removed under anesthesia.

Above: Mrs M.M. Van Beuren, of Gray Craig, Newport, Rhode Island. Mrs Van Beuren is a past president of the Pekingese Club of America.

Mammary Neoplasms: 25 per cent of all canine tumors are of mammary origin. About half of all reported cases are benign. They are highly recurrent and, when cancerous, fatalities are high. Age or number of litters has nothing to do with the condition itself or the seriousness.

Mange: The loss of a patch of hair usually signals the onset of mange, which is caused by any number of types of microscopic mites. The veterinarian will usually take scrapings to determine which of the types it is. Medicated baths and dips plus internal and external medication is essential as it spreads rapidly and with care can be confined to one part of the body. Antibiotics are prescribed.

Mastitis (mammary gland infection): After the birth of her young, a bitch may be beset by an infection causing inflammation of the mammary glands which produce milk for the puppies. Soreness and swelling make it painful for her when the puppies nurse. An abscess may form and she will usually run a fever. Hot compresses and antibiotics are necessary and in some instances hormone therapy.

Meningitis: Inflammation affecting the membranes covering the brain and/or spinal cord. It is a serious complication which may result from a severe case of distemper, tuberculosis, hardpad, head injury, etc. Symptoms are delirium, restlessness, high temperature, and dilated pupils in the eyes. Paralysis and death are almost certain.

Metritis: This infection, or inflammation of the uterus, causes the dog to exude a bloody discharge. Vomiting and a general lassitude are symptoms. Metritis can occur during the time the bitch is in season or right after giving birth. Antibiotics are used, or in severe cases hysterectomy.

Monorchidism: Having only one testicle.

Motion Sickness: On land, on sea, or in the air, your dog may be susceptible to motion sickness. Yawning, or excessive salivation, may signal the onset, and there is eventual vomiting. One or all of the symptoms may be present and recovery is miraculously fast once the motion ceases. Antinauseant drugs are available for animals which do not outgrow this condition.

Myeloma: Tumor of the bone marrow. Lameness and evidence of pain are symptoms as well as weight loss, depression and palpable tumor masses. Anemia or unnatural tendency to bleed in severe cases may be observed. The tumors may be detected radiographically, but no treatment has yet been reported for the condition.

Neonatal K-9 Herpesvirus Infection: Though K-9 herpesvirus infection, or CHV, has been thought to be a disease of the respiratory system in adult dogs, the acute necrotizing and hemorraghic disease occurs only in infant puppies. The virus multiplies in the respiratory system and female genital tracts of older dogs. Puppies may be affected in the vaginal canal. Unfortunately the symptoms resemble other neonatal infections, even hepatitis, and only after autopsy can it be detected.

Nephrotic Syndrome: Symptoms may be moist or suppurative dermatitis, edema or hypercholesteremia. It is a disease of the liver and may be the result of another disease. Laboratory data and biopsies may be necessary to determine the actual cause if it is other than renal disease. Cure is effected by eradicating the original disease. This is a relatively uncommon disease in dogs, and is detected by tests of the liver and urine.

Neuritis: Painful inflammation of a nerve.

Nosebleed (epistaxis): A blow or other injury which causes injury to the nasal tissues is usually the cause. Tumors, parasites, foreign bodies, such as thorns or burrs or quills, may also be responsible. Ice packs will help stem the tide of blood, though coagulants may also be necessary. Transfusions in severe cases may be indicated.

Orchitis: Inflammation of the testes.

Osteogenesis Imperfecta: or "brittle bones" is a condition that can be said to be both hereditary and dietary. It may be due to lack of calcium or phosphorus or both. Radiographs show "thin" bones with deformities throughout the skeleton. Treatment depends on cause.

Osteomyelitis (enostosis): Bone infection may develop after a bacterial contamination of the bone, such as from a compound fracture. Pain and swelling denote the infection and wet sores may accompany it. Lack of appetite, fever and general inactivity can be expected. Antibiotics are advised after X-ray determines severity. Surgery eliminates dead tissue or bone splinters to hasten healing.

Otitis: Inflammation of the ear.

Pancreatitis: It is difficult to palpate for the pancreas unless it is enlarged, which it usually is if this disease is present. Symptoms to note are as in other gastronomic complaints such as vomiting, loss of appetite, anorexia, stomach pains and general listlessness. This is a disease of older dogs though it has been diagnosed in young dogs as well. Blood, urine and stool examination and observation of the endocrine functions of the dog are in order. Clinical diseases that may result from a serious case of pancreatitis are acute pancreatitis which involves a complete degeneration of the pancreas, atrophy, fibrous and/or neoplasia, cholecystitis. Diabetes mellitus is also a possibility.

Patellar Luxation: "Trick knees" are frequent in breeds that have been "bred down" from Standard to Toy size, and is a condition where the knee bone slips out of position. It is a condition that can recur at any time as a result of a jump or excessive exercise. If it is persistent, anti-inflammatory drugs may be given or in some cases surgery can correct it.

Peritonitis: Severe pain accompanies this infection or inflammation of the lining of the abdominal cavity. Extreme sensitivity to touch, loss of appetite and vomiting occur. Dehydration and weight loss is rapid and anemia is a possibility. Antibiotics should kill the infection and a liquid diet for several days is advised. Painkillers may be necessary or drainage tubes in severe cases.

Phlebitis: Inflammation of a vein.

Placenta: The afterbirth which accompanies and has been used to nourish the fetus. It is composed of three parts; the chorion, amnion, and allantois.

Polycythemia Vera: A disease of the blood causing an elevation of hemoglobin concentration. Blood-letting has been effective. The convulsions that typify the presence can be likened to epileptic fits and last for several minutes. The limbs are stiff and the body feels hot. Mucous membranes are congested, the dog may shiver, and the skin has a ruddy discoloration. Blood samples must be taken and analyzed periodically. If medication to reduce the production of red blood cells is given, it usually means the dog will survive.

Proctitis: Inflammation of the rectum.

Above: Mexican, Canadian and American Ch. Chun-Chu-Fu's Kow-Kow's Victoria, bred and owned by Shirley Stone, Burbank, California. His sire was Ch. Bettina's Kow-Kow ex Chun-Chu-Fu's Khi-Ku's Starbrite.

Right: Mrs Elizabeth Mirylees, owner of the famous Beaupres Pekingese Kennels in Herefordshire, England, with some of her magnificent dogs, photographed on the patio of her home.

Below: Judge Ted Wurmser awards Best of Winners at the Greater Miami Kennel Club Show in January, 1973 to Betty Shoemaker's Gwynne's Treasured Truffle. This lovely 7¼ pound Peke was sired by Kumquat of Mingulay ex Linsown May Queen. Earl Graham photograph.

Prostatitis: Inflammation of the prostate gland.

Psittacosis: This disease which affects birds and people has been diagnosed in rare instances in dogs. A soft, persistent cough indicates the dog has been exposed and a radiograph will show a cloudy portion on the affected areas of the lung. Antibiotics such as aureomycin have been successful in the known cases and cure has been effected in two to three weeks' time. This is a highly contagious disease, to the point where it can be contracted during a post mortem.

Ch. Regent of Ashcroft, owned by Mrs W.A. Martel.

Pyometra: This uterine infection presents a discharge of pus from the uterus. High fever may turn to below normal as the infection persists. Lack of appetite with a desire for fluids and frequent urination are evidenced. Antibiotics and hormones are known cures. In severe cases, hysterectomy is necessary.

Rabies (hydrophobia): The most deadly of all dog diseases. The Pasteur treatment is the only known cure for humans. One of the viral diseases that affects the nervous system and damages the brain. It is contracted by the intake, through a bite or cut, of saliva from an infected animal. It takes days or even months for the symptoms to appear, so it is sometimes difficult to locate, or isolate, the source. There are two reactions in a dog to this disease. In the paralytic rabies the dog cannot swallow and salivates from a drooping jaw, and progressive paralysis eventually overcomes the entire body. The animal goes into coma and eventually dies. In the furious type of rabies the dog turns vicious, eats strange objects, in spite of a difficulty in swallowing, foams at the mouth, and searches out animals or people to attack—hence the expression "mad dog." Vaccination is available for dogs that run loose. Examination of the brain is necessary to determine actual diagnosis.

Rectal Prolapse) Diarrhea, straining from constipation or heavy infestations of parasites are the most common cause of prolapse which is the expulsion of a part of the rectum through the anal opening. It is cylindrical in shape, and must be replaced as soon as possible to prevent damage. Change in diet, medication to eliminate the cause, etc. will effect a cure.

Retinal Atrophy: A disease of the eye that is highly hereditary and may be revealed under ophthalmoscopic examination. Eventual blindness inevitably results. Dogs with retinal atrophy should not be used for breeding. Particularly prominent in certain breeds where current breeding trends have have tended to change the shape of the head.

Rhinitis: Acute or chronic inflammation of the mucous membranes of the nasal passages. It is quite common in both dogs and cats. It is seldom fatal, but requires endless "nursing" on the part of the owner for survival, since the nose passages must be kept open so the animal will eat. Dry leather on the nose though there is excessive discharge, high fever, sneezing, etc., are symptoms. Nose discharge may be bloody and the animal will refuse to eat, making it listless. The attacks may be recurrent and medication must be administered.

Rickets: The technical name for rickets is osteomalacia and is due to not enough calcium in the body. The bones soften and the legs become bowed or deformed. Rickets can be cured if caught in early stages by improvement in diet.

Ringworm: The dread of the dog and cat world! This is a fungus disease where the hair falls out in circular patches. It spreads rapidly and is most difficult to get rid of entirely. Drugs must be administered "inside and out!" The cure takes many weeks and much patience. Ultraviolet lights will show hairs green in color so it is wise to have your animal, or new puppy, checked out by the veterinarian for this disease before introducing him to the household. It is contracted by humans.

Root Canal Therapy: Injury to a tooth may be treated by prompt dental root canal therapy which involves removal of damaged or necrotic pulp and placing of opaque filling material in the root canal and pulp chamber.

Salivary Cyst: Surgery is necessary when the salivary gland becomes clogged or non-functional, causing constant salivation. A swelling becomes evident under the ear or tongue. Surgery will release the accumulation of saliva in the duct of the salivary gland, though it is at times necessary to remove the salivary gland in its entirety. Zygomatic salivary cysts are usually a result of obstructions in the four main pairs of salivary glands in the mouth. Infection is more prevalent in the parotid of the zygomatic glands located at the rear of the mouth, lateral to the last upper molars. Visual symptoms may be protruding eyeballs, pain when moving the jaw, or a swelling in the roof of the mouth. If surgery is necessary, it is done under general anesthesia and the obstruction removed by dissection. Occasionally, the zygomatic salivary gland is removed as well. Stitches or drainage tubes may be necessary or dilation of the affected salivary gland. Oral or internal antibiotics may be administered.

Scabies: Infection from a skin disease caused by a sarcoptic mange bite.

Scurf (dandruff): A scaly condition of the body in areas covered with hair. Dead cells combined with dried sweat and sebaceous oil gland materials.

Seborrhea: A skin condition also referred to as "stud tail," though studding has nothing to do with the condition. The sebaceous or oil-forming glands are responsible. Accumulation of dry skin, or scurf, is formed by excessive oily deposits while the hair becomes dry or falls out altogether.

Septicemia: When septic organisms invade the bloodstream, it is called septicemia. Severe cases are fatal as the organisms in the blood infiltrate the tissues of the body and all the body organs are affected. Septicemia is the result of serious wounds, especially joints and bones. Abscess may form. High temperature and/or shivering may herald the onset, and death occurs shortly thereafter since the organisms reproduce and spread rapidly. Close watch on all wounds, antibiotics and sulfur drugs are usually prescribed.

Shock (circulatory collapse): The symptoms and severity of shock vary with the cause and nervous system of the individual dog. Severe accident, loss of blood, and heart failure are the most common cause. Keep the dog warm, quiet and get him to a veterinarian right away. Symptoms are vomiting, rapid pulse, thirst, diarrhea, "cold, clammy feeling" and then eventually physical collapse. The veterinarian might prescribe plasma transfusion, fluids, perhaps oxygen, if pulse continues to be too rapid. Tranquilizers and sedatives are sometimes used as well as antibiotics and steroids. Relapse is not uncommon, so the animal must be observed carefully for several days after initial shock.

Sinusitis: Inflammation of a sinus gland that inhibits breathing.

Snakebite: The fact must be established as to whether the bite was poisonous or nonpoisonous. A horse-shoe shaped double row of toothmarks is a non-poisonous bite. A double, or two-hole puncture, is a poisonous snake bite. Many veterinarians now carry anti-venom serum and this must be injected intramuscularly almost immediately. The veterinarian will probably inject a tranquilizer and other antibiotics as well. It is usually a four-day wait before the dog is normal once again, and the swelling completely gone. During this time the dog should be kept on medication.

Spirochetosis: Diarrhea which cannot be checked through normal anti-diarrhea medication within a few days may indicate spirochetosis. While spirochete are believed by some authorities to be present and normal to gastro-intestinal tracts, unexplainable diarrhea may indicate their presence in great numbers. Large quantities could precipitate diarrhea by upsetting the normal balance of the organ, though it is possible for some dogs which are infected to have no diarrhea at all.

Spondylitis: Inflammation and loosening of the vertebrae.

Stomatitis: Mouth infection. Bleeding or swollen gums or excessive salivation may indicate this infection. Dirty teeth are usually the cause. Antibiotics and vitamin therapy are indicated; and, of course, scraping the teeth to eliminate the original cause. See also **Gingivitis.**

Strongylidosis: Disease caused by strongyle worms that enter the body through the skin and lodge in the wall of the small intestine. Bloody diarrhea, stunted growth, and thinness are general symptoms, as well as shallow breathing. Heavy infestation or neglect leads to death. Isolation of an affected animal and medication will help eliminate the problem, but the premises must also be cleaned thoroughly since the eggs are passed through the feces.

Suppository: A capsule comprised of fat or glycerine introduced into the rectum to encourage defecation. A paper match with the ignitible sulfur end torn off may also be used. Medicated suppositories are also used to treat inflammation of the intestine.

Tachycardia: An abnormal acceleration of the heartbeat. A rapid pulse signaling a disruption in the heart action. Contact a veterinarian at once.

Tapeworm: There are many types of tapeworms, the most common being the variety passed along by the flea. This is a white, segmented worm which lives off the wall of the dog's intestine and keeps growing by segments. Some of these are passed and can be seen in the stool or adhering to the hairs on the rear areas of the dog or even in his bedding. It is a difficult worm to get rid of since, even if medication eliminates segments, the head may remain in the intestinal wall to grow again. Symptoms are virtually the same as for other worms: debilitation, loss of weight, occasional diarrhea, and general listlessness. Medication and treatment should be under the supervision of a veterinarian.

Tetanus (lockjaw): A telarius bacillus enters the body through an open wound and spreads where the air does not touch the wound. A toxin is produced and affects the nervous system, particularly the brain or spine. The animal exhibits a stiffness, slows down considerably and the legs may be extended out beyond the body even when the animal is in a standing position. The lips have a twisted appearance. Recovery is rare. Tetanus is not common in dogs, but it can result from a bad job of tail docking or ear cropping, as well as from wounds received by stepping on rusty nails.

Thallotoxicosis or thallium poisoning: Thallium sulfate is a cellular-toxic metal used as a pesticide or rodenticide and a ready cause of poisoning in dogs. Thallium can be detected in the urine by a thallium spot test or by spectrographic analysis by the veterinarian. Gastro-intestinal disturbances signal the onset with vomiting, diarrhea, anorexia, stomach cramps. Sometimes a cough or difficulty in breathing occurs. Other intestinal disorders may also manifest themselves as well as convulsions. In mild cases the disease may be simply a skin eruption, depending upon the damage to the kidneys. Enlarged spleens, edema or nephrosis can develop. Antibiotics and a medication called dimercaprol are helpful, but the mortality rate is over 50 per cent.

Thrombus: A clot in a blood vessel or the heart.

Tick Paralysis: Seasonal attacks of ticks or heavy infestations of ticks can result in a dangerous paralysis. Death is a distinct reality at this point and immediate steps must be taken to prevent total paralysis. The onset is observed usually in the hindquarters. Lack of coordination, a reluctance to walk, and difficulty in getting up can be observed. Complete paralysis kills when infection reaches the respiratory system. The paralysis is the result of the saliva of the tick excreted as it feeds.

A lovely English parti-color from the nineteen thirties. . . Hei-Chu-Tzu of Caversham, owned by Mrs I.M. de Pledge.

The important Pekingese Cha Ming Ayree of Orchard Hill, owned by Mrs Richard Quigley, of Lock Haven, Pennsylvania.

Toad Poisoning: Some species of toads secrete a potent toxin. If while chasing a toad your dog takes it in his mouth, more than likely the toad will release this toxin from its parotid glands which will coat the mucous membranes of the dog's throat. The dog will salivate excessively, suffer prostration, cardiac arrhythmia. Some tropical and highly toxic species cause convulsions that result in death. Caught in time, there are certain drugs that can be used to counteract the dire effects. Try washing the dog's mouth with large amounts of water and get him to a veterinarian quickly.

Tonsillectomy: Removal of the tonsils. A solution called epinephrine, injected at the time of surgery, makes excessive bleeding almost a thing of the past in this otherwise routine operation.

Toxemia: The presence of toxins in the bloodstream, which normally should be eliminated by the excretory organs.

Trichiasis: A diseased condition of the eyelids, the result of neglect of earlier infection or inflammation.

Uremia: When poisonous materials remain in the body, because they are not eliminated through the kidneys, and are recirculated in the bloodstream. A nearly always fatal disease—sometimes within hours—preceded by convulsions and unconsciousness. Veterinary care and treatment are urgent and imperative.

Urinary Bladder Rupture: Injury or pelvic fractures are the most common causes of a rupture in this area. Anuria usually occurs in a few days when urine backs up into the stomach area. Stomach pains are characteristic and a radiograph will determine the seriousness. Bladder is flushed with saline solution and surgery is usually required. Quiet and little exercise is recommended during recovery.

Ventriculocordectomy: Devocalization of dogs, also known as aphonia. In diseases of the larynx this operation may be used. Portions of the vocal cords are removed by manual means or by electrocautery. Food is withheld for a day prior to surgery and premedication is administered. Food is again provided 24 hours after the operation. At the end of three or four months, scar tissue develops and the dog is able to bark in a subdued manner. Complications from surgery are few, but the psychological effects on the animal are to be reckoned with. Suppression of the barking varies from complete to merely muted, depending on the veterinarian's ability and each individual dog's anatomy.

Whipworms: Parasites that inhabit the large intestine and the cecum. Two to three inches in length, they appear "whiplike" and symptoms are diarrhea, loss of weight, anemia, restlessness or even pain, if the infestation is heavy enough. Medication is best prescribed by a veterinarian. Cleaning of the kennel is essential, since infestation takes place through the mouth. Whipworms reach maturity within thirty days after intake.

Above: English Ch. Tai Yang of Newnham, owned by Mrs Herbert Cowell. A popular winner in the nineteen twenties.

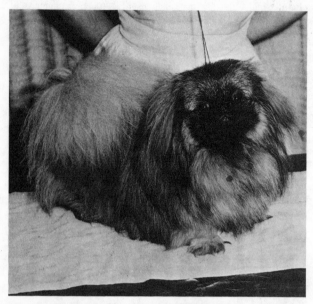

Above: Ch. Chun-Chu-Fu's Royal Peter, a Tri-International Champion, photographed here at 10 months of age. Bred and owned by Shirley Stone of Burbank, California, his sire was Canadian and American Ch. Calartha Mandarin of Jehol ex Canadian, Mexican and U.S. Ch. Chun-Chu-Fu's Golden Melodee.

A famous breeder of the early nineteen hundreds, Isabel K. Benjamin. Inset top right: Mrs Benjamin as a young girl.

Mary de Pledge, owner of the very, very famous English kennel, Caversham, photographed with a member of her second favorite breed!

GLOSSARY OF DOG TERMS

ACHILLES HEEL: The major tendon attaching the muscles of the calf from the thigh to the hock.

AKC: The American Kennel Club. Address: 51 Madison Avenue, N.Y., N.Y. 10010.

ALBINO: Pigment deficiency, usually a congenital fault, which renders skin, hair and eyes pink.

AMERICAN KENNEL CLUB: Registering body for canine world in the United States. Headquarters for the stud book, dog registrations, and federation of kennel clubs. It also creates and enforces the rules and regulations governing dog shows in the U.S.A.

ALMOND EYE: The shape of the eye opening, rather than the eye itself, which slants upwards at the outer edge, hence giving it an almond shape.

ANUS: Anterior opening found under the tail for purposes of alimentary canal elimination.

ANGULATION: The angles formed by the meeting of the bones.

APPLE-HEAD: An irregular roundness of topskull. A domed skull.

APRON: On long-coated dogs, the longer hair that frills outward from the neck and chest.

BABBLER: Hunting dog that barks or howls while out on scent.

BALANCED: A symmetrical, correctly proportioned animal; one having correct balance of one part in regard to another.

BARREL: Rounded rib section; thorax, chest.

BAT EAR: An erect ear. broad at base, rounded or semi-circular at top, with opening directly in front.

BAY: The howl or bark of the hunting dog.

BEARD: Profuse whisker growth.

BEAUTY SPOT: Usually roundish colored hair on a blaze of another color. Found mostly between the ears.

BEEFY: Overdevelopment or overweight in a dog, particularly hindquarters.

BELTON: A color designation particularly familiar to Setters. An intermingling of colored and white hairs.

BITCH: The female dog.

BLAZE: A type of marking. White stripe running up the center of the face between the eyes.

BLOCKY: Square head.

BLOOM: Dogs in top condition are said to be "in full bloom."

BLUE MERLE: A color designation. Blue and gray mixed with black. Marbled-like appearance.

BOSSY: Overdevelopment of the shoulder muscles.

BRACE: Two dogs which move as a pair in unison.

BREECHING: Tan-colored hair on inside of the thighs.

BRINDLE: Even mixture of black hairs with brown, tan or gray.

BRISKET: The forepart of the body below the chest.

BROKEN COLOR: A color broken by white or another color.

BROKEN-HAIRED: A wiry coat.

BROKEN-UP FACE: Receding nose together with deep stop, wrinkle, and undershot jaw.

BROOD BITCH: A female used for breeding.

BRUSH: A bushy tail.

BURR: Inside part of the ear which is visible to the eye.

BUTTERFLY NOSE: Parti-colored nose or entirely flesh color.

BUTTON EAR: The edge of the ear which folds to cover the opening of the ear.

C.A.C.I.B.: Award made in European countries to International champion dogs.

CANINE: Animals of the Canidae family which includes not only dogs but foxes, wolves, and jackals.

CANINES: The four large teeth in the front of the mouth often referred to as fangs.

CASTRATE: The surgical removal of the testicles on the male dog.

CAT-FOOT: Round, tight, high-arched feet said to resemble those of a cat.

CHARACTER: The general appearance or expression said to be typical of the breed.

CHEEKY: Fat cheeks or protruding cheeks.

CHEST: Forepart of the body between the shoulder blades and above the brisket.

CHINA EYE: A clear blue wall eye.

CHISELED: A clean cut head, especially when chiseled out below the eye.

CHOPS: Jowls or pendulous lips.

CLIP: Method of trimming coats according to individual breed standards.

CLODDY: Thick set or plodding dog.

CLOSE-COUPLED: A dog short in loins; comparatively short from withers to hipbones.

COBBY: Short-bodied; compact.

COLLAR: Usually a white marking, resembling a collar, around the neck.

CONDITION: General appearance of a dog showing good health, grooming and care.

CONFORMATION: The form and structure of the bone or framework of the dog in comparison with requirements of the Standard for the breed.

CORKY: Active and alert dog.

COUPLE: Two dogs.

COUPLING: Leash or collar-ring for a brace of dogs.

COUPLINGS: Body between withers and the hipbones indicating either short or long coupling.

COW HOCKED: When the hocks turn toward each other and sometimes touch.

CRANK TAIL: Tail carried down.

Left: Ch. Major Mite of Honan, America's greatest winning Pekingese of his time. No other American-bred Pekingese had amassed seven Bests In Shows, twice American bred, 37 Toy Groups. Mite was Best In Show at the Pekingese Club of America in 1949, Best In Show at the Chicago Pekingese Specialty in 1947, Best In Show there again in 1948. He was sire of many champions for his owner, Mrs Nathan S. Wise, Bond Hill Kennels, Cincinnati, Ohio.

CREST: Arched portion of the back of the neck.

CROPPING: Cutting or trimming of the ear leather to get ears to stand erect.

CROSSBRED: A dog whose sire and dam are of two different breeds.

CROUP: The back part of the back above the hind legs. Area from hips to tail.

CROWN: The highest part of the head; the topskull.

CRYPTORCHID: Male dog with neither testicle visible.

CULOTTE: The long hair on the back of the thighs.

CUSHION: Fullness of upper lips.

DAPPLED: Mottled marking of different colors with none predominating.

DEADGRASS: Dull tan color.

DENTITION: Arrangement of the teeth.

DEWCLAWS: Extra claws, or functionless digits on the inside of the four legs; usually removed at about three days of age.

DEWLAP: Loose, pendulous skin under the throat.

DISH-FACED: When nasal bone is so formed that nose is higher at the end than in the middle or at the stop.

DISQUALIFICATION: A dog which has a fault making it ineligible to compete in dog show competitions.

DISTEMPER TEETH: Discolored or pitted teeth as a result of having had distemper.

DOCK: To shorten the tail by cutting.

DOG: A male dog, though used freely to indicate either sex.

DOMED: Evenly rounded in topskull; not flat but curved upward.

DOWN-FACED: When nasal bone inclines toward the tip of the nose.

DOWN IN PASTERN: Weak or faulty pastern joints; a let-down foot.

DROP EAR: The leather pendant which is longer than the leather of the button ear.

DRY NECK: Taut skin.

DUDLEY NOSE: Flesh-colored or light brown pigmentation in the nose.

ELBOW: The joint between the upper arm and the forearm.

ELBOWS OUT: Turning out or off the body and not held close to the sides.

EWE NECK: Curvature of the top of neck.

EXPRESSION: Color, size and placement of the eyes which give the dog the typical expression associated with his breed.

FAKING: Changing the appearance of a dog by artificial means to make it more closely resemble the Standard. White chalk to whiten white fur, etc.

FALL: Hair which hangs over the face.

FEATHERING: Longer hair fringe on ears, legs, tail, or body.

FEET EAST AND WEST: Toes turned out.

FEMUR: The large heavy bone of the thigh.

FIDDLE FRONT: Forelegs out at elbows, pasterns close, and feet turned out.

FLAG: A long-haired tail.

FLANK: The side of the body between the last rib and the hip.

FLARE: A blaze that widens as it approaches the topskull.

FLASHY: Term used to describe outstanding color-pattern of dog.

FLAT BONE: When girth of the leg bones is correctly elliptical rather than round.

FLAT-SIDED: Ribs insufficiently rounded as they meet the breastbone.

FLEWS: Upper lips, particularly at inner corners.

FOREARM: Bone of the foreleg between the elbow and the pastern.

FOREFACE: Front part of the head; before the eyes; muzzle.

FROGFACE: Usually overshot jaw where nose is extended by the receding jaw.

FRINGES: Same as feathering.

FRONT: Forepart of the body as viewed head-on.

FURROW: Slight indentation or median line down center of the skull to the top.

GAY TAIL: Tail carried above the top line.

GESTATION: The period during which bitch carries her young; normally 63 days.

GOOSE RUMP: Too steep or sloping a croup.

GRIZZLE: Blueish-gray color.

Right: Copplestone Miss Pinkcoat, bred by A.R. Charlton and imported to this country from England by Betty Shoemaker of the Cumlaude Kennels, Bridgetown, New Jersey. Miss Pinkcoat's sire was Mr. Redcoat of Kanghe ex Kailyn of Brintoy.

GUN-SHY: When a dog fears gun shots.

GUARD HAIRS: The longer stiffer hairs which protrude through the undercoat.

HARD-MOUTHED: The dog that bites or leaves tooth marks on the game he retrieves.

HARE-FOOT: A narrow foot.

HARLEQUIN: A color pattern, patched or pied coloration, predominantly black and white.

HAW: A third eyelid or membrane at the inside corner of the eye.

HEEL: The same as the hock.

HEIGHT: Vertical measurement from the withers to the ground; or shoulders to the ground.

KNUCKLING-OVER: An insecurely knit pastern joint often causing irregular motion while dog is standing still.

LAYBACK: Well placed shoulders.

LAYBACK: Receding nose accompanied by an undershot jaw.

LEATHER: The flap of the ear.

LEVEL BITE: The front or incisor teeth of the upper and low jaws meeting exactly.

LINE BREEDING: The mating of dogs of the same breed related to a common ancestor. Controlled inbreeding. Usually grandmother to grandson, or grandfather to granddaughter.

LIPPY: Lips that do not meet perfectly.

LOADED SHOULDERS: When shoulder blades are out of alignment due to over-

MUZZLE: The head in front of the eyes—this includes nose, nostril and jaws as well as the foreface.

MUZZLE-BAND: White markings on the muzzle.

MOLARS: Rear teeth used for actual chewing.

NOSE: Scenting ability.

NICTITATING EYELID: The thin membrane at the inside corner of the eye which is drawn across the eyeball. Sometimes referred to as the third eyelid.

OCCIPUT: The upper crest or point at the top of the skull.

OCCIPITAL PROTUBERANCE: The raised occiput itself.

OCCLUSION: The meeting or bringing together of the upper and lower teeth.

Left: Ch. Ming of Downshire, the first California champion bitch, and Ch. Ah Moy of Downshire, third American-bred Pekingese champion. These two Pekes were the property of Miss Lydia Hopkins of the Sherwood Hall Kennels in California, which did so much winning in the "teens" of this century.

HOCK: The tarsus bones of the hind leg which form the joint between the second thigh and the metatarsals.

HOCKS WELL LET DOWN: When distance from hock to the ground is close to the ground.

HOUND: Dogs commonly used for hunting by scent.

HOUND-MARKED: Three-color dogs; white, tan and black, predominating color mentioned first.

HUCKLEBONES: The top of the hipbones.

HUMERUS: The bone of the upper arm.

INBREEDING: The mating of closely related dogs of the same standard, usually brother to sister.

INCISORS: The cutting teeth found between the fangs in the front of the mouth.

ISABELLA: Fawn or light bay color.

KINK TAIL: A tail which is abruptly bent appearing to be broken.

weight or overdevelopment on this particular part of the body.

LOIN: The region of the body on either side of the vertebral column between the last ribs and the hindquarters.

LOWER THIGH: Same as second thigh.

LUMBER: Excess fat on a dog.

LUMBERING: Awkward gait on a dog.

MANE: Profuse hair on the upper portion of neck.

MANTLE: Dark-shaded portion of the coat or shoulders, back and sides.

MASK: Shading on the foreface.

MEDIAN LINE: Same as furrow.

MOLERA: Abnormal ossification of the skull.

MONGREL: Puppy or dog whose parents are of two different breeds.

MONORCHID: A male dog with only one testicle apparent.

OLFACTORY: Pertaining to the sense of smell.

OTTER TAIL: A tail that is thick at the base, with hair parted on under side.

OUT AT SHOULDER: The shoulder blades are set in such a manner that the joints are too wide, hence jut out from the body.

OUTCROSSING: The mating of unrelated individuals of the same breed.

OVERHANG: A very pronounced eyebrow.

OVERSHOT: The front incisor teeth on top overlap the front teeth of the lower jaw. Also called pig jaw.

PACK: Several hounds kept together in one kennel.

PADDLING: Moving with the forefeet wide, to encourage a body roll motion.

PADS: The underside, or soles, of the feet.

PARTI-COLOR: Variegated in patches of two or more colors.

331

PASTERN: The collection of bones forming the joint between the radius and ulna, and the metacarpals.

PEAK: Same as occiput.

PENCILING: Black lines dividing the tan colored hair on the toes.

PIED: Comparatively large patches of two or more colors. Also called parti-colored or piebald.

PIGEON-BREAST: A protruding breastbone.

PIG JAW: Jaw with overshot bite.

PILE: The soft hair in the undercoat.

PINCER BITE: A bite where the incisor teeth meet exactly.

PLUME: A feathered tail which is carried over the back.

POINTS: Color on face, ears, legs and tail in contrast to the rest of the body color.

Ho Dynasty's Sunny Jim pictured winning on the West Coast. Sunny Jim is a full brother to Yama and Rubaiyat. Owned by the late Mrs. Gilma Blauvelt-Moss of New Jersey and Gloria Wallace and Kay Crow of California.

POMPON: Rounded tuft of hair left on the end of the tail after clipping.

PRICK EAR: Carried erect and pointed at tip.

PUPPY: Dog under one year of age.

QUALITY: Refinement, fineness.

QUARTERS: Hind legs as a pair.

RACY: Tall, of comparatively slight build.

RAT TAIL: The root thick and covered with soft curls—tip devoid of hair or having the appearance of having been clipped.

RINGER: A substitute for close resemblance.

RING TAIL: Carried up and around and almost in a circle.

ROACH BACK: Convex curvature of back.

ROAN: A mixture of colored hairs with white hairs. Blue roan, orange roan, etc.

ROMAN NOSE: A nose whose bridge has a convex line from forehead to nose tip. Ram's nose.

ROSE EAR: Drop ear which folds over and back revealing the burr.

ROUNDING: Cutting or trimming the ends of the ear leather.

RUFF: The longer hair growth around the neck.

SABLE: A lacing of black hair in or over a lighter ground color.

SADDLE: A marking over the back, like a saddle.

SCAPULA: The shoulder blade.

SCREW TAIL: Naturally short tail twisted in spiral fashion.

SCISSORS BITE: A bite in which the upper teeth just barely overlap the lower teeth.

SELF COLOR: One color with lighter shadings.

SEMIPRICK EARS: Carried erect with just the tips folding forward.

SEPTUM: The line extending vertically between the nostrils.

SHELLY: A narrow body which lacks the necessary size required by the Breed Standard.

SICKLE TAIL: Carried out and up in a semicircle.

SLAB SIDES: Insufficient spring of ribs.

SLOPING SHOULDER: The shoulder blade which is set obliquely or "laid back."

SNIPEY: A pointed nose.

SNOWSHOE FOOT: Slightly webbed between the toes.

SOUNDNESS: The general good health and appearance of a dog.

SPAYED: A female whose ovaries have been removed surgically.

SPECIALTY CLUB: An organization to sponsor and promote an individual breed.

SPECIALTY SHOW: A dog show devoted to the promotion of a single breed.

SPECTACLES: Shading or dark markings around the eyes or from eyes to ears.

SPLASHED: Irregularly patched, color on white or vice versa.

SPLAY FOOT: A flat or open-toed foot.

SPREAD: The width between the front legs.

SPRING OF RIBS: The degree of rib roundness.

SQUIRREL TAIL: Carried up and curving slightly forward.

STANCE: Manner of standing.

STARING COAT: Dry harsh hair; sometimes curling at the tips.

STATION: Comparative height of a dog from the ground—either high or low.

STERN: Tail of a sporting dog or hound.

STERNUM: Breastbone.

STIFLE: Joint of hind leg between thigh and second thigh. Sometimes called the ham.

STILTED: Choppy, up-and-down gait of straight-hocked dog.

STOP: The step-up from nose to skull between the eyes.

STRAIGHT-HOCKED: Without angulation; straight behind.

SUBSTANCE: Good bone. Or a dog in good weight, a well muscled dog.

SUPERCILIARY ARCHES: The prominence of the frontal bone of the skull over the eye.

SWAYBACK: Concave curvature of the back between the withers and the hip-bones.

TEAM: Four dogs usually working in unison.

THIGH: The hindquarter from hip joint to stifle.

THROATINESS: Excessive loose skin under the throat.

Ch. Calcutta Mandarin of Jehol and Ch. Rikki of Calcutta, owned by Vera Crofton of Topanga, California.

THUMB-MARKS: Black spots in the tan markings on the pasterns.

TICKED: Small isolated areas of black or colored hairs on a white background.

TIMBER: Bone, especially of the legs.

TOPKNOT: Tuft of hair on the top of head.

TRIANGULAR EYE: The eye set in surrounding tissue of triangular shape. A three-cornered eye.

TRI-COLOR: Three colors on a dog, white, black and tan.

TRUMPET: Depression or hollow on either side of the skull just behind the eye socket; comparable to the temple area in man.

TUCK-UP: Body depth at the loin.

TULIP EAR: Ear carried erect with slight forward curvature along the sides.

TURN-UP: Uptilted jaw.

TYPE: The distinguishing characteristics of a dog to measure its worth against the Standard for the breed.

UNDERSHOT: The front teeth of the lower jaw overlapping or projecting beyond the front teeth of the upper jaw.

UPPER ARM: The humerus bone of the foreleg between the shoulder blade and forearm.

VENT: Tan-colored hair under the tail.

WALLEYE: A blue eye also referred to as a fish or pearl eye.

WEAVING: When the dog is in motion, the forefeet or hind feet cross.

WEEDY: A dog too light of bone.

WHEATEN: Pale yellow or fawn color.

WHEEL-BACK: Back line arched over the loin; roach back.

WHELPS: Unweaned puppies.

WHIP TAIL: Carried out stiffly straight and pointed.

WIRE-HAIRED: A hard wiry coat.

WITHERS: The peak of the first dorsal vertebra; highest part of the body just behind the neck.

WRINKLE: Loose, folding skin on forehead and/or foreface.

INDEX